CHILD DEVELOPMENT AND EDUCATION

CHILD DEVELOPMENT AND EDUCATION

Third Edition

Teresa M. McDevitt
University of Northern Colorado

Jeanne Ellis Ormrod
University of Northern Colorado (Emerita)
University of New Hampshire

PEARSON

Merrill
Prentice Hall

Upper Saddle River, New Jersey
Columbus, Ohio

Library of Congress Cataloging-in-Publication Data

McDevitt, Teresa M.

  Child development and education / Teresa M. McDevitt, Jeanne Ellis Ormrod.—3rd ed.
    p. cm.
  Includes bibliographical references and index.
  ISBN 0-13-118817-8
    1. Child development. 2. Adolescent psychology. 3. Educational psychology.
I. Ormrod, Jeanne Ellis. II. McDevitt, Teresa M. Child development and education.
III. Title.

LB1115.M263 2007
305.231—dc22

                                                    2006046027

Vice President and Executive Publisher: Jeffery W. Johnston
Publisher: Kevin M. Davis
Development Editor: Autumn Crisp Benson
Editorial Assistant: Sarah N. Kenoyer
Production Editor: Mary Harlan
Copy Editors: Sue Snyder Kopp, Mary Benis
Design Coordinator: Diane C. Lorenzo
Photo Coordinator: Lori Whitley
Text Design: Kristina D. Holmes
Illustrations: Carlisle Editorial Services
Cover Design: Bryan Huber
Production Manager: Laura Messerly
Director of Marketing: David Gesell
Marketing Manager: Autumn Purdy
Marketing Coordinator: Brian Mounts

This book was set in Garamond by Carlisle Publishing Services. It was printed and bound by Courier Kendallville, Inc. The cover was printed by Phoenix Color Corp.

Photo Credits: Photo credits are listed on page P-1, facing the Name Index.

Pearson Education Ltd.   Pearson Education Australia Pty. Limited
Pearson Education Singapore Pte. Ltd. Pearson Education North Asia Ltd.
Pearson Education Canada, Ltd.   Pearson Educación de Mexico, S.A. de C.V.
Pearson Education–Japan   Pearson Education Malaysia Pte. Ltd.

10 9 8 7 6 5 4 3 2 1
ISBN: 0-13-118817-8

Dedication

To our children and husbands,
Connor, Alexander, and Eugene Sheehan
and
Christina, Alex, Jeffrey, and Richard Ormrod

About the Authors

Teresa M. McDevitt (left) is a psychologist with specializations in child development and educational psychology. She received a Ph.D. and M.A. in child development from Stanford University's Psychological Studies in Education program, an Ed.S. in educational evaluation from Stanford University, and a B.A. in psychology from the University of California, Santa Cruz. Since 1985 she has served the University of Northern Colorado in a variety of capacities—in teaching courses in child and adolescent psychology, human development, educational psychology, program evaluation, and research methods; in advisement of graduate students; in administration and university governance; and in research and grant writing. Her research focuses on child development, families, and teacher education. She has published articles in such journals as *Child Development, Learning and Individual Differences, Child Study Journal, Merrill-Palmer Quarterly, Youth and Society,* and *Science Education,* among others. She has gained extensive practical experiences with children, including raising two children with her husband and working in several positions with children—as an early childhood teacher of toddlers and preschool children, an early childhood special education teacher, and a volunteer in school and community settings. Teresa enjoys spending time with her children and husband and, when she has the chance, traveling internationally with her family.

Jeanne Ellis Ormrod (right) is an educational psychologist with specializations in learning, cognition, and child development. She received a Ph.D. and M.S. in educational psychology at The Pennsylvania State University and an A.B. in psychology from Brown University; she also earned licensure in school psychology through postdoctoral work at Temple University and the University of Colorado, Boulder. She was Professor of Educational Psychology at the University of Northern Colorado from 1976 until 1998, when she moved east to return to her native New England. She is now affiliated with the University of New Hampshire, where she teaches courses in educational psychology and research methods. She is the author or coauthor of several other Merrill/Prentice Hall books, including *Educational Psychology: Developing Learners, Human Learning, Essentials of Educational Psychology, Case Studies: Applying Educational Psychology,* and *Practical Research.* She has worked as a middle school geography teacher and school psychologist and has conducted research in cognitive development, memory, problem solving, spelling, and giftedness. When Jeanne is not teaching, writing, reading professional books and journals, or monitoring the diverse activities of her three grown children, she enjoys racquetball, boating, and occasional travel to diverse cultural settings.

Preface

As psychologists and teacher educators, we have been teaching child and adolescent development for many years. A primary goal in our classes has been to help students translate developmental theories into practical implications for teaching and caring for youngsters. In past years, the child development textbooks available to our students have often been quite thorough in their descriptions of theory and research, but they have offered few concrete suggestions for working with infants, children, and adolescents.

With this book, now in its third edition, we bridge the gap between theory and practice. We draw from innumerable theoretical concepts, from research studies conducted around the world, and from our own experiences as parents, teachers, psychologists, and researchers to identify strategies for promoting children's and adolescents' physical, cognitive, and social-emotional growth. Like the second edition, this book focuses on the entire span of childhood, from infancy through late adolescence. Unlike the broad-based applications of the second edition, however, the implications of this book are primarily educational in focus. As we wrote the third edition, we took to heart requests from several readers that we base the majority of our applications in classrooms, child care centers, and other educational settings. We also heeded advice from readers that we streamline our discussions, zeroing in more quickly, clearly, and concretely on the key concepts and core principles that are truly central to understanding how children and adolescents develop and how adults can enhance youngsters' growth and well-being. Users of the second edition will note, for example, that our introductory overviews have been shortened and made more concise. We hope that the outcome of our efforts is a more useful book for prospective teachers and other educational professionals.

Several features of the book make it different from other comprehensive textbooks about child and adolescent development. In particular, the book

- Continually relates abstract theories to educational strategies in schools
- Not only describes but also *demonstrates* developmental phenomena
- Guides observation of children and adolescents
- Directs analysis of what children and adolescents say, do, and create
- Offers ideas for effective teaching of, and working with, children and adolescents

In the next few pages, we provide examples of how the book accomplishes these goals.

The Only Comprehensive Development Text Written Specifically for Educators

This book focuses on concepts and principles that are important to both developmental theorists and educational practitioners. More so than any other text, McDevitt/Ormrod spells out the practical implications of developmental theory and research and provides concrete applications for those who teach and work with children and adolescents. The result is a text that is uniquely useful to those who are interested in practical applications of developmental scholarship.

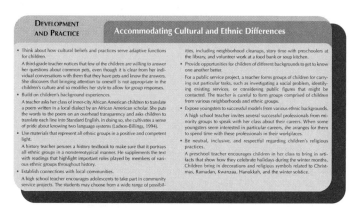

Development and Practice

In addition to discussing applications throughout the text itself, we provide *Development and Practice* features that offer concrete strategies for facilitating children's development. To help readers move from research to practice, each strategy is followed by an example of a professional using that strategy in a classroom or other setting. You will find examples of the *Development and Practice* feature on pages 221, 351, 479, and 507 of this text.

Observation Guidelines

To work productively with children and adolescents, one must first be able to see them accurately. Knowledge of development provides an essential lens through which professionals must look if they are to understand children. One of the foundational goals of this text is to help educators observe developmental nuances in the infants, children, and adolescents with whom they work. To this end, throughout the book we give readers *Observation Guidelines*. As you can see on pages 136, 169, 180, and 419, these tables offer specific characteristics to look for, present illustrative examples, and provide specific recommendations for practitioners.

NEW Applying Concepts in Child Development

New to this edition, an *Applying Concepts in Child Development* table appears at the end of each chapter (pages 30–31, 60, 94, 144, 187–188, 229–230, 273–274, 312–313, 354–355, 400, 438–439, 484–485, 527–528, and 568–569). These tables provide scenarios connected to developmental concepts; some cells in the table are intentionally left blank to allow readers to practice applying their knowledge of development in making educational decisions. Sample responses for the tables are available in the *Study Guide and Reader* so students may compare their own responses with those of an expert.

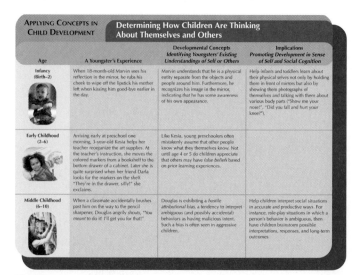

The Difference Between Reading About Development and Seeing It

Another central focus of this text is to illustrate concepts and research with frequent examples of real children and adolescents. Authentic case studies begin and end each chapter, and there are often separate, shorter vignettes within the chapter body. In addition to these types of illustrations, the text, much more than any similar text, also makes frequent use of real artifacts from children's journals, sketchbooks, and schoolwork. It is among real children and adolescents in the midst of the work they produce that developmental content becomes meaningful to educators and other practitioners. More than any other text, McDevitt/Ormrod brings this context to life.

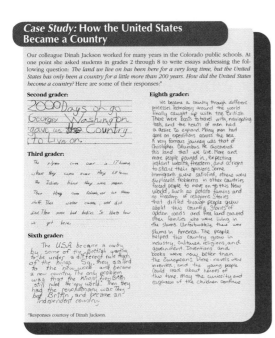

Case Study: How the United States Became a Country

Our colleague Dinah Jackson worked for many years in the Colorado public schools. At one point she asked students in grades 2 through 8 to write essays addressing the following question: *The land we live on has been here for a very long time, but the United States has only been a country for a little more than 200 years. How did the United States become a country?* Here are some of their responses:[a]

Second grader:

2000 Days ok go George Washington gave us the Country to Live on.

Third grader:

Sixth grader:

Eighth grader:

[a]Responses courtesy of Dinah Jackson.

Case Studies

Each chapter begins with a case that, by being referenced throughout the chapter, illustrates and frames that chapter's content. A chapter-ending case provides readers with an opportunity to apply chapter content. The questions that accompany each of these end-of-chapter cases help the reader in this application process; examples of answers to these questions appear in the Appendix. The ending case study analyses may be especially helpful in helping future teachers prepare for the *Praxis™ Principles of Learning and Teaching* tests and other licensure exams. You will find examples of the case studies on pages 92–93, 277, 397–398, and 566–567.

Listen to Brendan and Robin talk about recreational opportunities and friendly neighbors in the "Neighborhood" clips for early and late adolescence on Observation CD 2.

Observation CD-ROMs

Integrated into every chapter are video clips from a set of 3 CDs that accompanies this book. You can see examples of this integration on pages 203, 248, 347, and 537. Activities on the CDs allow students to explore 14 topics—such as Memory, Friendship, and Families—from the perspective of children from five age groups. The opportunity to see children and adolescents at different levels of development perform the same task or talk about a topic, such as what it means to be a friend, is unique and extremely powerful in demonstrating developmental differences.

NEW Interpreting Children's Artifacts and Actions

New to this edition, the *Interpreting Children's Artifacts and Actions* feature gives readers practice in evaluating and interpreting children's work and statements. You will find examples of this feature on pages 107, 225, and 545. Not only does this feature provide readers with additional authentic illustrations of chapter content, but it also offers readers an opportunity to apply their knowledge of child development in an authentic context. And since interpreting real children's work is a core assessment task of those who educate children and adolescents, this feature gives readers direct, concrete practice in assessment.

INTERPRETING CHILDREN'S ARTIFACTS AND ACTIONS — Comparing Self-Descriptions

When her children were younger, Jeanne once asked them to desc____ read their self-des____ more developmen____

Jeff (age 6): I lik____ things. I do good____ eyes. Yellow hair.

Alex (age 9): I h____ I like wearing sho____

curly. I was adopted. I was born in Denver. I

INTERPRETING CHILDREN'S ARTIFACTS AND ACTIONS — Fish in a Boat

Combining his pen-and-ink drawing skills and computer technology, 14-year-old Brady created this cartoon of fish rowing a boat upside-down at the water's surface. As you look at the cartoon, identify a logical reasoning skill it requires and the Piagetian stage that this skill reflects.

START BAILING, HOWARD, WE'RE TAKING ON AIR FAST!

New and Expanded Content

New Coverage of Content Domains

The "Development of Literacy" chapter in the second edition has become "Development in the Content Domains" (Chapter 10) and now includes coverage of development in reading, writing, mathematics, science, history, geography, art, and music.

CHAPTER 10: DEVELOPMENT IN THE CONTENT DOMAINS
Case Study: Phyllis and Benjamin Jones
Reading
    Emergent Literacy
    Phonological Awareness
    Word Recognition
    Reading Comprehension
    Metacognition in Reading
    Diversity in Reading Development
    Promoting Reading Development
Writing
    Handwriting
    Spelling
    Syntax and Grammar
    Composition Skills
    Metacognition in Writing
    Diversity in Writing Development
    Promoting Writing Development
Mathematics
    Number Sense and Counting
    Mathematical Concepts and Principles
    Basic Arithmetic Operations
    More Advanced Problem-Solving Procedures
    Metacognition in Mathematics
    Diversity in Mathematics Development
    Promoting Development in Mathematics
Science
    Children's Theories about the Physical and Biological
      Worlds
    Scientific Reasoning Skills
    Metacognition in Science
    Diversity in Science Development
    Promoting Development in Science
Development in Other Content Domains
    History
    Geography
    Art
    Music
Using Content Area Standards to Guide Instruction
Case Study: Beating the Odds
Summary
Applying Concepts in Child Development

Biological Beginnings and Physical Development Chapters

The previous edition's chapter on physical development has been expanded into two chapters. Chapter 3, "Biological Beginnings," focuses on genetic foundations of child development, prenatal development, and birth. Chapter 4, "Physical Development," focuses on brain development, other physical changes, and children's health.

CHAPTER 4: PHYSICAL DEVELOPMENT
Case Study: The Softball League
Principles of Physical Development
The Brain and Its Development
    Structures and Functions
    Developmental Changes
    Applications of Research on Brain Development
Physical Development During Childhood
    Infancy (Birth–Age 2)
    Early Childhood (Ages 2–6)
    Middle Childhood (Ages 6–10)
    Early Adolescence (Ages 10–14)
    Late Adolescence (Ages 14–18)
Physical Well-Being
    Eating Habits
    Physical Activity
    Rest and Sleep
    Health-Compromising Behaviors
Special Physical Needs
    Chronic Illness
    Serious Injuries and Health Hazards
    Physical Disabilities
    Pro
Case Study:
Summary
Applying Co

CHAPTER 3: BIOLOGICAL BEGINNINGS
Case Study: Expecting Zoe
Genetic Foundations of Child Development
    Structure and Operation of Genes
    Formation of Reproductive Cells
    Genetic Basis of Individual Traits
    The Awakening of Genes
    The Blending of Heredity and Environment
    Acknowledging Nature and Nurture in
      Children's Lives
Prenatal Development
    Phases of Prenatal Growth
    Medical Care
    Supporting Parents, Protecting Babies
Birth of the Baby
    Preparation for Birth
    The Birth Process
    Complications and Interventions
    Enhancing Caregivers' Sensitivity to
      Newborn Infants
Case Study: Understanding Adam
Summary
Applying Concepts in Child Development

Supplementary Materials

For Students

 Where the Web Meets Textbooks for Student Savings!

SafariX Textbooks Online is an exciting new choice for students looking to save money. As an alternative to purchasing the print textbook, students can subscribe to the same content online and save up to 50% off the suggested list price of the same text. With a SafariX WebBook, students can search the text, make notes online, print out reading assignments that incorporate lecture notes, and bookmark important passages for later review. The ISBN for the Safari X WebBook for this text is 0-13-175429-7.

Study Guide and Reader

Features in the *Study Guide and Reader* (ISBN: 0-13-225448-4) that help students focus their learning include (1) a chapter overview to give students an overall picture of chapter topics, (2) discussions of common student beliefs and misconceptions to alert students to widely held beliefs that may affect their mastery of developmental concepts and theories, (3) focus questions for students to answer as they read the chapter and test themselves about their comprehension of chapter content, (4) application exercises to give students practice in recognizing concepts and principles in action in the classroom and other settings, (5) more than 40 supplementary readings and research study descriptions to extend the content found in the textbook, (6) chapter glossary, and (7) sample test questions.

 Teacher Preparation Classroom

This new interactive Web site offers students a wealth of course-specific resources and activities to enrich and deepen their preparation as teachers. Organized around the major courses pre-service teachers take, the Teacher Prep site provides more than 150 video clips, each tied to a course topic and framed by learning goals and Praxis-type questions; more than 250 student/teacher artifacts, each tied to a course topic and framed by learning goals and application questions; over 500 strategies and lesson plans; over 500 *Educational Leadership* research articles; and other resources to equip students with the quality tools needed to excel in their courses and prepare them for their first classroom.

CD-ROMs: "Observing Children and Adolescents: Guided Interactive Practice in Understanding Development"

This unique set of three CDs is packaged with every copy of the textbook and integrated into every chapter. In more than 50 activities students view video clips of real children from infancy through adolescence, reflect on their observations, and record their interpretations. Students can explore 14 topics, including Memory, Intrinsic Motivation, Cognitive Development, Emotional Development, Families, Friendship, and Intelligence. Viewing these clips and responding to a series of questions across five age groups will familiarize students with the abilities and concerns of children at every developmental level—and reinforce key concepts.

Companion Website

Our Website at **www.prenhall.com/mcdevitt** helps students master course content with Practice Quizzes and Essay Questions, explore topics in depth in Web Links, and more.

Interactive Computer Simulations in Child Development

This problem-solving simulation CD-ROM (ISBN: 0-13-092969-7) allows students to participate in two "virtual" experiments—manipulating variables with a virtual pendulum to learn more about Piaget's theory of cognitive development, and assessing moral reasoning using Kohlberg's theory of moral development—and then apply their knowledge.

For Instructors

NEW **Multimedia Presentation Software**

The multimedia presentation software (ISBN: 0-13-118818-6) consists of DVDs that contain materials from the ancillaries offered with the text and are organized around PowerPoint® presentations. This technology enables professors to use available ancillaries in a classroom setting and to show appropriate video clips or present examples, scenarios, or problems to help facilitate classroom discussion or to supplement lectures. Professors can also create their own PowerPoint presentations or modify existing ones.

Instructor's Manual

This manual (ISBN: 0-13-119115-2) contains an outline of the primary chapter headings and sections, with a corresponding list of instructional materials to be used for each section; and suggestions and resources for learning activities, supplemental lectures, case study analyses, group activities, and handouts. Each element has been carefully crafted to provide opportunities to support, enrich, and expand upon what your students read in the text.

Multimedia Guide

The *Multimedia Guide* (ISBN: 0-13-119119-5) will help you enrich your students' interpretation and understanding of what they see in the videos, on the Simulations CD, on the Observing Children and Adolescents CDs, and on the Companion Website. Observation Record tables, similar to the Observation Guidelines tables in the text, help students record their observations and apply their knowledge of development. The *Multimedia Guide* is available online at the Instructor Resource Center at www.prenhall.com

Test Bank and TestGen

The Test Bank (ISBN: 0-13-119117-9) contains an average of 60 items per chapter, the majority of them newly constructed by co-author Jeanne Ormrod. These test items are categorized and marked as either lower-level items that ask students to identify or explain concepts they have learned or higher-level items that require students to apply their knowledge of developmental concepts and research to specific classroom situations. The computerized test bank software (TestGen) (ISBN: 0-13-119125-X) gives instructors electronic access to the test questions printed in the Test Bank and allows them to create and customize exams. TestGen is available in both Macintosh and PC/Windows versions.

Online PowerPoint Slides

The PowerPoint slides, available on the Instructor Resource Center at **www.prenhall.com,** include key concept summarizations, diagrams, and other graphic aids to enhance learning. They are designed to help students understand, organize, and remember concepts and developmental theories.

NEW OneKey Course Management

OneKey is Prentice Hall's exclusive new resource for instructors and students. OneKey is an integrated online course management resource featuring everything students and instructors need for work in or outside of the classroom, including the *Study Guide and Reader*, Companion Website material, *Instructor's Manual, Multimedia Guide, Test Bank, Observing Children and Adolescents* CDs, and PowerPoint slides. OneKey is available in WebCT and BlackBoard. The ISBNs for the OneKey Student Access Kits are Web CT Student Access Kit (0-13-175320-7) and BlackBoard Student Access Kit (0-13-228439-1). For more information about OneKey, instructors should contact their local Prentice Hall representative prior to placing their textbook order.

The Videotape Package

Insights Into Learning   One-hour videotapes include

- *Using Balance Beams in Fourth Grade* (ISBN: 0-13-095278-8). Students problem solve using weights on a balance beam and defend solutions.
- *Finding Area in Elementary Math* (ISBN: 0-13-095277-X). Fifth-graders find the area of an irregular shape using problem-solving steps. A teacher presents transfer tasks and probes students' reasoning.
- *Designing Experiments in Seventh Grade* (ISBN: 0-13-095279-6). Students conduct small-group experiments and discuss how factors affect a pendulum's oscillation rate, then a teacher conducts a lesson on separating and controlling variables.

Double-Column Addition: A Teacher Uses Piaget's Theory (ISBN: 0-13-751413-1) Second graders construct creative strategies for adding and subtracting two-digit numbers and reveal a true understanding of place value.

A Private Universe   (ISBN: 0-13-859646-8) This video illustrates the pervasiveness of misconceptions in high school students and in graduates and faculty at Harvard about the seasons of the year and the phases of the moon. One student's explanations are portrayed both before and after instruction. Questions probing her reasoning after instruction reveal she still holds some prior misconceptions.

Acknowledgments

Although we are listed as the sole authors of this textbook, in fact many individuals have contributed in significant ways to its content and form. Our editor, Kevin Davis, recognized the need for an applied child development book and nudged us to write one. Kevin has been the captain of our ship throughout all three editions of the book, charting our journey and alerting us when we drifted off course. We thank Kevin for his continuing encouragement, support, insights, task focus, and high standards.

We have been equally fortunate to work with Julie Peters (development editor for the first and second editions) and Autumn Benson (development editor for the third edition). Julie and Autumn have seen us through the day-to-day challenges of writing the book—for instance, offering creative ideas for improving the manuscript, locating artifacts to illustrate key concepts, pushing us to condense when we were unnecessarily wordy, insisting that certain concepts be clarified and illustrated, being a willing ear whenever we needed to vent our frustrations and, in general, coordinating our writing efforts until books went into production. We thank both Julie and Autumn for their advice, support, and good humor, and also for their willingness to drop whatever else they were doing to come to our assistance at critical times.

Others at Merrill Education have also been key players in bringing the book to fruition. Sue Snyder Kopp and Mary Benis worked diligently to keep the manuscript focused, concise, and clear. Mary Harlan guided the manuscript through the production process; without a complaint, she let us continue to tweak the book in innumerable small ways even as production deadlines loomed dangerously close. Autumn Benson and Becky Savage secured permissions for the excerpts and figures we borrowed from other sources and were flexible and dependable when we added to our list at the eleventh hour. Lori Whitley sifted through many piles of photos to identify those that could best capture key developmental principles in a visual form. Marketing whizzes Autumn Purdy, Brian Mounts, Ann Davis, Amy June, Joe Hale, Amy Judd, Suzanne Stanton, Barbara Koontz, and others helped us get out the word about the book. Prentice Hall sales representatives across the country offered us encouragement and relayed invaluable recommendations they had heard from faculty using the book.

We are also deeply indebted to the first two authors of the three compact disks that comprise *Observing Children and Adolescents: Guided Interactive Practice in Understanding Development*. Jayne Downey labored diligently and effectively to translate a good concept into a better reality. Jayne shared our desire to represent children and adolescents in a natural and positive light so that adults could understand them more deeply and sympathetically; among the many tasks she undertook were to recruit children and families, secure the services of interviewers, draft questions and set up tasks for children, film children in their homes, edit video clips, and interpret children's thoughts and actions. Stuart Garry brought his technological know-how, in-depth knowledge of developmental theory, artistic talents, and keen attention to detail to bear in designing the CDs themselves. Others were vital contributors, as well. Jason Cole expertly programmed the complex package. We extend our appreciation to Greg Pierson, Director of University Schools, and to Keli Cotner, Director of the Campus Child Care Center at the University of Northern Colorado, for granting permission and assistance to Jayne Downey in filming classrooms and facilities. Dana Snyder and Kelle Nolke, teachers at University Schools, kindly assisted with videotaping in their classroom; Dana Snyder also permitted her own lessons to be taped. We also acknowledge the excellent job done by interviewers Stacey Blank, Tara Kaysen, Addie Lopez, Laura Sether, and Lisa Blank. Thanks, too, to Randy Lennon at the University of Northern Colorado, for making equipment available for editing. Finally, the children and families were especially generous in allowing Jayne and the interviewers to come into their homes and to film the children.

We greatly appreciate Rebecca Pettit's willingness to take on both the *Instructor's Manual* and the *Multimedia Guide* for the third edition. These two resources offer many excellent suggestions and scaffolds for novice and experienced instructors alike.

Children, Adolescents, Teachers, and Other Professionals Equally important contributors to the book were the many young people and practitioners who provided the work samples, written reflections, other artifacts, and verbal responses that appear throughout the fourteen chapters and in the observation CD package. The work of the following young people contributed immeasurably to the depth and richness of our discussions:

Davis Alcorn	Eddie Garcia	Sarah Luffel	Bianca Sanchez
Jacob Alcorn	Palet Garcia	Jessica Lumbrano	Daniela Sanchez
Curtis Alexander	Veronica Garcia	Krista Marrufo	Corwin Sether
Kyle Alexander	James Garrett III	Steven Merrick	Alex Sheehan
David Alkire	Mayra de la Garza	Margaret Mohr	Connor Sheehan
Geoff Alkire	Amaryth Gass	Tchuen-Yi Murry	Aftyn Siemer
Brenda Bagazuma	Andrew Gass	Mike Newcomb	Karma Marie Smith
Andrew Belcher	Tony Gass	Malanie Nunez	Alex Snow
Katie Belcher	Dana Gogolin	Dustin O'Mara	Sam Snow
Kayla Blank	Ivy Gogolin	Alex Ormrod	Connor Stephens
Madison Blank	Kenton Groissaint	Jeff Ormrod	Megan Lee Stephens
Brent Bonner	Acadia Gurney	Tina Ormrod	Joe Sweeney
Diamond Bonner	Amanda Hackett	Shir-Lisa Owens	Emma Thompson
Ricco Branch	Jared Hale	Isiah Payan	Grace Tober
Marsalis Bush	Cody Havens	Isabelle Peters	Sarah Toon
Eric Campos	Tyler Hensley	Michelle Pollman	David Torres
Leif Carlson	Elisabet Deyanira	Laura Prieto-Velasco	Joseph Torres
Zoe Clifton	Hernandez	Ian Rhoades	Samuel Torres
Wendy Cochran	Lauryn Hickman	Talia Rockland	Madison Tupper
Jenna Dargy	Sam Hickman	Oscar Rodriguez	Danielle Welch
Noah Davis	William Hill	Elizabeth Romero	Brady Williamson
Shea Davis	Brandon Jackson	Corey Ross	Joey Wolf
Brandon Doherty	Rachel Johnson	Katie Ross	Lindsey Woollard
Daniel Erdman	Jordan Kemme	Trisha Ross	Anna Young
Rachel Foster	Marianne Kies	Amber Rossetti	

We also thank the children in the first- and second-grade classroom of Dana Snyder and Kelle Nolke at the Laboratory School, Greeley, Colorado (now University Schools).

To ensure that we included children's work from a wide variety of geographic locations and backgrounds, we contacted organizations north and south, east and west to obtain work samples that would reflect ethnic, cultural, and economic diversity. We want to thank these individuals for their assistance and coordination efforts: Don Burger at Pacific Resources for Education and Learning (PREL), Michelle Gabor of the Salesian Boys' and Girls' Club, Rita Hocog Inos of the Commonwealth of the Northern Mariana Islands Public School System, Bettie Lake of the Phoenix Elementary School District, Heidi Schork and members of the Boston Youth Clean-Up Corps (BYCC), Ann Shump of the Oyster River School District. Furthermore we thank the many teachers, counselors, principals, and other professionals—a child welfare case worker, a neurologist, a public health educator—who were so helpful in our efforts to identify artifacts, anecdotes, dialogues, and professional strategies to illustrate developmental concepts; key among them were Janet Alcorn, Rosenna Bakari, Trish Belcher, Paula Case, Michael Gee, Jennifer Glynn, Evie Greene, Diana Haddad, Betsy Higginbotham, Betsy Hopkins, Dinah Jackson, Jesse Jensen, Mike McDevitt, Erin Miguel, Michele Minichiello, Andrew Moore, Dan Moulis, Tina Ormrod, Annemarie Palincsar, Kellee Patterson, Elizabeth Peña, Jrene Rahm, Nancy Rapport, Gwen Ross, Karen Scates, Cindy Schutter, Karen Setterlin, Jean Slater, Julie Spencer, Nan Stein, Sally Tossey, Pat Vreeland, and Cathy Zocchi.

Colleagues and Reviewers In addition, we received considerable encouragement, assistance, and support from our professional colleagues. Developmentalists and educational psychologists at numerous institutions around the country have offered their careful and insightful reviews of one or more chapters. We are especially indebted to the following reviewers of this edition:

Thomas M. Batsis, Loyola Marymount University

Doris Bergen, Miami University

Donna M. Burns, The College of St. Rose

Deborah K. Deemer, University of Northern Iowa

Karen Drill, University of Illinois at Chicago

Linda L. Haynes, University of South Alabama

Joyce Juntune, Texas A&M University

Sharon McNeely, Northeastern Illinois University

Carol A. Marchel, Winthrop University

Marilyn K. Moore, Illinois State University

Andrew R. Whitehead, East Stroudsburg University of Pennsylvania

We continue to appreciate the guidance of reviewers for earlier editions of the book. These individuals helped to guide our early efforts:

Karen Abrams, Keene State College

Jan Allen, University of Tennessee

Lynley Anderman, University of Kentucky

David E. Balk, Kansas State University

Tom Batsis, Loyola Marymount University

Heather Davis, University of Florida

Teresa DeBacker, University of Oklahoma

Eric Durbrow, The Pennsylvania State University

William Fabricius, Arizona State University

Daniel Fasko, Morehead State University

Sherryl Browne Graves, Hunter College

Michael Green, University of North Carolina–Charlotte

Glenda Griffin, Texas A&M University

Deborah Grubb, Morehead State University

Melissa Heston, University of Northern Iowa

James E. Johnson, The Pennsylvania State University

Michael Keefer, University of Missouri–St. Louis

Judith Kieff, University of New Orleans

Nancy Knapp, University of Georgia

Mary McLellan, Northern Arizona University

Sharon McNeely, Northeastern Illinois University

Kenneth Merrell, University of Iowa

Tamera Murdock, University of Missouri–Kansas City

Bridget Murray, Indiana State University

Kathy Nakagawa, Arizona State University

Virginia Navarro, University of Missouri–St. Louis

Larry Nucci, University of Illinois–Chicago

Jennifer Parkhurst, Duke University

Sherrill Richarz, Washington State University

Kent Rittschof, Georgia Southern University

Linda Rogers, Kent State University

Richard Ryan, University of Rochester

Sue Spitzer, California State University, San Bernardino

Benjamin Stephens, Clemson University

Bruce Tuckman, The Ohio State University

Kathryn Wentzel, University of Maryland–College Park

Allan Wigfield, University of Maryland–College Park

Thomas D. Yawkey, The Pennsylvania State University.

Increasingly, we have heard from colleagues at other institutions who have taken the time to let us know what they think about the book and how it might be improved. We are grateful for such very helpful feedback. In addition, faculty and administrators at the University of Northern Colorado—especially Marlene Strathe, Steven Pulos, Randy Lennon, Kathy Cochran, Allen Huang, Mark Alcorn, Eugene Sheehan, and Kay Norton—unselfishly provided information, advice, resources, and time.

Our Families Finally, our families have been supportive and patient over the extended period we have been preoccupied with reading, researching, writing, and editing. Our children gave of themselves in anecdotes, artwork, and diversions from our work. Our husbands picked up the slack around the house and gave us frequent emotional boosts and comic relief. Much love and many thanks to Eugene, Connor, and Alex (from Teresa) and to Richard, Tina, Alex, and Jeff (from Jeanne).

T.M.M.
J.E.O.

Teacher Preparation Classroom

TEACHER PREP

MERRILL
PRENTICE HALL

See a demo at
www.prenhall.com/teacherprep/demo

Your Class. Their Careers. Our Future. Will Your Students Be Prepared?

We invite you to explore our new, innovative and engaging website and all that it has to offer you, your course, and tomorrow's educators! Organized around the major courses pre-service teachers take, the Teacher Preparation site provides media, student/teacher artifacts, strategies, research articles, and other resources to equip your students with the quality tools needed to excel in their courses and prepare them for their first classroom.

This ultimate on-line education resource is available at no cost, when packaged with a Merrill text, and will provide you and your students access to:

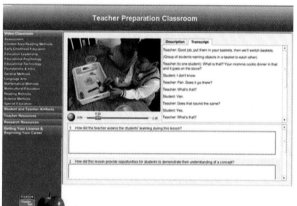

Online Video Library. More than 150 video clips—each tied to a course topic and framed by learning goals and Praxis-type questions—capture real teachers and students working in real classrooms, as well as in-depth interviews with both students and educators.

Student and Teacher Artifacts. More than 200 student and teacher classroom artifacts—each tied to a course topic and framed by learning goals and application questions—provide a wealth of materials and experiences to help make your study to become a professional teacher more concrete and hands-on.

Research Articles. Over 500 articles from ASCD's renowned journal *Educational Leadership.* The site also includes Research Navigator, a searchable database of additional educational journals.

Teaching Strategies. Over 500 strategies and lesson plans for you to use when you become a practicing professional.

Licensure and Career Tools. Resources devoted to helping you pass your licensure exam; learn standards, law, and public policies; plan a teaching portfolio; and succeed in your first year of teaching.

How to ORDER *Teacher Prep* for you and your students:
For students to receive a *Teacher Prep* Access Code with this text, instructors **must** provide a special value pack ISBN number on their textbook order form. To receive this special ISBN, please email **Merrill.marketing@pearsoned.com** and provide the following information:
- Name and Affiliation
- Author/Title/Edition of Merrill text

Upon ordering *Teacher Prep* for their students, instructors will be given a lifetime *Teacher Prep* Access Code.

Brief Contents

PART I   *Theory and Practice in Child Development*

CHAPTER 1:   Making a Difference in the Lives of Children and Adolescents   2

CHAPTER 2:   Using Research to Understand Children and Adolescents   33

PART II   *Foundations of Development*

CHAPTER 3:   Biological Beginnings   62

CHAPTER 4:   Physical Development   96

CHAPTER 5:   Family, Culture, and Community   146

PART III   *Cognitive Development*

CHAPTER 6:   Cognitive Development: Piaget and Vygotsky   190

CHAPTER 7:   Cognitive Development: Cognitive Processes   232

CHAPTER 8:   Intelligence   276

CHAPTER 9:   Language Development   314

CHAPTER 10:   Development in the Content Domains   356

PART IV   *Social and Emotional Development*

CHAPTER 11:   Emotional Development   402

CHAPTER 12:   Development of Self and Social Understanding   440

CHAPTER 13:   Development of Motivation and Self-Regulation   486

CHAPTER 14:   Peers, Schools, and Society   530

Contents

PART I   Theory and Practice in Child Development

CHAPTER 1

Making a Difference in the Lives of Children and Adolescents   2

Case Study: Tonya   3
The Field of Child Development   4
   Three Developmental Domains   5
   Effects of Context on Development   5
Basic Issues in Development   6
   Nature and Nurture   6
   Universality and Diversity   8
   Qualitative and Quantitative Change   9
   Applying Basic Lessons from Child Development   10
Theories of Child Development   12
   Biological Theories   12
   Behaviorism and Social Learning Theories   12
   Psychodynamic Theories   13
   Cognitive-Developmental Theories   14
   Cognitive Process Theories   14
   Sociocultural Theories   15
   Developmental Systems Theories   16
   Taking an Eclectic Approach   17
Developmental Periods   18
   Infancy (Birth–2 Years)   18
   Early Childhood (2–6 Years)   19
   Middle Childhood (6–10 Years)   20
   Early Adolescence (10–14 Years)   21
   Late Adolescence (14–18 Years)   22
From Theory to Practice   22
   Preparing for Developmentally Appropriate Practice   22
   Strengthening the Commitment   27
Case Study: Latisha   28
Summary   29
Applying Concepts in Child Development   30

CHAPTER 2

Using Research to Understand Children and Adolescents   33

Case Study: The After-School Program   32
Principles of Research   34
   Ethical Protection of Children   35
   The Scientific Method   35
   Research Participants   35

Analyzing Developmental Research   36
   Data Collection Techniques   36
   Research Designs   42
   Becoming a Thoughtful Consumer of Research   46
Conducting Research in Schools   48
   Collecting Information on the Job   48
   Observing Children   49
   Listening to Children   53
   Interpreting Assessments   54
   Conducting Action Research   56
   Ethical Guidelines for Teacher-Researchers   57
Case Study: The Study Skills Class   58
Summary   59
Applying Concepts in Child Development   59

PART II   Foundations of Development

CHAPTER 3

Biological Beginnings   62

Case Study: Expecting Zoe   63
Genetic Foundations of Child Development   64
   Structure and Operation of Genes   64
   Formation of Reproductive Cells   66
   Genetic Basis of Individual Traits   68
   The Awakening of Genes   72
   The Blending of Heredity and Environment   73
   Acknowledging Nature and Nurture in Children's Lives   74
Prenatal Development   74
   Phases of Prenatal Growth   75
   Medical Care   78
   Supporting Parents, Protecting Babies   83
Birth of the Baby   85
   Preparation for Birth   85
   The Birth Process   86
   Complications and Interventions   88
   Enhancing Caregivers' Sensitivity to Newborn Infants   90
Case Study: Understanding Adam   92
Summary   93
Applying Concepts in Child Development   94

CHAPTER 4

Physical Development   96

Case Study: The Softball League   97
Principles of Physical Development   98

The Brain and Its Development   100
  Structures and Functions   101
  Developmental Changes   104
  Applications of Research on Brain
    Development   108
Physical Development During Childhood   110
  Infancy (Birth–Age 2)   111
  Early Childhood (Ages 2–6)   111
  Middle Childhood (Ages 6–10)   114
  Early Adolescence (Ages 10–14)   114
  Late Adolescence (Ages 14–18)   118
Physical Well-Being   119
  Eating Habits   119
  Physical Activity   125
  Rest and Sleep   128
  Health-Compromising Behaviors   131
Special Physical Needs   136
  Chronic Illness   139
  Serious Injuries and Health Hazards   137
  Physical Disabilities   139
  Promoting Physical Well-Being in All
    Children   140
Case Study: Lucy   142
Summary   142
Applying Concepts in Child Development   143

CHAPTER 5

Family, Culture, and Community   146
  Case Study: Cedric and Barbara Jennings   147
  Cradles of Child Development   148
    Family   148
    Culture   149
    Community   149
  Family Structures   152
    Mothers and Fathers   152
    Divorced Parents   153
    Single Parents   154
    Parents and Stepparents   155
    Extended Family   155
    Adoptive Parents   156
    Foster Care   156
    Other Heads of Family   157
    Accommodating Diverse Family Structures   157
  Family Processes   159
    Families' Influences on Children   160
    Children's Influences on Families   163
    Risk Factors in Families   166
    Forming Partnerships with Families   167
  Life in the Community for Children and Families   174
    Ethnicity, Culture, and Gender   174
    Community Resources   182
    Educating Children from Low-Income
      Families   184
  Case Study: Four-Year-Old Sons   186
  Summary   186
  Applying Concepts in Child Development   187

PART III   Cognitive Development

CHAPTER 6

**Cognitive Development: Piaget
and Vygotsky   190**
  Case Study: Museum Visit   191
  Piaget's Theory of Cognitive Development   192
    Key Ideas in Piaget's Theory   193
    Piaget's Stages of Cognitive Development   196
    Current Perspectives on Piaget's Theory   201
    Key Ideas in Neo-Piagetian Theories   203
    Applying the Ideas of Piaget and His Followers   205
  Vygotsky's Theory of Cognitive Development   209
    Key Ideas in Vygotsky's Theory   209
    Current Perspectives on Vygotsky's Theory   213
    Applying the Ideas of Vygotsky and His
      Followers   218
  Comparing Piagetian and Vygotskian Perspectives   221
    Common Themes   222
    Theoretical Differences   224
  Case Study: Adolescent Scientists   232
  Summary   228
  Applying Concepts in Child Development   229

CHAPTER 7

**Cognitive Development: Cognitive
Processes   232**
  Case Study: How the United States Became
    a Country   233
  Basic Cognitive Processes   234
    Key Ideas in Information Processing Theory   234
    Sensation and Perception   236
    Attention   238
    Working Memory and the Central Executive   239
    Long-Term Memory   240
    Thinking and Reasoning   243
    Facilitating Basic Cognitive Processes   244
  Metacognition and Cognitive Strategies   246
    Learning Strategies   246
    Problem-Solving Strategies   249
    Strategy Development as "Overlapping Waves"   250
    Metacognitive Awareness   250
    Self-Regulated Learning   252
    Epistemological Beliefs   253
    Interdependence of Cognitive and Metacognitive
      Processes   255
    Promoting Metacognitive and Strategic
      Development   260
  Adding a Sociocultural Element to Information
    Processing Theory   260
    Intersubjectivity   260
    Social Construction of Memory   261

Collaborative Use of Cognitive Strategies 262
*Enhancing Information Processing Through Social
Interaction* 262
Children's Construction of Theories 263
Children's Theories of the Physical World 263
Facilitating Children's Theory Construction 265
Comparing and Critiquing Contemporary Approaches to
Cognitive Development 265
Exceptionalities in Information Processing 267
Learning Disabilities 268
Attention-Deficit Hyperactivity Disorder 268
Autism 269
*Working with Children Who Have Information
Processing Difficulties* 269
Case Study: The Library Project 271
Summary 272
Applying Concepts in Child Development 273

CHAPTER 8

Intelligence 276
Case Study: Gina 277
Defining Intelligence 277
Theoretical Perspectives of Intelligence 278
Spearman's g 278
Cattell's Fluid and Crystallized Intelligences 279
Gardner's Multiple Intelligences 279
Sternberg's Triarchic Theory 281
Distributed Intelligence 282
Measuring Intelligence 283
Tests of General Intelligence 284
Specific Ability Tests 288
Dynamic Assessment 288
*Assessing the Abilities of Infants and Young
Children* 289
Effects of Heredity and Environment on
Intelligence 291
Evidence for Hereditary Influences 291
Evidence for Environmental Influences 292
*How Nature and Nurture Interact in Their
Influence on Intelligence* 295
Developmental Trends in IQ Scores 296
Group Differences in Intelligence 298
Gender Differences 298
Socioeconomic Differences 299
Ethnic and Racial Differences 299
Critique of Current Perspectives on Intelligence 301
Implications of Theories and Research on
Intelligence 302
Exceptionalities in Intelligence 304
Giftedness 305
Mental Retardation 308
Case Study: Fresh Vegetables 310
Summary 311
Applying Concepts in Child Development 312

CHAPTER 9

Language Development 314
Case Study: Mario 315
Theoretical Perspectives of Language
Development 316
Early Theories: Modeling and Reinforcement 316
Nativism 317
Information Processing Theory 318
Sociocultural Theory 319
Functionalism 320
Critiquing Theories of Language Development 320
Trends in Language Development 323
Semantic Development 323
Syntactic Development 328
Development of Listening Skills 331
Development of Speaking Skills 335
Development of Pragmatics 340
Development of Metalinguistic Awareness 344
Development of a Second Language 347
The Timing of Second-Language Learning 347
Bilingualism 347
Approaches to Teaching a Second Language 348
Diversity in Language Development 349
Gender Differences 349
Socioeconomic Differences 349
Ethnic Differences 349
Exceptionalities in Language Development 350
Speech and Communication Disorders 350
*Sensory Impairments and Language
Development* 351
Case Study: Boarding School 353
Summary 353
Applying Concepts in Child Development 354

CHAPTER 10

Development in the Content Domains 356
Case Study: Phyllis and Benjamin Jones 357
Reading 358
Emergent Literacy 358
Phonological Awareness 359
Word Recognition 359
Reading Comprehension 360
Metacognition in Reading 362
Diversity in Reading Development 364
Promoting Reading Development 366
Writing 368
Handwriting 370
Spelling 370
Syntax and Grammar 370
Composition Skills 370
Metacognition in Writing 371
Diversity in Writing Development 373
Promoting Writing Development 373

Mathematics 374
   Number Sense and Counting 374
   Mathematical Concepts and Principles 375
   Basic Arithmetic Operations 375
   More Advanced Problem-Solving Procedures 378
   Metacognition in Mathematics 379
   Diversity in Mathematics Development 379
   Promoting Development in Mathematics 382
Science 384
   Children's Theories about the Physical and
     Biological Worlds 384
   Scientific Reasoning Skills 385
   Metacognition in Science 386
   Diversity in Science Development 388
   Promoting Development in Science 388
Development in Other Content Domains 390
   History 390
   Geography 391
   Art 392
   Music 394
Using Content Area Standards to Guide Instruction 395
Case Study: Beating the Odds 397
Summary 398
Applying Concepts in Child Development 399

PART IV Social and Emotional Development

CHAPTER 11

Emotional Development 402

Case Study: Merv 403
Erikson's Theory of Psychosocial Development 404
   Lessons Learned from Life's Challenges 404
   Contemporary Perspectives on Erikson's Theory 406
Attachment 407
   Developmental Course of Children's
     Attachments 408
   Individual Differences in Children's
     Attachments 410
   Origins of Attachment Security 411
   Multiple Attachments 413
   Attachment Security and Later Development 414
   Implications of Attachment Research 415
Emotion 417
   Developmental Changes in Emotions 418
   Group Differences in Emotions 422
   Promoting Children's Emotional Development 424
   Emotional Problems in Children and
     Adolescents 426
Temperament and Personality 431
   Elements of Temperament and Personality 431
   Helping Children to Be Themselves 435

Case Study: The Girly Shirt 437
Summary 437
Applying Concepts in Child Development 438

CHAPTER 12

Development of Self and Social Understanding 440

Case Study: Kellen 441
Sense of Self 442
   Effects of Children's Sense of Self 442
   Factors Influencing Sense of Self 443
   General Trends in Children's Sense of Self 444
   Changing Nature of the Self Over Childhood and
     Adolescence 447
   Diversity in Sense of Self 451
   Enhancing Children's Sense of Self 454
Social Cognition 458
   Theory of Mind 458
   Social Information Processing 462
   Social-Cognitive Bias and Prejudice 463
   Diversity in Social Cognition 464
   Fostering the Development of Social Cognition 464
Interpersonal Behaviors 466
   Interpersonal Behaviors at Different Ages 466
   Development of Prosocial Behavior and
     Aggression 466
   Diversity in Interpersonal Behaviors 475
   Fostering Effective Interpersonal Skills 482
Case Study: Gang Mediation 482
Summary 483
Applying Concepts in Child Development 484

CHAPTER 13

Development of Motivation and Self-Regulation 486

Case Study: Derrika 487
Motivation 487
   Effects of Extrinsic Rewards and Punishments 488
   Development of Intrinsic Motivation 489
   Development of Goals 492
   Development of Attributions 495
   Diversity in Motivation 498
   Motivating Children and Adolescents 500
Self-Regulation 508
   Developmental Trends in Self-Regulation 508
   Conditions That Foster Self-Regulation 509
   Diversity in Self-Regulation 510
   Promoting Self-Regulation 510
Moral Reasoning and Behavior 515
   Developmental Trends in Morality 515
   Factors Affecting Moral Development 519
   Diversity in Moral Development 522
   Promoting Moral Development 523

Case Study: Spencer   525
Summary   526
Applying Concepts in Child Development   527

CHAPTER 14

Peers, Schools, and Society   530
Case Study: Sharing at the Zoo   531
Peers   532
    Functions of Peer Relationships   532
    Peer Acceptance   533
    Friendships   534
    Social Groups   539
    Romance and Sexuality   542
Schools   549
    The School as a Community   549
    Socialization in Schools   551
    Transitions to New Schools   553
Society   555
    Services for Children and Adolescents   555
    Television and the Interactive Technologies   561

Case Study: Aaron and Cole   566
Summary   567
Applying Concepts in Child Development   567

APPENDIX

Analyses of the Ending Case Studies   A-1

Glossary   G-1

References   R-1

Photo Credits   P-1

Name Index   N-1

Subject Index   S-1

NOTE: Every effort has been made to provide accurate and current Internet information in this book. However, the Internet and information posted on it are constantly changing, so it is inevitable that some of the Internet addresses listed in this textbook will change.

Special Features

Development and Practice

Engaging in Developmentally Appropriate Practice with Infants, Children, and Adolescents 26

Getting a Flavor for Conducting Research as a Teacher 57

Showing Sensitivity to the Needs of Newborn Infants 90

Accommodating the Physical Needs of Infants and Children 115

Accommodating the Physical Needs of Adolescents 118

Making Schools Family-Friendly 174

Accommodating Cultural and Ethnic Differences 179

Facilitating Discovery Learning 206

Scaffolding Children's Efforts at Challenging Tasks 221

Providing Appropriate Stimulation for Infants 238

Getting and Keeping Children's Attention 245

Addressing the Unique Needs of Gifted Children and Adolescents 308

Maximizing the Development of Children and Adolescents with Mental Retardation 310

Promoting Listening Skills in Young Children 334

Working with Children Who Have Speech and Communication Disorders 351

Working with Children Who Have Hearing Impairments 352

Promoting Phonological Awareness and Letter Recognition in Young Children 361

Promoting Effective Reading Comprehension Strategies 362

Offering Warm and Sensitive Care to Infants and Toddlers 416

Encouraging Social Perspective Taking 465

Teaching Social Skills 479

Helping Children Meet Their Social Goals 505

Encouraging and Supporting Students at Risk 507

Teaching Self-Management Skills 515

Easing School Transitions 555

Enhancing Students' Before- and After-School Experiences 559

Basic Developmental Issues

Illustrations in the Three Domains 11

Biological Beginnings 79

Physical Development 130

Considering Family, Culture, and Community 151

Contrasting Piaget and Vygotsky 226

Contrasting Contemporary Theories of Cognitive Development 266

Contrasting Theories of Intelligence 283

Contrasting Contemporary Theories of Language Development 321

Developmental Progressions in the Content Domains 396

Attachment and Emotional Development 430

Prosocial Behavior and Aggression 475

Contrasting Extrinsic and Intrinsic Motivation 499

Social Contexts of Child Development 565

Developmental Trends

Accomplishments and Diversity at Different Age Levels 24–25

Prenatal Development 85

Physical Development at Different Age Levels 120–121

Chronic Health Conditions in Children and Adolescents 138–139

The Family's Concerns for Children of Different Ages 172–173

Thinking and Reasoning Skills at Different Age Levels 223

Basic Information Processing Abilities at Different Age Levels 247

Cognitive Strategies and Metacognition at Different Age Levels 256–257

Intelligence at Different Age Levels 297

Language Skills at Different Age Levels 345–346

Reading at Different Age Levels 363–364

Writing at Different Age Levels 372

Mathematics at Different Age Levels 380–381

Science at Different Age Levels 387

Emotional and Personal Development at Different Age Levels 434

Sense of Self at Different Age Levels 455

Social Cognition and Interpersonal Skills at Different Age Levels 477–478

Motivation at Different Age Levels 501–502

Moral Reasoning and Behavior at Different Age Levels 520

Peer Relationships at Different Age Levels 548–549

Observation Guidelines

Learning from Children and Adolescents 51

Indicators of Health in Newborn Infants 91

Assessing Physical Development in Infancy 113

Assessing Health Behaviors of Children and Adolescents 136

Identifying Family Conditions 169

Identifying Cultural Practices and Beliefs 180

Assessing Cognitive Advancements in Infants and Toddlers 198

Assessing Reasoning Skills 207

Observing Young Children's Play Activities 222

Assessing Cognitive Processing and Metacognition 267

Seeing Intelligence in Children's Daily Behavior 305

Identifying Cultural Differences in Sociolinguistic Conventions 341

Assessing Emergent Literacy in Young Children   360
Assessing Young Children's Attachment Security   412
Assessing the Emotions of Children
   and Adolescents   419
Noticing Temperament in Infants and Toddlers   432
Observing the Social Aspects of Young Children's
   Play   467
Assessing Children's Prosocial Development   473
Recognizing Intrinsic Motivation in Children's
   Behavior   493
Noticing Children's Level of Peer Acceptance   535

Interpreting Children's Artifacts and Actions

Emma's Story   20
My Butt's Too Big   50
It's an Image Thing   53
I Went to Davis's House   55
My Baby is Real!   82
I Can See Clearly Now, My Brain is Connected   106
It Hurts So Much It's Funny!   107
How Many Can I Do Today?   127
My Dad, My Hero   162

Fish in a Boat   208
Wet Head Experiment   225
Flash Card   254
Interview with Aletha   258
Pumpkin and Bat   270
Sunflower   303
Solar System   306
Connor's Vocabulary   323
Figure of Speech   335
Pseudowriting Samples   369
Arithmetic Errors   376
Simplifying a Fraction   384
I Love Mommy   409
Comparing Self-Descriptions   446
Hermit Crab   450
Bosnia   461
Kiley's Goals   504
Tears of Pearls   514
This Is Who I Am   545
Video Games: Good or Bad?   563

CHILD DEVELOPMENT
AND EDUCATION

Making a Difference
in the Lives of Children
and Adolescents

chapter 1

Case Study: Tonya

Case Study: Tonya

The Field of Child Development

Basic Issues in Development

Theories of Child Development

Developmental Periods

From Theory to Practice

Case Study: Latisha

Summary

Applying Concepts in Child Development

When Mary Renck Jalongo thinks back to her years as a novice teacher, one student often comes to mind:

Not only was she big for her age, she was older than anyone else in my first-grade class because she had been retained in kindergarten. Her name was Tonya and she put my patience, my professionalism, and my decision making on trial throughout my second year of teaching. Tonya would boss and bully the other children, pilfer items from their desks, or talk them into uneven "trades."

Matters worsened when I received a hostile note from a parent. It read, "This is the fourth time that Tommy's snack cake has been taken from his lunch. What are you going to do about it?"

What I did was to launch an investigation. First, I asked if anyone else was missing items from lunchboxes and discovered that many other children had been affected. Next, I tried to get someone to confess—not in the way that *my* teachers had done it, by sitting in the room until the guilty party or an informant cracked, but simply by asking the perpetrator to leave a note in my classroom mailbox. My classroom was antiquated, but it included an enclosed hallway, now equipped with coat racks and shelves that led to a restroom. Apparently, while I was preoccupied teaching my lessons, a child was stealing food. Three days later, several other children reported that they had seen Tonya "messing around people's lunchboxes." I asked her, but she denied it. At recess, I looked in her desk and found it littered with empty food wrappers. Then Tonya and I discussed it again in private and examined the evidence.

I consulted my principal about what to do. He suggested that I punish her severely; a month without recess seemed warranted, he said. I thought it might be better to call her mother, but they had no telephone and the principal assured me that, based on her failure to attend previous school functions, Tonya's mother would not come to school. Then I said I would write a note and set up a home visit. He strongly advised against that, telling me that Tonya's mother had a disease, that the house was a mess, and that she had a live-in boyfriend.

All these things were true, but I understand them differently now. Tonya's mother had lupus and was at a debilitating stage of the disease that prevented her from working, much less maintaining a spotless home. Tonya's family now consisted of mother, unofficial stepfather (also permanently disabled), and a three-year-old brother. They lived on a fixed income, and Tonya qualified for free lunches.

As a first-year teacher [at this school], I was reluctant to go against the principal's wishes, but I did draw the line at harsh punishment. When I asked Tonya *why* she took things from the other children's lunches, she simply said, "'Cause I was hungry." I asked her if she ate breakfast in the morning, and she said, "No. I have to take care of my little brother before I go to school." I asked her if having breakfast might solve the problem and she said, "Yes. My aunt would help." And so, my first big teaching problem was solved by an eight-year-old when instead of foraging for food each morning, Tonya and her brother walked down the block to her unmarried aunt's house before school and ate breakfast.

There was still the matter of repairing Tonya's damaged reputation with the other children, who had accumulated a variety of negative experiences with her and had labeled her as a thief. I stood with my arms around Tonya's shoulder in front of the class and announced that Tonya had agreed not to take things anymore, that she could be trusted, and that all was well.

Two weeks later, a child's candy bar was reported missing, and the class was quick to accuse Tonya. I took her aside and inquired about the missing candy bar. "No," she said firmly, "I didn't eat it." As I defended Tonya's innocence to her peers, I noticed how Tonya, the child who had learned to slouch to conceal her size, sat up tall and proud in her seat.

(continued)

I must confess that I was wondering if Tonya might be lying when Kendra, the child who reported the stolen candy bar, said she was ill and wanted to go home. Then, with a candor only possible in a young child, Kendra said, "I have a stomachache, and you want to know why? Because I just remembered that *I* ate my candy bar on the bus this morning." (Jalongo, Isenberg, & Gerbracht, 1995, pp. 114–116)[a]

[a]From *Teachers' Stories: From Personal Narrative to Professional Insight* (pp. 114–116), by M. R. Jalongo, J. P. Isenberg, & G. Gerbracht, 1995, San Francisco: Jossey-Bass. Copyright © 1995 by Jossey-Bass, Inc. Adapted by permission of John Wiley & Sons, Inc.

ary Jalongo, the teacher in the opening case study, understood that a child's development is enhanced with age-appropriate instruction and sensitive, loving care. By encouraging Tonya and her brother to eat breakfast with their aunt, Ms. Jalongo helped satisfy Tonya's physical needs and also paved the way for closer ties to extended family. By repairing Tonya's damaged reputation among the other children, Ms. Jalongo helped Tonya to earn their acceptance. Feeling comfortable physically and secure emotionally, Tonya was better prepared to tackle academic assignments and to develop a healthy sense of who she was and how she fit into the world around her. Because her actions were guided by knowledge of child development, Ms. Jalongo was able to make a difference in Tonya's life. This chapter introduces you to the field of child development, preparing you to make increasingly deep insights into the needs of children and adolescents.

The Field of Child Development

The study of human development helps us to understand how human beings change from the time of conception, through maturation into adulthood, and on into old age and death. This book covers the early part of the human journey—beginning at conception and including birth, infancy, childhood, and adolescence. The field of **child development** seeks to identify and explain persistent, cumulative, and progressive changes in the physical, cognitive, and social-emotional development of children and adolescents.

As you will learn throughout this book, a child's developmental journey is guided by three factors:

- *Nature*—the genetic inheritance of that particular child
- *Nurture*—the influence of the environment in which the child lives
- *The child's own activity*—what the child does, the choices and efforts that he or she makes

As you will also discover in your study, development includes changes that are common to most children and adolescents as well as those that are specific to particular individuals. At times, we will talk about changes that nearly everyone undergoes, such as acquiring complex language skills and developing consideration for other people's feelings. At other times, we will discuss changes that differ considerably among youngsters. For example, over time, some children spontaneously develop effective study skills, but others gain little insight into learning strategies without explicit instruction.

To portray the many factors that contribute to children's growth, scholars of child development draw from an array of academic disciplines. In this book, our descriptions of children's development draw on research primarily in psychology but also in biology, sociology, anthropology, and applied fields, such as early intervention, education, child and family studies, juvenile justice, counseling, social work, and medicine.

Our primary goal in this book is to help you to support healthy, optimal development in children and adolescents. We pursue this goal by focusing on two specific objectives. First,

child development
Study of the persistent, cumulative, and progressive changes in the physical, cognitive, and social-emotional development of children and adolescents.

we want you to learn how children and adolescents think, feel, and act at various ages. This information can help you understand the children and adolescents with whom you work. Second, we want you to be able to apply what you learn in your classroom, school, and community. Child development is an applied field that has a wealth of implications. This field can help you to define suitable instructional goals, select beneficial teaching methods, and communicate effectively with children. And, as you will learn, your guidance will be most useful when it is in harmony with the broad spectrum of children's needs and with their individual physical, intellectual, and social-emotional abilities.

Three Developmental Domains

The study of child development is organized into three *domains*, or broad areas of study: physical development, cognitive development, and social-emotional development. **Physical development** is, of course, concerned with the physical changes of the body and the brain. It includes such things as genetics, a fetus's growth in the mother's womb, birth, brain development, and the acquisition of such motor skills as throwing a ball and using scissors. It also encompasses behaviors that promote and impede health and environmental factors that influence physical growth. **Cognitive development** refers to the changes that occur in children's reasoning, concepts, memory, and language—changes that are cultivated by children's experiences in families, schools, and communities. **Social-emotional development** includes changes in emotions, self-concept, motivation, social relationships, and moral reasoning and behavior—advancements that depend in part on children's many social experiences with other people.

Although the three domains may appear to be independent areas, they are in fact closely interrelated. For example, physical growth in the brain allows cognitive advancements to take place. An increase in the ability to look at situations from multiple perspectives (a cognitive ability) enhances social skills. Children always develop as integrated wholes, never as fragmented beings. Thus, in their everyday work with children, educators often address more than one domain at a time. For instance, a preschool teacher might read a book about holidays to children, facilitating their language and literacy development, and then ask children to march to holiday music, addressing needs for physical activity and emotional expression.

Effects of Context on Development

All areas of development depend on the **context** of children's lives—children's experiences in families, schools, neighborhoods, cultural and ethnic groups, and society at large. Environmental factors such as family income level, religious affiliation, popular media, and even historical events influence children's development. Child development research has shown, for example, that some sort of "family" or other cluster of close, caring relationships is a critical condition for optimal development. In the opening case, we learned a few things about Tonya's family—that Tonya assumed responsibilities beyond her years in caring for her younger brother, that her mother was physically unable to give her much support, and that her aunt was able to provide the physical (and perhaps psychological) nurturance she so desperately needed.

Schools, too, play a significant role in development, not only by fostering cognitive and academic skills but also by communicating messages about children's abilities and worth and by providing an arena in which children can practice social skills. For example, while attending school, Tonya received a great many messages (often unflattering ones) about her likability and trustworthiness, and her limited social experiences led her to bully classmates rather than to cooperate with them. Fortunately, Ms. Jalongo remedied the situation and arranged for her to be seen—and to see herself—in a positive light.

In preparing to teach and work with children, you are about to become a vital part of the developmental context of children and adolescents. Your potential role in that context will be strengthened by a thorough foundation in child development. As you can see in Figure 1-1, this book provides such a foundation in its coverage of the three areas of development (physical, cognitive, and social-emotional domains), the contexts in which children and adolescents grow, and the research methods that reveal the nature of youngsters' developmental journeys.

Study Guide and Reader
To see how a program can address the broad spectrum of children's needs, look at the description of Head Start learning objectives in Supplementary Reading 1-1.

physical development
Physical and brain growth and age-related changes in motor skills.

cognitive development
Systematic changes in reasoning, concepts, memory, and language.

social-emotional development
Systematic changes in emotions, self-concept, motivation, social relationships, and moral reasoning and behavior.

context
The broad social environments, including family, schools and community services, neighborhoods, culture, ethnicity, and society at large, that influence children's development.

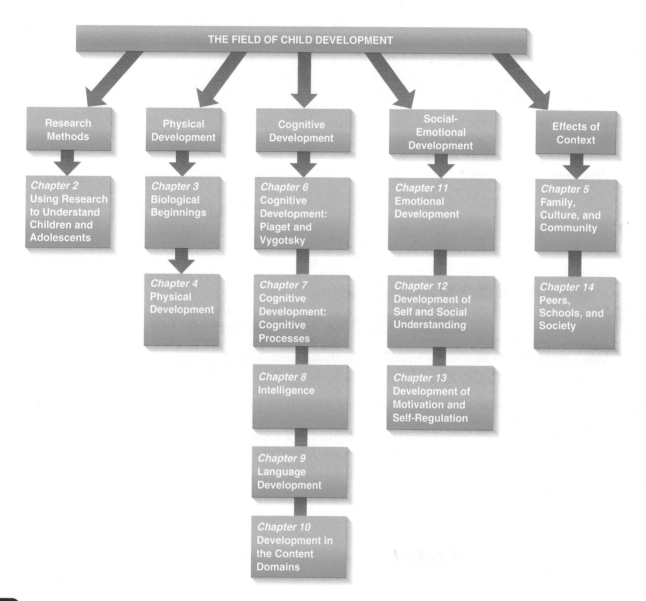

Figure 1-1

Overview of the book

Basic Issues in Development

In their attempts to explain the changes that take place during childhood, developmental theorists have grappled with, but not yet resolved, three key issues. First, they wonder how strongly heredity and environment influence development. Second, they speculate about the developmental paths that are true for everyone or, conversely, unique to individuals. Third, they debate about the developmental changes that can be characterized as major transformations or, alternatively, as a series of gradual trends. Let's now look more closely at these three issues, which are referred to as questions of (a) nature and nurture, (b) universality and diversity, and (c) qualitative and quantitative change.

Nature and Nurture

In the study of development, **nature** refers to the inherited (genetic) characteristics and tendencies that influence development. Some inherited characteristics appear in virtually everyone. For instance, almost all children have the capacity to learn to walk, understand language, imitate others, use simple tools, and draw inferences about how other people view the world. Thus all children have a set of universal human genes that, when coupled with a reasonable environment, permit them to develop as reasonably capable members of the human species.

Other kinds of genes create differences among people. Children's stature, eye color, and facial appearance are largely determined by genes. Children's **temperament**—their charac-

nature
Inherited characteristics and tendencies that affect development.

temperament
A child's characteristic ways of responding to emotional events, novel stimuli, and personal impulses.

teristic ways of responding to emotional events, novel stimuli, and their own impulses—seems to be in part affected by their individual genetic makeup (Rothbart, Ahadi, & Evans, 2000; D. C. Rowe, Almeida, & Jacobson, 1999). Similarly, being slow or quick to learn from instruction and everyday experiences has some genetic basis (Petrill & Wilkerson, 2000; Plomin, 1989).

Inherited characteristics and tendencies are not always evident at birth. Many physical features emerge gradually through the process of **maturation,** the genetically guided changes that occur over the course of development. Environmental support, such as food, reasonably safe and toxin-free surroundings, and responsive care from others, is necessary for maturation to take place; nature never works alone.

Thus nature's partner is **nurture,** the environmental conditions that influence development. Children's experiences in the environment affect all aspects of their being, from the health of their bodies to the curiosity of their minds. Nurture affects children's development through multiple channels: physically through nutrition, activity, and stress; intellectually through informal experiences and formal instruction; and socially through adult role models and peer relationships. With good environmental support, children thrive. Unfortunately, the conditions of nurture are *not* always nurturing. For example, children who grow up in an abusive family must look outside the family for stable, affectionate care.

Historically, many theorists saw nature and nurture as separate and rival factors. Some theorists believed that biological factors are ultimately responsible for growth. Other theorists assumed that children become whatever the environment shapes them to be. Increasingly, developmental theorists have come to realize that nature and nurture are both important and that they intermesh dynamically in the lives of children. Consider these principles of how nature and nurture exert separate and combined effects:

● *The relative effects of heredity and environment vary for different areas of development.* Some abilities are strongly influenced by genetically controlled systems in the brain. For example, the ability to distinguish among speech sounds develops without training and under a wide range of environmental conditions (Flavell, 1994; Gallistel, Brown, Carey, Gelman, & Keil, 1991). In contrast, abilities in traditional school subject areas (e.g., reading, geography) and advanced artistic and physical skills (e.g., playing the piano, playing competitive soccer) rest heavily on instruction and practice (Gardner, Torff, & Hatch, 1996; Olson, 1994; R. Watson, 1996).

● *Inherited tendencies make children more or less responsive to particular environmental influences.* Because of their genetic makeup, some children are easily affected by certain conditions in the environment, whereas others are less affected (Rutter, 1997). For example, children who are, by nature, inhibited may be quite shy around other people if they have few social contacts. If their parents and teachers encourage them to make friends, however, they may become more socially outgoing (Arcus, 1991; J. Kagan, 1998). In contrast, children who have more extroverted temperaments may be sociable regardless of the environment in which they grow up: They will persistently search for peers with whom they can talk, laugh, and spend time.

● *Environment may play a greater role in development when environmental conditions are extreme rather than moderate.* When youngsters have experiences typical for their culture and age-group, heredity often plays a strong role in their individual characteristics. Thus, when children grow up with adequate nutrition, a warm and stable home environment, and appropriate educational experiences, heredity affects how quickly and thoroughly they acquire new skills. But when they have experiences that are quite unusual—for instance, when they experience extreme deprivation—the influence of environment outweighs that of heredity (D. C. Rowe, Almeida, & Jacobson, 1999). For example, when children grow up deprived of adequate nutrition and stimulation, they may fail to develop advanced intellectual skills, even though they had the potential for such development when they were born (Plomin & Petrill, 1997; D. C. Rowe, Jacobson, & Van den Oord, 1999). Similarly, when malnourished, children tend to remain short in stature regardless of their genetic potential to be tall (J. S. Kagan, 1969).

● *Timing of environmental exposure matters.* When children are changing rapidly in any area, they are especially prone to influence by the environment. For example, early in a mother's pregnancy, her use of certain drugs may damage the quickly growing organs and

Connecting Concepts ⎯⎯⎯⎯⎯⎯⎯
Maturational changes in children's bodies and motor skills are discussed in Chapter 4.

Expert coaching (nurture) can enhance children's natural abilities (nature).

maturation
Genetically guided changes that occur over the course of development.

nurture
Environmental conditions that affect development.

limbs of the developing fetus. Just prior to birth, exposure to the same drugs may adversely affect the baby's brain, which at that point is forming the connections that will permit survival and the ability to learn in the outside world.

In a few cases environmental stimulation *must* occur during a particular period for an emerging ability to become functional (Blakemore, 1976; Hubel & Wiesel, 1965). In such cases there is a *critical period* for stimulation. For example, at birth, certain areas of the brain are tentatively reserved for processing visual patterns—lines, shapes, contours, depth, and so forth. In virtually all cases, infants do encounter adequate stimulation to preserve these brain circuits. However, when cataracts are present at birth and not removed for a few years, a child's vision is obstructed, and areas of the brain that otherwise would be devoted to vision lose some of this capacity (Bruer, 1999).

In many and probably most other developmental areas, however, children may be most receptive to a certain type of stimulation at one point in their lives but be able to benefit from it to some degree later as well. Tonya, in the introductory case study, may have encountered only limited exposure to language as a result of her mother's weakened condition. Immersed later in a rich verbal environment, Tonya would have a second chance to expand her verbal talents. Thus educational experiences at a later time can often make up for experiences missed at an earlier period (Bruer, 1999). Many theorists use the term **sensitive period** (rather than *critical period*) when referring to such a long time frame of heightened sensitivity to particular environmental experiences.

● *Children's natural tendencies affect their environment.* In addition to being affected by nature and nurture, children's own behaviors influence their growth. Youngsters make many choices, seek out information, and, over time, refine their ideas (Flavell, 1994; Piaget, 1985). For example, children often request information ("What *cooperate* mean, Mommy?") and experiences ("Uncle Kevin, can I play on your computer?"). Children even help create environments that exacerbate their genetic tendencies. For example, children with irritable dispositions might pick fights and provoke others to lash back at them, creating a more aggressive climate in which to grow.

As children get older, they become increasingly able to seek stimulation that suits their tendencies. For example, imagine that Marissa has an inherited talent for verbal skills—learning vocabulary, comprehending stories, and so on. As a baby, she relies on her parents to talk to her. As a toddler, she asks her parents for particular kinds of stimulation ("Read book, Daddy!"). In elementary school she reads to herself from books supplied by her teachers. As a teenager, she takes the bus to the library and selects her own books. Marissa's experience would suggest that genetic tendencies become more powerful as children grow older—an expectation that is in fact consistent with genetic research (Scarr & McCartney, 1983).

Universality and Diversity

Developmental changes that occur in just about everyone are said to reflect a certain degree of **universality.** For instance, unless physical disabilities are present, all young children learn to sit, walk, and run, almost invariably in that order. Other developmental changes are highly individual, reflecting **diversity.** As an illustration, the first words of some children are social gestures such as "bye-bye," and only later do these children add words for objects and actions. Other children initially learn words for objects and physical properties and later try social expressions.

Theorists differ in their beliefs that developmental accomplishments are universal among all human beings or unique to particular individuals. Some propose that maturation and shared genes create universality in development (e.g., Gesell, 1928). They point out that despite widely varying environments, virtually all human beings acquire fundamental motor skills, proficiency in language, the ability to inhibit immediate impulses, and so on. Certain consistencies in children's environments provide an additional route to universality. The developmental psychologist Jean Piaget believed that children acquire similar ways of thinking because they are all apt to encounter many similar phenomena. In all corners of the world, children observe that objects always fall down rather than up and that people usually get angry when someone intentionally hurts them.

Yet other theorists have been impressed by diversity in child development (e.g., Baltes, Reese, & Lipsitt, 1980; R. M. Lerner, 1989). Many of the theorists who emphasize diversity

———————— Connecting Concepts

Chapter 3 examines sensitive periods during prenatal development in the formation of brain and body parts. Chapter 9 presents evidence for sensitive periods in certain aspects of language development.

Although some developmental states are universal, others (e.g., tastes in clothing and music) reflect diversity in children's talents, temperaments, interests, relationships, and experiences. Art by Ricco, age 13.

sensitive period
A period in development when certain environmental experiences have a more pronounced influence than is true at other times.

universality
In a particular aspect of human development, the commonalities seen in the way virtually all individuals progress.

diversity
In a particular aspect of human development, the varied ways different individuals progress.

view environment (nurture) as weighing heavily in how we develop. They propose that factors as global as the historical period of one's childhood and as personal as one's family relationships help to shape how a person develops. Some of these theorists also see *culture as* a significant source of diversity: Children differ in the competencies they acquire based on the particular tools, communication systems, and values that pervade their lives (Rogoff, 1990; Wertsch & Tulviste, 1994).

Earlier we mentioned that the relative influences of nature and nurture vary from one area of development to another. The same is true for universality and diversity. For instance, development tends to be more universal in some aspects of physical development, such as the sequences in which puberty unfolds. Diversity tends to be more prevalent in other areas, such as in many aspects of cognitive and social-emotional development. Yet there is always *some* diversity, even in physical development. Obviously, children vary in height, weight, and skin color, and some are born with physical disabilities or become injured. Throughout the book you will find instances of developmental universality, but just as often you will see divergences among developmental pathways.

Teachers need to keep in mind not only typical age trends but also the diversity in children's abilities and developmental progress.

Qualitative and Quantitative Change

Sometimes development reflects dramatic changes in the essence or underlying structure of a characteristic. Such major reorganizations are called **qualitative changes.** For instance, when children learn to run, they propel their bodies forward in a way that is distinctly different from walking—they are not simply moving faster. When they begin to talk in two-word sentences rather than with single words, they are, for the first time, using rudimentary forms of grammar. But not all development involves dramatic change. In fact, development frequently occurs as a gradual progression, or *trend,* with many small additions to behaviors and thought processes. These progressions are called **quantitative changes.** For example, children grow taller gradually over time, and with both age and experience they slowly learn about such diverse realms as the animal kingdom and society's rules for showing courtesy.

Stage theories.   Theorists who emphasize qualitative changes use the term **stage** to refer to a period of development characterized by a particular way of behaving or thinking. According to a **stage theory** of development, individuals progress through a series of stages that are qualitatively different from one another.[1] Stage theories often assume that children act and reason in one stage at a time; during periods of transition, children waiver between two stages until they become proficient at the next level.

Most stage theories are *hierarchical.* In other words, each stage is seen as providing the essential foundation for stages that follow. Hierarchical stage theories tend to focus on a single dimension of development. For example, after observing children in a wide variety of logical tasks and thought-provoking situations, Jean Piaget proposed a stage theory to describe the development of logical thinking and reasoning. His observations led him to conclude that as infants, children interact with the world primarily through trial-and-error behavior. As children mature, they begin to represent, symbolically "manipulate," and make predictions about the world in their minds. They know, for example, that a rubber ball will bounce when they drop it on a wooden floor. Later they begin to derive logical deductions about concrete, real-world objects and situations. And once they reach adolescence, they become capable of thinking systematically about abstract ideas—for instance, by thinking about the unseen physical factors (e.g., *momentum, gravity*) influencing a ball's bounce. At each stage, Piaget suggested, children subsume their earlier thinking processes into more advanced, qualitatively different ones.

Connecting Concepts —————
Piaget's stages are described in Chapter 6.

qualitative change
Relatively dramatic developmental change that reflects considerable reorganization or modification of functioning.

quantitative change
Developmental change that involves a series of minor, trendlike modifications.

stage
A period of development characterized by a qualitatively distinct way of behaving or thinking.

stage theory
Theory that describes development as involving a series of qualitatively distinct changes.

---

[1] Note that developmentalists use the term *stage* in a somewhat narrower way than other people use it in everyday speech. Parents and other adults often make comments like "He's at the terrible twos stage" or "She's at that stage when she really worries about what her friends think." Such comments reflect the idea that children are behaving typically for their age-group, but they don't necessarily imply that a qualitative change has taken place.

——————— Connecting Concepts
Erikson's stages are described in
Chapter 11.

Another eminent stage theorist, Erik Erikson, focused on a set of primary developmental tasks that individuals face as they grow. During their childhood years, youngsters learn first to trust others and then to act self-sufficiently. In their adolescent and adult years, people form *identities* that define who they are and later form intimate relationships with others. In Erikson's theory, stages are "soft": People do not fully replace earlier developments with new modes of thinking (Kohlberg, Levine, & Hewer, 1983). Instead, earlier struggles persist—and sometimes intrude into—new challenges. For example, a young adult who has failed to develop a clear identity may enter romantic relationships with considerable confusion (J. Kroger, 2003).

Many stage theories also assume *universal* progressions: All children purportedly go through the same sequence of changes, although the ages at which individual children pass through each stage vary according to environmental support. Piaget was a strong believer in universal progressions in children's thinking. In contrast, Erikson believed that people deal with and resolve the social-emotional dilemmas in their lives in distinctly individual ways.

Over the years, developmental psychologists have offered a variety of stage theories to explain children's development. However, research does not entirely support the idea that young people proceed through one stage at a time or that they always move in the same direction (e.g., Ceci & Roazzi, 1994; Kurtines & Gewirtz, 1991; Metz, 1995). For example, a 9-year-old girl may show an advanced ability to plan ahead while playing chess (her hobby) but may have difficulty planning ahead while writing a complex essay (an unfamiliar activity). Nor do stage progressions always appear to be universal across cultures and educational contexts (e.g., Glick, 1975; Triandis, 1995). For example, youngsters raised in vastly different cultures often learn to think in significantly different ways (Rogoff, 2003). Given these and other research findings, few contemporary developmental theorists support strict versions of stage theories (Parke, Ornstein, Rieser, & Zahn-Waxler, 1994).

Many theorists now believe that qualitative changes do exist—not as inevitable, universal, and hierarchical patterns—but rather as dynamic states of thinking and acting that evolve as children mature and try new things. It is obvious, for example, that the actions of adolescents differ consistently from those of 2-year-old children. Fifteen-year-olds are not simply taller and more knowledgeable about the world; they go about their day-to-day living in qualitatively different ways. Maturation-based developments, such as the brain's increases in memory capacity, plus ever-expanding knowledge and experience, permit both gradual and occasionally dramatic changes in thinking and behaving (Case & Okamoto, 1996; Flavell, 1994).

Applying Basic Lessons from Child Development

As you read this book, you will find that the three basic developmental issues surface periodically within individual chapters. Nature and nurture, universality and diversity, and qualitative and quantitative change are also presented in Basic Developmental Issues tables in each chapter. The first of these tables, "Illustrations in the Three Domains," provides examples of how the basic developmental issues are reflected in the domains of physical, cognitive, and social-emotional development.

Much of developmental research deals with these three basic issues. Keeping them in mind as you learn about how children and adolescents progress in specific domains will help you understand development more fully. But these big ideas also have several practical implications for your teaching and working with children:

● *To best help children, keep in mind the influences of both nature and nurture on their growth and development.* A child's fate is never sealed—it always depends on care from adults and the child's own efforts. Again and again, nurture matters. But so does nature. How children respond to instruction and guidance depends, in part, on their genetic endowment. So when children show unusual talents, foster these talents. And when children's natural inclinations become stumbling blocks to positive growth, provide extra support.

● *To better understand children's capabilities and needs, become familiar with general developmental trends and common variations.* General trends at a particular age level affect the daily work of educators. For example, a caregiver familiar with Erikson's stages understands that an infant girl new to his care will take time to trust him—in the meantime, she

BASIC DEVELOPMENTAL ISSUES	Illustrations in the Three Domains		
Issue	**Physical Development**	**Cognitive Development**	**Social-Emotional Development**
Nature and Nurture	Nature guides the order and timing in which specific parts of the brain are formed. Genetic factors also determine certain individual dispositions, such as a tendency toward thinness or a susceptibility to diabetes. All growth depends on nurture. The effects of nutrition on health and the impact of training on athletic performance show that nurture can actively direct the course of development (Chapters 3 and 4).	Some aspects of intelligence, learning, and language seem to be genetically based. However, many contemporary theorists emphasize the significance of environmental influences (nurture), such as informal learning experiences, adult modeling and mentoring, family relationships, and formal schooling (Chapters 5, 6, 7, 8, 9, and 10).	Individual differences in temperament appear to be partly controlled by heredity (nature). Environmental influences (nurture) are evident in the development of self-esteem. Becoming aggressive, on the one hand, or helpful and empathic, on the other, occurs due to the combined influences of nature and nurture (Chapters 11 and 12).
Universality and Diversity	The emergence of key physical features (e.g., gender-specific characteristics appearing during puberty) is universal. Diversity is evident in the ages at which children and adolescents undergo key physical developments, as well as in their general state of physical health (Chapter 4).	The basic components of human language (e.g., an ability to combine words using grammar) and learning (e.g., the mechanisms that allow new information to be compared to previous experiences) are universal. Diversity is evident in the fact that some children have more effective ways of learning and remembering academic information than do others (Chapters 7, 8, and 9).	The need for peer affiliation represents a universal aspect of development in children and adolescents. However, there are considerable individual differences in the kinds of social groups that young people join (Chapter 14).
Qualitative and Quantitative Change	Some aspects of physical development (e.g., transformations in prenatal development and at puberty) reflect dramatic qualitative change. Most of the time, however, physical development occurs gradually as a result of many small changes (e.g., young children slowly grow taller) (Chapters 3 and 4).	Children's logical reasoning skills show some qualitative change; for instance, children acquire new, more sophisticated ways of solving problems. Quantitative change occurs as children gradually gain knowledge in various academic disciplines (Chapters 6, 7, and 10).	Some evidence suggests that with appropriate social experience, children's understanding of morality undergoes qualitative change, often in conjunction with changes in logical reasoning ability. In a more quantitative manner, children gradually come to understand how other people's minds work and discover that others' knowledge, beliefs, and desires may be different from their own (Chapters 12 and 13).

need lots of reassurance. Likewise, an elementary teacher familiar with Piaget's theory knows that children have difficulty with abstract ideas and so arranges many concrete, hands-on experiences when teaching academic concepts. Both the infant caregiver and the elementary teacher are effectively applying an understanding of children's typical age-related needs. At the same time, many variations in developmental pathways—the timing, appearance, and nature of changes—are normal and to be expected. By growing familiar with the developmental diversity among children, you can learn to give individual youngsters the specific support they need.

● *When assessing children's development, look for both quantitative and qualitative changes.* As you teach children academic concepts, the benefits of physical activity, ways to get along with peers, and so on, you might find that children often learn information in a *quantitative* fashion. That is, they soak up facts and skills rapidly and incrementally. You can support such learning by exposing children to rich and varied resources. On other occasions children might need to revamp their basic ways of thinking before they can progress. Much of the momentum for *qualitative* change comes from the child, but teachers and other professionals can support new ways of thinking by exposing children to increasingly sophisticated reasoning. For example, a class discussion about school rules can prompt children to realize that breaking rules not only leads to punishment but also upsets other people. With this new insight, many children become more considerate of others.

As you work with children, you will most certainly marvel at the complex ways these three basic developmental issues manifest themselves. Such issues have also intrigued the scholars who have proposed theoretical models of children's development. We turn now to the most influential of these theories.

Theories of Child Development

To guide their hypotheses and questions, research methods, and interpretations of data, developmental scholars construct **theories,** organized systems of principles and explanations. Seven theoretical approaches have dominated academic discussions of child development since the field emerged. We examine them here, one by one, and then refer to them selectively in later chapters as they become relevant to particular topics.

Biological Theories

Biological theories focus on how genetics and physiology contribute to development. Historically, biological theorists have emphasized *maturation* of children's bodies and motor abilities (Gesell, 1928). According to this perspective, children walk when they are physiologically ready, and puberty begins when a biological clock triggers the appropriate hormones. The timing of such changes varies somewhat among children, but the sequence of changes is virtually universal.

The most important contribution of biological theories has been to uncover children's natural tendencies. Biological scholars argue that many childhood tendencies have a genetic basis. When genes increase children's chances for survival, these genes are passed on to the next generation. As a result, characteristics of children reflect adaptations to environments our ancestors inhabited eons ago. For example, our ancestors' children had to be prepared to form bonds with protective caregivers, or they would not survive their early years. They also had to prefer certain flavors (e.g., the sweet taste of mother's milk and fresh berries) over others (e.g., the taste of contaminated water and that of spoiled meat) so they would not eat things that could poison them. When they grew older and could no longer be carried, children had to be strong and fast enough to outrun predators and their parents' enemies.

A limitation of early biological perspectives was that they neglected the effects of children's experiences on development. Although early biological theorists believed that the environment played an evolutionary role in selecting the specific traits that were passed on in the human species, they assumed that nurture, except under extreme conditions such as malnutrition, did not play a decisive role in an individual child's development. Contemporary biological theorists, however, realize that genes are flexible instructions that blend with environmental experiences to affect the child. Thus many biological perspectives are now more balanced in their regard for nature, nurture, and children's activity (Bjorklund, 2003).

Two key principles that a practitioner can take away from biological theories are that (a) children's maturational levels impose limits on their abilities and interests and (b) children's physiological states protect their survival and prepare them for responsible adult roles. Understanding the natural inclinations of children and adolescents can help teachers and other practitioners better guide young people and structure appropriate activities for them. For example, if you accept the idea that preschool children are predisposed to tumble around, you will understand that they need safe playground equipment. Similarly, if you know that school-age children are naturally drawn to the work of adults, you will be more likely to provide them with opportunities to participate in authentic adultlike tasks.

Behaviorism and Social Learning Theories

Whereas biological theorists see heredity (nature) as the principal driving force behind development, advocates of **behaviorism and social learning theories** propose that developmental change is almost exclusively due to environmental influences (nurture). Conducting research with humans and other species (e.g., dogs, rats, pigeons), these theorists have shown that many behaviors can be modified through environmental stimuli. As a proponent of a perspective known as *behaviorism,* B. F. Skinner suggested that children actively "work" for rewards such as food, praise, or physical contact, and tend to avoid behaviors that lead to punishment. Other behavioral theorists have revealed how

---

Connecting Concepts
Typical physical developments are described in Chapters 3 and 4.

---

theory
Organized system of principles and explanations regarding a particular phenomenon.

biological theory
Theoretical perspective that emphasizes genetic factors and physiological structures and functions of the body and brain.

behaviorism and social learning theory
Theoretical perspective that focuses on environmental stimuli and learning processes that lead to behavioral change.

children learn emotional responses (e.g., fear of dogs) based on their experiences (e.g., receiving a painful dog bite).

The primary contribution of behaviorism has been to identify environmental influences on children's behavior. Such a view has important practical applications, particularly when children have learned a maladaptive behavior—for example, when a toddler bites others or a second grader feels terrified when he arrives at school and has to separate from his parents.

A serious limitation of behaviorism is that it focuses exclusively on children's visible, external behaviors, with little consideration for how internal thought processes might influence those behaviors. In contrast, *social learning theorists* view children's beliefs and goals as crucial influences on children's actions. Researchers and theorists in the social learning tradition have shown that behavior is not just a response to a reward or punishment in the immediate environment. Children can anticipate the consequences of their actions and choose their behaviors accordingly, whether or not they have ever been rewarded or punished for particular actions. Moreover, children (and adults as well) learn a great deal by observing what other people do and what consequences (e.g., rewards and punishments) follow those behaviors. Social learning theorists such as Albert Bandura have integrated both behaviorist principles and thought processes in a perspective known as *social cognitive theory*. You will come across Bandura's ideas in later discussions of children's sense of self, interpersonal behaviors, and motivation.

A wide range of practical applications have been derived from behaviorism and social learning theory, and you will encounter many of them as you read this book. For now, let's look at three overarching principles. First, rewards and punishments do influence children's actions and feelings. Ms. Jalongo, in the opening case study, realized that punishing Tonya harshly for stealing would do Tonya more harm than good. Second, children's actions are affected by what they see others doing. For example, children often imitate others' behaviors—whether they be the hoop shots of a famous basketball player or a teacher's condescending actions toward the school custodian. And third, social cognitive theory helps explain children's motivation to complete schoolwork and treat peers kindly in the absence of adult supervision. In later chapters we identify helpful applications of behavioral principles for guiding and motivating children and adolescents.

Psychodynamic Theories

Psychodynamic theories focus on the interaction between certain inborn traits and the environment. These theories assert that early experiences play a critical role in later characteristics and behavior. They typically focus on social and personality development and, often, on abnormal development.

Sigmund Freud, the earliest psychodynamic theorist, argued that young children continually find themselves embroiled in internal conflicts between sexual and aggressive impulses, on the one hand, and desires to gain approval from parents and society, on the other. As an outgrowth of their internal motives and their social experiences in families, children progress through a series of qualitatively distinct stages, ideally learning to channel their impulses in socially appropriate ways. Another psychodynamic theorist, Erik Erikson, believed that people grow when they resolve their internal struggles. Compared to Freud, Erikson focused less on sexual and aggressive impulses and more on other parts of the developing personality, such as desires to feel competent and sure of one's own identity.

Psychodynamic perspectives have made a lasting contribution by highlighting the significance of children's social-emotional needs. Several psychodynamic ideas remain influential today: Early social experiences can direct later development; forceful and repeated efforts may be needed to dislodge children from an unhealthy path; and children wrestle with particular issues during certain phases of life.

A significant weakness of psychodynamic theories has been the difficulty of supporting claims with research data. For one thing, it is difficult to verify what internal conflicts a particular person might have, in part because many of our conflicts are presumed to be subconscious. If we ourselves are not consciously aware of a conflict, we are unlikely to talk about that conflict with another person. In addition, generalizations cannot necessarily be made from the studies that the theorists themselves conducted. For example, Freud developed his ideas from in-depth interviews with troubled adults—individuals whose childhoods did not necessarily reflect typical developmental pathways. Critics point out that desires to

---

Connecting Concepts ——————
You will read about children's sense of self and interpersonal behaviors in Chapter 12 and about their motivation in Chapter 13.

Connecting Concepts ——————
Children's emotional development is examined in Chapter 11.

psychodynamic theory
Theoretical perspective that focuses on how early experiences and internal conflicts affect social and personality development.

restrain sexual urges (Freud's theory) and define one's personal identity (Erikson's theory) may be principal motives for some people but not others. Finally, research has refuted several ideas central to psychoanalytical perspectives. For example, Freud recommended that children perform mildly aggressive acts as a way to release inborn aggressive tendencies, yet research indicates that encouraging such acts actually *increases* aggressive behavior (A. P. Goldstein, 1999; Mallick & McCandless, 1966).

Despite these serious problems, psychodynamic theories do remind educators that children can have mixed and confusing emotions. Adults can help children by teaching them to express their feelings in ways that both honestly reflect their experiences and are acceptable to other people.

Cognitive-Developmental Theories

Cognitive-developmental theories emphasize thinking processes and how they change, qualitatively, over time. According to these views, children play an active role in their own development. They seek out new and interesting experiences, try to understand what they see and hear, and work actively to reconcile any discrepancies between new information and what they previously believed to be true. Through these reflections, children's thinking becomes more logical and abstract over time.

The earliest and best known cognitive-developmental theorist was Jean Piaget. With a career that spanned decades and spawned thousands of research studies around the world, Piaget focued primarily on children's cognitive development. He investigated the nature of children's logical thinking about such topics as numbers and physical causality and examined their self-reflections about their own psychological processes. A second cognitive-developmental theorist, Lawrence Kohlberg, is known for his extensive research on moral reasoning.

Piaget, Kohlberg, and their colleagues concluded from their studies that children pass through a number of identifiable developmental stages as they move toward mature thought. For cognitive developmentalists, taking a developmental perspective means looking sympathetically at children and understanding the logic of their current level of thinking. Although adultlike reasoning may be the eventual, desired outcome for young people, cognitive developmentalists believe that it is a mistake to hurry children beyond their current capacities—that one cannot simply make a child think in ways beyond his or her current cognitive stage. They also believe that adults who try to push children beyond their current stage create unnecessary stress and fail to take advantage of the reasoning skills of which children *are* capable.

Many cognitive-developmental ideas are well regarded by the current generation of developmental scholars. For example, contemporary child development experts recognize that children's thinking often reflects a reasonable attempt to make sense of novel and puzzling information. However, cognitive-developmental theories have also undergone vigorous critiques. A central criticism, mentioned earlier, is that researchers rarely find that children's development reflects clear-cut stage progressions. Instead, children often move back and forth between more and less sophisticated ways of thinking. Critics point out, for example, that simply because children do not think abstractly about a particular topic does not mean that they are *incapable* of abstract reasoning, especially with the support of an adult. As we pointed out in our earlier example of the chess player, children are sometimes able to reason at a very high level in certain areas yet, at the same time, are incapable of advanced reasoning on other topics.

Perhaps the most important principle for practice that emerges from cognitive-developmental theories is that teachers need to understand children *as children*. To facilitate children's learning, educators must listen closely to children's conversations, observe their actions, and gently probe them about their thinking. Only when adults understand children's thinking can they hope to enhance it. Cognitive-developmental scholars also recommend that instruction emphasize opportunities for active interaction with other people and the environment. Methods that are based in drill and practice or highly structured training fail to encourage children's curiosity and should be minimized.

Cognitive Process Theories

Cognitive process theories focus on basic thinking processes. For instance, cognitive process theorists examine how people interpret and remember what they see and hear and how these processes change during childhood and adolescence.

Children develop, in part, by actively seeking out new and interesting experiences. Art by Margot, age 6.

———————— **Connecting Concepts**

Piaget's descriptions of children's thinking are summarized in Chapter 6, and Kohlberg's views on children's moral development are presented in Chapter 13.

cognitive-developmental theory
Theoretical perspective that focuses on major transformations to the underlying structures of thinking.

cognitive process theory
Theoretical perspective that focuses on the precise nature of human mental operations.

Cognitive process researchers conduct detailed analyses of what children think and do. For instance, they have studied the eye movements of children scanning pictures, the length of time children take to read various kinds of text, and children's strategies for completing puzzles. Such analyses are guided by clear models of how children attend to information, find it meaningful, and use it later. Cognitive process theories now dominate much of the research in cognitive development. You will see the influence of cognitive process theories in our later discussions of information processing, intelligence, language development, learning in the academic domains, and reasoning about the social world.

A key contribution of cognitive process theories has been to describe children's thinking with painstaking detail, but critics suggest that there is a price to pay for taking a myopic view of specific processes. Cognitive process researchers can easily overlook the larger issue of *why* children think as they do. Cognitive process approaches often neglect the social-emotional factors and contexts of children's lives, factors that many other modern developmental theorists consider significant.

Another contribution of cognitive process theories has been the wealth of concrete, research-tested instructional strategies they have provided. Many teachers have found these strategies and applications to be inordinately helpful. For example, cognitive process theories offer concrete techniques for keeping children's attention, making the most of children's limited memory capabilities, challenging children's misconceptions on particular topics, and teaching children to become independent and effective learners.

Sociocultural Theories

Cognitive developmentalists and cognitive process theorists have focused squarely on how intellectual skills develop within an individual. By and large, both have paid little attention to the roles played by the broader social and cultural contexts within which individuals live. **Sociocultural theories,** on the other hand, try to explain the impact of social and cultural systems on development. These theories see development as the process of children becoming full adult participants in the society into which they are born. As children participate in their cultural activities and gradually assume higher levels of responsibility, their knowledge and thought processes become increasingly mature. Naturally, the activities in which children participate vary from culture to culture, as do the particular adult roles toward which children are being ushered. Therefore, the process of development varies considerably from culture to culture.

Lev Vygotsky is the pioneering figure credited with advancing our knowledge of how children's minds are shaped by everyday experiences in social settings. He believed that side by side with adults and others in their community, children take part in activities that impart particular values and cultivate specific intellectual skills. For example, when children learn to use such symbolic systems as alphabets and number systems, their minds are transformed, and they come to think about words, language, and numerical patterns in entirely new ways. Because different cultures impart different ways of thinking about and performing daily tasks—they teach different writing systems, scientific concepts, religious beliefs, and so on—children's thoughts and behaviors develop in culturally specific ways.

The last two decades have seen a virtual explosion of research conducted within sociocultural perspectives. This research is often well received by teachers because it focuses on real children in real settings and gives teachers a sense of the tangible steps they can take to support children's learning. Another strength of sociocultural theories is that they show concretely how specific cultural groups encourage children to use distinctly different modes of thinking.

As with any theoretical approach, however, sociocultural theories have limitations. Sociocultural theorists have described children's thinking with less precision than have theorists working within cognitive process perspectives. In some cases theorists have taken for granted that children learn important skills simply by taking part in an activity; in reality, however, some children merely go through the motions and take little responsibility for completing a task. Sociocultural theorists have not yet adequately explained how children take on increasing responsibility over time.

Sociocultural theories offer important applications for educators and other adults. A key principle is that children learn by being engaged in authentic adult tasks. A child helping his mother or child care provider bake cookies learns how to measure ingredients, mix batter

Connecting Concepts ———————
Chapter 7 examines developmental trends in children's cognitive processes.

Connecting Concepts ———————
Vygotsky's theory is presented in Chapter 6.

sociocultural theory
Theoretical perspective that focuses on children's learning of tools and communication systems through practice in meaningful tasks with other people.

From the perspective of sociocultural theories, children and adolescents learn a lot from participating in routine, purposeful activities with adults.

without tipping over the bowl, and cooperate with others (Gauvain, 2001). A student in an elementary classroom learns to read, write, and perform basic mathematical operations. A student in a secondary classroom learns how to interpret maps, analyze a body of data, and think critically about social and economic problems. With the assistance of more advanced individuals, children begin to tackle culture-specific, real-world tasks that were previously beyond their capabilities.

In addition, teachers need to consider how children's cultural beliefs and practices will influence their interpretations of academic material and classroom events. When a classroom includes children from diverse cultural backgrounds, it is especially important to make rules for behavior explicit and to explain their underlying rationales. At the same time, teachers can validate children's existing cultural perspectives and traditions by incorporating them into certain lessons and classroom routines.

Developmental Systems Theories

Developmental systems theories help clarify how multiple factors combine to steer children's development. From systems perspectives, no single factor predominates in directing the course of development. Genes, children's own efforts at understanding, social experiences, rewards from adults, cultural tools, and more all combine to govern children's physical, cognitive, and social-emotional development (D. H. Ford & Lerner, 1992; R. M. Lerner, 1998; Thelen & Smith, 1998).

Urie Bronfenbrenner has been the most widely known and influential systems theorist. In his *bioecological perspective* on human development, Bronfenbrenner analyzed the interacting effects of children's environments, which include immediate and extended families, neighborhoods, schools, parents' workplaces, mass media, community services, and political systems and policies (Bronfenbrenner, 1979, 2005). In the bioecological model, children partly determine their own environment by demonstrating their natural and acquired skills and temperaments. The child who is quiet and reflective triggers a different style of instruction from the teacher than does the child who is disruptive and inattentive.

According to Bronfenbrenner, a reciprocal relationship exists between the child and his or her environment. In fact, there is a dynamic relationship between all systems in which a child develops. For example, if parents and teachers develop mutually respectful relationships, they may swap information back and forth and magnify their support of a child. If parent-teacher relationships are poor, adults may blame one another for a struggling child's limitations, with the result that no one teaches needed skills to the child.

The strength of developmental systems theories is that they capture it all—nature, nurture, and the child's own activity. Ironically, the integrative character of these theories also creates their weaknesses. It is difficult to make predictions about any single factor in development because the effects of each factor are so intertwined with other elements of the developmental context.

Like other theoretical perspectives, developmental systems theories offer valuable ideas that can guide teachers in their interactions with children. A dynamic relationship between developing children and the contexts in which they develop—their families, schools, peer groups, and so on—suggests that teachers and other school personnel need to adjust their services to the complex circumstances of children's lives. For example, a girl may resist attention from a school counselor because she has previously learned in her family that adults cannot be trusted to be consistently sensitive and warm. The counselor must persistently communicate that she cares about the girl and wants to help. Developmental systems theories also confirm the value of continual, informal monitoring of children's well-being. Youngsters can change dramatically after a major transition (e.g., moving to a new school), requiring educators to keep tabs on youngsters' evolving perceptions and feelings.

Taking an Eclectic Approach

Table 1-1 summarizes the seven theoretical perspectives. With so many theories, it is tempting to ask, Which one is right? The answer is that, to some extent, they all are. Each

---

— Connecting Concepts
The interactive effects of family, community, and culture are examined in Chapter 5.

---

developmental systems theory
Theoretical perspective that focuses on the multiple factors, including systems inside and outside children, that combine to influence children's development.

TABLE 1-1	Theories of Child Development	
Theoretical Perspectives	**Theoretical Positions**	**Representative Theorists**[a]
Biological Theories	*Description:* Theories emphasize genetic factors and physiological structures and functions of the body. *Nature and Nurture:* Characteristics and behaviors that enhance an individual's chances for survival and reproduction are supported by genetic instructions. Adequate nutrients, supportive social relationships, and exploration in the physical environment are essential to normal growth. *Universality and Diversity:* Universally, children form bonds with caregivers, express themselves with language, infer other people's intentions and feelings, and use tools. Diversity in appearance and ability occurs through variations in genes and experience. *Qualitative and Quantitative Change:* Qualitative changes are seen in sensitive periods of development. In other respects the child grows gradually, reflecting a quantitative transformation.	Charles Darwin Arnold Gesell Konrad Lorenz John Bowlby Mary Ainsworth Sandra Scarr Robert Plomin David Bjorklund
Behaviorism and Social Learning Theories	*Description:* Theories focus on environmental stimuli and learning processes that lead to behavioral change. *Nature and Nurture:* Emphasis is on nurture. When children act, the environment may respond with rewards or punishments. Children modify their actions based on their experiences, goals, and perception of whether an action will lead to a desirable or undesirable response. *Universality and Diversity:* Children typically work for some common rewards (e.g., food, praise, physical contact). Because environments vary in how they respond to children's actions, diversity in behavior is expected. *Qualitative and Quantitative Change:* Development is quantitative: Children undergo countless incremental changes in behaviors.	John B. Watson Ivan Pavlov B. F. Skinner Albert Bandura
Psychodynamic Theories	*Description:* Theories focus on how early experiences and internal conflicts affect social and personality development. *Nature and Nurture:* Sexual and aggressive urges are inborn. Family and society affect how children control and express instinctual urges; social relationships also affect children's basic trust in others and sense of self. *Universality and Diversity:* Universally, children struggle with strong feelings (e.g., aggression and sexuality, according to S. Freud) and personal challenges (e.g., the belief that they can or cannot make things happen, according to Erikson). Relationships with other people are highly varied and result in diversity in resolutions to life's challenges. *Qualitative and Quantitative Change:* Through a series of qualitatively distinct stages, children learn to resolve mixed feelings.	Sigmund Freud Anna Freud Erik Erikson
Cognitive-Developmental Theories	*Description:* Theories focus on major transformations in the cognitive structures that underlie thinking. *Nature and Nurture:* Children are biological organisms strongly motivated to make sense of their personal worlds (nature). Access to a reasonably complex physical and social environment is vital to development (nurture). Young people actively contribute to their own intellectual development. *Universality and Diversity:* Universality is emphasized. Variations among youngsters are most common at the highest stages of development, which may depend on particular kinds of experiences (e.g., exposure to puzzling phenomena or moral dilemmas, particular kinds of instruction). *Qualitative and Quantitative Change:* Children's thinking undergoes a series of defined transformations in the very essence of reasoning; new ways of thinking build on previous structures but are increasingly abstract and systematic. Quantitative additions to the knowledge base occur within stages.	Jean Piaget Bärbel Inhelder Lawrence Kohlberg David Elkind Robbie Case John Flavell
Cognitive Process Theories	*Description:* Theories focus on the precise nature of human cognitive operations. *Nature and Nurture:* Both nature and nurture are important. Children are born with basic capacities to perceive, interpret, and remember information; these capacities change with maturation of the brain, experiences in the natural and social worlds, and children's reflections on these experiences. *Universality and Diversity:* The desire to make sense of the world is universal. Diversity is present in the kinds of educational experiences children have and, to some degree, in their natural intellectual talents. *Qualitative and Quantitative Change:* The methods by which children perceive, interpret, and remember information gradually change in both qualitative and quantitative ways.	Robbie Case John Flavell Robert Siegler Ann L. Brown Henry Wellman Albert Bandura
Sociocultural Theories	*Description:* Theories focus on children's acquisition of tools and communication systems through practice in meaningful tasks with other people. *Nature and Nurture:* Emphasis is on nurture. Children learn to use tools favored by their families and communities as they take part in meaningful tasks with others (nurture). However, being a social and cultural being is part of children's genetic inheritance (nature). *Universality and Diversity:* All children learn language, beliefs espoused in their communities, practical life skills, and so on. However, variation is present in the particular tools that various cultures and societies use. *Qualitative and Quantitative Change:* Children gradually take on responsibility in social groups. As children become increasingly able to regulate their own thinking, they shift qualitatively in how they carry out tasks. For example, having been taught basic mathematical systems and rules of writing, young people can eventually use these tools independently and appropriately during academic lessons.	Lev Vygotsky A. R. Luria James Wertsch Barbara Rogoff Patricia Greenfield Mary Gauvain

(continued)

TABLE 1-1	Theories of Child Development (continued)	
Theoretical Perspectives	**Theoretical Positions**	**Representative Theorists**[a]
Developmental Systems Theories	*Description:* Theories focus on the multiple factors and systems that interact in their influences on children's development. *Nature and Nurture:* Multiple factors inside the child (nature) and outside the child (nurture) combine to influence developmental patterns. The child's own activity is also an essential factor in development. *Universality and Diversity:* Developmental changes occur in all individuals from conception to death. Some changes are common at particular ages, yet individual children may face slightly different obstacles when acquiring new abilities, such as learning to walk. The ways in which children encounter various challenges do not lead to universal outcomes and depend more heavily on particular historical events and life events. *Qualitative and Quantitative Change:* Most change is quantitative, but shifts in action occur that result in entirely new ways of behaving. For example, a baby may use her arm to swat awkwardly at a toy and later learn to pick it up with a precise, effective finger grip.	Urie Bronfenbrenner Arnold Sameroff Richard Lerner Kurt Fischer Esther Thelen Gilbert Gottlieb Paul Baltes

[a]A few theorists have contributed to two or more theoretical perspectives. For example, John Flavell and Robbie Case have made important contributions to both cognitive-developmental and cognitive process theories. Albert Bandura has made contributions to social learning and cognitive process perspectives.

perspective provides unique insights that no other approach can offer. At the same time, no single theory can adequately explain all aspects of child development. In a sense, any theory is like a lens that brings certain phenomena into sharp focus but leaves other phenomena blurry or out of the picture. We urge you to take an eclectic attitude as you read the variety of theoretical explanations you find in this book, looking for the most useful ideas that each theory has to offer.

Developmental Periods

We can make our task of exploring child development more manageable by dividing the developmental journey into specific time periods. Age cutoffs are somewhat arbitrary, yet we know that children act in very different ways at specific age levels. In our upcoming discussions, we consider five periods: infancy (birth–2 years), early childhood (2–6 years), middle childhood (6–10 years), early adolescence (10–14 years), and late adolescence (14–18 years). Here we summarize each period, identifying typical needs and accomplishments of youngsters and their implications for teachers and other practitioners.

Infancy (Birth–2 Years)

Infancy is a truly remarkable period. It is a time when basic human traits, such as emotional bonds to other human beings, nonverbal communication and language expression, motor exploration of the physical environment, and systematic approaches to learning about people and objects burst onto the scene.

A newborn baby is completely dependent on others. But baby is equipped with an arsenal of skills—including a distinctive cry, physical reflexes, an interest in human faces, and a brain alert to novelty and sameness—that gain comfort and stimulation from caregivers. In a matter of weeks, the baby smiles broadly during good-humored exchanges with a caregiver. As the caregiver responds warmly and consistently, attachment grows.

A sense of security nourishes infants' desire to learn. Babies want to know everything: what keys taste like, what older family members do in the kitchen, and what happens when they drop their bowl of peas. Infants' growing facility with language builds on interests in concrete experiences, such as a parent's laughter and the sensation of warm water in the bathtub.

During the first 2 years, many dramatic developmental changes occur.

Intellectual curiosity fuels babies' drive to use physical skills. Babies reach, crawl, and climb to get objects they desire. The urge to explore coincides with a budding sense of mastery ("I *can* do it!") and independence ("*I* can do it!"). Emotional reactions, such as a legitimate fear of heights and uneasiness in the presence of strangers, constrain physical exploration and occasionally prompt withdrawal.

Professional viewpoints. Caregivers who work effectively with infants realize that each baby is unique, develops at his or her own rate, and is hungry for loving interaction. Such caregivers emphasize *quality* of care, giving individualized, responsive, and affectionate attention to growing babies and their families (Chazan-Cohen, Jerald, & Stark, 2001).

In addition, knowledgeable infant caregivers design the physical environment so infants can explore objects and surroundings freely. In the "Environments: Infancy" video clip on Observation CD 1 (see description in the margin), you can observe one setting where crawling infants can speed up and down cushioned ramps and walking infants (*toddlers*) can swagger around open spaces.[2] When infants stumble, furniture poses little threat since it has been crafted with soft, rounded edges. Caregivers also design environments to foster infants' cognitive and social abilities. In the video clip, notice a mirror that attracts attention; colorful toys with complex textures that beg to be touched; mobiles over cribs that encourage inspection; a tunnel that invites entering, exiting, and playing peek-aboo games; and simple books for examination while cuddling with caregivers in a rocking chair.

High-quality early care prepares an infant for the expanded learning opportunities of early childhood. The infant is ready to venture from the caregiver's lap.

In the "Environments: Infancy" clip on Observation CD 1, see a setting that is safe and interesting for infants. You can use the three-CD set *Observing Children and Adolescents: Guided Interactive Practice in Understanding Development* (version 2.0) to enhance your understanding of developmental concepts and your observation skills with children.

Early Childhood (2–6 Years)

Early childhood is a period of incredible creativity, fantasy, wonder, and play. Preschool-aged children see life as a forum for imagination and drama: They reinvent the world, try on new roles, and work hard to play their parts in harmony with one another.

Language and communication skills develop rapidly during early childhood. New vocabulary, sensitivity to communication rules, and facility with syntax (grammar) are noticeable advancements. Language builds on daily increases in knowledge about the world and, especially, the habits and patterns of daily life.

Physical changes are apparent as well. High levels of energy radiate from preschool-aged children's activities. The cautious movements of infancy give way to fluid rolling, tumbling, running, and skipping.

Socially and emotionally, preschoolers are often endearing, trusting, and affectionate. They become progressively more interested in others, eagerly spend time with playmates, infuse fantasy into play, and contend with aggressive and self-centered impulses.

Preschool children learn a lot from handling concrete objects, using their imaginations, and talking with others.

Professional viewpoints. Effective teachers of young children inspire and channel children's natural energy. They are respectful of young children's curiosity, spontaneity, and desire to try on new roles.

Environments for young children can be designed to encourage the active and purposeful learning that is advocated by the National Association for the Education of Young Children (Bredekamp & Copple, 1997). For example, in the "Environments: Early Childhood" video clip on Observation CD 1, you can see a classroom where children draw and paint creatively. Play structures encourage children to climb, hide, stand tall, and spot one another. Tables and chairs make it possible for children to sit and talk together during mealtimes and group activities. A dramatic play area, furnished with kitchen appliances and dress-up clothes, encourages imagination. Elsewhere in the room children can sit and look at books and take turns on a computer. Mats let children recharge their batteries with sleep and rest; a separate bathroom area is available for toilet needs and hand washing. Outdoors, children can scoot on vehicles, ride bicycles, and play in the sand.

In the "Environments: Early Childhood" clip on Observation CD 1, you can observe a setting that encourages creative movement, pretend play, and hands-on learning in young children.

---

[2]Appreciation is extended to Greg Pierson, University Schools, and Keli Cotner, Campus Child Care Center, both of Greeley, Colorado, for granting permission to film their facilities.

Given ample chances to explore the environment and converse with others, young children gain valuable knowledge about themselves and their world. They become ready to complete the realistic tasks of middle childhood.

Middle Childhood (6–10 Years)

Middle childhood is a time of sustained attention to real-world activities. Although pretending is not abandoned, it plays less of a role than it did earlier. Instead, children display motivation and persistence in mastering the customs, tools, and accumulated knowledge of their community and culture. For example, children of this age often learn to read and write, cook and clean house, apply rules in games and sports, care for younger brothers and sisters, and use computer technology. At school in particular, there are plenty of tools to learn, as 7-year-old Emma demonstrates in her story in the following Interpreting Children's Artifacts and Actions exercise.

INTERPRETING CHILDREN'S ARTIFACTS AND ACTIONS   Emma's Story

Seven-year-old Emma wrote a story she called "The Adventures of Emily and Rose." As you examine the following excerpt from her story, look for evidence that Emma is learning the tools of literacy.

Emily and the Flowers

Once upon a time, a little girl named Emily wanted to play. But she had to play inside because it rained outside all week. She was so sad. One day the rain stopped. She was so happy because now she could play. She went outside. She saw all of these beautiful flowers.

With help from her teacher and a parent volunteer, Emma used word-processing software to make a professional-looking copy and illustrated certain scenarios using a pencil and colored markers. As she wrote the story, she drew on patterns she had noticed in other stories. For example, she borrowed a common introductory phrase, "Once upon a time," and included a character (Emily) who faced a problem (rain, which eventually stopped to allow play). Emma's story illustrates the creative work of which children of this age are capable when given appropriate support.

Serious commitments to peers, especially to playmates of the same age and gender, also emerge during middle childhood. Friendships are important, and children learn much from spending time together and from getting into—and out of—scuffles. Children also begin to compare their performance to that of others: Why do I have fewer friends than Maria does? Am I good enough to be picked for the baseball team? When they routinely end up on the losing side in such comparisons, children are more hesitant to try new challenges.

In the elementary school years, children internalize many admonishments they've heard repeatedly ("Don't play near the river," "Keep an eye on your little brother"). They gain a sense of what is expected of them, and most are inclined to live up to these expectations. Rules of games and classroom conduct become important. Basic motor skills are stable during middle childhood, and many children gain proficiency in athletic skills.

Middle childhood is a time of sustained attention to realistic tasks.

Professional viewpoints.   In middle childhood, children do their best thinking when they are familiar with a topic and can rely on concrete objects to bolster their reasoning. Teachers can nurture children's skills by asking them to sort and analyze objects and events; to gain proficiency in basic elements of reading, writing, mathematics, science, and other subjects; and to focus on the connections between the academic concepts they are learning and what they already know (National Council for Accreditation of Teacher Education, 2000).

In the "Environments: Middle Childhood" video clip on Observation CD 1, you can see a classroom that provides tangible support for children's academic learning. For example, maps are visible in several places, suggesting the importance of the world's geography. Frequently used words are posted on cabinets for children to refer to while writing. Small objects are stored in plastic canisters and drawers; children can manipulate, count, and classify objects according to shape and other properties. Books, a computer, chalkboards, and other resources are available to extend children's learning. Tables and chairs permit group work, and sofas encourage relaxation while reading.

Having learned to think systematically, children are ready for the next big tasks, growing an adult body and speculating on what it means to hold a job, date, become intimate, and raise a family. This transition between childhood and adulthood takes time and effort, and there are growing pains along the way.

In the "Environments: Middle Childhood" clip on Observation CD 1, view a setting that supports children's academic learning with concrete objects, displays of language rules, tables and chairs for group work, couches for relaxed reading, and other resources.

Early Adolescence (10–14 Years)

In early adolescence, youngsters slowly lose their childlike bodies and make strides toward reproductive maturation. Physical changes are accompanied by equally dramatic reorganizations in learning processes and relationships with parents and peers.

The physical changes of puberty are orderly and predictable, but boys and girls alike often experience them personally as puzzling, disconcerting events. Young adolescents sometimes look and feel awkward, and hormonal changes can lead to mood swings. In addition, adolescents reflect on their changing selves and worry about how other people and their peers perceive them. They wonder, What are they thinking of me? How does my hair look? Am I one of the "cool" kids? Peers become a sounding board through which adolescents gain assurance that their appearance and behaviors are acceptable.

Adolescents begin to think in a far-reaching, logical, and abstract manner. The interests of young adolescents broaden well beyond family and peer group. Feeling powerful and idealistic, adolescents challenge the existing order, wondering why schools, neighborhoods, governments, and the earth's ecosystem cannot be improved overnight.

Diversity is present in every developmental phase, but individual differences are especially pronounced in early adolescence. Although the physical changes of puberty occur in a fairly predictable manner, the age at which they emerge can vary considerably from one individual to the next. Thus not all young adolescents begin puberty during the 10–14

Early and late adolescence are times for many physical, cognitive, and social-emotional changes.

On Observation CD 1, watch the "Environments: Early Adolescence" clip to see a setting that encourages young adolescents to focus on academic learning, work together in groups, talk privately with advisors, and follow a code of conduct emphasizing kindness and respect.

age range. Some, girls especially, may begin puberty before 10. Others, boys in particular, may not begin puberty until the end of this age span.

Professional viewpoints.   The National Middle School Association (NMSA) offers guidelines for meeting the developmental needs of young adolescents at school (National Middle School Association, 2003). First, every student should be supported by one adult (an *advisor*) who keeps an eye on the student's academic and personal development, perhaps within the context of a "home base" period or other group meeting time. The advisor-student relationship, when stable and positive, can help young adolescents weather the rapid developmental changes they are likely to experience. In addition, NMSA suggests that large middle schools be subdivided into "houses" or other small units in which students share several classes with the same classmates and get to know a few teachers well. NMSA also advocates teaching techniques that are varied, engaging, and responsive to students' cultural backgrounds, prior knowledge, and individual talents.

An environment designed to meet the developmental needs of young adolescents is shown in the "Environments: Early Adolescence" video clip on Observation CD 1. Classrooms are equipped with a rich array of resources, including overhead projectors, a television and video cassette recorder, clocks, an easel, chalkboards, maps, binders, and a computer. Adolescents' artwork, papers, and a diorama are displayed for all to admire. A code of conduct reminds adolescents to treat themselves, others, and the environment with kindness and respect. A small room is set aside with two chairs and desks, allowing private conversations with familiar adults. Hallways are clean and uncluttered, school colors are obvious, and rows of lockers give adolescents places to store personal supplies and congregate between classes.

First steps toward maturity are often hesitant ones. With affection from parents and teachers, young adolescents gradually gain confidence that the adult world is within reach.

Late Adolescence (14–18 Years)

As teenagers continue to mature, they lose some of the gawky, uneven features of early adolescence and blossom into attractive young adults. And resembling young adults, older adolescents often feel entitled to make decisions. Common refrains often include the word *my:* "It's *my* hair, *my* body, *my* clothes, *my* room, *my* education, *my life!*"

Late adolescence can be a confusing time to make decisions due to the abundance of mixed messages that society communicates. For instance, teenagers may be encouraged to abstain from sexual activity, yet they continually encounter inviting, provocative sexual images in the media. Similarly, parents and teachers urge healthy eating habits, yet junk food is everywhere—in vending machines at school, at the refreshment stand at the movie theater, and often in kitchen cabinets at home.

Fortunately, many high school students make wise decisions. They try hard in school, explore career possibilities, gain job experience, and refrain from seriously risky behaviors. Others, however, are less judicious in their choices: They experiment with alcohol, drugs, sex, and violence and in general think more about here-and-now pleasures than long-term consequences.

Peer relationships remain a high priority in late adolescence. Affiliations with age-mates can be either a good or bad influence, depending on typical pastimes of the group. At the same time, most adolescents continue to savor their ties with trusted adults and preserve fundamental values championed by parents and teachers, such as the importance of a good education and the need to be honest and fair.

Individual differences in academic achievement are substantial during the high school years. Indeed, wide variations in students' abilities are among the biggest challenges faced by high schools today. Some low-achieving students drop out of high school altogether, perhaps to shield themselves from the stigma of academic failure. Many of the low achievers who stay in school hang out with students who share their own pessimistic views of education.

Professional viewpoints.   Older adolescents, who are beginning to take on grown-up re-sponsibilities, need intelligent, behind-the-scenes support from adults. The National Associ-ation of Secondary School Principals (2004) urges schools to become student-centered and personalized in their services.

School environments can help meet adolescents' needs for personalized attention by doing several things. As you can see in the "Environments: Late Adolescence" video clip on Observation CD 1, classrooms can sometimes be arranged so students face one another, making it hard for anyone to remain anonymous. Of course, physical arrangements must be adapted to instructional formats, and what matters more than layout is that teachers communicate affection, respect, and high expectations to *all* adolescents. In the science classrooms in this clip, numerous types of equipment, resources, and materials are pres-ent; these can be used flexibly to meet individual learning needs. Statements of responsi-bility and citizenship are posted on a wall. A mural contains images appealing to a range of interests, including music, drama, and athletics. The message seems to be that *everyone* belongs here.

The five periods of development just identified appear in Developmental Trends tables throughout the book. These tables summarize key developmental tasks, achievements, and variations at different age levels. In addition, they suggest implications for teachers and other practitioners who work with young people in each developmental period. The first of these tables, "Accomplishments and Diversity at Different Age Levels," gives an overview of the do-mains of physical, cognitive, and social-emotional development.

Watch the "Environments: Late Adoles-cence" clip on Observation CD 1 to see a setting that encourages adolescents to become proficient in primary subjects, achieve deeper understandings in areas of personal interest, and follow a code of conduct emphasizing responsibility and citizenship.

From Theory to Practice

The practical applications in this book build on the following core concept: Children are nur-tured most effectively when adults understand how children *generally* progress but also show sensitivity to children's *individual* needs. In other words, teachers engage in **development-ally appropriate practice,** instruction and caregiving adapted to the age, characteristics, and developmental progress of individual youngsters.

Developmentally appropriate practice enables growing children to be active learners, recognizes that adult-level functioning is not always either realistic or valuable for children to imitate, and encourages children to work together in an ethical and democratic fashion (Kohlberg & Mayer, 1972). Developmentally appropriate practice also represents an opti-mistic expectation that children *can* grow in positive directions.

By knowing the characteristics and thinking abilities of children at a particular age, adults can offer effective instruction and services. Development and Practice features, which appear throughout the book, provide illustrations of educators guiding young people of various ages. The first of these, "Engaging in Developmentally Appropriate Practice with Infants, Children, and Adolescents," appears on page 26.

Melanie (age 11) perceives Mrs. Lorenzo's classroom as warm and supportive. Teachers and other professionals who are affectionate, respectful, and mindful of children's strengths can make a difference in children's lives.

Preparing for Developmentally Appropriate Practice

In later chapters we pinpoint concrete strategies that relate to specific aspects of develop-ment. Here we offer four general strategies that will help you nurture children's potential for positive growth.

● *Look for and capitalize on children's strengths.* Individual children have different strengths, depending on their genes, present environment, and past experiences. Age is also a factor in a child's strengths. As an infant, a child may, for instance, be a careful observer of patterns of light and then at later ages proceed to become a determined explorer in the sand, an industrious builder of blocks, a leader among middle school classmates, and, eventually, an insightful critic of society.

It is not always easy for adults to see children's strengths, as adults are inclined to evaluate children according to their own standards of maturity. Sometimes children make life difficult for adults, as Tonya initially did in our introductory case study. Children who struggle or act out may provoke adults to dwell on children's limitations. With extra ef-fort, a change in tactics, and a solid faith in children's capacity for positive growth, edu-cators can find what children are able to accomplish and help them build upon these resources.

Study Guide and Reader ——————
Learn more about how the field of child development offers helpful guidance for teachers and other practitioners in Supplementary Reading 1-2.

developmentally appropriate practice Instruction and other services adapted to the age, characteristics, and develop-mental progress of individual children.

DEVELOPMENTAL TRENDS

Accomplishments and Diversity at Different Age Levels

Age	What You Might Observe	Diversity	Implications
Infancy (Birth–2) 	**Physical Development** • Motor skills including rolling over, sitting, crawling, standing, walking • Growing ability to reach, grab, manipulate, and release objects • Rudimentary self-feeding by the end of infancy • Rapid brain growth **Cognitive Development** • Ability to distinguish among different faces • Rapid growth in communication, including crying, using gestures and facial expressions, synchronizing attention with caregivers, babbling, forming one-word sentences, constructing multiple-word sentences • Ability to imitate simple gestures with a model present, moving to complex imitation of actions and patterns from memory • Growing ability to remember people and things out of sight **Social-Emotional Development** • Formation of close bonds with responsive and affectionate caregivers • Use of words to name people, things, needs, and desires • Playing side by side with peers but also interacting at times • Increasing awareness of ownership and boundaries of self ("Me!" "Mine!") • Developing sense of power and will ("No!")	• Considerable diversity exists in age when, and in manner in which, babies develop motor skills. • Self-feeding and self-help skills emerge later when families encourage children to rely on others for meeting basic needs. • Children's temperaments and physical abilities affect their exploration of the environment. • In unsafe environments, families may limit children's exploration. • Some young children learn two or three languages, especially when knowing more than one language is valued by caregivers. • Ability to pretend is displayed early by some children and later by others. • Nonverbal communication varies with culture. For instance, a child may be discouraged from making eye contact with an elder as a sign of respect. • Children who have few experiences with peers may appear tentative, detached, or aggressive. • Infants and toddlers who spend time in multiage settings interact differently than do those accustomed to same-age groups. • Some children are encouraged by families to share possessions, and others are encouraged to respect individual rights of property.	• Provide a safe, appropriate, sensory-rich environment so infants can move, explore surroundings, and handle objects. • Hold infants gently, and care for their physical needs in an attentive manner. • Learn and respond sensitively to each infant's manner of approaching or resisting new people, objects, and events. • Encourage but do not rush infants to learn motor skills, such as walking. • Learn what each family wants for its children, and try to provide culturally sensitive care. • Recognize that children's early images of themselves are influenced by unconscious messages from adults (e.g., "I enjoy holding you" or "I'm sad and unable to attend to your needs"). • Speak to infants regularly to enrich their language development. • Find out which languages families speak at home. • Communicate regularly with families about infants' daily activities, including how much and what they eat and drink, how well they sleep, and what their moods are during the day.
Early Childhood (2–6) 	**Physical Development** • Increasing abilities in such motor skills as running and skipping, throwing a ball, building block towers, and using scissors • Increasing competence in basic self-care and personal hygiene **Cognitive Development** • Dramatic play and fantasy with peers • Ability to draw simple figures • Some knowledge of colors, letters, and numbers • Recounting of familiar stories and events **Social-Emotional Development** • Developing understanding of gender • Emerging abilities to defer immediate gratification, share toys, and take turns • Modest appreciation that other people have their own desires, beliefs, and knowledge • Some demonstration of sympathy for people in distress	• Children master coordinated physical skills (e.g., skipping) at different ages. • Individual differences in fine motor proficiency and gross motor agility are substantial. • Some children enter kindergarten having had few social experiences with age-mates; others have been in group child care since infancy. • Family and cultural backgrounds influence the kinds of skills that children have mastered by the time they begin school. • Some children have had a lot of experience listening to storybooks, but others have been read to rarely. • Many children at this age have difficulty following rules, standing quietly in line, and waiting for their turns.	• Provide sensory-rich materials that encourage exploration (e.g., water table, sand box, textured toys). • Arrange a variety of activities (e.g., assembling puzzles, coloring, block construction, dance) that permit children to exercise fine motor and gross motor skills. • Encourage children to engage in cooperative and fantasy play by providing props and open play areas. • Read to children regularly to promote vocabulary and preliteracy skills. • Give children frequent opportunities to play, interact with peers, and make choices. • Communicate expectations for behavior so that children learn to follow the rules of group settings. • Communicate regularly with families about children's academic and social progress.

(continued)

DEVELOPMENTAL TRENDS

Accomplishments and Diversity at Different Age Levels (continued)

Age	What You Might Observe	Diversity	Implications
Middle Childhood (6–10) 	**Physical Development** • Ability to ride a bicycle • Successful imitation of complex physical movements • Participation in organized sports **Cognitive Development** • Development of basic skills in reading, writing, mathematics, and other academic subject areas • Ability to reason logically when aided by concrete objects **Social-Emotional Development** • Increasing awareness of how one's own abilities compare with those of peers • Desire for time with age-mates, especially friends of the same gender • Increasing responsibility in household chores • Adherence to rules in games • Understanding of basic moral rules	• Children begin to compare their academic and physical performance to that of others, and children who perceive they are doing poorly may lose motivation to achieve. • Many children are unable to sit quietly for long periods. • Individual differences are evident in children's performance in academic areas. • Children differ in temperament and sociability; some are outgoing, others are more reserved and shy. • A few children may show disturbing levels of aggression toward others.	• Tailor instructional methods (e.g., cooperative groups, individualized assignments, choices in activities) and materials to meet diversity in children's talents, background knowledge, and interests. • Address deficiencies in basic skills (e.g., in reading, writing, and math) before they develop into serious delays. • Provide moderately challenging tasks that encourage children to learn new skills, perform well, and seek additional challenges. • Provide the guidance necessary to help children interact more successfully with peers (e.g., by suggesting ways to resolve conflicts and finding a "buddy" for a newcomer to a school or club). • Prohibit bullying and enforce codes of conduct.
Early Adolescence (10–14) 	**Physical Development** • Onset of puberty • Significant growth spurt **Cognitive Development** • Emerging capacity to think and reason about abstract ideas • Preliminary exposure to advanced academic content in specific subject areas **Social-Emotional Development** • Continued (and perhaps greater) interest in peer relationships • Emerging sexual interest in the opposite gender or same gender, depending on orientation • Challenges to parents, teachers, and other authorities regarding rules and boundaries • Occasional moodiness	• Young adolescents exhibit considerable variability in the age at which they begin puberty. • Academic problems often become more pronounced during adolescence; students who encounter frequent failure become less engaged in school activities. • Adolescents seek out peers whose values are compatible with their own and who will give them recognition and status. • Some young adolescents begin to engage in deviant and risky activities (e.g., unprotected sex, cigarette smoking, use of drugs and alcohol).	• Suggest and demonstrate effective study strategies as adolescents begin to tackle difficult subject matter. • Give struggling adolescents the extra academic support they need to be successful. • Provide a regular time and place where young adolescents can seek guidance and advice about academic or social matters (e.g., offer your classroom or office as a place where students can occasionally eat lunch). • Provide opportunities for adolescents to contribute to decision making in clubs and recreation centers. • Hold adolescents accountable for their actions, and impose appropriate consequences when they break rules.
Late Adolescence (14–18) 	**Physical Development** • Achievement of sexual maturity and adult height • For some teens, development of a regular exercise program • Development of specific eating habits (e.g., becoming a vegetarian, consuming junk food) **Cognitive Development** • In-depth study of certain academic subject areas • Consideration of career tracks and job prospects **Social-Emotional Development** • Dating • Increasing independence (e.g., driving a car, making choices for free time) • Frequent questioning of existing rules and societal norms	• Some adolescents make poor choices regarding the peers with whom they associate. • Older adolescents aspire to widely differing educational and career tracks (e.g., some aspire to college, others anticipate seeking employment immediately after high school, and still others make no plans for life after high school). • Some teens participate in extracurricular activities; those who do are more likely to stay in school until graduation. • Some teens become sexually active, and some become parents. • Teenagers' neighborhoods and communities offer differing opportunities and temptations.	• Communicate caring and respect for all adolescents. • Allow choices in academic subjects and assignments, but hold adolescents to high standards for performance. • Provide the guidance and assistance that low-achieving students may need to be more successful. • Help adolescents explore higher education opportunities and a variety of career paths. • Encourage involvement in extracurricular activities. • Arrange opportunities for adolescents to make a difference in their communities through volunteer work and service learning projects.

DEVELOPMENT AND PRACTICE

Engaging in Developmentally Appropriate Practice with Infants, Children, and Adolescents

Infancy

- Set up a safe and stimulating environment for exploration.

  A caregiver in an infant center designs her environment so infants can safely crawl, walk, and climb both inside and on the playground. A quiet corner is reserved for small infants not yet able to move around. Various materials and toys are carefully arranged to be in reach and to invite use. Duplicates of heavily used toys are available.

- Arrange clean and quiet areas for meeting physical needs.

  A teacher in an early intervention program sets up his environment so that he can help toddlers meet their physical needs in a hygienic and quiet area. He talks to children during caregiving routines such as feeding, diapering, and toileting, explaining what's happening and praising children when they take small steps toward self-care.

- Provide culturally sensitive care, and support families' home languages.

  A family child care provider who is bilingual in Spanish and English uses both languages with infants and toddlers in her care. She has cloth and cardboard books in both languages (some of the books are homemade), as well as recordings of songs and stories.

Early Childhood

- Provide reassurance to children who have difficulty separating from their families.

  A child care provider establishes a routine for the morning. After children say goodbye to their parents, they stand at the window with him, watch their parents walk to their cars, and then find an activity to join.

- Create a classroom environment that permits children to explore their physical and cultural world.

  A preschool teacher makes several "stations" available to children during free-choice time. The stations include a water table and areas for playing with blocks, completing puzzles, doing arts and crafts, engaging in dramatic play, and listening to books on tape.

- Introduce children to the world of literature.

  A preschool teacher reads to the children at least once each day. She chooses books with entertaining stories and vivid illustrations that readily capture the children's attention, interest, and imagination.

Middle Childhood

- Encourage family members to become active participants in their children's activities.

  A religious educator invites children's parents and other family members to contribute in some small way to one of the classes. Different parents assist with musical performances, bake cookies, and give hands-on help during lessons.

- Ensure that all students acquire basic academic skills.

  A second-grade teacher individualizes reading instruction for her students based on their current knowledge and skills. She works on mastery of let-

ter identification and letter-sound correspondence with some, reading of simple stories with others, and selection of appropriate books with a few students who are already reading independently. She makes sure that all children have regular opportunities to listen to stories in small groups and on tape.

- Give children the guidance they need to establish and maintain positive relationships with their peers.

  When two children are quarreling, their teacher gives them several suggestions that can help them identify a reasonable compromise.

Early Adolescence

- Design a curriculum that is challenging and motivating and that incorporates knowledge and skills from several content areas.

  A middle school teacher designs a unit on "war and conflict," integrating writing skills and knowledge of social studies. He encourages students to bring in newspaper clippings about current events and to write about political debates.

- Assign every young adolescent an advisor who looks after the adolescent's welfare.

  During homeroom with her advisees, a seventh-grade teacher personally makes sure that each student is keeping up with assignments. She also encourages her advisees to talk with her informally about their academic and social concerns.

- Show sensitivity to youngsters who are undergoing the physical changes of puberty.

  A sports coach makes sure that adolescents have privacy when they dress and shower after team practice.

Late Adolescence

- Expect students to meet high standards for achievement, but give them the support and guidance they need to meet those standards.

  An English composition teacher describes and then posts the various steps involved in writing—planning, drafting, writing, editing, and revising—and asks his students to use these steps for their essays. He then monitors his students' work, giving feedback and suggestions as necessary and making sure that students execute each step in a way that enhances the quality of their writing.

- Encourage adolescents to give back to their communities.

  A high school requires all students to participate in 50 hours of volunteer work or service learning in their town.

- Educate adolescents about the academic requirements of jobs and colleges.

  A high school guidance counselor posts vacant positions in the area, listing the work experience and educational requirements for each.

● *Recognize that children's immaturity serves a purpose.* Human beings take longer to reach physical maturity than do members of any other species. Such a lengthy childhood allows children to learn what they need to know to become effective participants in adult society—from survival skills to the basic patterns, beliefs, and tools of their culture (Gould, 1977; Leakey, 1994).

When we compare children's abilities to our own, children inevitably come up short. For example, we might describe preschoolers as being self-centered and limited in the ability to think beyond immediate circumstances. Yet focusing on the personal relevance of new information is actually a reasonable way to make sense of new information, particularly for a small being with restricted world knowledge. From a developmental perspective, the "weaknesses" youngsters display and the "mistakes" they make often serve a purpose and promote development over the long run (Bjorklund & Green, 1992; Bruner, 1972).

● *Meet diverse needs.* Almost all children follow similar developmental pathways, but exceptions are everywhere, sometimes as a product of different cultures and environments and sometimes as a result of variability in genetic makeup. Regardless of their origin, children's differences require thoughtful accommodation. For example, children can learn a lot from one another's traditions, beliefs, and behaviors. However, children do not always notice the strengths of peers who come from backgrounds different than their own. Helping them avoid stereotypic thinking and cope with discrimination, racism, prejudice, and oppression are important agendas for teachers and other school

Teachers can effectively meet the needs of children when they learn about children's backgrounds, cultures, and families. Art by Belinda, age 12.

professionals (García Coll et al., 1996). In addition, some children have personal experiences—perhaps growing up in poverty or losing a family member to death or incarceration—that present them with unusual challenges. These experiences, as well, necessitate sensitivity and practical measures. Finally, perceptive adults routinely encounter variations in young people's temperaments and talents. Groups of youngsters never fit a single developmental mold, and adults need to plan activities that respect culture, group differences, and individual needs (Dahlberg, Moss, & Pence, 1999).

● *Nudge children toward advanced thinking and behaving.* To some extent, adults must *meet children where the children are,* at their current level of functioning. But to promote development, adults must also introduce tasks of increasing complexity. A school counselor, for instance, may work with a shy child to set specific goals that will promote her inclusion by peers. One such goal might be to stand close to a small group of children and make a point of saying something complimentary or relevant to their conversation. Initially, children may need occasional reminders and words of praise for such behaviors, but eventually they will initiate these behaviors on their own, without any prodding from adults.

Note that we intentionally say *nudge,* rather than *push,* children toward more advanced levels. Unreasonable expectations—expectations for behavior well beyond what children are currently capable of doing—will often lead to unnecessary failure, accompanied by stress, rather than the positive benefits that gentle prodding is likely to produce. At the same time, nudging children toward higher levels of responsibility does not mean that caregivers should be indulgent or lax in discipline. Children benefit from firm expectations for responsible behavior when these expectations are within reach.

By introducing tasks that involve increasing difficulty and responsibility, caregivers nudge children toward more advanced ways of thinking and behaving.

Strengthening the Commitment

A commitment to developmentally appropriate practice isn't something that can be applied automatically or that necessarily lasts forever. Teachers and other practitioners must continually discern the group-based characteristics and individual needs of young people. Furthermore, researchers continue to advance the frontiers of knowledge about child development. Therefore, educators can—and must—continue to learn more about youngsters' needs. Following are two useful things you can do:

Study Guide and Reader ————
Learn more about how teachers can help one another gain insight into children's needs in Supplementary Reading 1-3.

Find guidance through professional organizations such as Zero to Three (National Center for Infants, Toddlers and Families) and professional journals such as the *Zero to Three* journal, *Child Development* (published by the Society for Research in Child Development), *Journal of Early Adolescence*, and a host of others.

● *Continue to take courses in child development.* Additional coursework is one sure way of keeping up to date (a) on the latest theoretical perspectives and research results on child and adolescent development and (b) on their practical implications for work with young people. Such coursework has been shown to enhance professional effectiveness with children (Darling-Hammond, 1995).

● *Obtain new perspectives from colleagues.* If you ask colleagues the right questions—in particular, regarding what children's strengths are and how you can nurture them—you will continue to learn effective ways to help children. In addition, many professional organizations hold regular meetings at which you can hear researchers and practitioners exchange ideas. Such meetings enable teachers and other practitioners to learn about the latest research findings and theoretical advances in development and to discover new methods for supporting youngsters. Professional organizations also publish journals with new research findings and standards for instruction, care, and guidance of young people.

Throughout this chapter we have maintained that developmental journeys are not predetermined at the onset. Instead, developmental paths depend significantly on caring adults. As you will discover throughout this book, you can do much to help children navigate their individual developmental journeys. You can definitely make a difference in the lives of children.

Case Study: Latisha

Latisha, who is 13 years old, lives in a housing project in an inner-city neighborhood in Chicago. An adult asks her to describe her life and family, her hopes and fears, and her plans for the future. She responds as follows:

My mother works at the hospital, serving food. She's worked there for 11 years, but she's been moved to different departments. I don't know what my dad does because he don't live with me. My mother's boyfriend lives with us. He's like my step father.

In my spare time I just like be at home, look at TV, or clean up, or do my homework, or play basketball, or talk on the phone. My three wishes would be to have a younger brother and sister, a car of my own, and not get killed before I'm 20 years old.

I be afraid of guns and rats. My mother she has a gun, her boyfriend has one for protection. I have shot one before and it's like a scary feeling. My uncle taught me. He took us in the country and he had targets we had to like shoot at. He showed us how to load and cock it and pull the trigger. When I pulled the trigger at first I feel happy because I learned how to shoot a gun, but afterward I didn't like it too much because I don't want to accidentally shoot nobody. I wouldn't want to shoot nobody. But it's good that I know how to shoot one just in case something happened and I have to use it.

Where I live it's a quiet neighborhood. If the gangs don't bother me or threaten me, or do anything to my family, I'm OK. If somebody say hi to me, I'll say hi to them as long as they don't threaten me. . . . I got two cousins who are in gangs. One is in jail because he killed somebody. My other cousin, he stayed cool. He ain't around. He don't be over there with the gang bangers. He mostly over on the west side with his grandfather, so I don't hardly see him. . . . I got friends in gangs. Some of them seven, eight years old that's too young to be in a gang. . . . They be gang banging because they have no one to turn to. . . . If a girl join a gang it's worser than if a boy join a gang because to be a girl you should have more sense. A boy they want to be hanging on to their friends. Their friends say gangs are cool, so they join.

The school I go to now is more funner than the school I just came from. We switch classes and we have 40 minutes for lunch. The Board of Education say that we can't wear gym shoes no more. They say it distracts other people from learning, it's because of the shoe strings and gang colors.

My teachers are good except two. My music and art teacher she's old and it seems like she shouldn't be there teaching. It seem like she should be retired and be at home, or traveling or something like that. And my history teacher, yuk! He's a stubborn old goat. He's stubborn with everybody.

(continued)

When I finish school I want to be a doctor. At first I wanted to be a lawyer, but after I went to the hospital I said now I want to help people, and cure people, so I decided to be a doctor. (J. Williams & K. Williamson, 1992, pp. 11–12)[a]

- In what ways do we see the contexts of family, school, neighborhood, and culture affecting Latisha's development?
- Based on your own experiences growing up, what aspects of Latisha's development would you guess are probably universal? What aspects reflect diversity?
- What clues do we have that Latisha's teachers can almost certainly have a positive impact on her long-term development and success?

Once you have answered these questions, compare your responses with those presented in the appendix.

[a]From "'I Wouldn't Want to Shoot Nobody': The Out-of-School Curriculum as Described by Urban Students," by J. Williams and K. Williamson, 1992, *Action in Teacher Education, 14*(2), pp. 11–12. Adapted with permission of Association of Teacher Educators.

Summary

The Field of Child Development

The field of child development examines how human beings change from the time of conception, throughout infancy and childhood, and on into adolescence. Each child's developmental journey is guided by three factors: nature, nurture, and the child's own activity. Developmental theorists typically focus on the progression of children in three domains—physical, cognitive, and social-emotional—and look at how a variety of environmental contexts affect children's developmental course.

Basic Developmental Issues

Developmental theorists wrestle with three basic issues regarding children's development. First, they wonder how much development is influenced by nature (heredity) and how much by nurture (environment). Second, they speculate about the extent to which developmental paths are universal (true for everyone) or diverse (unique to individuals). And third, they debate about whether developmental changes can be characterized as qualitative (involving major transformations) or quantitative (reflecting gradual trends). Clearly, development is influenced by nature *and* nurture, some aspects of development are universal and others reflect diversity, and the course of development is characterized by both qualitative and quantitative change.

Theories of Child Development

Developmentalists have proposed a wide variety of explanations as to how and why children and adolescents change over time. These explanations can be categorized into seven general theoretical frameworks: biological, behaviorist and social learning, psychodynamic, cognitive-developmental, cognitive process, sociocultural, and developmental systems perspectives. These perspectives often focus on different domains of development and may place greater or lesser importance on nature versus nurture, universality versus diversity, and qualitative versus quantitative change.

Developmental Periods

Infancy (birth to 2 years) is a remarkable time of rapid growth and emergence of basic human traits, including emotional bonds to other people, language, and increasing motor mobility. Early childhood (2–6 years) is a time of imaginative play, rapid language development, advances in gross motor and fine motor skills, and expansion of social skills. During middle childhood (6–10 years), children tackle in earnest the tasks that they will need to participate effectively in adult society; they also develop friendships and internalize many of society's rules and prohibitions. In early adolescence (10–14 years), youngsters are preoccupied with the physical changes of puberty and sensitive about how they appear to others; at the same time, they are beginning to think in abstract and logical ways. Late adolescence (14–18 years) is a period of intensive interaction with peers and greater independence from adults. Although many older adolescents make wise choices, others engage in risky and potentially dangerous behaviors.

Commitment to Developmentally Appropriate Practice

Effective care of youngsters is based on an understanding of universal developmental pathways and respect for individual differences. As a future educator, you can identify and capitalize on individual children's strengths and nudge children toward increasing responsibility. Through ongoing education, conversations with colleagues, and participation in professional organizations, you can keep up to date on advancements in child development and maintain an optimistic outlook on your ability to help children.

Applying Concepts in Child Development

In this chapter you learned the value of identifying children's strengths. In the section "Preparing for Developmentally Appropriate Practice," you read that these strengths provide the foundation for future growth. The following table describes five experiences by youngsters that reflect one or more underlying developmental strengths. For each experience, the table identifies youngsters' developmental strengths, an implication for building on these strengths, or both. Notice that some of the cells have been left empty to give you a chance to make your own notes. After completing the cells, compare your responses with those in Table 1-1 in the *Study Guide and Reader*.

APPLYING CONCEPTS IN CHILD DEVELOPMENT	Identifying Developmental Strengths in Youngsters		
Age	A Youngster's Experience	Developmental Concepts *Identifying Developmental Strengths*	Implications *Building on Developmental Strengths*
Infancy (Birth–2)	An 8-month-old baby, Marita, has an ear infection and fever. She is in distress and cries often, reaching out for caregivers.	Marita is communicating her distress, having learned that caregivers can comfort her when she is hurt, tired, or scared. The baby's developmental strengths are her *expectation that others will help her* and her *ability to communicate her distress.*	
Early Childhood (2–6)	A 3-year-old child, Sydney, asks questions constantly. Sydney wants to know why the sky is blue, why leaves are green, why a doll is broken, and why it is time for a nap.	Sydney has an insatiable and healthy curiosity. The child has also learned that he can engage adults in conversations by asking a series of questions. Sydney's developmental strengths are a *desire for new knowledge* and the possession of *rudimentary conversation skills.*	Answer the child's questions when you can, tell him politely when you are *not* able to answer his questions, and read him books and arrange other educational experiences that address his most pressing interests.
Middle Childhood (6–10)	A group of 9-year-old boys and girls are playing football at recess. The game appears to be fun, but it is punctuated with arguments over whose turn it is to play particular positions and whether or not there has been a touchdown, the ball is in or out, or a tackle has been too rough.		Tell the children that their football game looks fun and that they seem to be working out their differences. Make sure that no one is bullying other children, and intervene if necessary.
Early Adolescence (10–14)	Between classes, middle school students talk in the hallways, pass notes, and laugh. Boys and girls congregate in separate groups, eye one another, and seem to be self-conscious.	These young adolescents are learning to relate to one another in entirely new ways. Their developmental strengths are the *exuberant way in which they approach peer relationships* and the *heightened interest they show in social networks.*	Permit free talk during passing times between classes, but ask one teacher or staff member to be nearby to intervene if necessary (e.g., if youngsters are inclined to harass one another). Be a receptive listener to young adolescents who feel slighted or ridiculed by peers.

(continued)

APPLYING CONCEPTS IN CHILD DEVELOPMENT

Identifying Developmental Strengths in Youngsters (continued)

Age	A Youngster's Experience	Developmental Concepts *Identifying Developmental Strengths*	Implications *Building on Developmental Strengths*
Late Adolescence (14–18) 	A group of high school students believes that school is "dumb" and their classes are boring. They see their teachers as hypocritical and out-of-touch. They have some specific thoughts on how rules and classes should be changed. They decide to write a letter to the newspaper and demand that either the school be changed or they be allowed to graduate early.	These adolescents are questioning the way schools are designed. Their developmental strengths are *an ability to see how the world could be different* and their *idealism* that school could be improved dramatically.	

Key Concepts

child development (p. 4)
physical development (p. 5)
cognitive development (p. 5)
social-emotional development (p. 5)
context (p. 5)
nature (p. 6)
temperament (p. 6)

maturation (p. 7)
nurture (p. 7)
sensitive period (p. 8)
universality (p. 8)
diversity (p. 8)
qualitative change (p. 9)
quantitative change (p. 9)
stage (p. 9)

stage theory (p. 9)
theory (p. 12)
biological theory (p. 12)
behaviorism and social learning theory (p. 12)
psychodynamic theory (p. 13)
cognitive-developmental theory (p. 14)

cognitive process theory (p. 14)
sociocultural theory (p. 15)
developmental systems theory (p. 16)
developmentally appropriate practice (p. 23)

Companion Website

Now go to our Companion Website at www.prenhall.com/mcdevitt to assess your understanding of chapter content with a Practice Quiz, apply what you've learned in Essay Questions, and broaden your knowledge with links to related Developmental Psychology Web sites.

Using Research to Understand Children and Adolescents

chapter 2

Case Study: The After-School Program

Case Study: The After-School Program

Principles of Research

Analyzing Developmental Research

Conducting Research in Schools

Case Study: The Study Skills Class

Summary

Applying Concepts in Child Development

Nicholas Cutforth worried about children in his community being left unsupervised after school. He read research studies and found that his fears were justified: Having a lot of unsupervised time increases the chances that young people will experiment with drugs, sex, and violent activities (Cutforth, 1997).

Nicholas decided to act. He launched an after-school program for fourth- and fifth-grade children attending school in an economically disadvantaged neighborhood of Denver, Colorado. It would give children a safe place to go, opportunities for sport and exercise, and coaching in social skills (Cutforth, 1997).

But would the program *really* help children? To answer this question, Nicholas studied the program's effects over a 3-year period, focusing on its impact on children's social skills. Each year he revised the program based on his findings.

In the first year, the program operated one afternoon a week and focused on fitness exercises, cooperative games, and group sports. Social lessons such as reminders to consider the feelings of others were also integrated into the physical activities. After each session, the children and Nicholas wrote in journals about their experiences. Children articulated a range of reactions, for example:

> I like playing basketball. . . .
> I didn't like today. (Cutforth, 1997, p. 133)

Nicholas's own journal included mixed reactions. He grew concerned about his inability to manage the children:

> The kids knew I was getting angry and that only made things worse. . . .
> Ricardo had been in trouble in school and never really settled down in class today. How can I deal with all his problems when I have 19 other kids to teach? (pp. 133–134)

At the end of the first year, Nicholas interviewed the children. Some children reported that they learned valuable social lessons:

> The program taught me to control my temper and now I don't lose it so fast. . . .
> I learned to have faith in myself. (p. 134)

However, other children talked about physical activities alone and did not mention social lessons:

> I learned how to play basketball. . . .
> I'm better at volleyball. (p. 134)

Nicholas concluded that his own weak management skills prevented him from cultivating children's social-emotional development. He needed help!

In the second year, Nicholas recruited two graduate students from the local university and three sixth-grade boys who had participated in the program the previous year to help run the program, which had been increased to two sessions per week. Nicholas was pleased with the results. Compared to children in the first-year program, children in the second-year program interacted more cooperatively and attended more frequently. The middle school helpers also reported that they learned from the experience, as in this report:

> It's great fun helping the kids and teaching them self-control skills. When I was in the program last year, I learned to encourage my team members. Now I'm trying to teach the kids what I learned. (p. 135)

(continued)

During the third year of the program, the three middle school boys asked Nicholas if they could continue as volunteers. Five additional children who had just completed the program wanted to become assistants as well. At this point, Nicholas decided to call the child assistants "apprentice teachers" and to instruct them in basic techniques for teaching and coaching, conflict resolution, communication, and time management. He also arranged enrichment activities, such as visits to a local university. Nicholas wondered if being an apprentice teacher might lead the boys to resist negative peer pressure and to take on productive roles in society. He wrote a comprehensive research plan for the new intervention. Nicholas continued to gain new insights as he collected and examined data on the children's experiences.

Research is a dependable way for educators to learn about child development. In the opening case study, Nicholas identified a problem and used two types of research to help solve it. He examined reports from developmental scholars, and he conducted his own observations, interviews, and analyses of data from children. By considering these two sources of information, Nicholas was able to implement an effective program for children. Nicholas's efforts show the powerful role that research data can play in helping teachers and other practitioners understand children's needs. This chapter teaches you how to analyze others' research and conduct your own insightful analyses of children. To make the most of research, both as a consumer and as a producer, you first need to learn basic principles of child development research.

Principles of Research

There are three basic principles all researchers must follow to make a meaningful contribution to knowledge about child development. First and foremost, researchers must obey a strict ethical code. Second, they must follow the steps of the scientific method. Finally, they must select children and adolescents who come from a particular group and can provide the desired information. We examine each of these principles in turn.

Ethical Protection of Children

A paramount concern for researchers is that they conduct their research in an ethical manner, in particular that they are honest and respectful of the rights of the children in their studies (American Psychological Association, 2002; Society for Research in Child Development, 2004). To protect children's rights, researchers follow these specific ethical standards:

- *Do no harm.* Researchers prioritize the welfare of children over their own desires for information. They avoid procedures that cause children stress, embarrassment, or pain.
- *Obtain consent.* Children's and parents' permission is obtained before information is collected. If researchers will not intrude on children's customary activities—for example, if they plan to observe children's spontaneous play at the park—they might consult supervisors and authorities trained in research ethics rather than seek consent directly from children and families (Stringer & Dwyer, 2005).
- *Preserve children's privacy.* Researchers usually describe group trends in their results. When researchers single out a particular child, they identity the child with a fictitious name and withhold other identifying information.
- *Be honest.* Children generally expect adults to be honest. Researchers do not exploit or undermine this assumption. Thus deception with children is almost always avoided.

- *Communicate openly.* After children provide information, researchers respond to any questions or concerns children or parents might have. When researchers write up their results, they often send families a brief description of their findings. Researchers also share the results with other investigators and, if appropriate, the general public.

In addition to protecting children, researchers must ensure they are collecting accurate, unbiased data. To do so, they use the scientific method.

If you were a teacher standing close to these children, would you be able to figure out why they were laughing? Your effectiveness in supporting children depends in part on your perceptive analyses of their behavior.

The Scientific Method

The **scientific method** is a powerful strategy for gaining knowledge because it requires researchers to think critically about the data they collect and the conclusions they draw. The scientific method includes these general steps:

1. *Pose a question.* Researchers clearly state the question they want to answer. When they can make predictions about the outcomes of their study, they also state hypotheses.
2. *Design an investigation.* Once the question is clear, researchers must figure out what kinds of information will help answer the question and, if applicable, test hypotheses.
3. *Collect data.* Researchers recruit children and then gather information using carefully defined procedures.
4. *Analyze the data.* Researchers organize the data, categorize children's responses, look for themes, and when appropriate, perform statistical tests. After making sense of the data, they draw conclusions relevant to the research question.
5. *Share the results.* Researchers make reasonable claims about the meaning and significance of the results. They present the findings to colleagues at conferences and in professional journals.

To use the scientific method effectively, developmental researchers need to have access to children and adolescents who are willing to serve as research participants. This element of the research is especially significant, and so we examine it further.

Research Participants

In deciding whom to recruit for their study, researchers identify a particular population about which they want to draw conclusions. They then select a subgroup, or **sample,** of that population. For example, imagine that a team of developmental psychologists wants to know how older adolescents think about employment. Perhaps these scholars are interested in all adolescents in public high schools in San Francisco, California. With the help of administrators in San Francisco schools, the researchers obtain a list of homeroom teachers and randomly select 10 percent of these teachers. Next, researchers ask the selected teachers to distribute letters, consent forms, and surveys to students and parents. If the return rate for the materials is fairly high, the researchers can be reasonably confident that their *sample* of adolescents is representative of the larger *population* of adolescents in public schools in San Francisco.

Ideally, individuals in the sample reflect the characteristics of the population. Yet this is not always the case. For example, many potential participants may decide not to join the study. Furthermore, developmental researchers, who historically have come primarily from a middle-class European American background, have found it easier to recruit children from similar backgrounds. The unfortunate result is that we have less information about youngsters from ethnic and racial minority groups, language environments other than English-only families, and low-income communities (e.g., Coll et al., 1996; C. B. Fisher, Jackson, & Villarruel, 1998). Currently, many developmental researchers are studying hard-to-find populations, such as migrant and homeless families. These outreach efforts will eventually strengthen conclusions about the universality and diversity of child development.

In some kinds of research, however, generalizing to a larger population is not the goal. Rather, developmental scholars study a child or small group of children intensively with the

scientific method
Multistep process of answering a carefully defined research question by using critical thinking and analysis of the evidence.

sample
The specific participants in a research study; their performance is often assumed to indicate how a larger population of individuals would perform.

aim of portraying, with depth and insight, life as the child or children experience it. When teachers and other practitioners study children in their care, as Nicholas did in the introductory case study, they are hoping to analyze these children's experiences in enough depth that they can draw conclusions about the experiences of *these children*—not about children in general.

Researchers may adapt the basic processes of following ethical standards, thinking scientifically, and recruiting participants in distinct ways that fit their particular research questions. Having this flexibility means that researchers make many decisions as they carry out their studies. Usually they make good choices, implementing sound methods that allow them to effectively answer their questions. Occasionally, though, researchers collect information haphazardly or make unwarranted interpretations of their data. Because investigations do vary in quality, it is important to analyze research reports critically rather than simply taking researchers' conclusions at face value. In the next section we examine developmental research in greater detail.

Analyzing Developmental Research

High-quality developmental research offers you a world of trustworthy knowledge about child development. To interpret developmental research sensibly, you need to become familiar with common data collection techniques and research designs.

Data Collection Techniques

Researchers rely on four primary techniques for collecting information: self-reports, tests and other assessment tasks, physiological measures, and observations of behavior. Each of these four techniques offers a unique window into the minds and habits of children and adolescents.

Self-reports.   Researchers often ask children to explain their beliefs, attitudes, hopes, and frustrations. In fact, some of the most informative research data come in the form of children's and adolescents' own statements about themselves—that is, in the form of **self-reports.** Self-reports take two primary forms, interviews and questionnaires.

During face-to-face **interviews,** researchers ask questions to explore the reasoning of individual children in considerable depth. When interviewers succeed in making children feel safe and comfortable, they can learn a lot about how children think about things. In the "Research: Early Adolescence" video clip on Observation CD 1, the interviewer gently but persistently asks 12-year-old Claudia a series of questions about why she grouped seashells in a particular way. The interviewer begins the discussion in this way:

Interviewer:	All right. Why did you make the groups that you did?
Claudia:	Mm, some, they were the ones that looked the most alike.
Interviewer:	How did you decide which shells to put where?
Claudia:	Um, I looked at them, like, and how they looked on every side. And I put them with the ones that looked closest like each other.
Interviewer:	Okay. So what were you looking for when you were grouping them?
Claudia:	Um, details.

Up until this point, Claudia describes her reasoning in a fairly general way. After a series of questions and requests for information from the interviewer, Claudia elaborates:

Interviewer:	Why are those in a group?
Claudia:	Um, they looked kind of the same. Feel like they both, they have the little thing there. And they fold over like that and have a tip.
Interviewer:	Okay. What makes them different from the other ones?
Claudia:	They're longer kind of. And they're smoother than the other ones.
Interviewer:	Oh, okay. And then those ones at the far corner over there. Now tell me about those ones.

Seven-year-old Grace drew this picture of an apple tree. What kinds of interview questions might you ask Grace if you wanted to learn more about her understanding of apple trees?

Listen to an interviewer use several different types of requests to elicit information from Claudia in the "Research: Early Adolescence" clip on Observation CD 1.

self-report
Data collection technique whereby participants are asked to describe their own characteristics and performance.

interview
Data collection technique that obtains self-report data through face-to-face conversation.

Claudia: They were smaller than these, so I put them together. And they both pretty much, or all of 'em pretty much, had the same kind of thing.

Interviewer: Like what?

Claudia: Like, they all had the cone at the top. The kind of pocket area.

Developmental researchers use **questionnaires** when they need to gather responses from a large number of participants. When young people complete questionnaires, they typically read questions or statements and choose from defined options that express feelings, attitudes, or actions. For example, in studies of adolescent-parent conflict, researchers have asked adolescents to identify issues (from a list of items) that provoke disagreement with their parents. From such data, researchers have learned that most adolescent-parent conflicts center on everyday concerns, including schoolwork, social life, and chores (Caplow, Bahr, Chadwick, Hill, & Williamson, 1982; Lynd & Lynd, 1929; Montemayor, 1983).

Both interviews and questionnaires have advantages. Valuable insights emerge from interviews in which researchers ask children to express their views, probe their understandings in a thorough yet sensitive fashion, and confirm what children say with other types of data. Questionnaires are an efficient way to determine group trends in youngsters' experiences. Self-reports have definite limitations, though. Interviews are time-consuming and highly dependent on an interviewer's skills. Questionnaires exceed many children's reading abilities and do not allow researchers to probe, nor do they allow children to express confusion or mixed feelings. In addition, when researchers are unfamiliar with children's typical ways of thinking, they may unintentionally create response options that are out of sync with children's actual ideas. Despite such difficulties, self-report techniques can give researchers vivid glimpses into the thoughts and actions of growing youths.

Tests and other assessment tasks. A **test** is an instrument designed to assess knowledge, abilities, or skills in a fairly consistent fashion from one individual to the next. Tests allow adults to draw inferences about children's internal processes—their learning, reasoning, and ideas. Some tests involve paper and pencil, whereas others do not, but all typically yield a result in the form of a number (e.g., a score on an intelligence test) or category (e.g., "alert" or "proficient").

Tests are prevalent in Western society, even at the moment of birth. For example, at 1 minute and 5 minutes after an infant is born, medical personnel commonly administer the *Apgar scale,* scoring infants from 0 to 2 on color, heart rate, reflexes, muscle tone, and respiration (yielding a maximum of 10 points). Low Apgar scores predict serious medical risks. In one study, infants with 5-minute Apgar scores of 3 or less were far more likely to die within 28 days after birth than were infants with Apgar scores of 7 to 10 (B. M. Casey, McIntire, & Leveno, 2001).

Tests are also used to gauge the effectiveness of early interventions and new educational programs. For example, in a study by F. A. Campbell and Ramey (1994), intelligence tests and other measures of cognitive development were administered at regular intervals to children from ages 3 months to 12 years. Test scores indicated that children who participated in a child care program beginning as infants made greater cognitive gains than nonparticipants, with these gains lasting at least through age 12 (when data collection ended). A second intervention, beginning at age 5 and lasting for 3 years, was less effective. Thus these tests were valuable in revealing that interventions may be most effective when they begin at a young age.

Developmental scholars also measure children's abilities in ways that we would not necessarily think of as "tests." They make use of a variety of other **assessments,** such as asking children to perform certain tasks and then examining the understandings and skills revealed by the children's performance. For instance, developmental scholars conducting separate investigations might record children's efficiency in navigating through a maze, their accuracy in detecting emotional expressions, and their understanding of commonly used

Fourteen-year-old Connor took these notes in his history class. How might you design an interview that examines Connor's understanding of the abstract concepts he recorded (e.g., "popular sovereignty" and "social contract")?

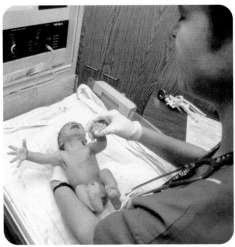

Infants are administered tests from the moment they are born. Minutes after birth, the Apgar scale helps physicians determine a newborn's physical condition.

questionnaire
Data collection technique that obtains self-report data through a paper-pencil inventory.

test
Instrument designed to assess knowledge, understandings, abilities, or skills in a consistent fashion across individuals.

assessment
Task that children complete and researchers use to make judgments of children's understandings and skills.

Observe an interviewer assess Alicia's comprehension of proverbs in the "Cognitive Development: Late Adolescence" clip on Observation CD 1.

———————— Connecting Concepts
Chapters 6 and 7 examine children's thinking processes in greater detail.

———————— Connecting Concepts
Chapter 4 examines brain development during childhood and adolescence.

physiological measure
Direct assessment of physical development or physiological functioning.

habituation
Changes in children's physiological responses to repeated displays of the same stimulus, reflecting loss of interest.

observation
Data collection technique whereby a researcher carefully observes and documents the behaviors of participants in a research study.

verbal expressions. In the "Cognitive Development: Late Adolescence" video clip on Observation CD 1, an interviewer assesses 14-year-old Alicia's comprehension of proverbs:

Interviewer: What does it mean when someone says, "Better to light a candle than to curse the darkness"?

Alicia: Well, it means, probably, that you're actually getting somewhere than just complaining about it and not doing anything about it.

Interviewer: What does it mean when someone says, "An ant may well destroy a dam"?

Alicia: I think it probably means that even though they're really small, they can still change things.

An advantage of tests and other assessment tasks is that they provide clues to children's thinking. From her responses, we know that Alicia grasps the essential meaning of the expressions presented. Assessments tell us only so much, however—we cannot tell *how* Alicia was able to decipher the proverbs. Had she previously encountered them, or did she apply strong reasoning skills on the spot? Single tests and assessments can rarely tell us how children have come to particular ideas or how they might change their skills if given particular kinds of instruction.

Physiological measures.   To learn about children's physical development, researchers often turn to **physiological measures,** indications of such bodily conditions as heart rate, hormone levels, bone growth, brain activity, eye movements, body weight, and lung capacity. Physiological measures provide valuable information about children's health and physical growth.

In addition, physiological measures have made it possible to make significant advances to our knowledge of infants' cognitive development. For example, researchers have learned a great deal about infants' attention, perception, and memory by exploiting babies' tendency to respond differently to familiar and unfamiliar stimuli. When infants are shown the same object or pattern repeatedly, they grow accustomed to it and lose interest (M. Bornstein, 1989). This tendency, called **habituation,** can be assessed through changes in heart rate, sucking, and eye movements. Habituation studies have shown that infants can detect differences between similar musical melodies and between pictures of dots that differ in number (Aldridge, Stillman, & Bower, 2001; Chang & Trehub, 1977; Hayne, Rovee-Collier, & Borza, 1991; McCall & Kagan, 1967; Xu & Spelke, 2000). Likewise, fetuses (prospective babies still in their mothers' wombs) become "bored" (they stop reacting) when they feel the same low-intensity vibration repeatedly on their mothers' abdomens (van Heteren, Boekkooi, Jongsma, & Nijhuis, 2001).

New medical technologies have also improved our understanding of brain development. We have learned of fascinating developmental patterns through animal research, analyses of brains of youngsters who died during childhood, and new technologies that can be safely implemented with living children. An example of the last of these is magnetic resonance imaging (MRI), which measures blood flow and permits comparison of parts of the brain (M. H. Johnson, 1999). One recent investigation examined MRI data on the brains of healthy individuals from age 7 to age 30 (Sowell, Delis, Stiles, & Jernigan, 2001). Compared to children's brains, adults' brains show fewer but stronger connections in areas of the brain that support judgment, restraint, and the ability to plan for the future (Figure 2-1).

An advantage of physiological measures is that they give precise indications of how children's bodies and brains are functioning. A disadvantage is that the meaning of the data they yield is not always clear. For example, are the infant habituation studies measuring distinctions that infants make thoughtfully or unconsciously? Another limitation is that many physiological tests cannot be administered often because they cause discomfort (e.g., some brain-scan procedures can be quite noisy) or may be harmful if done too frequently (as is the case with X-rays).

Observations.   Researchers conduct **observations** when they carefully watch the behavior of youngsters. Observations can offer rich portraits of "slices" of children's lives, particularly when they take place over an extended time and are supplemented with interviews, tests, and other data.

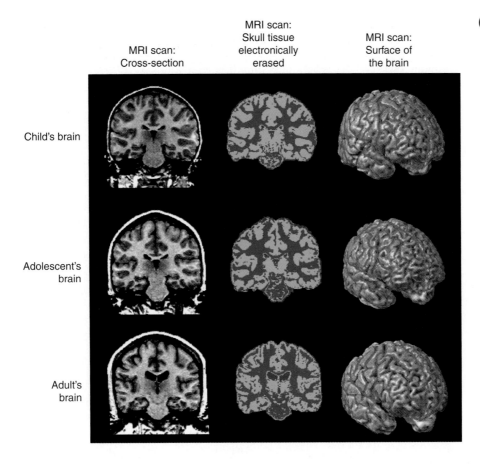

MRI scan:
Cross-section

MRI scan:
Skull tissue
electronically
erased

MRI scan:
Surface of
the brain

Child's brain

Adolescent's
brain

Adult's
brain

Figure 2-1

Images of three brains from magnetic resonance imaging (MRI): a child's brain (top row), an adolescent's brain (middle row), and an adult's brain (bottom row). Comparisons of the three brains in the middle column reveal how parts of the brain mature with age. The green reveals a decrease in the proportion of volume in the cortex—the wrinkled, caplike structure devoted to advanced psychological processes—that is made up of neurons ("gray matter"). This decrease may reflect increasing specialization in brain function in adults relative to children. The blue reveals an increase of the proportion of cells that insulate and protect neurons ("white matter"), which may reflect faster, more efficient processing. The red reveals increases in cerebrospinal fluid, which fills in the gaps around the brain, protecting and nourishing it; this fluid expands in volume when brain connections become more efficient and take up less space.

From E. R. Sowell, P. M. Thompson, D. Rex, D. Kornsand, K. D. Tessner, T. L. Jernigan, and A. W. Toga, "Mapping Sulcal Pattern Asymmetry and Local Cortical Surface Gray Matter Distribution *in vivo:* Maturation in the Perisylvian Cortices," 2002, *Cerebral Cortex, 12,* pp. 17–26. Reprinted by permission of Oxford University Press.

Researchers who conduct observations generally keep a detailed record of significant events that take place in a particular setting, such as a neighborhood playground or family home. The following observation records interactions between a father and his 5-year-old daughter, Anna:

11:05 AM   Anna looks at her father, who is sitting on the couch reading the newspaper: "Wanna play Legos, Dad?" Dad says, "Sure" and puts down the paper and gets on the floor. Anna pushes a pile of Legos toward Dad and says, "Here. You can build the factory with the volcanoes."

11:06 AM   Dad looks puzzled and says, "What factory?" Anna laughs and says, "The one where they make molten steel, silly!" Dad says "Oh, I forgot" and picks up a gray Lego and fits a red one to it." (Pellegrini, 1996, p. 22)

Although they hope to describe events as faithfully as possible, observers must make decisions about what to include and what to ignore. The observer who writes about Anna and her father may focus on the pair's negotiations over what to play and what to pretend. Other events, such as Anna dropping toys or her father scratching his head, would receive less attention.

Observations are frequently used to document characteristics and behaviors (e.g., hairstyles, dress codes, "bullying" behaviors) that young people display in public settings. They are also helpful for studying actions that individuals may be unaware of or unable to articulate (e.g., the types of questions that teachers direct toward boys and girls) and behaviors that violate social rules (e.g., temper tantrums, petty thefts). Observations of children's everyday actions in natural settings likewise tell us a lot about children's interests. By observing 7-month-old Madison in the "Emotional Development: Infancy" video clip on Observation CD 2, you can see Madison's interest in the visual properties of toys and books.

The strength of observations is their ability to tell us what children actually do—not simply what children *say* they do or what parents report about their children's actions. Observations have their weaknesses, however. For one thing, the presence of an observer might actually change the behaviors under investigation. Children will sometimes be deterred from

Observe Madison studying objects visually in the "Emotional Development: Infancy" clip on Observation CD 2. What might developmental scholars learn from Madison's eye movements?

When Claudia sorts seashells in the "Research: Early Adolescence" clip on Observation CD 1, might the unfamiliar adult filming her affect her thoughts, feelings, and actions?

showing typical behaviors because they are distracted by the presence of an observer. They may misbehave or, alternatively, stay on task more than usual. Some young people become self-conscious or even anxious in the presence of a stranger. To minimize these reactions, researchers often spend considerable time in a setting before they observe formally. That way, children grow accustomed to researchers and eventually carry on as they normally would.

Another weakness of observations is that researchers' expectations can influence their conclusions. For example, if an observer perceives children to be hostile, she may categorize an interaction between two boys as "hitting," whereas another observer who perceives children as friendly may see the same scuffle as "energetic play." Researchers handle this problem by spending as much time as possible in the setting, carefully defining the events and behaviors they observe, and discussing their observations with other observers.

The four data-gathering techniques just described—self-reports, tests and other assessment tasks, physiological measures, and observations of behavior—must be implemented with care to ensure the accuracy of the data collected.

Accuracy in data collection.   As researchers collect data, they continually ask themselves how they know they are getting accurate information. In other words, researchers are concerned with **validity,** the extent to which their data collection method actually assesses what they want to assess. Researchers must show that they are examining the essential parts of a well-defined domain. For instance, researchers who see mathematical skill as being comprised of both computational proficiencies (adding, subtracting, multiplying, dividing) and problem-solving abilities (making sense of situations by determining their underlying mathematical patterns) must make a point to include *both* types of competencies in their assessments.

Researchers must also rule out the influence of other, irrelevant traits. For instance, do scores on a test of mathematical ability reflect children's knowledge of a particular culture—for instance, are there too many questions about American sports? Does a test of scientific reasoning assess children's desire to please the experimenter as much as it assesses finesse in thinking skills? Only when researchers can say no to such questions do they have some assurance that their methods are valid.

The validity of data is also enhanced when investigators reflect on the perspectives of research participants. Skilled researchers recognize that young people bring their own expectations and agendas to interactions with adults. Some participants (adolescents especially) may give responses to shock a researcher or in some other way undermine the research effort. Others may tell a researcher what they think the researcher wants to hear. Furthermore, children and adolescents may understand words and phrases differently than researchers do. Probing sensitively, searching for confirmation through a variety of sources, and reassuring children that they are not personally being evaluated are strategies researchers use to improve the validity of data.

Ten-year-old Laura drew this picture of a field of poppies. How might you validly and reliably conduct observations to learn about Laura's techniques in planning, drawing, and coloring her pictures?

Researchers must also ask whether their data collection techniques are yielding consistent, dependable results—in other words, whether their methods have **reliability.** Data are reliable when the same kind of result is obtained in a variety of circumstances. In general, reliability is lower when unwanted influences (usually temporary in nature) affect the results. Children and adolescents, like adults, inevitably perform differently on some occasions than on others; they may be more or less rested, attentive, cooperative, honest, and articulate. Their performance is also influenced by characteristics of the researcher (e.g., gender, educational background, ethnic origin, appearance) and conditions in the research setting (e.g., how quiet the room is, how instructions are worded, what kinds of incentives are given for participation).

Sometimes the assessment instrument itself influences the reliability of scores, as occurs when two different forms of an instrument yield dissimilar conclusions about children. This could happen if one form is more difficult or if two researchers interpret the same data differently. When the researchers are making subjective judgments (e.g., about the sophistication of children's artistic skills), they must establish clear criteria or they run the risk of making undependable judgments.

validity
Extent to which a data collection technique actually assesses what the researcher intends for it to assess.

reliability
Extent to which a data collection technique yields consistent, dependable results—results that are only minimally affected by temporary and irrelevant influences.

In summary, a variety of factors can distort the meaning of data (see Table 2-1). Researchers generally cannot rule out *all* threats to validity and reliability, but they can show that they have taken reasonable precautions to minimize distortions.

TABLE 2-1

Distortions of Information Collected from Children and Adolescents

Source of Information	Possible Distortion	Example	Implication
Self-Reports (interviews and questionnaires)	Memory of research participants	In a study of children's informal experiences with science in their families, a 9-year-old forgets about his family's frequent trips to the local natural history museum.	When soliciting information from children (perhaps about their life experiences or their understandings of concepts), begin with general questions and then ask specific follow-up questions to probe children's meaning.
	Interpretations by research participants	When asked if she has encountered any sexual harassment at her school, a teenager focuses only on unwanted physical contacts. She does not share the researcher's more comprehensive definition, which also includes verbal harassment.	When asking children and adolescents for their opinions and experiences, define your terms carefully.
	Defensiveness of research participants	In an anonymous survey, a young adolescent prefers not to admit that she has experimented with marijuana.	Respect children's right to privacy, but recognize that they may not always be honest with you about sensitive issues.
Tests and Other Assessment Tasks	Response style of research participants	Children rush through a test, responding quickly and not very carefully, so that they can have a longer recess.	Encourage children to work carefully and thoroughly on tests, and give them reasons and incentives for performing at their best.
	Cultural bias in test content	Some children taking a mathematics test have difficulty with two questions—one asking them to calculate the perimeter of a football field and another asking them to calculate the area of a baseball diamond—because they have little familiarity with these sports.	Carefully screen test content and eliminate any items that may either penalize or offend children from particular backgrounds.
	Participants' familiarity with test format	Some children in a third-grade class have never taken tests involving a matching-item format and so skip all items using this format.	Give children ample practice with the test formats you will be using.
Physiological Measures	Participants' attention to stimuli	In a study on infants' habituation, half of the babies tested are sleepy and do not attend to the array of objects shown to them.	When you want to draw conclusions about whether infants can make distinctions among stimuli, present them with tasks only when they are rested, fed, and alert.
	Participants' motivation	In a study of lung capacity of adolescents, participants are not motivated to perform at their best.	Establish rapport with participants, and encourage them to do their best on physical tasks.
	Instrumentation problems	A computer operator examining brain images fails to separate pictures of brain matter from those of surrounding tissues. The result is that the estimates of brain matter are confounded with the data on total brain volume.	Ensure that physiological data are produced according to the highest technical standards. Do not interpret information you are not adequately trained to analyze.
Observations	Bias of observers	In a study of gender differences in sharing behavior, an observer expects girls to share their possessions more often than boys and so is more apt to notice such actions in girls.	Think about your own biases about children and how they may color what you "see."
	Attention limitations of observers	In a study of nonverbal communication in older adolescents, a researcher misses a third of the smiles, gestures, winks, and other subtle communication behaviors that they display.	Keep in mind that you can take in only a limited amount of information in any given period of time.
	Effects of the observer's presence	During a researcher's observations of an after-school science club, young adolescents are unusually quiet, businesslike, and on task.	Be alert to ways that children might change their behavior when they know that you are watching.

Source: Distortions in self-reports, tests, and observations identified by Hartmann & George, 1999.

Using multiple data collection techniques.   In addition to eliminating possible distortions, researchers sometimes strengthen their conclusions by using several different measurement techniques. The information collected is often more persuasive as a result.

The value of multiple data sources is demonstrated nicely in research with children in Brazil. Regina Campos and her colleagues (1994) interviewed children and adolescents who worked, and in some cases also lived, on the streets of a large city. These researchers supplemented open-ended interviews and group discussions with structured interviews and in-depth observations of youths. As an example, researchers learned through self-reports that young people who lived on the streets faced more serious problems than those who lived at home: 75 percent of the street-based youths but only 15 percent of the home-based youths reported engaging in illegal activities. The observations they conducted gave depth to these verbal reports. A member of the research team aptly captures the desperation of drug dependency:

> I was in the square, the kids were sniffing thinner. L.A. was very agitated because the can had finished. L.R. said, "Look at that, just because the thinner's gone, he's in the mood, the first neck-lace that appears, he'll grab it." D.R. added, "It's true, when the thinner's gone they all get nerv-ous until they get money for another can; when they buy it they . . . are calm again." (R. Campos et al., 1994, p. 325)

Having carefully collected information from children, researchers must also consider the meaning of the data within the broader context of the study. To a large extent, the research design directs the interpretation of the data.

Research Designs

The *research design* translates the research question into concrete elements in a study. The design specifies the schedule of data collection and strategies for analyzing the data. In child development research, the design typically focuses on one of these themes: the effects of new treatments on children, the elements of children's development that occur together, those aspects of children's behavior that change with time and those that stay the same, and the nature of children's everyday experiences.

Studies that identify causal relationships.   In an **experimental study,** a researcher manipulates one aspect of the environment and measures its impact on children. Experiments typically involve an intervention, or *treatment,* of some sort. Participants are divided into two or more groups, with separate groups receiving different treatments or perhaps with one group (a **control group**) receiving either no treatment or a presumably ineffective one. Following the treatment(s), the researcher looks at the groups for differences in the children's behavior.

In a true experimental design, participants are assigned to groups on a *random* basis; they have essentially no choice in the treatment (or lack thereof) that they receive.[1] Random assignment increases the likelihood that any differences among the groups (perhaps differences in motivations or personalities of group members) are due to chance alone. With the exception of administering a particular treatment, the experimenter makes all conditions of the research experience identical or very similar for all of the groups. The researcher thus tries to ensure that the only major difference among the groups is the experimental treatment. Therefore, any differences in children's subsequent behaviors are almost certainly the *result* of treatment differences.

A classic study illustrates the use of an experimental design (Bandura, Ross, & Ross, 1963). Preschool-aged children (2½ to 5½ years old) were brought to a playroom and ran-domly assigned to one of four conditions. Children in the *Real-Life Aggression* condition watched an adult (serving as a model) act aggressively toward an inflated Bobo doll (a 5-foot

experimental study
Research study in which a researcher manipulates one aspect of the environment (a treatment), controls other aspects of the environment, and assesses the treatment's effects on participants' behavior.

control group
A group of participants in a research study who do not receive the treatment under investigation; often used in an experimental study.

---

[1]Ethical considerations may lead researchers to give an alternative treatment to members of the control group. The researcher offers something of value to children in the control group while not compro-mising the experimental comparison. In other circumstances researchers make the experimental treat-ment available to children in the control group *after* the study has been completed.

Photographs of children, aged 3 to 6 years, imitating aggressive acts made by an adult model, from a study by Bandura, Ross, and Ross (1963). Researchers found that children who viewed aggressive models behaved more aggressively than those who did not view aggressive acts. Experimental studies, such as this one, are useful to adults working with children because they clearly identify causal effects. From "Imitation of Film-Mediated Aggressive Models," by A. Bandura, D. Ross, and S. A. Ross, 1963, *Journal of Abnormal and Social Psychology, 66*, pp. 3-11. Reprinted with permission.

plastic figure). The model punched the doll in the "nose," sat on it, hit it with a mallet, tossed it in the air, and kicked it. The model also made verbally aggressive comments such as, "Sock him in the nose." Children in the *Human Film-Aggression* condition watched a movie of a model performing the same actions. Children in the *Cartoon Film-Aggression* condition watched a televised "cartoon" character (a woman dressed as a black cat) doing the same things, but in this case the film was accompanied by cartoon music. In the *Control* condition, children had no exposure to aggressive models.

Following exposure to a treatment or control condition, the experimenter met with each child individually. She gave the children some appealing toys but then told them that these were her very best toys and that she was going to save them for some other children.[2] After this attempt to frustrate the children, the experimenter did paperwork and moved to a corner of the room to become "as inconspicuous as possible" (p. 5). Researchers behind a one-way mirror observed children's responses, focusing on their aggressive behavior.

The results of the study are more complicated than we can fully describe here, but the gist is that children in the treatment groups were more aggressive than were children in the control group. In addition, children imitated specific aggressive acts more often in the live model condition than they did in the cartoon model condition (recall the rather specific and unusual acts of aggression the models used, such as sitting on the doll and punching it in the nose).

Experiments are unique among research designs because of the degree to which outside influences are controlled and therefore eliminated as possible explanations for the results obtained. For this reason, experiments are the method of choice when a researcher wants to identify possible cause-effect relationships.

In many situations experiments are impossible, impractical, or unethical. When random assignment isn't a viable strategy, researchers may conduct a **quasi-experimental study,** in which they administer one or more experimental treatments but do not randomly assign participants to treatment and control groups (D. T. Campbell & Stanley, 1963). For example, a team of researchers might examine the effects of an after-school recreation program on aggressive behavior in middle school students. The researchers establish the program at one middle school and then enlist a second middle school to serve as a control group. Before starting the program, the researchers collect data to ensure that students at the two schools share certain characteristics (e.g., type of community and

Connecting Concepts —————
Factors affecting children's aggression are examined more thoroughly in Chapter 12.

---

[2]An act of deception such as this would be carefully reviewed ahead of time by a panel of researchers with expertise in ethics. When deception is permitted, researchers are required to take other measures that protect children's welfare. For example, at the end of a study, they might explain to participants why and how the study was conducted and help them feel at ease about their experiences.

quasi-experimental study
Research study in which one or more experimental treatments are administered but in which random assignment to groups is not possible.

Consider the following questions:

- Do children with high self-esteem achieve at higher levels in school than do children with low self-esteem?
- How is children's aggressiveness related to their popularity?

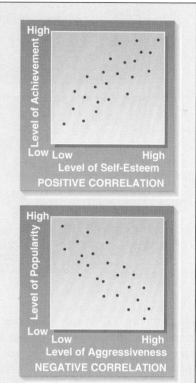

These two questions ask about relationships between two variables—between self-esteem and school performance and between aggressiveness and popularity. The nature of such relationships is sometimes expressed with a statistic known as a *correlation coefficient.*

A correlation coefficient is a number between –1 and +1; most correlation coefficients are decimals (either positive or negative) somewhere between these two extremes. A correlation coefficient simultaneously tells us about the direction and strength of the relationship between two variables.

Direction of the relationship. The sign of the coefficient (+ or –) tells us whether the relationship is positive or negative. In a *positive correlation,* as one variable increases, the other variable also increases. In children, self-esteem is positively related to academic achievement (Marsh, 1990a). In a *negative correlation,* as one variable increases, the other variable decreases. Aggression and popularity are negatively correlated: Children who are more aggressive are less popular with their peers (e.g., Coie, Dodge, Terry, & Wright, 1991).

Strength of the relationship. The size of the coefficient tells us how strong the relationship is. A number close to either +1 or –1 (e.g., +.89 or –.76) indicates a *strong correlation:* The two variables are closely related, so knowing the level of one variable allows us to predict the level of the other variable with considerable accuracy. A number close to 0 (e.g., +.15 or –.22) indicates a *weak correlation:* Knowing the level of one variable allows us to predict the level of the other variable, but we cannot predict with much accuracy. Coefficients in the middle range (e.g., those in the .40s and .50s, whether positive or negative) indicate a *moderate correlation.*

In the graphs above, each dot shows the degree to which a person exhibits the separate factors.

Figure 2-2

Correlation coefficients as statistical summaries of relationships

family income levels). The researchers cannot, however, make sure that the groups are similar in every respect. The possibility exists that some other variable (e.g., presence of gangs at one school but not the other) may account for any later difference in students' aggressive behavior.

Studies that identify associations.   Some studies are aimed at uncovering patterns that exist naturally in children's lives. In an investigation examining associations, researchers collect information on one variable, such as the amount of time per week parents read to children, and see if it is related to another variable, such as the size of children's vocabulary. A **correlation** is a specific type of association indicating the extent to which two variables are related to each other. If a correlation exists, one variable changes when the other variable does, in a somewhat predictable fashion. The direction (positive or negative) and strength of a correlation are often summarized by a statistic known as a **correlation coefficient,** which we describe in Figure 2-2.

In a **correlational study** investigators do not change anything, as they do in an experiment. Instead, they look for naturally occurring associations among existing characteristics, behaviors, or other variables. For example, in a study with 8- to 11-year-old children, Shavers (2000) found an association between children's exposure to community violence and children's expressions of aggression. Children who had seen a lot of violence in their neighborhoods tended to act aggressively themselves. Because these data are correlational in nature, they do not give definitive clues as to what factors might lead children exposed to violence to become aggressive themselves. Although community violence might have triggered aggression in children, other conditions, such as parents' difficulty in supervising children, could have been the cause. Or perhaps a third factor, such as high unemployment rates, provoked both community violence and unrest in children. The complicated and uncertain manner in which variables are associated in real life means we can never draw definitive conclusions about causation from correlational data alone.

correlation
Extent to which two variables are related to each other, such that when one variable increases, the other either increases or decreases in a somewhat predictable fashion.

correlation coefficient
A statistic that indicates the nature of the relationship between two variables.

correlational study
Research study that explores relationships among variables.

Studies that show developmental change and stability.   Some investigations, known as *developmental studies,* examine how children grow, change, or stay the same as they become older and have more experiences. In a **cross-sectional study** a researcher compares individuals at two or more age levels at the same point in time and assesses the same characteristic or behavior for each age-group. For example, in a study with first- and third-grade boys, Coie, Dodge, Terry, and Wright (1991) found that first graders were more likely to be targets of aggression than were third graders.

Cross-sectional designs are frequently used to discover how children's and adolescents' thinking abilities, social skills, and other characteristics change over time. Their major weakness is that, even though they reveal differences between age levels, they do not necessarily indicate that age itself is the reason for the differences. For example, in the study about targets of aggression just described, suppose that the third-grade group had taken part in a conflict resolution program but the program was eliminated before the first-grade children could participate. In such a case, age differences in aggression might reflect program exposure more than maturational factors.

Another option for studying developmental stability and change is the **longitudinal study,** in which a researcher studies one group of children or adolescents over a lengthy period of time, often for several years and sometimes even for decades. Longitudinal designs allow us to examine the persistence of certain characteristics over time and the factors in children's early lives that forecast their later performance. An example of a longitudinal study is Eron's (1987) investigation into factors potentially related to aggressive behavior. Eron collected data at three points in time, first when the participants were in third grade, a second time 10 years later, and a third time 12 years after that. Factors evident when the participants were children, including a punitive style of discipline by their parents, children's preference for watching violent television shows, and children's lack of a guilty conscience about hurting others, predicted their aggressiveness and criminal behavior 10 and 22 years later.

To strengthen inferences that can be made about change and stability in child development, some researchers have creatively modified developmental designs. To address questions about short-term learning, some researchers have tried *microgenetic methods,* which you might think of as brief but thorough longitudinal designs. Researchers implementing microgenetic methods may study children's actions and strategies while learning a new task over a few hours, days, or weeks (Siegler & Stern, 1998; Vygotsky, 1978). Other variations include a combination of cross-sectional and longitudinal designs. For instance, a *cohort-sequential design* replicates a longitudinal study with new *cohorts*—that is, with one or more additional groups of people born in certain subsequent years. To illustrate, Suhr (1999) conducted a cohort-sequential study to examine children's scores in mathematics, reading recognition, and reading comprehension. Scores were collected every 2 years for children who were born in 1980, 1981, 1982, and 1983. Suhr found that growth in skills was rapid between ages 5 and 10 but slowed down after 10. Because the data included children from four different birth years, Suhr could be reasonably confident that the spurt of learning that occurred between 5 and 10 years is a reasonably accurate result and not an anomaly of one particular group.

Studies that describe children's experiences in natural contexts.   In a **naturalistic study** a researcher examines development in natural contexts, as children and adolescents behave and interact in their families, peer groups, schools, clubs, and elsewhere. Some of these studies, known as *ethnographies,* look at the everyday rules of behavior, beliefs, social structures, and other cultural patterns of an entire group of people—perhaps a community, a classroom, or family. Other naturalistic studies take the form of *case studies,* wherein the researcher looks at a single child or adolescent in considerable depth over a period of time. (The latter are not to be confused with the case studies in this book, which are more limited in scope.)

Naturalistic studies vary greatly in nature, as the methods they incorporate are limited only by the researcher's imagination. However, a description by Ember and Ember (1994) of the Kapauku, who lived in the central highlands of western New Guinea, can give you a feel for the naturalistic approach. War and homicides were frequent among the Kapauku, and the Embers attributed such aggressiveness to the childhood experiences of the Kapauku:

> At about 7 years of age, a Kapauku boy begins to be under the father's control, gradually sleeping and eating only with the men and away from his mother. His father gives him a garden plot to cultivate and later a pig to raise. The father tries to train his son to be a brave warrior. His

cross-sectional study
Research study in which the performance of individuals at different ages is compared.

longitudinal study
Research study in which the performance of a single group of people is tracked over a period of time.

naturalistic study
Research study in which individuals are observed in their natural environment.

training begins when the father engages his son in mock stick fights. Gradually the fights become more serious and possibly lethal when the father and son shoot real war arrows at each other. Groups of boys play at target shooting; they also play at hitting each other over the head with sticks. Boys from neighboring villages (in the same political unit) play at war by fighting with blunt arrows and sticks. (Ember & Ember, 1994, pp. 639–640)

This brief description of the Kapauku would have been possible only after extended observations in this society. Often naturalistic researchers spend a great deal of time observing and talking with the people they study. Researchers learn as much as they can about the rules by which people live, trying to capture the details of people's relationships, conversations, and beliefs. When describing any particular aspect of people's lives (in this case, aggressive actions), researchers reflect on how it fits within the broader culture and community.

In the description of research designs in this section, we included several studies focusing on one topic, children's aggression. Each individual developmental research design has its own strengths and weaknesses (Table 2-2). Together, these designs give us a more complete picture of children's aggression. More generally, the designs each contribute unique insights to our knowledge of child development.

Becoming a Thoughtful Consumer of Research

As you read this chapter, you may be studying research methods in child development for the very first time. Nevertheless, if you ask yourself a few simple questions, you can begin to distinguish studies that are worthy of your consideration from those that are not. Following are several questions to keep in mind:

● *What is your primary concern?* Unless you have a plan, it is easy to end up with research material that does not meet your needs. Jotting down notes about your interests and bringing them to a reference librarian is a reasonable tactic for beginning your search of research reports. Librarians can help you identify promising electronic databases and choose keywords that will pick up articles and other resources directly related to your concerns.

● *Were the data published in a reputable journal?* Research that is technically strong and theoretically significant tends to be published in selective journals. Research studies that are seriously flawed are published (if at all) in journals with lax standards. Concentrate your search in the former. To find reputable journals, you can check to see if national or international professional organizations sponsor journals related to your topic. For example, the American Psychological Association, the Society for Research in Child Development, and the American Educational Research Association publish several high-quality journals. Alternatively, you can ask university professors or reference librarians to recommend journals. Finally, you can examine reference lists in the back of textbooks (such as this one) that are informed by developmental research.

● *Do the data have high validity for the purpose of the research?* With articles in hand, you can examine the assurances researchers give on the accuracy of measures. For example, a team of developmental psychologists investigating children's writing skills might use a test of writing ability that has been carefully constructed and previously tested on a large population similar to the sample in the team's study.

● *Do the data have high reliability?* The data should have been influenced only minimally by temporary characteristics and chance factors. Reliability is especially an issue with young children, whose limited language skills, short attention spans, and relative inexperience with tests may lead to considerable variation in performance from one day to the next. Reliability is also a concern when researchers must make subjective judgments. For example, observers asked to distinguish between aggression and rough-and-tumble play must be trained to notice behaviors and facial expressions that effectively differentiate between these dissimilar interactions (Pellegrini, 1996).

● *Are the conclusions really supported by the data?* Experimental studies often enable researchers to draw conclusions about cause-effect relationships, but other designs rarely do. If you are reading about data from quasi-experimental and correlational studies, you

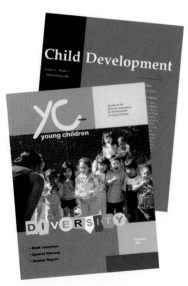

Many professional journals are available to help you learn more about infant, child, and adolescent development.

TABLE 2-2

Developmental Research Designs

Design	Strengths and Limitations	Example
Studies That Identify Causal Relationships	Strengths • Experiments offer clear information about the environmental causes of children's behaviors. • Rigorous procedures allow others to replicate the study. Limitations • Experiments conducted in artificial settings may not accurately capture conditions in the real world. • Cause-effect relationships in quasi-experiments are speculative at best.	In an experimental study, children who see an aggressive model later act more aggressively than do children who see a nonviolent model. This study demonstrates that showing an aggressive model causes an increase in children's own aggression, but the research does not reveal the natural conditions under which this effect is most likely to occur.
Studies That Identify Associations	Strengths • Correlational studies are relatively inexpensive to conduct. • Many relationships can be examined in a single study. • Children can be examined in their natural environments. Limitation • Cause-effect relationships cannot be determined from correlational data.	In a correlational investigation, children's exposure to community violence forecasts their own high levels of aggression. However, the study does not provide conclusive evidence that exposure to community violence actually causes children to become aggressive.
Studies That Show Developmental Change and Stability	Strengths • Cross-sectional designs offer an efficient snapshot of how characteristics or behaviors probably change with age. • Longitudinal studies allow prediction of later characteristics from earlier characteristics. Limitations • In cross-sectional designs, age differences can be explained in a variety of ways, including physiological maturation, exposure to different schooling experiences, and important historical events. • Longitudinal studies are expensive, time-consuming, and of questionable relevance to other populations of children.	In one study, individuals who are extremely aggressive in middle childhood tend to become unusually aggressive adults. This association does not clarify the reason for the association or indicate that it would occur in other populations.
Studies That Describe Children in Natural Contexts	Strength • Naturalistic studies capture the complexities and subtle nuances of children's environments and experiences. Limitations • Naturalistic studies are difficult and time-consuming to conduct, as they generally require extensive and in-depth data collection. • Results do not determine which factors affect children.	Cross-cultural comparisons reveal that some societies offer children more frequent and extreme experiences with violence than do others. However, the specific ways in which these experiences affect children are not clear.

should expect that authors are careful when talking about what factors *cause* children to respond in certain ways. If you are reading about naturalistic research, you should expect that authors explain procedures that give their study integrity (e.g., conducting observations over a reasonably long period of time, checking patterns they initially notice by obtaining additional information, and interpreting events with references to meaningful cultural patterns).

● *How substantial are the results?* Sometimes researchers observe dramatic effects from interventions, which make their findings compelling. For example, in a classic study by Palincsar and Brown (1984), six seventh-grade students with poor reading comprehension skills participated in twenty 30-minute sessions involving *reciprocal teaching,* a procedure in which students learn to ask themselves and one another thought-provoking questions about what they are reading. After this relatively short intervention, the students showed remarkable improvement in their reading comprehension skills, sometimes even surpassing the performance of their classmates (A. L. Brown & Palincsar, 1987; Palincsar & Brown, 1984). Such a strong effect has inspired other educators to try this strategy for promoting reading

Connecting Concepts
Reciprocal teaching is described in more depth in Chapter 6.

comprehension. In research on some other interventions (e.g., a comparison of two counseling techniques), the difference may be statistically significant but small. A very small effect is generally not worthy of your serious consideration.

● *Are the results consistent with other data?* Keep in mind that our knowledge base about children is fallible and ever-changing. The new research findings that appear each year sometimes support what we have previously thought to be true and sometimes call into question our earlier conclusions. Ideally, we must look for consistent patterns across many studies and not rely too heavily on the results of any single study.

● *How might researchers' biases have influenced their interpretations?* Much as researchers strive to be impartial, their interpretations are influenced by their expectations. For example, researchers are more likely to dwell on findings that support, rather than contradict, their hypotheses. As a reader, you cannot always know the biases of the researcher, but you can be skeptical of conclusions that are only modestly supported by data.

● *Do the conclusions seem reasonable in light of your own experiences?* Sometimes researchers and theorists offer advice that flies in the face of what common sense tells us is appropriate. For example, John Watson, a trailblazing psychologist in the early twentieth century, warned mothers about the perils of excessive "mother love" and advised them not to "hug or kiss" their children or "let them sit in your lap" (J. Watson, 1928, pp. 81, 87). His ideas about parenting are questionable today, yet he touted his position with vigor to a generation of parents and nursery school teachers. Unfortunately, some parents and teachers followed his advice. As a newcomer to the technically rich world of developmental research, you may find it difficult to determine what constitutes a reasonable application of research. However, you will definitely want to be doubtful of claims that sound outrageous or incompatible with your own experiences with children.

—————— Connecting Concepts
Chapter 5 describes the qualities of effective parenting.

● *Are the results generalizable to infants, children, or adolescents with whom you work?* Fortunately, researchers typically describe the specific characteristics (e.g., age, gender, ethnicity, family income level) of the participants in their studies. If their samples are different in important ways from the children in your charge, be cautious in your use of their results.

Now that you have a general understanding of the basic principles and methods of research, you can begin to read developmental investigations with a critical eye. You are also ready to conduct your own analyses of the things children do, say, and write.

Conducting Research in Schools

As you have seen, academic researchers work diligently to collect information about children and adolescents in ways that are ethical, sensitive, valid, and reliable. Teachers and other school professionals do the same, although their strategies are somewhat different. In this final section we consider techniques for gathering information in schools. We conclude the section by offering ethical guidelines for classroom data collection.

Collecting Information on the Job

As you interact with children and adolescents, you can use some of the same methods of data collection used by researchers. Unlike researchers, however, you will usually not have the luxury of controlled conditions for collecting information. Your primary motivations, of course, will be to effectively teach and nurture young people.

Because you will likely have a busy classroom of children and many demands on your attention, you must take extra care to think critically about the information you collect. We recommend these tactics:

● *Continually question the validity and reliability of the information you collect.* Validity and reliability are and must be ongoing concerns not only for researchers but also for teachers and other practitioners. Educators must be appropriately cautious when interpreting data they have gathered about children.

● *Form multiple hypotheses.* In your efforts to observe children and adolescents, never be content with a single interpretation, no matter how obvious that explanation might seem to you. Always consider multiple possible reasons for the behaviors you observe and resist the temptation to settle on one of them as "correct" until you've had a chance to eliminate other possibilities. In essence, try to behave as a developmental scholar would: Hold your opinions in abeyance until the data are fairly compelling. In this regard, teachers and some other professionals actually have an advantage over scholars. Whereas researchers often see children for only brief periods, educators and other practitioners can deepen their understanding of children's needs as new information becomes available.

● *Realize you may be wrong.* As you interact with children, search for evidence that both confirms your expectations and makes you change your ideas. Teresa recalls the case of an infant she cared for who was agitated one day. Teresa initially figured the infant was cranky because of being sick (as were so many children in the child care center that day). Later Teresa realized she was wrong. While changing the baby's diaper, she discovered an abscess (an inflamed sore) on the baby's bottom. Naturally, she regretted that she had not immediately investigated other causes for the baby's discomfort. These kinds of mistakes, which can be highly distressing to caregivers, are common. Knowing that you may sometimes be wrong about children's states, you can constantly look for clues from children that will help you understand them more fully.

● *Always use multiple sources of information.* Because no single source of data ever has "perfect" validity and reliability, teachers and other school personnel must use many sources of information—self-reports, tests, observations, homework, in-class creations, attendance patterns, and anything else that might be of value—to understand and draw conclusions about children's development. For example, they may look at facial expressions and body language for signs of comprehension, insight, engagement, or boredom (D. E. Hunt, 1981; Pinnegar, 1988). In the classroom, teachers can examine children's work, listen to their discussions, and consider the questions they ask, all the while trying to determine exactly what children are learning and how they are interpreting their experiences (Heuwinkel, 1998; S. M. Wilson, Shulman, & Richert, 1987).

As educators gain experience with children and adolescents, they become better able to draw inferences about youngsters' perspectives on life. They must remember, however, that no single behavior or statement is likely to be a completely trustworthy reflection of a young person's understandings and values.

● *Use all your senses.* Through years of experience working with children and adolescents, educators often develop strong intuitions about how youngsters feel and think in particular situations. Beginning teachers and caregivers do not have the benefit of years of experience, but they can be as open as possible to the clues children transmit, intentionally or not, as to their feelings and interests. For example, adults who care for infants can often guess fairly accurately which baby is crying from hunger, pain, fear, or exhaustion. But they need not rely on a mysterious sixth sense—they can keep written records of diaper changes, ounces of formula consumed, duration of naps, and so on. When infants become agitated, caregivers can refer to these records to help determine the nature of the unmet physical or emotional need.

Observing Children

If you carefully watch children and adolescents in classrooms, clubs, and other natural settings, you can learn a lot about their interests, values, and abilities. Here are some suggestions to enhance your observation skills:

● *Consider children's developmental states.* When you sense an unmet need, analyze the situation using your knowledge of child development. Your emerging familiarity with typical characteristics of different age-groups can help you target your observations of children. Often, by noticing recurrent themes in children's actions and statements, you can get a sense of their thoughts and feelings. In the following exercise, consider developmental pressures that lead some girls to become self-conscious.

INTERPRETING CHILDREN'S ARTIFACTS AND ACTIONS   My Butt's Too Big

An expert in recreation observed a group of 15-year-old girls during a leadership training program. Among the activities were a high-ropes course and rock climbing. As you read the author's notes of her observations, speculate about the developmental factors that help to explain the girls' concerns.

References to weight, height, and overall appearance were made throughout the trip and were most often self-directed and self-critical. This was most pronounced in "Swiss Seating," where the girls were taught how to tie their seat harnesses for the high ropes course. Comments included, "I don't *even* want to know how big this makes my butt look," "Like I really want to call attention to *these* thighs," and "Remind me not to eat ever again."

Another concern was that of "looking stupid." Comments indicated that the girls were actually restricting their own behavior to avoid looking uncoordinated or like a "rookie." . . . One girl hung on the rock face in the same position for a full 10 minutes waiting for others to tell her what to do so that she would not "look retarded by doing the wrong moves."

. . . There was universal relief that no males were present on the trip: "I'd hate for a guy to see me in this thing [seat harness]. There's just some things I don't want them to know." The girls frequently made comments like, "There's no way I'd do this in front of a guy. My butt's too big." (Hurtes, 2002, p. 115)

These girls were decidedly self-conscious about how they looked in front of others. This feeling is a typical sentiment of adolescence and may occur because adolescents are critical of their own bodies and assume other people are equally judgmental.

Throughout the book you will find several tools you can use to improve your ability to make insightful inferences about children. The Interpreting Children's Artifacts and Actions exercises are one such tool. Observation Guidelines tables will also assist you in spotting particular developmental abilities in children and adolescents. The first of these, "Learning from Children and Adolescents," suggests some general things to look for in your work with young people.

● *Observe how children respond to the demands of particular settings.* Teachers can see children in varied settings, such as in the classroom and cafeteria and on the playground. As you observe children and adolescents in particular settings, ask yourself what they are doing, why they might be behaving as they are, how they might be interpreting events, and how the setting may be affecting their behavior.

● *Observe youngsters' nonverbal behaviors.* Careful observation of children's posture, actions, and emotional expressions can provide important information about their preferences and abilities. For example, an infant caregiver may learn that one 18-month-old toddler slows down, pulls at his ear, and seeks comfort when he's sleepy, whereas another child of the same age speeds up, squirms, and becomes irritable when ready for a nap. During an interview with a teenage boy, a school counselor senses that he is withdrawn and despondent. In response, the counselor inquires sympathetically about his feelings toward family members, teachers, and friends at school.

● *Separate observations from inferences.* To learn to observe objectively, you can practice making separate records of what you see and what you think it means. Here are some observation notes from a student teacher, Ana, who recorded her observations in a "Notetaking" column and her interpretations in a "Notemaking" one:

Teachers and caregivers can collect valuable information about children by observing their choices and reactions in everyday environments—what they look at, what they choose to play with, what they find distressing, and what makes them laugh.

OBSERVATION GUIDELINES

Learning from Children and Adolescents

Characteristic	Look For	Example	Implication
What Children Do	• Exploration of the environment through manipulation of objects, attention, and attempts to make sense of events in conversations with other people (may indicate inquisitiveness for certain kinds of information) • Preferred activities during free time (may show children's foremost desires and interests) • Interest in people, including initiating interactions as well as responding to those initiated by others (may indicate comfort levels in social situations) • Quiet periods of self-absorption (may indicate thoughtful self-reflection or sadness) • Facial expressions (reflecting enjoyment, excitement, sadness, confusion, anger, or frustration) • Tenseness of limbs (might indicate intense concentration or excessive anxiety) • Slouching in seat (might indicate fatigue, boredom, or resistance to an activity)	Whenever his teacher engages the class in a discussion of controversial issues, James participates eagerly. When she goes over the previous night's homework, however, he crosses his arms, slouches low in his seat, pulls his hat low over his eyes, and says nothing.	Provide a safe environment with interesting and attractive objects for active exploration. Make changes to the environment based on the preferred activities of children who inhabit it. Use children's body language as a rough gauge of interest, and modify activities that do not appear to be engaging children's attention and interest. Speak individually and confidentially with children who often show signs of sadness or anger.
What Children Say	• Verbal expressions of likes and dislikes • Thoughtful and insightful questions about the topic at hand (indicates high task engagement and motivation) • Questions that have already been answered (might indicate inattentiveness or lack of understanding) • Complaints about the difficulty of an assignment (might indicate low motivation, lack of ability or confidence, or an overloaded schedule of academic and social obligations)	In a whining tone, Danielle asks, "Do we really have to include *three* arguments in our persuasive essays? I've been thinking really hard and can only come up with one!"	Read between the lines in the questions children ask and the comments they make. Consider what their questions and comments indicate about their existing knowledge, skills, motivation, and self-confidence.
What Children Produce in Assessments and Artifacts	• Careful and thorough work (indicates high motivation) • Unusual and creative ideas, artwork, or constructions (indicates high motivation and a willingness to take risks) • Numerous sloppy errors (might indicate that a child did an assignment hurriedly, has poor proofreading skills, or has a learning disability)	When Martin's social studies teacher gives several options for how students might illustrate the idea of *democracy,* Martin creates a large poster of colorful, cartoon-like characters engaging in such activities as voting, free speech, and making new laws.	When looking at and evaluating children's work, don't focus exclusively on "right" and "wrong" answers. Examine a variety of artifacts when drawing inferences about children's abilities and interests.

Notetaking

A child is working at the computer. There are fourteen students working at their desks. Six students are working with another teacher (aide) in the back of the room. It is an English reading/writing group she is working with—speaking only in English. I see a mother working with one child only and she is helping the student with something in English. There is a baby in a carriage nearby the mother. I hear classical music playing very lightly. I can only hear the music every once in a while when the classroom is really quiet. I stand up and move around the room to see what the children at their desks are working on. They are writing scary stories. The baby makes a funny noise with her lips and everyone in the class laughs and stares for a few seconds, even the teacher. . . .

Notemaking

The class seems to be really self-directed. . . . I am not used to seeing students split up into different groups for Spanish and English readers because in my class they are Spanish readers, but it is really good for me to see this because it happens in a lot of upper grade settings, and I will be working in an upper grade bilingual setting next placement. I really like the idea of putting on music during work times. I know that when I hear classical music it really helps me to relax and calm as well as focus. I think that it has the same effect on the students in this class. I'm noticing more and more that I really cherish the laughter in a classroom when it comes from a sincere topic or source. It is also nice to see the students *and* the *teacher* laughing. . . .

(C. Frank, 1999, pp. 11–12)[3]

Teachers can learn a lot from watching children's facial expressions, postures, and other nonverbal behaviors. These two girls appear to be enjoying their time together on the computer.

[3]From *Ethnographic Eyes: A Teacher's Guide to Classroom Observation* (pp. 11–12), by Carolyn Frank, 1999, Portsmouth, NH: Heinemann. Copyright 1999 by Carolyn Frank. Reprinted with permission.

It is impossible to separate objective observations completely from interpretations. Nonetheless, trying to notice the nuances in children's activities without jumping to conclusions can help you become a more perceptive observer. By distinguishing what you see from what it might mean, you can also learn about your own values as a teacher, as Ana might have done when rereading her "Notemaking" comments.

● *Try out different kinds of observations.* The kinds of observations you conduct will depend on what you hope to gain from watching and listening to children. *Running records* are narrative summaries of a child's activities during a single period of time (Nicolson & Shipstead, 2002). Running records provide teachers and other professionals with opportunities to focus on a particular child and draw conclusions about the child's emerging developmental abilities. In Figure 2-3 you can see an excerpt from a running record prepared by a language specialist for a child with a hearing impairment. After writing this running record, the language specialist concluded that Taki understood some aspects of spoken language when she followed directions. However, Taki needed help when completing the Listening Lotto game. These kinds of conclusions can offer professionals good ideas about next steps. Possibly, the language specialist observing Taki realized she might need to look further into Taki's hearing ability.

Anecdotal records are brief incidents observed and described by teachers and other professionals (Nicolson & Shipstead, 2002). Anecdotal records are typically made when an adult notices a child take an action or make a statement that is developmentally significant. For example, anecdotal records are sometimes made of children's fears, accomplishments, physical milestones, social interaction patterns, and ways of thinking. Anecdotal records tend to be far briefer than running records, and they may be written up later in the day. In other words, the adult does not typically generate anecdotal records by sitting down and writing notes; instead, he or she may simply be struck by a child's statement or action and record and reflect on it later. Anecdotal records can help identify individual needs. Teachers can also accumulate notes about children and share them with family members during conferences, informal conversations, and meetings. Figure 2-4 shows teacher-prepared anecdotal records for three young children.

Teachers sometimes use *checklists* and *rating scales* when they wish to evaluate the degree to which children's behaviors reflect specific criteria. Checklists allow observers to note whether a child's actions or work products reflect specific standards. For example,

Figure 2-3
Running record for Taki during Listening Lotto. Note that developmentalists often list a child's age in both years and additional months, separating the two numbers by a semicolon. For instance, Taki's age of 5 years and 1 month is indicated as "5;1."
From *Through the Looking Glass: Observations in the Early Childhood Classroom* (3rd ed.) (pp. 118–119), by S. Nicolson and S. G. Shipstead, 2002, Upper Saddle River, New Jersey: Merrill/Prentice Hall. Copyright 2002 by Pearson Education. Reprinted with permission.

Center/Age level:	Center for Speech and Language/3- to 6-Year-Olds		
Date:	7/17	Time:	10:20–10:26 AM
Observer:	Naoki	Child/Age:	Taki/5;1
		Teacher:	Camille

	Comments
Taki is seated on the floor with Kyle (4;8) and Camille, the teacher, in a corner of the classroom; both children have their backs to the center of the room. Taki sits with her right leg tucked under her bottom and her left leg bent with her foot flat on the floor. The Listening Lotto card is in front of her on the floor, and she holds a bunch of red plastic markers in her right hand. Camille begins the tape.	10:20
The first sound is of a baby crying. Taki looks up at Camille, who says, "What's that?" Taki looks at Kyle, who has already placed his marker on the crying baby. Camille says, "That's a baby crying," and points to the picture on Taki's card. Taki places the marker with her left hand as the next sound, beating drums, begins.	No intro of game. Hearing aid working.
Taki looks at Kyle as the drumming continues. Camille points to the picture of the drums on Taki's card, and Taki places her marker.	Understands process.
The next sound is of a toilet flushing. Taki looks at Kyle and points to the drums. Kyle says, "Good, Taki. We heard drums banging." Taki smiles. Camille says, "Do you hear the toilet flushing?" as she points to the correct picture. Taki places her marker and repositions herself to sit cross-legged. She continues to hold the markers in her right hand and place them with her left.…	10:22 Kyle supportive of Taki.

Conclusions: Taki's receptive language was on display when she followed the teacher's directions in Listening Lotto (put markers on the appropriate spots), but she did not demonstrate success on her own. Her fine motor control was in evidence as she adeptly handled small markers.

10/5 Tatiana (2;0):	While sitting on the floor in the art area peeling the wrappers off crayons, she looked up as the caregiver grew near and said, "I making the crayons all naked."
1/15 Maggie (4;8):	I listened as Maggie chattered on and on while the two of us cleaned up the block area. Finally I winked and said, "It all sounds like baloney to me." Maggie quickly asked, "What's baloney?" I replied, "It's a word that means you made all that up!" She thought for a few seconds and said, "No, it's salami!"
2/24 Matthew (7;4):	While discussing *In a Dark, Dark Room and Other Scary Stories* by Alvin Schwartz, Matthew thoughtfully shared, "Do you know what kind of scary things I like best? Things that are halfway between real and imaginary." I started to ask, "I wonder what …" Matthew quickly replied, "Examples would be aliens, shadows, and dreams coming true." (Nicolson & Shipstead, 2002, p. 139)

Figure 2-4

Anecdotal records for young children
From *Through the Looking Glass: Observations in the Early Childhood Classroom* (3rd ed.) (p. 139), by S. Nicolson and S. G. Shipstead, 2002, Upper Saddle River, New Jersey: Merrill/Prentice Hall. Copyright 2002 by Pearson Education. Reprinted with permission.

Figure 2-5 shows a checklist a debate teacher can use to evaluate a student's oral presentation. Rating scales are similar to checklists, but these ask observers not simply *whether* a child shows a particular behavior but rather *how often or consistently* the child shows the behavior. Using the rating scale in Figure 2-6, a teacher can indicate how often a child shows particular behaviors relating to being on task during independent seatwork (Pellegrini, 1996).

One means of recording observations is not necessarily better than another. Instead, each observational system has a distinct purpose. As you gain experience in observing youngsters, you are likely to see how your own understanding of individual children grows when you use several observational methods and supplement them by listening to children.

Listening to Children

From a young age, children are motivated to tell adults what makes them happy, relieved, or satisfied, on the one hand, and distressed, angry, or sad, on the other. It is up to adults to set aside the time, put youngsters at ease, and let them speak their minds. Here's how you can gain access to children's perspectives:

● *Let children know you care.* The surest way into a child's heart is, of course, to express affection sincerely and consistently. When you have earned a child's trust, the child is likely to articulate what's on his or her mind. In the excerpts in the following exercise, several high school boys willingly express their struggles.

INTERPRETING CHILDREN'S ARTIFACTS AND ACTIONS

The Image Thing

Interviewers asked high school boys about their struggles in life and their means for seeking help. As you read three of the responses, consider the kinds of pressures the boys experienced, and the ease with which they expressed their feelings.

For guys, image is probably the biggest thing . . . your appearance as a guy or how you fit in, in terms of athletics or whatever, what group you're part of, probably good athletics, pretty much kind of a smart kid, you know, well liked by people. . . . It's kind of the untouched, unspoken pressure. . . .

They [his sisters] all have this, I don't want to call it a cop out, but it's always like a fail-safe that they can get married and be a housewife and they don't have the pressure to have to have a job and to have to support a family. . . . I don't have that. . . .

You definitely have to have an image. And if you don't have your own image, and if you're not one of the persons that wears those khakis and the freaking ugly ass checkered shirts every goddamn day, then you have to have an image to stand out. You have to be someone; you have to be someone that stands out, you know someone cool, and there are kids that try to do that. (Timlin-Scalera, Ponterotto, Blumberg, & Jackson, 2003, p. 344)

Directions: On the space in front of each item, place a plus sign (+) if performance is satisfactory; place a minus sign (–) if the performance is unsatisfactory.

_____ 1. States the topic at the beginning of the report.

_____ 2. Speaks clearly and loudly enough to be heard.

_____ 3. Uses language appropriate for the report.

_____ 4. Uses correct grammar.

_____ 5. Speaks at a satisfactory rate.

_____ 6. Looks at the class members when speaking.

_____ 7. Uses natural movements and appears relaxed.

_____ 8. Presents the material in an organized manner.

_____ 9. Holds the interest of the class.

Figure 2-5

Checklist for evaluating an oral presentation
From *Writing Instructional Objectives for Teaching and Assessment* (7th ed.) (pp. 82–83), by Norman E. Gronlund, 2004, Upper Saddle River, NJ: Merrill/Prentice Hall. Copyright 2004 by Pearson Education. Reprinted with permission.

Directions: For each item, indicate how frequently the child shows this type of behavior during seatwork by circling the appropriate description.

1. Settles quietly during beginning of task.

| Never | Seldom | Sometimes | Frequently | Always |

2. Shows strong interest in completing task.

| Never | Seldom | Sometimes | Frequently | Always |

3. Concentrates on task despite difficulties and interruptions.

| Never | Seldom | Sometimes | Frequently | Always |

4. Works through task from beginning until end.

| Never | Seldom | Sometimes | Frequently | Always |

Figure 2-6

Rating scale of a child's concentration during seatwork
Adapted from *Observing Children in Their Natural Worlds: A Methodological Primer*, by A. D. Pellegrini, 1996, Mahwah, NJ: Erlbaum. Used with permission.

Connecting Concepts

One interview from Wilson and Corbett's study appears in the discussion of *self-regulated learning* in Chapter 7.

The three boys seem to have experienced pressures to fit into a group, prepare for future jobs, and distinguish themselves as individuals. The boys admitted feelings of vulnerability, which we would not expect unless they felt reasonably safe. Perhaps it is telling that author Timlin-Scalera had worked at the school for 7 months before she began collecting data. Usually children and adolescents do not disclose their fears and concerns unless an adult has established a trusting relationship with them.

● *Develop your interviewing skills.* Too often, conversations between adults and children are short, ask-a-question-and-get-an-answer exchanges. Lengthier dialogues, perhaps with an individual child or a small group of children, can be far more informative. To find out what young people believe, adults must not only encourage them to talk but also follow up with probing questions and frequent reassurances that their ideas and opinions are important and valued. For example, one expert urges teachers

> to become skilled at letting the children expose their ideas and also at getting the children to feel that they want to share their ideas with the teacher and the other children. Children must feel it is enjoyable to express themselves and to be thrilled by others' ideas. To achieve this means that both the teacher and the children must learn to communicate on equal terms and to share their experiences. (Pramling, 1996, p. 570)

Getting children to talk takes experience, but there are a few things you can do (Graue & Walsh, 1998). For instance, try a combination of open-ended questions ("How was your day?") and close-ended questions ("Did you watch TV when you went home from school?"). Also, include some general requests for information that are not in question form ("Tell me more about that"). Try not to ask a long series of questions, or your probing may seem like an inquisition. Sometimes it is appropriate to ask children how *other children* view life; this can be an effective way to help them feel safe in speaking their minds. For example, rather than asking children how they feel about achievement tests, ask them how *other children* feel ("How did kids at your school feel last week when they took the state achievement test?").

When talking with children, always consider factors that affect how they respond. Certainly the relationship between adult and child is significant, but so are other variables, including ethnicity and gender (Holmes, 1998). A child's age is also significant. Many younger children become confused with abstract terms, and some adolescents may hide their true feelings.

● *Ask children and adolescents about their experiences.* Unless adults listen to young people, they cannot fully understand young people's experiences. Sometimes children see the world in the same way as adults, but at other times they have vastly different viewpoints. For example, B. L. Wilson and Corbett (2001) found that sixth-grade students in six schools in Philadelphia shared many values with adults. The students stated that they wanted teachers to push them to complete assignments (even when they resisted), to maintain order (even when they misbehaved), and to ensure they understood material (even when they struggled). Despite their apparent desire to succeed, these youngsters were unaware of what it took to do well when subjects became difficult, and they were naive about skills needed for success in college.

When educators learn how youngsters actually experience school and other services, they can better help youngsters meet their needs. For example, from Wilson and Corbett's study, we realize that teachers need to be persistent in explaining concepts, teaching study skills, and preparing adolescents for the reality of college. Children also have much to say to other school professionals, such as school counselors. Children have told adults, for example, that they dislike frequent changes in the social workers assigned to them and resent adults' failures to protect their confidentiality (Munro, 2001).

Interpreting Assessments

In addition to observing and listening, you can gain a sense of how children think by examining their schoolwork and the many other products they create—artwork, scribbled notes to friends, and so forth. To learn from the artifacts children create, you might follow these recommendations:

● *Remember that validity and reliability apply to all assessments.* Never overinterpret any single product the child has made. For example, a frowning self-portrait is not indisputable proof that the child artist is unhappy or has low self-esteem. Perhaps he is simply having a bad day or does not like the teacher who asked him to draw the picture. Consider multiple explanations as you examine the artifact in the following exercise.

INTERPRETING CHILDREN'S ARTIFACTS AND ACTIONS   I went to davis's house

The note at right was written by 9-year-old Alex. He left it on the kitchen counter for his parents when they were out for a walk. As you examine it, consider what Alex understands about the mechanics of English.

I went to davis's house

Alex

Alex is inconsistent in his punctuation. Notice how he capitalizes the pronoun and one proper noun ("I" and "Alex") and fails to capitalize the other proper noun ("davis"). He marks possession properly ("davis's") and indents his name, as he might in a letter. Possibly, Alex's understanding of punctuation is emerging but incomplete. However, what if you learned that Alex's parents are lax about punctuation when they write informal notes yet conscientious in their punctuation in formal writing? Might Alex be imitating a *style* of informal writing rather than trying to follow all rules of punctuation? To answer that question, we would need additional writing samples from Alex, ideally with details of the circumstances in which he prepared them.

● *Keep in mind both the advantages and limitations of paper-pencil tests.* Paper-pencil tests are often an efficient way of determining what children have and have not learned. Furthermore, a well-designed test can reveal a great deal about children's thinking processes. However, appraisals of children that rely exclusively on test scores often paint a lopsided picture of their abilities. For instance, children who have limited reading and writing skills (perhaps because they have a learning disability, or perhaps because they have only recently begun to learn English) are likely to perform poorly. Furthermore, paper-pencil tests, by their very nature, cannot provide certain kinds of information. For instance, they tell us little if anything about children's self-confidence, motor skills, ability to work well with others, or expertise at using equipment.

● *In addition to examining children's work, assess environments to determine the extent to which they support children's efforts.* Some assessment strategies can identify the strengths, priorities, and limitations of families, classrooms, and other settings. For instance, special educators, social workers, and family educators can talk with families to learn more about children's resources and needs. In addition, assessment strategies are vital to prevention programs and other community services. For instance, teams of community members planning a program to prevent substance abuse may need to identify conditions in the community that increase and decrease drug use by youngsters (U.S. Department of Health and Human Services, 2001).

Conducting Action Research

To understand and address challenges in meeting children's needs, teachers can conduct systematic studies of children's learning and adjustment at school, with the goal of seeking more effective strategies and interventions for them. Such research, referred to as **action research,** takes numerous forms, such as assessing the effectiveness of a new teaching technique, gathering information about adolescents' opinions on a schoolwide issue, or conducting an in-depth case study of a particular child (Cochran-Smith & Lytle, 1993; G. E. Mills, 2003). In our introductory case study, Nicholas conducted research in order to implement and evaluate a new program for fourth and fifth graders.

Action research employs the following steps (G. E. Mills, 2003):

1. *Identify an area of focus.* The teacher-researcher begins with a problem and gathers some preliminary information that might shed light on the problem. Usually this involves perusing the research literature for investigations of related problems and perhaps also surfing the Internet or conducting informal interviews of colleagues or students. He or she then identifies one or more research questions and develops a research plan (data collection techniques, necessary resources, schedule, etc.) for answering those questions. At this point, the teacher seeks guidance from supervisors and experts in research ethics (if applicable).

2. *Collect data.* The teacher-researcher collects data relevant to the research questions. Such data might be obtained from questionnaires, interviews, observations, achievement tests, children's journals or portfolios, or existing records (e.g., school attendance patterns, rates of referral for discipline problems, hours spent by volunteers on school projects). Many times, the teacher-researcher uses two or more of these sources in order to address research questions from various angles.

3. *Analyze and interpret the data.* The teacher-researcher looks for patterns in the data. Sometimes the analysis involves computing particular statistics (e.g., percentages, averages, correlation coefficients). At other times it involves an in-depth, nonnumerical inspection of the data. In either case, the teacher-researcher relates the patterns observed to the original research questions.

4. *Develop an action plan.* The final step distinguishes teachers' research from the more traditional research studies we considered earlier: The teacher-researcher uses the information collected to select a new practical strategy—for instance, to change instructional techniques, counseling practices, home visiting schedules, or school policies.

A good example of research by a teacher is a case study conducted by Michele Sims (1993). Initially concerned with why middle school students of average intelligence struggle to comprehend classroom material, Sims began to focus on one of her students, a quiet boy named Ricardo. She talked with Ricardo, had conversations with other teachers and with university faculty, wrote her ideas in her journal, and made notes of Ricardo's work. The more she learned, the better she understood who Ricardo was as an individual and how she could better foster his development. She also became increasingly aware of how often she and her fellow teachers overlooked the needs of quiet students:

action research
Systematic study of an issue or problem by a teacher or other practitioner, with the goal of bringing about more productive outcomes for children.

> We made assumptions that the quiet students weren't in as much need. My colleague phrased it well when she said, "In our minds we'd say to ourselves—'that child will be all right until we get back to him.'" But we both wanted desperately for these children to do more than just survive. (Sims, 1993, p. 288)

DEVELOPMENT AND PRACTICE

Getting a Flavor for Conducting Research as a Teacher

- Keep a journal of your observations and reflections.

  A high school English teacher keeps a daily log of students' comments and insights about the novels they are reading.

- Talk with your colleagues about what you are observing and hypothesizing.

  A school counselor notices that girls in a school club are excited about their participation. She asks colleagues for their ideas about why the girls are so interested.

- Encourage children and families to contribute to your inquiry.

  A teacher in an infant room hears parents complain that their employers do not grant them time off to care for their children when they are sick. She asks three parents who have been most vocal to help her look into federal and corporate policies regarding family leave.

- Collect information and write about children you seem unable to reach.

  A middle school teacher keeps a journal of her observations of students who sit in the back of the room and appear to be mentally "tuned out." After a few weeks she begins to form hypotheses about strategies that might capture the interest and attention of these students.

- Conduct informal research on topics on which children or families can help.

  A career counselor examines his community's employment rates and enlists the help of adolescents to survey local businesses about possible needs that youngsters could serve in after-school jobs.

Action research serves many positive functions. It can solve problems, broaden perspectives on adults' relationships with children, foster a community spirit among adults caring for children, and make schools and communities more humane (Noffke, 1997). For individual teachers, conducting research is also a good way to improve their abilities to grasp and meet the needs of youngsters. The Development and Practice feature "Getting a Flavor for Conducting Research as a Teacher" suggests some initial steps you can take.

Ethical Guidelines for Teacher-Researchers

Regardless of how you collect data from children, you must protect children's well-being. We recommend that you learn as much as possible at college about your legal and ethical responsibilities as a school professional. In addition, we offer the following guidelines:

● *Be tentative in your conclusions.* Never put too much weight on any single piece of information. Instead, collect a variety of data sources—such as writing samples, test scores, projects, informal observations of behavior—and look for general trends. Even then, be cautious in the conclusions you draw, and consider multiple hypotheses to explain the patterns you see. Finally, when sharing your perceptions of children's talents and abilities with parents, acknowledge that these are your *interpretations,* based on the data you have available, rather than irrefutable facts.

● *Administer and interpret tests or research instruments only if you have adequate training.* Many instruments, especially psychological assessments, physiological measures, and standardized achievement tests, must be administered and interpreted by individuals trained in their use. In untrained hands they yield results that are highly suspect and, in some cases, potentially harmful.

● *Be sensitive to children's perspectives.* Children are apt to notice any unusual attention you give them. For instance, when Michele Sims was collecting data about Ricardo, she made the following observation:

> I'm making a conscious effort to collect as much of Ricardo's work as possible. It's difficult. I think this shift in the kind of attention I'm paying to him has him somewhat rattled. I sense he has mixed feelings about this. He seems to enjoy the conversations we have, but when it comes to collecting his work, he may feel that he's being put under a microscope. Maybe he's become quite accustomed to a type of invisibility. (Sims, 1993, p. 285)

When data collection makes children feel so self-conscious that their performance is impaired, a teacher-researcher must seriously consider whether or not the value of the information collected outweighs possible detrimental effects.

● *Keep your supervisor informed of your research initiatives.* You and your principal (or other supervisor) are ultimately responsible for your actions with children. Furthermore, supervisors are knowledgeable about policies in your school, district, and community that relate to research. In addition, school leaders can give you a fresh set of eyes when it comes to interpreting the data you eventually collect.

● *Maintain confidentiality.* It may be appropriate for teachers to share results of their research with colleagues. Some also make their findings known to an audience beyond the walls of their institution; for instance, they may make presentations at conferences or write journal articles describing what they have learned. However, you must never broadcast research findings in ways that violate children's anonymity. Teachers must likewise protect their data sources from examination by onlookers. For example, it would be unwise to leave a notebook containing running records or completed checklists on a table where other children and adults would have access to them.

Knowledge about children comes from a variety of sources—not only from research but also from one's own intuition, conversations with other teachers, and observations of children. None of these sources is adequate in and of itself. Each becomes more powerful and effective when complemented by other approaches. Effective teachers and other practitioners draw from as many resources as possible when deciding how best to meet the needs of children.

Case Study: The Study Skills Class

In spring semester, Deborah South is asked to teach study skills to a class of 20 low-achieving and seemingly unmotivated eighth graders. Later she describes a problem she encountered and her attempt to understand the problem through action research (South, 2003):

My task was to somehow take these students and miraculously make them motivated, achieving students. I was trained in a study skills program before the term started and thought that I was prepared. . . .

Within a week, I sensed we were in trouble. My 20 students often showed up with no supplies. Their behavior was atrocious. They called each other names, threw various items around the room, and walked around the classroom when they felt like it. . . .

Given this situation, I decided to do some reading about how other teachers motivate unmotivated students and to formulate some ideas about the variables that contribute to a student's success in school. Variables I investigated included adult approval, peer influence, and success in such subjects as math, science, language arts, and social studies, as well as self-esteem and students' views of their academic abilities.

I collected the majority of the data through surveys, interviews, and report card/attendance records in an effort to answer the following questions:

- How does attendance affect student performance?
- How are students influenced by their friends in completing schoolwork?
- How do adults (parents, teachers) affect the success of students?
- What levels of self-esteem do these students have?

As a result of the investigation, I learned many things. For example, for this group of students attendance does not appear to be a factor—with the exception of one student, their school attendance was regular. Not surprisingly, peer groups did affect student performance. Seventy-three percent of my students reported that their friends never encouraged doing homework or putting any effort into homework.

Another surprising result was the lack of impact of a teacher's approval on student achievement. Ninety-four percent of my students indicated that they never or seldom do their homework to receive teacher approval. Alternatively, 57 percent indicated that they often or always do their homework so that their families will be proud of them.

One of the most interesting findings of this study was the realization that most of my students misbehave out of frustration at their own lack of abilities. They are not being obnoxious to *gain* attention, but to *divert* attention away from the fact that they do not know how to complete the assigned work.

When I looked at report cards and compared grades over three quarters, I noticed a trend. Between the first and second quarter, student performance had increased. That is, most students were doing better than they had during the first quarter. Between the second and third quarters, however, grades dropped dramatically. I tried to determine why that drop would occur, and the only common experience shared by these 20 students was the fact that they had been moved into my class at the beginning of the 3rd quarter. . . .

When I presented my project to the action research class during our end-of-term "celebration," I was convinced that the "cause" of the students' unmotivated behavior was my teaching. . . . This conclusion, however, was not readily accepted by my critical friends and colleagues . . . who urged me to consider other interpretations of the data. (pp. 1–2)[a]

- What methods did Deborah use to collect her data? What were the potential strengths and limitations of each method?
- Deborah tentatively concluded that her own teaching led to the dramatic drop in grades from the second quarter to the third. Is her conclusion justified? Why or why not?

Once you have answered these questions, compare your responses with those presented in the appendix.

[a]From "What Motivates Unmotivated Students?" by D. South. In *Action Research: A Guide for the Teacher Researcher* (2nd ed., pp. 1–2), by G. E. Mills, 2003, Upper Saddle River, NJ: Merrill/Prentice Hall. Reprinted with permission of the author.

Summary

Principles of Research with Children

Research with children needs to be guided by strong ethical standards, the scientific method, and access to children and adolescents who can supply needed information. The manner in which researchers integrate these principles into their investigations depends on the kinds of methods they use.

Developmental Research Methods

Developmental researchers use various methods for collecting data, including interviews and questionnaires, tests and other assessment tasks, physiological measures, and observations. Regardless of the method, the data should be accurate measures of the characteristics or behaviors being studied (a matter of *validity*) and should be only minimally influenced by temporary, irrelevant factors (a matter of *reliability*). Developmental researchers also use a research design that matches their question. Designs differ in the extent to which they allow researchers to draw conclusions about cause-effect relationships, find associations that already exist, trace age trends over time, and observe children and adolescents in their natural environments. To make the most of developmental studies, you must judge whether the conclusions are warranted and applicable to your own work with young people.

Gathering Information in Schools

Teachers and caregivers often gather data about children and adolescents. Educators can learn a great deal from their everyday observations of youngsters, conversations with them, and assessments of the products they create.

Applying Concepts in Child Development

In this chapter you learned that a single piece of information from children is often consistent with more than one interpretation. The following table describes information collected about the experiences of five youngsters. For each of these experiences, the table identifies factors that affect interpretations about the information, offers an implication for making appropriate conclusions about the information, or both. Apply what you have learned about data collection techniques to fill in the empty cells. When you're done, compare your responses with those in Table 2-1 in the *Study Guide and Reader*.

APPLYING CONCEPTS IN CHILD DEVELOPMENT   Learning from Children and Adolescents

Age	A Youngster's Experience	Developmental Concepts *Considering the Accuracy of Information*	Implications *Drawing Appropriate Conclusions*
Infancy (Birth–2) 	An 18-month old baby, Harriet, is drowsy when an unfamiliar adult tries to examine her recognition of common household words, such as *ball*. The girl fails to point to particular objects when the adult asks her to do so.	The fact that Harriet is not alert, the task is somewhat artificial, and the adult is a stranger raises questions about *the task's validity as an indication of the child's ability.*	
Early Childhood (2–6)	Four-year old Seth takes a children's picture book, points at each page, and tells the teacher what each page says.		The researcher realizes that more observations are needed to determine whether Seth can read. It may also be helpful to talk with the boy about his interests and abilities in reading.
Middle Childhood (6–10) 	A teacher is conducting action research on her students' performance in mathematics. One 9-year-old boy, Ryan, turns in a blank paper each time the class does math worksheets. Ryan has recently moved from another state, and the teacher does not yet know what Ryan's skills are. He is very quiet.	The teacher examines each child's written work, talking with children individually about their interests in math and watching them as they perform mathematical operations. The teacher appreciates that she is just getting to know Ryan and that there are many reasons why he might not be completing the math problems. His failure to complete the work may not be a *reliable* indication of his current knowledge and skills, and the inference that Ryan is not able to do the work may not be *valid*.	The teacher cannot draw firm conclusions about Ryan's mathematical skills. There are countless reasons why he is not doing well on the worksheets—perhaps he has not yet been exposed to multiplication, feels anxious about math, or is bored with the task. Alternatively, he might be shy and worried about being in the new classroom. The teacher realizes that she needs more information before she can draw any conclusions about Ryan's abilities.
Early Adolescence (10–14)	Twelve-year-old Mary completes a survey related to sexual harassment at school. Mary reports that she has experienced each and every action, such as being touched inappropriately while walking down the school hall and being the recipient of unwanted comments about her physical appearance.	The researcher realizes that Mary may be exaggerating the amount of sexual harassment she has experienced at school. It is also possible that Mary is giving an accurate report of her experiences. Both *validity* and *reliability* of responses are in question.	The researcher determines that it will be necessary to look at all students' responses before concluding that sexual harassment is pervasive at school. Because Mary's responses are somewhat unexpected, the researcher may choose to follow it up with informal interviews among a few girls. The researcher may also want to look into the school's policies and procedures to see if the school is inadvertently condoning sexual harassment.
Late Adolescence (14–18) 	Seventeen-year-old Melinda has had a brain scan. Her scan seems to show that some brain areas, especially those circuits devoted to planning ahead and using good judgment, are less mature than those in typical adult brains.	Adolescent brains are undergoing continuous refinement as they change with maturational processes and experience. The results of a single brain scan should not be taken too seriously, however. Any single result *cannot* be assumed to be completely *valid* or *reliable*.	

Key Concepts

scientific method (p. 35)
sample (p. 35)
self-report (p. 36)
interview (p. 36)
questionnaire (p. 37)
test (p. 37)

assessment (p. 37)
physiological measure (p. 38)
habituation (p. 38)
observation (p. 38)
validity (p. 40)
reliability (p. 40)

experimental study (p. 42)
control group (p. 42)
quasi-experimental study (p. 43)
correlation (p. 44)
correlation coefficient (p. 44)
correlational study (p. 44)

cross-sectional study (p. 45)
longitudinal study (p. 45)
naturalistic study (p. 45)
action research (p. 56)

Now go to our Companion Website at www.prenhall.com/mcdevitt to assess your understanding of chapter content with a Practice Quiz, apply what you've learned in Essay Questions, and broaden your knowledge with links to related Developmental Psychology Web sites.

Biological Beginnings

Case Study: Expecting Zoe

Genetic Foundations of
    Child Development

Prenatal Development

Birth of the Baby

Case Study: Understanding
    Adam

Summary

Applying Concepts in Child
    Development

Case Study: Expecting Zoe

Soon after deciding they wanted a child, Charles and Cynthia were thrilled to learn Cynthia was pregnant. Their shared joy, however, soon gave way to distress. Cynthia experienced nausea and had a hard time finding adequate energy to carry on with daily routines. Charles and Cynthia became worried that, at age 36, she was at risk for complications and miscarriage. That she bled a little bit every now and then fueled their concern. Midwives examined Cynthia and sent her for additional medical tests. Cynthia was frightened during the initial moments of an ultrasound examination:

> The technician covered the monitor that was facing me until she could have a look. This scared me even more. About two seconds after she put the wand on my belly, she said, "Your baby is fine." We then watched in amazement as we saw the baby with its beating heart squirming around the screen. (Cancellaro, 2001, pp. 27–28)[a]

The couple's fears eased somewhat during the second 3 months of Cynthia's pregnancy. About the 15th week of her pregnancy, Cynthia's nausea subsided, her tummy expanded, and she began to wear maternity clothes. During her 17th week of pregnancy, Cynthia underwent an amniocentesis procedure. No genetic disorders were detected, and Cynthia and Charles learned they were expecting a girl. An ultrasound test showed that the fetus now had recognizably human features:

> The last time we'd seen her on screen she looked like a little space creature. Now she actually looked like a baby, an adorable baby, kicking her feet, spreading her fingers, even sucking her thumb. (p. 48)

During the final 3 months of her pregnancy, Cynthia settled easily into preparations for the baby's arrival. Throughout her pregnancy Cynthia had eaten healthfully. For exercise, she had walked and participated in prenatal yoga. When she felt tired, she had rested. Having remained health conscious, Cynthia now prepared for a natural childbirth.

One evening (2 weeks before her projected delivery date), fluid leaked from Cynthia's body. She was in the beginning stages of labor. The contractions began. Cynthia and Charles went to the birthing center. Gratified to learn her cervix had already dilated to 4 centimeters, Cynthia sat in a Jacuzzi and tried to relax between contractions. But 6 hours and many intense contractions later, her cervix had opened no farther. Accepting advice from her midwife, Cynthia received an intravenous injection of Stadol, a pain reliever. The medicine slightly diminished Cynthia's pain but also dashed her hopes for an entirely natural childbirth. Nevertheless, she continued to breathe through the contractions.

Eventually, Cynthia dilated fully and began to push. But after pushing for more than 3 hours, the baby was not proceeding through the birth canal. Cynthia was brought to an operating room, and it was determined that medical intervention was needed. A doctor attached a device to the baby's head to help with the extraction. Once the baby's head was visible, Cynthia did the rest of the pushing unassisted.

Pink and healthy, Zoe Elizabeth was born! Both parents were overwhelmed with awe and love for their new baby.

[a]Excerpts from *Pregnancy Stories: Real Women Share the Joys, Fears, Thrills, and Anxieties of Pregnancy from Conception to Birth,* by Cecelia A. Cancellaro © 2001 by Cecelia A. Cancellaro. Reprinted with permission by New Harbinger Publications, Inc. www.newharbinger.com

While Cynthia and Charles were managing the emotional highs and lows of pregnancy, Zoe-to-be was growing quietly and changing constantly. Over the 9 months of her prenatal development, Zoe was transformed from a single cell, charged with a unique genetic makeup, into a fully formed baby, ready to live, learn, and, ultimately, to love. At birth, Zoe moved from a warm bath of nutrients in Cynthia's womb to the bright lights and cool, dry air of the hospital. In the moments after birth, Zoe took her first breaths and looked into the faces of her adoring parents. Zoe had a healthy beginning because of good conditions from both nature and nurture. In this chapter we discuss how genes (nature) and the environment (nurture) work together to direct children's growth, how physical changes in prenatal development occur in a predictable sequence, and how the amazing childbirth process progresses. We also suggest that specific kinds of support from professionals can enhance the quality of children's biological beginnings.

Genetic Foundations of Child Development

Like Zoe, every child has a unique profile of hereditary instructions that support his or her life, growth, human traits, and individuality. These guidelines are contained in a child's **genes,** the basic units of heredity.

Structure and Operation of Genes

Each gene gives instructions to the body to create a particular protein. Various proteins create a child's physical characteristics through the many life-sustaining reactions they direct in the child's body. For example, some proteins guide the production of new cells with particular properties (e.g., elastic skin cells or message-sending brain cells). Other proteins tell the body to grow, fight infection, repair damage, carry chemical signals throughout the body, regulate other genes, and so forth.

In recent decades scientists have made substantial progress in defining the formation and purpose of many genes. The number of genes a human being has remains difficult to determine because other biological materials, such as bacteria, exist in cells and resemble the complex structures of genes. Current estimates range from between 20,000 and 140,000 genes (Antequerra & Bird, 1993; Aparicio, 2000; Claverie, 2001; International Human Genome Sequencing Consortium, 2004; Liang et al., 2000). We do know that a human's thousands of genes (whatever their precise number turns out to be) are laid out in an orderly way, side by side, in rodlike structures called **chromosomes.** Genes are dispersed among 46 chromosomes, which reside in the center of virtually every cell in the body (National Human Genome Research Institute, 2003). Chromosomes are organized into 23 distinct pairs that are easily seen with a high-powered microscope (Figure 3-1). One chromosome of each pair is inherited from the mother, the other from the father.

Genes are made up of deoxyribonucleic acid, or **DNA.** A DNA molecule is structured like a ladder that has been twisted many times into a spiral staircase (see Figure 3-2). Pairs of chemical substances comprise each step of the staircase, and a sequence of these steps makes up a protein-coding gene. Scientists use location on the staircase to determine the identity of particular genes. The hierarchical relationships among cells, chromosomes, genes, and DNA molecules are represented in Figure 3-3.

Genes set the stage for both universality and diversity among children. In fact, the vast majority of genes are universal among children (National Human Genome Research Institute, 2003; Venter et al., 2001). Among these universal genes are those that make it possible for children to develop basic human abilities, such as communicating with language, walking and running, and forming social relationships. Unless children have extremely serious genetic defects or grow up in an especially deprived or abusive environment, they all develop basic human capacities (Bugental & Goodnow, 1998). The remaining (small) proportion of genes varies among children. Genes that vary predispose individual children to be relatively tall or short, heavy or thin, active or sedentary, eager to learn new things or content to rely on existing knowledge, emotionally agreeable or combative, and healthy or vulnerable to disease. As you will see, the environment and children's own activities also moderate the impact of such genes.

gene
Basic unit of heredity in a living cell; segments of genes are contained on chromosomes.

chromosome
Rodlike structure that resides in the nucleus of every cell of the body and contains genes that guide growth and development; each chromosome is made up of DNA.

DNA
A spiral-staircase shaped molecule that guides the production of proteins needed by the body for growth and development; short for *deoxyribonucleic acid.*

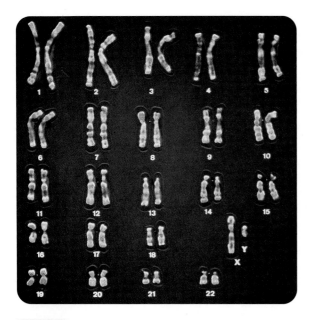

Figure 3-1

Photograph of human chromosomes that have been extracted from a human cell, colored, magnified, and arranged in order of size.

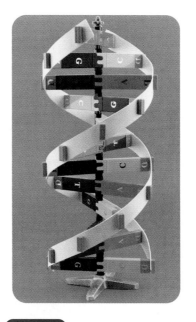

Figure 3-2

A DNA molecule is structured like a ladder that has been twisted successively into a spiral staircase.

In one respect, genes are the start of a long chain of events (see Figure 3-4). Genes directly affect the operations of individual cells; single cells grow together in communities that become organs, brain circuits, and other systems of the body; and these physiological systems influence the child's behavior, relationships, and learning. Thus genes are powerful, but they are *not* simple recipes or blueprints for traits. Rather, the proteins that originate from genetic instructions are released into the child's cells; their effects depend partly (largely, in some cases) on the child's health and activity. To illustrate, an 8-year-old boy genetically predisposed to asthma may rarely have respiratory flare-ups because his family gives him proper medical care and shields him from dogs and cats, which are his personal triggers for wheezing and coughing.

In another respect, the causal chain operates in reverse, with the environment and child's experiences initiating a sequence of processes that ultimately affect gene expression (look again at Figure 3-4). That is, the environment provides opportunities for learning and exposure to nutrition and toxins; these experiences affect brain and body; and the health and operations of bodily systems activate (or suppress) particular genes. For example, a 12-year-old girl grows up in a weight-conscious family and an appearance-obsessed society; she develops an eating disorder that curtails her body's progress through puberty. In effect, the girl's environmental experiences and her own actions delay the activation of genes that would, under conditions of adequate nutrition, permit her normal sexual development.

Notice in Figure 3-4 that *time* also affects genetic expression. In fact, only a subset of genes is active in a cell at any given moment. Basically, cells can sense the body's maturational state, and they use this information to select particular genes for activation. Other genes remain dormant until it is their turn to be called into action. This fact helps explain the order of maturational changes in physical appearance and motor skills. To illustrate, hormones for growth are produced in cells during childhood, whereas hormones for puberty are produced later, during adolescence. It also explains why some diseases and mental health conditions seem to appear out of nowhere: Genes that make people vulnerable to some conditions remain silent until maturational states elicit their effects.

In summary, genes do their work as part of a complex system of physical processes. Soon we will tell you more about how genes contribute to a child's individual traits, but first we need to explain how a child receives his or her genetic makeup in the first place.

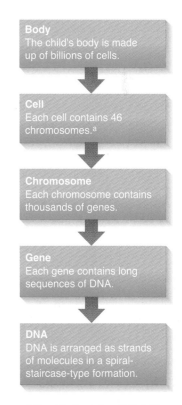

Body
The child's body is made up of billions of cells.

Cell
Each cell contains 46 chromosomes.[a]

Chromosome
Each chromosome contains thousands of genes.

Gene
Each gene contains long sequences of DNA.

DNA
DNA is arranged as strands of molecules in a spiral-staircase-type formation.

[a] Reproductive cells, with their 23 chromosomes, are exceptions.

Figure 3-3

Genetic structures in the body are organized hierarchically.

Figure 3-4

The effects of genes are mediated by the child's experience and activity. Genes interact directly with cells and indirectly with other systems in the body and with the environment. The environment affects the child's experience; experience, in turn, influences the child's brain and body and indirectly affects the operation of cells and expression of genes. These direct and indirect effects can change over time, as new genes come into play and the child's activity, experience, nutrition, relationships, and exposure to toxins change.

Sources: G. Gottlieb, 1992; T. D. Johnston & Edwards, 2002.

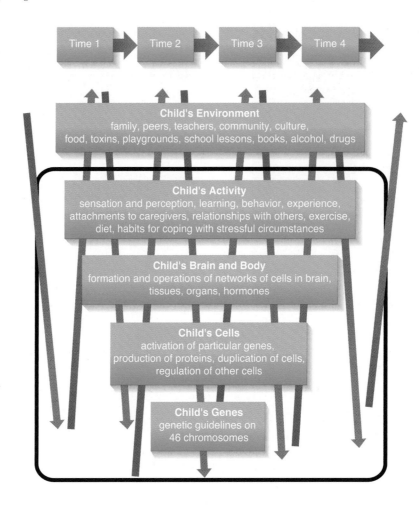

Formation of Reproductive Cells

As we have said, normal human cells contain 46 chromosomes. There is an important exception: Male and female reproductive cells, called **gametes,** have only 23 chromosomes each—half of each chromosome pair. Gametes, which take the form of *sperm* in men and *ova* in women, are created by a process of cell division called **meiosis** (see Figure 3-5).

Meiosis.   During meiosis, nature forms new reproductive cells so that a child has some genetic characteristics from both parents as well as some novel features. Meiosis begins when the 46 chromosomes within a male or female *germ cell* (a precursor to a gamete) pair up into 23 matched sets. The germ cell then duplicates each chromosome, and pairs of chromosomes line up side by side. Next, segments of genetic material are exchanged between each pair. This *crossing-over* of genetic material shuffles genes between paired chromosomes and produces new hereditary combinations that do not exist in either parent's chromosomes.

After crossing-over takes place, the pairs of duplicated chromosomes separate and the cell divides into two new germ cells with half from each pair. Chance determines which of the duplicated chromosomes from each of the 23 pairs moves to one or the other of the two new cells. This step thus provides a second route to genetic individuality. During this first cell division, one of the two new female germ cells gets the bulk of the cell matter and is strong and healthy—that is, it is *viable*—whereas the second, smaller cell disintegrates. Both new male germ cells are viable.

A second cell division takes place, and the duplicated chromosomes separate. Each new cell receives one of the duplicate chromosomes from each pair. The resulting male germ cells are ready to mature and become male gametes (sperm). The female germ cell undergoes this second division only after being fertilized by a sperm. When the female cell divides, once

gamete
Reproductive cell that, in humans, contains 23 chromosomes rather than the 46 chromosomes present in other cells in the body; a male gamete (sperm) and a female gamete (ovum) join at conception.

meiosis
The process of cell reproduction and division by which gametes are formed.

General Process of Meiosis

Each germ cell has 46 chromosomes. Chromosomes begin to move together and pair up into 23 matched sets in the germ cells.

Each chromosome replicates (duplicates) itself. Notice that the single strands in the previous step have doubled in this step.

Crossing-over occurs: Pairs of duplicated chromosomes temporarily unite and exchange segments of chromosomes. This shuffling of genes between paired chromosomes—known as *crossing-over*—ensures unique combinations of genes that differ from those of both the mother and the father.

The pairs of doubled chromosomes separate and the cell divides, forming two new cells, each containing 23 double-structured chromosomes. Chromosomes randomly join with others in one of the two new cells. This process is called the *first meiotic division*. It further ensures genetic individuality.

The second meiotic division takes place. The cell divides in two and the double-structured chromosomes are separated. Chromosomes are now single-structured: the new cell now has one chromosome from each pair, and a total of 23 chromosomes. Resulting cells are now gametes that mature and become ready to unite at conception.

During conception, the sperm enters the ovum.

The two sets of 23 chromosomes, one from the father and one from the mother, unite to form a zygote.

Sperm in Men

Production of sperm begins for boys at puberty. During an initial phase, germ cells (precursors to sperm) are formed. *Only one pair from the 23 pairs of chromosomes is shown here.*

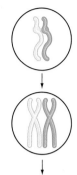

In the male, these first three steps have occurred sometime after puberty and continue to occur throughout the male's reproductive years.

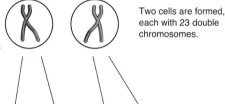

Two cells are formed, each with 23 double chromosomes.

There are now four male gametes (sperm).

Ova in Women

Production of ova begins for girls during prenatal development. During an initial phase, germ cells (precursors to ova) are formed. *Only one pair from the 23 pairs of chromosomes is shown here.*

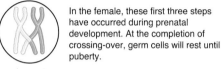

In the female, these first three steps have occurred during prenatal development. At the completion of crossing-over, germ cells will rest until puberty.

Meiosis resumes during puberty. With each ovulation, the germ cell will complete the first meiotic division producing two cells, each with 23 double chromosomes. One cell receives the majority of cell material and becomes viable. The other cell may reproduce but neither it nor its progeny will be a viable gamete.

Only one potentially viable ovum, which has 23 chromosomes, remains. This step of the second meiotic division occurs only if the ovum is fertilized with a sperm.

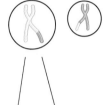

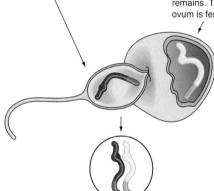

Figure 3-5

Reproductive cells. *Meiosis* is the multistep process of forming gametes, cells that join in reproduction to form a new organism. During meiosis, one-of-a-kind combinations of genes are produced during two distinct phases: crossing-over (when genes are exchanged between chromosomes) and cell division (when particular chromosomes randomly combine with others in new cells). Human variability is also enhanced at *conception,* when chance affects which gametes unite and combine their genetic instructions. During conception, the sperm enters the ovum and the two sets of 23 chromosomes are fused to form a zygote. The new offspring has some characteristics from both parents as well as some new chromosome structures not present in either parent.
Sources: K. L. Moore & Persaud, 2003; Sadler, 2000.

These monozygotic twins share the same genetic instructions. Identical twins are usually quite similar in physical appearance and share many psychological characteristics, such as being particularly intelligent or gregarious. However, despite their many similarities, identical twins make their own choices, experience some different environments, form some separate friendships and, as a result, develop into two distinctly unique individuals.

again, only one of the two new cells, a female gamete (an ovum), is viable. The process of meiosis thus produces one ovum and four sperm.[1]

The process of meiosis ensures that some traits are preserved across generations and other entirely new traits are created. Children share some features with both of their parents because they inherit half of their chromosomes from each parent. Children are unlike their parents (and siblings) in other respects because parts of chromosomes change slightly during meiosis; the chromosome structures that children inherit are *not* exact duplicates of parents' chromosomes.[2] Furthermore, a single gene transmitted from parent to child (and shared by both) may operate differently in the two family members because other genes (not shared by both) may intensify or weaken that gene's effects.

Gender.   When one sperm and one ovum unite at conception, the 23 chromosomes from each parent come together and form a new being (the **zygote**) with 46 chromosomes. The 23rd chromosome pair determines the gender of the individual: Two *X chromosomes* (one each from the mother and father) produce a female, and a combination of an *X chromosome* and a *Y chromosome* (from the mother and father, respectively) produces a male. If you look at the photograph of human chromosomes in Figure 3-1, you can see the XY pair near the bottom right corner, which makes this individual a male.

How twins are created.   Occasionally a zygote splits into two separate cell clusters, resulting in two offspring instead of one. *Identical,* or **monozygotic twins,** come from the same fertilized egg and so have the same genetic instructions. At other times, two ova simultaneously unite with two sperm cells, again resulting in two offspring. These **dizygotic twins,** also known as *fraternal* twins, are as similar to one another as ordinary siblings. They share some genetic traits but not others.

Because monozygotic and dizygotic twins differ in the degree to which they share genes, researchers have studied them extensively. Twin studies permit rough estimates of the relative effects of heredity and environment on human characteristics. In many cases monozygotic twins are quite similar to one another in terms of how sociable they are and how they express emotion, whereas dizygotic twins are less similar (Plomin & DeFries, 1985). Even so, identical twins are not identical in all psychological characteristics—an indication that environment, experience, children's own choices, and even random factors also affect development.

Genetic Basis of Individual Traits

So far, you have learned that children have both uniform genes (that make them resemble one another in their human abilities) and variable genes (that contribute to their individuality). Uniform human genes, carried by all parents, are transmitted to every child. Genes that vary among children are transmitted through systematic patterns of inheritance as well as through less common mechanisms and by biological errors during meiosis and other cell divisions. Let's look more closely at how children receive traits that contribute to their individuality.

Common mechanisms of genetic transmission.   When the two sets of 23 chromosomes combine into matched pairs during conception, the corresponding genes inherited from each parent pair up. Each gene pair includes two forms of the protein-coding instructions—two **alleles**—related to a particular physical characteristic. Sometimes the two genes in an allele pair give the same instructions ("Have dark hair!" "Have dark hair!"). At other times, they give very different instructions ("Have dark hair!" "Have blond hair!"). When two genes give dif-

zygote
Cell formed when a male sperm joins with a female ovum; with healthy genes and nurturing conditions in the uterus, it may develop into a fetus and be born as a live infant.

monozygotic twins
Twins that began as a single zygote and so share the same genetic makeup.

dizygotic twins
Twins that began as two separate zygotes and so are as genetically similar as two siblings conceived and born at different times.

alleles
Genes located at the same point on corresponding (paired) chromosomes and related to the same physical characteristic.

---

[1] Sperm are produced continuously throughout a male's reproductive years. During sexual intercourse, between 200 and 600 million sperm are deposited in the woman's vagina (K. L. Moore & Persaud, 2003). In girls, up to 2 million germ cells are present at birth. Many subsequently decay, and between 40,000 and 400,000 remain at the beginning of adolescence. About 400 ova will be released during ovulation over the woman's lifetime (Sadler, 2000).

[2] In any given parent, each event of meiosis begins with the exact same chromosomes from that parent. The process of meiosis tweaks the structure of chromosomes slightly; no two meiotic events change chromosomes in precisely the same way.

ferent instructions, one gene is often more influential than its counterpart. A **dominant gene** manifests its characteristic, in a sense overriding the instructions of a **recessive gene** with which it is paired. A recessive gene influences growth and development primarily when its partner is also recessive. For example, genes for dark hair are dominant and those for blond hair are recessive. Thus a child with a dark hair gene and a blond hair gene will have dark hair, as will a child with two dark hair genes. Only when two blond hair genes are paired together will a child have blond hair.

However, when two genes of an allele pair "disagree," one gene doesn't always dominate completely. Sometimes one gene simply has a stronger influence than the other, a phenomenon known as **codominance.** *Sickle cell disease,* a blood disease, is an example. The disease develops in its full-blown form only when a person has two (recessive) alleles for it. Nevertheless, when an individual has one recessive allele for sickle cell disease and one "healthy" allele, he or she may experience temporary, mild symptoms when short of oxygen (L. W. Sullivan, 1987).

In reality, the influence of genes is often even more complex. Many physiological traits and most psychological ones are dependent on multiple genes rather than on a single pair of alleles. In **polygenic inheritance** many separate genes each exert some influence on the expression of a trait. Height is an example: An individual's adult height is not determined by a single allele pair, but rather by several genes that each contributes small effects (J. M. Tanner, 1990). (Of course, height and other complex traits are also affected by nutrition, activity, and other environmental influences.)

Problems in genetic instructions.   Sometimes problems occur in the genetic instructions that children receive (see Table 3-1). There are two primary types of genetic disorders, chromosome abnormalities and single-gene defects. A child with a *chromosome abnormality* may have an extra chromosome, a missing chromosome, or a wrongly formed chromosome. Because each chromosome holds thousands of genes, a child with a chromosomal abnormality tends to have many affected genes, and the result can be major physical problems and mental retardation (Burns, Brady, Dunn, & Starr, 2000). Chromosomal abnormalities occur when chromosomes divide unevenly during meiosis. They can also occur after meiosis, when the zygote's cells divide unevenly, leaving the growing zygote with some cells with normal chromosomes and others with abnormal chromosomes. Chromosomal abnormalities may be caused by a variety of factors, including parents' exposure to viruses, radiation, and drugs.

Positive attitudes of educators, advocacy by parents, and federal legislation have improved educational services and opportunities for many children with chromosomal abnormalities, genetic defects, and other disabilities.

Chromosome abnormalities occur in 1 per 150 births (Burns et al., 2000). One such abnormality, an extra 21st chromosome or an extra piece of one, causes *Down syndrome.* Children with Down syndrome typically show delays in mental growth and are susceptible to heart defects and other health problems. Apparently, the extra 21st chromosome causes biochemical changes that redirect brain development (N. R. Carlson, 1999). The severity of disabilities caused by Down syndrome and many other chromosomal abnormalities varies considerably from one child to the next.

A second type of genetic disorder occurs when a child inherits a *single-gene defect* from one or both parents. Resulting physical problems tend to be more specific and subtle than those caused by chromosomal abnormalities (Burns et al., 2000). Nonetheless, some single-gene defects are quite serious. The usual pattern of inheritance is that children who inherit a dominant-gene defect show the problem. Those who inherit a recessive-gene defect show the problem only if both genes in the allele pair are defective (transmission is slightly different in X-chromosome-linked defects).

Some genetic problems do not fit neatly into the categories of chromosomal abnormality or single-gene defect. For instance, some conditions may be mild or severe depending on the particular sequence of chemical compounds on a gene. An example is *Fragile X syndrome,* which results from a genetic defect on the X chromosome. When this defect is small and limited, people who carry the problem gene are able to produce some of a particular protein needed by the body, and as a result they may show no symptoms or only mild learning disabilities. But the defect can intensify as it is passed from one generation to the next and lead to Fragile X syndrome (Hagerman & Lampe, 1999). Children with Fragile X

dominant gene
Gene that overrides any competing instructions in an allele pair.

recessive gene
Gene that influences growth and development primarily when the other gene in the allele pair is identical to it.

codominance
Situation in which the two genes of an allele pair, although not identical, both have some influence on a characteristic.

polygenic inheritance
Situation in which many genes combine in their influence on a particular characteristic.

TABLE 3-1

Common Chromosomal and Genetic Disorders in Children

Disorder	Incidence	Characteristics[a]	Implications for Care
Chromosome Abnormalities. Children with chromosome abnormalities are born with an irregular number of chromosomes (more than or fewer than 46) or with one or more chromosomes that have irregular structures (deletions from or duplications to parts of an individual chromosome, or with a part of one chromosome moved to another location).			
Down syndrome	1 per 700–1,000 births	Children with Down syndrome have one extra chromosome. Physical characteristics include a protruding tongue, thick lips, flat nose, short neck, wide gaps between toes, short fingers, specific health problems, and risks for heart problems and hearing loss. Mental retardation can range from mild to severe. Children often have good visual discrimination skills and may be better at understanding verbal language than producing it.	Provide explicit instruction in any delayed skills (e.g., in language). Address health issues such as heart problems and potential feeding difficulties.
Klinefelter syndrome	1 per 500–1,000 boys	Only boys have Klinefelter syndrome; they have one Y chromosome and two X chromosomes. Diagnosis may not occur until adolescence, when testes fail to enlarge. Affected boys tend to have long legs, to grow modest breast tissue, and to remain sterile. They tend to show lower than average verbal ability and some speech and language delays.	Offer an enriched verbal environment. Medical treatment may be given to support development of male sexual characteristics.
Turner syndrome	1 per 2,500–5,000 girls	Only girls have Turner syndrome; they have one X chromosome and are missing the second sex chromosome. Affected girls have broad chests, webbed necks, short stature, and specific health problems. They do not show normal sexual development. They may show normal verbal ability but lower than average ability in processing visual and spatial information.	Provide instruction and support related to visual and spatial processing. Hormone therapy helps with bone growth and development of female characteristics.
Prader-Willi syndrome	1 per 10,000–25,000 births	A deletion from a gene segment on chromosome 15 is inherited from the father. Children with this syndrome tend to become obese and show mental retardation; they also have small hands and feet and are short in stature. They may develop maladaptive behaviors such as throwing frequent temper tantrums and picking at their own skin. Beginning at ages 1–6, children may eat excessively, hoard food, and eat unappealing substances.	Create developmentally appropriate plans to help children regulate eating, decrease inappropriate behaviors, and increase acceptable emotional expression. Seek medical care as necessary.
Angelman syndrome	1 per 10,000–30,000 births	A deletion from a gene segment on chromosome 15 is inherited from the mother. Children with this syndrome show mental retardation, a small head, seizures, and jerky movements. They have unusual, recurrent bouts of laughter not associated with happiness.	Provide appropriate educational support suited to children's skills and developmental levels. Seek medical care as necessary.
Single-Gene Defects. Children with single-gene defects have a problem on a dominant gene (an error on one of the 22 paired chromosomes, that is, on any chromosome except X or Y[b]), a recessive defect on both chromosomes in one of the 22 matched pairs, or a problem in a recessive gene on the X chromosome (boys) or a problem in a gene on both X chromosomes (girls).			
Neurofibromatosis	Mild form occurs in 1 per 2,500–4,000 births; severe form occurs in 1 per 40,000–50,000 births	Children with this dominant-gene defect develop benign and malignant tumors in the central nervous system. The condition may be caused by an error in a gene that would normally suppress tumor growth. Learning disabilities are somewhat common and mental retardation occurs occasionally. Most individuals experience only minor symptoms, such as having colored and elevated spots on their skin.	Address learning disabilities; offer adaptive services to children with mental retardation. Tumors may need to be removed or treated. Surgery or braces may be needed if the spine becomes twisted.

(continued)

[a]This table describes typical symptoms for children with particular chromosomal and genetic problems. Children's actual level of functioning depends on the medical treatments they receive; their experiences with families, teachers, other caregivers, and other children; and their health and other genes they might possess. New medical treatments and educational interventions are constantly being tested, and many will increase quality of life for these children.

[b]X-linked dominant defects also occur but are rare. For example, children who receive the gene for Hypophosphatemia on the X chromosome produce low levels of phosphate and, as a result, have soft bones that are easily deformed.

TABLE 3-1

Common Chromosomal and Genetic Disorders in Children (continued)

Disorder	Incidence	Characteristics[a]	Implications for Care
Huntington disease (HD)	3 to 7 per 100,000 births	Children with this dominant-gene defect develop a progressive disorder of the central nervous system. Signs typically appear by age 35 to 45, though age of first symptoms has varied between 2 and 85 years. HD may be caused by the production of a protein that destroys brain cells. Early signs include irritability, clumsiness, depression, and forgetfulness. Eventually, loss of control over movements of arms, legs, torso, or facial muscles occurs, speech becomes slurred, and severe mental disturbances arise.	Remove sharp edges from the physical environment. When memory deteriorates, provide visual instructions about daily tasks. Medication may be given to alleviate movement problems and depression.
Phenylketonuria (PKU)	1 per 15,000 births, with rates highest in people of Celtic origin (e.g., from Ireland and Scotland)	Children with this recessive-gene defect are at risk for developing mental retardation, eczema, seizures, and motor and behavioral problems such as aggression, self-mutilation, and impulsiveness. When children have both recessive genes for PKU, their livers cannot produce an enzyme that breaks down phenylalanine (an amino acid); this substance accumulates and becomes toxic to the brain.	Provide educational materials to enhance planning and memory skills and compensate for limitations. When phenylalanine is restricted from diet, children develop much more normally, and mental retardation is avoided. Subtle problems may still result (e.g., awkward pencil grip and learning disabilities).
Sickle cell disease	1 per 500–600 children of African (Black) descent; rates are also elevated in people of Mediterranean descent	Children with this recessive-gene defect develop problems with blood circulation. The disease causes red blood cells to grow rigid, and passage of blood through small vessels causes pain. Children may experience many serious conditions, including stroke, infection, tissue damage, and fatigue. Symptoms become obvious during the first or second year of life.	Be alert to medical crises, such as strokes. Offer comfort to children who are tired or in pain. Treatments include blood transfusions, medication for pain and infections, and other medicines to reduce frequency of medical crises.
Cystic fibrosis (CF)	1 per 3,300 children from European American backgrounds and 1 per 9,500 children from Hispanic American backgrounds	Children with this recessive-gene defect have glands that produce large amounts of abnormally thick, sticky mucus, which creates serious problems for breathing and digestion. CF is usually noticed in infancy due to persistent coughing, wheezing, pneumonia, and big appetite with little weight gain. Many individuals with CF now live well into their 40s.	Be aware of symptoms that require medical care. The condition is often treated with physical therapy, medication, and bronchial drainage.
Tay-Sachs disease	1 per 2,500–3,600 children among Ashkenazi Jews (of Eastern European ancestry)	Children with this recessive-gene defect develop a fatal, degenerative condition of the central nervous system. They lack an enzyme required to break down a fatty substance in brain cells. At about 6 months of age, children slow down in development, lose vision, display an abnormal startle response, and go into convulsions. Other functions are gradually lost, and children become mentally retarded, cannot move, and die by age 3 or 4.	Offer love and attention as you would to other children. Be alert to new accommodations that may be needed in the environment, such as stabilizing and securing the surroundings when children lose sight. There is no known cure or treatment.
Thalassemia (Cooley's anemia)	1 in 800–2,500 individuals of Greek or Italian descent in the U.S.; rates are lower in other groups	Children with this recessive-gene defect develop a disease of blood cells in which oxygen is not transmitted effectively. They become pale, fatigued, and irritable within their first 2 years of life. Individuals with serious forms of the condition may develop feeding problems, diarrhea, and enlargement of the spleen and heart, infections, and unusual facial features and bone structures. Young people severely impaired by this condition sometimes die by early adulthood.	Help children to cope with their health problems. Treatment may include blood transfusions, antibiotics, and occasionally bone marrow transplants.
Duchenne muscular dystrophy	1 per 3,000 to 4,000 boys	Only boys acquire this X-linked recessive-gene defect, which causes a progressive muscular weakness because of a gene's failure to produce an essential protein needed by muscle cells. Between ages 2 and 5, affected boys begin to stumble and walk on their toes or with another unusual gait. They may lose the ability to walk between ages 8 and 14 and may later die from respiratory and cardiac problems.	Watch for respiratory infections and heart problems. Treatments include physical therapy, orthopedic devices, surgery, and medications to reduce muscle stiffness.

Sources: Blachford, 2002; Burns et al., 2000; Cody & Kamphaus, 1999; Dykens & Cassidy, 1999; Massimini, 2000; K. L. Moore & Persaud, 2003; Nilsson & Bradford, 1999; M. P. Powell & Schulte, 1999; J. T. Smith, 1999; Waisbren, 1999; Wynbrandt & Ludman, 2000.

syndrome develop severe learning disabilities, emotional problems, and mental retardation. Their physical characteristics include prominent ears, long faces, double-jointed thumbs, and flat feet, and they typically possess other health conditions, such as being prone to sinus and ear infections (Hagerman & Lampe, 1999). In addition, these children tend to be socially anxious, sensitive to touch and noise, and inclined to avoid eye contact and to repeat certain activities over and over again (e.g., spinning objects, waving their arms, saying the same phrase). The problems of girls with Fragile X are generally less serious than comparable symptoms in boys because girls have a second X chromosome that usually is healthy enough to produce some of the missing protein. Boys, on the other hand, have a Y chromosome that is unable to produce this protein.

Other physical problems can occur when several genes act together to make a developing fetus vulnerable to poor nutrition, trauma, and other adverse conditions. *Spina bifida* (in which the spinal cord is malformed) and *cleft palate* (in which a split occurs in the roof of the mouth) are examples of such conditions, which tend to run in some families but do not follow simple patterns of genetic transmission. It appears that affected children have genes that make them susceptible to particular environmental threats, such as their mother's vitamin deficiency or illness, during their prenatal development (K. L. Moore & Persaud, 2003).

All children require individualized care, but those with chromosomal abnormalities, single-gene defects, and other genetic conditions and birth defects may need interventions tailored to their conditions. In several places in this book, you will find specific recommendations for supporting the learning of children with disabilities. Because these children ultimately are more similar to, than different from, children without such problems, it also makes sense for teachers to draw on their understandings of fostering typical developmental progressions.

The Awakening of Genes

Earlier we explained that only some genes are active in cells at any particular time. As a result, some genes have an almost immediate influence on the development of physical characteristics, but many others don't manifest themselves until later in *maturation,* when provoked to do so by hormones and other factors (J. M. Tanner, 1990). Height is again an example. Children's length at birth is determined largely by prenatal conditions in the mother's uterus and is only minimally influenced by heredity. By 18 months of age, however, we see a definite correlation between children's heights and the heights of their parents, presumably because genetic factors have begun to exert their influence (J. M. Tanner, 1990).

Some emerging characteristics are tightly controlled by genetic instructions, a phenomenon known as **canalization** (Waddington, 1957). For instance, basic motor skills are highly canalized: Crawling, sitting, and walking appear under a wide range of circumstances. They almost invariably appear without training or encouragement. Only extremely unusual environmental conditions can stifle them, such as when a young child exposed to heavy doses of a toxic substance (e.g., lead paint) is seriously delayed in mastering basic motor and psychological skills (Gottlieb, 1991, 1992).

Many skills are *not* canalized, however. Most of the abilities that children acquire at school—reading, writing, mathematical problem solving, and so on—are modified by experiences children have both in and out of the classroom. Social skills tend also to rely on environmental support. For example, figuring out other people's intentions, learning to anticipate others' actions, and taking turns during conversation are competencies that are refined with social experience.

Another developmental factor in genetic expression is the operation of *sensitive periods.* In Chapter 1 we explained that a sensitive period is an age range during which certain environmental experiences are especially important for normal development. The timing of sensitive periods is dictated by heredity, which determines *when* particular kinds of environmental stimulation can come into play.

Sensitive periods are observed in some aspects of physical development, perceptual abilities, brain development, and language acquisition. For example, children are especially sensitive to language input during infancy and early childhood. With regular opportunities for participation in conversations, young children easily learn one or more languages. Children deprived of language during early childhood require considerable intervention if they are to learn a first language later in life. Sensitive periods also play a role in the effects of harmful

----

Connecting Concepts

Chapters 7 and 8 offer instructional strategies that may be especially beneficial for children with learning disabilities, mental retardation, and other cognitive disabilities.

----

canalization
Tight genetic control of a particular aspect of development.

substances. That is, some environmental substances may be highly detrimental at one phase of development yet exert little or no effect at other phases. Later in this chapter you will learn that prenatal development includes sensitive periods for the formation of limbs, organs, facial structures, and brain connections.

In other areas, such as learning to read and engage in productive social relationships, there is no single restricted time frame for learning. Children who have had inadequate experiences or instruction in these areas can frequently make up for lost time. However, educators should not simply wait for children to catch up when they lag behind peers in fundamental academic and social skills. Such competencies represent vital personal resources that build cumulatively over time, and without appropriate intervention, delayed children may easily fall further behind and come to see themselves as incapable.

The Blending of Heredity and Environment

Numerous environmental and personal factors influence genetic expression. These include nutrition, illness, medication, stressful events, temperature, exposure to light, intensity of stimulation, and opportunities for physical activity (B. Brown, 1999; T. D. Johnston & Edwards, 2002; J. D. Wilson & Foster, 1985). For example, Guatemalan children raised in the United States tend to grow taller than their parents did in Guatemala, presumably because of more abundant and diverse nutritional resources in the United States (Bogin, 1988). The environment may also affect the hormones that provoke genes into action. For example, stressful events suppress the release of certain hormones and so can hinder growth in tissues of the body and nervous system (B. Brown, 1999). Long-term, excessive stress can also lead to the death of neurons in the hippocampus, a component of the brain essential for memory and other cognitive functions (Lombroso & Sapolsky, 1998). In such a circumstance, stress undermines a biological system that, under optimal conditions, would have been directed by genes to become stronger.

Complex psychological traits, such as personality characteristics and intellectual talents, are the outcomes of numerous genes (nature) and environmental experiences (nurture). For instance, there appear to be genetic origins to becoming particularly cheerful, outgoing, moody, anxious, or aggressive, and to becoming a risk taker (Bouchard, 2004; Henderson, 1982; Rothbart & Bates, 1998; Tellegren, Lykken, Bouchard, & Wilcox, 1988). Yet these traits are clearly influenced as well by the environment (Plomin, Owen, & McGuffin, 1994). We're not born wild or shy; instead, we're born with certain tendencies that our environments may or may not encourage. For example, children who, from birth, have displayed high energy levels are inclined to seek out new sensations, become impulsive, and act somewhat aggressively (Goldsmith & Gottesman, 1996). Caregivers may increase the aggression of impetuous children by carrying out punitive and bitter exchanges with them, allowing them to hit others, and failing to appeal to their empathy for other people's distress (Goldsmith & Gottesman, 1996; G. R. Patterson, 1986, 1995).

There are at least three mechanisms by which the child's genetic makeup affects his or her experiences in particular environments (Scarr, 1992, 1993; Scarr & McCartney, 1983). A *passive gene-environment relation* occurs when parents' genetic tendencies correlate with the kind of setting in which they raise their children. Especially when their children are young, parents select environments based on their own preferences and genetic tendencies. For example, a father with a strong imagination and a love of drama may bring his son to theater performances. The father's drive toward dramatic expression has some genetic basis, and the child may share this genetically based talent. Thus the boy's genes correlate with his environment, but the association is considered passive because the boy is not determining the environment—his father is. In an *evocative gene-environment relation,* children's own characteristics elicit specific kinds of reactions from the environment. For example, a calm and compliant child may have a soothing effect on caregivers, who respond with warmth. A child who is quick to argue may instead provoke hostile reactions from both adults and peers. Finally, an *active gene-environment relation* occurs when children have particular talents that influence environments made accessible to them. For instance, an athletic youngster may join a baseball team, organize neighborhood games, request sports equipment from parents, and otherwise create occasions for practicing athletic skills.

Connecting Concepts
Chapter 9 discusses sensitive periods in language development in more depth.

Some aspects of temperament, such as fearfulness, have a genetic basis but are also influenced by the environment. Although this boy is hesitant about separating from his mother in the morning, she has worked out a daily transition that calms his fears.

We are all products of nature and nurture. Genes do not direct the appearance, behavior, or even cell functioning in any simple, predetermined fashion. Genes operate in concert with one another; are affected by nutrition, stress, and other environmental agents; and are activated by hormones and physiological events. Furthermore, they may be influential at particular points in development, suddenly bringing out characteristics that seem to come "from nowhere." In general, a child's genes provide rough guidelines that may be either stretched or compressed, depending on the influence of other genes and the child's health, schooling, interpersonal relationships, and environmental resources.

Acknowledging Nature and Nurture in Children's Lives

Genetic influence may seem like a very abstract topic compared to the world of real children in schools and community settings. Nevertheless, anyone working closely with children and adolescents must understand the power of genetic factors. At the same time, recognition that the environment also guides human development should inspire everyone's optimism about children's potential for positive growth. With these points in mind, we offer the following recommendations:

● *Expect and make allowances for individual differences.* Teachers and other practitioners who value a multitude of physical characteristics, personality types, and talents can put youngsters at ease. Children who are tall and short, chubby and thin, coordinated and clumsy, shy and outgoing, and calm and irritable all have a rightful place in the hearts of adults who teach and nurture them.

Some young people have genetically based temperaments that make them somewhat prone to withdraw from social contact, act impulsively, or respond aggressively to conflict. Adults can help these young people learn social skills for forming healthy relationships.

● *Remember that environmental factors influence virtually every aspect of development.* Children's development is *not* simply an outgrowth of biology (Eisenberg, 1998). Even when children have inherited the potential for certain talents, temperaments, and deficits, their paths can be steered one way or another by environmental factors—physical conditions, social interactions, educational experiences, and so on. For instance, children who are genetically predisposed to be irritable, distractible, or aggressive can, with guidance, learn more adaptive and socially productive ways of responding (e.g., DeVault, Krug, & Fake, 1996; T. R. Robinson, Smith, Miller, & Brownell, 1999).

● *Intervene when children struggle.* There is an extended window of time for learning many things, but we cannot leave it to chance that delayed children will catch up on their own. Basic intellectual, social, and emotional skills affect many aspects of life, making it important to offer extra guidance when children's progress is unusually slow. Furthermore, without appropriate intervention, children who straggle far behind peers may come to doubt their capability for future learning, leading to even more serious problems, such as dropping out of school.

● *Encourage children to make growth-promoting choices.* Especially as they grow older, youngsters actively seek experiences compatible with their natural tendencies. Adults can help them find activities and resources that allow them to cultivate their talents and remediate their weaknesses. For instance, a socially outgoing boy with an excessive amount of energy and little self-control may be inclined to interrupt adults and peers. His teachers may need to remind him to hold his tongue and give others a chance to speak. They might also encourage the boy to join the drama club, a sports team, or other groups in which he can exercise leadership skills while increasing his self-control.

From a biological standpoint, the child is a complex, coordinated system with interacting parts and processes—notably, genes, body, environment, and the child's initiative and activity. This system originates before birth, during the prenatal period.

Prenatal Development

prenatal development
Growth that takes place between conception and birth.

During **prenatal development,** the period of growth between conception and birth, a simple, single cell changes into a complex human being. During this remarkable developmental journey, the new being undergoes a series of changes, takes nourishment from the mother, and resides in an environment especially suited to its emerging yet fragile capabilities.

Phases of Prenatal Growth

During its prenatal growth, the developing baby-to-be must accomplish a range of tasks, including growing new cells, moving through the mother's body, settling into an interior wall of the mother's uterus, taking in nutrition and expelling wastes, forming and refining basic body structures, and activating rudimentary learning abilities. Prenatal development is divided into three phases: the period of the *zygote*, the period of the *embryo*, and the period of the *fetus*.

Development of the zygote.   During the middle of a woman's menstrual cycle, an *ovum* (female gamete) emerges from one of her two *ovaries* (see Figure 3-6). Several protective cells surround the ovum. The ovum enters the adjacent *fallopian tube*, a narrow and curved pipe that connects the ovary to the uterus. The ovum is guided toward the uterus by fringelike cell structures in the fallopian tube. When a man ejaculates, he releases millions of sperm into the woman's vagina, but only about 250 will find their way into the uterus and move toward the fallopian tube (K. L. Moore & Persaud, 2003). As the ovum is gently ushered down the fallopian tube, sperm swim vigorously against the current to reach it. When a conception takes place, a single sperm attaches to and eventually enters the ovum. The ovum cooperates by rearranging its exterior layers so that no other sperm can enter. The ovum and the sperm then combine their chromosomes, and the zygote, a new being, is formed.

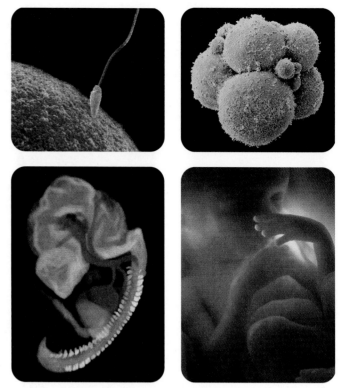

Human prenatal development begins at conception (top left) and then progresses through the periods of the zygote (top right), embryo (bottom left), and fetus (bottom right).

The zygote creates new cells as it travels through the fallopian tube and toward the uterus. In a process called **mitosis,** the zygote duplicates its cells such that all of these new cells share its original 46 chromosomes. During mitosis, the spiral staircase of DNA straightens itself up, splits down the middle, and each half re-creates the original structure. After two exact copies of each chromosome are formed, one copy from each pair moves to opposite sides of the cell, the cell breaks open, and two new cells are formed. This process of mitosis continues throughout the lifespan and permits both growth and replacement of cells.

In the zygote, mitosis takes place in the following manner. The first cell divides into two cells; these two cells divide to make four cells; four divide into eight; and by the time the zygote has 16 cells, it is entering the uterus (see Figure 3-6). These cells align themselves as the exterior lining of a sphere (see the *blastocyst* in Figure 3-6). Now about a week old, the zygote attaches itself to the wall of the uterus. The zygote separates into two parts, a tiny being that will develop further into an embryo, and the *placenta,* the spongy structure in the uterus that provides nourishment. Cells begin to specialize and merge with other similar cells to form distinct structures, such as the nervous system and brain. The implanted zygote releases hormones, telling the ovaries that a conception has occurred and that menstruation should be prevented. In 2 short weeks the new being has initiated growth, taken a journey, and found a hospitable home.

Development of the embryo.   The period of the **embryo** extends from Weeks 2 through 8 after conception. Tasks of the embryonic period are to instigate life-support systems and form basic bodily structures. The placenta becomes larger, stronger, and more refined as it goes about its job of supplying food, liquid, and oxygen; removing wastes; and secreting hormones that sustain the pregnancy. An *umbilical cord* forms and connects the embryo to the placenta.

The embryo itself undergoes rapid structural changes and increases in size. During prenatal development, growth tends to occur from top to bottom (head first, feet last) and from inside to outside (torso before limbs, arms and legs before hands and feet). Consistent with these trends, the head and heart are among the first structures to develop (see Figure 3-7). The growth of the neural tube that will give rise to the brain and spinal cord is well under way early in this period. Neurons—the cells that form connections to and in the brain— emerge and move to their proper places. Buds of limbs begin to develop, and by the 8th week, fingers and toes are recognizably distinct as separate digits. Also during the period of the embryo, internal organs appear and begin to develop.

mitosis
The process of cell duplication by which chromosomes are preserved and a human being or other biological organism can grow.

embryo
During prenatal Weeks 2 through 8, the developing being that is in the process of forming major body structures and organs.

Figure 3-6

Development of the zygote
Based on K. L. Moore, Persaud, & Shiota,
2000.

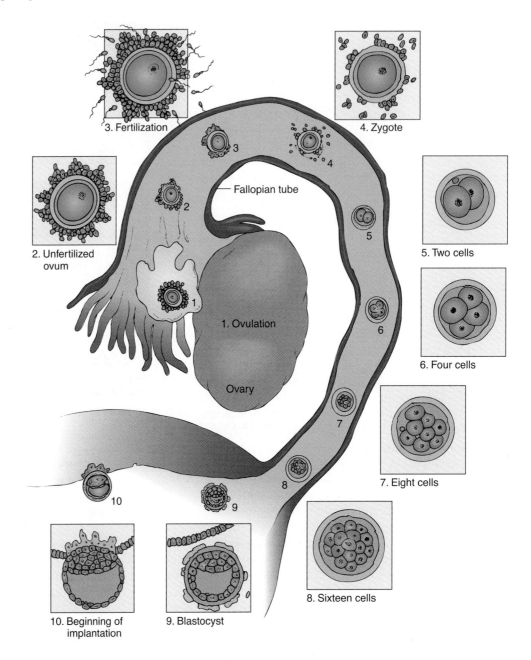

3. Fertilization

4. Zygote

2. Unfertilized
ovum

Fallopian tube

5. Two cells

6. Four cells

1. Ovulation

Ovary

7. Eight cells

8. Sixteen cells

10. Beginning of
implantation

9. Blastocyst

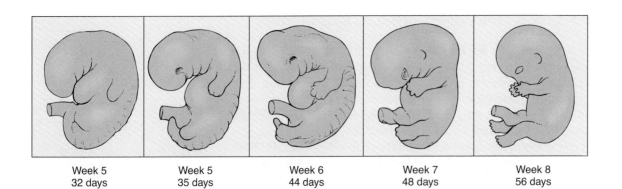

| Week 5 | Week 5 | Week 6 | Week 7 | Week 8 |
| 32 days | 35 days | 44 days | 48 days | 56 days |

Figure 3-7

Development of the embryo
Based on K. L. Moore, Persaud, & Shiota, 2000.

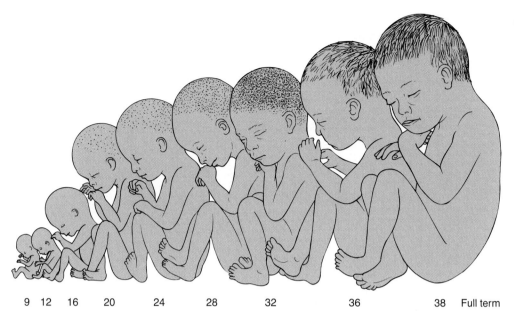

Figure 3-8
Development of the fetus
Based on K. L. Moore, Persaud, & Shiota, 2000.

9 12 16   20   24   28   32   36   38 Full term

Development of the fetus.   The period of the **fetus** lasts from Week 9 until birth. During this period, the developing being grows rapidly, receiving finishing touches that will permit life outside the womb (see Figure 3-8). The many organs and structures that were initiated earlier are now expanded, and they become coordinated with other systems in the body. The fetus's body is elaborated through a series of specific changes:

- *Third month.* The head is large in comparison to the rest of the body but now slows down in rate of growth. The eyes move to their proper place, and the fetus becomes increasingly human looking. The external genitalia grow. The fetus begins to show reflexes and muscular movement, but these are small and not yet felt by the mother.
- *Fourth month.* The fetus grows rapidly in length (height). Weight increases slowly. Hair grows on the head and eyebrows.
- *Fifth month.* The fetus continues to grow rapidly in length. Fine hair covers the body. The mother can usually feel the fetus's movement by now.
- *Sixth month.* The fetus's skin is red and wrinkled; the body is lean. Fingernails are present. The respiratory system and central nervous system are still developing and coordinating their operations.
- *Seventh month.* Eyes open and eyelashes are present. Toenails grow. The body begins to fill out.
- *Eighth month.* Skin is pink and smooth. Fat grows under the skin. The testes (in males) descend. (K. L. Moore & Persaud, 2003; Sadler, 2000).

With its basic body structures formed, the fetus spends the weeks before birth getting larger and heavier. On average, the fetus at 6 months weighs approximately 1 pound, 13 ounces; at 7 months, 2 pounds, 14 ounces; and at 8 months, 4 pounds, 10 ounces (K. L. Moore & Persaud, 2003). Birth weights vary, of course, but on average, the newborn infant weighs 7 pounds, 8 ounces. These last few weeks of weight gain increase the chances of an infant's survival after birth. In fact, infants rarely survive when they are born before they have progressed through at least 6 months of prenatal development or weigh less than 1 pound, 2 ounces. (We examine the health and treatment of early and small infants later in this chapter.)

The brain also expands and matures during the final weeks and months of prenatal growth. Structurally, the outer layers of the brain (those closest to the skull) bunch up and form folds and creases, creating a staggering number of potential circuits for transmitting information. Functionally, the fetus's brain is being prepared to carry out vital reflexes, such as sucking, swallowing, and looking away from bright lights. In the weeks before birth, the fetus's brain also activates circuits for sensing stimulation and learning from it. For example, it appears that fetuses can hear sounds in the womb. In one study, pregnant mothers who were

fetus
During prenatal Week 9 until birth, the developing being that is growing in size and weight and in sensory abilities, brain structures, and organs needed for survival.

a few days before their deliveries were randomly assigned to one of two treatments, music-exposure and nonexposure conditions (James, Spencer, & Stepsis, 2002). Both groups of mothers had earphones placed on their abdomens. In the music-exposure condition, a single song, "Little Brown Jug," was played repeatedly over a 4-hour period. In the nonexposure group, no sound was emitted from the earphones. The fetuses were studied during the conditions. Compared to fetuses not exposed to the music, fetuses exposed to the song showed more fluctuations in their heart rates. Greater fluctuations in heart rate suggest that, in some primitive way, the fetuses were attending to the music. Remarkably, the researchers also found evidence that the infants retained their memory of the music. After birth, both the music-exposed and nonexposed fetuses (now infants) listened for a half-hour as "Little Brown Jug" played repeatedly in their earphones. Compared to the infants who had not previously been exposed to this music, infants who were exposed prior to birth were more likely to stay awake longer and to fluctuate in heart rate during the hour after music exposure.

Fetuses may also learn to recognize some flavors, presumably because substances from the mother's diet are transmitted into the womb's fluid and swallowed by the fetus. In one study, pregnant women were assigned to one of two conditions during the last weeks of their pregnancy. One group of women drank carrot juice and water during 4 days over each of 3 weeks (Mennella, Jagnow, & Beauchamp, 2001). The other group drank water but no carrot juice over the same time frame. After their infants were born and had begun to eat cereal, the researchers asked the mothers to add carrot juice to the infants' cereal. Infants who had been exposed to carrots during their prenatal development showed fewer negative facial expressions while eating the carrot-flavored cereal than did infants of mothers who had drunk only water.

These and other studies suggest that rudimentary abilities to learn and remember simple patterns are present before birth (DeCasper & Spence, 1986; Kisilevsky et al., 2003; van Heteren, Boekkooi, Jongsma, & Nijhuis, 2000). As you will see in later chapters, these initial and amazing learning abilities continue to evolve systematically over years and even decades.

In summary, the formation of a human life is the outcome of countless changes. The body grows step by step, carefully managed by nature, constantly drawing from nurture. In spectacular feats of coordination, new cells extend body parts so that these structures become increasingly defined—for example, simple paddles turn into elongated arms, these arms add hands, and eventually hands add fingers. Prenatal development and genetic expression show a wonderful balance between nature and nurture, universality and diversity, and qualitative and quantitative change, as you can see in the Basic Developmental Issues table "Biological Beginnings."

Medical Care

Prospective parents invariably hope for healthy children. To enhance their chances of giving birth to strong, well-formed infants, prospective mothers can seek medical care before getting pregnant. When they do become pregnant, women can shield their developing offspring from harmful substances and obtain ongoing medical care.

Preparing for pregnancy. A woman can increase her chances of having a healthy infant by caring for herself *before* becoming pregnant. Physicians and nurses advised of a woman's wish for a child may suggest that she watch her diet, take approved vitamin supplements, exercise moderately, and avoid alcohol and drugs. They may also ask her about her prescriptions and over-the-counter medicines, since some can be harmful to fetuses. For example, some acne and wrinkle creams and oral preparations appear to cause serious problems in the facial structure, heart, and neural tubes of fetuses (Sadler, 2000). These and other potentially dangerous substances are not recommended for women who are pregnant or likely to conceive. Medical personnel may also address particular health problems that can be activated or complicated by pregnancy, such as hypertension or diabetes. Finally, a physician or nurse may discuss any concerns that the woman has about her age (Sherwen, Scoloveno, & Weingarten, 1999). Pregnant women under age 17 may be at risk for having a baby with low birth weight. Advanced age in mothers and fathers (35 or older for mothers, 40 or older for fathers) is associated with slightly elevated risks for genetic problems.

A man and woman concerned about conceiving a child with significant birth defects may consult a genetic counselor. Prospective parents are most likely to work with a genetic counselor when they have had several miscarriages, have given birth to a child with a genetic de-

Conecting Concepts

You will learn more about brain development in Chapter 4 and about learning in Chapters 6 and 7.

BASIC DEVELOPMENTAL ISSUES | Biological Beginnings

Issue	Genetic Foundations	Prenatal Development
Nature and Nurture	Nature forms gametes (sperm and ovum) and fuses them to form a future child with a genetic makeup that, in turn, becomes a permanent, influential agent of nature for the child. Nurture is evident in environmental effects on the parents' chromosomes, as occurs when radiation and illness create errors in reproductive cells. During and after prenatal development, nature and nurture weave together: Genes do their work in the context of the child's physiology, nutrition, and experience.	Nature and nurture are closely intertwined during the baby-to-be's prenatal development. The effects of nature are evident in predictable, ordered changes to body structures and in the formation and operation of supporting physical structures, such as the placenta, that make growth possible. The effects of nurture are seen with nutrition, protection from harmful substances, and the mother's stress management.
Universality and Diversity	The vast majority of children are born with 46 chromosomes. Most genes take the form of uniform instructions for necessary proteins to build human bodies and brains. Some genes vary systematically across children and permit individual differences in height, weight, physical appearance, motor skills, intellectual abilities, and temperament. Errors in chromosomes and genes are another source of diversity.	In healthy prenatal beings, there is considerable universality in the sequence of changes. The small being proceeds through phases of the zygote, embryo, and fetus, and ultimately is born after approximately 9 months. Diversity occurs because of variations in mothers' health, exposure to harmful substances, genetic vulnerabilities of the fetus, and the efficiency with which physical structures in the womb sustain life.
Qualitative and Quantitative Change	Qualitative changes are made possible by the careful sequence with which particular genes are triggered into action. At appropriate times, selected genes are activated and create qualitative changes in the child's body, such as growth in particular areas of the body and the transformations of puberty. When genes direct the body to grow larger and to undergo maturational processes, they also permit quantitative changes, such as increases in height and weight.	The future baby undergoes a series of predictable transformations: The zygote moves through the fallopian tubes, grows new cells, and burrows into the inside wall of the uterus; the embryo creates many new cells, which form the basic organs and structures of the body; and the fetus builds and refines these preliminary structures, activates physiological processes needed for survival, and puts on weight. Quantitative changes are present in the rapid production of new cells, particularly in the brain and body prior to birth.

fect or chromosomal abnormality, or are aware of family history of a genetic disorder, mental retardation, or birth defects (Meyerstein, 2001). The genetic counselor examines the family's medical records, other pertinent records, and information the couple provides about the health of siblings, parents, and other biological relatives. Diagnostic tests may be conducted, including an analysis of the potential parents' chromosomes. Genetic counselors inform the couple of medical facts, inheritance patterns, estimated risks for having a child with a birth defect or disorder, ways to deal with risks, and health care and reproductive options. Counselors may recommend that prenatal diagnostic tests be conducted during a pregnancy. Genetic counselors also provide supportive counseling and make appropriate referrals to mental health professionals (Meyerstein, 2001; Sherwen et al., 1999).

Avoiding harmful substances. During prenatal development, babies-to-be are sometimes exposed to potentially harmful substances, or **teratogens.** Examples of teratogens include many prescription and nonprescription drugs; alcohol; infectious agents such as rubella, syphilis, and human immunodeficiency virus (HIV); and some environmental chemicals, such as lead and polychlorinated biphenyls (K. L. Moore & Persaud, 2003).

Prenatal development includes a series of sensitive periods for forming physical structures. These physical structures are most vulnerable to teratogens when the structures are first emerging, growing speedily, and laying the foundation upon which more refined extensions must build. Thus the timing of exposure to teratogens partly determines their impact on the developing being (see Figure 3-9).

A newly formed *zygote* has not yet begun to form separate body parts and tends not to sustain structural defects when exposed to teratogens. Occasionally exposure to teratogens can cause death of the zygote, but more often a few cells will die or become damaged and these cells will be replaced with healthy cells (K. L. Moore & Persaud, 2003). During the

To protect their children, pregnant women can eat healthfully, see their doctor, reduce their stress, and avoid potentially harmful substances, such as alcohol and cigarettes.

teratogen
Potentially harmful substance that can cause damaging effects during prenatal development.

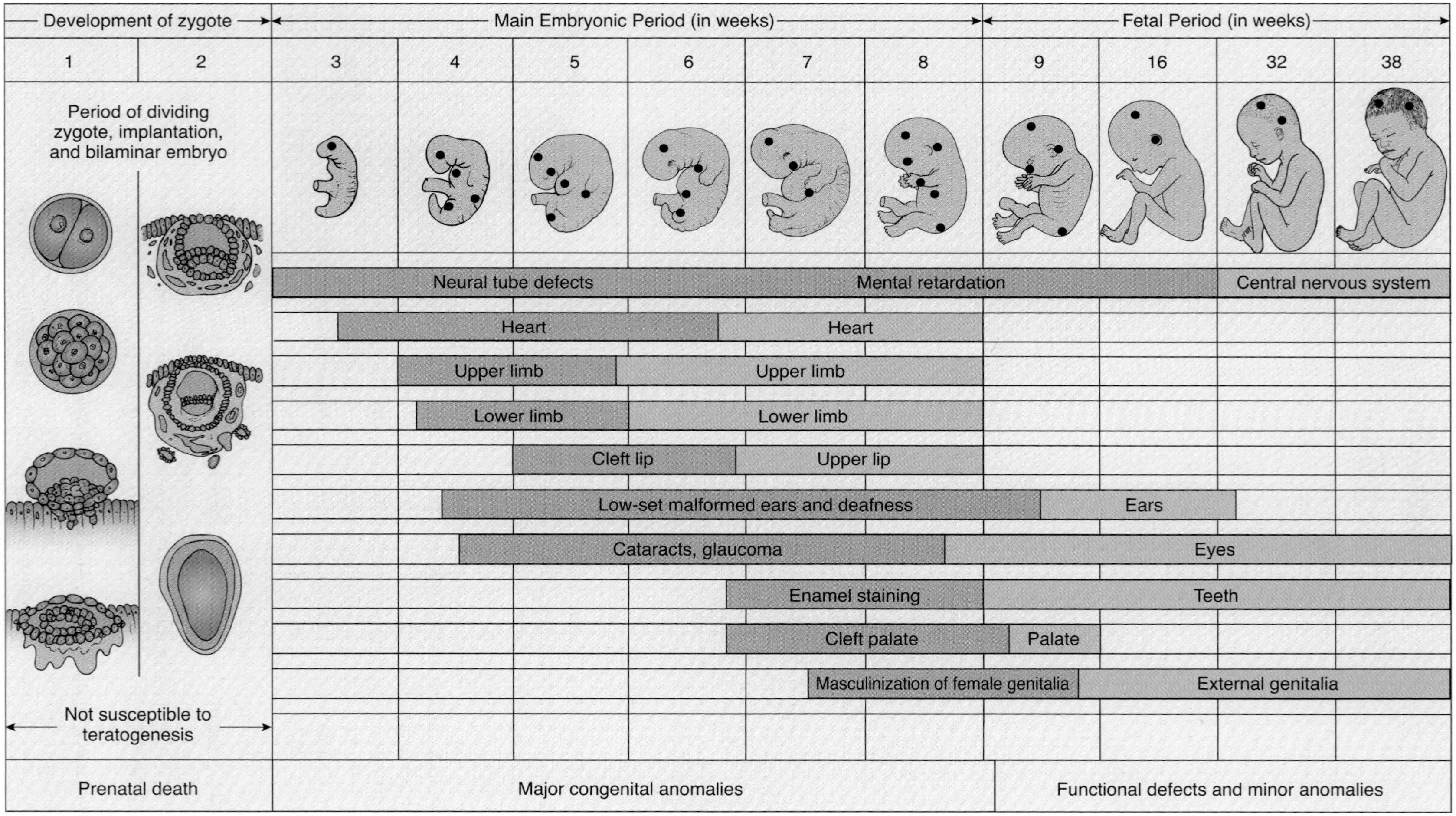

Figure 3-9

Sensitive periods in prenatal development. The effects of teratogens depend in part on timing of exposure. Black dots indicate sites that are growing rapidly and are particularly susceptible to damage from teratogens.

Adapted from *Before We are Born: Essentials of Embryology and Birth Defects* (6th edition), K. L. Moore & T. V. N. Persaud, p. 130, copyright © 2003, with permission from Elsevier.

embryonic period, however, damage can be serious. The principal structures of the body, including the limbs and the internal organs, are formed during the period of the embryo, and exposure to drugs, alcohol, and other teratogens can cause major structural problems. For example, limbs are particularly sensitive to harm 24 to 36 days after conception (K. L. Moore & Persaud, 2003). Keep in mind that during this early, critical phase of the pregnancy, women may not yet know they are pregnant. Finally, growth during the *fetal period* is less susceptible to serious structural damage, although there are some exceptions: Notably, the brain continues to grow until (and after) birth, and as a result, the fetus's brain can be damaged late in pregnancy.

The genetic makeup of both mother and baby moderates the effects of teratogens. For example, phenytoin is an anticonvulsant medication prescribed for some people who have epilepsy. Between 5 percent and 10 percent of children exposed to phenytoin as embryos develop a small brain, mental retardation, wide spaces between eyes, a short nose, and other distinctive facial features (K. L. Moore & Persaud, 2003). About a third of exposed embryos show minor congenital problems, and half are unaffected. Presumably, genetic factors are partly responsible for these different outcomes.

Amount of teratogens is also important. The greater the exposure, the more severe and widespread the effects. Clearly, women who are pregnant must exercise caution in the food and substances they ingest and the toxins they encounter in the environment. In fact, this need for caution extends to all women who are sexually active and capable of becoming pregnant, because women are not always aware that they are carrying a rapidly growing embryo or fetus. Here are some examples of particular teratogens and their potential effects on offspring:

- *Alcohol.* Women who drink alcohol during pregnancy can give birth to infants with *fetal alcohol syndrome.* Cells in the brain are disrupted, physical and motor development is delayed, facial abnormalities occur, mental retardation is common, and children become impulsive and exhibit other behavioral problems. In less severe cases, children may develop learning disabilities or minor physical problems.
- *Nicotine.* Women who smoke cigarettes are more likely to give birth to small, lightweight babies and (less often) to lose their infants through miscarriage.
- *Marijuana.* Use of marijuana is associated with premature birth and low birth weight. Exposed infants may experience tremors and oversensitivity to certain kinds of stimuli.
- *Cocaine.* Women using cocaine during pregnancy are more likely to give birth prematurely and have babies with low birth weight, small head size, lethargy, and irritability.
- *Heroin.* Pregnant women who use heroin may miscarry or give birth prematurely. After birth, exposed infants may be irritable, suffer respiratory complications, and even die, and those who survive may have small head size.
- *HIV infection and AIDS.* Pregnant women with the HIV virus are at risk for passing on the virus to their children, and children who become infected may initially show delays in motor skills, language, and cognitive development, and ultimately develop more serious health impairments. (Chasnoff, Burns, Burns, & Schnoll, 1986; E. Hunt, Streissguth, Kerr, & Olson, 1995; Korkman, Autti-Raemoe, Koivulehto, & Granstroem, 1998; Kraemingk & Paquette, 1999; Mayes & Bornstein, 1997; Oser & Cohen, 2003; Teeter & Semrud-Clikeman, 1997)

Maternal anxiety can also create problems for the fetus. For example, pregnant women who experience high levels of stress risk having infants with low birth weights and irritable dispositions who, later in life, experience difficulty focusing attention and dealing with negative emotions (Huizink, Mulder, & Buitelaar, 2004; Van den Bergh & Marcoen, 2004).

Implementing medical procedures.   Once a woman is pregnant, she and her partner may obtain diagnostic information about the status of their offspring. An *ultrasound examination* (also known as ultrasonography) has become a routine part of the obstetric care of pregnant women. Ultrasound devices emit high-frequency sound waves that bounce off tissues of varying densities (Sherwen et al., 1999). The device is passed over the woman's abdomen or inserted in her vagina. The echoes to the waves are converted to two-dimensional images of the fetus, and these are displayed on a television monitor. Ultrasound examinations provide good estimates of the age of the fetus, detect multiple fetuses, and reveal major abnormalities (K. L. Moore & Persaud, 2003; Sherwen et al., 1999). Ultrasounds are also used as anatomical guides during the implementation of other prenatal tests. Finally, ultrasound examinations confirm the reality of the pregnancy for expectant parents, as you can see in the following exercise.

INTERPRETING CHILDREN'S ARTIFACTS AND ACTIONS   My Baby Is Real!

One of the first artifacts of childhood is often available before birth: images of fetuses produced during ultrasound examinations. As you read the following reflections of six parents, identify their feelings about these images and any apprehension they had about the results of the examination.

1. Yes, when (she) got pregnant I didn't really understand it. But after we had the ultrasound I did. . . . It was the most exciting thing I have done as far as the baby is concerned. It was more exciting than when I heard that we were going to have a baby. (a father; Ekelin, Crang-Svalenius, & Dykes, 2004, p. 337)[a]
2. That you can see so much! Awesome. Small, small fingers and everything looked perfect. And just everything works. There is a little heart beating and you can see so much even if the baby is only 18 cm (long). That there actually is something so almost completely developed it just has to grow. That such good technology exists—it's unbelievable . . . they can see so much. (a mother; p. 339)
3. And it became so very alive and I felt very close to the baby. Yes, it felt like a fine moment, it was a very philosophic . . . emotional moment . . . it felt very good. (a father; p. 339)
4. This is definitely one of the top ten on the list of fantastic memories in my life I think. I really believe that. It is really completely fantastic. It's really a big thing I think. (a father; p. 340)
5. . . . all I can say is that even if there should be some fault, if an arm or leg was missing I would never for my life be able to take it away. And even if it had Down's syndrome or something like that I would never manage to have an abortion. Never in my life. (a mother; p. 339)
6. I hadn't thought much about it. But it was there a little, little bit. We know a couple whose first child had spina bifida so they

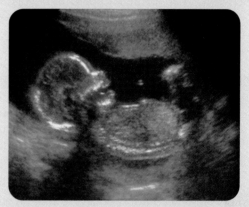

Seeing an ultrasound image of their developing baby can be a memorable experience for expectant parents.

chose not to have that baby. So there is that possibility but it feels very far away for some reason. It won't affect us. The power of life makes one just believe that everything will be fine. (a father; p. 338)

[a]Excerpts reprinted from *Midwifery, 20,* M. Ekelin, E. Crang-Svalenius, & A. K. Dykes, "A Qualitative Study of Mothers' and Fathers' Experiences of Routine Ultrasound Examination in Sweden," pp. 335–344, copyright © 2004, with permission from Elsevier.

Ultrasound examinations provoked many strong feelings in the prospective parents quoted in the exercise. Several parents (1–4) expressed an overriding sense of joy upon receiving confirmation that their offspring were well formed and recognizably human. Two parents (5, 6) were somewhat apprehensive as they contemplated the problems their offspring potentially could face. If the ultrasound had uncovered possible problems, the medical staff would likely have advised the parents about diagnostic medical tests.

Several prenatal diagnostic techniques are generally implemented only with high-risk pregnancies. *Chorionic villus sampling* (CVS) is an invasive diagnostic procedure performed sometime between 7 and 12 weeks after fertilization (K. L. Moore et al., 2000). A needle is inserted into the woman's abdomen or a tube is guided through her cervix (see the left side of Figure 3-10), and tiny amounts of chorionic villi (blood vessels that grow on the membrane surrounding the developing embryo or fetus) are collected. Abnormalities detected by CVS include chromosomal abnormalities, X-chromosome-linked disorders such as Tay-Sachs disease, and some diseases of the blood, such as sickle cell disease (Sherwen et al., 1999). Test results are typically available within a few days. The procedure

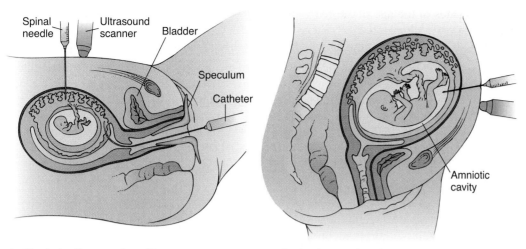

Figure 3-10

Prenatal diagnostic methods. In both chorionic villus sampling (A) and amniocentesis (B), an ultrasound procedure guides the test.

Based on K. L. Moore et al., 2000.

A. Chorionic villus sampling with a 7-week-old embryo

B. Amniocentesis with a 13-week-old fetus

entails a small risk for damage to an arm or leg of the embryo or fetus, and miscarriage is possible but unlikely (Sadler, 2000).

Amniocentesis is an invasive diagnostic procedure performed sometime between 13 and 18 weeks after fertilization (K. L. Moore et al., 2000). A needle is inserted into the woman's abdomen to draw a small amount of fluid from the uterus (see the right side of Figure 3-10). The fluid is analyzed for high concentrations of a fetal protein, which are present when fetuses have *neural tube defects* and some abdominal problems (Sadler, 2000). Fetal cells floating in the amniotic fluid are also analyzed for possible chromosomal abnormalities. Other problems detected by amniocentesis are biochemical defects, prenatal infections, and blood diseases (Sherwen et al., 1999). Results from cell cultures usually take 2 to 4 weeks to analyze. Risks associated with amniocentesis are trauma to the fetus, infection, and miscarriage (fetal loss rates are 0.5%; Sadler, 2000; Sherwen et al., 1999).

Other tests are performed occasionally. For example, the mother's blood can be tested for the presence of fetal cells. Normally, not many fetal cells cross the placenta into the mother's circulation, but some do, and the mother's blood can be tested for high rates of fetal protein, which might indicate a neural tube defect in the fetus. In consultation with the mother, a physician may also use a *fetoscope,* an instrument with a tiny camera and light, to examine the fetus for defective limbs or other deformities. Corrective surgery can be performed in rare circumstances.

When couples learn that their offspring has a chromosomal abnormality or other serious defect, they may seek support from counselors and medical personnel. Depending on their values and circumstances, some couples choose to terminate the pregnancy, concerned that they will not be able to care adequately for a child with special needs. Other couples want practical tips and emotional support in preparing for the birth of their disabled child, believing in the fetus's right to life and their ability to be caring parents for the child.

Supporting Parents, Protecting Babies

If you have the opportunity to work with prospective parents, you can educate them about prenatal development and their future child's need for protection. Here are some specific tactics to take:

● *Encourage women to review their health before becoming pregnant.* Women who are planning a pregnancy or capable of becoming pregnant should consult their physician. In particular, women who take over-the-counter or prescription medications need to talk with their doctor about risks for a pregnancy and alternative ways of managing chronic conditions.

● *Remind sexually active women to take care of themselves.* Women may be several weeks along (or longer) in a pregnancy before they become aware of it. Consequently, women who might be pregnant should watch their diet, restrict their exposure to teratogens such as alcohol, and avoid X-rays.

● *Encourage pregnant women to seek medical care.* Nurses and other medical personnel will examine risks, reassure prospective mothers, and treat ongoing medical conditions safely. Under the guidance of their doctor, pregnant women often follow an exercise program. Getting regular exercise can help pregnant women keep up their stamina, prepare for birth, and limit stress to within reasonable levels. Pregnant women should also be encouraged to follow a diet that supports their own health as well as the nutritional needs of the fetus. Getting adequate rest is another important goal for pregnant women, even though doing so is not always possible, especially when they have other children, jobs, and other responsibilities.

● *Urge pregnant women to stay clear of teratogens.* Smokers can be encouraged to reduce the number of cigarettes they smoke or, better, to quit smoking altogether. Expectant women who drink alcohol or take drugs need to be confronted with the dreadful and permanent damage these substances might cause in their unborn children. Obviously, pregnant women who are dependent on alcohol or drugs need immediate professional help.

● *Encourage pregnant women to relax.* Women who seem particularly anxious during pregnancy may benefit from help in dealing with stress. They can try relaxation techniques and consult with medical personnel or mental health professionals.

● *Ask pregnant women to speak their minds.* Many pregnant women have experiences they want to share. For example, they may have concerns about possible birth defects or simply want to communicate excitement, as when they first feel the fetus stir within them. Many women appreciate sympathetic listeners who let them talk about their changing and sometimes conflicting feelings.

● *Ask fathers to verbalize their experiences.* Many fathers are mystified with the physical changes their partners undergo during pregnancy. Some fathers feel excluded during pregnancy—although they had an obvious hand in ushering in the new being, they may believe they are not needed for further development. In reality, fathers can play an enormously important role in supporting expectant mothers. And many prospective fathers gain just as much as mothers from having a sensitive listener with whom to share their worries and hopes related to the baby.

● *Advise new parents about appropriate care when children have been exposed to teratogens.* Sadly, the brains and bodies of many children are impaired due to prenatal exposure to drugs, alcohol, infection, and other teratogens. Some of these effects are lasting, but even so, affected children certainly benefit from responsive, predictable, and developmentally appropriate care. For example, children who have been exposed to cocaine and other serious teratogens often develop good language, communication, and interpersonal skills when they receive high-quality care (J. V. Brown, Bakeman, Coles, Platzman, & Lynch, 2004). Special educational services may likewise enhance the academic and social skills of teratogen-exposed children.

● *Intervene when mothers continue to use drugs and alcohol after the birth.* For their own sake and that of their children, women who continue to abuse substances after their babies are born need professional treatment. Many of these mothers also may need guidance with parenting skills (J. V. Brown et al., 2004). Community counselors and family educators can advise families about helpful programs in their area.

Unlike many developmental accomplishments, such as learning to talk, walk, and ride a bicycle, many aspects of prenatal development cannot be observed directly. Nonetheless, scientific evidence provides accurate benchmarks as to what is happening to the baby-to-be during the various phases of growth. In addition, as the pregnancy proceeds, there are some observable changes in mothers and fetuses. The Developmental Trends table "Prenatal Development" provides a useful synopsis of key prenatal developments and observable signs of growth.

After many months of pregnancy, most prospective parents are eager to meet their son or daughter, face-to-face. It is time for birth.

DEVELOPMENTAL TRENDS	Prenatal Development		
Phase of Prenatal Growth	What You Might Observe	Diversity	Implications
Zygote (conception to 2 weeks following)	• The zygote begins to develop at conception, with the fusing of sperm and ovum. The being's first cell divides into two cells, two divide into four, four divide into eight, and so forth. The zygote is a ball of cells as it travels down the fallopian tube and into the uterus. • No signs of pregnancy are noticeable to the prospective mother.	• Couples vary in their chances of conceiving a child. • Some children are conceived with the assistance of reproductive technologies. • A large number of zygotes perish because errors in chromosomes cause them to be seriously malformed and unable to grow. • Hormonal factors in the woman can also cause loss of zygotes.	• Encourage prospective parents to plan for a pregnancy by first taking stock of their health, talking with a physician and, if they have concerns about potential genetic problems in their children, seeing a genetic counselor. • Persuade prospective parents to follow a physician's recommendations regarding use of prescription medications, over-the-counter drugs, and consumption of vitamins. • Persuade sexually active women to avoid alcohol and drugs.
Embryo (2 through 8 weeks after conception)	• Body parts and organs are being formed as the embryo develops rapidly. At the end of the period, the little being shows a head structure and limbs that are recognizably human. • The prospective mother may notice that her menstrual period is late. She may experience early signs of pregnancy, such as nausea, fatigue, a sense of abdominal swelling, and tender breasts.	• The embryo is especially susceptible to damage from harmful substances. The extent of harm done to the embryo by teratogens will depend on the timing and duration of exposure, the amount of the dose, and the biological vulnerability of the embryo. • Miscarriage (or spontaneous loss of the embryo) is fairly common during this period.	• Encourage a prospective mother to see a physician if she believes she might be pregnant. • Encourage pregnant women to shield themselves from potentially harmful substances. Educate prospective mothers and fathers about the impact of teratogens on the developing embryo.
Fetus (9 weeks after conception until birth)	• Organs and body parts continue to grow and mature. • The mother can feel the fetus moving, lightly at first and actively over time. • The mother's abdomen swells and she gains weight.	• Many pregnant women feel strong and healthy during the final months of pregnancy, but some continue to experience nausea and fatigue. • Fetuses vary in many respects, including their movements, growth rates and birth weights, and readiness for survival at birth.	• Advise pregnant women to follow the advice of their physician regarding diet and exercise. • Listen to prospective mothers and fathers talk about their hopes, fears, and expectations related to the baby. • Continue to advocate for abstinence from alcohol and drugs; discourage cigarette smoking. • Encourage pregnant women to manage their stress levels. • Tell pregnant women about prepared childbirth classes in their area.

Source: K. L. Moore & Persaud, 2003.

Birth of the Baby

The events leading up to, and culminating in, a human childbirth provoke a range of feelings in parents—excitement, fear, pain, fatigue, and joy, to name a few. These events are managed best when families prepare ahead of time, take advantage of adequate medical care, and hold reasonable expectations about the baby's abilities and needs.

Preparation for Birth

Parents are highly individual in their feelings about pregnancy and birth, although some anxiety is common. For example, a first-time mother may be eager to have her baby but anxious about the pain she will experience during delivery. A couple may be worried about the birth, having previously suffered several miscarriages. Another couple with a strained relationship may have mixed feelings about raising a child together. Such feelings may influence the actual birth experience (Niven, 1992). Excessive levels of stress not only make for an unpleasant experience for parents but also can prolong the early stages of labor, raise the mother's blood pressure, and decrease oxygen to the baby. Parents can reduce their anxiety by seeking out information, getting organized for the baby, and preparing other children in their family for the new arrival.

Health-care providers and family educators can give useful information and reassurance to parents during the pregnancy. For example, they may teach relaxation techniques; offer tips for posture, movement, and exercise; and persuade women to eliminate potentially risky behaviors, such as drinking alcohol and smoking cigarettes. *Prepared childbirth classes* also are potentially very helpful. These programs emphasize the natural aspects of birth and the woman's control over the process. They typically include the following elements:

- Relaxation and breathing techniques that encourage the mother to stay focused, manage pain, reduce fear, and use muscles effectively during the various phases of the labor
- Support from a spouse, partner, friend, or family member who coaches the mother throughout labor and delivery, reminds her to use the breathing techniques she has learned, massages her, and otherwise encourages her
- Education about the physiology and mechanics of delivery, types of positions during delivery, and pain medications and other medical interventions used with some women (Dick-Read, 1944; Lamaze, 1958; Sherwen et al., 1999)

The pregnant woman and her partner, if she has one, may also prepare for birth by deciding where it will occur and who will attend to it. Hospitals offer the latest technology, well-trained medical staff, arrangements for insurance coverage, and pain medication, but they have disadvantages. Hospitals are perceived by some parents as instituting unnecessary and invasive treatments and as creating an impersonal climate that separates rather than unites family members during a momentous occasion. Community birth centers are homelike, inexpensive, and welcoming of extended contact with the newborn; however, they are less appropriate for women with high-risk deliveries, those who need emergency care, and those whose insurance does not cover costs. Home settings offer families a familiar and comforting environment, allow family members to participate, are inexpensive, and give extended contact with the newborn. They have disadvantages similar to those of community birth centers and offer no pain medication, few emergency procedures, and minimal access to trained birth attendants (Sherwen et al., 1999). Many hospitals have responded to concerns about their lack of family orientation by setting aside hospital birthing rooms that are attractive, comfortable, and large enough to accommodate several family members. In North America, physicians most often deliver babies, but other common attendants include certified nurse midwives, certified midwives who are not nurses, and lay midwives without formal training (Sherwen et al., 1999).

The Birth Process

Amazingly, medical researchers are still not able to pinpoint the cascade of changes that are necessary to trigger the uterine contractions that begin a woman's labor (Demarest & Charon, 1996; Sherwen et al., 1999). Presently, medical researchers believe that a combination of factors precipitates labor, including hormonal changes in the mother's body and maturation of the fetus's body.

Typically, the mother's uterus begins preparations for birth 38 to 40 weeks into the pregnancy. Here is the incredible sequence of events that constitutes the birth process:

- As the pregnancy advances, the mother experiences *Braxton Hicks contractions.* These irregular contractions exercise the mother's uterine muscles without causing the cervix to open.
- In most cases (95%), the baby settles in a head-downward position, which will facilitate its passage through the birth canal. When babies are in breech position (positioned to come out buttocks or legs first) or in a sideways position (a shoulder would likely come out first), the delivery is monitored closely and often requires a cesarean delivery.
- A few events may occur in the days immediately before labor begins. The mother may experience a descent of the baby into the pelvis, experience a rush of energy, lose 1 to 4 pounds as her hormonal balance changes, and notice vaginal secretions. Sleep is difficult at this time. Accordingly, health providers may help mothers use relaxation techniques and reassure them that sleep disturbances prior to labor do not usually interfere with its progression.
- In the *first stage of labor*, the mother experiences regular uterine contractions that widen the cervix opening (see Figure 3-11, picture A). These contractions last until

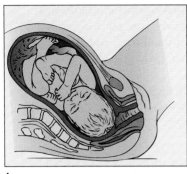
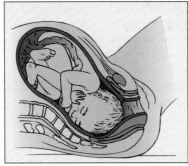
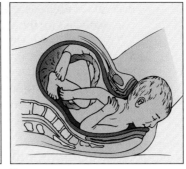

A.   B.   C.

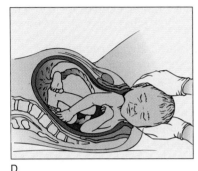
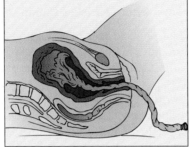

D.   E.

Figure 3-11

Stages of a normal birth. In the first stage of labor, the mother's cervix dilates (A). After numerous contractions the cervix opens completely, the baby's head moves down the vagina, and the second stage of labor begins (B). The second stage continues with the mother pushing with each contraction, the baby moving down the vagina, and the baby's head appearing (C). Gradually, the shoulders and rest of the body emerge (D). The third stage of labor is the delivery of the placenta (E). Based on Demarest & Charon, 1996.

the cervix is dilated to about 10 centimeters (approximately 4 inches). Mothers experience pain, especially in their pelvis and back. This first stage typically takes about 12 to 16 hours for mothers who are having their first baby and 6 to 8 hours for mothers who have previously delivered one or more babies. Medical personnel keep track of the opening of the cervix and monitor the fetal heartbeat. They may offer the mother pain medication and encourage her to walk around. At the beginning of the first stage of labor, contractions are spaced widely apart (e.g., every 15 to 30 minutes) and mild to moderate in intensity. When the cervix dilates to 3 centimeters, an "active" phase begins and lasts until full dilation. Contractions become stronger and longer (they last 30 to 60 seconds) and occur every 2 to 3 minutes.

- In the *second stage of labor*, the cervix is fully dilated, the baby proceeds down the birth canal, and the child is born (see Figure 3-11, pictures B, C, and D). This stage may take about half an hour, but in first pregnancies it often lasts up to 2 hours. Contractions come often and hard. They appear every other minute and last for a minute at a time. Mothers must push hard to help move the baby down and out. Medical personnel continue to watch the fetal heartbeat. The doctor may use forceps or call for a cesarean delivery if uterine contractions slow down or the baby cannot move quickly enough. Too fast is not good either, however, because the pressure might tear the mother's tissues or damage the baby's head. Thus the doctor or midwife may place a hand on the part of the baby coming out and ease out the baby methodically. Medical personnel may also help rotate the baby's head so that it can get past the mother's pelvic bones. As the head comes out, the doctor or midwife checks to make sure the umbilical cord is not wrapped around the head, and if it is, the cord is moved. The nose and mouth are cleansed of fluids. The mother continues to push to release the baby's shoulders and the rest of the body. The baby is gently wiped dry, and after the blood has drained from the umbilical cord into the baby's body, the cord is clamped and cut. The baby is born! The baby is placed on the mother, and the father or other coach may take a turn holding him or her.

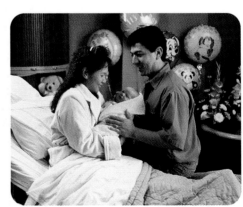

Many parents feel an overwhelming sense of joy when their baby arrives.

- In the *third stage of labor*, the placenta and fetal membranes (the afterbirth) are expelled by the uterus (see Figure 3-11, picture E). Usually, this process happens naturally and without assistance, although medical personnel must watch to make sure it happens. The mother is checked to see if lacerations have occurred or if medical treatment is needed.
- Oftentimes the baby is alert immediately after birth and looks around the room—a stunning and memorable event for parents and other family members (Demarest & Charon, 1996; Sherwen et al., 1999).

Complications and Interventions

Medical personnel, midwives, and the mother's partner can do many things to comfort the mother as she goes through labor and delivery. Following are some examples of interventions that are typical in many Western societies (Enkin et al., 2000; Sherwen et al., 1999):

- Midwives, coaches, and medical staff may help relieve the mother's pain by using methods that do not require medication. For example, some mothers are assisted by a warm whirlpool path, visual images of the cervix opening, music, hypnosis, biofeedback, and massage.
- Physicians sometimes offer *analgesics,* medicines that reduce pain without loss of consciousness. Medications injected into the mother's spine (such as *epidural analgesia)* are an especially common method for labor relief. Generally, these medications are not offered early in labor, as they may slow progress, but also not too late, as physicians want the medicine to be metabolized (used and broken down in the body) by mother and baby prior to birth. Some analgesic medications can increase the need for other medical interventions, such as use of forceps and cesarean deliveries, and they may reduce breathing in the newborn.
- Physicians may offer *anesthetics* to women in active labor if extreme pressure must be applied (such as occurs in the use of forceps) or when a cesarean delivery must be performed. Anesthetics cause loss of sensation and in some cases also lead to loss of consciousness.
- Women sometimes take *opioids* (also known as narcotics), medicines that reduce the sensation of pain by changing the way it is perceived by the brain. Opioids have several disadvantages, including limited effectiveness in reducing pain, occasional side effects such as nausea and drowsiness, and tendency to adversely affect the baby's breathing and breastfeeding.
- Physicians may *induce labor*—that is, start it artificially—with medications (e.g., Pitocin). Candidates for an induced labor include women past their due dates and those with diabetes or pregnancy-induced hypertension.
- During a *cesarean delivery,* the baby is removed surgically from an incision made in the mother's abdomen and uterine wall. Almost 30 percent of babies born in the United States are delivered through cesarean surgery, a rate which many people suggest is higher than it should be (Centers for Disease Control and Prevention, 2005d). Cesarean deliveries are performed when the physician believes the safety of the mother, child, or both is at stake. Examples of conditions that might lead to a cesarean delivery are fetal distress, health problems of the mother, failure to progress in labor, infections in the birth canal, and presence of multiple babies.

Babies at risk.   Some babies are born before they are able to cope with the demands of life outside the womb. Two categories of babies require special care:

- *Babies born early*. The **premature infant** is born before the end of 37 weeks after conception (Sherwen et al., 1999). Premature labor may be triggered by several factors, including infection, multiple gestations (such as the presence of twins or triplets), abnormalities in the fetus, death of the fetus, abnormalities in the mother's uterus or cervix, and serious disease in the mother (Demarest & Charon, 1996). Extremely early babies (born after only 32 weeks or fewer of prenatal growth) face serious risk factors, including higher than typical rates of death during infancy. Premature infants are also at risk immediately after birth for health

premature infant
Infant born early (before 37 weeks of prenatal growth) and sometimes with serious medical problems.

problems, including breathing problems, anemia, brain hemorrhages, feeding problems, and temperature instability.

- *Babies born small for date.* Some infants are small and light given the amount of time they have had to develop in the mother's uterus. These babies are at risk for many problems, including neurological deficiencies, structural problems with body parts, breathing difficulties, vision problems, and other serious health problems (Sadler, 2000). These children may have chromosomal abnormalities, or they may have been exposed to infections or harmful substances during their prenatal development.

Developmental care for babies at risk.   Babies born especially early or small may not have the physical maturity to breathe independently, regulate their body's changes in temperature, or suck adequately to meet nutritional needs. Despite these challenges, babies can often survive with access to life-sustaining devices and medicines. Physicians and nurses also strive to create a therapeutic atmosphere that is nurturing and developmentally appropriate. The following guidelines are recommended for those who care for a fragile infant:

- Reduce the infant's exposure to light and noise.
- Regulate the amount of handling of the infant by medical staff.
- Position the baby to increase circulation.
- Encourage parents to participate in the care of the infant.
- Inform parents about the infant's needs.
- Arrange activities such as diapering and changing clothes so that interruptions to sleep and rest are minimized.
- Encourage parents to cuddle with the infant and carry him or her often and for long periods.
- Swaddle the baby in a blanket with arms bent and hands placed near the mouth to permit sucking on fingers or hands.
- Massage the baby.
- Educate parents about caring for the child as he or she grows older. (Als et al., 1994; T. Field, 2001; Sherwen et al., 1999)

Study Guide and Reader ——————
Learn more about massage of fragile infants in Supplementary Reading 3-1.

When fragile babies become strong enough to leave the hospital and go home with their families, they may need continued specialized treatments. Their families, as well, may benefit from support because these babies often show a lot of distress and are not easily soothed. If parents of premature and other health-impaired infants learn to fulfill infants' needs confidently and tenderly, however, these infants are likely to calm down and develop healthy habits for responding to distress (J. M. Young, Howell, & Hauser-Cram, 2005). Furthermore, fragile infants who repeatedly relax in the arms of their caregivers will have the chance to participate in pleasing interactions, form close bonds with caregivers, and gain needed mental energy for exploring the environment.

As with all children, the developmental journeys of premature and sick newborn infants are typically *not* destined to be rocky ones (Bronfenbrenner, 2005). In fact, many premature and small infants go on to catch up with peers in their motor, intellectual, and communication skills, particularly when families, educators, and other professionals meet their special needs (Sheffield, Stromswold, & Molnar, 2005). Others have intellectual delays or persisting medical problems, such as visual problems or asthma, and these children as well benefit from appropriate medical care, hope and advocacy from families, and educational services that help them progress academically and socially. As they grow older, these children may require continued services, such as speech therapy and other individualized educational interventions (Sheffield et al., 2005). Without sensitive care and, if needed, effective intervention, premature and low-birth-weight infants will continue to be physically distressed and may face later problems in coping with negative emotions and in learning at school (Nomura, Fifer, & Brooks-Gunn, 2005; Shenkin, Starr, & Deary, 2004).

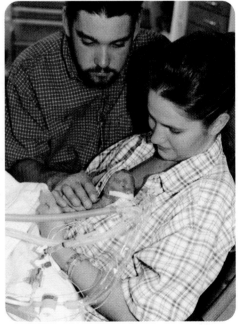

Responsive care of fragile infants entails careful consideration of their physical, social-emotional, and intellectual needs.

Responsive care of fragile infants—as well as healthy infants—entails careful consideration of infants' physical, social-emotional, and intellectual needs. In our final section in this chapter, we relay some ideas for helping caregivers identify and meet the psychological needs of these wondrous little people.

DEVELOPMENT AND PRACTICE

Showing Sensitivity to the Needs of Newborn Infants

- Carefully observe the sensory abilities of newborn infants.

  A pediatric nurse watches a newborn infant scanning her parents' faces. The nurse explains to parents that infants have limited visual acuity right from birth, but they can see some things, are especially attracted to human faces, and develop stronger vision in their first few months.

- Observe the physiological states of newborn infants.

  A family educator talks with parents about their newborn infants, commenting that infants commonly sleep for long periods but usually have brief periods each day when they are receptive to quiet interaction.

- Notice the kinds of stimuli that attract infants' attention.

  A mother watches her newborn infant while he is awake and alert. She notices that her son intently observes her face as well as other stimuli, such as the edges of the bassinet.

- Encourage parents to articulate their growing awareness of infants' preferences for being soothed.

A mother's physician asks her how she is getting along with her new baby. When she reports that the baby cries a lot, the doctor asks her about the kinds of attention the baby finds most comforting. The doctor also explains that most infants find it soothing to be held tenderly, and some infants also calm down while riding in a car or stroller. The doctor suggests that the mother keep informal records of the infant's fussy times and the kinds of care that eventually soothe the infant.

- Model sensitive care for new parents.

  A family educator shows a new father how to hold the baby, change her diaper, and interact quietly and sensitively with her.

- Offer appropriate care to fragile infants.

  A hospital offers life-saving care to fragile infants and attends to their sensory abilities and psychological needs by reducing light, noise, and unnecessary medical procedures, and massaging the infants a few times daily.

Enhancing Caregivers' Sensitivity to Newborn Infants

To give infants a healthy start on life, parents and other caregivers must recognize infants' abilities, interests, and styles of self-expression. Family educators and other professionals can support infants indirectly—yet powerfully—when they teach family members how to observe their infants closely and respond sympathetically to infants' individual needs. To get a sense of how you might enhance caregivers' awareness of infant needs, examine the illustrations in the Development and Practice feature "Showing Sensitivity to the Needs of Newborn Infants." Also consider these recommendations:

● *Talk about infants' sensory and perceptual abilities.* Infants learn a lot about the world from their sensory and perceptual abilities. **Sensation** refers to the infant's detection of a stimulus; for example, a newborn baby may sense a father's stroking movements on her hand. Infants (and adults, for that matter) sense many things that they don't necessarily focus on or think about. When infants do attend to and interpret a sensation, **perception** takes place, such as when the baby, now 6 months old, watches a moving image and perceives it to be his father.

At birth, many newborn infants look intently at the faces of parents and others, giving people the impression that infants are learning from the beginning of life. In fact, they are. What newborn infants actually *perceive* cannot be determined with certainty, but researchers have established that newborn infants are able to *sense* basic patterns and associations. The majority of infants can see well-defined contrasts and shapes, such as large black and white designs on checkerboards, but it takes time for the various parts of the eye to work efficiently and to connect with brain structures necessary for making sense of visual stimuli. During the first year of life, vision improves dramatically. Infants can see best from a distance of about 6–12 inches, develop a preference for looking at faces, and are increasingly able to explore the visual properties of objects (Courage & Adams, 1990; D. L. Mayer & Dobson, 1982; van Hof-van Duin & Mohn, 1986). The sense of hearing is actually more advanced at birth than is vision. Recall that late in prenatal development, fetuses begin to hear and recognize repeated vocal and musical patterns. Typically developing infants are also born with the ability to experience touch, taste, and smell. Sensory and perceptual abilities continue to develop, and these abilities will, of course, make critical contributions to infants' subsequent learning about the world.

● *Point out the physiological states of newborn infants.* Unless they have previously had a child or been around newborn infants, parents may be surprised at how their infants act, how long they sleep, and how they respond to stimuli. Family educators and medical personnel can educate parents by explaining the nature of infants' **states of arousal,** the physiological conditions of sleepiness and wakefulness that infants experience throughout

──────── **Connecting Concepts**
Chapter 7 describes the early development of visual sensation and perception in more detail. It also offers suggestions for providing appropriate stimulation for infants.

sensation
Physiological detection of stimuli in the environment.

perception
Interpretation of stimuli that the body has sensed.

state of arousal
Physiological condition of sleepiness or wakefulness.

OBSERVATION GUIDELINES

Indicators of Health in Newborn Infants

Characteristic	Look For	Example	Implication
Adjustment After Birth	• First breaths are taken within a half minute after birth (the doctor may suction fluid from the mouth and throat). • Attempts to nurse or suck on a bottle's nipple occur within a few hours after birth (the baby may lose a few ounces of weight the first few days). • First urination and bowel movements occur within first 2 days. • Head may be elongated after birth but gradually regains round appearance; skin may be scratched and contain discolored spots that disappear within a few days.	Immediately after birth, Trinisha begins crying. Her head is misshapen and she has some blotchy spots on her skin. Her mother places Trinisha on her chest, and the baby quiets down, opens her eyes, and scans the room.	Before birth, encourage parents to arrange for appropriate medical care for their newborn babies. After birth, reassure parents about the appearance of newborn infants.
States of Arousal	• *Quiet sleep:* The infant lies still with closed eyelids and relaxed facial muscles. • *Active sleep:* Although the infant is sleeping, eyes may open and shut and move from side to side, facial expressions change and include grimaces, and breathing is irregular. • *Drowsiness:* The infant's eyelids may open and close without focus, and breathing is regular and rapid. • *Quiet alert:* The infant is awake, calm, happy, and engaged with the world. • *Active waking:* The infant wriggles and shows bursts of vigorous movements, breathing is irregular and skin is flushed, and the infant may moan or grunt. • *Crying:* The infant cries and thrashes, and the face is flushed and distressed.	In the first few days after birth, baby Yolance spends most of his time sleeping. Some of his sleep appears peaceful, and at times he appears to be dreaming. When Yolance is awake, he sometimes looks intently at people and objects close to him. At other times, he appears agitated, and these episodes tend to escalate into loud and persistent crying.	Help parents to notice the distinct states of arousal that infants experience. Encourage them to develop a sensitive style of responding to infants' distress. Help parents recognize when infants are in the quiet, alert state, as this is a good time to interact calmly with babies.
Reflexes	• *Rooting:* When touched near the corner of the mouth, the infant turns toward the stimulus, as if in search of breast or bottle. • *Sucking:* When a nipple or finger touches the infant's mouth, he or she begins to suck it. • *Grasping:* The infant grasps onto a finger or other small object placed in his or her hand. • *Moro reflex:* When startled, the infant stretches arms outward and then brings them together as in a hugging, embracing motion. • *Babinski reflex:* When the inner side of the infant's foot is rubbed from heel to toe, the infant's big toe moves upward and the other toes fan inward toward the bottom of the foot. • *Stepping:* When the baby is held upright under the arms with feet dangling and touching a hard surface, the legs take rhythmic steps. • *Tonic neck reflex:* When the infant is lying on his or her back and the head is moved toward one side, the arm on that side extends out and away from the body, and the arm on the other side is flexed close to the head with clenched fist (resembling a fencing position).	Little Josefina lies on her back on a blanket as her mother washes the dishes. When her mother accidentally drops and breaks a dish, Josefina appears alarmed, extends her arms, and seems to be grasping for something in midair.	Gently demonstrate infants' reflexes to family members. Explain that reflexes show that infants' brains and bodies are operating as they should. Family members, including the baby's siblings, may use the grasping reflex as a way to interact with the baby.

Sources: C. W. Snow & McGaha, 2003; Wolff, 1966.

the day. Infant practitioners can also point out infants' **reflexes,** their automatic motor responses to stimuli. One example of a reflex is an infant blinking his eyes when his father moves him close to a bright light. Take a look at the Observation Guidelines table "Indicators of Health in Newborn Infants" for the kinds of physical conditions you might mention to parents.

● *Encourage families to watch infants' responses to particular stimuli.* Infants give off clues about what they like and dislike, find interesting, and experience as pleasant or painful. However, it may take a while for caregivers to decipher infants' signals and the circumstances

reflex
Automatic motor response to stimuli.

that elicit them. Educators and other practitioners can advise families that infants will most likely express their interests when they are in a quiet but alert state. When infants are drowsy, asleep, or agitated, they tend not to show curiosity. When they are rested, comfortable, and awake, they may scan the visual environment, intently study the properties of objects, such as a mobile over the crib, and smile at familiar vocalizations from a parent. By observing the textures, tastes, sounds, and visual properties that attract infants' sustained attention, parents and other caregivers can guess about the concepts that infants are identifying. Maybe they're learning that the blanket feels soft, the juice tastes sweet, the melody is pleasing, and the rubber duck is attractive.

● *Ask families about the kinds of stimulation that infants find soothing.* Babies have distinct preferences for how they like to be comforted. For example, different babies may relax to varying sensations—listening to the rumble of the clothes dryer, nursing at mother's breast, sleeping on father's chest, or going for a ride in the car. When families have not found the antidote to their infants' fussy periods, they may appreciate suggestions from practitioners about a range of techniques for soothing.

● *Model sensitive interactions with infants.* Not all caregivers are naturally inclined to interact in a gentle, reassuring manner with infants. Educators and other practitioners can show parents and other caregivers how to slow their pace, hold the baby gently but firmly, speak quietly, and watch for signs that the baby is ready to interact (e.g., the baby looks into caregivers' faces) or distressed by the interaction (e.g., the baby looks away).

● *Show parents how to care for the baby.* First-time parents may appreciate some hands-on tips for administering to the physical needs of a new baby. Unless they have seen a baby being bathed, nursed, fed a bottle, diapered, or carried, new parents may not know how to perform these caretaking functions.

● *Offer early and continued support to parents of fragile infants.* Infants who are at risk for one reason or another—for example, those who are premature or have serious disabilities—can require unusually high vigilance from parents. Infants might cry often, be difficult to console, or need an intensive course of treatment. Some infants with health problems may be sluggish and seek out little interaction from their parents. In such cases family members may have practical questions about optimal care for their children, and they may also benefit from counseling and other services.

Case Study: Understanding Adam

———— Study Guide and Reader
To learn more about the learning problems that Adam faced in school, go to Supplementary Reading 8-1.

Michael Dorris adopted Adam at age 3. As a small child, Adam was sweet and affectionate but delayed in size and prone to seizures. Michael noticed intellectual delays but believed that Adam would catch up over time. When Adam was 5, Michael took a new job and enrolled his son in a child care center. Michael hoped that Adam's teachers would be able to teach Adam basic skills, such as using the toilet and tying his shoes, that so far had exceeded Adam's grasp.

In the excerpt that follows, Michael is beginning to come to grips with the full impact of Adam's disabilities:

Every morning and late afternoon, as I drove him to and from his school, I talked a steady stream, pointing out interesting sights, asking about his activities, recounting tales of my adventures at work. At its midpoint our route traversed a railroad track, and this was the only thing on Adam's mind. He had noticed it shortly after we moved to the area and identified it with "The Little Engine That Could."

"Choo choo train!" he sang the first time we rumbled over it, and I, delighted at this recognition, chimed in.

"Choo choo!"

That night, on the way home, he watched for the crossing and when it came in sight, he said, "Choo choo." He did the same the next morning and the next evening, and the next and the next. For the two years he attended his day care, he never once failed to chime it, but he rarely said anything else. I would be talking to him about all the positive features of dry pants—the trips we could take without diaper bags, the luxury of rash-free skin, the approval and celebration of children and adults alike—and in the middle of it he'd say "choo choo" and cut me off. I could be close to the punch line of a story—"Who's been sleeping in my bed and is *still in it?*"

"Choo choo."

At such times I might reply with an attitude that was annoyed and frustrated, or, alternatively cajoling and happy.

"Choo choo," my five-year-old son would obstinately rejoin.

. . . Adam always crossed those tracks in the same way, as if he had never done so before. . . . It was as if he were hanging from the rung of a ladder by his hands and refused to go forward, preferring to dangle in one spot until he dropped. He had grasped a single connection in the universe that resonated to him, and it was enough, it was sufficient, it obscured from his view everything behind it.

. . . [T]here was never more than a single, solitary thing on Adam's mind at any one time. Ideas did not compete for his attention; he was loyal, sticking with a fascination until he wore it out. . . .

. . . For years I assumed I was fighting the effects of his medication, battering the barriers of his late start, scaling self-protective walls erected against the neglect he experienced as an infant. It was not until the following summer, when Adam was still five years old, that I began to have an inkling that my real adversary was the lingering ghost of Adam's biological mother, already dead . . . of acute alcohol poisoning. (Dorris, 1989, pp. 43–45)[a]

- Adam was eventually diagnosed with *fetal alcohol syndrome* (FAS). What characteristics do children with FAS have?
- What conditions lead to FAS? In other words, how was it that Adam came to develop FAS?
- Adam eventually learned many practical skills, such as how to read and hold down a simple job. What kinds of support would Adam have needed to achieve a good quality of life?

Once you have answered these questions, compare your responses with those in the appendix.

[a]From *The Broken Cord,* by Michael Dorris, copyright 1989 by Michael Dorris. Used by permission of Harper & Row Publishers, Inc., New York.

Summary

Genetic Foundations of Child Development

All children have a set of genetic instructions that influence their characteristics at birth as well as the many physical features that emerge as they grow. Most of the genes that children inherit are ones they share with other children, giving them a common human heritage. Other genes contribute to children's individuality by disposing them to look and act in certain unique ways.

Genes exert their effects on children through complex and interactive processes in cells and bodily systems; the effects of genes are mediated by children's health, other physiological processes, and children's experience in particular environments. Acknowledging the powerful effects of nature, teachers and other professionals can show that they value children's individual genetic profiles, such as their unique combinations of particular temperaments, physical features, and exceptional talents. Practitioners can also express their confidence that, whatever children's natural abilities, children have the potential to achieve high personal and academic standards.

Prenatal Development

At conception, the new being inherits a unique genetic makeup and begins the lifelong process of growing, changing, and interacting in and with the environment. Development begins at conception, when the *zygote,* a one-celled being, divides multiple times and becomes a ball of cells that burrows into the uterus. From Weeks 2 through 8 after conception, the *embryo* grows rapidly, forming structures needed to sustain future growth and developing rudimentary organs and body parts. Between Week 9 and birth, the *fetus* continues to grow rapidly, now putting the finishing touches on the body and brain and becoming sufficiently heavy and strong to live in the outside world.

Professionals can support healthy prenatal growth of children by informing prospective parents (and all sexually active women) about the damaging effects of teratogens to unborn children; the need to evaluate their health and medical regimens before a pregnancy; and the value of stress reduction, a healthful diet, appropriate exercise, and ongoing medical care during pregnancy.

Birth of the Baby

The birth of the baby is an exciting event for parents and other family members, who can ease their anxiety and the mother's pain by preparing for childbirth. Birth is a multistage process that is often helped along by family members and professionals in the medical community, such as doctors, nurses, and midwives. The health and medical needs of newborn infants depend on their birth weight, size, prior exposure to teratogens, the mother's health, and the newborn infants' genetic vulnerabilities. Family educators and other professionals can help parents develop realistic expectations about their newborn infants and respond sensitively to their physical and psychological needs.

Applying Concepts in Child Development

In this chapter you learned that children's biological beginnings are important determinants of their long-term abilities and health. The following table describes factors that affect the health of babies-to-be and newborn infants. For each of these health circumstances, the table identifies a factor that affects an offspring's health, offers an implication for working with children and families, or both. Apply what you've learned about children's biological beginnings to fill in the empty cells in the table. When you're done, compare your response with those in Table 3-1 in the *Study Guide and Reader.*

APPLYING CONCEPTS IN CHILD DEVELOPMENT
Promoting Healthy Beginnings for Children and Their Families

Period of Development	The Experiences of Children and Families	Developmental Concepts *Identifying Factors That Affect Children's Beginnings*	Implications *Helping Children and Families to Experience Healthy Beginnings*
Prior to Conception	Kuri and Taro want to have a child. They go to the doctor to discuss their desire to plan for a healthy pregnancy.	The *health of any children conceived by a couple* depends on several factors, including the mother's health prior to the pregnancy and her diet, actions, stress levels, and exposure to teratogens during the pregnancy. The health of their children's genes is mostly beyond parents' control, although some parents may choose to terminate a pregnancy when diagnostic prenatal tests reveal a serious problem.	Encourage prospective parents to talk with their doctor before conception and to make the necessary adjustments to their lifestyle. For example, the woman will want to find out whether any medicines she takes can affect the health of her offspring. Couples concerned about possible birth defects may choose to see a genetic counselor.
During the First Few Weeks of Pregnancy	A pregnant woman, Antoinette, does not know she is pregnant and continues to drink large amounts of alcohol and to smoke a pack of cigarettes each day. Antoinette contracts a cold virus and takes over-the-counter medicines.		Encourage women who are sexually active and able to conceive children to shield themselves from teratogens as a matter of course.
From 9 Weeks After Conception Until Birth	A pregnant woman, Larissa, is highly anxious about giving birth to a child because she does not have a job or supportive partner. Late in her pregnancy, Larissa and her mother go to prepared childbirth courses at their local community college.	*Excessive stress* can be harmful to both the mother and her unborn child. *Preparation for childbirth* can reassure parents about the birth process and help them express their preferences for the birth, including who will be present and how they might respond to various scenarios.	
At Birth	Kia and Bello give birth to a premature baby, Riley, 6 weeks early. He weighs only 4 pounds, 2 ounces. Riley receives intensive medical care and is strong enough to go home with his parents 2 weeks later.		Offer appropriate and nurturing care to babies at risk. Address the medical needs of fragile infants, and help parents care for infants in a responsive manner. As premature infants grow, provide them with services, intervention, and educational experiences that help them flourish.

Key Concepts

gene (p. 64)
chromosome (p. 64)
DNA (p. 64)
gamete (p. 66)
meiosis (p. 66)
zygote (p. 68)

monozygotic twins (p. 68)
dizygotic twins (p. 68)
alleles (p. 68)
dominant gene (p. 69)
recessive gene (p. 69)
codominance (p. 69)

polygenic inheritance (p. 69)
canalization (p. 72)
prenatal development (p. 74)
mitosis (p. 75)
embryo (pp. 75)
fetus (pp. 77)

teratogen (p. 79)
premature infant (p. 88)
sensation (p. 90)
perception (p. 90)
state of arousal (p. 90)
reflex (p. 91)

Companion
Website

Now go to our Companion Website at www.prenhall.com/mcdevitt to assess your understanding of chapter content with a Practice Quiz, apply what you've learned in Essay Questions, and broaden your knowledge with links to related Developmental Psychology Web sites.

Physical Development

chapter 4

Case Study: The Softball League

Principles of Physical Development

The Brain and Its Development

Physical Development During Childhood

Physical Well-Being

Special Physical Needs

Case Study: Lucy

Summary

Applying Concepts in Child Development

Case Study: **The Softball League**

Two brothers, Tom (age 13) and Phillip (age 15) are talking with psychologist William Pollack about the impact of organized sports on their lives:

"There used to be nothing to do around here," Tom told me [Dr. Pollack], referring to the small, economically depressed town where he and his brother live.

"There was like just one bowling alley, and it was closed on weekends. We had nothing to do, especially during the summer," Phillip agreed.

"Not quite a year ago," Tom explained, "three of our best friends died of an OD."

Indeed, the autumn before, three teenage boys in the same sleepy town had all drunk themselves into oblivion and then overdosed on a lethal cocktail of various barbiturates. Sure, the town had always had its problems—high unemployment, poorly funded schools, and many broken families. But this was different. Three boys, the oldest only sixteen, were gone forever.

The mood in the town was sullen the summer following the deaths, and Tom and Phillip were resolved to change things. "We went to the mayor and to the priest at our church, and we asked if we could set up a regular sports program for kids around here," Phillip explained.

"A softball league," Tom added.

"What a great idea," I told the boys.

"Yeah. At first we were just ten guys," said Tom.

"But then, like, everybody wanted to sign up—girls too," explained Phillip. "Now there are too many kids who want to play. More than a hundred. But the state government offered to help with some money and coaches."

"So it is making a difference, to have this new league?" I asked the boys.

"Hell, yeah," Phillip replied. "Now, we've got a schedule. We've got something to do."

"I'm not sure I'd be here anymore if it wasn't for the league," added Tom. "For a long time I couldn't deal with things. Now I've got a place to go." (Pollack, 1998, p. 274)[a]

[a]From *Real Boys: Rescuing Our Sons from the Myths of Boyhood*, by William Pollack © 1998 by William Pollack. Used by permission of Random House, Inc.

Organized sports allow children and adolescents alike to exercise, improve physical skills, and make productive use of leisure time. Art by Eric, age 12.

As children develop, they undergo numerous physical changes. They grow taller and stronger. They become increasingly proficient with such complex motor skills as using scissors, riding a bicycle, and playing softball. They go through puberty. Their brains mature. Physical changes do not happen automatically, of course. Most depend at least partly on good choices by children and on appropriate support from adults. In the introductory case study, Tom and Phillip showed good judgment when they arranged for a sports league and asked community leaders to help. The result was that Tom, Phillip, and other youngsters were able to practice athletic skills, forge friendships, and have fun. In this chapter we examine physical development, focusing on age-related changes in body and brain during childhood and adolescence; influences of youngsters' behaviors on their health; and actions educators and other practitioners can take to support the health of all children, including children with special physical needs.

Principles of Physical Development

As with all aspects of child development, physical growth is the outcome of nature and nurture. Human genes tell children's bodies to complete a particular sequence of changes, according to a defined timetable. For instance, certain spots in the cartilage and bones of children's legs periodically swell with new cells, and children grow taller. Agents of nurture—nutrition, affectionate relationships, and opportunities for physical activity and sleep—feed growth and energize children's learning. This blending of nature and nurture is manifested in these principles of physical growth:

● *Children's bodies are dynamic systems.* As dynamic systems, children's bodies are composed of interconnected parts that change over time. For example, maturation of brain and muscles, nutrition, and activity level all influence motor skills. As one or more of these factors change, new possibilities arise. For example, children continually discover that their bodies permit new skills, such as standing erect without support at age 1, balancing on a bicycle at age 5, and doing pull-ups at age 10. Over time, children progress toward more mature levels, but as they do, they may occasionally persist with particular motor actions for long periods or temporarily return to primitive styles of behaving.

Observe Madison reaching for objects in the "Emotional Development: Infancy" clip on Observation CD 2.

To illustrate how dynamic systems operate, let's look at infants' ability to reach for objects with their arms and hands. Infants move their limbs spontaneously from birth and even before (in later stages of pregnancy, many women feel their developing babies thumping against their insides). When they are about 3½ to 4 months old, infants first try to reach for objects (Thelen & Smith, 1998). Their initial efforts are shaky but gradually improve. After some small improvements, though, infants often exhibit *declines* in speed, directness, and smoothness in reaching. Possibly, they must figure out how to integrate changes in muscle tone or deal with some other new factor. By 12 months, however, most can reach easily and quickly. In the "Emotional Development: Infancy" video clip on Observation CD 2, you can see 7-month-old Madison adeptly reach for objects and transfer objects from one hand to the other.

Even nearly universal accomplishments, such as reaching for objects, show dramatic individual differences in pathways to proficiency. For example, infants who make large and vigorous movements spontaneously in their first few months of life must learn to control such movements before they can successfully reach for objects (Thelen, Corbetta, & Spencer, 1996; Thelen et al., 1993). In contrast, infants who generate few and slow movements spontaneously in their first few months have a different set of problems to solve: They must learn to apply muscle tone while extending arms forward and holding them stiffly.

● *Different parts of the body mature at different rates.* Specific parts of the body grow at varying rates, and in young children some parts are closer than others to their ultimate adult size. Heads are proportionally closer to adult size than are trunks, which are more advanced than arms and legs. In the upper limbs, the hand is closer to adult size than the forearm; the forearm is closer than the upper arm. Likewise in the lower limbs, the foot is more advanced than the calf, which is more advanced than the thigh. Figure 4-1 illustrates how relative body proportions change throughout childhood and adolescence.

Internally, different systems grow at different rates as well (J. M. Tanner, 1990). For instance, the lymphoid system (e.g., tonsils, adenoids, lymph nodes, and the lining of the small intestines) grows rapidly throughout childhood and then slows somewhat in adolescence. This system helps children resist infection, which is particularly important during the early and middle childhood years when children are exposed to many contagious illnesses for the first time. In contrast, reproductive organs expand slowly until adolescence, when there's a substantial burst of growth.

The outcome of separate systems growing at distinct rates is that the body as a whole increases in size, albeit somewhat unevenly among its parts. Typical growth curves for height and weight reveal rapid increases in the first 2 years, slow but steady growth during early and middle childhood, an explosive spurt during adolescence, and a leveling off to mature levels by early adulthood (Hamill et al., 1979). Patterns of growth are similar for boys and girls, although girls tend to have their adolescent growth spurts about a year and a half earlier, and boys, on average, end up a bit taller and heavier.

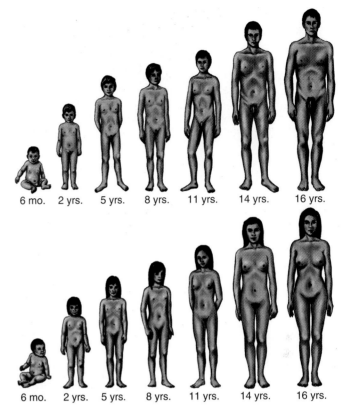

6 mo. 2 yrs. 5 yrs. 8 yrs. 11 yrs. 14 yrs. 16 yrs.

6 mo. 2 yrs. 5 yrs. 8 yrs. 11 yrs. 14 yrs. 16 yrs.

Figure 4-1

Physical development during childhood and adolescence. Children grow taller and heavier as they develop, and the characteristics and relative proportions of their bodies change as well.
Based on The Diagram Group, 1983.

● *Functioning becomes increasingly differentiated.* As you learned in Chapter 3, every cell in the body (with the exception of sperm and ova) contains the same genetic instructions. But as cells grow, they take on specific functions, some aiding with digestion, others transporting oxygen, still others transmitting information to various places in the body, and so on. Thus individual cells "listen" to only a subset of the many instructions they have available. This progressive shift from having the *potential* to become many things to manifesting a specific working process or form is known as **differentiation.**

Differentiation characterizes other aspects of physical development as well. For instance, during prenatal development, the arms first protrude as simple buds from the torso but then they become longer, sprout globular hands, and differentiate into fingers. Motor skills, too, become increasingly differentiated: They first appear as global, unsteady actions but gradually evolve into precise, controlled motions. You can see a clear developmental progression toward fine motor control by comparing the writing-implement grips of 16-month-old Corwin, 4-year-old Zoe, and 9-year-old Elena in video clips on Observation CD 2.

● *Functioning becomes increasingly integrated.* As cells and body parts differentiate, they must also work together. Their increasingly coordinated efforts are known as **integration** (J. M. Tanner, 1990). As examples, the various parts of the eye coordinate their mechanical movements so as to permit vision; separate areas of the brain form connections that allow exchanges between thoughts and feelings; and fingers become longer and more adept at synchronizing movements for handling small objects (see Figure 4-2).

● *Each child follows a unique growth curve.* Children's bodies appear to pursue predetermined heights—perhaps not as specific as 4′9″ or 6′2″, but definite ballpark targets for height, nonetheless. Growth curves are especially evident when things go temporarily awry in children's lives. Circumstances such as illness or poor nutrition may briefly halt height increases. But when health and adequate nutrition are restored, children grow rapidly. Before you know it, they're back on track—back to where we might have expected them to be, given their previous rate of growth. Exceptions to this self-correcting tendency occur when severe malnutrition is present very early in life or extends over a lengthy time period. For instance, children who are seriously undernourished during the prenatal phase

Observe a developmental differentiation in hand grip by comparing three children holding writing utensils: Corwin in the "Literacy: Infancy" clip, Zoe in the "Neighborhood: Early Childhood" clip, and Elena in the "Neighborhood: Middle Childhood" clip, all on Observation CD 2.

differentiation
An increase from general to more specific functioning over the course of development.

integration
An increasing coordination of body parts over the course of development.

Development of a boy at ages 1, 5, 9, 13, and 17. Notice the gradual, systematic changes: The boy grows taller, his face becomes more angular, his trunk elongates, and his hair color darkens. The boy is wearing the same T-shirt in all five photos.

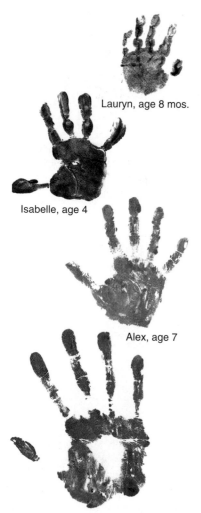

Lauryn, age 8 mos.

Isabelle, age 4

Alex, age 7

Connor, age 15

Figure 4-2

As children develop, their body parts become increasingly distinct (*differentiated*) as well as progressively coordinated (*integrated*). These handprints are shown at 25 percent of actual size.

---

neuron
Cell that transmits information to other cells; also called nerve cell.

axon
Armlike part of a neuron that sends information to other neurons.

tend not to catch up completely, and they are at risk for later mental and behavioral deficiencies, motor difficulties, and psychiatric problems (e.g., schizophrenia) (A. L. Brown et al., 1996; Chavez, Martinez, & Soberanes, 1995; Sigman, 1995).

● *Physical development is characterized by both quantitative and qualitative changes.* Many physical changes are outcomes of a series of minor refinements. Motor skills, which may seem to the casual observer to appear overnight, are in most cases the result of numerous gradual advancements. For example, when Teresa's son Alex was 4, he wanted to snap his fingers like his older brother. Alex diligently practiced finger snapping several times a day for 2 months yet was unable to make the desired sound. With practice, however, his movements became more adept, and one day, much to his delight—snap—he got it right. In Alex's eyes, the accomplishment was a quantum leap forward, but in reality it was probably the result of repeated practice. Because the desired movements improved gradually, Alex's mastery of the snap might be considered a quantitative change in motor proficiency.

Qualitative changes in physical development are seen as well. To illustrate, Figure 4-3 shows how both walking and throwing a ball change over time. For example, during their initial attempts at walking, toddlers must concentrate on balance and upright posture, and they take short steps, make flat-footed contact with toes turned outward, and flex their knees as their feet contact the ground (Gallahue & Ozmun, 1998). A few years later, they increase their stride, make heel-toe contact, swing their arms a bit, lift themselves vertically as they proceed, and show increased pelvic tilt. The mature pattern of walking, achieved between ages 4 and 7, is characterized by a reflexive arm swing, a narrow base of support, a relaxed and long stride, minimal vertical lift, and a decisive heel-toe contact.

General principles of physical development come to life in individual children according to children's genetic heritage, experience, and support from adults. We now turn to more specific aspects of physical development, beginning with the brain, the most complex system of the body.

The Brain and Its Development

The brain is an extraordinary organ that regulates the activities of other systems in the body, senses information in the environment, and guides the child's movement. The child's brain also permits advanced human abilities: It forms associations between environmental stimuli and mental concepts, fills everyday experience with emotional meaning, translates thoughts and feelings into words and behaviors, and determines actions needed to achieve desired outcomes.

Altogether, the brain has approximately 100 billion **neurons,** cells that transmit information to other cells (Naegele & Lombroso, 2001). Neurons are connected to one another by their axons and dendrites. **Axons** are long, armlike structures that *send* information to other

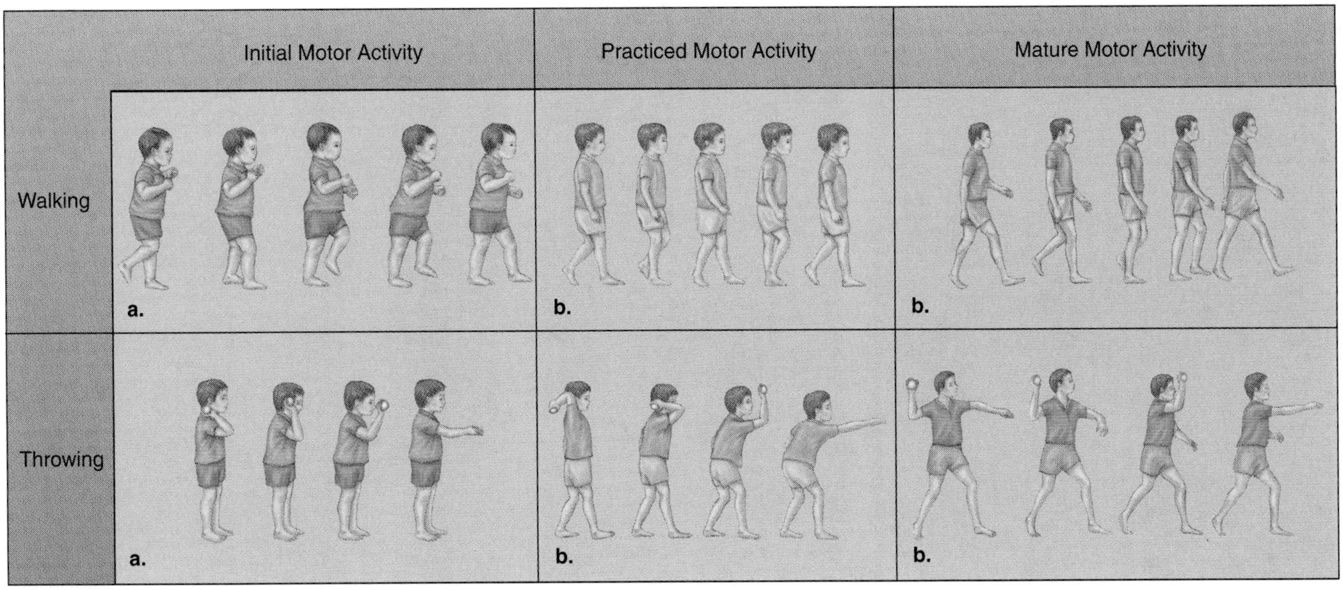

Figure 4-3

Developmental sequences showing qualitative change in walking and overhand throwing. In *walking,* children tend to progress from (a) difficulty maintaining balance and using short steps with flat-footed contact, to (b) a smoother pattern, where arms are lower and there is heel-toe contact, to (c) a relaxed gait, with reflexive arm swing. In *overhand throwing,* the trend is from (a) stationary feet and action mainly from the elbow, to (b) ball held behind head, arm swung forward and high over shoulder, and a definite shift forward with body weight, to (c) movement of foot on same side as throwing arm; definite rotation through hips, legs, spine, and shoulders; and a step with foot opposite to the throwing arm as weight is shifted.
Based on Gallahue & Ozmun, 1998.

neurons. **Dendrites** are branchlike appendages that reach out to *receive* information from other cells (Figure 4-4). The dendrites and axons of neurons come together at junctions called **synapses.** Neurons communicate by electrically charging one another to "fire," or in some cases by preventing firing, by sending chemical substances out of the axons and across the synapses that join the cells.

Most neurons have hundreds or even thousands of synapses linking them with other neurons (R. F. Thompson, 1975), so obviously a great deal of cross-communication occurs. Communication among areas of the brain is made possible by groups of neurons growing together and forming communities. Following the principle that there is strength in numbers, communities of neurons called *circuits* are laid out as side-by-side wires that reach out to other groups of neurons. The outcome is that important processes of the brain (such as feeling emotions, paying attention, and learning new ideas) are supported by robust structures.

Neurons are assisted by other kinds of brain cells, called **glial cells.** Glial cells give neurons structural support and protect the connections among neurons. They also produce chemicals that neurons need to function properly, repair injured neurons, and dispose of seriously damaged neurons (N. R. Carlson, 1999; Teeter & Semrud-Clikeman, 1997).

Structures and Functions

The brain is organized into three main parts—the hindbrain, the midbrain, and the forebrain (Figure 4-5)—and each of these parts is organized further into specialized systems with identifiable functions.

- The **hindbrain** controls basic physiological processes that sustain survival, including breathing, blood pressure, sleep, arousal, balance, and movement (thank your hindbrain for your slow, methodical breathing as you sleep blissfully at night).
- The **midbrain** connects the hindbrain to the forebrain and acts as a kind of relay station between the two; for instance, it sends messages to the forebrain about priorities for attention ("Hello! Alarm clock ringing! Hello! Alarm clock ringing!").
- The **forebrain** produces complex thinking, emotional responses, and the driving forces of motivation ("It's 6:00 AM? Ugh! I can sleep another 10 minutes if I skip breakfast!").

dendrite
Branchlike part of a neuron that receives information from other neurons.

synapse
Junction between two neurons.

glial cell
Cell in the brain or other part of the nervous system that provides structural or functional support for one or more neurons.

hindbrain
Part of the brain controlling the basic physiological processes that sustain survival.

midbrain
Part of the brain that coordinates communication between the hindbrain and forebrain.

forebrain
Part of the brain responsible for complex thinking, emotions, and motivation.

Figure 4-4

Neurons in the brain. The neuron on the left is receiving information from other cells. Next, it will fire and incite other neurons to fire. Arrows show the direction of messages being sent.
Based on N. R. Carlson, 1999.

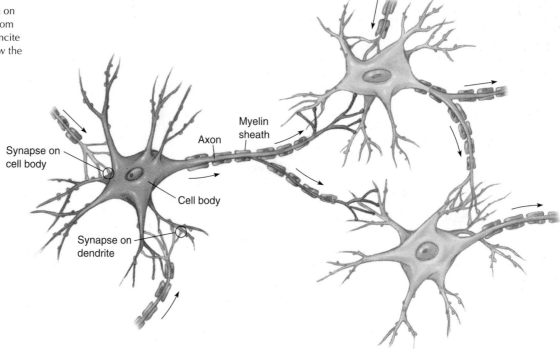

Figure 4-5

Structure of the human brain. The human brain is an enormously complex and intricate structure with three main parts: the hindbrain, midbrain, and forebrain.
Based on N. R. Carlson, 1999.

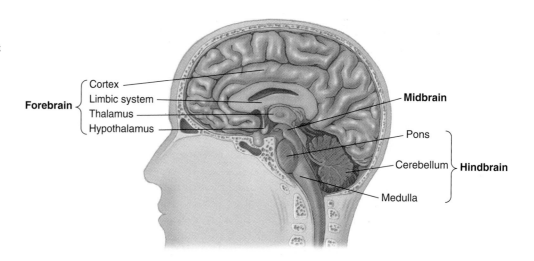

cortex
Part of the forebrain that houses conscious thinking processes (executive functions).

executive functions
Purposeful and goal-directed intellectual processes (e.g., reasoning, decision making) made possible by higher brain structures.

The *forebrain* is of special relevance to educators and other practitioners because it allows children to learn and to develop individual personalities. The forebrain contains the **cortex,** a wrinkled cap that rests on the midbrain and hindbrain. The cortex is where interpreting, reasoning, communicating, planning, decision making, and other purposeful, conscious thinking processes (collectively known as **executive functions**) take place. The cortex is also the seat of many personality traits, such as being enthusiastic and sociable or quiet and introverted, and of habitual ways of responding to physical events and novel information. For example, a 10-year-old girl's cortex would control the way she snuggles up to her father on the sofa in the evening, her exuberant style in social groups, her understanding of how to read, her knowledge of basketball and, of course, much more.

Physiologically, the cortex is extremely convoluted. Bundles of neurons repeatedly fold in on themselves. This physical complexity permits a huge capacity for storing information as well as for transmitting information throughout the brain. Consistent with the principle of differentiation, various parts of the cortex develop specific functions, which we now examine.

Areas of specialization within the cortex.   The cortex consists of regions (called *lobes*) that specialize in particular functions, such as decision making and planning (front), understanding and production of language (sides), and visual processing (rear). In addition, the cortex is divided into two halves, or *hemispheres*. The **left hemisphere** controls the right side of the body, and the **right hemisphere** manages the left side. In most people the *left hemisphere* dominates in *analysis,* breaking up information into its constituent parts and extracting order in a sequence of events (N. R. Carlson, 1999; Uba & Huang, 1999). Talking, understanding speech, reading, writing, mathematical problem solving, and computer programming are all beneficiaries of left-hemisphere processing. It is usually the *right hemisphere* that excels in *synthesis,* pulling together information into a coherent whole (especially nonlinguistic information such as body language, three-dimensional images, and other visual patterns). The right hemisphere therefore usually dominates when we attempt to recognize faces, detect geometrical patterns, read maps, and draw. It is also key to our appreciation of musical melodies, humor, and emotions.

The specializations of the two hemispheres are assured by the physical layout of neural circuits. The left hemisphere has neurological connections to fewer regions of the brain than does the right; this layout permits the application of rules in specific, structured domains, such as language and mathematics. The left hemisphere does its work close to home, so to speak. The right hemisphere is more amply connected with distant areas in the brain, permitting associations to all kinds of thinking and feeling (Goldberg & Costa, 1981; Semrud-Clikeman & Hynd, 1991; Teeter & Semrud-Clikeman, 1997).

Although these particular functions of the hemispheres (i.e., left focusing on analysis, right on synthesis) apply to most people, left-handed individuals often have reversed patterns, with the right hemisphere dominant in analysis and the left hemisphere more involved in synthesis (N. R. Carlson, 1999). And other individuals (particularly those who use both hands equally well) blend psychological functions within hemispheres (Sheehan & Smith, 1986).

The two hemispheres, despite their separate specialties, are in constant communication, trading information through a thick bundle of connecting neurons. Therefore, no single mental activity is exclusively the domain of one hemisphere or the other (N. R. Carlson, 1999). Both hemispheres always work together. For example, the right hemisphere may process a complex emotion, such as mixed feelings experienced at a high school graduation, while the left hemisphere searches for words to communicate the feelings.

Supplementing the numerous circuits existing *within* the cortex are connections *between* the cortex and other parts of the brain. As an illustration, basic, "energizing" activities that reside partly in areas of the brain outside the cortex (e.g., certain aspects of attention, emotions, and motivation) regularly interact with more reflective, "intellectual" processes that take place in the cortex. For example, children who feel relaxed may readily grasp a classroom lesson, but children who are sad or angry may not. Yet especially as children get older, they can use thinking processes to control their emotions to some degree. For instance, a child who initially feels anxious during a challenging lesson may convince himself that he has the ability to understand the material and should relax and focus on the teacher's explanation.

These and other developmental changes in the brain's connections occur with maturation and experience. Before we examine developmental changes in the brain more fully, we consider some of the problems that can occur in the brain's structure and processes.

Malformations in brain development.   In some cases people's brains have unusual circuits or missing or distorted structures, malformations that can interfere with learning and behavior. Neurological conditions may affect children's abilities to pay attention, learn efficiently, control impulses, deal with negative emotions, and so forth.

Some neurological disorders are not obvious at birth, or even in the first few years of life. For example, **schizophrenia,** a serious psychiatric disorder that affects one in a hundred people, often does not surface until adolescence or adulthood (N. R. Carlson, 1999). Individuals with schizophrenia display such symptoms as thought disorders (e.g., irrational ideas and disorganized thinking), hallucinations (e.g., "hearing" nonexistent voices), delusions (e.g., worrying that "everyone is out to get me"), and social withdrawal (e.g., avoiding eye contact or conversation with others). Such symptoms appear to result, at least in part, from structural abnormalities or overactive synapses in certain parts of the brain (N. R.

Connecting Concepts ——————
Various aspects of such *self-regulation* are discussed in Chapters 7, 11, and 13.

left hemisphere
Left side of the cortex; largely responsible for sequential reasoning and analysis, especially in right-handed people.

right hemisphere
Right side of the cortex; largely responsible for simultaneous processing and synthesis, especially in right-handed people.

schizophrenia
A psychiatric condition characterized by irrational ideas and disorganized thinking.

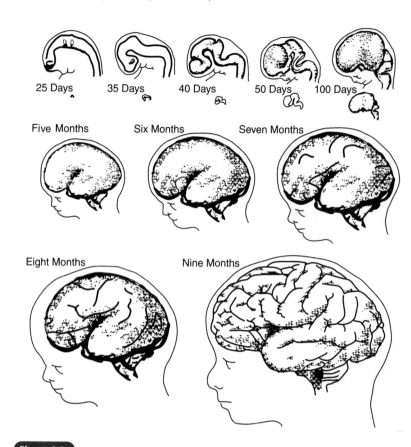

25 Days   35 Days   40 Days   50 Days   100 Days

Five Months   Six Months   Seven Months

Eight Months   Nine Months

Figure 4-6

Changes in the human brain during prenatal development. During the first few months, the basic structures appear (in the top row of drawings, the relative size of the brains has been increased to show detail of the structures). During the middle months of prenatal development, these structures become more distinct. During the final few weeks prior to birth, the cortex folds in and out of itself, preparing the fetus for learning as a baby.

From "The Development of the Brain" by W. Maxwell Cowan, 1979, *Scientific American, 241*, p. 106. Illustration copyright 1979 by Tom Prentiss. Reproduced by permission.

Carlson, 1999; Giedd, Jeffries, et al., 1999; L. K. Jacobsen, Giedd, Berquin, et al., 1997; L. K. Jacobsen, Giedd, Castellanos, et al., 1997).

What factors cause serious malformations in brain development? Errors in genetic instructions can cause mental retardation; these learning delays occur when genes trigger problems in brain chemistry and architecture. Other neurological abnormalities may be due to a mother's drug or alcohol use, illness, or stress during pregnancy. For example, prenatal exposure to rubella (German measles) can reduce the number of neurons formed, lead to small brains, and ultimately produce mental retardation (C. A. Nelson, 2006). Still other neurological problems are caused by oxygen deprivation or other complications during childbirth and by inadequate nutrition or exposure to lead paint before or after birth (see Chapter 3's discussion of *teratogens*). In cases of schizophrenia, a variety of factors, including genes, viral infections during prenatal development, and childbirth complications may share responsibility (N. R. Carlson, 1999).

Now that you have a general understanding of the brain's structure and functions, we turn to the specific transformations that occur during particular developmental periods.

Developmental Changes

The magnificent intricacy of the human brain is made possible by a lengthy process in which its parts are formed, refined, and connected. In fact, nature and nurture sculpt the brain throughout the child's prenatal development, infancy, childhood years, and adolescence.

Prenatal development.   During prenatal development, the brain's most basic parts are formed. The brain begins as a tiny tube approximately 25 days after conception. This seemingly simple tube grows longer in places and folds inward to form pockets, as illustrated in Figure 4-6 (Cowan, 1979; Rayport, 1992). Three bulges can be recognized early on; these bulges become the forebrain, midbrain, and hindbrain.

Neurons reproduce in the inner portion of the tube. Between the 5th and 20th weeks of prenatal development, they do so at the astonishing rate of 50,000 to 250,000 new cells per second (Cowan, 1979; M. Diamond & Hopson, 1998). The vast majority of neurons that will ever be used by a person are formed during the first 7 months of prenatal development (M. H. Johnson, 1998; Rakic, 1995).

Newly formed neurons move, or *migrate,* to specific brain locations where they will do their work. Some young neurons push old cells outward, creating brain structures underneath the cortex. Others actively seek out their destination, climbing up pole-like glial cells and ultimately giving rise to the cortex. Once in place, neurons send out axons in efforts to connect with one another. Groups of axons grow together as teams, reaching toward other groups of neurons (their targets) that attract them by secreting certain chemicals. As axons get close to their targets, they generate branches that become synapses with the target cells. The target cells do their part as well, forming small receptors so that they can receive stimulation.

Only about half of neurons ultimately make contact with other cells. Those that make contact survive; the others die. Nature's tendency to overproduce neurons and eliminate those that fail to connect ensures that the brain invests in workable connections (M. Diamond & Hopson, 1998; P. R. Huttenlocher, 1990).

Infancy and early childhood.   Beginning at birth, the infant's brain has two important tasks: (a) ensuring survival outside the womb and (b) learning about people, things, language, sensations, emotions, and events. Coming from healthy prenatal environments, most newborns are well prepared to breathe, suck, swallow, cry, and form simple associations. With survival taken

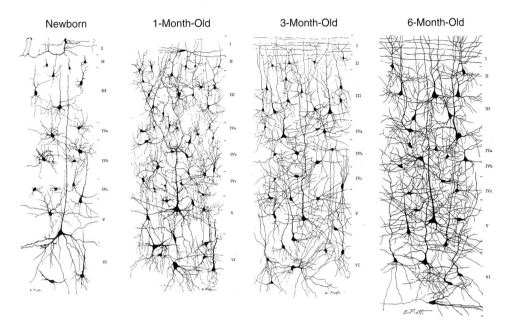

Newborn   1-Month-Old   3-Month-Old   6-Month-Old

Figure 4-7

Drawings of the cellular structure of an infant's visual cortex. Comparison of these drawings at four different ages reveals the rapid and extensive growth of dendrites during infancy. Drawings were based on Golgi stain preparations from Conel (1939–1975).

Reprinted by permission of the publisher from *The Postnatal Development of the Human Cerebral Cortex*, Vols. I–VIII, by Jesse LeRoy Conel, Cambridge, MA: Harvard University Press, Copyright © 1939, 1975 by the President and Fellows of Harvard College.

care of, the brain forms countless connections (synapses) among neurons—connections that make learning possible. Neurons sprout large numbers of dendrites that stretch in different directions, reaching out toward neighboring neurons (M. H. Johnson, 1998). (In Figure 4-7 you can see the rapid development of dendrites in areas of the cortex that support vision.) In the first 3½ years of life, so many new synapses appear (a phenomenon called **synaptogenesis**) that their number far exceeds adult levels (Bruer, 1999). Then, following this fantastic proliferation of synapses, frequently used connections become stronger and connections not often used wither away in a process known as **synaptic pruning.** Particular regions of the brain take their turns growing and shedding synapses. For instance, synaptic pruning occurs early in the second year in parts of the cortex that handle vision, but a bit later in other parts of the cortex (Bruer, 1999; P. R. Huttenlocher, 1990).

Why do children's growing brains create a great many synapses, only to eliminate a sizeable proportion of them later on? In the case of synapses, more is not necessarily better (Bruer & Greenough, 2001; Byrnes, 2001). Psychologists speculate that by generating more synapses than will ever be needed, human beings have the potential to adapt to a wide variety of conditions and circumstances. As children encounter certain regularities in their environment, some synapses are actually a nuisance because they are inconsistent with typical environmental events and typical behavior patterns. Synaptic pruning, then, may be Mother Nature's way of making the brain more efficient.

Early brain development is also marked by **myelination,** a process in which glial cells grow around the axons of neurons to form a fatty coating (*myelin*) that insulates axons and enables them to conduct electrical charges more quickly and efficiently. Just as synaptic proliferation and pruning proceed through areas of the brain in a particular order, myelination occurs in a predictable sequence (Yakolev & Lecours, 1967). It actually begins during the prenatal period, coating neurons involved in basic survival skills. In infancy it occurs with neurons that activate sensory abilities, followed by those involved in motor skills, and eventually those responsible for complex thinking processes (M. Diamond & Hopson, 1998).

From a neurological perspective, infancy and early childhood are noteworthy because the brain connections formed become the foundation of many later abilities. For example, in the first months of life, neurological circuits permit very basic skills in visually scanning objects, recognizing faces, distinguishing novel and familiar stimuli, and detecting sounds used by caregivers (M. H. Johnson, 1999). When these rudimentary abilities first appear, they seem rather automatic and reflexlike. A 2-month-old baby may visually track a ball thrown by his older brother, but he is unlikely to reflect on what he's seeing. With maturation and experience, growing children begin to *think* about their perceptions and use them to guide behavior. In the "Emotional Development: Infancy" video clip on Observation CD 2, you can observe 7-month-old Madison intently studying the properties of a blue toy. Although you cannot see the neurons firing in her brain, Madison certainly appears to be thinking about the visual properties of objects.

Observe Madison using her emerging perceptual skills to learn about the properties of a toy in the "Emotional Development: Infancy" clip on Observation CD 2.

synaptogenesis
A universal process in brain development whereby many new synapses appear, typically in the first 3½ years of life.

synaptic pruning
A universal process in brain development whereby many previously formed synapses wither away, especially if they have not been used frequently.

myelination
The growth of a fatty sheath around neurons that allows them to transmit messages more quickly.

Middle childhood.   During the elementary school years, the two hemispheres become increasingly distinct (Sowell et al., 2002). Furthermore, the brain continues to distinguish groups of neurons that are used regularly from those that are seldom used. It nurtures the active connections, those relating to core skills, understandings, and emotional responses, and allows the underutilized ones to shrivel. Synaptic pruning of weak connections becomes a major force of change during childhood. Yet even as unused synapses are being pruned back, new ones continue to be formed with learning, especially in the cortex (National Research Council, 1999). In addition, the process of myelination continues, protecting neurons and speeding up transmission of messages (Yakovlev & Lecours, 1967).

These neurological patterns—in which often-used connections are solidified and become more efficient and many new synapses are formed—explain the rapid and sustained learning of children. Children quickly become knowledgeable about whatever strikes their fancy—comic books, dance movements, cake decorating, or hunting strategies, for example. Likewise, they learn much about the habits and motives of people in their lives; this knowledge helps them to fit comfortably into family and peer groups. Children also become fluent in their native tongue, flexibly and expertly using sophisticated words and grammatical structures.

Most neurological development in middle childhood occurs in the cortex (B. J. Casey, Giedd, & Thomas, 2000; Sowell, Delis, et al., 2001). It appears that the building of neurological circuits that support executive functions peaks during middle childhood (6 to 8 years) and continues to be refined into adolescence (Passler, Isaac, & Hynd, 1985).

The net result of neurological changes in childhood is that children become capable of completing more psychological operations simultaneously. For example, they can keep a greater number of ideas in mind at once. You can see this capacity being tapped in the "Memory: Early Childhood" video clip on Observation CD 1. In the clip 6-year-old Brent listens to 12 words and tries to recall them (he is able to recall 6 words). A year or so earlier he probably would have recalled fewer words, and in a few more years, he likely will recall more.

Yet in part because their brain circuits are still under construction, children in the elementary grades have limited ability to plan realistically for the future. Despite good intentions, they cannot easily sustain commitments to goals, especially when other events and motives intervene. For example, they occasionally forget things when they leave home in the morning. In addition, their emotions are being processed at lower levels of the brain because the cortex is not yet fully developed. Thus it takes many years of neurological maturation (and encouragement from caregivers) before youngsters are able to express their feelings in a manner that is both genuine and culturally appropriate.

Observe Brent as he tries to keep a few words in mind in the "Memory: Early Childhood" clip on Observation CD 1.

——————— **Connecting Concepts**
Chapter 7 explores the increasing capacity of children's memories in greater depth.

Adolescence.   The cortex continues to change in important ways during adolescence (B. J. Casey et al., 2000; Sowell, Delis, et al., 2001). For instance, myelination continues in parts of the brain used in sophisticated thought processes, such as planning ahead and juggling several ideas simultaneously (Benes, 2001; Bruer 1999). Such developments allow youngsters to imagine the future and work toward long-term goals. Adolescents see the world in new ways, looking beyond its surface elements and detecting abstract principles. In the following Interpreting Children's Artifacts and Actions exercise, you can see how one adolescent reflects on her expanding intellectual abilities.

INTERPRETING CHILDREN'S ARTIFACTS AND ACTIONS

I Can See Clearly Now, My Brain Is Connected

As you read 16-year-old Sarah's self-reflection, consider the potential role that neurological development might play in Sarah's new intellectual abilities.

I remember walking by a building and I looked at its "For Rent" sign and, for the first time, I had all these weird thoughts. . . . I didn't just think of it as a building, but I thought, gee, someone had to paint that sign and someone had to make that building—probably there were dozens of people who worked on the building to get it there. And, to me, it was the first time that I really realized what a big world it was and that it has a lot of people in it and I began to think: Where do I fit in? (Strauch, 2003, pp. 110–111)

In her observations of the building, Sarah saw not only its material qualities but also its ties to society and to herself personally. The ability to probe beneath the surface of phenomena requires considerable brain power, and particularly the capacity to hold and compare several ideas in mind simultaneously. This capacity grows steadily over childhood and culminates in abstract thinking in adolescence. Ironically, the brains of adolescents unleash these high-brow abilities at the same time that they incite new passions, a taste for adventure, and cravings for danger (Strauch, 2003). In the next Interpreting Children's Artifacts and Actions exercise, "It Hurts So Much It's Funny," you can see how two adolescents revel in their reckless actions.

INTERPRETING CHILDREN'S ARTIFACTS AND ACTIONS
It Hurts So Much It's Funny!

Sherie, 14, and Rachel, 13, trade stories of daring in front of Diane, an educator and interviewer. They laugh uproariously as they tell their stories. As you read, speculate about why nature provokes adolescents to throw caution to the wind.

Rachel: You know what was wicked funny? I was racing down the road with Wanda on bikes and her tire was already so flat and she was racing, okay, and all of a sudden her tire goes boom, and she flew off.

Sherie: You know what hurt? When we lived, when we were camping out on Pleasant Pond? I was riding my bike . . . and it flipped over and the handle jabbed right in my stomach. It hurt so bad, it was awful . . . it hurt wicked . . .

Rachel: [My sister] pushed me into the road so I got run over.

Sherie: [*laughing hard, as are the others*]: She had a broken arm in third grade.

Diane: She pushed you in the road?

Rachel: Yes! I was on the sled and she pushed me in the road.

Diane: Oh well, she didn't mean for you to get run over.

Rachel: She was mad at me that day anyway. . . . Hey, I was on *her* sled so I didn't care. It got totaled. (L. M. Brown, 1998, p. 50)

Possibly, the two girls were amused that they acted foolishly yet lived to tell about it. This goofiness may be nature's way of hastening young people's departure from the nest. Fortunately, continued development in the front part of the cortex eventually helps adolescents envision the effects their actions might have for them, giving them a motivation to curtail seriously dangerous behaviors. Myelination in the front region of the cortex, where planning, executive functions, and other complex cognitive processes occur, continues well beyond puberty (Giedd, Blumenthal, et al., 1999; Kolb & Fantie, 1989).

Continued maturation of the cortex also helps adolescents reflect on their own and others' feelings. That is, adolescents become increasingly able to analyze emotions at higher levels of the brain, rather than responding to emotions spontaneously, as they did in childhood (Killgore, Oki, & Yurgelun-Todd, 2001). Because these analytical abilities take some time to mature and also depend on experience, adolescents may be thoughtful one moment and rash the next. In the "Emotional Development: Late Adolescence" video clip on Observation CD 2, you can listen to 15-year-old Greg describe both impulsive reactions to anger and more controlled responses:

Interviewer: What are some things kids do when they're angry?
Greg: Hit lockers at school. They just get mad . . .
Interviewer: Okay.
Greg: And they don't want you to be around 'em. They just are not pleasant to be around.
Interviewer: Okay. What are some things that kids can do to calm themselves down?
Greg: I don't know. Usually give it a night, 'cause they, if they're mad they usually don't get unmad by the end of the day.

Listen to Greg describe both impulsive and controlled reactions to anger in the "Emotional Development: Late Adolescence" clip on Observation CD 2.

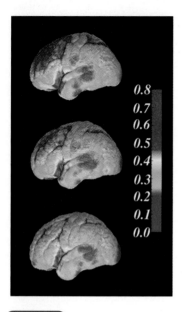

Figure 4-8

As humans develop, their brains become more efficient. The images show the average proportion of gray matter (neurons) in the left hemisphere in brains of children (top), adolescents (middle), and adults (bottom). Researchers collected magnetic resonance images (MRIs) of individuals' brains, then took averages for each age-group and coded the proportion of gray matter in the cortex, which is reflected in the images. Warm colors (red and yellow) show high proportions of gray matter, and cool colors (blue and green) show low proportions. Notice the decreased amount of red and yellow (neurons) in the adult's brain as compared to the child's brain. This shows a developmental decline in the proportion of the cortex devoted solely to neurons. With development, unused neurons die out and active neurons become stronger and more efficient due to increases in myelination.

From "Mapping Sulcal Pattern Asymmetry and Local Cortical Surface Gray Matter Distribution *in vivo:* Maturation in the Perisylvian Cortices," by E. R. Sowell, P. M. Thompson, D. Rex, D. Kornsand, K. D. Tessner, T. L. Jernigan, and A. W. Toga, 2002, *Cerebral Cortex, 12,* pp. 17–26. Reprinted by permission of Oxford University Press.

While bouncing back and forth between an expanding intellect and a drive toward risk taking, adolescents are also benefiting from some changes that have been under way for years. For example, neurological pathways that support motor skills and speech reach an adultlike form during late childhood and adolescence (Paus et al., 1999). Also, circuits connecting language centers within the cortex continue to grow during adolescence, although at a slower rate than they did earlier (P. M. Thompson et al., 2000).

These and other neurological changes clearly show that teenagers' brains are works in progress. In fact, the brain evolves in systematic ways well into adulthood (Sowell, Thompson, Holmes, Jernigan, & Toga, 1999). Myelination and the process of synaptic pruning continue in adulthood, as shown vividly in the brain scans in Figure 4-8. As a result, adults' brains are more efficient, compared to children's brains, both in terms of the connections (axons, dendrites, and synapses) and the insulation of these connections (through myelination).

We summarize key neurological changes during developmental periods in Table 4-1, where we also suggest implications for educators who work with youngsters in particular age-groups. Some general applications from research on brain development are also discussed in the following section.

Applications of Research on Brain Development

We sometimes hear colleagues talk about the implications of brain research for how children should be taught and guided at school. In fact, research in brain development is still in its infancy (Bruer, 1997; R. E. Mayer, 1998; O'Boyle & Gill, 1998). We don't always know, for example, what it means for an area of the brain to increase in size or activity during a particular developmental period: Are such changes the result of maturational developments or the outcome of repeated practice—or both? How much experience is needed to activate new circuits? To what degree can weak circuits be strengthened with instruction? Because so many questions persist, it makes sense to derive educational applications from those neurological findings that are backed up with psychological research on children's learning. Here are some recommendations that integrate what we know about brain development with research on other aspects of child development:

● *Give children many opportunities to learn spontaneously.* In their everyday, informal experiences, children learn a great deal about the physical world, social relationships, language, and practices of their culture. They don't necessarily have to be taught everything they need to learn, although they do need to be exposed to it. In many cases opportunities for play and informal experimentation are just as beneficial as, and sometimes even more beneficial than, planned and systematic instruction (R. D. Brown & Bjorklund, 1998; Bruer, 1999; Chafel, 1991).

In fact, because some neurological changes do not take place until middle childhood or later, youngsters may not even be able to benefit from certain kinds of educational experiences until middle childhood at the earliest. Sustaining attention on a single topic and inhibiting inappropriate actions are capacities that improve with experience but also depend on brain development. Accordingly, some expectations may be quite reasonable for older children yet unreasonable for younger ones.

● *Be optimistic that everyday experiences and classroom instruction can have an impact throughout childhood and adolescence.* Some educators exaggerate the need for structured sensory experiences during infancy and early childhood. Certainly some kinds of stimulation *are* necessary for normal development of some functions, notably visual processing and depth perception. For instance, cats, monkeys, and people who have reduced or abnormal visual stimulation in their first few months sometimes develop lifelong difficulties with visual perception, apparently as a result of irreversible neurological change (Bruer, 1999). On the other hand, everyday experience provides sufficient stimulation for normal development in these visual areas of the brain (Bruer, 1999; Greenough, Black, & Wallace, 1987).

Furthermore, there is little evidence that sensitive periods exist for areas of the brain that support learning and performance in reading, mathematics, music, or other culture-specific intellectual pursuits (Bruer, 1999; Greenough et al., 1987). We know from countless studies,

TABLE 4-1

Developmental Changes in the Brain

Developmental Period	Distinctive Neurological Changes	Implications
Prenatal Development	*The brain's basic parts are constructed:* • The primary structures of the brain emerge within the first few months of prenatal growth. • Neurons, the building blocks of the brain, are formed. They migrate to the places where they will do their work. • The cortex becomes convoluted, and the brain prepares circuits for reflexes and rudimentary learning processes.	• Encourage pregnant women to obtain adequate nutrition; to protect themselves from toxins, drugs, alcohol, injury, and excessive stress; and to obtain prenatal care from a physician. • Educate adolescents (especially adolescent girls at risk for an early pregnancy) about health threats to unborn children.
Infancy	*The brain activates circuits for reflexes, sensation and perception, engagment with caregivers, and detection of patterns in the world:* • Many new connections form among neurons. Dendrites form and expand their reach and complexity, initially in brain areas that support basic biological functions and later in areas that permit learning. • During the first year of life, synapses grow in density, especially in areas of the brain devoted to vision and hearing. • Synaptic pruning begins in certain areas. • Myelination occurs during infancy and continues throughout childhood, adolescence, and adulthood.	• Provide infants with the nutrition they need to build healthy bodies and brains. • Offer infants stimulating environments that include rich visual patterns and human voices, but don't overdo it. Infants are hungry to learn about the world, but they need to do it in their own ways, on their own timetable. • Carefully observe infants' reactions to stimuli to determine their preferences. Comment on the properties of objects, such as stripes and bright colors, that attract their attention. • Talk to infants. They are able to learn a lot about language even when they are still unable to talk themselves. • Form stable and affectionate relationships with infants—their brains are as busy forming emotional circuits as they are learning to perceive objects, physical events, and properties of language.
Childhood	*The brain strengthens neurological circuits used regularly and allows underutilized connections to shrivel:* • Synaptic pruning occurs with gusto in waves through distinct parts of the brain. • The front part of the cortex (closest to the forehead), used for learning new information, controlling behavior, and planning ahead, undergoes synaptic pruning throughout childhood, adolescence, and into adulthood. • Myelination continues to protect neurons and speed up the transmission of signals. • The two hemispheres of the brain take on distinct responsibilities. • Although synapses are pruned during childhood, adolescence, and adulthood, new synapses continue to be formed, reflecting learning through experience.	• Take advantage of children's growing awareness of patterns in their environment. For example, ask children to think about the nature and origin of the seasons, tidal movements, and holidays. • Encourage children to learn more than one language—most children can easily learn two or more languages (see Chapter 9). • In informal contexts, expose children to advanced cultural and aesthetic systems, such as music, poetry, and geometric patterns; exposure to these systems may lay the groundwork for ways of thinking that children can use in the future.
Adolescence	*The brain fortifies connections for coping with emotions and guiding actions toward long-term goals:* • Having begun in childhood, synaptic pruning in the front part of the cortex continues, allowing improvements in memory and attention. • Myelination continues to protect neurons and speed up firing of neurons, especially in the front of the cortex, where planning and other complex cognitive processes occur. • The cortex matures, helping adolescents integrate information from different sensory systems and engage in planning, decision making, and higher-order thinking. • The two hemispheres of the brain continue to become specialized for different purposes. • Circuits that support motor and speech functions continue to mature during late childhood and adolescence. • Growth of circuits connecting language centers of the cortex slows down. • The brain strengthens the ability of higher centers of the brain to analyze and regulate emotions.	• Acknowledge the positive features of adolescents' newfound passions, such as creative artwork, interests in politics, and fascination with sports. • Ask adolescents to think about the consequences of their actions for the future. • Encourage adolescents to use their developing ability to think abstractly. For example, adolescents can systematically test hypotheses in science, contemplate the complex motivations of characters in literature, and envision multiple causes of political conflict in history classes. • Provide opportunities for adolescents to participate in physical activity and, when they show an interest, to seek advanced training. • Encourage adolescents to attend to the emotional expressions, experiences, and plights of other people.

Sources: N. R. Carlson, 1999; B. J. Casey et al., 2000; Cowan, 1979; M. Diamond & Hopson, 1998; P. R. Huttenlocher, 1979, 1990; P. R. Huttenlocher & de Courten, 1987; M. H. Johnson, 1998; Killgore et al., 2001; National Research Council, 1999; Paus et al., 1999; Rakic, 1995; Sowell, Delis, et al., 2001; Sowell et al., 2002; Sowell, Thompson, et al., 2001; P. M. Thompson et al., 2000; Yakovlev & Lecours, 1967.

as well as from our own everyday observations, that human beings continue to learn new information and skills quite successfully throughout the lifespan (Mühlnickel, Elbert, Taub, & Flor, 1998; C. A. Nelson, 1999; Ramachandran, Rogers-Ramachandran, & Stewart, 1992; Sowell et al., 1999).

You can therefore reasonably assume that the brain remains adaptable throughout childhood and adolescence. You *can* have an important impact with children of any age if you offer such brain-friendly experiences as properly designed instruction, exposure to rich cultural experiences (e.g., visits to museums, libraries, and the like), and constructive social relationships. Early years are learning years, but so are later ones.

● *Accommodate individual differences in neurological functioning.* Individualizing instruction is especially important for children who have neurological exceptionalities. For example, children who have difficulty distinguishing among the various sounds of speech may have brain circuits that are not sufficiently formed to permit this activity. Intensive training in speech processing seems to benefit these children, presumably because of its effects on brain pathways (C. A. Nelson, 1999). Special educators, school psychologists, and other specialists can often recommend effective strategies for working with children who have various neurological deficits.

● *Provide extra guidance to children who have had early exposure to drugs and alcohol.* Children who were exposed to alcohol, cocaine, and other drugs during prenatal development often have unique needs. For instance, these youngsters may need assistance in understanding abstract ideas, inhibiting inappropriate responses (such as impulsively hitting bothersome peers), and applying rules to multiple settings (e.g., "keep your hands to yourself" applies to the lunchroom and playground as well as to the classroom) (Lutke, 1997).

Ultimately, adults must remember that, with proper guidance and instruction, many children of alcohol- and drug-abusing parents can lead productive and fulfilling lives. One 17-year-old girl with fetal alcohol syndrome expressed this idea eloquently:

> There are two things I want you to know: Do not call me a victim, and do not tell me what I cannot do. Help me to find a way to do it. (Lutke, 1997, p. 188)

● *Encourage children and adolescents to think about the consequences of their actions.* To take full advantage of emerging abilities to temper impulses, young people need to practice these skills. Long-term planning and self-control do not appear on the scene—or in the brain—fully formed. Therefore, you can encourage young people to plan in a range of areas, such as keeping track of homework assignments, planning to meet graduation requirements, determining the steps needed to land certain jobs, and deciding the optimal time to raise a family.

● *Help children who have been neglected or abused to form warm, trusting, and stable relationships.* First relationships leave impressions on children's brains (Siegel, 1999). That is, children develop expectations, apparently inscribed in their brains, regarding how relationships unfold (e.g., whether caregivers are affectionate or rejecting), how emotions progress (e.g., whether anger defuses or escalates into a turbulent outburst), and how they should judge themselves (e.g., whether they are intrinsically worthy people or not). These expectations do not necessarily remain permanent features in the brain, but they do tend to persist unless children's later relationships are substantially and consistently different from their previous experiences. With patience and faith in children's resilience, responsive adults can help ill-treated children learn new ways of relating to others.

Physical Development During Childhood

As you have seen, changes take place in size, bodily proportions, and neurological structures throughout childhood and adolescence. With these changes come new opportunities to practice motor skills, develop healthy habits, engage in physical activity, and relate to peers in unprecedented ways. We describe physical growth during the developmental periods in more detail in the next few pages.

———— Connecting Concepts
The ability to distinguish among various sounds of speech is an important factor in learning to read (see Chapter 10).

———— Connecting Concepts
Chapter 3 introduces the cause and effects of fetal alcohol syndrome.

———— Connecting Concepts
Chapter 11 describes the types of *attachments* that young children form with parents and other caregivers. Chapter 12 explores how children's self-judgments become an important part of their *sense of self.*

Infancy (Birth–Age 2)

Infancy is an impressive period of rapid growth and development. However, even at birth, infants display remarkable reflexes. Before the umbilical cord is cut, the first reflex, *breathing,* begins, providing oxygen and removing carbon dioxide. Breathing and a few other reflexes begin in infancy and operate throughout life. Other reflexes, such as automatically grasping small objects placed in the hands and responding to loud noises by flaring out arms and legs, last only a few months. Reflexes are evidence of normal neurological development, and their absence is a matter of concern to physicians (Touwen, 1974).

Crying allows infants to express discomfort and seek relief. The time infants spend crying tends to decrease by the fourth or fifth month (St. James-Roberts & Halil, 1991). Parents and other caregivers are physiologically primed to respond to cries, especially to intense cries indicating extreme pain (R. M. Wood & Gustafson, 2001). Sensitive caregivers learn to identify urgency in infants' crying and to use information about infants' habits, daytime schedules, and time elapsed since last feeding to determine how—and how quickly—to respond.

Some infants, however, are difficult to soothe. About 1 or 2 in every 10 infants exhibit **colic,** persistent crying for long periods during the first 3 months of life (Hide & Guyer, 1982). The causes of colic are uncertain but may include abdominal distress and disturbances in the brain's regulation of sleeping and waking (American Academy of Pediatrics [AAP] Committee on Nutrition, 1998; Papousek & Papousek, 1996). Rates do not differ between breast- and bottle-fed babies, but colic is somewhat more common among infants who have eaten cereal and other solid foods during their first 3 months (Hide & Guyer, 1982). For some infants, intolerance of cow's milk seems to perpetuate colic.

Because infants cannot use words to communicate physical needs, practitioners must seek information from families about their babies' sleeping, eating, drinking, diapering, and comforting preferences and habits (Greenman & Stonehouse, 1996). Figure 4-9 is a service plan that might be completed by a family member and submitted to a caregiver. Of course, even the most detailed plan cannot predict how a particular infant will behave throughout each day. Caregivers must respond to infants' changing needs by attending to signals that indicate comfort and distress. We offer ideas of what to look for in the Observation Guidelines table "Assessing Physical Development in Infancy."

As they grow older, infants add motor skills to their physical repertoire. Motor skills at first appear slowly, then more rapidly. In the first 12 to 18 months, infants learn to hold up their heads, roll over, reach for objects, sit, crawl, and walk. In the second year, they walk with increasing balance and coordination, manipulate small objects, and begin to run, jump, and climb. In the "Cognitive Development: Infancy" video clip on Observation CD 1, you can observe 16-month-old Corwin walking confidently and competently. Corwin holds his arms high to maintain balance, but he is also agile enough to walk quickly and stay upright while reaching down into a bag.

Motor skills emerge in a particular order, following *cephalocaudal* and *proximodistal* trends (Robbins, Brody, Hogan, Jackson, & Green, 1928). The **cephalocaudal trend** refers to the vertical growth of skills, which proceeds from the head downward. Infants first learn to control their heads, then shoulders and trunk, and later their legs. The **proximodistal trend** refers to the inside-outside pattern in which growth progresses outward from the spine. Infants, for example, first learn to control their arms, then their hands, and finally, their fingers.

Early Childhood (Ages 2–6)

Visit a local playground, and you are likely to see preschool children engaged in nonstop physical activity. Physical movement is a hallmark of early childhood, and dramatic changes occur in both gross motor skills and fine motor skills. **Gross motor skills** (e.g., running, hopping, tumbling, climbing, and swinging) permit large movement through and within an environment. **Fine motor skills** (e.g., drawing, writing, cutting with scissors, and manipulating small objects) involve more limited, controlled, and precise movements, primarily with the hands.

Connecting Concepts
In Chapter 3 we examine infants' reflexes and recommend that practitioners point them out to new parents.

Observe Corwin walk with good balance in the "Cognitive Development: Infancy" clip on Observation CD 1.

colic
Persistent crying by infants; it is most prevalent in the first 3 months of life.

cephalocaudal trend
Vertical ordering of motor skills and physical development; order is head first to feet last.

proximodistal trend
Inside-outside ordering of motor skills and physical development; order is inside first and outside last.

gross motor skills
Large movements of the body that permit locomotion through and within an environment.

fine motor skills
Small, precise movements of particular parts of the body, especially the hands.

Infant/Toddler Needs and Services Plan

Date: _____

Child's Name: _____ Birth Date/Age of Child _____ _____

Parent(s) Name: _____

Primary Caregiver: _____

Homebase: _____

Sleeping Routine

Pre-nap routines/rituals: _____

_____

How many naps per day (typical):   a.m. _____ to _____ p.m. _____ to _____

Length of nap: _____

What position does your child prefer: _____

Waking behavior/routine: _____

Special concerns: _____

Eating Routine

Solid Food: _____ Time of day you want given: _____

Special meals to be served in homebase: _____

Allergies: _____

Food dislikes or eating problems: _____

Food likes and eating preferences: _____

Special diet/requests: _____

Special concerns: _____

Bottle/Cup Routine

Circle: Bottle   Cup

Formula: Brand _____   Amount _____

Time of day you want given _____

Juice: Type _____   Amount _____

Time of day you want given _____

Milk: _____   Amount _____

Time of day you want given _____

Breast Milk: _____   Amount _____

Time of day you want given _____

Introducing Solid Foods

We recommend introducing infant cereal at 4–6 months, vegetables, fruits, and their juices at 5–7 months, protein such as cheese, yogurt, cooked beans, meat, fish, chicken, and egg yolk at 6–8 months, whole egg at 10–12 months, and milk at 12 months. We also can introduce the use of a cup and spoon at 8–10 months.

If you do not wish to follow our recommendations, please sign:

_____

Comforting/Distress

Does your child have a security object?   Name? _____

Does your child use a pacifier?   When? _____

Other information? _____

Diapering Routine

Please circle which type of diaper to use: Disposable   Cloth

If the child needs lotion or ointment, please specify which brand: _____

Does you child have any services that are different from those provided by the center's routine program? i.e., special exercises, special materials, accommodation of special services.

_____

_____

_____

Other Information

_____

_____

_____

The Needs and Services Plan will be updated every three months or sooner if requested by parent/guardian.

Parent Signature _____ Date _____

Staff Signature _____ Date _____

Date of change _____ Parent Initials _____ Staff Initials _____

Date of change _____ Parent Initials _____ Staff Initials _____

Date of change _____ Parent Initials _____ Staff Initials _____

Figure 4-9

Service plan for infants and toddlers

From *Prime Times: A Handbook for Excellence in Infant and Toddler Programs,* by Jim Greenman and Anne Stonehouse (Redleaf Press, 1996). Copyright © 1996 by Jim Greenman and Anne Stonehouse. Reprinted with permission from Redleaf Press, St. Paul, Minnesota, www.redleafpress.org. To order, call 800-423-8309.

Observe Acadia and Cody playing actively and spontaneously at the park in the "Physical Activity: Early Childhood" clip on Observation CD 1.

During the preschool years, children typically learn such culture-specific motor skills as riding a tricycle and throwing and catching a ball. Motor skills become smoother and better coordinated over time as a result of practice, longer arms and legs, and genetically guided increases in muscular control. Optimism and persistence in motor tasks play a role as well. For instance, when Teresa's son Alex was 4, he repeatedly asked his parents to throw him a softball as he stood poised with his bat. Not at all deterred by an abysmal batting average (about .05), Alex would frequently exclaim, "I almost got it!" His efforts paid off, as he gradually did learn to track the ball visually and coordinate his swing with the ball's path.

A lot of chatter, fantasy, and sheer joy accompanies gross motor activity in early childhood. You can observe creative and cooperative interactions between two 4-year-old children, Acadia and Cody, as they play on climbing equipment in the "Physical Activity: Early Childhood" video clip on Observation CD 1. The children practice a variety of gross mo-

OBSERVATION GUIDELINES

Assessing Physical Development in Infancy

Characteristic	Look For	Example	Implication
Eating Habits	• Ability to express hunger to adults • Developing ability to suck, chew, and swallow • Ability to enjoy and digest food without abdominal upset • Cultural and individual differences in how families feed infants	Wendy Sue is a listless eater who doesn't seem as interested in food as other infants in her child care program. The caregiver tells the director she is worried, and the two decide to talk with the parents. It is possible that professional intervention might be needed.	To understand an infant's health, talk with parents and families. Find out what they believe about appropriate care of infants.
Mobility	• Developing ability to coordinate looking and feeling • Growing ability to move toward objects • Temperamental factors that might affect exploration • Physical challenges that might affect exploration, including hearing and visual impairments • Temporary declines in exploration, such as when separating from parents	Due to neurological damage at birth, Daniel's left arm and leg are less strong than those on his right side. His new teacher at his child care center notices that he is reluctant to move around in the center. During a home visit, the teacher finds that Daniel's movements are somewhat lopsided, but he crawls around energetically. The teacher realizes that Daniel needs to feel secure in the program before he can explore freely there.	Set up the environment so infants will find it safe, predictable, attractive, and interesting. Help individual children find challenges and opportunities that meet their abilities.
Resting Patterns	• Methods babies use to put themselves to sleep • Families' expectations for sleeping arrangements • Difficulties in falling asleep • Evidence that families understand risk factors for sudden infant death syndrome (SIDS)	Angie cries a lot when falling asleep, in part because she is used to sleeping on her stomach. Her teacher explains to her parents that he places babies on their backs in order to reduce the risk of SIDS. He rubs Angie's head to soothe her and help her adjust to her new sleeping position.	Talk to parents about risk factors for SIDS (see the upcoming section "Rest and Sleep"). Explain why you place babies on their backs when they are falling asleep.
Health Issues	• Possible symptoms of infections, such as unusual behavior, irritability, fever, and respiratory difficulty. • Suspicious injuries and unusual behaviors that may indicate abuse • Possible symptoms of prenatal drug exposure, including difficulty sleeping, extreme sensitivity, and irritability • Physical disabilities requiring accommodation	A child care teacher enjoys having Michael, age 18 months, in her care. Michael has cerebral palsy, making it difficult for him to scoot around. His teacher encourages him to move toward objects, but she also brings things to him to examine and play with. When he has a fever, she calls his mother or father, as she would with any child.	Remain alert to signs of illness and infection in children. Contact family members when infants have a fever or show other unusual physical symptoms.

tor skills (running, climbing, throwing a ball), all in the name of play. Often young children infuse pretend roles into their physical play. For example, they may become super-heroes and villains, cowboys and cowgirls, astronauts and aliens. During *chase play,* a young child may run after another child, pretending to be a lion or other predator (Steen & Owens, 2000).

Young children also make strides in fine motor skills. When given drawing tools, many begin to scribble sometime around age 2 (see Figure 4-10) and gradually master circles, other shapes, and alphabet letters in the preschool and early elementary years. Some children spend considerable time drawing and cutting as early as 3½ or 4 (see Figure 4-11), and they may form their own creative shapes (e.g., by combining circles and lines to represent human beings) as well as mimic adults' cursive writing with wavy lines or connected loops (J. J. Beaty, 1998; R. Kellogg, 1967; McLane & McNamee, 1990).

We often find large individual differences in young children's fine motor skills. Some children, such as those born with certain chromosomal conditions (e.g., Down syndrome) and those exposed to alcohol during prenatal development, tend to progress more slowly than

Figure 4-10

This drawing by Tina, age 2½, shows early practice in making circular shapes.

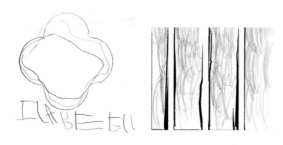

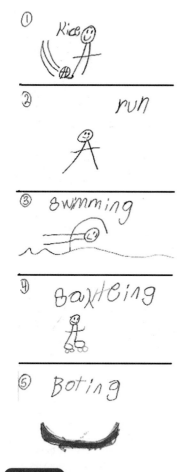

Figure 4-11

Isabelle, age 3½, traced shapes and wrote her name in the artwork on the left. Learning to spell her name, Isabelle included two *E*s and two *L*s. In the artwork on the right, she practiced her cutting, attempting to follow the black lines, and correcting her work in the third rectangle from the left, showing her desire to meet a standard of straightness.

Figure 4-12

When asked to choose five things he liked to do, 6-year-old Alex selected five athletic activities: kicking, running, swimming, skating, and boating.

puberty
Physiological changes that occur during adolescence and lead to reproductive maturation.

growth spurt
Rapid increase in height and weight during puberty.

age-mates (H. M. Barr, Streissguth, Darby, & Sampson, 1990; Bruni, 1998; Goyen, Lui, & Woods, 1998). Furthermore, some evidence indicates that certain fine motor activities (e.g., cursive handwriting) may be easier for girls than boys (M. R. Cohen, 1997). Fortunately, explicit instruction and practice can help children improve fine motor skills, although some differences in dexterity inevitably persist (Bruni, 1998; Case-Smith, 1996).

Middle Childhood (Ages 6–10)

Over the course of middle childhood, youngsters typically show slow but steady gains in height and weight. Now children's bodies grow larger without altering the basic structures. As a result, proportions of separate body parts change less than in infancy or early childhood. With these slow, continuous gains come a few losses: Children lose their 20 primary ("baby") teeth one by one, replacing them with permanent teeth that at first appear oversized in the small mouths of 6-, 7-, and 8-year-olds. Girls mature somewhat more quickly than do boys, erupting permanent teeth sooner and progressing toward skeletal maturity earlier.

In middle childhood, children build on their emerging physical capabilities. Many gross motor skills, once awkward, are now executed fluidly. Whereas preschoolers may run for the sheer joy of it, elementary school children put running to use in organized games and sports. They intensify their speed and coordination in running, kicking, catching, and dribbling. Becoming proficient in athletic skills can be gratifying for children. As you can see in Figure 4-12, 6-year-old Alex chose five athletic movements when asked by his teacher to identify five things he liked to do. You can also observe the pleasure that 9-year-old Kyle and 10-year-old Curtis experience as they practice basketball skills in the "Physical Activity: Middle Childhood" video clip on Observation CD 1.

Children within this age range also improve in fine motor skills. Their drawings, supported by physiological maturation and cognitive advances, are more detailed, and their handwriting becomes smaller, smoother, and more consistent (see Chapter 10). They also begin to tackle such fine motor activities as sewing, model building, and arts and crafts projects.

As children progress through middle childhood, they become increasingly sensitive about their physical appearance. Consider this fourth grader's self-critical viewpoint:

> I am the ugliest girl I know. My hair is not straight enough, and it doesn't even have the dignity to be curly. My teeth are crooked from sucking my thumb and from a wet-bathing-suit-and-a-slide accident. My clothes are hand-me-downs, my skin is a greenish color that other people call "tan" to be polite, and I don't say the right words, or say them in the right way. I'm smart enough to notice that I'm not smart enough; not so short, but not tall enough; and definitely, definitely too skinny. (Marissa Arillo, in Oldfather & West, 1999, p. 60)

For many children, self-consciousness increases as they get close to puberty. And it is not only the children themselves who notice their physical appearance: Other people do as well. In fact, people generally respond more favorably to children they perceive to be physically attractive. In a variety of cultures, physical attractiveness is correlated with, and probably a causal factor in, self-esteem (Chu, 2000; Harter, 1999). Thus, although many children exaggerate their own physical flaws, the reality is that appearance is influential in social relationships, and it does affect how children feel about themselves.

In the Development and Practice feature "Accommodating the Physical Needs of Infants and Children," we give examples of strategies for meeting individual and group needs for physical care, creating a hazard-free environment, and integrating physical activity into the curriculum.

Early Adolescence (Ages 10–14)

The most obvious aspect of physical change in early adolescence is the onset of **puberty.** Ushered in by a cascade of hormones, puberty involves a series of biological changes that lead to reproductive maturity. It is marked not only by the maturation of sex-specific characteristics but also by a **growth spurt,** a rapid increase in height and weight. The hormonal

DEVELOPMENT AND PRACTICE

Accommodating the Physical Needs of Infants and Children

- Meet the physical needs of individual infants rather than expecting all to conform to a universal and inflexible schedule.

  A caregiver in an infant program keeps a schedule of times infants receive their bottles and naps. That way, she can plan her day to rotate among individual infants, giving each as much attention as possible.

- View meeting the physical needs of infants as part of the overall curriculum for their care and education.

  An infant-toddler caregiver understands the importance of meeting physical needs in ways that establish and deepen relationships with each child. She uses one-to-one activities such as diaper changing and bottle feeding as occasions to interact.

- Make sure the classroom is free of sharp edges, peeling paint, and other environmental hazards to which young children may be particularly vulnerable.

  After new carpet is installed in his classroom, a preschool teacher notices that several children complain of stomachaches and headaches. He suspects that the recently applied carpet adhesive may be to blame and, with the approval of the preschool's director, asks an outside consultant to evaluate the situation. Meanwhile, he conducts most of the day's activities outdoors or in other rooms.

- Provide frequent opportunities for children to engage in physical activity.

  A preschool teacher schedules "Music and Marching" for mid-morning, "Outdoor Time" before lunch, and a nature walk to collect leaves for an art project after naptime.

- Plan activities that will help children develop their fine motor skills.

  An after-school caregiver invites children to make mosaics that depict different kinds of vehicles. The children glue a variety of small objects (e.g., beads, sequins, beans, colored rice) onto line drawings of cars, trains, boats, airplanes, bicycles, and so on.

- Design physical activities so that students with widely differing skill levels can successfully participate.

  During a unit on tennis, a physical education teacher has children practice the forehand stroke using tennis rackets. First, she asks them to practice bouncing and then hitting the ball against the wall of the gymnasium. If some students master these basic skills, she asks them to see how many times in succession they can hit the ball against the wall. When they reach five successive hits, she tells them to vary the height of the ball from waist high to shoulder high (Logsdon, Alleman, Straits, Belka, & Clark, 1997).

- Integrate physical activity into academic lessons.

  When teaching about molecules and temperature, a fifth-grade teacher asks children to stand in a cluster in an open area of the classroom. To show children how molecules behave when something is cold, she asks them to stay close together and move around just a little bit. To show them how molecules behave when something is hot, she asks them to spread farther apart and move more actively.

- Give children time to rest.

  After a kindergarten class has been playing outside, their teacher offers a snack of apple slices, crackers, and milk. Once they have cleaned up their milk cartons and napkins, the children gather around him on the floor while he reads them a story.

- Respect children's growing ability to care for their own bodies.

  In an after-school program, a teacher allows the children to go to the restroom whenever they need to. He teaches children to hang a clothespin with their name on an "out rope" when they leave the room and then remove the pin when they return.

---

increases of adolescence have other physiological repercussions as well, such as increased oil production in the face (often manifested as acne), increased activity in the sweat glands, mood swings, and emotional sensitivity (Buchanan, 1991).

Girls typically progress through puberty before boys do. Puberty begins in girls sometime between ages 8 and 13 (on average, at age 10). It starts with a growth spurt, "budding" of the breasts, and the emergence of pubic hair. Whereas such changes are typically gradual, the onset of menstruation, **menarche,** is an abrupt event that can be either positive or frightening, depending on a girl's awareness and preparation. The first menstrual period tends to occur rather late in puberty, usually between 9 and 15 years of age. Nature apparently delays menstruation, and with it the possibility of conception, until girls are physically strong and close to their adult height and therefore physiologically better able to have a successful pregnancy.

For boys, puberty gets its start between 9 and 14 years (on average, at 11½ years), when the testes enlarge and the scrotum changes in texture and color. A year or so later, the penis grows larger and pubic hair appears; the growth spurt begins soon after. At about 13 to 14 years, boys have their first ejaculation experience, **spermarche,** often while sleeping. Boys seem to receive less information from parents about this milestone than girls do about menstruation, and little is known about their feelings about it. Later developments include growth of facial hair, deepening of the voice, and eventually the attainment of adult height. (The course of puberty for both boys and girls is depicted in Figure 4-13.)

Notice that for girls the growth spurt is one of the first signs of puberty, but for boys it occurs relatively late in the sequence. The result of this discrepancy is that boys end up taller: They have a longer period of steady prepubescent growth, and they grow a bit more than

Observe Kyle and Curtis practicing basketball skills in the "Physical Activity: Middle Childhood" clip on Observation CD 1. (See the description on p. 114 of the pleasure the boys experience from physical activity.)

menarche
First menstrual period in an adolescent female.

spermarche
First ejaculation in an adolescent male.

IN GIRLS	IN BOYS
Initial elevation of breasts and beginning of growth spurt (typically between 8 and 13 years; on average, at 10 years)	Enlargement of the testes and changes in texture and color of scrotum (typically between 9 and 14 years; on average, at 11½ years)
Appearance of pubic hair (sometimes occurs before elevation of breasts)	Increase in penis size and appearance of pubic hair
Increase in size and structure of uterus, vagina, labia, and clitoris	(average, at 12½ years)
Further development of breasts	*Spermarche*, or first ejaculation
Peak of growth spurt	Peak of growth spurt, accompanied by more rapid penis growth
Menarche, or onset of menstrual cycle (typically between 9 and 15 years)	Appearance of facial hair
	Deepening voice, as size of larynx and length of vocal cords increase
Completion of height gain (about two years after menarche) and attainment of adult height	Completion of penis growth
	Completion of height gain and attainment of adult height
Completion of breast development and pubic hair growth	Completion of pubic hair growth

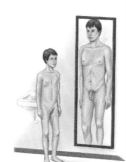

Figure 4-13

Maturational sequences of puberty

girls do during their adolescent growth spurt. With the onset of puberty, boys also gain considerably more muscle mass than girls, courtesy of the male hormone *testosterone* (J. R. Thomas & French, 1985).

To some extent, biology affects psychology in young adolescents. Continuing development of the cortex allows more complex thought, as we have seen, and hormonal fluctuations and additional changes in the brain affect emotions. Adolescents' rapidly changing physical characteristics can be a source of either excitement or dismay. For instance, Anne Frank looked positively on puberty, as this entry in her diary shows:

> I think what is happening to me is so wonderful, and not only what can be seen on my body, but all that is taking place inside. I never discuss myself or any of these things with anybody; that is why I have to talk to myself about them.
>
> Each time I have a period—and that has only been three times—I have the feeling that in spite of all the pain, unpleasantness, and nastiness, I have a sweet secret, and that is why, although it is nothing but a nuisance to me in a way, I always long for the time that I shall feel that secret within me again. (A. Frank, 1967, p. 146)

Others are not at all happy with their changing bodies. In *Reviving Ophelia,* therapist Mary Pipher (1994) describes ninth-grader Cayenne's perspective:

> She hated her looks. She thought her hair was too bright, her hips and thighs too flabby. She tried to lose weight but couldn't. She dyed her hair, but it turned a weird purple color and dried out. She felt almost every girl was prettier. She said, "Let's face it. I'm a dog." (p. 32)[1]

Curiously, psychology also affects biology, in that life experiences influence biological growth in adolescence. Family conflict seems to accelerate puberty in girls, although not in boys (Kenneth, Smith, & Palermiti, 1997). However, pubertal maturation seems to be delayed in girls who grow up in low-income families, perhaps because of less adequate nutrition (Tremblay, 1999).

---

[1]From *Reviving Ophelia* by Mary Pipher, Ph.D., copyright 1994 by Mary Pipher, Ph.D. Used by permission of Putnam Berkeley, a division of Penguin Putnam Inc.

During the adolescent growth spurt, appetites increase considerably.
© Zits Partnership. King Features Syndicate.

Accompanying the physical changes of puberty are changes in adolescents' cognitive capacities, social relationships, and feelings about themselves (Brooks-Gunn, 1989; Brooks-Gunn & Paikoff, 1992). Puberty also seems to loosen restraints on problem behaviors. For example, the onset of puberty in boys is associated with increased aggression (Olweus, Mattson, Schalling, & Low, 1988), alcohol and cigarette use (Reifman, Barnes, & Hoffman, 1999), and experimentation with such behaviors as lying, shoplifting, and burglary (Cota-Robles & Neiss, 1999). As we suggested earlier in this chapter, adolescents' risk taking may be based partly in new brain circuits. The teenage brain, it seems, provokes young people to try new things, be daredevils, and affiliate with like-minded peers.

Also influencing risky behaviors is a phenomenon known as the **personal fable:** Young teenagers tend to imagine themselves as unique, invincible members of the human race (Elkind, 1981a). Because they are like no one else (or so they think), they wrongly assume they are not vulnerable to dangers that harm others. Their sense of invulnerability may lead them to take foolish risks, such as experimenting with drugs and alcohol and having unprotected sexual intercourse (DeRidder, 1993; S. P. Thomas, Groër, & Droppleman, 1993).

Considerable variation exists in the timing of puberty within groups of girls and boys, and this causes problems for some teenagers. Researchers have focused primarily on the potential vulnerabilities of *early-maturing girls* and *late-maturing boys*. Early-maturing girls become heavier and more curvaceous at younger ages. Some of these girls feel dissatisfied with their bodies, which do not resemble the slim, angular professional models idealized in the popular media. Early-maturing girls are also sometimes less happy and more likely to engage in precocious sexual activity and other risky behaviors than are later-maturing girls (C. D. Hayes & Hofferth, 1987; C. E. Irwin & Millstein, 1992; Stattin & Magnusson, 1989; Susman, Nottelmann, Inoff-Germain, Dorn, & Chrousos, 1987).

Late-maturing boys, on the other hand, are still "boys" when some of their peers are beginning to show signs of adultlike masculinity. Research indicates that they get off to a slower start than other boys in important aspects of development. For instance, they tend to be less athletically inclined and less popular with peers, and they less frequently seek leadership positions at school (R. T. Gross & Duke, 1980; H. F. Jones, 1949; Simmons & Blyth, 1987). On the plus side, they are less likely to engage in risk-taking behaviors such as smoking, drinking, and delinquent activities (P. D. Duncan, Ritter, Dornbusch, Gross, & Carlsmith, 1985; Susman et al., 1985).

Connecting Concepts
Chapter 12 will tell you more about the emergence and decline of the personal fable during adolescence.

The rapid physical changes of puberty are accompanied by new intellectual abilities and social relationships.

personal fable
Belief held by many adolescents that they are unique beings invulnerable to normal risks and dangers.

The timing of puberty does not necessarily establish lifelong patterns, however. Many adolescents learn constructive lessons from the trials and tribulations of their teenage years. The ability of adolescents to adjust positively to puberty depends to a large degree on their culture, parents, and school setting (Blyth, Simmons, & Zakin, 1985; Hill, Holmbeck, Marlow, Green, & Lynch, 1985; A. C. Peterson & Taylor, 1980; Stattin & Magnusson, 1989). In some cultures puberty is joyously welcomed by formal celebrations, such as the bar mitzvahs and bat mitzvahs for 13-year-olds of the Jewish faith and *quinceañeras* for 15-year-old girls in Mexican and Mexican American communities.

Connecting Concepts
In Chapter 14 we will look at social aspects of adolescent sexuality.

School personnel can help youngsters adjust by giving some advance warning about physiological changes and reassuring youngsters that considerable variations in timing are well within the "normal" range. In the Development and Practice feature "Accommodating the Physical Needs of Adolescents," we give additional examples of strategies for accommodating both the changes of puberty and the diversity that exists among young adolescents.

Late Adolescence (Ages 14–18)

At about age 15 for girls and age 17 for boys, the growth spurt ends, and in the later teenage years, most adolescents reach sexual maturity. (However, because of individual differences, especially among boys, some show few signs of puberty until the high school years.) With sexual maturation comes increasing interest in sexual activity, including hugging, kissing and, for many teens, more intimate contact as well (Delamater & MacCorquodale, 1979). Later in this chapter we will consider health risks associated with unprotected sexual contact among peers.

As you have learned, the brain continues to refine its pathways during adolescence, permitting more thoughtful control of emotions and more deliberate reflection about possible consequences of various behaviors. Perhaps as a result, the false sense of invulnerability associated with the personal fable tends to decline in later adolescence (Durkin, 1995; Lapsley, Jackson, Rice, & Shadid, 1988). Nevertheless, many older adolescents continue to engage in behaviors that could undermine their long-term physical health—for instance, smoking cigarettes or abusing alcohol and drugs. (B. J. Guthrie, Caldwell, & Hunter, 1997; Wallander, Eggert, & Gilbert, 2004). You can see examples of the risky behaviors that some high school students try in Table 4-2.

The Developmental Trends table "Physical Development at Different Age Levels" summarizes the key characteristics of each age-group and provides implications for teachers and other professionals. In the next section we examine more closely the practices that contribute to good health and, conversely, the choices that undermine it.

TABLE 4-2

Percentage of U.S. Students Grades 9–12 Who Reported Engaging in Risky Behaviors

Risky Behavior	Girls	Boys
Substance Use		
Alcohol (in last 30 days)	45.8	43.8
Tobacco (in last 30 days)	24.6	30.3
Marijuana (in last 30 days)	19.3	25.1
Cocaine (in last 30 days)	3.5	4.6
Inhalants (in last 30 days)	3.4	4.3
Heroin (in lifetime)	2.0	4.3
Methamphetamine (in lifetime)	6.8	8.3
Ecstasy (MDMA; in lifetime)	10.4	11.6
Illegal steroids (in lifetime)	5.3	6.8
Sexual Behaviors		
Had sexual intercourse (in lifetime)	45.3	48.0
Sexually active (had intercourse in past 3 months)	34.6	33.8
No condom use during last intercourse (among sexually active adolescents)	42.6	31.2
Alcohol or drug use at last sexual intercourse (among sexually active adolescents)	21.0	29.8
Had four or more sexual partners (in lifetime)	11.2	17.5
Behaviors That Contribute to Unintentional Injuries		
Rarely or never wore seat belts in car	14.6	21.5
Bicycle riding without helmets (among those who rode bicycle in last 12 months)	84.2	87.2
Rode with a driver who had been drinking alcohol (in last 30 days)	31.1	29.2
Drove car after drinking alcohol (in last 30 days)	8.9	15.0

Source: Centers for Disease Control and Prevention, 2004.

Physical Well-Being

With age, children and adolescents become more aware of "good health" (Figure 4-14). But they also become progressively motivated to make their own decisions and, even in late adolescence, don't always make choices that are best for their health. In the following sections, we consider issues related to health and well-being, including eating habits, physical activity, rest and sleep, and health-compromising behaviors. We also identify strategies that adults can use to encourage young people to develop healthful lifestyles.

Eating Habits

As you have learned, children's nutrition affects their physical growth, brain development, and sexual maturation. Their diet also influences their energy level, concentration, and long-term health problems. Given the importance of nutrition, an essential question is, How do children learn to eat well?

Good eating habits start at birth. Breastfeeding is the preferred method of feeding infants because breast milk is rich in needed vitamins and provides infants with antibodies against illnesses (AAP, 2005). Breast milk is also easier to digest than infant formula, and breastfed babies have fewer allergies, colds, stomachaches, and other common ailments (Beaudry, Dufour, & Marcoux, 1995; Dewey, Heinig, &

Figure 4-14

As children grow older, they become more knowledgeable about what "good health" entails. Grace (age 11) drew this rendition of healthy and unhealthy people.

Modeled after Mayall, Bendelow, Barker, Storey, & Veltman, 1996.

DEVELOPMENTAL TRENDS

Physical Development at Different Age Levels

Age	What You Might Observe	Diversity	Implications
Infancy (Birth–2) 	• Emergence of reflexes • Initial increase followed by decline in crying • Rapid growth and change in proportions of body parts • Increasing ability to move around, first by squirming; then rolling, crawling, creeping, or scooting; finally by walking • Increasing ability to coordinate small muscles of hands and eyes • Increasing self-help skills in such areas as feeding, dressing, washing, toileting, and grooming	• Children vary in timing and quality of gross motor skills (e.g., rolling over, crawling, and sitting up) depending on genetic and cultural factors. • Children vary in timing of mobility as well as in methods they use to get around (some children never crawl or creep). • Fine motor skills and eye-hand coordination may appear earlier or later depending on genetic makeup and encouragement from caregivers. • Self-help skills appear earlier when encouraged, but virtually all children learn them eventually, and sooner is not necessarily better.	• Celebrate each child's unique growth patterns, but watch for unusual patterns or differences that may require accommodation or intervention. • Provide a choice of appropriate indoor and outdoor experiences to help children practice their developing fine and gross motor skills. • Don't push infants to reach milestones. Allow them to experience each phase of physical development thoroughly. • Be aware of serious developmental delays that call for professional intervention.
Early Childhood (2–6) 	• Loss of rounded, babyish appearance, with arms and legs lengthening and taking on more mature proportions • Boundless physical energy for new gross motor skills, such as running, hopping, tumbling, climbing, and swinging • Acquisition of fine motor skills, such as functional pencil grip and use of scissors • Transition away from afternoon nap, which may initially be marked by periods of fussiness in the afternoon	• Children differ considerably in the ages at which they master various motor skills. • Boys are more physically active than girls, but girls are healthier overall; these differences continue throughout childhood and adolescence. • Some home environments (e.g., small apartments, as well as larger houses in which parents restrict movement) limit the degree to which children can engage in vigorous physical activity; others may present hazardous environmental conditions (e.g., lead paint, toxic fumes). • Children with mental retardation may have delayed motor skills.	• Provide frequent opportunities to play outside or (in inclement weather) in a gymnasium or other large indoor space. • Intersperse vigorous physical exercise with rest and quiet time. • Encourage fine motor skills through puzzles, blocks, doll houses, and arts and crafts. • Choose activities that accommodate diversity in gross and fine motor skills.
Middle Childhood (6–10) 	• Steady gains in height and weight • Loss and replacement of primary teeth • Refinement and consolidation of gross motor skills and integration of such skills into structured play activities • Participation in organized sports • Increasing fluency in fine motor skills, such as handwriting and drawing	• Variations in weight and height are prominent at any single grade level. • Children begin to show specific athletic talents and interests. • Gender differences appear in children's preferences for various sports and physical activities. • Some neighborhoods do not have playgrounds or other safe play areas that foster gross motor skills. • Some children have delays in fine motor skills (e.g., their handwriting may be unusually uneven and irregular) as a result of neurological conditions or lack of opportunity to practice fine motor tasks. • Some children spend much of their nonschool time in sedentary activities, such as watching television or playing video games.	• Integrate physical movement into academic activities. • Provide daily opportunities for children to engage in self-organized play activities. • Teach children the basics of various sports and physical games, and encourage them to participate in organized sports programs. • Encourage practice of fine motor skills, but don't penalize children whose fine motor precision is delayed.

(continued)

DEVELOPMENTAL TRENDS

Physical Development at Different Age Levels (continued)

Age	What You Might Observe	Diversity	Implications
Early Adolescence (10–14) 	• Periods of rapid growth • Beginnings of puberty • Self-consciousness about physical changes • Some risk-taking behavior	• Onset of puberty may vary over a span of several years; puberty occurs earlier for girls than for boys. • Leisure activities may or may not include regular exercise. • Young teens differ considerably in strength and physical endurance, as well as in their specific talents for sports. Noticeable gender differences occur, with boys being faster, stronger, and more confident about their physical abilities than girls. • Peer groups may or may not encourage risky behavior.	• Be a role model by showing a commitment to physical fitness and good eating habits. • Provide privacy for changing clothes and showering during physical education classes. • Explain what sexual harassment is, and do not tolerate it, whether it appears in the form of jokes, teasing, or physical contact. • Encourage after-school clubs and sponsored leisure activities that help teenagers spend their time constructively. • Explain to adolescents that risky behaviors can cause them real harm.
Late Adolescence (14–18) 	• In girls, completion of growth spurt and attainment of mature height • In boys, ongoing increases in stature • Ravenous appetites • Increasing sexual activity • Some serious risky behaviors (e.g., drinking alcohol, taking illegal drugs, engaging in unprotected sexual contact, driving under the influence of drugs or alcohol), due in part to greater independence and acquisition of drivers' licenses	• Gender differences in physical abilities increase; boys are more active in organized sports programs. • Boys more actively seek sexual intimacy than girls do. • Some teens struggle with issues related to sexual orientation. • Some teens begin to taper off their earlier risky behaviors and make better decisions. • Eating disorders may appear, especially in girls. • Adolescents are less likely than younger children to get regular medical care.	• Make sure that adolescents know "the facts of life" about sexual intercourse and conception. • Encourage abstinence when adolescents are not sexually active. • When adolescents are sexually active and committed to remaining so, encourage them to use protective measures and to restrict the number of partners. • Encourage young people to form goals for the future (e.g., going to college, developing athletic skills) that motivate productive actions and discourage incompatible risky behaviors. • Develop and enforce policies related to sexual harassment.

Sources: Black, Hutcheson, Dubowitz, & Berenson-Howard, 1994; Bredekamp & Copple, 1997; W. Dennis, 1960; Eaton & Enns, 1986; C. P. Edwards, Gandini, & Giovaninni, 1996; Eisenberg, Martin, & Fabes, 1996; Gallahue & Ozmun, 1998; Gerber, 1998; Hopkins & Westra, 1998; Jacklin, 1989; M. C. Linn & Hyde, 1989; Logsdon, Alleman, Straits, Belka, & Clark, 1997; National Research Council, 1993a; Pellegrini & Smith, 1998; Sadker & Sadker, 1994; Sheridan, 1975; Simons-Morton, Taylor, Snider, Huang, & Fulton, 1994; J. M. Tanner, 1990; J. R. Thomas & French, 1985; Wigfield, Eccles, & Pintrich, 1996.

Nommsen-Rivers, 1995; Isolauri, Sutas, Salo, Isosonppi, & Kaila, 1998). Of course, some mothers cannot easily breastfeed, others do not want to, and still others (e.g., mothers who carry the human immunodeficiency virus) cannot do so safely, since it is possible to pass on infections in breast milk. As an alternative, families may select one of the iron-fortified formulas that have been commercially prepared to match the digestive abilities of infants (AAP Committee on Nutrition, 1998, 1999). These formulas tend to be derived from the proteins of cow's milk or soybeans, and they are carefully regulated so they fulfill infants' unique needs for calories, vitamins, and minerals. Other specialty formulas are available for infants with food allergies and intolerances. Professional caregivers generally try to support families' preferences but also suggest beneficial strategies, such as introducing nutritious soft cereals and fruits at around 4 to 6 months of age and avoiding hard foods that infants cannot easily swallow.

Unfortunately, practitioners often encounter children who are poorly fed, perhaps because parents have few financial resources, are homeless, are physically or mentally ill,

As children gain increasing independence from adults, they also gain more control over what they do and do not eat. Unfortunately, many adolescents choose relatively nonnutritious meals that are high in fat and sodium.

or simply do not have access to appropriate nutrition. Even in more fortunate financial circumstances, parents may rush to work in the morning and neglect to feed either themselves or their children. When children are underfed or given only nonnutritious foods, the outcomes can be quite serious. For example, anemia (iron deficiency), the most common nutritional deficiency in children worldwide, is associated with developmental delays and behavioral disturbances (Centers for Disease Control and Prevention, 1997).

As children make more of their own decisions about what and when to eat, their nutrition may deteriorate. For instance, in a large-scale study of American children, 24 percent of children aged 2 to 5 had a good diet and only 6 percent of adolescents aged 13 to 18 did (Federal Interagency Forum on Child and Family Statistics, 1999). Many children become less inclined to eat breakfast as they get older, and this practice may result in difficulty concentrating in school (Centers for Disease Control and Prevention, 2005c). Furthermore, the particular foods youngsters choose to eat may lack essential nutrients. In general, adolescents (especially boys) eat far too much "bad" stuff, such as high-fat and high-sodium foods, and far too little "good" stuff, such as fruits, vegetables, and whole grains (T. N. Robinson & Killen, 1995; Simons-Morton, Baranowski, Parcel, O'Hara, & Matteson, 1990; Subar et al., 1992). In fact, only about 20 percent of young people eat enough fruits and vegetables, and just 40 percent of children 2–17 years old meet the U.S Department of Agriculture's recommendations for fiber (found in fruits, vegetables, whole grains, and dried beans and peas) (Centers for Disease Control and Prevention, 2004, 2005c).

Part of the problem is that children don't understand how eating habits relate to health. At age 5, children know that some foods (e.g., fruits, vegetables, milk) are good for them but have no idea why (Carey, 1985). Figure 4-15 shows a school assignment in which 7-year-old Alex reveals his emerging understanding of food groups. The ability to categorize foods does not automatically produce insights about what each food type contributes to physiological processes, however. For instance, by ages 9 to 11, the vast majority of children still have not learned that the body breaks food down into the essential nutrients it needs to grow and thrive (Carey, 1985). Such ignorance can continue well into adolescence. For example, Jeanne's son Jeff, at 17, maintained that he could get through an entire day on a few donuts and several cans of cola.

Another factor contributing to poor diets is the eating habits children learn at home. Many parents and other family members do not have time to plan nutritious menus, shop for fresh produce, and prepare healthful meals. Educators cannot dictate the eating habits of children at home, but they can advocate for proper diets at school. In fact, many school leaders currently are examining meals served in school cafeterias and insisting that food-service contractors offer meals that are low in sodium and fat and high in fresh fruits and vegetables. Numerous educators are also restricting the contents of vending machines, eliminating carbonated beverages and junk food and replacing them with bottled water, juice, milk, and snacks that have reasonable nutritional value, such as yogurt and beef jerky (Centers for Disease Control and Prevention, 2005b).

Overweight youth.   About 16 percent of children and adolescents between 6 and 18 years are overweight (Centers for Disease Control and Prevention, 2005c; Federal Interagency Forum on Child and Family Statistics, 2004). For many overweight children, problems with weight begin in early childhood. Amazingly, 8.6 percent of American children as young as 2 to 6 years old are overweight (Centers for Disease Control and Prevention, 1997).

Some children are seriously overweight. Children are considered **obese** if their body weight exceeds their "ideal" weight (a figure that takes into account their age, gender, height, and body build) by 20 percent or more (Rallison, 1986). The prevalence of childhood obesity has increased over the last few decades (Gortmaker, Dietz, Sobol, & Wehler, 1987). As many as 15 percent of children and adolescents aged 6 to 19 are obese (American Obesity Association, 2005). Some obese children outgrow their baby fat, but others

obesity
Condition in which a person weighs at least 20 percent more than what is optimal for good health.

do not. Approximately 40 percent of obese 7-year-olds are obese as adults, and 70 percent of obese 10- to 13-year-olds become obese adults (L. H. Epstein, Wing, & Valoski, 1985). Childhood obesity is a concern because it may lead to serious health risks in adulthood, including diabetes, high blood pressure, high cholesterol, asthma, arthritis, and overall poor health (Centers for Disease Control and Prevention, 2005c; Kedesdy & Budd, 1998). It has social consequences as well. Peers may torment obese youngsters, calling them names and excluding them from enjoyable activities.

Obesity seems to have some genetic basis, but environmental factors, such as family eating patterns and restricted exercise, also play a role (Kedesdy & Budd, 1998). Fortunately, interventions, including dietary counseling, calorie restriction combined with increases in physical activity, and behavioral techniques (e.g., setting specific goals, monitoring progress toward goals, and recognizing and rewarding progress), are often effective (Kedesdy & Budd, 1998). Such interventions are more successful with obese children than with obese adults, possibly because children continue to grow in height whereas adults do not, and children have a briefer history of poor eating habits (cf. L. H. Epstein, 1990).

Eating disorders.   Whereas some young people eat too much, others eat too little and develop eating disorders that seriously threaten their health. People with **anorexia nervosa** eat little, if anything. In contrast, people with **bulimia** eat voraciously, especially fattening foods, and then purge their bodies by taking laxatives or forcing themselves to vomit. Adolescents in particular are at risk for developing eating disorders. In a recent national survey of students in grades 9 through 12, extreme weight control methods, such as not eating, taking diet pills, vomiting, and taking laxatives, were widespread (Centers for Disease Control and Prevention, 2004). For example, about 8 percent of the girls and 3 percent of the boys had vomited or taken laxatives during the last month in order to lose weight.

Individuals with eating disorders often have a distorted body image (believing they are "fat" even when they appear grossly thin to others), and they may exercise compulsively to lose additional weight (Attie, Brooks-Gunn, & Petersen, 1990; Kedesdy & Budd, 1998). In addition to jeopardizing physical health, eating disorders may slow down the bodily changes associated with puberty (Rallison, 1986).

Many experts believe that society's obsession with thinness is partly to blame for anorexia nervosa and bulimia (Attie et al., 1990; C. B. Fisher & Brone, 1991; Streigel-Moore, Silberstein, & Rodin, 1986). It is fashionable for girls and women in particular to be slender; thin is "in." Psychological factors also come into play. Individuals may use their thinness to gain attention, stifle their growing sexuality, or maintain a sense of control in the face of overbearing parents. In some cases inherited conditions predispose people to eating disorders (Attie & Brooks-Gunn, 1989; C. B. Fisher & Brone, 1991). Eating disorders that appear before puberty are associated with loneliness and depression (Alessi, Krahn, Brehm, & Wittekindt, 1989; Attie et al., 1990).

Occasionally school personnel and other adults unwittingly contribute to eating disorders. Consider the case of Heidi, a 16-year-old with bulimia (Pipher, 1994). Heidi was a gymnast whose coach weighed her weekly and insisted that she remain thin. One day, Heidi, the coach, and the other gymnasts went to a restaurant, where Heidi ate a double cheeseburger and onion rings. After eating, she regretted the meal, imagined the next day's weigh-in, went to the bathroom, and forced herself to vomit. Here's how she described the experience:

"It was harder than you would think. My body resisted, but I was able to do it. It was so gross that I thought, 'I'll never do that again,' but a week later I did. At first it was weekly, then twice a week. Now it's almost every day. My dentist said that acid is eating away the enamel of my teeth."

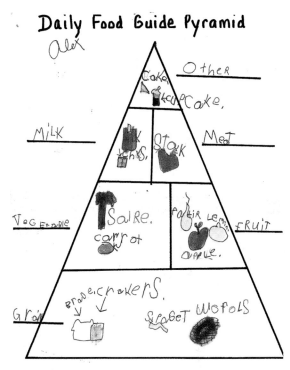

Figure 4-15

Children may learn about food groups before they understand why they should consume more of some foods and less of others. Alex (age 7) drew this picture of food groups for a lesson at school. He placed bread, crackers, spaghetti, and waffles in *grains,* the bottom layer of the food group; celery and carrots in *vegetables;* pears, lemons, and apples in *fruits;* milk and cheese in the *milk* group; steak in *meat;* and in the top, restricted portion of the food pyramid, cake and cupcakes (his favorites!).

Study Guide and Reader

Learn more about problems in body image and eating disorders in Supplementary Reading 4-1.

anorexia nervosa

Eating disorder in which a person eats little or nothing for weeks or months and seriously jeopardizes health.

bulimia

Eating disorder in which a person, in an attempt to be thin, eats a large amount of food and then purposefully purges it from the body by vomiting or taking laxatives.

Heidi began to cry. "I feel like such a hypocrite. People look at me and see a small, healthy person. I see a person who gorges on food and is totally out of control. You wouldn't believe how much I eat. I shove food into my mouth so fast that I choke. Afterwards, my stomach feels like it will burst." (p. 167)[2]

Anorexia nervosa and bulimia are not easily corrected simply by encouraging individuals to change their eating habits. Young people with these conditions frequently require intensive and long-term intervention by medical and psychological specialists (Linscheid & Fleming, 1995). Educators should be alert to common symptoms such as increasing thinness, complaints of being "too fat," and a lack of energy. When they suspect an eating disorder, they should consult with a counselor, school psychologist, or principal.

Promoting better eating habits.   We end this section with thoughts about what teachers and other practitioners can do to foster better nutrition and eating habits:

● *Provide between-meal snacks when children are hungry.* Children need periodic snacks as well as regular meals. Crackers, healthy cookies, and fruit slices can reinvigorate active children. Nutritious snacks are particularly important for children who are growing rapidly and for those who receive inadequate meals at home. In providing snacks, educators must be aware of food allergies, family food preferences, and possible limitations in chewing and swallowing hard substances.

● *Offer healthful foods at school.* Teachers and other school personnel can advocate for healthful foods and drinks on the cafeteria line and in the vending machines at school. When children are permitted to bring snacks, teachers can send home written recommendations for children and their families (e.g., carrot sticks, pretzels, and granola bars). As a fourth grader, Teresa's son Alex was advised that chocolate (a culinary passion for him) was *not* a good idea for a mid-morning snack. He began to bring other snacks instead, such as granola bars (and as you might suspect, he was happy to find granola bars sprinkled with chocolate chips).

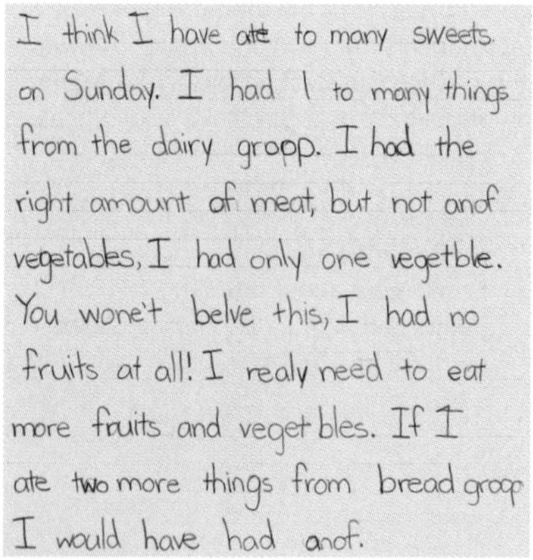

● *Regularly review the basics of good nutrition, and ask children to set goals for improving their eating habits.* Well planned school-based programs can be quite effective in changing children's eating habits and reducing their fat, sodium, and cholesterol intake (Bush et al., 1989; C. L. Perry et al., 1989; Resnicow, Cross, & Wynder, 1991). Such programs are more likely to be successful when they ask youngsters to set specific goals (e.g., reducing consumption of salty snacks), encourage them to chart their progress toward these goals, show them that they can stick with new eating patterns, and take cultural practices into account (Schinke, Moncher, & Singer, 1994; D. K. Wilson, Nicholson, & Krishnamoorthy, 1998).

A reasonable first step is to introduce children to basic food groups and ask them to evaluate their own diets based on recommended servings for each group. Figure 4-16 shows a third grader's analysis of her eating habits over the weekend.

● *Educate children about eating disorders.* Teachers and other professionals can take the glamour out of being excessively thin by educating youngsters about eating disorders. For instance, Teresa's son Connor first learned about anorexia nervosa when his third-grade teachers talked about eating disorders as part of a unit on the human body.

● *Follow up when you suspect serious nutritional problems.* Malnutrition can occur as a result of many factors. When low family income is the cause, practitioners can help families to obtain free or reduced-cost lunches at school. When parental neglect or mental illness is possibly involved, teachers may need to report their suspicions to principals, counselors, or school nurses to find the best approach for protecting vulnerable children.

● *Convey respect for the feelings of children and adolescents.* Children and adolescents who struggle with obesity or eating disorders are certainly as distressed as their peers—and often even more so—when others make unflattering comments about their appearance. Adults can insist that classrooms, child care centers, and after-school programs are "no-tease zones" regarding weight and other physical conditions.

I think I have ate to many sweets on Sunday. I had 1 to many things from the dairy groop. I had the right amount of meat, but not anof vegetabues, I had only one vegetble. You wone't belve this, I had no fruits at all! I realy need to eat more fruits and vegetbles. If I ate two more things from bread groop I would have had anof.

Figure 4-16

Charlotte (age 8) reflects on her eating habits over the weekend.

---

[2]From *Reviving Ophelia* by Mary Pipher, Ph.D., copyright 1994 by Mary Pipher, Ph.D. Used by permission of Putnam Berkeley, a division of Penguin Putnam Inc.

In addition, children who are eligible for free lunches at school may be embarrassed about their limited financial circumstances. In response, educators can minimize the extent to which these children feel that they stand out. For instance, a considerate staff member at one school took subsidized lunches and placed them in students' own lunchboxes, enabling children to avoid a potential stigma when eating with classmates from higher-income families (Mayall et al., 1996).

Physical Activity

Infants and toddlers are highly motivated to master new physical skills. As they wiggle, squirm, reach, and grasp, they exercise physical skills and also learn a lot about the world. For young children, physical activity is so enjoyable—and increasingly controllable—that they become even more active during early childhood. Activity level then decreases in middle childhood and adolescence, sometimes by as much as 50 percent (D. W. Campbell, Eaton, McKeen, & Mitsutake, 1999; Rowland, 1990).

Infants are highly motivated to master new physical skills and to explore their environment.

A common feature of physical activity in early and middle childhood is **rough-and-tumble play,** or good-natured "fighting." Children wrestle each other to the ground, push and shove, and roll around together. Perhaps in our evolutionary past, rough-and-tumble play prepared children for the fights they were likely to encounter as adolescents and adults (A. P. Humphreys & Smith, 1987). In today's world it seems to serve other purposes, such as providing breaks from demanding intellectual tasks and establishing who is dominant in a group of children (Bjorklund & Brown, 1998; Pellegrini & Smith, 1998). Whatever the functions of rough-and-tumble play, children often derive considerable pleasure from it, and when adults insist that they stop fighting, children are likely to maintain that they are just "playing" or "messing around."

In schools and child care centers, rough play is rarely considered acceptable, in large part because of the risk of injury. Yet children do need outlets for their seemingly boundless energy. Unfortunately, at most schools, opportunities for physical activity are quite limited. Even in physical education classes, children spend much of their time listening and watching demonstrations and waiting in line for their turn to try a new skill. Elementary students spend less than 10 percent of physical education class time in moderate or vigorous physical activity, and middle school students spend only 17 percent of class time in such activity (Simons-Morton, Taylor, Snider, & Huang, 1993; Simons-Morton et al., 1994).

As youngsters reach adolescence, exercise can help them maintain physical fitness and cope effectively with life's frustrations and stresses (J. D. Brown & Siegel, 1988). However, school tasks become increasingly sedentary in middle school and high school, and so adolescents are most likely to find opportunities for vigorous activity outside school walls (Pate, Long, & Heath, 1994). Many do not get the exercise they need. For instance, in a recent national survey with high school students, only 55 percent of girls and 70 percent of boys participated in vigorous exercise—physical activities that made them sweat or breathe hard (Centers for Disease Control and Prevention, 2004).

Throughout childhood, and especially in adolescence, boys tend to be more active than girls. Boys are more active on the playground and have more difficulty sitting still in class (Eaton & Enns, 1986; Sallis, 1993). During early and middle childhood, gender differences in the proficiency of motor skills are typically quite small and are probably due more to environmental factors (such as opportunities to practice specific skills) than hereditary influences (Gallahue & Ozmun, 1998; J. R. Thomas & French, 1985). After puberty, however, boys have a significant advantage over girls in many physical activities, especially those requiring height and muscular strength (Eisenberg et al., 1996; M. C. Linn & Hyde, 1989; J. R. Thomas & French, 1985).

Organized sports. In this chapter's opening case study, Tom and Phillip established a softball league that became a valuable forum for exercise. Organized sports offer the means for maintaining and enhancing physical strength, endurance, and agility. They also promote social development by fostering communication, cooperation, and leadership skills.

Organized sports can have a downside when adults promote unhealthy competition, put excessive pressure on children to perform well, and encourage athletically talented children at the expense of their less gifted teammates. Well-meaning parents and coaches can bolster children's athletic skills, but they can also rob children of their intrinsic enjoyment of sports (R. E. Smith & Smoll, 1997).

rough-and-tumble play
Playful physical "fighting" typical in early and middle childhood.

Regular recess and breaks for physical movement not only promote children's physical well-being but also lead to improved attention and concentration in more cognitively oriented activities. Art by Grace, age 11.

Generally speaking, boys are more confident than girls about their ability to play sports, and boys are almost twice as likely as girls to belong to an organized sports team (Sadker & Sadker, 1994; Wigfield et al., 1996). For boys especially, participation in sports is a prestigious activity, and talented athletes are usually quite popular with classmates (Sadker & Sadker, 1994).

Encouraging physical activity.   Researchers still have much to learn about how adults can best promote healthful physical activity in children and adolescents (W. C. Taylor, Beech, & Cummings, 1998). Preliminary information suggests that interventions with small groups and school-based programs can be effective in increasing youngsters' physical activity (W. C. Taylor et al., 1998). Here are some specific strategies educators can follow to promote physical activity:

● *Be "pro-ACTIVE."* Teachers can incorporate physical movement into many activities, particularly at the elementary school level. Regular breaks that include physical activity can actually increase children's attention to more sedentary, cognitively demanding tasks (Pellegrini & Bjorklund, 1997; Pellegrini & Bohn, 2005).

● *Provide appropriate equipment and guidance so children can safely engage in physical activity.* Open space, playground equipment, balls, and other athletic props encourage physical exercise. Equipment should be chosen carefully to allow children to experiment freely yet safely, ideally minimizing times when adults have to say no to certain activities (M. B. Bronson, 2000). Equipment and exercise facilities should also be properly designed and sized to fit children's body sizes and abilities (Frost, Shin, & Jacobs, 1998).

Expectations should not exceed the developmental abilities of children. For example, swimming "lessons" for infants are questionable because infants who paddle around independently can swallow a potentially fatal amount of water (AAP Committee on Sports Medicine and Fitness and Committee on Injury and Poison Prevention, 2000). Swimming lessons for babies can also create a false sense of security, leading families to believe erroneously that small children don't need supervision around water. Figure 4-17 shows a swim record given by an instructor to parents of a 3½-year-old child; notice that the expectations are realistic for many children of preschool age.

By the middle elementary years, children can organize many physical activities and games themselves. Coaches, teachers, recreation directors, and other practitioners should tolerate some bickering as children fuss over rules and in other ways learn to get along. Even so, adults may occasionally need to intervene to minimize physical aggression, remind children to follow safety rules, and integrate children who do not readily join in.

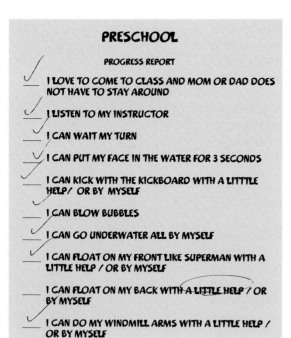

PRESCHOOL

PROGRESS REPORT

✓ I LOVE TO COME TO CLASS AND MOM OR DAD DOES NOT HAVE TO STAY AROUND

✓ I LISTEN TO MY INSTRUCTOR

✓ I CAN WAIT MY TURN

✓ I CAN PUT MY FACE IN THE WATER FOR 3 SECONDS

✓ I CAN KICK WITH THE KICKBOARD WITH A LITTLE HELP/ OR BY MYSELF

✓ I CAN BLOW BUBBLES

✓ I CAN GO UNDERWATER ALL BY MYSELF

✓ I CAN FLOAT ON MY FRONT LIKE SUPERMAN WITH A LITTLE HELP / OR BY MYSELF

✓ I CAN FLOAT ON MY BACK WITH A LITTLE HELP / OR BY MYSELF

✓ I CAN DO MY WINDMILL ARMS WITH A LITTLE HELP / OR BY MYSELF

Figure 4-17

Progress report for a 3½-year-old girl in a preschool swimming class. Standards appear developmentally appropriate for this age level. Depending on a child's cultural experiences and individual temperament, the first standard, not wanting parents poolside, might be a difficult one to meet.

● *Make exercise an enjoyable activity.* By the time they reach high school, many young people have had some unpleasant experiences with physical exercise and, as a result, associate exercise with discomfort, failure, embarrassment, competitiveness, boredom, injury, or regimentation (Rowland, 1990). Furthermore, many adolescents do not see physical exercise as a regular part of the daily lives of their parents or other family members. Youngsters are more likely to engage in a physical activity if they enjoy it and find it reasonably challenging (W. C. Taylor et al., 1998). They may have intrinsic interest in developing particular skills (e.g., in karate), take pleasure in physical self-expression (e.g., through dance), or appreciate the camaraderie they gain from team sports and other group activities.

● *Plan physical activities with diversity in mind.* Not everyone can be a quarterback, and not everyone likes football. In fact, it's probably a minority of youngsters who are drawn to competitive sports at all. But nearly all children and adolescents can find enjoyment in physical activity in some form. Offering a range of activities, from dance to volleyball, and modifying them for children with special needs can maximize the number of students who participate. For example, a child who is unusually short might look to such activities as soccer, cycling, or gymnastics that do not require exceptional height (Rudlin, 1993). Similarly, a girl in a wheelchair might go up to bat in a softball game and then have a classmate run the bases for her.

● *Focus on self-improvement rather than on comparison with peers.* Focusing on one's own improvement is, for most children, far more motivating than focusing on how well one's performance stacks up against that of peers. Focusing too much on comparison with others may lead children and adolescents to believe that physical ability is largely a matter of "natural talent," when in fact most physical skills depend on considerable practice (Ames, 1984; Proctor & Dutta, 1995).

One obvious way to promote self-improvement is to teach skills in progression, from simple to complex (Gallahue & Ozmun, 1998). For example, a preschool teacher might ask children to hop on one foot as they pretend to be the "hippity hop bunny." Once they have mastered that skill, the teacher can demonstrate more complex skills, such as galloping and skipping. Carefully sequenced lessons give children feelings of success and make physical activities enjoyable. Even in competitive sports, the emphasis should be more on how well children have "played the game"—on whether they worked well together, treated members of the opposing team with respect, and were all-around good sports—than on whether they won or lost (Gallahue & Ozmun, 1998).

Another tactic is to ask children to chart their progress on particular athletic skills and exercises (Centers for Disease Control and Prevention, 2002). In the following exercise, see how one teenage boy kept track of three activities over a 5-day period.

Adults can help adolescents to see how enjoyable and worthwhile exercise can be.

Connecting Concepts
Chapter 12 examines the benefits to children of keeping track of their own progress in academic and other domains.

INTERPRETING CHILDREN'S ARTIFACTS AND ACTIONS   How Many Can I Do Today?

Fifteen-year-old Connor kept a record of his performance on three activities: sit-ups, push-ups, and up-downs. As you examine his record, look for evidence that these activities were appropriate for him.

Your Name: Connor   Your Age: 15   Adult Supervising: MOM

Record of Physical Activity

	Activity 1: Sit ups		Activity 2: Push ups		Activity 3: up-downs	
Day 1-5: Exercise	How many did you do?	How did it feel?	How many did you do?	How did it feel?	How many did you do?	How did it feel?
1	37	Good	26	Hard to keep Back Straight	21	Hard to Keep Balance
2	22	Stomach Sore from yesterday. Sore	30	Easy	25	Harder
3	26	Stomach is better OK	22	Sore	23	Sore
4	15	Hurt really Bad!	20	Sore	25	Hard
5	30	tried to beat #1 But to sore to	31	Beat It	25	use a lot of energy
Day 6: Reflect	What parts of your body did you use? Stomach muscles!		What parts of your body did you use? Upper Body.		What parts of your body did you use? A Full body work out	
	What did you do to prevent injury? Stopped when it hurt.		What did you do to prevent injury? Tried to keep Balance		What did you do to prevent injury? Stopped when I needed to	

Record of 15-year-old Connor's physical activity.
Form adapted from *Planning for Physical Activity* (a BAM! Body and Mind Teacher's Corner resource) by the Centers for Disease Control and Prevention, Fall 2002.
Retrieved January 19, 2003, from http://www.bam.gov/teachers/activities/planning.htm

Connor reported that he enjoyed the challenge of trying to beat his own records. However, notice the drop in sit-ups on the second day, as compared to the first day. Connor complained that his stomach muscles hurt after his first attempts and only gradually recovered. The activities seem to be appropriate because he indicated on the form that he stopped when the exercises began to hurt, and an adult supervised his efforts.

● *Make sure that children don't overdo it.* Becoming excessively involved in exercise can present medical problems for children. The soft and spongy parts of bones in growing children are susceptible to injury from repeated use, and especially from excessive weight-bearing forces (R. H. Gross, 2004; Micheli, 1995). Weight-training machines are almost always designed for larger adult-size bodies, exacerbating children's chances for injury. Overuse injuries are also seen in distance running, distance swimming, and gymnastics (Gallahue & Ozmun, 1998). Furthermore, excessive concern about being successful in athletics can lead youngsters to make health-compromising choices (taking steroids, gaining or losing weight too quickly, etc.), as the earlier case of Heidi, the 16-year-old gymnast, illustrates. Medical experts recommend that children be discouraged from concentrating solely on one sport before adolescence, that they never be encouraged to "work through" injuries such as "shin splints" or stress fractures, and that they receive regular care from a physician who can monitor the health effects (such as unmet nutritional needs and delays in sexual maturation) of intensive training (AAP Committee on Sports Medicine and Fitness, 2000).

Rest and Sleep

Resting and sleeping are essential to growth and health. Sleep actually helps young people grow, because growth hormones are released at higher rates as children snooze. In addition to promoting growth, sleep may help the brain maintain normal functioning and promote its development (N. R. Carlson, 1999).

————— Connecting Concepts
Chapter 3 describes infants' states of arousal.

Infancy.   Newborn babies spend a long time sleeping, 16 to 18 hours a day according to some estimates (Wolff, 1966). Gradually, infants develop wake-sleep cycles that correspond to adults' day-night cycles (St. James-Roberts & Plewis, 1996). They begin to sleep through the night when they are ready to, depending in part on sleeping arrangements and other factors. Teresa recalls that her sons as infants were oblivious to a pediatrician's guideline that they should be able to sleep through the night by 10 weeks of age and 10 pounds in weight. Infants' sleeping habits are affected not only by individual differences but also by varying cultural practices, suggesting that there is no single "best" way to put babies to sleep (Shweder et al., 1998).

Although there may be no best way, there is definitely one *wrong* way to put babies to sleep. Medical experts advise caregivers *not* to place babies on their stomachs for sleeping. This position puts babies at risk for **sudden infant death syndrome (SIDS),** a death that occurs (usually during sleep) without an apparent medical cause. SIDS is a leading cause of death among infants from 1 month through 1 year in age (AAP Task Force on Infant Sleep Position and Sudden Infant Death Syndrome, 2000; CJ Foundation for SIDS, 2002). During the period that SIDS is most common (between 2 and 4 months), infants' brains are developing circuits that control arousal, breathing, heart rate, and other basic physiological functions. Small delays in neurological development may prove fatal if infants are under stress, for example if they have a respiratory infection (F. M. Sullivan & Barlow, 2001). Perhaps infants who die suddenly do not wake when breathing becomes difficult, or they may be unable to clear their throats, a reflex known to be less active when infants sleep on the stomach. It is quite possible that there are multiple causes of SIDS (Sullivan & Barlow, 2001).

sudden infant death syndrome (SIDS)
Death of an infant in the first year of life, typically during sleep, that cannot be explained by a thorough medical examination; it peaks between birth and 4 months.

Infant caregivers must be well aware of current recommendations not only for reducing the risk of SIDS but for preventing suffocation more generally. These include placing babies on their backs (face up) to sleep, refraining from smoking nearby, keeping babies at a comfortable temperature, using a firm mattress, and avoiding soft surfaces and loose bedding (AAP Task Force on Infant Sleep Position and SIDS, 2000; CJ Foundation for SIDS, 2002).

Recommendations regarding sleeping position do *not* rule out placing babies on their stomachs while awake. In fact, medical experts recommend that caregivers allow infants some supervised time on their stomachs. "Tummy time" can help infants exercise neck and upper body muscles. It can also relieve pressure on the back part of the head and thereby help it to grow normally (AAP Task Force on Infant Sleep Position and SIDS, 2000).

Early childhood through adolescence.   Time spent sleeping decreases steadily over the course of childhood and adolescence. Two-year-olds typically need 12 hours of sleep, 3- to 5-year-olds need 11 hours, 10- to 13-year-olds need 10 hours, and 14- to 18-year-olds need 8½ hours (Roffwarg, Muzio, & Dement, 1966). These figures, of course, are averages. The number of hours of sleep children of a particular age need to feel rested varies greatly.

Occasional sleep problems are normal occurrences in childhood. Nightmares are common between ages 3 and 6, and children may ask adults to help them battle the demons of the night that seem so real. More seriously, one-fourth of all children have chronic problems sleeping (Durand, 1998). Pronounced sleep disturbances (e.g., waking repeatedly during the night) may be due to serious health problems, excessive stress, use of street drugs, or side effects from prescribed medications. For instance, repeated nightmares are especially common among children who have been victims of abuse or other traumatic incidents (Durand, 1998; Vignau et al., 1997). Also, children with certain disabilities (e.g., cerebral palsy, severe visual impairment, autism, attention-deficit hyperactivity disorder) often have difficulty sleeping (Durand, 1998).

When children and adolescents get insufficient sleep, they are likely to be irritable and have difficulty with changes in routine. Any aggressive tendencies may worsen (Durand, 1998). In a study with preschool children, children's sleep patterns were associated with their adjustment in school (J. E. Bates, Viken, Alexander, Beyers, & Stockton, 2002). What seemed most detrimental was a failure to establish regular sleep habits, with frequent changes in bedtime and in the number of hours children slept. In another study, disrupted sleep in older children (7- to 12-year-olds) adversely affected performance in simple tasks that required concentration (Sadeh, Gruber, & Raviv, 2002).

Our own experience tells us that adolescents are less likely than younger children to get sufficient sleep. Although they require less sleep than they did in their earlier years, they are still growing rapidly, and their bodies need considerable time to rest (Mitru, Millrood, & Mateika, 2002). However, out-of-school obligations—extracurricular activities, part-time jobs, social engagements, and homework assignments—may keep teenagers up until the wee hours of the morning. In some cases adolescents make up for lost sleep at school. It's not uncommon for high school teachers (and college professors as well) to find students napping during class time—a practice hardly conducive to classroom learning!

Accommodating children's needs for rest and sleep.   Educators often have youngsters in their classrooms who do not sleep easily and soundly, including some who are truly sleep-deprived. With this in mind, we offer the following suggestions:

● *When appropriate, provide time for sleep during the day.* Infants and toddlers *must* sleep during the day. It is common practice, and most certainly good practice, to include an afternoon naptime in the schedule of preschoolers who attend child care or school in the afternoon. A few older children and adolescents—for instance, those with brain injuries or other chronic health conditions—may need an hour or two of sleep as well, perhaps on a couch in the school nurse's office (D. L. Jackson & Ormrod, 1998).

● *Include time for rest in the daily schedule.* Young children typically give up their afternoon nap sometime between ages 2 and 5, but for quite some time after that, they need to recharge their batteries with quiet and restful activities (e.g., listening to stories or music) in the afternoon. Children at any age level learn most effectively when they take an occasional, restful break from intense activity.

● *Watch for children who appear sleepy, irritable, or distractible.* Teachers and other practitioners can speak tactfully with family members when they think chronic fatigue is causing children to have trouble concentrating, maintaining reasonably good spirits, and resisting aggressive impulses.

BASIC DEVELOPMENTAL ISSUES   Physical Development

Issue	Physical Growth	Motor Skills	Physical Health and Activity
Nature and Nurture	Genetic instructions specify the particular changes that occur as bodies grow larger, and they also provide individual targets for mature height and weight. Yet normal progressions depend on healthful environments and experiences, such as adequate nutrition, movement, stimulation, affection, and protection from toxic substances.	Nature sets firm boundaries as to the motor skills a child can execute at any age range. For instance, a 6-month-old cannot run and a 10-year-old cannot clear 15 feet in the standing high jump. However, organized sports programs and other opportunities for regular exercise allow children to expand, refine, and polish their developing motor skills.	Nature influences children's activity level (e.g., 3-year-olds tend to be more physically active than 17-year-olds) and susceptibility to infection and illness. Children learn habits of eating and exercise from their parents and others in their community.
Universality and Diversity	Children tend to show similar sequences in physical development (e.g., in the emergence of sexual characteristics associated with puberty) across a wide range of environments and cultures. However, the rate of development differs considerably from one child to the next, with differences being partly the result of genetic diversity and partly the result of cultural and other variations in food, exercise, and so on.	Motor skills often develop in the same, universal sequence. For example, children can, on average, pick up crumbs at age 1, scribble with a crayon at age 2, and build a tower 10 blocks high at age 4 (Sheridan, 1975). Diversity is present in the specific ages at which children master motor skills, due in part to genetic differences and in part to variations in environmental support.	All children and adolescents need good nutrition, plenty of rest, and a moderate amount of physical activity to be healthy. Huge variation is present in the activity levels and eating habits of youngsters. In addition, children differ in their susceptibility to illness.
Qualitative and Quantitative Change	Many physical advancements are the result of a series of quantitative physiological changes (e.g., gradual increases in physical strength and dexterity). Qualitative changes are revealed in the new physical characteristics that emerge with puberty.	As a general rule, children must practice motor skills for a long time before they can execute them easily and gracefully, and a series of quantitative improvements allow more complex skills to emerge. Some motor skills, such as walking and throwing a ball, also change qualitatively with maturity and practice.	During the middle childhood years, children gradually gain control over what they eat and how they spend their leisure time (a quantitative change). Reorganization in thinking about safety and danger sometimes occurs in adolescence. Young people may shift from a preoccupation with safety to a thrill-seeking mind-set (a qualitative change).

● *Encourage youngsters to make steady progress on assignments so they don't wait to start a lengthy one the night before it is due.* At the high school level, adolescents may have several hours of homework each night. Add to this workload extracurricular events, social activities, family commitments, and a part-time job, and you have adolescents who are seriously overstretched. When an out-of-school task is lengthy and complex, as a major project or research paper might be, teachers can encourage regular progress by giving interim deadlines for various *parts* of the project.

● *Recognize that sleep problems can be a sign of illness or emotional stress.* Words of acknowledgement and kindness ("You look tired today, Darragh. Did you sleep all right last night?") may give children permission to share their troubles and, as a result, take the first step toward resolving them.

As you have seen, the advances that occur in physical development take many forms and depend on several distinct factors, including maturational processes, experience, and nutrition. In the Basic Developmental Issues table "Physical Development," we summarize how physical development shows nature and nurture, qualitative and quantitative change, and universality and diversity. Because good health comes not only from health-promoting habits but also from avoiding negative substances, we now focus on the important topic of health-compromising behaviors.

Health-Compromising Behaviors

Especially as they grow older and gain increasing independence from adult supervision, children and adolescents face many choices about how to spend their leisure time. They often make decisions without adequate knowledge about how certain behaviors are likely to affect their health and physical well-being. Here we look at three health-compromising behaviors: cigarette smoking, alcohol and drug use, and sexual activity.

Cigarette smoking.   An alarming percentage of young people smoke cigarettes (see Table 4-2). European American teens are at most risk (almost one-third of White teens smoke or use some other form of tobacco), although adolescents from other ethnic groups also smoke (Centers for Disease Control and Prevention, 2004). Unfortunately, many teens continue to use tobacco when they become adults.

Because the health risks are so well publicized, it is difficult for many adults to understand why adolescents choose to smoke. Undoubtedly, "image" is a factor. Teens may smoke cigarettes to look older, rebel, and affiliate with certain peer groups. Advertising plays a role as well. The majority of teen smokers make purchases from only a few cigarette brands, perhaps because of the youthful, fun-loving images that certain tobacco companies cultivate in the media. Regardless of the reasons adolescents begin smoking, those who continue to smoke may develop health problems that they might otherwise avoid.

Alcohol and drug use.   Alcohol and drugs are among the most serious threats to physical health that adolescents face today. Occasionally a single episode with a particular drug leads to permanent brain damage or even death. (Recall the mention in our introductory case study of three boys who died in an attempt to get "high.") Losing judgment under the influence of alcohol and drugs, adolescents may put themselves at risk in other ways, such as engaging in unprotected sexual activity. Those who are intravenous drug users may share needles, putting themselves at risk of contracting HIV/AIDS (described later in the chapter) and other diseases (Thiede, Romero, Bordelon, Hagan, & Murrill, 2001). Figure 4-18 lists substances used by some adolescents.

Given the hazards of alcohol and drugs, why do adolescents so frequently use them? For some, it's a matter of curiosity: After hearing about alcohol and drugs so often, not only from their peers but also from adults and the media, teens may simply want to experience the effects firsthand. Also, adolescence is a time when young people seek self-definition (Who shall I be? How does it feel to be a certain kind of me?), and experimentation with new roles and behaviors, including drug use, is common (Durkin, 1995; Shedler & Block, 1990).

Adult behaviors, too, influence substance abuse. Many adolescents who use drugs or alcohol have parents who have done little to promote adolescents' self-confidence, willingness to abide by society's rules, or ability to stay focused on long-term goals in the presence of immediate, conflicting interests (Botvin & Scheier, 1997; Jessor & Jessor, 1977). Furthermore, drug and alcohol use is more typical when people in the local community are relatively tolerant of such behavior (Poresky, Daniels, Mukerjee, & Gunnell, 1999).

Peer group norms and behaviors are yet another factor affecting substance abuse (J. A. Epstein, Botvin, Diaz, Toth, & Schinke, 1995; B. M. Segal & Stewart, 1996). To a great extent, use of alcohol and drugs is a social activity (Durkin, 1995), and teenagers may partake simply as a means of "fitting in." In other cases teens inclined to violate social norms may actively seek out peer groups similarly disposed to trouble (A. M. Ryan, 2000).

In North American society, many teenagers try alcohol or drugs at one time or another. If these substances give them pleasure, satisfy a desire for thrills, alleviate anxieties, or deaden feelings of pain and depression, teens may begin to use them regularly. Unfortunately, some eventually develop an **addiction** to, or biological and psychological dependence on, drugs or alcohol. They grow physiologically accustomed to using the substance and need increasing quantities to produce a desired effect. If they try to stop, addicts experience intense cravings and severe physiological and psychological reactions (Hussong, Chassin, & Hicks, 1999). Teenagers who are impulsive and disruptive, perform

Connecting Concepts ————
Adolescents' search for the "real me" is discussed in Chapter 12.

addiction
Physical and psychological dependence on a substance, such that increasing quantities must be taken to produce the desired effect and withdrawal produces adverse physiological and psychological effects.

Alcohol depresses the central nervous system and impairs coordination, perception, speech, and decision making; for instance, heavy drinkers may talk incoherently and walk with a staggering gait. Teens who drink excessively are more likely to have car accidents and commit rape.

Methylene dioxymethamphetamine (MDMA, or "ecstasy") gives its users a sense of euphoria and exuberance, sensory enhancements and distortions, and feelings of being at peace with the world and emotionally close to others (it is sometimes called the "hug drug"). However, the sense of euphoria often leads its users to ignore bodily distress signals, such as muscle cramping and dehydration; more serious effects include convulsions, impaired heart function, and occasionally death. It is often available at dance clubs ("raves"), where its effects are intensified by music and flashing lights.

Inhalants are attractive to many adolescents because they cause an immediate "high" and are readily available in the form of such household substances as glue, paint thinner, aerosol paint cans, and nail polish remover. These very dangerous substances can cause brain damage and death.

Marijuana delays reaction time, modifies perception, and instills a mild feeling of euphoria, but it can also heighten fears and anxieties. Teens who smoke marijuana may have red eyes, dry mouths, mood changes, loss of interest in former friends and hobbies, and impaired driving.

Methamphetamine ("speed") is a stimulant that gives users a sense of energy, alertness, confidence, and well-being.

Overdoses are possible, addiction frequently occurs, and changes to the brain and heart may occur. People who use speed regularly combat psychiatric problems, such as believing that "everyone is out to get me."

Cocaine (including *crack*, a particularly potent form) overstimulates neurons in the brain and gives users a brief sense of intense euphoria; it can also cause tremors, convulsions, vomiting, respiratory problems, and heart failure. Cocaine users may be energetic, talkative, argumentative, and boastful; long-time users may appear anxious and depressed. Crack users are prone to violence and crime.

Lysergic acid diethylamide (LSD) is a psychedelic drug that gives its users the sensation of being on an exotic journey, or "trip." It is usually swallowed as a chemical on a piece of paper or as a drop of liquid placed on the tongue. It can impair judgment, provoke anxiety, trigger underlying mental problems and, in the case of "bad trips," cause serious distress.

Prescription medications are used by a growing number of adolescents because of their physical effects on the body. Prescription painkillers, such as OxyContin and Vicodin, are potentially addictive narcotics that reduce sensations of discomfort and increase feelings of pleasure and well-being. Anabolic steroids are another type of medication for which there is an illicit market among teenagers. Some adolescents use nonprescribed doses of steroids to increase muscle development, but they also inadvertently experience unwanted side effects and serious health problems.

Figure 4-18

Effects and symptoms of adolescent substance abuse

Sources: G. R. Adams, Gullotta, & Markstrom-Adams, 1994; Atwater, 1996; DanceSafe, 2000a, 2000b; S. S. Feldman & Wood, 1994; L. D. Johnston, O'Malley, & Bachman, 2000; L. D. Johnston, O'Malley, Bachman, & Schulenberg, 2005; Kulberg, 1986; L. Smith, 1994; J. M. Taylor, 1994.

poorly in school, find little value in education, and have family members with mental illness or substance-abuse problems are especially at risk for becoming dependent on alcohol and drugs (A. L. Bryant & Zimmerman, 1999; Chassin, Curran, Hussong, & Colder, 1996; Flannery, Vazsonyi, Torquati, & Fridrich, 1994; Wills, McNamara, Vaccaro, & Hirky, 1996).

Sexual activity. Teenagers get mixed messages about the acceptability of sexual activity. Social and religious norms often advocate abstinence, yet television and films depict explicit sexual behavior. Peers may urge participation in sexual activity, and teens themselves experience sexual desires. Schools usually do little to help teens sort out these messages and feelings. Although they often include information about male and female anatomy, procreation, and birth in their health or biology curricula, they rarely offer much guidance about how to make sense of one's emerging sexuality or how to behave in romantic relationships (Pipher, 1994).

Many teenagers do become sexually active. On average, about 4 or 5 in every 10 high school students in the United States report having had sexual intercourse (Centers for Disease Control and Prevention, 2004; see Table 4-2). In many cases sexual activity is carried out in a high-risk fashion. For example, 1 in 4 sexually active teenagers reports having used no contraception during his or her first intercourse (Abma, Martinez, Mosher, & Dawson, 2004). More than 1 in 10 high school students have had four or more sexual partners (Centers for Disease Control and Prevention, 2004). From the perspective of physical health, early sexual activity is problematic because it can lead to sexually transmitted infection, pregnancy, or both.

Sexually transmitted infections (STIs).   Sexually transmitted infections vary in their severity. Syphilis, gonorrhea, and chlamydia can be treated with antibiotics, but teens do not always seek prompt medical help when they develop symptoms. Without treatment, serious problems can occur, including infertility and sterility, heart problems, and birth defects in future offspring. Genital herpes has no known cure, but medication can make its symptoms less severe.

Undoubtedly the most life-threatening STI is acquired immune deficiency syndrome (AIDS), a medical condition in which the immune system is weakened, permitting severe infections, pneumonias, and cancers to invade the body. AIDS is caused by a virus, human immunodeficiency virus (HIV), which can be transmitted through the exchange of bodily fluids, including blood and semen, during just a single contact. Half of all new HIV infections in the United States occur in young people between 13 and 24 years of age (Futterman, Chabon, & Hoffman, 2000). Sexual transmission is the primary means of HIV transmission during adolescence (AAP Committee on Pediatric AIDS and Committee on Adolescence, 2001).

The only good news about this deadly disease is that it has spurred public awareness campaigns that have led some groups to use safer sex practices, such as less intimate contact with new acquaintances and more frequent use of latex condoms (Catania et al., 1992; J. A. Kelly, 1995). Safe sexual practices are not universal, however. As noted earlier, many adolescents believe that they are invulnerable to normal dangers, and they may falsely believe that their partner is "safe" (J. D. Fisher & Fisher, 1992; J. A. Kelly, Murphy, Sikkema, & Kalichman, 1993; S. M. Moore & Rosenthal, 1991). Many young people (especially heterosexual youngsters) believe that only members of "high-risk groups" can spread HIV (Amirkhanian, Tiunov, & Kelly, 2001; L. S. Wagner, Carlin, Cauce, & Tenner, 2001). Young people with disabilities (e.g., youngsters with mental retardation) are at especially high risk for acquiring HIV because they tend to have limited knowledge of sex and contraception, are more likely to engage in high-risk sexual behavior, and are more vulnerable to sexual abuse by others (Mason & Jaskulski, 1994).

Pregnancy.   Despite popular beliefs to the contrary, teenage pregnancy rates are now lower than they were throughout much of the 20th century (Coley & Chase-Lansdale, 1998). Nevertheless, in the United States approximately 8 out of every 100 teenage girls between 15 and 19 years become pregnant each year (National Campaign to Prevent Teen Pregnancy, 2005a). Many of these pregnancies end in abortion or miscarriage, but others, of course, go to full term (Chase-Lansdale & Brooks-Gunn, 1994; Henshaw, 1997). In 2003 the birthrate for American girls aged 15 to 19 was 4.2 births per 100 girls (National Campaign to Prevent Teen Pregnancy, 2005b). Most girls who become teenage mothers come from low-income families that are often headed by single parents with low levels of education. Pregnant girls may believe that life offers them few if any educational or career options (Coley & Chase-Lansdale, 1998). Many look to sex and motherhood to supply the emotional closeness they don't find in other relationships (Coley & Chase-Lansdale, 1998). Some teenage girls believe that their families want them to have babies (Stack & Burton, 1993). Thirteen-year-old Janice, who is pregnant, explains:

> I'm not having this baby for myself. The baby's grandmother wants to be a "mama" and my great-grandfather wants to see a grandchild before he goes blind from sugar. I'm just giving them something to make them happy. (Stack & Burton, 1993, p. 161)

When young mothers have not fully matured physically, and especially when they do not have access to adequate nutrition and health care, they are at greater risk for medical complications during pregnancy and delivery. Problems arise after delivery as well. On average, teenage mothers have more health problems, are less likely to complete school or keep a steady job, live in greater poverty, and have more impaired psychological functioning than their peers (Coley & Chase-Lansdale, 1998; Upchurch & McCarthy, 1990).

Addressing health-compromising behaviors.   Schools and community organizations can do a great deal to address behaviors that put children and adolescents at physical risk. We offer a few thoughts on appropriate support:

Children and adolescents are less likely to engage in health-compromising behaviors when they have constructive alternatives for their leisure time.

● *Provide healthy options for free time.* Children and adolescents are less likely to engage in health-compromising behaviors when they have better things to do with their time. For instance, in our opening case study, a softball league afforded a productive form of recreation. Community leaders can advocate for after-school youth centers, community athletic leagues, and public service programs for young people. As an example, the *First Choice* program, which has been implemented at more than 50 sites in the United States, is targeted at students who are at risk of dropping out of school or getting in serious trouble with the law (Collingwood, 1997). The program focuses on fitness and prevention of drug use and violence. Elements that appear to contribute to its success include physical activity classes, a peer fitness leadership training program, parent support training, and coordination with mental health agencies and recreational facilities.

● *Ask adolescents to keep their long-term goals continually in mind.* Youngsters need personally relevant reasons to stay away from illegal substances and to make wise choices about sexual activity. Having firm long-term goals and optimism about the future can help them resist negative peer and media pressure.

● *Prevent problems.* It is much easier to teach children and adolescents to resist cigarettes, alcohol, and drugs than it is to treat dependence on these substances. One important approach is to establish a "no tolerance" policy on school grounds, in after-school programs, and in community centers. Youngsters are less likely to smoke, drink, or take drugs if they think they might be caught (Voelkl & Frone, 2000). On the other hand, scare tactics, simple lessons about the detrimental effects of tobacco and drugs, and attempts to enhance self-esteem are relatively ineffective. What seem to work better are programs that strive to change *behaviors* of children and adolescents. Such programs might ask young people to make a public commitment to stay clean and sober, teach them how to resist peer pressure, and give them strategies for solving social problems, curbing impulsive behaviors, and coping with anxiety (Botvin & Scheier, 1997; Forgey, Schinke, & Cole, 1997).

The effects of intervention programs diminish over time. Therefore, youngsters' resistance to tobacco, alcohol, and drugs needs to be established *before* they face temptation and then boosted *along the way* as they confront temptation and peer pressure. Ideally, prevention programs should take into consideration the cultures in which young people are growing up.

● *Implement programs that have demonstrated success with the population of young people with whom you work.* Obviously, the kinds of programs educators can implement are determined largely by their professional duties and the needs of youngsters with whom they work. One effective drug prevention program was developed by staff members in the Forest Hills School District in Cincinnati, Ohio, and implemented by coaches there (see Figure 4-19). It has since been tried elsewhere and featured by the U.S. Drug Enforcement Agency. This comprehensive program enlists participation by school coaches, principals, other school staff, team captains, parents, and the adolescents themselves (U.S. Drug Enforcement Administration, 2002). Coaches speak openly and often with athletes about substance use. Peer pressure is also used to discourage alcohol and drug use. When athletes do break the rules, they are given defined consequences, but in a way that communicates hope that they will try harder next time. The pledges for students to sign and a sample letter from coaches to parents about a drug or alcohol violation in Figure 4-19 will give you a flavor of the program.

● *Encourage adolescents to protect themselves.* Approaches to preventing adolescent pregnancy and transmission of STIs among adolescents are somewhat controversial. Many parents, for example, object to schools' advocacy of the use of condoms and other forms of "safe sex." (And, of course, at the present time condom use is no guarantee of protection against either infection or pregnancy.) Evidence suggests, however, that having condoms available in schools moderately increases condom use for those students who are already sexually active (and so may offer some protection against HIV infection) and does not necessarily increase rates of sexual activity (Guttmacher et al., 1997).

Student's Pledge	**Sample Letter from Coach to Parent about a Drug or Alcohol Violation**
As a participant in the _____ High School Athletic Program, I agree to abide by all training rules regarding the use of alcohol, tobacco, and other drugs. Chemical dependency is a progressive but treatable disease, characterized by continued drinking or other drug use in spite of recurring problems resulting from that use. Therefore, I accept and pledge to abide by the training rules listed in the athletic handbook and others established by my coach.	Dear Parent:

Student's Pledge

As a participant in the _____ High School Athletic Program, I agree to abide by all training rules regarding the use of alcohol, tobacco, and other drugs. Chemical dependency is a progressive but treatable disease, characterized by continued drinking or other drug use in spite of recurring problems resulting from that use. Therefore, I accept and pledge to abide by the training rules listed in the athletic handbook and others established by my coach.

To demonstrate my support, I pledge to:

1. Support my fellow students by setting an example and abstaining from the use of alcohol, tobacco, and other drugs.

2. Not enable my fellow students who use these substances. I will not cover up for them or lie for them if any rules are broken. I will hold my teammates responsible and accountable for their actions.

3. Seek information and assistance in dealing with my own or my fellow students' problems.

4. Be honest and open with my parents about my feelings, needs, and problems.

5. Be honest and open with my coach and other school personnel when the best interests of my fellow students are being jeopardized.

Student _____ Date _____

**PARENTS: We ask that you co-sign this pledge to show your support.

Sample Letter from Coach to Parent about a Drug or Alcohol Violation

Dear Parent:

Your daughter _____ has violated the _____ High School extra-curricular activities code of conduct. She voluntarily came forward on Thursday afternoon and admitted her violation of the code, specifically, drinking alcohol. The code is attached.

We respect her honesty and integrity and hope you do as well. Admitting a mistake such as this is very difficult for her. Not only does she have to deal with authorities such as us, she must face you, her parents, as well as her peers—which is probably the most difficult. We understand that no one is perfect and that people do make mistakes. Our code, and the resulting consequences of violating the code, is a nationally recognized model and is designed to encourage this type of self-reporting where the student can seek help and shelter from guilt without harsh initial penalties. She has admitted to making a mistake and is willing to work to alleviate the negative effects of the mistake.

As you can see in the enclosed code, we require that your daughter complete 10 hours of drug and alcohol in-service education and counseling. In addition, she must sit out 10 practice days of competition. She is still part of the team and must attend practices and competition; she is just not allowed to compete or participate in games for 10 days.

We hope you understand and support our effort to provide a healthy athletic program for the students. If you have any questions, please call either one of us at the high school.

Sincerely,

Figure 4-19

Team Up drug prevention materials from high school athletic coaches

From *Team Up: A Drug Prevention Manual for High School Athletic Coaches,* by the U.S. Drug Enforcement Administration, 2002, Washington, DC: U.S. Department of Justice Drug Enforcement Administration.

Use of condoms among sexually active adolescents is far from universal, in part because of interpersonal factors (e.g., reluctance to use a condom or to ask that a partner use one) and situational factors (e.g., impaired judgment due to alcohol or drugs) (Manderson, Tye, & Rajanayagam, 1997). Programs that encourage sexual abstinence are a less-controversial alternative and can be effective in the short run, although their effectiveness over the long is uncertain (McKay, 1993).

Overall, it appears that messages to adolescents need to be tailored to the current risks they face (Centers for Disease Control and Prevention, 2005a). For example, adolescents who have not yet been sexually intimate can be encouraged to remain abstinent. Those who are currently sexually active and choose to remain so may benefit from being advised to use protective measures and limit their numbers of partners.

● *Encourage adolescents with infections to abstain from sex or to use precautions.* Sadly, many adolescents already are infected with HIV or other STIs. Obviously, they need medical treatment and care. They must also be encouraged to stop the spread of the infection. When infected adolescents remain sexually active, precautions are essential. Unfortunately, this is a message these youngsters are not prepared to hear. For instance, although estimates vary, in the United States perhaps 40 to 70 percent of HIV-infected teenagers engage in unprotected sex (Belzer et al., 2001; Murphy et al., 2001).

The four areas we've discussed in this section—eating habits, physical activity, rest and sleep, and health-compromising behaviors—all have major effects on youngsters' physical development. In the Observation Guidelines table "Assessing Health Behaviors of Children and Adolescents," we identify characteristics and behaviors that bear on good and poor health. (Obviously, practitioners should not make inferences about health or provide treatment for which they are not trained.) We turn now to children who have special physical needs and the practices that can help them achieve their full potential.

OBSERVATION GUIDELINES	Assessing Health Behaviors of Children and Adolescents		
Characteristic	**Look For**	**Example**	**Implication**
Eating Habits	• Frequent consumption of junk food (candy, chips, carbonated beverages, etc.) • Unusual heaviness or thinness, especially if these characteristics become more pronounced over time • Lack of energy • Reluctance or inability to eat anything at lunchtime	Melissa is a good student, an avid runner, and a member of the student council. She is quite thin but wears baggy clothes that hide her figure, and she eats only a couple pieces of celery for lunch. Her teacher and principal suspect an eating disorder and meet with Melissa's parents to share their suspicion.	Observe what children eat and drink during the school day. Seek free or reduced-rate breakfasts and lunches for children from low-income families. Consult with specialists and parents when eating habits are seriously compromising children's health.
Physical Activity	• Improvements in speed, complexity, and agility of gross motor skills (e.g., running, skipping, jumping) • Restlessness and fidgeting (reflecting a need to release pent-up energy) • Bullying and other socially inappropriate behaviors during playtime • Cooperation and teamwork during organized sports activities • Overexertion (increasing the risk of injury)	During a class field day, a fifth-grade teacher organizes a soccer game with her students. Before beginning the game, she asks them to run up and down the field, individually accelerating and decelerating while kicking the ball. She then has them practice kicking the ball in ways that allow them to evade another player. Only after such practice does she begin the game (Logsdon et al., 1997).	Incorporate regular physical activity into the daily schedule. Choose tasks and activities that are enjoyable and allow for variability in skill levels. Make sure youngsters have mastered necessary prerequisite skills before teaching more complex skills.
Rest and Sleep	• Listlessness and lack of energy • Inability to concentrate • Irritability and overreaction to frustration • Sleeping in class	A teacher in an all-day kindergarten notices that some of his students become cranky during the last half-hour or so of school, and so he typically reserves this time for storybook reading and other quiet activities.	Provide regular opportunities for rest. When a youngster seems unusually tired day after day, talk with him or her (and perhaps with parents) about how lack of sleep can affect attention and behavior. Jointly seek possible solutions to the problem.
Health-Compromising Behaviors	• The smell of cigarettes on clothing • Physiological symptoms of drug use (e.g., red eyes, dilated pupils, tremors, convulsions, respiratory problems) • Distortions in speech (e.g., slurred pronunciation, fast talking, incoherence) • Poor coordination • Impaired decision making • Mood changes (e.g., anxiety, depression) • Dramatic changes in behavior (e.g., unusual energy, loss of interest in friends) • Signs of sensory distortions or hallucinations • Rapid weight gain and a tendency to wear increasingly baggy clothes (in girls who may be pregnant)	A school counselor notices a dramatic change in James's personality. Whereas he used to be energetic and eager to engage in activities, he now begins to "zone out" during counseling sessions. He slumps in his chair, looking down or staring out the window. His limited speech is unintelligible. The counselor suspects drug use and asks him about his demeanor. James denies that anything is wrong, so the counselor confronts him directly about her suspicions, refers him to a drug treatment center, and consults with her supervisor about additional steps to take.	Educate children and adolescents about the dangers of substance abuse and unprotected sexual activity; teach behaviors that will enable youngsters to resist temptations, tailoring instruction to their cultural backgrounds. Encourage participation in enjoyable and productive leisure activities that will enable young people to socialize with health-conscious peers. Consult with the counselor, psychologist, or social worker when you suspect that a youngster is pregnant or abusing drugs or alcohol.

Special Physical Needs

Some children have long-term physical conditions that affect school performance, friendships, and leisure activities. Here we look at chronic illness, serious injuries, and physical disabilities in children and adolescents. We then identify strategies for accommodating these conditions.

Chronic Illness

All children get sick now and then, but some have ongoing, long-term illnesses as a result of genetic legacies (e.g., cystic fibrosis), environmentally contracted illnesses (e.g., AIDS), or an interaction between the two (e.g., some forms of cancer). In the United States, two-thirds of chronically ill children and adolescents attend their neighborhood schools for part or all of the school day (R. Turnbull, Turnbull, Shank, & Smith, 2004). Some chronically sick youngsters show few if any symptoms at school, but others have noticeable limitations in strength, vitality, or alertness.

As children get older, they tend to learn how to manage their symptoms. For instance, most children with diabetes can monitor blood sugar levels and take appropriate follow-up action. Yet children sometimes forget to take prescribed medication, and they are not always completely reliable in assessing their status. For example, children with asthma may not realize when they are having a severe reaction (Bearison, 1998). Accordingly, educators may need to keep an eye on children's symptoms, seek family help when conditions deteriorate, and obtain medical assistance in cases of emergency.

Teachers can also help chronically ill children develop social skills and relationships. Some children who are ill feel so "different" that they are hesitant to approach peers (R. Turnbull et al., 2004). Furthermore, they may blame their physical condition (perhaps accurately, perhaps not) for any problems they have in social relationships (Kapp-Simon & Simon, 1991). As a result, they may become isolated, with few opportunities to develop interpersonal skills. Absences from school are common among chronically ill children because of hospitalization, doctor visits, and flare-ups of their condition.

Unfortunately, some healthy children actively avoid or reject peers who have serious illnesses. To some extent, such reactions reflect ignorance. Many children, young ones especially, have naive notions about illness. For instance, preschoolers may believe that people catch colds from the sun or get cancer by being in the same room as someone with cancer (Bibace & Walsh, 1981). As children get older, their conceptions of illness gradually become more complex, they grow more attuned to their own internal body cues, and they can differentiate among types of illness (Bearison, 1998).

Finally, teachers and other professionals may be able to help sick children address their mental health needs. Children with chronic illnesses are prone to anxiety and depression, and they may have trouble separating from their families when they arrive at school (Shapiro & Manz, 2004). Practitioners can offer sensitive support to struggling, sick children by giving them extra time to say goodbye to families in the morning and, when children seem especially sad or withdrawn, making appropriate referrals to counselors. Actual needs of chronically ill youngsters vary significantly by developmental level, as do the accommodations that best address their needs, as you can see in the Developmental Trends table "Chronic Health Conditions in Children and Adolescents."

Serious Injuries and Health Hazards

Injuries represent a major threat to children and adolescents. Every year, more young people die from accidental injuries than from cancer. In fact, for children and adolescents between 1 and 19 years of age, injuries are the leading cause of death (Deal, Gomby, Zippiroli, & Behrman, 2000). As children get older, their increasing independence makes them susceptible to certain kinds of injuries. For example, injuries from firearms and motor vehicle accidents increase throughout the adolescent years (Centers for Disease Control, 1996).

Although some injuries quickly heal, others have long-term effects that must be accommodated. For instance, each year in the United States, approximately 475,000 children aged birth to 14 sustain traumatic brain injuries from playground falls, bicycle mishaps, skiing accidents, and other traumatic events (Langlois, Rutland-Brown, & Thomas, 2004). Depending on location and severity, brain injuries can have temporary or lasting effects on physical functioning (e.g., seizures, headaches, poor motor coordination, fatigue) and psychological processes (e.g., impairments in perception, memory, concentration, language, decision making, or anger management). Thus assistance for children with brain injuries must be tailored to each individual's unique needs. For one child assistance may mean minimizing distractions in the classroom, for another it may mean allowing extra

DEVELOPMENTAL TRENDS

Chronic Health Conditions in Children and Adolescents

Age	What You Might Observe	Diversity	Implications
Infancy (Birth–2) 	• Irregular sleep and wake cycles • Trouble being soothed • Digestive problems • Breathing problems	• Some genetic conditions, such as cystic fibrosis, may be diagnosed during infancy. • Some infants initially show normal developmental advances, such as making eye contact, babbling, and smiling, and then slow down in their physical growth as illnesses progress.	• Provide emotional support to families when they struggle with the news that their children have a chronic or serious illness. • Determine the kinds of physical care that infants find comforting and soothing.
Early Childhood (2–6) 	• Eating problems • Regular medication schedule • Some toileting problems • Susceptibility to other illnesses, such as the common cold • Belief that "being bad" is the cause of getting sick	• Children may have special nutritional needs. • Some children may need to take dietary supplements. • Children may fail to take prescribed medicines when their parents believe medication is unnecessary or cannot afford to purchase it.	• Encourage children to adhere to diets advised by medical personnel. • Allow children to use the toilet whenever necessary. • Safeguard small children from environmental substances that exacerbate their symptoms (e.g., shield children with asthma from secondhand smoke).
Middle Childhood (6–10) 	• Frequent teasing and inappropriately personal questions from other children • Periods of health followed by flare-ups of the condition • Some efforts by the child to manage symptoms at school (e.g., a child with asthma monitors his or her lung function with a peak flow meter) • Greater than average number of absences from school	• The nature of the illness will affect the child's ability to manage it and other children's reactions to it. • Absences from school vary depending on the child's illness, frequency of flare-ups, and the family's anxiety about the illness. • Some children are hospitalized occasionally or regularly. • Many children show some adverse reactions to particular treatments (e.g., becoming nervous or jittery after taking asthma medicine).	• Ask families for ideas about how you can support the child's physical well-being. • Advise family members of significant changes in the child's symptoms and health-management routines. • Insist that other children show understanding of children with chronic illnesses while also preserving sick children's right to privacy. • When children are absent due to hospitalizations, keep in touch through phone calls, e-mail, and notes from classmates. • Allow children (particularly those with diabetes) to eat nutritious snacks regularly throughout the school day.
Early Adolescence (10–14) 	• Heightened concern about physical appearance • Some self-consciousness about being different due to illness • Growing knowledge of how to monitor health conditions • Transition from family care to self-care of chronic illnesses • Some feeling of being invincible to threats to health	• Some adolescents who were previously conscientious about their treatment regimens now become inconsistent in adhering to good medical routines. • Some adolescents with chronic health conditions may need accommodations at school or in particular classes, such as physical education. • Some adolescents show irregular physical features that reflect the progression of their disease (e.g., adolescents with cystic fibrosis may develop enlarged and rounded fingertips). • Adolescents with diabetes may have an increase in symptoms when they are growing rapidly.	• Offer reassurance that all adolescents are valued members of the class and school. • Advise adolescents about the supportive services of school counselors. • Continue to encourage contact with classmates and teachers when adolescents are hospitalized or recuperating at home. • Talk privately with adolescents about seeing the school nurse as needed (e.g., to take inhaled medications).

(continued)

Chronic Health Conditions in Children and Adolescents (continued)

Age	What You Might Observe	Diversity	Implications
Late Adolescence (14–18) 	• Growing knowledge of health conditions and their optimal management • Some difficulties in physical education classes (e.g., breathing problems, fatigue, and weakness with heat) • Some negative feelings when illness necessitates continued dependence on parents (e.g., being unable to obtain a driver's license because of a seizure disorder)	• Some adolescents who regularly miss school due to illness feel isolated and lonely at school. • Some adolescents face declining health as well as the prospect of dying in early adulthood. • Some adolescents manage their health conditions effectively and make plans that realistically address their conditions. • Adolescents who engage in risky behaviors or follow chaotic lifestyles may fail to take prescribed medicines. • Adolescents with some serious health conditions are vulnerable to depression.	• At the beginning of the year, develop a plan for dealing with school absences and making up missed academic work. • Consult with a school counselor to learn appropriate ways to help if an adolescent is terminally ill. • Encourage adolescents to assume increasing responsibility for management and treatment of their condition.

Sources: Annett, 2004; Lemanek, 2004; Quittner, Modi, & Roux, 2004; Shapiro & Manz, 2004; R. A. Smith, Martin, & Wolters, 2004; Wallander et al., 2004; J. Williams, 2004; Young-Hyman, 2004.

time to complete assignments, and for yet another it may mean adjusting expectations for performance, at least for the first few weeks or months (R. Turnbull et al., 2004).

Many childhood injuries are avoidable, of course, and schools can play a key role in educating children about preventive measures. Adults can teach children to use seat belts while riding in motor vehicles, wear helmets while biking and skating, and install smoke detectors at home (e.g., Klassen, MacKay, Moher, Walker, & Jones, 2000). Educators should also be aware of youngsters who are more vulnerable than others. For instance, children with Down syndrome are particularly susceptible to sprains and dislocations because of poor muscle tone and excessive mobility in their joints (P. L. Krebs, 1995).

Finally, educators can learn about hazardous substances that may be present in their community. For example, children can come into contact with lead from a variety of sources: in the womb if their mothers have lead in their bodies; in dirt, dust, or sand if it is present in their play areas; and in paint chips in older homes (Agency for Toxic Substances and Disease Registry, 1999). Depending on the amount of lead they ingest, children may develop blood anemia, kidney damage, colic, muscle weakness, and brain damage. Young children can be affected more seriously by exposure to some substances because their brains and bodies are growing quickly (Kroger, Schettler, & Weiss, 2005). Some health problems may disappear if toxic substances are removed, but there can be lasting declines in intelligence. Obviously, teachers and child care providers will want to do all they can to protect children from harmful substances at school and in other community settings.

Physical Disabilities

Children with physical disabilities, such as cerebral palsy, muscular dystrophy, congenital heart problems, or blindness, have the same basic needs as other children, namely a good diet, regular physical activity, and adequate rest and sleep. In addition, they may need specially adapted equipment (e.g., a wheelchair, a speech synthesizer, or a computer printer that produces Braille) and an environmental layout that permits safe movement. Some children with physical disabilities, especially those with multiple handicaps, have cognitive as well as physical impairments, but many others have intellectual capabilities similar to those of their nondisabled peers (R. Turnbull et al., 2004).

Because physical activity and exercise are central to health, fitness, and mood, adults must find ways to adapt physical activities for children with special physical needs. Basically, such adaptation involves giving as much support as necessary to enable successful movement. For example, a teacher can assist students who are visually impaired by guiding their bodies into correct positions and by inserting bells or other noisemakers inside playground balls (D. H. Craft, 1995). It is also essential to communicate reasonable expectations for success in physical skills.

Promoting Physical Well-Being in All Children

Children are diverse in the physical strengths on which they can build and in the weaknesses that delay their developmental progress. Those with chronic illnesses, serious injuries, and physical disabilities often require individualized accommodations so they can learn effectively and achieve optimal health. There are some general guidelines that apply to *all* children but especially to those with special physical needs:

Adults can help all children participate in physical activity to the fullest extent possible.

● *Help every child participate in all activities to the fullest extent possible.* In recent years children with special needs have increasingly joined their nondisabled peers in everyday school activities. In a practice called **inclusion,** children and adolescents with disabilities and other exceptional needs are educated for all or part of the school day within the general education classroom. Many educators have found that when they keep an open mind about what their students can accomplish, and especially when they think creatively about how they can adapt activities to the needs of individual students, almost all students can participate meaningfully in virtually all classroom activities (Logan, Alberto, Kana, & Waylor-Bowen, 1994; Salisbury, Evans, & Palombaro, 1997). For example, a workshop class can set up a buddy system so an adolescent with limited fine motor control can participate in wood carving. Likewise, a physical education class can make it possible for a child with cerebral palsy to get into and out of the swimming pool safely by using a ramp.

● *Seek guidance from parents or guardians and from specialized organizations.* Parents and guardians often have helpful suggestions about adjustments that would enable their children to participate more fully in school and extracurricular activities. And professional organizations—most are easily found on the Internet—offer a wealth of ideas about adapting instruction and equipment for children with chronic physical conditions and disabilities. Two broadly focused organizations are the American Alliance for Health, Physical Education, Recreation and Dance (with a subspecialty organization, Adapted Physical Activity Council) and the National Consortium for Physical Education and Recreation for Individuals with Disabilities. Specific disabilities are the focus of other organizations, such as the American Athletic Association for the Deaf, Wheelchair Sports USA, and the U.S. Association for Blind Athletes.

● *Encourage children to monitor their health conditions.* Children gradually learn to cope with the everyday demands of chronic health conditions, but they may need reminders to check on critical physiological states (e.g., to test blood glucose levels if diabetic), go to the nurse's office at appropriate times (e.g., to take medicines), and look after their recurring physical needs (e.g., to eat nutritious snacks and use the toilet regularly).

● *Encourage children and their families to follow protective measures.* Caregivers and teachers can teach young children how to handle emergencies, such as how and under what circumstances to make an emergency phone call (M. C. Roberts, Brown, Boles, & Mashunkashey, 2004). In elementary school, teachers can explain (and enforce) safety rules for climbing and using slides. Child care centers and schools can distribute safety brochures on topics such as seat belts, bicycle helmets, fire and smoke safety, and so forth. In addition, educators and other practitioners can encourage families to implement safety measures. For example, child care centers might distribute tokens for pizza or movies when children arrive at the center buckled up in a safety seat (M. C. Roberts et al., 2004).

inclusion
Practice of educating all students, including those with severe and multiple disabilities, in neighborhood schools and general education classrooms.

● *Design environments to minimize injuries.* Careful attention to classrooms, child care centers, and playgrounds can reduce children's injuries (M. C. Roberts et al., 2004). For example, an infant caregiver can make sure she purchases cribs with slats close together to prevent babies' heads from getting stuck between them. The caregiver can also examine toys for choking hazards, set the temperature of water heaters below what would cause scalding, and confirm that the refrigerator door will not lock from the inside (M. C. Roberts et al., 2004). An elementary school principal can ensure that a playground has no sharp edges and that the ground's surface is built with soft, cushioning materials. A high school safety team can ensure that smoke detectors are installed properly and regularly checked for working batteries.

● *Know what to do in a health emergency.* Some children have conditions that may occasionally result in life-threatening situations. For example, a child with diabetes may go into insulin shock, a child with asthma may have trouble breathing, or a child with epilepsy may have a seizure. When teachers learn that a child has a chronic health condition, they should consult with parents and school medical personnel to find out (ahead of time) how to respond to such emergencies.

● *Educate peers about a disability.* Peers are more likely to show kindness to a child with a physical or health impairment if they understand the nature of the disability. Peers should know, for example, that cancer cannot be spread through breathing the same air and that epileptic seizures, though frightening, are only temporary. Keep in mind, however, that a teacher should talk about a child's physical condition *only* when the child and his or her parents have given permission for the teacher to do so (Shapiro & Manz, 2004).

● *Keep lines of communication open with children who are hospitalized or homebound.* Sometimes children's physical conditions keep them hospital-bound or homebound for lengthy periods of time. In such circumstances, children can often participate in classroom lessons, activities, and social events by telephone or computer hook-up. When they cannot, they may be especially appreciative of correspondence and photographs from classmates and other important people in their lives.

● *Teach social skills to children who find themselves excluded from friendship groups.* Children with chronic health conditions often miss a lot of school. School absences and the stresses of the condition (and occasional overprotection from parents) can put a strain on children's peer relationships. Teachers can keep an eye out for the inclusion of chronically ill children, particularly when they reenter school after repeated or lengthy absences. Teachers can also coach children to try particular social skills, such as listening sympathetically, resolving conflicts, and gaining entry into an existing group of children (Kapp-Simon & Simon, 1991).

● *Address any problems in learning that accompany children's illnesses.* Depending on their health conditions and the medicines they take, children with chronic illnesses may develop learning disabilities, attention problems, and difficulty with learning in an organized and strategic manner (Shapiro & Manz, 2004). Teachers can address learning disabilities and teach children how to organize their work, set interim goals for complex assignments, and so forth.

Connecting Concepts ———
Chapter 7 presents strategies for working with children who have learning disabilities and other information processing difficulties.

● *Use precautions when caring for children who are sick or injured.* Educators can teach children basic safety precautions, such as sneezing into one's elbow, staying away from a friend's bloody knee, and washing hands after using the toilet. Adults also need to take precautions themselves. Appropriate barrier precautions for blood (e.g., latex gloves) are advisable when children skin their knees, have open wounds, and the like. Experts also direct caregivers to wash their hands after changing diapers and wiping noses (AAP Committee on Pediatric AIDS and Committee on Infectious Diseases, 1999).

The health of children and adolescents affects not only their physical development but also other domains. Children who are sick may have diminished energy for tackling challenging academic tasks. Moreover, health and fitness indirectly affect social development, as our final case study illustrates.

Case Study: Lucy

In her early teenage years, Lucy had leukemia. After a long hospitalization, plus radiation and chemotherapy treatments that resulted in temporary hair loss, Lucy's disease finally went into remission. Eventually, Lucy was healthy enough to return to school, but her life at school was quite different from what it once had been. Her therapist, Mary Pipher (1994), explains:

> It had been hard for her to return to school. Everyone was nice to Lucy, almost too nice, like she was a visitor from another planet, but she was left out of so many things. Her old friends had boyfriends and were involved in new activities. When she was in the hospital they would visit with flowers and magazines, but now that she was better, they didn't seem to know what to do with her.
>
> Frank [her father] said, "Lucy's personality has changed. She's quieter. She used to clown around. Now she is more serious. In some ways she seems older; she's suffered more and seen other children suffer. In some ways she's younger; she's missed a lot."
>
> Lucy had missed a great deal: ninth-grade graduation, the beginning of high school, parties, dating, sports, school activities and even puberty (the leukemia had delayed her periods and physical development). She had lots of catching up to do. She'd been so vulnerable that her parents were protective. They didn't want her to become tired, to eat junk food, to forget to take her medicines or to take any chances. Her immune system was weak and she could be in trouble with the slightest injury. Lucy, unlike most teens, didn't grimace at her parents' worries. She associated them with staying alive. (p. 84)[a]

- Lucy's illness delayed the onset of puberty. What other effects might her illness have had on her development relative to peers? As you ponder this question, consider her cognitive and social development as well as her physical development.
- In some respects, Lucy probably developed more quickly than most students her age. What particular strengths might Lucy have had as a result of having combated a life-threatening illness?
- As a teacher working with this age-group, what strategies might you use to ease Lucy's return to school?

Once you have answered these questions, compare your responses with those presented in the appendix.

[a]From *Reviving Ophelia* by Mary Pipher, Ph.D., copyright 1994 by Mary Pipher, Ph.D. Used by permission of Putnam Berkeley, a division of Penguin Putnam Inc.

Summary

Principles of Physical Development

Different systems of the body grow at different rates. Over time, physiological functioning becomes both increasingly differentiated (e.g., different cells take on different roles) and increasingly integrated (e.g., different body parts work more closely together). Children's bodies seem to aim for certain targets in physical growth, even if growth is temporarily deterred by illness or inadequate nutrition.

Development of the Brain

The human brain is a complex organ that regulates basic physiological functions (e.g., heart rate), sensations of pleasure and pain, motor skills and coordination, emotional responses, and intellectual processes. The brain consists of millions of interconnected circuits of neurons that make up the distinct parts of the brain. During prenatal development, neurons are created and these cells migrate to places where they will do their work. During infancy, the brain creates many connections among neurons; areas of the brain that support perceptual learning show particularly rapid growth. During early and middle childhood, the brain protects those connections that are used most often and lets the others die out; particular refinements also solidify language skills and higher learning functions. During adolescence, the brain grows in areas that play key roles in forethought and judgment.

Physical Development Across Childhood

Predictable changes in physical functioning occur during childhood and adolescence. During infancy, survival mechanisms (e.g., reflexes) are implemented, crying time peaks and then decreases, feeding moves from milk to a combination of milk and soft solids, and motor skills permit exploration. Early childhood is marked by vigorous physical activity and the acquisition of new motor skills. Middle childhood is a time of consolidation, when growth rate slows down and children put motor skills to purposeful use. Puberty begins in early adolescence and extends over several years' time. Adult height and sexual maturation are attained in late adolescence.

Physical Well-Being

Health depends on several factors, including eating habits, physical activity, and rest and sleep. Some children and adolescents show patterns of behavior (e.g., eating disorders, overreliance on sedentary activities, overcommitments that result in insufficient sleep) that may jeopardize their physical well-being. In adolescence, additional health-compromising behaviors may emerge as youths struggle with such temptations as cigarette smoking, alcohol, drugs, and unprotected sexual activity.

Special Physical Needs

Youngsters with chronic illness, serious injuries, and physical disabilities often benefit from modifications in instruction, equipment, and their physical environment. Ultimately, educators should strive to make experiences as "normal" as possible for these children.

Applying Concepts in Child Development

In this chapter you learned about many aspects of physical development in children and adolescents. The following table describes issues related to the physical well-being of youngsters at five different age levels. For each of these issues, the table identifies one or more concepts related to physical development, offers an implication for working with children of that age-group, or both. Apply what you've learned about brain development, typical physical changes, and factors affecting children's physical well-being to fill in the empty cells in the table. When you're done, compare your responses with those in Table 4-1 in the *Study Guide and Reader*.

APPLYING CONCEPTS IN CHILD DEVELOPMENT	Supporting Physical Development		
Age	**A Youngster's Experience**	**Developmental Concepts** *Factors Affecting Physical Well-Being*	**Implications** *Supporting Physical Well-Being*
Infancy (Birth–2)	Thirteen-month old Naima appears to her caregiver to be a healthy, spirited child. The caregiver is surprised when Naima's parents point out that Naima occasionally seems to struggle in her motor development, as when she recently began to walk but then returned to crawling for a few weeks. They wonder if they should take her to the doctor.	Naima is showing sequences of progress and typical regressions in her motor skills. Naima's progress and occasional regressions suggest a *dynamic system* at work. Children act on the world, discover that their bodies permit new skills, make preliminary progress in mastering these skills, and often show declines in proficiency as they figure out how to deal with one or more changing factors (e.g., increases in muscle tone).	Reassure parents that infants make substantial progress in motor skills over brief periods. Explain that some retreats are common and usually reflect the child's adjustment to a new factor, such as weight gain, a temporary illness, or a change in muscle tone. Of course, Naima's parents may be noticing something that is unusual about their daughter, so be sure to encourage them to follow up with their doctor if they are worried about her.
Early Childhood (2–6)	In an orientation meeting for families at a child care center, one father asks how the center will help his 3-year-old son Jules develop a "strong brain." Jules's father brings in a newspaper article about the importance of providing enriching educational experiences for young children.		Reassure parents that you are eager to support children in all aspects of their development, including their brain development. Further explain that a well-rounded preschool environment with lots of hands-on experiences, opportunities for pretend play, stories and puzzles, stable relationships with teachers and peers, healthful snacks, and outdoor play will offer ample enrichment for children's growing brains.

(continued)

APPLYING CONCEPTS IN CHILD DEVELOPMENT

Supporting Physical Development (continued)

Age	A Youngster's Experience	Developmental Concepts *Factors Affecting Physical Well-Being*	Implications *Supporting Physical Well-Being*
Middle Childhood **(6–10)** 	Seven-year-old Roy is overweight. His doctor recently gave his mother a brochure on obesity in children. It seems that a range of factors contribute to Roy's obesity—his parents are both overweight, Roy has developed a preference for fatty foods, and he spends most of his free time at home watching television and playing video games. His parents ask Roy's teacher, Mr. McGinnis, how much exercise Roy gets at school and wonder if a lack of physical activity is the problem. They also make a passing comment that it may simply be Roy's destiny to be a "big, chunky guy."	*Obesity* is a serious health risk in childhood. It predicts health problems in adulthood. Being obese as a child is predicted by familial weight problems, poor eating habits, and restricted physical activity. Because Roy is only 7 years old, he has a good chance of changing his eating habits and increasing his physical activity levels.	
Early Adolescence **(10–14)** 	Thirteen-year old Helen used to be known as the school "brainiac," but recently she has *not* been acting intelligently. In the last year, Helen has matured physically and now appears several years older than most of her peers. In fact, Helen has been spending her weekend nights doing dangerous things with friends, such as drinking alcohol, driving with older boys she barely knows, and stealing cosmetics at a local store. When her parents recently confronted her with their suspicions, Helen replied that they should not worry.	It is common for young adolescents to engage in some *risky behaviors*. Helen may be an *early-maturing adolescent* who is allowing herself to be ushered into high-risk behaviors by older teenagers. Helen also seems to be affected by the *personal fable* because she discounts any potential harm that could come to her as a result of her risky actions.	
Late Adolescence **(14–18)** 	Ms. Comstock thinks about the high school seniors she has in her literature courses. Her students appear to be attractive, bright young adults. But from private conversations with them, Ms. Comstock knows that these teenagers can be introspective and thoughtful one moment yet rash and impulsive the next. And although they certainly seem smart enough to stay on top of their homework assignments, they nevertheless frequently forget to complete projects on time. For a second, she would love to see inside their brains. She wonders: Do they have the bodies of adults and the brains of children?	Brains continue to develop rapidly and systematically during adolescence and, in fact, into the adult years. *Brain development* during adolescence builds on the many changes of childhood. It refines the front part of the cortex, which supports planning, emotional control, reasoning, and judgment.	Continue to communicate expectations to adolescents that they have the ability to act thoughtfully and appropriately, but also give them the scaffolding they need to be successful. For example, because it is difficult for them to keep long-term goals in mind, ask youngsters to turn in *parts* of assignments before handing in the final projects.

Key Concepts

differentiation (p. 99)
integration (p. 99)
neuron (p. 100)
axon (p. 100)
dendrite (p. 101)
synapse (p. 101)
glial cell (p. 101)
hindbrain (p. 101)
midbrain (p. 101)

forebrain (p. 101)
cortex (p. 102)
executive functions (p. 102)
left hemisphere (p. 103)
right hemisphere (p. 103)
schizophrenia (p. 103)
synaptogenesis (p. 105)
synaptic pruning (p. 105)
myelination (p. 105)

colic (p. 111)
cephalocaudal trend (p. 111)
proximodistal trend (p. 111)
gross motor skills (p. 111)
fine motor skills (p. 111)
puberty (p. 114)
growth spurt (p. 114)
menarche (p. 115)
spermarche (p. 115)

personal fable (p. 117)
obesity (p. 122)
anorexia nervosa (p. 123)
bulimia (p. 123)
rough-and-tumble play (p. 125)
sudden infant death syndrome
    (SIDS) (p. 128)
addiction (p. 131)
inclusion (p. 140)

Companion
Website

Now go to our Companion Website at www.prenhall.com/mcdevitt to assess your understanding of chapter content with a Practice Quiz, apply what you've learned in Essay Questions, and broaden your knowledge with links to related Developmental Psychology Web sites.

Family, Culture, and Community

chapter 5

Case Study: Cedric and Barbara Jennings

Case Study: Cedric and Barbara Jennings

Cradles of Child Development

Family Structures

Family Processes

Life in the Community for Children and Families

Case Study: Four-Year-Old Sons

Summary

Applying Concepts in Child Development

Cedric Lavar Jennings is a senior at Ballou High School, an inner-city school in Washington, D.C. Throughout his school career his grades have been exemplary, and he has recently learned that he has been accepted at Brown University for the following year.

Cedric and his mother, Barbara, have been a family of two since Cedric's birth and are very close. They live in a lower-income neighborhood, where crack cocaine dealers regularly do business and gunshots are frequent background noise at night. Despite such an environment, Cedric has flourished, in large part because of his mother's support. Not only is he a high achiever, but he is also a very likeable young man with a strong moral code.

One night, Barbara and Cedric attend the Parent-Teacher-Student Association meeting at Ballou. After the meeting they go to Cedric's homeroom, where the homeroom teacher is handing out first-semester grade reports. Cedric is appalled to discover a B on his grade sheet. In *A Hope in the Unseen,* Suskind (1998) reports what happens next:

"I got a B in physics! I can't believe it."

He begins ranting about the cheating in his class, about how he thinks a lot of other kids cheated. . . . Barbara remembers that he mentioned something about this a week ago—but she dismissed the whole matter.

Squeezed into a school desk next to him, she wants to tell Cedric that it doesn't matter. None of it. Some small hubbub about cheating and grades is meaningless now that he's been admitted to Brown, the top college acceptance of any Ballou student in years.

But, of course, he knows all that, too. And the more dismissive her look, the more rabid he becomes. Then she gets it: it's about her watching over him, defending him, always being there. ". . . I mean, what are *we* going to do?!" he shouts at the end of his furious soliloquy about what's right and fair and just.

She's up. "Well, Lavar [she usually calls him by his middle name], we'll just have to go have a word with that teacher." A second later, they're stomping together through the halls, headed for the physics classroom of an unsuspecting Mr. Momen. They find that he is alone. He turns and offers greetings as they enter, but Cedric launches right in—the whole diatribe, offered with added verve from his rehearsal with his mom.

Mr. Momen, a wry, sometimes sarcastic man in his mid-forties, mournfully shakes his head, a helmet of gray-flecked hair. "Cedric, you got a B for the marking period," he says in precise, accented English. "The test for you is irrefutable. The curve says yours is a B, and that, for you, is a B for the marking period. So, okay. That's it, yes?"

"But kids are cheating! You leave the room and they open the book. Lots of them. You don't know what goes on. You shouldn't leave the room, that's when it starts. It ends up that I get penalized 'cause I won't cheat."

"Cedric, stop. I can't, myself, accuse all of them of cheating," says Mr. Momen, shrugging.

Barbara watches the give-and-take, realizing that the teacher has artfully shoved Cedric into a rhetorical corner by placing her son's single voice against the silent majority—his word against theirs.

Years of practice at this have taught her much: choose your words meticulously and then let them rumble up from some deep furnace of conviction. "My son doesn't lie," she says, like an oracle, "not about something like this."

The silent majority vanishes. She stands, straight and motionless, a block of granite. Momen looks back at her, eye to eye. Soon, the silence becomes unbearable. He's forced to move. "I guess he could take a retest I make for him," he says haltingly. "It will be a hard test, though, that I will make for you, Cedric."

(continued)

"Fine," says Barbara, closing the deal. "Thank you, Mr. Momen. We can go now," she says. Once they're in the hallway, she whispers to Cedric, "You *will* be getting an A on that test, Lavar. You understand?" She doesn't expect an answer.

After a week of ferocious study, Cedric does get his A on the special test—scoring 100— and an A for the marking period. He brings home the paper and lays it on the dining room table, like a prize, a trophy.

Barbara looks at it for a moment. "On the next stop, you know you'll be on your own. I won't be there to come to the rescue," she says, feeling as though a clause of their partnership has expired.

"Well, then," he says a little tersely, tapping the paper once with his index finger, "I guess this paper is sort of your diploma." (pp. 113–115)[a]

[a]From *A Hope in the Unseen,* by Ron Suskind, copyright © 1998 by Ron Suskind. Used by permission of Broadway Books, a division of Random House, Inc.

Cedric knew that his mother would back him up when he needed her. Like Cedric, most children can depend on their families for food and shelter, love and reassurance, and guidance and advocacy. As children's first teachers, families instruct children in how to relate to other people and achieve such cultural ideals as trying hard in school, being truthful, and fighting against oppression. Of course, children grow up not only in a family but also in society. Ideally, the family's principles are validated when children participate in productive cultural activities and community events.

In this chapter you will learn how children's psychological growth is nurtured in three important contexts: family, culture, and community. You will also learn that teachers and other school personnel can exert a positive impact on children by taking to heart the lessons children learn at home and in society, and by forging effective partnerships with children's parents and guardians.

Cradles of Child Development

Connecting Concepts
You will learn about other contexts of development—namely, peers, schools, child care settings, and the media—in Chapter 14.

A happy and healthy childhood largely depends on a loving relationship with families, regular exposure to the traditions of a culture, and participation in a responsive community. Let's look more closely at these three contexts and their primary contributions to children's development.

Family

Every child needs at least one adult who passionately promotes his or her health, education, and welfare, preferably for life (Bronfenbrenner, 2001). Typically, a child's *family* has this dedication.

A **family** consists of two or more people who live together and are related by enduring factors such as birth, marriage, adoption, or long-term mutual commitment. Families with children usually have one or two adults (most often the parents) who serve as heads of the family and care for the children for many years. *Heads of family* have authority over children and are responsible for children's welfare.

Obviously, families do many things for their children. Biological parents give children the genetic legacy that will guide their physical development throughout life. After birth, parents provide hands-on care. If this care is reasonably sensitive, children form close bonds with their caregivers, and these bonds energize children to explore the world (Ainsworth, 1963, 1973; Bowlby, 1969/1982).

As youngsters grow, their families continue to feed and clothe them. But just as importantly, family members are key figures in the **socialization** of youngsters. That is, by encouraging certain behaviors and beliefs (and *dis*couraging others), parents and

family
Two or more people who live together and are related by enduring factors such as birth, marriage, adoption, or long-term mutual commitment.

socialization
Systematic efforts by other people and by institutions to prepare youngsters to act in ways deemed by society to be appropriate and responsible.

other heads of family help children act and think in ways their society deems appropriate and responsible. Heads of family use a variety of means to socialize children (Damon, 1988). For instance, they teach and model proper ways of behaving in various situations. They reward certain behaviors and punish others. They arrange for children to gain certain kinds of experiences and steer them clear of less productive ones. And by nurturing close emotional bonds with children, they enhance children's motivation to comply with rules and requests.

Culture

Culture refers to the characteristic *behaviors* and *beliefs* of a specific, and usually long-standing, social group. Cultural behaviors include the everyday routines that families and children carry out as they maintain households, work and play, use tools, and relate to one another. Cultural behaviors also include the periodic rituals, such as worshipping and celebrating holidays, that families perform together.

Parents and other family members play a major role in children's socialization.

The effects of culture can be observed by comparing the customs of people in distinct groups or separate regions. For instance, cultural groups exhibit differences in meal practices (what, how, and with whom they eat), division of responsibility in families (who obtains food, prepares dinner, disciplines the children, etc.), and social practices (how and with whom children play, how marital partners are selected). Cultural groups also show different communication styles. For example, in some cultures children are expected to take a turn in adults' conversations, and in other cultures children are shooed away to the sidelines of adults' discussions, where children are allowed to play among themselves or eavesdrop on the adults (M. Cole, 2006; Rogoff, 2003).

Belief systems, although not as obvious as behaviors, are an equally important part of a group's cultural heritage. Consider the following ideas:

- Babies are innocent at birth.
- As children grow, they should become increasingly self-reliant and independent.
- If people want something, they should say so.
- Competition among individuals is healthy and productive.

Beliefs like these reflect some of the core ideas of mainstream Western culture (Hollins, 1996; Shweder et al., 1998), but they are far from universal. For example, adults in some cultural groups think that infants are not innocent but, rather, that they display inappropriate impulses that must be eradicated (Shweder et al., 1998). And whereas some cultural groups value competition over cooperation, many others take the opposite position (Dien, 1998; Hollins, 1996; Webb & Palincsar, 1996).

The two bookends of culture—behaviors and beliefs—are closely related. Common behavioral practices are grounded in beliefs about what is true, healthy, appropriate, and rational (Shweder et al., 1998). Adults within a culture, therefore, can justify their typical ways of raising children by asserting familiar values. As one example, consider how families defend their sleeping practices. Many European American parents have their children sleep alone in their own rooms or beds, and they explain that the practice assures nighttime privacy for adults and fosters independence in children. Other parents, particularly in certain other cultures, sleep beside their children and say that co-sleeping arrangements foster a sense of closeness and solidarity among family members (Shweder et al., 1998).

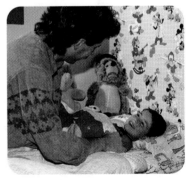

Cultures differ in their practices and beliefs related to children's sleeping.

Ultimately, by growing up in a *culture,* children experience human life as predictable and meaningful. Culture also adds an intellectual dimension to life by exposing children to the accumulated wisdom, advanced discoveries, and creative works of society.

Community

A child's **community** includes the local neighborhood and the surrounding vicinity. It gives the child and family a bridge to the outside world. The community is significant

culture
Behaviors and belief systems that characterize a social group and provide a framework for how group members decide what is normal and appropriate.

community
The local neighborhood and surrounding vicinity of a child and his or her family.

Listen to Brendan and Robin talk about recreational opportunities and friendly neighbors in the "Neighborhood" clips for early and late adolescence on Observation CD 2.

developmentally because it supplies playmates and outlets for children's recreation. Particularly when they are young, children tend to make friends with other youngsters who play with them in the neighborhood or join them at a local school, sports team, or other nearby institution. As they grow older, youngsters generally decide how to spend their spare time based on opportunities that are convenient and affordable. You can see how important recreational opportunities are to youngsters by listening to 14-year-old Brendan in the "Neighborhood: Early Adolescence" video clip on Observation CD 2. Here's how Brendan describes his neighborhood:

There's a lot of people. Nice people. And there's fun stuff to do around here. . . . We play football or sports in the backyards, and we have playgrounds and a basketball court.

Communities also affect children indirectly in that they fortify parents with social networks and services. For example, parents may have their own friends who occasionally step in to supervise children's activities, model and offer advice on effective parenting strategies, and provide the emotional support that parents need, especially in times of trouble (Bronfenbrenner, 2005; Cochran, 1993; McLoyd, 1990; Simons, Lorenz, Wu, & Conger, 1993). Many institutions within the community—health clinics, social service agencies, homeless shelters, houses of worship, and so on—also back up families' efforts to keep children on productive pathways.

Finally, communities tell children what society expects them to become as adults. The activities in which local adults engage—whether productive employment and community volunteerism, on the one hand, or drug trafficking and gang affiliation, on the other—convey to youngsters what behaviors are typical, if not desirable. For example, when most adults in a neighborhood have stable, well-paid jobs, children are more likely to stay in school and aspire to similar types of employment (Jencks & Mayer, 1990). Adults in the community who are friendly to neighborhood children can be especially influential role models when children's own parents are punitive and hostile (Silk, Sessa, Morris, Steinberg, & Avenevoli, 2004). More generally, when adults reach out to other people, perhaps doing errands for sick neighbors or hosting a block party, young people take notice. In the "Neighborhood: Late Adolescence" video clip on Observation CD 2, 15-year-old Robin is impressed by friendly gestures from her neighbors:

Next door there is these two, this old couple. They're really, really nice . . . we went over to their house for a Christmas party one time. The entire neighborhood came.

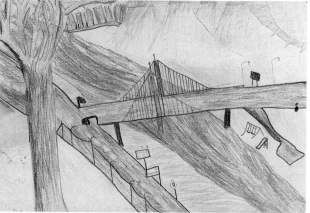

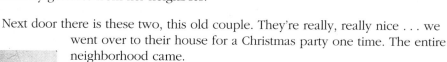

As children gain increasing mobility with age, their neighborhoods expand, as shown in these drawings by (top) Marsalis, age 7½, and (bottom) James, age 13. Marsalis stays very close to home, but James can easily travel a mile or more on his bicycle.

In summary, families care for children, culture gives meaning to children's lives, and the community connects children to external social contacts and resources. Essentially, family, culture, and community serve as fountains of nurture that children draw from as they grow, learn, and act in the world. The many layers that make up children's environment—for example, with families at the core, schools and child care centers providing essential services, and society's laws and values indirectly influencing children through their direct effects on families—are represented in Figure 5-1.

The Basic Developmental Issues table "Considering Family, Culture, and Community" provides examples of nature and nurture, universality and diversity, and qualitative and quantitative change in each of these settings. As you inspect the table, notice that these three environments are similar in their common function of nurturing children. Except under unusual circumstances, such as extreme poverty or absolute isolation, children's contexts supply reasonably healthy relationships and adequate resources. How children respond to these contexts changes with their age. In their first years, children rely primarily on families for social interaction, but children's worlds gradually expand with peer relationships and exchanges in schools, neighborhoods, and community groups. We now explore the people in the center of children's lives—the members of their families.

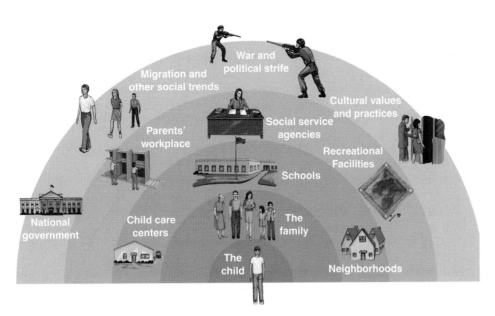

Figure 5-1
Children's development depends on their exposure to numerous social *systems*—organizations, institutions, and settings comprised of people who interact regularly. Central, of course, are children's families, but other systems affect children's development either directly (as neighborhoods and schools do) or indirectly through their impact on family, culture, or community.
Based on Bronfenbrenner, 2005.

BASIC DEVELOPMENTAL ISSUES	Considering Family, Culture, and Community		
Issue	**Family**	**Culture**	**Community**
Nature and Nurture	As agents of nature, parents give their children genes for basic human traits and for their own individual characteristics (such as dispositions to be physically healthy or frail). As agents of nurture, families care for children, serve as role models, engage children in affectionate relationships, and permit children's participation in routine family activities.	The general capacity for culture has evolved over millions of years and is inscribed in the human genetic code. For example, children's desire to learn from others probably has a genetic basis. In the daily lives of children and families, cultural traditions and beliefs nurture children in that they give meaning, purpose, and predictability to children's relationships, activities, tool use, and communication systems.	Human beings are a social species with natural inclinations to congregate in communities. When a community contains friendly neighbors, decent housing, accessible playmates, safe playgrounds, and reasonably stable and well-paying jobs for heads of family, the community can be an especially nurturing context for children's development.
Universality and Diversity	Children universally need one or more adults to advocate enthusiastically and steadfastly for their welfare, and families usually serve in this role. Families differ considerably in their structures (that is, membership) and styles of expressing affection and authority. Children cope well in a variety of families, but children face serious problems when families are neglectful or abusive.	Children need (and almost always have) opportunities to participate in meaningful cultural activities. Cultural diversity occurs in beliefs (such as whether or not children are perceived to be capable of reasoning at a young age) and behaviors (such as how men and women each contribute to household maintenance).	Communities universally create a link to the outside world for children and families. Communities vary in population density, other geographical features, and degree of support for children and families. For instance, some communities are safe and academically enriching, and others are dangerous and stark environments.
Qualitative and Quantitative Change	Some changes in family roles occur in a trendlike, quantitative fashion, such as when children gradually become more responsible for their own behavior. For example, children may slowly learn the steps in preparing a meal (e.g., washing the vegetables, buttering the bread, and grilling the meat). Some changes facilitate entirely new ways of thinking and behaving (a qualitative transformation), such as when a 12-year-old boy is asked to look after his 8-year-old sister for the first time.	Some cultures view development in terms of abrupt qualitative changes; for instance, rituals signify passage from childhood to adulthood and may be accompanied by an immediate and major change in young people's roles in the community. Other cultures view development as a series of small, gradual steps; for instance, children are given gradual increases in independence.	Children's experiences in communities show a few qualitative changes. For example, getting a driver's license or part-time job can shift youngsters' behaviors in fairly dramatic ways—they can suddenly make many choices about pastimes and purchases on their own. Many changes are probably gradual in form, such as children gradually learning about a city's neighborhoods as they systematically venture farther from home during bicycle rides.

Listen to Joey, Kent, Crystal, and Robin, the children interviewed in the four "Families" video clips on Observation CD 3, speak affectionately about their very different families.

—————— **Connecting Concepts**

Children's emotional bonds to parents, known as *attachments,* are discussed in more depth in Chapter 11.

—————— **Study Guide and Reader**

Learn more about the roles of fathers in children's lives in Supplementary Reading 5-1.

family structure

In a family with children, the family's makeup; specifically, the children in a family home and the adults who live with and care for the children.

coparents

The two (or more) parents who share responsibility for rearing their children.

Family Structures

A child's **family structure** refers to the makeup of the family—the people who live with the child in a family home, including any other children residing there and the adult or adults who care for the child and any siblings. Individual children live in one of several possible family structures. Consider these statistics compiled on American children by the U.S. Census Bureau (Fields, 2001):

- 62 percent live with both biological parents
- 25 percent live in a one-parent family
- 7 percent live with a biological parent and a stepparent
- 4 percent live without a parent in their household (they may live with grandparents, other relatives, or foster parents, or have some other living arrangement)
- 2 percent live in a two-parent family in which one or both parents have adopted them

Keep in mind that some children's circumstances defy such cut-and-dried categories. For instance, when children have divorced parents, their living arrangements may include moving back and forth between two different households. And adopted children live in other family structures as well as in two-parent families. For example, approximately 16 percent of adopted children live in single-parent families (Fields, 2001).

Children benefit from the care they receive from many types of families. In the "Families" video clips on Observation CD 3, you can listen to four children describe families that similarly radiate warmth even though they differ in structure. Children eagerly soak up affection from sensitive, caring family members, often with little concern for how their family's makeup compares to society's stereotypes of what a "proper" family is. Nevertheless, different family structures afford somewhat distinct benefits and challenges for children, and these characteristics merit thoughtful consideration by educators. In the sections that follow, we look at children's experiences in particular types of families and the strategies that educators can use to support a broad base of children and families.

Mothers and Fathers

When a mother and father are present in the home, children tend to form close bonds with both parents (M. E. Lamb, Chuang, & Cabrera, 2005). Being nurtured by two people is certainly beneficial for children—it gives them two loving role models and magnifies the affection they receive.

Within a two-parent family, both parents are important to the children, but a mother and father may take on slightly different roles. Mothers typically spend more time in physical care (feeding, bathing, scheduling doctors' appointments, etc.) and display more affection (e.g., kisses, hugs, smiles) toward their children (Belsky, Gilstrap, & Rovine, 1984; Engle & Breaux, 1998; Hossain & Roopnarine, 1994; Parke & Tinsley, 1987). Mothers also spend more time interacting with children while reading, playing peekaboo, and playing with toys (Parke & Tinsley, 1981).

In contrast, fathers are generally more physically playful with children, and they help children get along with people outside the family (Bridges, Connell, & Belsky, 1988; Engle & Breaux, 1998; M. E. Lamb, 1976; M. E. Lamb et al., 2005; Pettit, Brown, Mize, & Lindsey, 1998). Nevertheless, fathers are not simply playmates; fathers spend substantial amounts of time caring for their children and are quite competent in feeding, bathing, and nurturing children (Endicott, 1992; M. E. Lamb, 1976; M. E. Lamb, Frodi, Hwang, Frodi, & Steinberg, 1982; Mackey, 2001). In many societies fathers become more involved as children grow older, especially in disciplining children and modeling subtle masculine qualities, such as being a source of support and dependability for one's family (Engle & Breaux, 1998; Munroe & Munroe, 1992).

Mothers and fathers also influence children through two elements of their own relationship. First, they are spouses, joined as intimate partners; and second, they act as **coparents,** united in their responsibility for raising children (Schoppe-Sullivan, Mangelsdorf, Frosch, & McHale, 2004). Both as a married couple and as coparents, a man and woman have much to work out on a daily basis. Fortunately, many children gain valuable lessons in cooperation and conflict resolution (J. P. McHale & Rasmussen, 1998). Parents are role models for airing differences constructively and searching for solutions that are mutually beneficial. And when husband and wife have a good relationship, they are inclined to shower affection on children (M. Dube, Julien, Lebeau, & Gagnon, 2000; Ward & Spitze, 1998). Not surprisingly, children of happily married couples tend to perceive their lives as enjoyable and satisfying, and when they reach adulthood, they are able to establish close relationships with their own partners (S. S. Feldman, Gowen, & Fisher, 1998; Gohm, Oishi, Darlington, & Diener, 1998).

A 5-year-old boy drew this picture of his traditional two-parent family: (clockwise, from right) his father, himself, his mother, and his older brother. Also included are the family goldfish and the family's house and driveway.

In comparison, the lessons some other children receive are less beneficial. For instance, some children are regularly disturbed by parents' heated arguments. Such loud and bitter exchanges are poor models for dealing with conflict. Arguments also put parents into a foul mood, which can quickly spill over into their parenting interactions with children. In fact, when parents argue frequently, their interactions with children are often tense, harsh, and inconsistent (Almeida, Wethington, & Chandler, 1999; Gable, Belsky, & Crnic, 1992; Hetherington & Clingempeel, 1992; S. G. O'Leary & Vidair, 2005). Marital conflict is associated with assorted problems in youngsters, including physical aggression, depression, anxiety, and difficulties in intimate relationships (Forehand, Biggar, & Kotchick, 1998; Hetherington et al., 1999; L. F. Katz & Low, 2004; Tallman, Gray, Kullberg, & Henderson, 1999; Webster-Stratton & Hammond, 1999).

Largely because of troubled marriages, children who begin life in two-parent families do not necessarily remain in that situation. We look now at how children fare during and following the divorce of parents.

Divorced Parents

Once an infrequent occurrence, divorce is now fairly commonplace. In the United States approximately 1 in 5 first marriages ends in divorce or separation within 5 years of the wedding; one-third of first marriages are disrupted within 10 years (Bramlett & Mosher, 2002). Divorce rates are higher among adults with low educational levels, low family income, and no religious affiliation, and among those who had children prior to the marriage (Bramlett & Mosher, 2002). Divorce rates also are higher for White and Black Americans than for Hispanic and Asian Americans (U.S. Census Bureau, 2005).

For children, the divorce of parents is not a single event but instead a series of occurrences, each one requiring adjustment. Ongoing marital friction often precedes a divorce (Furstenberg & Cherlin, 1991). Recall that exposure to heated conflict is difficult for children to deal with, so even before the divorce, children may struggle. Nevertheless, children do not typically see their parents' divorce as inevitable or desirable; they are, after all, one family. Thus news of the divorce can be a crushing blow for children. Some children are truly caught offguard because they have been reassured previously that "Mommy still loves Daddy" or "We're trying to work things out" (Wallerstein & Kelly, 1980). Moreover, at the time of the announcement, parents may not be able to offer children adequate reassurance, burdened as they are with their own distress.

Children must make another adjustment when custody arrangements are determined. Parents may go through mediation to determine custody and visitation rights. Sometimes divorcing parents cannot reach agreement, and so the courts prescribe an arrangement that meets the children's needs (Hetherington & Stanley-Hagen, 1997).

The months after divorce continue to be difficult for many children and parents (Hetherington, Cox, & Cox, 1978). Custodial parents often struggle to manage all the tasks involved in maintaining an organized household, including shopping, cooking, cleaning, paying bills, and monitoring children's activities and homework (Wallerstein & Kelly, 1980). Financial setbacks can further complicate the picture. Parents who previously owned a house may have to sell it, and so, on top of everything else, children must move to new (and inevitably smaller) quarters and lose proximity to close friends and neighbors (Furstenberg & Cherlin, 1991; J. R. Harris, 1998).

As the coparents begin to establish separate households, children learn how their parents will get along (or not) and what role each parent will now play with them. One parent may withdraw from the children and eventually invest, both emotionally and financially, in a new life and perhaps a new family. Thus one unfortunate consequence of some divorces is that children lose contact with one of their parents, more often their father (Furstenberg & Cherlin, 1991). However, this trend is by no means universal. Many fathers actively seek joint custody arrangements after a divorce (R. A. Thompson, 1994). Continued contact between fathers and children is facilitated by fathers continuing to live nearby and remaining committed to their parenting role, and by mothers and fathers going through mediation about custody arrangements and keeping a lid on disputes after the divorce (Emery, Laumann-Billings, Waldron, Sbarra, & Dillon, 2001; R. W. Leite & McKenry, 2002; R. A. Thompson, 1994). Sometimes noncustodial fathers redefine their roles with children, perhaps becoming

One in 4 children grows up in a family headed by a single parent.

fun-loving companions (e.g., taking regular trips to the movies, amusement parks, etc.) rather than nurturers and disciplinarians (Asmussen & Larson, 1991).

Every family experiencing divorce is unique, but some general factors appear to affect children's adjustment to the change. Divorce can be more difficult for boys than girls, especially when mothers assume custody, do not remarry, and establish negative and coercive ways of interacting with their sons (Hetherington, 1988, 1989). Divorce can be especially overwhelming for young children, who may erroneously believe that their own naughty behavior caused the family's breakup (Fausel, 1986; Wallerstein, 1984). Older children and adolescents usually find their parents' divorce quite painful, yet most cope reasonably well with the change, at least over the long run, and especially if they have easygoing temperaments and age-appropriate social skills (Forehand et al., 1991; Hetherington, Bridges, & Insabella, 1998). Even so, about 25 percent of adolescents from divorced families subsequently have some difficulty establishing intimate relationships with peers (Hetherington et al., 1998).

Coparents and other adults help children to adjust positively by maintaining affectionate relationships with them, holding firm and consistent expectations for their behavior, willingly listening to their concerns, and encouraging them to continue to see familiar friends and other family members (Hetherington, 1988, 1989; Hetherington et al., 1998; Hetherington & Clingempeel, 1992). And, of course, children are likely to flourish when coparents establish reasonably productive relationships with one another and agree on expectations and disciplinary measures (Hetherington et al., 1978).

In a few cases divorce is actually beneficial for children's development. Some children rise to the challenge, comforting parents and siblings and filling in as needed around the house. Furthermore, a peaceful, single-parent home may be infinitely preferable to a household in which two parents engage in continual, intense bickering or in which one parent is abusive or irresponsible (Grych & Finchman, 1997).

Single Parents

Single parents carry out the tasks of parenting with the realization that much responsibility falls on their shoulders. This realization often leads single parents to see their children's needs as a top priority.

Generally, single-parent families cope well, particularly if they have a reasonable standard of living and the support of a stable network of family and friends (J. R. Harris, 1998). In fact, the simpler structure of single-parent families provides some advantages: Children may be shielded from intense conflict between parents, observe strong coping skills in their custodial parent, and enjoy the intimacy of a small family. Consider what Cedric Jennings (from our introductory case study) wrote in his application to Brown University:

> [B]eing a black male in a single parent home is sometimes tough without that male figure to help in the growing process. But I thank God for my loving mother. I even see some of my peers that have a mother and father, but are heading in the wrong direction. Some of them are into drug-dealing and others try to be "cool" by not doing good in school and not going to classes. But my mother has instilled so many positive values in me it would be hard to even try to get on the wrong track. (Suskind, 1998, p. 107)[1]

---

[1]From *A Hope in the Unseen,* by Ron Suskind, copyright © 1998 by Ron Suskind. Used by permission of Broadway Books, a division of Random House, Inc.

Single-parent families do experience unique challenges, though. Approximately 90 percent of single parents are women, and many single parents, mothers especially, have limited incomes (Fields, 2001). Single parents, mothers and fathers alike, express reservations about their ability to "do it all"—to juggle children, home, and work responsibilities (R. A. Thompson, 1994). Unless they have the support of extended family members, neighbors, or friends, single parents may have difficulty coping when they are tired, sick, or emotionally taxed, and they may be unable to offer children the rich range of roles, activities, and relationships that seem to maximize positive developmental outcomes (Garbarino & Abramowitz, 1992b). Fortunately, many single parents are well aware of their personal limitations, and so they reach out to others.

Parents and Stepparents

Many divorced parents eventually remarry. When they do, they and their children become members of a **blended family,** a family in which an original parent-and-children family structure expands to include a new parent figure and any children in his or her custody. Blended families are also formed when a remarried parent who already has a child goes on to have another child with the new spouse.

For a family to blend successfully, it must establish its own identity and traditions. It must decide how to spend money, divide household chores, prepare and serve meals, and celebrate holidays. It must also develop productive ways of expressing and resolving conflicts and determining rules and disciplinary techniques.

As is true for all family structures, children in blended families experience benefits and challenges. A new adult may bring additional income to the family and can help with household duties. Children can forge relationships with a new parent figure and, possibly, with new brothers and sisters. Yet children may feel that they must now share a parent's time and affection with the new spouse. They may believe, too, that the new stepparent is interfering with a possible reunion of the divorced parents and that by showing affection to the stepparent, they are betraying their nonresident parent (Papernow, 1988).

Most children in blended families eventually adjust reasonably well to their new family situation (D. A. Dawson, 1991; Furstenberg & Cherlin, 1991; Hetherington et al., 1998). Relationships between stepparents and children are not always as close and affectionate as those between biological parents and children, and stepparents may have greater difficulty disciplining children (Furstenberg, Nord, Peterson, & Zill, 1983; Hetherington et al., 1999). Yet in many (probably most) instances, stepparents soon become important parts of children's lives. Figure 5-2 is a Mother's Day poem by 9½-year-old Shea for her stepmother Ann, who at the time had been a family member for about 3 years. It reveals clearly the close relationship that had developed between Shea and Ann.

Extended Family

Many children have strong ties with relatives, including grandparents, aunts, uncles, and others. You can get a sense of the importance of extended family by listening to 6-year-old Joey in the "Families: Early Childhood" video clip on Observation CD 3:

Joey: Grandma helps me to do my homework. . . . My uncle helps me by
               making homework.
Interviewer: Oh he does? He gives you homework?
Joey: Yeah.

Children commonly enjoy close relationships with their grandparents. In the United States, 7.5 percent of all children live with at least one grandparent (Fields, 2001). In many cases grandparents supplement parents' care, but in other cases grandparents are the full-time caregivers. For example, when a child's parents are young and economically poor, neglectful, imprisoned, or incapacitated by illness or substance abuse, grandparents often

---

MOM is WOW

She is great at hide-and-seek
She takes me to look at an antique
I get to see her three times a week

MOM is WOW

She helped teach me multiplication
She encourages my imagination
She is involved when it comes to participation

MOM is WOW

She's a great stepmom, I guarantee
She lets us watch Disney TV
She is an important part of the family tree

MOM is WOW

No matter what, she is never late
If I have a question, she will demonstrate
When it comes to stepmoms, she's great

MOM is WOW

Figure 5-2

In her fourth-grade class, 9½-year-old Shea wrote a Mother's Day poem for her stepmother. Shea's teacher provided the "Mom is wow" structure for students to follow.

Listen to Joey talk about activities he enjoys with family members in the "Families: Early Childhood" clip on Observation CD 3.

blended family
Family created when one parent-child(ren) family combines with another parent figure and any children in his or her custody; also, the structure that emerges when a parent already with a child remarries and has another child with the new spouse.

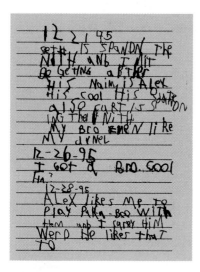

Figure 5-3

In his journal, 7-year-old Connor communicates his excitement about becoming a big brother. Eight-month-old Alex is placed in Connor's family on Dec. 20, and in the first journal entry the following day, Connor hopes that Alex will become his brother (when the court finalizes the adoption). Right away, Connor finds the baby to be both cool and cute. After a few days (Dec. 28 entry), Connor is aware of some of Alex's likes, such as playing peekaboo and being carried by him. (In his journal, Connor also talks about his friends spending the night.)

——————— Connecting Concepts
You will learn more about problems in forming close bonds with family members in Chapter 11.

become primary guardians (L. M. Burton, 1992). Custodial grandparents sometimes worry that they do not have adequate energy and financial resources to raise a second generation of children, yet their mature outlook and extensive parenting skills often lead them to be more competent caregivers than the noncustodial parents would be (Cox, 2000; A. Kornhaber, 1996). For example, grandmothers are less punitive and more responsive to children's needs than teen mothers are, and children cared for by grandmothers generally have more economic stability, show greater self-reliance, and seem better able to avoid drug abuse and vandalism (Chase-Lansdale, Brooks-Gunn, & Zamsky, 1994; R. D. Taylor & Roberts, 1995; M. Wilson, 1989).

In some families, other extended family members assume central roles in the lives of children (Harrison, Wilson, Pine, Chan, & Buriel, 1990; Stack & Burton, 1993). In American society, aunts, uncles, and cousins may step forward to raise children when they are the only viable caregivers. And in some other areas of the world, male members of the extended family, such as uncles, regularly serve as primary father figures for children (Engle & Breaux, 1998).

Adoptive Parents

Two or three out of every 100 children in the United States are adopted (Fields, 2001; Kreider, 2003; Zill, 1985). Half of these adoptions involve a child's relatives or stepparents; the other half are arranged through agencies, attorneys, and other intermediaries (Stolley, 1993).

Adoption can be a positive event for children, who can form ties with loving parents. It can also be a blessing for adoptive parents, who find themselves—sometimes overnight—with a child. In Figure 5-3, 7-year-old Connor conveys his excitement on becoming a big brother to 8-month-old Alex.

The last few decades have seen several changes in adoption practices (Center for the Future of Children, 1993). One growing practice is *open adoption,* in which the birth mother (and perhaps also the birth father) meet and choose the adopting family with help from an agency. Another is *international adoption,* whereby orphaned or relinquished children living in one country are adopted by families in another country. Many adoption agencies are now more flexible in evaluating potential adoptive parents; the result is an increasing number who are single, older, gay, lesbian, or from lower-income groups. The adoption of increasing numbers of older children is another trend. Occasionally these children have physical or mental disabilities or may require special services due to poor care earlier in life (Rutter & O'Connor, 1999).

Although adopted children are at slightly greater risk for emotional, behavioral, and academic problems than children reared by biological parents, most adopted children thrive and grow up to be well-adjusted individuals (Brodzinsky, 1993). Adopted children seem to cope best when family members talk openly about the adoption yet provide the same love and nurturance that they would offer any biological offspring.

In extreme cases children may have been abused or neglected or had several different placements before being adopted, and these children sometimes find it difficult to form positive relationships with their new families (D. Howe, 1995; L. M. Singer, Burkowski, & Waters, 1985). Professional intervention can be helpful (and is sometimes critical) for adoptive families when children's past unstable family life now leads them to resist forming close bonds with new family members.

Foster Care

In *foster care,* children are placed with families through a legal but temporary arrangement. Tragically, parents' substance abuse is often a major factor in determining the need for foster care placement. Approximately half of children enter foster care because their primary caregiver has maltreated them (R. Collins, 1999).

Largely because of their previously unstable family life, children in foster care exhibit higher rates of emotional and behavioral difficulties than do other children (Shealy, 1995). Ideally, foster parents receive ample support that helps them maintain their resolve (and self-control) as they care for troubled children. One promising tactic has been to train *therapeutic foster parents* to be professional caregivers; these parents care for only one or two children, are given ongoing emotional support themselves, have access to crisis intervention services, are encouraged to keep their focus on children's social and educational needs, and are advised by case managers who also have reasonably small workloads (R. P. Hawkins, 1989).

The majority of U.S. children in foster care are reunited with their families within a year (U.S. Department of Health and Human Services, 2000). However, some children in foster care become available for adoption. Unfortunately, because of heavy caseloads in agencies, crowded court dockets, and the preferences of numerous adoptive parents for newborn infants, foster children may be shuffled among numerous temporary arrangements before being placed into permanent homes (McKenzie, 1993; U.S. Department of Health and Human Services, 2000). Such a transitory existence is particularly detrimental when children have already faced challenges—perhaps neglect, abuse, abandonment, or early exposure to drugs or HIV. Fortunately, many children in foster care are eventually adopted, often by their foster parents and sometimes by other adults who are eager to adopt older children.

International adoptions have become increasingly common. Many adoptive parents encourage their children to learn about their native culture as well as the culture of their adoptive family.

Other Heads of Family

Our discussion of family structures has not been exhaustive; some children experience variations on these configurations or live in other family arrangements altogether. For instance, a growing number of children live with *gay and lesbian parents*. When Jeanne's daughter Tina was a teaching intern, 4 of the 15 students in her first-grade class had two gay or lesbian parents. Children who have gay and lesbian parents are as intelligent and well adjusted as other children, and most grow up to be heterosexual adults (Bailey, Bobrow, Wolfe, & Mikach, 1995; Faks, Filcher, Masterpasqua, & Joseph, 1995; Golombok & Tasker, 1996; C. J. Patterson, 1992). Children of homosexual parents may notice that their parents are stigmatized by society, but the children usually cope with such prejudice without too much difficulty (C. J. Patterson & Chan, 1997).

Some children spend considerable time in a *cohabiting family,* in which a parent has an intimate nonmarital partner living in the home. About 5 percent of children in the United States live with parents who are cohabiting with partners (Fields, 2001). Little is known about the experiences of children with cohabiting parents; however, we can expect that like children in other family settings, children living with cohabiting parents adjust favorably when their family circumstances are stable and when both adults in the household maintain warm and consistent relationships with them (S. R. Aronson & Huston, 2004).

Adolescent parents often need and receive support from government and social agencies. Although many adolescent parents are sensitive and reliable caregivers to their children, some single adolescent mothers experience a lot of stress and lack awareness of children's emotional, cognitive, and social needs (Borkowski et al., 2002). Teenage parents who are anxious and simultaneously hold unrealistic ideas about child development can become inattentive, inconsistent, and critical with their children. The unhappy result is that their children face risks for developmental delays. For example, children of adolescent mothers are less likely to become securely attached to their mothers, and they may show delayed language development and lower-than-average academic achievement (Borkowski et al., 2002). Nonetheless, many adolescent parents are competent caregivers, and practitioners can better the odds for these teens and their children when they effectively educate and support the teens and provide developmentally appropriate care for their children.

Accommodating Diverse Family Structures

Most teachers and other school professionals place high value on being inclusive and respectful of families, and they do what they can to help children adjust to changes in family membership. Following are some specific tactics educators can use to support all children and their varied families:

● *When organizing activities, make them flexible enough to be relevant to a wide variety of family circumstances.* School assignments and extracurricular activities sometimes involve one or more family members. For instance, in the elementary grades, children may make cards for Mother's Day and Father's Day. In high school biology classes, students may be asked to trace the occurrence of physical traits (e.g., brown hair and blond hair) in several generations of their family. Such tasks, though well intentioned, may exclude youngsters

Model, discuss, and encourage acceptance of all family structures.

whose family structures don't fit the traditional mold. With a little creativity, teachers can easily broaden activities so that they accommodate diverse family structures. For instance, the biology teacher can be more inclusive by presenting data on several generations of a hypothetical biological family and asking all class members to analyze the data. As another example, recall the Mother's Day poem Shea wrote to her stepmother (Figure 5-2). Shea's teacher gave her enough time to write two poems, one for her mother and one for her stepmother.

● *Encourage acceptance of diverse family structures.* Occasionally children tease classmates from nontraditional families. For instance, some children of gay and lesbian parents may be ridiculed because of their parents' sexual orientation, and adopted children may hear other children question the closeness of their bonds with adoptive parents (Hare, 1994; Shelley-Sireci & Yanni, 2005). At the preschool and elementary levels, teachers can counteract such attitudes by reading stories about children in a variety of family structures and by expressing the view that loving families are formed in many ways. In the secondary grades, adolescents tend to be more informed and accepting about diverse family structures; nevertheless, teachers should keep an ear open for, and emphatically discourage, any derogatory comments about other youngsters' family circumstances.

● *Include fathers and other heads of family.* When children live in two-parent families, people outside the family often direct communication about children to mothers alone. Educators can try to equalize communications to mothers and fathers when both are present in the home. By doing so, they can validate the incredibly influential roles that mothers and fathers alike play in children's lives. It is also important to acknowledge the presence of other heads of family, such as grandparents serving as guardians. And whenever possible, extended family members should be welcome at school open houses, plays, and concerts.

● *Be supportive when children undergo a major family transition.* Many events, including divorce, remarriage, departure of a parent's nonmarital partner, death of a family member, or movement from one foster family to another, can change a child's family life dramatically. In each case one or more old relationships may end, and new relationships may begin. During family transitions, children also may move to new residences and, as a result, lose some sources of social and emotional support (Adam, 2004). Adjustment to major family transitions takes time, and teachers and caregivers should be prepared to offer long-term support (Hetherington, 1999). Children and heads of family are likely to appreciate kind words and understanding, especially in the early months.

● *Remain patient while children are figuring out how to adjust to new family structures.* Youngsters may find that they must learn to adapt to moving between two houses and following two sets of rules. Consider 16-year-old Selina's articulation of the tensions that arise when she prepares to change households:

> It gets to about five o'clock on Sunday and I get like a really awful feeling and then . . . aah, packing up again . . . I don't complain about it. That's just the way it is. There's no *point* complaining about it, nothing's going to change. . . . [But] usually on a Sunday around that time . . . we're upset because we're having to move and everyone's tempers . . . you know, you get quite irritable. (Smart, Neale, & Wade, 2001, p. 128)[2]

In such circumstances adults can express sympathy for children's frustration but also encourage them to come up with a plan for keeping track of belongings (including homework) as they move between houses.

● *Let children say what they want to say; don't pry.* Children often prefer to keep family matters to themselves. They may feel that teachers and counselors are inappropriately interested in their personal lives (Smart et al., 2001). It is desirable, therefore, for adults to offer reassurance without being too inquisitive. When children do bring up family problems, help them consider options for dealing with the problems.

---

[2]From *The Changing Experiences of Childhood: Families and Divorce* (p. 128) by C. Smart, B. Neale and A. Wade, 2001, Malden, MA: Blackwell Publishers. Copyright 2001 by Carol Smart, Bren Neale and Amanda Wade. Reprinted by permission.

● *Reach out to students who are living in foster care.* Children in foster care may be emotionally overburdened and have trouble asking for assistance and comfort. Furthermore, they may have profound academic and social needs and may sometimes engage in behaviors that upset experienced professionals. Nevertheless, children in foster care almost invariably benefit when adults articulate clear and consistent expectations and offer ongoing personal support.

How heads of family treat one another and their children affects the skills and dispositions that children develop. In fact, family *processes* overshadow family *structure* in the power of their effects on children. Let's turn to the research on the nature and consequences of relationships within the family.

Family Processes

Family processes—the frequent interchanges that family members have with one another—serve as lessons for children on how to respond to authority figures, get along with others, and prepare for school. In this section we examine influences within families, including the effects of families on children and those of children on families. We also look into risk factors for families and offer suggestions on how to establish productive working relationships with families.

Children learn a lot from participating in routine activities with parents.

Families' Influences on Children

As powerful agents of socialization, parents and other heads of family implement four particularly influential practices: encouraging children to participate in everyday routines; using parenting styles that blend affection with discipline; creating an environment that prepares children for school; and providing children with financial resources and being role models as employed workers.

Guided participation in everyday activities. **Guided participation,** the child's active engagement in adults' everyday activities, is an important way that parents support children's learning. In a (typically) nurturing manner, parents allow children to participate with them in their regular duties, such as cooking and eating, taking trips to stores, and going to places of worship. With parental guidance, children are motivated to participate in these routines and to take on increasing levels of responsibility (Rogoff, 1990, 2003).

Parents also influence children through the experiences they arrange for children outside the home. Especially when children are young, parents organize such activities as playdates at friends' houses and other outings (Gauvain, 1999, 2001). Through such repeated activities, parents often encourage children to look ahead and plan for the future. When children are young, parents may ask them what they will do later in the day or what they might need ("It looks like it might rain. Did you pack a jacket?"). As they grow older, parents may help youngsters think through complex tasks ("That assignment requires you to turn in a summary and a critique. I wonder how long each will take to complete.").

Such guided participation is *universal.* All cultures direct families to arrange for children's inclusion in meaningful events. *Diversity* comes into play in the particular routines that families carry out. Consider the financial lessons of two boys in different cultures. The first boy accompanies his father to the bank and watches his father deposit funds, earmarked for college, into the boy's savings account. This boy learns about family expectations for higher education and the (literal) value of a college education. Hundreds of miles away, the second boy counts fish with his father after a day at sea; father and son speculate on how the recent storm may have affected the catch. This boy learns about weather patterns, ocean streams, the behavior of fish, and the need to set aside profits for scarce times. Both boys learn to save money, but in other respects the family's socialization is quite different.

Parenting styles. Throughout the world most parents manage to find acceptable, balanced ways to show their love and wield their authority (R. H. Bradley, Corwyn, McAdoo, & Coll,

Connecting Concepts
Chapter 6 examines guided participation as an important factor in cognitive development.

guided participation
Active engagement in adult activities, typically with considerable direction and structure from an adult or other more advanced individual; children are given increasing responsibility and independence as they gain experience and proficiency.

2001; Rohner & Rohner, 1981). However, parents vary in how they express affection and implement discipline; that is, they develop characteristic **parenting styles.** Initial research into parenting styles in U.S. families, conducted by Diana Baumrind (1967, 1971, 1980, 1989, 1991), identified three unique styles—*authoritarian, authoritative,* and *permissive.* A fourth style—*uninvolved*—has since been identified by other researchers in the field. The results suggest these patterns:

- Parents who use an **authoritarian style** expect complete and immediate compliance. They neither negotiate expectations nor provide reasons for their requests ("Clean your room because I told you to—and I mean *now*!). Authoritarian parents also tend to be somewhat cool, aloof, and punitive with children, and they expect children to act in a mature fashion at a fairly young age. Children of authoritarian parents tend to be withdrawn, mistrusting, and unhappy. They have low self-esteem, little self-reliance, and poor social skills, and in some cases they are overly aggressive with others (Coopersmith, 1967; Lamborn, Mounts, Steinberg, & Dornbusch, 1991; Maccoby & Martin, 1983; Simons, Whitbeck, Conger, & Conger, 1991).

- Parents who use an **authoritative style** also seek mature behavior from their children, but they do so in a warmer manner that incorporates give-and-take, explanations for why rules should be followed, and respect for children's viewpoints ("OK, maybe you don't need to sort through your backpack *every* night, but can we both agree you'll do it every Wednesday and Saturday?"). Children of authoritative parents are generally mature, friendly, energetic, confident in tackling new tasks, and able to resist distractions. They have high self-esteem, are self-reliant, and have good social skills. Furthermore, they achieve at high levels academically, are well-behaved at school, and adjust reasonably well to traumatic events (Coopersmith, 1967; Dekovic & Janssens, 1992; Dornbusch, Ritter, Leiderman, Roberts, & Fraleigh, 1987; Hetherington & Clingempeel, 1992; Lamborn et al., 1991; R. C. Loeb, Horst, & Horton, 1980; L. Steinberg, Elmen, & Mounts, 1989).

- Parents who use a **permissive style** care about their children, but they exercise little control over children's behaviors. Permissive parents relinquish decisions to children (even fairly young ones) about when to go to bed, what chores (if any) to do around the house, and what curfews to abide by ("Fine. Just ignore what I say!"). Children in such families are typically immature, impulsive, demanding and dependent on parents and, not surprisingly, disobedient when parents ask them to do something they do not want to do. These children tend to have difficulty in school, to be aggressive with peers, and to engage in delinquent acts as adolescents (Lamborn et al., 1991; Pulkkinen, 1982).

- Some parents are not only permissive but also indifferent to their children. **Uninvolved parents** make few demands on their children, and they respond to children in an uncaring and rejecting manner. Their children frequently exhibit serious difficulties in many areas, including problems with school achievement, emotional control, tolerance for frustration, and delinquency (Lamborn et al., 1991; Simons, Robertson, & Downs, 1989).

Overall, the research suggests that the authoritative style is the most effective pattern for many U.S. children. On the playground and in the community, children of authoritative parents know that rules exist for a reason, exceptions are sometimes possible, and everyone has a right to an opinion (Hinshaw, Zupan, Simmel, Nigg, & Melnick, 1997). Even so, authoritative parenting is far from universal and may not be optimal or possible in some environments. The effects of a particular style may depend on other dynamics in the family. For example, many Asian American families make high demands for obedience and discourage negotiation over rules (and so appear "authoritarian"), but they do so within the context of a close, supportive mother-child relationship (Chao, 1994, 2000). This parenting style is bolstered in some families by principles of Confucianism, which teach children that parents are right and that obedience and emotional restraint are essential for family harmony (Chao, 1994). In fact, some Chinese American children may feel bad when their parents fail to use an involved, directive style, which they see as an expression of love. Moreover, the

parenting style
General pattern of behaviors that a parent uses to nurture and guide his or her children.

authoritarian style
Parenting style characterized by strict expectations for behavior and rigid rules that children are expected to obey without question.

authoritative style
Parenting style characterized by emotional warmth, high expectations and standards for behavior, consistent enforcement of rules, explanations regarding the reasons behind these rules, and the inclusion of children in decision making.

permissive style
Parenting style characterized by emotional warmth but few expectations or standards for children's behavior.

uninvolved style
Parenting style characterized by a lack of emotional support and a lack of standards regarding appropriate behavior.

children of very controlling Asian American parents often do quite well in school (Chao, 1994; Dornbusch et al., 1987; Lin & Fu, 1990).

Similarly, research yields mixed results as to whether authorita*tive* or authorita*rian* parenting is more effective in some African American families (Baumrind, 1982; Deater-Deakard, Dodge, Bates, & Pettit, 1996; D. Rowe, Vazsonyi, & Flannery, 1994; Steinberg, Lamborn, Darling, Mounts, & Dornbusch, 1994). Positive outcomes have been found in some children whose parents use the authoritarian style, which is fairly common among African American families, but the benefits may be due to other socialization factors. Quite possibly other important family dimensions—a strong emphasis on spirituality, active involvement of extended family members, ongoing resistance to oppression, cultural pride, and so on—have not been taken into account in researchers' classifications of parenting styles (H. C. Stevenson, 1995; R. D. Taylor & Roberts, 1995).

Study Guide and Reader ——————
Learn more about cultural variations in parents' styles of expressing authority and affection in Supplementary Reading 5-2.

Other aspects of families' lives may make the authoritative style ineffective or impossible to implement. When families live in dangerous neighborhoods, for example, parents may better serve children by being directive, particularly if parents simultaneously communicate the consequences of disregarding strict rules (Hale-Benson, 1986; McLoyd, 1998b). In other circumstances parents are strict not because they are consciously preparing children to survive in hazardous environments, but rather because economic hardship and other family stresses provoke them to be short-tempered with children (Bronfenbrenner, Alvarez, & Henderson, 1984; L. F. Katz & Gottman, 1991; Russell & Russell, 1994).

In a range of cultural settings, most heads of family are sufficiently capable as nurturers and disciplinarians that they inspire reasonably mature, socially competent behavior in children. Through a variety of tactics, and most certainly by being affectionate, parents persuade children that they are trying to be helpful and supportive. As a result, children usually accept parents' authority, even though they may sporadically (and sometimes recurrently) haggle with parents (Hoffman, 1994). In contrast, when children see parents as demeaning, cruel, or hostile, children tend *not* to accept parents' guidance. A key implication for educators is that children from any cultural background who have experienced harsh punishments or uninvolved parenting may exhibit assorted behavior problems both at home and in the classroom. With these children, teachers must typically make special efforts to communicate rules, give reasonable consequences when rules are disobeyed, reward good behavior, and encourage consideration of other people's perspectives, needs, and feelings.

Parents find many ways to express affection and guide their children.

Educators and counselors may also be able to help by teaching effective disciplinary techniques and other child-rearing strategies to parents. For example, in one intervention with an ethnically diverse sample of low-income parents of 2- and 3-year-old children, parents were randomly assigned to either receive or not receive parent training (D. Gross et al., 2003). Those who received training became more self-confident in their parenting, were more positive in their interactions with toddlers, and used less coercive discipline strategies. In addition, their children showed fewer behavior problems in the classroom.

Families as little schoolhouses.   Before they ever set foot in a classroom, children begin to acquire academic foundations at home. For instance, they learn the elementary purposes and patterns of language, and may be exposed to reading materials, art, music, computer technology, and scientific and mathematical thinking (Hess & Holloway, 1984; Scott-Jones, 1991). When children enter school, their families continue to offer views on schooling—how to behave, what goals to strive for, how hard to try, and so on. Increasingly, parents also influence children by selecting a school from among many choices, including public, private, or charter schools; home schooling arrangements; or schools that embody particular cultural values, such as African-centered education (Madhubuti & Madhubuti, 1994).

Many parents deliberately prepare their children for academic endeavors. Some, especially those who are well educated and financially comfortable, immerse their children in highly verbal and technologically rich environments that include sophisticated language, stimulating books and toys, and age-appropriate computer programs. They also encourage their children to manipulate complex objects and engage in exploratory play, and they take trips to museums and other educationally enriching sites. Numerous studies indicate that enriched home environments are associated with children's advanced cognitive, linguistic, and academic skills (e.g., R. H. Bradley & Caldwell, 1984; Brooks-Gunn, Klebanov, & Duncan, 1996; A. W. Gottfried, Gottfried, Bathurst, & Guerin, 1994; Jimerson, Egeland, & Teo, 1999). These associations between academically strong home environments and children's academic success are probably due to a variety of factors, including parents' persistent efforts to teach academic skills, the fact that intelligence has some genetic basis (high-ability parents tend to have high-ability children), and the availability of academic resources in advantaged communities.

—————— Connecting Concepts
See Chapter 8 for a discussion of both genetic and environmental influences on intelligence.

Parents also influence children by carrying out activities that have an academic focus (such as reading and writing) in front of children. For example, children observe and later imitate the literate behaviors of their parents (Bandura, 1986). In this manner, children are more competent, enthusiastic readers if their parents read frequently at home (Hess & McDevitt, 1989). In many cases families supplement their deeds with words about the value of an education. For instance, families may tell children that a good education is the best way to secure a decent job. In the excerpt in the following exercise, 13-year-old Connor describes what he has learned from his father about doing well in school.

INTERPRETING CHILDREN'S ARTIFACTS AND ACTIONS   My Dad, My Hero

Thirteen-year-old Connor had the assignment "Write an essay describing your idol" as part of an interdisciplinary unit on choices and responsibilities. What did Connor learn about what it takes to do well in school?

Choosing my idol was very easy for me. It was easy for me because of how successful he is now and where he came from. In Ireland in the mid Fifties my idol was born. He was born to a poor family. His father was a company sergeant in the Irish army. His father volunteered for the United Nations and went all the way to the Congo to maintain peace. He was injured in an attack on the Leopoldville air force base in the Congo. . . .

My idol lived in a two-bedroom apartment on the military grounds. His Mom stayed home to look after him and his sister. My idol worked very hard in school. He made good choices. While some of his friends were playing soccer he was working hard and studying. Now after all that hard work he is a Dean of Education. He has two excellent children (especially the older one). He is my Father.

My dad got as far as he is in many ways. The one he thinks is the most important thing in getting him the furthest in life is the fact that his parents every night made him study and do homework. Sometimes he did not like having to do all the homework because he missed out on the fun. Now he says it is the education that got him so far. All of his friends would walk by his house and have a good time and ask him if he could come out. . . . He says that I should do my homework before friends and do it right because an education is very important. . . .

After working hard in secondary (high) school, he got a scholarship to go to college. Without the scholarship he could not have gone to college because his family could not afford to send him. . . .

What have I learned from my Dad's experiences? He came from a poor background to be very successful. From his background you could not have predicted his job or his success (or how wonderful his children are). What were the keys to his success? He studied hard, had goals and priorities, and was persistent. If I could do something similar I would probably study as hard as I could. Also I would try as hard as he did in school. He is trying to teach me the same values and work ethic. I would like to have his values. However, sometimes it's hard for me to devote time to studying. There's lots of distractions, especially friends, Nintendo, and sports. I'm trying my best.

From his father, Connor has learned the value of hard work. Connor seems to apply this standard to his own life, concluding that he, too, should try hard and resist temptations. Connor also comments that his grandparents insisted that his father do his homework. In this manner, families play another important role through their involvement (or lack of involvement) in children's schooling. At home, many heads of family discuss school activities with children, assist with homework, and praise children or give feedback about in-class projects. At school, heads of family may confer with teachers about children's classroom progress, volunteer in the classroom, participate in parent advisory groups, join fund-raising initiatives, and so forth. Students whose parents are involved in school activities have better attendance records, higher achievement, and more positive attitudes toward school than students whose parents are not actively involved. This difference exists even when the prior school performance of the two groups of students has been the same (Chavkin, 1993; Eccles & Harold, 1993; J. L. Epstein, 1996; Hoover-Dempsey & Sandler, 1997; Jimerson et al., 1999).

Parents' employment.   Most parents, both married and single, are employed either outside or inside the home (U.S. Census Bureau, 2000a, 2000b). By being employed, heads of family earn income to meet children's basic needs for food, clothing, and shelter. When income is plentiful, families can also give children access to books and academic supplies, travel, home computers, recreation, and so forth.

Parents' employment is developmentally influential in a second way: It occupies parents' time and so creates the need for other adults to supervise children's activities. When children are young, working parents usually choose one of these arrangements for children's care: looking after the children themselves while in the workplace; placing children with relatives, particularly grandparents; enrolling children in an organized facility, such as a child care center or preschool; or employing a non-relative to provide care in the child's or a provider's own home (U.S. Census Bureau, 2003). When children reach middle childhood and early adolescence, employed parents tend to rely primarily on schools to care for youngsters during the day. They may also have children participate in enrichment activities (e.g., classes in music, art, or computer skills) and sports programs, or arrange for supervision by other family members (e.g., an older sibling).

About 15 percent of parents of school-age children rely on children to care for themselves after school (U.S. Census Bureau, 2003). Children's frequent self-care is a concern because children are typically less able than adults to anticipate and avoid dangerous situations (a child may answer the front door without first looking through the peephole, for example). Children also are less inclined than adults to think about long-term consequences of their choices (a hungry child might automatically grab a bag of potato chips rather than make a sandwich, for example). And some children become fearful and lonely when left alone (T. J. Long & Long, 1982). Nevertheless, many children in self-care do well: They check in with parents by phone, make nutritious snacks, do chores, and begin their homework. Self-care arrangements appear more effective when parents explain safety procedures, convey expectations for behavior when home alone, and monitor children's activities by phone (Galambos & Maggs, 1991; Steinberg, 1986).

Some children come home to an empty house or apartment after school and tend to their own needs until their parents finish work.

Parents' employment also influences children's development by transmitting certain values about work and social roles. In the workplace, parents encounter certain kinds of decision-making practices that filter down to the home front (Crouter, 1994; Kohn, 1977). Middle-income jobs often require extensive consultation with others, and people employed in such positions typically have a fair amount of autonomy. Lower-income jobs more often emphasize following rules, such as coming to work on time and sticking to strict routines. Parents in both income groups seem to prepare their children to fit into jobs with income levels similar to their own, with middle-income parents valuing self-direction in their children and lower-income parents preferring conformity to authority.

Employed parents can serve as role models by showing that they are responsible, working citizens who contribute to the greater good of society. For instance, girls whose mothers are employed outside the home are likely to perceive women as having numerous career options and rewarding lives (E. Williams & Radin, 1993). Daughters also seem to develop their own career aspirations in part from watching their mothers' professional accomplishments.

Work can interfere with effective parenting, however, especially when job pressures elevate stress levels at home and when parents must work excessively long hours (Crouter & Bumpus, 2001; MacDermid, Lee, & Smith, 2001; Moorehouse, 1991). Jobs that do not permit parents to take off time when they give birth, adopt children, or have sick children also can adversely affect parents and children (R. Feldman, Sussman, & Zigler, 2004; Kamerman, 2000; Ruhm, 1998).

Children's Influences on Families

While children are being exposed to parents' guidance, they are also busily expressing their own wants and needs, often quite emphatically (recall Cedric's outraged response to his B in physics: ". . . what are *we* going to do?!"). Through their requests, demands, and actions, children influence parents and other family members.

Figure 5-4

Ten-year-old Samuel thanks his mother for all she has taught him.

Figure 5-5

Six-year-old Alex wrote this sympathy card to his father the day Alex's grandfather (his father's father) died. Children reciprocate the affection their parents give them; this includes offering comfort when they see their parents are distressed.

———————— Connecting Concepts

Chapter 11 describes common dimensions of children's temperaments and personalities.

Children's effects on parents.   Socialization of children involves *reciprocal influences,* whereby children and their parents simultaneously affect one another's behaviors and together create the environment in which they all live. Parents set the tone, to some degree, but children contribute immensely to family dynamics.

Reciprocal influences are evident in parent-child interactions from the very beginning (R. Q. Bell, 1988). Babies demand comfort by crying, but they also coo, chatter, lure their parents into contact in a most disarming manner, and in other ways tell parents that they are important people in babies' lives. A father intent on sweeping the kitchen floor, for example, may find it hard to resist the antics of his 6-month-old daughter who wriggles, chatters, and smiles at him.

Reciprocal influences continue as children grow. For example, preschoolers and parents play games that require both parties to take turns and imitate one another (Kohlberg, 1969). During middle childhood and adolescence, youngsters and their parents take cues from each other's actions. In Figure 5-4, 10-year-old Samuel thanks his mother for teaching him how to behave. Realizing that his mother's underlying motive is to help him, Samuel is likely to listen to her requests in the future. She, in turn, is likely to respond with gratitude to his gestures of appreciation. During adolescence, youngsters may bring home their enthusiasm for new hobbies, interests, and technologies. For instance, when Jeanne's son Alex was a high school senior, he encouraged her to take an art history class with him, and their increased appreciation for diverse art forms led to many mother-son conversations.

When parents do their part to establish a warm climate for the family, children usually reciprocate with affectionate gestures. The note in Figure 5-5, in which 6-year-old Alex offers comfort to his father on the day that Dad's own father (Alex's grandfather) has died, illustrates a child's affectionate response. In contrast, when parents establish a negative climate, children may learn to accuse and ridicule their parents. Some family members intensify demands as they interact, as shown in this interchange:

Mother:	I told you to clean your room. This is a *disaster.*
Daughter:	Get outta *my* room!
Mother:	[raises her voice] You clean up that mess or you're grounded! [stamps her foot]
Daughter:	Hah! You can't make me!
Mother:	For a month! [shouting now]
Daughter:	You stink! [stomps out of her room and marches to the front door]
Mother:	For two months! [shouting louder]
Daughter:	As if you'd notice I was gone! [slams door]

During this exchange, things go from bad to worse: The daughter is blatantly disobedient, the mother intensifies her demands, and both mother and daughter become increasingly angry. Such exchanges are common in some troubled families (G. R. Patterson & Reid, 1970). When patterns of negative interaction become habitual, it is difficult for family members to learn new ways of responding to one another. However, both parents and children can grow and change, often in response to counseling and other interventions.

Various aspects of children's temperaments and personalities may be partly responsible for the types of routine exchanges that families develop. For example, children who are inclined to be agreeable may elicit calm responses from parents, whereas more spirited, irritable, or rebellious children may provoke parents to clamp down firmly on misbehavior (Eisenberg & Fabes, 1994; J. R. Harris, 1995, 1998; Scarr, 1993). Because children within any single family often have different temperaments, their parents may use distinct styles with each of them—a tendency that children may misinterpret as favoritism toward a sibling (Kowal, Krull, & Kramer, 2004).

Children's natural talents also influence the kinds of experiences parents provide for them (Scarr, 1992, 1993). For example, a father with an extensive vocabulary and advanced verbal reasoning may genetically endow his daughter with similar talents. As her verbal skills blossom, the young girl asks her parents to read to her, explain the meanings of challenging words, and discuss complex ideas. On the surface, her parents promote their daughter's verbal abilities through their actions. But their daughter also influences parents, instigating and shaping her own opportunities for learning.

Some of children's influences on parents are environmental in origin—children educate parents about what they have learned at school and in the community. A good example comes from the field of political socialization (M. McDevitt & Chaffee, 1998). In one intervention, approximately half of all classrooms in San Jose, California, participated in "Kids Voting USA," a program in citizenship education for students from kindergarten through grade 12, and the other half served as a control group. Not only did the children in the program learn more about political issues and practices, but they also apparently brought their knowledge and excitement about politics home. Their parents began to pay more attention to the news, talked more often about politics, and formed stronger opinions about candidates and political issues. In such compelling educational experiences, interest seems to "trickle up" from children to parents.

Siblings' responses to one another.   Children have an impact not only on their parents but also on any siblings present in the family. Approximately 80 percent of children in the United States live in a household with at least one sibling (Fields, 2001).

Siblings serve many purposes for children. First and foremost, the presence of brothers and sisters creates the possibility that close sibling relationships will supplement parent-child bonds. Children often rely on siblings for comfort when anxious or upset (Bank, 1992; Stewart, 1983). Other functions of siblings depend on the relative ages of children. In mainstream Western society, older siblings often look after young children when parents do brief errands. In many other societies, older children are the primary caregivers for younger brothers and sisters for a significant part of the day (Parke & Buriel, 1998; Weisner & Gallimore, 1977). Older siblings also serve as role models and playmates for younger children (R. Barr, 1999). In addition, older siblings may teach young children new skills (e.g., tying shoes), although they are less likely than parents to be patient tutors (Perez-Granados & Callanan, 1997). To observe how the relative ages of siblings affect a young person, listen to 15-year-old Robin talk about her relationships with her siblings in the "Families: Late Adolescence" video clip on Observation CD 3:

> [My older brother] is kind of like my Dad. He's really nice to me. . . . With my brother, I usually like to play sports. With my little brother, I always play video games with him. My little sister, we like to argue with each other.

The intellectual and social influences of siblings may also depend on their *birth order*—that is, on whether children were born first, second, or somewhere later down the line. Older siblings tend to have a slight advantage academically, perhaps because of the exclusive time they had with their parents before any brothers or sisters came along, and also possibly because they themselves benefit from teaching younger siblings (G. H. Brody, 2004; Zajonc & Mullally, 1997). Younger siblings show greater skill in interacting with peers, possibly as a result of negotiating with older siblings and learning how to outmaneuver them to gain favor with parents (Dunn, 1984; N. Miller & Maruyama, 1976). Even preschool-age siblings discuss their needs and desires with one another, and such discussions may give them practice in inferring the perspectives of other people (Dunn, 1993; Perner, Ruffman, & Leekam, 1994; Ruffman, Perner, Naito, Parkin, & Clements, 1998).

Sibling rivalry is often a fact of life in families with multiple children. Children regularly compete for limited resources, including parents' attention, and occasionally become downright combative over seemingly trivial issues (such as who gets to select first from a full plate of freshly baked cookies: "Lem*me* go first!" "No, it's *my* turn!"). Competition among siblings probably has some benefits, including creating a motivation to learn new skills (so as to keep up with or outsmart siblings). However, resentment may brew if one child feels slighted by a parent who appears to favor another (G. H. Brody, Stoneman, & McCoy, 1994). Children may also feel jealous when, with age, their siblings increasingly form friendships outside the family circle (Dunn, 1996).

Despite their importance for many children, siblings are by no means essential for healthy development. *Only children*—children without brothers or sisters—are often stereotyped as spoiled and egotistical, but research findings on their adjustment are favorable. On average, only children perform well in school and enjoy particularly close relationships with their parents (Falbo, 1992; Falbo & Polit, 1986).

When children do have siblings, teachers can often take advantage of their close-knit relationships, especially when children face a loss or challenge. For instance, in times of family

Listen to Robin characterize her relationships with siblings in the "Families: Late Adolescence" clip on Observation CD 3.

My brother helps me play football.

Children learn many things from their brothers and sisters. Art by Alex, age 10.

crisis (e.g., the death of a grandparent or a parent's imprisonment), children may appreciate contact with siblings, perhaps on the playground, in the lunchroom, or in the nurse's office.

Educators can also show their sensitivity to the importance of siblings during schoolwide events. For example, many schools welcome the entire family during back-to-school nights, and school personnel might make durable toys and child-friendly snacks available for younger siblings. During conferences, teachers should avoid making comparisons between students and their siblings. And when making classroom placements, teachers and other school personnel can listen respectfully to families' perspectives on siblings' needs. For instance, some parents of twins favor keeping them together in the classroom, especially in the early grades and when the children have had little experience being separated (Preedy, 1999; N. L. Segal & Russell, 1992). At the same time, teachers will have their own experiences with siblings and can share these with parents, for example, as when a teacher notices that twins have become disruptive by being together in the classroom.

Risk Factors in Families

As you have seen, "good" families—those that foster children's physical, cognitive, and social-emotional development—come in a wide variety of packages, and they use many, probably countless, distinct styles. In sometimes strikingly different ways, a multitude of psychologically healthy families adequately meet children's basic needs.

Unfortunately, not all families provide optimal environments for children. **Child maltreatment** is the most serious outcome of an unhealthy family environment. Maltreatment takes four major forms (English, 1998; R. A. Thompson & Wyatt, 1999). *Neglect* occurs when caregivers fail to provide food, clothing, shelter, health care, or affection and do not adequately supervise children's activities (the uninvolved parents we described earlier are neglectful when they are truly disengaged from their children). Caregivers engage in *physical abuse* when they intentionally cause physical harm to children, perhaps by kicking, biting, shaking, or punching them. If spanking causes serious bruises or injuries, it, too, is considered physical abuse. Caregivers engage in *sexual abuse* when they seek sexual gratification from children through acts such as genital contact or pornographic photography. They engage in *emotional abuse* when they consistently ignore, isolate, reject, denigrate, or terrorize children or when they corrupt children by encouraging them to engage in substance abuse or criminal activity. Sadly, some parents and other caregivers submit children to more than one form of abuse, as one woman's recollection illustrates:

> My father used to do the weirdest things to me. I hate him. He was in the navy, back in the war and stuff like that. I guess he picked up weird things like that. He used to put me in the corner and put a bag over my head and every time he'd walk by he'd kick me—just like a dog. My mom told me once he put a tick on my stomach and let the tick suck my blood. Things like that—really gross, things that a father would never do to their (sic) daughter. He'd stick toothpicks up my fingernails until it would bleed. [Did he sexually abuse you, too?] Oh, yeah. When I was six. Had to get me to the hospital. I had twenty stitches. I just can't talk about it. (Belenky, Clinchy, Goldberger, & Tarule, 1986, p. 159)

Tragically, children can suffer long-term consequences from being neglected or assaulted by family members (English, 1998; Emery & Laumann-Billings, 1998; Gershoff, 2002; Leiter & Johnsen, 1997; R. A. Thompson & Wyatt, 1999). Infants without adequate nutrition may experience permanent retardation of their physical growth. Neglected toddlers have difficulty trusting others and forming healthy relationships with peers and adults. When they reach school age, children who have been abused and neglected tend to do poorly in school and to be absent frequently; they are also more likely to experience emotional problems, commit crimes (e.g., shoplifting), and engage in alcohol and substance abuse. Children who endure sexual abuse may become infected with sexually transmitted diseases and face emotional problems. Physically abused children are more likely than nonabused children to become aggressive themselves, have poor social skills, show little empathy for the distress of others and, in their adulthood, partake in criminal and antisocial behavior.

The occurrence of child maltreatment seems to be related to characteristics of both the adult perpetrator and child victim. Adults who maltreat children usually suffer from serious psychological problems, such as having low self-esteem or being anxious, depressed, aggressive, or impulsive (National Research Council, 1993b; R. A. Thompson & Wyatt, 1999).

child maltreatment
Adverse treatment of a child in the form of neglect, physical abuse, sexual abuse, or emotional abuse.

Some neglectful and abusive parents have serious substance abuse problems (Bishop et al., 2001; Kienberger-Jaudes, Ekwo, & Van Voorhis, 1995; R. A. Thompson & Wyatt, 1999). Many have little contact with family or friends (R. A. Thompson & Wyatt, 1999). Some abusive parents are quite naive about children's development and become angry when children fail to fulfill unrealistic expectations (English, 1998). Children most likely to be maltreated are those who are very young (premature infants are especially at risk), have disabilities, and are irritable and not easily soothed (English, 1998; L. Little, 2000a; P. Sullivan & Knutson, 1998; R. A. Thompson & Wyatt, 1999).

> *Dear Diary,*
> *Father was home early from the bar. He was really drunk this time. I was just sitting down reading a book when he started hitting me. My mom tried to help me but it was no use. Finnaly went to a corner when he fainted. After that mom and I left for Aunt Mary. Maybe we'll be safe there.*

Like the father described in this child's diary entry, many family members who are abusive suffer from serious psychological problems.

Educators and others working with children and adolescents must, by law, contact proper authorities (e.g., Child Protective Services) when they suspect child abuse or neglect. Child Protective Services may be able to verify the maltreatment and to provide the family with counseling, parent education, housing assistance, substance abuse treatment, home visits, and referrals for other services. Almost one-fifth of child victims are placed in foster care after an investigation or assessment for child maltreatment (U.S. Department of Health and Human Services, 2004). Unfortunately, reports to Child Protective Services do not always lead to immediate services for maltreated children or their families. Sometimes authorities cannot find sufficient evidence to substantiate suspicions, and at other times high caseloads prevent authorities from giving prompt assistance (Larner et al., 1998; Wolock, Sherman, Feldman, & Metzger, 2001).

As they wait for intervention, maltreated children desperately need stable, caring relationships with adults outside the family. Teachers can offer comfort and address children's reactions to maltreatment, such as being inattentive, disruptive, or withdrawn at school. When authorities do intervene, continued sensitivity from teachers is essential, as children now may need to adjust to changes in family structure (e.g., a child might be placed with a foster family) or family climate (e.g., a mother might become depressed when she learns she might lose custody of her children).

Forming Partnerships with Families

Parents and teachers have much in common. They both take on tough (but gratifying) responsibilities that demand long hours, an unwavering devotion to children, clear objectives, and flexible methods. Of course, parents and teachers occasionally find themselves on opposite sides of the table, as initially happened in our introductory case. When teachers and families ultimately communicate effectively (and Barbara and Mr. Momen eventually did, with help from Cedric), they are likely to magnify their positive effects on children. Ideally, then, teachers and parents (and other heads of family) become partners that collaborate in support of children's learning (Hidalgo, Siu, Bright, Swap, & Epstein, 1995). We offer the following recommendations on forming constructive partnerships with families:

Parents and guardians can support their children's education by participating in school activities, as these mothers are doing by helping out at a school-sponsored carnival.

● *Encourage families to get involved in their children's education.* Parents and other family members are more likely to become involved in children's education when they believe that (a) their involvement is important, (b) they can exert a positive influence on their children's educational achievement, and (c) school personnel want their involvement (R. M. Clark, 1983; Hoover-Dempsey & Sandler, 1997; Lareau, 1989). Thus many teachers encourage families to help children make progress toward academic objectives. When Teresa's son Alex was in fourth grade, he brought home a weekly newsletter from school. Every issue contained the same reminder that children should read nightly for 20 minutes (and by implication, that parents should verify that this reading took place). With older students, teachers may use slightly different tactics, ones that foster family involvement but play down the directive role of parents. For example, Teresa recalls that when her son Connor was in middle school, she and her husband received a booklet containing tear sheets with suggestions on how parents might contribute to school activities (such as driving on field trips, volunteering in the classroom, and bringing in treats for special events); it was easy to go through the booklet, choose a few activities, and send the sheets back to school.

Study Guide and Reader ⎯⎯⎯⎯⎯
Learn more about encouraging family involvement with a parent club in Supplementary Reading 5-3.

● *Address barriers to involvement.* Although most parents and other primary caregivers want what is best for their children, many do not participate in school meetings. Some parents have exhausting work schedules and lack adequate child care. Some families have difficulty communicating in English. Still others may believe that it is inappropriate to bother teachers with questions about their children's progress. And some parents are actively involved when their children are in elementary school but increasingly withdraw as their children move to middle and secondary levels (J. L. Epstein, 1996; Finders & Lewis, 1994; Roderick & Camburn, 1999). A few parents avoid school because of their own painful memories. One father put it this way:

> They expect me to go to school so they can tell me my kid is stupid or crazy. They've been telling me that for three years, so why should I go and hear it again? They don't do anything. They just tell me my kid is bad.
>
> See, I've been there. I know. And it scares me. They called me a boy in trouble but I was a troubled boy. Nobody helped me because they liked it when I didn't show up. If I was gone for the semester, fine with them. I dropped out nine times. They wanted me gone. (Finders & Lewis, 1994, p. 51)

Certainly, it is not easy to override parents' deep-seated reservations about schools, but teachers can communicate their genuine desire to visit with parents at school or have them become involved in some other way.

● *Get to know families.* As you have learned, families come in many forms and are equally diverse in their styles of parenting. Thus an important first step is to determine who the guardians are and whether other family members care for children on a daily basis. The Observation Guidelines table "Identifying Family Conditions" lists characteristics of families that teachers can identify and accommodate.

● *Ask family members about talents they would be willing to share.* Many family members have special abilities (such as woodworking, calligraphy, storytelling) that they would happily demonstrate at school. Likewise, some parents are bilingual, and they might step forward to translate school materials for other parents who speak little English (Finders & Lewis, 1994). To benefit from these talents, you may wish to ask families at the beginning of the year about their interests in sharing particular kinds of expertise with the school.

● *Use a variety of communication formats.* Families appreciate hearing about children's accomplishments, and they deserve to know about behaviors that consistently interfere with children's learning and adjustment. Likewise, teachers can learn a lot about a child's needs from talking with family members. Here are a few helpful forms of communication:

Meetings: In most schools, parent-teacher-student conferences are scheduled one or more times a year. These meetings are an excellent forum for celebrating children's successes and identifying areas that need additional attention. For example, at one conference it may be mutually agreed that the teacher will find new assignments that better match the child's needs, the child will begin keeping track of due dates for homework, and the family will reserve a quiet place at home for the child to do homework uninterrupted.

Written communications: Educators can use structured forms to let parents know what their children are doing. Prepared forms that specify activities and leave space for individual comments can be helpful. In Figure 5-6, teachers describe 2½-year-old Sam's first day in the toddler room, including information about their program and how Sam fared. More formal newsletters communicate school- and community-wide events, resources, and policies.

Telephone conversations: Telephone calls are useful when issues require immediate attention. For example, teachers might call parents to express concern when a student's behavior deteriorates unexpectedly. But they might also call to express their excitement about an important step forward. Parents, too, should feel free to call teachers. Keep in mind that many parents are at work during the school day; hence it is often helpful for teachers to take calls at home during the early evening hours.

Figure 5-6

A structured daily activity form completed for 2½-year-old Sam. Parents often appreciate information about what their children did and learned during the day.

OBSERVATION GUIDELINES

Identifying Family Conditions

Characteristic	Look For	Example	Implication
Family Structure	• Single versus multiple caregivers • Presence or absence of siblings • Extended family members living in the home • Nonrelatives living in the home • Children's attachments to and relationships with other family members	Alexis's chronic kidney disease flare-ups cause fatigue and irritability. At such times, she finds comfort in being with her older sister at recess and lunch. Alexis's teachers have observed the girls' close relationship and provide opportunities for them to be together when Alexis is ill.	Accept all heads of family as valued, legitimate caregivers of children. Include extended family members (especially those who appear to be regular caregivers) at school functions. Give youngsters time to be with siblings in times of personal or family crisis.
Cultural Background	• Language(s) spoken at home • Children's loyalty to and sense of responsibility for other family members • Children's attitudes toward cooperation and competition • Children's and parents' communication styles (whether they make eye contact, ask a lot of questions, are open about their concerns, etc.)	Carlos is very reserved in class. He follows instructions and shows that he wants to do well in school. However, he rarely seeks his teacher's help. Instead, he often asks his cousin (a classmate) for assistance.	Remember that most children and parents are interested in academic achievement, despite what their behaviors may make you think. Adapt instructional styles to children's preferred ways of interacting and communicating. Consider how families' cultural knowledge and skills might enrich the classroom.
Family Livelihood	• Presence of a family business (e.g., farm, cottage industry) that requires children's involvement • Children in self-care for several hours after school • Older children and adolescents with part-time jobs (e.g., grocery store work, paper routes) • Parental unemployment	April completes several chores on the family farm before going to school each morning. She keeps records of the weight and health of three calves born last year. She constructs charts to show their progress as a project for her seventh-grade science class.	Take young people's outside work commitments into account when assigning homework. For example, give students at least 2 days to complete short assignments and at least a week for longer ones.
Parenting Styles	• Parents' warmth or coldness toward their children • Parents' expectations for their children's behavior and performance • Parents' willingness to discuss issues and negotiate solutions with their children • Possible effects of children's temperaments on parents' disciplinary styles • Children's interpretations of parents' motives in disciplining them • Cultural values, such as honoring one's elders, that give meaning to parents' discipline • Dangers and opportunities in the community that influence the effects of a given parenting style	At a parent-teacher conference, Julia's parents express their exasperation about trying to get Julia to do her homework: "We've tried everything—reasoning with her, giving ultimatums, offering extra privileges for good grades, punishing her for bad grades—but nothing seems to work. She'd rather hang out with her friends every night."	Acknowledge that most parents have their children's best interests at heart and use disciplinary methods they have seen others use. Recognize that parents often adapt their parenting styles to children's temperaments. Communicate high expectations, show sensitivity to children's needs, and give reasons for your requests.
Disruptive Influences	• Change in family membership (e.g., as a result of death, divorce, remarriage, or cohabitation) • Change of residence • Physical or mental illness in parents or other family members • Parental alcoholism or substance abuse • Economic poverty • Long-term stress in the family	Justin has had trouble concentrating since his parents' divorce, and he no longer shows much enthusiasm for class activities.	Show compassion for children undergoing a significant family transition. Listen patiently if children would like to talk. Realize that some families may quickly return to healthy functioning but others may be in turmoil for lengthy periods. Seek the assistance of a counselor when children have unusual difficulty.
Maltreatment	• Frequent injuries, usually attributed to "accidents" • Age-inappropriate sexual knowledge or behavior • Extreme withdrawal, anxiety, or depression • Excessive aggression and hostile behaviors • Untreated medical or dental needs • Chronic hunger • Poor hygiene and grooming • Lack of warm clothing in cold weather	Johnny often has bruises on his arms and legs, which his mother says are the result of a "blood problem." He recently broke his collarbone, and soon after that, he had a black eye. "I fell down the stairs," he explained, but refused to say more.	Immediately report any signs of child maltreatment to a school counselor or principal. Contact Child Protective Services for advice about additional courses of action that should be followed.

Hello!

How much money would it take for you to agree to go back to your 7th grade year of school? You couldn't pay me enough!!!

Disrespect and thoughtless comments to peers seem to be on the upswing in the 7th grade at [our school]. Today we had a town meeting, and I had one of my serious chats with the class about the importance of treating others properly. I strongly encouraged students to step back and evaluate their own behavior. I asked them to think about whether their parents would be proud of how they treat others. I also asked if they personally were proud of how they treat others.

I think most of you know me well enough by now to know that I have a low tolerance for people who treat others poorly. If your child is having trouble with peers, please encourage him or her to talk with me. If s/he is struggling with taking that first step, I hope you would take the time to call me to discuss it. Unless I'm aware of concerns, I can't work on making things better.

It takes a village.

Nancy

Figure 5-7

Professionals who work with families can sometimes stay in touch by electronic mail. In this e-mail message a counselor alerts parents to the social climate at school.

Courtesy of Nancy S. Rapport.

When you suspect you have views that conflict with those of a child's parents or guardians, share your perspectives about the child's needs and ask family members to do the same.

─────── **Study Guide and Reader**
Learn more about parents' ideas and how they may differ from those of teachers in Supplementary Reading 5-4.

E-mail and Web sites: Increasingly, educators find that they can maintain regular contact with parents electronically—for instance, by sending e-mail messages and creating Web pages that list events and assignments. In Figure 5-7, you can see an e-mail message sent by a school counselor to parents. Notice that the counselor not only advises parents of a problem but asks for their help in encouraging proper behavior. Such electronic communication, of course, can be used only when parents have easy access to computer technology and the Internet.

Parent discussion groups: In some instances teachers, counselors, and principals may want to assemble a group of parents to discuss mutual concerns. For example, school leaders might want to use a discussion group as a sounding board for evaluating possible school improvement plans.

● *When two or more family members are primary caregivers, encourage everyone to stay in touch.* For example, when two parents are actively involved in a child's life—whether they live in the same household or not—teachers should try to get to know both parents and show respect for the role that each plays in the child's development. All too often, fathers are left out of the picture, yet in today's society fathers tend to be more involved in children's lives than their own fathers were with them (Tamis-LeMonda & Cabrera, 1999).

● *When first meeting with parents and other heads of family, establish rapport.* Although some parents feel confident and comfortable when they talk with teachers, others may be anxious, uncertain, or distrustful. Educators can look for signs of discomfort, use friendly body language, comment optimistically about children's abilities, display a sense of humor, and treat parents as authorities who can help them learn about children's needs.

● *Be a listener as well as a talker.* Most parents want to be heard rather than just "talked at" (Hoover-Dempsey & Sandler, 1997), yet some may be reluctant to voice their perspectives without some encouragement. Educators can often encourage input by asking specific questions (e.g., "What does Kira like to do in her free time?") and assuring parents that they should feel free to call whenever they have questions or concerns.

● *Help parents see that the concerns they have about their children often are natural responses to children's developmental challenges.* For example, parents may worry about separating from their babies in the child care center; handling oppositional behaviors of young children; teaching indispensable academic skills during middle childhood; and helping young adolescents cope with puberty. You can see an expanded list of parents' concerns and ways teachers might address them in the Developmental Trends table "The Family's Concerns for Children of Different Ages" on pages 172–173. Teachers can also play an enormously helpful role in casting children's developmental abilities in a positive light, as you can see in a middle school teacher's handout for parents in Figure 5-8.

● *Step into their shoes.* Families sometimes live very different lives than those of the professionals who work with them. By talking with community leaders, reading the research on local groups, and listening sympathetically to parents, educators can learn a lot about various families' lives. For example, by seeking information about homeless families who reside in temporary shelters, teachers would learn about the many efforts these parents make to protect their children (Torquati, 2002). With these insights, teachers would likely see value in reassuring parents about the school's procedures for ensuring a safe, stimulating environment for children.

● *Remember that most parents view their children's behavior as a reflection of their own competence.* Parents typically feel proud when their children are successful in school and get along well with friends. In contrast, parents may respond to their children's academic failures or behavior problems with embarrassment, shame, anger, or denial. Teachers are more likely to have productive discussions with parents if they avoid placing blame and instead propose that they all—students, parents, and teachers—work as teams to find solutions.

● *Be alert for possible cultural differences.* When conferring with parents about children's problematic classroom behaviors, educators should keep in mind that people from different cultural groups usually have distinct ideas about how children should be disciplined. For example, many Chinese American parents believe that Western schools are too lenient in correcting inappropriate behavior (Hidalgo et al., 1995). In some Native American and Asian cultures, a child's misbehaviors may be seen as bringing shame on the family or community; thus a common disciplinary strategy is to ignore or ostracize the child for an extended period of time (Pang, 1995; Salend & Taylor, 1993). As educators talk with family members who have different cultural views, they can listen with an open mind and try to find common ground on which to develop strategies for helping children (Salend & Taylor, 1993).

● *Accommodate language and literacy differences.* When a child's parents speak a language other than English, educators often try to include in conversations someone who can converse fluently with the parents in their native tongue (and ideally, someone whom the parents trust). Educators should also have newsletters and other written messages translated whenever it is reasonable to do so.

● *Reflect on and curb your biases.* Teachers and other practitioners are occasionally influenced by stereotypes of certain cultural or socioeconomic groups. For example, some caregivers in child care settings have negative views of low-income families and may inadvertently communicate these biases to parents (Holloway, Fuller, Rambaud, & Eggers-Péirola, 1997; Kontos, Raikes, & Woods, 1983; Kontos & Wells, 1986). Practitioners can effectively work with children and parents from diverse backgrounds only when they actively reflect on their existing assumptions about particular groups and strive to look for the unique qualities and characteristics—and especially the *strengths*—that each child and parent is apt to have.

● *Inform parents of services available to them.* Families in trouble often appreciate hearing about agencies that offer supportive services. For example, families who have been found to be seriously maltreating their children may be at risk for having the children placed in foster care. In such cases teachers and other professionals must protect children, but often they can also advise parents about potentially helpful services, such as outlets for family recreation and parent groups (Staudt, 2001).

● *When appropriate, visit families in their homes.* Home visits are a widely used way of supporting parents' efforts at home, especially with young children (Gomby, Culross, & Behrman, 1999). Home visiting programs typically focus on educating parents about children's needs and preventing such problems as neglect or abuse. To make home visits maximally effective, educators can present themselves as friendly and nonjudgmental, make an effort to establish rapport with parents and other family members, and offer practical suggestions for helping children to learn. One educator considers home visits a vital first step in communicating with migrant families:

> At the beginning of the school year, [Name] Elementary went house by house in their whole zone. . . . Everybody—the counselors, the librarian, the clerks, the paraprofessionals—went to visit families. Everybody's home was visited at least once by somebody in the school in a positive fashion. OK? They told [parents] "*Mire Señora, queremos que sepa que en la escuela nos importa su hija o hijo y queremos saber dónde vive y si le podemos ayudar en algo, estamos para servirle.* [Look, Miss, we want you to know that we care about your daughter or son and we

---

Adolescent Development

Eleven . . . is a time of breaking up, of discord and discomfort. Gone is the bland complaisance of the typical ten-year-old. Eleven is a time of loosening up, of snapping old bonds, of trial and error as the young child tests the limits of what authority will and will not permit

Louise Bates Ames, Ph.D.
Your Ten- to Fourteen-Year-Old
Gesell Institute of Human Development

To understand your adolescent, you need to consider . . .
. . . the child s basic individuality.
. . . what is expected of anyone of his or her particular age level.
. . . what environment your child finds himself or herself in.

Eleven-year-olds can be . . .
egocentric,
energetic,
always "loving" or "hating";

as well as . . .
not as cooperative or accepting as in the past
more angry than in the past
inattentive
hungry all the time
more interested in the clothes they wear (but not in cleaning them!)
uncertain
more apt to cry
fearful
rebellious
very interested and involved in family activities

Figure 5-8

Teachers can be valuable sources of information about child and adolescent development. In this flier for parents, middle school teacher Erin Miguel describes several common characteristics of young adolescents.
Reprinted with permission of Erin Miguel, Jones Middle School, Columbus, Ohio.

DEVELOPMENTAL TRENDS	The Family's Concerns for Children of Different Ages		
Age	**Topics**	**Diversity**	**Implications**
Infancy (Birth–2) 	**Physical Development** • Ensuring infants' basic safety by structuring the environment so they cannot put themselves in danger (e.g., by tumbling down stairs, swallowing cleaning supplies) • Meeting infants' physical needs (e.g., feeding on a baby's schedule, diapering, and easing baby into a sleep schedule that conforms to adults' patterns) • Giving proper nutrition to match physiological needs and pace of growth **Cognitive Development** • Offering face-to-face interactions • Talking with infants and responding enthusiastically to their babbling • Encouraging infants to take turns in conversations and simple games • Providing appropriate sensory stimulation **Social-Emotional Development** • Watching for infants' preferences and abiding by these—for example, after noticing that an infant enjoys watching vehicles, selecting picture books with trucks to share with the child • Arranging for consistent, stable, responsive caregivers to whom children can become emotionally attached • Affirming infants' feelings so that they begin to understand emotions • Responding with reasonable promptness to infants' cries so that they learn that they can rely on parents	• Some parents may promote independence in infants by encouraging them to try self-help actions, such as picking up bits of food and feeding themselves; others may prefer to do these things for infants. • Nap time may depend on parents' beliefs about how much sleep children need and the proper way to help them fall asleep. • Parents may differ in how much they talk with infants. Some may verbalize frequently; others may soothe infants and focus on nonverbal gestures. • Families differ in beliefs about out-of-home care. Some parents resist commercial child care and will leave infants only for brief periods with familiar relatives. Other parents are comfortable with employed caregivers. • Concerns of parents depend partly on the temperament and health status of infants. When infants are difficult to soothe or are sick, parents may be quite concerned.	• Complete daily records of infants' physical care so that parents are aware of how their infants' needs were met and the kind of day they had. • Talk with parents about the developmental milestones (e.g., rolling over, sitting up, uttering a first word) you notice in infants. For example, point out when you notice a new tooth breaking through the gums. • Post a chart of typical developmental milestones (e.g., rolling over, sitting up, uttering a first word) so that parents can think about what their infants might be presently learning. Select a chart that emphasizes the variation in ages at which infants attain developmental milestones. • Ask parents to share their concerns about their infants, and offer reassurance when appropriate.
Early Childhood (2–6) 	**Physical Development** • Ensuring children's basic safety (e.g., protecting them from street traffic and household chemicals) • Helping children with self-care routines (e.g., dressing, brushing teeth, bathing) • Finding appropriate outlets for physical energy **Cognitive Development** • Answering children's seemingly incessant questions • Channeling curiosity into constructive activities • Reading stories and in other ways promoting a foundation for literacy • Preparing for transition to formal schooling **Social-Emotional Development** • Curbing temper tantrums • Promoting sharing among siblings and peers • Addressing conflicts and aggressive behavior • Forming relationships with new caregivers in child care and preschool	• Some parents, worrying about their children's safety, are exceptionally reluctant to leave them in the care of others. • Low-income families have little or no discretionary income with which to purchase books and other supplies for cognitive enrichment. • Some kindergartners and first graders have had little or no prior experiences with other children; for instance, they may be only children or may not have previously attended child care or preschool. • Some parents (especially those from higher-income, professional backgrounds) may overdo efforts to maximize children's cognitive development, giving children too many intellectually challenging activities and too few chances to relax or play.	• Suggest possible approaches to teaching young children about self-care habits, social skills, and impulse control. • Keep parents regularly informed about their children's progress in both academic and social skills. • Provide books and other stimulating materials that parents can check out and use at home. • When highly educated parents seem overly concerned about maximizing their children's cognitive development, suggest literature (e.g., John Bruer's *The Myth of the First Three Years*) that encourages a balance between stimulation and relaxation.

DEVELOPMENTAL TRENDS

The Family's Concerns for Children of Different Ages (continued)

Age	Topics	Diversity	Implications
Middle Childhood (6–10) 	**Physical Development** • Fostering healthy eating habits • Using safety equipment (e.g., seatbelts in the car, helmets for cycling or skateboarding) • Establishing exercise routines and limiting television and video games **Cognitive Development** • Helping children acquire habits and expectations that will aid them in their academic work • Promoting mastery of basic academic skills • Enhancing children's education through family involvement and outings **Social-Emotional Development** • Giving children increasing independence and responsibility (e. g., for waking up on time, doing homework) • Monitoring interactions with siblings, playmates • Instilling moral values (e.g., honesty, fairness)	• Some parents may be overly stressed from work responsibilities. • Some neighborhoods have few if any playgrounds or other places where children can safely play. • Children's special talents and interests influence their choices of activities outside the home. • Some children look after themselves for long periods after school, and they may or may not use this time wisely.	• Obtain and distribute literature about safety measures from local police, fire departments, and pediatricians' offices. • Provide resource materials (perhaps through a parent library in the classroom) that parents can use to assist their children with academic subject matter. • Encourage parents' involvement in school activities and parent-teacher groups. • Suggest facilities and programs in the community (e.g., youth soccer leagues, scout organizations) that provide free or inexpensive opportunities for after-school recreation and skill development.
Early Adolescence (10–14) 	**Physical Development** • Recognizing and dealing with early stages of puberty • Encouraging physical fitness • Affording basic clothing during periods of rapid growth **Cognitive Development** • Supporting school-based changes in expectations for academic performance • Accepting that adolescents want the world to be better than parents and other adults have made it **Social-Emotional Development** • Showing sensitivity to self-consciousness about appearance • Accommodating requests for more leisure time with peers • Dealing with increased conflict as adolescents seek greater autonomy	• Children differ markedly in the age at which they begin puberty. • Different families have different decision-making styles. • Some parents may have considerable difficulty allowing their children greater independence. • Overt parent-teenager conflicts are rare in some cultures, especially in those that cultivate respect for elders (e.g., many Asian cultures). • Some young teens may have little access to safe and well-equipped recreational facilities. • Peer groups encourage varying behaviors and values.	• Identify and inform parents about age-appropriate athletic and social programs in the community. • Collaborate with colleagues and teachers to establish a homework hotline through which students can get ongoing support and guidance for home assignments. • Share with parents your impressions about reasonable expectations for independence and responsibility in young adolescents.
Late Adolescence (14–18) 	**Physical Development** • Keeping track of teenagers' whereabouts • Encouraging high school students to maintain realistic schedules that allow adequate sleep • Worrying about risky driving • Concern about possible alcohol and drug use **Cognitive Development** • Encouraging youth to persist with increasingly challenging academic subject matter • Understanding adolescents' expanding capacity for logical, systematic thinking • Educating adolescents about employment prospects and college requirements **Social-Emotional Development** • Worrying about the loss of parental control over teenagers' social activities • Finding a reasonable balance between supervision and independence • Monitoring adolescents' part-time jobs	• Alcohol and drugs are readily available in most communities, but their use is more frequent and socially acceptable in some neighborhoods than in others. • Some parents refuse to believe that their children may be engaged in serious health-compromising behaviors, even when faced with evidence. • Families differ in their knowledge of, and experiences with, higher education; some may be unable to counsel their children about options in postsecondary education. • Parents differ in the extent to which they encourage teenagers' part-time employment.	• Suggest ways in which adolescents can maintain regular contact with their families when they are away from home for lengthy periods (e.g., by making regular phone calls home). • Provide information about possible careers and educational opportunities after high school; include numerous options, including part-time and full-time vocational programs, community colleges, and four-year colleges and universities.

Sources: W. A. Collins, 1990; Maccoby, 1980, 1984; Montemayor, 1982; Mortimer, Shanahan, & Ryu, 1994; Paikoff & Brooks-Gunn, 1991; Pipher, 1994; Warton & Goodnow, 1991; Youniss, 1983.

DEVELOPMENT AND PRACTICE

Making Schools Family-Friendly

- Help children and their families feel that they are valued members of the school.

  A caregiver of infants and toddlers provides storage boxes ("cubbies") for each child. On the outside, the child's name is posted and photographs of the child and his or her family are displayed. Children regularly point to their parents and other family members throughout the day.

- Recognize the significance of families in children's lives.

  A music teacher asks students to bring in the lyrics from their favorite family songs. She posts the words of songs on a bulletin board labeled "My Family and Me."

- Acknowledge the strengths of families' varying backgrounds.

  When planning a lesson on the history of farming in Colorado, a middle school social studies teacher asks families if they could bring in any farm tools (or photographs of tools) that they use while planting and harvesting crops.

- Use a variety of formats to communicate with parents.

  A fourth-grade teacher works with the children in his class to produce a monthly newsletter for parents. Two versions of the newsletter are created, one in English and one in Spanish.

- Tell parents about children's many strengths, even when communicating information about shortcomings.

  A school counselor talks on the phone with the parents of a student. She describes several areas in which the student has made considerable progress but also asks for advice about strategies that might help him stay on task and be more agreeable with peers.

- Be sensitive to parents' concerns about their children.

  A school counselor talks with worried parents of a 16-year-old girl who has begun smoking and possibly experimenting with drugs. Thinking about the girl's interest in photography, the counselor tells the parents about the school's after-school photography club, with hopes that the companionship of more academically oriented peers might get her back on the right track.

- Encourage all parents and guardians to get involved in school activities.

  A high school principal sends home a book of "coupons" printed with assorted activities that parents and other family members might do to help the school (e.g., tutoring in the classroom, baking goodies for a school open house, serving on the parent advisory group). She accompanies the book with a letter expressing her hope that all parents will return a coupon that commits them to least one activity.

want to know where you live and if we can help you in any way, we are here to serve you.]" And we began to get parents who said, "They care to come out here on an afternoon, when it's hot, you know, and visit? They really care about us!" (G. R. López, Scribner, & Mahitivanichcha, 2001, p. 264)

None of the strategies just described will, in and of itself, guarantee a successful working relationship with parents and other heads of families. Meetings with parents occur somewhat infrequently. Written communication is ineffective with parents who have limited literacy skills. Some families prefer not to be visited at home. And, of course, not everyone has a telephone, let alone e-mail. Despite the difficulty with staying in touch, effective teachers and other practitioners do their best to form productive partnerships with families (e.g., see the Development and Practice feature "Making Schools Family-Friendly").

Life in the Community for Children and Families

By now you are familiar with the idea that children and their families are strongly influenced by people in the community. In this section we focus on several aspects of the community, beginning with an analysis of how children's ethnicity, culture, and gender determine many of their opportunities and much of their outlook on life. We then examine the kinds of communities that children live in and the hardships children face when they and their families live in economic poverty. We end this section with recommendations for educating children who live in low-income families.

Ethnicity, Culture, and Gender

A child's **ethnicity** is his or her affiliation with a group of individuals who share values, beliefs, behaviors and, often, common ancestors. An ethnic group may be comprised of people of the same race, national origin, or religious background.

Culture and ethnicity are overlapping concepts. Often a single society (such as citizens of the United States) may be comprised of several ethnic groups. Conversely, one ethnic group can be composed of individuals from numerous cultural groups. For example, people who are *Hispanic* tend to be Spanish- or Portuguese-speaking (or descended from individuals who spoke these languages), and they may originate from one of several very different regions (Spain, Mexico, Central and South American countries, Spanish-speaking Caribbean

ethnicity
Membership in a group of people with common ancestors and shared values, beliefs, and behaviors.

nations or Portugal); as a result, Hispanics share a few common values but have many distinct cultural practices (C. B. Fisher, Jackson, & Villarruel, 1998). The implication of this heterogeneity is that knowing a child comes from a Hispanic American background gives only a rough idea as to what his or her cultural values might be.

Ethnicity also overlaps, to some degree, with race. In some ethnic groups, members may come from a single race, but this is not always the case. In general, *ethnicity* has a stronger association with cultural dimensions, and *race* connotes physical similarities such as skin color or eye shape (C. B. Fisher et al., 1998). As we have suggested, a child's ethnic group may furnish some values and traditions. A child's race, which often is apparent to others, can be an especially strong factor in how he or she is treated—whether the child encounters discrimination or privilege, for instance.

Membership in a particular racial or ethnic group is not always a good indication of children's cultural beliefs.

Today many children are *multiethnic,* claiming ancestry from more than a single ethnic group. For instance, a child whose mother has African American and Native American heritage and whose father immigrated from England may be exposed to a variety of family traditions (E. W. King, 1999). Multiethnic children may affiliate with two or more ethnic groups and selectively carry out particular traditions depending on the context (e.g., eating contemporary American foods in restaurants and traditional Vietnamese dishes at family gatherings).

Culture, ethnicity, and families.   Families play a major role in imparting cultural beliefs and practices. For instance, in some ethnic groups, including those found in many Hispanic, Native American, and Asian communities, obligation to family is especially important. Children raised in these cultures are likely to feel responsibility for their family's well-being and a strong sense of loyalty to other family members (Abi-Nader, 1993; García, 1994; Hidalgo et al., 1995). For example, Chinese families who immigrate to the United States typically strive to instill in their children honor of family, respect for elders, and eagerness to achieve academically (Chao, 2000). Cultures that emphasize family obligation often require cooperation within social groups and actively discourage competition (Hollins, 1996; Okagaki & Sternberg, 1993).

In many Western cultures, parents value school achievement and encourage children to do well in school (Banks & Banks, 1995; Delgado-Gaitan, 1992; B. J. Duran & Weffer, 1992; Hossler & Stage, 1992; A. H. Yee, 1992). The specific forms of this encouragement differ to some degree from one ethnic group to another. Many Asian American parents transmit the belief that high academic achievement comes only with considerable effort and persistence (Hess, Chang, & McDevitt, 1987). In many Latino cultures, being well educated does not refer solely to having a good formal education; it also means being successful in social situations and showing respect to others (Okagaki & Sternberg, 1993; Parke & Buriel, 1998). In some traditional Native American and Polynesian communities, children are expected to excel in art, dance, and other cultural traditions more than in such academic pursuits as reading or mathematics (Kirschenbaum, 1989; N. Reid, 1989; Wise & Miller, 1983).

Culture, gender, and families.   Most cultures socialize girls and boys somewhat differently. For instance, European American parents are likely to encourage daughters to engage in stereotypically feminine behaviors (e.g., playing with dolls, helping other people) and freely express emotions. Meanwhile, they are apt to encourage sons to undertake stereotypically masculine activities (e.g., playing with blocks, engaging in rough-and-tumble play) and hide feelings that convey weakness, such as fear and sadness (Bornstein, Haynes, Pascual, Painter, & Galperin, 1999; Lippa, 2002; Lytton & Romney, 1991). Parents also tend to assign household chores based on traditional male and female roles. For example, they ask their daughters to wash dishes and clean the house and ask their sons to mow the lawn and take out the garbage (Eisenberg et al., 1996; S. M. McHale, Bartko, Crouter, & Perry-Jenkins, 1990). Parents are also more likely to enroll sons, rather than daughters, in competitive sports leagues and programs for gifted students (Eccles, Wigfield, & Schiefele, 1998).

Group and individual differences exist in how families socialize children to become men and women. Although most cultural groups make clear distinctions between what "men do" and what "women do," some cultures permit boys and girls to act similarly. For instance, some lower-income African American parents encourage sons and daughters to be emotionally expressive, and they communicate that both men and women can be powerful and helpful people (P. T. Reid, 1985). Yet differences in socialization exist within any single group, with some parents being far more traditional in their views of appropriate male and female behaviors than others. To some degree, parents who endorse gender stereotypes have children with similar beliefs (Tenenbaum & Leaper, 2002). But children also have their own predispositions to act (or not act) in stereotypically masculine or feminine ways, and these tendencies may or may not be consistent with their parents' traditional or egalitarian biases (Liben & Bigler, 2002).

Ethnicity, immigration, and social change.   Cultural and ethnic differences become salient when people move from one environment to another—for instance, when they immigrate to a new country. When different cultural groups exist in the same region, the two groups interact and learn about one another (C. B. Fisher et al., 1998). As people participate in the customs and take on the values of a new culture, **acculturation** occurs. Acculturation takes four different forms:

- **Assimilation.** Some people totally embrace values and customs of the new culture, giving up their original cultural identity in the process (LaFromboise, Hardin, Coleman, & Gerton, 1993). Assimilation is typically a gradual process that occurs over several generations (Delgado-Gaitan, 1994).
- **Selective adoption.** Immigrants may acquire some customs of the new culture while also retaining other customs from their homeland. For instance, families may begin to celebrate some of the holidays of their new culture while continuing to observe holidays from their country of origin.
- **Rejection.** Sometimes people move to a new culture without taking on any of their new community's cultural practices (U. Kim & Choi, 1994). Complete rejection of a new culture is probably possible only when an individual has little need to interact with people in that culture.
- **Bicultural orientation.** Some people retain their original culture yet also acquire beliefs and master practices of their new culture, and they readily adjust behaviors to fit the particular contexts in which they find themselves (Hong, Morris, Chiu, & Benet-Martínez, 2000).

In previous decades total assimilation was considered by many people in the United States to be the optimal situation for immigrants and, more generally, members of ethnic minority groups. The route to success was presumed to entail blending into the "melting pot" in which people of diverse backgrounds became increasingly similar. More recently, however, researchers have discovered that when young immigrants give up their family's cultural traditions, they are at greater risk for dangerous behaviors, such as using alcohol and drugs, having unprotected sex, and engaging in criminal activities (Caetanno, 1987; Gilbert & Cervantes, 1986; Neff, Hoppe, & Perea, 1987; Vega, Gil, Warheit, Zimmerman, & Apospori, 1993; Ventura & Tappel, 1985). Children and adolescents who reject traditional cultural values often find themselves in conflict with their parents and may lack the strong positive values they need to resist temptation (C. B. Fisher et al., 1998).

Increasingly, the idea that the United States is a melting pot is giving way to the idea that the country can be more productively thought of as a "mosaic" of cultural and ethnic pieces that all legitimately contribute to the greater good of society (C. B. Fisher et al., 1998). Consistent with this view, immigrant children appear to adjust most successfully when they learn certain aspects of their new culture while also retaining aspects of their original culture—that is, when they show a pattern of either *selective adoption* or *bicultural orientation*. For instance, adolescent immigrants who maintain allegiance to traditional values enjoy close, unstressed relationships with parents and support from extended family. As a general rule, they do well in school, have few behavioral or mental health problems, and express high life satisfaction (C. B. Fisher et al., 1998; Fuligni, 1998; U. Kim & Choi, 1994).

Challenges faced by children from minority cultural backgrounds.   When children come from cultural backgrounds different from mainstream culture, they not only must tackle basic developmental tasks (such as mastering language and learning about the physical world), but also must face other challenges as well. For example, children from diverse cultural back-

---

———————— **Connecting Concepts**

As you'll learn in Chapter 6, *assimilation* has a different meaning in Piaget's theory of cognitive development. The terms *cultural assimilation* and *cognitive assimilation* are two distinct concepts.

---

acculturation
Process of taking on the customs and values of a new culture.

assimilation
Form of acculturation in which a person totally embraces a new culture, abandoning a previous culture in the process.

selective adoption
Form of acculturation in which a person assumes some customs of a new culture while also retaining some customs of a previous culture.

rejection
Form of acculturation in which a person refuses to learn or accept any customs and values from a new cultural environment.

bicultural orientation
Form of acculturation in which a person is familiar with two cultures and selectively draws from the values and traditions of one or both cultures depending on the context.

grounds follow customs very different from those followed by people in the dominant cultural group, leading to misunderstandings on both sides. To illustrate, in many ethnic minority groups in the United States, parents rarely engage children in the question-answer sessions ("What does a doggie say?" "Wuff!" "That's right! A dog says, 'Ruff, ruff!'") seen in many European American homes and in most American classrooms (Losey, 1995; L. S. Miller, 1995). Unaccustomed to this communication pattern, children may be puzzled when questioned in this way at school or in community settings. Teachers and caregivers not familiar with a child's culture may think something is wrong when the child doesn't respond as expected.

Another challenge many ethnic minority children face is that they and their parents are subjected to *discrimination,* inequitable treatment as a result of their group membership. As an example, compared to European Americans with comparable incomes and credit histories, African Americans and Hispanic Americans tend to be given less information about loan options when applying for mortgages (M. A. Turner et al., 2002). Also, African Americans and Hispanic Americans have, on average, lower-paying jobs than European Americans and are underrepresented in managerial positions and professional occupations (Federal Glass Ceiling Commission, 1995). Due in part to such discrimination, ethnic minority families are more likely than European American families to live in undesirable neighborhoods and to lack sufficient income to purchase books, magazines, and computers.

Coping mechanisms.   Because of discrimination, racism, and segregation, ethnic minority children and their families must develop coping strategies that allow them to adjust effectively under adverse circumstances (Garcia Coll et al., 1996; McAdoo & Martin, 2005; Varela et al., 2004). One coping strategy is to develop a strong **ethnic identity,** an awareness of being a member of a particular group and the commitment to adopting certain values and behaviors characteristic of the group. Youngsters develop a sense of ethnic identity out of the array of messages they receive from families, peers, community, and the media. For instance, they may hear tales of ancestors' struggles and victories in a discriminatory setting, and they may see media portrayals of their ethnic group in particular roles—perhaps as leaders and trailblazers for humane causes or, alternatively, as violent and deviant troublemakers (C. B. Fisher et al., 1998). Eventually, many youngsters form a coherent set of beliefs about their cultural group, become proud of their cultural traditions, and reject demeaning messages from other people (Luster, 1992; Ogbu, 1994; Phinney, 1990; Spencer, Noll, Stoltzfus, & Harpalani, 2001).

A second important coping strategy is to take advantage of confidence-building strategies that are present in some form in every culture. As an illustration, many African American families cultivate positive personal qualities, such as deep religious convictions, that sustain children in difficult environmental conditions, including high unemployment and poverty (McCreary, Slavin, & Berry, 1996). Close bonds with extended family members also help many African American children resist negative peer pressure (Giordano, Cernkovich, & DeMaris, 1993).

School performance.   Despite the challenges they face, many children and adolescents from diverse cultural and ethnic backgrounds manage to hold their own in the classroom. On average, children of immigrant families perform as well academically as native-born children of similar income backgrounds, and they stay in school longer. Children of Asian families and those of highly educated parents are especially successful (Davenport et al., 1998; Flynn, 1991; Fuligni, 1998; McDonnell & Hill, 1993). Not all ethnic groups enjoy academic success, however. African Americans, Native Americans, and Hispanic Americans have historically performed at somewhat lower levels in the classroom than their classmates of European descent (L. S. Miller, 1995). Furthermore, students in these three groups are more likely to be identified as having special educational needs and to drop out prior to graduation (Portes, 1996; Rumberger, 1995; U.S. Department of Education, Office of Civil Rights, 1993).

The lower school achievement of members of some ethnic minority groups occurs because of several factors, including environmental stresses associated with economic hardship,

Connecting Concepts ————
Such question-answer sessions are described in more detail in Chapter 9.

Connecting Concepts ————
Possible roots of such discrimination—*social-cognitive biases*—are described in Chapter 12.

Children often adjust well when they remain knowledgeable about their ethnic heritage and also master customs of mainstream society.

ethnic identity
Awareness of being a member of a particular ethnic or cultural group and willingness to adopt certain behaviors characteristic of that group.

TABLE 5-1	**Percentages of U.S. Children Who Belong to Ethnic Groups**				
	Estimates for Year			**Projections for Year**	
Ethnicity	**1980**	**1990**	**2000**	**2010**	**2020**
White	74	69	61	56	53
Black	15	15	16	15	15
Hispanic	9	12	17	21	24
Asian/Pacific Islander	2	3	4	4	5
American Indian/Alaska Native; multiple race; or any other race	1	4	4	5	6

Note: Figures are for U.S. children 17 years and under. Accumulated percentages may not equal 100 due to rounding error. Data from 2000 and after are not fully comparable to data from previous years due to changes in Census categories.
Source: Federal Interagency Forum on Child and Family Statistics, 2005.

limited access to good schools and educational opportunities, failures of schools to recognize children's cultural strengths, low expectations from some teachers, and (in the case of recent immigrants from non-English-speaking countries) language barriers (Graham, 1989; Holliday, 1985; McLoyd, 1998b; H. W. Stevenson, Chen, & Uttal, 1990).

Creating supportive environments for ethnic minority children.   In the United States the number of children from ethnic minority backgrounds is increasing at a proportionally high rate and is expected to continue to do so (see Table 5-1). Teachers can expect that, regardless of the community in which they work, they will have the opportunity to work with youngsters from diverse ethnic groups. You can see some illustrations of adults nurturing the cultural and ethnic strengths of youngsters in the Development and Practice feature "Accommodating Cultural and Ethnic Differences." Here are some related strategies for helping children from diverse ethnic backgrounds achieve academic and social success:

● ***Seek guidance from cultural authorities.*** Educators who have become experts on a culture's traditions offer helpful viewpoints on how schools and community groups can build on children's diverse experiences. For instance, Madhubuti and Madhubuti (1994) describe African-centered schools in which group learning activities play a key role, African and African American history and traditions are incorporated into curricula, and African American role models are regularly invited into the classroom. Other specialists in African American education recommend acknowledging students' feelings of inequity and disenfranchisement, describing struggles and contributions of students' ancestors, and conducting class discussions about how, together, students can work toward a better society (Asante, 1991; Bakari, 2000; Beauboeuf-LaFontant, 1999; Ladson-Billings, 1994; Mitchell, 1998).

● ***Accept the validity of cultural viewpoints that differ from your own.*** All professionals make assumptions that come from the cultural environments—mainstream or not—in which they grew up. Like all human beings, teachers favor their own attitudes and see their ideas as the way things "should" be, particularly if they belong to the dominant culture (P. J. Miller & Goodnow, 1995). As a result, a teacher may perceive students from other cultural groups as being in some way less capable (e.g., less mature or socially competent) than students from his or her own cultural group, even when the two groups of students actually have similar ability (K. Alexander, Entwisle, & Thompson, 1987; Hong et al., 2000).

Furthermore, although very few professionals intentionally discriminate against young people based on the color of their skin (Sleeter & Grant, 1999), their actions sometimes perpetuate group differences. For instance, some teachers rarely modify or individualize instruction for students with diverse needs; instead, they present instruction in a take-it-or-leave-it manner. Clearly, teaching children in a culturally sen-

Adults naturally make assumptions based on the cultural environment in which they grew up. They should be aware of this tendency and accept that others' cultural viewpoints are also valid.

DEVELOPMENT AND PRACTICE

Accommodating Cultural and Ethnic Differences

- Think about how cultural beliefs and practices serve adaptive functions for children.

  A third-grade teacher notices that few of the children are willing to answer her questions about common pets, even though it is clear from her individual conversations with them that they have pets and know the answers. She discovers that bringing attention to oneself is not appropriate in the children's culture and so modifies her style to allow for group responses.

- Build on children's background experiences.

  A teacher asks her class of inner-city African American children to translate a poem written in a local dialect by an African American scholar. She puts the words to the poem on an overhead transparency and asks children to translate each line into Standard English. In doing so, she cultivates a sense of pride about knowing two language systems (Ladson-Billings, 1994).

- Use materials that represent all ethnic groups in a positive and competent light.

  A history teacher peruses a history textbook to make sure that it portrays all ethnic groups in a nonstereotypical manner. He supplements the text with readings that highlight important roles played by members of various ethnic groups throughout history.

- Establish connections with local communities.

  A high school teacher encourages adolescents to take part in community service projects. The students may choose from a wide range of possibil-

ities, including neighborhood cleanups, story time with preschoolers at the library, and volunteer work at a food bank or soup kitchen.

- Provide opportunities for children of different backgrounds to get to know one another better.

  For a public service project, a teacher forms groups of children for carrying out particular tasks, such as investigating a social problem, identifying existing services, or considering public figures that might be contacted. The teacher is careful to form groups comprised of children from various neighborhoods and ethnic groups.

- Expose youngsters to successful models from various ethnic backgrounds.

  A high school teacher invites several successful professionals from minority groups to speak with her class about their careers. When some youngsters seem interested in particular careers, she arranges for them to spend time with these professionals in their workplaces.

- Be neutral, inclusive, and respectful regarding children's religious practices.

  A preschool teacher encourages children in her class to bring in artifacts that show how they celebrate holidays during the winter months. Children bring in decorations and religious symbols related to Christmas, Ramadan, Kwanzaa, Hanukkah, and the winter solstice.

sitive way requires more than giving lip service to cultural diversity; it requires a genuine commitment to modifying interactions with children so they can achieve their full academic potential. This commitment entails not only a willingness to work with children but also a dedication to learning children's values and traditions (Bakari, 2000).

● *When it is appropriate to do so, accommodate the practices and values of children's cultures.* Some teachers, in an effort to treat everyone equitably, try to be "color-blind" in their treatment of children. But in fact, practitioners are most effective with youngsters when they tailor their practices to children's cultural backgrounds (Diller, 1999; Kottler, 1997; Pérez, 1998; L. Weiner, 1999). The Observation Guidelines table "Identifying Cultural Practices and Beliefs" lists some values and styles of approaching tasks that teachers and other school personnel can identify and accommodate.

● *Include numerous cultural perspectives in curricula and programs for young people.* As societies become the multicultural mosaic we spoke of earlier, it is essential that curricula and instructional methods reflect this diversity (Sleeter & Grant, 1991). **Multicultural education** is one model of schooling that tries to transmit the experiences of numerous cultural groups—and also those of men and women, people of varying sexual orientations, and people with disabilities (Banks, 1995; García, 1995; Hollins, 1996; NCSS Task Force on Ethnic Studies Curriculum Guidelines, 1992). Following are examples of what teachers might do:

- In history, look at wars and other major events from diverse perspectives (e.g., the Spanish perspective of the Spanish-American War and Native American groups' views of pioneers' westward migration in North America).
- In social studies, examine discrimination and oppression.
- In literature, present the work of minority authors and poets.
- In art, consider creations and techniques by artists from around the world.
- In music, teach songs from many cultures and nations.
- In physical education, teach games or folk dances from other countries and cultures. (Asai, 1993; Boutte & McCormick, 1992; Casanova, 1987; Cottrol, 1990; K. Freedman, 2001; Koza, 2001; NCSS Task Force on Ethnic Studies Curriculum Guidelines, 1992; Pang, 1995; Sleeter & Grant, 1999; Ulichny, 1994)

multicultural education
Education that regularly includes the perspectives and experiences of numerous cultural groups.

OBSERVATION GUIDELINES

Identifying Cultural Practices and Beliefs

Characteristic	Look For	Example	Implication
Individualism	• Independence, assertiveness, and self-reliance • Eagerness to pursue individual assignments and tasks • Willingness to compete against others • Pride in one's own accomplishments	When given the choice of doing a project either by herself or with a partner, Melissa decides to work alone. She is thrilled when she earns a third-place ribbon in a statewide competition.	Provide time for independent work, and accommodate children's individual achievement levels. Give feedback about personal accomplishments in private rather than in front of peers.
Collectivism	• Willingness to depend on others • Emphasis on group accomplishments over individual achievements • Preference for cooperative rather than competitive tasks • Concern about bringing honor to one's family • Strong sense of loyalty to other family members	Tsusha is a talented and hard-working seventh grader. She is conscientious about bringing home her graded work assignments to show her parents, but she appears uncomfortable when praised in front of classmates.	Stress group progress and achievement more than individual successes. Make frequent use of cooperative learning activities.
Behavior Toward Authority Figures	• Looking down in the presence of an authority figure (common in some Native American, African American, Mexican American, and Puerto Rican children) *vs.* looking an authority figure in the eye (common in some children of European American descent) • Observing an adult quietly (an expectation in some Native American and some Hispanic groups) *vs.* asking questions when one doesn't understand (common in some European American groups)	A Native American child named Jimmy never says a word to his teacher. He looks frightened when his teacher looks him in the eye and greets him each morning. One day, the teacher looks in another direction and says, "Hello, Jimmy" as he enters the classroom. "Why hello Miss Jacobs," he responds enthusiastically (Gilliland, 1988, p. 26).	Recognize that different cultures show respect for authority figures in different ways; don't misinterpret lack of eye contact or nonresponse as an indication of disinterest or disrespect.
Cognitive Tools	• Focus on the abstract properties of objects and ideas (common in some European American communities) • Preference for personal anecdotes about objects and events (common in some Native American and African American groups)	During a science lesson, a teacher asks children to categorize rocks and minerals and guess how they were formed. Francisco talks about volcanoes and sandstone, whereas Seymour makes groups of specimens similar to those in his grandmother's rock garden.	When presenting natural substances and materials, refer both to abstract concepts and ideas and to objects and experiences in children's everyday lives.
Valued Activities	• Hopes for high achievement in traditional academic areas (common in many cultural groups in Western countries) • Devaluing of school achievement as representative of White culture (evident in some students from minority groups) • Expectations for excellence in culture-specific activities, such as art or dance (often seen in traditional Native American and Polynesian communities)	Clarence is obviously a very bright young man, but he shows considerable ambivalence about doing well in his high school classes. He often earns high marks on quizzes and tests, but he rarely participates in class discussions or turns in homework assignments.	Show how academic subject matter relates to children's lives. Acknowledge youngsters' achievement in nonacademic as well as academic pursuits. Allow young people to keep their accomplishments confidential from age-mates so that they can maintain credibility with peers who don't value school achievement.
Conceptions of Time	• Concern for punctuality and acknowledgment of deadlines for assignments (common for some students of European descent) • Lack of concern for specific times and schedules (observed in some Hispanic and Native American communities)	Lucy and her parents are diligent about going to parent-teacher conferences, but they often arrive well after their scheduled time.	Encourage punctuality as a way of enhancing children's long-term success in mainstream Western society. At the same time, recognize that not all children are especially concerned about clock time. Be flexible when parents seem to disregard strict schedules.

Sources: Banks & Banks, 1995; Basso, 1984; Garcia, 1994; Garrison, 1989; Gilliland, 1988; Grant & Gomez, 2001; Heath, 1983; Irujo, 1988; Kirschenbaum, 1989; Losey, 1995; McAlpine & Taylor, 1993; L. S. Miller, 1995; Ogbu, 1994; N. Reid, 1989; Shweder et al., 1998; Tharp, 1994; Torres-Guzmán, 1998; Trawick-Smith, 2003; Triandis, 1995.

Children can begin to learn about different cultures and common human bonds in early and middle childhood. One example of a lesson in diversity is represented in Figure 5-9. In this artwork, 9-year-old Dana shows her understanding of different sources of light in two very different settings, that of a large, modern city and that of the Masai, a cattle-herding tribe of east Africa. As children grow older, they become increasingly able to learn details about different people's perspectives and circumstances. Figure 5-10 shows 13-year-old Carol's notes on the distinct perspectives of different groups discussed in her American history class. In previous lessons Carol learned about lasting contributions Native Americans have made to American government, art, language, food, and sports. Here, Carol focuses on the "New Arrivals" who came to the New World in the 1600s, writing about the separate experiences of men and women, and of European settlers, African settlers, and enslaved Africans.

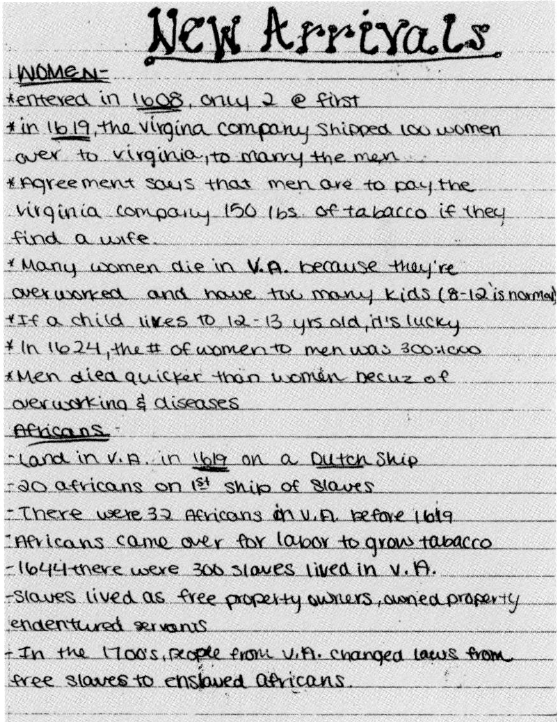

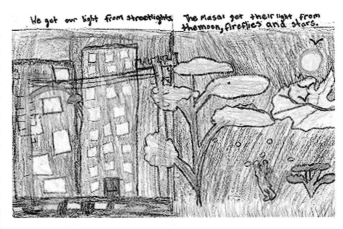

Figure 5-9

Nine-year-old Dana learned about how different people use natural and artificial light. Art by Dana.

As teachers explore cultures with youngsters, they can look for commonalities as well as differences. For example, they might study how various cultural groups celebrate the beginning of a new year, discovering that "out with the old and in with the new" is a common theme (Ramsey, 1987). At the secondary level, classes might explore issues faced by adolescents of all cultures: gaining the respect of elders, forming trusting relationships with peers, and finding a meaningful place in society (Ulichny, 1994).

● ***Foster respect for diverse cultures and ethnic groups.*** In addition to taking children's cultural backgrounds into account when interacting with them, teachers should convey that all cultural perspectives have merit. They should select materials that represent cultural groups in a positive and competent light—for instance, by choosing books and movies that portray people of varying ethnic backgrounds as legitimate participants in society rather than as exotic "curiosities" who live in a separate world. Educators should also avoid (or at least comment critically on) materials that portray members of minority groups in an overly simplistic, romanticized, exaggerated, or otherwise stereotypical fashion (Banks, 1994; Boutte & McCormick, 1992; Pang, 1995).

● ***Create opportunities for children with diverse backgrounds to interact.*** When youngsters have positive interactions with people from backgrounds other than their own, they gain further respect for different cultures. In culturally heterogeneous schools, teachers and school counselors might promote friendships among students from different groups by using cooperative learning activities, teaching simple phrases in other students' native languages, and encouraging schoolwide participation in extracurricular activities. In culturally homogeneous schools, professionals might take youngsters beyond school boundaries—perhaps engaging them in community service projects or arranging a visit to a culturally inclusive center for the arts.

● ***Recognize that children may follow practices from two or more cultures.*** Earlier we introduced the idea that immigrant children often adjust well when they hold onto their family's cultural beliefs rather than fully replacing these beliefs with ideas favored by the dominant society. Teachers often find that children are selective in the customs they absorb from their new communities. The same principle holds for multiethnic children. Children raised by parents from different ethnic cultures are likely to value traditions from both sides of the family.

New Arrivals

WOMEN-
*entered in 1608, only 2 @ first
*in 1619, the virgina company shipped 100 women over to virginia, to marry the men
*Agreement says that men are to pay the virginia company 150 lbs. of tabacco if they find a wife.
*Many women die in V.A. because they're overworked and have too many kids (8-12 is normal)
*If a child likes to 12-13 yrs old, it's lucky
*In 1624, the # of women to men was 300:1000
*Men died quicker than women becuz of overworking & diseases

Africans
-Land in V.A. in 1619 on a Dutch ship
-20 africans on 1st ship of slaves
-There were 32 Africans in V.A. before 1619
-Africans came over for labor to grow tabacco
-1644 there were 300 slaves lived in V.A.
-Slaves lived as free property owners, owned property endentured servants
-In the 1700's, people from V.A. changed laws from free slaves to enslaved Africans.

Figure 5-10

Thirteen-year-old Carol took these notes in her American history class. Throughout the unit, her teacher made a point of discussing the perspectives of different groups. Carol's notes show that she learned about the hardships faced by men and women in the New World in the 1600s; she also learned about European settlers, African settlers, and enslaved Africans.

● ***When cultural conflicts occur, find constructive ways to address them.*** Occasionally, children and families follow cultural practices that are contradictory—at least on the surface—to those adhered to in the classroom. When this happens, it is a good idea to learn more about these practices. Investing such an effort can better prepare adults to appreciate why children act as they do and to make reasonable accommodations for children's cultural practices ("OK, avoiding certain foods shows their religious devotion; I can certainly offer other snack choices").

Showing respect for diverse cultural perspectives does not necessarily mean that "anything goes" or that there are no moral judgments to be made. No one, for example, needs to embrace a cultural practice in which some people's basic human rights are blatantly violated. Showing respect does mean, however, that adults and children must try to understand another cultural group's behaviors within the entirety of that culture's beliefs and assumptions (M. N. Cohen, 1998).

Community Resources

As a bridge to the outside world, a community offers social and material resources that sustain children and their families. Of course, the particular assets that are available to children vary by community. Here we examine the nature of the community and the impact of the family's income on children's lives. In addition, we offer specific recommendations for working with children from low-income families.

Figure 5-11

Six-year-old Lee created this drawing after visiting an art museum. In it, he represents some of the themes he perceived in the museum's paintings, including warfare, religion, and community.

Type of community.   Communities vary in their population density and geographical features, such as climate, natural resources, and predominant cultures. These and other features in the community pervade the lives of families and affect the development of children. For instance, children who live in large cities often have ready access to ongoing events and resources related to music, art, drama, science, sports, and diverse cultures. Experiencing cultural events firsthand can be exciting and motivating for children. In Figure 5-11, 6-year-old Lee displays his enthusiasm for an art museum he visited in a large city.

Not every child in a big city can take advantage of its splendors, however. Some families can afford to live in nicely maintained houses, enroll their children in well-staffed schools, and pay for children to visit museums and attend concerts and sports events. Others cannot. Forced to live in unsafe neighborhoods, economically poor families and their children regularly encounter such problems as drugs, violence, crime, and racial segregation (Massey & Denton, 1993). Disadvantaged families often must send their children to dilapidated schools with records of low achievement. Secondary school principals in inner-city public schools are more likely than their counterparts in rural and suburban schools to see poverty, inadequate academic skills, student apathy, and lack of parent involvement as serious problems affecting their schools (National Center for Education Statistics, 1999b).

Families living in rural settings, particularly farming communities, often foster a cooperative spirit and strong work ethic (García, 1994). Many farm families structure chores so that all family members contribute to the family's economic livelihood. Furthermore, farm families periodically help others in the community with seasonal projects, such as harvesting crops. A downside of rural environments is that options for recreation can be limited, leading some young people to seek excitement through unproductive activities. For instance, school principals in rural areas and small towns are more likely than principals in central cities and suburban areas to identify student alcohol abuse as a serious problem (National Center for Education Statistics, 1999b). Students may also find it challenging when they must travel many miles to attend school each day and so cannot participate in extracurricular activities.

On average, families in suburban communities have higher incomes than those who live in inner cities or rural areas, and their schools are often better funded. Children and their families often have easy access to the educational and cultural resources of the big city, yet everyone has a bit of backyard and privacy. However, economic resources are not equally distributed in suburban communities, and not all young people have an optimistic outlook about their chances for future success (Gaines, 1991). Furthermore, some youngsters in suburban schools can be snooty with peers who fail to measure up to their standards for dress and behavior, creating a painfully unwelcome climate for those who are rejected.

socioeconomic status (SES)
One's general standing in an economically stratified society, encompassing family income, type of job, and education level.

Family income.   A child's experience in a community is strongly affected by the family's personal and financial resources. This idea is captured in the notion of the family's **socioeconomic status (SES),** its standing in the community based on such variables as the family's income level, the prestige of parents' jobs, and parents' levels of education. A family's socioeconomic status—whether high-SES, middle-SES, or low-SES—gives us a sense of how much flexibility family members have with regard to where they live and what they buy, how much influence they have in political decision making, what educational opportunities they can offer children, and so on.

In many respects, family income is only a modest contributor to children's development. After all, it is the family's guidance and relationships that directly affect children; material resources are of secondary importance. Evidence of this developmental prioritization comes from children of affluent families: Despite attending good schools and living in safe neighborhoods, these children are at risk for emotional problems and substance abuse when parents put excessive pressure on them or are not involved in their day-to-day activities (Luthar & Latendresse, 2005). However, it is equally important to recognize that at the other end of the financial spectrum, economically poor families sometimes have so little in physical comfort and financial security that their ability to nurture may be compromised (Hoover-Dempsey & Sandler, 1997; Jimerson et al., 1999; McLoyd, 1998b; Seaton et al., 1999; Walberg & Paik, 1997). Because children of economically disadvantaged families have many unmet developmental needs (some of which can be addressed in schools), we now examine the hardships faced by these children and the strategies that effectively nurture them.

Children living in economic poverty. Approximately 18 percent of American children live in poverty (Federal Interagency Forum on Child and Family Statistics, 2005). Poverty can be detrimental to youngsters of any age, but it seems most troublesome for infants and young children (Baydar, Brooks-Gunn, & Furstenberg, 1993; Brooks-Gunn & Duncan, 1997; Center for the Future of Children, 1997; G. J. Duncan, Yeung, Brooks-Gunn, & Smith, 1998).

Children and adolescents in low-income neighborhoods may have fewer choices for recreation than their economically advantaged peers.

Children and adolescents living in poverty face serious challenges. Typical problems include these:

- *Poor nutrition and health care.* Some children are poorly fed and have little access to adequate health care; as a result, they may suffer from malnutrition and other chronic health problems.
- *Inadequate housing and material goods.* Many children live in tight quarters, perhaps sharing one or two rooms with several other family members. Some children have no place to live at all, except perhaps the family car or a homeless shelter. Some poor children are reluctant to come to school because they lack bathing facilities and presentable clothing. And even the most basic school supplies may be beyond their reach.
- *Toxic environment.* Compared to their economically advantaged peers, children in poor families are more likely to be exposed to factory pollution, toxic waste dumps, allergens that trigger asthma, and excessive noise.
- *Gaps in background knowledge.* Teachers typically assume that children have had certain kinds of experiences before they begin school—for instance, that they have been read to, have seen many kinds of animals at farms or zoos, and have had ample opportunities to explore their physical environment. However, some children who live in extreme poverty miss out on such foundational experiences. At home, poor children are less often spoken to and they receive less overall cognitive stimulation than do children from economically advantaged families.
- *Increased probability of disabling conditions.* Children who live in poverty are more likely to have physical, mental, or social-emotional disabilities.
- *Emotional stress.* Children function less effectively when under stress, and many poor children and their families live in chronically stressful conditions, constantly worrying about where their next meal is coming from or how long the landlord will wait before evicting them for not paying the rent. Experiencing chronic emotional stresses, low-income parents may lose their patience with children and become punitive and insensitive. In addition, poor children are more likely to be subjected to maltreatment by parents or other adults and to encounter violent crimes in their neighborhoods.

- *Lower quality schools.* Schools in low-income neighborhoods and communities are often poorly funded and equipped, and they have high teacher turnover rates. Furthermore, some teachers at these schools have lower expectations for students—and offer a less demanding curriculum, assign less homework, and set lower standards for performance—than teachers of middle-SES students.
- *Public misconceptions.* People from economically advantaged backgrounds often have mixed feelings about low-SES families: They may feel pity yet simultaneously believe that poor people are responsible for their misfortunes, perhaps because of laziness, promiscuity, or overdependence on social welfare programs. (Cases & Okamoto, 1996; Center for the Future of Children, 1997; Chafel, 1997; Coe, Salamon, & Molnar, 1991; G. W. Evans, 2004; Gershoff, Aber, & Raver, 2005; Gollnick & Chinn, 2002; Linver, Brooks-Gunn, & Kohen, 2002; Maccoby & Martin, 1983; McLoyd, 1998a, 1998b; L. S. Miller, 1995; Murdock, 1999; Parke et al., 2004; Pawlas, 1994; Portes, 1996; Sidel, 1996; R. A. Thompson & Wyatt, 1999; Trueba, 1988; U.S. Department of Education, 1997)

Obviously, poverty creates serious threats to children's welfare. Sadly, many children and adolescents find the challenges of poverty so overwhelming that they engage in behaviors—dropping out of school, abusing drugs and alcohol, participating in criminal activities—that create further problems. However, many children and adolescents from poor families do well despite the adversities they face. They are relatively hardy to life's hardships (Kim-Cohen, Moffitt, Caspi, & Taylor, 2004). These youngsters show **resilience,** an ability to thrive despite adverse environmental conditions. For instance, almost half of low-income high school graduates subsequently enroll in college (National Center for Education Statistics, 2003). Let's examine strategies educators use to nurture this resilience in low-income youngsters.

Educating Children from Low-Income Families

Adults who want to "make a difference" in children's lives are especially likely to do so in schools and other institutions serving low-SES populations. But to be effective, teachers and other adults must be committed to their jobs, think creatively about how they can make the most of limited resources, and show a contagious enthusiasm for learning (L. W. Anderson & Pellicer, 1998; Ogden & Germinario, 1988). Experts offer these recommendations for working with children from low-income families:

● *Invest in children's strengths.* When teachers concentrate on youngsters' weaknesses, youngsters become easily discouraged and may soon resign themselves to the idea that their efforts are in vain. In contrast, focusing on what's *right* with children can generate—in both adults and children—optimism, enthusiasm, and a definite commitment to learning. For instance, children from lower-SES backgrounds are often clever at improvising with everyday objects (Torrance, 1995). If they work part-time to help their families make ends meet, they may have a good understanding of the working world. If they are children of single, working parents, they may know far more than peers about cooking, cleaning, and taking care of younger siblings (Whiting & Edwards, 1988). And many children of poor immigrant families have two parents at home to support them; are physically healthy; and have families with a strong sense of obligation to their welfare, a cohesive community upon which to draw, and a clear commitment to working hard (Shields & Behrman, 2004).

● *Foster a sense of belonging.* Children from low-income backgrounds may appreciate teachers' efforts to build a *sense of community*—a sense that the group (e.g., class or school) has shared goals, respects one another's efforts, and believes that everyone makes an important contribution (L. W. Anderson & Pellicer, 1998; J. Downey, 2000). For example, teachers can assign chores on a rotating basis, use cooperative learning activities, involve children and adolescents in cross-grade tutoring, and encourage everyone's participation in extracurricular activities (J. Downey, 2000). Because youngsters often feel more connected to their community when, in some small way, they give something back, educators can also sponsor community service projects. For example, members of a school might conduct a neighborhood cleanup, volunteer in a nursing home, serve as readers at the local library, or raise funds to benefit community causes (Ladson-Billings, 1994). In Figure 5-12 you can see a mural painted by teenagers as part of the city of Boston's Mural Crew.

─────── **Connecting Concepts**

In Chapter 14 you will learn that early childhood interventions are an effective way to help economically disadvantaged children get off to a good start.

─────── **Connecting Concepts**

The strategies teachers can follow to foster a sense of community in their classroom and school are described in Chapter 14.

resilience

Ability of some youngsters (often enhanced with environmental support) to thrive despite adverse environmental conditions.

Figure 5-12

Saturday in Jamaica Plain. The Mural Crew program of the Boston Youth Clean-up Corps (BYCC) enlists groups of teenagers to beautify the city with public works of art.
Artists: Antonio, Gabe, Awurama, Agapito, Nikia, Alyssa, and Jon. Supervising artists: Heidi Schork and Teig Grennan.

● *Convey clear and consistent expectations for children's behavior.* For all children, and especially for those who have had more than their share of life's challenges, knowing what's expected is important. Hence adults need to describe their expectations in clear, concrete terms (J. Downey, 2000). For instance, when finishing lunch in the cafeteria, children might be asked explicitly to "empty the napkins and leftovers into the trash bin, put the trays and dishes on the counter, and go quietly outside." When working in cooperative groups, young people might be reminded, "Everyone needs to participate in the discussions and contribute to the group project."

● *Show relevance of academic skills to children's lives and needs.* Finding personal relevance in classroom activities and subject matter is important for any child, but it may be especially critical for children from low-SES backgrounds (L. W. Anderson & Pellicer, 1998; Lee-Pearce, Plowman, & Touchstone, 1998). Helping children see how they can use skills in their everyday lives makes learning more meaningful as well as more motivating.

● *Introduce children to institutions in their community.* When children have not had the opportunity to see institutions in their society, they can often learn a lot from brief visits. For instance, teachers sometimes take their classes on field trips to a zoo, museum, post office, fire station, and so forth, and thereby create new knowledge for children to build on in academic lessons. When field trips are too expensive or logistically impossible, an alternative is to bring the community to children—for instance, by having a representative of the local zoo bring some of the zoo's smaller residents for the children to observe or by asking a police officer to describe the many public services that the police department provides.

● *Communicate high expectations for children's success.* Children from low-SES backgrounds often do not expect much of their own academic skills. Typically, they also have lower aspirations for higher education and possible careers (M. S. Knapp & Woolverton, 1995; S. M. Taylor, 1994). Yet teachers can communicate a can-do attitude, encourage students to challenge themselves, and provide support to help students reach their goals. Offering help sessions for challenging classroom material, finding low-cost academic enrichment programs available during the summer, and helping adolescents fill out applications for college scholarships are just a few examples of such support.

● *Give homeless children school supplies and help them ease into new communities.* Educators who work with children of homeless families can help them adjust to their new settings. For example, teachers, principals, and school counselors might pair homeless children with classmates who can explain school procedures and introduce them to peers;

provide a notebook, clipboard, or other portable "desk" on which children can do their homework at the shelter; find adult or teenage volunteers to tutor them at the shelter; ask civic organizations to donate school supplies; meet with parents at the shelter rather than at school; and share copies of homework assignments, school calendars, and newsletters with shelter officials (Pawlas, 1994).

● *Find good role models for children and adolescents.* Youngsters from some low-income neighborhoods encounter few good role models (Torrance, 1995). Young people are more likely to be optimistic about their future when they meet—and ideally establish close, trusting relationships with—people from their community who have succeeded despite limited financial resources.

Case Study: Four-Year-Old Sons

A common behavior displayed by preschoolers is asking a lot of *why* questions. Consider how two mothers of 4-year-old boys interpret their sons' incessant questioning. Elizabeth describes her son Charles as

> . . . mouthing off; just always mouthing off. Whenever I say anything to him, he asks me "Why?" Like I say we're going to the store and he says "Why?" Or I tell him "Don't touch the bug 'cuz it's dead" and he says "Why?" Like he's just trying to get me mad by never listening to me. He never accepts what I say. He mouths off all the time instead of believing me. It's like he just wants to tease me. You know, he tests me. (Belenky, Bond, & Weinstock, 1997, pp. 129–130)

In contrast, Joyce describes her son Peter this way:

> Well, you know, he's got such an active mind, always going; like he's never satisfied with just appearances—he's always trying to figure out how things tick, why they do. So if I ask him to do something or tell him to do something, he's always asking why. He really wants to understand what's the goal—what's the purpose—how come? He's really trying to piece the world all together . . . and understand it all. It's wonderful. Or if I say, "We're going to the store," he wants to know why. He's real interested in figuring out how one thing leads to another. It's great, because sometimes he helps me realize that I haven't really thought through why I'm saying what I am. And so we do think it through. (Belenky et al., 1997, p. 130)

● How do the two mothers interpret their sons' questions differently? How might their interpretations help us to predict their disciplinary styles?
● How might Elizabeth and Joyce have developed their particular parenting styles?
● What kinds of educational opportunities might these mothers create at home for their children? What might teachers do to encourage each mother's involvement at school?

Once you have answered these questions, compare your responses with those presented in the appendix.

Summary

Cradles of Child Development

Family, culture, and community provide essential foundations for child development. These three contexts teach children who they are as human beings, how they should relate to others, and what they can aspire to become as adults. The three settings are interrelated in their effects on children.

Family Structures

Families come in many forms, including two-parent families, single-parent families, blended families, adoptive families, foster families, extended families, and numerous other types. Many youngsters experience one or more changes in family structure (e.g., as a result of divorce, remarriage, or death of a parent) at some point during their childhood or adolescence. Individual family structures offer unique benefits and challenges for children, but ultimately the quality of family relationships exceeds family structure in developmental significance. Teachers can be inclusive of families by recognizing the existence of many structures and inviting families of all kinds to become involved at school.

Family Processes

Parents influence children's development through the relationships they build with children, the activities they include children in, and their manner of showing affection and disciplining children. In addition, parents may affect children's development through their employment outside the home; for instance, some children of working parents care for themselves during after-school hours. Children influence their families, in turn, by virtue of their temperaments, interests, and abilities. Children also influence one another as siblings, but having a sibling is not vital to normal, healthy development.

Most families provide safe and nurturing environments for children. However, some families maltreat children, either by neglecting them or by subjecting them to physical, sexual, or emotional abuse. Such maltreatment can have negative long-term effects on children's development.

Effective partnerships between educators and families rest squarely on good communication. Teachers can use several methods of communication, and they can try to get parents actively involved in children's education and activities.

Family, Culture, and Community Life

Children and families are profoundly affected by their experiences in ethnic groups and cultural traditions. To a large extent, children's ethnicity affects their values, actions, and styles of communicating. Boys and girls are socialized somewhat differently, depending on their ethnicity and the particular beliefs of their families. Children also are influenced by their community's character and by the incomes of their families. Educators can build on children's experiences in the community and, importantly, help economically disadvantaged children by providing support, resources, and acknowledgement of children's personal strengths.

Applying Concepts in Child Development

In this chapter you learned that children and adolescents are strongly influenced by the family, culture, and community in which they grow. The following table describes family experiences of five children and adolescents. For each of these youngsters, the table identifies one or more developmental concepts related to families, offers an implication for working with the youngsters and their families, or both. Apply what you've learned about families to fill in the empty cells in the table. When you're done, compare your responses with those in Table 5-1 in the *Study Guide and Reader*.

APPLYING CONCEPTS IN CHILD DEVELOPMENT	Accommodating Children's Families		
Age	A Youngster's Experience	Developmental Concepts *Identifying Family Conditions*	Implications *Working Effectively with Children's Families*
Infancy (Birth–2)	Eight-month-old Yves sits in his high chair at the child care center. Yves is hungry but cries rather than feeding himself the diced peaches and turkey on his tray. His caregiver, Mrs. Phillipe, talks with Yves's mother and learns that during meal times at home, she holds Yves and places soft, tiny bits of food directly into his mouth.	Little Yves encounters different feeding customs at home and at the child care center. These different practices may be rooted in dissimilar *cultural beliefs* about desirable qualities in social groups (e.g., for being close to one another or showing independence) and in *cultural behaviors* in caring for infants (e.g., encouraging infants to relax as caregivers tend to them or, in contrast, fostering their self-care).	
Early Childhood (2–6)	Tawaia is the fourth and youngest child in the Hume family. At 4 years, Tawaia seems to her teacher, Ms. Brookhart, to be socially perceptive. Ms. Brookhart notices Tawaia's ability to charm her friends into sharing their toys with her. Ms. Brookhart also observes that Tawaia can hold her ground during verbal tussles with other children, occasionally selecting insults that aptly push the other children's hot buttons.		Show sensitivity to the bonds that children have with siblings, allowing them to comfort one another during times of family loss. Try not to compare children to their siblings, though, and also do *not* assume that children without siblings are lonely or spoiled.

(continued)

APPLYING CONCEPTS IN CHILD DEVELOPMENT — Accommodating Children's Families (continued)

Age	A Youngster's Experience	Developmental Concepts *Identifying Family Conditions*	Implications *Working Effectively with Children's Families*
Middle Childhood (6–10) 	Nine-year-old Michael is the only child of his single mother, Ms. Clementine. Michael seems to be mature for his age, particularly in the chores he does around the house, including making dinner twice a week when his mother is at work. Michael feels protective toward his mother, whom he knows to be hard working and devoted to him.	Children in *single-parent families* often have close relationships with their parents. Michael enjoys such a close bond with his mother, and he also seems to have been coached by her in making constructive use of his time in *self-care*, when she is at work and he is home alone.	
Early Adolescence (10–14)	Mr. Drake, a middle school math teacher, holds an advising meeting with one of his students, Janice, and her parents, Mr. and Mrs. Lee. During the conference, Janice answers questions for the family, and Mr. and Mrs. Lee quietly smile and nod their heads. Later Mr. Drake notices that Mr. and Mrs. Lee fail to take him up on his suggestion that they participate in one of the school's many parent-staffed events.	Mr. and Mrs. Lee may hold different *cultural beliefs* from Mr. Drake about the appropriate roles of parents in children's academic learning. Janice's parents are respectful of Mr. Drake but may not feel it is appropriate for them to ask questions of him during meetings. Furthermore, they may be more inclined to help Janice with her homework at home than to become involved at school events.	Invite families to participate as they can in school activities, but also make certain to acknowledge the important roles that families play in supporting children's academic learning at home.
Late Adolescence (14–18) 	Mr. Vogel notices that one of his students, Christy, has suddenly become quiet and withdrawn during homeroom period. He talks with her privately and learns that her parents have recently told her they are getting a divorce. Christy explains that her parents have been arguing constantly over the last year, and she finds the divorce to be traumatic.	Changes in *family structure* can be unsettling for children and adolescents for months and sometimes longer. Adolescents tend to adjust to *parents' divorce* somewhat more easily than do younger children, but adolescents still generally need time to sort through the changes, make sense of their parents' conflicts, and regroup with new custody arrangements.	Listen sensitively when children inform you that they are troubled by a family disruption. Help children sort through the practical issues that inevitably arise when children face a change in living arrangements or find that they must move back and forth between their parents' houses.

Key Concepts

family (p. 148)
socialization (p. 148)
culture (p. 149)
community (p. 149)
family structure (p. 152)
coparents (p. 152)

blended family (p. 155)
guided participation (p. 159)
parenting style (p. 160)
authoritarian style (p. 160)
authoritative style (p. 160)
permissive style (p. 160)

uninvolved style (p. 160)
child maltreatment (p. 166)
ethnicity (p. 174)
acculturation (p. 176)
assimilation (p. 176)
selective adoption (p. 176)

rejection (p. 176)
bicultural orientation (p. 176)
ethnic identity (p. 177)
multicultural education (p. 179)
socioeconomic status (p. 182)
resilience (p. 184)

Now go to our Companion Website at www.prenhall.com/mcdevitt to assess your understanding of chapter content with a Practice Quiz, apply what you've learned in Essay Questions, and broaden your knowledge with links to related Developmental Psychology Web sites.

Cognitive Development:
Piaget and Vygotsky

chapter 6

Case Study: Museum Visit

Piaget's Theory of Cognitive
Development

Vygotsky's Theory of
Cognitive Development

Comparing Piagetian and
Vygotskian Perspectives

Case Study: Adolescent
Scientists

Summary

Applying Concepts in Child
Development

Case Study: Museum Visit

Four-year-old Billy[a] is fascinated by dinosaurs. He and his mother have read many books about dinosaurs, and so he already has some knowledge about these creatures and the geological time periods in which they lived. As Billy and his mother visit a dinosaur exhibit at a natural history museum, they have the following conversation:

Mother: This is a real dinosaur rib bone. Where are your ribs? Where are your ribs? No that's your wrist. Very close.

Billy: Oh, yeah, right here.

Mother: Yeah, that's right. Here. Protecting your heart . . . and your lungs. And this was one from a dinosaur from the Jurassic period, also found from our country. In a place called Utah.

Mother: And this one . . . [Mother picks up a piece of fossilized dinosaur feces, known as *coprolite*] Oh! You're not . . . guess what that is. Look at it and guess what that is.

Billy: Um, what?

Mother: Guess. What's it look like?

Billy: His gum? What? Mom!

Mother: It's dinosaur poop.

Billy: Ooooo! (laughs)

Mother: That's real dinosaur poop.

Billy: I touched it! (laughs)

Mother: It's so old that it doesn't smell anymore. It turned to rock. It's not mushy like poop. It's like a rock. And that's from the Cretaceous period but we don't know what dinosaur made it. And this was also found in our country in Colorado. I think that's pretty funny.

Billy: What's this?

Mother: So this one . . . Oh, that's called . . . that's a stone that dinosaurs . . . remember in your animal book it says something about how sometimes chickens eat stones to help them digest—it helps them mush up their food in their tummy?

Billy: Yeah.

Mother: Well, dinosaurs ate stones to mush up their food in their tummy and this was one of the stones that they ate. They're so big, that to them this was a little stone. Right? And that also comes from Colorado. (dialogue from Crowley & Jacobs, 2002, p. 346)

[a]"Billy" is a pseudonym.

Like Billy in the opening case, many young children find dinosaurs fascinating. Art by Corey, age 6.

This brief conversation about dinosaur fossils gives us a glimpse into how a 4-year-old might think about new objects and how an adult might help him interpret and make better sense of them. In other words, the conversation is an example of **cognition** in action. Cognition encompasses all the mental activities in which a human being engages, including perception, categorization, understanding, memory, logical reasoning, and problem solving. These processes evolve and change in many ways over the course of childhood and adolescence. Furthermore, cognitive processes may differ considerably even among children of the same age. For example, whereas Billy has enough knowledge of geological time periods to understand his mother's references to the *Jurassic* and *Cretaceous* periods, many of his age-mates are apt to find these words nonsensical and meaningless.

cognition
The various mental activities in which a person engages.

To some extent, cognitive development depends on physiological maturation. As you discovered in Chapter 4, the brain undergoes a series of genetically controlled changes during infancy, childhood, and adolescence that allow increasingly sophisticated thinking processes. But environmental events—both informal experiences (e.g., encounters with new, intriguing objects) and more formal, planned interventions (e.g., classroom lessons)—also play an essential role in fostering children's cognitive capabilities. In addition, as will become clear very shortly, much of children's cognitive development is the result of their own efforts to make sense of their world.

In this chapter we'll consider two early theories—those of Jean Piaget and Lev Vygotsky—that have greatly enhanced our understanding of how children's thinking changes with age. Both theories have much to say about how parents, teachers, and other adults can help children think and learn more effectively.

Piaget's Theory of Cognitive Development

Jean Piaget was especially curious about the nature of knowledge and how children acquire it. To determine where knowledge comes from and the forms that it takes at different ages, he observed the everyday actions of infants and children and drew inferences about the thinking and reasoning that seemed to underlie their behavior. In his lab in Geneva, Switzerland, Piaget pioneered the **clinical method,** a procedure in which an adult presents a task or problem and asks a child a series of questions about it, tailoring these questions to responses the child has previously made. In one task, for example, an adult shows a child a box containing about a dozen wooden beads, two of which are white and the rest brown. The adult first shows the beads to a 6-year-old, whom we'll call Brian.[1] The following discussion ensues:

Adult:	Are there more wooden beads or more brown beads?
Brian:	More brown ones, because there are two white ones.
Adult:	Are the white ones made of wood?
Brian:	Yes.
Adult:	And the brown ones?
Brian:	Yes.
Adult:	Then are there more brown ones or more wooden ones?
Brian:	More brown ones.
Adult:	What color would a necklace made of the wooden beads be?
Brian:	Brown and white. (Here [Brian] shows that he understands that all the beads are wooden.)
Adult:	And what color would a necklace made with the brown beads be?
Brian:	Brown.
Adult:	Then which would be longer, the one made with the wooden beads or the one made with the brown beads?
Brian:	The one with the brown beads.
Adult:	Draw the necklaces for me.

Brian draws a series of black rings for the necklace of brown beads. He then draws a series of black rings plus two white rings for the necklace of wooden beads.

Adult:	Good. Now which will be longer, the one with the brown beads or the one with the wooden beads?
Brian:	The one with the brown beads. (dialogue from Piaget, 1952a, pp. 163–164)

Brian has difficulty with a question that, to us, seems quite simple. Even though all the beads are wooden and only some (albeit the majority) are brown, he concludes that there are more brown beads than wooden ones. In contrast, 8-year-old "Natalie" answers the question easily. Logically, she says, there must be more wooden beads than brown beads:

Adult:	Are there more wooden beads or more brown beads?
Natalie:	More wooden ones.
Adult:	Why?

clinical method
Procedure in which an adult probes a child's reasoning about a task or problem, tailoring questions in light of what the child has previously said or done in the interview.

---

[1]Piaget identified children in his studies by abbreviations. We've substituted names throughout the text to allow for easier discussion.

Natalie: Because the two white ones are made of wood as well.

Adult: Suppose we made two necklaces, one with all the wooden beads and one with all the brown ones. Which one would be longer?

Natalie: Well, the wooden ones and the brown ones are the same, and it would be longer with the wooden ones because there are two white ones as well. (dialogue from Piaget, 1952a, p. 176)

Natalie exhibits **class inclusion,** the recognition that an object can belong both to a particular category and to one of its subcategories simultaneously.

Drawing from such interviews with preschoolers, school-age children, and adolescents, as well as from in-depth observations of the behaviors of infants and toddlers, Piaget (e.g., 1928, 1952b, 1959, 1985) developed a theory of cognitive development that has contributed a great deal to our understanding of how children and adolescents think and learn.

Key Ideas in Piaget's Theory

Central to Piaget's theory are the following principles and concepts:

● *Children are active and motivated learners.* In the opening case study, Billy seems quite eager to make sense of the fossils he sees in the natural history museum. Piaget proposed that children are naturally curious about their world and actively seek out information to help them interpret and understand it (e.g., Piaget, 1952b). They often experiment with the objects they encounter, manipulating them and observing the effects of their actions. For example, we authors think back (without much nostalgia) to the days when our children were in high chairs, experimenting with their food (poking, squishing, rolling, dropping, and throwing it) as readily as they would eat it.

Many contemporary theorists share Piaget's view that much of a human being's motivation for learning and development comes from within. It appears that growing children are naturally inclined to try to make sense of—and as a result, can deal more effectively with—the people, objects, and events around them (e.g., Fischer, 2005; K. Nelson, 1996a). You can see an example of such *intrinsic motivation* in the "Cognitive Development: Early Childhood" video clip on Observation CD 1, in which 2-year-old Maddie encounters an intriguing new object and actively manipulates it to discover some of its properties.

Observe Maddie experiment with a new object in the "Cognitive Development: Early Childhood" clip on Observation CD 1.

● *Children organize what they learn from their experiences.* Children don't just amass the things they learn into a collection of isolated facts. Instead, they pull their experiences together into an integrated view of how the world operates. For example, by observing that food, toys, and other objects always fall down (never up) when released, children begin to construct a basic understanding of gravity. As they interact with family pets, visit zoos, look at picture books, and so on, they develop an increasingly complex understanding of animals. Piaget depicted learning as a very *constructive* process: Children create (rather than simply absorb) their knowledge about the world.

In Piaget's terminology, the things that children learn and can do are organized as **schemes,** groups of similar thoughts or actions that are used repeatedly in response to the environment. Initially, children's schemes are largely behavioral in nature, but over time they become increasingly mental and, eventually, abstract. For example, an infant may have a scheme for putting things in her mouth, a scheme that she uses in dealing with a variety of objects, including her thumb, her toys, and her favorite blanket. A 7-year-old may have a scheme for identifying snakes, one that includes their long, thin bodies, their lack of legs, and their slithery nature. As a 13-year-old, Jeanne's daughter Tina had her own opinion about what constitutes fashion, a scheme that allowed her to classify various articles of clothing on display at the mall as being either "totally awesome" or "really stupid."

Observe Corwin repeating "putting-in" and "taking-out" schemes in the "Cognitive Development: Infancy" clip on Observation CD 1.

Piaget proposed that children use newly acquired schemes over and over in both familiar and novel situations. For example, in the "Cognitive Development: Infancy" video clip on Observation CD 1, you can observe 16-month-old Corwin repeatedly taking a toy out of a paper bag and then putting it back in. In the process of repeating their schemes, children refine them and begin to use them in combination with one another. Eventually, they integrate schemes into larger systems of mental processes called **operations.** This integration allows them to think in increasingly sophisticated ways. For instance, 8-year-old Natalie's reasoning about the "beads" problem shows greater integration than 6-year-old

class inclusion
Recognition that an object simultaneously belongs to a particular category and to one of its subcategories.

scheme
In Piaget's theory, an organized group of similar actions or thoughts that are used repeatedly in response to the environment.

operation
In Piaget's theory, an organized and integrated system of logical thought processes.

Piaget's belief that children construct rather than absorb knowledge has stood the test of time. This drawing reflects 6-year-old Laura's conception of underwater ocean life, including her belief that sea creatures exhale in a manner similar to people.

——————— Connecting Concepts

Note that Piaget's concept of assimilation is quite different from the process of *cultural assimilation* described in Chapter 5.

constructivism
Theoretical perspective proposing that learners construct a body of knowledge and beliefs, rather than absorbing information at face value.

individual constructivism
Theoretical perspective that focuses on how people construct meaning from events on their own.

assimilation
In Piaget's theory, process of dealing with a new event in a way that is consistent with an existing scheme.

accommodation
Process of dealing with a new event by either modifying an existing scheme or forming a new one.

Brian's: Although both children understand that some beads are both brown and wooden, only Natalie takes both characteristics into account simultaneously to conclude that there must be more wooden beads than brown beads. Brian apparently can consider only one characteristic at a time. As a result, he compares the brown beads only with the remaining wooden beads (the white ones) and so concludes that there are more brown ones than wooden ones.

Piaget's idea that children don't just absorb their experiences—that they actively try to interpret and make sense of events and then integrate what they've learned into comprehensive, personally constructed understandings—figures prominently in many contemporary views of learning and cognitive development. The perspective that people construct rather than absorb knowledge is generally known as **constructivism.** Here we are specifically talking about **individual constructivism,** in which a single individual creates new understandings. Later in the chapter we'll encounter *social constructivism,* in which two or more people are actively and collaboratively involved in the process.

● *Children adapt to their environment through the processes of assimilation and accommodation.* According to Piaget, children's developing schemes allow them to adapt in ever more successful ways to their environment. Such adaptation occurs as a result of two complementary processes: assimilation and accommodation. **Assimilation** entails dealing with an object or event in a way that is consistent with an existing scheme. For example, an infant may assimilate a ball into her putting-things-in-the-mouth scheme. A 7-year-old may quickly identify a new slithery object in the backyard as a snake. A 13-year-old may readily label a schoolmate's clothing as being either quite fashionable or "soooo *yesterday.*"

Yet sometimes children cannot easily interpret a new object or event using their existing schemes. In these situations one of two forms of **accommodation** will occur. Children will either modify an existing scheme to account for the new object or event or else form an entirely new scheme to deal with it. For example, an infant may have to open her mouth wider than usual to accommodate a large plastic ball or teddy bear's paw. The 13-year-old may have to revise her existing scheme of fashion according to changes in what's hot and what's not. The 7-year-old may find a long, slithery thing with a snakelike body that cannot possibly *be* a snake because it has four legs. After some research, he will develop a new scheme—*salamander*—for this creature.

We see instances of both assimilation and accommodation in the opening case study. Billy initially thinks that the piece of coprolite is a large wad of dinosaur gum—that is, he mistakenly assimilates the object into his "chewing gum" scheme. But with his mother's help, he creates a new scheme, "fossilized dinosaur poop," that more accurately accounts for what he is seeing. Later Mother helps Billy assimilate a large stone into a "stones-that-help-digestion" scheme he has previously acquired. In the process, however, he must also modify this scheme so that it applies to dinosaurs as well as to chickens.

Although children's schemes change over time, the two processes through which their schemes are acquired and modified—assimilation and accommodation—remain the same throughout the course of development. Assimilation and accommodation typically work hand in hand as children develop knowledge and understanding of the world. Children interpret each new event within the context of their existing knowledge (assimilation) but at the same time may modify their knowledge as a result of the new event (accommodation). Accommodation rarely happens without assimilation. People of any age can benefit from (accommodate to) new experiences only when they can relate those experiences to their current knowledge and beliefs.

Although Piaget was vague about how assimilation and accommodation might actually work (e.g., Klahr, 1982), contemporary developmentalists embrace the principle that children's new ideas are based on their earlier ones. Developmentally speaking, new knowledge, skills, and cognitive processes don't just appear out of thin air.

● *Interaction with the physical environment is critical for cognitive development.* Without new experiences, children have no reason to modify, and so improve on, their existing schemes. By exploring and manipulating the world around them—by conducting many little "experiments" with various objects and substances—children learn the nature of such physical characteristics as volume and weight, discover principles related to force and gravity, acquire a better understanding of cause-effect relationships, and so on. Activities such as fiddling with sand and water, playing games with balls and bats, and experimenting in a science laboratory help children construct a more complete and accurate understanding of how the physical world operates. The following anecdote from a preschool teacher illustrates this process:

> Tommy . . . had built a tower on a base of three regular blocks on end, with a round, flat piece of Masonite on top. Then on top of this were three more blocks and Masonite, supporting in turn a third story. . . . The tower was already taller than Tommy, and he had a piece of triangular Masonite in hand and was gently testing the tower's steadiness against his taps. Small taps and the tower would lean, settle, and become still. Again and again he varied the strength and place of the taps; watched, waited, tapped again, and finally—on purpose—did hit hard enough to topple the structure. Then the entire process of building the tower and testing it was repeated. (F. P. L. Hawkins, 1997, p. 200)

Teachers and other adults can help children learn new information more effectively by building on children's prior knowledge and experiences.

Likewise, as 9-year-old Kyle and 10-year-old Curtis bounce, throw, and catch a basketball in the "Physical Activity: Middle Childhood" video clip on Observation CD 1, they are undoubtedly refining their understanding of such physical phenomena as force and inertia.

As it turns out, *perception* of the physical world may be more important than actual physical manipulation of it. For example, children with significant physical disabilities make major cognitive advancements despite their fairly limited experiences with physical objects (Bebko, Burke, Craven, & Sarlo, 1992). In one way or another, however, children must have some sort of experience with the physical world—encounters with various physical phenomena (e.g., pressure, inertia, oscillation), exposure to cause-effect relationships, and so on—if they are to get a good sense of how it works.

As Curtis and Kyle play basketball (see the "Physical Activity: Middle Childhood" clip on Observation CD 1), what laws of physics might they be observing in action?

● *Interaction with other people is equally critical.* Although Piaget believed that children themselves construct their knowledge and understandings of the world, nevertheless they have much to learn from interacting with others. For example, as you will discover shortly, preschoolers often have difficulty seeing the world from anyone's perspective but their own. By conversing, exchanging ideas, and arguing with others, they gradually come to realize that different individuals see things differently and that their own view of the world is not necessarily a completely accurate or logical one. Elementary school children may begin to recognize logical inconsistencies in what they say and do (e.g., recall Brian's insistence that there were more brown beads than wooden beads) when someone else points out the inconsistencies. And through discussions with peers or adults about social and political issues, high school students may slowly modify their newly emerging idealism about how the world "should" be.

● *The process of equilibration promotes increasingly complex forms of thought.* Piaget proposed that children are sometimes in a state of **equilibrium:** They can comfortably interpret and respond to new events using existing schemes. But equilibrium doesn't continue indefinitely. As children grow, they frequently encounter situations for which their current knowledge and skills are inadequate. These situations create **disequilibrium,** a sort of mental "discomfort" that spurs them to try to make sense of what they observe. By replacing, reorganizing, or better integrating their schemes (in other words, through accommodation), children eventually are able to understand and address previously puzzling events. The movement from equilibrium to disequilibrium and back to equilibrium again is known as **equilibration.** Equilibration and children's intrinsic desire to achieve equilibrium promote the development of more complex levels of thought and knowledge.

Let's return to the case of Brian and the "beads" problem. The adult asks Brian to draw two necklaces, one made with the wooden beads and one made with the brown beads. The adult hopes that after Brian draws a brown-and-white necklace that is longer than an all-brown necklace, he will notice that his drawings are inconsistent with his statement that there are more brown beads. The inconsistency might lead Brian to experience disequilibrium,

equilibrium
State of being able to address new events using existing schemes.

disequilibrium
State of being unable to address new events with existing schemes.

equilibration
Movement from equilibrium to disequilibrium and back to equilibrium; a process that promotes the development of increasingly complex forms of thought and knowledge.

perhaps to the point where he would reevaluate his conclusion and realize that the number of all the brown beads plus two white ones *must* be greater than the number of brown beads alone. In this case, however, Brian apparently is oblivious to the inconsistency, remains in equilibrium, and so has no need to revise his thinking at this time.

● *Children think in qualitatively different ways at different age levels.* Piaget was a *stage theorist:* He proposed that as a result of both brain maturation and a wide variety of environmental experiences, children proceed through a sequence of four stages of cognitive development. Each stage builds on the accomplishments of any preceding stages, and so children progress through the four stages in a particular order. Piaget suggested that the stages are *universal*—that they describe the cognitive development of children throughout the world.

As you will discover later in the chapter, many psychologists question the notion that cognitive development is either as stagelike or as universal as Piaget believed. Nevertheless, Piaget's stages provide helpful insights into the nature of children's thinking at different age levels, and so we will look at them more closely.

Piaget's Stages of Cognitive Development

——————— Study Guide and Reader
Piaget broke the sensorimotor stage into six discrete substages. These are described in Supplementary Reading 6-1.

Piaget's four stages are summarized in Table 6-1. The age ranges associated with the stages are *averages:* Some children reach a stage a bit earlier, others a bit later. Also, children are occasionally in *transition* from one stage to the next, displaying characteristics of two adjacent stages at the same time.

Observe Madison's explorations of objects in the "Emotional Development: Infancy" clip on Observation CD 2.

Sensorimotor stage (birth until age 2).   In the first month of life, infants' behaviors are little more than biologically built-in responses to particular stimuli—that is, they are *reflexes* (e.g., sucking on a nipple)—that help keep them alive. In the second month infants begin to exhibit voluntary behaviors that they repeat over and over, reflecting the development of perception- and behavior-based *sensorimotor schemes.* Initially, such behaviors focus almost exclusively on infants' own bodies (e.g., putting one's fist in one's mouth), but eventually they involve nearby objects as well. For much of the first year, infants' behaviors are largely spontaneous and unplanned. For example, as 7-month-old Madison explores a variety of toys in the "Emotional Development: Infancy" video clip on Observation CD 2, she is clearly intrigued by each toy's physical properties, but she shows little concern about how she might use a toy to accomplish particular goals.

Observe Corwin's goal-directed behavior and object permanence in the "Cognitive Development: Infancy" clip on Observation CD 1.

Late in the first year, after repeatedly observing that certain actions lead to certain consequences, infants gradually acquire knowledge of cause-effect relationships. At this point, they begin to engage in **goal-directed behavior:** They behave in ways that they know will bring about desired results. At about the same time, they acquire **object permanence,** an understanding that physical objects continue to exist even when they are out of sight. In the "Cognitive Development: Infancy" video clip on Observation CD 1, 16-month-old Corwin shows object permanence when he looks for a toy elephant that his mother repeatedly hides. His searches under a pillow are directed toward a particular goal: finding the elephant.

Piaget believed that for much of the sensorimotor period, children's thinking is restricted to objects in their immediate environment—that is, to the here and now. But in the latter half of the second year, young children develop **symbolic thought,** the ability to represent and think about objects and events in terms of internal, mental entities, or *symbols.* They may "experiment" with objects in their minds, first predicting what will happen if they do something to an object and then putting their plans into action. They may also recall and imitate behaviors they have seen other people exhibit—for instance, "talking" on a toy telephone or "driving" with a toy steering wheel.

goal-directed behavior
Intentional behavior aimed at bringing about an anticipated outcome.

object permanence
Realization that objects continue to exist even when they are out of sight.

symbolic thought
Ability to represent and think about external objects and events in one's mind.

The acquisitions of the sensorimotor stage are basic building blocks on which later cognitive development depends. The Observation Guidelines table "Assessing Cognitive Advancements in Infants and Toddlers" on page 198 presents some of the behaviors you might look for as you work with infants and toddlers.

Preoperational stage (age 2 until age 6 or 7).   The ability to represent objects and events mentally (i.e., symbolic thought) gives children in the preoperational stage a more extensive

TABLE 6-1		**Piaget's Four Stages of Cognitive Development**	
Stage	**Proposed Age Range**[a]	**General Description**	**Examples of Acquisitions**
Sensorimotor	Birth to age 2	Schemes are based largely on behaviors and perceptions. Especially in the early part of the stage, children cannot think about things that are not immediately in front of them, and so they focus on what they are doing and seeing at the moment.	• *Trial-and-error experimentation:* Exploration and manipulation of objects to determine their properties • *Goal-directed behavior:* Intentional behavior to bring about a desired result • *Object permanence:* Realization that objects continue to exist even when removed from view • *Symbolic thought:* Representation of physical objects and events as mental entities (*symbols*)
Preoperational	Age 2 through age 6 or 7	Thanks in part to their rapidly developing symbolic thinking abilities, children can now think and talk about things beyond their immediate experience. However, they do not yet reason in logical, adultlike ways.	• *Language:* Rapid expansion of vocabulary and grammatical structures • *Extensive pretend play:* Enactment of true-to-life or fanciful scenarios with plots and assigned roles (e.g., mommy, doctor, Superman) • *Intuitive thought:* Some logical thinking based on "hunches" and "intuition" rather than on conscious awareness of logical principles (especially after age 4)
Concrete Operations	Age 6 or 7 through age 11 or 12	Adultlike logic appears but is limited to reasoning about concrete, real-life situations.	• *Distinction between one's own and others' perspectives:* Recognition that one's own thoughts and feelings may be different from those of others and do not necessarily reflect reality • *Class inclusion:* Ability to classify objects as belonging to two or more categories simultaneously • *Conservation:* Realization that amount stays the same if nothing is added or taken away, regardless of alterations in shape or arrangement
Formal Operations	Age 11 or 12 through adulthood	Logical reasoning processes are applied to abstract ideas as well as concrete objects and situations. Many capabilities essential for advanced reasoning in science and mathematics appear.	• *Reasoning about abstract, hypothetical, and contrary-to-fact ideas:* Ability to draw logical deductions about situations that have no basis in physical reality • *Separation and control of variables:* Ability to test hypotheses by manipulating one variable while holding other variables constant • *Proportional reasoning:* Conceptual understanding of fractions, percentages, decimals, and ratios • *Idealism:* Ability to envision alternatives to current social and political practices (sometimes with little regard for what is realistically possible in a given time frame)

[a]The age ranges presented in the table are *averages:* Some children reach a stage a bit earlier, others a bit later.

worldview than they had during the sensorimotor stage. They can now recall past events and envision future ones and begin to tie their experiences together into an increasingly complex understanding of the world.

Language skills virtually explode during the early part of the preoperational stage. The words in children's rapidly increasing vocabularies provide labels for newly developed mental schemes and serve as symbols that enable children to think about objects and events even when not directly in sight. Furthermore, language provides the basis for a new form of social interaction, verbal communication. Children can express their thoughts and receive information from other people in a way that was not possible during the sensorimotor stage.

The emergence of symbolic thought is reflected not only in rapidly expanding language skills but also in the changing nature of children's play. Preschoolers often engage in fantasy and make-believe, using realistic objects or reasonable substitutes to act out the roles and behaviors of the people they see around them. Piaget proposed that such pretend play enables children to practice using newly acquired symbolic schemes and familiarize

OBSERVATION GUIDELINES

Assessing Cognitive Advancements in Infants and Toddlers

Characteristic	Look For	Example	Implication
Repetition of Gratifying Actions	• Repetition of actions involving the child's own body • Repetition of actions on other objects • Evidence that the child repeats an action because he or she notices and enjoys it	Myra waves her arms, stops, and waves her arms again. She makes a sound and repeats it, as if she enjoys listening to her own voice.	Provide a variety of visual, auditory, and tactile stimuli; for instance, play "This little piggy" with an infant's toes, hang a mobile safely over the crib, and provide age-appropriate objects (e.g., rattles, plastic cups). Be patient and responsive when infants repeat seemingly "pointless" actions (e.g., dropping favorite objects).
Exploration of Objects	• Apparent curiosity about the effects that different behaviors have on objects • Use of multiple behaviors (feeling, poking, dropping, shaking, etc.) to explore an object's properties • Use of several sensory modalities (e.g., seeing, listening, feeling, tasting)	Paco reaches for his caregiver's large, shiny earring. The caregiver quickly removes the earring from her ear and holds its sharp end between her fingers while Paco manipulates the silver loop and multicolored glass beads that hang from it.	Provide objects that infants can explore using multiple senses, making sure the objects are free of dirt and toxic substances and are large enough to prevent swallowing.
Experimentation	• Creativity and flexibility in the behaviors the child uses to discover how things work • Specific problems that the child tackles and the approaches he or she uses to solve them	Jillian drags a stepstool to her dresser so that she can reach the toys on top of it. One by one, she drops the toys, watching how each one lands and listening to the sound it makes on impact.	Childproof the environment so that experiments and problem solving are safe. Provide objects that require a sequence of actions (e.g., stacking cups, building blocks, pull toys). Closely supervise toddlers' activities.
Imitation and Pretending	• Imitation of actions modeled by another person • Imitation of actions when the model is no longer present • Using one object to stand for another	Darius holds a doll and sings to it the way his mother sings to him. He combs the doll's hair with a spoon and uses an empty plastic vitamin bottle to feed the doll.	Engage children in reciprocal, imitative games (e.g., peekaboo, hide-and-seek). Provide props that encourage pretend play (miniature shopping carts, plastic carpentry tools, dolls, etc.).

themselves with the various roles they see others assume in society. This idea is illustrated in the following scenario, in which 5-year-olds Jeff and Scott construct and operate a "restaurant":

> In a corner of Jeff's basement, the boys make a dining area from several child-sized tables and chairs. They construct a restaurant "kitchen" with a toy sink and stove and stock it with plastic dishes and "food" items. They create menus for their restaurant, often asking a parent how to spell the words but sometimes using their knowledge of letter-sound relationships to guess how a particular word might be spelled.
>
> Jeff and Scott invite their mothers and fathers to come to the new restaurant for lunch. After seating their "customers," the boys pretend to write their meal orders on paper tablets and then scurry to the kitchen to assemble the requested lunch items. Eventually, they return to serve the meals (hamburgers, French fries, and cookies—all of them plastic—plus glasses of imaginary milk), which the adults "eat" and "drink" with gusto. After the young waiters return with the final bills, the adults pay for their "meals" with nickels and leave a few pennies on the tables as tips.

With the emergence of symbolic thought, young children are no longer restricted to the here and now and so can think and act far more flexibly than they did previously. At the same time, preoperational thinking has some definite limitations, especially as compared to the concrete operational thinking that emerges later. For example, Piaget described young children as exhibiting **egocentrism,** an inability to view situations from another person's perspective. Young children may have trouble understanding how a thoughtless remark may have hurt someone else's feelings. They may play games together without ever checking to

——————— **Study Guide and Reader**
Several perspectives on one form of egocentrism—*egocentric speech*—are presented in Supplementary Reading 6-2.

egocentrism
Inability of a child in Piaget's preoperational stage to view situations from another person's perspective.

be sure that they are all playing according to the same rules. And they may say things without considering the perspective of the listener—for instance, leaving out critical details as they tell a story and giving a fragmented version that a listener cannot possibly understand. Here we see one reason why, in Piaget's view, social interaction is so important for development. Only by getting repeated feedback from other people can children learn that their thoughts and feelings are unique to them—that their own perception of the world is not always shared by others.

Preoperational thinking is also illogical (at least from an adult's point of view), especially during the preschool years. For example, recall 6-year-old Brian's insistence that there were more brown beads than wooden beads, reflecting an inability to engage in class inclusion. Following is another example of the "logic" that characterizes preoperational thought:

> We show 4-year-old Lucy the three glasses at the top of Figure 6-1. Glasses A and B are identical in size and shape and contain an equal amount of water. We ask Lucy if the two glasses of water contain the same amount, and she replies confidently that they do. We then pour the water in Glass B into Glass C. We ask her if the two glasses of water (A and C) still have the same amount. "No," Lucy replies. She points to Glass A and says, "That glass has more because it's taller."

Lucy's response illustrates a lack of **conservation:** She does not realize that because no water has been added or taken away, the amount of water in the two glasses must be equivalent. Young children often confuse changes in appearance with changes in amount. Piaget suggested that such confusion occurs, in general, because children in the preoperational stage depend more on perception than on logic when they reason. In the "Cognitive Development: Early Childhood" video clip on Observation CD 1, notice how 2-year-old Maddie is easily swayed by appearance when the "fishy crackers" in one row are spaced farther apart than those in the other row.

As children approach the later part of the preoperational stage, perhaps at around age 4 or 5, they show early signs of being logical. For example, they sometimes draw correct conclusions about classification problems (e.g., the wooden beads problem) and conservation problems (e.g., the water glasses problem). But they base their reasoning on hunches and intuition rather than on any conscious awareness of underlying logical principles, and so they cannot yet explain *why* their conclusions are correct. When children move into the concrete operations stage, they become increasingly able both to make logical inferences and to explain the reasoning behind their conclusions.

Concrete operations stage (age 6 or 7 until age 11 or 12). At about age 6 or 7, children's thinking processes begin to take the form of logical operations through which they can integrate various qualities and perspectives of an object or event. Such operational thought enables a number of more advanced abilities. For example, children now realize that their own perspectives and feelings are not necessarily shared by others and may reflect personal opinions rather than reality. Accordingly, they know they can sometimes be wrong and begin to seek out external validation for their ideas, asking such questions as "What do you think?" and "Did I get that problem right?"

Children in the concrete operations stage are capable of many forms of logical thought. For instance, they can easily classify objects into two categories simultaneously. (Recall 8-year-old Natalie's ease in solving the wooden beads versus brown beads problem.) And they are capable of conservation: They readily understand that if nothing is added or taken away, amount stays the same despite any changes in shape or arrangement. As an example, in the "Cognitive Development: Middle Childhood" video clip on Observation CD 1, 10-year-old Kent has no difficulty determining that two rows of 10 M&M candies each must contain the same number of M&Ms, even though those in one row are spaced farther apart than those in the other.

Children continue to develop their newly acquired logical thinking capabilities throughout the elementary school years. For instance, over time they become capable of dealing with increasingly complex conservation tasks. Some forms of conservation, such as conservation of liquid and conservation of number (the latter illustrated by Kent's M&Ms problem), appear at age 6 or 7. Other forms may not appear until several years later. Consider the task

A   B   C
Before

A   B   C
After

Figure 6-1

Conservation of liquid: Do Glasses A and C contain the same amount of water after the water in B is poured into C?

Observe Maddie's age-typical lack of conservation of number in the "Cognitive Development: Early Childhood" clip on Observation CD 1.

Study Guide and Reader ———

Tables contrasting Piaget's preoperational, concrete operational, and formal operational stages are presented in Supplementary Reading 6-3.

conservation
Realization that if nothing is added or taken away, amount stays the same regardless of any alterations in shape or arrangement.

Figure 6-2

Conservation of weight: Balls A and B initially weigh the same. When Ball B is flattened into a pancake shape, how does its weight now compare with that of Ball A?

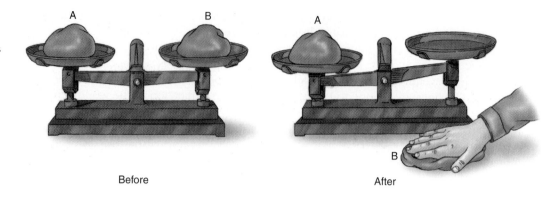

Before   After

Observe how Kent easily conserves number but has difficulty with abstract proverbs in the "Cognitive Development: Middle Childhood" clip on Observation CD 1.

involving conservation of weight depicted in Figure 6-2. Using a balance scale, an adult shows a child that two balls of clay have the same weight. One ball is removed from the scale and smashed into a pancake shape. The child is then asked if the pancake weighs the same as the unsmashed ball or if the two pieces of clay weigh different amounts. Children typically do not achieve conservation of weight—that is, they do not realize that the flattened pancake weighs the same as the round ball—until sometime between the ages of 9 and 12 (Sund, 1976).

Although children displaying concrete operational thought show many signs of logical thinking, their cognitive development is not yet complete. For example, they have trouble understanding and reasoning about abstract or hypothetical ideas (hence the term *concrete operations* stage). In language, this weakness may be reflected in an inability to interpret the underlying meaning of proverbs (observe 10-year-old Kent's difficulty in the "Cognitive Development: Middle Childhood" video clip on Observation CD 1). In mathematics, it may be reflected in confusion about such concepts as *pi* (π), *infinity,* and *negative number.* And in social studies, it may limit children's comprehension of such abstract notions as *democracy, communism,* and *human rights.*

Formal operations stage (age 11 or 12 through adulthood).   Sometime around puberty, children enter the formal operations stage. At this point, Piaget suggested, they become capable of thinking and reasoning about things that have little or no basis in physical reality—that is, about abstract concepts, hypothetical ideas, and statements that contradict what they know to be true in the real world. Also emerging are scientific reasoning abilities that enable children to identify cause-effect relationships in physical phenomena. As an example, consider the following task:

> An object suspended by a rope or string—a pendulum—swings indefinitely at a constant rate. Some pendulums swing back and forth very quickly, whereas others swing more slowly. Design an experiment that can help you determine what factor or factors affect a pendulum's oscillation rate.

To successfully tackle this problem, you must first *formulate hypotheses* about possible variables affecting a pendulum's swing. For instance, you might consider (a) the weight of the suspended object, (b) the length of the string that holds the object, (c) the force with which the object is pushed, and (d) the height from which the object is initially released. You must then *separate and control variables,* testing one factor at a time while holding all others constant. For instance, to test the hypothesis that weight makes a difference, you should try different weights while keeping constant the length of the string, the force with which you push each weight, and the height from which you release it. Similarly, if you hypothesize that the length of the string is critical, you should vary the length of the string while continuing to use the same weight and starting the pendulum in motion in the same manner. If you carefully separate and control variables, your observations should lead you to conclude that only *length* affects a pendulum's oscillation rate.

Once formal operational thinking appears, more advanced verbal and mathematical problem solving is also possible. For instance, adolescents become able to see beyond literal interpretations of such proverbs as "A rolling stone gathers no moss" and "An ant may well destroy a dam" to identify their underlying messages. (Notice how easily 14-year-old Alicia interprets these proverbs in the "Cognitive Development: Late Adolescence" video clip on Observation CD 1.) Adolescents become better able to understand such concepts as *negative number* and *infinity* because they can now comprehend how numbers can be below zero and how two parallel lines will never touch even if they go on forever. And they can understand the nature of proportions (e.g., fractions, ratios, decimals) and correctly use proportions when working on mathematical problems.

Because adolescents capable of formal operational reasoning can deal with hypothetical and contrary-to-fact ideas, they can envision how the world might be different from, and possibly better than, the way it actually is. Thus they may be idealistic about social, political, religious, and ethical issues. Many adolescents begin to show concern about world problems and devote some of their energy to worthy issues such as global warming, world hunger, or animal rights. Curiously, however, their devotion may sometimes be more evident in their talk than in their actions (Elkind, 1984). Furthermore, they often offer recommendations for change that seem logical but aren't practical in today's world. For example, they may argue that racism would disappear overnight if people would just begin to "love one another," or they may propose that a nation help bring about world peace by disbanding its armed forces and discarding all its weapons. Piaget suggested that adolescent idealism reflects an inability to separate one's own logical abstractions from the perspectives of others and from practical considerations. It is only through experience that adolescents eventually begin to temper their optimism with some realism about what is possible in a given time frame and with limited resources.

Observe Alicia interpret proverbs in the "Cognitive Development: Late Adolescence" clip on Observation CD 1.

As adolescents become increasingly able to reason about abstract, hypothetical, and contrary-to-fact ideas, they also become more idealistic about how the world should be.

Current Perspectives on Piaget's Theory

Piaget's theory has sparked a great deal of research about children's cognitive development. In general, this research supports Piaget's proposed *sequence* in which different abilities emerge (Flavell, 1996; Siegler & Richards, 1982). For example, the ability to reason about abstract ideas emerges only after children are already capable of reasoning about concrete objects and events, and the order in which various conservation tasks are mastered is much as Piaget described. Contemporary developmental theorists question the *ages* at which various abilities actually appear, however. They are also finding that children's logical reasoning capabilities may vary considerably depending on their previous knowledge, experiences, and cultural background. And while modern-day developmentalists agree with many of Piaget's basic ideas—for instance, they concur with his notions of constructed (rather than absorbed) knowledge and the motivating nature of disequilibrium—they are less certain about the stagelike nature of cognitive development.

Capabilities of different age-groups. Infants and preschoolers are apparently more competent than Piaget's descriptions of the sensorimotor and preoperational stages suggest. For instance, infants show preliminary signs of object permanence as early as 2½ months old and continue to firm up this understanding over a period of many months (Baillargeon, 2004; L. B. Cohen & Cashon, 2006). Preschoolers don't always show egocentrism. If we ask them to show us their artwork, they hold it so that we (rather than they) can see it, and they can often recognize the emotions that others are feeling (Lennon, Eisenberg, & Carroll, 1983; Newcombe & Huttenlocher, 1992). And under some circumstances preschoolers are capable of conservation and class inclusion (M. Donaldson, 1978; R. Gelman & Baillargeon, 1983; Rosser, 1994).

Piaget may have underestimated the capabilities of elementary school children as well. Many elementary students occasionally show some ability to think abstractly and hypothetically (S. Carey, 1985; Metz, 1995). Also, some older elementary school children can separate and control variables, especially when given hints about the importance of controlling all variables except the one they are testing (Danner & Day, 1977; Metz, 1995; Ruffman, Perner, Olson, & Doherty, 1993). And even first graders can understand simple proportions (e.g., fractions such as ½, ⅓, and ¼) if they can relate these concepts to every-day objects (Empson, 1999).

Yet Piaget probably *over*estimated what adolescents can do. Formal operational thinking processes emerge much more gradually than Piaget suggested, and even high school students don't use them as regularly as Piaget would have us believe (Flieller, 1999; Kuhn, Amsel, & O'Loughlin, 1988; Pascarella & Terenzini, 1991; Schauble, 1996). Furthermore, adolescents may demonstrate formal operational thought in one content domain while thinking more concretely in another (Klaczynski, 2001; Lovell, 1979; Tamburrini, 1982). Evidence of formal operations typically emerges in the physical sciences earlier than in such subjects as history and geography. Students often have difficulty thinking about abstract and hypothetical ideas in history and geography until well into the high school years.

A related issue is whether formal operations is really the final stage of cognitive development, as Piaget suggested. Some theorists have proposed that many adults progress to a fifth, postformal stage in which they can envision multiple approaches to the same problem and recognize that each approach may be valid from a particular perspective (Commons, Richards, & Armon, 1984; Sinnott, 1998). Other theorists disagree, arguing that adult life simply poses different kinds of problems than the academically oriented ones that adolescents encounter at school (Schaie & Willis, 2000).

Effects of prior knowledge and experience. Piaget believed that once children acquire a particular reasoning skill, they can apply it in virtually any context. Yet it is becoming increasingly apparent that for people of all ages, the ability to think logically in a particular situation depends on knowledge and background experiences relevant to the situation. Children as young as age 4 or 5 begin to show conservation after having experience with conservation tasks, especially if they can actively manipulate the task materials and discuss their reasoning with someone who already exhibits conservation (D. Field, 1987; Halford & Andrews, 2006; R. E. Mayer, 1992). Similarly, concrete manipulatives can help children as young as 9 grasp the nature of proportions (Fujimura, 2001). Children aged 10 and 11 can solve logical problems involving hypothetical ideas if they are taught relevant problem-solving strategies, and they become increasingly able to separate and control variables when they have numerous experiences that require them to do so (S. Lee, 1985; Schauble, 1990). Junior high and high school students, and adults as well, often apply formal operational thought to topics about which they have a great deal of knowledge and yet think concretely about topics with which they are unfamiliar (Girotto & Light, 1993; M. C. Linn, Clement, Pulos, & Sullivan, 1989; Schliemann & Carraher, 1993).

As an illustration of how prior knowledge affects formal operational thinking, consider the fishing pond in Figure 6-3. In a study by Pulos and Linn (1981), 13-year-olds were shown a similar picture and told, "These four children go fishing every week, and one child, Herb, always catches the most fish. The other children wonder why." If you look at the picture, it is obvious that Herb is different from the three other children in several ways, including the bait he uses, the length of his fishing rod, and his location by the pond. Children who were experienced fishermen more effectively separated and controlled variables for this situation than they did for the pendulum problem described earlier, whereas the reverse was true for non-fishermen. In the "Cognitive Development" video clips for middle childhood and late adolescence, on Observation CD 1, 10-year-old Kent and 14-year-old Alicia both consider the problem as they look at the picture in Figure 6-3. Notice how Kent, who appears to have some experience with fishing, considers several possible variables, whereas Alicia, who is older but admittedly a nonfisherman, considers only two:

Figure 6-3

What are some possible reasons why Herb is catching more fish than the others?

Based on Pulos & Linn, 1981.

Kent: He has live . . . live worms, I think. Fish like live worms more, I guess 'cause they're live and they'd rather have that than the lures, plastic worms. . . . Because he might be more patient or that might be a good side of the place. Maybe since Bill has a boombox thing [referring to the radio], I don't think they would really like that because . . . and he doesn't really have anything that's extra. . . . But he's the standing one. I don't get that. But Bill, that could scare the fish away to Herb because he's closer. . . .

Alicia: Because of the spot he's standing in, probably. . . . I don't know anything about fishing. Oh, OK! He actually has live worms for bait. The other girl's using saltine crackers [she misreads *crickets*]. . . . She's using plastic worms, he's using lures, and she's using crackers and he's actually using live worms. So obviously the fish like the live worms the best.

Observe how experience with fishing affects Kent's and Alicia's ability to identify variables in the "Cognitive Development" clips for middle childhood and late adolescence, on Observation CD 1.

One general experience that promotes more advanced reasoning is formal education. Going to school and the specific nature of one's schooling are associated with mastery of concrete operational and formal operational tasks (Artman & Cahan, 1993; Flieller, 1999; Rogoff, 2003). For instance, you may be happy to learn that taking college courses in a particular area (in child development, perhaps?) leads to improvements in formal reasoning skills related to that area (Lehman & Nisbett, 1990).

Effects of culture.   Piaget suggested that his stages were universal, that they applied to children and adolescents around the globe. Yet research indicates that the course of cognitive development differs somewhat from one culture to another. For example, Mexican children whose families make pottery for a living acquire conservation skills much earlier than Piaget proposed (Price-Williams, Gordon, & Ramirez, 1969). Apparently, making pottery requires children to make frequent judgments about needed quantities of clay and water—judgments that must be fairly accurate regardless of the specific shape or form of the clay or water container. In other cultures, especially in some where children don't attend school, conservation appears several years later than it does in Western cultures, and formal operational reasoning may never appear at all (M. Cole, 1990; Fahrmeier, 1978). In such contexts some logical reasoning skills may simply have little relevance to people's daily activities (J. G. Miller, 1997).

Does cognitive development occur in stages?   As you have seen, Piaget was not completely on target about when certain abilities develop and, in some cases, about whether they develop at all. He also overestimated the extent to which children generalize newly acquired reasoning skills to a broad range of tasks and contexts.

In light of all the evidence, does it still make sense to talk about discrete stages of cognitive development? Most contemporary developmental theorists doubt that cognitive development is as stagelike as Piaget proposed (e.g., Flavell, 1994; Kuhn & Franklin, 2006; Siegler & Alibali, 2005). Children exhibit certain developmental *trends* in their thinking (e.g., a trend toward increasingly abstract thought), to be sure. But the sophistication of their reasoning in any given situation depends largely on the particular context in which they find themselves and on their prior knowledge and experiences relative to the task at hand. Thus children don't necessarily reason in consistently logical or illogical ways at any single point in time.

A perspective known as *information processing theory,* described in Chapter 7, characterizes the general trends in cognitive processes we are likely to see as children develop. Yet some psychologists believe that, by entirely rejecting Piaget's notion of stages, we may be throwing the baby out with the bath water. These psychologists have combined some of Piaget's ideas with concepts from information processing theory to construct **neo-Piagetian theories** of how children's learning and reasoning capabilities change over time.

Key Ideas in Neo-Piagetian Theories

Neo-Piagetian theorists do not always agree about the exact nature of children's thinking at different age levels or about the exact mechanisms that promote cognitive development. Nevertheless, several ideas are central to neo-Piagetian approaches:

neo-Piagetian theory
Theoretical perspective that combines elements of Piaget's theory with more contemporary research findings and suggests that development in specific content domains is often stagelike in nature.

——————— Connecting Concepts
You'll learn more about the development of working memory in Chapter 7.

● *Cognitive development is constrained by the maturation of information processing mechanisms in the brain.* Neo-Piagetian theorists have echoed Piaget's belief that cognitive development depends somewhat on brain maturation. One prominent neo-Piagetian, Robbie Case, has suggested that a mechanism in the brain known as **working memory** is especially important for cognitive development (e.g., Case, 1985). Working memory is that part of the human memory system in which people hold and actively think about new information. (For instance, you are using your working memory right now to make sense of what you're reading about cognitive development.) Children's working memory capacity increases—and so their ability to think about several things simultaneously also increases—with age (more on this point in Chapter 7). Neo-Piagetian theorists propose that children's limited working memory capacity at younger ages restricts their ability to acquire complex thinking and reasoning skills (Case & Okamoto, 1996; Fischer & Bidell, 1991; Lautrey, 1993).

● *Children acquire cognitive structures that affect their thinking in particular content domains.* Neo-Piagetian theorists reject Piaget's notion that children develop increasingly integrated systems of mental processes (operations) that they can apply equally to a wide variety of tasks and content domains. Instead, they suggest, children acquire more specific systems of concepts and thinking skills that influence reasoning related to specific topics.

For example, Robbie Case has proposed that integrated networks of concepts and cognitive processes, called **central conceptual structures,** form the basis for much of children's thinking, reasoning, and learning in certain areas (Case & Okamoto, 1996; Case, Okamoto, Henderson, & McKeough, 1993). A central conceptual structure related to *number* underlies children's ability to reason about and manipulate mathematical quantities. This structure reflects an integrated understanding of how such mathematical concepts as numbers, counting, addition, and subtraction are interrelated. A central conceptual structure related to *spatial relationships* underlies children's performance in such areas as drawing, construction and use of maps, replication of geometric patterns, and psychomotor activities (e.g., writing in cursive, hitting a ball with a racket). This structure enables children to align objects in space according to one or more reference points (e.g., the *x*- and *y*-axes used in graphing). And a central conceptual structure related to *social thought* underlies children's reasoning about interpersonal relationships, their knowledge of common patterns in human interaction, and their comprehension of short stories and other works of fiction. This structure includes children's general beliefs about human beings' thoughts, desires, and behaviors. Case has found evidence indicating that the three conceptual structures probably develop in a wide variety of cultural and educational contexts (Case & Okamoto, 1996).

——————— Connecting Concepts
Chapter 10 describes Case's central
conceptual structure for number in
greater depth.

● *Development in specific content domains can sometimes be characterized as a series of stages.* Although neo-Piagetian theorists reject Piaget's notion that a single series of stages characterizes all of cognitive development, they speculate that cognitive development in specific content domains often has a stagelike nature (e.g., Case, 1985; Case & Okamoto, 1996; Fischer & Immordino-Yang, 2006). Children's entry into a particular stage is marked by the acquisition of new abilities, which children practice and gradually master over time. Eventually, they integrate these abilities into more complex structures that mark their entry into a subsequent stage.

Even in a particular subject area, however, cognitive development is not necessarily a single series of stages through which children progress as if they were climbing rungs on a ladder. In some cases development might be better characterized as progression along "multiple strands" of skills that occasionally interconnect, consolidate, or separate in a weblike fashion (Fischer & Immordino-Yang, 2006; Fischer, Knight, & Van Parys, 1993). From this perspective, children may acquire more advanced levels of competence in a particular area through any one of several pathways. For instance, as they become increasingly proficient in reading, children may gradually develop their word decoding skills, their comprehension skills, and so on—and they may often combine these skills when performing a task—but the rate at which each skill is mastered will vary from one child to the next.

working memory
Component of memory that enables people to actively think about and process a small amount of information.

central conceptual structure
Integrated network of concepts and cognitive processes that forms the basis for much of one's thinking, reasoning, and learning in a specific content domain.

According to Robbie Case's neo-Piagetian perspective, children develop central conceptual structures in number, spatial relationships, and social thought (and perhaps in other areas as well). These structures affect children's reasoning and performance on a variety of relevant tasks.

Applying the Ideas of Piaget and His Followers

Piaget's theory and the subsequent research and theories it has inspired have numerous practical implications for educators and other professionals. These implications include the following:

● *Provide opportunities for children to experiment with physical objects and natural phenomena.* Children of all ages can learn a great deal by exploring the natural world in a hands-on fashion. In infancy this might involve having regular access to objects with visual and auditory appeal, such as mobiles, rattles, stacking cups, and pull toys (note the plastic tower, books, and musical octopus in the "Emotional Development: Infancy" video clip on Observation CD 2). At the preschool level, this might involve playing with water, sand, wooden blocks, and age-appropriate manipulative toys. During the elementary school years, hands-on exploration might entail throwing and catching balls, going on nature walks, working with clay and watercolor paints, and constructing Popsicle-stick structures.

Despite their increased capabilities for abstract thought in adolescence, teenagers also benefit from opportunities to manipulate and experiment with concrete materials—perhaps equipment in a science lab, cameras and film, food and cooking utensils, or wood and woodworking tools. Such opportunities allow teens to discover laws of the natural world firsthand and to tie their newly emerging abstract ideas to the physical, concrete world.

Children and adolescents often remember information more effectively when they discover it for themselves rather than simply reading or hearing about it (de Jong & van Joolingen, 1998; M. A. McDaniel & Schlager, 1990; D. S. McNamara & Healy, 1995). On the downside, however, youngsters sometimes misinterpret what they observe, thereby either learning the wrong thing or confirming their existing misconceptions about the world (Hammer, 1997; Schauble, 1990). Consider the case of Barry, an 11th grader whose physics class was studying the idea that an object's mass and weight do *not,* in and of themselves, affect the speed at which the object falls. Students were asked to design and build an egg container that would keep an egg from breaking when dropped from a third-floor window. They were told that on the day of the egg drop, they would record the time it took for the eggs to reach the ground. Convinced that heavier objects fall faster, Barry added several nails to his egg's container. Yet when he dropped it, classmates timed its fall at 1.49 seconds, a time very similar to that for other students' lighter containers. He and his teacher had the following discussion about the result:

Teacher: So what was your time?
Barry: 1.49. I think it should be faster.

See examples of age-appropriate objects for exploration in the "Emotional Development: Infancy" clip on Observation CD 2.

DEVELOPMENT AND PRACTICE

Facilitating Discovery Learning

• Identify a concept or principle that students can learn about through interaction with their physical or social environment.

A fifth-grade teacher realizes that through a series of hands-on measurement tasks, her students can derive a general formula for calculating the area of a triangle.

• Make sure students have the necessary prior knowledge for discovering new ideas and principles.

A first-grade teacher asks students what they already know about air (e.g., people breathe it, wind is air that moves). After ascertaining that the students have some awareness that air has substance, she and her class conduct an experiment in which a glass containing a crumpled paper towel is turned upside-down and completely immersed in a bowl of water. The teacher eventually removes the glass from the water and asks students to explain why the paper towel didn't get wet.

• Show puzzling results to create disequilibrium.

A science teacher shows her class two glasses of water. In one glass an egg floats at the water's surface. In the other glass an egg rests on the bottom. The students give a simple and logical explanation for the difference: One egg has more air inside and so must be lighter. But then the teacher switches the eggs into opposite glasses. The egg that the students believe to be "heavier" now floats, and the "lighter" egg sinks to the bottom. The students are quite surprised and demand to know what is going on. (Ordinarily, water is less dense than an egg, so an egg placed in it will quickly sink. But in this demonstration, one glass contains salt water—a mixture denser than an egg and so capable of keeping it afloat.)

• Structure and guide a discovery session so that students proceed logically toward discoveries you want them to make.

A seventh-grade science teacher asks students to speculate about variables that might influence the rate at which a pendulum swings. His students offer three possibilities: length of the pendulum, weight of the object at the bottom, and angle at which the pendulum is initially dropped. The students work in small groups to test each of these hypotheses. When one group fails to separate and control variables, the teacher asks its members to look closely at their data: "What did you change between test one and test two? . . . Which caused the faster swing? . . . Why can't you come to a conclusion by looking at the numbers?" He continues to ask questions until the students realize they have confounded length and weight in their experimentation.

• Have students record their discovery session findings.

A biology teacher has students make sketches of the specific organs they observe as they dissect an earthworm.

• Help students relate their findings to concepts and principles in the academic discipline they are studying.

After students in a social studies class have collected data on average incomes and voting patterns in different counties within their state, their teacher asks, "How can we interpret these data using what we've learned about the relative wealth of members of the two major political parties?"

Sources: Bruner, 1966; de Jong & van Joolingen, 1998; N. Frederiksen, 1984; D. T. Hickey, 1997; R. E. Mayer, 2004; Minstrell & Stimpson, 1996; E. L. Palmer, 1965; B. Y. White & Frederiksen, 1998.

Teacher: Why?
Barry: Because it weighed more than anybody else's and it dropped slower.
Teacher: Oh really? And what do you attribute that to?
Barry: That the people weren't timing real good. (C. Hynd, 1998, p. 34)

Psychologists and educators have offered numerous suggestions for making discovery sessions effective. The Development and Practice feature "Facilitating Discovery Learning" presents and illustrates several recommendations.

————— Study Guide and Reader
Supplementary Reading 6-4 illustrates the use of Piaget's clinical method in assessing children's and adolescents' reasoning.

● *Explore children's reasoning with problem-solving tasks and probing questions.* By presenting a variety of Piagetian tasks involving either concrete or formal operational thinking skills and probing students' reasoning with a series of follow-up questions—that is, by using Piaget's clinical method—adults can gain valuable insights into how children think about their world. The Observation Guidelines table "Assessing Reasoning Skills" lists some of the characteristics you might look for.

In probing children's reasoning, however, teachers and other practitioners need not stick to traditional Piagetian tasks. On the contrary, Piaget's clinical method is applicable to a wide variety of content domains and subject matter. For example, in the "Research: Early Adolescence" video clip on Observation CD 1, you can hear an interviewer asking 12-year-old Claudia a series of questions to probe her reasoning during a categorization task (e.g., "How did you decide which shells to put where?" "What makes [those shells] different from the other ones?").

Observe the use of probing questions in the "Research: Early Adolescence" clip on Observation CD 1.

● *Keep Piaget's stages in mind when interpreting children's behavior and when planning activities, but don't take the stages too literally.* Although Piaget's four stages are not always accurate descriptions of children's and adolescents' thinking capabilities, they do provide a rough idea of the cognitive processes you are apt to see at various age levels (Kuhn, 1997; Metz, 1997). For example, infant caregivers should remember that repetitive behaviors,

OBSERVATION GUIDELINES

Assessing Reasoning Skills

Characteristic	Look For	Example	Implication
Egocentrism[a]	• Difficulty understanding others' perspectives • Describing events without giving listeners sufficient information to understand them • Playing group games without initially agreeing about rules	In her attempt to show Jeremy how to play a computer game, Luisa continually leaves out critical details in her instructions. Yet she doesn't seem to understand why Jeremy is confused.	Let children know when you don't understand what they are telling you. Ask them to share their ideas and opinions with one another.
Concrete Thought	• Heavy reliance on concrete manipulatives to understand concepts and principles • Difficulty understanding abstract ideas	Tobey solves arithmetic word problems more easily when he can draw pictures of them.	Use concrete objects and examples to illustrate abstract situations and problems.
Abstract Thought	• Ability to understand strictly verbal explanations of abstract concepts and principles • Ability to reason about hypothetical or contrary-to-fact situations	Ilsa can imagine how two parallel lines might go on forever without ever coming together.	When working with adolescents, occasionally use verbal explanations (e.g., short lectures) to present information, but assess their understanding frequently to make sure they understand.
Idealism	• Idealistic notions about how the world should be • Inability to take other people's needs and perspectives into account when offering ideas for change • Inability to adjust ideals in light of what can realistically be accomplished	Martin advocates a system of government in which all citizens contribute their earnings to a common "pool" and then withdraw money only as they need it.	Engage adolescents in discussions about challenging political and social issues.
Scientific Reasoning Skills	• Identifying multiple hypotheses for a particular phenomenon • Separation and control of variables	Serena proposes three possible explanations for a result she has obtained in her physics lab.	Have middle school and high school students design and conduct simple experiments. Include experiments about issues related to their backgrounds and interests.
Mathematical Reasoning Skills	• Understanding and using abstract mathematical symbols (e.g., π, the variable x in algebraic equations) • Understanding and using proportions in mathematical problem solving	Giorgio uses a 1:240 scale when drawing a floor plan of his school building.	Initially, introduce abstract mathematical concepts and tasks using simple examples (e.g., when introducing proportions, begin with fractions such as 1/3 and 1/4). Progress to more complex examples only when youngsters appear ready to handle them.

[a]Consistent with common practice, we use the term *egocentrism* to refer to the egocentric thinking that characterizes preoperational thought. Piaget actually talked about different forms of egocentrism at each of the four stages of development. For instance, he described the idealism of adolescence as a form of egocentrism that reflects an inability to distinguish one's own logical conclusions from the perspectives of others and from constraints of the real world.

even those that make a mess or cause inconvenience (dropping food, throwing toys), are one important means through which infants master basic motor skills and learn cause-effect relationships. Preschool teachers should not be surprised to hear young children arguing that the three pieces of a broken candy bar constitute more candy than a similar, unbroken bar (a belief that reflects lack of conservation). Elementary school teachers should recognize that their students are likely to have trouble with proportions (e.g., fractions, decimals) and with such abstract concepts as *historical time* in history, and *place value, negative number,* and *pi* in mathematics (Barton & Levstik, 1996; Byrnes, 1996; Tourniaire & Pulos, 1985). And educators and other professionals who work with adolescents should expect to hear passionate arguments that reflect idealistic yet unrealistic notions about how society should operate. The following exercise, "Fish in a Boat," provides practice in using Piaget's stages to interpret one young adolescent's drawing.

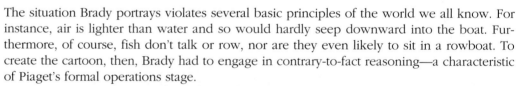

INTERPRETING CHILDREN'S ARTIFACTS AND ACTIONS   **Fish in a Boat**

Combining his pen-and-ink drawing skills and computer technology, 14-year-old Brady created this cartoon of fish rowing a boat upside-down at the water's surface. As you look at the cartoon, identify a logical reasoning skill it requires and the Piagetian stage that this skill reflects.

START BAILING, HOWARD, WE'RE TAKING ON AIR FAST!

The situation Brady portrays violates several basic principles of the world we all know. For instance, air is lighter than water and so would hardly seep downward into the boat. Furthermore, of course, fish don't talk or row, nor are they even likely to sit in a rowboat. To create the cartoon, then, Brady had to engage in contrary-to-fact reasoning—a characteristic of Piaget's formal operations stage.

Piaget's stages also provide guidance about strategies that are apt to be effective in teaching children at different age levels. For instance, given the abstract nature of historical time, elementary school teachers planning history lessons should probably talk only sparingly about specific dates before the recent past (Barton & Levstik, 1996). Also, especially in the elementary grades (and to a lesser degree in middle and high school), instructors should find ways to make abstract ideas more concrete for their students. As one simple example, a third-grade teacher, realizing that *place value* might be a difficult concept for 8- and 9-year-olds to comprehend, showed her students how to depict two-digit numbers with blocks, using ten-block rows for the number in the tens column and single blocks for the number in the ones column. In Figure 6-4 one of her students, 8-year-old Noah, depicts the number 34 using this approach.

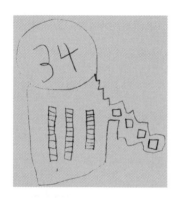

Figure 6-4

Noah's depiction of the number 34

● *Present situations and ideas that children cannot easily explain using their existing knowledge and beliefs.* Events and information that conflict with youngsters' current understandings create disequilibrium that may motivate them to reevaluate and perhaps modify what they "know" to be true. For instance, if they believe that "light objects float and heavy objects sink" or that "wood floats and metal sinks," an instructor might present a common counterexample: a metal battleship (floating, of course) that weighs many tons.

● *Use familiar content and tasks when asking children to reason in sophisticated ways.* Earlier we presented evidence to indicate that children and adolescents display more advanced reasoning skills when they work with topics they know well. With such evidence in mind, teachers and other practitioners might ask the youngsters they are working with to do the following:

- Conserve liquid within the context of a juice-sharing task.
- Separate and control variables within the context of a familiar activity (perhaps fishing, designing an effective paper airplane, or using various combinations of ingredients in baking cookies).
- Consider abstract ideas about subject matter that has already been studied in depth in a concrete fashion.

● *Plan group activities in which young people share their beliefs and perspectives with one another.* As noted earlier, Piaget proposed that interaction with peers helps children realize that others often view the world very differently than they themselves do and that their own ideas are not always completely logical or accurate. Interactions with age-mates that involve differences of opinion—situations that create **sociocognitive conflict**—can cause disequilibrium that may spur children to reevaluate their current perspectives.

Children are more likely to think in sophisticated ways about objects and situations with which they are familiar.

Many contemporary psychologists share Piaget's belief in the value of sociocognitive conflict (e.g., N. Bell, Grossen, & Perret-Clermont, 1985; De Lisi & Golbeck, 1999; Webb & Palincsar, 1996). They have offered several reasons why interactions with peers may help promote cognitive growth:

- Peers speak at a level that children can understand.
- Whereas children may accept an adult's ideas without argument, they are more willing to challenge and disagree with the ideas of their peers.
- When children hear competing views held by peers—individuals who presumably have knowledge and abilities similar to their own—they may be motivated to reconcile the contradictions. (Champagne & Bunce, 1991; Damon, 1984; Hatano & Inagaki, 1991)

When using group interaction to help children and adolescents acquire more sophisticated understandings, keep in mind that youngsters can also acquire misinformation from one another (Good, McCaslin, & Reys, 1992). It is essential, then, that teachers monitor group discussions and correct for any misconceptions or misinterpretations that young people may pass on to their peers.

Although children learn a great deal from their interactions with others, cognitive development is, in Piaget's theory, largely an individual enterprise: By assimilating and accommodating to new experiences, children develop increasingly more advanced and integrated schemes over time. Thus Piaget's perspective depicts children as doing most of the mental "work" themselves. In contrast, another early developmental theory—that of Russian psychologist Lev Vygotsky—places much of the responsibility for children's development on the adults in their society and culture. We turn to this theory now.

Vygotsky's Theory of Cognitive Development

In the "Museum Visit" case at the beginning of the chapter, a mother helps her 4-year-old son Billy make sense of several dinosaur artifacts. For instance, she points out how dinosaur ribs and human ribs serve the same function ("Protecting your heart . . . and your lungs"). She relates some of the artifacts to scientific concepts that Billy already knows (*Jurassic, Cretaceous*) and substitutes everyday language ("dinosaur poop") for an unfamiliar scientific term (*coprolite*).

Vygotsky proposed that adults, like Billy's mother, promote children's cognitive development by engaging them in meaningful and challenging activities, helping them perform those activities successfully, and talking with them about their experiences. Because he emphasized the importance of society and culture for promoting cognitive growth, his perspective is known as a **sociocultural theory.**

Key Ideas in Vygotsky's Theory

Vygotsky acknowledged that biological factors play a role in development. Children bring certain characteristics and dispositions to the situations they encounter, and their responses to those situations vary accordingly. Furthermore, children's behaviors, which are

sociocognitive conflict
Situation in which one encounters and has to wrestle with ideas and viewpoints different from one's own.

sociocultural theory
Theoretical perspective that focuses on children's learning of tools and communication systems through practice in meaningful tasks with other people.

From Vygotsky's perspective, parents and other adults promote children's cognitive development in part by conveying how their culture interprets the world.

influenced in part by inherited traits, affect the particular experiences that they have (Vygotsky, 1997). However, Vygotsky's primary focus was on the role of nurture, and especially on the ways in which a child's social and cultural environments foster cognitive growth. Following are central ideas and concepts in Vygotsky's theory:

● *Through both informal interactions and formal schooling, adults convey to children the ways in which their culture interprets the world.* In their interactions with children, adults share the *meanings* they attach to objects, events and, more generally, human experience. In the process, they transform, or *mediate*, the situations children encounter. Meanings are conveyed through a variety of mechanisms, including language, mathematical symbols, art, music, and so on.

For example, imagine yourself as a 2-year-old. Today your mother is doing things—blowing up balloons, wrapping boxes in brightly colored paper and ribbon, and so on—that are not part of her normal routine. Soon several of your older brother's playmates arrive carrying brightly wrapped packages. The older children play games for a while, and then your brother opens all the packages. Later your mother brings in a large cake with lighted candles on top, and your brother blows out the candles. Fortunately, Mom occasionally stops to tell you what is going on. It is your brother's *birthday,* she says, and he's having a *party* to celebrate. By blowing out the candles on his cake, your brother is trying to make a wish come true. Mom's explanations are essential to your making sense of the occasion, because a birthday celebration and the various rituals it includes are culture-specific phenomena.

Informal conversations are one common method by which adults pass along culturally appropriate ways of interpreting situations. But no less important in Vygotsky's eyes is formal education, where teachers systematically impart the ideas, concepts, and terminology used in various academic disciplines. Although Vygotsky, like Piaget, saw value in allowing children to make some discoveries themselves, he also saw value in having adults pass along the discoveries of previous generations (Karpov & Haywood, 1998; Vygotsky, 1962).

Increasingly, contemporary developmental psychologists are recognizing the many ways in which culture shapes children's cognitive development. A society's culture ensures that each new generation benefits from the wisdom that preceding generations have accumulated. It guides children in certain directions by encouraging them to pay attention to particular stimuli (and not to others) and to engage in particular activities (and not in others). And it provides a lens through which children come to construct culturally appropriate interpretations of their experiences.

We see the effects of culture in many of children's everyday activities both in and out of school—for instance, in the books they read, the jokes they tell, the roles they enact in pretend play, and the extracurricular activities they pursue. As one example, consider the game of Monopoly. Through this popular board game, children learn about buying and mortgaging real estate, paying rent and taxes, and making business decisions within a capitalistic society. Furthermore, they practice skills in mathematics (e.g., making change, calculating percentages) and negotiation (e.g., selling and exchanging properties). Happily, children seem able to adapt the game to fit their own ability levels. For example, 14-year-olds use more complicated mathematical procedures when playing the game than 8-year-olds do (Guberman, Rahm, & Menk, 1998).

● *Every culture passes along physical and cognitive tools that make daily living more effective and efficient.* Not only do adults teach children specific ways of interpreting experience, but they also pass along specific tools that can help children tackle the various tasks and problems they are apt to face. Some tools, such as shovels, sewing machines, and computers, are physical objects. Others, such as writing systems, maps, and spreadsheets, are largely symbolic. Still others, such as engaging in meditation, using rules of subtraction to calculate change from a dollar, and determining the fastest route from one place to another, may have little physical ba-

Playing Monopoly provides an opportunity to practice mathematical skills and such adult activities as buying and mortgaging real estate, paying rent and taxes, and negotiating trades with other businesspeople.

sis at all. In Vygotsky's view, acquiring tools that are strictly symbolic or mental—**cognitive tools**—greatly enhances children's cognitive abilities.

Different cultures pass along different cognitive tools. Thus Vygotsky's theory leads us to expect greater diversity among children than Piaget's theory does. For instance, recall a point made earlier in the chapter: Children acquire conservation skills at a younger age if conservation of clay and water is important for their family's pottery business. Similarly, children are more likely to acquire map-reading skills if maps (perhaps of roads, subway systems, and shopping malls) are a prominent part of their community and family life (Trawick-Smith, 2003; Whiting & Edwards, 1988). Children are more apt to have a keen sense of time if cultural activities are tightly regulated by clocks and calendars (K. Nelson, 1996a). And in the opening case study, Billy can relate museum exhibits to certain geological periods—cognitive tools that can help him organize prehistoric artifacts—only because aspects of his culture (children's books, museums, etc.) have enabled him to acquire those tools.

● *Thought and language become increasingly interdependent in the first few years of life.* One very important cognitive tool is language. For us as adults, thought and language are closely interconnected. We often think by using the specific words that our language provides. For example, when we think about household pets, our thoughts contain such words as *dog* and *cat*. In addition, we usually express our thoughts when we converse with others. In other words, we "speak our minds."

But Vygotsky proposed that thought and language are separate functions for infants and young toddlers. In these early years, thinking occurs independently of language, and when language appears, it is first used primarily as a means of communication rather than as a mechanism of thought. Sometime around age 2, thought and language become intertwined: Children begin to express their thoughts when they speak, and they begin to think in words (see Figure 6-5).

When thought and language first merge, children often talk to themselves, a phenomenon known as **self-talk** (also known as *private speech*). Vygotsky suggested that self-talk serves an important function in cognitive development. By talking to themselves, children learn to guide and direct their own behaviors through difficult tasks and complex maneuvers in much the same way that adults have previously guided them. Self-talk eventually evolves into **inner speech,** in which children "talk" to themselves mentally rather than aloud. They continue to direct themselves verbally through tasks and activities, but others can no longer see and hear them do it.

Recent research has supported Vygotsky's views regarding the progression and role of self-talk and inner speech. The frequency of children's audible self-talk decreases during the preschool and early elementary years, but this decrease is at first accompanied by an increase in whispered mumbling and silent lip movements, presumably reflecting a transition to inner speech (Bivens & Berk, 1990; R. E. Owens, 1996; Winsler & Naglieri, 2003). Furthermore, self-talk increases when children are performing more challenging tasks, at which they must exert considerable effort to be successful (Berk, 1994; Schimmoeller, 1998). Even adults occasionally talk to themselves when they face new challenges.

● *Complex mental processes begin as social activities. As children develop, they gradually internalize the processes they use in social contexts and begin to use them independently.* Vygotsky proposed that many thought processes, including the use of cognitive tools, have their roots in social interactions. As children discuss objects and events with adults and other knowledgeable individuals—often within the context of the everyday activities of their culture—they gradually incorporate into their own thinking the ways in which the people around them talk about and interpret the world, and they begin to use the words, concepts, symbols, and strategies that are typical for their culture.

The process through which social activities evolve into internal mental activities is called **internalization.** The progression from self-talk to inner speech we just described illustrates this process: Over time, children gradually internalize adults' directions so that they are eventually giving *themselves* directions.

Not all mental processes emerge as children interact with adults, however. Some develop as children interact with peers. For example, children frequently argue with one another about a variety of matters—how best to carry out an activity, what games to play, who did what to whom, and so on. According to Vygotsky, childhood arguments help children

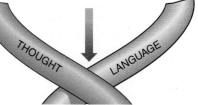

In infancy, thought is nonverbal in nature, and language is used primarily as a means of communication.

At about 2 years of age, thought becomes verbal in nature, and language becomes a means of expressing thoughts.

With time, children begin to use *self-talk* to guide their own thoughts and behaviors.

Self-talk gradually evolves into *inner speech*, whereby children guide themselves silently (mentally) rather than aloud.

Figure 6-5

Vygotsky proposed that thought and language initially emerge as separate functions but eventually become intertwined.

---

cognitive tool
Concept, symbol, strategy, or other culturally constructed mechanism that helps people think more effectively.

self-talk
Talking to oneself as a way of guiding oneself through a task.

inner speech
"Talking" to oneself mentally rather than aloud.

internalization
In Vygotsky's theory, the gradual evolution of external, social activities into internal, mental activities.

In Vygotsky's view, complex cognitive processes begin in social contexts. Children gradually internalize these processes and can eventually use them independently.

discover that there are often several ways to view the same situation. Eventually, he suggested, children internalize the "arguing" process, developing the ability to look at a situation from several different angles *on their own.*

● *Children appropriate their culture's tools in their own idiosyncratic manner.* Children do not necessarily internalize *exactly* what they see and hear in a social context. Rather, they often transform ideas, strategies, and other cognitive tools to make them uniquely their own. You may sometimes see the term **appropriation** used to refer to this process of internalizing but also adapting the ideas and strategies of one's culture for one's own use.

● *Children can perform more challenging tasks when assisted by more advanced and competent individuals.* Vygotsky distinguished between two kinds of abilities that children are apt to have at any particular point in their development. A child's **actual developmental level** is the upper limit of tasks that he or she can perform independently, without help from anyone else. A child's **level of potential development** is the upper limit of tasks that he or she can perform with the assistance of a more competent individual. To get a true sense of children's cognitive development, Vygotsky suggested, teachers should assess children's capabilities both when performing alone *and* when performing with assistance.

Children can typically do more difficult things in collaboration with adults than they can do on their own. For example, with the assistance of a parent or teacher, they may be able to read more complex prose than they are likely to read independently. They can play more difficult piano pieces when an adult helps them locate some of the notes on the keyboard or provides suggestions about what fingers to use. And notice how a student who cannot independently solve division problems with remainders begins to learn the correct procedure through an interaction with her teacher:

Teacher: [writes 6)‾44‾ on the board] 44 divided by 6. What number times 6 is close to 44?
Child: 6.
Teacher: What's 6 times 6? [writes 6]
Child: 36.
Teacher: 36. Can you get one that's any closer? [erasing the 6]
Child: 8.
Teacher: What's 6 times 8?
Child: 64 . . . 48.
Teacher: 48. Too big. Can you think of something . . .
Child: 6 times 7 is 42. (A. L. Pettito, 1985, p. 251)

● *Challenging tasks promote maximum cognitive growth.* The range of tasks that children cannot yet perform independently but *can* perform with the help and guidance of others is, in Vygotsky's terminology, the **zone of proximal development (ZPD).** A child's zone of proximal development includes learning and problem-solving abilities that are just beginning to emerge and develop. Naturally, any child's ZPD will change over time. As some tasks are mastered, other, more complex ones appear on the horizon to take their place.

Vygotsky proposed that children learn very little from performing tasks they can already do independently. Instead, they develop primarily by attempting tasks they can accomplish only in collaboration with a more competent individual—that is, when they attempt tasks within their zone of proximal development. In a nutshell, it is the challenges in life, not the easy successes, that promote cognitive development.

Whereas challenging tasks are beneficial, impossible tasks, which children cannot do even with considerable structure and assistance, are of no benefit whatsoever (Vygotsky, 1987b). (For example, it is pointless to ask a typical kindergartner to solve for *x* in an algebraic equation.) A child's ZPD therefore sets a limit on what he or she is cognitively capable of learning.

● *Play allows children to stretch themselves cognitively.* Recall the scenario of Jeff and Scott playing "restaurant," presented earlier in the chapter. The two boys take on several adult roles (restaurant manager, waiter, cook) and practice a variety of adultlike behaviors: assembling the necessary materials for a restaurant, creating menus, keeping track of customers'

appropriation
Gradual adoption of (and perhaps also adaptation of) other people's ways of thinking and behaving for one's own purposes.

actual developmental level
Upper limit of tasks that a child can successfully perform independently.

level of potential development
Upper limit of tasks that a child can successfully perform with the assistance of a more competent individual.

zone of proximal development (ZPD)
Range of tasks that one cannot yet perform independently but can perform with the help and guidance of others.

orders, and tallying final bills. In real life such a scenario would, of course, be impossible. Very few 5-year-old children have the cooking, reading, writing, mathematical, or organizational skills necessary to run a restaurant. Yet the element of make-believe brings these tasks within the boys' reach (e.g., Lillard, 1993). In Vygotsky's words:

> In play a child is always above his average age, above his daily behavior, in play it is as though he were a head taller than himself. (Vygotsky, 1978, p. 102)

Many contemporary psychologists share Vygotsky's and Piaget's belief that play provides an arena in which youngsters can practice the skills they will need in later life. Not only does play promote social skills (e.g., cooperation and conflict resolution strategies), but it also helps children experiment with new combinations of objects, identify cause-effect relationships, and learn more about other people's perspectives (Chafel, 1991; Lillard, 1998; Rubin, Fein, & Vandenberg, 1983; Zervigon-Hakes, 1984).

To some degree, play probably serves different purposes for different age-groups. For infants, one primary goal of play activities seems to be to discover what objects are like and can do, as well as what people can do *to* and *with* the objects. Through such discoveries, infants learn many basic properties of the physical world (Morris, 1977). Through more social games, such as peekaboo and pat-a-cake, infants practice imitation and acquire rudimentary skills in cooperation and turn taking (Bruner & Sherwood, 1976; Flavell, Miller, & Miller, 2002).

Vygotsky suggested that make-believe play allows children to practice adult roles. And when they use one object to stand for another (e.g., when they use plastic crates for train cars), they become increasingly able to distinguish between objects and their symbolic representations.

When play takes on an element of make-believe sometime around age 2, children begin to substitute one object for another and eventually perform behaviors involving imaginary objects—for instance, "eating" imaginary food with an imaginary fork (O'Reilly, 1995; Pederson, Rook-Green, & Elder, 1981). As Vygotsky suggested, such pretense probably helps children distinguish between objects and their symbolic representations and respond to internal representations (e.g., to the concept of *fork*) as much as to external objects (Bodrova & Leong, 1996; Haight, 1999; Karpov, 2003). When, in the preschool years, children expand their pretend play into elaborate scenarios—sometimes called **sociodramatic play**—they can also practice roles such as "parent," "teacher," or "waiter," and they learn how to behave in ways that conform to cultural standards and expectations. Furthermore, children engaging in sociodramatic play are apt to gain a greater appreciation of what other people might be thinking and feeling (Göncü, 1993; Karpov, 2003; Lillard, 1998).

As children reach school age, role-playing activities gradually diminish, and other forms of play take their place. For instance, elementary school children often spend time constructing things from cardboard boxes or Legos, playing cards and board games, and engaging in team sports. Many of these activities continue into adolescence. Although such forms of play do not mimic adult roles in as obvious a manner as "house" and "restaurant," they, too, serve a purpose. Especially in group games and sports, children must follow a specific set of rules. By adhering to restrictions on their behavior, children learn to plan ahead, to think before they act, to cooperate and compromise, to solve problems, and to engage in self-restraint—skills critical for successful participation in the adult world (Bornstein, et al., 1999; Christie & Johnsen, 1983; Sutton-Smith, 1979).

Play, then, is hardly a waste of time. Instead, it provides a valuable training ground for the adult world. Perhaps for this reason it is seen in children worldwide.

Current Perspectives on Vygotsky's Theory

Vygotsky focused more on the processes through which children develop than on the abilities seen in children of particular ages. He did identify stages of development but portrayed them in only the most general terms. From our perspective, the stages are not terribly informative (we refer you to Vygotsky, 1997, pp. 214–216, if you would like to learn more about them). In addition, Vygotsky's descriptions of developmental processes were often imprecise and lacking in detail (Gauvain, 2001; Haenan, 1996; Wertsch, 1984).

sociodramatic play
Play in which children take on roles and act out a scenario of events.

For these reasons, Vygotsky's theory has been more difficult for researchers to test and either verify or disprove than has Piaget's theory.

Despite such weaknesses, many contemporary theorists and practitioners have found Vygotsky's theory both insightful and helpful. Although they have taken Vygotsky's notions in many different directions, we can discuss much of their work within the context of several general ideas: social construction of meaning, scaffolding, participation in adult activities, and acquisition of teaching skills.

Social construction of meaning.   Contemporary psychologists have elaborated on Vygotsky's proposal that adults help children attach meaning to the objects and events around them. They point out that an adult (e.g., a parent or teacher) often helps a child make better sense of the world through joint discussion of a phenomenon or event that the two of them have mutually experienced (Crowley & Jacobs, 2002; Eacott, 1999; Feuerstein, 1990). Such an interaction, sometimes called a **mediated learning experience,** encourages the child to think about the phenomenon or event in particular ways: to attach labels to it, recognize principles that underlie it, draw certain conclusions from it, and so on. For instance, in the opening case study, Billy's mother mediates Billy's understanding of dinosaur artifacts by helping him recognize the protective function of dinosaur ribs and the role that stones played in dinosaur digestion. In such a conversation, the adult must, as Billy's mother does, consider the prior knowledge and perspectives of the child and tailor the discussion accordingly (Newson & Newson, 1975).

In addition to co-constructing meanings with adults, children often talk among themselves to derive meaning from their experiences. As we authors reflect back on our own childhood and adolescent years, we recall having numerous conversations with friends in our joint efforts to make sense of our world, perhaps within the context of identifying the optimal food and water conditions for raising tadpoles, deciding how best to carry out an assigned school project, or figuring out why certain teenage boys were so elusive.

School is one obvious place where children and adolescents can toss around ideas about a particular issue and perhaps reach consensus about how best to interpret and understand the topic in question. As an example of how members of a classroom might work together to construct meaning, let's consider a discussion in Keisha Coleman's third-grade class. The students are debating how they might solve the problem $-10 + 10 = ?$. They are using a number line like the following to facilitate their discussion:

Several students, including Tessa, agree that the solution is "zero" but disagree about how to use the number line to arrive at that answer. Excerpts from a discussion between Tessa and her classmate Chang (as facilitated by Ms. Coleman) follow:

Tessa:	You have to count numbers to the right. If you count numbers to the right, then you couldn't get to zero. You'd have to count to the left.
[Ms. Coleman]:	Could you explain a little bit more about what you mean by that? I'm not quite sure I follow you. . . .
Tessa:	Because if you went that way [points to the right] then it would have to be a higher number. . . .
Chang:	I disagree with what she's trying to say. . . . Tessa says if you're counting right, then the number is—I don't really understand. She said, "If you count right, then the number has to go smaller." I don't know what she's talking about. Negative ten plus ten is zero. . . . What do you mean by counting to the right?
Tessa:	If you count from ten up, you can't get zero. If you count from ten left, you can get zero.
Chang:	Well, negative ten is a negative number—smaller than zero.
Tessa:	I know.
Chang:	Then why do you say you can't get to zero when you're adding to negative ten, which is smaller than zero?
Tessa:	OHHHH! NOW I GET IT! This is positive. . . . You have to count right.
[Ms. Coleman]:	You're saying in order to get to zero, you have to count to the right? From where, Tessa?
Tessa:	Negative 10. (P. L. Peterson, 1992, pp. 165–166)

— Connecting Concepts
An additional application of Vygotsky's ideas is *dynamic assessment,* described in Chapter 8.

mediated learning experience
Discussion between an adult and a child in which the adult helps the child make sense of an event they have mutually experienced.

The class continues in its efforts to pin down precisely how to use the number line to solve the problem. Eventually, Tessa offers a revised and more complete explanation. Pointing to the appropriate location on the number line, she says, "You start at negative 10. Then you add 1, 2, 3, 4, 5, 6, 7, 8, 9, 10." She moves her finger one number to the right for each number she counts. She reaches the zero point on the number line when she counts "10" and concludes, "That equals zero" (P. L. Peterson, 1992, p. 168). Notice that at no time does Ms. Coleman impose her own interpretations either on the problem itself or on what Tessa and Chang have to say about it. Instead, she lets the two children struggle to make sense of the problem and, eventually, to agree on how best to solve it.

In recent years many theorists have become convinced of the value of joint meaning-making discussions in helping children acquire more complex understandings of their physical, social, and academic worlds. This perspective, generally known as **social constructivism,** is reflected in advocacy for instructional practices that involve frequent student interaction—class discussions, cooperative learning activities, peer tutoring, and so on—in elementary and secondary classrooms.

Scaffolding.   Theorists have given considerable thought to the kinds of assistance that can help children successfully accomplish challenging tasks and activities. The term **scaffolding** is often used to describe the guidance or structure provided by more competent individuals to help children perform tasks in their ZPD. To understand this concept, think of the scaffolding used in the construction of a new building. The *scaffold* is an external structure that provides support for the workers (e.g., a place where they can stand) until the building itself is strong enough to support them. As the building gains substance and stability, the scaffold becomes less necessary and is gradually removed.

In much the same way, an adult guiding a child through a new task may initially provide a scaffold to support the child's early efforts. In the teacher-student dialogue about the division problem 6)44 presented earlier, the teacher provides clues about how to proceed, such as searching for the multiple of 6 closest to, but still less than, 44. Similarly, adults provide scaffolding when they demonstrate the use of particular tools or procedures, give hints about how to approach a difficult problem, or divide a complex task into smaller, easier steps (Rosenshine & Meister, 1992; D. Wood, Bruner, & Ross, 1976). In the example that follows, notice how a mother helps her 4-year-old daughter Sadie assemble a toy from Duplo blocks (larger versions of Legos) by following a set of instructions:

Appropriate scaffolding often enables children to perform tasks they cannot otherwise do.

Mother:	Now you need another one like this on the other side. Mmmmmm . . . there you go, just like that.
Sadie:	Then I need this one to go like this? Hold on, hold on. Let it go. There. Get that out. Oops!
Mother:	I'll hold it while you turn it. (*Watches Sadie work on toy.*) Now you make the end.
Sadie:	This one?
Mother:	No, look at the picture. Right here (*points to plan*). That piece.
Sadie:	Like this?
Mother:	Yeah. (Gauvain, 2001, p. 32; reprinted with permission.)

As children become more adept at performing new tasks, scaffolding like that provided by Sadie's mother should be gradually phased out so that the children eventually perform the tasks on their own.

Participation in adult activities.   Virtually all cultures allow—and in fact usually require—children to be involved in adult activities to some degree. Children's early experiences are often at the fringe of an activity. As children acquire greater competence, they gradually take a more central role in the activity until, eventually, they are full-fledged participants (Gaskins, 1999; Guberman, 1999; Lave & Wenger, 1991).

In most cases children's early involvement in adult activities is scaffolded and supervised through what is sometimes known as **guided participation** (Rogoff, 2003). For

social constructivism
Theoretical perspective that focuses on people's collective efforts to impose meaning on the world.

scaffolding
Support mechanism, provided by a more competent individual, that helps a child successfully perform a task within his or her zone of proximal development.

guided participation
Active engagement in adult activities, typically with considerable direction and structure from an adult or other more advanced individual; children are given increasing responsibility and independence as they gain experience and proficiency.

Through their annual cookie drives, Girl Scouts are introduced to adult business practices in marketing, salesmanship, accounting, and taking inventory.

example, when our own children were preschoolers, we authors often had them help us bake cookies by asking them to measure, pour, and mix ingredients, but we stood close by and offered suggestions about how to get the measurements right, minimize spilling, and so on. (Mothers in Mayan communities do very much the same thing when teaching their daughters how to make tortillas; Rogoff, 2003.) Similarly, when taking our children to the office with us, we had them press the appropriate buttons in the elevator, check our mailboxes, open envelopes, or deliver documents to the department secretary, but we kept a close eye on what they were doing and provided guidance as necessary. In later years we gave them increasing responsibility and independence. For example, by the time Jeanne's son Jeff reached high school, he was baking and decorating his own cakes and cookies, and he ran errands around the community—for example, making trips to the library and post office—to help Jeanne as she worked on the articles and books she was writing.

Parents are not the only ones who engage children in adult activities. For example, schools sometimes invite students to be members of faculty decision-making committees, and parent-teacher organizations ask students to help with school fund-raising efforts. Girl Scout troops introduce girls to salesmanship, accounting, and other adult business practices during annual cookie drives (Rogoff, 1995, 2003). Many local newspapers take on high school students as cub reporters, movie reviewers, and editorial writers, especially during the summer months.

In some instances adults work with children and adolescents in formal or informal **apprenticeships,** one-on-one relationships in which the adults teach the young people new skills, guide their initial efforts, and present increasingly difficult tasks as proficiency improves and the ZPD changes. Many cultures use apprenticeships as a way of gradually introducing children to particular skills and trades in the adult community—perhaps weaving, tailoring, or midwifery (Lave & Wenger, 1991; Rogoff, 1990). Apprenticeships are also common in teaching a child how to play a musical instrument (D. J. Elliott, 1995).

In apprenticeships, children learn not only the behaviors but also the language of a skill or trade (Lave & Wenger, 1991). For example, when master weavers teach apprentices their art, they might use such terms as *warp, weft, shuttle,* and *harness* to focus attention on a particular aspect of the process. Similarly, when teachers guide students through scientific experiments, they use words like *hypothesis, evidence,* and *theory* to help the students evaluate their procedures and results (Perkins, 1992). Furthermore, an apprenticeship can show children how adults typically think about a task or activity—a situation known as a **cognitive apprenticeship** (J. S. Brown, Collins, & Duguid, 1989; Rogoff, 1990; W. Roth & Bowen, 1995). For instance, an adult and child might work together to accomplish a challenging task or solve a difficult problem (perhaps sewing a patchwork quilt, solving a mathematical brainteaser, or collecting data samples in biology fieldwork). In the process of talking about various aspects of the task or problem, the adult and child together analyze the situation and develop the best approach to take, and the adult models effective ways of thinking about and mentally processing the situation.

Although apprenticeships can differ widely from one context to another, they typically have some or all of the following features (A. Collins, Brown, & Newman, 1989):

- *Modeling.* The adult carries out the task, simultaneously thinking aloud about the process, while the child observes and listens.
- *Coaching.* As the child performs the task, the adult gives frequent suggestions, hints, and feedback.
- *Scaffolding.* The adult provides various forms of support for the child, perhaps by simplifying the task, breaking it into smaller and more manageable components, or providing less complicated equipment.
- *Articulation.* The child explains what he or she is doing and why, allowing the adult to examine the child's knowledge, reasoning, and problem-solving strategies.
- *Reflection.* The adult asks the child to compare his or her performance with that of experts, or perhaps with an ideal model of how the task should be done.

apprenticeship
Mentorship in which a novice works intensively with an expert to learn how to accomplish complex tasks in a particular domain.

cognitive apprenticeship
Mentorship in which an expert and a novice work together on a challenging task and the expert suggests ways to think about the task.

- *Increasing complexity and diversity of tasks.* As the child gains greater proficiency, the adult presents more complex, challenging, and varied tasks to complete.
- *Exploration.* The adult encourages the child to frame questions and problems on his or her own and thereby to expand and refine acquired skills.

From a Vygotskian perspective, gradual entry into adult activities increases the probability that children will engage in behaviors and thinking skills within their ZPD. It also helps children tie newly acquired skills and thinking abilities to the specific contexts in which they are apt to be useful later on (Carraher, Carraher, & Schliemann, 1985; P. Light & Butterworth, 1993).

In an apprenticeship, children learn both the skills and the language associated with a particular activity.

Acquisition of teaching skills.   As children learn new skills from more experienced members of their community, they may also learn how to teach those skills to someone else (Gauvain, 2001). With age and experience, they become increasingly adept at teaching others what they have learned. In a study in rural Mexico (Maynard, 2002), Mayan children were observed as they worked with younger siblings in such everyday activities as preparing food and washing clothes. The children's earliest form of "instruction" (perhaps around age 4 or 5) was simply to let a younger brother or sister join in and help. At age 6 or 7, children tended to be directive and controlling, giving commands and taking over if something wasn't done correctly. By the time they were 8, however, they were proficient teachers, using a combination of demonstrations, explanations, physical guidance, and feedback to scaffold their siblings' efforts.

For another example of how skillfully children can teach one another, let's return to the game of Monopoly. Four 8-year-old girls are playing the game while a researcher videotapes their interactions (Guberman et al., 1998). One girl, Carla, has limited math skills and little experience playing the game. On her first turn, she lands on Connecticut Avenue:

Nancy:	Do you want to buy it?
Carla:	Hmmmm . . . [There is a long pause and some unrelated discussion among the players.] How much is it again? Twelve hundred . . .
Nancy:	A hundred and twenty dollars.
Carla:	A hundred and twenty [She starts to count her money] . . . a hundred [She is referring to a $10 bill] . . .
Sarah:	You give her one of these and one of these. [She holds up first a $100 bill and then a $20 bill of her own money.] (Guberman et al., 1998, p. 436; format adapted)

Notice how Nancy and Sarah scaffold Carla's initial purchase. Nancy asks her to consider buying the property and tells her the purchase price. When it is clear that Carla is having trouble counting out $120 (she thinks that a $10 bill is worth $100), Sarah gives her sufficient guidance that she can identify the needed bills by color alone. Later in the game, as Carla becomes more competent, the other girls reduce their support. For instance, at one point Carla lands on Virginia Avenue, with a purchase price of $160:

Carla hesitates making the payment, looking through her money. Eventually, she takes a $100 bill from her money and appears unsure how to continue.

Nancy: Just a fifty and a ten.

Carla gives a $50 bill and a $10 bill to the banker. (Guberman et al., 1998, p. 437; format adapted)

When children teach others, the "teachers" often benefit as much as the "students" (D. Fuchs, Fuchs, Mathes, & Simmons, 1997; Inglis & Biemiller, 1997; Webb & Palincsar, 1996). For instance, when young people study something with the expectation that they will be teaching it to someone else, they are more motivated to learn it, find it more interesting, and learn it more effectively (Benware & Deci, 1984; Semb, Ellis, & Araujo, 1993). Furthermore, when children who are relatively weak in a particular skill (compared to their age-mates) have the opportunity to guide younger children in that skill, they develop greater ability to guide themselves as well, presumably because they internalize the directions they have been giving someone else (Biemiller, Shany, Inglis, & Meichenbaum, 1998).

Applying the Ideas of Vygotsky and His Followers

Vygotsky's work and the recent theoretical advances it has inspired have numerous implications for teaching and working with children and adolescents:

● *Help children acquire the basic cognitive tools of various activities and academic disciplines.* Virtually every adult activity involves certain concepts and ways of thinking, and mastering them enables children to engage more successfully in the activity. For instance, children can become better musicians when they can read music and understand what *keys, chords,* and *thirds* are. They develop their carpentry skills when they know how to interpret blueprints and understand such terms as *plumb* and *right angle.* Furthermore, through such disciplines as science, mathematics, and social studies, our culture passes along key concepts (e.g., *molecule, negative number, democracy*), symbols (e.g., H_2O, π, x^3), and visual representations (e.g., graphs, maps) that can help growing children organize and interpret the physical and social worlds in which they live. Literature, poetry, music, and fine arts help children impose meaning on the world as well—for example, by capturing the thoughts and feelings that characterize human experience.

● *Use group learning activities to help children internalize cognitive strategies.* As we've seen, Vygotsky suggested that children are apt to internalize—and so eventually use independently—the processes they first use in social interaction. We find an example of the benefits of social interaction in **reciprocal teaching,** an approach to reading instruction that has had great success in enhancing children's reading comprehension skills (A. L. Brown & Palincsar, 1987; Palincsar & Brown, 1984, 1989). This approach is designed to foster four effective reading strategies:

- *Summarizing:* Identifying the main ideas of a reading passage
- *Questioning:* Asking oneself questions to check comprehension of ideas
- *Clarifying:* Taking steps to better understand a confusing point
- *Predicting:* Anticipating what points an author is apt to make in later sentences or paragraphs

A teacher and several students meet in a group to read a piece of text, occasionally stopping to discuss and process the text aloud. Initially, the teacher leads the discussion, asking questions about the text to promote summarizing, questioning, clarifying, and predicting. He or she gradually turns this "teaching" role over to different students, who for a short time take charge of the discussion and ask one another the same kinds of questions that their teacher has modeled. Eventually, the students can read and discuss a text almost independently of the teacher, working together to make sense of it and checking one another for comprehension and possible misunderstandings.

As an illustration, consider the following reciprocal teaching session for a group of six first graders reading a passage about snowshoe rabbits. In this particular case the teacher reads the text in small segments (at higher grade levels, the children themselves take turns reading). After each segment, the teacher pauses while the children discuss and make sense of the segment. As you read the dialogue, look for examples of summarizing, questioning, clarifying, and predicting (there is at least one instance of each).

The children were reading about the snowshoe rabbit, and it was the 16th day of dialogue. The teacher had just read a segment of text describing the season in which baby rabbits are born and the ways in which the mother rabbit cares for her babies. A student named Kam is the dialogue leader.

Kam: When was the babies born?
Teacher: That's a good question to ask. Call on someone to answer that question.
Kam: Robby? Milly?
Milly: Summer.
Teacher: What would happen if the babies were born in the winter? Let's think.

Several children make a number of responses, including: "The baby would be very cold." "They would need food." "They don't have no fur when they are just born."

reciprocal teaching
Approach to teaching reading in which students take turns asking teacherlike questions of their classmates.

Kam:	I have another question. How does she get the babies safe?
Kris:	She hides them.
Kam:	That's right but something else. . . .
Teacher:	There is something very unusual about how she hides them that surprised me. I didn't know this.
Travis:	They are all in a different place.
Teacher:	Why do you think she does this?
Milly:	Probably because I heard another story, and when they're babies they usually eat each other or fight with each other.
Teacher:	That could be! And what about when that lynx comes?

Several children comment that that would be the end of all the babies.

Travis:	If I was the mother, I would hide mine, I would keep them all together.
Kris:	If the babies are hidden and the mom wants to go and look at them, how can she remember where they are?
Teacher:	Good question. Because she does have to find them again. Why? What does she bring them?
Milly:	She needs to bring food. She probably leaves a twig or something.
Teacher:	Do you think she puts out a twig like we mark a trail?

Several children disagree and suggest that she uses her sense of smell. One child, recalling that the snowshoe rabbit is not all white in the winter, suggests that the mother might be able to tell her babies apart by their coloring.

Teacher:	So we agree that the mother rabbit uses her senses to find her babies after she hides them. Kam, can you summarize for us now?
Kam:	The babies are born in the summer. . . .
Teacher:	The mother . . .
Kam:	The mother hides the babies in different places.
Teacher:	And she visits them . . .
Kam:	To bring them food.
Travis:	She keeps them safe.
Teacher:	Any predictions?
Milly:	What she teaches her babies . . . like how to hop.
Kris:	They know how to hop already.
Teacher:	Well, let's read and see. (dialogue courtesy of A. Palincsar)

Notice how the teacher scaffolds the children's teaching strategies, in part by giving hints ("Kam, can you summarize for us now?") and in part by modeling effective questions ("What would happen if the babies were born in the winter?"). Notice, too, how the children support one another in their meaning-making efforts (Kris: "She hides them." Kam: "That's right but something else. . . . ").

Reciprocal teaching has been used successfully with a wide variety of students, ranging from first graders to college students, to teach effective reading and listening comprehension skills. In many cases students become far more effective readers—sometimes even surpassing the achievement of their peers—and apply their new reading strategies when studying a wide variety of subject areas (Alfassi, 1998; A. L. Brown & Palincsar, 1987; Palincsar & Brown, 1984, 1989; Rosenshine & Meister, 1994).

● *Present challenging tasks, and provide sufficient scaffolding that children can accomplish them successfully.* To promote cognitive development, teachers and other adults must present some tasks and assignments that a child can perform successfully only with assistance—that is, tasks within the child's ZPD. Children at any single age level are likely to have different zones of proximal development and so may need different tasks and assignments. In other words, instruction is most effective when it is individually tailored to children's unique strengths and limitations.

Children need some degree of support in tackling challenges, of course. Figure 6-6 shows a simple worksheet that scaffolds 4-year-old Hannah's early efforts to write the numerals 1

Figure 6-6

In this simple worksheet a preschool teacher scaffolds 4-year-old Hannah's efforts to write numerals.

	TASK PERFORMANCE	TASK INSTRUCTIONS
Step 1	The adult performs the task, modeling it for the child.	The adult verbalizes instructions.
Step 2	The child performs the task.	The adult verbalizes instructions.
Step 3	The child performs the task.	The child repeats the instructions aloud.
Step 4	The child performs the task.	The child whispers the instructions.
Step 5	The child performs the task.	The child thinks silently about the instructions.

Figure 6-7

Five steps for teaching children to scaffold their own efforts through self-talk

—————— Connecting Concepts
You'll see an example of varying assessment contexts in the discussion of *dynamic assessment* in Chapter 8.

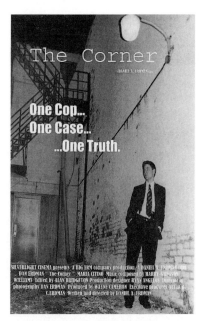

In an authentic activity for his senior project, 18-year-old Daniel wrote a story and screenplay, selected a cast, and directed, produced, and promoted his own film.

authentic activity
Instructional activity similar to one that a child might eventually encounter in the outside world.

to 5. The Development and Practice feature "Scaffolding Children's Efforts at Challenging Tasks" presents several additional examples. One of the strategies listed in this feature—*teach children how to talk themselves through a complex new procedure*—makes use of Vygotsky's concept of *self-talk* to enable children to create their *own* scaffolding. Teaching children how to give themselves instructions and thereby guide themselves through a new task might proceed through five steps (Meichenbaum, 1977, 1985):

1. *Cognitive modeling.* An adult model performs the desired task while verbalizing instructions that guide performance.
2. *Overt, external guidance.* The child performs the task while listening to the adult verbalize the instructions.
3. *Overt self-guidance.* The child repeats the instructions aloud (*self-talk*) while performing the task.
4. *Faded, overt self-guidance.* The child whispers the instructions while performing the task.
5. *Covert self-instruction.* The child silently thinks about the instructions (*inner speech*) while performing the task.

In this sequence of steps, depicted in Figure 6-7, the adult initially serves as a model both for the behavior itself and for the process of self-guidance. Responsibility for performing the task is soon turned over to the child. Eventually, responsibility for guiding the performance is turned over as well.

● *Assess children's abilities under a variety of work conditions.* Teachers and others who hope to foster children's cognitive development need to know not only what the children can and cannot do, but also under what conditions they are most likely to accomplish various tasks successfully (Calfee & Masuda, 1997). By asking children to work under varying conditions—sometimes independently, sometimes in collaboration with one or more peers, and sometimes with adult instruction and support—one can get a better sense of the tasks that are in each child's ZPD.

● *Provide opportunities to engage in authentic activities.* As we've already seen, children's participation in adult activities plays a critical role in their cognitive development. Many theorists have suggested that adults can better promote learning and cognitive development by having children engage in **authentic activities**—activities similar to those that the children may eventually encounter in the adult world—rather than in more traditional academic tasks (e.g., D. T. Hickey, 1997; E. H. Hiebert & Fisher, 1992; Lave, 1993). Following are some examples:

- Writing an editorial
- Participating in a debate
- Designing an electrical circuit
- Conducting an experiment
- Writing a computer program
- Creating and distributing a class newsletter
- Performing in a concert
- Planning a family budget
- Conversing in a foreign language
- Making a videotape
- Constructing a museum display
- Developing a home page for the Internet

By placing classroom activities in real-world contexts, teachers can often enhance students' mastery of the information and skills they're studying (A. Collins et al., 1989; De Corte, Greer, & Verschaffel, 1996). For example, students may show greater improvement in writing skills when they practice writing stories, essays, and letters to real people, rather than completing short, artificial writing exercises (E. H. Hiebert & Fisher, 1992). Likewise, they may gain a more complete understanding of how to use and interpret maps when they construct their own maps than when they engage in workbook exercises involving map interpretation (Gregg & Leinhardt, 1994).

● *Give children the chance to play.* So far, many of our suggestions—teaching cognitive tools, presenting difficult tasks, engaging children in authentic activities, and so on—imply that children's cognitive development depends largely on formal instruction and involves some amount of "work." Yet informal play activities have value as well. Thus many developmental theorists advocate including play in children's daily schedules, especially in the preschool years (Chafel, 1991; Hirsh-Pasek, Hyson, & Rescorla, 1990; Van

DEVELOPMENT AND PRACTICE

Scaffolding Children's Efforts at Challenging Tasks

- Ask questions that get children thinking in appropriate ways about a task.

  As students in a high school science class begin to plan their experiments for an upcoming science fair, their teacher encourages them to separate and control variables by asking them to consider the following questions: *What do I think causes the phenomenon I am studying? What other possible variables might cause or influence it? How can I be sure that these variables are not influencing the results I obtain?*

- Provide explicit guidance about how to accomplish a task, and give frequent feedback.

  When an outdoor educator takes 12-year-olds on their first camping trip, he has the children work in pairs or threesomes to pitch their tents. Although he has previously shown the children how to pitch a tent, this is the first time they've actually done it themselves, and so he provides written instructions that they can follow. In addition, he circulates from campsite to campsite to check on each group's progress and provide assistance as necessary.

- Provide a calculator, computer software (word processing program, spreadsheet, etc.), or other technology that makes some aspects of the task easier.

  Children in a third-grade class have mastered basic addition, subtraction, and multiplication facts. They are now applying their knowledge of arithmetic to determine how much money they would need to purchase a number of recreational items from a mail-order catalog. Because the list of items is fairly lengthy (it includes six soccer balls, four catcher's mitts, three gymnastic mats, etc.), their teacher gives them calculators to do the necessary multiplication and addition.

- Teach children how to talk themselves through a complex new procedure.

  A physical education teacher shows beginning tennis players how to use self-instructions to remember correct form when swinging the racket:

  1. Say *ball* to remind yourself to look at the ball.
  2. Say *bounce* to remind yourself to follow the ball with your eyes as it approaches you.
  3. Say *hit* to remind yourself to focus on contacting the ball with the racket.
  4. Say *ready* to get yourself into position for the next ball to come your way.

- Divide a complex task into several smaller, simpler tasks, and perhaps ask children to tackle it in small groups.

  A fourth-grade teacher has his students create a school newspaper that includes news articles, a schedule of upcoming events, a couple of political cartoons, and classified advertisements. Several students work together to create each feature, with different students assuming different roles (e.g., fact finder, writer, editor) and occasionally switching roles.

- Gradually withdraw guidance as children become more proficient.

  A child care provider has the 2-year-olds in her care take turns distributing the crackers, fruit, and napkins at snack time, and she asks all of them to bring their dishes and trash to the kitchen after they have finished eating. Initially, she must show the children how to carry the food so that it doesn't spill. She must also remind them to make sure that every child gets a serving and to clean up when they are done. As the year progresses, such explicit guidance and reminders are no longer necessary, although she must occasionally say, "I think two of you have forgotten to bring your cups to the kitchen. I'm missing the one with Big Bird on it and the one with Cookie Monster."

Sources: Gallimore & Tharp, 1990; Good et al., 1992; Lajoie & Derry, 1993; Lou et al., 1996; Meichenbaum, 1985; P. F. Merrill et al., 1996; Rogoff, 1990; Rosenshine & Meister, 1992; Stevens & Slavin, 1995; D. Wood et al., 1976; S. G. Ziegler, 1987 (tennis example).

Hoorn, Nourot, Scales, & Alward, 1999). Following are several suggestions for promoting preschoolers' play (Frost et al., 1998):

- Partition the classroom into small areas (e.g., a corner for blocks, a "housekeeping" area, an art table) that give children numerous options. (For example, look at the environments for infants and young children in the "Environments" video clips on Observation CD 1.)
- Provide realistic toys (e.g., dolls, dress-up clothes, plastic dishes) that suggest certain activities and functions, as well as more versatile objects (e.g., Legos, wooden blocks, cardboard boxes) that allow children to engage in fantasy and imagination.
- Provide enough toys and equipment to minimize potential conflicts, but keep them limited enough in number that children must share and cooperate.

By observing children during play, teachers also can gain insights into the abilities and skills that individual children have acquired. Examples of things to look for are presented in the Observation Guidelines table "Observing Young Children's Play Activities."

Observe the variety of play areas for infants and young children in the "Environments" clips on Observation CD 1.

Connecting Concepts ————
An Observation Guidelines table in Chapter 12 offers additional suggestions regarding the social aspects of young children's play.

Comparing Piagetian and Vygotskian Perspectives

Together, Piaget's and Vygotsky's theories and the research they've inspired give us a more complete picture of cognitive development than either theory provides alone. The Developmental Trends table "Thinking and Reasoning Skills at Different Age Levels" draws on elements of both perspectives to describe characteristics of children and adolescents in different age ranges.

OBSERVATION GUIDELINES

Observing Young Children's Play Activities

Characteristic	Look For	Example	Implication
Exploratory Play with Objects	• Interest in exploring objects in the environment • Ability to manipulate objects • Use of multiple senses in exploratory play	When Tyler sees a new jack-in-the-box among the supply of toys in the playroom, he picks it up, inspects it on all sides, and begins to turn the crank (although not enough to make "Jack" pop out). After Tyler leaves it to play with something else, Sarah picks it up. Rather than visually inspecting it, however, she sniffs it, then puts the crank in her mouth and begins to suck and chew on it.	Provide a wide variety of toys and other objects for infants and toddlers to explore and experiment with, making sure that all are safe, clean, and nontoxic. Anticipate that children may use these things in creative ways (and not necessarily in the ways their manufacturers intended) and will move frequently from one object to another.
Group Play	• Extent to which children play with one another • Extent to which children in a play group coordinate their play activities	Lamarr and Matthew are playing with trucks in the sandbox, but each boy seems to be in his own little world.	Give children opportunities to play together, and provide toys that require a cooperative effort.
Use of Symbolic Thought and Imagination	• Extent to which children use one object to stand for another • Extent to which children incorporate imaginary objects into their play	Julia tells her friend she is going to the grocery store, then opens an imaginary car door, sits on a chair inside her "car," steers an imaginary steering wheel, and says, "Beep, beep" as she blows an imaginary horn.	When equipping a play area, include objects (e.g., wooden blocks, cardboard boxes) that children can use for a variety of purposes.
Role Taking	• Extent to which children display behaviors that reflect a particular role • Extent to which children use language (e.g., tone of voice, specific words and phrases) associated with a particular person or role • Extent to which children coordinate and act out multiple roles within the context of a complex play scenario	Mark and Alisa are playing doctor. Alisa brings her teddy bear to Mark's "office" and politely says, "Good morning, Doctor. My baby has a sore throat." Mark holds a Popsicle stick against the bear's mouth and instructs the "baby" to say "Aaahhh."	Provide toys and equipment associated with particular roles (e.g., toy medical kit, cooking utensils, play money).

Piaget's and Vygotsky's theories share common themes that continue to appear in more contemporary views of cognitive development. At the same time, they have important differences that have led modern researchers to probe more deeply into the mechanisms through which children's thinking processes develop.

Common Themes

If we look beyond the very different vocabulary Piaget and Vygotsky often used to describe the phenomena they observed, we notice three themes that their theories share: challenge, readiness, and the importance of social interaction.

Challenge. We see the importance of challenge most clearly in Vygotsky's concept of the *zone of proximal development:* Children benefit most from tasks that they can perform only with the assistance of more competent individuals. Yet challenge, albeit of a somewhat different sort, also lies at the heart of Piaget's theory: Children develop more sophisticated knowledge and thought processes only when they encounter phenomena they cannot adequately understand using their existing schemes—in other words, phenomena that create *disequilibrium.*

Readiness. According to both theories, any child will be cognitively ready for some experiences but not ready for others. From Piaget's perspective, children can accommodate to new objects and events only when they can also assimilate them into existing schemes. That is, there must be some overlap between the "new" and the "old." In addition, Piaget argued that children cannot learn from an experience until they have begun the transition into a stage that allows them to deal with and conceptualize that experience appropriately.

DEVELOPMENTAL TRENDS

Thinking and Reasoning Skills at Different Age Levels

Infancy (Birth–2)

- Physical exploration of the environment becoming increasingly complex, flexible, and intentional
- Growing awareness of simple cause-effect relationships
- Emergence of ability to represent the world mentally (e.g., as reflected in make-believe play)

- Temperamental differences (e.g., the extent to which infants are adventure-some vs. more timid and anxious) influence exploratory behavior.
- Infants and toddlers who are emotionally attached to their caregivers are more willing to venture out and explore their environment (see Chapter 11).
- In some cultures adults encourage infants to focus more on people than on the physical environment. When people rather than objects are the priority, children may be less inclined to touch and explore their physical surroundings.

- Set up a safe, age-appropriate environment for exploration.
- Provide objects that stimulate different senses—for instance, things that babies can look at, listen to, feel, and smell.
- Suggest age-appropriate toys and activities that parents can provide at home.

Early Childhood (2–6)

- Rapidly developing language skills
- Reasoning that is, by adult standards, illogical
- Limited perspective-taking ability
- Frequent self-talk
- Sociodramatic play
- Little understanding of how adults typically interpret events

- Shyness may reduce children's willingness to talk with adults and peers and to engage in cooperative sociodramatic play.
- Adultlike logic is more common when children have accurate information about the world (e.g., about cause-effect relationships).
- Children learn to interpret events in culture-specific ways.

- Provide numerous opportunities for children to interact with one another during play and other cooperative activities.
- Introduce children to a variety of real-world environments and situations through field trips and picture books.
- Talk with children about their experiences and possible interpretations.

Middle Childhood (6–10)

- Conservation, class inclusion, and other forms of adultlike logic
- Limited ability to reason about abstract or hypothetical ideas
- Emergence of group games and team sports that involve coordinating multiple perspectives
- Ability to participate to some degree in many adult activities

- Development of logical thinking skills is affected by the importance of those skills in a child's culture.
- Formal operational reasoning may occasionally appear for simple tasks and familiar contexts, especially in 9- and 10-year-olds.
- Physical maturation and psychomotor skills affect willingness to play some games and team sports.

- Use concrete manipulatives and experiences to illustrate concepts and ideas.
- Supplement verbal explanations with concrete examples, pictures, and hands-on activities.
- Allow time for organized play activities.
- Introduce children to various adult professions, and provide opportunities to practice authentic adult tasks.

Early Adolescence (10–14)

- Emerging ability to reason about abstract ideas
- Increasing scientific reasoning abilities (e.g., formulating and testing hypotheses, separating and controlling variables)
- Emerging ability to reason about mathematical proportions
- Emerging idealism about political and social issues, but often without taking real-world constraints into consideration
- Increasing ability to engage in adult tasks

- Adolescents can think more abstractly when they have considerable knowledge about a topic.
- Adolescents are more likely to separate and control variables for situations with which they are familiar.
- Development of formal operational reasoning skills is affected by the importance of those skills in one's culture.
- The idealistic notions that young people espouse may reflect their religious, cultural, or socioeconomic backgrounds.

- Present abstract concepts and principles central to various academic disciplines, but tie them to concrete examples.
- Have students engage in scientific investigations, focusing on familiar objects and phenomena.
- Assign mathematics problems that require use of simple fractions, ratios, or decimals.
- While demonstrating how to do a new task, also talk about how to effectively *think* about the task.

Late Adolescence (14–18)

- Abstract thought and scientific reasoning skills more prevalent, especially for topics about which adolescents have considerable knowledge
- Idealistic notions tempered by more realistic considerations
- Ability to perform many tasks in an adultlike manner

- Abstract thinking tends to be more common in some content areas (e.g., mathematics, science) than in others (e.g., history, geography).
- Formal operational reasoning skills are less likely to appear in cultures that don't require those skills.
- Teenagers' proficiency in particular adult tasks varies considerably from individual to individual and from task to task.

- Study particular academic disciplines in depth; introduce complex and abstract explanations and theories.
- Encourage discussions about social, political, and ethical issues; elicit multiple perspectives regarding these issues.
- Involve adolescents in activities that are similar or identical to the things they will eventually do as adults.
- Explain how experts in a field think about the tasks they perform.

Vygotsky, too, proposed that there are limits on the tasks that children can reasonably handle at any particular time. As children acquire some capabilities, other, slightly more advanced ones begin to emerge, initially in an immature form. Children's newly forming abilities fall within their ZPD and can be fostered through adult assistance and guidance.

Teachers and other professionals who work with children must be very careful when considering the concept of *readiness,* however. Historically, many practitioners have assumed that biological maturation and background experiences (or the lack thereof) put an upper limit on what children can do and that some children may not be "ready" for a formal instructional setting such as kindergarten. In fact, all children are ready to learn *something.* The issue is not whether a child is ready, but what a child is ready for and how best to facilitate his or her cognitive development in both academic and nonacademic settings (Stipek, 2002; R. Watson, 1996).

Importance of social interaction.   In Piaget's eyes, the people in a child's life can present information and arguments that create disequilibrium and foster greater perspective taking. For instance, when young children disagree with one another, they begin to realize that different people may have different yet equally valid viewpoints, and they gradually shed the egocentrism that characterizes the preoperational stage.

In Vygotsky's view, social interactions provide the very foundation for thought processes: Children internalize the processes they use when they converse with others until, ultimately, they can use them independently. Furthermore, tasks within the ZPD can, by definition, be accomplished only when others assist in children's efforts.

Theoretical Differences

Following are four questions that capture key differences between Piaget's and Vygotsky's theories of cognitive development.

To what extent is language essential for cognitive development?   According to Piaget, language provides verbal labels for many of the concepts and other schemes that children have already developed. It is also the primary means through which children interact with others and begin to incorporate multiple perspectives into their thinking. Yet in Piaget's view, much of cognitive development occurs independently of language.

For Vygotsky, however, language is absolutely critical for cognitive development. Children's thought processes are internalized versions of social interactions that are largely verbal in nature. Through two language-based phenomena—self-talk and inner speech—children begin to guide their own behaviors in ways that others have previously guided them. Furthermore, in their conversations with adults, children learn the meanings that their culture ascribes to particular events and gradually begin to interpret the world in culture-specific ways.

The truth of the matter probably lies somewhere between Piaget's and Vygotsky's perspectives. Piaget clearly underestimated the importance of language: Children acquire more complex understandings of phenomena and events not only through their own interactions with the world but also (as Vygotsky suggested) by learning how others interpret those phenomena and events. On the other hand, Vygotsky may have overstated the case for language. Some concepts clearly emerge *before* children have verbal labels to attach to them (Halford & Andrews, 2006; L. M. Oakes & Rakison, 2003). Furthermore, verbal exchanges may be less important for cognitive development in some cultures than in others. For instance, adults in some rural communities in Guatemala and India place heavy emphasis on gestures and demonstrations, rather than on verbal instructions, to teach and guide children (Rogoff, Mistry, Göncü, & Mosier, 1993).

What kinds of experiences promote development?   Piaget maintained that children's independent, self-motivated explorations of the physical world form the basis for many developing schemes, and children often construct these schemes with little guidance from others. In contrast, Vygotsky argued for activities that are facilitated and interpreted by more competent individuals. The distinction, then, is one of self-exploration versus guided exploration and instruction. Children almost certainly need both kinds of experiences: opportunities to

INTERPRETING CHILDREN'S ARTIFACTS AND ACTIONS — Wet Head Experiment

In this three-page artifact, 10-year-old Amaryth documents her experimentation with water and a penny. She is trying to answer the question, *Which side of a penny can hold more water on its surface?* As you look at the artifact, identify elements of both Piaget's and Vygotsky's approaches at work during the activity.

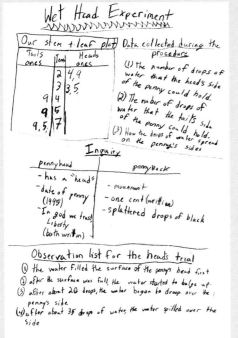

manipulate and experiment with physical phenomena on their own and opportunities to draw upon the wisdom of prior generations (Brainerd, 2003; Karpov & Haywood, 1998). Often a combination of the two is possible, as illustrated in the Interpreting Children's Artifacts and Actions exercise "Wet Head Experiment," above.

The hands-on, exploratory nature of Amaryth's experimentation—and in particular, her drop-by-drop placement of water on the two sides of the penny—reflects Piaget's view that interaction with the physical world is essential for cognitive development. Furthermore, on page 3, Amaryth offers two possible hypotheses for the superior water-holding capacity of the "tails" side, revealing an emerging ability to think about hypothetical as well as concrete ideas. Meanwhile, Amaryth uses strategies and concepts that her teacher has taught her—for instance, systematically recording observations, identifying patterns in data using a stem-and-leaf plot, and thinking about the *reliability* of the methodology—reflecting Vygotsky's idea that culture passes along cognitive tools that enhance children's thinking and reasoning.

What kinds of social interactions are most valuable? Both theorists saw value in interacting with people of all ages. However, Piaget emphasized the benefits of interactions with peers (who could create conflict), whereas Vygotsky placed greater importance on interactions with adults and other more advanced individuals (who could support children in challenging tasks and help them make appropriate interpretations).

Some contemporary theorists have proposed that interactions with peers and interactions with adults play different roles in children's cognitive development (Damon, 1984; Rogoff, 1991; Webb & Palincsar, 1996). When children's development requires that they abandon old perspectives in favor of new, more complex ones, the sociocultural conflict that often occurs among age-mates (and the multiple perspectives that emerge from it) may be optimal for bringing about such change. But when children's development instead requires that they learn new skills, the thoughtful, patient guidance of a competent adult may be more beneficial (Gauvain, 2001; Radziszewska & Rogoff, 1991).

How influential is culture?   In Piaget's mind, the nature of children's logical thinking skills and the progression of these skills over time are largely independent of the specific cultural context in which children are raised. In Vygotsky's view, however, culture is of paramount importance in determining the specific thinking skills that children acquire. Vygotsky was probably more on target here. Earlier in the chapter we presented evidence to indicate that children's reasoning skills do not necessarily appear at the same ages in different countries. In fact, some reasoning skills (especially those involving formal operational thought) may never appear at all.

Teachers and other practitioners must keep in mind, however, that there isn't necessarily a single "best" or "right" way for a culture to promote cognitive development (Rogoff, 2003). Despite their diverse instructional practices, virtually all of the world's cultures have developed a myriad of strategies for helping growing children acquire the knowledge and skills they will need to be successful participants in adult society.

In the Basic Developmental Issues table "Contrasting Piaget and Vygotsky," we compare the two perspectives in terms of our three general themes: nature and nurture, universality and diversity, and qualitative and quantitative change. Obviously, neither theorist was completely "right" or completely "wrong." Both offered groundbreaking insights into the nature of children's learning and thinking, and as you will discover in the next chapter, both have influenced more recent theories of cognitive development. In fact, Piaget's and Vygotsky's theories complement each other to some extent, with the former helping us understand how children often reason on their own and the latter providing ideas about how adults can help them reason more effectively. The final case study describes how four young adolescents reason about a classic Piagetian task—the pendulum problem—and illustrates the kinds of scaffolding that a teacher might provide to help them reason in a more "formal operational" fashion.

BASIC DEVELOPMENTAL ISSUES	Contrasting Piaget and Vygotsky	
Issue	**Piaget**	**Vygotsky**
Nature and Nurture	Piaget believed that biological maturation probably constrains the rate at which children acquire new thinking capabilities. However, his focus was on how interactions with both the physical environment (e.g., manipulation of concrete objects) and the social environment (e.g., discussions with peers) promote cognitive development.	Vygotsky acknowledged that children's inherited traits and talents affect the ways in which they deal with the environment and hence affect the experiences they have. But his theory primarily addresses the environmental conditions (e.g., engagement in challenging activities, guidance of more competent individuals, exposure to cultural interpretations) that influence cognitive growth.
Universality and Diversity	According to Piaget, the progression of children's reasoning capabilities is similar across cultures. Once children have mastered certain reasoning processes, they can apply those processes to a wide range of tasks. Children differ somewhat in the ages at which they acquire new abilities.	From Vygotsky's perspective, the specific cognitive abilities that children acquire depend on the cultural contexts in which the children are raised and the specific activities in which they are asked and encouraged to engage.
Qualitative and Quantitative Change	Piaget proposed that children's logical reasoning skills progress through four qualitatively different stages. Any particular reasoning capability continues to improve in a gradual (quantitative) fashion throughout the stage in which it first appears.	Vygotsky acknowledged that children undergo qualitative changes in their thinking but did not elaborate on the nature of these changes. Much of his theory points to gradual and presumably quantitative improvements in skills. For instance, a child may initially find a particular task impossible, later be able to execute it with adult assistance, and eventually perform it independently.

Case Study: Adolescent Scientists

Scott Sowell has just introduced the concept of *pendulum* in his seventh-grade science class. When he asks his students to identify variables that might influence the frequency with which a pendulum swings, they suggest three possibilities: the amount of weight at the bottom, the length of the pendulum, and the "angle" from which the weight is initially dropped.

Mr. Sowell divides his students into small groups and gives each group a pendulum composed of a long string with a paperclip attached to the bottom (Figure A). He also provides extra paperclips that the students can use to increase the weight at the bottom. He gives his students the following assignment: ***Design your own experiment. Think of a way to test how each one of these variables affects the frequency of swing. Then carry out your experiment.***

Jon, Marina, Paige, and Wensley are coming to grips with their task as Mr. Sowell approaches their table.

Marina: We'll time the frequency as the seconds and the . . . um . . . what? [She looks questioningly at Mr. Sowell.]

Mr. S.: The frequency is the number of swings within a certain time limit.

The group agrees to count the number of swings during a 15-second period. After Jon determines the current length of the string, Wensley positions the pendulum 25 degrees from vertical. When Jon says "Go" and starts a stopwatch, Wensley releases the pendulum. Marina counts the number of swings until, 15 seconds later, Jon says "Stop." Jon records the data from the first experiment: length = 49 cm, weight = 1 paperclip, angle = 25°, frequency = 22.

The group shortens the string and adds a second paperclip onto the bottom of the first clip. The students repeat their experiment and record their data: length = 36 cm, weight = 2 paperclips, angle = 45°, frequency = 25.

Wensley: What does the weight do to it?

Marina: We found out that the shorter it is and the heavier it is, the faster it goes.

Mr. Sowell joins the group and reviews its results from the first two tests.

Mr. S.: What did you change between Test 1 and Test 2?

Marina: Number of paperclips.

Mr. S.: OK, so you changed the weight. What else did you change?

Wensley: The length.

Marina: And the angle.

Mr. S.: OK, so you changed all three between the two tests. So what caused the higher frequency?

Wensley: The length.

Marina: No, I think it was the weight.

Jon: I think the weight.

Paige: The length.

Mr. S.: Why can't you look at your data and decide? [The students look at him blankly.] Take a look at the two tests. The first one had one paperclip, and the second had two. The first test had one length, and the second test had a shorter length. Why can't you come to a conclusion by looking at the two frequencies?

Marina: All of the variables changed.

Mr. Sowell nods in agreement and then moves on to another group. The four students decide to change only the weight for the next test, so they add a third paperclip to the bottom of the second. Their pendulum now looks like Figure B. They continue to perform experiments but are careful to change only one variable at a time, or so they think. In reality, each time the group adds another paperclip, the pendulum grows longer. Mr. Sowell visits the students once again.

Mr. S.: One thing you're testing is length, right? And another thing is weight. Look at your system. Look at how you might be making a slight mistake with

Figure A

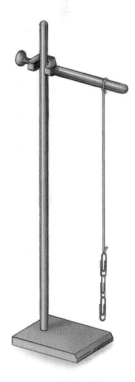

Figure B

(continued)

Marina: weight and length. [He takes two paperclips off and then puts one back on, hanging it, as the students have done, at the bottom of the first paperclip.]
Marina: It's heavier *and* longer.
Mr. S.:   Can you think of a way to redesign your experiments so that you're changing only weight? How can you do things differently so that your pendulum doesn't get longer when you add paperclips?
Jon: Hang the second paperclip from the bottom of the string instead of from the first paperclip.

When Mr. Sowell leaves, the students add another paperclip to the pendulum, making sure that the overall length of the pendulum stays the same. They perform another test and find that the pendulum's frequency is identical to what they obtained in the preceding test. Ignoring what she has just seen, Marina concludes, "So if it's heavier, the frequency is higher."

- In what ways does Mr. Sowell scaffold the students' efforts during the lab activity?
- With which one of Piaget's stages is the students' reasoning most consistent?
- Use one or more of Piaget's ideas to explain why Marina persists in her belief that, despite evidence to the contrary, weight affects a pendulum's frequency.
- Drawing from current perspectives on Piaget's theory, identify a task for which the students might be better able to separate and control variables.

Once you have answered these questions, compare your responses with those presented in the appendix.

Summary

Piaget's Theory

Piaget portrayed children as active and motivated learners who, through numerous interactions with their physical and social environments, construct an increasingly complex understanding of the world around them. He proposed that cognitive development proceeds through four stages: (a) the sensorimotor stage (when cognitive functioning is based primarily on behaviors and perceptions); (b) the preoperational stage (when symbolic thought and language become prevalent, but reasoning is "illogical" by adult standards); (c) the concrete operations stage (when logical reasoning capabilities emerge but are limited to concrete objects and events); and (d) the formal operations stage (when thinking about abstract, hypothetical, and contrary-to-fact ideas becomes possible).

Developmental researchers have found that Piaget probably underestimated the capabilities of infants, preschoolers, and elementary school children and overestimated the capabilities of adolescents. Furthermore, children's reasoning on particular tasks depends somewhat on their prior knowledge, experience, and formal schooling relative to those tasks. Contemporary developmentalists doubt that cognitive development can really be characterized as a series of general stages that pervade children's thinking in diverse content domains. A few theorists, known as neo-Piagetians, propose that children acquire more specific systems of concepts and thinking skills relevant to particular domains and that these systems may change in a stagelike manner. Many others instead suggest that children exhibit more gradual trends in a variety of abilities.

However, virtually all contemporary theorists acknowledge the value of Piaget's research methods and his views about motivation, the construction of knowledge, and the appearance of qualitative changes in cognitive development.

Vygotsky's Theory

Vygotsky proposed that adults promote children's cognitive development both by passing along the meanings that their culture assigns to objects and events and by assisting children with challenging tasks. Social activities are often precursors to, and form the basis for, complex mental processes: Children initially use new skills in the course of interacting with adults or peers and slowly internalize these skills for their own, independent use. Often children first experiment with adult tasks and ways of thinking within the context of their early play activities.

Contemporary theorists have extended Vygotsky's theory in several directions. For instance, some suggest that adults can help children benefit from their experiences through joint construction of meanings, guided participation, and cognitive apprenticeships. Others recommend that adults engage children and adolescents in authentic, adultlike tasks, initially providing enough scaffolding that youngsters can accomplish those tasks successfully and gradually withdrawing it as proficiency increases. And most developmentalists believe that children's play activities prepare them for adult life by allowing them to practice a variety of adultlike behaviors and to develop skills in planning, cooperation, problem solving, and self-restraint.

Comparing Piagetian and Vygotskian Perspectives

Challenge, readiness, and social interaction are central to the theories of both Piaget and Vygotsky. However, the two perspectives differ on the role of language in cognitive development, the relative value of free exploration versus more structured and guided activities, the relative importance of interactions with peers versus adults, and the influence of culture.

Applying Concepts in Child Development

In this chapter you learned that challenging tasks and situations promote cognitive development. The following table describes experiences of five children and adolescents. For each of these experiences, the table identifies one or more developmental concepts related to challenge, offers an implication for working with children of that age-group, or both. Apply what you've learned about Piagetian and Vygotskian perspectives to fill in the empty cells in the table. When you're done, compare your responses with those in Table 6-1 in the *Study Guide and Reader.*

APPLYING CONCEPTS IN CHILD DEVELOPMENT	Examining Challenges That Promote Cognitive Development		
Age	**A Youngster's Experience**	**Developmental Concepts** *Identifying the Nature of the Challenge*	**Implications** *Facilitating Cognitive Growth*
Infancy (Birth–2)	Eighteen-month-old Julia is becoming frustrated that the tower she's trying to build with wooden blocks keeps toppling over. Her caregiver sits on the floor beside her and helps her stack the blocks in such a way that the tower is more stable.	Building a block tower is in Julia's *zone of proximal development:* She can do it successfully only with assistance.	
Early Childhood (2–6)	Four-year-old Jacob is trying to put together a simple picture puzzle. His progress is slow, but he persists. As he works, he continually makes comments such as, "Nope, doesn't fit," "Where's that green one?" and "Maybe if I turn it this way. . . ."	Jacob is engaging in *self-talk* as a way of guiding himself through a difficult task.	Encourage rather than discourage self-talk, because it enables children to perform some difficult tasks without the assistance of others.
Middle Childhood (6–10)	"Metal always sinks, because metal is heavier than water," 9-year-old Rachel emphatically states. Her teacher shows her a postcard of a large cargo ship and says, "This ship is made almost entirely of metal. Why is it floating?" Rachel pauses, squinches her face, and thinks. "Wow, I don't know. Why *does* it float? That doesn't make sense!"		Present information that conflicts with what children currently believe as a way of helping them acquire more sophisticated understandings of the world.
Early Adolescence (10–14)	As part of an assignment for his eighth-grade journalism class, 14-year-old Jamal shadows a local newspaper reporter for a day. The reporter gives Jamal a steno pad similar to the one she herself uses and encourages him to take notes as she interviews the mayor and police chief. Periodically she looks at Jamal's notes and offers suggestions on how he might improve them. At the end of the day, Jamal helps the reporter write a story for the paper using the notes they've both taken.	As a newcomer to the world of journalism, Jamal does not have the training he would need to write a newspaper story on his own. However, he can certainly contribute in meaningful ways to a story. The reporter is engaging Jamal in *guided participation* in an adult activity.	Engage children and adolescents in typical adult activities, for instance by introducing authentic activities in the classroom or by giving them opportunities to take on tasks in community agencies and businesses.

(continued)

APPLYING CONCEPTS IN CHILD DEVELOPMENT

Examining Challenges That Promote Cognitive Development (continued)

Age	A Youngster's Experience	Developmental Concepts *Identifying the Nature of the Challenge*	Implications *Facilitating Cognitive Growth*
Late Adolescence (14–18) 	A high school social studies teacher in a wealthy school district presents some alarming statistics about the number of people living in poverty in the local community. When he asks his students to suggest some possible solutions to the situation, a heated debate ensues: "Some people are just lazy." "No they aren't! We just need to find them all jobs so they can earn a decent living." "Some people can't work because they have disabilities. How about if every rich family 'adopted' a poor family and helped it out?"	The students' diverse opinions about the problem reflect *sociocognitive conflict* that should promote disequilibrium and motivate the students to think about the matter more deeply. Yet some of the responses (e.g., finding jobs for everyone, asking rich families to "adopt" poorer ones) may be unrealistic, consistent with the *idealism* so typical of adolescence.	

Key Concepts

cognition (p. 191)
clinical method (p. 192)
class inclusion (p. 193)
scheme (p. 193)
operation (p. 193)
constructivism (p. 194)
individual constructivism (p. 194)
assimilation (p. 194)
accommodation (p. 194)
equilibrium (p. 195)
disequilibrium (p. 195)

equilibration (p. 195)
goal-directed behavior (p. 196)
object permanence (p. 196)
symbolic thought (p. 196)
egocentrism (p. 198)
conservation (p. 199)
neo-Piagetian theory (p. 203)
working memory (p. 204)
central conceptual
    structure (p. 204)
sociocognitive conflict (p. 209)

sociocultural theory (p. 209)
cognitive tool (p. 211)
self-talk (p. 211)
inner speech (p. 211)
internalization (p. 211)
appropriation (p. 212)
actual developmental level (p. 212)
level of potential
    development (p. 212)
zone of proximal development
    (ZPD) (p. 212)

sociodramatic play (p. 213)
mediated learning
    experience (p. 214)
social constructivism (p. 215)
scaffolding (p. 215)
guided participation (p. 215)
apprenticeship (p. 216)
cognitive apprenticeship (p. 216)
reciprocal teaching (p. 218)
authentic activity (p. 220)

Companion Website

Now go to our Companion Website at www.prenhall.com/mcdevitt to assess your understanding of chapter content with a Practice Quiz, apply what you've learned in Essay Questions, and broaden your knowledge with links to related Developmental Psychology Web sites.

Cognitive Development: Cognitive Processes

Case Study: How the United States Became a Country

Case Study: How the United States Became a Country

Basic Cognitive Processes

Metacognition and Cognitive Strategies

Adding a Sociocultural Element to Information Processing Theory

Children's Construction of Theories

Comparing and Critiquing Contemporary Approaches to Cognitive Development

Exceptionalities in Information Processing

Case Study: The Library Project

Summary

Applying Concepts in Child Development

Our colleague Dinah Jackson worked for many years in the Colorado public schools. At one point she asked students in grades 2 through 8 to write essays addressing the following question: *The land we live on has been here for a very long time, but the United States has only been a country for a little more than 200 years. How did the United States become a country?* Here are some of their responses:[a]

Second grader:

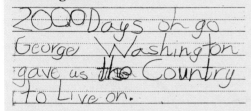

2000 Days oh go George Washington gave us the Country to Live on.

Third grader:

The pilgrims came over in 17 hundred, when they came over they bilt houses. The Idians thout they were mean. Then they came friends, and tot them stuff. Then winter came, and alot died. Then some had babies. So thats how we got here.

Sixth grader:

The U.S.A. became a country by some of the British wanting to be under a different rule than of the kings. So, they sailed to the "new world" and became a new country. The only problem was that the kings from Britin still ruled the "new world". Then they had the revolutionary war. They beat Britin, and became an independent country.

Eighth grader:

We became a country through different processes. Technology around the world finally caught up with the British. There were boats to travel with, navigating tools, and the hearts of men had a desire to expand. Many men had gone on expeditions across the sea. A very famous journey was that of Christopher Columbus. He discovered this land that we live. More and more people poured in, expecting instant wealth, freedom, and a right to share their opinions. Some immigrants were satisfied, others were displeased. Problems in other countries forced people to move on to this New World, such as potato famins and no freedom of religions. Stories that drifted through people grew about this country. Stories of golden roads and free land coaxed other families who were living in the slums. Unfortunately, there were slums in America. The people helped this country grow in industry, cultures, religions, and government. Inventions and books were now better than the Europeans. Dime-novels were invented, and the young people could read about heroes of this time. May the curiosity and eagerness of the children continue

[a]Responses courtesy of Dinah Jackson.

These four compositions illustrate important changes in children's knowing and thinking as they grow older. Perhaps most obvious is an increase in knowledge. The sixth and eighth graders know considerably more—not only about the origins of their country but also about correct spelling and rules of punctuation and capitalization—than the second and third graders do. Furthermore, whereas the third grader describes the nation's history as a list of seemingly unrelated facts, the sixth and eighth graders have pulled what they have learned into an integrated whole that "hangs together." In addition, the younger children's descriptions reflect very simplistic and concrete understandings (e.g., the country was a gift from George Washington, the Pilgrims came over and built houses). In contrast, the eighth grader uses abstract concepts (e.g., technological progress, freedom of religion, overly optimistic expectations for wealth) to explain immigration to the United States.

In the preceding chapter, we looked at two early theories of cognitive development, those of Jean Piaget and Lev Vygotsky. In this chapter our focus is on contemporary theories and research. As you will discover as you read the chapter, contemporary developmental psychologists often build on and extend Piaget's and Vygotsky's ideas in their explanations of how children and adolescents think and learn and in their recommendations for helping young people think and learn more effectively.

Basic Cognitive Processes

Do children become better able to pay attention as they grow older? Do they learn and remember things more effectively as they move through the school grades? How does the nature of their knowledge change over time? Such questions reflect the approach of **information processing theory,** a theoretical perspective that addresses how human beings receive, think about, mentally modify, and remember information, and how such cognitive processes change over the course of development.

Information processing theory emerged in the late 1950s and early 1960s and has continued to evolve in the decades that have followed. Many early information processing theorists tried to draw parallels between how people think and how computers operate. Accordingly, they borrowed computer terminology to describe human thought processes. For example, they described people as *storing* (i.e., putting) information in memory and then *retrieving* it from memory (i.e., finding it) when they need it at a later time.

Increasingly, however, researchers have found that people often think in distinctly non-computer-like ways. Much of information processing theory now has a *constructivist* flavor similar to that of Piaget's theory. Many contemporary theorists recognize that human beings actively construct their own unique understandings of the world. As an example, consider the second grader's explanation in the opening case study:

2000 Days oh go George Washington gave us the Country to Live on.

Almost certainly, no one has ever told her that the United States was a gift from George Washington. Instead, she uses something she has learned—that Washington was a key figure in the country's early history—to construct what is, to her, a logical explanation of her country's origin. Furthermore, not knowing how to spell *ago,* she uses two words she does know (*oh* and *go*) to construct a reasonable (albeit incorrect) spelling.

Key Ideas in Information Processing Theory

Figure 7-1 presents a model of what the human information processing system might look like. Although information processing theorists don't always agree about the specific mechanisms involved in learning and remembering information, many of them agree on the following points:

● *Input from the environment provides the raw material for cognitive processing.* Human beings receive input from the environment through the senses (e.g., by seeing, hearing, or touching) and translate that raw input into more meaningful information. The first part of this process, detecting stimuli in the environment, is *sensation*. The second part, interpreting those stimuli, is *perception*.

information processing theory
Theoretical perspective that focuses on the specific ways in which people mentally think about ("process") the information they receive.

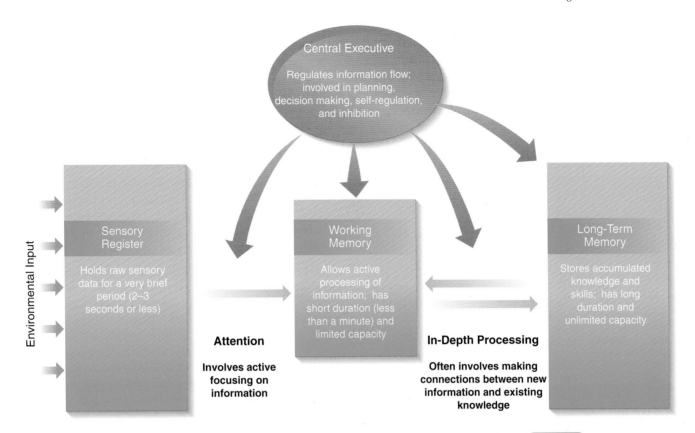

Figure 7-1
A model of the human information processing system

Because even the simplest interpretation of an environmental event takes time, many theorists believe that human memory includes a mechanism that allows people to remember raw sensory data for a very short time (perhaps 2 to 3 seconds for auditory information and probably less than a second for visual information). This mechanism goes by a variety of names, but we'll refer to it as the **sensory register.**

● *In addition to a sensory register, human memory includes two other storage mechanisms: working memory and long-term memory.* In Chapter 6 we introduced the concept of **working memory,** the component of memory in which people actively think about information. For instance, working memory is where children try to solve a problem or make sense of what they are reading. It can keep information for only a very short time (probably less than a minute) and so is sometimes called *short-term memory.*[1] Furthermore, working memory appears to have a limited capacity—only a small amount of "space" in which people can hold and think about events or ideas. As an illustration, try computing the following division problem in your head:

$$59\overline{)49,383}$$

Did you find yourself having trouble remembering some parts of the problem while you were dealing with other parts? Did you ever arrive at the correct answer of 837? Most people cannot solve a multistep division problem like this unless they can write the problem on paper. There simply isn't "room" in working memory to hold all the numbers in your head while simultaneously trying to solve the problem.

Long-term memory is the component that allows human beings to save the many things they've learned from their experiences. For instance, it might include such knowledge as where cookies are stored in the kitchen and how much 2 and 2 equal, as well as such skills as how to ride a bicycle and how to use a microscope. Things in long-term memory

Connecting Concepts
The distinction between sensation and perception is discussed in greater detail in Chapter 3.

sensory register
Component of memory that holds incoming information in an unanalyzed form for a very brief time (2–3 seconds or less).

working memory
Component of memory that enables people to actively think about and process a small amount of information.

long-term memory
Component of memory that holds knowledge and skills for a relatively long period of time.

---

[1]In everyday language, people often use the term "short-term memory" to refer to memory that lasts for a few days or weeks. Notice how, in contrast, information processing theorists characterize short-term memory as lasting *less than a minute.*

don't necessarily last forever, but they do last for a lengthy period of time, especially if they are used frequently. In addition, long-term memory appears to have an unlimited capacity, "holding" as much information as a person could possibly need to save.

To think about information previously stored in long-term memory, people must retrieve and reflect on it in working memory. Thus, although people's capacity to keep information in long-term memory may be boundless, their ability to *think about* what they've stored is limited to whatever they can hold in working memory at any one time.

● *Attention is essential to the learning process.* Most information processing theorists believe that attention is the primary process through which information moves from the sensory register into working memory. Thus it plays a key role in the interpretation, storage, and recall of information. In the "Memory: Middle Childhood" video clip on Observation CD 1, you can see what happens when a child isn't paying attention. Ten-year-old David remembers 3 of the 12 words that the interviewer reads to him. He sees his lapse in attention as the reason he did not recall more words: "My brain was turned off right now."

In the "Memory: Middle Childhood" clip on Observation CD 1, observe David's realization that attention affects his memory of a word list.

● *A variety of cognitive processes are involved in moving information from working memory to long-term memory.* Whereas attention is instrumental in moving information from the sensory register to working memory, other, more complex processes are needed if people are to remember information for longer than a minute or so. Some theorists suggest that repeating information over and over (*rehearsing* it) is sufficient for its long-term storage. Others propose that people store information effectively only when they connect it to concepts and ideas that already exist in long-term memory—for instance, when they use what they already know either to *organize* or expand (i.e., *elaborate*) on the new information. The three processes just listed—rehearsal, organization, and elaboration—are examples of the *executive functions* described in Chapter 4. We will look at their development more closely later in this chapter.

● *People control how they process information.* Some sort of cognitive "supervisor" is almost certainly necessary to ensure that a person's learning and memory processes work effectively. This mechanism, sometimes called the **central executive,** oversees the flow of information throughout the memory system and is critical for planning, decision making, self-regulation, and inhibition of unproductive thoughts and behaviors. Although the central executive is probably closely connected to working memory, information processing theorists haven't yet pinned down its exact nature.

● *Cognitive development involves gradual changes in various components of the information processing system.* Information processing theorists reject Piaget's notion of discrete developmental stages. Instead, they believe that children's cognitive processes and abilities develop through steady and gradual *trends*. In the following sections, we look at developmental trends in sensation and perception, attention, working memory and the central executive, long-term memory, and thinking and reasoning.

Sensation and Perception

Most sensory and perceptual development occurs in infancy. Researchers have reached the following conclusions about infants' sensory and perceptual abilities:

● *Some sensory and perceptual capabilities are present at birth. Others emerge within the first few weeks or months of life.* As you discovered in Chapter 3, even newborns can sense and discriminate among different sights, sounds, tastes, and smells (Bijeljac-Babic, Bertoncini, & Mehler, 1993; Flavell et al., 2002; Rosenstein & Oster, 1988; Steiner, 1979). And their ability to perceive—that is, to *interpret*—the information their senses give them appears quite early. For instance, newborns have some ability to determine the direction from which a sound is coming. And within the first week they seem to understand that objects maintain the same shape and size even when they are rotated or moved farther away and so *look* different (Morrongiello, Fenwick, Hillier, & Chance, 1994; Slater, Mattock, & Brown, 1990; Slater & Morison, 1985).

Many sensory and perceptual capabilities, such as visual acuity, visual focusing, color discrimination, and the ability to locate the source of sounds, continue to improve during the first few months—and in some cases the first year or two—of life (R. J. Adams, 1987;

central executive
Component of the human information processing system that oversees the flow of information throughout the system.

Ashmead, Davis, Whalen, & Odom, 1991; Aslin, 1993; Hillier, Hewitt, & Morrongiello, 1992). Visual acuity changes markedly during the first year. At birth it is less than 20/600, but by 8 months of age it is around 20/80 (Courage & Adams, 1990). Infants can nevertheless do a great deal with their limited eyesight. For instance, within the first few days of life, they can recognize the contours of their mother's face and can imitate facial expressions depicting happiness, sadness, and surprise (T. Field, Woodson, Greenberg, & Cohen, 1982; M. H. Johnson & de Haan, 2001; Walton, Bower, & Bower, 1992). However, visual perception is probably not fully developed until the preschool years, when the part of the cortex that handles visual information becomes similar to that of an adult (T. L. Hickey & Peduzzi, 1987).

● *Infants show consistent preferences for certain types of stimuli, especially social ones.* As early as the first week of life, infants are drawn to new and interesting stimuli and events (Haith, 1990). Also key among their early preferences are social stimuli. For instance, within 3 days of birth, they recognize their mother's voice and will suck on a synthetic nipple more vigorously if doing so turns on a recording of their mother speaking (DeCasper & Fifer, 1980). Within the first month, they show a preference for looking at faces over other objects, and by 3 months, this preference exists even when the other objects are perceptually similar in other characteristics, such as symmetry and contrast (L. B. Cohen & Cashon, 2006; Dannemiller & Stephens, 1988; M. H. Johnson & Morton, 1991). By 4 months, infants also seem to prefer looking at human forms of movement (e.g., walking) over other movements (Bertenthal, 1993; Bertenthal & Pinto, 1993). This early inclination to focus on social stimuli is, of course, highly beneficial: Infants must depend on others not only for their survival but also for learning language and other essential aspects of their culture.

● *Perceptual development is the result of both biological maturation and experience.* Both nature and nurture appear to be essential for perceptual development (e.g., Held, 1993; M. H. Johnson, 1998). We find an example of this principle in research on depth perception. To determine when infants acquire depth perception, researchers often use a *visual cliff,* a large glass table with a patterned cloth immediately beneath the glass on one side and the same pattern on the floor under the other side (see Figure 7-2). In a classic early study (E. J. Gibson & Walk, 1960), infants aged 6 to 14 months were placed on a narrow platform between the "shallow" and "deep" sides of a visual cliff. Their mothers stood at one end of the table and actively coaxed them to crawl across the glass. Although most of the infants willingly crawled off the platform to the "shallow" side, very few of them ventured onto the "deep" side. By age 6 months, then, infants can apparently perceive depth and know that sharp drop-offs are potentially dangerous.

Figure 7-2

By refusing to crawl to the "deep" side of this glass-covered table (known as a *visual cliff*), infants show a fear of heights.

Is fear of heights the result of biology or experience? Certainly neurological maturation is involved in depth perception to some degree. Visual acuity must be sufficiently sharp and the brain must be sufficiently developed to enable infants to perceive edges and inclines. Some species that can walk almost immediately after birth (e.g., chicks, lambs, baby goats) show avoidance and fear of the deep side of the visual cliff when they are less than 24 hours old (E. J. Gibson & Walk, 1960), suggesting that an inborn fear of heights is fairly common in the animal kingdom. But researchers have found that experience is also important. Infants who have had experience with self-locomotion, either through crawling or using a walker, show greater fear of drop-offs than infants without such experience (Bertenthal, Campos, & Kermoian, 1994; J. J. Campos, Bertenthal, & Kermoian, 1992).

From an evolutionary perspective, it makes sense that both heredity and environment should play a role in perceptual development. Because perception of one's surroundings is essential for survival, the human species has undoubtedly evolved some biologically built-in perceptual mechanisms. At the same time, the specific environments to which humans must adapt vary from place to place, and so the human brain has evolved to be responsive to local circumstances (J. J. Gibson, 1979; Greenough & Black, 1992; Thelen & Smith, 1998). This is not to say, however, that parents and other caregivers should give infants as much stimulation as possible. The kinds of experiences that ensure optimal perceptual development are

DEVELOPMENT AND PRACTICE

Providing Appropriate Stimulation for Infants

• Give infants some choice and control in their sensory experiences.

A home child care provider offers a variety of simple toys and other objects for the infants in her care to explore and play with. She often places several items within reach, and she respects infants' occasional rejection and apparent dislike of certain items.

• Be aware of the dangers of too much stimulation.

A teacher in an infant child care center realizes that the center is often busy and noisy. Knowing that too much stimulation can be unsettling, he monitors the sights, sounds, textures, and even smells that are present at any one time. He tries to tone down the environment a bit when introducing a new stimulus for an infant to experience or explore.

• Read cues.

A father helps his daughter's child care provider understand the signals she typically gives. "She often turns away when she's had enough of something," he explains. "But at other times, she just acts sleepy. You know she's overstimulated if you put her in a quiet place and she perks up. If she's truly tired, then she quickly goes to sleep."

• Avoid the "better baby" trap.

A child care provider recently attended a workshop on the latest "brain research," where several presenters made a strong pitch for certain new products, claiming that the products are essential for maximizing intellectual growth. Fortunately, she knows enough about cognitive development to realize that children benefit equally from a wide variety of toys and that an intensive "sensory stimulation" approach is probably not in children's best interest.

• Recognize that temperamental and cultural differences determine the optimum amount of stimulation for each child.

A teacher in a child care center has noticed that some of the toddlers in her group seem to respond to a good deal of sensory input by getting excited and animated, whereas others fuss, go to sleep, or in some other way indicate that they are on overload. Although she herself prefers a quiet, peaceful room, one of her coworkers enjoys lively salsa music and often plays it while the children are awake. The two teachers respect their own differences and often compare notes about how different children respond to quiet versus more active environments.

those that children with normal sensory abilities are apt to encounter in any reasonably nurturing environment (Bruer, 1999). The Development and Practice feature "Providing Appropriate Stimulation for Infants" offers suggestions for things that infant caregivers might reasonably do.

Attention

The development of attention is due, in part, to brain maturation and, in particular, to the continuing development of the cortex in the first few years of life (Ridderinkhof & van der Molen, 1995; Ruff & Rothbart, 1996). The increasing involvement of the cortex undoubtedly contributes to the following developmental trends:

Observe how Corwin's attention is drawn to a novel object in the "Cognitive Development: Infancy" clip on Observation CD 1.

● *Children's attention is affected by stimulus characteristics and, later, also by familiarity.* In the "Cognitive Development: Infancy" video clip on Observation CD 1, 16-month-old Corwin is captivated by an unusual, multicolored toy he finds in a paper bag. Like all human beings, infants and toddlers quickly turn their attention to new, unusual, and perhaps intense stimuli—for instance, a flash of light, loud noise, or sudden movement (e.g., Bahrick, Gogate, & Ruiz, 2002). Once they have gained some knowledge about their everyday world, familiarity comes into play as well. In particular, they are most likely to be drawn to objects and events that are moderately different, but not too different, from those they have previously experienced (McCall, Kennedy, & Applebaum, 1977; L. M. Oakes, Kannass, & Shaddy, 2002). This tendency to prefer novelty in moderation is consistent with Piaget's belief that children can accommodate to (and so benefit from) new stimuli only to the extent that they can also assimilate those stimuli into their existing schemes.

● *Children attend differently to people than to inanimate objects.* By the time infants are 4 weeks old, they show distinct ways of attending to their primary caregivers. In particular, they attend longer and may engage in a repetitive cycle of paying attention, looking away, paying attention again, looking away again, and so on. Undoubtedly their attention is influenced by the fact that the person who is the focus of their attention responds to them—for instance by moving, showing emotion, and coordinating actions with the infants' own behaviors (Brazelton, Koslowski, & Main, 1974). In fact, adults often work hard to engage the attention of infants, and as you will discover later in the chapter, the attention-sharing sessions of infants and adults play an important role in cognitive development.

● *With age, distractibility decreases and sustained attention increases.* Once they are captivated by an object or event, infants as young as 6 months are less distractible than they would be otherwise (Richards & Turner, 2001). How long young children can sustain their attention is partly a function of their temperament. Some toddlers can become quite engrossed in an activity when the task is self-chosen, intriguing, and free from interference by others. By and large, however, young children's attention moves quickly from one thing to another. Preschool and kindergarten children in free-play situations typically spend only a few minutes engaged in one activity before they move on to another (Dempster & Corkill, 1999; Ruff & Lawson, 1990). (As an example, notice how quickly 2½-year-old Maddie loses interest in the conservation task in the "Cognitive Development: Early Childhood" video clip on Observation CD 1.) Such distractibility isn't necessarily a bad thing, as it may draw young children to other potentially valuable learning activities. But it can be frustrating for adults who have particular agendas in mind.

As children move through the elementary school years, they become better able to focus and sustain their attention on a particular task, and they are less distracted by irrelevant stimuli (Higgins & Turnure, 1984; Lane & Pearson, 1982; Ruff & Lawson, 1990). For example, in one experimental study (Higgins & Turnure, 1984), children in three age-groups (preschool, second grade, and sixth grade) were given age-appropriate tasks to complete. Some children worked on the tasks in a quiet room, others worked in a room with a little background noise, and still others worked with a great deal of background noise. Preschool and second-grade children performed most effectively under the quiet conditions and least effectively under the very noisy conditions. But the sixth graders performed just as well in a noisy room as in a quiet room. Apparently, the older children were able to ignore the noise, whereas the younger children were not.

● *Attention becomes increasingly purposeful.* By the time children are 3 or 4 months old, they show some ability to anticipate where an object of interest will be and to focus their attention accordingly (Haith, Hazen, & Goodman, 1988). In the preschool years they begin to use attention specifically to help them learn and remember something, and their ability to use it effectively continues to improve during the elementary and middle school years (DeMarie-Dreblow & Miller, 1988; Hagen & Stanovich, 1977; P. Miller & Seier, 1994). Indeed, children's learning increasingly becomes a function of what they think they need to remember.

As an illustration of the purposeful nature of attention, imagine that you have the six cards shown in Figure 7-3 in front of you on a table. You are told to remember only the *colors* of the cards. Now the cards are flipped over, and you are asked where the green card is, where the purple card is, and so on. You are then asked to name the picture that appeared on each card. Chances are, you will remember the colors far more accurately than the pictures.

In one study (Maccoby & Hagen, 1965), children in grades 1 through 7 were asked to perform a series of tasks similar to the one just described. The older children remembered the background colors more accurately than the younger children did. Yet the older children were no better than younger ones at remembering the objects pictured on the cards. In fact, the oldest group in the study remembered the *fewest* objects. These results suggest that older children are better at paying attention to and learning the things they need to know, but they are not necessarily better at learning information irrelevant to their goals.

Working Memory and the Central Executive

Working memory and the central executive (which, as noted earlier, are probably closely connected) are largely responsible for what children pay attention to, how they think about it, and how well they remember it. Three developmental trends in these components of the human information processing system enable youngsters to handle increasingly complex cognitive tasks with age:

● *Processing speed increases.* As young people move through childhood and adolescence, they execute many cognitive processes more quickly and efficiently in working

Observe Maddie's age-typical shifts in attention in the "Cognitive Development: Early Childhood" clip on Observation CD 1.

Figure 7-3

Imagine that you are told to remember the colors of each of these cards. After the cards are flipped over, do you think you would remember where each color appeared? Would you also remember what pictures appeared on each card, even though you were not asked to remember the pictures?
Modeled after stimuli used by Maccoby & Hagen, 1965.

———— Connecting Concepts
Chapter 4 describes the nature and progression of myelination in the brain.

———— Connecting Concepts
Chapter 10 describes reading development in more detail.

memory (Fry & Hale, 1996; Kail, 1993; Luna, Garver, Urban, Lazar, & Sweeney, 2004). Some of this increased speed and efficiency is undoubtedly due to the genetically driven *myelination* of neurons in the brain. Yet experience and practice are involved as well. By frequently practicing certain mental and physical tasks, children and adolescents eventually become able to perform them very quickly and with little or no conscious effort—a phenomenon known as **automatization.** Once thoughts and actions become automatized, they take up very little "space" in working memory, enabling children to devote more working memory capacity to other, more challenging tasks and problems.

As one simple example of the benefits of automatization, consider how children's reading ability improves over time. When children first begin to read, they often devote considerable mental effort to identifying the words on the page—remembering what the letter configuration f-r-i-e-n-d spells, sounding out an unfamiliar word such as *elementary,* and so on—and so may remember little about the meaning of what they've read. But with increasing exposure to a variety of reading materials, word identification gradually becomes an automatized process, such that children immediately recognize most of the words they encounter. At this point, children can focus their efforts on what is ultimately the most important part of the reading process: understanding the ideas that an author is trying to communicate.

Automatization increases the likelihood that a child will respond to a particular situation in a particular way. In many instances the child will have practiced and automatized the best response for that situation—"best," at least, for that child's environment and culture. Because different environments and cultures sometimes require very different responses, children need to learn the most effective ways of responding within the contexts in which they are growing up. Thus the *non*automatized cognitive processes of young children may, to some degree, be a blessing rather than a curse, allowing them to practice and ultimately to automatize the processes that are most likely to serve them well in their own circumstances (Bjorklund & Green, 1992).

● *The capacity of working memory increases with age.* When people of various ages are asked to hold several separate items of information—perhaps a series of digits or several unrelated words—in working memory, older children can remember more items than younger children can, and adults can remember even more. Much of this increase in working memory capacity is probably due to the fact that cognitive processes become faster and more efficient with age and so take up less "room." But the actual physical "space" of working memory may increase somewhat as well (Fry & Hale, 1996; Gathercole & Hitch, 1993; Kail, 1993).

● *The central executive increasingly takes charge of cognitive processes.* Thanks in large part to continuing maturation of the cortex, youngsters gain increasing control of their cognitive processes throughout childhood and adolescence (Luna et al., 2004; G. R. Lyon & Krasnegor, 1996; Zelazo, Müller, Frye, & Marcovitch, 2003). With such control come a variety of new abilities. For instance, youngsters become better able to plan and direct their future actions and activities. They can better inhibit inappropriate thoughts and behaviors. And they can reflect on and think *about* their thinking, as we'll see in our discussion of *metacognition* later in the chapter. Keep in mind, however, that the central executive is still a "work in progress" even in adolescence and does not fully mature until adulthood.

Long-Term Memory

Some knowledge in long-term memory is almost certainly universal. For instance, children all over the globe soon learn that people typically have two legs but cats and dogs have four. Other knowledge is, of course, more dependent on children's unique experiences and on the cultural contexts in which they grow up. For example, in the four children's compositions in the opening case study, we consistently see a European American perspective on the early days of the United States: The focus is on immigration and early European colonization. Were we to ask Native American children how the United States came into being, we might get a very different perspective, perhaps one based on invasion, confiscation, or demolition.

Several developmental phenomena related to long-term memory enhance children's ability to understand and respond to their world:

automatization
Process of becoming able to respond quickly and efficiently while mentally processing or physically performing certain tasks.

● *The capacity to remember information in long-term memory appears very early and improves with age.* At birth, and probably even *before* birth, children have some ability to learn and remember their experiences (DeCasper & Spence, 1986; Kisilevsky et al., 2003). In infancy and the toddler years, the capacity for long-term memory manifests itself in a variety of ways. For instance, when a ribbon connected to a mobile is tied to a 2-month-old baby's foot, the baby easily learns that kicking makes the mobile move and remembers the connection over a period of several days—even longer if he or she is given an occasional reminder (Rovee-Collier, 1999). Infants aged 3 to 6 months show evidence that they remember the order in which they've seen a sequence of three mobiles (Gulya, Rovee-Collier, Galluccio, & Wilk, 1998). At age 6 months, they can also recall and imitate actions they have seen 24 hours earlier, and their memory for such actions increases in duration in the months that follow (Bauer, 2006; Collie & Hayne, 1999). By the time children reach their second birthday, they are able to retain a complex sequence of actions for a year or more (Bauer, 2006).

● *Children increasingly have conscious awareness of past events.* Despite the findings just described, children typically have little if any *conscious* recall of things that happened during their first 2 years—a phenomenon known as **infantile amnesia.** For much of the preschool period, recall of past events continues to be rather sketchy. The immaturity of certain brain structures in the early years may be partly responsible (Bauer, 2002; Siegel, 1999). Furthermore, early experiences may be stored in memory in a form that children cannot easily retrieve (C. A. Nelson, 1995; Newcombe, Drummey, Fox, Lie, & Ottinger-Albergs, 2000).

When children gain proficiency in language, and particularly when people around them engage them in conversations about what they are experiencing, their conscious memory for past events improves dramatically (McGuigan & Salmon, 2004; C. A. Nelson & Fivush, 2004; K. Nelson, 1996b). It appears that talking about events enables children to store the events in a verbal (language-based) form, making the events easier to recall at a later time.

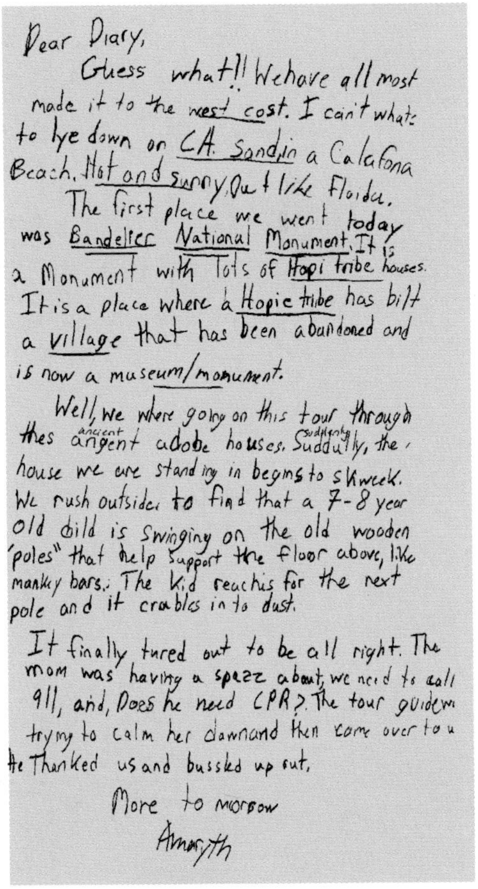

● *The amount of knowledge stored in long-term memory increases many times over.* This trend is an obvious one, and the four essays in the opening case study illustrate it clearly. Yet the obviousness of the trend does not diminish its importance in cognitive development. In particular, long-term memory provides the **knowledge base** from which children draw as they encounter, interpret, and respond to new events. As their knowledge base grows, children can interpret new events with greater sophistication and respond to them more effectively (Siegler & Alibali, 2005). Children vary considerably in the specific experiences they have, of course, and this diversity leads to the development of unique knowledge bases on which children build while learning new things. For example, in Figure 7-4, 10-year-old Amaryth describes a day when her family visited a national monument that was once a Hopi village. Travel opportunities such as this will undoubtedly enhance Amaryth's ability to learn about Native American civilizations in her history and social studies classes.

● *Children's knowledge about the world becomes increasingly integrated.* Children begin categorizing their experiences as early as 3 or 4 months of age (we'll return to this point in our discussion of *organization* a bit later). Even so, much of what young children know about the world consists of separate, isolated categories and facts. In contrast, older children's knowledge includes many associations and interrelationships among concepts and ideas (Bjorklund, 1987). This developmental change is undoubtedly one reason why older children can think more logically and draw inferences more readily: They have a more cohesive understanding of the world around them.

As an example, let's return to the essays in the opening case study. Notice how the third grader presents a chronological list of events without any attempt at tying them together:

The Idiuns thout they were mean. Then they came friends, and tot them stuff. Then winter came, and alot died. Then some had babies.

Connecting Concepts

The study involving memory for the song "Little Brown Jug," described in Chapter 3, illustrates how children can remember some things they experience even before birth.

Dear Diary,
Guess what!! We have all most made it to the west cost. I can't wate to lye down on CA. sand in a Calafona Beach. Hot and sunny. Out like Floida.

The first place we went today was Bandelier National Monument. It is a Monument with lots of Hopi tribe houses. It is a place where a Hopie tribe has bilt a village that has been abandoned and is now a museum/monument.

Well, we where going on this tour through thes angient adobe houses. Suddenly, the house we are standing in begins to shwek. We rush outside to find that a 7-8 year old child is swinging on the old wooden "poles" that help support the floor above, like mankey bars. The kid reachis for the next pole and it crables into dust.

It finally tured out to be all right. The mom was having a spezz about; we need to call 911, and, Does he need CPR?. The tour guidem trying to calm her down and then came over to us. He Thanked us and bussed up out.

More to morrow
Amaryth

Figure 7-4

Children who have had diverse experiences (museum trips, travel to historical sites, etc.) have a broad knowledge base on which to build when they study classroom subject matter.

infantile amnesia
General inability to recall events that have occurred in the early years of life.

knowledge base
One's knowledge about specific topics and the world in general.

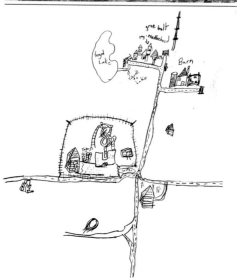

In contrast, the eighth grader frequently identifies or implies cause-effect relationships among events:

> More and more people poured in, expecting instant wealth, freedom, and a right to share their opinions. Some immigrants were satisfied, others were displeased. Problems in other countries forced people to move on to this New World, such as potato famins and no freedom of religions. Stories that drifted through people grew about this country. Stories of golden roads and free land coaxed other families who were living in the slums.

Another example of increasing integration is seen in children's knowledge of their local communities (Forbes, Ormrod, Bernardi, Taylor, & Jackson, 1999). In Figure 7-5 we present maps that three children drew of their hometown. The first grader's map includes only a few features of her town (her house, her school, nearby mountains) that she knows well, and the spatial relationships among the features are inaccurate. The third grader's map shows many features of his immediate neighborhood and their proximity to one another. The seventh grader's map encompasses numerous town landmarks and their relative locations on major streets. It also makes greater use of symbols—for instance, single lines for roads, squares for buildings, and distinctive letter *M*s to indicate McDonald's restaurants.

Children and adults alike sometimes organize their knowledge into schemas and scripts. **Schemas** (similar, but not identical, to Piaget's *schemes*) are tightly integrated sets of ideas about specific objects or situations. For example, you might have a schema for what a typical horse looks like (it's a certain height, and it has an elongated head, a mane, four legs, etc.) and a schema for what a typical office contains (it probably has a desk, chair, file cabinets, bookshelves, and books). **Scripts** encompass knowledge about the predictable sequence of events related to particular activities. For example, you probably have scripts related to how weddings typically proceed, and even many 3-year-olds can tell you what typically happens when you go to McDonald's (K. Nelson, 1997). Schemas and scripts help children make sense of their experiences and predict what is likely to happen in familiar contexts on future occasions.

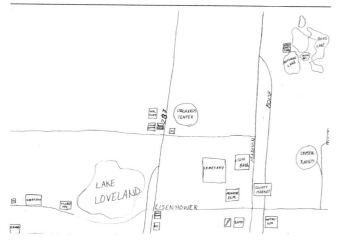

Schemas and scripts increase in number and complexity as children grow older (Farrar & Goodman, 1992; Flavell et al., 2002). Like Piaget's schemes, children's earliest schemas and scripts may be behavioral and perceptual in nature. For instance, toddlers can act out typical scenarios (scripts) with toys long before they have the verbal skills to describe what they are doing (Bauer & Dow, 1994). As children get older, these mental structures presumably become less tied to physical actions and perceptual qualities.

Schemas and scripts often differ somewhat from one culture to another. Such cultural differences may influence the ease with which children can understand and remember the information and events they encounter (Lipson, 1983; Pritchard, 1990; R. E. Reynolds, Taylor, Steffensen, Shirey, & Anderson, 1982). For example, in one study (R. E. Reynolds et al., 1982), eighth graders read a letter written by a young teenager, Sam, to his friend Joe. In it, Sam describes an incident in the school cafeteria earlier in the day:

Figure 7-5

Three maps of Loveland, Colorado, drawn by a first grader (top), a third grader (middle), and a seventh grader (bottom).

Maps courtesy of Dinah Jackson.

> I got in line behind Bubba. As usual the line was moving pretty slow and we were all getting pretty restless. For a little action Bubba turned around and said, "Hey Sam! What you doin' man? You so ugly that when the doctor delivered you he slapped your face!" Everyone laughed, but they laughed even harder when I shot back, "Oh yeah? Well, you so ugly the doctor turned around and slapped your momma!" It got even wilder when Bubba said, "Well man, at least my daddy ain't no girl scout!" We really got into it then. After a while more people got involved—4, 5, then 6. It was a riot! People helping out anyone who seemed to be getting the worst of the deal. (R. E. Reynolds et al., 1982, p. 358; italics omitted)

schema
Tightly integrated set of ideas about a specific object or situation.

script
Schema that involves a predictable sequence of events related to a common activity.

Many European American children incorrectly interpreted the incident as involving physical aggression, but African American children saw it for what it really was: a friendly exchange of mock insults common among male youths in some African American communities.

● *Children's growing knowledge base facilitates more effective learning.* As a general rule, older children and adults learn new information and skills more easily than do younger children. A key reason is that they have more existing knowledge (including more schemas and scripts) that they can use to help them understand and organize new material (Eacott, 1999; Halford, 1989; R. Kail, 1990). When the tables are turned—when children know more about a particular topic than adults do—the children are often the more effective learners (Chi, 1978; Lindberg, 1991; Schneider, Korkel, & Weinert, 1989). For example, when Jeanne's son Alex was about 5 or 6, the two of them used to read books about lizards together. Alex always remembered more from the books than Jeanne did, because he was a self-proclaimed "lizard expert" and Jeanne knew very little about reptiles of any sort.

Thinking and Reasoning

From an information processing perspective, many developmental changes in thought processes reflect qualitative changes in the mental *strategies* that children use to learn and problem-solve. We'll discuss such strategies a bit later in the chapter. For now, we look at a few general developmental trends in thinking and reasoning:

As these children play "store," they show that they already have a well-developed script for what typically happens at the checkout counter.

● *Thought increasingly makes use of symbols.* As you should recall from Chapter 6, Piaget proposed that infants' and toddlers' schemes are predominantly sensorimotor—that is, based on perceptions and behaviors. Near the end of the sensorimotor stage (at about 18 months, Piaget suggested), children begin to think in terms of **symbols,** mental entities (e.g., words) that do not necessarily reflect the perceptual and behavioral qualities of the objects or events they represent.

Piaget was probably correct in believing that sensorimotor representations of objects and events precede symbolic representations. However, the shift from one to the other is much more gradual than Piaget thought. Long before children reach school age, they begin to use such symbols as words, numbers, pictures, and miniature models to represent and think about real-life objects and events (DeLoache, Miller, & Rosengren, 1997; J. Huttenlocher, Newcombe, & Vasilyeva, 1999; K. Nelson, 1996a). Yet when children begin elementary school, they may initially have only limited success in dealing with the wide variety of symbols they encounter. For instance, elementary school teachers often use blocks and other concrete objects to represent numbers or mathematical operations, but not all kindergartners and first graders make the connection between the objects and the concepts they stand for (DeLoache et al., 1997; Uttal et al., 1998). Maps, too, are largely symbolic in nature, and children in the early grades often interpret them too literally, perhaps thinking that a road that is red on a map is actually painted red (Liben & Downs, 1989b). As children grow older, their use of symbols to think, remember, and solve problems grows in frequency and sophistication.

● *Logical thinking abilities improve with age.* Although most information processing theorists reject Piaget's idea of discrete stages in logical thinking, they do agree that logical thinking improves—and often changes qualitatively—over time. Some logical thinking is evident even in infancy. Children as young as 6 months old can perceive a cause-effect relationship in a sequence of events. For instance, when 6-month-olds see one object hit another and the second object moves immediately after the impact, they seem to understand that the first object has essentially "launched" the second one (L. B. Cohen & Cashon, 2006).

By preschool age, children can draw logical inferences from language-based information—for instance, drawing appropriate conclusions about events depicted in children's stories (M. Donaldson, 1978; R. Gelman & Baillargeon, 1983). However, preschoolers and elementary school children do not always draw *correct* inferences, and they have difficulty distinguishing between what *must* be true versus what *might* be true given the evidence before them (Galotti, Komatsu, & Voelz, 1997; Pillow, 2002). The ability to draw logical conclusions improves in adolescence. Yet even at this point, reasoning is often influenced by personal motives and biases (Klaczynski, 2001; Kuhn & Franklin, 2006). Although the trend is toward more logical thinking with age, any given child or adolescent is apt to reason more logically on some occasions than others (Klaczynski, 2001; Kuhn, 2001a).

● *Gestures sometimes foreshadow the emergence of more sophisticated thinking and reasoning.* As children make the transition to more advanced forms of reasoning—perhaps

Connecting Concepts
Chapter 10 describes the development of reasoning processes in specific content domains, such as mathematics, science, and social studies.

symbol
Mental entity that represents an external object or event, often without reflecting its perceptual and behavioral qualities.

about traditional Piagetian tasks or mathematical problems—they often show such reasoning in their gestures before they show it in their speech (Goldin-Meadow, 1997, 2001). The following scenario illustrates this trend:

> [A] 6-year-old child [is] attempting to justify her belief that the amount of water changed when it was poured from a tall, skinny glass into a short, wide dish. The child says, "It's different because this one's tall and that one's short," thus making it clear that she has focused on the heights of the two containers. However, in the very same utterance, the child indicates with her hand shaped like a C first the diameter of the glass and then, with a wider C, the larger diameter of the dish. The child speaks about the heights but has also noticed—not necessarily consciously—that the containers differ in width as well. (Goldin-Meadow, 1997, p. 13)

Gestures, like the 6-year-old's C-shaped hand gestures, appear to provide a way for children to "experiment" (cognitively) with new ideas. Gestures may also alleviate the strain on working memory as children first begin to wrestle with more complex ways of thinking (Goldin-Meadow, 2001; Goldin-Meadow, Nusbaum, Kelly, & Wagner, 2001).

Facilitating Basic Cognitive Processes

Our discussion of information processing theory thus far leads to several implications for working with children and adolescents:

See examples of safe environments for young children in the "Environments" clips for infancy and early childhood, on Observation CD 1.

● *Provide a variety of choices for infants and young children.* In the first few years of life, children learn many things about the physical world through direct contact—by looking, listening, feeling, tasting, and smelling. Thus infants, toddlers, and preschoolers should have a wide variety of toys and other objects to manipulate and play with, and their environment should be set up for safe movement and exploration (you can see examples in the infancy and early childhood clips of the "Environments" module on Observation CD 1). Children need enough options that they can identify activities and playthings that are within their current abilities yet also encourage cognitive growth.

In the "Intrinsic Motivation: Early Childhood" clip on Observation CD 3, hear Joey describe a challenge that he and most young children face: keeping attention on academic tasks.

● *Help children pay attention to the things that are important for them to learn and remember.* As we've seen, attention is a critical factor in learning. Yet many children, young ones especially, are easily distracted by the sounds and sights around them. For example, in the "Intrinsic Motivation: Early Childhood" video clip on Observation CD 3, 6-year-old Joey gives a plausible explanation for why it is sometimes hard to pay attention at school: "The noise."

Despite adults' best efforts, children and adolescents—even highly motivated high school students—cannot keep their minds on a single task indefinitely. Furthermore, some youngsters (perhaps because of a seemingly boundless supply of physical energy or perhaps because of a cognitive, emotional, or behavioral disability) have a more difficult time paying attention than others. Several strategies for helping children focus their attention productively are presented in the Development and Practice feature "Getting and Keeping Children's Attention."

In the "Memory: Late Adolescence" clip on Observation CD 1, observe how Hilary connects new information to what she already knows.

● *Relate new information to children's existing knowledge.* People of all ages learn new information more effectively when they can relate it to what they already know (Ormrod, 2004). Yet children and adolescents don't always make meaningful connections on their own. For instance, they may not realize that subtraction is simply the reverse of addition or that Shakespeare's *Romeo and Juliet* is in some ways similar to modern-day ethnic clashes in Europe, Asia, and North America. By pointing out such connections, adults can foster more effective learning and the development of a more integrated knowledge base. In the "Memory: Late Adolescence" video clip on Observation CD 1, 16-year-old Hilary explains how she makes some connections on her own and how her teacher helps her make additional ones:

> When I'm trying to study for a test, I try to associate the things that I'm trying to learn with familiar things. Like, if I have a Spanish vocabulary test, I'll try to . . . with the Spanish words, I'll try to think of the English word that it sounds like, because sometimes it does sound like the English word. And then our Government teacher is teaching us the amendments and we're trying to memorize them. He taught us one trick for memorizing Amendment 2, which is the right to bear arms. He said, "Bears have two arms, so that's Amendment 2."

DEVELOPMENT AND PRACTICE

Getting and Keeping Children's Attention

- Capture interest and attention with bright colors, intriguing sounds, and objects that invite manipulation and exploration.

  A child care provider purchases several musical instruments (e.g., a xylophone, toy guitar, and set of drums) for toddlers to play with. And as long as none of the children are napping, she lets the older ones in her care compose simple songs on the family piano.

- Minimize distractions, especially when working with young children.

  A school psychologist is administering a battery of tests to a 7-year-old boy who is suspected of having a significant learning disability. Before the testing session, the psychologist puts away the kachina doll and Russian nesting dolls that decorate her office shelves. She also removes all of the testing materials from sight, putting items in front of the boy only as it is time to use them.

- Present stimulating activities and lessons in which children *want* to pay attention.

  In a unit on nutrition, a high school biology teacher has students determine the nutritional value of various menu items at a popular local fast-food restaurant.

- Get children physically involved in tasks and lessons.

  A middle school history teacher plans a day late in the school year when all of his classes will "go back in time" to the American Civil War. In

preparation for the event, the students spend several weeks learning about the Battle of Gettysburg, researching typical dress and meals of the era, gathering appropriate clothing and equipment, and preparing snacks and lunches. On the day of the "battle," students assume various roles: Union and Confederate soldiers, government officials, journalists, merchants, housewives, doctors and nurses, and so on.

- Incorporate a variety of activities into the daily schedule.

  After explaining how to calculate the area of squares and rectangles, a fourth-grade teacher has her students practice calculating area in a series of increasingly challenging word problems. She then breaks the class into small cooperative groups. Each group is given a tape measure and calculator and asked to determine the area of the classroom floor, excluding those parts of the floor covered by several built-in cabinets that extend into the room. To complete the task, the students must divide the room into several smaller rectangles, compute the area of each rectangle separately, and add the subareas together.

- Provide frequent breaks from sedentary activities.

  To provide practice with the alphabet, a kindergarten teacher occasionally has students make letters with their bodies: one child standing with arms extended up and out to make a Y, two children bending over and joining hands to form an M, and so on.

● *Remember that children can think about only a small amount of information at any one time.* Although working memory capacity increases somewhat during childhood and adolescence, young and old people alike can mentally manipulate only a very limited amount of material in their heads at once. Thus teachers and other adults who instruct children should pace any presentation of new information slowly enough that their students have time to "process" it all. They might also write complex directions or problems on a chalkboard or ask children to write them on paper. And they can teach more effective strategies for learning and solving problems (we'll say more about such strategies shortly).

● *Consider not only what children say, but also what they do, when determining what they know or are ready to learn.* Earlier we described a 6-year-old who said that a tall, thin glass had more water than a short, wide dish because of the height difference between the two containers. At the same time, she showed through her gestures that the tall container had a smaller diameter than the short one. Such discrepancies in what children say and do suggest a possible readiness for developing new ideas and logical reasoning skills—for instance, a readiness for acquiring conservation of liquid (Goldin-Meadow, 1997).

In some instances adults might assess children's current knowledge by asking them to draw rather than describe what they have learned. For example, Figure 7-6 shows 8-year-old Noah's knowledge of how a seed becomes a plant. His picture clearly reflects his understanding that roots typically go down before a stalk grows up and that leaves gradually increase in size and number.

● *Give children ongoing practice in using basic information and skills.* Some information and skills are so fundamental that growing children must become able to retrieve and use them quickly and effortlessly. For instance, to read well, children must be able to recognize most of the words on the page without having to sound them out or look them up in the dictionary. To solve mathematical word problems, they should have such number facts as "2 + 4 = 6" and "5 × 9 = 45" on the tips of their tongues. And to write well, they should be able to form letters and words without having to stop and think about how to make an uppercase *G* or spell the word *the*.

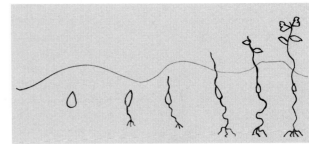

Figure 7-6

Noah's picture of how a seed becomes a plant

Ultimately, children and adolescents can automatize basic information and skills only by using and practicing them repeatedly (J. C. Anderson, 1983; Schneider & Shiffrin, 1977). This is definitely *not* to say that teachers should fill each day with endless drill-and-practice exercises involving isolated facts and procedures. Automatization can occur just as readily when the basics are embedded in a variety of stimulating, challenging (and perhaps authentic) activities.

The Developmental Trends table "Basic Information Processing Abilities at Different Age Levels" summarizes the information processing capabilities of children and adolescents. We now focus on two manifestations of the *central executive* aspect of the information processing system: metacognition and cognitive strategies.

Metacognition and Cognitive Strategies

As an adult with many years of formal education behind you, you have probably learned a great deal about how you think and learn. For example, you may have learned that you cannot absorb everything in a textbook the first time you read it. You may also have learned that you remember information better when you try to make sense of it based on what you already know, rather than when you simply repeat it over and over again in a "thoughtless" manner. The term **metacognition** refers both to the knowledge that people have about their own cognitive processes and to their intentional use of certain cognitive processes to improve learning and memory.

As children develop, the specific mental processes they use to learn information and solve problems—their **cognitive strategies**—become increasingly sophisticated and effective. Their awareness of their own thinking, their ability to direct and regulate their own learning, and their beliefs about the nature of knowledge and learning also change in significant ways. In the upcoming pages, we look at these trends more closely.

Learning Strategies

Toddlers as young as 18 months show some conscious attempts to remember something. For example, when asked to remember where a Big Bird doll has been hidden in their home, they may stare or point at its location until they are able to go get it (DeLoache, Cassidy, & Brown, 1985). Yet overall, young children rarely make a point of trying to learn and remember something. For instance, 4- and 5-year-olds can remember a set of objects more successfully by playing with the objects than by intentionally trying to remember them (L. S. Newman, 1990).

As they progress through the elementary and secondary grades, children and adolescents develop **learning strategies**—techniques that they intentionally use to learn something—that help them remember information more effectively. Three that appear during the school years are rehearsal, organization, and elaboration.

Rehearsal.   What do you do if you need to remember a telephone number for a few minutes? Do you repeat it to yourself over and over as a way of keeping it in your working memory until you can dial it? Such repetition of information as a way of remembering it is known as **rehearsal.**

Rehearsal is rare in preschoolers but increases in frequency and effectiveness throughout the elementary school years. By age 7 or 8, many children spontaneously rehearse individual pieces of information as a way of more easily remembering the information. By age 9 or 10, they become more strategic, combining several items into a single list as they rehearse. For example, if they hear the list "cat . . . dog . . . horse," they might say "cat" after the first item, say "cat, dog" after the second, and say "cat, dog, horse" after the third. Combining separate items in this manner helps children remember them more effectively (Bjorklund & Coyle, 1995; Gathercole & Hitch, 1993; Kunzinger, 1985).

Organization.   Take a minute to study and remember the following 12 words, then cover them up and try to recall as many as you can.

shirt	table	hat
carrot	bed	squash
pants	potato	stool
chair	shoe	bean

metacognition
Knowledge and beliefs about one's own cognitive processes, as well as efforts to regulate those cognitive processes to maximize learning and memory.

cognitive strategy
Specific mental process that people use to acquire or manipulate information.

learning strategy
Specific mental process used in acquiring new information.

rehearsal
Attempt to learn and remember information by repeating it over and over.

Basic Information Processing Abilities at Different Age Levels

Age			
Infancy (Birth–2) 	• Some ability to learn evident from birth • Adultlike hearing acuity within hours after birth • Considerable improvement in visual acuity over the first year • Preference for moderately complex stimuli • Attention easily drawn to intense or novel stimuli • Some ability to integrate information (e.g., learning that certain kinds of toys are stored in certain places in the playroom)	• Attention spans are partly due to differences in temperament, but persistent inability to focus on any one object may signal a cognitive disability. • Exploration tendencies vary considerably: Some children may constantly seek new experiences, whereas others may be more comfortable with familiar objects.	• Change some toys and materials regularly to capture infants' interests and provide new experiences. • Provide objects that can be easily categorized (e.g., colored blocks, plastic farm animals). • Allow for differences in interest, attention span, and exploratory behavior; offer choices of toys and activities.
Early Childhood (2–6) 	• Short attention span • Distractibility • Some understanding and use of symbols • Limited knowledge base with which to interpret new experiences	• Pronounced disabilities in information processing (e.g., ADHD, dyslexia) begin to reveal themselves in children's behavior. • Children's prior knowledge differs markedly depending on their cultural and socioeconomic backgrounds.	• Change activities often. • Keep unnecessary distractions to a minimum. • Provide a variety of experiences (field trips to the library, fire department, etc.) that enrich children's knowledge base.
Middle Childhood (6–10) 	• Increasing ability to attend to important stimuli and ignore irrelevant stimuli • Increasingly symbolic nature of thought and knowledge • Gradual automatization of basic skills • Increasing exposure to environments beyond the home and family, leading to an expanding knowledge base • Knowledge of academic subject matter relatively unintegrated, especially in science and social studies	• Many children with learning disabilities or ADHD have short attention spans and are easily distracted. • Some children with learning disabilities have a smaller working memory capacity than their peers. • Mild cognitive disabilities may not become evident until the middle or upper elementary grades.	• Intersperse sedentary activities with physically more active ones to help children maintain attention. • Provide many opportunities to practice basic knowledge and skills (e.g., number facts, word recognition), often through authentic, motivating, and challenging tasks. • Begin to explore hierarchies, cause and effect, and other interrelationships among ideas in various disciplines. • Consult experts when learning or behavior problems might reflect a cognitive disability.
Early Adolescence (10–14) 	• Ability to attend to a single task for an hour or more • Basic skills in reading, writing, and mathematics (e.g., word identification, common word spellings, basic math facts) largely automatized • Growing (although not necessarily well integrated) knowledge base related to various topics and academic disciplines	• Many adolescents with information processing difficulties have trouble paying attention for a typical class period. • Many adolescents with sensory or physical disabilities (e.g., those who are blind or in a wheelchair) have a more limited knowledge base than their peers, due to fewer opportunities to explore the world around them.	• Provide variety in learning tasks as a way of keeping young adolescents' attention. • Frequently point out how concepts and ideas are related to one another, both within and across content domains. • Provide extra guidance and support for those with diagnosed or suspected information processing difficulties.
Late Adolescence (14–18) 	• Ability to attend to a single task for lengthy periods • Extensive and somewhat integrated knowledge in some content domains	• High school students have choices in course selection, leading to differences in the extent of their knowledge base in various content areas.	• Occasionally give assignments that require adolescents to focus on a particular task for a long period. • Consistently encourage adolescents to think about the "hows" and "whys" of what they are learning. • Assess learning in ways that require adolescents to depict relationships among ideas.

Observe how Brent, Colin, and Hilary organize a word list in the "Memory" clips for early childhood, early adolescence, and late adolescence, on Observation CD 1.

In what order did you remember the words? Did you recall them in their original order, or did you rearrange them somehow? If you are like most people, you grouped the words into three semantic categories—clothing, furniture, and vegetables—and recalled them category by category. In other words, you used **organization** to help you learn and remember the information. In the "Memory" video clips on Observation CD 1, you can observe Brent, Colin, and Hilary organizing the 12 words into categories. For example, 6-year-old Brent recalls vegetables first, then a type of furniture, then three items of clothing: "Beans, squash, stool, shirt, pants, hat . . . I forget."

As early as 3 or 4 months old, children begin to organize their experiences into categories (Halford & Andrews, 2006; Quinn, 2002). As they approach their first birthday, some of their categories seem to be based on perceptual similarity (e.g., *balls* are round, *blocks* are cubes), but they also show emerging knowledge of more abstract categories (e.g., *animals* and *furniture*) (Pauen, 2002; Sugarman, 1983). By age 2, children may physically pick up objects and group them by theme or function, perhaps using categories such as "things for the feet" or "kitchen things" (Fenson, Vella, & Kennedy, 1989; Mandler, Fivush, & Reznick, 1987).

More consistent and intentional use of organization to facilitate learning and memory appears a bit later. Under certain circumstances, preschoolers intentionally organize information to help them remember it. For instance, imagine that a researcher shows you twelve identical containers, several small pieces of candy, and several wooden pegs (see Figure 7-7). The experimenter places either a piece of candy or a wooden peg in each container and then closes the container to hide its contents. How can you remember which containers hold candy? An easy yet effective strategy is to divide the containers into two groups, one with candy and one with pegs, as the researcher fills them. Many 4-year-old children spontaneously use this strategy (DeLoache & Todd, 1988).

As children move through the elementary, middle school, and secondary grades, they increasingly organize information to help learn it (Lucariello, Kyratzis, & Nelson, 1992; Nguyen & Murphy, 2003; Plumert, 1994; Pressley & Hilden, 2006). Their organizational patterns become more sophisticated, reflecting a variety of semantic, hierarchical, and often fairly abstract categories. They can also be more flexible in their organizational schemes. For example, consider the alternatives that 17-year-old Paul identifies for organizing shells in the "Intelligence: Late Adolescence" video clip on Observation CD 1:

> Yeah, I could do them by color, smoothness. Some are rough, some got little jagged edges on them. Some are just smooth. And these big ones they could do like patterns and stuff.

Notice Paul's ability to consider multiple organizational structures for sorting shells in the "Intelligence: Late Adolescence" clip on Observation CD 1.

Elaboration.   If we authors tell you that we've both spent many years living in Colorado, you will probably conclude that we either live or have lived in or near the Rocky Mountains. You might also infer that we have, perhaps, done a lot of skiing, hiking, or camping. In this situation you aren't only learning the information we told you, you're also learning some information that you yourself supplied. This process of **elaboration**—embellishing on new information based on what you already know—typically facilitates learning and memory, sometimes quite dramatically.

Children begin to elaborate on their experiences as early as the preschool years (Fivush, Haden, & Adam, 1995). As a strategy that they *intentionally* use to help them learn, however, elaboration appears relatively late in development (usually around puberty) and gradually increases throughout the teenage years (Schneider & Pressley, 1989). Even in high school, it is primarily students with high academic achievement who use their existing knowledge to help them learn new information. Low-achieving high school students are much less likely to use elaboration strategies as an aid to learning, and many students of all ability levels resort to rehearsal for difficult, hard-to-understand material (J. E. Barnett, 2001; Pressley, 1982). The following interview with 15-year-old "Beth," who earns mostly As in her classes but must work hard to get them, illustrates how infrequently some high school students elaborate on classroom subject matter:

Adult: Once you have some information that you think you need to know, what types of things do you do so that you will remember it?

Beth: I take notes . . . [pause].

Adult: Is that all you do?

organization
Process of identifying interrelationships among pieces of information as a way of learning them more effectively.

elaboration
Process of using prior knowledge to embellish on new information and thereby learn it more effectively.

Beth: Usually. Sometimes I make flash cards.

Adult: What types of things do you usually put on flash cards?

Beth: I put words I need to know. Like spelling words. I put dates and what happened then.

Adult: How would you normally study flash cards or your notes?

Beth: My notes, I read them over a few times. Flash cards I look at once and try to remember what's on the other side and what follows it. (interview courtesy of Evie Greene)

Notice how Beth emphasizes taking notes and studying flash cards, approaches that typically require little or no elaboration. In fact, using flash cards is little more than rehearsal.

Environmental and cultural influences on learning strategy development.
Environment appears to play a major role in determining the kinds of strategies children develop. For example, children are more likely to use effective learning strategies when teachers and other adults teach and encourage their use (Ormrod, 2004; Pressley & Hilden, 2006). They are also more likely to use effective strategies when they discover that using them enhances learning success (Fabricius & Hagen, 1984; Starr & Lovett, 2000). In contrast, when young people find that assigned learning tasks are quite easy for them, they have little reason to acquire more effective strategies.

Culture, too, makes a difference. Children in African schools have better strategies for remembering orally transmitted stories than children in American schools (E. F. Dube, 1982). Children in China and Japan rely more heavily on rehearsal than their counterparts in Western schools, perhaps because their schools place a greater emphasis on rote memorization and drill-and-practice (D. Y. F. Ho, 1994; Purdie & Hattie, 1996). Children in typical Western schools appear to have better strategies for learning lists of words (e.g., rehearsal, organization) than unschooled children in developing nations, probably because list-learning tasks are more common in school settings (M. Cole & Schribner, 1977; Rogoff, 2003).

This is not to say that schooling aids the development of *all* learning strategies, however. For instance, in one study (Kearins, 1981), unschooled children in Australian aborigine communities more effectively remembered the spatial arrangements of objects than children who attended Australian schools. The aborigine children lived in a harsh desert environment with little rainfall, and so their families moved frequently from place to place in search of new food sources. With each move, the children had to quickly learn the spatial arrangements of subtle landmarks in the local vicinity in order to find their way home from any direction.

Figure 7-7

While you watch, a researcher randomly places either a small candy or a wooden peg into each of 12 containers and closes its lid. What simple strategy could you use to help you remember which containers hold candy?
Modeled after DeLoache & Todd, 1988.

Problem-Solving Strategies

By the time children are 12 months old, they have some ability to think about and solve problems. Imagine that an infant sees an attractive toy beyond her reach. One end of a string is attached to the toy, and its other end is attached to a cloth closer at hand. But between the cloth and the infant is a foam rubber barrier. The infant puts two and two together, realizing that to accomplish her goal (getting the toy), she has to do several things in sequence. She removes the barrier, pulls the cloth toward her, grabs the string, and reels in the toy (Willatts, 1990). This ability to break a problem into two or more subgoals and work toward each one in turn continues to develop during the preschool and elementary school years (e.g., Klahr & Robinson, 1981; Welsh, 1991).

As children get older, their problem-solving strategies become increasingly mental rather than behavioral. Often their mental problem solving involves applying certain *rules* to a problem, with more complex and effective rules evolving over time. As an example, consider the balancing task depicted in Figure 7-8. The top half of the figure shows a metal beam balancing on a fulcrum at its midpoint. In the bottom half of the figure, we hold the beam steady while hanging 3- and 6-pound weights at particular locations (9 notches to the left of the fulcrum and 4 notches to the right, respectively). Will the beam continue to be balanced when we let go of it, or will one side fall?

The equipment: Balance and weights

The problem

Figure 7-8

A beam without weights balances on a fulcrum located at its center. After weights are hung from the beam in the manner shown here, will the beam continue to balance? If not, which side of the beam will drop?

Children acquire a series of increasingly complex rules to solve such a problem (Siegler, 1976, 1978). Initially (perhaps at age 5), they consider only the amount of weight on each side of the beam. Comparing 6 pounds to 3 pounds, they would predict that the right side of the beam will fall. Later (perhaps at age 9), they begin to consider distance as well as weight. They realize that weights located farther from the fulcrum have a greater effect, but their reasoning is not precise enough to ensure correct solutions. For the problem in Figure 7-8, they would merely guess at how greater distance compensates for greater weight. Eventually (perhaps in high school), they may develop a rule that reflects a multiplicative relationship between weight and distance:

> *For the beam to balance, the product of weight and distance on one side must equal the product of weight and distance on the other side. In cases where the two products are unequal, the side with the larger product will fall.*

Applying this rule to the problem in Figure 7-8, they would determine that the product on the left side ($3 \times 9 = 27$) is greater than the product on the right side ($6 \times 4 = 24$) and so would correctly predict that the left side will fall.

Strategy Development as "Overlapping Waves"

Children tend to acquire a new cognitive strategy gradually over time. Initially, they are likely to use it infrequently and ineffectively. With time and practice, they become more adept at applying it efficiently, flexibly, and successfully to tackle challenging tasks (P. A. Alexander, Graham, & Harris, 1998; Siegler & Alibali, 2005).

By the time children reach elementary school, they may have several strategies to choose from when dealing with a particular learning or problem-solving task, and the specific strategy they use may vary from one occasion to another. Some strategies are apt to be developmentally more advanced than others, yet because children initially have trouble using the more advanced ones effectively, they may resort to less efficient but more dependable "backup" strategies. For example, even after children have learned their basic math facts ($2 + 4 = 6$, $9 - 7 = 2$, etc.), they sometimes resort to counting on their fingers to solve simple addition and subtraction problems. Eventually, however, children acquire sufficient proficiency with their new strategies that they can comfortably leave their less efficient ones behind (P. A. Alexander et al., 1998; Siegler & Alibali, 2005).

From an information processing perspective, then, development of strategies does not occur in discrete, one-step-at-a-time stages. Instead, each strategy develops slowly and increases in frequency and effectiveness over a lengthy period, perhaps over several months or years. Later it may slowly disappear if a better strategy emerges to take its place. You might think of the rise and fall of various strategies as being similar to the *overlapping waves* depicted in Figure 7-9 (Siegler, 1996; Siegler & Alibali, 2005).

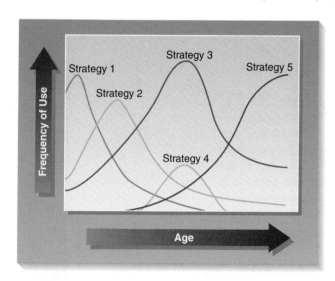

Figure 7-9

Strategic development as overlapping waves: Children gradually replace simple cognitive strategies with more advanced and effective ones. Here we see how five different strategies for dealing with the same task might change in frequency over time.
From *Children's Thinking* (4th ed., p. 98), by R. Siegler and M. W. Alibali, 2005, Upper Saddle River, NJ: Prentice Hall. Copyright 2005 by Prentice Hall. Adapted with permission of Prentice-Hall, Inc., Upper Saddle River, NJ.

metacognitive awareness
Extent to which one is able to reflect on the nature of one's own thinking processes.

Metacognitive Awareness

In addition to acquiring new cognitive strategies, children acquire increasingly sophisticated knowledge about the nature of thinking. This **metacognitive awareness** includes (a) awareness of the existence of thought and then, later, awareness about (b) one's own thought processes, (c) the limitations of memory, and (d) effective learning and memory strategies.

Awareness of the existence of thought.   By the time children reach age 3, they are aware of thinking as an entity in its own right (Flavell, Green, & Flavell, 1995). Their initial understanding of thought is quite simplistic, however. They are likely to say that a person is "thinking" only when he or she is actively engaged in a challenging task and has a thoughtful or puzzled facial expression. They also view thinking and learning as relatively passive activities (e.g., the mind acquires and holds information but doesn't do much with it), rather than as the active, constructive processes they actually are (Flavell et al., 1995; Wellman, 1990).

Awareness of one's own thought processes.   Young children have only a limited ability to look inward at their own thinking and knowledge (Flavell, Green, & Flavell, 2000). Although many preschoolers have the words *know, remember,* and *forget* in their vocabularies, they don't fully grasp the nature of these mental phenomena in themselves. For instance, 3-year-olds use the term *forget* simply to mean "not knowing" something, regardless of whether they knew the information at an earlier time (T. D. Lyon & Flavell, 1994). And when 4- and 5-year-old children are taught a new piece of information, they may say that they've known it for quite some time (M. Taylor, Esbensen, & Bennett, 1994). The following interview, which a kindergarten teacher aide conducted with a bright 5-year-old whom we'll call "Ethan," illustrates the relatively superficial awareness that young children have of their own thought processes:

Aide: When you learn a new song, like "The Horne Street School Song," how do you remember the words?

Ethan: I just remember. I didn't know how to sing it for a while until I listened to the words enough to remember them.

Aide: When I ask you during group time to "put on your thinking caps," what do I mean?

Ethan: It means think. You think hard until you know what you are trying to think about. . . . I don't really know how you think, you just do. . . .

Aide: How do you remember to give Mommy and Papa papers that we send home?

Ethan: My good memory.

Aide: Why do you have a good memory?

Ethan: It's just good. It started when I turned three. I still had it when I was four, and now when I am five. (interview courtesy of Betsy Hopkins)

During the elementary and secondary school years, children and adolescents become better able to reflect on their own thought processes and so are increasingly aware of the nature of their thinking and learning (Wellman & Hickling, 1994). (You can observe this progression firsthand by listening to the four children in the "Memory" video clips on Observation CD 1.) To some extent, adults can foster such development by talking about the mind's activities—for instance, by referring to "thinking caps" or describing someone's mind as "wandering" (Wellman & Hickling, 1994).

Awareness of memory limitations.   Young children tend to be overly optimistic about how much they can remember. As they grow older and encounter a wide variety of learning tasks, they discover that some things are more difficult to learn than others (Flavell et al., 2002; B. L. Schwartz & Perfect, 2002). They also begin to realize that their memories are not perfect and that they cannot possibly remember everything they see or hear. For example, in one study (Flavell, Friedrichs, & Hoyt, 1970), preschoolers and elementary school children were shown pictures of 1 to 10 objects and asked to predict how many objects they could remember for a short time period. The average predictions of each of four age-groups, and the average number of objects the children actually did remember, were as follows:

In the "Memory" clips on Observation CD 1, listen to Brent, David, Colin, and Hilary reflect on their thought processes and predict their performance on a memory task.

Age-Group	Predicted Number	Actual Number
Preschool	7.2	3.5
Kindergarten	8.0	3.6
Grade 2	6.0	4.4
Grade 4	6.1	5.5

Notice that children in all four age-groups predicted that they would remember more objects than they actually did. But the older children were more realistic about the limitations of their memories than the younger ones. In the "Memory" video clips on Observation CD 1, you can observe similar overestimations by 6-year-old Brent and 10-year-old David. Both boys predict they will recall all 12 words presented, but Brent remembers just 6 and David recalls only 3. In contrast, 12-year-old Colin and 16-year-old Hilary predict their performance quite accurately.

Young children's overly optimistic assessment of their memory capabilities may actually be beneficial for their cognitive development. In particular, it may give them the necessary confidence to try new and difficult learning tasks—challenges that, from Vygotsky's perspective, promote cognitive growth (Bjorklund & Green, 1992).

Knowledge about effective learning and memory strategies.   Imagine that it's winter and you live in a cold climate. Just before you go to bed, some friends ask you to go ice skating with them after class tomorrow. What might you do to be sure you will remember to take your ice skates to class with you? Older children typically generate more strategies than younger children for remembering to take a pair of skates to school. Yet even 5- and 6-year-olds can often identify one or more effective strategies—perhaps writing a note to themselves, recording a reminder on a tape recorder, or leaving their skates next to their school bag (Kreutzer, Leonard, & Flavell, 1975).

Not only do children acquire more effective learning strategies (e.g., organization, elaboration) as they grow older, but they also become increasingly aware of what strategies are effective in different situations (S. B. Lovett & Flavell, 1990; Schneider & Lockl, 2002; Short, Schatschneider, & Friebert, 1993). Consider the simple idea that when you don't learn something the first time you try, you need to study it again. This is a strategy that 8-year-olds use but 6-year-olds do not (Masur, McIntyre, & Flavell, 1973). Similarly, tenth graders are more aware than eighth graders of the advantages of using elaboration to learn new information (H. S. Waters, 1982). Even so, many children and adolescents seem relatively uninformed about which learning strategies work most effectively in different situations (Kuhn, Garcia-Mila, Zohar, & Andersen, 1995; J. W. Thomas, 1993). The following interview with "Amy," a 16-year-old with a history of low school achievement, illustrates how metacognitively naive some adolescents are:

Adult: What is learning?
Amy: Something you do to get knowledge.
Adult: What is knowledge?
Amy: Any information that I don't know.
Adult: What about the things you already know?
Amy: That doesn't count.
Adult: Doesn't count?
Amy: As knowledge, because I already know it.
Adult: How do you know when you have learned something?
Amy: When I can repeat it, and it is the same as what the teacher said or what I read, and I can remember it forever or a really long time. (interview courtesy of Jennifer Glynn)

Notice how Amy thinks she has learned something when she can repeat what a teacher or textbook has told her. She says nothing about *understanding* classroom subject matter. And curiously, she thinks of knowledge as things that she *doesn't* know.

Self-Regulated Learning

As children and adolescents gain awareness of their learning and memory processes, they become more capable of **self-regulated learning**—that is, they begin to control and direct their own learning. Self-regulated learning involves strategies such as these:

- Setting goals for a learning activity
- Planning an effective use of learning and study time
- Keeping attention on the subject matter to be learned, and motivating oneself to persist in learning it
- Identifying and using appropriate learning strategies
- Monitoring progress toward goals, evaluating the effectiveness of learning strategies, and adjusting goals or learning strategies as necessary
- Evaluating the final knowledge gained from the learning activity (Schunk & Zimmerman, 1997; Winne, 1995a; Wolters, 2003)

As you can see, self-regulated learning is a complex, multifaceted process. For example, effective learners use a variety of strategies to keep their minds on their work, perhaps engaging in encouraging self-talk ("Good job, you're making progress") or turning a study task into an enjoyable game (Wolters, 2003, p. 194).

—————— Connecting Concepts
Self-regulated learning is an aspect of *self-regulation*, described more generally in Chapter 13.

self-regulated learning
Directing and controlling one's own cognitive processes in order to learn successfully.

One especially important aspect of self-regulated learning is **comprehension monitoring,** checking one's own understanding frequently while learning something new. Comprehension-monitoring skills continue to improve throughout the school years, and so youngsters become increasingly aware of when they actually know something. Young children (e.g., those in the early elementary grades) often overestimate how much they know or understand (Schneider & Lockl, 2002). As a result, they don't study new material as much as they should, and they seldom ask questions when they receive incomplete or confusing information (Dufresne & Kobasigawa, 1989; Markman, 1977; T. M. McDevitt, Spivey, Sheehan, Lennon, & Story, 1990). Yet even adolescents sometimes have difficulty assessing their own knowledge accurately. For instance, they may overestimate how well they will perform on an exam (e.g., Hacker, Bol, Horgan, & Rakow, 2000).

In its "mature" form, then, self-regulated learning is virtually nonexistent in elementary school students, and even many secondary students have difficulty effectively regulating their own learning (M. B. Bronson, 2000; Zimmerman & Risemberg, 1997). For example, in a study at a middle school in inner-city Philadelphia (B. L. Wilson & Corbett, 2001), the vast majority of students planned to graduate from high school and attend college. Yet few of them had a good understanding of what it would take to do well in their classes, as this interview with one student reveals:

Effective learners engage in self-regulated learning. For instance, they set goals for themselves, choose effective learning strategies, and monitor their learning progress.

Adult:	Are you on track to meet your goals?
Student:	No. I need to study more.
Adult:	How do you know that?
Student:	I just know by some of my grades. [mostly Cs]
Adult:	Why do you think you will be more inclined to do it in high school?
Student:	I don't want to get let back. I want to go to college.
Adult:	What will you need to do to get better grades?
Student:	Just do more and more work. I can rest when the school year is over. (dialogue from B. L. Wilson & Corbett, 2001, p. 23)

Notice how simplistic the student's notion of studying is: "Just do more and more work." Nowhere in the interview does the student mention effective learning and self-regulation strategies, such as setting goals, organizing and elaborating on classroom material, or monitoring progress.

Epistemological Beliefs

As someone who learns new things every day, you undoubtedly have ideas about what "knowledge" and "learning" are. Such ideas are collectively known as **epistemological beliefs.** Included in people's epistemological beliefs are their views about the certainty, structure, and source of knowledge; about the speed with which learning occurs; and about the nature of learning ability. As children and adolescents develop, many (though not all) of them change their beliefs about knowledge and learning. Typical changes are shown in Table 7-1. For example, most children in the elementary grades think that the absolute truth about any topic is "out there" somewhere, waiting to be discovered (Astington & Pelletier, 1996). As they reach the high school and college years, some begin to realize that knowledge is a subjective entity and that two or more perspectives on a topic may each have some merit (W. G. Perry, 1968; Schommer, 1994b, 1997). Additional changes may also occur in high school. For example, 12th graders are more likely than 9th graders to believe that knowledge consists of complex interrelationships (rather than discrete facts), that learning happens slowly (rather than quickly), and that learning can be enhanced by practice and better strategies (Schommer, 1997). Some high school students continue to have very superficial views of knowledge and learning, however. For instance, recall how 16-year-old Amy defined *learning* simply as "something you do to get knowledge" and *knowledge* as "any information that I don't know."

Students' epistemological beliefs influence the ways in which they study and learn (Hofer & Pintrich, 1997; Purdie, Hattie, & Douglas, 1996; Schommer, 1997). When students believe that knowledge consists of discrete facts that are indisputably right or wrong, that one either has that knowledge or doesn't, and that learning happens quickly if at all, they may focus on rote memorization of the subject matter and easily give up if they find themselves struggling to understand it. In contrast, when students believe that knowledge is a complex body of information that is learned gradually with time and effort, they are apt to use a wide variety of learning

comprehension monitoring
Process of checking oneself to make sure one understands what one is studying.

epistemological beliefs
Beliefs regarding the nature of knowledge and knowledge acquisition.

TABLE 7-1

Developmental Changes in Epistemological Beliefs

With regard to . . .	Children initially believe that . . .	As they develop, they may eventually begin to realize that . . .
The certainty of knowledge	Knowledge about a topic is a fixed, unchanging, absolute "truth."	Knowledge about a topic (even that of experts) is tentative and dynamic; it continues to evolve as ongoing inquiry and research add new insights and ideas.
The simplicity and structure of knowledge	Knowledge is a collection of discrete, largely unrelated facts.	Knowledge is a set of complex and interrelated ideas.
The source of knowledge	Knowledge comes from outside the learner, for instance from a teacher or "authority" of some kind.	Knowledge is derived and constructed by learners themselves.
The speed of learning	Knowledge is acquired quickly, and in an all-or-nothing fashion, or else not at all. As a result, people either know something or they don't.	Knowledge is acquired gradually over time. Thus people can have greater or lesser degrees of knowledge about a topic.
The nature of learning ability	People's ability to learn is a stable quality over which they have little control.	People's ability to learn can improve with practice and the use of better strategies.

Sources: Astington & Pelletier, 1996; Hammer, 1994; Hofer & Pintrich, 1997, 2002; Hogan, 1997; Kuhn & Franklin, 2006; M. C. Linn, Songer, & Eylon, 1996; W. G. Perry, 1968; Schommer, 1994a, 1994b, 1997.

strategies, and they persist until they've made sense of what they're studying (D. L. Butler & Winne, 1995; Kardash & Howell, 1996; Schommer, 1994b). Not surprisingly, then, students with more advanced epistemological beliefs achieve at higher levels in the classroom (Schommer, 1994a).

More advanced levels of achievement may, in turn, bring about more advanced views about knowledge and learning (Schommer, 1994b; Strike & Posner, 1992). The more that students get beyond the "basics" and explore the far reaches of a discipline—whether it be science, mathematics, history, or some other content domain—the more they discover that learning involves acquiring an integrated and cohesive set of ideas, that even the experts don't know everything about a topic, and that truly complete and accurate "knowledge" of how the world operates may ultimately be an unattainable goal.

We speculate, however, that less sophisticated epistemological beliefs may have some benefits for young children. Children may initially be more motivated to learn about a topic if they think there are absolute, unchanging facts (and sometimes there are!) that they can easily learn and remember. And it is often very efficient to rely on parents, teachers, and the library as authoritative sources for desired information.

We can sometimes get a sense of children's and adolescents' epistemological beliefs by looking at the artifacts they produce in the classroom. The following exercise, "Flash Card," provides an example.

INTERPRETING CHILDREN'S ARTIFACTS AND ACTIONS

Flash Card

Twelve-year-old Jennie makes several flash cards to help her study for a science test. An example appears to the right. As you look at what Jennie has written, speculate on her beliefs about the nature of knowledge and learning.

Definitions: Assn # 5

Physical environment - things in the environment that are not living: rocks, water, etc.

Limiting factors - factors of the nonliving physical environment that limit where organisms live.

biological environment - an environment which consists of other plants + animals.

habitat - where an organism lives.

niche - the way an organism fits into its environment.

dispersal - a spreading out of animals from their habitat.

The flash card focuses entirely on definitions, suggesting that Jennie views science as a collection of discrete, right-or-wrong facts. If she has copied the definitions from a textbook, chalkboard, or teacher handout (as seems likely), then she may also think of knowledge as something that is best acquired from an authority figure. Her use of flash cards to prepare for the test suggests that she sees learning as a relatively superficial, "thoughtless" enterprise that involves little more than rehearsal. If the upcoming test will assess students' learning by asking for verbatim repetition of definitions and other facts—rather than, say, asking students to apply what they've learned to new situations—then Jennie's teacher might actually be encouraging such simplistic epistemological beliefs.

Interdependence of Cognitive and Metacognitive Processes

Developmental changes in various areas we've described—for instance, in attention, memory, strategies, metacognitive awareness, self-regulated learning, and epistemological beliefs—are clearly interdependent. For instance, children's improving ability to pay attention and their increasing self-regulatory efforts to control their own attention enable them to learn more from instructional materials and activities. Their growing knowledge base, in turn, enhances their ability to use such learning strategies as organization and elaboration while reading and studying. As learning and problem-solving strategies become more effective and efficient, these strategies require less working memory capacity and so enable children to deal with more complex tasks and problems.

As adolescents' beliefs about the nature of knowledge become more sophisticated, so, too, are their learning strategies apt to change in light of those beliefs. For example, if high school students conceptualize "knowledge" about a topic as a unified body of ideas and interrelationships, they are more likely to use such strategies as organization and elaboration, rather than simple rehearsal, to master the topic. Furthermore, their growing comprehension-monitoring abilities give them feedback about what they are and are not learning and so may enhance their awareness of which learning strategies are effective and which are not.

The Developmental Trends table "Cognitive Strategies and Metacognition at Different Age Levels" summarizes developmental changes in children's cognitive strategies, metacognitive awareness, self-regulated learning, and epistemological beliefs.

Promoting Metacognitive and Strategic Development

Metacognition is at the very heart of cognition, and so metacognitive development is central to cognitive development. Children are more likely to acquire and use effective strategies when they are aware of the various strategies they use and monitor how well each one helps them reach their goals (Kuhn, 2001b). Following are several suggestions for fostering the development of metacognition and cognitive strategies:

● *Model and teach effective cognitive strategies.* Adults can often foster more effective problem-solving strategies by modeling them for children. Infants as young as 10 months can overcome obstacles to obtain an attractive toy if an adult shows them how to do it (Z. Chen, Sanchez, & Campbell, 1997; Want & Harris, 2001). Engaging television programs in which young children are encouraged to join on-screen characters in solving various problems (e.g., as is done in Nickelodeon's *Blue's Clues*) also help young children acquire new problem-solving strategies (Crawley, Anderson, Wilder, Williams, & Santomero, 1999).

Learning strategies, too, can clearly be modeled and taught. For instance, 4- and 5-year-olds can be taught to organize objects into categories as a way of helping them remember the objects (Carr & Schneider, 1991; Lange & Pierce, 1992). As children encounter increasingly challenging learning tasks at school and elsewhere, simple categorization alone is, of course, not enough. By the time they reach high school, students will need to learn—and often must be explicitly taught—strategies such as elaboration, comprehension monitoring, goal setting, note taking, and time management. Ideally, such instruction should be integrated into lessons about academic topics, rather than in a separate course or unit (Hattie, Biggs, & Purdie, 1996; Pressley, El-Dinary, Marks, Brown, & Stein, 1992). Once adolescents become proficient in advanced strategies, they are apt to find these strategies more rewarding than

Study Guide and Reader ⎯⎯⎯
Supplementary Reading 7-1 discusses the effects of *modeling* in more detail.

DEVELOPMENTAL TRENDS

Cognitive Strategies and Metacognition at Different Age Levels

Age Level			
Infancy (Birth–2) 	• Use of one object to obtain another (in the second year) • Emerging ability to plan a sequence of actions to accomplish a goal (appearing sometime around age 1) • General absence of intentional learning strategies; however, toddlers may look or point at a location to remember where a desired object is hidden • Little awareness and knowledge of thought processes (may have some awareness that other people have intentions, however; see Chapter 12)	• Willingness to engage in trial-and-error and other exploratory behavior is partly a function of temperamental differences. • Emergence of early problem-solving strategies is somewhat dependent on opportunities to experiment with physical objects. • Children with significant physical disabilities may have limited opportunities to explore and experiment.	• Model tool use and other simple problem-solving strategies. • Pose simple problems for infants and toddlers to solve (e.g., place desired objects slightly out of reach), but monitor children's reactions to make sure they are not unnecessarily frustrated in their efforts to solve problems.
Early Childhood (2–6) 	• Some rehearsal beginning in the preschool years, but with little effect on learning and memory • Occasional use of organization with concrete objects • Some ability to learn simple strategies modeled by others • Awareness of thought in oneself and others, albeit in a simplistic form; limited ability to reflect on the specific *nature* of one's own thought processes • Belief that learning is a relatively passive activity • Overestimation of how much information one can typically remember	• Children's awareness of the mind and mental events depends partly on the extent to which adults talk with them about thinking processes. • Many young children with autism have little conscious awareness of the existence of thought, especially in other people.	• Model strategies for simple memory tasks (e.g., pinning permission slips on jackets to remind children to get their parents' signatures). • Talk often about thinking processes (e.g., "I *wonder* if . . . ," "Do you *remember* when . . . ?").
Middle Childhood (6–10) 	• Use of rehearsal as the predominant intentional learning strategy • Gradual increase in organization as a learning strategy • Emerging ability to reflect on the nature of one's own thought processes • Frequent overestimation of one's own memory capabilities • Little if any self-regulated learning	• Chinese and Japanese children rely more heavily on rehearsal than their peers in Western schools; this difference continues into adolescence. • Children with cognitive disabilities are less likely to organize material as they learn it. • A few high-achieving children are capable of sustained self-regulated learning, especially in the upper elementary grades.	• Encourage children to repeat and practice the things they need to learn. • Ask children to study information that is easy to categorize, as a way of promoting organization as a learning strategy (Best & Ornstein, 1986). • Ask children to engage in simple, self-regulated learning tasks; give them suggestions about how to accomplish the tasks successfully.
Early Adolescence (10–14) 	• Emergence of elaboration as an intentional learning strategy • Few and relatively ineffective study strategies (e.g., poor note-taking skills, little if any comprehension monitoring) • Increasing flexibility in the use of learning strategies • Emerging ability to regulate one's own learning • Belief that knowledge about a topic consists of a collection of discrete facts	• Adolescents differ considerably in their use of effective learning strategies. • Some adolescents, including many with cognitive disabilities, have few strategies for engaging effectively in self-regulated learning.	• Ask questions that encourage adolescents to elaborate on new information. • Teach and model effective strategies within the context of various subject areas. • Assign homework and other tasks that require independent learning; provide sufficient structure to guide students' efforts. • Give adolescents frequent opportunities to assess their own learning.

DEVELOPMENTAL TRENDS

Cognitive Strategies and Metacognition at Different Age Levels (continued)

Late Adolescence (14–18)

- Increase in elaboration
- Growing awareness of which cognitive strategies are most effective in different situations
- Increasing self-regulatory learning strategies (e.g., comprehension monitoring)
- Increasing realization that knowledge involves understanding interrelationships among ideas

- High-achieving teenagers are most likely to use sophisticated learning strategies (e.g., elaboration); others typically resort to simpler, less effective strategies (e.g., rehearsal).
- Many teenagers with cognitive disabilities have insufficient reading skills to learn successfully from typical high school textbooks; furthermore, their study skills tend to be unsophisticated and relatively ineffective.

- Continue to teach and model effective learning strategies both in and out of school.
- Assign more complex independent learning tasks, giving the necessary structure and guidance for those who are not yet self-regulating learners.
- Present various subject areas as dynamic entities that continue to evolve with new discoveries and theories.

simple rehearsal. In the "Memory: Late Adolescence" video clip on Observation CD 1, 16-year-old Hilary describes her feelings about rehearsal this way:

> Just felt like I was trying to memorize for a test or something. . . . Sometimes it's kind of boring or repetitious, [just] going over it.

Small-group learning and problem-solving activities, especially when structured to encourage effective cognitive processes, can also promote more sophisticated strategies (e.g., A. King, 1999; Palincsar & Herrenkohl, 1999). One approach is to teach children how to ask one another thought-provoking questions about the material they are studying. The following exchange shows two fifth graders using such questions as they study material about tide pools and tidal zones:

Hear Hilary express her view of rehearsal in the "Memory: Late Adolescence" clip on Observation CD 1.

Janelle: What do you think would happen if there weren't certain zones for certain animals in the tide pools?

Katie: They would all be, like, mixed up—and all the predators would kill all the animals that shouldn't be there and then they just wouldn't survive. 'Cause the food chain wouldn't work—'cause the top of the chain would eat all the others and there would be no place for the bottom ones to hide and be protected. And nothing left for them to eat.

Janelle: O.K. But what about the ones that had camouflage to hide them? (A. King, 1999, p. 95)

Notice how Janelle's questions don't ask Katie to repeat what she has already learned. Instead, Katie must use what she's learned to speculate and draw inferences; in other words, she must engage in elaboration. Questioning like Janelle's appears to promote both better recall of facts and increased integration of ideas, undoubtedly because it encourages more sophisticated learning strategies (Kahl & Woloshyn, 1994; A. King, 1999; E. Wood et al., 1999).

Why are collaborative learning and problem-solving activities so beneficial? For one thing, group members scaffold one another's efforts, providing assistance on difficult tasks and monitoring one another's progress toward a particular goal. Second, group members must describe and explain their strategies, thereby allowing others to observe and possibly model them. Third, in a Vygotskian fashion, group members may internalize their group-based strategies. For instance, when they engage in mutual question asking, they may eventually ask *themselves,* and then answer, equally challenging questions as they read and study.

One effective way of acquiring new learning strategies is to practice them first in a group situation.

● *Ask children to describe their beliefs about thinking and learning.* At several points in the chapter, we've presented interviews in which children describe their views about thinking, learning, and studying. Such interviews can often shed light on young people's study strategies and epistemological beliefs. They can be especially helpful when youngsters are having trouble mastering new knowledge and skills. The following exercise, "Interview with Aletha," gives you practice in making sense of children's comments about thinking and learning.

INTERPRETING CHILDREN'S ARTIFACTS AND ACTIONS   Interview with Aletha

As an assignment for one of Jeanne's classes, a college student conducted the following interview with 9-year-old "Aletha," a fourth grader. As you read the interview, try to ascertain Aletha's beliefs about the nature of human learning and memory. Also look for evidence that Aletha is becoming a self-regulating learner.

Adult: What is paying attention?
Aletha: What they are talking about is interesting and it's fun. Before we learn about anything new, my teacher asks us questions [about the new topic] and nobody knows the answers. When we are done, she asks us questions and you know all the answers. It's cool! To learn new things you have to pay attention. If you don't, then you won't know what's going on. If you are talking with your friends or fiddling, you are not paying attention, so the teacher will call on you and you won't know the answer. If you are not listening, then you are not paying attention. When it's interesting, I'm really paying attention. It's hard if

you're not interested, but that's not how it works. You have to pay attention.
Adult: How do you pay attention if it's not interesting?
Aletha: I think of questions in my head and I have to pay attention to see if the teacher answers my questions before I want the answers. Then I have something to say when the teacher calls on me.
Adult: Can you do other things when you pay attention?
Aletha: Some things. You can't read a book because it's hard to do both. Sometimes in science we watch movies and we are allowed to keep notes because we have a test on the movie later. I write the stuff down so I can memorize it. That was easy [to take notes], but it's hard because I had to write while I was listening.
Adult: Is paying attention just listening?
Aletha: Not necessarily. You can listen and not have a clue. But if you don't listen, you obviously won't get it.
(interview courtesy of an anonymous student)

Aletha knows that attention is critical for getting information into memory ("To learn new things you have to pay attention"). She also knows that paying attention involves more than just directing her eyes and ears in a particular direction—that it involves a certain amount of mental effort as well ("It's hard if you're not interested, but that's not how it works. You have to pay attention"). In her own way, she also knows that working memory has a limited capacity ("You can't read a book because it's hard to do both," "it's hard because I had to write while I was listening"). Furthermore, by asking herself questions that she hopes her teacher will answer, she increases the odds that she will keep her attention focused on the lesson and can monitor her ongoing comprehension of the lesson—two signs of self-regulated learning. Aletha's metacognitive development is hardly complete, however: Her view of learning from an educational film is to "memorize" her notes.

● *Give children frequent feedback about their progress, and help them see the relationship between their strategies and their learning and problem-solving success.* Children are likely to acquire and use new strategies only if they realize that these strategies are more effective than those they've previously been using (Pressley, Ross, Levin, & Ghatala, 1984; M. K. Reid & Borkowski, 1987). For example, a teacher might ask students to study similar sets of information in two different ways—perhaps to study one using rehearsal and another using elaboration. The teacher might then assess students' recollection of both sets of information: Presumably the more effective strategy will have promoted better learning and memory. With repeated, concrete comparisons of the effectiveness of different strategies, children will gradually discard the less effective ones and rely more heavily on those that will serve them well in the years to come.

● *Provide opportunities for children to evaluate their own learning, and help them develop mechanisms for doing so effectively.* As noted earlier, self-regulating learners monitor their progress throughout a learning task and then evaluate their ultimate success in mastering what they've been studying. Theorists have offered several recommendations for promoting self-monitoring and self-evaluation:

- Teach children to ask themselves, and then answer, questions about the topic (Rosenshine, Meister, & Chapman, 1996).
- Have children set specific goals for each learning session and then describe how they've met them (Morgan, 1985).
- Provide specific criteria that children can use to judge their performance (Winne, 1995b).
- On some occasions, delay feedback, so that children first have the opportunity to evaluate their own performance (D. L. Butler & Winne, 1995; Schroth, 1992).
- Encourage children to evaluate their performance realistically, and then reinforce them (e.g., with praise or extra-credit points) when their evaluations match an adult's evaluation or some other external standard (McCaslin & Good, 1996; Schraw, Potenza, & Nebelsick-Gullet, 1993; Zuckerman, 1994).
- Have children compile portfolios that include samples of their work, along with a written reflection on the quality and significance of each sample (Paris & Ayres, 1994; N. E. Perry, 1998; Silver & Kenney, 1995).

By engaging in ongoing self-monitoring and self-evaluation of their performance, children should eventually develop appropriate standards for their performance and apply those standards regularly to their accomplishments—true hallmarks of a self-regulating learner.

● *Expect and encourage increasingly independent learning over time.* Self-regulated learning is a complex endeavor that involves many abilities (goal setting, attention control, flexible use of cognitive strategies, comprehension monitoring, etc.) and takes many years to master. Throughout the elementary and secondary school years, teachers and other adults must encourage and scaffold it in age-appropriate ways. For instance, they might provide examples of questions that encourage elaboration (e.g., "Explain why _____," "What is a new example of _____?"). They might provide a general organizational framework that children can follow while taking notes. They might provide guidance about how to develop a good summary (e.g., "Identify or invent a topic sentence," "Find supporting information for each main idea"). Such scaffolding is most likely to be helpful when children are studying subject matter they find difficult to comprehend yet can comprehend if they apply appropriate strategies—in other words, when the subject matter is within their zone of proximal development (Pressley et al., 1992). As children develop increasing proficiency with each self-regulating strategy, the scaffolds can gradually be removed.

Connecting Concepts —————
The concept *zone of proximal development* is described in Chapter 6.

● *Promote more sophisticated epistemological beliefs.* For optimal learning and achievement, especially in the secondary and postsecondary school years, young people must be aware that knowledge is not a cut-and-dried set of facts and that effective learning is not simply a process of mindlessly repeating those facts over and over. One way to foster more advanced epistemological beliefs is to talk specifically about the nature of knowledge and learning—for example, to describe learning as an active, ongoing process of finding interconnections among ideas and eventually constructing one's own understanding of the world (Schommer, 1994b). But probably an even more effective approach is to provide experiences that lead children and adolescents to discover that knowledge is dynamic rather than static and that successful learning sometimes occurs only through effort and persistence. For example, teachers might give their students complex problems that have no clear-cut right or wrong answers, have students read conflicting accounts and interpretations of historical events, or ask students to compare several different, yet possibly equally credible, explanations of a particular scientific phenomenon (Britt, Rouet, Georgi, & Perfetti, 1994; Leinhardt, 1994; M. C. Linn et al., 1996; Schommer, 1994b).

Having children interact with one another may also influence their views of the nature of knowledge and learning (Kuhn, Shaw, & Felton, 1997; C. L. Smith, Maclin, Houghton, & Hennessey, 2000). Heated discussions about controversial topics (e.g., pros and cons of capital punishment, or various interpretations of a classic work of literature) should help children gain an increased understanding that there is not always a simple "right" answer to a question or issue. Furthermore, by wrestling and struggling as a group with difficult subject matter, children may begin to understand that one's knowledge about a topic is likely to evolve and improve gradually over time. In addition, group methods of inquiry are a critical feature of how the adult world tackles challenging issues and problems. By providing opportunities for children to formulate questions and problems, discuss and critique one another's explanations and analyses, and compare and evaluate potential solutions, adults give children practice in these all-important skills (P. Bell & Linn, 2002; Bendixen & Rule, 2004; Kuhn & Weinstock, 2002).

As a brief aside, we should note that although some children have frequent opportunities to exchange ideas with adults at home (e.g., at the family dinner table), other children, including many who are at risk for academic failure and dropping out of school, rarely have opportunities to discuss academic subject matter at home. Discussions about puzzling phenomena or controversial topics at school and in after-school activities may fill a significant void in the cognitive experiences of these children (Pogrow & Londer, 1994).

Adding a Sociocultural Element to Information Processing Theory

At several points in our discussion of information processing theory, we've touched on the importance of children's social and cultural environments. For instance, we've noted that children show a preference for social stimuli (e.g., human faces, their mother's voice) very early in life. We've seen how talking with children about an event can enhance their memory of it. And we've discovered that different cultures encourage somewhat different learning strategies. With such findings in mind, some theorists have suggested that a combination of information processing and sociocultural perspectives (such as those of Vygotsky and his followers) provides a better explanation of how cognitive development occurs than either perspective can provide alone. In particular, information processing theory may tell us a great deal about *what* changes over time, and sociocultural views (notions about internalization, mediated learning experiences, guided participation, and the like) may help us explain *how* those changes occur (Gauvain, 2001; Ornstein & Haden, 2001).

This blend of information processing and sociocultural approaches is still in its infancy, but researchers have made considerable progress in three areas: intersubjectivity, social construction of memory, and collaborative use of cognitive strategies.

Intersubjectivity

For two people to interact and communicate, they must have shared understandings on which to build. For instance, each member of the pair should have some awareness of what the other person sees, knows, thinks, and feels. Such mutual understanding is known as **intersubjectivity** (Newson & Newson, 1975; Rommetveit, 1985; Trevarthen, 1980). The beginnings of intersubjectivity are seen at about 2 months of age, when infants and their caregivers focus on and interact with each other, making eye contact, exchanging smiles, taking turns vocalizing, and so on (Adamson & McArthur, 1995; Kingstone, Smilek, Ristic, Friesen, & Eastwood, 2003).

Sometime around 9 or 10 months of age, intersubjectivity becomes more complex, taking the form of **joint attention.** At this point, an infant and caregiver can focus on a single object, with both members of the pair monitoring the *other's* attention to the object and coordinating their behaviors toward the object (Adamson & McArthur, 1995; Carpenter, Nagell, & Tomasello, 1998; Trevarthen & Hubley, 1978). You can see joint attention in action as 16-month-old Corwin and his mother read a book together in the "Literacy: Infancy" video clip on Observation CD 2.

Early in the second year, infants also begin to show **social referencing,** looking at someone else for clues about how to respond to or feel about a particular object or event (Feinman, 1992; Klinnert, Emde, Butterfield, & Campos, 1986). Children are most likely to engage in social referencing when they encounter a new and uncertain situation. For example, in one study (Klinnert, 1984), 1- and 1½-year-old infants were shown three new toys to which their mothers had been instructed to respond with a happy, fearful, or neutral expression. Upon seeing each new toy, most infants looked at their mother and chose actions consistent

Connecting Concepts
Vygotsky's sociocultural theory is described in Chapter 6.

Observe joint attention in the "Literacy: Infancy" clip on Observation CD 2.

intersubjectivity
Awareness of shared understandings and perceptions that provide the foundation for social interaction.

joint attention
Phenomenon in which two people (e.g., a child and caregiver) simultaneously focus on the same object or event, monitor each other's attention, and coordinate their responses.

social referencing
Looking at someone else (e.g., a caregiver) for clues about how to respond to a particular object or event.

with her response. They typically moved toward the toy if Mom showed pleasure but moved away from it if she showed fear.

As information processing theorists tell us, attention is critical to learning and cognitive development. As we bring the sociocultural perspective into the picture, we see that awareness of a *partner's* attention is critical as well (D. A. Baldwin, 2000; Gauvain, 2001). For instance, when an adult uses a word that an 18-month-old toddler has never heard before, the toddler will often look immediately at the speaker's face and follow the speaker's line of vision to the object being referenced. In this way, children probably learn many object labels (D. A. Baldwin, 2000). In general, a child can learn from a person with more experience only if both people are focusing on the same thing and *know* that they are sharing their focus. Because intersubjectivity is so critical for children's ability to learn from more experienced members of their community, it appears to be a universal phenomenon across cultures (Adamson & Bakeman, 1991).

Social Construction of Memory

In Chapter 6 we explained how adults often help children construct meaning from events (see "Social Construction of Meaning," p. 214). An adult can also help a child reconstruct events that the two of them have previously experienced and stored in their respective long-term memories. Almost as soon as children are old enough to talk, their parents begin to engage them in conversations about past events (Fivush, Haden, & Reese, 1996; Gauvain, 2001; Ratner, 1984). Initially, the parents do most of the work, reminiscing, asking questions, prompting recall, and so on, but by the time children are 3, they, too, are active participants in the conversations (Fivush et al., 1996).

Discussions about past events have several benefits (Gauvain, 2001). First, as noted earlier in the chapter, children are more likely to remember the experiences they talk about. Second, because adults focus on certain aspects of events and not others, children learn what things are important to remember. Third, because adults are apt to interpret events in particular ways (e.g., finding some things amusing and others distasteful), children acquire perspectives and values appropriate for their culture. For example, when European American mothers recall past events with their 3-year-olds, they often refer to the thoughts and feelings of the participants. In contrast, Asian mothers are more likely to talk about social norms and expectations, such as what someone should have done instead. Such differences are consistent with the priorities and values of these cultures (Bauer, 2006; Mullen & Yi, 1995).

Yet another benefit of reminiscing about past events is that children learn to use a *narrative* structure for telling stories: They recall events in a temporal sequence, and they include information about particular people's intentions and actions (Gauvain, 2001). Many children acquire a rudimentary narrative structure before they are 2, and this structure enhances their memory of what they have experienced (Bauer & Mandler, 1990).

Connecting Concepts ─────────
Chapter 9 looks more closely at the development of narratives.

Talking about events occasionally has a downside, however, especially for young children (Bruck & Ceci, 1997; Ghetti & Alexander, 2004; Leichtman & Ceci, 1995). Imagine that a man identified as "Sam Stone" briefly visits a preschool classroom. He comments on the story the teacher is reading to the children, strolls around the perimeter of the room, waves good-bye, and leaves. Later an adult asks, "When Sam Stone got that bear dirty, did he do it on purpose or was it an accident?" and "Was Sam Stone happy or sad that he got the bear dirty?" When asked such questions, children may recall that Sam soiled a teddy bear, even though he never touched a stuffed animal during his visit (Leichtman & Ceci, 1995, p. 571). Such susceptibility to leading questions is more common in 3- and 4-year-olds than in 5- and 6-year-olds. Older children are less likely to be swayed by the power of suggestion (Leichtman & Ceci, 1995). When teachers and other professionals ask young children to describe events they have witnessed—say, a fight on the playground or a possible theft in the classroom—they should be careful to ask questions that do not communicate any foregone conclusions about what children may have experienced or witnessed. For instance, one might simply say, "Tell me what happened as best as you can remember it." Furthermore, adults should, whenever possible, seek additional evidence that might either corroborate or cast doubt on young children's recollections.

When asking children to describe a past event, adults must be careful not to ask leading questions that may influence what children "remember."

Collaborative Use of Cognitive Strategies

Earlier in the chapter we mentioned that children acquire more sophisticated cognitive strategies when adults model and teach those strategies. A sociocultural perspective suggests that adults should go a step further, engaging children in activities that require collaborative use of particular strategies. Through joint discussion and use of strategies—typically with considerable adult guidance and scaffolding at first—children gradually internalize those strategies and begin using them independently (Freund, 1990; Gauvain, 2001). The following example illustrates such internalization:

> Ben, age 4, shuffles into the family room with a jar of pennies that he has been saving. He announces to his mother that he wants to count them to see how much money he has. With mother looking on, Ben dumps the coins on the coffeetable and begins to count the pennies, one by one. All is going well until he counts some pennies a second time. Mother interrupts and suggests that he put the pennies in rows so that he doesn't count any twice. Ben agrees to do this, but he aligns his rows poorly. Mother shows him how to straighten them by making a few sample rows herself. She also tells him that it is important to put 10 coins in each row and no more. They finish building the rows together and then they count the pennies: there are 47. A few days later Ben tells his mother that his father gave him some more pennies so he needs to count them again. Mother looks on as Ben dumps the pennies on the coffeetable and begins, on his own, to set up rows of 10. (Gauvain, 2001, p. 140; reprinted with permission)

Strategies associated with self-regulated learning, too, may have their roots in social interaction. At first, other people (e.g., parents, teachers) might help children through a particular learning task by setting goals for the activity, keeping children's attention focused on the task, monitoring learning progress, and so on. Developmentally speaking, a reasonable bridge between other-regulated learning and self-regulated learning is **co-regulated learning,** in which an adult and one or more children share responsibility for directing the various aspects of the learning process (McCaslin & Good, 1996). For instance, the adult and children might mutually agree on the specific goals of a learning endeavor, or the adult might describe the criteria that indicate successful learning and then have children evaluate their own performance in light of those criteria. Initially, the adult might provide considerable scaffolding for the children's learning efforts. The scaffolding can gradually be removed as children become more effectively self-regulating.

Enhancing Information Processing Through Social Interaction

In this and the preceding chapter, we've identified numerous implications of the sociocultural and information processing perspectives. Following are additional implications that emerge when we consider both perspectives simultaneously:

● *Regularly engage infants in social exchanges.* In the early months, social interaction with infants may simply involve making eye contact, smiling and talking, extending a finger to be grabbed, and so on. Later it is more likely to involve jointly looking at, manipulating, experimenting with, and talking about objects. Such activities, simple though they may be, foster the mutual awareness (intersubjectivity) so essential for later information sharing and perspective taking.

● *Talk with children about their experiences.* Children begin to talk about their experiences almost as soon as they begin to speak, and by age 2 they do it fairly often (van den Broek, Bauer, & Bourg, 1997). Adults should join in: Talking with children about joint experiences not only enhances children's memories of what they are seeing and doing but also helps children interpret their experiences in culturally appropriate ways.

● *Involve children and adolescents in joint activities that require new strategies.* Information processing theorists point out that a good deal of cognitive development involves the acquisition of increasingly effective and efficient cognitive strategies. Vygotsky suggested that children often internalize the processes they first use in a social context and that they are most likely to benefit from challenging tasks when they have the guidance and support of more experienced individuals. Taken together, the two perspectives highlight the importance of having adults work closely with youngsters to scaffold the use and eventual mastery of sophisticated approaches to learning and problem solving.

co-regulated learning
Process through which an adult and child share responsibility for directing various aspects of the child's learning.

Children's Construction of Theories

Some developmental psychologists suggest that children gradually combine their understandings into integrated belief systems, or *theories,* about particular topics. This approach to cognitive development is known as **theory theory.** No, you're not seeing double here. Although the term *theory theory* may seem rather odd, to us it suggests that many psychologists, dry as their academic writings might sometimes be, do indeed have a sense of humor.

Children's theories about the world begin to emerge quite early in life. As an illustration, by 6 or 7 months of age, children appear to have some understanding that human beings and other animals are different from inanimate objects—for instance, that living and nonliving entities move in distinctly different ways (L. B. Cohen & Cashon, 2006; P. L. Harris, 2006). As children grow older, they increasingly understand that the *insides* of living creatures are as important as, and perhaps more important than, outside appearance (S. A. Gelman & Kalish, 2006). Even though they have not yet learned about genetics, DNA, and the like, they realize that biological entities are defined primarily by their origins. For example, consider the following problem:

> These fruits are red and shiny, and they're used to make pies and cider, and everybody calls these things apples. But some scientists . . . looked way deep inside them with microscopes and found out these weren't like most apples. These things had the inside parts of pears. They had all the cells of pears and everything like that, and when they looked to see where they came from they found that these came off of pear trees. And, when the seeds from this fruit were planted, pear trees grew. So what are these: apples or pears? (Keil, 1989, pp. 305–306)

Children as young as 8 or 9 typically say that the fruits are pears, not apples. Here is one child's explanation:

Child: Because the seeds, when you plant the seeds a pear tree would grow, and if it were an apple, an apple tree would grow. They've got the insides of a pear and an apple wouldn't have the insides of a pear if it wasn't a pear.

Adult: Then how come it looks like this?

Child: It's been sitting out for a long time and it turned red. (dialogue from Keil, 1989, p. 171)

In contrast, children understand that nonliving, human-made objects are largely defined by their functions, not their internal makeup. For instance, if bowling balls are reshaped into objects that hold liquid for drinking, children conclude that these objects are cups rather than bowling balls. One child explained such a conclusion this way:

Child: They're used for the same purpose as cups and they look like cups and you can drink from them and you can't bowl with them, they're definitely cups!

Adult: Can they still be cups if they're made out of the same stuff as bowling balls?

Child: Yeah . . . and if you could melt down a glass and make it into a bowling ball without breaking it to bits, it would still be a bowling ball and not a cup. (dialogue from Keil, 1989, p. 174)

It appears that within the first 3 years of life, children begin to form theories about the physical world, the biological world, the social world, and the nature of thinking (Torney-Purta, 1994; Wellman, Cross, & Watson, 2001; Wellman & Gelman, 1998). As they grow older, they expand on and refine their theories, integrating many of the facts, concepts, and beliefs they acquire and incorporating numerous hierarchical and cause-effect relationships (Keil, 1994; McCauley, 1987; Wellman & Gelman, 1998). Let's explore children's theories of the physical world as an example.

Children's Theories of the Physical World

Young infants are amazingly knowledgeable about the physical world. For example, by age 3 or 4 months, they show signs of surprise when one solid object passes directly through another one, when an object seems to be suspended in midair, or when an object appears to move immediately from one place to another without traveling across the intervening space to get there (Baillargeon, 1994; Spelke, 1994; Spelke, Breinlinger, Macomber, & Jacobson,

Connecting Concepts ————
We'll explore children's theories about other people's thoughts, feelings, and actions—collectively known as *theory of mind*—in Chapter 12.

theory theory
Theoretical perspective proposing that children construct increasingly integrated and complex understandings of physical and mental phenomena.

1992). Such findings suggest that young infants know that objects (a) are substantive entities with definite boundaries, (b) fall unless something holds them up, and (c) move in a continuous manner across space. These findings also suggest to some theorists that infants have some basic knowledge about the physical world that is biologically built-in and present at birth (Baillargeon, 2004; Flavell et al., 2002; Spelke, 2000).

The idea that some knowledge and inclinations might be biologically preprogrammed is known as **nativism.** Built-in knowledge would have an evolutionary advantage, of course—it would give infants a head start in learning about their environment—and evidence for it has been observed in other species as well (S. A. Gelman & Kalish, 2006; Spelke, 2000). Nevertheless, the extent to which the human brain is hard-wired with certain knowledge, or at least with predispositions to acquire that knowledge, is, at present, an unresolved issue (K. Nelson, 1996a; Newcombe, 2002).

Whatever their origins may be, children's early conceptions of objects provide a foundation for constructing an integrated and increasingly elaborate theory of the physical world. But especially in the preschool and early elementary years, children's theories develop with little or no direct instruction from adults and so often include naive beliefs and misconceptions about how the world operates. Consider the following conversation with a 7-year-old whom we'll call "Rob":

Connecting Concepts

As you will discover in Chapter 9, nativism also figures prominently in some theories of language development.

Adult: How were the mountains made?
Rob: Some dirt was taken from outside and it was put on the mountain and then mountains were made with it.
Adult: Who did that?
Rob: It takes a lot of men to make mountains, there must have been at least four. They gave them the dirt and then they made themselves all alone. [*sic*]
Adult: But if they wanted to make another mountain?
Rob: They pull one mountain down and then they could make a prettier one. (dialogue from Piaget, 1929, p. 348; format adapted)

The belief that people play a significant role in influencing physical phenomena (e.g., making clouds move, causing hurricanes) is common in the early elementary years, and some cultures actually promote it (O. Lee, 1999; Piaget, 1960a). Children in the elementary grades may also believe that natural objects and phenomena have a particular purpose. For instance, they may believe that pointy rocks exist so that animals can scratch themselves when they have an itch (Kelemen, 1999, 2004; Piaget, 1929). Another widely held misconception is that the sun revolves around the earth—that at night, it "goes" to the other side of the world (Vosniadou & Brewer, 1987).

Some misconceptions persist well into adolescence. For example, many high school and college students believe that an object continues to move only if a force continues to act on it and that an object dropped from a moving train or airplane will fall straight down (diSessa, 1996; McCloskey, 1983). In reality, of course, an object continues to move at the same speed in a particular direction unless a force acts to change its speed or direction (reflecting the law of inertia), and an object dropped from a moving train or plane not only falls but also continues to move forward (reflecting the laws of gravity and inertia).

Several factors probably contribute to inaccuracies in children's theories about the world (Astuti, Solomon, & Carey, 2004; E. M. Evans, 2001; Glynn, Yeany, & Britton, 1991). Sometimes misconceptions result from how things appear to be. For example, from our perspective here on earth, the sun looks as if it moves around the earth, rather than vice versa. Sometimes misconceptions are encouraged by common expressions in language (e.g., the sun "rises" and "sets"). Various cultural mechanisms—fairy tales, television shows, religious teachings, occasionally even textbooks—may also play a role. For example, after cartoon "bad guys" run off the edge of a cliff, they usually remain suspended in air until they realize that there's nothing solid holding them up.

Earlier in the chapter we presented the principle that *children's growing knowledge base facilitates more effective learning.* But when children's "knowledge" is inaccurate, it often has a counterproductive effect, in that *children's erroneous beliefs about a topic interfere with their understanding of new information related to the topic.* For example, consider the fact that many children in the early elementary grades believe that the earth is flat rather than

Children's early theories often include naive beliefs and misconceptions about the world. When 4-year-old Isabelle is asked "How were lakes made?" she offers an unlikely—but in her mind quite plausible—explanation: "You get a bucket and you fill it up with water. You get lots and lots of buckets." She illustrates her theory with the picture shown here.

nativism
Theoretical perspective proposing that some knowledge is biologically built-in and present at birth or soon thereafter.

round. When adults tell them the earth is actually round, they may interpret that information within the context of what they already "know" and so think of the earth as being *both* flat and round—in other words, shaped like a pancake (Vosniadou, 1994).

Facilitating Children's Theory Construction

Theory theory yields several practical implications for parents, teachers, and other adults who work with young people:

● *Encourage and answer children's* **why** *and* **how** *questions.* As you may know from your own experience, young children ask many *why* and *how* questions: "Why is the sky blue?" "How does a telephone call know which house to go to?" Such questions often pop up within the context of shared activities with adults (Callanan & Oakes, 1992, p. 214). Although adults may find them bothersome, they typically reflect children's genuine desire to make sense of their world and enhance their theories about what causes what and why things are the way they are (Elkind, 1987; Kemler Nelson, Egan, & Holt, 2004).

● *When teaching a new topic, determine what children already know and believe about it.* Adults can more successfully address children's misconceptions when they know what those misconceptions are (K. J. Roth & Anderson, 1988; C. Smith, Maclin, Grosslight, & Davis, 1997; Vosniadou & Brewer, 1987). For example, when beginning a new curriculum unit, teachers should probably assess students' existing beliefs about the topic, perhaps simply by asking a few informal questions that probe what students know and *mis*know.

● *When children have misconceptions about a topic, work actively to help them acquire more accurate understandings.* Even as children encounter more accurate and adult-like perspectives about the world, their existing misconceptions do not necessarily disappear. In fact, because early "knowledge" influences the interpretation of subsequent experiences, misconceptions are often quite resistant to change even in the face of blatantly contradictory information (Chinn & Brewer, 1993; Kuhn, 2001b; Shuell, 1996). Thus teachers and other adults must make a concerted effort to help youngsters revise their early, inaccurate theories to incorporate more accurate and productive world views. In other words, they must help youngsters undergo **conceptual change.** Theorists and researchers have offered several strategies for promoting conceptual change:

- Ask questions that challenge children's current beliefs.
- Present phenomena that children cannot adequately explain within their existing perspectives.
- Engage children in discussions of the pros and cons of various explanations of observed phenomena.
- Explicitly point out what the differences between children's beliefs and "reality" are.
- Show how the scientifically accepted explanation of an event or phenomenon makes more sense than any alternative explanation children themselves can offer.
- Have children study a topic for an extended period of time so that accurate explanations are mastered rather than learned in a superficial, rote manner. (Chan, Burtis, & Bereiter, 1997; Chinn & Brewer, 1993; diSessa, 1996; Posner, Strike, Hewson, & Gertzog, 1982; Prawat, 1989; K. J. Roth, 1990; Slusher & Anderson, 1996; Vosniadou & Brewer, 1987)

Comparing and Critiquing Contemporary Approaches to Cognitive Development

The Basic Developmental Issues table "Contrasting Contemporary Theories of Cognitive Development" compares information processing theory and theory theory with respect to nature and nurture, universality and diversity, and qualitative and quantitative change. Yet even as you think about the contrasts, keep in mind that various theoretical perspectives of cognitive development aren't necessarily mutually exclusive. For instance, recall how we combined elements of information processing theory and sociocultural theory earlier in the chapter. Recall, too, how neo-Piagetian theorists have drawn on elements of both Piaget's

conceptual change
Revision of one's knowledge and understanding of a topic in response to new information about the topic.

BASIC DEVELOPMENTAL ISSUES

Contrasting Contemporary Theories of Cognitive Development

Issue	Information Processing Theory	Theory Theory
Nature and Nurture	Focus is on how environmental input is interpreted, stored, integrated, and remembered and on how formal instruction can best facilitate more effective learning and cognitive development. Information processing difficulties (learning disabilities, ADHD, autism) often have biological origins.	From interactions with their physical and social environments, children construct integrated understandings and beliefs about various physical, social, and mental phenomena. However, rudimentary understandings of the physical world—or at least predispositions to divide up and interpret the world in particular ways—may be biologically built-in and present at birth.
Universality and Diversity	The components of the information processing system (e.g., working memory, long-term memory, central executive) are universal. However, some people use their information processing capabilities more effectively than others. People's prior knowledge and their mastery of various cognitive strategies influence the degree to which they can learn new information and skills effectively.	Any biologically built-in knowledge and predispositions are universal across cultures. However, informal experiences, formal schooling, and community practices and beliefs—things that are apt to differ from one culture to the next—lead children to embellish on their initial understandings in somewhat culture-specific ways.
Qualitative and Quantitative Change	Over the course of development, children and adolescents acquire a variety of new cognitive strategies that are qualitatively different from earlier ones. Each strategy evolves gradually over a lengthy period and becomes increasingly efficient and effective—a trend that reflects quantitative change.	As children gain more information about their world, they may add to their theories in a quantitative manner. Under certain conditions, however, new and compelling experiences spur children to overhaul their theories in a way that reflects qualitative change.

theory and information processing theory (see Chapter 6). Teachers typically find a variety of theories to be useful in helping them understand and work effectively with children and adolescents.

Contemporary theories have extended our understanding of cognitive development far beyond Piaget's and Vygotsky's early ideas. Information processing theory has made significant inroads into the question of how human beings mentally process and learn new information and how cognitive processes change over the course of childhood and adolescence. Theory theory helps us understand why children's naive beliefs (e.g., "The world is flat") may persist even in the face of contradictory evidence. Together such approaches lead us to conclude that cognitive development involves more gradual changes and that the evolution of children's reasoning capabilities is more domain-specific than Piaget suggested.

Yet much work remains to be done on the nature and course of cognitive development. Perhaps the biggest challenge for today's theorists is to explain in precise terms how and why cognitive development occurs (Gauvain, 2001; Siegler & Alibali, 2005). Theorists have made some progress on this front, to be sure—for instance, children appear to have an innate need to adapt to their environment, and they almost certainly acquire more complex strategies as adults nurture such strategies—but we do not yet have a detailed understanding of how various aspects of heredity and environment work in concert to transform newborn infants into cognitively sophisticated adults. To arrive at such an understanding, developmentalists must eventually pull together the concepts and research findings of multiple theoretical perspectives and research methodologies.

Although we do not yet have a complete picture of cognitive development, existing theories and research findings tell us a great deal about what to look for in children's development and how to work effectively with various age-groups (see the Observation Guidelines table "Assessing Cognitive Processing and Metacognition"). What we have learned about cognitive development can also help us identify children who may be having difficulties in processing certain kinds of information, as we shall see now.

OBSERVATION GUIDELINES

Assessing Cognitive Processing and Metacognition

Characteristic	Look For	Example	Implication
Intersubjectivity	• Reciprocal interaction with caregivers • Attempts to coordinate one's own actions toward an object with the actions of another person • Social referencing (i.e., responding to an object or event based on how an adult responds to it)	A child care provider is obviously frightened when a large dog appears just outside the fenced-in play yard, and she yells at the dog to go away. Fifteen-month-old Owen observes her reaction and begins to cry.	Regularly engage young infants in affectionate and playful interactions (smiles, coos, etc.). Remember that your own actions and reactions toward objects and events will communicate messages about the value, appeal, and safety of those objects and events.
Attention	• Sustained attention to human beings and inanimate objects • Ability to stay on task for an age-appropriate period • On-task behavior when distracting stimuli are present	During after-lunch story time, a second-grade teacher has been reading Roald Dahl's *Charlie and the Chocolate Factory.* Most of the children are quiet and attentive the entire time, but Ben fidgets and squirms, and soon he finds a new form of entertainment: making silly faces at nearby classmates.	Monitor children's ability to pay attention in an age-appropriate fashion. If children have exceptional difficulty staying on task, minimize distractions, teach them strategies for focusing their attention more effectively, and give them opportunities to release pent-up energy appropriately.
Automatization of Basic Skills	• Retrieval of simple facts in a rapid, effortless fashion • Ability to use simple problem-solving strategies quickly and efficiently	Elena easily solves the problem $$\frac{4}{12} = \frac{x}{36}$$ because she realizes that $\frac{4}{12}$ is the same as $\frac{1}{3}$.	Give children numerous opportunities to use and practice essential facts and skills; do so within the context of interesting and motivating activities.
Learning Strategies	• Use of rehearsal in the elementary grades • Use of more integrative strategies (e.g., organization, elaboration) in the secondary grades • Flexible use of strategies for different learning tasks	Terri studies each new concept in her high school physics class by repeating the textbook definition aloud three or four times. Later she can barely remember the definitions she has studied, and she is unable to apply the concepts when trying to solve physics problems.	Show struggling learners that their difficulties may be due to ineffective strategies, and teach them strategies that can help them learn more successfully.
Self-Regulated Learning Capabilities	• Initiative in identifying and seeking out needed information • Intentional efforts to keep attention focused on an assigned task • Effective planning and time management • Realistic appraisal of what has and has not been learned	At wrestling practice one day, John tells his coach that he has just read several articles about the pros and cons of using steroids to increase muscle mass. "I'm a little confused about why most experts advise against them," he says. "Can you help me understand their logic?"	When youngsters fail to complete independent assignments in a timely or thorough manner, provide more structure for subsequent tasks. Gradually remove the structure over time as they become better able to regulate their own learning and performance.
Beliefs About Knowledge and Learning	• Optimism that knowledge and ability improve with practice and persistence • Attempts to understand interrelationships among ideas (e.g., cause and effect, similarities and differences) • Eagerness to evaluate and compare various perspectives and theories	Several middle school students are studying for a test on westward migration in North America during the 1800s. Some students focus on cause-effect relationships among events. Others make a list of facts from the textbook and study them in a piecemeal fashion.	Convey the message that mastering a topic is an ongoing, lifelong enterprise that requires effort and persistence. Especially when working with adolescents, communicate that knowledge about a topic includes an understanding of how different ideas interrelate and a recognition that competing perspectives may all have some merit.

Exceptionalities in Information Processing

All human beings learn and process information in a somewhat unique, idiosyncratic manner. But the information processing capabilities of some individuals are different enough that they require the use of specially adapted instructional practices and materials. Here we consider three kinds of exceptionalities in information processing: learning disabilities, attention-deficit hyperactivity disorder, and autism.

Children with learning disabilities typically have less effective learning and memory skills than their classmates and so may need extra structure and guidance to help them study effectively.

─────── **Study Guide and Reader**
Supplementary Reading 7-2 describes the kinds of information processing difficulties you might see in children with learning disabilities.

Learning Disabilities

A **learning disability** is a significant difficulty in one or more specific cognitive processes that cannot be attributed to general mental retardation, a behavioral disorder, or sensory impairment. The difficulty interferes with academic achievement to such a degree that special educational services are warranted (Mercer, Jordan, Allsopp, & Mercer, 1996; National Joint Committee on Learning Disabilities, 1994).

Many learning disabilities appear to have a biological basis. Some children with learning disabilities have minor abnormalities in parts of the brain involved in language processing (Manis, 1996). Others seem especially vulnerable to "interference" from signals in the brain that are irrelevant to the task at hand (Dempster & Corkill, 1999). Furthermore, learning disabilities often run in families (J. G. Light & Defries, 1995; Oliver, Cole, & Hollingsworth, 1991).

Children with learning disabilities are a diverse group, with a wide variety of talents, ability levels, and personalities. Yet many of them do seem to have certain characteristics in common. They may have few effective learning and problem-solving strategies at their disposal and so take a rather "passive" approach to learning tasks—for instance, mindlessly staring at a textbook instead of actively thinking about what the words mean (Brownell, Mellard, & Deshler, 1993; Mercer, 1997). Some of them appear to have less working memory capacity than their age-mates, making it more difficult to engage in several cognitive processes simultaneously (Swanson, 1993). In the elementary grades they are apt to exhibit poor attention and motor skills and have trouble acquiring one or more basic skills (J. W. Lerner, 1985). They may also begin to show emotional problems, due at least partly to frustration about their repeated academic failures.

In the secondary grades, difficulties with attention and motor skills diminish, but students can become especially susceptible to emotional problems (J. W. Lerner, 1985). Besides dealing with the usual social issues of adolescence (e.g., dating, peer pressure), they must also deal with the more stringent demands of the junior high and high school curriculum. Learning in secondary schools is highly dependent on reading and learning from relatively sophisticated textbooks, yet many high school students with learning disabilities have significant reading difficulties (R. Turnbull, Turnbull, Shank, & Smith, 2004). Perhaps for these reasons, adolescents with learning disabilities are often among those students most at risk for academic failure and dropping out of school (Barga, 1996).

Attention-Deficit Hyperactivity Disorder

Children with **attention-deficit hyperactivity disorder (ADHD)** have either or both of the following characteristics (American Psychiatric Association, 1994; Barkley, 1998; Landau & McAninch, 1993):

- *Inattention.* Children may be easily distracted by either external stimuli or their own thoughts. They may daydream, have trouble listening to and following directions, or give up easily when working on difficult tasks.
- *Hyperactivity and impulsivity.* Children may seem to have an excess amount of energy. They may be fidgety, move around at inappropriate times, talk excessively, or have difficulty working or playing quietly. They may also show such impulsive behaviors as blurting out answers, interrupting others, making careless mistakes, and acting without thinking about potential consequences of their behavior.

A deficit in executive functioning (i.e., in the central executive we spoke of earlier), and more specifically in the inhibition of inappropriate responses, may be at the heart of ADHD (Barkley, 1998; B. J. Casey, 2001). The condition appears to have a biological and possibly genetic origin (Barkley, 1998; Landau & McAninch, 1993). It seems to run in families, is three times as likely to be identified in boys as in girls, and is more frequently shared by identical twins than by fraternal twins (Conte, 1991; Faraone et al., 1995; Gillis, Gilger, Pennington, & DeFries, 1992).

In addition to inattentiveness, hyperactivity, and impulsivity, children identified as having ADHD may have difficulties with cognitive processing, academic achievement, interpersonal skills, or classroom behavior (Barkley, 1998; Claude & Firestone, 1995; Gresham & MacMillan, 1997; Grodzinsky & Diamond, 1992). In adolescence, hyperactivity diminishes and attention span and impulse control improve (E. L. Hart, Lahey, Loeber, Applegate, & Frick, 1995). Even so, adolescents with ADHD have greater difficulty than their peers in successfully meeting the challenges of the teenage years—the physical changes of puberty, more

learning disability
Significant deficit in one or more cognitive processes, to the point where special educational services are required.

attention-deficit hyperactivity disorder (ADHD)
Disability characterized by inattention, by hyperactivity and impulsive behavior, or by all three characteristics.

complex classroom assignments, increasing demands for independent and responsible behavior, and so on—and are more prone to tobacco and alcohol use, traffic accidents, and dropping out (Barkley, 1998; Whalen, Jamner, Henker, Delfino, & Lozano, 2002).

Autism

On the surface, **autism** appears to be more of a disability in social and emotional functioning than in cognitive processing. Probably its most central characteristic is a marked impairment in social interaction. Many children with autism form weak if any emotional attachments to other people and prefer to be alone (Denkla, 1986; Schreibman, 1988). They tend to show deficits in intersubjectivity; for instance, they seldom make eye contact or engage in joint attention (Gauvain, 2001; P. L. Harris, 2006). Several other characteristics are also common, including communication impairments (e.g., absent or delayed speech), repetitive behaviors (e.g., continually rocking or waving hands), narrowly focused and odd interests (e.g., an unusual fascination with watches), and a strong need for a predictable environment (American Psychiatric Association, 1994; Dalrymple, 1995; R. Turnbull et al., 2004).

Despite autism's apparent "antisocial" nature, an abnormality in information processing may be at its root. In many instances, areas of the brain that play a key role in thinking about social information are impaired (Dawson, Carver, et al., 2002; Leslie, 1991). Furthermore, some children with autism appear to have either an undersensitivity or an oversensitivity to sensory stimulation, or perhaps an inability to screen out sensory information (Grandin & Johnson, 2005; R. C. Sullivan, 1994; D. Williams, 1996). Consider this autobiographical account from a woman with autism:

> From as far back as I can remember, I always hated to be hugged. I wanted to experience the good feeling of being hugged, but it was just too overwhelming. It was like a great, all-engulfing tidal wave of stimulation, and I reacted like a wild animal. . . .
>
> When I was little, loud noises were also a problem, often feeling like a dentist's drill hitting a nerve. They actually caused pain. I was scared to death of balloons popping, because the sound was like an explosion in my ear. Minor noises that most people can tune out drove me to distraction. (Grandin, 1995, pp. 63, 67)

Autism is almost certainly caused by a brain abnormality (Dawson, Munson, et al., 2002; Gillberg & Coleman, 1996). Its origins are often genetic, and it is more commonly seen in males than females (Bristol et al., 1996; Bryson, 1997). You can best think of autism as a *spectrum* of disorders, with some instances of the condition being more severe than others. For example, children with *Asperger syndrome* share some features of autism—especially difficulties in thinking about and responding to social situations—but they achieve developmental milestones in language at typical ages and tend to display fewer of the repetitive behaviors associated with more severe forms of the condition.

Even youngsters with severe forms of autism may have strengths in certain areas (American Psychiatric Association, 1994). Some have exceptional visual-spatial thinking skills (Grandin & Johnson, 2005; D. Williams, 1996). In a few instances, youngsters with autism possess an extraordinary ability, such as exceptional musical or artistic talent, that is quite remarkable in contrast to other aspects of their mental functioning (Grandin & Johnson, 2005; Treffert, 1989; Winner, 2000b).

Working with Children Who Have Information Processing Difficulties

Children within any one of the three categories just described are apt to be more different than they are similar. Hence teachers and other practitioners who work with them must consider the unique needs of each child. Yet several general suggestions are applicable to many children with information processing difficulties:

● *Examine children's work for clues about specific processing difficulties.* Writing samples, math homework, and other academic work can be a rich source of information about cognitive deficits that may hinder children's ability to learn and master classroom subject matter. For example, a child who solves a subtraction problem this way:

$$\begin{array}{r} 85 \\ -\ 29 \\ \hline 64 \end{array}$$

autism
Disability characterized by infrequent social interaction, little awareness of one's own and others' thoughts, communication impairments, repetitive behaviors, narrowly focused interests, and a strong need for a predictable environment.

may be applying an inappropriate rule ("Always subtract the smaller number from the larger one") to subtraction. A child who reads the sentence *I drove the car* as *I drove the cat* may be having trouble using context clues in reading words and sentences. The following exercise, "Pumpkin and Bat," can give you a taste of what error analysis might involve.

INTERPRETING CHILDREN'S ARTIFACTS AND ACTIONS   Pumpkin and Bat

A few days before Halloween, Nathan, age 7, created and illustrated the writing sample to the right. Writing in small print, his first-grade teacher clarified what he intended to say: "I drew this pumpkin" and "A bat." As you look at Nathan's work, identify one or more patterns of errors in his word spellings, and speculate about cognitive processing difficulties that such errors might reflect.

With the exception of the *L* in the first line, Nathan correctly captured some of the sounds in the words he was trying to spell. For example, he acknowledged the *d* in *drew,* the *s* in *this,* and the *b* and *t* in *bat.* But he omitted several other consonants, as well as all of the vowel sounds except for the initial *I.* We might suspect that Nathan has difficulty hearing all the distinct sounds in spoken words and matching them with the letters he sees in written words. Such difficulties are common in young elementary school students who have significant reading disabilities (Hulme & Joshi, 1998; Stanovich, 2000; Swanson, Mink, & Bocian, 1999).

Connecting Concepts
You'll learn more about Nathan's disability, known as *dyslexia,* in Chapter 10.

● *Help children keep their attention on the task at hand.* Many children with information processing difficulties are easily distracted. Thus adults who work with them should minimize the presence of other stimuli likely to compete for their attention, perhaps by finding a quiet room for tasks requiring considerable concentration or pulling down window shades when appealing alternatives lurk outside. Many children also benefit from specific training in attention-focusing strategies, such as keeping one's eyes directed toward a speaker or moving to a new location if the current one presents too many distracting sights and sounds (Buchoff, 1990).

● *Teach strategies for controlling hyperactivity and impulsivity.* All children, but especially those with information processing difficulties, need regular opportunities to release pent-up energy, perhaps in the form of recess, sports, or hands-on activities (Panksepp, 1998; Pellegrini & Bohn, 2005). In addition, after a period of high activity, adults might give children a "settling-in" time that allows them to calm down gradually (Pellegrini & Horvat, 1995). As an example, when children return from lunch, many elementary teachers begin the afternoon by reading a chapter from a high-interest storybook.

Teaching children to use self-talk can help them resist the tendency to respond too quickly and impulsively to situations and problems. For example, notice how one formerly impulsive child learned to talk himself through matching tasks in which he needed to find two identical pictures among several very similar ones:

When children have information processing difficulties, adults should minimize the presence of distracting stimuli that may compete for their attention. This girl, who has autism, works best in a classroom that is not crowded or noisy.

I have to remember to go slowly to get it right. Look carefully at this one, now look at these carefully. Is this one different? Yes, it has an extra leaf. Good, I can eliminate this one. Now, let's look at this one. I think it's this one, but let me first check the others. Good, I'm going slow and carefully. Okay, I think it's this one. (Meichenbaum & Goodman, 1971, p. 121)

● *Provide extra scaffolding for studying, doing homework, and completing other learning tasks.* Children with information processing difficulties often need considerable support for learning tasks, especially those they complete on their own (e.g., T. Bryan, Burstein, & Bryan, 2001). Such support might take a variety of forms—suggestions for taking notes, handouts that list major ideas, memory tricks for remembering particular tidbits of information (e.g., using *HOMES* to remember the five Great Lakes: Huron, Ontario, Michigan, Erie, and Superior), "Things to Do" lists with items that students can check off after completing specific tasks, and so on.

● *Keep the daily schedule and physical environment relatively predictable.* Some novelty in activities does wonders for maintaining children's interest and motivation (Renninger, Hidi, & Krapp, 1992). But a day with surprises around every corner may arouse excessive anxiety in some children, and such anxiety interferes with effective information processing (Eysenck, 1992; Lazarus, 1991). Furthermore, many children with autism find comfort and security in the predictability of their surroundings. To maintain some sense of predictability, teachers and others who work with children who have disabilities might schedule certain activities at the same time each day or on a particular day of each week (Dalrymple, 1995). When there is a change in the schedule (perhaps because of a fire drill or field trip), adults should give children advance warning of the change and indicate when the schedule will be back to normal (Dalrymple, 1995). And if the group includes one or more children with autism, furniture and equipment should be rearranged infrequently, if at all.

● *Teach social skills.* Some children with learning disabilities have difficulty processing social information, some with ADHD behave so impulsively that they alienate their peers, and as a general rule children with autism have significant impairments in social interaction. These children stand to benefit from specific training in social skills, which can enhance their interpersonal effectiveness (e.g., C. E. Cunningham & Cunningham, 1998; G. Williams, Donley, & Keller, 2000). In Chapters 12, 13, and 14, we identify a variety of strategies for promoting effective interaction with others.

Conneting Concepts
Chapter 12 explores social information processing and offers strategies for teaching social skills.

Children with learning disabilities, ADHD, and autism are not the only ones who have trouble processing and learning information. As a general rule, *children and adolescents process information less effectively than adults do.* The final case study provides a clear example.

Case Study: The Library Project

In the final year of her teacher education program, Jessica Jensen is a teacher intern in four eighth-grade social studies classes. She has recently assigned a month-long group project that involves considerable library research. Midway through the project, Jess writes the following entry in her journal:

Within each group, one student is studying culture of the region, one has religion, one has economy, and one government. The point is for the students to become "experts" on their topic in their region. There are a lot of requirements to this assignment. I'm collecting things as we go along because I think a project this long will be difficult for them to organize. . . .

So we spent all week in the library. I collected a minimum of two pages of notes yesterday, which will be a small part of their grade. The one thing that surprised me in our work in the library was their lack of skills. They had such difficulty researching, finding the information they needed, deciding what was important, and organizing and taking notes. As they worked, I walked around helping and was shocked. The librarian had already gotten out all of the appropriate resources. Even after they had the books in front of them, most did not know what to do. For instance, if they were assigned "economy," most looked in the index for that particular word. If they didn't find it, they gave up on the book. After realizing this, I had to start the next day with a brief lesson on researching and cross-referencing. I explained how they could look up *commerce, imports, exports,* and how these would

(continued)

all help them. I was also shocked at how poor their note-taking skills were. I saw a few kids copying paragraphs word for word. Almost none of them understood that notes don't need to be in full sentences. So, it was a long week at the library.

Next week is devoted to group work and time to help them work on their rough drafts. With the difficulty they had researching, I can imagine the problems that will arise out of turning their notes into papers. (journal entry courtesy of Jessica Jensen)

- Initially, the intern realizes that her students will need some structure to complete the project successfully. In what ways do she and the librarian structure the assignment for the students?
- What specific strategies do the students use as they engage in their library research? In what ways are their strategies less effective than an adult's might be?
- How does the students' prior knowledge (or lack thereof) influence the effectiveness of their strategies?

Once you have answered these questions, compare your responses with those presented in the appendix.

Summary

Information Processing Theory

Information processing theory focuses on how children receive, think about, mentally modify, and remember information, and on how these cognitive processes change over the course of development. Information processing theorists propose that cognitive capabilities improve gradually with age and experience. Infants have many sensory and perceptual capabilities at birth or soon thereafter. In general, however, children are less efficient learners than adults are. For instance, they have shorter attention spans, a smaller working memory capacity, and a smaller and less integrated knowledge base to which they can relate new information and events.

Metacognition and Cognitive Strategies

The term *metacognition* encompasses both the knowledge that people have about their own cognitive processes and their intentional use of certain cognitive processes to facilitate learning and memory. Children's metacognitive knowledge and cognitive strategies improve throughout the school years. For instance, children become more proficient in such learning strategies as rehearsal, organization, and elaboration, and they acquire increasingly powerful and effective ways of solving problems. With age, they become more aware of the nature of thinking, learning, and knowledge, and they develop strategies for regulating their own learning.

Integrating the Sociocultural and Information Processing Perspectives

Information processing theory can tell us a great deal about what abilities change over time, and sociocultural views can help us explain how those changes occur. Combining elements of both perspectives, then, can give us a more complete picture

of cognitive development than we might get from either one alone. For example, children learn what to pay attention to in part by watching what other people pay attention to. And adults can help children become more effective, self-regulating learners by giving them control of a learning activity in a gradual, step-by-step manner.

Theory Theory

Some theorists propose that children gradually construct integrated belief systems (theories) about the physical world, the biological world, the social world, and mental events. Such theories are not always accurate, however. For instance, children's theories about the physical world may include erroneous beliefs about the solar system and laws of motion. To the extent that children's theories include misconceptions, they may interfere with children's ability to acquire more sophisticated understandings.

Critiquing Theories of Cognitive Development

Contemporary theories (e.g., information processing theory, theory theory) have added considerably to Piaget's and Vygotsky's early notions of children's thinking and knowledge-building processes. Taken together, various theoretical perspectives give us a more complete picture of cognitive development than any single perspective can give us alone.

Exceptionalities in Information Processing

The information processing capabilities of some children are different enough that they require the use of specially adapted instructional practices and materials. Children with learning disabilities have significant difficulties in one or more specific cognitive processes. Children with attention-deficit hyperactivity disorder (ADHD) either (a) have exceptional difficulty focusing attention on assigned tasks or (b) are unusually hyperactive and impulsive for their age-group, and many children exhibit problems in both of these areas. Children with autism exhibit a marked impairment in social interaction, perhaps as a result of deficits in certain areas of the brain or of extreme undersensitivity or oversensitivity to sensory stimulation.

Applying Concepts in Child Development

In this chapter you've learned about a wide variety of cognitive and metacognitive processes that influence children's and adolescents' ability to interpret and respond effectively to their environment. The following table describes behaviors that youngsters at five different age levels exhibit. For each of these behaviors, the table identifies one or more relevant cognitive or metacognitive processes, offers an implication for working with children of that age-group, or both. Apply what you've learned about basic information processing, metacognition, and theory construction to fill in the empty cells in the table. When you're done, compare your responses with those in Table 7-1 in the *Study Guide and Reader*.

APPLYING CONCEPTS IN CHILD DEVELOPMENT	Identifying Children's Cognitive Processes		
Age	**A Youngster's Experience**	**Developmental Concepts** *Identifying Cognitive Processes*	**Implications** *Promoting Effective Processes*
Infancy (Birth–2)	One Monday morning, 13-month-old Miguel meets his child care provider's new kitten for the first time. Miguel isn't sure what to make of this creature. When he sees that his caregiver is happily petting the kitten, he smiles and reaches out to touch the kitten's head.	Miguel is engaging in *social referencing,* checking to see how a trusted adult reacts to the new kitten and then responding in a similar way. Social referencing is an aspect of *intersubjectivity,* in which participants in a social situation have some awareness of what other participants are looking at, thinking, or feeling.	As you introduce infants to new people, animals, and objects, model appropriate ways of interacting with and responding to them.
Early Childhood (2–6)	A kindergarten teacher is reading Mercer Mayer's *What Do You Do with a Kangaroo?* to his class. As he often does during story time, he picks up a globe and points to the spot where the story takes place—in this case, Australia. "Most kangaroos live here in Australia," he says. "How come they don't fall off the world?" 5-year-old Andrea asks.		Listen carefully to children's comments for clues regarding their beliefs about their physical and social worlds. With age-appropriate explanations, nudge them toward more accurate understandings.
Middle Childhood (6–10)	Although 10-year-old Kendall seems quite capable of doing typical fifth-grade work, he rarely stays on task for more than a few minutes during the school day. He is especially distractible during small-group activities and on other occasions when class activities are fairly noisy. He tends to remember very little of the material that is presented during such times.	*Attention* is critical for getting information into working memory and then (with further processing) into long-term memory. Distractibility is common for children in the preschool and early elementary years, but it is unusual for a boy as old as Kendall. Quite possibly Kendall has an undiagnosed *learning disability* or *attention-deficit hyperactivity disorder.*	
Early Adolescence (10–14)	When Faith was in elementary school, she was a conscientious student who earned mostly As and Bs. Now, as a 13-year-old seventh grader, she often forgets to do her homework—sometimes she doesn't even know what her homework assignments are—and her grades have slipped to Cs and Ds. "I need to get my grades up," she tells the school counselor, "because I want to go to college. Next year I promise to work harder."	Faith apparently has not acquired many *self-regulated learning* skills: setting goals, planning study time, and so on. Such skills become increasingly important as students move through the grade levels and are expected to work more independently.	When students show a decline in academic achievement in middle school or junior high, assume that lack of self-regulation skills, rather than lack of motivation, is the culprit. But don't expect students to acquire self-regulated learning skills on their own. Instead, actively *teach* goal setting, self-motivation strategies, comprehension monitoring, and so on.

(continued)

APPLYING CONCEPTS IN CHILD DEVELOPMENT

Identifying Children's Cognitive Processes (continued)

Age	A Youngster's Experience	Developmental Concepts *Identifying Cognitive Processes*	Implications *Promoting Effective Processes*
Late Adolescence (14–18) 	After failing the first exam in his Advanced Placement biology class, 17-year-old John tells his science teacher, "I've never done so poorly on a test before, and I studied really hard for it. I repeated everything over and over until I knew it cold!" The teacher looks at John's notebook for the class and responds, "I think I see what the problem is. Your class notes are nothing more than facts and definitions. But my test asked you to apply what you've learned to real-life situations and problems."		Especially at the high school level, encourage students to organize and make sense of information, rather than simply to repeat it verbatim. Help them discover that true mastery of a topic involves understanding how concepts and ideas relate to one another and to real-world situations and problems.

Key Concepts

information processing theory (p. 234)
sensory register (p. 235)
working memory (p. 235)
long-term memory (p. 235)
central executive (p. 236)
automatization (p. 240)
infantile amnesia (p. 241)
knowledge base (p. 241)

schema (p. 242)
script (p. 242)
symbol (p. 243)
metacognition (p. 246)
cognitive strategy (p. 246)
learning strategy (p. 246)
rehearsal (p. 246)
organization (p. 248)
elaboration (p. 248)

metacognitive awareness (p. 250)
self-regulated learning (p. 252)
comprehension monitoring (p. 253)
epistemological beliefs (p. 253)
intersubjectivity (p. 260)
joint attention (p. 260)
social referencing (p. 260)

co-regulated learning (p. 262)
theory theory (p. 263)
nativism (p. 264)
conceptual change (p. 265)
learning disability (p. 268)
attention-deficit hyperactivity disorder (ADHD) (p. 268)
autism (p. 269)

Now go to our Companion Website at www.prenhall.com/mcdevitt to assess your understanding of chapter content with a Practice Quiz, apply what you've learned in Essay Questions, and broaden your knowledge with links to related Developmental Psychology Web sites.

Intelligence

chapter 8

Case Study: Gina

Defining Intelligence

Theoretical Perspectives of Intelligence

Measuring Intelligence

Effects of Heredity and Environment on Intelligence

Developmental Trends in IQ Scores

Group Differences in Intelligence

Critique of Current Perspectives on Intelligence

Implications of Theories and Research on Intelligence

Exceptionalities in Intelligence

Case Study: Fresh Vegetables

Summary

Applying Concepts in Child Development

Case Study: Gina

Seventeen-year-old Gina has always been an enthusiastic and self-motivated learner. As a toddler, she talked early and often. As a 4-year-old, she asked her mother to identify a few words in a reading primer her aunt had given her, used the words to deduce many letter-sound relationships, and then deciphered additional words in the primer on her own. By the time she reached kindergarten, she was reading first- and second-grade-level storybooks.

In elementary school Gina consistently achieved straight As on her report cards until finally, in sixth grade, she broke the pattern by getting a B in history. Since then, she has earned a few more Bs, but As continue to dominate her record. Her performance has been highest in her advanced math courses, where she easily grasps the abstract concepts and principles that many of her classmates find difficult to understand.

Gina has other talents as well. She won her high school's creative writing contest 2 years in a row. She has landed challenging roles in her school's drama productions. And as the president of the National Honor Society during her senior year, she has masterfully coordinated a schoolwide peer tutoring program to assist struggling students.

Gina's teachers describe her as a "bright" young woman. Her friends affectionately call her a "brainiac." Test results in her school file bear out their assessments: An intelligence test that she took in junior high school yielded a score of 140, and this year she performed at the 99th percentile on college aptitude tests.

This is not to say that Gina is strong in every arena. She shows little artistic ability in her paintings or clay sculptures. Her piano playing is mediocre despite 5 years of weekly lessons. In athletic events she has little stamina, strength, or flexibility. She is shy and unsure of herself at social events. And she hasn't earned an A in history since fifth grade, in large part because her idea of how best to learn involves simply memorizing people, places, and dates.

In our discussion of cognitive development in the two preceding chapters, we focused primarily on what cognitive abilities and processes are typical for children in various age-groups. As we examine intelligence in this chapter, we focus more on differences among children in any *single* age-group. Psychologists don't all agree about the nature of intelligence. However, many use the term when they talk about the extent to which a person can consistently learn and perform effectively in a wide variety of situations. Gina's performance reflects such consistency: She has earned high marks throughout her school career, and she achieves at high levels in many areas. Yet intelligence is not necessarily a permanent, set-in-concrete characteristic that youngsters either do or don't have. As you will see, children's intelligence can, and often does, change with age and experience. Furthermore, children can behave more or less "intelligently" depending on the circumstances and the topic at hand.

Defining Intelligence

Theorists define and conceptualize intelligence in a variety of ways, but most agree that it has several distinctive qualities:

- It is *adaptive,* such that it can be used flexibly to respond to a variety of situations and problems.

- It involves *learning ability:* People who are intelligent in particular domains learn new information and behaviors more quickly and easily than people who are less intelligent in those domains.
- It involves the *use of prior knowledge* to analyze and understand new situations effectively.
- It involves the complex interaction and coordination of *many different mental processes.*
- It is *culture-specific.* What is "intelligent" behavior in one culture is not necessarily intelligent behavior in another culture. (Greenfield, 1998; Laboratory of Comparative Human Cognition, 1982; Li, 2004; Neisser et al., 1996; Sternberg, 1997, 2004; Sternberg & Detterman, 1986)

With these qualities in mind, we offer one possible (but intentionally broad) definition of **intelligence:** the ability to apply past knowledge and experiences flexibly to accomplish challenging new tasks.

Children apply their intellectual abilities in a wide variety of academic and social contexts. Because intelligence is adaptive, it helps children survive and thrive in their particular culture. For example, in mainstream Western culture, strong verbal skills are typically encouraged, as they are likely to help children succeed in society. But not all cultures value chattiness. In some cultures, talking a lot is interpreted as a sign of immaturity or low intelligence (Crago, 1988; Minami & McCabe, 1996; Sternberg, 2003). One researcher working at an Inuit school in northern Quebec asked a teacher about a boy whose language seemed unusually advanced for his age-group. The teacher replied:

> "Do you think he might have a learning problem? Some of these children who don't have such high intelligence have trouble stopping themselves. They don't know when to stop talking." (Crago, 1988, p. 219)

In North America and western Europe, intelligence is largely thought of as an ability that influences children's academic achievement and adults' professional success. Such a view is hardly universal, however. Many African and Asian cultures think of intelligence as involving social as well as academic skills—maintaining harmonious interpersonal relationships, working effectively together to accomplish challenging tasks, and so on (Li, 2004; Sternberg, 2004). And in Buddhist societies in China, Taiwan, and elsewhere, intelligence also involves acquiring strong moral values and making meaningful contributions to society (Li, 2004).

Theoretical Perspectives of Intelligence

Some psychologists have suggested that intelligence is a single, general ability that people "have" to varying degrees and apply to a wide range of tasks. Historically, considerable evidence has supported this idea (McGrew, Flanagan, Zeith, & Vanderwood, 1997; Neisser et al., 1996). Although different measures of intelligence yield somewhat different results, they all correlate with one another: Individuals who score high on one measure tend to score high on others as well. Even tests with two different kinds of content (e.g., a verbal test assessing knowledge of vocabulary and a nonverbal test assessing ability to analyze geometric designs) tend to correlate with one another (N. Brody, 1985; Carroll, 1992; Spearman, 1904).

Yet the correlations among various intelligence measures are sometimes only moderate ones. Children who get the highest scores on one test do not always get the highest scores on another test. For instance, youngsters who demonstrate exceptional ability in some areas of the school curriculum may exhibit only average performance in others (recall Gina's high performance in math and writing but average performance in art and music). Therefore, not all psychologists believe that intelligence is a single entity that people "have" in varying amounts. Instead, some argue, people can be more or less intelligent in different situations and on different kinds of tasks. In this section we present five theoretical perspectives on the single-entity versus multiple-abilities nature of intelligence.

Spearman's *g*

In the early 1900s, Charles Spearman (1904, 1927) proposed that intelligence comprises both (a) a single, pervasive reasoning ability (a *general factor*) that is used on a wide variety of

intelligence
Ability to apply past knowledge and experiences flexibly to accomplish challenging new tasks.

tasks and (b) a number of narrow abilities (*specific factors*) involved in executing particular tasks. From Spearman's perspective, children's performance on any given task depends both on the general factor and on any specific factors that the task involves. For example, measures of various language skills (vocabulary, word recognition, reading comprehension, etc.) are all highly correlated, presumably because they all reflect both general intelligence and the same specific factor: verbal ability. A measure of language skills will correlate less with a measure of mathematical problem solving, because the two measures are apt to tap into somewhat different specific abilities.

Many contemporary psychologists believe that sufficient evidence supports Spearman's concept of a general factor—often known simply as Spearman's **g**—in intelligence and that the ability to process information quickly may be at its core. Researchers often find substantial correlations between measures of information processing speed (e.g., reaction times to familiar stimuli) and IQ scores (N. Brody, 1992; Fry & Hale, 1996; Vernon, 1993). For example, children who, as infants, habituate very quickly to new visual stimuli tend to have substantially higher IQ scores in childhood and adolescence (Dougherty & Haith, 1997; McCall & Mash, 1995; S. A. Rose & Feldman, 1995; L. A. Thompson, Fagan, & Fulker, 1991).

Not all psychologists agree that a *g* factor exists, however. Some suggest that the evidence for a single general factor in intelligence can be either strong or weak depending on the specific abilities measured and on the statistical methods used to analyze the data (Neisser, 1998a; Sternberg & Grigorenko, 2000).

Spearman's concept of *g* reflects the idea that intelligence may involve a general ability to think and reason about a wide variety of tasks.

Connecting Concepts
Recall the discussion of *habituation* in Chapter 2.

Cattell's Fluid and Crystallized Intelligences

Raymond Cattell (1963, 1987) has found evidence for two distinctly different components of general intelligence (*g*). First, children differ in **fluid intelligence** (*g*ᶠ), their ability to acquire knowledge quickly and adapt to new situations effectively. Second, they differ in **crystallized intelligence** (*g*ᶜ), the knowledge and skills they have accumulated from their experiences, schooling, and culture. These two components may be more or less relevant to different kinds of tasks. Fluid intelligence relates more to novel tasks, especially those that require rapid decision making and are largely nonverbal in nature. Crystallized intelligence is more important for familiar tasks, especially those that are heavily dependent on language and prior knowledge.

According to Cattell, fluid intelligence is largely the result of inherited biological factors, whereas crystallized intelligence depends on both fluid intelligence and experience and so is influenced by both heredity and environment (Cattell, 1980, 1987). Fluid intelligence peaks in late adolescence and begins to decline gradually in adulthood. In contrast, crystallized intelligence continues to increase throughout childhood, adolescence, and most of adulthood (Cattell, 1963).

Both Spearman and Cattell have acknowledged that neither a single *g* factor nor a distinction between *g*ᶠ and *g*ᶜ can account for all aspects of intelligent behavior. More domain-specific abilities clearly play a role as well, as we will see in the next two theoretical perspectives.

Gardner's Multiple Intelligences

Howard Gardner concedes that a general factor may very well exist in intelligence, but he questions its usefulness in explaining people's performance in particular situations (Gardner, 1995). In his view, children and adults have at least eight distinctly different abilities, or *multiple intelligences,* which are described and illustrated in Table 8-1. Gardner suggests that there may also be a ninth, "existential" intelligence dedicated to philosophical and spiritual issues (e.g., Who are we? Why do we die?). However, evidence for it is weaker than that for the other intelligences (Gardner, 1999, 2000a), and so it is not included in the table.

Gardner presents some evidence to support the existence of multiple intelligences. For instance, he describes people who are quite skilled in one area (perhaps in composing music) and yet have seemingly average abilities in the other areas. He also points out that people who suffer brain damage sometimes lose abilities that are restricted primarily to one intelligence. One person might show deficits primarily in language, whereas another might have difficulty with tasks that require spatial reasoning.

g
General factor in intelligence that influences performance in a wide variety of tasks and content domains.

fluid intelligence
Ability to acquire knowledge quickly and thereby adapt effectively to new situations.

crystallized intelligence
Knowledge and skills accumulated from one's prior experience, schooling, and culture.

TABLE 8-1	Gardner's Multiple Intelligences	
Type of Intelligence[a]	**Examples of Relevant Behaviors**	
Linguistic Intelligence Ability to use language effectively	• Making persuasive arguments • Writing poetry • Identifying subtle nuances in word meanings	
Logical-Mathematical Intelligence Ability to reason logically, especially in mathematics and science	• Solving mathematical problems quickly • Generating mathematical proofs • Formulating and testing hypotheses about observed phenomena[b]	
Spatial Intelligence Ability to notice details of what one sees and to imagine and manipulate visual objects in one's mind	• Conjuring up mental images • Drawing a visual likeness of an object • Making fine discriminations among very similar objects	
Musical Intelligence Ability to create, comprehend, and appreciate music	• Playing a musical instrument • Composing a musical work • Showing a keen awareness of the underlying structure of music	
Bodily-Kinesthetic Intelligence Ability to use one's body skillfully	• Dancing • Playing basketball • Performing pantomime	
Interpersonal Intelligence Ability to notice subtle aspects of other people's behaviors	• Correctly perceiving another's mood • Detecting another's underlying intentions and desires • Using knowledge of others to influence their thoughts and behaviors	
Intrapersonal Intelligence Awareness of one's own feelings, motives, and desires	• Discriminating among such similar emotions as sadness and regret • Identifying the motives guiding one's own behavior • Using self-knowledge to relate more effectively with others	
Naturalist Intelligence Ability to recognize patterns in nature and differences among natural objects and life-forms	• Identifying members of particular plant or animal species • Classifying natural forms (e.g., rocks, types of mountains) • Applying one's knowledge of nature in such activities as farming, landscaping, or animal training	

Sources: Gardner, 1983, 1993, 1999, 2000a; Gardner & Hatch, 1990.

[a]Gardner has also suggested the possibility of an existential intelligence dedicated to philosophical and spiritual issues, but he acknowledges that evidence is weaker for it than for the eight intelligences described here.

[b]This example may remind you of Piaget's theory of cognitive development. Many of the stage-relevant characteristics that Piaget described fall within the realm of logical-mathematical intelligence.

In Gardner's theory of multiple intelligences, the ability to draw lifelike renditions of three-dimensional objects falls in the domain of spatial intelligence. Art by Oscar, seventh grade (top), and Daniela, eighth grade (bottom).

According to Gardner, the multiple intelligences may take somewhat different forms in different cultures, depending on how each culture shapes and molds the raw talents of its growing children. For example, in Western culture, spatial intelligence might be reflected in painting, sculpture, or geometry. But among the Gikwe bushmen of the Kalahari Desert, it might be reflected in the ability to recognize and remember many specific locations over a large area (perhaps over several hundred square miles), identifying each location by the rocks, bushes, and other landmarks found there (Gardner, 1983).

Gardner's perspective offers the possibility that the great majority of children are intelligent in one way or another. Many educators have wholeheartedly embraced such an optimistic view of human potential and propose that all students can successfully master classroom subject matter when instructional methods capitalize on each student's intellectual strengths (e.g., L. Campbell, Campbell, & Dickinson, 1998; M. Kornhaber, Fierros, & Veenema, 2004). In psychological circles, however, reviews of Gardner's theory are mixed. Some psychologists do not believe that Gardner's evidence is sufficiently compelling to support the notion of eight or nine distinctly different abilities (N. Brody, 1992; Kail, 1998; Sternberg, 2003). Others agree that people may have a variety of relatively independent abilities but argue for intelligences other than the ones Gardner has described (e.g., Horn & Noll, 1997; Sternberg et al., 2000). Still others reject the idea that abilities in specific domains, such as in music or bodily movement, are really "intelligence" per se (Bracken, McCallum, & Shaughnessy, 1999; Sattler, 2001).

Sternberg's Triarchic Theory

In speculating about the nature of intelligence, Robert Sternberg has made a number of distinctions that involve *threes* of something—hence the term *triarchic*. For one thing, he suggests that people may be more or less intelligent in three different domains (Sternberg, 1998, 2004; Sternberg et al., 2000). *Analytical intelligence* involves making sense of, analyzing, contrasting, and evaluating the kinds of information and problems often seen in academic settings and on intelligence tests. *Creative intelligence* involves imagination, invention, and synthesis of ideas within the context of new situations. *Practical intelligence* involves applying knowledge and skills effectively to manage and respond to everyday problems and social situations.

In addition, Sternberg proposes that intelligent behavior involves an interplay of three factors, all of which vary from one occasion to the next: (a) the environmental *context* in which the behavior occurs, (b) the way in which one's prior *experiences* are brought to bear on a particular task, and (c) the *cognitive processes* required by the task (Sternberg, 1985, 1997, 2003). These three factors are summarized in Figure 8-1.

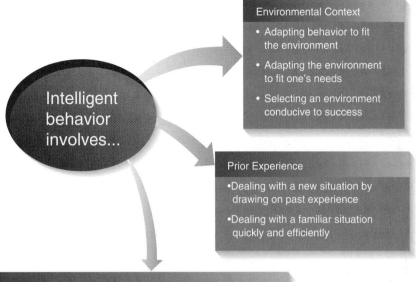

Role of environmental context. As noted earlier, intelligence involves adaptation. In Sternberg's view such adaptation might take one of three forms: (a) modifying a response to deal successfully with specific environmental conditions, (b) modifying the environment to better fit one's own strengths and needs, or (c) selecting an alternative environment more conducive to success. Furthermore, behavior may be more or less intelligent in different cultural contexts. For example, learning to read is an adaptive response in some cultures yet largely irrelevant to others.

Sternberg has identified three general skills that are especially adaptive in Western culture. One is *practical problem-solving ability,* such as the ability to identify exactly what the problem *is* in a particular situation, reason logically about the problem, and generate a multitude of possible problem solutions. A second skill is *verbal ability,* such as the ability to speak and write clearly, develop and use a large vocabulary, and understand and learn from what one reads. A third is *social competence,* such as the ability to relate effectively to other human beings, be sensitive to others' needs and wishes, and provide leadership.

Role of prior experience. Intelligent behavior sometimes involves the ability to deal successfully with a brand-new situation. At other times it involves the ability to deal with familiar situations rapidly and efficiently. In both cases a child's prior experiences play a critical role. When children encounter a new task or problem, they must draw on past experience and consider the kinds of responses that have been effective in similar circumstances. When they deal with more familiar tasks, basic knowledge and skills related to the task must be sufficiently *automatized* that the task can be completed quickly and effortlessly.

Role of cognitive processes. In addition to considering how context and prior experience affect behavior, we must also consider how a child thinks about (mentally processes) a particular task or situation. Sternberg suggests that numerous cognitive processes are involved in intelligent behavior: interpreting a new situation in productive ways, sustaining concentration on a task, separating important information from irrelevant details, identifying

Figure 8-1

In Sternberg's triarchic model of intelligence, three different factors influence intelligent behavior.

Connecting Concepts

As you learned in Chapter 7, automatization results from using information and skills over and over again.

possible problem-solving strategies, finding relationships among seemingly different ideas, making effective use of external feedback, and so on. Some of these processes facilitate *knowledge acquisition* relevant to a task at hand, others are directly involved in the actual *performance* of the task, and still others comprise *metacognition* that oversees the entire endeavor (Sternberg, 2004). Different cognitive processes are likely to be relevant to different situations, and so a child may behave more or less "intelligently" depending on the specific cognitive processes needed at the time.

——————— Connecting Concepts
See Chapter 7 for an in-depth discussion of metacognition.

To date, research neither supports nor refutes the notion that intelligence has the various triarchic components that Sternberg describes. Certain aspects of Sternberg's theory (e.g., how various factors work together, what specific roles metacognition plays) are described in such general terms that they are difficult to test empirically (Sattler, 2001; Siegler & Alibali, 2005). And Sternberg himself acknowledges that most of the research supporting his theory has been conducted by his own research team (Sternberg, 2003), rather than by outsiders who might be more objective or critical. Nevertheless, Sternberg's perspective helps us understand intelligence in terms of the specific cognitive processes that may underlie it. Furthermore, it reminds us that a child's ability to behave intelligently may vary considerably, depending on the particular context and specific knowledge and skills that a task requires. Some theorists believe that context makes all the difference in the world—a belief that is clearly evident in the concept of distributed intelligence.

Distributed Intelligence

Implicit in our discussion so far has been the assumption that intelligent behavior is something that children and adolescents engage in with little if any help from external resources. But some psychologists point out that youngsters are far more likely to behave intelligently when they have the support of their physical, social, and cultural environments (Pea, 1993; Perkins, 1995; Sternberg & Wagner, 1994). For example, it's easier for many adolescents to solve for *x* in the equation

——————— Connecting Concepts
Such forms of support should remind you of the *scaffolding* discussed in Chapter 6.

$$\frac{7}{25} = \frac{x}{375}$$

if they have pencil and paper, or perhaps even a calculator, with which to work out the problem. And they are more likely to write a convincing persuasive essay if they brainstorm with their peers about arguments to make in support of a particular opinion.

The concept of distributed intelligence reminds us that children and adolescents often perform more intelligently when they work with others to tackle problems, have symbolic tools such as charts and equations to represent and transform information, and use computers to organize and manipulate data.

This idea that intelligent behavior depends on physical, social, and cultural support mechanisms is sometimes referred to as **distributed intelligence.** Children and adolescents can "distribute" their thinking (and therefore think more intelligently) in at least three ways (Pea, 1993; Perkins, 1992, 1995). First, they can use physical objects, and especially technology (e.g., calculators, computers), to handle and manipulate large amounts of information. Second, they can work with others to explore ideas and solve problems. Third, they can represent and think about the situations they encounter using the various symbolic tools their culture provides—for instance, the words, diagrams, charts, mathematical equations, and so on that help them simplify or make better sense of complex topics and problems.

From this perspective, intelligence is not a characteristic that resides "inside" a person, nor is it something that can be easily measured and then summarized with a single test score. Instead, it is a highly variable and context-specific ability that virtually anyone can possess when appropriate environmental supports are available. Theorists have only begun to explore the implications of a "distributed" view of intelligence, however. Much work remains to be done, both in identifying the specific ways in which the environment can support intelligent behavior and in determining how great an effect such support is likely to have.

distributed intelligence
Thinking facilitated by physical objects and technology, social support, and concepts and symbols of one's culture.

The five perspectives just presented provide widely diverging views of human intelligence. Their differences with respect to the three themes—nature and nurture, universality and diversity, and qualitative and quantitative change—are presented in the Basic Developmental Issues table "Contrasting Theories of Intelligence."

BASIC DEVELOPMENTAL ISSUES	**Contrasting Theories of Intelligence**				
Issue	**Spearman's General Factor (g)**	**Cattell's Fluid and Crystallized Intelligence**	**Gardner's Multiple Intelligences**	**Sternberg's Triarchic Theory**	**Distributed Intelligence**
Nature and Nurture	Spearman did not specifically address the issue of nature versus nurture. Subsequent researchers have found evidence that *g* is probably influenced by both heredity and environment.	Cattell proposed that fluid intelligence is largely the result of inherited factors. Crystallized intelligence is influenced by both heredity (because it depends partly on fluid intelligence) and environmental experiences.	Gardner believes that heredity provides some basis for individual differences in the various intelligences. However, culture influences the form that each intelligence takes, and formal schooling influences the extent to which each intelligence flourishes.	Sternberg emphasizes the roles of environmental context (e.g., culture) and prior experience in intelligent behavior. Thus his focus is on nurture.	Environmental support mechanisms (physical tools, social interaction, and the symbolic representations of one's culture) influence a person's ability to behave intelligently.
Universality and Diversity	Spearman assumed that the existence of *g* is universal across cultures. However, people vary both in their general intellectual ability and in more specific abilities.	The distinction between fluid and crystallized intelligence is applicable across cultures. People within a particular culture differ in their fluid and crystallized abilities. In addition, the nature of crystallized intelligence (i.e., what specific knowledge and skills are important) varies from one culture to another.	According to Gardner, the various intelligences are products of human evolution and so are seen worldwide. However, any particular intelligence will manifest itself differently in different environments and cultures.	The three factors that influence intelligent behavior (context, experience, cognitive processes) are universal. Different cultures may value and require different skills, however, so intelligence may take particular forms in each culture.	The physical, social, and symbolic support mechanisms at one's disposal vary widely from situation to situation and from one cultural group to another.
Qualitative and Quantitative Change	Spearman derived his theory from various tests of cognitive abilities. Implicit in such tests is the assumption that abilities change quantitatively over time.	Cattell, too, based his theory on numerical measures of various abilities. Thus his emphasis was on quantitative changes in both fluid and crystallized intelligence. For instance, some evidence indicates a quantitative increase in fluid analytical abilities in childhood and adolescence and a gradual decline in adulthood.	Growth in each intelligence has both quantitative and qualitative elements. For example, in logical-mathematical intelligence, children gain skills in increments (quantitatively) but also acquire new (and qualitatively different) abilities.	The effects of relevant prior experiences, more automatized knowledge and skills, and more efficient cognitive processes involve quantitative change. The acquisition of new strategies over time involves qualitative change.	Intelligent behavior is context-specific. Some contexts enhance intelligence quantitatively (e.g., children might remember more from a textbook when they not only read it but also can listen to an audiotape of the book). Other contexts enhance intelligence qualitatively (e.g., children are more likely to elaborate on textbook content when they are taught how to ask one another thought-provoking questions about the material; see Chapter 7).

Measuring Intelligence

Although psychologists have not been able to agree on what intelligence is, they have been trying to measure it for more than a century. In the early 1900s, school officials in France asked the psychologist Alfred Binet to develop a way of identifying students who would have exceptional difficulty in regular classrooms and would therefore be in need of special educational services. To accomplish the task, Binet devised a test that measured general knowledge, vocabulary, perception, memory, and abstract thought. He found that students who performed poorly on his test tended to perform poorly in the classroom as well. Binet's test was the earliest version of what we now call an **intelligence test.** Today intelligence tests are widely used to assess children's cognitive functioning and predict academic achievement, especially when a child may possibly have special educational needs.

Tests of General Intelligence

Most intelligence tests in use today have been developed to do the same thing that Alfred Binet's first test was intended to do: identify people with special needs. In many cases intelligence tests are used as part of a diagnostic battery of tests to determine why certain children are showing developmental delays or academic difficulties and whether they require special interventions or educational services. In other instances intelligence tests are used to identify children with exceptionally high ability who are probably not being challenged by the regular school curriculum and may require more in-depth instruction or advanced classwork to nurture their cognitive growth.

Intelligence tests typically include a wide variety of questions and problems for children to tackle. By and large, the focus is not on what children have specifically been taught at school, but rather on what they have learned and deduced from their general, everyday experiences.

Examples of general intelligence tests.   To give you a feel for the nature of general intelligence tests, we briefly describe three of them.[1]

Wechsler Intelligence Scale for Children.   One widely used intelligence test is the fourth edition of the *Wechsler Intelligence Scale for Children,* or *WISC-IV* (Wechsler, 2003), designed for children and adolescents aged 6 to 16. The WISC-IV consists of 15 subtests, with various subtest scores being combined to obtain composite scores in Verbal Comprehension, Perceptual Reasoning, Working Memory, and Processing Speed. Many of the subtest scores are also combined to determine a total score, known as a Full Scale IQ. Examples of items like those on the WISC-IV are presented in Figure 8-2.

Stanford-Binet Intelligence Scales.   A second commonly used instrument is the *Stanford-Binet Intelligence Scales* (Roid, 2003; Thorndike, Hagen, & Sattler, 1986). The Stanford-Binet can be used with children as young as 2, adolescents, and adults. The individual being assessed is asked to perform a wide variety of tasks, some involving verbal material and responses (e.g., defining vocabulary words, finding logical inconsistencies in a story, or interpreting proverbs) and others involving concrete objects or pictures (e.g., remembering a sequence of objects, copying geometric figures, or identifying absurdities in pictures). The Stanford-Binet yields an overall IQ score, and its most recent edition (Roid, 2003) also yields Verbal and Nonverbal IQs, plus more specific scores in Fluid Reasoning, Knowledge, Working Memory, Visual-Spatial Processing, and Quantitative Reasoning.

Universal Nonverbal Intelligence Test.   The WISC-IV and Stanford-Binet depend heavily on language: Even when tasks involve reasoning about strictly nonverbal, visual material, the child is usually given verbal instructions about how to complete them. In contrast, some measures of intelligence involve no language whatsoever. An example is the *Universal Nonverbal Intelligence Test,* or *UNIT* (Bracken & McCallum, 1998). Designed for children and adolescents aged 5 to 17, the UNIT consists of six subtests involving memory or reasoning

---

intelligence test
General measure of current cognitive functioning, used primarily to predict academic achievement over the short run.

[1]Many intelligence tests are described on their publishers' Web sites. You can learn more about some of them by visiting the Companion Website for this text. Go to www.prenhall.com/mcdevitt, choose Chapter 8, and click on *Web Links.*

Figure 8-2

Items similar to those found on the *Wechsler Intelligence Scale for Children®—Fourth Edition*

Copyright © 2003 by Harcourt Assessment, Inc. Reproduced by permission. All rights reserved.

Following are descriptions of 6 of the 15 subtests on the WISC-IV, along with items similar to those included in the subtests.

Similarities
This subtest is designed to assess a child's verbal reasoning and concept formation.

- In what way are a lion and a tiger alike?
- In what way are an hour and a week alike?
- In what way are a circle and a triangle alike?

Comprehension
This subtest is designed to assess a child's understanding of general principles and social situations.

- What should you do if you see someone forget his book when he leaves a restaurant?
- What is the advantage of keeping money in a bank?
- Why is copper often used in electrical wires?

Information
This subtest is designed to assess a child's general knowledge about a broad range of topics.

- How many wings does a bird have?
- What is steam made of?
- What is pepper?

Letter-Number Sequencing
This subtest is designed to assess a child's working memory capacity. In each item, a letter-number sequence is presented, and the child is asked to repeat first the numbers (in numerical order) and then the letters (in alphabetical order).

- Q-3 [Response: 3-Q]
- M-3-P-6 [Response: 3-6-M-P]
- 5-J-4-A-1-S [Response: 1-4-5-A-J-S]

Arithmetic
This subtest is designed to assess a child's ability to solve orally presented arithmetic problems within a certain time limit, tapping into both working memory capacity and knowledge of arithmetic.

- Sam had three pieces of candy and Joe gave him four more. How many pieces of candy did Sam have altogether?
- Three women divided eighteen golf balls equally among themselves. How many golf balls did each person receive?
- If two buttons cost $.15, what will be the cost of a dozen buttons?

Block Design
This subtest is designed to assess a child's ability to analyze and reproduce geometric designs, thus tapping into visual-spatial ability. The child looks at a series of designs, such as the one below, and is asked to re-create them using blocks that are solid red on two sides, solid white on two sides, and diagonally red and white on the remaining two sides.

regarding visual stimuli (see Figure 8-3). Its content (e.g., people, mice, cheese) was chosen from objects and symbols presumed to be universal across all industrialized cultures. Instructions are given entirely through gestures, pantomime, and modeling, and the child responds by either pointing or manipulating objects.

Nonverbal tests such as the UNIT are especially useful for children who have hearing impairments or language-related learning disabilities, as well as for children for whom English is a second language. For instance, children who are deaf and children who have been raised speaking a language other than English perform better on the UNIT than on more traditional language-based intelligence tests (Krivitski, McIntosh, Rothlisberg, & Finch, 2004; Maller, 2000; McCallum 1999).

IQ scores. In the early 20th century, some psychologists began to calculate scores for intelligence tests by comparing a child's *mental age* (referring to the age-group of students whose performance was most similar to the child's performance) with his or her chronological age (W. Stern, 1912; Terman, 1916). The mathematical formula involved division, and so

Symbolic Memory is primarily a measure of short-term visual memory and complex sequential memory for meaningful material. The task is to view a sequence of universal symbols for 5 seconds and then recreate it from memory using the Symbolic Memory Cards.

Spatial Memory is primarily a measure of short-term visual memory for abstract material. The task is to view a pattern of green and/or black dots on a 3 × 3- or 4 × 4-cell grid for 5 seconds and then recreate the pattern from memory using green and black chips on a blank Response Grid.

Object Memory is primarily a measure of short-term recognition and recall of meaningful symbolic material. The examinee is presented a randomly arranged pictorial array of common objects for 5 seconds, after which the stimulus page is removed, and a second pictorial array is presented containing all of the previously presented objects and additional objects to serve as foils. The task requires the examinee to identify objects presented in the first pictorial array by placing a response chip on the appropriate pictures.

Cube Design is primarily a measure of visual-spatial reasoning. The task requires the examinee to use two-colored cubes to construct a three-dimensional design that matches a stimulus picture.

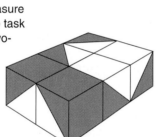

Analogic Reasoning is primarily a measure of symbolic reasoning. The task requires the examinee to complete matrix analogies that employ both common objects and novel geometric figures by pointing to one of four multiple choice options.

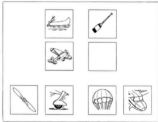

Mazes is primarily a measure of reasoning and planful behavior. The examinee uses paper and pencil to navigate and exit mazes by tracing a path from the center starting point of each maze to the correct exit, without making incorrect decisions en route. A series of increasingly complex mazes is presented.

 Figure 8-3

Items similar to those on the Universal Nonverbal Intelligence Test (UNIT)

the resulting score was called an *intelligence quotient,* or **IQ,** score.[2] Even though we still use the term *IQ,* intelligence test scores are no longer based on the old formula. Instead, they are determined by comparing a person's performance on the test with the performance of others in the same age-group. Scores near 100 indicate average performance: People with a score of 100 have performed better than half of their age-mates on the test and not as well as the other half. Scores well below 100 indicate below-average performance on the test, and scores well above 100 indicate above-average performance.

Figure 8-4 shows the percentage of people getting scores at different points along the scale (e.g., 12.9% get scores between 100 and 105). Notice how the curve is high in the middle and low at both ends. This shape tells us that many more people obtain scores close to 100 than scores very much higher or lower than 100. For example, if we add up the percentages in different parts of Figure 8-4, we find that approximately two-thirds (68%) of individuals in any particular age-group score within 15 points of 100 (i.e., between 85 and 115). In contrast, only 2 percent score as low as 70, and only 2 percent score as high as 130.[3]

Figure 8-4 does not include scores below 70 or above 130. Such scores are possible but relatively rare. For instance, Gina, in the opening case study, once obtained a score of 140 on an intelligence test. A score of 140 is equivalent to a percentile rank of 99.4. In other words, only 6 people out of every 1,000 would earn a score as high as or higher than Gina's.

Validity and reliability of general intelligence tests. In Chapter 2 we introduced you to the concepts of validity and reliability. In general, the *validity* of an intelligence test is the extent to which it actually measures intelligence. The *reliability* of an intelligence test is the extent to which it yields consistent, dependable scores.

Researchers take a variety of approaches in their efforts to determine the validity of intelligence tests. For instance, they look for evidence that older children perform better on the test items than younger children—a result consistent with the assumption that children think more intelligently with age. (Note that children's *IQ scores* do *not* necessarily increase with age; more on this point later.) As an example of such age differences, observe how three children define the word *freedom* in the "Intelligence" video clips for middle childhood, early adolescence, and late adolescence, on Observation CD 1:

Kate (age 8):   You want to be free. Or you want to play something . . . and you got caught and they have to keep you like in jail or something like in a game and you want to get free.

Ryan (age 13):   It means that you can, like, do stuff that you want.

Paul (age 17):   Basically something that everyone has these days or should have. It's the right to be able to make your own decisions and choose for yourself what you want to do or want to be.

Notice how, with age, the responses get increasingly abstract and complex. Kate limits her definition to a specific behavior, getting out of "jail" in a game. Ryan defines the term more abstractly and broadly, implying that it has relevance to a wide variety of situations. Paul offers an abstract definition as well, but his is more specific and precise than Ryan's.

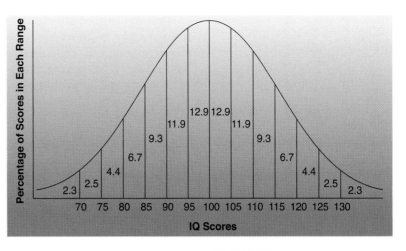

Figure 8-4

Percentage of IQ scores in different ranges

Connecting Concepts ——————
Validity and reliability are important for virtually any measure of human characteristics (see Chapter 2).

Notice how children's word definitions become increasingly sophisticated with age in the "Intelligence" clips for middle childhood, early adolescence, and late adolescence, on Observation CD 1.

---

[2] Alfred Binet himself objected to the use of intelligence quotients, believing that his tests were too imprecise to warrant such scores. Lewis Terman, an American psychologist, was largely responsible for popularizing the term *IQ* (Montagu, 1999a).

[3] This symmetrical and predictable distribution of scores happens by design rather than by chance. If you have some knowledge of descriptive statistics, you probably recognize Figure 8-4 as a normal distribution. IQ scores are based on a normal distribution with a mean of 100 and, for most tests, a standard deviation of 15.

IQ score
Score on an intelligence test, determined by comparing one's performance with the performance of same-age peers.

Researchers also examine the validity of intelligence tests by determining how closely IQ scores correlate with school achievement and other indicators of intelligence. Many research studies indicate that traditional measures of general intelligence, such as the WISC-IV and the Stanford-Binet, have considerable validity in this respect. On average, children and adolescents who earn higher scores on these tests have higher academic achievement and complete more years of education than their lower-scoring peers (N. Brody, 1997; Gustafsson & Undheim, 1996; P. E. Williams, Weiss, & Rolfhus, 2003a). To a lesser extent, IQ scores also predict later performance in the adult workplace (Sattler, 2001; Sternberg, 1996). We have less information about the UNIT, because it has only recently arrived on the scene, but emerging evidence indicates that it, too, has some validity as a measure of intelligence (Farrell & Phelps, 2000; Fives & Flanagan, 2002; Krivitski et al., 2004; McCallum & Bracken, 1997; E. L. Young & Assing, 2000).

To determine the reliability of intelligence tests, researchers look at various indications of consistency, especially the extent to which the same test yields similar scores on two different occasions, the extent to which different subtests within a particular test yield similar results for a particular child, and the extent to which two different examiners score a child's performance in the same way. The WISC-III, Stanford-Binet, and UNIT are highly reliable in these respects (Anastasi & Urbina, 1997; Sattler, 2001; P. E. Williams, Weiss, & Rolfhus, 2003b; E. L. Young & Assing, 2000).

Specific Ability Tests

Whenever we summarize a child's performance with a single IQ score, as we often do with general intelligence tests, we are to some extent buying into Spearman's concept of *g*. In contrast, **specific ability tests** have been developed to assess certain cognitive abilities more precisely. Some of these tests, called *aptitude tests,* are designed to assess a person's potential to learn in particular content domains, such as mathematics or auto mechanics. Others focus on specific aspects of cognitive processing (e.g., memory for auditory information, ability to think and reason about spatial relationships) and are often used in identifying learning disabilities.

Specific ability tests are more consistent with a multidimensional view of intelligence, such as Spearman's concept of specific abilities or Gardner's concept of multiple intelligences. They typically have high reliability and a reasonable degree of validity, at least in terms of how accurately they seem to measure the specific abilities they're designed to assess. However, they get mixed reviews on whether they predict children's performance in particular domains more accurately than do general measures of intelligence (Anastasi & Urbina, 1997; R. J. Cohen & Swerdlik, 1999; McGrew et al., 1997; Neisser et al., 1996).

Dynamic Assessment

The approaches described so far focus on what children can *currently* do with little or no assistance from anyone else. In contrast, **dynamic assessment** focuses on assessing children's ability to learn in new situations, usually with an adult's assistance (Feuerstein, 1979; Feuerstein, Feuerstein, & Gross, 1997; Lidz, 1997; Tzuriel, 2000). Typically, dynamic assessment involves (a) identifying one or more tasks that children cannot initially do independently, (b) providing in-depth instruction and practice in behaviors and cognitive processes related to the task(s), and then (c) determining the extent to which each child has benefited from the instruction (Feuerstein, 1979, 1980; Kozulin & Falik, 1995; Lidz & Gindis, 2003; Tzuriel, 2000). Accordingly, dynamic assessment is sometimes called *assessment of learning potential.*

Dynamic assessment is consistent with several theoretical perspectives. As Sternberg has pointed out, intelligence involves adaptation to new situations. And as the concept of distributed intelligence reminds us, intelligent behavior is heavily context-dependent. But Vygotsky's theory of cognitive development is probably most relevant here. As you learned in Chapter 6, Vygotsky proposed that we can get a more complete picture of children's cognitive development when we assess not only their *actual developmental level* (the upper limit of tasks they can successfully accomplish on their own) but also their *level of potential development* (the upper limit of tasks they can accomplish when they have the assistance of more competent individuals).

——— Connecting Concepts

See Chapter 6 for an in-depth discussion of Vygotsky's theory.

specific ability test
Test designed to assess a specific cognitive skill or the potential to learn and perform in a specific content domain.

dynamic assessment
Systematic examination of how a child's knowledge or reasoning may change as a result of learning a specific task or performing it with adult guidance.

Learning Strategies Checklist	None of the time	Some of the time	Most of the time
Attention/Discrimination			
• initiates focus with minimum cues	0	1	2
• maintains focus with minimum cues	0	1	2
• responds to relevant cues, ignores irrelevant cues	0	1	2
Comparative Behavior			
• comments on features of task	0	1	2
• uses comparative behavior to select item	0	1	2
• talks about same/different	0	1	2
Planning			
• talks about overall goal	0	1	2
• talks about plan	0	1	2
Self-Regulation/Awareness			
• waits for instructions	0	1	2
• seeks help when difficult	0	1	2
• corrects self	0	1	2
• rewards self	0	1	2
Transfer			
• applies strategies within tasks	0	1	2
• applies strategies between tasks	0	1	2
Motivation			
• persists even when frustrated	0	1	2
• shows enthusiasm	0	1	2

Figure 8-5

Example of a checklist for evaluating a child's approach to learning during a dynamic assessment
Copyright © 1993 by E. Peña. Reprinted with permission.

Dynamic assessment is a fairly new approach to assessing intelligence, and so psychologists are only beginning to discover its strengths and weaknesses. On the plus side, it often yields more optimistic evaluations of children's abilities than traditional measures of intelligence and may be especially useful in assessing the abilities of children who have been raised outside of mainstream Western culture (Sternberg, 2004; Swanson & Lussier, 2001; Tzuriel, 2000). Furthermore, dynamic assessment can provide a wealth of qualitative information about children's cognitive strategies and approaches to learning and so may be helpful in guiding future instruction (Feuerstein, 1979; Hamers & Ruijssenaars, 1997; Tzuriel, 2000). Figure 8-5 presents a checklist that one psychologist has used during a dynamic assessment of children's learning and problem-solving skills. Although a few of the items on the checklist are specific to the tasks the clinician presented, most of them are sufficiently generic that they might be applied in a wide variety of circumstances.

Yet disadvantages of dynamic assessment are also emerging. It often involves considerable training before it can be used appropriately, and it typically requires a great deal of time to administer (Anastasi & Urbina, 1997; Tzuriel, 2000). Furthermore, questions have been raised about how best to determine the validity and reliability of dynamic assessment instruments, and those instruments that have been evaluated have fared poorly in comparison to more traditional approaches (Swanson & Lussier, 2001; Tzuriel, 2000). Accordingly, when educators and psychologists use dynamic assessment to assess children's capabilities, they should do so cautiously and always within the context of other data.

Assessing the Abilities of Infants and Young Children

If an adult is to assess a child's cognitive abilities accurately, the child must, of course, be a cooperative participant in the process—for instance, by staying alert, paying attention, and maintaining interest in the assessment tasks. Yet infants and young children are not always able to cooperate. Infants may be sleepy, fussy, or afraid of the stranger conducting the assessment. Young children may have short attention spans, lose interest in the test questions and materials, or misinterpret instructions. Because of such factors, which can vary considerably from one occasion to the next, test scores for infants and young children tend to have lower reliability than those of older children and adolescents (Anastasi & Urbina, 1997; Bracken & Walker, 1997; Fleege, Charlesworth, & Burts, 1992; Wodtke, Harper, & Schommer, 1989).

Nevertheless, teachers, child care providers, and other professionals sometimes need to monitor the cognitive development of infants and young children, perhaps to identify significant developmental delays that require intervention or perhaps to determine readiness for various kinds of educational experiences. Here we briefly describe the nature of tests available for infants, toddlers, and preschoolers.

The Bayley Scales of Infant Development, designed for children aged 1 month to 3½ years, are sometimes used when significant developmental delays are suspected.

Tests for infants and toddlers.   Infants born in hospital settings are typically assessed as soon as they are born. At both 1 minute and 5 minutes after birth, a doctor or nurse evaluates their color, heart rate, reflexes, muscle tone, and breathing, giving each characteristic a rating between 0 and 2. A perfect score on this *Apgar Scale* is 10. A more in-depth assessment for young infants from birth until 2 months is the *Neonatal Behavioral Assessment Scale* (Brazelton Institute, 2000). Often used to identify significant neurological abnormalities, it assesses alertness and attention, the quality of visual and auditory processing, and a variety of reflexes and behaviors.

Perhaps the most widely used test for older infants and toddlers is the *Bayley Scales of Infant Development* (Bayley, 2005). Designed for children aged 1 month to 3½ years, it includes five scales. Three scales—for cognitive development (attention, memory, concept formation, etc.), language, and motor skills—are assessed through interactions with the child. Two additional scales—for social-emotional functioning and adaptive behavior—are assessed through parent questionnaires.

Tests of cognitive abilities for infants and toddlers might better be called *developmental assessments* than intelligence tests per se. They appear to assess current cognitive functioning reasonably well and can be helpful in identifying significant cognitive disabilities if used in combination with other information (Sattler, 2001). However, measures of cognitive growth in the first few years of life often have little or no relationship to intelligence in later years (Hayslip, 1994; McCall, 1993; Neisser et al., 1996). "Bright" babies do not necessarily become the brightest fourth graders, and toddlers who appear slow to learn may eventually catch up to, or even surpass, their peers (more about this point in the discussion of IQ stability later in the chapter).

In the "Intelligence: Infancy" video clip on Observation CD 1, you can observe 14-month-old Corwin stacking blocks and identifying pictures of various objects and animals. Such tasks are typical of developmental tests for toddlers. An examiner administering such a test might also rate Corwin on such characteristics as attention, engagement in the test activities, and emotional regulation.

Observe tasks similar to those on infant tests of cognitive abilities in the "Intelligence: Infancy" clip on Observation CD 1.

Tests for preschoolers.   As you've previously learned, the Stanford-Binet Intelligence Scales can be used for children as young as 2. Another commonly used test for young children is the third edition of the *Wechsler Preschool and Primary Scale of Intelligence,* or WPPSI-III (Wechsler, 2002). Suitable for children aged 2½ to 7, the WPPSI-III has 14 subtests, some similar to those on the WISC-IV and others (e.g., naming a pictured object) more appropriate for young children. In addition to an overall IQ, it yields a Verbal IQ (based on subtests that depend heavily on a child's language skills), a Performance IQ (based on subtests that require only minimal use of language), a score for General Language, and (for children aged 4 and older) a measure of Processing Speed.

As measures of intelligence for young children, both the Stanford-Binet and WPPSI-III correlate with other measures of intelligence and provide reasonable estimates of children's current cognitive functioning. In other words, they have some validity and reliability (Lichtenberger & Kaufman, 2003; McCallum, 1991; Sattler, 2001). Although young children's IQ scores correlate somewhat with their scores in later years, the correlations are modest at best—no doubt because many young children have high energy levels, short attention spans, and little interest in sitting still for more than a few minutes. Thus measures of IQ obtained in the preschool years should *not* be used to make predictions about children's academic performance over the long run (Bracken & Walker, 1997).

Other tests for preschoolers, known as *school readiness tests,* are designed to determine whether children have acquired cognitive skills—for instance, knowledge of colors, shapes, and letters—that many kindergarten and first-grade teachers view as essential foundations for their curricula. Although widely used in school districts, such tests have come under fire in recent years, for several reasons. First, the scores they yield correlate only moderately at best with children's academic performance even a year or so later (La Paro & Pianta, 2000; Stipek, 2002). Second, many assess only cognitive development, whereas social and emotional development should also be considerations in determining a child's readiness for formal education (Miller-Jones, 1989; Pellegrini, 1998). Finally, by age 5, most children are probably ready for some sort of structured educational program. Rather than determining whether children can adapt to a particular educational curriculum and environment, it is probably more beneficial to determine how the school curriculum and environment can be adapted to fit each child's particular needs (Lidz, 1991; Stipek, 2002).

As you can see, we must be careful how we interpret and use the results of intelligence tests and other measures of cognitive abilities. As a general rule, and especially when test results are used to make decisions about young children, educators and other practitioners should use test scores only in combination with other information—observations of the children in a variety of settings, interviews with parents and teachers, and so on. Practitioners should also reserve judgment about the extent to which IQ scores reflect children's inherited abilities, on the one hand, or their environments and background experiences, on the other. In the next section we sift through the data concerning the relative effects of heredity and environment.

Effects of Heredity and Environment on Intelligence

It is often difficult to separate the relative influences of heredity and environment on human characteristics. People who have similar genetic makeup (e.g., brothers and sisters, parents and their children) typically live in similar environments as well. So when we see similarities in IQ among members of the same family, it is hard to know whether those similarities are due to the genes or to the environments that family members share. Nevertheless, a significant body of research tells us that both heredity and environment affect intelligence.

Evidence for Hereditary Influences

Earlier we mentioned that measures of information processing speed correlate with IQ scores. Speed of processing depends on neurological efficiency and maturation, which are genetically controlled. From this standpoint, then, we have some support for a hereditary basis for intelligence (Perkins, 1995). The fact that children with certain genetic defects (e.g., Down syndrome) have, on average, significantly lower IQ scores than their nondisabled peers (Keogh & MacMillan, 1996) provides further evidence of heredity's influence. But perhaps the most convincing evidence comes from twin studies and adoption studies.

Twin studies.   Numerous studies have used monozygotic (identical) twins and dizygotic (fraternal) twins to get a sense of how strongly heredity affects IQ. Because monozygotic twins begin as a single fertilized egg which then separates, they are genetically equivalent human beings. In contrast, dizygotic twins are conceived as two separate fertilized eggs. They share about 50 percent of their genetic makeup, with the other 50 percent being unique to each twin. If identical twins have more similar IQ scores than fraternal twins, we can reasonably conclude that heredity influences intelligence.

Most twins are raised together by the same parent(s) and in the same home, and so they share similar environments as well as similar genes. Yet even when twins are raised separately (perhaps because they have been adopted and raised by different parents), they typically have similar IQ scores (Bouchard & McGue, 1981; N. Brody, 1992; Mackintosh, 1998;

Plomin & Petrill, 1997). In a review of many twin studies, Bouchard and McGue (1981) found these average (median) correlations:

—————— Connecting Concepts
Correlation coefficients are described in Figure 2-2 in Chapter 2.

	Correlations of Twins' IQs
Identical twins raised in the same home	.86
Identical twins raised in different homes	.72
Fraternal twins raised in the same home	.60

The correlation of .72 indicates that identical twins raised in different environments tend to have very similar IQ scores. In fact, these twins are more similar to each other than are fraternal twins raised in the *same* home.[4]

Even when identical twins are raised by different families, they typically have similar IQ scores, indicating that intelligence has a biological component. However, twins raised in different homes are somewhat less similar than twins raised in the same home, indicating that environment affects intelligence as well.

Adoption studies.   Another way to separate the effects of heredity and environment is to compare adopted children with both their biological and adoptive parents. Adopted children tend to be similar to their biological parents in genetic makeup. Their environment, of course, more closely matches that of their adoptive parents. Researchers have found that adopted children's IQ scores are more highly correlated with their biological parents' IQs than with their adoptive parents' IQs. In other words, in a group of people who place their infants up for adoption, those with the highest IQs tend to have offspring who, despite being raised by other people, also have the highest IQs. Furthermore, the IQ correlations between adopted children and their biological parents become stronger, and those between the children and their adoptive parents become weaker, as the children grow older, especially during late adolescence (Bouchard, 1997; McGue, Bouchard, Iacono, & Lykken, 1993; Plomin, Fulker, Corley, & DeFries, 1997; Plomin & Petrill, 1997). (If you find this last research result puzzling, we'll offer an explanation shortly.)

Keep in mind that twin studies and adoption studies do not completely separate the effects of heredity and environment (W. A. Collins, Maccoby, Steinberg, Hetherington, & Bornstein, 2000; Wahlsten & Gottlieb, 1997). For example, adopted children have shared a common environment for at least 9 months—the 9 months of prenatal development—with their biological mothers. Likewise, monozygotic twins who are raised in separate homes have shared a common prenatal environment and often have similar, if not identical, postnatal environments as well. Furthermore, twin studies and adoption studies do not allow researchers to examine the ways in which heredity and environment might interact in their effects on measured intelligence. Any interactive effects are often added to the "heredity" side of the scoreboard (A. Collins et al., 2000; Turkheimer, 2000). Despite such glitches, twin and adoption studies point convincingly to a genetic component in intelligence (Bouchard, 1997; N. Brody, 1992; E. Hunt, 1997; Neisser, 1998a; Petrill & Wilkerson, 2000).

This is not to say that children are predestined to have an intelligence level similar to that of their biological parents. In fact, most children with high intelligence are conceived by parents of average intelligence rather than by parents with high IQ scores (Plomin & Petrill, 1997). Children's genetic ancestry, then, is hardly a surefire predictor of what their own potential is likely to be. Environment also makes an appreciable difference, as we shall now see.

Evidence for Environmental Influences

Numerous sources of evidence converge to indicate that environment has a significant impact on IQ scores. We find some of this evidence in twin studies and adoption studies. Studies of the effects of nutrition, toxic substances, home environment, early intervention, and formal schooling provide additional support for the influence of environment. Also, a steady increase in performance on intelligence tests over the past several decades—known as the *Flynn effect*—is almost certainly attributable to environmental factors.

—————————

[4]In our teaching experiences, we have found that some students erroneously interpret the higher correlations as indicating that identical twins have higher intelligence. This is, of course, not the case. The size of each correlation indicates the *strength of the relationship* between twins' IQs, not the level of twins' intelligence per se.

Twin studies and adoption studies revisited.   Let's look once again at the IQ correlations for identical twins raised in the same home versus in different homes. The median correlation for twins raised in different homes is .72, whereas that for twins raised in the same home is .86. In other words, twins raised in different homes have less similar IQs than twins raised in the same home. The distinct environments that different families provide do have some influence on intellectual development.

Adoption studies, too, indicate that intelligence is not determined entirely by heredity (Capron & Duyme, 1989; Devlin, Fienberg, Resnick, & Roeder, 1995; Waldman, Weinberg, & Scarr, 1994). For instance, in one study (Scarr & Weinberg, 1976), some children of poor parents (with unknown IQs) were adopted by middle-class parents with IQs averaging 118–121. Other children remained with their biological parents. IQ averages of the children in the two groups were as follows:

	Average IQs
Adopted children	105
Nonadopted children	90

Although the adopted children's IQ scores were, on average, lower than those of their adoptive parents, they were about 15 points higher than the scores for the control group children, who were raised by their biological parents.

Effects of early nutrition.   Severe malnutrition, either before birth or during the early years of life, can limit neurological development and have a long-term impact on cognitive development and intelligence (Ricciuti, 1993; S. A. Rose, 1994; Sigman & Whaley, 1998). Attention, memory, abstract reasoning, and general school achievement are all likely to suffer from inadequate nutrition. Children sometimes recover from short periods of poor nourishment (due, perhaps, to war or illness), but the adverse effects of long-term deprivation are more enduring (Sigman & Whaley, 1998).

Some research studies have examined the effects of providing medically approved food supplements and vitamins to infants and young children who would not otherwise have adequate nutrition. Such interventions are most likely to enhance children's development of motor skills, but in some instances cognitive development is enhanced as well (Pollitt & Oh, 1994; Sigman & Whaley, 1998).

Effects of toxic substances.   A variety of toxic substances, or *teratogens,* in children's prenatal or early postnatal environments—for instance, alcohol, drugs, radiation, lead-based paint dust—affect neurological development and thus also affect children's later IQ scores (e.g., Michel, 1989; Neisser et al., 1996; Streissguth, Barr, Sampson, & Bookstein, 1994; Vogel, 1997; Vorhees & Mollnow, 1987). An example of such effects is fetal alcohol syndrome, in which children whose mothers consumed large amounts of alcohol during pregnancy show poor motor coordination, delayed language, and mental retardation (Dorris, 1989).

Effects of home environment.   One likely explanation for the beneficial effects of adoption is that adoptive parents, who typically have adequate financial resources and high levels of education, can provide a more stimulating home environment than the biological parents might have been able to offer. Correlational studies indicate that stimulating home environments—those in which parents interact frequently with their children, make numerous learning and reading materials available, encourage the development of new skills, use complex sentence structures in conversation, and so on—are associated with higher IQ scores in children (Bradley & Caldwell, 1984; Brooks-Gunn et al., 1996; McGowan & Johnson, 1984). Furthermore, when two biologically *un*related children of the same age are raised by the same parents (typically because one or both children are adopted), the children's IQs tend to be more similar than we would expect by chance alone—a relationship that can be attributed only to the influence of a common home environment (N. L. Segal, 2000).

We find especially compelling evidence for the beneficial effects of stimulating home environments in an ongoing project in Romania (C. A. Nelson, 2005). As a result of previous government policies, most Romanian orphans were at one time placed in large institutions to be raised. After a change in government and the intervention of a team of developmental psychologists, some institutionalized infants (randomly selected) were placed with adults

Connecting Concepts
Chapter 3 describes fetal alcohol syndrome in more depth and illustrates it in an ending case study about a boy named Adam.

Study Guide and Reader
Further information about Adam is presented in Supplementary Reading 8-1.

Connecting Concepts
Keep in mind that correlational studies alone do not necessarily reveal a causal relationship (see Chapter 2).

willing to serve as foster parents. (Sadly, the intervention team could not find foster families for all of the infants.) As researchers periodically assessed the children's physical and cognitive development, they found dramatic differences between the two groups. Despite adequate nutrition, children remaining in an institution throughout infancy and the preschool years had smaller head circumferences and less brain activity than the foster children. When intelligence was assessed, the institutionalized children had an average IQ of 64 (indicating mental retardation), whereas the foster children, on average, had IQs in the normal range.

Effects of early intervention.   Unfortunately, not all children live in homes that provide ongoing stimulation and nurturance. When children live in impoverished or neglectful home environments, enriching preschool programs and other forms of early intervention can make an appreciable difference. For instance, high-quality child care and preschool programs (e.g., Head Start) frequently lead to short-term IQ gains and other cognitive and academic benefits (Bronfenbrenner, 1999; NICHD Early Child Care Research Network, 2002b; Zigler, 2003). The effects of such programs don't continue indefinitely, however. Without follow-up interventions during the elementary school years, cognitive advantages (e.g., higher IQ scores and academic achievement) often diminish over time and in some cases disappear altogether (Brooks-Gunn, 2003; Farran, 2001).

We must not be disheartened by such results. Publicly funded preschool programs such as Head Start often enroll the most economically disadvantaged children in the community. To study the long-term effects of these programs, researchers sometimes have difficulty finding an appropriate control group. For instance, they may compare children who attended the programs with children who, though not attending preschool, grew up in more advantaged circumstances (Schnur, Brooks-Gunn, & Shipman, 1992). Furthermore, early intervention often leads to long-term improvements in areas not reflected in IQ test scores. For instance, children who attend intensive, developmentally appropriate academic preschool programs are, later on, more likely to have high achievement motivation and self-esteem, less likely to exhibit serious behavior problems or need special education services, and more likely to graduate from high school (F. A. Campbell & Ramey, 1995; McCall & Plemons, 2001; Spencer et al., 2001; Washington & Bailey, 1995).

Early intervention is most effective in fostering intellectual development when it is tailored to children's existing abilities and interests. But bombarding infants and small children with constant or intense stimulation is *not* effective. As you discovered in Chapter 6, children seem to have a natural desire to learn about their environment, and most eagerly explore their surroundings. But they can handle only so much information—and certainly only so much *new* information—at any one time. Furthermore, pushing young children into exceptionally challenging (perhaps age-inappropriate) activities can cause stress, depression and, in some cases, physical harm (Elkind, 1987). And ultimately, a secure, supportive relationship with one or more caregivers or teachers is just as important as age-appropriate toys and activities (S. Loeb, Fuller, Kagan, & Carrol, 2004; NICHD Early Child Care Research Network, 2002b).

Effects of formal schooling.   The very act of attending school leads to small increases in IQ. In Western societies, children who begin their educational careers early and attend school regularly have higher IQ scores than children who do not. When children must start school later than they would otherwise for reasons beyond their families' control, their IQs are at least 5 points lower for every year of delay. Furthermore, children's IQ scores decline slightly (usually only temporarily) over the course of the summer months, when children are not attending school. And other things being equal, children who drop out have lower IQ scores than children who remain in school, losing an average of almost 2 IQ points for every year of high school not completed (Ceci, 2003; Ceci & Williams, 1997).

The benefits of schooling for intellectual growth are seen in a wide variety of cultures. One probable reason why school attendance affects IQ is that it encourages acquisition of more advanced cognitive processes—rehearsal, organization, metacognition, and so on (M. Cole, 2006). And as Vygotsky pointed out, school provides a systematic means through which children can acquire many concepts and perspectives that previous generations have developed to tackle day-to-day tasks and problems effectively.

The Flynn effect.   The last few decades have seen a slow, steady increase in people's average performance on IQ tests throughout the industrialized world (Flynn, 1987, 1999, 2003;

Research indicates that stimulating preschool experiences often increase IQ in economically disadvantaged children, at least over the short run.

──────── **Connecting Concepts**
Vygotsky's concepts of *cognitive tool* and *mediated learning experience* are especially relevant to this point (see Chapter 6).

Neisser, 1998b). This trend is commonly known as the **Flynn effect.** A similar change has been observed in children's performance on traditional Piagetian tasks (Flieller, 1999). Such improvements are difficult to attribute to heredity because the same gene pool (albeit with an occasional mutation) is passed along from one generation to the next, and so the cause is almost certainly environmental. Theorists disagree as to the likely explanations, however. Better nutrition, smaller family sizes, higher quality home environments, better schooling (for parents as well as children), and more enriching and informative stimulation (increased access to television, reading materials, etc.) are all possibilities (Daley, Whaley, Sigman, Espinosa, & Neumann, 2003; Flynn, 2003; Neisser, 1998b).

How Nature and Nurture Interact in Their Influence on Intelligence

Clearly both nature and nurture influence intelligence. What is less clear is *how much* influence each of these factors has. A few theorists have tried to estimate nature's contribution (the *heritability* of IQ) from the correlations obtained in twin and adoption studies (e.g., McGue et al., 1993; Plomin et al., 1997). But most psychologists now believe that it may ultimately be impossible to separate the relative effects of heredity and environment. They suggest that the two combine to influence children's cognitive development and measured IQ in ways that we can probably never disentangle (e.g., W. A. Collins et al., 2000; Flynn, 2003; Rogoff, 2003; Turkheimer, 2000). Theorists have made the following general points about how nature and nurture interact as they affect intellectual development:

● *Heredity establishes a range rather than a precise figure.* Heredity does not dictate that a child will have a particular IQ score. Instead, it appears to set a range of abilities within which children will eventually fall, with the actual ability level each one achieves depending on his or her specific environmental experiences (Weinberg, 1989). Heredity may also affect how susceptible or impervious a child is to particular environmental influences (Rutter, 1997). For example, high-quality instruction may be more important for some children than for others. In the opening case study, Gina learned how to read before she attended school, and with only minimal help from her mother. Yet other, equally intelligent children may learn to read *only* when they have systematic reading instruction tailored to their individual needs.

Connecting Concepts
For an example of how some intelligent children learn to read only with high-quality instruction, see the description of Kellen in the opening case in Chapter 12.

● *Genetic expression is influenced by environmental conditions.* Genes are not entirely self-contained, independent "carriers" of developmental instructions. Rather, the particular instructions they transmit are influenced by the supportive or nonsupportive nature of children's environments. In an extremely impoverished environment—one with a lack of adequate nutrition and little if any stimulation—heredity may have little to say about the extent to which children develop intellectually. In an ideal environment—one in which nutrition, parenting practices, and educational opportunities are optimal and age-appropriate—heredity can have a significant influence on children's IQ scores (Ceci, 2003; D. C. Rowe et al., 1999; Turkheimer, Haley, Waldron, D'Onofrio, & Gottesman, 2003).

Connecting Concepts
For more on how environmental factors affect genetic expression, see the section "The Blending of Heredity and Environment" in Chapter 3.

Intelligence is almost certainly the result of many genes, each contributing a small amount to measured IQ (Sattler, 2001). These genes may "kick in" at different points in development, and their expression will be influenced by particular environmental conditions at those times. Thus we do not have a single heredity-environment interaction, but rather a number of heredity-environment interactions all contributing to intellectual growth (Simonton, 2001).

● *Especially as they get older, children choose their environments and experiences.* Children may actively seek out environmental conditions that match their inherited abilities—a phenomenon known as **niche-picking** (Flynn, 2003; Halpern & LaMay, 2000; Scarr & McCartney, 1983). For example, children who, genetically speaking, have exceptional quantitative reasoning ability may enroll in advanced mathematics courses, delight in tackling mathematical brainteasers, and in other ways nurture their inherited talents. Children with average quantitative ability are less likely to take on such challenges and so have fewer opportunities to develop their mathematical skills. In such circumstances the relative effects of heredity and environment are difficult to tease apart.

Earlier we mentioned that the IQ correlations between adopted children and their biological parents become stronger over time. We now have a possible explanation for this

Flynn effect
Gradual increase in intelligence test performance observed in many countries over the past several decades.
niche-picking
Tendency to actively seek out environments that match one's inherited abilities.

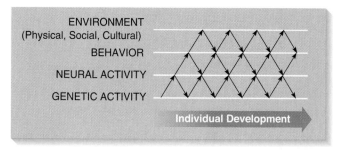

ENVIRONMENT
(Physical, Social, Cultural)

BEHAVIOR

NEURAL ACTIVITY

GENETIC ACTIVITY

Individual Development

Figure 8-6

Bidirectional influences among genetic
activity, neural activity, behavior, and
environment

From *Individual Development and Evolution:
The Genesis of Novel Behavior* (p. 186), by
G. Gottlieb, New York: Oxford University
Press, Inc. Copyright © 1991 by Gilbert
Gottlieb. Reprinted with permission.

finding. Children gain increasing independence as they get older.
Especially as they reach adolescence, they spend less time in their
home environments, and they make more of their own decisions
about the kinds of opportunities to pursue—decisions undoubtedly based, in part, on their natural talents and tendencies (McGue
et al., 1993; Petrill & Wilkerson, 2000).

You might think of intelligence as being the result of four factors (Gottlieb, 1991, 1992). *Genetic activity* affects *neural activity*
(i.e., the operation of neurons in the brain), which in turn affects
behavior, which in turn affects the *environment*. But influence
moves in the opposite direction as well: The environment affects behavior, and these two
(through stimulation, nutritional intake, physical activity, etc.) affect neural activity and genetic expression. The continuing interplay of genetics, neural activity, behavior, and environment is depicted in Figure 8-6.

Developmental Trends in IQ Scores

In one sense, children definitely become more "intelligent" as they develop: They know
more, can think in more complex ways, and can solve problems more effectively. However,
IQ scores are based not on how much children develop over time, but rather on how well
children perform in comparison with their age-mates. By definition, the average IQ score for
any age-group is 100. On average, then, IQ does not increase with age.

Nevertheless, IQ scores do change in two important ways over the course of development:

● *IQ scores become increasingly stable.* As noted previously, children's early performance
on infant measures of cognitive development are not terribly predictive of their later intelligence.
We've already encountered two reasons for the poor predictive powers of infant tests. First, infants are not always cooperative participants in the assessment process. Second, the various
genes contributing to intelligence kick in at different times over the course of development. But
in addition, the types of items on intelligence tests for young children are often considerably different than items on tests for older children and adolescents. The Developmental Trends table
"Intelligence at Different Age Levels" identifies some commonly used indicators of intelligence
at various age levels, along with important considerations to keep in mind for each level.

As children progress through the school years, their IQ scores tend to hover within an
increasingly limited range. Although children continue to develop cognitively, each child's
relative intelligence in comparison with peers changes less as time goes on (N. Brody, 1992;
Neisser et al., 1996; Sattler, 2001). As an example, look once again at the chapter's opening
case study. Gina obtained an IQ score of 140 (equivalent to the 99th percentile) in junior high
school and performed at a similar level on college aptitude tests several years later.

Despite the increasing stability of IQ scores, we must remember that these scores simply
reflect youngsters' performance on a particular test at a particular time. Some change (sometimes as much as 10 to 20 points' worth, and occasionally even more) can
reasonably be expected over the years. The longer the time interval between
two administrations of an intelligence test, the greater the change in IQ we
are likely to see, especially when young children are involved (B. S. Bloom,
1964; Humphreys, 1992; McCall, 1993; Sattler, 2001). IQ scores and other
measures of cognitive ability are most likely to increase when children are
highly motivated and independent learners and when they have ongoing exposure to stimulating activities, high-quality instruction, and a variety of
reading materials (e.g., Echols, West, Stanovich, & Kehr, 1996; Sameroff,
Seifer, Baldwin, & Baldwin, 1993; Schellenberg, 2004).

● *IQ scores become increasingly accurate predictors of future academic achievement.* As IQ scores become more stable with age, their usefulness in predicting classroom performance also increases. Yet educators
should remember two things about the relationship between IQ and
academic achievement. First, intelligence does not necessarily *cause*
achievement. Even though children with high IQs typically perform well in

Adults should never base their expectations for children's
achievement solely on intelligence test scores. Many students
achieve at higher levels than their IQ scores predict.

DEVELOPMENTAL TRENDS	Intelligence at Different Age Levels		
Age	**What You Might Observe**	**Diversity**	**Implications**
Infancy (Birth–2) 	• Success on test items that involve early developmental accomplishments (e.g., recognition memory, visual preferences, eye-hand coordination) • Distractibility and short attention span • Variability in performance from one assessment to the next • Performance dependent on examiner's ability to establish a positive relationship with the infant	• Temperamental differences (e.g., a tendency to be shy or cautious) affect infants' willingness to interact with the examiner and test materials. • Compared to full-term infants, infants born prematurely are less physically developed and more easily fatigued and so tend to obtain somewhat lower test scores. However, with good medical care and families' responsive involvement, many premature infants gradually develop into healthy, intelligent individuals. • Exposure to drugs or alcohol before birth may adversely affect test performance.	• Create a secure and comfortable examiner-child relationship before beginning an assessment. • Use results only to identify significant developmental delays requiring immediate intervention; refrain from making long-term predictions about intellectual growth. • Communicate honestly with parents about their child's test performance, while also describing the test's strengths and weaknesses as an assessment tool.
Early Childhood (2–6) 	• Success on test items that involve naming objects, stacking blocks, drawing circles and squares, remembering short lists, and following simple directions • Short attention span, influencing test performance • Variability in test scores from one occasion to the next	• Significant developmental delays in the early years may indicate mental retardation or other disabilities. • On average, children from lower-income families perform at lower levels on measures of cognitive development than children from middle-income families; however, enriching preschool experiences can narrow and occasionally eliminate the gap.	• Use IQ tests primarily to identify significant delays in cognitive development; follow up by seeking intervention programs for children with such delays. • Provide preschool experiences that foster children's language skills, knowledge of numbers and counting, and visual-spatial thinking.
Middle Childhood (6–10) 	• Success on test items that involve defining concrete words, remembering sentences and short sequences of digits, understanding concrete analogies, recognizing similarities among objects, and identifying absurdities in illogical statements • Some consistency in test scores from one occasion to the next • Noticeable differences among children in mastery of classroom subject matter	• For this age range, many intelligence tests become increasingly verbal in nature; thus proficiency with the English language can significantly affect test performance. • Children with learning disabilities may perform poorly on some parts of an intelligence test. • Children from some ethnic minority groups may perform poorly in situations where the examiner has not established rapport.	• Individualize instruction to match children's varying abilities to learn in particular content domains. • Do *not* assume that poor performance in some domains necessarily indicates limited ability to learn in other areas. • Take children's cultural and linguistic backgrounds into account when interpreting IQ scores.
Early Adolescence (10–14) 	• Success on test items that involve defining commonly used abstract words, drawing logical inferences from verbal descriptions, and identifying similarities between opposite concepts • Considerable individual differences in the ability to understand abstract material	• Some adolescents (especially those from certain ethnic minority groups) may not perceive high test performance as having personal benefits and so may not be motivated to perform at their best. • Some adolescents who are gifted may try to hide their talents; cultures that stress traditional male and female roles may actively discourage females from achieving at high levels.	• Expect considerable diversity in adolescents' ability to master abstract classroom material, and individualize instruction accordingly. • Make sure that school enrichment programs include students from ethnic minority groups; do not rely exclusively on IQ scores to identify students as gifted (see Observation Guidelines table on p. 305).
Late Adolescence (14–18) 	• Success on test items that involve defining infrequently encountered words, identifying differences between similar abstract words, interpreting proverbs, and breaking down complex geometric figures into their component parts • Relative stability in most adolescents' IQ scores • Increasing independence to seek out opportunities consistent with existing ability levels (niche-picking)	• Concerns about appearing "too smart" may continue into the high school years. • Some members of minority groups may underperform because their awareness of negative group stereotypes creates debilitating anxiety during a test (see the discussion of *stereotype threat* on p. 301).	• Provide challenging activities for teenagers who are gifted. • Encourage bright adolescents from lower-income families to pursue a college education, and help them with the logistics of college applications (e.g., applying for financial aid).

Sources: Bayley, 2005; Brooks-Gunn, 2003; Brooks-Gunn et al., 1996; Colombo, 1993; G. A. Davis & Rimm, 1998; S. I. Greenspan & Meisels, 1996; Lukasson et al., 2002; Mayes & Bornstein, 1997; McLoyd, 1998b; Ogbu, 1994; Steele, 1997; Terman & Merrill, 1972; A. Thomas & Chess, 1977; Thorndike et al., 1986; Wechsler, 2002, 2003.

school, we cannot say conclusively that their high achievement is actually the result of their intelligence. Intelligence certainly plays an important role in school performance, but many other factors—motivation, quality of instruction, family resources and support, peer group norms, and so on—are also involved. Second, the relationship between IQ scores and achievement is an imperfect one, with many exceptions. For a variety of reasons, some children with high IQ scores do not perform well in the classroom. And other children achieve at higher levels than would be predicted from their IQ scores alone. Educators and other adults should never base their expectations for children's achievement solely on intelligence test scores.

Group Differences in Intelligence

By design, intelligence tests reveal individual differences in children's general cognitive ability. But what do these tests reveal about *group* differences? In this section we examine research findings related to possible gender, socioeconomic, ethnic, and racial differences in intelligence test performance.

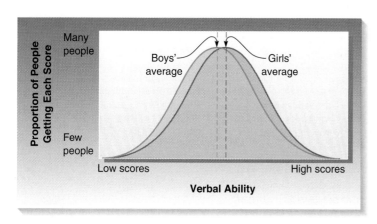

Figure 8-7

Typical "difference" between girls and boys in verbal ability

As you read the upcoming pages, please keep two principles in mind. First, *there is a great deal of individual variability within any group.* We will describe how children of different groups perform on average, yet some children are very different from that "average" description. Second, *there is almost always a great deal of overlap between any two groups.* As an example, consider gender differences in verbal ability. Research studies often find that girls have slightly higher verbal performance than boys (Halpern & LaMay, 2000; Lueptow, 1984; Maccoby & Jacklin, 1974). Yet the difference is typically quite small, with a great deal of overlap between the two groups. Figure 8-7 shows the typical overlap between girls and boys on measures of verbal ability. Notice that many of the boys perform at higher levels than some of the girls, despite the average advantage for girls. Obviously, we could not use such data to make predictions about how particular girls and boys would perform in classrooms and other settings.

Gender Differences

Apart from a greater frequency of mental retardation in boys than girls, there are rarely any significant gender differences in IQ scores (Halpern, 1997; Neisser et al., 1996). This finding is at least partly a function of how intelligence tests are developed: As a general rule, test constructors eliminate any test items on which one gender performs better than the other.

Average differences in more specific cognitive abilities are sometimes found but are usually small. Girls are often slightly better at such verbal tasks as reading and writing (Halpern, 2004; Hedges & Nowell, 1995; Maccoby & Jacklin, 1974). Especially after puberty, boys perform somewhat better on some tasks involving visual-spatial thinking (which require people to imagine two- or three-dimensional figures and mentally manipulate them), and adolescents with extremely high mathematical ability are more likely to be male than female (Benbow, Lubinski, Shea, & Eftekhari-Sanjani, 2000; Eisenberg et al., 1996; Halpern, 1997; Hegarty & Kozhevnikov, 1999). In such domains, however, there is typically a great deal of overlap between the two genders.

Some gender differences in specific intellectual abilities may be partly due to hormonal differences or subtle anatomical differences in the brain (Halpern, 2004; Halpern & LaMay, 2000; O'Boyle & Gill, 1998). Environmental factors appear to play a role as well. In many cultures boys and girls have distinctly different experiences growing up. For instance, in mainstream Western cultures boys are more likely to have toys that require physical manipulation in space (building blocks, model airplanes, footballs, etc.), and such items can foster the development of visual-spatial skills. In contrast, girls are more likely to have dolls, housekeeping items (e.g., dishes, plastic food), and board games—items that are apt to encourage verbal communication with peers (Halpern, 1992; Liss, 1983; Sprafkin, Serbin, Denier, & Connor,

1983). Researchers occasionally observe other patterns of gender differences in particular ethnic groups—for instance, Hispanic girls may demonstrate better visual-spatial ability than Hispanic boys—and such findings are almost certainly due to environment rather than heredity (Huston, 1983; Schratz, 1978).

In recent years, perhaps because of the push for more equitable educational opportunities, males and females have become increasingly similar in their abilities (Eisenberg et al., 1996; Gustafsson & Undheim, 1996; Jacklin, 1989). For all intents and purposes, educators should expect boys and girls to have similar potential in virtually all subject areas. Boys and girls don't always *believe* they have similar abilities, however, as you will discover in Chapter 12.

Connecting Concepts ——————
Chapter 12 describes several differences between boys' and girls' self-perceptions about ability.

Socioeconomic Differences

Intelligence test scores are correlated with socioeconomic status. On average, children from lower-SES families earn somewhat lower IQ scores, and they also perform at lower levels in school, than children from middle-SES families (Brooks-Gunn, 2003; McLoyd, 1998b; Neisser et al., 1996). Children who grow up in persistently impoverished conditions are at greatest risk for poor performance in these respects, but even children who endure only short-term poverty suffer to some degree (McLoyd, 1998b).

Connecting Concepts ——————
Chapter 5 discusses the nature of *socioeconomic status.*

Several factors probably contribute to differences in IQ and school achievement among socioeconomic groups (Berliner, 2005; McLoyd, 1998b; L. S. Miller, 1995). Poor nutrition, lack of health care, and greater-than-average exposure to environmental toxins can impede neurological development. Parents who work long hours (especially single parents) may have little time to spend with their children and may be unable to find or afford high-quality child care (Marshall, 2004). Some parents with limited educational backgrounds may have little knowledge about how best to help children acquire academic skills (P. P. Edwards & Garcia, 1994; Portes, 1996). And a family without a dependable income must, in general, place higher priority on survival and physical well-being than on toys, books, and other materials that nurture children's cognitive growth. Once children begin school, they may lack the knowledge and skills (e.g., familiarity with letters and numbers) upon which more advanced learning depends. Their lower school attendance rates, due to health problems, family crises, and frequent changes of residence, further decrease their opportunities for acquiring the academic skills so critical for their school success.

In addition, teachers—especially those who have grown up in middle-SES families—often have lower academic expectations for children from lower-income homes. As a result, they may give these children less time and attention, fewer opportunities to learn, and less challenging assignments (K. Alexander et al., 1987; McLoyd, 1998b; Rosenthal, 1994). Unwittingly, then, teachers may exacerbate any socioeconomic differences in cognitive ability that already exist.

High-quality preschool programs can boost IQ scores (at least over the short run) and enhance school achievement, and the benefits seem to be greatest for children from low-SES families (e.g., Magnuson, Meyers, Ruhm, & Waldfogel, 2004). Programs that teach parents how to provide stimulating activities for, and interact effectively with, their growing children can also make a difference (F. A. Campbell & Ramey, 1994; Ceci, 2003). And when teachers have high expectations for students from lower-income backgrounds, the students are more likely to perform at high levels (Midgley, Feldlaufer, & Eccles, 1989; M. Phillips, 1997).

Ethnic and Racial Differences

Some measures of early cognitive functioning in infants reveal no differences among ethnic groups (Fagan & Singer, 1983). However, ethnic and racial differences in intelligence and more specific cognitive abilities appear in the preschool years and persist throughout childhood and adolescence. On average, Asian Americans and European Americans outperform African Americans and Hispanic Americans (N. Brody, 1992; Bruer, 1997; McCallum, 1999; Neisser et al., 1996). In some studies Asian Americans score at the highest levels of all, outscoring European Americans by 1 to 5 IQ points (N. Brody, 1992; Flynn, 1991).

Speculations about the source of such differences have prompted considerable debate. In their 1994 book *The Bell Curve,* Richard Herrnstein and Charles Murray used three consistently observed group differences—European American families have higher incomes than

African American families, children from upper- and middle-income families have higher IQ scores than children from lower-income families, and European American children have higher IQ scores than African American children—to conclude that European Americans have a genetic advantage over African Americans. As you might suspect, the book generated considerable controversy and a great deal of outrage.

Scholars have poked many holes in the logic used in *The Bell Curve* (Jacoby & Glauberman, 1995; Marks, 1995; Montagu, 1999b). They find numerous weaknesses in the research studies (most of which were correlational rather than experimental studies) and statistical analyses upon which Herrnstein and Murray based their conclusions. Critics argue that any innate differences in intelligence have not had sufficient time to emerge in human evolution, nor does it seem logical that some groups would evolve to be less adaptive (i.e., less intelligent) than others. They point out, too, that the very concept of *race*, though widely used to categorize people in our society, has no simple basis in biology: It is virtually impossible to identify a person's "race" by analyzing his or her DNA.

In past years some theorists have suggested that cultural bias in intelligence tests explains ethnic and racial differences in IQ scores. Today, however, most theorists believe that the tests themselves are not the primary culprits and suggest that other environmentally based factors—perhaps including socioeconomic status, discrimination, and motivation—are to blame. Let's look at each of these possible explanations.

Cultural bias.   A test has **cultural bias** when one or more of its items either offend or unfairly penalize people of a particular ethnic background, gender, or socioeconomic status, to the point that the validity of the test results is affected. Certain characteristics of intelligence tests may lead some children to attain scores that underestimate their intelligence and ability to achieve long-term academic and professional success. For instance, many contemporary intelligence tests focus on abstract thinking and other cognitive processes important in industrialized Western societies but less relevant to other cultures (J. G. Miller, 1997; Ogbu, 1994). Lack of familiarity with a test's questions and tasks may also hamper children's performance (Heath, 1989; Neisser et al., 1996). Facility with the English language is a factor as well: Children for whom English is a second language perform relatively poorly on test items that are primarily verbal in nature (E. C. Lopez, 1997).

Despite such considerations, cultural bias does not appear to be the primary factor accounting for group differences in IQ. Publishers of intelligence tests routinely employ individuals from diverse backgrounds to ensure that test content is fair and appropriate for students of all races and ethnicities (Linn & Miller, 2005). When children's native language is English, English-based intelligence tests have similar reliability and validity (e.g., they predict future academic performance equally well) for different ethnic and racial groups (R. T. Brown, Reynolds, & Whitaker, 1999; Neisser et al., 1996; Sattler, 2001). Group differences are observed even when tests are intentionally designed to minimize culture-specific content, as is true for the nonverbal UNIT test described earlier (McCallum, 1999; Neisser, 1998a).

Socioeconomic status.   One likely reason for the lower IQ scores of African American and Hispanic American children is that, on average, these children grow up in families and neighborhoods with lower incomes than do European American children (Brooks-Gunn et al., 1996; McLoyd, 1998b). As we've seen, socioeconomic status can affect the quality of prenatal and postnatal nutrition, availability of stimulating toys and books, quality of educational experiences, and a host of other environmental factors influencing intellectual development and test performance. Keep in mind, however, that children from low-income families have many strengths—perhaps creativity with common materials or greater familiarity with everyday household tasks—that their economically advantaged classmates may *not* have.

Discriminatory practices.   Even when different ethnic and racial groups have similar economic resources, systematic and long-term discrimination (e.g., exclusion from better schools and jobs, lower expectations for classroom performance) can limit minority children's opportunities for intellectual growth (Ogbu, 1994). Widespread discrimination may cause heredity to have an indirect effect on intelligence, in that inherited skin color or other physical

---

—————— **Connecting Concepts**
Chapter 2 explains how correlational and experimental studies are different.

—————— **Connecting Concepts**
Chapter 5 describes some of the strengths of children from low-SES backgrounds.

cultural bias
Extent to which an assessment instrument offends or unfairly penalizes some individuals because of their ethnicity, gender, or socioeconomic status.

characteristics (rather than inherited intellectual potential per se) elicit responses from society that affect intellectual development. Following is a helpful analogy:

> Consider a culture in which red-haired children are beaten over the head regularly, but all other children are treated well. . . . The effect of a red-hair gene on red hair is a "direct" genetic effect because the gene affects the color via an internal biochemical process. By contrast. . . . the red-hair genes affect IQ *indirectly*. (N. Block, 1999, pp. 466–467, emphasis added)

Motivation. Many children try to perform at their best on intelligence tests (Flynn, 1991; Ogbu, 1994). But others, including some African American and Hispanic American youngsters, may have little motivation to do well. Some may give minimal answers (e.g., "I don't know") as a way of shortening a testing session that they find confusing and unsettling (Zigler & Finn-Stevenson, 1992). Others may view school achievement of any sort as a form of "acting White" and therefore as something that interferes with their *ethnic identity*—that is, with their sense of "what it means" to belong to a particular ethnic group (Ogbu, 1994). Still others may exhibit a phenomenon known as **stereotype threat:** They perform more poorly, unintentionally and perhaps as a result of excessive anxiety, if they believe that members of their group typically do not do well on particular kinds of tests (McKown & Weinstein, 2003; Osborne & Simmons, 2002; Steele, 1997).

Connecting Concepts
In many cases, however, a strong ethnic identity leads to *high* academic achievement, as you'll discover in Chapter 12.

Undoubtedly, the factors just described have different influences (and in some cases, no influence at all) on how individual children perform on an intelligence test. An encouraging trend is that various ethnic and racial groups have, in recent years, become increasingly similar in IQ scores and other measures of cognitive ability. Such a trend can be attributed only to more equitable environmental conditions across society (Ceci, Rosenblum, & Kumpf, 1998; Huang & Hauser, 1998; Neisser et al., 1996).

Critique of Current Perspectives on Intelligence

At present, the psychological study of intelligence is a virtual minefield of explosive issues: What is intelligence? How should we measure it? How much is it influenced by hereditary (and so presumably unchangeable) factors? Can enriching experiences significantly improve it? The answers to such questions have major implications for educational practice, political decision making, and social policy, but they have not yet been completely answered. In addition, several fundamental concerns about contemporary research and practice related to intelligence and intelligence tests must be raised:

Motivation to do well on an intelligence test increases the IQ scores that children earn, especially on group-administered paper-pencil tests.

● ***Research has relied too heavily on traditional intelligence tests.*** Existing intelligence tests have been designed primarily to identify individuals who may require special interventions or educational services, and in this context they can be quite helpful. Yet researchers have used them in other ways as well—for instance, to make cross-group comparisons, draw conclusions about the relative effects of heredity and environment in intellectual development, and evaluate the effectiveness of preschool programs for low-income children—without due consideration of the appropriateness of IQ tests for such purposes. Traditional intelligence tests are probably too limited to help researchers completely answer broad theoretical questions about the origins and development of intelligence. As psychologist Robert Sternberg once put it, "there is more to intelligence than IQ" (1996, p. 15).

● ***IQ scores are too often interpreted out of context.*** Over the years, the use of intelligence tests has been quite controversial. In earlier decades (as recently as the 1970s), IQ scores were frequently used as the sole criterion for identifying children as having mental retardation. In part as a result of this practice, children from racial and ethnic minority groups were disproportionately represented in special education classes, where their potential for academic achievement was not always recognized or effectively nurtured.

Most clinical and school psychologists, counselors, and other specialists now have sufficient training in psychoeducational assessment to understand that a single IQ score should never warrant a diagnosis of "mental retardation" or any other condition. Decisions about

stereotype threat
Reduction in performance (often unintentional) as a result of a belief that one's group typically performs poorly.

special educational placement and services must always be based on multiple sources of information about a child. Yet many other people (including many teachers) seem to view IQ scores as precise measures of permanent characteristics. For instance, we often hear remarks such as "She has an IQ of such-and-such" spoken in much the same matter-of-fact manner as someone might say "She has brown eyes."

For most children, IQ scores are reasonably accurate reflections of their current cognitive development and learning potential. But for a few children, IQs may be poor summaries of what they can do at present or are likely to do in the future. Teachers and other professionals must be extremely careful not to put too much stock in any single IQ score, especially when working with children from diverse backgrounds.

Some cultures value and nurture abilities that are not reflected in traditional intelligence tests.

● *Assessment of intelligence focuses almost exclusively on skills valued in mainstream Western culture.* The items found on traditional intelligence tests focus on cognitive skills (logical reasoning, abstract thought, etc.) that are valued primarily in middle-class North American, European, and Australian societies (Sternberg, 1996, 2004). Such a bias enhances the tests' ability to predict students' school achievement because schools in these societies place heavy emphasis on the same set of skills.

Yet other cultural and socioeconomic groups value and nurture other abilities that may be equally beneficial for children's long-term academic and professional success. For example, cooperation is a valued skill in Mexican culture, and so Mexican American children often show exceptional skill in cooperating with peers (Abi-Nader, 1993; Okagaki & Sternberg, 1993; Vasquez, 1990). African American children may show particular talent in oral language—more specifically, in colorful speech, creative storytelling, or humor (Torrance, 1989). In Navajo culture, intelligence may be reflected in a child's ability to help the family and tribe, to perform cultural rituals, or to demonstrate expert craftsmanship (Kirschenbaum, 1989). In parts of Polynesia, it might be reflected in art, music, or dance (N. Reid, 1989). Ultimately, we can gain a better understanding of children's intellectual abilities only when we broaden the ways in which we assess those abilities.

● *Intelligence tests overlook dispositions and metacognitive strategies that are important contributors to intellectual functioning.* Most descriptions and measures of intelligence focus on specific things that a child *can* do (abilities), with little consideration of what a child is *likely* to do (dispositions). Intelligence tests don't evaluate the extent to which children view a situation from multiple perspectives, examine data with a critical eye, regulate their own learning, and metacognitively reflect on their thoughts and actions. Yet such qualities are often just as important as intellectual ability in determining success in academic and real-world tasks (Kuhn, 2001a; Perkins, 1995; Perkins, Tishman, Ritchhart, Donis, & Andrade, 2000).

● *Many theorists have placed higher priority on assessing current intelligence than on developing future intelligence.* Implicit in the practice of intelligence testing is the assumption that intelligence is a relatively fixed, and perhaps largely inherited, ability. In our view, there has been entirely too much focus on sorting children and entirely too little on fostering their development. Fortunately, some psychologists and educators are now calling for a shift in focus from the *assessment* of intelligence to the *development* of intelligence (Boykin, 1994; P. D. Nichols & Mittelholtz, 1997; Sternberg et al., 2000). As theorists and researchers gain a better understanding of the nature of intelligence and the environmental factors that promote it, societies and schools can, we hope, shift to a more proactive approach, one in which all children are given the opportunities and resources they need to maximize their intellectual growth.

Implications of Theories and Research on Intelligence

Given existing knowledge about the nature and development of intelligence, as well as our concerns about shortcomings in the field, we offer the following suggestions to teachers and other practitioners who work with infants, children, and adolescents:

● *Maintain a healthy skepticism about the accuracy of IQ scores.* Intelligence tests can, in many cases, provide a general idea of children's current cognitive functioning. Yet IQ scores are rarely dead-on measures of what children can do. As we have seen, the scores of young children can vary considerably from one testing to the next and are not always accurate predictors of children's future academic success. Furthermore, the scores of children from diverse ethnic and linguistic groups are often affected by background experiences, motivation, and English proficiency. We cannot stress this point enough: IQ scores should *never* be used as the sole criterion in making diagnoses and decisions about children.

● *Support early intervention programs in your community.* Early intervention is especially important for infants and toddlers with developmental disabilities, as well as for those living in low-income neighborhoods or unstable family settings. Such intervention can take the form of regular checkups and nutritional support for pregnant women, stimulating infant care and preschool programs, or suggestions and materials for helping inexperienced parents nurture their children's cognitive growth at home. Intervention is most effective when it integrates a variety of services into a single support network and considers children's physical, social, and emotional needs as well as their cognitive development (S. Loeb et al., 2004; Shonkoff & Phillips, 2000). Ideally, then, teachers who work with young children at risk for academic difficulties should closely coordinate their efforts with health care professionals, social workers, and other professionals who are actively involved in nurturing children's development.

● *Be open-minded about the ways in which children might demonstrate intelligence.* As we've seen, some psychologists believe that human intelligence isn't a single entity—that it is, instead, a collection of relatively separate abilities that children may have to varying degrees. Take a multiple-intelligences perspective as you try the following "Sunflower" exercise.

INTERPRETING CHILDREN'S ARTIFACTS AND ACTIONS   Sunflower

To the right are 10-year-old Amaryth's drawings of a sunflower and an insect that she found on it. Identify one or more of Gardner's multiple intelligences that Amaryth put to use in creating the drawings. You may want to refer back to Table 8-1 (p. 280) as you do this exercise.

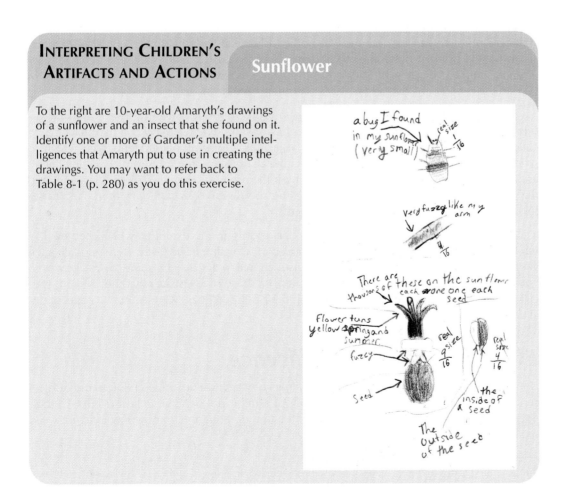

Amaryth certainly needed to rely on her naturalist intelligence to detect patterns in the sunflower's seeds. She also made good use of her spatial intelligence to measure the insect and various parts of the sunflower and then to magnify the objects as she sketched them (notice her references to "real size"). And to some degree she drew on her linguistic intelligence as she tried to capture in words the very nonverbal nature of what she was seeing. For example, notice how she used an analogy to describe the sunflower's stem ("very fuzzy like my arm").

To the extent that intelligence is culture-dependent, intelligent behavior is likely to take different forms in children from different cultural backgrounds (Gardner, 1995; Neisser et al., 1996; Perkins, 1995; Sternberg, 1985). The Observation Guidelines table "Seeing Intelligence in Children's Daily Behavior" presents a variety of behaviors that may reflect higher intelligence than children's IQ scores reveal.

● *Capitalize on children's individual strengths and abilities when teaching new topics and skills.* Gardner's theory, in particular, encourages educators to use a variety of approaches in instruction, building on the diverse abilities that different children may have (Gardner, 1999, 2000b; M. Kornhaber et al., 2004). For instance, the following scenario illustrates how some children may learn more effectively when they can use their visual-spatial skills:

> In third grade, Jason loved to build with blocks, legos, toothpicks, popsicle sticks, anything that fit together. During a unit on ancient history, Jason built an object for every culture studied. He fashioned Babylonian ziggurats out of legos, Egyptian pyramids with toothpicks and small marshmallows, the Great Wall of China from miniature clay bricks which he made, the Greek Parthenon from styrofoam computer-packing, Roman bridges out of popsicle sticks and brads, and Mayan temples with molded plastic strips resurrected from an old science kit. While appearing apathetic during most classroom activities, Jason was highly animated during his building projects. History came alive for Jason when he could build the structures of each era and culture studied. (L. Campbell et al., 1998, p. 79)

● *Promote more "intelligent" cognitive strategies.* Look back once again at the chapter's opening case study. Gina's relative weakness in history is due largely to her ineffective study strategies. In fact, teachers, parents, and other adults can promote more effective learning, studying, and problem solving—and in doing so can promote more intelligent behavior—by teaching children more sophisticated and effective cognitive and metacognitive strategies (Perkins, 1995; Perkins & Grotzer, 1997; Sternberg, 2002).

● *Give children the support they need to think more intelligently.* The notion of distributed intelligence tells us that intelligent behavior should be relatively commonplace when children have the right physical tools, social groups, and symbolic systems with which to work (Barab & Plucker, 2002; Pea, 1993). Rather than asking the question, "How intelligent are these children?" educators might instead ask themselves, "How can I help these children think as intelligently as possible? What tools and social networks can I give them? What useful concepts and procedures can I teach them?"

Children and adolescents often differ considerably in the extent to which they display intelligent thinking and behavior. For the most part, educators can easily accommodate such variability within the context of normal instructional practices. In some cases, however, young learners have ability levels so different from those of age-mates that they require special educational services to help them reach their full potential. We turn now to exceptionalities in intelligence.

Exceptionalities in Intelligence

No matter how we define or measure intelligence, we find that some children and adolescents show exceptional talent and others show significant cognitive delays relative to their peers. The two ends of the intelligence continuum are commonly known as *giftedness* and *mental retardation.*[5]

---

[5]In the United States, different states may establish somewhat different criteria for these two categories, especially with regard to determining eligibility for special educational services.

OBSERVATION GUIDELINES

Seeing Intelligence in Children's Daily Behavior

Characteristic	Look For	Example	Implication
Oral Language Skills	• Sophisticated vocabulary • Colorful speech • Creative storytelling • Clever jokes and puns	LaMarr entertains his friends with clever "Your momma's so fat . . ." jokes.	Look for unusual creativity or advanced language development in children's everyday speech.
Learning Ability	• Ability to learn new information quickly • Exceptional knowledge about a variety of topics • Ability to find relationships among diverse ideas • Excellent memory	Four-year-old Gina teaches herself to read using several reading primers she finds at home. Initially, her mother identifies a few words for her. From these words she deduces many letter-sound correspondences that enable her to decipher additional words.	Make note of situations in which children learn and comprehend new material more quickly than their peers. Look for creative analogies and interconnections.
Problem-Solving Skills	• Ability to solve challenging problems • Flexibility in applying previously learned strategies to new kinds of problems • Ability to improvise with commonplace objects and materials	A fourth-grade class plans to perform a skit during an upcoming open house. When the children puzzle about how to hang a sheet from the ceiling (to serve as a stage curtain), Jeff suggests that they turn their desks to face the side of the classroom rather than the front. This way, the sheet can be hung from a light fixture that runs the length of the room.	Present unusual tasks and problems for which children have no ready-made strategies.
Cognitive and Metacognitive Strategies	• Use of sophisticated learning strategies • Desire to understand rather than memorize • Effective comprehension monitoring	Shannon, a sixth grader, explains that she learned the countries on South America's west coast (Colombia, Ecuador, Peru, Chile) by creating the sentence, "*Co*lin *e*ats *p*eas and *ch*ocolate."	Ask children to describe how they think about the things they are trying to learn and remember.
Curiosity and Inquisitiveness	• Voracious appetite for knowledge • Tendency to ask a lot of questions • Intrinsic motivation to master challenging subject matter	Alfredo reads every book and article he can find about outer space. He has a particular interest in black holes.	Find out what children like to do in their free time.
Leadership and Social Skills	• Ability to persuade and motivate others • Exceptional sensitivity to other people's feelings and body language • Ability to mediate disagreements and help others reach reasonable compromises	As a high school student, Gina organizes and directs a schoolwide peer tutoring program.	Observe how children interact with their peers at play, in cooperative group work, and in extracurricular activities.

Sources: B. Clark, 1997; A. W. Gottfried et al., 1994; Lupart, 1995; Maker, 1993; Maker & Schiever, 1989; Perkins, 1995; Torrance, 1989, 1995; R. Turnbull et al., 2004; Winner, 1997.

Giftedness

Gina, described in the opening case study and revisited in the Observation Guidelines table, is an example of someone who is gifted (you may also see the term *gifted and talented*). In general, **giftedness** is unusually high ability or aptitude in one or more areas (e.g., math, science, creative writing, art, or music) to the point where special educational services are necessary to help a youngster meet his or her full potential (e.g., Gromko, 2004; U.S. Department of Education, 1993). When we try to pin down giftedness more precisely, we find considerable disagreement about how to do so (K. R. Carter, 1991; Keogh & MacMillan, 1996). Many school districts identify students as gifted primarily on the basis of general IQ scores, often using 125 or 130 as a minimum cutoff point. But some experts argue that multiple criteria—perhaps creativity and motivation as well as IQ scores—should be applied when determining children's eligibility for special services (Council for Exceptional Children, 1995; Renzulli & Reis, 1986; Sternberg & Zhang, 1995).

Children who are gifted are typically very different from one another in their particular strengths and talents, but as a group they tend to share certain characteristics. Typically, they

giftedness
Unusually high ability in one or more areas, to the point where children require special educational services to help them meet their full potential.

process information more quickly and remember it more easily, have more advanced reasoning and metacognitive skills, and use more effective learning and problem-solving strategies (K. R. Carter & Ormrod, 1982; Steiner & Carr, 2003; Winner, 1997, 2000). Often they have an exceptional drive to learn, seek out new challenges, make their own discoveries, and master tasks with little instruction from others (D. A. Greenspan, Solomon, & Gardner, 2004; Winner, 2000). They tend to set extremely high standards for their performance, sometimes to the point of unrealistic perfectionism (W. D. Parker, 1997). Most have high self-esteem, good social skills, and above-average emotional adjustment, although a few extremely gifted children have social or emotional difficulties because they are so very different from their peers (A. W. Gottfried et al., 1994; Keogh & MacMillan, 1996; Silverman, 1994). In the following "Solar System" exercise, you can observe several qualities of giftedness firsthand.

INTERPRETING CHILDREN'S ARTIFACTS AND ACTIONS   Solar System

As an assignment for one of Jeanne's classes, a graduate student conducted the following interview with her 7½-year-old daughter, whom we'll call "Mia." As you read the interview, look for characteristics that suggest exceptional intelligence.

Mom: What are you learning in science?
Mia: The solar system.
Mom: What are you learning about the solar system?
Mia: The planets.
Mom: What are you learning about the planets?
Mia: There are only eight planets.
Mom: How do you know that?
Mia: The teacher taught us a poem to help us remember.
Mom: What was the poem?
Mia: My Very Educated Mother Just Served Us Nine Pizzas.
Mom: What does that stand for?
Mia: Mercury, Venus, Earth, Mars, Jupiter, Saturn, Uranus, Neptune, Pluto. (She counts the planets on her fingers a couple of times.) Oops, there are nine planets, not eight. I made a mistake.
Mom: Anything else you want to share?
Mia: Yeah. Pluto is the farthest planet from the sun and the smallest planet. Earth and Mars are the only planets to have moons. Mars has two moons and the Earth has only one. . . . [Pluto] has the largest orbit around the sun, and it was discovered in 1936, and it takes 284 years to go around the sun one time.

Mom: How do you know all that?
Mia: I picture outside space in my head and I can see all the planets outside in space, and I keep looking until I see Pluto.
Mom: How do you remember when Pluto was discovered and how long it takes for Pluto to go one time around the sun?
Mia: I remember 1936 because I was born in 1996, that sounds a lot like 1936. To remember that it is 284 days [she previously said 284 *years,* so apparently misspeaks here], I just hear the teacher saying it in my head and thinking that is a really long time.
Mom: Any other facts you want to share?
Mia: Venus is the second planet away from the sun. It's always very cloudy there and really hot. It's the hottest planet.
Mom: While you were talking with me, all these ideas came to your head. How did you remember all this information?
Mia: I was thinking I was a spaceman and I just lifted off from Earth and crash-landed on Venus. I was dying there. So I recharged my ship and came back to Earth.
Mom: Why were you dying there?
Mia: All the clouds around Venus were trapping the heat in. It was very hot, so I wanted to leave. (interview courtesy of an anonymous student)

You undoubtedly noticed the sheer *quantity* of what Mia remembers about the solar system. Her knowledge is quite remarkable for a 7-year-old. You may also have picked up on her metacognitive skills: Mia can easily reflect on and describe her own thought processes. In addition, Mia seems to have depended more on elaboration than on rehearsal to remember facts about the planets. For instance, to remember that Venus is cloudy and hot, she imagined this scenario: "I was a spaceman and I just lifted off from Earth and crash-landed on Venus. . . . All the clouds around Venus were trapping the heat in. It was very hot, so I wanted to leave." Given Mia's obvious engagement with the subject matter during the lesson, we might guess that she is a highly motivated and self-regulating learner. All of these qualities—exceptional knowledge and memory, advanced metacognitive skills, effective learning strategies, high motivation, and self-regulated learning—are telltale signs of giftedness.

Giftedness may be partly an inherited characteristic. Some individuals who are gifted show unusual brain development, perhaps advanced development in the right hemisphere

——————— Connecting Concepts
As you learned in Chapter 7, intentional use of elaboration usually doesn't emerge until puberty.

or greater involvement of both hemispheres in performing certain kinds of tasks (Winner, 2000). Environmental factors probably play a significant role as well (B. Clark, 1997; A. W. Gottfried et al., 1994; Shavinina & Ferrari, 2004). For instance, children who are gifted are more likely to be firstborn or only-born children, who generally have more attention and stimulation from their parents than other children do. Children who are gifted also tend to have many opportunities to practice and enhance their abilities from a very early age, long before they have been identified as being gifted. And they are more likely to seek out enriching opportunities—an example of the *niche-picking* phenomenon described earlier.

As is true for Gina in the opening case study, a child's giftedness is often evident throughout childhood and adolescence. Some children show signs of advanced cognitive and linguistic development as early as 18 months of age (A. W. Gottfried et al., 1994). Yet others are "late bloomers": Their talents become evident relatively late in the game, perhaps as environmental conditions bring such talents to fruition.

Fostering the development of children who are gifted.   Gifted students tend to be among our schools' greatest underachievers. When required to progress at the same rate as their nongifted peers, they achieve at levels far short of their capabilities (K. R. Carter, 1991; Gallagher, 1991; Reis, 1989). Drawing on Vygotsky's theory of cognitive development, we could say that children who are gifted are unlikely to be working within their zone of proximal development if they are limited to the same tasks assigned to their peers, diminishing their opportunities to develop more advanced cognitive skills. In the "Intrinsic Motivation: Middle Childhood" video clip on Observation CD 1, 9-year-old Elena reveals her desire for challenge in her description of PEAK, a program at her school for students who are gifted:

In the "Intrinsic Motivation: Middle Childhood" clip on Observation CD 1, observe Elena's desire for a challenging curriculum.

Adult: What do you like best about school?
Elena: I like PEAK. . . . It's for smart kids who have, like, good ideas for stuff you could do. And so they make it more challenging for you in school. So instead of third-grade math, you get fourth-grade math.

Many students with special gifts and talents become bored or frustrated when their school experiences don't provide tasks and assignments that challenge them and help them develop their unique abilities (Feldhusen, 1989; Feldhusen, Van Winkle, & Ehle, 1996; Winner, 2000). They may lose interest in school tasks and put in only the minimum effort they need to get by in the classroom, as Geoff, a gifted 11th grader, reveals in the letter shown in Figure 8-8.

Dear Mr. P—— [the school principal]:

I have found in recent months that it is time for me to make the next step in my life. This step is graduation. I would like to graduate a year early in May, this year, with the class of 2002.

This is a step I have chosen as the best for me for several reasons. The first reason is that I would like to spend a semester studying abroad in Austria. I have chosen Austria because it is a country where German is spoken and this is the language I have been learning for four years. . . .

I have also decided to graduate because several people have suggested that this is my best option, as they believe that I am at a maturity level that indicates I should move on. These people, among others, are primarily my parents, my advisor, and the school counselor. They suggest that I am ready to graduate, but perhaps not ready for college, which is why I've chosen to do a foreign exchange and give myself time to further mature and prepare for college.

Besides these reasons, I personally believe that I would have extreme difficulty attending school next year and succeeding.

I have been told that this same thing is seen every year, when seniors become tired of attending, as they lack the motivation to succeed. I am afraid that this would happen to me, but on a higher level, as I already feel that I am losing motivation. Attending school next year could mean dire consequences for my transcript, my G.P.A., and my life.

When speaking with [the school counselor], we decided that I need to finish an internship and one job shadow, and I will have the credits necessary to graduate by the end of the school year. I plan to set up several internships over a period of five days in five different fields of engineering, so I can get an idea of what each field is like. . . .

I hope you understand my reasons for leaving and I am sure that you will support me in my decision to graduate early. It will be difficult to change in such a gigantic way, but it will be very beneficial for me in the end.

Sincerely,

Geoff A——

Figure 8-8

Many students who are gifted lose interest in school when not sufficiently challenged by classroom activities. Here are excerpts from a letter in which Geoff, an 11th grader, requests permission to graduate early. School officials found his rationale convincing and complied with his request.

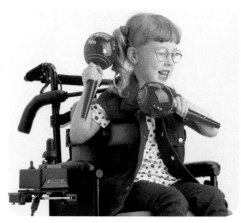

Some children who are gifted also have disabilities—possibly learning disabilities, emotional disorders, or physical challenges. This girl's teacher must take both her giftedness and her physical disability into account when planning instruction.

Yet some children and adolescents try to hide their exceptional talents. They may fear that peers will ridicule them for their high academic abilities and enthusiasm for academic topics, especially at the secondary school level (Covington, 1992; DeLisle, 1984). Girls in particular are likely to hide their talents, especially if they have been raised in cultures that do not value high achievement in females (Covington, 1992; G. A. Davis & Rimm, 1998; M. L. Nichols & Ganschow, 1992). Gifted Asian Americans, because of cultural traditions of obedience, conformity, and respect for authority, may be reluctant to engage in creative activities and may willingly comply when asked to perform unchallenging assignments (Maker & Schiever, 1989).

Several strategies for helping children and adolescents with exceptional abilities maximize their potential are presented and illustrated in the Development and Practice feature "Addressing the Unique Needs of Gifted Children and Adolescents."

Keep in mind that a child can be gifted and also have a disability. For example, some children with exceptional gifts and talents have learning disabilities, ADHD, autism, emotional disorders, or physical or sensory challenges (e.g., Hettinger & Knapp, 2001; Moran & Gardner, 2006). In such situations teachers and other practitioners must, when planning instruction, address the disabilities as well as the areas of giftedness. A few gifted children—for example, those with a limited English background or those who have specific learning disabilities—may even need some training in basic skills (Brown-Mizuno, 1990; C. R. Harris, 1991; Udall, 1989).

Mental Retardation

Children with **mental retardation** show developmental delays in most aspects of their academic and social functioning. A child must exhibit two characteristics before a diagnosis of mental retardation is appropriate (American Association on Mental Retardation, 1992; Keogh & MacMillan, 1996; R. Turnbull et al., 2004):

- *Significantly below-average general intelligence.* Children with mental retardation perform poorly on traditional intelligence tests, with IQ scores being no higher than 65 or 70 (reflecting performance in the bottom 2 percent of the age-group). In addition, they learn slowly and perform quite poorly on school tasks in comparison with age-mates, and they show consistently poor achievement across virtually all academic subject areas.

- *Deficits in adaptive behavior.* Low intelligence test scores and poor academic performance are insufficient evidence to classify children as having mental retardation. An additional criterion is a deficit in **adaptive behavior,** which includes *practical intelligence* (management of the ordinary activities of daily living) and *social intelligence* (appropriate conduct in social situations). In these areas children and adolescents with mental retardation often exhibit behaviors typical of individuals much younger than themselves.

——— **Study Guide and Reader**
Supplementary Reading 8-2 provides more detail on the nature of adaptive behavior as a criterion for diagnosing mental retardation.

mental retardation
Disability marked by significantly below-average general intelligence and deficits in adaptive behavior.

adaptive behavior
Behavior related to daily living skills and appropriate conduct in social situations.

Children and adolescents with mental retardation show impairments in many aspects of information processing, including attention, working memory, executive functioning, learning strategies, and metacognition. They have trouble generalizing what they learn to new situations and often exhibit a sense of helplessness about their ability to learn new things (Borkowski & Burke, 1996; Butterfield & Ferretti, 1987; Dempster & Corkill, 1999; Seligman, 1975; R. Turnbull et al., 2004). Their play activities are the kinds that would ordinarily be observed in much younger children (F. P. Hughes, 1998; Malone, Stoneham, & Langone, 1995).

Mental retardation is often caused by abnormal genetic conditions (e.g., Down syndrome). Sometimes mental retardation runs in families, such that many family members' abilities fall at the lower end of the normal distribution of intelligence (Kail, 1998). Yet heredity is not always to blame. Some instances of mental retardation are due to noninherited biological causes, such as severe malnutrition or substance abuse during the mother's pregnancy (e.g., recall our earlier discussion of fetal alcohol syndrome), oxygen deprivation associated with a difficult birth, or environmental toxins (Keogh & MacMillan, 1996; McLoyd, 1998b; Streissguth et al., 1994; Vogel, 1997). Conditions in the home, such as parental neglect or an extremely impoverished and unstimulating home life, may also be at fault (Batshaw & Shapiro, 1997; Feuerstein, 1979; M. M. Wagner, 1995). Undoubtedly as a result of such factors as malnutrition, ingestion of lead dust in old buildings, and other environmental hazards, children from poor, inner-city neighborhoods are overrepresented among school children who are identified as having mental retardation (U.S. Department of Education, Office of Civil Rights, 1993).

Fostering the development of children with mental retardation.   The great majority of children and adolescents with mental retardation attend school, and many of them are capable of mastering a wide variety of academic and vocational skills. The Development and Practice feature "Maximizing the Development of Children and Adolescents with Mental Retardation" presents and illustrates several effective strategies.

Teachers and other adults must remember that children with mental retardation have many strengths and that they are more likely to master new knowledge and skills when instruction builds on what they know and do well. In *Expecting Adam,* Martha Beck (1999) describes how her son Adam, who has Down syndrome, learned the alphabet. Soon after Adam turned 3, Beck and her husband began regular drills on alphabet letters, but they made little progress until they stumbled on a different instructional approach 3 years later:

> [F]rom the time he started preschool at three, we kept running Adam through the alphabet, repeating the name of each letter, along with its major sound, thousands and thousands of times in the strained voices of tourists who believe they can overcome any language barrier by sheer volume.
>
> It didn't work. When quizzed without prompting, Adam never recognized the letters on his own. By the time he was six I was ready to give up.
>
> Then one day John [Adam's father] was holding up a plastic letter and making its sound, which happened to be "EEEEEEE," when Adam suddenly perked up and said, "Wizbef!" This is the way he pronounces his sister Elizabeth's name. . . . During that day, we discovered that Adam's learning capacity went way beyond anything we expected—as long as everything he learned related directly to someone he cared about. He had absolutely no interest in, for example, "E is for egg." But E for Elizabeth—now *that* was crucial information.
>
> In the end we all learned the alphabet this way. The symbols we had been trying to link to abstract sounds ended up as a parade of personalities: Adam first, of course, and then Billy, Caleb, Diane, Elizabeth, Francine, Grandpa . . . As we figured out how he learned, the landscape of our son's mind began to reveal itself to us. Instead of a rationally constructed structure of empirical observations, logical conclusions, and arbitrary symbols, Adam's mental world seems to be more like a huge family reunion. It is a gathering of people, all linked by Adam's affection into a complex universe of relationships and characteristics. In this world, Adam learned as fast as anyone I know. Long before he could read or write even the most basic words (or so I thought), Adam came home to tell me, in his garbled tongue, about the new boy who had just moved into his class, and who had become Adam's friend. When I couldn't understand his pronunciation of the boy's name, Adam grabbed a pencil in his stubby, grubby little-boy fingers, and wrote "Miguel Fernando de la Hoya" on a piece of paper—a piece of paper, needless to say, which I intend to frame. (M. Beck, 1999, pp. 314–315)[6]

---

[6]From EXPECTING ADAM by Martha Beck, copyright © 1999 by Martha Beck. Used by permission of Times Books, a division of Random House, Inc.

DEVELOPMENT AND PRACTICE

Maximizing the Development of Children and Adolescents with Mental Retardation

- Encourage infants to use the strengths they have, and offer opportunities and support for acquiring new knowledge and skills.

  An 18-month-old who has mental retardation and physical disabilities has recently begun attending an infant care center. His caregiver thinks creatively about how to help him interact with his physical environment. For example, she glues Popsicle sticks to the pages of cardboard books so that he can easily grab them and turn the pages. To help him feel secure in his infant chair, she puts skid-proof material on the seat of the chair and cushions at the sides to keep him upright.

- Introduce new material at a slower pace, and provide many opportunities for practice.

  A fourth-grade teacher gives a student only two new addition facts a week, primarily because any more than two seem to overwhelm him. Every day, the teacher has the student practice writing the new facts and review addition facts learned in previous weeks.

- Explain tasks concretely and in very specific language.

  An art teacher gives a student explicit training in the steps she needs to take at the end of each painting session: (1) Rinse the paintbrush at the sink, (2) put the brush and watercolor paints on the shelf in the back room, and (3) put the painting on the counter by the window to dry. Initially, the

teacher needs to remind the student of every step in the process. However, with time and practice, the student eventually carries out the process independently.

- Give explicit guidance about how to study.

  A teacher tells a student, "When you study a new spelling word, it helps if you repeat the letters out loud while you practice writing the word. Let's try it with *house,* the word you are learning this morning. Watch how I repeat the letters—H . . . O . . . U . . . S . . . E—as I write the word. Now you try doing what I just did."

- Give feedback about specific behaviors rather than about general areas of performance.

  A vocational educator tells a student, "You did a good job in wood shop this week. You followed my instructions correctly, and you put away the equipment when I asked you to do so."

- Encourage independence.

  A life skills instructor shows a student how to use her calculator to figure out how much she needs to pay for lunch every day. The instructor also gives the student considerable practice in identifying the correct bills and coins to use when paying various amounts.

Sources: Fletcher & Bray, 1996; Patton, Blackbourn, & Fad, 1996; Perkins, 1995; R. Turnbull et al., 2004.

Although usually a long-term condition, mental retardation is not necessarily a lifelong disability, especially when the presumed cause is environmental rather than genetic (Beirne-Smith, Ittenbach, & Patton, 1998; Landesman & Ramey, 1989). Our final case study illustrates just how much of a difference environment can make.

Case Study: Fresh Vegetables

Twelve-year-old Steven had no known genetic or other organic problems but had been officially labeled as having mental retardation based on his low scores on a series of intelligence tests. His prior schooling had been limited to just part of one year in a first-grade classroom in inner-city Chicago. His mother had kept him home after a bullet grazed his leg while he was walking to school one morning. Fearing for her son's safety, she would not let him outside the apartment after that, not even to play, and certainly not to walk the six blocks to the local elementary school.

When a truant officer finally appeared at the door one evening 5 years later, Steven and his mother quickly packed their bags and moved to a small town in northern Colorado. They found residence with Steven's aunt, who persuaded Steven to go back to school. After considering Steven's intelligence and achievement test scores, the school psychologist recommended that he attend a summer school class for students with special needs.

Steven's summer school teacher soon began to suspect that Steven's main problem might simply be a lack of the background experiences necessary for academic success. One incident in particular stands out in her mind. The class had been studying nutrition, and so she had asked her students to bring in some fresh vegetables to make a large salad for their morning snack. Steven brought in a can of green beans. When a classmate objected that the beans weren't fresh, Steven replied, "The hell they ain't! Me and Momma got them off the shelf this morning!"

If Steven didn't know what *fresh* meant, the teacher reasoned, then he might also be lacking many of the other facts and skills on which any academic curriculum is inevitably based. She and the teachers who followed her worked hard to help Steven make up for all those years in Chicago during which he had experienced and learned so little. By the time Steven reached high school, he was enrolling in regular classes and maintaining a 3.5 grade-point-average.[a]

- Did Steven have mental retardation? Why or why not?
- The school psychologist recommended that Steven be placed in a special class for students with special needs. Was such a class an appropriate placement for Steven? Why or why not?

Once you have answered these questions, compare your responses with those presented in the appendix.

[a]Adapted from D. L. Jackson & Ormrod, 1998.

Summary

Characterizing Intelligence

Intelligence involves effective learning processes and adaptive behavior and may manifest itself differently in different cultures. Some theorists believe that intelligence is a single entity (a general factor, or g) that influences children's learning and performance across a wide variety of tasks and subject areas. This belief is reflected in the widespread use of IQ scores as general estimates of academic ability. In contrast, other theorists (e.g., Gardner, Sternberg) propose that intelligence consists of a number of somewhat independent abilities and therefore cannot be accurately reflected in a single IQ score. There is growing recognition that children are more likely to behave "intelligently" when they have physical, social, and symbolic support systems to help them in their efforts.

Measuring Intelligence

Most intelligence tests have been developed primarily to identify individuals who have special needs (e.g., those who are gifted or have mental retardation). Contemporary intelligence tests include a variety of tasks designed to assess what people have learned and deduced from their everyday experiences. Performance on these tests is usually summarized by one or more IQ scores, which are determined by comparing an individual's performance with the performance of others of the same age. In some instances specific ability tests or dynamic assessment may be more useful for evaluating children's capabilities in specific areas or predicting their ability to benefit from certain kinds of instruction. Tests for infants and young children are often helpful in identifying those who have significant developmental delays. However, results of tests given to small children should not be used to make long-term predictions about cognitive development.

Hereditary and Environmental Influences

Studies with twins and adopted children indicate that intelligence may be partly an inherited characteristic. But environmental conditions, including nutrition, toxic substances, home environment, enriching preschool programs, and formal schooling, can also have a significant impact on IQ scores. Heredity and environment interact in their influence, to the point where it may be virtually impossible to separate the relative effects of each on children's intellectual development.

Developmental Trends and Group Differences

Performance on intelligence tests predicts school achievement to some degree, with IQ scores becoming increasingly stable and having greater predictive power as children grow older. Nevertheless, some children's IQ scores change considerably over time, especially during the early years.

On average, children from low-income families earn lower IQ scores than children from middle-income families. Males and females perform similarly on general tests of intelligence, although slight gender differences are sometimes observed on measures of specific cognitive abilities. Average differences in IQ scores are frequently found among various ethnic and racial groups, with substantial evidence indicating that environmental factors are at the root of these differences.

Critique of Current Perspectives

Research on intelligence has relied heavily on traditional intelligence tests, which emphasize skills valued in mainstream Western culture and overlook dispositions and metacognitive strategies as important contributors to intellectual performance. Some theorists are now calling for a shift in focus from the assessment of intelligence to its *nurturance*.

Implications of Theory and Research on Intelligence

Used within the context of other information, intelligence tests can often provide a general idea of children's current cognitive functioning. Yet educators and other practitioners should remain optimistic about every child's potential for intellectual growth. They should anticipate that different children will be intelligent in different ways and should capitalize on children's unique strengths and abilities to promote learning and achievement. And they should give children the social support and the physical and symbolic tools that can enhance intelligent thinking and performance.

Exceptionalities in Intelligence

Children and adolescents identified as being gifted show exceptional achievement or promise in one or more content domains. Giftedness may reflect itself differently in different cultures, but in general, gifted individuals demonstrate rapid learning, advanced reasoning, and sophisticated cognitive strategies. In contrast, mental retardation is characterized by low general intellectual functioning and deficits in adaptive behavior. In individual children, either kind of exceptionality may have genetic roots, environmental causes, or both. Children with unusually high or low intelligence maximize their cognitive development when instruction is geared to specific strengths and weaknesses.

Applying Concepts in Child Development

In this chapter you encountered five different perspectives on the nature of intelligence: Spearman's general factor (*g*) and specific factors, Cattell's fluid intelligence and crystallized intelligence, Gardner's multiple intelligences, Sternberg's triarchic theory, and distributed intelligence. The following table presents descriptions of children and adolescents at each age level, one or more theoretical perspectives that some of the descriptions reflect, and potential educational implications. Apply what you've learned about intelligence to fill in the empty cells in the table. When you're done, compare your responses with those in Table 8-1 in the *Study Guide and Reader*.

APPLYING CONCEPTS IN CHILD DEVELOPMENT · Using Various Theories of Intelligence to Understand Youngsters' Behaviors

Age	A Youngster's Experience	Developmental Concepts *Applying Theories of Intelligence to Patterns in Youngsters' Behaviors*	Implications *Helping Youngsters Reach Their Full Potential*
Infancy (Birth–2)	When Meghan was born, features of her face, fingers, and toes made it clear that she has Down syndrome. Now almost 2, Meghan has just a few words in her speaking vocabulary, and she learns new things more slowly than her age-mates. She has only recently learned to walk and also shows delays in learning to feed and dress herself.		When children show delays in many different areas, identify a variety of interventions that can support their development in each domain. For example, when working with children with mental retardation, provide explicit instruction not only in cognitive and linguistic skills but also in adaptive behaviors.
Early Childhood (2–6)	Five-year-old Robin has discovered many addition and subtraction facts on her own and is now insisting that her mother help her understand what multiplication is. Robin also enjoys taking apart small household gadgets (e.g., ballpoint pens, flashlights) to see how they work. Yet she is a physically awkward child who has had trouble learning such skills as tying shoes, and she seems at a loss about how to play with the other children in her kindergarten class.	Robin shows strengths and weaknesses consistent with Gardner's theory of *multiple intelligences*. In particular, she seems to be stronger in logical-mathematical intelligence than in bodily-kinesthetic intelligence and interpersonal intelligence.	Provide experiences that help children develop both their strong and weak areas. Use their strengths as a way of getting them actively engaged in activities in which they can also work on their weaknesses. For example, if a child is strong in math and science but weak in social skills, have the child practice social skills in a cooperative group project with one or two classmates who also have high logical-mathematical intelligence.
Middle Childhood (6–10)	When it comes to learning and remembering things about African American history, 9-year-old Tyrone is like a sponge, absorbing almost everything he reads. He explains his good memory this way: "When I'm reading something, I keep asking myself questions about it and then try to answer them. If I can't answer a question, I go back and read the stuff again."	Tyrone's ability to engage in comprehension monitoring and reflect on his thought processes is unusual for a 9-year-old (see Chapter 7). The role of specific cognitive and metacognitive processes in intelligence is most evident in Sternberg's *triarchic theory*.	

<table>
<tr><th colspan="2">APPLYING CONCEPTS IN CHILD DEVELOPMENT</th><th colspan="3">Using Various Theories of Intelligence to Understand Youngsters' Behaviors (continued)</th></tr>
</table>

Age	A Youngster's Experience	Developmental Concepts *Applying Theories of Intelligence to Patterns in Youngsters' Behaviors*	Implications *Helping Youngsters Reach Their Full Potential*
Early Adolescence (10–14) 	For a science fair project, 13-year-old Jacquita interviews more than 100 students about their eating habits—how often they eat fresh fruits and vegetables, how often they go to fast-food restaurants, and so on. At first, Jacquita has difficulty organizing and making sense of her data. But after her teacher shows her how to use a computer spreadsheet, she easily summarizes her findings and creates several bar graphs for her science fair poster.		Give youngsters the symbolic and physical tools they need to think and act intelligently. For example, share with students the many symbolic systems adults in Western societies use to collect, analyze, and interpret data—questionnaires, spreadsheets, statistical procedures, etc.—and teach students how to use calculators, computers, and other physical tools to make the use of symbolic systems easier and more efficient.
Late Adolescence (14–18) 	Mark is quite motivated to do well in his high school classes. Class material doesn't always come easily to him, but he studies hard and so gains a firm grasp of the subject matter. He is especially knowledgeable about current events, as he spends much of his leisure time reading the local newspaper and such news magazines as *Time* and *The Economist*.	Cattell's theory is relevant here. It appears that Mark has average or above-average, but not exceptional, *fluid intelligence*. However, he has accumulated considerable knowledge (especially about current events), reflecting high *crystallized intelligence*.	Help children and adolescents acquire an in-depth and well integrated knowledge base about topics that will be especially useful in adult life. For example, teach classroom subject matter in ways that promote true understanding and integration of ideas, rather than mindless memorization of discrete facts.

Key Concepts

intelligence (p. 278)
g (general factor in intelligence) (p. 279)
fluid intelligence (p. 279)
crystallized intelligence (p. 279)

distributed intelligence (p. 282)
intelligence test (p. 284)
IQ score (p. 287)
specific ability test (p. 288)

dynamic assessment (p. 288)
Flynn effect (p. 295)
niche-picking (p. 295)
cultural bias (p. 300)

stereotype threat (p. 301)
giftedness (p. 305)
mental retardation (p. 308)
adaptive behavior (p. 308)

Companion Website

Now go to our Companion Website at www.prenhall.com/mcdevitt to assess your understanding of chapter content with a Practice Quiz, apply what you've learned in Essay Questions, and broaden your knowledge with links to related Developmental Psychology Web sites.

Language Development

chapter 9

Case Study: Mario

Case Study: Mario

Theoretical Perspectives of Language Development

Trends in Language Development

Development of a Second Language

Diversity in Language Development

Exceptionalities in Language Development

Case Study: Boarding School

Summary

Applying Concepts in Child Development

As a young boy growing up in rural Vermont, Mario had the good fortune to learn two languages. At home, his parents spoke Spanish almost exclusively, in part because they wanted to pass their cultural heritage along to their son. Most of Mario's early exposure to English was in the English-speaking child care centers and preschools he attended off and on from the time he was 2.

When Mario was 5, his dominant language was Spanish, but he was proficient in English as well. After his first 2 months in kindergarten, his teacher wrote the following in a report to Mario's parents:

> [Mario is] extremely sociable. He gets along fine with all the children, and enjoys school. He is quite vocal. He does not seem at all conscious of his speech. His slight accent has had no effect on his relations with the others. Whenever I ask the class a question, he is always one of the ones with his hand up.
>
> His greatest problem seems to be in the give and take of conversation. Since he always has something to say, he often finds it difficult to wait his turn when others are talking. When he talks, there are moments when you can see his little mind thinking through language—for he sometimes has to stop to recall a certain word in English which he might not have at his finger tips. (Fantini, 1985, p. 28)[a]

The "slight accent" in Mario's English led a speech therapist to recommend speech therapy, which Mario's parents declined. In fact, all traces of an accent disappeared from Mario's speech by age 8, and his third-grade teacher was quite surprised to learn that he spoke a language other than English at home.

Standardized tests administered over the years attested to Mario's proficiency in English. Before he began kindergarten, his score on a standardized English vocabulary test was at the 29th percentile, reflecting performance that, though a little on the low side, was well within an average range. Later, when he took the California Achievement Test in the fourth, sixth, and eighth grades, he obtained scores at the 80th percentile or higher (and mostly above the 90th percentile) on the reading, writing, and spelling subtests. When Mario spent a semester of fifth grade at a Spanish-speaking school in Bolivia, he earned high marks in Spanish as well, with grades of 5 on a 7-point scale in reading, writing, and language usage.

As Mario grew older, his vocabulary and written language skills developed more rapidly in English than in Spanish, in large part because most of his school instruction was in English. His father described the situation this way:

> [B]y about fifth grade (age ten), he had entered into realms of experience for which he had no counterpart in Spanish. A clear example was an attempt to prepare for a fifth grade test on the topic of "The Industrial Revolution in England and France." It soon became clear that it was an impossibility to try to constrain the child to review materials read and discussed at school—in English—through Spanish. With this incident, [use of English at home] became a fairly well established procedure when discussing other school topics, including science, mathematics, and the like. (Fantini, 1985, p. 73)

[a]Excerpts from *Language Acquisition of a Bilingual Child: A Sociolinguistic Perspective,* by A. E. Fantini, 1985. Clevedon, England: Multilingual Matters. (Available from the SIT Bookstore, School for International Training, Kipling Road, Brattleboro, VT 05302.) Reprinted with permission.

A cquiring the language of one's culture is, from an objective standpoint, an extremely complex and challenging undertaking. To understand and use a language effectively, children must master four basic components of the language. First, they must master **phonology:** They must know how words sound and be able to produce them. (Although Mario had a "slight accent" at age 5, he completely mastered English pronunciations by age 8.) Second, children must master **semantics,** the meanings of a large number of words. (Mario ultimately learned more English words than Spanish words because most of his schooling was in English.) Third, children must have a good command of **syntax,** knowing how words can legitimately be combined to form understandable phrases and sentences. (Mario's language development was all the more remarkable because he learned syntactic rules for two languages instead of one.) And finally, children must master the **pragmatics** of language, using social conventions and linguistic strategies that enable effective communication with others. (In kindergarten Mario had difficulty with turn taking, an important aspect of effective communication.)

As was true for Mario in his early years, young children do not yet have all the linguistic knowledge and skills they will eventually need to participate fully in adult society. Yet within the first 3 or 4 years of life, most children acquire sufficient proficiency in all four aspects of language to carry on productive conversations with those around them. How they accomplish this monumental task in such a short time is one of the great mysteries of child development. In this chapter we often revisit Mario as we explore the multifaceted nature of human language and its development over childhood and adolescence. We begin our discussion by looking at several theoretical perspectives on how children acquire their first language—that is, their **native language.**

Theoretical Perspectives of Language Development

Theorists have offered numerous explanations for how children learn their native language. Here we describe early theories based on modeling and reinforcement plus four more contemporary perspectives: nativism, information processing theory, sociocultural theory, and functionalism.

Early Theories: Modeling and Reinforcement

Some early theorists suggested that language development is largely the result of modeling—that children simply imitate the speech of others. Imitation is certainly involved in language development to some degree. Infants occasionally imitate the sounds that parents and other caregivers make (Tronick, Cohn, & Shea, 1986). Older children, too, sometimes pick up other people's words, expressions, rhymes, and song lyrics (R. E. Owens, 1996; Peters, 1983). When Mario began attending an English-speaking preschool, he came home using such expressions as "Shut up!" and "Don't do dat!" which he had apparently acquired by listening to his classmates (Fantini, 1985, p. 97).

The behaviorist B. F. Skinner (1957) suggested that *reinforcement* also plays a role, in that parents and other adults in a child's environment praise or in some other way reward increasingly complex language use. In Skinner's view, when infants make a variety of speech sounds in a seemingly random fashion, adults respond favorably to—and so encourage children to repeat—only those sounds used in the local language. As children grow older, Skinner proposed, adults begin to reinforce the use of single words, then the use of multiword combinations, and eventually only word combinations that are, from an adult's perspective, grammatically correct.

As complete explanations of how children acquire language, however, these early theories have not held up under the scrutiny of research. The speech of young children includes many phrases (e.g., "Allgone milk") that people around them neither say nor reinforce (N. Chomsky, 1959; V. Cook & Newson, 1996; D. Lightfoot, 1999). Moreover, parents usually reinforce their children's statements based on what is factually accurate rather than what is grammatically correct (R. Brown & Hanlon, 1970; O'Grady, 1997). Even in the elementary and secondary school years, the great majority of grammatical errors in children's speech go

—————— Connecting Concepts

You'll learn more about the effects of reinforcement in Chapter 13.

phonology
The sound system of a language; how words sound and are produced.

semantics
The meanings of words and word combinations.

syntax
Rules used to put words together into sentences.

pragmatics
Conventions and strategies used in effective and socially acceptable verbal interactions.

native language
The first language a child learns.

uncorrected (Bohannon, MacWhinney, & Snow, 1990). And children may continue to produce grammatically incorrect sentences despite feedback that the sentences need revision, as the following dialogue illustrates:

Child: Nobody don't like me.
Mother: No, say "nobody likes me."
Child: Nobody don't like me.

[Eight repetitions of this dialogue]

Mother: No, now listen carefully; say "nobody likes me."
Child: Oh! Nobody don't likes me. (McNeill, 1966, p. 68)

Clearly, then, neither modeling nor reinforcement sufficiently explains how children eventually acquire an adultlike form of their native language.

Although parents and other adults certainly model and reinforce children's early efforts at speech, modeling and reinforcement alone do not adequately account for language development.

Nativism

In an approach known as **nativism,** some theorists have turned to biology to explain language development. One early pioneer, Noam Chomsky (1965, 1972, 1976), proposed that growing children have a biologically built-in mechanism—a **language acquisition device**—that enables them to learn many complex aspects of language in a very short time. This mechanism provides certain "prewired" knowledge and skills that make the task of learning language much simpler than it would be if children had to start from scratch.

Many psychologists share Chomsky's belief that human beings, though certainly not born knowing any particular language, nevertheless inherit some predispositions that assist them in acquiring linguistic knowledge and skills. Beginning at a very early age, infants can detect subtle differences among very similar speech sounds. They can divide a steady stream of sound into small segments (e.g., syllables) and identify common patterns in what they hear. They seem to have a few built-in concepts (e.g., colors such as red, pink, and yellow) that predispose them to categorize their experiences in certain ways. And possibly they also have a *Universal Grammar,* a set of parameters that predispose them to form certain kinds of grammatical structures but not others (H. S. Cairns, 1996; Gopnik, 1997; Hirsh-Pasek & Golinkoff, 1996; D. Lightfoot, 1999; O'Grady, 1997).

Several lines of research converge to support the belief that language has roots in biology. First, children from diverse cultural and linguistic backgrounds tend to reach milestones in language development at similar ages. Virtually all children, even those who are congenitally deaf and have never heard a human voice, begin to produce speechlike syllables at about 6 or 7 months of age on average (Kuhl & Meltzoff, 1997; J. L. Locke, 1993). (We look at this *babbling* more closely later in the chapter.) In general, children who have regular exposure to a language—regardless of which language they are learning and whether the language is spoken or manually signed—make similar progress in producing meaningful words and stringing them together into appropriate, interpretable sequences (Crago, Allen, & Hough-Eyamie, 1997; L. A. Pettito, 1997).

A second body of evidence comes from brain research (Aitchison, 1996; J. L. Locke, 1993; Strozer, 1994). For most people, the left hemisphere of the cortex dominates in speech and language comprehension. Two specific regions of the left cortex of the brain seem to specialize in language functions (see Figure 9-1). *Broca's area,* located near the forehead, plays a key role in producing speech. *Wernicke's area,* behind the left ear, is heavily involved in understanding speech. But remember a point made in Chapter 4: No single mental activity—language included—is exclusively the domain of one hemisphere or the other. The right hemisphere is actively involved in sifting through multiple possible meanings of an ambiguous statement, perceiving humor and sarcasm, and using manual languages such as American Sign Language (Beeman & Chiarello, 1998; Neville & Bavelier, 2001; Ornstein, 1997). In addition, the right hemisphere dominates in language activities for a sizable number of left-handers, as well as for children who incur serious injuries in their left hemispheres before age 1 (Kolb & Whishaw, 1996; Ornstein, 1997; Stiles & Thal, 1993).

Additional evidence for the nativist view comes from the finding that there appear to be *sensitive periods* in certain aspects of language development (Bortfeld & Whitehurst, 2001; Bruer, 1999; J. L. Locke, 1993). Children who have little or no exposure to *any* language in

Connecting Concepts
You have also seen the influence of nativism in the discussion of *theory theory* in Chapter 7.

Connecting Concepts
Chapter 4 provides an overview of the left and right hemispheres in right-handed and left-handed individuals.

nativism
Theoretical perspective proposing that some knowledge is biologically built-in and present at birth or soon thereafter.
language acquisition device
Biologically built-in mechanism hypothesized to facilitate language learning.

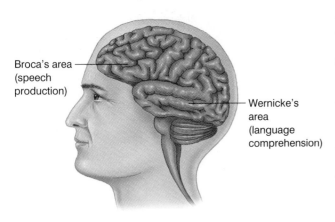

Figure 9-1

Primary language specialization centers in the brain

Broca's area (speech production)

Wernicke's area (language comprehension)

the early years often have trouble acquiring language later on, even with intensive language instruction (Curtiss, 1977; Newport, 1990). The phonological and syntactic aspects of language development seem to be most at risk when opportunities for learning a language are delayed. Youngsters typically learn how to pronounce a second language flawlessly only if they study it before mid-adolescence or, even better, in the preschool or early elementary years, as Mario did (Bialystok, 1994a; Collier, 1989; Flege, Munro, & MacKay, 1995). They may also have an easier time mastering complex aspects of a second language's syntax when they are immersed in the language within the first 5 to 10 years of life (Bialystok, 1994a, 1994b; J. S. Johnson & Newport, 1989). From a nativist perspective, the predictable timing of such sensitive periods suggests the influence of genetically driven maturational processes.

Researchers have yet to obtain clear evidence that human beings do, in fact, inherit a neurological mechanism that is specifically dedicated to learning language. Even if research eventually confirms the existence of such a mechanism, however, we wouldn't necessarily know what cognitive processes underlie language learning, nor would we know why virtually all children worldwide seem highly motivated to acquire language (Pinker, 1987). The theoretical perspectives that follow better address these issues.

Information Processing Theory

Information processing theorists focus on the specific cognitive processes that children use as they acquire language. From an information processing perspective, one essential ingredient in language learning is attention (M. Harris, 1992; Hirsh-Pasek & Golinkoff, 1996). Infants pay attention to human speech and speech-related events from a very early age. Within a few days after birth, they show a preference for human voices over other sounds, can distinguish between familiar and unfamiliar voices, and in some instances expend considerable effort to hear a familiar one (DeCasper & Fifer, 1980; Fifer & Moon, 1995; J. L. Locke, 1993). They are also more likely to look at speakers who use the short, simple, rhythmic language that adults frequently use when talking to young children (R. P. Cooper & Aslin, 1990; Fernald, 1992; P. S. Kaplan, Goldstein, Huckeby, & Cooper, 1995). Adults seem to know (perhaps unconsciously) that attention is critical for language learning. For instance, when talking with young children, they are apt to point to the people or objects under discussion and make sure that the children are looking in the appropriate direction (M. Harris, 1992).

Reasoning is another critical player in language development (Atkinson, 1992; H. S. Cairns, 1996; Cromer, 1993; Karmiloff-Smith, 1993). For instance, young children seem to form hypotheses about the meanings of words based on the context in which the words are used. In one study (T. K. Au & Glusman, 1990), researchers showed preschoolers an unfamiliar animal and consistently called it a *mido*. Later they presented a collection of odd-looking animals (including some midos) and asked the children to find a *theri* in the set (see Figure 9-2). Although the children had no information to guide their selection, they always chose an animal other than a mido. Apparently, they deduced that because the midos already had a name, a theri had to be a different kind of animal.

Working memory, too, is important in children's acquisition and use of language. Effective communication involves knowledge not only about spoken language but also about appropriate eye contact, gestures, and tone of voice (T. M. McDevitt & Ford, 1987). Given the limited capacity of working memory, a simple conversation might potentially involve coordinating so many skills that any meaningful exchange of information would be impossible. But fortunately, children soon automatize many aspects of language (e.g., word pronunciations, simple syntax, retrieval of common word meanings), freeing up working memory capacity for more complex language tasks. In many situations effective communication is also facilitated by previously developed schemas and scripts (e.g., "Hi, how are you?" "Fine, thanks. How are you?") that occur frequently in social interaction and can be used with little thought or effort.

——————— Connecting Concepts

Information processing theory is described in depth in Chapter 7.

Even in the first few weeks of life, most infants enjoy listening to the human voice, and they will expend considerable effort to hear a familiar one.

——————— Connecting Concepts

Working memory, automatization, schemas, and scripts are described in Chapter 7.

Figure 9-2
Children are more likely to attach new words to objects for which they don't already have labels. In this situation, a child is likely to choose either the purple crocodile-like creature or the yellow dinosaur-like creature as being a theri.
After T. K. Au & Glusman, 1990.

This is a *mido.*   Which one of these is a *theri*?

Some information processing theorists use the concept of automatization to make a counterargument to nativists' claim that sensitive periods in second-language learning reflect biologically built-in time frames. Perhaps what appear to be predetermined "best" times for learning particular aspects of language are simply the result of the brain's tendency to adapt fairly quickly to its environment. Becoming proficient in one's native language early on—attending to and practicing particular speech sounds, zeroing in on certain syntactic formats, and so on—may enhance automatization in the use of that language, but perhaps at the expense of learning a second, very different language (Elman et al., 1997; Merzenich, 2001).

Sociocultural Theory

Whereas information processing theorists consider the cognitive processes involved in acquiring and using language, sociocultural theorists look more at how social interactions foster language development. From a sociocultural perspective, words are apt to be used first in a social context and then, through the process of internalization, gradually become part of children's thought processes (K. Nelson, 1996a). *Intersubjectivity*—a mutual awareness of what conversation partners are looking at or thinking about—is critical if children are to learn new words in their interactions with others (Baldwin, 2000; Gauvain, 2001). Earlier we noted that adults can gain children's attention by pointing at certain objects and by speaking in a simplistic, high-pitched, singsong manner. Children, too, contribute to a state of mutual attention by observing where adults are looking. By considering both the direction of an adult's gaze and the content of his or her speech, a child can often infer the meanings of new words. As an illustration, imagine that a father and his 3-year-old daughter are in the produce section of the local supermarket. "Oh good," the father exclaims, "a carambola. I love carambolas!" If the daughter has never heard the word *carambola* before, she will likely look at her father's face and then follow his gaze to the object in question (in this case, a yellow-green, star-shaped fruit). But she is apt to do this only if she realizes that her father is probably looking at what he is talking about.

As early as the second year, children use what they know or can surmise about other people's thoughts to assist them in learning word meanings. For example, in one study (Baldwin, 1993), 18-month-olds were looking at one new toy while an adult looked at another. When the adult exclaimed, "A modi!" the children typically turned their attention to see what the

Connecting Concepts
See Chapter 7 for more information about intersubjectivity.

adult was looking at. A short time later, when the children were asked to get the modi, they were most likely to choose the toy the adult had been looking at, even though they themselves had been looking at something different when they first heard the word.

Functionalism

Another important question involves motivation: Why do children *want* to learn the language of their society? Some psychologists argue that over the course of evolution, human beings developed language skills in large part because language serves several useful functions—hence the term **functionalism**—for the species. Language helps children acquire knowledge, establish productive interpersonal relationships, control their own behavior, and influence the behavior of others (E. Bates & MacWhinney, 1987; L. Bloom & Tinker, 2001; Budwig, 1995; Pinker, 1997). From a very early age, children seem to be aware of the power of language in controlling the actions of others and, in the process, helping them satisfy their own needs and desires (e.g., L. Bloom & Tinker, 2001). For instance, when Mario attended preschool as a 3-year-old, he quickly learned such expressions as "No do dat no more!" and "Get auto here!" (Fantini, 1985, pp. 97–98). We can reasonably guess that such language enabled Mario to control his classmates' behaviors in ways that more gentle speech might not have.

Functionalists point out that language development is closely intertwined with—and in fact critical for—development in other domains (L. Bloom & Tinker, 2001; Langacker, 1986). For instance, as you discovered in Chapter 6, language enhances cognitive development in several ways: by providing symbols with which children can mentally represent and remember events, allowing children to exchange information and perspectives with others, and enabling children to internalize processes they first use in a social context. Language is essential for social and moral development as well. Through conversations and conflicts with adults and peers, children learn socially acceptable ways of behaving toward others (see Chapter 12) and, in most cases, eventually establish a set of principles that guides their moral decision making (see Chapter 13).

Language is so important for the human species that children seem to have the ability not only to learn it but also to *create* it. We find an example in a study of children attending a school for the deaf in Nicaragua (Senghas & Coppola, 2001). Before coming to the school, the children had little or no exposure to sign language, and teachers at the school focused primarily on teaching them how to lip-read and speak Spanish. Although many of the children made little progress in Spanish, they became increasingly adept at communicating with one another through a variety of hand gestures, and they consistently passed this sign language along to newcomers. Over a period of 20 years, the children's language became increasingly systematic and complex, with a variety of syntactic rules taking shape. Many of the innovations originated with children age 10 or younger—a finding that lends further support to the idea that young minds are especially proficient in acquiring language.

Critiquing Theories of Language Development

The Basic Developmental Issues table "Contrasting Contemporary Theories of Language Development" summarizes how nativism, information processing theory, sociocultural theory, and functionalism differ with respect to the broad themes of nature and nurture, universality and diversity, and qualitative and quantitative change. Another important difference among various theoretical perspectives is one of focus: Nativism focuses on syntactic development, information processing and sociocultural theories look more closely at semantic development, and functionalism considers how motivation fits into the overall picture. Therefore, theorists often shift from one perspective to another or combine elements of two or more perspectives, depending on the particular aspect of language development they are discussing.

A key source of controversy remains, however. Most nativists propose that children inherit a mechanism whose sole function is to facilitate the acquisition of language, whereas other theorists (especially those who take an information processing or functionalist approach) believe that language development arises out of more general cognitive abilities that

functionalism
Theoretical perspective of language development that emphasizes the purposes language serves for human beings.

BASIC DEVELOPMENTAL ISSUES

Contrasting Contemporary Theories of Language Development

Issue	Nativism	Information Processing Theory	Sociocultural Theory	Functionalism
Nature and Nurture	By and large, children develop language only when they are exposed to it; thus environmental input is essential. But children also appear to rely on a biological mechanism that includes predetermined "knowledge" about the nature of language and possibly also includes skills that help them decipher the linguistic code.	Most information processing theorists assume that language learning involves a complex interplay between inherited inclinations and abilities, on the one hand, and experiences that facilitate effective language learning (e.g., attention-getting actions by parents, frequent practice in using words), on the other.	Sociocultural theorists don't necessarily discount the role of heredity, but they focus on the social contexts that promote development and the cultural legacy (e.g., culture-specific interpretations of words and phrases) that a society passes along from one generation to the next.	As their needs and desires become increasingly ambitious and complex, children propel their own language development through their efforts to communicate more effectively. Their needs and desires are probably the result of both heredity and environment.
Universality and Diversity	Although human languages differ in many respects, most have certain things in common (e.g., most include both nouns and verbs). Furthermore, children in different language communities reach milestones in language development at similar ages. Diversity exists primarily in the specific phonological, semantic, syntactic, and pragmatic features of various languages.	Information processing mechanisms that affect language acquisition (e.g., attention, automatization) are universally relevant across cultures. Children's unique language experiences, which differ among and within cultures, lead both to differences in the language(s) that children speak and to differences in children's knowledge of a particular language (e.g., the precise meanings they assign to specific words).	Some mechanisms that promote language development (e.g., intersubjectivity) may be universal across cultures. At the same time, different societies cultivate many culture-specific linguistic practices.	The drive to understand and be understood by others is universal. Different cultural groups may be more responsive to, and so nurture, some ways of communicating more than others.
Qualitative and Quantitative Change	Children often acquire specific syntactic structures in a predictable sequence, with noticeable, stagelike changes in linguistic constructions occurring after each new acquisition (e.g., Dale 1976; O'Grady, 1997).	Many changes in language development—for instance, children's ever-enlarging vocabularies, ongoing refinement of word meanings, increasing automatization in pronunciation and other skills, and expanding working memory capacities (enabling production of longer and more complex sentences)—come about in a trendlike, quantitative fashion.	The nature of adult-child relationships that nurture language development may change both quantitatively and qualitatively over time. For example, qualitative change occurs in the development of intersubjectivity. Initially, intersubjectivity involves only an interaction between an adult and a child. Later it involves a mutual focus on, as well as shared understandings of, an object (see Chapter 7).	With development, children's needs and desires change in both quality and intensity. Thus both qualitative and quantitative changes are to be expected.

promote learning and development across a wide variety of domains. Research evidence points to a language-specific developmental mechanism for at least *some* aspects of language learning (Flavell et al., 2002; Maratsos, 1998; Siegler & Alibali, 2005; Trout, 2003). Children of all cultures learn language very quickly, and they acquire complex syntactic structures even when those structures are unnecessary for effective communication. In addition, children with mental retardation show marked differences in language development depending on their particular disability (N. G. S. Harris, Bellugi, Bates, Jones, & Rossen, 1997). Let's compare children who have Down syndrome with children who have *Williams syndrome,* a genetic disorder characterized by distinctive facial features, poor muscle tone, and abnormalities in the circulatory system. Children with both conditions typically have low measured IQ scores (often between 50 and 70), putting them in the bottom 2 percent of their peer group. Yet children with Down syndrome usually have delayed language development (consistent with their cognitive development), whereas children with Williams syndrome have such good language skills that they are often initially perceived as having normal intellectual abilities. A difference in language skills between two groups makes sense only if a language-specific mechanism guides language development somewhat independently of other aspects of cognitive development.

Other theoretical issues related to language development also remain unanswered. Two that have potential implications for teachers, caregivers, and other practitioners are the following:

● *Which comes first, language comprehension or language production?* Psychologists studying language development frequently make a distinction between expressive and receptive language skills. **Receptive language** is the ability to understand what one hears and reads. That is, it involves language *comprehension.* In contrast, **expressive language** is the ability to communicate effectively either orally or on paper. In other words, it involves language *production.*

A widely held assumption is that receptive language skills must precede expressive language skills. After all, it seems reasonable that children must understand what words and sentences mean before they use them in their own speech and writing. For example, in the "Intelligence: Infancy" video clip on Observation CD 1, 14-month-old Corwin readily responds to his mother's questions and commands even though his own use of words is minimal.

Yet many theorists don't believe the relationship between receptive and expressive language is so clear-cut (R. E. Owens, 1996). Children sometimes use words and expressions whose meanings they don't completely understand. Teresa recalls a 3-year-old preschooler who talked about the "accoutrements" in her purse, presumably after hearing others use the word in a similar context. Although the girl used the word appropriately in this situation, she did not understand all its connotations. That is, her production exceeded her comprehension. Ultimately, receptive and expressive language skills probably develop hand in hand, with language comprehension facilitating language production and language production also enhancing language comprehension.

● *What role does infant-directed speech play in language development?* Earlier we mentioned that infants seem to prefer the short, simple, rhythmic speech that adults often use when they talk to young children. Such **infant-directed speech** (also called *motherese* or *caregiver speech*) is different from normal adult speech in several ways (Kuhl & Meltzoff, 1997; Littlewood, 1984). It is spoken more slowly and distinctly and at a higher pitch. It uses a limited vocabulary and consists of sentences with few words and simple grammatical structures. It has exaggerated shifts in tone that help convey a speaker's message. It involves frequent repetition and is generally concerned with objects and events that take place in close temporal and physical proximity to the child. You can hear examples in the infancy video clips of the "Cognitive Development," "Intelligence," and "Literacy" modules on Observation CDs 1 and 2.

Adults often use infant-directed speech when they converse with young children, and they adapt their use of it to the age of the listening child (Rondal, 1985). Logically, such speech should facilitate language development, because its clear pauses between words, simple vocabulary and syntax, exaggerated intonations, and frequent repetition should make it easier for children to decipher what they hear. The problem with this hypothesis is that infant-directed speech is not a universal phenomenon. Adults in some cultures do not think of young children as suitable conversation partners and so speak to them rarely if at all. Despite these circumstances, the children successfully acquire the language of their community (Heath, 1983; Ochs & Schieffelin, 1995; O'Grady, 1997).

If infant-directed speech isn't essential for language development, what, then, is its purpose? One possibility is simply that it enhances adults' ability to communicate effectively with young children (O'Grady, 1997). Many parents interact frequently with their infants and toddlers and undoubtedly want to be understood (e.g., M. Harris, 1992). Infant-directed speech

In the "Intelligence: Infancy" clip on Observation CD 1, notice how Corwin has greater facility with receptive language than with expressive language.

Hear Corwin's mother use infant-directed speech in the infancy clips of the "Cognitive Development," "Intelligence," and "Literacy" modules on Observation CDs 1 and 2.

receptive language
Ability to understand the language one hears or reads.

expressive language
Ability to communicate effectively through speaking and writing.

infant-directed speech
Short, simple, high-pitched speech often used when talking to young children.

may also be part of parents' and other adults' attempts to establish and maintain affectionate relationships with children (Trainor, Austin, & Desjardins, 2000).

Trends in Language Development

Children's first form of communication is crying. Soon thereafter, they also begin to communicate by smiling, cooing, and pointing. On average, they begin using recognizable words sometime around their first birthday, and they are putting these words together by their second birthday. During the preschool years, their vocabulary grows considerably, and their sentences become longer. By the time they enroll in elementary school, at age 5 or 6, they use language that seems adultlike in many respects. Yet throughout the elementary and secondary school years, children and adolescents learn thousands of new words, and they become capable of comprehending and producing increasingly complex sentences. They also continue to develop skills for conversing appropriately with others, and they acquire a better understanding of the nature of language.

In the following sections, we explore the development of semantics, syntax, listening, speaking, pragmatics, and metalinguistic awareness over the course of infancy, childhood, and adolescence.

Semantic Development

Young children appear to understand some words as early as 8 months of age, and they typically say their first word at about 12 months (Fenson et al., 1994; M. Harris, 1992; O'Grady, 1997; Tincoff & Jusczyk, 1999). In the "Literacy: Infancy" video clip on Observation CD 2, you can hear 16-month-old Corwin say several words, including "mooo," "boon" (for *balloon*), "two," and "bye." By the time children are 18 months old, many have 50 words in their expressive vocabularies (O'Grady, 1997). There is considerable variability from child to child, however. For example, Mario did not say his first Spanish word until he was 16 months old, and by his second birthday he was using only 21 words (Fantini, 1985).

To get a sense of the types of words children are apt to have in their early working vocabularies, try the following exercise, "Connor's Vocabulary."

Hear Corwin's early words in the "Literacy: Infancy" clip on Observation CD 2.

INTERPRETING CHILDREN'S ARTIFACTS AND ACTIONS   Connor's Vocabulary

As a specialist in child development, Teresa kept ongoing records of her son Connor's early speech. In the box to the right are the words and phrases Connor was using at 18 months old. As you examine the list, look for patterns in Connor's expressive language.

Words:	night-night	hot	uice (for *juice*)
ball	book	boy	bath
mo (for *more*)	ah-dooo (for	eye	hole
no	*cock-a-*	toes	up
do (for *dog*)	*doodle-doo*)	balloo (for	bike
at (for *cat*)	birdie	*balloon*)	pie
moo (for *cow*	ho-ho (for	bubble	bock (for
or *moon*)	*Santa Claus*)	E, O (for the	*block*)
duck (for *truck,*	dowel (for	letters on	
duck, stuck)	*towel*)	signs)	**Two-Word**
bus	tea	woo-woo (for	**Combinations:**
Mama	milk	a dog	bye-bye duck
Dada	nana (for	barking)	bye-bye Dada
my	*banana*)	knock-knock	my nana
bye-bye	boat	doll	
hi	bowl	uh-oh!	

Connor's speaking vocabulary included 43 words, some of which he was beginning to combine into 2-word "sentences." At least 30 of the words (70%) were definitely nouns, and a few others ("ah-dooo," "ho-ho," "woo-woo") might have occasionally been used as labels for roosters, Santa Claus, and dogs. Such a preponderance of nouns is typical for toddlers worldwide (Bornstein & Cote, 2004). Most of Connor's other words can be categorized as actions ("bye-bye," "night-night," "knock-knock," "up") or descriptors ("mo" [more], "my," "hot," "uh-oh!"). As a group, the words Connor used as a 1½-year-old were undoubtedly related to objects and events he encountered frequently in his everyday world. And at least three of them—"mo" [more], "no," and "up"—must have communicated Connor's desires quite clearly to his parents and other caregivers (recall our earlier discussion of functionalism).

At some point during the end of the second year or beginning of the third year, a virtual explosion in speaking vocabulary occurs, with children learning 30 to 50 words a month and, later, as many as 20 new words each day (M. Harris, 1992; O'Grady, 1997). Mario, for example, was using more than 500 words by the time he was 3 (Fantini, 1985). In the preschool years, children also begin to organize their knowledge of various words into general categories (e.g., *juice, cereal,* and *morning* are all related to breakfast), hierarchies (e.g., *dogs* and *cats* are both *animals*), and other cross-word relationships (S. A. Gelman & Kalish, 2006; M. Harris, 1992).

When children are 6, their linguistic knowledge typically includes 8,000 to 14,000 words, of which they use about 2,600 in their own speech (Carey, 1978). By the sixth grade, their receptive vocabulary includes, on average, 50,000 words. By high school, it includes approximately 80,000 words (G. A. Miller & Gildea, 1987; Nippold, 1988; R. E. Owens, 1996). Thus children learn several thousand new words each year and so, on average, must learn numerous new words *every day* (W. E. Nagy, Herman, & Anderson, 1985). The rapid increase in vocabulary throughout childhood and adolescence is especially remarkable when we consider what word knowledge includes: Children must know not only what each word means but also how to pronounce it and how to use it in appropriate contexts (H. S. Cairns, 1996).

The dramatic increase in the number of words that children can use and understand is the most obvious aspect of semantic development. Yet several other principles characterize semantic development as well:

● *Children initially focus on lexical words; grammatical words come a bit later.* All languages have two main categories of words (Shi & Werker, 2001). **Lexical words** have some connection, either concrete or abstract, to objects or events in people's physical, social, and psychological worlds. They include nouns (e.g., *horse, freedom*), verbs (e.g., *swim, think*), adjectives (e.g., *handsome, ambiguous*), and adverbs (e.g., *quickly, intentionally*). All 43 of the words in Connor's vocabulary at 18 months were lexical words. **Grammatical words** (also known as *function words*) have little meaning by themselves but affect the meanings of other words or the interrelationships among words or phrases. They include articles (e.g., *a, the*), auxiliary verbs (e.g., the *have* in *I have swum*), prepositions (e.g., *before, after*), and conjunctions (e.g., *however, unless*). By the time children are 6 months old, they can distinguish between lexical words and grammatical words and, like Connor, show a distinct preference for lexical words (Shi & Werker, 2001).

● *Over time, children continue to refine their understandings of lexical words.* Children's initial understandings of lexical words are often fuzzy. Children have a general idea of what certain words mean but define them imprecisely and may use them incorrectly. One common error is **undergeneralization,** in which children attach overly restricted meanings to words, leaving out some situations to which the words apply. For example, Jeanne once asked her son Jeff, then 6, to tell her what an *animal* is. He gave this definition:

It has a head, tail, feet, paws, eyes, nose, ears, lots of hair.

Like Jeff, young elementary school children often restrict their meaning of *animal* primarily to nonhuman mammals, such as dogs and horses, and insist that fish, birds, insects, and people are *not* animals (Carey, 1985; Saltz, 1971). Another frequent error is **overgeneralization:** Words are given meanings that are too broad and so are applied to inappropriate situations. For example, a child might say "I'm barefoot all over!" or "I'll get up so early that it will still be late" (Chukovsky, 1968, p. 3).

lexical word
Word that in some way represents an aspect of one's physical, social, or psychological world.

grammatical word
Nonlexical word that affects the meanings of other words or the interrelationships among words in a sentence.

undergeneralization
Overly restricted meaning for a word, excluding some situations to which the word applies.

overgeneralization
Too broad a meaning for a word, such that it is used in situations to which it doesn't apply.

In addition to undergeneralizing and overgeneralizing, children sometimes confuse the meanings of similar words. The following conversation illustrates 5-year-old Christine's confusion between *ask* and *tell:*

Adult:	Ask Eric his last name. [Eric Handel is a classmate of Christine's.]
Christine:	Handel.
Adult:	Ask Eric this doll's name.
Christine:	I don't know.
Adult:	Ask Eric what time it is.
Christine:	I don't know how to tell time.
Adult:	Tell Eric what class is in the library.
Christine:	Kindergarten.
Adult:	Ask Eric who his teacher is.
Christine:	Miss Turner. (dialogue from C. S. Chomsky, 1969, p. 55; format adapted)

Preschoolers are, in many respects, quite proficient in using their native language. Yet they still have much to learn; for instance, they may exhibit undergeneralization or overgeneralization in their initial understandings of words.

In a similar manner, young children often confuse comparative words, sometimes interpreting *less* as "more" or thinking that *shorter* means "longer" (R. E. Owens, 1996; Palermo, 1974).

● ***Children have difficulty with grammatical words throughout the elementary and middle school years.*** Children's mastery of a particular grammatical word typically evolves slowly over a period of several years. For instance, although 3-year-olds can distinguish between the articles *a* and *the*, children as old as 9 are occasionally confused about when to use each one (R. E. Owens, 1996; Reich, 1986). Children in the upper elementary and middle school grades have trouble with many conjunctions, such as *but, although, yet, however,* and *unless* (Nippold, 1988; R. E. Owens, 1996). As an illustration, consider the following two pairs of sentences:

Jimmie went to school, but he felt sick.
Jimmie went to school, but he felt fine.

The meal was good, although the pie was bad.
The meal was good, although the pie was good.

Even 12-year-olds have trouble identifying the correct sentence in pairs like these, reflecting only a vague understanding of the connectives *but* and *although* (E. W. Katz & Brent, 1968). (The first sentence is correct in both cases.)

● ***Understanding of abstract words emerges later than understanding of concrete words.*** Words like *but* and *although* may be especially difficult for elementary school children because their meanings are fairly abstract. Let's revisit a point made in Chapter 6: Youngsters are better able to think abstractly in adolescence than in early or middle childhood. Young children in particular are apt to define words (even fairly abstract ones) in terms of the obvious, concrete aspects of their world (Anglin, 1977; Ausubel, Novak, & Hanesian, 1978). For example, when Jeanne's son Jeff was 4, he defined *summer* as the time of year when school is out and it's hot outside. By the time he was 12, he knew that scientists define summer in terms of the earth's tilt relative to the sun—a much more abstract notion.

How children learn word meanings. Because many words encompass *categories* of objects, events, or relationships (proper nouns such as *Mama* and *Santa Claus* are an exception), an ability to categorize is an essential prerequisite for learning them. Infants begin categorizing objects in their world as early as 3 months of age (see Chapter 7). Sometime between 3 and 10 months, they can categorize spatial relationships that provide the basis for certain prepositions and directional words (e.g., *above* vs. *below, left* vs. *right*) (Quinn, 2003). By 10 to 12 months, they also distinguish between greater and lesser quantities of something, providing a foundation for learning words such as *more* and *less* (Feigenson, Carey, & Hauser, 2002).

An additional challenge in learning word meanings, and in acquiring syntax as well, is that children must mentally divide the continuous stream of speech they hear into the individual "pieces" that are words. Even in the simplified infant-directed speech described earlier, one word flows quickly into the next, without pause (Jusczyk, 1997). Despite such nonstop verbal action, infants begin to identify the specific words in speech by 7 or

Connecting Concepts ——
Chapter 6 describes Piaget's and contemporary researchers' views on the development of abstract thought.

Connecting Concepts ——
You can find more on the development of categories in the discussion of *organization* in Chapter 7.

Children are more likely to learn words that they hear frequently—a principle that programs such as *Sesame Street* effectively use to promote language development (Rice, Huston, Truglio, & Wright, 1990).

8 months of age (Aslin, Saffran, & Newport, 1998; Jusczyk, 1997). Exactly how they do it remains a mystery, but they probably rely on numerous clues, including the characteristic rhythm, stress patterns, and consistencies in word sequences they hear in their native language (Jusczyk, 2002).

Once children have such basics down, how do they zero in on the meanings of specific words? In some cases adults provide direct instruction at home and at school, perhaps by labeling objects or by asking questions ("Where is the _____?") while looking at picture books with children (Dunham, Dunham, & Curwin, 1993; Fukkink & de Glopper, 1998; Sénéchal, Thomas, & Monker, 1995). Sometimes older children also become involved in language instruction. In the following dialogue, 5-year-old Kris is playing with her 23-month-old cousin Amy. Kris holds up a stuffed dog:

Kris:	What is it?
Amy:	Doggie.
Kris:	What?
Amy:	Doggie.
Kris:	A doggie, yeah. (Picks up elephant.) What is this?
Amy:	Doggie.
Kris:	What?
Amy:	Baby.
Kris:	(Prompts Amy.) No. Uh–. Uh–.
Amy:	Pig.
Kris:	Uh–. Elephant.
Amy:	Elephant.
Kris:	Yeah elephant. (dialogue from P. J. Miller, 1982, p. 74; format adapted)

More often than not, however, caregivers, teachers, and other individuals do not explicitly identify what they are referring to when they use new words. As a result, youngsters probably learn most words by inferring their meaning from the contexts in which the words are used (Akhtar, Jipson, & Callanan, 2001; Pinker, 1987; Waxman, 1990). Young toddlers sometimes need numerous repetitions of a particular word before they understand and use it (M. Harris, 1992; Peters, 1983; Woodward, Markman, & Fitzsimmons, 1994). But by the time children are 2 or 3, they can often infer a word's general meaning after only one exposure—a process known as **fast mapping** (Heibeck & Markman, 1987; Pinker, 1982).

Young children seem to use a number of general "rules" to fast-map word meanings. Following are some examples:

- If I see several objects and know labels for all of them except one, a new word is probably the name of the unlabeled object. (Recall the research study involving the words *mido* and *theri* described earlier.)
- If someone uses a word while pointing to a particular object, the word probably refers to the *whole* object rather than to just a part of it.
- Generally speaking, when a word is used to refer to a particular object or action, it refers to *similar* objects or actions as well.
- If a word is preceded by an article (e.g., "This is a _____"), it refers to a category of objects. If it has no article in front of it (e.g., "This is _____"), it is the name of a *particular* object (i.e., it is a proper noun).
- Words for particular things (i.e., proper nouns) are more likely to refer to animate objects (e.g., people, pets) than to inanimate ones. (Akhtar, Carpenter, & Tomasello, 1996; T. K. Au & Glusman, 1990; S. A. Gelman & Taylor, 1984; Golinkoff, Hirsh-Pasek, Bailey, & Wenger, 1992; Golinkoff, Hirsh-Pasek, Mervis, Frawley, & Parillo, 1995; Haryu & Imai, 2002; Jaswal & Markman, 2001; Markman, 1989, 1992; Waxman, 2003)

As children get older, they continue to use such rules to draw inferences about word meanings. They also refine their understandings of words through repeated encounters with the words in different contexts and sometimes through direct feedback that they've used a word incorrectly (Carey & Bartlett, 1978).

In many cases learning a word's precise meaning involves identifying the **defining features** of the concept that the word represents—that is, identifying the characteristics that a particular object or event must exhibit in order to be classified as an instance of that concept.

fast mapping
Inferring a word's general meaning after a single exposure.

defining feature
Characteristic that must be present in all instances of a concept.

For example, a *circle* must be both round and two-dimensional. People who *walk* are people who stand upright, move their bodies by moving their feet, and have at least one foot on the ground at all times.

Words are most easily learned when they have defining features that are concrete and obvious. Words are harder to learn when their defining features are abstract, subtle, or difficult to pin down. Children, younger ones especially, are often misled by **correlational features,** attributes that are nonessential but frequently present and may be more readily observable than the defining features (Keil, 1989; Mervis, 1987). Consider how the three children in one family once defined *plant:*

Andrew (age 7): Something that people plant in a garden or somewhere.

Amaryth (age 10): A growing thing that's sometimes beautiful.

Tony (age 13): A life-form that uses sunlight and carbon dioxide to live.

Andrew focused on a feature that is true for some but not all plants: their location in a garden. In contrast, Amaryth mentioned one defining feature (growth) that is true of, but not unique to, plants, along with a correlational feature (beauty). Tony mentioned characteristics that a biologist might identify. Presumably Tony had learned these defining features in one of his science classes at school.

Fostering semantic development. Researchers have identified several strategies that teachers, parents, and other caregivers can use to help children learn word meanings:

● ***Talk regularly to, with, and around infants and toddlers.*** Even when young children do not yet talk themselves, they learn a great deal from hearing their native language. Initially, they learn its basic characteristics, such as its typical rhythms and stress patterns and the specific sounds (phonemes) that it does and does not include. Later, as they begin to mentally "divide" others' speech into individual words, they also begin to draw inferences about what some of those words mean. Although the simple sentences and attention-grabbing tones of parents may initially attract infants into conversation, over the long run it is the richness of other people's language—the wide variety of words, complex syntactic structures, and so on—that facilitates children's vocabulary development (B. Hart & Risley, 1995; Hoff & Naigles, 2002).

● ***Give definitions.*** By the time children are school age, they often learn words more easily when they are told what the defining features are—in other words, when they are given definitions (Tennyson & Cocchiarella, 1986). Definitions are especially valuable when defining features are abstract or otherwise not obvious. Children can usually learn what a *circle* is and what *red* means even without definitions, because roundness and redness are characteristics that are easily noticed. But the defining features of such words as *polygon* and *fragile* are more subtle, and for words like these, definitions can be very helpful. Ideally, children should be encouraged to define new vocabulary in their own words and use this vocabulary in a variety of contexts.

● ***Provide examples and nonexamples.*** Children often acquire a more accurate understanding of a word when they are shown several examples (Barringer & Gholson, 1979; Tennyson & Cocchiarella, 1986). Ideally, such examples should be as different from one another as possible so that they illustrate a word's entire range. To illustrate, if adults limit their examples of *animal* to dogs, cats, cows, and horses, children will understandably draw the conclusion that all animals have four legs and fur (a case of undergeneralization). If, instead, adults also present goldfish, robins, beetles, earthworms, and people as examples of *animal,* children are apt to realize that animals can differ considerably in physical appearance.

In addition to having examples, children benefit from having nonexamples of a word, especially those that are "near misses" (Winston, 1973). For instance, to learn what a *salamander* is, a child might be shown such similar animals as snakes and lizards and told that they are "not salamanders." By presenting nonexamples, including the near misses, adults minimize the extent to which children are likely to overgeneralize in their use of words.

Children acquire more accurate understandings of words when they see concrete examples.

correlational feature
Characteristic present in many instances of a concept but not essential for concept membership.

● *Give feedback when children use words incorrectly.* Misconceptions about word meanings sometimes reveal themselves in children's speech and writing. Astute teachers and caregivers listen closely not only to what children say but also to how they say it, and they also look at how children use words in their writing. For instance, a preschooler might mistakenly refer to a rhinoceros as a "hippo," an elementary school student might deny that a square is a rectangle, and a high school student might use the term *atom* when she is really talking about molecules. In such situations adults should gently correct the misconceptions, perhaps by saying something along these lines: "A lot of people get hippos and rhinoceroses confused, because both of them are large and gray. This animal has a large horn on its nose, so it's a rhinoceros. Let's find a picture of a hippo and see how the two animals are different."

● *Encourage children to read as much as possible.* Avid readers learn many more new words and so have larger vocabularies than do children who read infrequently (Fukkink & de Glopper, 1998; Stanovich, 2000; Swanborn & de Glopper, 1999). And when an adult reads storybooks to young children, the children are more likely to develop their vocabularies if the adult occasionally stops to ask about or explain potentially unfamiliar words (Brabham & Lynch-Brown, 2002).

(handwritten note) What dose worrisome meen? What is and dose prevaricate mean? Sobtruct!?

Regular reading promotes vocabulary development. On this page of her fifth-grade journal, 10-year-old Amaryth has jotted down unknown words in a book she is reading.

Syntactic Development

Which of the following sentences are grammatically correct?

- Growing children need nutritious food and lots of exercise.
- Experience students find to be many junior high school an unsettling.
- Allow class discussions to exchange ideas and perspectives students.
- Schizophrenia often does not appear until adolescence or adulthood.

You undoubtedly realized that the first and last sentences are grammatically correct and that the two middle ones are not. But *how* were you able to tell the difference? Can you describe the specific grammatical rules you used to make your decisions?

Rules of syntax—the rules we use to combine words into meaningful sentences—are incredibly complex (N. Chomsky, 1972). Much of our knowledge about syntax is in an unconscious form. Although we can produce acceptable sentences and can readily understand the sentences of others, we cannot always put our finger on exactly what it is we know about language that allows us to do these things. Even experts struggle to identify all the rules of English syntax (Aitchison, 1996).

Despite the complex and elusive nature of syntactic rules, children seem to pick up on them rather quickly. By the time children reach school age, they have mastered many of the basics of sentence construction (McNeill, 1970; Reich, 1986). Even so, they are apt to show gaps in their syntactic knowledge throughout the elementary school years and often into the secondary school years as well. Following are noteworthy aspects of syntactic development over the course of childhood and adolescence:

● *Some syntax appears in children's earliest word combinations.* Initially, children use only single words to express their thoughts. For instance, at 18 months, Connor would simply say "mo" if he wanted more of whatever he was eating or playing with at the time. And like many toddlers, he would stretch out his arms and plead "Up!" when he wanted to be carried or cuddled. Developmentalists sometimes use the word **holophrase** to refer to such one-word "sentences."

When children first begin combining words into two- and three-word sentences, they typically use lexical words (rather than grammatical words) almost exclusively. For instance, they might say "Give doggie" to mean *Give it to the doggie* or "Mommy pumpkin" to mean *Mommy is cutting a pumpkin* (R. Brown, 1973, p. 205). By using such **telegraphic speech,** children maximize the meaning their short sentences convey, just as many adults used to do when they sent telegrams and didn't want to pay extra for long messages.

Yet children show evidence that they are using simple syntactic rules even when their sentences are only two words long (R. Brown, 1973; H. S. Cairns, 1996; O'Grady, 1997). For example, their two-word combinations might reflect description ("Pillow dirty"), location ("Baby table"), or possession ("Adam hat"). As children's sentences increase in length, they

holophrase
A single word used to express a complete thought; commonly observed in children's earliest speech.

telegraphic speech
Short, grammatically incomplete sentences that include lexical (rather than grammatical) words almost exclusively; common in toddlers.

also increase in syntactic complexity—for instance, by including a subject, verb, and object (e.g., "I ride horsie") or describing both an action and a location ("Put truck window," "Adam put it box") (R. Brown, 1973, pp. 141, 205).

● *Young children rely heavily on word order when interpreting sentences.* By the time they are 1½, children have some understanding that, at least in English, word order affects meaning. For instance, they know that "Big Bird is washing Cookie Monster" means something different from "Cookie Monster is washing Big Bird" (Hirsh-Pasek & Golinkoff, 1996). Yet young children are sometimes misled by the order in which words appear (O'Grady, 1997). For instance, many preschoolers seem to apply a general rule that a pronoun refers to the noun that immediately precedes it. Consider the sentence "John said that Peter washed him." Many 4-year-olds think that *him* refers to *Peter* and so conclude that Peter washed himself. Similarly, kindergartners are apt to have trouble with the sentence "Because she was tired, Mommy was sleeping" because no noun appears before *she.*

● *Children's questions increasingly incorporate multiple syntactic rules.* In some languages it's very easy to ask questions. In Chinese, for instance, a person can change a statement into a question simply by adding *ma* to the end of the sentence. In English, however, asking questions is more complicated. At a minimum, it requires switching the order of the subject and verb ("Are you hungry?"). When past tense is involved, asking a question requires putting the auxiliary verb but *not* the main verb first ("Have you eaten yet?"). And when something other than a yes or no answer is called for, a question word (e.g., *who, what, where, how*) must also appear at the beginning ("What did you eat?").

Preschoolers are known for their many *what* and *why* questions. With age, their questions reflect an increasing ability to integrate multiple syntactic rules.

English-speaking children seem to master these question-asking rules one step at a time. Initially, their questions may be nothing more than telegraphic sentences with a rise in pitch at the end (e.g., "Kitty go home?") (R. Brown, 1973, p. 141). At about 2½ years, they attach question words to the beginning, and sometime in their third year, they add an auxiliary verb such as *is* or *does.* However, preschoolers often neglect one or more of the rules for asking questions. For instance, they may ask "What you want?" (forgetting to add the auxiliary verb) or "What you will do?" (forgetting to put the auxiliary verb before the subject) (de Villiers, 1995, pp. 516, 518). But by the time they are 5, most English-speaking children have mastered the correct syntax for questions (de Villiers, 1995).

● *Children tend to learn general rules for word endings before they learn the many exceptions.* Knowledge of syntax includes knowledge about when to use word endings (suffixes) such as *-s, -er,* and *-ed.* When children first learn the rules for using suffixes (e.g., *-s* indicates plural, *-er* indicates a comparison, and *-ed* indicates past tense), they often apply these rules indiscriminately, without regard for exceptions. Thus a child might say "I have two *foots,*" "Chocolate is *gooder* than vanilla," or "I *goed* to Grandma's house." This phenomenon, known as **overregularization,** is especially common during the preschool and early elementary years. It gradually diminishes as children master the irregular forms of various words: The plural of *foot* is *feet,* the comparative form of *good* is *better,* the past tense of *go* is *went,* and so on (Cazden, 1968; Marcus, 1996; Siegler, 1994).

Yet most high school students (and many adults as well) haven't completely mastered the irregularities of the English language (Marcus, 1996). For instance, throughout his high school years, Jeanne's son Jeff consistently said "I have *broughten . . .* " despite Jeanne's constant reminders that he should say "I have *brought. . . .* "

● *The ability to comprehend passive sentences evolves gradually during the preschool and elementary school years.* In a passive sentence, the subject of the sentence is the recipient, rather than the agent, of the action that the verb describes. Passive sentences frequently confuse young children, who may incorrectly attribute the action to the subject. Consider these two sentences:

The boy is pushed by the girl.

The cup is washed by the girl.

Preschoolers are more likely to be confused by the first sentence—that is, to think that the boy is the one doing the pushing—than by the second sentence (Karmiloff-Smith, 1979). The

overregularization
Use of a syntactic rule in situations where an exception to the rule applies.

first sentence has two possible "actors," but the second sentence has only one: Both boys and girls can push someone else, but cups can't wash girls. Complete understanding of passive sentences doesn't appear until sometime around fourth grade (O'Grady, 1997; R. E. Owens, 1996; Tager-Flusberg, 1993).

● *Children can be confused by sentences with multiple clauses.* Word order sometimes leads young children to misinterpret multiple-clause sentences (E. V. Clark, 1971; Sheldon, 1974). Consider the sentence "The horse kicked the pig after he jumped over the fence." Children as old as 6 often say that the horse kicked the pig *before* it jumped over the fence, even though the word *after* clearly communicates the opposite sequence (E. V. Clark, 1971).

Children begin to produce simple subordinate clauses, such as those that follow and modify nouns (e.g., "This is the toy *that I want*") at about age 4 (R. E. Owens, 1996). Sentences with one clause embedded in the middle of another clause are more difficult, especially if the noun tying the clauses together has a different function in each clause. Consider the sentence "The dog *that was chased by the boy* is angry" (R. E. Owens, 1996, p. 382). The dog is the subject of the main clause ("The dog . . . is angry") but is the recipient of the action in the embedded clause (" . . . [dog] was chased by the boy"). Seventh graders easily understand such sentences, but younger children overrely on word order to interpret them and so may conclude that the boy, rather than the dog, is angry (R. E. Owens, 1996).

● *Knowledge of syntactic rules continues to develop at the secondary level.* In middle school and high school, adolescents learn more subtle aspects of syntax, such as subject-verb and noun-pronoun agreement, correct uses of *that* versus *which* to introduce subordinate clauses, functions of punctuation marks such as colons and semicolons, and so on. They rarely develop such knowledge on their own, however. Instead, most of their syntactic development probably occurs as the result of formal instruction, especially through courses in language arts, English composition, and foreign languages.

● *Multilingual children readily distinguish among the syntactic structures used in different languages.* As Mario simultaneously learned Spanish and English, he also learned which syntactic rules applied to each language. Intrusions from one language to the other occurred infrequently even in the preschool years (he once pluralized the English word *balloon* with the Spanish suffix *-es,* saying "balloones") and disappeared altogether soon after (Fantini, 1985).

How children acquire syntactic knowledge.   Even infants have some awareness of patterns in speech. For example, in one study (Marcus, Vijayan, Bandi Rao, & Vishton, 1999), 7-month-olds heard a series of "sentences" each comprised of three nonsense syllables (e.g., *ga, na, ti, li*). Infants in Group 1 consistently heard them in a predictable "ABA" pattern (e.g., "Ga ti ga," "Li na li"), whereas infants in Group 2 consistently heard them in an "ABB" pattern (e.g., "Ga ti ti," "Li na na"). After habituating to these sentences, they heard another series of "sentences" with new nonsense syllables, with some sentences following the ABA pattern (e.g., "Wo fe wo") and others following the ABB pattern (e.g., "Wo fe fe"). The infants paid greater attention when listening to the pattern that was new for them, showing that the pattern they had heard before was "the same old thing," even though new sounds were involved.

Such sensitivity to patterns is undoubtedly essential for syntactic development. Some theorists suggest that acquiring syntax involves discovering the probabilities with which various word combinations appear in sentences (MacWhinney & Chang, 1995; Saffran, 2003; Sirois, Buckingham, & Shultz, 2000). As one simple example, children may notice that *the* is usually followed by names of things or by "describing" words (e.g., they might hear "the dog," "the picnic," or "the pretty hat"). In contrast, *the* is rarely followed by words that identify specific actions (e.g., they never hear "the do" or "the went"). In addition, children may engage in **semantic bootstrapping,** using word meanings as a basis for forming syntactic categories (E. Bates & MacWhinney, 1987; S. A. Gelman & Kalish, 2006; Pinker, 1984, 1987). For instance, they may notice that labels for people and concrete objects always serve particular functions in sentences, that action words serve other functions, that spatial-relationship and direction words serve still others, and so on. Through this process they may gradually acquire an intuitive understanding of nouns, verbs, prepositions, and other parts of speech— an understanding that allows them to use various kinds of words appropriately in sentences.

——————— **Connecting Concepts**
Recall the discussion of *habituation* in Chapter 2.

semantic bootstrapping
Using knowledge of word meanings to derive knowledge about syntactic categories and structures.

Although theorists do not yet have a clear understanding of how children acquire syntactic rules, most agree that syntactic development is largely a constructive and unconscious process, especially in the early years (Aitchison, 1996; H. S. Cairns, 1996; Karmiloff-Smith, 1993). Young children typically receive little if any direct instruction about how to form sentences. Instead, they apparently develop their own set of syntactic rules through their observations of other people's speech. They may occasionally misapply the rules (as is seen in overregularization), but with time and practice they become adept at using most rules appropriately (Dale, 1976; Marcus, 1996).

Formal language arts instruction brings some syntactic knowledge to a conscious level. Beginning in the upper elementary and middle school grades, children often learn to identify the various parts of a sentence (e.g., subject, direct object, prepositional phrase, subordinate clause) about which they acquired intuitive knowledge years earlier. They also study various verb tenses (e.g., present, past, present progressive) even though they have been using these tenses in their everyday speech for quite some time.

Fostering syntactic development. Especially as they are learning the more complex and subtle aspects of syntax, children and adolescents often benefit from ongoing instruction and practice in various syntactic structures. Following are several examples of how educators and caregivers can promote youngsters' syntactic development:

Especially in adolescence and adulthood, many advances in language development probably occur as a result of formal instruction.

● ***Expand on young children's telegraphic speech.*** When young children speak in telegraphic sentences, caregivers can engage in **expansion** by repeating the sentences in a more mature form. For example, when a toddler says, "Mommy lunch," mother might respond by saying, "Mommy is eating her lunch" (R. E. Owens, 1996, p. 224). Expansion gives children gentle feedback about the incompleteness of their own utterances and possibly encourages them to use more complex syntactic forms (R. E. Owens, 1996; Scherer & Olswang, 1984).

● ***Teach irregular forms of verbs and comparative adjectives.*** Children do not always hear the irregular forms of verbs and adjectives in everyday speech. For example, their young playmates may talk about what's *badder* or *worser*, and many adults confuse the past tenses of the verbs *lay* and *lie* (which are *laid* and *lay*, respectively). Some formal instruction in irregular forms may therefore be the only way that children discover which terms are correct and which are not.

● ***Describe various sentence structures, and give children considerable practice in their use.*** Having children examine and practice common syntactic structures (active and passive voice, independent and dependent clauses, etc.) has at least two benefits. First, children should be better able to vary their sentence structure as they write—a strategy associated with more sophisticated writing (Byrnes, 1996; Spivey, 1997). Second, learning the labels for such structures (e.g., *passive voice*) in English should help them acquire analogous structures in other languages they study at a later time.

● ***Provide ample opportunities for children to express their ideas in a relatively "formal" way, and give feedback about appropriate syntax.*** In typical everyday conversation, adults and children alike often use incomplete sentences and are lax in their adherence to grammatical rules (V. Cook & Newson, 1996; D. Lightfoot, 1999). But what's common in casual speech is often frowned upon in writing and public speaking. In formal and public situations (e.g., a letter to the editor of a local newspaper or a presentation to a large group), correct grammar is, in many people's minds, an indication that the writer or speaker is educated and well-informed and is therefore someone to take seriously (R. E. Owens, 1996; Purcell-Gates, 1995; H. L. Smith, 1998).

Development of Listening Skills

As you might guess, children's ability to understand what they hear is closely related to their semantic and syntactic development. In addition, the development of listening skills is characterized by the following trends:

expansion
Repetition of a child's short utterances in a more complete and grammatically correct form.

● *In the first year, infants learn to focus primarily on sounds important in their native language.* The basic elements of spoken language—all the consonants and vowels a language includes—are collectively known as **phonemes.** Phonemes are the smallest units of speech that indicate differences in meaning in a particular language. For instance, the word *bite* has three phonemes: a "buh" sound, an "eye" sound, and a "tuh" sound. If we change any one of these sounds—for instance, if we change *b* to *f* (*fight*), long *i* to long *a* (*bait*), or *t* to *k* (*bike*)—we get a new word with a different meaning.

Beginning on day one, infants can discriminate among a wide variety of phonemes, including many that they don't hear in the speech around them (Aldridge et al., 2001; Jusczyk, 1995; Werker & Lalonde, 1988). Before long, they show a noticeable preference for sounds and words they hear frequently. For instance, 5-month-olds pay more attention to their own names than to other, similar-sounding words (Mandel, Jusczyk, & Pisoni, 1995). When infants reach 8 or 9 months, they also seem to prefer listening to the sounds and rhythms of their native language (Jusczyk & Aslin, 1995; Saffran, Aslin, & Newport, 1996). For instance, Mario showed an early preference for Spanish rather than English (Fantini, 1985).

This early tuning-in to a particular language gradually alters what infants "hear" and "don't hear" in speech. By the time children are a year old, they primarily hear the differences that are important in their own languages (Jusczyk, 1997; Werker & Tees, 1999). For example, 1-year-old infants in English-speaking countries continue to hear the difference between "L" and "R," a distinction critical for making such discriminations as *lap* versus *rap* and *lice* versus *rice*. In contrast, Japanese children gradually lose the ability to tell the difference, presumably because the Japanese language treats the two sounds as a single phoneme. Similarly, babies in English-speaking societies lose the ability to distinguish among various "S" sounds that comprise two or more different phonemes in certain other languages.

As you can see, the first year of life is an important one for learning which differences among speech sounds are essential for understanding one's native language. Yet children continue to fine-tune their discriminative powers throughout early and middle childhood. For instance, they may have some difficulty distinguishing between words that differ by only one phoneme until they are 5 (Gerken, 1994; Rayner, Foorman, Perfetti, Pesetsky, & Seidenberg, 2001). Furthermore, they may continue to hear some sound differences not important in their own language until they are 8 to 10 years old (Siegler & Alibali, 2005).

● *Young children rely more heavily on context than older children, but youngsters of all ages take context into account.* Children do not necessarily need to focus on every sound, or even every word, when they listen to what other people say. For instance, 18-month-olds often know from the context what word a speaker is going to say after hearing only the first two phonemes (Fernald, Swingley, & Pinto, 2001). Furthermore, using various contextual clues, children often realize that what a speaker says is different from what the speaker actually means (M. Donaldson, 1978; Flavell et al., 2002; Paul, 1990). For example, kindergartners may correctly conclude that a teacher who asks "Whose jacket do I see lying on the floor?" is actually requesting the jacket's owner to pick it up and put it where it belongs. However, children raised in some cultural groups (e.g., children in some communities in the southeastern United States) rarely hear such indirect requests from parents and other family members. Those who don't are more likely to adhere to classroom rules when their teachers specifically tell them what needs to be done (Heath, 1983).

Sometimes young children are *too* dependent on context for determining the meaning of language, to the point where they don't listen carefully enough to understand a spoken message accurately. They may instead "hear" what they think the speaker means based on their beliefs about the speaker's intentions. As an example, look at the cows and horses in Figure 9-3. *Are there more cows or more black horses?* There are four cows but only three black horses, so obviously there are more cows. Yet if you ask 6-year-olds this question, they are apt to tell you that there are more black horses. In probing the children's reasoning, it becomes clear that most of them interpret the question as a request to compare only the *black* cows with the black horses. For example, one child defended his incorrect answer by saying, "There's more black horses 'cos there's only two black cows" (M. Donaldson, 1978, p. 44).

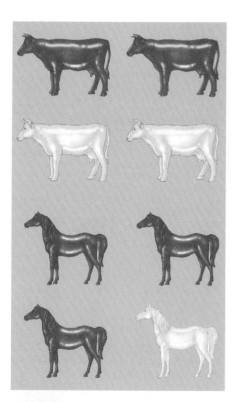

Figure 9-3

Are there more cows or more black horses?

phonemes
Smallest units of a spoken language that signify differences in meaning.

Older children and adolescents consider the context in a somewhat different way, in that they compare a message to the reality of the situation. Such a comparison enables them to detect sarcasm—to realize that the speaker actually means the exact opposite of what he or she is saying (Capelli, Nakagawa, & Madden, 1990). For instance, they understand that someone who says "Oh, that's just great!" in the face of dire circumstances doesn't think the situation is "great" at all.

● *Young children have an overly simplistic view of what "good listening" is.* Children in the early elementary grades believe they are good listeners if they simply sit quietly without interrupting the person speaking. Older children (e.g., 11-year-olds) are more likely to recognize that good listening also requires an understanding of what is being said (T. M. McDevitt et al., 1990).

● *Elementary school children do not always know what to do when they don't understand what they hear.* In a series of studies (T. M. McDevitt, 1990; T. M. McDevitt et al., 1990), children in grades 1, 3, and 5 were given the following dilemma:

> This is a story about a girl named Mary. Mary is at school listening to her teacher, Ms. Brown. Ms. Brown explains how to use a new computer that she just got for their classroom. She tells the children in the classroom how to use the computer. Mary doesn't understand the teacher's directions. She's confused. What should Mary do? (T. M. McDevitt, 1990, p. 570)

Some children responded that Mary should ask the teacher for further explanation. But others said that Mary should either listen more carefully or seek clarification of the procedure from other children. Many children, younger ones especially, believe it is inappropriate to ask a teacher for help, perhaps because they have previously been discouraged from asking questions in school or at home. Cultural background plays a role here as well. Many children growing up in Asian and Mexican American communities are reluctant to ask questions because they've been taught that initiating a conversation with an adult is disrespectful (Delgado-Gaitan, 1994; Grant & Gomez, 2001).

● *Older children and adolescents become increasingly able to find multiple meanings in messages.* As children move into the middle and secondary grades, they become aware that some messages are ambiguous and have two or more possible meanings (Bearison & Levey, 1977; Nippold, 1988; R. E. Owens, 1996). They also become better able to understand **figurative speech,** speech that communicates meaning beyond a literal interpretation of its words. For instance, they understand that idioms should not be taken at face value—for instance, that a person who "hits the roof" doesn't really hit the roof and that someone who is "tied up" isn't necessarily bound with rope. They become increasingly adept at interpreting similes and metaphors (e.g., "Her hands are like ice," "That man is the Rock of Gibraltar"). And in the late elementary years, they begin to draw generalizations from proverbs such as "Look before you leap" and "Don't put the cart before the horse." In the "Cognitive Development" video clips for middle childhood and late adolescence, on Observation CD 1, you can observe how children's ability to understand proverbs improves with age. For example, whereas 10-year-old Kent seems baffled by the old adage "A rolling stone gathers no moss," 14-year-old Alicia offers a reasonable explanation: "Maybe when you go through things too fast, you don't collect anything from it." Adolescents' ability to interpret proverbs in a generalized, abstract fashion continues to develop throughout the secondary school years (R. E. Owens, 1996).

Although children's ability to understand figurative language depends to some degree on their cognitive maturity, it may also depend on how much they have been exposed to such language. Many inner-city African American communities make heavy use of figurative language, such as similes, metaphors, and hyperbole (intentional exaggeration), in their day-to-day conversations, jokes, and stories (Hale-Benson, 1986; Ortony, Turner, & Larson-Shapiro, 1985; H. L. Smith, 1998). The following anecdote illustrates this point:

> I once asked my mother, upon her arrival from church, "Mom, was it a good sermon?" To which she replied, "Son, by the time the minister finished preaching, the men were crying and the women had passed out on the floor." (H. L. Smith, 1998, p. 202)

Observe the developmental progression in understanding figurative speech as you listen to Kent and Alicia interpret proverbs in the "Cognitive Development" clips for middle childhood and late adolescence, on Observation CD 1.

figurative speech
Speech that communicates meaning beyond a literal interpretation of its words.

DEVELOPMENT AND PRACTICE

Promoting Listening Skills in Young Children

- Present only small amounts of information at one time.

  A preschool teacher helps the 3- and 4-year-olds in her class make "counting books" to take home. She has previously prepared nine sheets of paper (each with a different number from 1 to 9) for each child. She has also assembled a variety of objects that the children can paste on the pages to depict the numbers (two buttons for the "2" page, five pieces of macaroni for the "5" page, etc.). As she engages the children in the project, she describes only one or two steps of the process at a time.

- Expect children to listen attentively only for short periods.

  A kindergarten teacher has learned that most of his students can listen quietly to a storybook for no more than 10 or 15 minutes at a stretch, and he plans his daily schedule accordingly.

- Discuss the components of good listening.

  A first-grade teacher explains to her students that "good listening" involves more than just sitting quietly, that it also involves paying attention and trying to understand what the speaker is saying. Later, after a police officer has visited her class to discuss bicycle safety, she asks the children to restate some of the safety precautions the officer mentioned.

- Discuss courses of action that children should take when they don't understand a speaker.

  A second-grade teacher encourages his students to ask questions whenever they don't understand something he tells them in class.

With such a rich oral tradition, it is not surprising that inner-city African American youth are especially advanced in their ability to comprehend figurative language (Ortony et al., 1985).

Cognitive factors influencing the development of listening comprehension.   Not only does children's ability to understand what they hear depend on their knowledge of word meanings and syntax, but it also depends on their general knowledge about the world. For instance, children can better understand a peer's description of a newly purchased Volkswagen Beetle if they have a schema for Volkswagen Beetles. They can better understand a friend's story about a trip to a fast-food restaurant if they have a script of what such visits typically entail. Children's schemas, scripts, and other knowledge about the world enable them to draw inferences from the things they hear, thus filling gaps in the information actually presented.

In addition, children's ability to understand and remember what they hear is limited to what they can reasonably hold in working memory (Anthony, Lonigan, & Dyer, 1996; L. French & Brown, 1977). When information exceeds their working memory capacity, it will, as a common expression puts it, "go in one ear and out the other." Because young children tend to have less working memory capacity than older children and adults, they will be especially limited in their ability to understand and remember what others tell them. Preschoolers, for instance, often have trouble remembering and following directions with multiple steps (L. French & Brown, 1977).

Children's general cognitive abilities play a role as well. Interpreting messages in nonliteral ways requires abstract thinking and an ability to draw analogies across diverse situations (R. E. Owens, 1996; Winner, 1988). Given what we know about the development of abstract thought, it is hardly surprising that children have difficulty understanding metaphors and proverbs in the preschool and early elementary years.

Promoting listening comprehension.   Parents, teachers, caregivers, and others who work with toddlers, preschoolers, and students in the primary grades must take into account the limited listening comprehension skills that young children are likely to have (see the Development and Practice feature "Promoting Listening Skills in Young Children"). Following are three more general suggestions for adults who work with children and adolescents at all age levels:

● ***Take children's semantic and syntactic development into account when speaking to them, and check frequently to be sure they understand.*** Using vocabulary and syntactic structures appropriate to the age-group is, of course, essential if adults want children to understand what they say. Furthermore, rather than assuming that their messages have been understood, adults should in some way assess children's understandings, perhaps by asking questions, having children restate ideas in their own words, or having them demonstrate what they've learned through actions or pictures. The following exercise, "Figure of Speech," provides practice in assessing children's understandings.

--- Connecting Concepts

Developmental changes in working memory are described in Chapter 7.

INTERPRETING CHILDREN'S ARTIFACTS AND ACTIONS   Figure of Speech

In response to an assignment in his third-grade class, 8-year-old Jeff drew his interpretation of the common expression *Your eyes are bigger than your stomach.* As you look at Jeff's drawing, what can you conclude about his language comprehension skills?

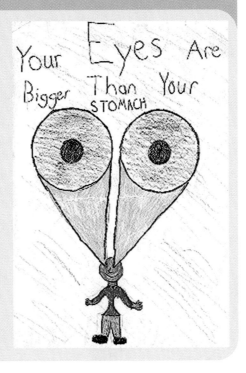

Jeff certainly understands the sentence's literal meaning, because the eyes are quite a bit larger than the person's very narrow waistline. The person he's drawn is a nonrealistic, "silly" one, so perhaps he has an inkling that the sentence is not intended to be taken entirely at face value. However, he misses the meaning that this common figure of speech usually conveys: that a person requests more food than he or she can possibly eat at a single sitting. This focus on the literal rather than figurative meaning of the sentence is hardly surprising. As you've learned, understanding figurative speech is far more common in adolescence than at younger ages.

● *Adjust the length of verbal presentations to the attention span of the age-group, and avoid information overload.* As information processing theory tells us, people of all ages can understand a message only when they are paying attention, and they can handle only a limited amount of information at a time. Given such limitations, children and adolescents alike often benefit from hearing something more than once (e.g., Wasik, Karweit, Burns, & Brodsky, 1998).

● *Encourage critical listening.* Sometime around age 3 to 6, children begin to realize that what people say is not necessarily what is true (e.g., Koenig, Clément, & Harris, 2004; K. Lee, Cameron, Doucette, & Talwar, 2002). Yet throughout the elementary and secondary school years, children and adolescents sometimes have difficulty separating fact from fiction in the messages they hear. Children who are taught not to believe everything they hear are more likely to evaluate messages for errors, falsehoods, and ambiguities. For example, when children are reminded that television commercials are designed to persuade them to buy something, they are less likely to be influenced by the commercials (T. M. McDevitt, 1990; D. F. Roberts, Christenson, Gibson, Mooser, & Goldberg, 1980).

Development of Speaking Skills

As children become more adept at understanding what other people say, they also become more adept at expressing their own thoughts, ideas, and wishes. When children first begin to speak, their objective is often to control someone else's behavior. For example, a toddler who yells "Elmo!" may very well be asking a parent to purchase the Elmo doll she sees on a shelf at the toy store. Over the next 2 or 3 years, however, children increasingly use speech to exchange information with others. By age 4, exchanging information appears to be the primary function of oral language (R. E. Owens, 1996).

Children begin to develop their speaking skills long before they utter their first word, however. Following are several trends that characterize the development of speaking skills in infancy, childhood, and adolescence:

● *In the first year of life, children become increasingly proficient in making speech sounds and increasingly language-specific in their vocalizations.* Between 1 and 2 months of age, infants typically begin **cooing,** making vowel sounds in an almost "singing" manner (e.g., "aaaaaaa," "oooooo"). Sometime around 6 months, they begin **babbling,** combining consonant and vowel sounds into syllables that they repeat over and over (e.g., "mamama-mama," "doodoodoo") without apparent meaning. With time, babbling becomes increasingly speechlike in nature, as infants combine different syllables into language-like utterances. Also with time, infants gradually drop the sounds they don't hear in the speech around them (J. L. Locke, 1993). In essence, infants first babble in a universal "language" that includes a wide variety of phonemes, but they later babble only in their native tongue.

● *Infants and toddlers sometimes use gestures to communicate.* As early as age 1, some children try to communicate through actions rather than words. An infant might put his fingers in his mouth to indicate that he wants something to eat. A toddler might wrinkle her nose and sniff as a way of "talking" about flowers. Such gestures seem to pave the way for later language development, but they are typically abandoned as children gain proficiency in language—unless, of course, children learn a manual language or grow up in a culture that encourages demonstrative gestures (Goodwyn & Acredolo, 1998; Goodwyn, Acredolo, & Brown, 2000; Namy & Waxman, 2002).

● *Pronunciation continues to develop in the early elementary years.* As we've discovered, children say their first word sometime around their first birthday, and by age 2 or so most children talk a great deal. Yet children typically do not master all the phonemes of the English language until they are about 8 years old (R. E. Owens, 1996). During the preschool years, they are likely to have difficulty pronouncing *r* and *th* (they might say "wabbit" instead of "rabbit" and "dat" instead of "that"). Most children have acquired these sounds by the time they are 6, but at this age they may still have trouble with such consonant blends as *str, sl,* and *dr* (R. E. Owens, 1996).

Recall the kindergarten teacher's reference to Mario's "slight accent." Mario mastered Spanish pronunciation by age 3. A few months later, he could produce many of the additional phonemes required for English. Nevertheless, Spanish sounds occasionally crept into Mario's English for several years thereafter (Fantini, 1985).

● *As children grow older, their conversations with others increase in length and depth.* Early conversations tend to be short. Most young children are quite willing and able to introduce new topics into a conversation, but they have difficulty maintaining a sustained interchange about any single topic (Brinton & Fujiki, 1984; K. Nelson, 1996a). As they grow older, they can carry on lengthier discussions about a single issue or event. And as they reach adolescence, the content of their conversations becomes increasingly abstract (R. E. Owens, 1996).

● *Children become increasingly able to adapt their speech to the characteristics of their listeners.* As early as age 3, preschoolers use simpler language with toddlers than they do with adults and peers (T. M. McDevitt & Ford, 1987; Shatz & Gelman, 1973). Yet preschoolers and elementary school children don't always take their listeners' visual perspectives and prior knowledge into account and so may provide insufficient information for listeners to understand what they are saying (Glucksberg & Krauss, 1967; T. M. McDevitt & Ford, 1987). We can recall numerous occasions when our own children yelled "What's this?" from another room, apparently unaware that we could not possibly see what they were looking at. To some extent, such speech may reflect the *egocentrism* that Piaget described. However, it may also be the result of young children's lack of proficiency in precisely describing the objects and events they are currently experiencing or have previously witnessed.

As children grow older, they become increasingly able to take other people's knowledge and perspectives into consideration and so are better able to make their meanings clear (Son-

——————— **Connecting Concepts**
Gestures also play a role in young children's reasoning (see Chapter 7).

As children grow older, they become better able to carry on lengthy conversations about a single topic.

——————— **Connecting Concepts**
Piaget's concept of *egocentrism* is discussed in Chapter 6.

cooing
Making and repeating vowel sounds (e.g., "oooooo"); common in early infancy.

babbling
Repeating certain consonant-vowel syllables over and over (e.g., "mamamama"); common in the latter half of the first year.

nenschein, 1988). They also become better able to read the subtle nonverbal signals (e.g., the puzzled brows, the lengthy silences) that indicate others' confusion about their messages (T. M. McDevitt & Ford, 1987).

● *Over time, children become more skillful at narratives.* Beginning in the preschool years, children can tell a story, or **narrative**—an account of a sequence of events, either real or fictional, that are logically interconnected (McKeough, 1995; Sutton-Smith, 1986). The following narrative, told by 4-year-old Lucy, is typical of children's early fiction:

> Once upon a time there was a girl who lived on a farm with a very good horse and she always rode to the country on the horse and they had a picnic together. (McKeough, 1995, p. 156)

Kindergartners and first graders can typically describe a sequence that reflects appropriate ordering of events and includes cause-effect relationships (Kemper, 1984; Kemper & Edwards, 1986; McKeough, 1995). Narratives become increasingly complex during the elementary years. Definite plot lines begin to emerge, as do descriptions of people's thoughts, motives, and emotions (Bauer, 2006; Kemper, 1984; R. E. Owens, 1996).

The exact nature of children's narratives varies somewhat from culture to culture. For example, in some African American communities, narratives may include several events that, on the surface, seem unrelated yet all contribute to a single underlying message—perhaps providing strategies for helping a baby brother (Hale-Benson, 1986; R. E. Owens, 1996; Trawick-Smith, 2003). Children from some backgrounds may have little or no exposure to certain kinds of narratives before beginning school (Heath, 1986). For example, in some lower-socioeconomic communities in the southern United States, children have few if any opportunities to describe events that they alone have experienced. These children are more likely to talk about events they have shared with their listeners (Heath, 1986).

● *Creative and figurative expressions emerge during the elementary years and continue into adolescence.* With age, children become increasingly creative in their language use. Elementary school children have widely shared expressions that they use to make choices ("Eenie, meenie, minie, mo"), challenge one another ("I double-dare you"), and establish standards for behavior ("Finders keepers, losers weepers") (R. E. Owens, 1996). In inner-city African American communities, creative word play may also appear in the form of **playing the dozens,** playful teasing of one another through exaggerated insults (e.g., "Your momma is so dumb that she climbed over a pane of glass to see what was on the other side"). Exaggeration (hyperbole) is evident in African American storytelling as well. In the following exchange, 12-year-old Terry and his neighbor Tony begin with a kernel of truth (a cat fight in the neighborhood) and then let their imaginations run wild:

Terry:	Didja hear 'bout Aunt Bess' cat las' night?
Tony:	No, what 'bout dat ol' cat?
Terry:	Dat cat get in a fight.
Tony:	A fight?
Terry:	Yeah, it kilt a dog.
Tony:	Ain't no cat can kill no dog.
Terry:	Dis cat, he kilt a big dog, dat ol' German shepherd stay down by ol' man Oak's place.
Tony:	What'd you do?
Terry:	Me? I kilt a horse.
Tony:	You ain't kilt no horse, (pause) more'n likely a mouse. Where?
Terry:	On Main Street. Yesterday.
Tony:	And you kilt one, for sure?
Terry:	Yea, me 'n dat ol' cat, we built a big fire, stirred it aroun', threw oil in it, got it goin' good, and I rod [*sic*] dat horse right in.
Tony:	Ya did?
Terry:	Yup.
Tony:	I know, it took a while to git de cat outta de fire, 'bout (pause) maybe a week or so, 'n Mr. Rowe [who owns a bicycle shop on Main Street] give us a bicycle, 'n we ride de horse, 'n my friend, Steve, he ride de horse, too, 'n we come back and foun' dat ol' cat done kilt dat big dog.
Terry:	Why?
Tony:	'Cause dat cat say "Wow, I'm de greates', ain't no dog kin git me," (pause) like ain't no fire gonna git *me* (pause) 'n my horse (pause) 'n my bicycle. (Heath, 1983, pp. 183–184; reprinted with the permission of Cambridge University Press)

Connecting Concepts ——————
You can see examples of narratives at various grade levels in the four compositions presented in the opening case study in Chapter 7.

Connecting Concepts ——————
Additional examples of playing the dozens appear in the story of Sam on page 242 of Chapter 7.

narrative
Verbal account of a temporal sequence of events that are logically interconnected; a story.

playing the dozens
Friendly, playful exchange of insults, common in some African American communities; also called *joaning* or *sounding.*

The use of figurative language in children's speech emerges during the elementary years and increases in frequency and sophistication during the secondary school years. Adolescents often use metaphors, similes, and phrases with double meanings. They are also likely to use sarcasm to communicate a message opposite from what their words mean literally (R. E. Owens, 1996).

● *Adolescents sometimes use their own teen "dialect" in conversing with peers.* Many adolescents express themselves in ways that are unique to their age-group, or perhaps to a small group of friends (R. E. Owens, 1996). For example, over the years, teenagers have used a variety of adjectives—*cool, boss, radical, awesome,* and so on—to describe something they really like. At age 16, Jeanne's son Alex insisted on addressing everyone (including his mother) as "Dude." Such expressions help adolescents establish themselves as belonging to a particular peer group in much the same way that their clothing and hairstyles do (J. R. Harris, 1995).

How children develop speaking skills.   Children's increasing proficiency in oral language is the result of many things: better muscular control of the lips and tongue, more semantic and syntactic knowledge, growing awareness of what listeners are apt to know and believe, acquisition of abstract reasoning ability, and so on. But to a considerable degree, the development of speaking skills also comes from practice, practice, practice.

Sometimes preschoolers' conversational partners are adults, who typically take the lead in discussions (R. E. Owens, 1996). In their interactions with peers, however, children can converse more as equal partners. Furthermore, when children assume the roles of "mommy," "teacher," "doctor," or "storekeeper" in play activities, they can experiment with the variety of linguistic styles and jargon that they associate with such roles (Christie & Johnsen, 1983; K. Nelson, 1986). Often, too, they use narratives to develop a story line for their play:

> You're the daddy. And you pretend to get dressed. You're going to take the baby to the zoo. (R. E. Owens, 1996, p. 347)

During the elementary and secondary school years, experience—in the form of both structured activities (e.g., oral presentations at school) and unstructured interactions (e.g., conversations with friends)—almost certainly continues to play a key role in the development of speaking skills. For instance, the prevalence of word play and figurative language in inner-city African American communities is probably largely responsible for the especially creative speech of the children who grow up in these communities (Ortony et al., 1985; H. L. Smith, 1998).

Promoting speaking skills.   To help children and adolescents develop their speaking skills, teachers and other adults should, of course, give them many and varied opportunities to speak in both structured and unstructured contexts. The following strategies may also be beneficial:

● *Regularly engage infants in "conversation."* In the "Infancy" video clips of the "Cognitive Development," "Intelligence," and "Literacy" modules on Observation CDs 1 and 2, you can observe several "conversations" that 16-month-old Corwin has with his mother. Although Corwin says few words distinctly enough to be understood, he knows how to take turns in the dialogue and understands enough of what his mother says to respond appropriately to her questions.

Most infants readily participate in verbal interactions with adults as early as 3 or 4 months of age. Even at this point they have some knowledge of turn taking: They may quietly listen when an adult speaks to them and vocalize when the adult stops (Ginsburg & Kilbourne, 1988). Young infants also tend to mimic the intonations (e.g., changes in pitch and stress) that a caregiver uses (Masataka, 1992). When a caregiver mimics *their* vocalizations, infants' speechlike sounds increase in frequency (K. Bloom, Russell, & Wassenberg, 1987). It appears, then, that experience with verbal interaction has benefits even for children who do not yet understand much of what they hear.

Another effective strategy is to teach infants gestures they can use to communicate their wishes. For instance, caregivers might teach babies signs for *more* and *please* (see Figure 9-4). Infants as young as 6 months old can successfully learn a few hand signs to communicate with caregivers (Goodwyn et al., 2000; R. H. Thompson, McKerchar, & Dancho, 2004).

Observe Corwin's turn taking with his mother in the "Infancy" clips of the "Cognitive Development," "Intelligence," and "Literacy" modules on Observation CDs 1 and 2.

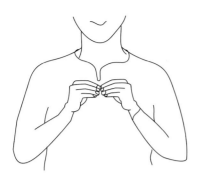

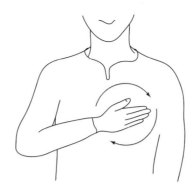

"More"

"Please"

Place your fingertips together in front of your chest, as if adding something to the top of a pile.

Hold your hand close to your heart with palm facing toward your chest, and move it clockwise (from an observer's viewpoint) to indicate pleasure.

Figure 9-4

Children as young as 6 months can be taught to communicate through simple gestures. Examples of useful gestures are the signs for *more* and *please* in American Sign Language.

● *Let children know when their message is difficult to understand.* People of all ages occasionally have trouble communicating their thoughts clearly to others. Young children may have particular difficulty because of their limited ability to consider the knowledge and perspectives of their listeners. Asking questions or expressing confusion when children describe events and ideas ambiguously or incompletely should gradually help them express their thoughts more precisely and take into account what their listeners do and do not know.

● *Ask children to tell stories.* Adults often ask questions that encourage children to respond in narrative form. For instance, a teacher might ask, "What did you do this weekend?" or "Do you remember what happened the last time someone brought a pet to show-and-tell?" Giving children opportunities to narrate events, either actual incidents or fictional creations, provides a context in which they can practice speaking for sustained periods and build on the rich oral traditions of many cultural groups (Hale-Benson, 1986; Hemphill & Snow, 1996; McCarty & Watahomigie, 1998).

Storytelling ability can be enhanced by specific training and practice (McKeough, 1995). Consider how 6-year-old Leanne's ability to tell a story improved over a 2-month period as a result of specific instruction about how to conceptualize and tell stories:

Before instruction:

A girl—and a boy—and a kind old horse. They got mad at each other. That the end. (McKeough, 1995, p. 170)

After instruction:

Once upon a time there was a girl. She was playing with her toys and—um—she asked her mom if she could go outside—to play in the snow. But her mom said no. And then she was very sad. And—and she had to play. So she she [sic] asked her mom if she could go outside and she said yes. She jumped in the snow and she was having fun and she had an idea and she jumped in the snow and she feeled happy. (McKeough, 1995, p. 170)

● *Encourage creativity in oral language.* Linguistic creativity can be expressed in many ways, including through stories, poems, songs, rap, jokes, and puns. Such forms of language not only encourage creative language use but also help children identify parallels between seemingly dissimilar objects or events. Recognizing commonalities enables children to construct similes, metaphors, and other analogies. Hyperbole can be encouraged as well, as long as children realize that they are intentionally stretching the truth. For the assignment shown in Figure 9-5, 6-year-old Morris was instructed to write a fact and then a "tall sentence" in which he should fantasize or exaggerate.

School provides an excellent context in which children and adolescents can develop their speaking skills.

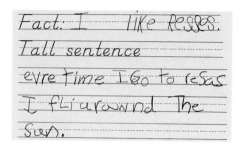

Figure 9-5

Morris (age 6) shows that he knows the difference between a fact ("I like recess") and a "tall sentence" ("Every time I go to recess I fly around the sun").

In addition, the playful use of language can help children discover general characteristics of language, as an event in Mario's childhood illustrates:

Seven-year-old Mario tells his parents a joke that he has heard at school earlier in the day. He relates the joke in English: "What did the bird say when his cage got broken?" His parents have no idea what the bird said, so he tells them, "Cheap, cheap!"

Mario's parents find the joke amusing, so he later translates it for the family's Spanish-speaking nanny: "*¿Qué dijo el pájaro cuando se le rompió la jaula?*" He follows up with the bird's answer: "*Barato, barato.*" Mario is surprised to discover that the nanny finds no humor in the joke. He knows that he has somehow failed to convey the point of the joke but cannot figure out where he went wrong. (Fantini, 1985, p. 72)[1]

The joke, of course, gets lost in translation. The Spanish word *barato* means "cheap" but has no resemblance to the sound that a bird makes. Only several years later did Mario understand that humor that depends on wordplay does not always translate from one language to another (Fantini, 1985). His eventual understanding of this principle was an aspect of his growing *metalinguistic awareness,* a topic we examine shortly.

Development of Pragmatics

The pragmatic aspects of language include verbal and nonverbal strategies for communicating effectively with others. Strategies for initiating conversations, changing the subject, telling stories, and arguing persuasively are all forms of pragmatic knowledge. Knowledge and use of behaviors that are considered polite and socially acceptable in verbal interactions—that is, knowledge and use of appropriate **sociolinguistic behaviors**—also fall within the domain of pragmatics.

Most children begin to acquire pragmatic skills—prefacing a request with "please," responding to other people's questions, and so on—long before they reach school age. Preschoolers also learn that certain ways that they might speak to their peers ("Shut up!" "Get auto here!") are unacceptable when talking to adults (Bryant, 2001). Children continue to refine their knowledge of pragmatics throughout the preschool years and elementary grades (Garvey & Berninger, 1981; R. E. Owens, 1996; Warren-Leubecker & Bohannon, 1989). Our own observations indicate that this process continues into the middle and high school years as well. However, children from different cultures often learn different social conventions, particularly in matters of etiquette, as you will see now.

Cultural differences in sociolinguistic behaviors.   Cultural differences in sociolinguistic behaviors sometimes lead to misunderstandings in cross-cultural interactions. For example, some Native American communities believe it unnecessary to say hello or good-bye (Sisk, 1989). When children from these communities fail to extend greetings, an adult may erroneously conclude that they are being rude. In other Native American communities, children learn to display steady, neutral facial expressions even as they experience strong feelings inside (Montgomery, 1989). An adult from a non–Native American background might easily misinterpret a child's lack of facial expression as a sign of boredom or disinterest.

Following are additional cultural differences that may lead to misunderstandings in classrooms and other group settings. These differences are summarized in the Observation Guidelines table "Identifying Cultural Differences in Sociolinguistic Conventions."

Talking versus being silent.   Relatively speaking, mainstream Western culture is a chatty one. People often say things to one another even when they have very little to communicate, making small talk as a way of maintaining interpersonal relationships and filling awkward silences (Irujo, 1988). In some African American communities as well, people speak frequently—for instance, spontaneously shouting out or moving about during church services (Lein, 1975).

In certain other cultures, however, silence is golden. Brazilians and Peruvians often greet their guests silently, Arabs stop talking to indicate a desire for privacy, and many Native American communities value silence in general (Basso, 1972; Menyuk & Menyuk, 1988;

---

sociolinguistic behaviors
Social and culturally specific conventions that govern appropriate verbal interaction.

[1]From *Language Acquisition of a Bilingual Child: A Sociolinguistic Perspective,* by A. E. Fantini, 1985. Clevedon, England: Multilingual Matters. (Available from the SIT Bookstore, School for International Training, Kipling Road, Brattleboro, VT 06302.) Reprinted with permission.

OBSERVATION GUIDELINES

Identifying Cultural Differences in Sociolinguistic Conventions

Characteristic	Look For	Example	Implication
Talkativeness	• Frequent talking, even about trivial matters, *or* • Silence unless something important needs to be said	When Muhammed abruptly stops talking to his peers and turns to read his book, the other children think his action is rude.	Don't interpret a child's sudden or lengthy silence as necessarily reflecting apathy or intentional rudeness.
Style of Interacting with Adults	• Willingness to initiate conversations with adults, *or* • Speaking to adults only when spoken to	Elena is exceptionally quiet in class, and she answers questions only when her teacher directs them specifically at her. At lunch and on the playground, however, she readily talks and laughs with her friends.	Keep in mind that some children won't tell you when they're confused. If you think they may not understand, take them aside and ask specific questions to assess what they have learned. Provide additional instruction to address any gaps in understanding.
Eye Contact	• Looking others in the eye when speaking or listening to them, *or* • Looking down or away in the presence of adults	Herman always looks at his feet when an adult speaks to him.	Don't assume that children aren't paying attention just because they don't look you in the eye.
Personal Space	• Standing quite close to a conversation partner, perhaps touching that person frequently, *or* • Keeping distance between oneself and others when talking with them	Michelle is noticeably uncomfortable when other people touch her.	Give children some personal space during one-on-one interactions. So that they might more effectively interact with others, teach them that what constitutes personal space differs from culture to culture.
Responses to Questions	• Answering questions readily, *or* • Failure to answer very easy questions	Leah never responds to "What is this?" questions, even when she knows the answers.	Be aware that some children are not accustomed to answering the types of questions many Western adults ask during instruction. Respect children's privacy when they are reluctant to answer questions about family life.
Wait Time	• Waiting several seconds before answering questions, *or* • Not waiting at all, and perhaps even interrupting others	Mario often interrupts his classmates during class discussions.	When addressing a question to an entire group, give children several seconds to think before calling on one child for an answer. When some children interrupt regularly, communicate a procedure (e.g., hand raising and waiting to be called on) to ensure that everyone has a chance to be heard.

Trawick-Smith, 2003). And as noted in Chapter 8, some cultures interpret talking a lot as a sign of immaturity or low intelligence.

Interacting with adults. In many European American families, children feel they can speak freely when they have comments or questions. Yet children raised in certain other cultures (e.g., in many Hispanic, Native American, and Southeast Asian cultures, as well as in some African American communities) learn very early that they should engage in conversation with adults only when their participation has been directly solicited. In such cultures, speaking directly and assertively to adults is seen as rude, perhaps even rebellious (Banks & Banks, 1995; Delgado-Gaitan, 1994; Grant & Gomez, 2001). For example, children in the Yup'ik culture of Alaska are expected to learn primarily by close, quiet observation of adults, and so they rarely ask questions or otherwise interrupt what adults are doing (García, 1994).

For some children in the Pacific Islands, one-on-one interactions with adults may remind them of scoldings they've received from their parents. Often these children are quite willing to respond in class as a group yet remain silent when called on individually (K. H. Au, 1980).

Making eye contact. Among many people from European American backgrounds, looking someone in the eye is a way of indicating that they are trying to communicate or are listening

In some cultures, looking an adult in the eye is a sign of respect. In other cultures, it is interpreted as *disrespect*.

intently. But in many African American, Hispanic, and Native American cultures, a child who looks an adult in the eye is showing disrespect. Children in such cultures are taught to look down in the presence of adults (Gilliland, 1988; Torres-Guzmán, 1998; Trawick-Smith, 2003). The following anecdote shows how accommodation to this culturally learned behavior can make a difference:

> A teacher [described a Native American] student who would never say a word, nor even answer when she greeted him. Then one day when he came in she looked in the other direction and said, "Hello, Jimmy." He answered enthusiastically, "Why hello Miss Jacobs." She found that he would always talk if she looked at a book or at the wall, but when she looked at him, he appeared frightened. (Gilliland, 1988, p. 26)

Maintaining personal space.   In some cultures, such as in some African American and Hispanic communities, people stand close together when they talk and may touch one another frequently (Hale-Benson, 1986; Slonim, 1991; Sue, 1990). In contrast, European Americans and Japanese Americans tend to keep a fair distance from one another—they maintain some **personal space**—especially if they don't know one another very well (Irujo, 1988; Trawick-Smith, 2003). Adults who work regularly with children must be sensitive to the personal space that children from various cultural backgrounds need in order to feel comfortable in interactions with others.

Responding to questions.   A common interaction pattern in many Western classrooms is the **IRE cycle:** A teacher *initiates* an interaction by asking a question, a student *responds* to the question, and the teacher *evaluates* the response (Mehan, 1979). Similar cycles are frequently found in parent-child interactions in middle-income European American homes. As we reflect back on our interactions with our own children as toddlers and preschoolers, we can recall many occasions when we asked them questions such as "How old are you?" and "What does a cow say?" and praised them for correct answers. But children from some backgrounds—for instance, many of those raised in lower-income homes, as well as those raised in some Mexican American, Native American, and Hawaiian communities—are unfamiliar with such question-answer sessions when they first come to school (Losey, 1995).

Furthermore, different cultural groups teach children to answer different kinds of questions. European American parents frequently ask their children to identify objects and characteristics (notice the kinds of questions that Mother asks Corwin in the "Literacy: Infancy" video clip on Observation CD 2). Yet in certain other cultures, parents rarely ask their children questions that they themselves know the answers to (Crago, Annahatak, & Ningiuruvik, 1993; Heath, 1980; Rogoff & Morelli, 1989). Parents in some African American communities in the southeastern United States are more likely to ask questions involving comparisons and analogies. For example, rather than asking "What's that?" they may instead ask "What's that like?" (Heath, 1980). Also, children in these communities are specifically taught *not* to answer questions that strangers ask about personal and home life (e.g., "What's your name?" "Where do you live?"). Teachers' comments about these children reflect a lack of understanding about the culture from which the children come:

In the "Literacy: Infancy" clip on Observation CD 2, hear the kinds of questions that European American mothers typically ask their young children.

> "I would almost think some of them have a hearing problem; it is as though they don't hear me ask a question. I get blank stares to my questions. Yet when I am making statements or telling stories which interest them, they always seem to hear me."

> "The simplest questions are the ones they can't answer in the classroom; yet on the playground, they can explain a rule for a ballgame or describe a particular kind of bait with no problem. Therefore, I know they can't be as dumb as they seem in my class." (Heath, 1980, pp. 107–108)

Meanwhile, parents describe the confusion their children are experiencing:

> "My kid, he too scared to talk, 'cause nobody play by the rules he know. At home I can't shut him up."

> "Miss Davis, she complain 'bout Ned not answerin' back. He says she asks dumb questions she already know about." (Heath, 1980, p. 107)

Waiting and interrupting.   Teachers frequently ask their students questions and then wait for an answer. But exactly how long do they wait? The typical **wait time** for many teachers

personal space
Personally and culturally preferred distance between two people during social interaction.

IRE cycle
Adult-child interaction pattern marked by adult initiation, child response, and adult evaluation; in Western cultures such a pattern is often seen in instructional settings.

wait time
The length of time a teacher pauses, after either asking a question or hearing a student's comment, before saying something.

is a second or even less, at which point they either answer a question themselves or call on another student (M. B. Rowe, 1974, 1987). Yet people from some cultures leave lengthy pauses before responding as a way of indicating respect, as this statement by a Northern Cheyenne illustrates:

> Even if I had a quick answer to your question, I would never answer immediately. That would be saying that your question was not worth thinking about. (Gilliland, 1988, p. 27)

For some cultural groups, then, students are more likely to participate in class and answer questions when given several seconds to respond (Grant & Gomez, 2001; Mohatt & Erickson, 1981; Tharp, 1989).

In contrast, children from certain other backgrounds, rather than pausing to show respect, may interrupt adults or peers who haven't finished speaking—an action that some of their teachers might interpret as rudeness. In some African American, Puerto Rican, and Jewish families, family discourse often consists of several people talking at once. In fact, people who wait for their turn might find themselves excluded from the discussion altogether (Condon & Yousef, 1975; Farber, Mindel, & Lazerwitz, 1988; Hale-Benson, 1986; Slonim, 1991). And in some Hawaiian communities, an interruption is taken as a sign of personal involvement in the conversation (Tharp, 1989).

How sociolinguistic behaviors develop.   As we've seen, even young infants exhibit turn taking in their "conversations" with others, in that they tend to remain quiet when an adult is talking. This tendency may be essential to language development (J. L. Locke, 1993) and so may reflect a biological predisposition. By and large, however, conversational etiquette and other sociolinguistic conventions are probably culturally transmitted.

Often adults teach sociolinguistic behaviors directly. Mario once explained to his parents how his kindergarten teacher encouraged students to take turns when speaking in class (we present an English translation of Mario's Spanish):

> [A]t school, I have to raise my hand . . . and then wait a long, long time. And then the teacher says: "Now you can speak, Mario," and she makes the other children shut up, and she says, "Mario's speaking now." (Fantini, 1985, p. 83)[2]

Children also learn many conventions through imitating the behaviors of others—perhaps copying the way their parents answer the telephone, greet people on the street, and converse with friends and relatives. In addition, the feedback youngsters receive from others (sometimes blatant, sometimes more subtle) may encourage them to behave in certain ways and not others. For instance, most young children eventually learn that they get along better with their peers when they ask for something nicely ("May I please have that?") rather than make demands ("Gimme dat!"). And older children and adolescents may discover that when they stand too close to others, their conversational partners act uneasy and may even back up to create a more comfortable distance.

Taking sociolinguistic differences into account.   When the sociolinguistic behaviors expected at home differ significantly from those expected at school and in other group settings, a sense of confusion, or **culture shock,** can result. Such culture shock can interfere with children's adjustment to the group setting and, ultimately, with their behavior and achievement as well (Banks & Banks, 1995; Ogbu, 1992; Phelan, Yu, & Davidson, 1994). Adults further compound the problem when, interpreting children's behaviors as being unacceptable or otherwise "odd," they jump too quickly to the conclusion that certain youngsters are unable or unwilling to make productive contributions to the group (Bowman, 1989; Hilliard & Vaughn-Scott, 1982).

Clearly, teachers and other practitioners must educate themselves about the diverse sociolinguistic patterns they are likely to encounter in day-to-day interactions with children. Furthermore, they must keep children's varying conversational styles in mind as they design group lessons and activities. For example, teachers might check their students'

---

[2]See footnote 1 on page 340.

culture shock
Sense of confusion that occurs when one encounters an environment with expectations for behavior very different from those in one's home environment.

understanding of classroom material by calling for group rather than individual responses or perhaps by having students write their responses on paper. They might also vary their questions to include those that different students are accustomed to answering at home. And they should allow sufficient wait time for all students to think about and respond to questions.

Some children lack pragmatic skills desirable in *any* culture. For example, we have known children who seemed so insistent on dominating a conversation that no one else could contribute to the discussion. When children haven't mastered basic conventions of conversational etiquette, they may have trouble establishing and maintaining productive relationships with adults and age-mates. In such cases educators can provide guided practice in missing skills. If difficulties persist despite ongoing efforts to address them, children should be evaluated by a speech-language pathologist, school psychologist, or other appropriate specialist.

Development of Metalinguistic Awareness

——————— Connecting Concepts
Metalinguistic awareness is an aspect of *metacognition,* described in Chapter 7.

Children's **metalinguistic awareness** is their conscious understanding of the nature and functions of language. For instance, it includes awareness that speech is comprised of smaller units (words, phonemes, etc.), that printed words have one-to-one correspondences to spoken words, and that language is an entity separate from its meaning. It also includes the ability to distinguish between what a person says and what he or she actually means (Yaden & Templeton, 1986).

In the late preschool or early elementary school years, children become consciously aware that words are the basic units of language, that spoken words are comprised of phonemes, and that different phonemes tend to be associated with different letters or letter combinations (Tunmer, Pratt, & Herriman, 1984). In the elementary years, children also become increasingly able to distinguish between grammatically acceptable and unacceptable sentences (Bowey, 1986; Hakes, 1980). As they move into the upper elementary and middle school grades, they begin to recognize the component parts of speech, at least partly as a result of formal instruction about nouns, verbs, and so on. More sophisticated aspects of metalinguistic awareness, such as recognizing that a word or phrase has multiple meanings, don't emerge until the middle school years and continue to develop throughout adolescence.

The Developmental Trends table "Language Skills at Different Age Levels" summarizes characteristics you are likely to see in children's linguistic knowledge and skills at various age levels.

How children develop metalinguistic awareness.   Theoretical accounts of metalinguistic development focus almost exclusively on the effects of experience. One factor that probably promotes metalinguistic awareness is "playing" with language through rhymes, chants, jokes, puns, and so on. For example, rhymes help children discover the relationships between sounds and letters. Jokes and puns help children discover that words and phrases can have more than one meaning (Bradley & Bryant, 1991; Cazden, 1976; Christie & Johnsen, 1983; R. E. Owens, 1996).

Children's early experiences with books also promote metalinguistic awareness (Yaden & Templeton, 1986). The very process of reading to children helps them realize that printed language is related to spoken language. In addition, some children's books playfully address the nature of language. An example is *Amelia Bedelia Goes Camping* (Parish, 1985), one in a series of books featuring a rather obtuse maid who takes everything her employers say quite literally. For instance, when they tell Amelia it's time to "hit the road," she hits the road with a stick—a behavior that our own children found quite amusing.

Formal language instruction further fosters metalinguistic awareness. By exploring parts of speech, various sentence structures, and the like, children and adolescents gain a better grasp of the underlying structure of language. By reading and analyzing poetry and classic literature, they discover a variety of mechanisms (similes, metaphors, symbolism, etc.) that a writer might use to convey multiple layers of meanings.

metalinguistic awareness
Extent to which one consciously understands and thinks about the nature of language.

Finally, research consistently indicates that knowledge of two or more languages (bilingualism) promotes greater metalinguistic awareness (X. Chen et al., 2004; Diaz & Klingler,

DEVELOPMENTAL TRENDS

Language Skills at Different Age Levels

Age	What You Might Observe	Diversity	Implications
Infancy (Birth–2) 	• Interest in listening to the human voice and in exchanging vocalizations with adults • Repetition of vowel sounds (cooing) at age 1–2 months and consonant-vowel syllables (babbling) at about 6 months • Understanding of some common words at about 8 months • Use of single words at about 12 months • Use of two-word combinations at about 18 months • Rapid increase in vocabulary in the second year	• In the latter half of the first year, babbling increasingly reflects phonemes of the native language. • Temperament may influence the development of expressive language; more cautious children may wait a bit before beginning to speak. • Chronic ear infections can interfere with early language development. • Infants with severe hearing impairments babble, but the quality of their babbling changes little over time. Spoken language progresses no further unless intensive training is provided.	• Engage young infants in "conversations," using simplified and animated speech (i.e., infant-directed speech) and responding when they vocalize. • Label and describe the objects and events children encounter. • Teach simple hand signs that preverbal infants can use to communicate. • Ask simple questions (e.g., "Is your diaper wet?" "What does a cow say?"). • Repeat and expand on children's early "sentences" (e.g., follow "Kitty eat" with "Yes, the kitty is eating").
Early Childhood (2–6) 	• Rapid advances in vocabulary and syntax • Incomplete understandings of many simple words (e.g., undergeneralization, overgeneralization, confusion between simple comparatives such as *more* vs. *less*) • Overregularization (e.g., *foots, gooder, goed*) • Overdependence on word order and context (instead of syntax) when interpreting messages • Superficial understanding of what "good listening" is • Difficulty pronouncing some phonemes and blends (e.g., *r, th, sl, dr*) • Increasing ability to construct narratives	• Children raised in bilingual environments may show slight delays in language development, but any delays are short-lived and usually not a cause for concern. • Major speech and communication disorders (e.g., abnormal syntactic constructions) reveal themselves in the preschool years.	• Read age-appropriate storybooks as a way of enhancing vocabulary. • Give children corrective feedback when their use of words indicates inaccurate understanding. • Work on simple listening skills (e.g., sitting quietly, paying attention). • Ask follow-up questions to make sure that children accurately understand important messages. • Ask children to construct narratives about recent events (e.g., "Tell me about your camping trip last weekend").
Middle Childhood (6–10) 	• Increasing understanding of temporal words (e.g., *before, after*) and comparatives (e.g., *bigger, as big as*) • Incomplete knowledge of irregular word forms • Literal interpretation of messages (especially before age 9) • Pronunciation mastered by age 8 • Consideration of a listener's knowledge and perspective when speaking • Sustained conversations about concrete topics • Construction of narratives with plots and cause-effect relationships • Linguistic creativity and wordplay (e.g., rhymes, word games)	• Some minor speech and communication disorders (e.g., persistent articulation problems) become evident and can be addressed by specialists. • African Americans often show advanced ability to use figurative language (e.g., metaphor, hyperbole). • Bilingual children are apt to show advanced metalinguistic awareness.	• Teach irregular word forms (e.g., the superlative form of *bad* is *worst*, the past tense of *bring* is *brought*). • Use group discussions as a way to explore academic subject matter. • Have children develop short stories that they present orally or in writing. • Encourage jokes and rhymes that capitalize on double meanings and homonyms (sound-alike words). • When articulation problems are evident in the upper elementary grades, consult with a speech-language pathologist.
Early Adolescence (10–14)	• Increasing awareness of the terminology used in various academic disciplines • Ability to understand complex, multi-clause sentences • Emerging ability to look beyond literal interpretations; comprehension of simple proverbs • Emerging ability to carry on lengthy conversations about abstract topics • Significant growth in metalinguistic awareness	• Frequent readers tend to have larger vocabularies. • Girls are more likely than boys to converse about intimate and confidential matters. • African American teens may bandy insults back and forth in a playful manner. • Adolescents may prefer to use their native *dialects* even if they have mastered *Standard English* (see discussion in "Ethnic Differences" section).	• Begin to use the terminology used by experts in various academic disciplines (e.g., *simile* in language arts, *theory* in science). • Use classroom debates to explore controversial issues. • Present proverbs and ask children to consider possible underlying meanings. • Explore the nature of words and language as entities in and of themselves.

(continued)

DEVELOPMENTAL TRENDS

Language Skills at Different Age Levels (continued)

Age	What You Might Observe	Diversity	Implications
Late Adolescence (14–18)	• Acquisition of many terms related to specific academic disciplines • Subtle refinements in grammar, mostly as a result of formal instruction • Mastery of a wide variety of connectives (e.g., *although, however, nevertheless*) • General ability to understand figurative language (e.g., metaphors, proverbs, hyperbole)	• Boys are apt to communicate their thoughts in a direct and straightforward manner; girls are more likely to be indirect and tactful. • A preference for one's native dialect over Standard English continues into the high school years.	• Consistently use the terminology associated with various academic disciplines. • Distinguish between similar abstract words (e.g., *weather* vs. *climate, velocity* vs. *acceleration*). • Explore complex syntactic structures (e.g., multiple embedded clauses). • Consider the underlying meanings and messages in poetry and fiction. • When teenagers have a native dialect other than Standard English, encourage them to use it in informal conversations and creative writing; encourage Standard English for more formal situations.

Sources: C. Baker, 1993; Bruer, 1999; Bruner, 1983; N. Chomsky, 1972; Eilers & Oller, 1994; Elias & Broerse, 1996; Fantini, 1985; Fenson et al., 1994; Fifer & Moon, 1995; Goodwyn et al., 2000; Hale-Benson, 1986; J. L. Locke, 1993; T. M. McDevitt, 1990; K. Nelson, 1973; O'Grady, 1997; Ortony et al., 1985; R. E. Owens, 1996; H. L. Smith, 1998; R. H. Thompson et al., 2004.

1991; Moran & Hakuta, 1995). By the time Mario was 5, he showed considerable awareness of the nature of language:

> Mario was well aware that things were called in one of several possible ways, that the same story could be retold in another language (he was capable of doing this himself), and he knew that thoughts were convertible or translatable through other forms of expression. . . . He knew that a [language] could be varied so as to make it sound funny or to render its messages less transparent, such as in Pig Spanish. . . .
>
> [As Mario grew older,] he became increasingly analytical about the medium which so many take for granted as their sole form of expression. He demonstrated interest, for example, in the multiple meaning of some words ("'right' means three things"); and in peculiar usages ("Why do you call the car 'she'?"); as well as intuitions about the origins of words ("'soufflé' sounds French"). (Fantini, 1985, pp. 53–54)[3]

Promoting metalinguistic development.   Factors that promote metalinguistic awareness—language play, reading experiences, formal instruction, and bilingualism—have several implications for teaching and working with children:

● ***Explore multiple meanings through ambiguities, jokes, riddles, and the like.*** Having fun with language can be educational as well as entertaining. For example, teachers and parents might ask children to identify the double meanings of such sentences as *He is drawing a gun* and *This restaurant even serves crabs* (Wiig, Gilbert, & Christian, 1978). Jokes and riddles provide another vehicle for exploring multiple meanings (Shultz, 1974; Shultz & Horibe, 1974):

> Call me a cab.
> Okay, you're a cab.

> Tell me how long cows should be milked.
> They should be milked the same as short ones, of course.

● ***Read literature that plays on the nature of language.*** One of our favorites is *The Phantom Tollbooth* (Juster, 1961), which has considerable fun with word meanings and common expressions. In one scene the main character (Milo) asks for a square meal and is served

---

[3]See footnote 1 on page 340.

(you guessed it) a plate "heaped high with steaming squares of all sizes and colors." Among the all-time classics in English wordplay are Lewis Carroll's *Alice's Adventures in Wonderland* and *Through the Looking Glass*. These books are packed with whimsical uses of double word meanings, homonyms, and idioms, as the following excerpt from *Through the Looking Glass* illustrates:

> "But what could [a tree] do, if any danger came?" Alice asked.
> "It could bark," said the Rose.
> "It says, 'Boughwough!'" cried a Daisy. "That's why its branches are called boughs."

● *Encourage children to learn a second language.* Promoting metalinguistic awareness is just one of several benefits of learning a second language. In the next section we look more closely at second language learning and bilingualism.

Development of a Second Language

As the adult workplace becomes increasingly international in scope, there is greater need than ever before for children to learn one or more languages in addition to their native tongue. Here we address three issues related to the development of a second language: the optimal timing for second-language learning, the nature of bilingualism, and approaches to teaching a second language.

The Timing of Second-Language Learning

As you discovered early in the chapter, there may be one or more sensitive periods for learning language—especially for acquiring flawless pronunciation and complex syntactic structures—that might make exposure to a second language in the first few years of life ideal. In general, early exposure to a second language is more important if the second language is very different from the first. For example, a native English speaker benefits more from an early start in Japanese or Arabic than from an early start in, say, French or German (Bialystok, 1994a; Strozer, 1994). However, any advantage young children may have because of biological "readiness" may be counterbalanced by the greater cognitive maturity, world knowledge, and metalinguistic sophistication on which adolescents and adults can build as they study a new language (Bialystok, 1994b; Collier, 1989; M. Long, 1995). Furthermore, people can learn the vocabulary of a particular language at virtually any age (Bruer, 1999). Thus people of all ages can acquire proficiency in a second language. Given research findings to date, there appears to be no definitive "best" time to begin.

Although there may be no hard-and-fast sensitive period for acquiring a second language, getting an early start on second-language instruction certainly has benefits (T. H. Cunningham & Graham, 2000; Diaz, 1983; A. Doyle, 1982; Reich, 1986). Learning a second language leads, on average, to higher achievement in reading, vocabulary, and grammar. Furthermore, it sensitizes youngsters to the international and multicultural nature of the world in which they live. Children who learn a second language during the elementary school years express more positive attitudes toward people who speak that language, and they are more likely to enroll in foreign language classes in high school. And in classrooms in which children speak only one of two different languages (perhaps some speaking only English and others speaking only Spanish), instruction in the second language promotes cross-communication and peer interaction.

Bilingualism

Bilingualism is the ability to speak two languages fluently. Bilingual individuals, like Mario, can switch easily from one language to the other, and they readily distinguish the contexts in which they should use each one. The teacher in the "Language: Classroom" video clip on Observation CD 2 is clearly bilingual: She consistently uses both spoken English and sign language as she talks.

At least half of the world's children are bilingual or multilingual, typically because they've been exposed to two or more languages regularly and from an early age (Hoff-Ginsburg, 1997). At one time many psychologists believed that bilingual environments were detrimental

Observe a bilingual teacher as she both talks and signs in the "Language: Classroom" clip on Observation CD 2.

bilingualism
Knowing and speaking two languages fluently.

to children's linguistic and cognitive development, but recent research has been quite favorable. Children raised in bilingual environments from birth or soon thereafter sometimes show initial delays in language development, but by elementary school they have caught up to their monolingual peers and easily keep the two languages separate (C. Baker, 1993; Bialystok, 2001; Lanza, 1992). Furthermore, as we have seen, bilingual children show greater metalinguistic sophistication than their monolingual peers. And when they are truly fluent in both languages, they tend to perform better in situations requiring advanced cognitive functioning—for instance, on intelligence tests and on tasks requiring creativity (Bialystok & Senman, 2004; Diaz & Klingler, 1991; García, 1994; Moran & Hakuta, 1995).

Being bilingual may also have cultural and personal advantages. In many Native American groups, the ancestral language is important for communicating oral history and cultural heritage and for conducting local business, yet adults in those groups realize that mastery of spoken and written English is essential for children's long-term success (McCarty & Watahomigie, 1998). Although Puerto Rican children will have more educational and professional opportunities if they know English, they often speak Spanish at home and with peers, partly as a way of showing respect to their elders and partly as a way of maintaining a sense of cultural identity (Nieto, 1995; Torres-Guzmán, 1998). Marisol, a high school student, put it this way:

> I'm proud of [being Puerto Rican]. I guess I speak Spanish whenever I can. . . . I used to have a lot of problems with one of my teachers 'cause she didn't want us to talk Spanish in class and I thought that was like an insult to us, you know? (Nieto, 1995, p. 127)

And in some cases, being bilingual is the only way children can maintain personal relationships with important people in their lives. For instance, some children are bilingual in English and American Sign Language as a way of communicating effectively with one parent who can hear and another who is deaf (L. A. Pettito, 1997).

Approaches to Teaching a Second Language

Just as children typically learn their native language through informal daily exposure, so, too, can they learn two languages simultaneously if, like Mario, they are raised in a consistently bilingual environment. But when children begin a second language at an older age, perhaps in the elementary grades or even later, they often learn it more quickly if their language-learning experiences are fairly structured (Strozer, 1994).

As you may have learned from your own experience, studying a foreign language for one 45-minute period several times a week hardly promotes mastery. Two more intensive approaches, immersion and bilingual education, can be quite effective, with each being useful in somewhat different situations. To keep our discussion simple, let's assume that students are living in an English-speaking country. If these students are native English speakers, total **immersion** in the second language—hearing and speaking it almost exclusively in the classroom throughout the day—helps students acquire proficiency fairly quickly, and any adverse effects on achievement in other academic areas appear to be short-lived (Collier, 1992; T. H. Cunningham & Graham, 2000; Genesee, 1985). But on average, non-English-speaking students studying English for the first time (e.g., recent immigrants) fare better in **bilingual education,** in which they receive intensive instruction in English while studying other academic subject areas in their native language (Willig, 1985; Wright & Taylor, 1995; Wright, Taylor, & Macarthur, 2000).

Why is immersion better for some students while bilingual education is better for others? Remember, language is an important foundation for cognitive development: It provides symbols for mentally representing the world, enables children to exchange ideas with others, helps them internalize sophisticated cognitive strategies, and so on. Students in an English-speaking country who are immersed in a different language at school still have many opportunities—at home, with their friends, and in the local community—to continue using and developing their English. In contrast, non-native English speakers may have few opportunities outside of their homes to use their native language. If they are taught exclusively in English, they may very well lose proficiency in their native language before developing

Bilingual education programs are especially effective when they encourage skills in students' native language as well as in English.

immersion
Approach to second-language instruction in which students hear and speak that language almost exclusively in the classroom.

bilingual education
Approach to second-language instruction in which students are instructed in academic subject areas in their native language while simultaneously being taught to speak and write in the second language.

adequate proficiency in English, and their cognitive development will suffer in the process. In such cases bilingual education, which is designed to foster growth in *both* languages, is more likely to promote cognitive as well as linguistic growth (Krashen, 1996; Pérez, 1998; Tse, 2001; Winsler, Díaz, Espinosa, & Rodriguez, 1999).

Diversity in Language Development

As is true in other developmental domains, children in any single cultural group vary in the ages at which they achieve milestones in language development. For example, shy or reserved children may begin to speak somewhat later than more outgoing ones (K. Nelson, 1973). In addition to idiosyncratic individual differences, we also see differences based on children's gender, socioeconomic status, and ethnicity.

Gender Differences

As infants and toddlers, girls are, on average, more verbally active than boys. Girls also begin to speak about a month earlier, form longer sentences sooner, and have a larger vocabulary (Halpern & LaMay, 2000; Reznick & Goldfield, 1992). Once they reach the school years, girls outperform boys on tests of verbal ability (see Chapter 8). This difference is quite small, however, and there is considerable overlap between the two groups (see Figure 8-7 in Chapter 8).

Qualitative differences exist as well, for children and adults alike. On average, males, who see themselves as information providers, speak more directly and bluntly. In contrast, females, who seek to establish and deepen relationships through their conversations, are more likely to be indirect, tactful, and polite (R. E. Owens, 1996; Tannen, 1990).

Socioeconomic Differences

As mentioned in the earlier discussion of nativism, children from diverse backgrounds tend to reach language milestones at similar ages. However, children from higher-income homes tend to have larger vocabularies (B. Hart & Risley, 1995; Hoff, 2003; Wasik & Bond, 2001). This difference appears to be at least partly due to the quantity and quality of language that mothers use with their children. Although mothers from all income levels tend to interact frequently with their children, on average mothers from higher-SES families talk with their babies more, ask more questions, elaborate more on topics and, in general, expose their children to a greater variety of words (B. Hart & Risley, 1995).

Ethnic Differences

As you've already learned, sociolinguistic conventions, use of figurative language, and narrative styles often differ from one ethnic group to another. In addition, children from different ethnic and cultural groups may use a form of English different from the **Standard English** typically considered acceptable at school. More specifically, they may speak in a **dialect**, a form of English (or, more generally, a form of any language) that includes some unique pronunciations and syntactic structures. Dialects tend to be associated either with particular geographical regions or with particular ethnic and cultural groups. An example is shown in Figure 9-6. In this narrative, an English-speaking fifth grader living in the Northern Mariana Islands of the Pacific Ocean mixes present and past tenses in his description of a past event, much as he is apt to do in his everyday speech.

Perhaps the most widely studied ethnic dialect is **African American English** (also known as *Black English Vernacular* and *Ebonics*). This dialect, which is actually a group of similar dialects, is used in many African American communities throughout the United States and is characterized by certain unique pronunciations, idioms, and grammatical constructions. For instance, a child might say, "He got ten dollar," "Momma she mad," or "I be going to dance tonight" (R. E. Owens, 1995, p. A–8). At one time many researchers believed that an African American dialect represented a less complex form of speech than Standard English, and so they urged educators to teach students to speak "properly" as quickly as possible. But psychologists now realize that African American dialects are, in fact, very complex languages that have their own predictable idioms and grammatical

Study Guide and Reader
Supplementary Reading 9-1 describes the ideal progression of bilingual education for children with limited English proficiency.

> Yesterday I really have bad day. Because I break the window. When I knock at the door, knowbody was there. Then I knock at the window very hard it break. My mom got made at me. Because I break the window. I brack the window because my sister don't want to open the door. So I break the window.

Figure 9-6

A local dialect is evident in this writing sample from a fifth grader who lives in the Northern Mariana Islands of the Pacific Ocean.
Writing sample courtesy of the Commonwealth of the Northern Mariana Islands Public School System and of the Pacific Resources for Education and Learning (PREL).

Standard English
Form of English generally considered acceptable in school (as reflected in textbooks, grammar instruction, etc.) and in the media.

dialect
Form of a language characteristic of a particular geographic region or ethnic group.

African American English
Dialect of some African American communities that includes pronunciations, grammatical constructions, and idioms different from those of Standard English.

rules and that these dialects promote communication and complex thought as readily as Standard English (DeLain, Pearson, & Anderson, 1985; Fairchild & Edwards-Evans, 1990; R. E. Owens, 1996).

Many children and adolescents view their native dialect as an integral part of their cultural identity (McAlpine, 1992; Ogbu, 1999; Tatum, 1997). Furthermore, when a local dialect is the language most preferred by residents of a community, it is often the most effective means through which youngsters can communicate in daily interactions. However, many people in mainstream Western culture associate higher social status with people who speak Standard English, and they perceive speakers of other dialects in a lesser light (Gollnick & Chinn, 2002; Purcell-Gates, 1995; H. L. Smith, 1998). In addition, children who know Standard English have an easier time learning to read (Charity, Scarborough, & Griffin, 2004). For such reasons, most experts recommend that all youngsters acquire proficiency in Standard English (Casanova, 1987; M. Craft, 1984; Ogbu, 1999).

Ultimately, children and adolescents function most effectively when they can use both their local dialect and Standard English in appropriate settings. For example, although teachers may wish to encourage Standard English in most written work or in formal oral presentations, they might find other dialects quite appropriate in creative writing or informal classroom discussions (Gollnick & Chinn, 2002; Ogbu, 1999; Warren & McCloskey, 1993). One teacher of African American children explains it this way:

> I don't want them to be ashamed of what they know but I also want them to know and be comfortable with what school and the rest of the society require. When I put it in the context of "translation" they get excited. They see it is possible to go from one to the other. It's not that they are not familiar with Standard English. . . . They hear Standard English all the time on TV. It's certainly what I use in the classroom. But there is rarely any connection made between the way they speak and Standard English. I think that when they can see the connections and know that they can make the shifts, they become better at both. They're bilingual! (Ladson-Billings, 1994, p. 84)

Exceptionalities in Language Development

In Chapter 7 you learned that some children with learning disabilities or autism may have difficulties with one or more aspects of language. Here we describe possible language difficulties for two additional groups of children: those with speech and communication disorders and those with sensory impairments.

Speech and Communication Disorders

Some children seem to develop normally in all respects except for language. Children with **speech and communication disorders** (also known as *specific language impairments*) have abnormalities in spoken language or in language comprehension that significantly interfere with their performance at school and elsewhere. Such disorders may involve problems in one or more of the following:

- Receptive language (e.g., inability to distinguish among different phonemes, difficulty understanding or remembering directions)
- Articulation (e.g., mispronunciations or omissions of certain sounds)
- Fluency (e.g., stuttering, or an atypical rhythm in speech)
- Syntax (e.g., abnormal syntactic patterns, or incorrect word order)
- Semantics (e.g., difficulty interpreting words that have two or more meanings; consistent use of words with imprecise meanings, such as *thing* or *that*)
- Pragmatics (e.g., talking for a long time without letting others speak) (American Speech-Language-Hearing Association, 1993; R. E. Owens, 1996; R. Turnbull et al., 2004)

speech and communication disorders
Disability characterized by abnormalities in producing or understanding spoken language, to the point where special educational services are required.

Speech and communication disorders are also suspected when children don't demonstrate age-appropriate language. However, speech patterns that reflect a regional or ethnic dialect and those that are due to a bilingual background do *not* fall within the realm of speech and communication disorders (recall the speech therapist who inappropriately recommended that Mario have speech therapy).

DEVELOPMENT AND PRACTICE

Working with Children Who Have Speech and Communication Disorders

- Be on the lookout for children who exhibit significant delays or other language problems unusual for their age-group.

  A preschool teacher consults with a speech-language pathologist about a 4-year-old girl who communicates only by pointing and gesturing. "She's certainly not shy," the teacher explains. "She often tries to get other children's attention by poking them, and she loves to sit on my lap during story time."

- Encourage children to speak.

  An 11-year-old has trouble pronouncing the *s* sound (e.g., he says "th-pethial" for *special*) and is meeting regularly with a speech therapist to address the problem. Nevertheless, his fifth-grade teacher encourages him to speak in class, especially in small-group settings. When he does so, she models acceptance of his disability, and if a classmate makes fun of his speech, she discreetly takes the classmate aside and explains that all children have strengths and weaknesses and that everyone in her class deserves respect and support.

- Listen patiently.

  A high school student often stutters when she speaks and may sometimes struggle for several seconds midway through a sentence to pronounce a particular word. Her teachers know she is able to complete her thoughts if they give her time.

- Ask for clarification when a message is unclear.

  An 8-year-old boy often says "this" or "that thing there" when referring to objects in the classroom. Suspecting that he may have an undiagnosed language disability, his third-grade teacher refers him to a school psychologist for evaluation, but she also asks him to call objects by their names.

- Provide guidance about how to talk effectively with others.

  A middle school student often dominates conversations in small-group discussions, rambling on at such length that her classmates have trouble getting a word in edgewise. Her teacher meets with her during lunch one day to remind her of the importance of letting everyone participate. Together they identify a strategy that will help her keep her comments to a reasonable period: Whenever she starts to speak, she will look at the second hand on her watch and be sure to yield the floor after a maximum of 30 seconds.

Sources: L. Bloom & Lahey, 1978; Patton et al., 1996; R. Turnbull et al., 2004.

Some children with speech and communication disorders have problems with reading and writing as well (J. R. Johnston, 1997; Tallal, 2003). Personal and social problems may also emerge. Some youngsters feel so self-conscious about their language disability that they are reluctant to speak to peers (Patton et al., 1996). And if they sound "odd" or are difficult to understand, they may suffer the ridicule of thoughtless classmates and have difficulty making friends (LaBlance, Steckol, & Smith, 1994; Rice, Hadley, & Alexander, 1993).

In some cases language disorders are inherited (Spinath, Price, Dale, & Plomin, 2004; Tomblin, 1997). In other instances they are associated with specific brain abnormalities (J. L. Locke, 1993). But often the exact cause of a speech or communication disorder is unknown (T. F. Campbell et al., 2003; Wang & Baron, 1997).

Although trained specialists typically work with children who have impaired communication skills, parents, teachers, and other adults can also facilitate the language development of these youngsters. Several recommendations are presented in the Development and Practice feature "Working with Children Who Have Speech and Communication Disorders."

Sensory Impairments and Language Development

Children with severe visual impairments (e.g., blindness) typically have normal syntactic development but are apt to have more limited vocabularies than their sighted age-mates (M. Harris, 1992). Because they cannot always see the objects and events around them, they simply don't have as many opportunities to make connections between words and their meanings.

Children with hearing impairments (e.g., deafness) are at risk for delays in both syntactic and semantic development, especially if an impairment was present at birth or appeared early in life (M. Harris, 1992). Furthermore, children who have been completely deaf from birth or soon thereafter typically need special training to develop proficiency in speaking. Yet these children are apt to show normal language development in *sign language* if family members and others use it as the primary means of communicating with them (M. Harris, 1992; Newport, 1990; L. A. Pettito, 1997). Deaf infants who are regularly exposed to sign language often begin to "babble" with their hands at 7 to 10 months. They are apt to sign their first word at around 18 to 22 months, with multiword phrases following soon thereafter. Like hearing children, children who use sign language appear to construct rules that guide their language use,

Happy Mother's Day!

Children with hearing loss can interact more effectively with their peers when everyone knows sign language. Here, Marianne, a hearing child, has created a Mother's Day card using the sign for "I love you."

DEVELOPMENT AND PRACTICE

Working with Children Who Have Hearing Impairments

- Intervene as early as possible to address correctable hearing impairments.

  Among the children in a preschool class for low-income children is a 3-year-old boy who is deaf. His mother expresses interest in a cochlear implant but cannot afford one. The boy's teacher and an audiologist who consults at the school locate a charitable organization that will pay for the cost of surgery. With the implant, the boy begins to hear the language around him, and both his receptive and expressive language rapidly develop.

- Communicate messages through multiple modalities.

  A 15-year-old who is deaf has a child-specific aide who accompanies her to all of her classes and manually translates the content of teachers' lectures and explanations. Even so, her teachers make sure that they com-

municate as much as possible through sight as well as sound. For example, they write important points on the chalkboard and illustrate key ideas with pictures and other graphics.

- Learn elements of American Sign Language and finger spelling, and teach them to children's peers.

  A teacher in a combined first- and second-grade class has several students who are deaf, and so she both speaks and signs to her class as she presents new information and describes assignments. All of her students know enough American Sign Language to converse easily with one another. (The teacher and students are depicted in the two "Language" clips on Observation CD 1.)

Sources: Bruer, 1999; Newport, 1990; Svirsky, Robbins, Kirk, Pisoni, & Miyamoto, 2000.

and they gradually expand on and refine these rules over time (Goldin-Meadow & Mylander, 1993; L. A. Pettito, 1997).

A case study of BoMee (Wilcox, 1994) illustrates just how much is possible when parents provide a linguistically rich environment through sign language. BoMee was born in Korea 8 weeks prematurely. Although she could hear at birth, early illnesses or medications apparently caused profound hearing loss shortly thereafter. At age 2½, BoMee was adopted by American parents, who communicated with her regularly in sign language. Within a few weeks after BoMee's arrival, they also began to sign their self-talk as a way of "thinking aloud." For instance, BoMee's mother might sign "What goes next in this recipe?" or "Where are my shoes?" Within a week, BoMee began signing her own self-talk, such as "Where my shoes are?" Soon self-talk was a regular feature in BoMee's problem-solving activities. On one occasion BoMee was trying to put a dress on her doll, but the dress was too small. She signed to herself:

> Hmmm, wrong me. This dress fit here? Think not. Hmmm. For other doll here. (Translation: *Hmmm, I'm wrong. Does this dress go on this doll? I don't think so. Hmmm. It goes on this other doll.*) (Wilcox, 1994, p. 119)

BoMee showed other normal linguistic behaviors as well. She simplified her language when she signed to her baby brother. And just as hearing children typically read aloud in the early stages of reading, BoMee signed "out loud" when she began to read.

Like Mario, BoMee may have had an advantage in the development of metalinguistic awareness. She was exposed to both English-based signs and American Sign Language (which have somewhat different vocabularies and syntactic structures) and quickly became bilingual in her knowledge of the two language systems. She understood very early that some people talked and others used sign language. Furthermore, shortly after her third birthday, she appropriately signed "This Little Piggy" in two different ways—in English-based signs and in American Sign Language—to people who understood only one of the two languages. Clearly, then, children with hearing loss can have very normal cognitive and linguistic development when their language environment is appropriate for them.

Children who have sensory impairments typically work with specialists to develop strategies for living successfully in a world of sighted, hearing people. Yet teachers, parents, and other adults can also help these children in many ways. Examples are presented in the Development and Practice feature "Working with Children Who Have Hearing Impairments."

Mastery of the basic underpinnings of language (i.e., semantics and syntax) and proficiency in the receptive and expressive aspects of spoken language (i.e., listening and speaking) are, of course, important in their own right. But they also provide the foundation for receptive and expressive skills in written language. We turn to development of reading, writing, and other academic domains in the next chapter.

Case Study: Boarding School

Some parts of Alaska are so sparsely settled that building local high schools makes little economic sense. So in certain Native American communities, older students are sent to boarding school for their high school education. A high priority for boarding school teachers is to help students master Standard English. With this information in mind, consider the following incident:

> Many of the students at the school spoke English with a native dialect and seemed unable to utter certain essential sounds in the English language. A new group of speech teachers was sent in to correct the problem. The teachers worked consistently with the students in an attempt to improve speech patterns and intonation, but found that their efforts were in vain.
>
> One night, the boys in the dormitory were seeming to have too much fun, and peals of laughter were rolling out from under the door. An investigating counselor approached cautiously and listened quietly outside the door to see if he could discover the source of the laughter. From behind the door he heard a voice, speaking in perfect English, giving instructions to the rest of the crowd. The others were finding the situation very amusing. When the counselor entered the room he found that one of the students was speaking. "Joseph," he said, "You've been cured! Your English is perfect." "No," said Joseph returning to his familiar dialect, "I was just doing an imitation of you." "But if you can speak in Standard English, why don't you do it all of the time?" the counselor queried. "I can," responded Joseph, "but it sounds funny, and I feel dumb doing it." (Garrison, 1989, p. 121)

- Why might Joseph prefer his native dialect to Standard English?
- Is Joseph bilingual? Why or why not?
- The counselor told Joseph that he had "been cured." What beliefs about Joseph's native dialect does this statement reflect?

Once you have answered these questions, compare your responses with those presented in the appendix.

Summary

Theoretical Perspectives

Although modeling, reinforcement, and feedback almost certainly play some role in language development, early theories based on such processes could not adequately account for the fact that most children acquire a very complex language system in a very short period, and with only limited guidance from adults. Several more recent theoretical perspectives have emerged, each focusing on somewhat different aspects of language development. *Nativists* propose that young children have certain "prewired" knowledge and skills that facilitate language acquisition. *Information processing theorists* apply general principles of cognition (e.g., the importance of attention, the process of automatization) to explain how some aspects of language may develop. *Sociocultural theorists* emphasize the role that social interactions play in language learning. *Functionalists* propose that children develop language primarily because it enhances their effectiveness in social groups and increases their ability to satisfy their own needs. Many theorists draw from elements of two or more of these perspectives when explaining how language develops. Nevertheless, some areas of incompatibility among the theories (e.g., whether children inherit some "preprogramming" that helps them learn language) remain unresolved.

Trends in Language Development

Children and adolescents continue to develop their linguistic knowledge and skills throughout the preschool and school years. For instance, school-age children add several thousand new words to their vocabulary each year. Over time, they rely less on word order and more on syntax to interpret other people's messages, and they can comprehend and produce sentences with increasingly complex syntactic structures. Their conversations with others increase in length, they become better able to adapt the content of their speech to the characteristics of their listeners, and they become more aware of the unspoken social conventions that govern verbal interactions in their culture. They also acquire a growing understanding of the nature of language as an entity in and of itself.

Learning a Second Language

Although research findings are mixed with regard to the "best" time to learn a second language, they consistently indicate that knowing two or more languages enhances achievement in reading and other language arts, promotes greater metalinguistic awareness, and fosters multicultural sensitivity. An *immersion* approach to teaching a second language is effective only when children have ample opportunity to continue developing their native language outside of school. In other situations *bilingual education* is usually preferable.

Diversity and Exceptionalities in Language Development

Subtle qualitative differences have been observed in the conversational styles of males and females. Children from higher-SES backgrounds tend to have larger vocabularies, probably because they are likely to be exposed to a wider variety of words. Different ethnic groups may show differences in sociolinguistic behaviors, storytelling traditions, use of figurative language, and dialects.

Some children have disabilities that affect their language development. Speech and communication disorders include abnormalities in articulation, fluency, syntax, receptive language, or other aspects of language that significantly interfere with children's performance and accomplishments in and out of school. Children with hearing impairments and (to a lesser extent) those with visual impairments may have more limited language proficiency because of reduced exposure to language or reduced awareness of the meaningful contexts in which it is used.

Applying Concepts in Child Development

In this chapter you discovered a variety of ways in which receptive language and expressive language change as children grow older. The following table describes language-related behaviors of children and adolescents in five different age ranges. For each youngster, the table indicates whether the behavior is typical for the age-group, suggests developmentally appropriate responses to the behavior, or both. Apply what you've learned about language development to fill in the empty cells in the table. When you're done, compare your entries with those in Table 9–1 in the *Study Guide and Reader*.

APPLYING CONCEPTS IN CHILD DEVELOPMENT — Assessing Developmental Progress in Language

Age	A Youngster's Experience	Developmental Concepts *Recognizing Typical and Unusual Behaviors for the Age-Group*	Implications *Facilitating Acquisition of Language Skills*
Infancy (Birth–2)	When a caregiver at a child care center exclaims, "Your daddy's here!" 10-month-old Midori looks eagerly in the direction of the door. But despite Midori's apparent understanding of the word *Daddy*, she does not yet say his name, not even a reasonable approximation such as "Dada." Sometimes she says "dadadadada," but with little regard for whether her father is present.	This behavior is typical for the age-group. Although children can understand some words as early as 8 months, on average they don't say their first word until sometime around their first birthday. Midori's repetition of the syllable *da*, apparently without reference to anything in her environment, is an instance of *babbling*.	Regularly engage infants in "conversations" in which they can practice vocalizing, taking turns, maintaining eye contact, and using other basic language skills. Simplify your language somewhat (e.g., use *infant-directed speech*), but use a variety of words in appropriate contexts.
Early Childhood (2–6)	Twenty kindergartners sit quietly and politely as the school principal describes the procedure they should follow during a fire drill. However, many of them are unable to describe the procedure after the principal leaves the room.	This behavior is typical for the age-group. Young children often think that being a "good listener" simply means sitting still and being quiet. They do not necessarily realize that listening also involves understanding and remembering what the speaker says.	
Middle Childhood (6–10)	Seven-year-old Arthur's sentences are rarely more than two or three words long.	Such speech is unusual for the age-group. Children typically begin putting two words together sometime around age 2, and their sentences become increasingly longer after that. By school age, their sentences are adultlike in many respects.	

APPLYING CONCEPTS IN CHILD DEVELOPMENT

Assessing Developmental Progress in Language (continued)

Age	A Youngster's Experience	Developmental Concepts *Recognizing Typical and Unusual Behaviors for the Age-Group*	Implications *Facilitating Acquisition of Language Skills*
Early Adolescence (10–14)	In an oral report in his seventh-grade history class, 14-year-old Roy says such things as "John Wesley Powell looked for *gooder* boats to use" and "He *goed* down the Grand Canyon in a canoe."	These errors are unusual for the age-group. Adding *-er* to irregular adjectives and *-ed* to irregular verbs are examples of *overregularization.* Overregularization of such common words as *good* and *go* is often seen in the early elementary years but is rare in adolescence.	When children's syntax and word usage are unusual, consider whether a local dialect or family communication patterns might be the cause. Encourage Standard English in formal situations, but allow the dialect in everyday conversation with family and friends. If dialect differences cannot account for what you observe, consult with a specialist about appropriate interventions.
Late Adolescence (14–18) 	When talking to members of a high school soccer team just before the first game of the season, a coach says, "Remember, ladies, a chain is only as strong as its weakest link." The girls nod in agreement and vow that they will all try to play their best.		Use a variety of common expressions when talking with adolescents, but check to be sure that your listeners can see beyond the surface meanings to understand your underlying messages.

Key Concepts

phonology (p. 316)
semantics (p. 316)
syntax (p. 316)
pragmatics (p. 316)
native language (p. 316)
nativism (p. 317)
language acquisition device (p. 317)
functionalism (p. 320)
receptive language (p. 322)
expressive language (p. 322)

infant-directed speech (p. 322)
lexical word (p. 324)
grammatical word (p. 324)
undergeneralization (p. 324)
overgeneralization (p. 324)
fast mapping (p. 326)
defining feature (p. 326)
correlational feature (p. 327)
holophrase (p. 328)
telegraphic speech (p. 328)
overregularization (p. 329)

semantic bootstrapping (p. 330)
expansion (p. 331)
phonemes (p. 332)
figurative speech (p. 333)
cooing (p. 336)
babbling (p. 336)
narrative (p. 337)
playing the dozens (p. 337)
sociolinguistic behaviors (p. 340)
personal space (p. 342)
IRE cycle (p. 342)

wait time (p. 342)
culture shock (p. 343)
metalinguistic awareness (p. 344)
bilingualism (p. 347)
immersion (p. 348)
bilingual education (p. 348)
Standard English (p. 349)
dialect (p. 349)
African American English (p. 349)
speech and communication disorders (p. 350)

Companion Website

Now go to our Companion Website at www.prenhall.com/mcdevitt to assess your understanding of chapter content with a Practice Quiz, apply what you've learned in Essay Questions, and broaden your knowledge with links to related Developmental Psychology Web sites.

Development in the Content Domains

chapter 10

Case Study: Phyllis and Benjamin Jones

Reading

Writing

Mathematics

Science

Development in Other Content Domains

Using Content Area Standards to Guide Instruction

Case Study: Beating the Odds

Summary

Applying Concepts in Child Development

Case Study: Phyllis and Benjamin Jones

Phyllis Jones and her son Benjamin lived in a low-income, inner-city, African American neighborhood. Here is their story:

[Phyllis] finished high school and two years of college, and regrets that she did not go farther. She wishes she had "listened to her grandmother" who was "always pushing" her to study; instead, "I did enough just to get by." She is deeply concerned about her son's education, and determined that he will go farther than she did. She is particularly concerned about his learning to read, noting that "without reading, you can't do anything," and that "readers are leaders—I want Benjamin to read and read and read. . . . "

Mrs. Jones decided that the only way to be certain that Benjamin would learn to read was to teach him herself. She began buying books for him when he was an infant, and she asked friends and relatives to give him books as Christmas and birthday presents. Before he turned 3, she bought him a set of phonics tapes and workbooks, which she used to conduct regular lessons, helping Benjamin learn to recognize the forms and sounds of letters, combinations of letters, and eventually entire words. She also gave him lessons in letter formation, handwriting, and spelling. When Benjamin was 3, he began attending a Head Start program, while his mother continued to teach him at home. She tried to make these activities "fun for Benjamin." She was pleased with his interest in reading and writing, and sometimes frustrated that he did not learn as quickly as she wanted him to.

Benjamin sometimes pretended to read magazines, newspapers, and books. His mother was gratified by his enthusiasm, commenting on his "reading" of *The Gingerbread Man,* "you can hear the laughter and joy in his voice." But she also told Benjamin he was "not really reading." On one occasion, she pointed to the print in the book Benjamin was pretending to read and said "these are what you read. Someday you will learn to read." Another time she commented, "Benjamin thinks he can read. What he'll do is recite some words from a story and exclaim with great joy 'I can read! I can read!' I explained to him that he isn't reading. Reading is looking at a book and saying the words that are written there. But I say one day he will read—soon, just like Tony [an older friend of Benjamin's]." By the time Benjamin was 4, his mother noted that he knew "all of his alphabet by sight. Praise God!"

When Benjamin turned 4, Mrs. Jones began taking him to a reading program at the storefront church she attended. This program was designed for older children, but she thought he would "pick up something." She also continued to work on reading and writing at home, using index cards to make a card game to teach Benjamin how to write his name. When he was about 4½, Benjamin began sounding out words that he noticed around him, such as "off" and "on." His mother commented, "now he wants to know what everything spells and wants to guess at some of them. He asked me on the bus if E-M-E-R-G-E-N-C-Y spelled 'emergency'." On another occasion, when she picked Benjamin up at Head Start, "he said, 'Guess what we did today? I'll give you a hint—it begins with J. Then he said the word was J-E-M, which was supposed to be 'gym'." His mother was delighted with his interest in reading: "Hurrah! I hope it carries through the rest of his life." By the end of his second year in Head Start, when he had just turned 5, Benjamin could read a number of simple words by sounding them out and had a small sight vocabulary. His mother took great pride in these achievements: "Hallelujah! He can read!" (McLane & McNamee, 1990, pp. 103–105)[a]

[a]Reprinted by permission of the publisher from *Early Literacy* by Joan Brooks McLane and Gillian Dowley McNamee, pp. 103–105, Cambridge, MA: Harvard University Press. Copyright © 1990 by Joan Brooks McLane and Gillian Dowley McNamee.

hyllis Jones knew how important reading and writing are for success in the adult world, and so she provided a solid foundation on which Benjamin's reading and writing development could build. Like Phyllis, many parents in industrialized countries share with their children basic elements of reading, writing, arithmetic, geography, music, and so on. For instance, they may teach their children letters and numbers, show them globes and road maps, and sing or play music for them.

By the time children reach age 5 or 6, schools take over much of the responsibility for passing along the rich cultural heritage of modern-day societies. In this chapter we look at how knowledge and skills in a variety of academic disciplines—reading, writing, math, science, history, geography, art, and music—develop over the course of childhood and adolescence. We also identify strategies for promoting children's development in various content domains.

Reading

Children's literacy skills—their skills in reading and writing—obviously build on their knowledge of spoken language. The thousands of words and innumerable grammatical structures that children master in speech are basic elements of written language as well. However, written language differs from spoken language in important ways. To learn to read and write, children must learn the relationships between how words sound and are produced in speech, on the one hand, and how they look and are written on paper, on the other. Children must also master nuances of the written symbol system that have no counterparts in spoken language, such as punctuation marks and appropriate uses of upper- and lowercase letters (Dyson, 1986; Liberman, 1998; Paris & Cunningham, 1996).

Reading is a complex, multifaceted process that continues to develop throughout childhood and adolescence. In the upcoming sections, we look at children's acquisition of basic knowledge about written language (emergent literacy) and examine the development of four critical aspects of reading: phonological awareness, word recognition, comprehension, and metacognition.

Emergent Literacy

Through early exposure to reading and writing, young children learn many things about written language (Paris & Cunningham, 1996; Pérez, 1998; Weiss & Hagen, 1988). For instance, they learn that

- Print has meaning and conveys information
- Different kinds of printed matter (storybooks, newspapers, telephone books, grocery lists, etc.) serve different purposes
- Spoken language is represented in a consistent way in written language (e.g., specific alphabet letters are associated with specific sounds, words are always spelled the same way)
- Written language includes some predictable elements and conventions (e.g., fairytales often begin with "Once upon a time," and in English, writing proceeds from left to right and from the top of the page to the bottom)

Such basic knowledge about written language, which lays a foundation for reading and writing development, is known as **emergent literacy.**

Parents and other adults promote emergent literacy in numerous ways (McLane & McNamee, 1990; Teale, 1978). They provide easy access to reading and writing materials. They model reading and writing behavior. They take children on frequent trips to the library. They talk about the things they've read and written. They demonstrate that reading and writing are useful and enjoyable activities. But perhaps most importantly, they read to children regularly (L. Baker, Scher, & Mackler, 1997; Serpell, Baker, & Sonnenschein, 2005). Reading to children is especially valuable when parents and other caregivers talk with children about what they are reading together (Panofsky, 1994). By doing so, adults engage children in the *social construction of meaning* we discussed in Chapter 6.

Some parents and child care providers introduce children to books quite early, pointing at pictures and labeling objects (C. E. Snow & Ninio, 1986). We think back to the books we bought for our own children long before they were walking or talking. Some consisted of nothing more than a few cloth, plastic, or otherwise indestructible pages that depicted a simple item (perhaps

When children grow up in literacy-rich environments, they begin to engage in pre-reading and pre-writing activities quite early.

emergent literacy
Knowledge and skills that lay a foundation for reading and writing; typically develops in the preschool years from early experiences with written language.

a cat, doll, or truck) on each page. Although these books hardly had spellbinding plots, they often captured our infants' attention, at least temporarily. In the "Emotional Development: Infancy" video clip on Observation CD 2, you can see 7-month-old Madison manipulate two simple books, one made of cloth and the other made of stiff cardboard pages containing family photographs.

Children who are read to frequently during the preschool years learn to read more easily once they reach elementary school (Sénéchal & LeFevre, 2002; Whitehurst et al., 1994). Associating literacy activities with pleasure may be especially important. Children who enjoy their early reading experiences are more likely to read frequently on their own later on (L. Baker et al., 1997). Thus authentic literacy activities (e.g., reading children's stories) are often more beneficial for young children than activities involving drill and practice of isolated skills.

By observing young children as they interact with books and writing implements, teachers and caregivers can infer a great deal about what children have learned about the nature of written language. For instance, children may pretend to read storybooks, as Benjamin Jones did, or recognize certain letters of the alphabet, as 4-year-old Carrie does in the "Literacy: Early Childhood" video clip on Observation CD 2. The Observation Guidelines table "Assessing Emergent Literacy in Young Children" offers several ideas about what to look for.

Phonological Awareness

Before Benjamin Jones was 3, his mother Phyllis began teaching him to recognize the shapes and sounds of letters. Knowing letters and their sounds is an obvious prerequisite for learning to read (M. J. Adams, 1990; M. Harris & Giannouli, 1999). But in addition, children are more successful readers when they have **phonological awareness**—when they can hear the distinct, individuals sounds that make up words (Kirby, Parrila, & Pfeiffer, 2003; McBride-Chang & Kail, 2002; Stanovich, 2000). Phonological awareness includes abilities such as these:

- Hearing the specific syllables within words (e.g., hearing "can" and "dee" as separate parts of *candy*)
- Dividing words into discrete word sounds, or *phonemes* (e.g., hearing the sounds "guh," "ay," and "tuh" in *gate*)
- Blending separate phonemes into meaningful words (e.g., recognizing that, when put together, the sounds "wuh," "eye," and "duh" make *wide*)
- Identifying words that rhyme (e.g., realizing that *cat* and *hat* end with the same sounds)

Phonological awareness develops gradually during the preschool and early elementary years (Barron, 1998; Goswami, 1999; Lonigan, Burgess, Anthony, & Barker, 1998). Most children can detect the syllables within words by age 4, well before they begin school and start learning to read. Soon after, they begin to realize that many syllables can be divided into two parts: an *onset* (one or more consonants that precede the vowel sound) and a *rime* (the vowel sound and any consonants that follow it). By the time they are 6 or 7, many children can identify the individual phonemes in spoken words. This last ability seems to emerge hand in hand with learning to read (Goswami, 1999; M. Harris & Giannouli, 1999; Perfetti, 1992).

Phyllis Jones helped Benjamin acquire phonological awareness with the help of phonics workbooks and audiotapes. Yet parents and teachers can often cultivate phonological awareness just as effectively within the context of lively, enjoyable listening, reading, and spelling activities (Muter, 1998). The Development and Practice feature "Promoting Phonological Awareness and Letter Recognition in Young Children" (p. 361) presents several useful strategies.

Word Recognition

At age 4, Benjamin could sound out some of the printed words he encountered. Most 4-year-olds don't have as much knowledge of letter-sound relationships as Benjamin did, but they can correctly identify certain words that appear in familiar contexts. For example, many preschoolers correctly identify the word *stop* when it appears on a red, octagonal sign at the side of the road. They can "read" the word *Cheerios* on a cereal box. They know that a word at a fast-food restaurant is *McDonalds* when the *M* takes the form of the well-known golden arches (Ehri, 1994; Juel, 1991; Share & Gur, 1999).

Sometime around age 5, children begin to look more closely at words. Initially, they are apt to focus on one or two visually distinctive features, perhaps seeing the "tail" hanging

Observe appropriate books for infants in the "Emotional Development: Infancy" clip on Observation CD 2.

Observe Carrie's emergent literacy in the "Literacy: Early Childhood" clip on Observation CD 2.

Young readers often rely heavily on context clues to help them identify words. As they learn various letter-sound relationships, they become increasingly proficient at sounding out new words. With time and practice, they develop a sizable sight vocabulary and can recognize many words quickly and easily.

phonological awareness
Ability to hear the distinct sounds within words.

OBSERVATION GUIDELINES

Assessing Emergent Literacy in Young Children

Characteristic	Look For	Example	Implication
Attitudes Toward Books	• Frequent manipulation and perusal of books • Interest and attentiveness when adults read storybooks • Eagerness to talk about stories that are read	Martina often mentions the Berenstain Bears books that her father reads to her at home.	Devote a regular time to storybook reading, choose books with colorful pictures and imaginative story lines, and occasionally stop to discuss and interpret characters and events in a story. Make regular trips to the library.
Behaviors with Books	• Correct handling of books (e.g., holding them right-side up, turning pages in the appropriate direction) • Pretend reading • Use of picture content or memory of the story to construct a logical sequence of events when pretending to read • Asking "What does this say?" about particular sections of text	Rusty doesn't seem to know what to do with the books in his preschool classroom. He opens them haphazardly and apparently sees nothing wrong with ripping out pages.	If children have had only limited experience with books, occasionally read one-on-one with them. Let them hold the books and turn the pages. Ask them to make predictions about what might happen next in a story.
Word Recognition	• Recognition of product names when they appear in logos and other familiar contexts • Recognition of own name in print	Katherine sees a take-out bag from a local fast-food restaurant and correctly asserts that it says "Burger King."	Prominently label any coat hooks, storage boxes, and other items that belong to individual children. Write children's names in large letters on paper and encourage them to trace or copy the letters. When children are ready, ask them to put their first name (or first initial) on their artwork.
Writing Behaviors	• Production of letterlike shapes • Writing in a left-to-right sequence • Ability to write some letters correctly or almost correctly • Ability to write own name	Hank can write his name, but he frequently reverses the *N* and sometimes leaves it out altogether.	Give children numerous opportunities to experiment with writing implements (paper, crayons, markers, pencils, etc.) in both structured tasks and unstructured situations. Guide letter and word formation when children show an interest.
Knowledge About the Nature and Purposes of Written Language	• Awareness that specific words are always spelled in the same way • Correct identification of telephone books, calendars, and other reference materials • Pretend writing for particular purposes	When Shakira and Lucie pretend to grocery shop, they write several lines of squiggles on a piece of paper. They say that this is a list of items they need to get at the store.	Encourage play activities that involve pretend writing (e.g., writing and delivering "letters" to friends or classmates). Let children see you engaging in a wide variety of reading and writing activities.

Sources: Some ideas and examples from Dickinson, Wolf, & Stotsky, 1993; F. P. L. Hawkins, 1997; McLane & McNamee, 1990; D. W. Rowe & Harste, 1986; Share & Gur, 1999; Sulzby, 1985.

down at the end of *dog* or the two "ears" sticking up in the middle of *rabbit*. Soon after, they begin to use some of a word's letters for phonetic clues about what the word must be. For example, they might read *box* by looking at the *b* and *x* but ignoring the *o* (Ehri, 1991, 1994).

Once children have mastered letter-sound relationships, they rely heavily on these relationships as they read (Ehri, 1991, 1994). Doing so allows them to identify such simple words as *cat, bed, Dick,* and *Jane.* However, they have difficulty when they encounter words that violate general pronunciation rules. For instance, using the rule that *ea* is pronounced "ee" (as in *meat* and *treat*), they might read *head* as "heed" or *sweater* as "sweeter."

By the middle elementary grades, most children have a reasonable **sight vocabulary:** They can recognize a sizable number of words immediately and with little effort. That is, a good deal of word recognition has become *automatized*. When they encounter words that aren't in their sight vocabulary, they draw on letter-sound relationships, common spelling patterns, and context clues to decipher the words (Ehri & Robbins, 1992; W. E. Nagy, Berninger, Abbott, Vaughan, & Vermeulen, 2003; R. E. Owens, 1996).

────────── Connecting Concepts
Chapter 7 discusses the nature and importance of automatization.

Reading Comprehension

sight vocabulary
Words that a child can immediately recognize while reading.

In its most basic form, reading comprehension involves understanding the words and sentences on the page. But for advanced readers, it also means going *beyond* the page to identify main ideas, make inferences and predictions, detect an author's assumptions and biases,

DEVELOPMENT AND PRACTICE

Promoting Phonological Awareness and Letter Recognition in Young Children

- Read alphabet books that use colorful pictures, amusing poems, or entertaining stories to teach letters and letter sounds.

  A preschool teacher shares *Alphabet Adventure* (Wood & Wood, 2001) with her group of 4-year-olds. The children eagerly follow along as the main character, "Little i," looks for her lost dot, and they delight in finding various letters on each page.

- Have children think of words that rhyme.

  A kindergarten teacher challenges his students to think of at least five words that rhyme with *break*.

- Ask children to identify words that begin (or end) with a particular sound or group of sounds.

  A first-grade teacher asks, "Who can think of a word that begins with a 'str' sound? For example, *string* begins with a 'str' sound. What are some other words that begin with 'str'?"

- Say several words and ask children which one begins (or ends) in a different sound.

  A second-grade teacher asks, "Listen carefully to these four words: *end, dent, bend,* and *mend.* Which one ends in a different sound than the others? Listen to them again before you decide: *end, dent, bend,* and *mend.*"

- Show pictures of several objects and ask children to choose the one that begins (or ends) with a different sound from the others.

  A kindergarten teacher shows his class pictures of a dog, a door, a wagon, and a dragon. "Three of these things start with the same sound. Which one starts with a *different* sound?"

- Have children practice writing alphabet letters on paper and representing letters in other ways.

  A first-grade teacher has children make letters with their bodies. For example, one child stands with his arms outstretched like a Y, and two others bend over and clasp hands to form an M.

and so on (Perfetti, 1985). Thus reading comprehension is a very *constructive* process: Readers combine what they see on the printed page with their existing knowledge and beliefs—both about the world in general and about the structures and conventions of written language—to derive meaning from text (I. L. Beck, McKeown, Sinatra, & Loxterman, 1991; Smagorinsky, 2001; Weaver & Kintsch, 1991).

Several general trends characterize the development of reading comprehension in childhood and adolescence:

● *Children's growing knowledge base facilitates better reading comprehension.* As children grow older, they become better able to understand what they read, in part because they know more about the topics about which they are reading (Byrnes, 1996; Rayner et al., 2001). In fact, children's reading comprehension ability at *any* age is influenced by topic knowledge (Lipson, 1983; Pearson, Hansen, & Gordon, 1979). For example, when second graders read about spiders, those who already know a lot about spiders remember more and draw inferences more easily than peers who know less about the topic (Pearson et al., 1979).

● *Children acquire more knowledge about common structures in fictional and nonfictional texts.* Most 5- and 6-year-olds can distinguish between books that tell stories and books that provide information (S. L. Field, Labbo, & Ash, 1999). As children get older, they also learn how various kinds of text are typically organized, and such knowledge helps them make better sense of what they read. For instance, they gradually acquire a **story schema** that represents the typical components of fictional narratives, such as main characters, setting, plot, and problem resolution (Graesser, Golding, & Long, 1991; N. L. Stein & Glenn, 1979). When a work of fiction is organized in an unusual way (e.g., when it consists of a series of flashbacks), older children may use a story schema to mentally rearrange the text's elements into a structure that makes sense (Byrnes, 1996; N. L. Stein, 1982; Zwaan, Langston, & Graesser, 1995).

With age, children also begin to use common structures in nonfiction to enhance their comprehension (Byrnes, 1996). For instance, when reading a textbook, they may rely on headings and subheadings to help them identify key ideas and organize what they are studying. And when reading a persuasive essay, they may anticipate that the author will first present a particular point of view and then offer evidence to support it.

● *Children become increasingly able to draw inferences from what they read.* Especially as children reach the upper elementary grades, they become more adept at drawing inferences and so more effectively learn new information from what they read (Chall, 1996; Paris & Upton, 1976). However, they tend to take the things they read at face value, make little attempt to evaluate the quality of ideas, and often don't notice obvious contradictions (Chall, 1996; P. Johnston & Afflerbach, 1985; Markman, 1979).

As children reach adolescence and move into the secondary grades, they read written material with a more critical eye (Chall, 1996; R. E. Owens, 1996). They begin to recognize

Connecting Concepts
See Chapters 6 and 7 for discussions of constructive processes in learning and development more generally.

Study Guide and Reader
Not only does children's knowledge base enhance their literacy skills, but reading and writing further enhance their knowledge base (see Supplementary Reading 10-1).

story schema
Knowledge of the typical elements and sequence of a narrative.

DEVELOPMENT AND PRACTICE

Promoting Effective Reading Comprehension Strategies

- Teach reading comprehension skills in all subject areas and content domains.

  When a life skills instructor tells his students to read a section of their first-aid manual, he also suggests several strategies they might use to help them remember what they read. For example, as students begin each section, they should use the heading to make a prediction as to what the section will be about. At the end of the section, they should stop and consider whether their prediction was accurate.

- Model effective reading strategies.

  A girl in a seventh-grade history class reads aloud a passage describing how, during Columbus's first voyage across the Atlantic, many members of the crew wanted to turn around and return to Spain. Her teacher says, "Let's think of some reasons why the crew might have wanted to go home." One student responds, "Some of them might have been homesick." Another suggests, "Maybe they thought they'd never find their way back if they went too far."

- Encourage children to relate what they are reading to things they already know about the topic.

  Children in a third-grade classroom are each reading several books on a particular topic (e.g., dinosaurs, insects, outer space). Before they begin reading a book, their teacher asks them to write answers to three ques-

tions: (a) What do you already know about your topic? (b) What do you hope to learn about your topic? and (c) Do you think what you learn in your books will change what you already know about your topic?

- Ask children to identify key elements of the stories they read.

  A fourth-grade teacher instructs his students to ask themselves five questions as they read stories: (a) Who is the main character? (b) Where and when did the story take place? (c) What did the main characters do? (d) How did the story end? and (e) How did the main character feel?

- Suggest that children create mental images that capture what they are reading.

  When a high school English class reads Nathaniel Hawthorne's *The Scarlet Letter,* the teacher suggests that students close their eyes and imagine what the two main characters, Arthur Dimsdale and Hester Prynne, might look like. He then asks several students to describe their mental images.

- Scaffold children's early efforts to use complex strategies.

  A middle school science teacher asks her students to write summaries of short textbook passages. She gives them four rules to use as they develop their summaries: (a) Identify the most important ideas, (b) delete trivial details, (c) eliminate redundant information, and (d) identify relationships among the main ideas.

Sources: Gambrell & Bales, 1986; Pressley et al., 1994; Rinehart, Stahl, & Erickson, 1986; Short & Ryan, 1984; H. Thompson & Carr, 1995.

By the time they reach high school, many adolescents no longer take everything they read at face value. Instead, they begin to read text with a critical eye.

─────── **Connecting Concepts**
See Chapter 7 for a general discussion of metacognition.

─────── **Study Guide and Reader**
Supplementary Reading 10-2 describes six possible stages in reading development.

that different authors sometimes present different viewpoints on a single issue. They also become more aware of the subtle aspects of fiction, such as the underlying themes and symbolism of a novel.

The ability to draw inferences seems to be a key factor in children's reading comprehension. Some youngsters who have trouble understanding what they read appear to have less working memory capacity, which limits their ability to consider and integrate multiple pieces of information at once (Oakhill, Cain, & Yuill, 1998). In addition, many poor readers don't relate what they read to what they already know about a topic. Thus they are less likely to fill in missing details that would help them make sense of text (Cain & Oakhill, 1998).

Metacognition in Reading

As children gain more experience with reading, and especially with reading textbooks and other informational text, they develop a variety of strategies for comprehending written material. For instance, adolescents can more easily identify main ideas than elementary school children can (van den Broek, Lynch, Naslund, Ievers-Landis, & Verduin, 2003). High school students are more likely to monitor their comprehension as they read, and also to backtrack (i.e., reread) when they don't understand something the first time, than are children in the upper elementary and middle school grades (Garner, 1987; Hacker, 1995). Not all adolescents use effective metacognitive reading strategies, however, and those who engage in little metacognition often have considerable difficulty understanding and remembering what they read (Alvermann & Moore, 1991; Hacker, 1995).

With proper instruction and support, children and adolescents can learn to use effective metacognitive strategies and improve their reading comprehension as a result. One useful approach is *reciprocal teaching,* described in Chapter 6. The Development and Practice feature "Promoting Effective Reading Comprehension Strategies" presents additional suggestions.

In general, as young people move through the elementary and secondary grades, they read with greater fluency and flexibility and become able to read increasingly complex and challenging material. The Developmental Trends table "Reading at Different Age Levels" traces the development of reading over the course of childhood and adolescence.

DEVELOPMENTAL TRENDS

Reading at Different Age Levels

Age	What You Might Observe	Diversity	Implications
Infancy (Birth–2) 	• Physical exploration of simple cloth and cardboard books • Increasing enjoyment of storybooks; initially, toddlers focus more on pictures than on story lines • Attention to and enjoyment of rhythm and rhymes in spoken language	• Temperamental differences influence infants' and toddlers' ability to sit still and attend to books.	• Provide small, durable picture books of cloth, cardboard, or plastic. • Read books with catchy rhythms and rhymes to capture and maintain attention. • During story time, label and talk about the pictures in books. Recognize that toddlers may not be able to sit still for a lengthy story.
Early Childhood (2–6) 	• Incorporation of books and familiar story lines into play activities • Increasing knowledge of letters and letter-sound correspondences • Identification of a few words in well-known contexts (e.g., words on commercial products) • Use of a word's distinctive features (e.g., a single letter or overall shape) to read or misread it	• Children who have had little exposure to books and reading before starting school may have less knowledge about the nature of reading. Some cultures emphasize oral language more than written language. • When parents speak a language other than English, they may provide early literacy experiences in their native tongue; such experiences provide a good foundation for reading and writing in English. • Some children begin school knowing the alphabet and may have a small sight vocabulary as well. Others may need to start from scratch in learning letters and letter sounds.	• Read to young children using colorful books with high-interest content. • Teach letters of the alphabet through engaging, hands-on activities. • Teach letter-sound relationships through storybooks, games, rhymes, and enjoyable writing activities. • Encourage children to read words that can easily be identified from their contexts. • Encourage parents to read regularly to children.
Middle Childhood (6–10) 	• Ability to hear individual phonemes within words • Increasing proficiency in identifying unfamiliar words • Growing sight-word vocabulary, leading to greater reading fluency • Beginning of silent reading (at age 7 or 8) • Increasing ability to draw inferences • Tendency to take things in print at face value	• Children with deficits in phonological awareness have a more difficult time learning to read. • Children with hearing impairments may be slower to master letter-sound relationships. • On average, girls develop reading skills earlier than boys. • Children vary widely in their use of effective comprehension strategies.	• Explore "families" of words that are spelled similarly. • Assign well-written trade books (e.g., children's paperback novels) as soon as children are able to read and understand them. • Engage children in discussions about books. Focus on interpretation, inference drawing, and speculation. • For children who struggle with reading, explicitly teach phonological awareness and word identification skills, especially within the context of meaningful reading activities.
Early Adolescence (10–14) 	• Automatized recognition of most common words • Ability to learn new information through reading • Emerging ability to go beyond the literal meaning of text • Emerging metacognitive processes that aid comprehension (e.g., comprehension monitoring, backtracking)	• Adolescents with deficits in phonological awareness continue to lag behind their peers in reading development. • Individuals who were poor readers in elementary school often continue to be poor readers in adolescence. • Some individuals (e.g., some with mental retardation) may have excellent word identification skills yet not understand what they read. • Individuals with sensory challenges may have less general world knowledge that they can use to construct meaning from what they read.	• Assign age-appropriate reading materials in various content areas; provide scaffolding (e.g., questions to answer) to guide youngsters' thinking and learning as they read. • Begin to explore classic works of poetry and fiction. • Use reciprocal teaching to promote poor readers' comprehension skills (see Chapter 6). • Seek the advice and assistance of specialists to help promote the reading skills of youngsters who lag far behind their peers.

(continued)

DEVELOPMENTAL TRENDS

Reading at Different Age Levels (continued)

Age	What You Might Observe	Diversity	Implications
Late Adolescence (14–18) 	• Automatized recognition of many abstract and discipline-specific words • Ability to consider multiple viewpoints about a single topic • Ability to critically evaluate what is read • More sophisticated metacognitive reading strategies	• Poor readers draw few if any inferences from what they read and use few if any effective metacognitive processes. • As classroom learning becomes more dependent on reading textbooks and other written materials, adolescents with reading disabilities may become increasingly frustrated in their attempts to achieve academic success. • Girls are more likely than boys to enroll in advanced literature classes.	• Expect that many teenagers can learn effectively from textbooks and other reading materials, but continue to scaffold reading assignments, especially for poor readers. • Encourage adolescents to draw inferences and make predictions from what they read. • Critically analyze classic works of poetry and fiction. • Modify reading materials and paper-pencil assessments for individuals with delayed reading development.

Sources: Cain & Oakhill, 1998; Chall, 1996; Dryden & Jefferson, 1994; Ehri, 1994; Felton, 1998; M. Harris & Hatano, 1999; Hedges & Nowell, 1995; Hulme & Joshi, 1998; P. Johnston & Afflerbach, 1985; McBride-Chang & Treiman, 2003; McLane & McNamee, 1990; W. E. Nagy et al., 2003; R. E. Owens, 1996; L. Reese, Garnier, Gallimore, & Goldenberg, 2000; Share & Gur, 1999; Trawick-Smith, 2003; Trelease, 1982; R. Turnbull et al., 2004; Wigfield et al., 1996; Yaden & Templeton, 1986.

Diversity in Reading Development

To some extent, development of literacy skills goes hand in hand with overall intellectual development. Many (but not all) children who are later identified as intellectually gifted begin to read earlier than their peers, and some read frequently and voraciously (Piirto, 1999; R. Turnbull et al., 2004). Children with mental retardation learn to read more slowly than their age-mates, and they acquire fewer effective reading strategies. In some instances they may develop excellent word identification skills yet understand little or nothing of what they read (Cossu, 1999).

Children with visual or hearing impairments may be at a disadvantage when learning to read, in part because their general language development may be delayed (see Chapter 9). In addition, children who are visually impaired cannot see the printed page when caregivers read to them in the early years, and so they know less about the conventions of written language (the left-to-right progression of words, the use of punctuation, etc.) when they begin school (Tompkins & McGee, 1986). Children with hearing impairments who have learned a manual language (e.g., American Sign Language) rather than spoken language cannot take advantage of letter-sound relationships and may have limited knowledge of the idioms and other irregularities of day-to-day speech (Andrews & Mason, 1986; Chall, 1996). Many graduating high school students who are deaf read only at a fourth- or fifth-grade level (Chall, 1996).

Some children with learning disabilities have considerable difficulty learning to read. In its extreme form, this difficulty is known as **dyslexia,** a disability that often has biological roots (Galaburda & Rosen, 2001; Snowling, Gallagher, & Frith, 2003). Contrary to popular belief, dyslexia is typically *not* a problem of visual perception, such as reading words or letters backwards. Instead, many children with dyslexia have deficits in phonological awareness (Stanovich, 2000; Swanson et al., 1999). Others have deficits in the ability to identify visual stimuli quickly, which translates into difficulty automatizing connections between printed words and their meanings (Stanovich, 2000; Wimmer, Mayringer, & Landerl, 2000; Wolf & Bowers, 1999). Some children with reading disabilities may also have general information processing difficulties, such as a smaller working memory capacity or a tendency to process information at a slower-than-average rate (Wimmer, Landerl, & Frith, 1999; Wolf & Bowers, 1999).

We find further diversity in children's reading development as a function of their gender, socioeconomic status, ethnicity, and native language.

dyslexia
Inability to master basic reading skills in a developmentally typical time frame despite normal reading instruction.

Gender differences.   On average, girls read better than boys (Weaver-Hightower, 2003). And in the high school grades, girls are more likely than boys to enroll in advanced literature classes (Wigfield et al., 1996). Boys tend to have less interest in reading than girls do, in part because boys find fewer books at school that pique their curiosity and in part because many of them prefer more physically active pastimes (Freedman, 2003; Taylor & Lorimer, 2002–2003).

Socioeconomic differences.   As the opening case study illustrates, many low-income parents regularly read to their children and in other ways foster literacy development (Jimerson et al., 1999; McLane & McNamee, 1990). Yet many others have little knowledge of how to promote emergent literacy through storybook readings and other reading activities. On average, then, children from lower-income families come to school with fewer literacy skills than children from middle- and upper-income families. The difference among socioeconomic groups not only persists, but in fact *increases,* over the course of the elementary and secondary school years (Chall, 1996; Jimerson et al., 1999; Portes, 1996). Thus, as children from low-income families get older, they fall further and further behind their more economically advantaged peers.

Ethnic and cultural differences.   Ethnic and cultural groups differ considerably in their emphasis on engaging young children in reading activities. Some African American groups focus more on oral storytelling than on book reading (Trawick-Smith, 2003). Some Native American communities stress art, dance, and oral histories that carry on the group's cultural traditions (Trawick-Smith, 2003). Immigrant Hispanic parents often place higher priority on promoting their children's moral development (e.g., teaching them right from wrong) than on promoting early literacy skills (Gallimore & Goldenberg, 2001).

Storybook reading in the early years promotes the development of emergent literacy—basic knowledge about written language and literature that provides the foundation for learning how to read and write.

Even when young children have been regularly immersed in books, their cultural backgrounds influence their interpretations of what they read. As an example, Rosenna Bakari, a colleague of ours who specializes in African-centered education, describes an incident involving her 7-year-old daughter Nailah:

> [An event] that always stands out in my mind is a reading comprehension question that Nailah had in a workbook. The question asked why two brothers drew a line down the middle of a messy room to clean it. The answer was pretty obvious: The boys were dividing the room in half so that they could each clean their part. However, Nailah could not get to that answer no matter how I scaffolded her. When I told her the answer, she replied, "Why would they divide the room up? They should just both clean it together." I immediately realized that in her African-centered world, division rarely takes place. Most things in our house are communal. Each child is responsible for the other. So for her to get to that answer would have taken something beyond reasonable reading comprehension. She would have had to understand that there are people in the world who operate under different views about sharing and responsibility. That's a more difficult task for a seven-year-old. (R. Bakari, personal communication, 2002)

People from most ethnic groups in Western society value literacy and see it as essential for children's eventual success in the adult world (Gallimore & Goldenberg, 2001; Pérez, 1998). Educators must be sensitive to what children's early language and literacy experiences have been and use them as the foundation for reading instruction. For example, reading instruction may be more effective for native Hawaiian children when they can engage in *overlapping talk* (in which they frequently interrupt one another) as they discuss the stories they are reading. Such a conversational style is consistent with their speaking practices at home (K. H. Au & Mason, 1981). And children and adolescents from all backgrounds will respond more favorably to literature and textbooks that reflect their own culture's ways of living and thinking (Gollnick & Chinn, 2002).

Cross-linguistic differences.   The more regular and predictable a language's letter-sound relationships are, the more easily children learn to read (M. Harris & Hatano, 1999). Languages differ considerably in the extent to which spelling precisely captures how words are pronounced. Spanish, Portuguese, Italian, German, Finnish, and Swahili have highly regular and predictable spelling patterns, such that a word's spelling usually tells a reader exactly how the word is pronounced and its pronunciation tells a writer exactly how the word is spelled. English, French, and Greek are less regular, in that some sounds can be represented by two or more different letters or letter combinations. Some languages don't use an alphabet at all, so that predictable relationships between the forms of spoken and written language are few and far between. For instance, Chinese and Japanese are written as *characters* that represent entire syllables rather than individual phonemes.

Curiously, phonological awareness seems to be an important factor even in reading non-alphabetic languages such as Chinese and Japanese (McBride-Chang & Ho, 2000; J. C. Ziegler, Tan, Perry, & Montant, 2000). The underlying cause of this relationship has not been pinned down, but it may in some way be related to the fact that when people read, they mentally retrieve the sounds of written words as one way of connecting the words with their meanings (Rayner et al., 2001; J. C. Ziegler et al., 2000). Children in China, Taiwan, and Japan are often taught one or more alphabetic, phonetic systems for representing their language in writing before they are taught more traditional characters, and such training increases their phonological awareness (e.g., Hanley, Tzeng, & Huang, 1999).

Promoting Reading Development

Traditionally, reading is taught primarily in elementary school. Many teachers and other adults assume that middle school and high school students read well enough to learn successfully from textbooks and other printed materials. But as you have seen, this assumption is not always warranted. Even at the high school level, many adolescents have not yet mastered all of the skills involved in reading effectively. Furthermore, children who have trouble reading in elementary school often continue to be poor readers in the secondary grades (Felton, 1998) and so may be in particular need of ongoing instruction and support in reading skills. We offer the following general strategies for promoting reading development throughout childhood and adolescence:

● *Help parents of young children acquire effective storybook reading skills.* In the "Literacy: Infancy" video clip on Observation CD 2, Corwin's mother enthusiastically engages her son in a discussion about the book they are looking at:

In the "Literacy: Infancy" clip on Observation CD 2, observe the strategies Corwin's mother uses during picture book reading.

Mother:	Do you wanna see the cow? Would you like to read with Mama? You ready for the cow? Where is he? [turns the page] Huh! The cow says . . .
Corwin:	Mooo!
Mother:	What's that? [points to something in the book]
Corwin:	Boon.
Mother:	Balloon! We can count! One . . .
Corwin:	Two.
Mother:	Two! [reading book] This is my nose. Where's your nose?
Corwin:	[touches his nose]
Mother:	Nose! Where's your toes?
Corwin:	[grabs his toes]
Mother:	There's your toes!

Notice how the mother models enthusiasm for the book and uses its content to review object labels (*balloon, nose, toes*) and general world knowledge (numbers, what a cow says) with Corwin. Yet some parents have little awareness of how to read to young children, perhaps because they themselves were rarely read to when they were young. Such parents benefit from explicit instruction in strategies for reading to children—labeling and describing pictures, asking questions that encourage inferences and predictions, inviting children to make comments, and so on. When parents begin to use such strategies as they read to their children, their children acquire larger vocabularies, better knowledge of written language, and appreciation for literature (P. A. Edwards & Garcia, 1994; Gallimore & Goldenberg, 2001; H.-Z. Ho, Hinckley, Fox, Brown, & Dixon, 2001; Whitehurst et al., 1994).

● *Use meaningful and engaging activities to teach basic reading skills.* Explicit instruction in basic reading skills—relating letters to sounds, identifying simple words, finding main ideas, and so on—facilitates reading development, especially for poor readers (Hulme & Joshi, 1998; Rayner et al., 2001; Stanovich, 2000). To become truly effective readers, children must automatize the most basic aspects of reading, including letter-sound relationships and recognition of most words (M. J. Adams, 1990; Ehri, Nunes, Stahl, & Willows, 2001; Stanovich, 2000). As you should recall from Chapter 7, automatization develops primarily through practice, practice, and more practice.

One approach, of course, is to provide drill-and-practice activities—workbook exercises, flash cards, and so on—that help children automatize specific reading skills (e.g., see Figure 10-1). Unfortunately, many children find such activities dull and boring (E. H. Hiebert & Raphael, 1996; J. C. Turner, 1995). Instruction in basic skills does not *have* to be dull and boring, however. With a little thought, teachers, parents, and other adults can develop enjoyable, meaningful activities to teach almost any basic reading skill. For instance, to promote phonological awareness in young children, adults might conduct a game of "Twenty Questions" (e.g., "I'm thinking of something in the room that begins with the letter *B*") or ask children to bring something from home that begins with the letter *T*. To foster greater automatization in word recognition, they might simply engage children in a variety of authentic reading activities (Ehri, 1998; Share, 1995).

Under no circumstances should teachers postpone teaching reading comprehension until basic skills are automatized. To do so would be to communicate the message that reading is a meaningless, tedious task, rather than a source of enlightenment and pleasure (Serpell et al., 2005). Well-known children's book author Dr. Seuss was a master at writing and illustrating stories that young children find enjoyable and engaging. The following excerpt from his book *One Fish Two Fish Red Fish Blue Fish* helps children learn the -*ook* pattern:

> We took a look.
> We saw a Nook.
> On his head
> he had a hook.
> On his hook
> he had a book.
> On his book
> was "How to Cook."
> (Seuss, 1960, p. 30)

● *Identify and address reading problems early.* If children initially struggle with reading, they are apt to read as little as possible and so limit their opportunities for practice, improvement, and automatization of basic skills. As a result, the gap between them and their peers widens over time (Stanovich, 2000). To minimize the damage, then, children should make up any reading deficits early in the game, ideally in first grade or even earlier (e.g., A. E. Cunningham & Stanovich, 1997; Morris, Tyner, & Perney, 2000).

We urge you to be on the lookout for signs of reading disabilities in the early elementary grades. Perhaps the most telling sign is considerable difficulty in learning letter-sound relationships and applying them effectively in reading and writing tasks. Children with early reading difficulties benefit from deliberate and intensive training in letter recognition, phonological awareness, and word identification strategies (M. W. Lovett et al., 2000; Schneider, Roth, & Ennemoser, 2000; Stanovich, 2000).

● *Use high-interest works of fiction and nonfiction.* Children and adolescents read more energetically and persistently, use more sophisticated metacognitive strategies, and remember more content when they are interested in what they are reading (R. C. Anderson, Shirey, Wilson, & Fielding, 1987; J. T. Guthrie et al., 1998; Sheveland, 1994). For example, in the "Literacy: Late Adolescence" video clip on Observation CD 2, 14-year-old Alicia describes the importance of being able to choose what she reads:

> I really don't like it when the reading is required. I can't read books if they're required. I just avoid reading them because they don't seem very interesting. And even after you read them, even though they might be interesting, they're not as interesting as if you picked them up by yourself.

As much as possible, then, teachers, parents, and other adults should choose reading materials that are likely to be relevant to young people's own lives and concerns, and they should give youngsters some choices about what to read.

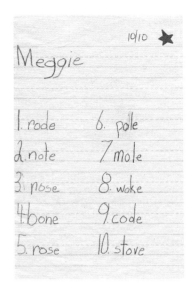

Figure 10-1

In this assignment, 7-year-old Meggie, a first grader, practices words with a long *o* sound and silent *e*. Instruction in specific letter-sound relationships and common spelling patterns helps children with both reading and spelling. However, too much focus on such drill and practice may lead children to conclude that reading and writing are meaningless, joyless activities.

Connecting Concepts
The writing sample in the "Pumpkin and Bat" exercise in Chapter 7 (p. 270) shows unusual difficulty with letter-sound relationships and signals a possible reading disability.

Observe Alicia's preference for self-chosen literature in the "Literacy: Late Adolescence" clip on Observation CD 2.

We Wear the Mask
by Paul Laurence Dunbar

We wear the mask that grins and lies,
It hides our cheeks and shades our eyes,–
This debt we pay to human guile;
With torn and bleeding hearts we smile,
And mouth with myriad subtleties.

Why should the world be overwise,
In counting all our tears and sighs?
Nay, let them only see us, while
We wear the mask.

We smile, but, O great Christ, our cries
To thee from tortured souls arise.
We sing, but oh the clay is vile
Beneath our feet, and long the mile;
But let the world dream otherwise,
We wear the mask!

Figure 10-2

Interpreting poetry through art. Jeff's brightly colored painting is the cheerful face ("mask") that its African American owner presents in public. The black face is the flip side of the mask, as viewed by the person wearing it. Depicted in the holes of the mask are a lynching (left eye); a whipping (right eye); an African American woman and a white baby (nostrils), reflecting white owners' rape of slaves; and a slave ship with someone being thrown overboard (mouth).

——————— **Study Guide and Reader**
Group discussions about literature can begin quite early, as illustrated in Supplementary Reading 10-3.

● *Conduct group discussions about stories and novels.* Children and adolescents often construct meaning more effectively when they discuss what they read with peers. For instance, adults can form "book clubs" in which children lead small groups of peers in discussions about specific books (Alvermann, Young, Green, & Wisenbaker, 1999; McMahon, 1992). They can hold "grand conversations" about a particular work of literature, asking youngsters to share their responses to questions with no single right answers—perhaps questions related to interpretations or critiques of various aspects of a text (Eeds & Wells, 1989; E. H. Hiebert & Raphael, 1996). By tossing around possible interpretations of what they are reading, children often model effective reading and listening comprehension strategies for one another (R. C. Anderson et al., 2001).

● *Have children use a variety of media to interpret what they read.* Group discussions are hardly the only mechanisms for fostering the interpretation of literature. Children might also perform skits to illustrate stories, write personal letters that one character in a story might send to another character, or create works of art that illustrate the setting or characters of a novel or the underlying meaning of a poem. Figure 10-2 shows how 16-year-old Jeff illustrated Paul Laurence Dunbar's poem "We Wear the Mask" as an assignment for his American literature class.

● *Encourage reading outside of school.* Reading beyond school walls—for instance, reading during the summer months—probably accounts for a significant portion of young people's growth in reading (D. P. Hayes & Grether, 1983; Stanovich, 2000). Providing books that children can take home to read or reread (perhaps accompanied by audiotapes) encourages outside reading and can significantly enhance reading comprehension skills (Koskinen et al., 2000). Visits to the local library can also encourage outside reading. In fact, when planning a library visit, teachers might extend an invitation for parents to accompany the group. In some cases such a visit may be the first time parents have ever been to a library (Heath, 1983).

Writing

Children begin attempting to write long before they reach school age, especially if they often see people around them writing. As early as 18 months of age, many toddlers can hold a pencil or crayon and scribble randomly (McLane & McNamee, 1990; Winner, 2006). In fact, in the "Literacy: Infancy" video clip on Observation CD 2, Corwin does so even sooner (at 16 months old) when his mother encourages him. Children's early efforts with pencil and paper are largely exploratory, reflecting experimentation with different kinds of marks on paper and other surfaces.

With the increasing motor coordination they acquire during the preschool years, children become better able to control their hand movements and can produce recognizable shapes. By age 4, their writing is clearly different from drawing (Graham & Weintraub, 1996; Sulzby, 1986). For instance, it may consist of wavy lines or connected loops that loosely resemble adults' cursive writing. Children's early writing—or more accurately, *pseudowriting*—often reveals considerable knowledge about written language, as the following exercise, "Pseudowriting Samples," illustrates.

Observe Corwin's early attempt at scribbling in the "Literacy: Infancy" clip on Observation CD 2.

INTERPRETING CHILDREN'S ARTIFACTS AND ACTIONS

Pseudowriting Samples

Two children in Cathy Zocchi's preschool class created the artifacts you see here. A 4-year-old boy wrote the "letter" on the left to his mother and told his teacher it said, "Dear Mommy, from Tommy." A 5-year-old girl wrote the second piece without explaining its meaning. As you look at the artifacts, identify aspects of written language that each child has mastered.

Both children have obviously learned that writing consistently proceeds horizontally across the page. (If we were to watch them writing, we could determine whether they also know that, in English, writing always proceeds from left to right and from the top of the page to the bottom.) Four-year-old Tommy has apparently seen enough examples of cursive writing to know that letters are sometimes connected to one another. The 5-year-old's writing more closely resembles printing than cursive writing and includes actual letters. The letters *M, N,* and *O* are most common, but on closer inspection, you can also find *A, B, D, U,* and *V.*

By the time children are 5, they frequently incorporate letters and letterlike forms in their pseudowriting (Graham & Weintraub, 1996). Some preschoolers don't yet realize that writing must take a particular form to have meaning, however, and even those who do are often unable to distinguish between true writing and meaningless marks on a page. For instance, children may scribble something and ask an adult, "What did I write?" (McLane & McNamee, 1990).

True writing is, of course, much more than simply putting letterlike forms on paper. To become skillful writers, growing children must not only master handwriting and spelling but also learn conventions of capitalization and punctuation, discover how to communicate thoughts clearly, and metacognitively regulate the entire writing effort. Unless some of these skills and processes are automatized, virtually any writing task exceeds the limits of a typical child's working memory capacity.

Writing involves many things: considering what the reader is likely to know, expressing thoughts coherently, spelling words correctly, adhering to conventions of grammar and punctuation, and so on. Children and adolescents don't have the working memory capacity to handle all of these tasks simultaneously unless some skills are automatized.

Handwriting

During the elementary school years, children's handwriting gradually becomes smaller, smoother, and more regular (Graham & Weintraub, 1996). Little if any improvement in handwriting occurs after elementary school, and for some youngsters handwriting quality actually declines during adolescence (Graham & Weintraub, 1996). Some legibility may be lost because adolescents write more quickly than younger children. In fact, rapid, automatized handwriting (or, as an alternative, automatized keyboarding) is an important factor in effective writing (Graham, Harris, & Fink, 2000; D. Jones & Christensen, 1999).

Spelling

As you might guess, phonological awareness is as important in spelling as it is in reading (P. Bryant, Nunes, & Aidinis, 1999; Griffith, 1991; Lennox & Siegel, 1998). Benjamin Jones showed phonological awareness when, as a 4-year-old, he captured both the "juh" and "mm" sounds in *gym* to spell "JEM."

Children learn the correct spellings of a few words (such as their names) almost as soon as they learn how to write letters of the alphabet. But in their early writing they tend to engage in considerable guesswork about how words are spelled, creating **invented spellings** that correctly capture certain sounds but may only vaguely resemble actual words (Treiman, 1998). Consider the invented spellings in this kindergartner's creation entitled "My Garden" (note that "HWS" is *house*):

THIS IS A HWS
THE SUN
WL SHIN
ND MI
GRDN
WL GRO (Hemphill & Snow, 1996, p. 192)

─────── **Study Guide and Reader**
Supplementary Reading 10-4 describes developmental trends in children's early spelling and offers strategies for promoting spelling development.

As children develop greater phonological awareness, their spellings increasingly represent most or all of the phonemes they hear (Gentry, 1982; Hemphill & Snow, 1996). Sometime around first or second grade, they also begin to incorporate common letter patterns (e.g., *-ight, -ound,* and *-ing* in English) into their spelling (P. Bryant et al., 1999; Nation & Hulme, 1998). All along, of course, they are learning more and more *correct* spellings, and eventually they automatize many of these spellings, retrieving them quickly and easily as they write (Rittle-Johnson & Siegler, 1999).

Syntax and Grammar

As children grow older, they use longer sentences in their writing. By the time they are 12 or 13, the syntactic structures they use in written work are considerably more complex than those they use in speech. With age, too, comes increasing automatization of punctuation and capitalization rules (Byrnes, 1996; Gillam & Johnston, 1992).

Composition Skills

When preschool children engage in early writing activities at home, they often do so with a particular purpose in mind, such as labeling a possession or writing a letter to a grandparent. Only when children enter kindergarten or first grade do most of them begin to write for writing's sake. Children's earliest compositions are usually narratives, such as recollections of personal experiences or short, fictional stories (Hemphill & Snow, 1996). Expository writing (e.g., research reports, persuasive essays) arrives on the scene considerably later (R. E. Owens, 1996), possibly because teachers typically don't ask for such writing until the upper elementary grades.

The nature and quality of children's and adolescents' writing change in many ways throughout the elementary and secondary school years, as reflected in the following trends:

● *Children develop their topics in greater depth as they grow older.* When children of various ages are asked to write about a particular topic, older ones tend to include more

invented spelling
A child's early, self-constructed word spelling, which may reflect only some of the word's phonemes.

ideas than younger ones do (Donovan, 1999; Scardamalia & Bereiter, 1986). Such growth continues throughout the school years. For instance, when writing persuasive essays, high school students include more arguments than elementary and middle school students do, and 12th graders include more arguments than 9th graders (Knudson, 1992; McCann, 1989).

● *Children increasingly take their audience into account when they write.* In our discussion of language development in the preceding chapter, we mentioned that children become increasingly able to adapt their speech to the characteristics of their listeners. The same is true for writing: With age and experience, children become better able to envision the audience to whom they are writing and tailor their text accordingly (R. T. Kellogg, 1994; Knudson, 1992; Perfetti & McCutchen, 1987).

● *With age comes an increasing ability to write a cohesive composition.* In the elementary grades, children use few if any devices to tie their compositions together. For instance, they may write a story by beginning with "Once upon a time," listing a sequence of events that lead only loosely to one another, and then ending with "They lived happily ever after" (McLane & McNamee, 1990). Their nonfiction, too, may be little more than a list of facts or events. Older children, and especially adolescents, are more capable of analyzing and synthesizing their thoughts when they write, and so they compose more cohesive, integrated texts (McCutchen, 1987; R. E. Owens, 1996; Spivey, 1997).

Study Guide and Reader ———————

Writing samples presented in Supplementary Reading 10-5 illustrate this and other developmental trends in writing.

● *Especially in adolescence, a knowledge-telling approach gradually evolves into a knowledge-transforming approach.* Young writers often compose a narrative or essay simply by writing down ideas in the order in which they come to mind. Such an approach is known as **knowledge telling** (Bereiter & Scardamalia, 1987; McCutchen, 1996). But with age, experience, greater automatization of basic writing skills, and an increasing ability to take the characteristics of potential readers into account, some adolescents (and a few younger children as well) begin to think of writing as a process of helping potential readers *understand* what they're saying. This approach, known as **knowledge transforming,** is illustrated by an eighth grader's response to the question *How did the United States become a country?*, shown in Figure 10-3.

Metacognition in Writing

Good writers think about a topic ahead of time and carefully plan how they are going to write about it. They also critically evaluate their work, looking not only for grammatical and spelling errors but also for omissions, ambiguities, logical flaws, and contradictions. Such editing skills emerge slowly and are incomplete even by the end of adolescence. Children and adolescents alike have considerable difficulty identifying problems in their own writing, particularly those related to clarity and cohesiveness (Beal, 1996; Berninger, Fuller, & Whitaker, 1996; Fitzgerald, 1987). Because they have trouble reading their own writing as another person might read it, they are apt to think they are expressing themselves more clearly than they really are (Bartlett, 1982; Beal, 1996). As a result, they often don't revise their work unless a teacher or other adult specifically urges them to do so. When they *do* rewrite, they tend to make only small, superficial changes (Beal, 1996; Cameron, Hunt, & Linton, 1996; Francis & McCutchen, 1994). More critical self-reflection and self-editing, if it develops at all, is apt to come later, perhaps in college writing classes.

The Developmental Trends table "Writing at Different Age Levels" identifies changes in writing seen during infancy and the preschool, elementary school, and secondary school years.

We became a country by way of common sense. The inhabitants on American soil thought it rather silly and ridiculus to be loyal to, follow rules and pay taxes to a ruler who has never seen where they live. King George III had never set foot (as far as I know) on American soil, but he got taxes and other things from those who lived here. When America decied to unit and dishonnor past laws and rules, England got angry. There was a war. When we won, drew up rules, and accepted states America was born.

In a more poetic sense, we became a country because of who lived here and what they did. They actions of heros, heroines, leaders, followers and everyday people made America famous, an ideal place to live. The different cultures and lifestyles made America unique and unlike any other place in the world. If you think about it, it's like visiting the worlds at Epcot in Florida. You can go from country to country without leaving home.

Figure 10-3

In her account of how the United States became a country, an eighth grader tries to help the reader understand what she is saying—an approach known as *knowledge transforming.* (We've kept her spelling errors intact.)
Essay courtesy of Dinah Jackson.

knowledge telling
Writing down ideas in whatever order they come to mind, with little regard for communicating the ideas effectively.

knowledge transforming
Writing ideas in such a way as to intentionally help the reader understand them.

Writing at Different Age Levels

Age	What You Might Observe	Diversity	Implications
Infancy (Birth–2) 	• Development of eye-hand coordination, including the *pincer grasp*, through which infants use thumb and forefinger to pick up and hold objects • Appearance of scribbling at 18 to 24 months • Interest in mimicking "writing"; gradual awareness that some objects are used for writing	• Individual differences appear in the development of fine motor skills. • Infants can imitate only what they see, so those who never see anyone writing are unlikely to mimic writing or understand that some objects are used for writing.	• Allow toddlers to manipulate small objects that do not present choking hazards. • Have a variety of tools available for scribbling and coloring (e.g., fat crayons or washable, nontoxic markers). • Tape writing paper to the table or floor to permit easier writing.
Early Childhood (2–6)	• Increasing muscular control in writing and drawing • Pseudowriting (e.g., wavy lines, connected loops) in preschool play activities • Ability to write own name (perhaps at age 4) • Ability to write most letters of the alphabet (at age 4 or later) • Invented spellings (at ages 5–6)	• Some cultures place greater emphasis on writing than others. • Some children have little if any exposure to written materials at home and so have less knowledge of letters. • Children with visual impairments have less awareness of print conventions (left-to-right progression, use of punctuation, etc.).	• Make writing implements (pencils, markers, paper) easily accessible. • Give children opportunities to write their names and a few other meaningful words. • Have children act out stories they have orally composed.
Middle Childhood (6–10)	• Gradual increase in smoothness of handwriting; gradual decrease in handwriting size • Increasing use of letter-sound relationships and common letter patterns when spelling words • Predominance of narratives in writing • Difficulty identifying problems (especially problems of clarity) in own writing	• Better readers tend to be better writers, presumably because general language ability provides a foundation for both reading and writing. • Children with deficits in phonological awareness have a more difficult time learning to spell. • Girls show higher achievement in writing and spelling beginning in the elementary years. • Children with dyslexia often have poor handwriting skills.	• Engage children in authentic writing activities (e.g., writing letters to relatives, creating a newsletter). • Provide regular practice in spelling, grammar, and punctuation (often within authentic activities). • Explore various ways in which particular phonemes and phoneme combinations are spelled in the English language. • Introduce expository forms of writing (e.g., descriptions, lab reports). • Build opportunities for editing into the schedule; offer suggestions about how children can improve their writing.
Early Adolescence (10–14)	• Automatized spelling of most common words • Increasing use of expository forms of writing • Use of longer and more complex syntactic structures • Reluctance to edit and revise unless strongly encouraged to do so	• Some older children and adolescents (e.g., those with learning disabilities) may have exceptional difficulty with spelling and sentence structure. • Some adolescents write often in their spare time (e.g., keeping diaries, writing notes to friends), whereas others write only when required to do so at school.	• Provide continuing instruction in spelling, punctuation, and grammar. • Introduce persuasive and argumentative forms of writing. • Suggest a specific audience for whom to write. • Give feedback on first drafts, including guidance on how to improve clarity and cohesiveness. • Encourage adolescents to use local dialects in creative writing projects.
Late Adolescence (14–18)	• Ability to write about a particular topic in depth • More organized and cohesive essays • Increasing tendency to knowledge-transform rather than knowledge-tell • More revisions than at younger ages, but with a focus on superficial rather than substantive problems	• Individuals with learning disabilities may focus largely on mechanics (spelling, use of correct grammar, etc.) while writing, perhaps because such skills are not yet automatized. • Individuals from some cultural backgrounds (e.g., those from some East Asian countries) may be reluctant to put their thoughts on paper unless they are certain that they are correct.	• Assign and scaffold lengthy writing projects. • Teach specific strategies for organizing and synthesizing ideas. • Show examples of effective writing (e.g., writing that illustrates knowledge transforming). • For teens who have language-based learning disabilities, downplay the importance of correct spelling and grammar when evaluating written work; teach strategies for overcoming or compensating for weaknesses.

Sources: Beal, 1996; Berninger et al., 1996; Byrnes, 1996; Cameron et al., 1996; Dickinson et al., 1993; Dien, 1998; Gentry, 1982; Graham & Weintraub, 1996; M. Harris & Hatano, 1999; Hedges & Nowell, 1995; Hemphill & Snow, 1996; R. Kellogg, 1967; MacArthur & Graham, 1987; McLane & McNamee, 1990; Rittle-Johnson & Siegler, 1999; Robin, Berthier, & Clifton, 1996; Rochat & Bullinger, 1994; Rochat & Goubet, 1995; Shanahan & Tierney, 1990; Smitherman, 1994; Spivey, 1997; Trawick-Smith, 2003; R. Turnbull et al., 2004; Yaden & Templeton, 1986.

Diversity in Writing Development

As is true for reading development, writing development tends to be correlated with general intelligence. Some children who are gifted exhibit extraordinary writing talent. In contrast, most children with mental retardation show general delays in writing skills. Some children with learning disabilities have problems in handwriting, spelling, or expressing themselves coherently on paper (R. Turnbull et al., 2004).

Children with writing disabilities typically focus their writing efforts more on addressing mechanical issues (spelling, grammar, etc.) than on communicating clearly (Graham, Schwartz, & MacArthur, 1993). The quality of their writing improves considerably when the mechanical aspects of writing are minimized (e.g., when they can dictate their stories and other compositions) and when they are given a specific series of steps to follow as they write (Hallenbeck, 1996; MacArthur & Graham, 1987; Sawyer, Graham, & Harris, 1992).

Group differences in writing.   Group differences in writing are most often found for gender: Girls tend to write and spell somewhat better than boys (Feingold, 1993; Weaver-Hightower, 2003). Girls are also more confident than boys about their writing abilities, even when no differences in the actual writing performance of the two groups exist (Pajares & Valiante, 1999).

Researchers have observed a few cultural differences that are apt to influence children's writing development. Some cultural groups rely more on other forms of visual representation than on traditional paper-and-pencil writing. For instance, the Yup'ik peoples of northern Canada frequently engage in *storyknifing,* in which they carve symbols and pictures in the mud while simultaneously telling tales about the family's or community's history (deMarrais, Nelson, & Baker, 1994). And those cultures that do rely heavily on writing may vary considerably in their writing practices. For instance, Vietnamese children are often reluctant to commit their ideas to paper unless they're confident that their ideas are correct and will not be misinterpreted (Dien, 1998).

Figure 10-4

Once infants are old enough to sit up on their own, they can begin to explore the properties of paper and paint, as 5-month-old Lauryn did in this early finger painting. Such activities should be closely supervised, of course, and only nontoxic substances used.

Promoting Writing Development

Psychologists and experienced educators have offered several suggestions for promoting children's and adolescents' writing development:

● *Provide tools for drawing and writing as soon as children are old enough to use them.* Quite early in life, children can begin to explore—and so discover what they can do with—drawing, writing, and painting tools (e.g., see Figure 10-4). As fine motor skills, cognitive abilities, and knowledge of written symbols continue to improve during the preschool years, children become increasingly able to produce recognizable shapes and letters. The "Environments: Early Childhood" video clip on Observation CD 1 shows an area of a preschool classroom equipped with numerous drawing and writing implements.

Observe a preschool drawing and writing center in the "Environments: Early Childhood" clip on Observation CD 1.

● *Present authentic writing tasks, and offer choices about writing topics.* Youngsters write more frequently, and in a more organized and communicative (e.g., knowledge-transforming) manner, when they can write for a "real" audience (not just for their teacher) and when they're interested in their topic (Benton, 1997; Garner, 1998; Sugar & Bonk, 1998). For example, when one high school English teacher noticed that several very capable students weren't completing assigned writing tasks, he began asking students to write about their personal experiences and share their work with others on the Internet. The students suddenly began writing regularly, presumably because they could write for a real audience and could now choose what they wrote about (Garner, 1998). In the "Literacy" video clips for middle childhood, early adolescence, and late adolescence on Observation CD 2, Daniel, Brendan, and Alicia all mention that they like to choose their writing topics. Daniel responds this way to the interviewer's question "Do you like to write?":

Observe students' preference for self-chosen writing topics in the "Literacy" clips for middle childhood, early adolescence, and late adolescence, on Observation CD 2.

> Sort of. . . . It depends on the kind of story and writing. I mean, I don't want it to be, like, an assignment that the teacher tells me to do, like a certain type of story she wants me to write. I want it to be from my ideas.

● *Scaffold children's writing efforts.* Such scaffolding can take a variety of forms, including the following:

- Ask young children (e.g., first graders) to dictate rather than write their stories.
- Help children brainstorm ideas for communicating effectively (e.g., by using examples, analogies, and similes; see Figure 10-5).
- Provide an explicit structure for children to follow as they write (e.g., for a persuasive essay, ask students to include a main argument, supporting arguments, and rebuttals to possible counterarguments).
- Suggest that children initially focus on communicating clearly and postpone attention to writing mechanics (e.g., spelling, punctuation) until later drafts.
- Provide specific questions that children should ask themselves as they critique their writing (e.g., "Are the ideas logically organized?").
- Ask children to collaborate on writing projects, or to read and respond to one another's work.
- Encourage use of word processing programs. (Benton, 1997; Chambliss, 1998; De La Paz, Swanson, & Graham, 1998; K. R. Harris & Graham, 1992; R. T. Kellogg, 1994; McLane & McNamee, 1990; Page-Voth & Graham, 1999; Sitko, 1998; Sperling, 1996; Treiman, 1993)

————————— **Study Guide and Reader**
Supplementary Reading 10-6 provides an example of how a teacher might scaffold youngsters' efforts in revising their writing.

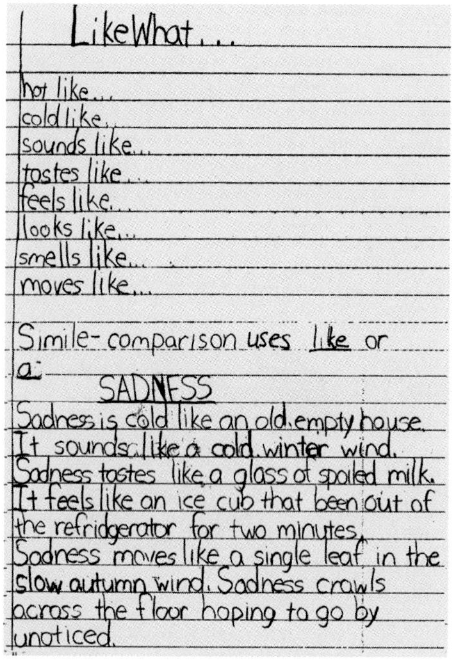

● *Include writing assignments in all areas of the curriculum.* Writing should not be a skill that only elementary teachers and secondary English teachers teach. In fact, writing takes different forms in different disciplines. Writing fiction is very different from writing a science laboratory report, which in turn is very different from writing an analysis of historical documents. Ideally, all teachers should teach writing to some degree, and especially at the secondary level, they should teach the writing skills specific to their own academic disciplines (Burnett & Kastman, 1997; Sperling, 1996).

Mathematics

Mathematics is actually a cluster of domains—arithmetic, algebra, geometry, statistics, and so on—that use somewhat different methods for representing and solving quantitative problems (De Corte et al., 1996). Much of our focus here will be on the development of knowledge and skills that are central to all of these domains, including counting, basic concepts and procedures, and metacognition.

Number Sense and Counting

By 5 or 6 months of age, infants have some awareness of quantity. Although they certainly aren't counting at this age, they do seem to notice the difference between a set of two objects and a set of three objects, as well as the difference between a set of 16 dots and a set of 32 dots (Canfield & Smith, 1996; Wynn, 1995; Xu & Spelke, 2000). As they approach their first birthday, they also show some understanding of *more* versus *less*. For example, 11-month-olds notice the difference between sequences of pictures that reflect increases versus decreases in quantity (Brannon, 2002).

Except for small groupings (e.g., sets of two or three objects), infants' awareness of quantity is fairly imprecise. The ability to count may be necessary to distinguish between similar quantities—say, between sets of seven versus eight objects (Geary, 2006; Siegler & Robinson, 1982). Many children begin counting before their third birthday, and most 3- and 4-year-olds can correctly count to 10 (Geary, 2006). Five-year-olds can often count far beyond 10 (perhaps to 50), although they may get confused about the order of such numbers as 70, 80, and 90 (Fuson & Hall, 1983). As children work with two- and three-digit written numbers in the elementary grades, they increasingly master the correct sequence of numbers well into the hundreds and beyond (Case & Okamoto, 1996).

When children first begin to count, they don't necessarily do so in a way that accurately determines amount (Geary, 2006; Wynn, 1990). For example, they may say two successive

| LikeWhat... |
| hot like... |
| cold like... |
| sounds like... |
| tastes like... |
| feels like... |
| looks like... |
| smells like... |
| moves like... |

Simile- comparison uses **like** or **a**:

SADNESS

Sadness is cold like an old empty house. It sounds like a cold winter wind. Sadness tastes like a glass of spoiled milk. It feels like an ice cub that been out of the refridgerator for two minutes. Sadness moves like a single leaf in the slow autumn wind. Sadness crawls across the floor hoping to go by unoticed.

Figure 10-5

After her class brainstorms the kinds of similes a writer might use, 11-year-old Charlotte practices using similes in a description of sadness.

numbers (e.g., "...three, four...") while pointing to a single object and so count it twice. Or, instead, they may point to two successive objects while saying only one number. But by the time they are 4 or 5, most children have mastered several basic principles of counting, including the following:

- *One-one principle.* Each object in the set being counted must be assigned one and only one number word. In other words, you say "one" while pointing to one object, "two" while pointing to the second, and so on until every object has been counted exactly once.
- *Cardinal principle.* The last number word counted indicates the number of objects in the set. In other words, if you count up to five when counting objects, then there are five objects in the set.
- *Order-irrelevance principle.* A set of objects has the same number regardless of the order in which individual objects are counted. (Gallistel & Gelman, 1992; R. Gelman & Gallistel, 1978; Griffin, Case, & Capodilupo, 1995)

Initially, children apply these principles primarily to small number sets (e.g., of 10 objects or fewer), but within a few years they can apply the principles to larger sets as well. As they do so, their ability to recognize that quantity stays the same regardless of changes in arrangement (*conservation of number*) also improves (Geary, 2006).

Mathematical Concepts and Principles

In addition to a basic understanding of numbers, mathematical reasoning requires an understanding of many concepts and principles. An especially critical one in the early elementary grades is the **part-whole principle,** the idea that any single number can be broken into two or more smaller numbers (e.g., 7 can be broken into 1, 2, and 4) and that any two or more numbers can be combined to form a larger number. This principle is probably central to children's understanding of addition and subtraction (Sophian & Vong, 1995).

Children also begin to encounter simple fractions (e.g., one-half, one-fourth) in the early elementary grades. By the upper elementary and middle school grades, a typical mathematics curriculum requires children to work regularly with a variety of proportions, including improper fractions (e.g., ¾), mixed numbers (e.g., 5⅓), decimals, and percentages. As you should recall from Chapter 6, Piaget suggested that children become capable of proportional reasoning when they enter the formal operations stage, sometime around age 11 or 12. Yet, in fact, many young adolescents struggle with fractions and other proportions (Byrnes, 1996; Geary, 2006). Part of the problem seems to be that they misapply their knowledge of whole numbers. For example, because 4 is greater than 3, they are apt to conclude that ¼ is greater than ⅓. And because 256 is greater than 7, they are apt to think that 0.256 must be greater than 0.7.

Middle school and high school math classes increasingly focus on abstract concepts, such as *pi* (π), *irrational number,* and *variable.* Mathematical principles, such as *the product of two negative numbers is a positive number* and *the angles of a triangle always have a total of 180°,* also become increasingly abstract. Because such concepts and principles tend to be far removed from the concrete realities with which children and adolescents are familiar, formal instruction about them is usually necessary (Byrnes, 1996; De Corte et al., 1996; Geary, 1994).

Basic Arithmetic Operations

Two of the most basic mathematical procedures are, of course, addition and subtraction. Infants seem to have a preliminary understanding of these processes well before their first birthday (McCrink & Wynn, 2004; Wynn, 1992). For example, imagine that two Mickey Mouse dolls are placed on a table in front of you. An experimenter lowers a screen to block your view of the dolls, and then you watch the experimenter take one of the dolls from behind the screen and put it away. You assume that only one doll remains on the table, but as the screen is raised, you still see *two* dolls there. Even 5-month-olds seem to be surprised by this outcome, indicating an awareness that something isn't as it should be.

Connecting Concepts

Chapter 6 describes several forms of conservation, including conservation of number.

part-whole principle
Idea that any single number can be broken into two or more smaller numbers, and that any two or more numbers can be combined to form a larger number; central to children's understanding of addition and subtraction.

Long before receiving formal instruction in addition and multiplication at school, young children often develop addition and multiplication strategies on their own by building on their finger-counting skills.

—————————— Connecting Concepts
The changing frequency of various addition and multiplication strategies over time reflects the *overlapping waves* idea presented in Chapter 7.

By age 2½ or 3, children clearly understand that adding objects to a set increases quantity and subtracting objects from a set decreases quantity (Huttenlocher, Jordan, & Levine, 1994). At age 4 or 5, they begin to apply their knowledge of counting to simple addition and subtraction problems, typically using procedures they develop on their own (Bermejo, 1996; Geary, 1994; Siegler & Jenkins, 1989). One early strategy is to use fingers to represent the objects in question. Consider the problem *If I have 2 apples and you give me 3 more apples, how many apples do I have altogether?* A child might put up two fingers and then three more fingers and count all the fingers to reach the solution, "5 apples." Somewhat later, children may begin to use a *min* strategy, in which they start with the larger number (for the apple problem, they would start with 3) and then add on, one by one, the smaller number (e.g., counting "three apples . . . then four, five . . . five apples altogether") (Siegler & Jenkins, 1989). They might do something similar for subtraction, starting with the original number of objects and then counting down the number of objects removed: "Five . . . then four, three . . . three apples left"). Still later, of course, children learn and retrieve many basic addition and subtraction facts (e.g., 2 + 3 = 5, 5 − 3 = 2) that allow them to bypass the more cumbersome counting strategies.

By the early elementary years, children use a variety of strategies for solving simple addition and subtraction problems, including physically counting objects, counting on fingers, and retrieving addition and subtraction facts from memory. As they get older, they increasingly rely on memory and depend less on fingers and other objects (Ashcraft, 1982; Siegler & Jenkins, 1989).

In North America, formal instruction in multiplication usually begins in second or third grade. Once again, children typically learn and use a mixture of strategies (Cooney & Ladd, 1992; Geary, 2006). When working with small numbers, they may simply use addition (e.g., solving "3 × 3" by adding 3 + 3 and then adding another 3 to the sum). Sometimes they count by twos, fives, or some other number (e.g., solving "5 × 4 = ?" by counting "five, ten, fifteen, twenty"). Sometimes they apply certain rules, such as *anything times zero is zero* or *anything times 1 is itself*. Gradually, retrieval of basic multiplication facts replaces such strategies (Cooney, Swanson, & Ladd, 1988).

Children often encounter simple division problems in the preschool years—for instance, when food or toys must be shared among two or more siblings or peers—and even some 3-year-olds may use counting to divide quantities somewhat equitably (K. Miller, 1989). With formal instruction, children become more efficient and precise. As they tackle division problems, children often rely on their knowledge of other arithmetic facts, especially multiplication facts (e.g., if 5 × 4 = 20, then 20 ÷ 5 = 4) (Geary, 1994).

When children encounter arithmetic problems involving two-digit or larger numbers, and especially when the problems involve "carrying" or "borrowing" across columns, they must also master the concept of *place value*. This idea that digits reflect different quantities depending on the column (whether they are in the ones column, tens column, and so on) is a fairly abstract one that many children have trouble with in the elementary grades (Fuson & Kwon, 1992; Geary, 2006). And if children don't understand place value, they are more apt to make errors when they tackle problems that require carrying or borrowing (Geary, 1994). As examples, consider the addition and subtraction problem solutions presented in the following exercise, "Arithmetic Errors."

INTERPRETING CHILDREN'S ARTIFACTS AND ACTIONS   Arithmetic Errors

For each of these problems, a child has correctly retrieved basic math facts but arrived at an incorrect solution. Identify the inappropriate strategy the child has used in each case.

$$\begin{array}{r} 26 \\ +47 \\ \hline 613 \end{array} \qquad \begin{array}{r} 603 \\ -305 \\ \hline 208 \end{array}$$

The child who solved the addition problem on the left simply put the sums of 6 + 7 (13) and 2 + 4 (6) side by side at the bottom. The child who solved the subtraction problem on the right apparently knew that borrowing was necessary to perform the subtraction in the ones column. Finding only a zero in the tens column, she instead borrowed "10" from the hundreds column. Thus she subtracted 13 − 5 in the ones column and 5 − 3 in the hundreds column. Such mistakes are less common when children not only know *how* to carry and borrow but also know *why* carrying and borrowing make sense.

A possible central conceptual structure for number.   Neo-Piagetian theorist Robbie Case and his colleagues (Case & Mueller, 2001; Case & Okamoto, 1996; Case et al., 1993; Griffin, Case, & Siegler, 1994) have suggested that during the preschool and elementary school years, children gradually develop a *central conceptual structure* that integrates

Connecting Concepts
Recall the discussion of *central conceptual structures* in neo-Piagetian theory in Chapter 6.

much of what they know about numbers, counting, addition, subtraction, and place value. In Case's view, 4-year-olds understand the difference between "a little" and "a lot" and recognize that adding objects leads to more of them and subtracting objects leads to fewer of them. Such knowledge might take the form depicted in the top half of Figure 10-6. Furthermore, many 4-year-olds can accurately count a small set of objects and conclude that the last number they count equals the total number of objects in the set (the cardinal principle). This process is depicted in the bottom half of Figure 10-6. Thus 4-year-olds can visually compare a group of 5 objects with a group of 6 objects and tell you that the latter group contains more objects, and they may also count accurately to either 5 or 6. Yet they cannot answer a question such as "Which is more, 5 or 6?" because the question involves knowledge of *both* more-versus-less and counting. It appears that they have not yet integrated their two understandings of number into a single conceptual framework.

By the time children are 6, they can easily answer simple "Which is more?" questions. Case proposed that at the age of 6, the two structures in Figure 10-6 have become integrated into the more comprehensive structure depicted in Figure 10-7. As illustrated in the figure, children's knowledge and reasoning about numbers now include several key elements:

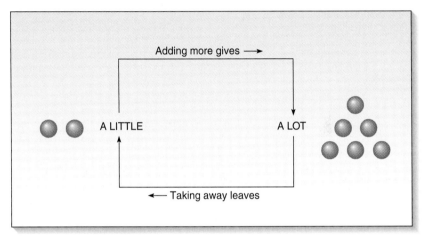

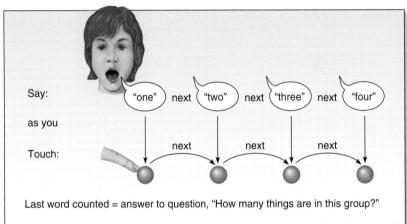

Figure 10-6

Hypothetical numerical structures at age 4
From "The Role of Central Conceptual Structures in the Development of Children's Thought" by R. Case, Y. Okamoto, in collaboration with S. Griffin, A. McKeough, C. Bleiker, B. Henderson, & K. M. Stephenson, 1996, *Monographs of the Society for Research in Child Development, 61*(1, Serial No. 246), p. 6. Copyright 1996 by the Society for Research in Child Development. Adapted with permission from the Society for Research in Child Development.

- Children understand and can say the verbal numbers "one," "two," "three," etc.
- They recognize the written numerals 1, 2, 3, and so on.
- They have a systematic process for counting objects: They say each successive number as they touch each successive object in a group. Eventually, children count by mentally "tagging" (rather than physically touching) each object.
- They also use their fingers for representing small quantities (e.g., 3 fingers equals 3 objects). Their use of fingers for both counting objects and representing quantities may be a key means through which they integrate the two processes into a single conceptual structure.
- They equate movement toward higher numbers with such concepts as "a lot," "more," and "bigger." Similarly, they equate movement toward lower numbers with such concepts as "a little," "less," and "smaller."

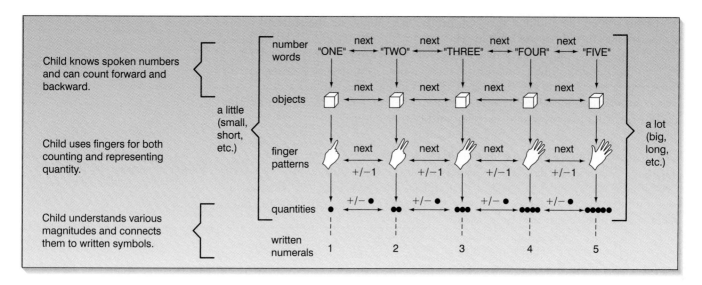

Figure 10-7

Hypothetical central conceptual structure at age 6
From "Differentiation, Integration, and Covariance Mapping as Fundamental Processes in Cognitive and Neurological Growth" by R. Case & M. P. Mueller, 2001, *Mechanisms of Cognitive Development: Behavioral and Neural Perspectives* (J. L. McClelland & R. S. Siegler, Eds.), p. 201. Mahwah, NJ: Erlbaum. Adapted with permission from Lawrence Erlbaum Associates.

- They understand that movement from one number to the next is equivalent to either adding one unit to the set or subtracting one unit from it, depending on the direction of movement.
- They realize that any change in one dimension (e.g., from 3 to 4) must be accompanied by an equivalent change along other dimensions (e.g., from "three" to "four" and from ••• to ••••).

In essence, the more comprehensive conceptual structure at age 6 forms a mental "number line" that children can use to facilitate their understanding and execution of such processes as addition, subtraction, and comparisons of quantities.

At age 8, Case proposed, children have sufficiently mastered this central conceptual structure that they can begin using two number lines simultaneously to solve mathematical problems. For instance, they can now answer such questions as "Which number is bigger, 32 or 28?" and "Which number is closer to 25, 21 or 18?" Such questions require them to compare digits in both the ones column and tens column, with each comparison taking place along a separate number line. In addition, 8-year-olds presumably have a better understanding of operations that require transformations across columns, such as "carrying 1" to the tens column during addition or "borrowing 1" from the tens column during subtraction.

Finally, at about age 10, children become capable of generalizing the relationships of two number lines to the entire number system. They now understand how the various columns (ones, tens, hundreds, etc.) relate to one another and can expertly move back and forth among the columns. They can also treat the answers to mathematical problems as mental entities in and of themselves and so can answer such questions as "Which number is bigger, the difference between 6 and 9 or the difference between 8 and 3?"

Case tracked the development of children's central conceptual structure for number only until age 10. He acknowledged, however, that children's understanding of numbers continues to develop well into adolescence. For instance, he pointed out that teenagers often have trouble with questions such as "What is a half of a third?" and suggested that their difficulty results from an incomplete conceptual understanding of division and the results (e.g., fractions) that it yields.

More Advanced Problem-Solving Procedures

By the time children reach middle school, most are relatively proficient in solving simple arithmetic problems with whole numbers (Byrnes, 1996). As they move through the middle school and high school grades, much of the math curriculum involves procedures for working with proportions (e.g., fractions, decimals), negative numbers, roots and exponents (e.g., $\sqrt{18}$, 4^3), and unknown variables (e.g., x, y). Children will be able to tackle more complex problems if, to some degree, they automatize these procedures so that they can use them quickly and efficiently (Geary, 1994).

Ideally, children must also *make sense of* these procedures, rather than simply learning to apply them in a rote, meaningless fashion. In other words, children's understanding of mathematical procedures should be closely tied to their understanding of mathematical concepts and principles, in much the same way that their understanding of addition and subtraction is closely connected to their understanding of numbers and counting (Geary, 1994; Hecht, Close, & Santisi, 2003; Rittle-Johnson, Siegler, & Alibali, 2001). In the "Intrinsic Motivation: Early Adolescence" video clip on Observation CD 3, 12-year-old Claudia justifies her love of math quite simply: "You can explain it all." When children can*not* make sense of mathematical procedures—perhaps because they haven't yet mastered the abstract concepts on which the procedures are based or perhaps because no one has shown them why certain manipulations are mathematically logical—they are apt to use the procedures incorrectly and have trouble applying them to real-world problems (Byrnes, 1996; Geary, 2006).

Listen to 12-year-old Claudia's views about math in the "Intrinsic Motivation: Early Adolescence" clip on Observation CD 3.

Metacognition in Mathematics

Not only should children understand what they're doing when they tackle mathematical problems, they should also plan, monitor, and evaluate their problem-solving efforts. Such metacognitive oversight might involve setting goals for a problem-solving task, checking to be sure all the needed information is at hand, and carefully scrutinizing a final solution to determine whether it's a logical one (Cardelle-Elawar, 1992; Carr & Biddlecomb, 1998; L. S. Fuchs et al., 2003). Only a child who metacognitively reflects on his or her problem-solving efforts will recognize that a sum of 613 is *not* a reasonable answer to the problem $26 + 47$.

Many elementary and secondary school students do not actively reflect on what they're doing as they solve mathematical problems (Carr & Biddlecomb, 1998). Furthermore, even in the high school grades students are apt to have fairly naive epistemological beliefs about the nature of mathematics and mathematical problem solving. The following misconceptions about math are typical:

- Mathematics is a collection of meaningless procedures that must simply be memorized and recalled as needed.
- Math problems always have one and only one right answer.
- There is only one right way to solve any particular math problem.
- One will either solve a problem within a few minutes or else not solve it at all. (De Corte, Op't Eynde, & Verschaffel, 2002; Schoenfeld, 1988, 1992)

Connecting Concepts ——————
See Chapter 7 for a general discussion of epistemological beliefs.

Such beliefs are often counterproductive when youngsters encounter unusual and complex problems for which they have no ready-made, prescribed procedures.

The Developmental Trends table "Mathematics at Different Age Levels" characterizes some of the mathematical knowledge and abilities commonly seen in infants, children, and adolescents.

Diversity in Mathematics Development

Virtually all children around the globe have a general awareness that objects and substances can vary in quantity and amount (Geary, 2006). But youngsters differ considerably in the extent to which they master mathematical concepts and procedures. Some children have learning disabilities that impede their ability to automatize math facts and solve simple math problems quickly (N. C. Jordan, Hanich, & Kaplan, 2003). Others have little exposure to numbers and counting at home and so come to school lacking knowledge in these fundamental areas (Griffin et al., 1995). In addition, researchers often find gender and cultural differences in mathematics development.

DEVELOPMENTAL TRENDS

Mathematics at Different Age Levels

Age	What You Might Observe	Diversity	Implications
Infancy (Birth–2) 	• Some awareness that adding or subtracting something affects quantity (appearing at around 5 months) • Discrimination between sequences that show increases versus decreases in amount	• Some toddlers have familiarity with small-number words (e.g., *two, three*), usually because their parents often use the words in parent-child interactions. • Children with visual impairments may have fewer opportunities to make more-versus-less comparisons.	• Use small-number words (e.g., *two, three*) when talking with infants and toddlers if doing so makes sense within the context of everyday activities. • Provide age-appropriate toys that encourage children to focus on size or quantity (e.g., nesting cups, stacking blocks).
Early Childhood (2–6) 	• Clear understanding that adding objects results in an increase and removing objects results in a decrease (by age 2½ or 3) • Appearance of counting (at around age 3) • Increasing ability to count correctly (perhaps to 50 by age 5) • Emergence of self-constructed addition and subtraction strategies (e.g., counting objects or using fingers) • Some familiarity with division in everyday sharing tasks	• Chinese children learn to count at a younger age than children whose native language is English. The more "transparent" nature of Chinese number words is thought to be at least partly responsible for this difference. • At age 5, Chinese- and Japanese-speaking children have a better grasp of place value than English-speaking children (apparently because Chinese and Japanese number words make place value more obvious). • On average, children from middle-income families begin counting at an earlier age than children from low-income families.	• In storybook reading sessions, occasionally read books that engage children in counting activities (e.g., *The Icky Bug Counting Book,* Pallotta & Masiello, 1992). • Use concrete manipulatives to help children learn counting and simple addition and subtraction.
Middle Childhood (6–10) 	• Increasing ability to count correctly into the hundreds and beyond • Acquisition of more efficient addition and subtraction strategies, including retrieval of number facts • Increasing mastery of multiplication and division strategies • Growing understanding of place value and its relevance to carrying and borrowing • Some understanding of simple fractions • Increasing ability to solve word problems	• Children vary considerably in the strategies they use at any given age level. For instance, some 8-year-olds have most basic math facts automatized, whereas others continue to rely heavily on fingers. • Children who speak certain Asian languages (e.g., Mandarin Chinese) master multidigit addition and subtraction at an earlier age than English-speaking children. • Some children begin to dislike math, typically because they have consistently been frustrated in their efforts to understand and master it.	• Help children understand the logic underlying basic mathematical procedures (e.g., show the relevance of *place value* to carrying and borrowing). • Provide frequent practice in basic arithmetic as a way of promoting automaticity. • Introduce number lines as a way of helping children understand how numbers relate to one another. • Have low-achieving fourth and fifth graders tutor first and second graders in basic math skills.
Early Adolescence (10–14) 	• Increasing ability to understand abstract concepts (e.g., π, x) • Emerging ability to understand and work with proportions • Naive epistemological beliefs about math (e.g., that it involves memorizing procedures without necessarily understanding them)	• Young adolescents who have not yet automatized basic arithmetic facts are apt to struggle when they encounter challenging math concepts and procedures. • Some adolescents tend to misapply their knowledge about whole numbers to problems involving fractions and decimals. • Young adolescents vary widely in their ability to understand and apply the abstract mathematical concepts that are typically introduced in the middle school grades.	• Conduct small-group activities in which students must devise and explain multiple approaches to solving a single problem. • Teach metacognitive strategies for solving problems (e.g., identify the goal to be achieved, break a complex problem into smaller steps).

(continued)

DEVELOPMENTAL TRENDS	Mathematics at Different Age Levels (continued)		
Age	**What You Might Observe**	**Diversity**	**Implications**
Late Adolescence (14–18)	• Increasing facility in working with abstract concepts and principles (e.g., *unknowns* such as *x* and *y*) • Difficulty translating word problems into algebraic expressions • Tendency for many teens to memorize and mindlessly apply mathematical procedures, rather than to reflect on and understand the procedures	• Individual differences in mathematical abilities increase in the high school years, due both to "tracking" based on students' existing abilities and to the prevalence of elective math courses in high school. • Boys show a slight advantage in overall math achievement and are more likely than girls to enroll in advanced math classes. • Girls have less confidence about their ability to do math even when they achieve at the same level as boys.	• Ask teenagers to apply their math skills to real-life contexts and problems. • Allow teens to use calculators when performing complex mathematical operations (this strategy allows them to devote most of their working memory capacity to the overall problem-solving effort). • Minimize competition for grades and other rewards for math achievement (this strategy is especially important for girls).

Sources: Brannon, 2002; Byrne & Shavelson, 1986; Byrnes, 1996; Cardelle-Elawar, 1992; Carr & Biddlecomb, 1998; Case & Okamoto, 1996; Cooney & Ladd, 1992; Cooney et al., 1988; Davenport et al., 1998; De Corte et al., 1996; De Corte et al., 2002; Eccles, 1989; Empson, 1999; Fuson & Hall, 1983; Fuson & Kwon, 1992; Gallistel & Gelman, 1992; Geary, 1994, 2006; Greeno, Collins, & Resnick, 1996; Griffin et al., 1995; Hegarty & Kozhevnikov, 1999; C. S. Ho & Fuson, 1998; J. Huttenlocher et al., 1994; Inglis & Biemiller, 1997; McCrink & Wynn, 2004; K. Miller, 1989; K. F. Miller, Smith, Zhu, & Zhang, 1995; Schoenfeld, 1988, 1992; Siegler & Jenkins, 1989; Wynn, 1990, 1992, 1995; Xu & Spelke, 2000.

Gender differences.   Average differences between boys and girls in mathematics development tend to be fairly small, with some researchers finding a slight advantage for one gender or the other depending on the age-group and task in question. However, boys show greater *variability* in math. More boys than girls have very high math ability, especially in high school, and more boys than girls have significant disabilities in math (Halpern & LaMay, 2000; Hedges & Nowell, 1995; Penner, 2003).

The prevalence of adolescent males at the upper end of the math-ability continuum may be partly due to biology, and in particular to sex-related hormones (e.g., estrogen, testosterone) that differentially affect brain development before and after puberty (Halpern, 1992; Hegarty & Kozhevnikov, 1999; Lippa, 2002). One area in which these hormones may come into play is in the development of **visual-spatial ability,** the ability to imagine and mentally manipulate two- and three-dimensional figures (see Figure 10-8). On average, boys and men perform better than girls and women on measures of visual-spatial ability, which may give them an advantage in certain kinds of mathematical tasks (Halpern, 2004; Halpern & LaMay, 2000).

Yet environmental factors also play a role in gender differences in mathematics. In many Western societies, mathematics has historically been viewed as a "male" domain more suitable for boys than for girls. Some parents pick up on this stereotype and more actively expect and encourage their sons (rather than daughters) to learn math (Bleeker & Jacobs, 2004; Eccles et al., 1993: Tiedemann, 2000). Perhaps partly as a result of such differential expectations and encouragement, boys tend to have greater confidence about their math ability than girls do, even when actual achievement levels for both genders have been similar (Herbert, Stipek, & Miles, 2003; Middleton, 1999; Vermeer, Boekaerts, & Seegers, 2000). In the high school grades, boys are also more likely to value math as a discipline and to enroll in advanced math classes (Davenport et al., 1998; Eccles et al., 1998).

Cultural differences.   One consistent finding is that Asian and Asian American students achieve at higher levels in math than students from other North American ethnic groups. Adult behaviors may partly account for this difference. Asian teachers provide more thorough explanations of mathematical concepts and assign more math homework than North American teachers do (Huntsinger, Jose, Larson, Krieg, & Shaligram, 2000; Perry, 2000). And Asian parents are more likely to believe that math achievement comes from hard work (rather than

visual-spatial ability
Ability to imagine and mentally manipulate two- and three-dimensional figures.

1. The figure on the left is a flag. Which one or more of the three figures on the right represent(s) the *same* side of the flag? Which one or more of them represent(s) the *flip* side?

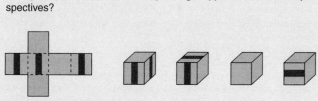

Model   a   b   c

2. When the figure on the left is folded along the dotted lines, it becomes a three-dimensional object. Which one or more of the four figures on the right represent(s) how this object might appear from different perspectives?

Model   a   b   c   d

3. When the object on the left is rotated in three-dimensional space, it can look like one or more of the objects on the right. Which one(s)?

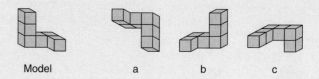

Model   a   b   c

Answer Key:

(1) Flags *a* and *b* are the flip side; flag *c* is the same side.
(2) Depending on the direction from which it is viewed, the object might look like either *a* or *d*.
(3) The object can be rotated to look like either *a* or *c*.

Figure 10-8

Three examples of tasks requiring visual-spatial ability

Three tasks modeled, respectively, after Thurstone & Jeffrey, 1956; G. K. Bennett, Seashore, & Wesman, 1982; and Shepard & Metzler, 1971.

being a "natural" talent) and so insist that children spend a good deal of their time at home on schoolwork (C. S. Ho & Fuson, 1998; Okagaki, 2001).

Many theorists speculate that the nature of number words in Asian languages (Chinese, Japanese, Korean) may also facilitate Asian children's mathematical development (Fuson & Kwon, 1992; K. F. Miller et al., 1995; Miura, Okamoto, Vlahovic-Stetic, Kim, & Han, 1999). In these languages the structure of the base-10 number system is clearly reflected in number words. For example, the word for 11 is literally "ten-one," the word for 12 is "ten-two," and the word for 21 is "two-ten-one." Furthermore, words for fractions reflect what a fraction *is*. For example, the word for ¼ is literally "of four parts, one." In contrast, English has many number words (e.g., *eleven, twelve, thirteen, twenty, thirty, one-half, one-fourth*) that "hide" the base-10 structure somewhat and don't give much information about the nature of proportions.

One thing that Asian languages and European languages have in common is a system for identifying virtually any possible number. But numbers and mathematics are cultural creations that are not universally shared across cultures. For example, the Oksapmin people in Papua New Guinea identify the numbers 1 through 29 using different body parts, progressing from the right hand and arm (1 is the right thumb) to the neck and head (14 is the nose) and then down the left arm (29 is the inside of the left forearm) (Saxe, 1981). Although such a system appears to be sufficient in Oksapmin culture, it does not lend itself well to multiplication, division, or more complex mathematical procedures. The Pirahã society in a remote region of Brazil has three words for number that, roughly translated, mean *one or a very small amount, two or a slightly larger amount,* and *many.* People in Pirahã culture have difficulty distinguishing among similar quantities greater than three or four, apparently because counting has little value in their day-to-day activities (Gordon, 2004).

Promoting Development in Mathematics

Mathematics probably causes more confusion and frustration for children and adolescents than any other academic subject. The hierarchical nature of the discipline may be partly to blame. To the extent that youngsters don't completely master math concepts and procedures at one grade level, they lack necessary prerequisites for learning math successfully in later grades. Yet developmental factors also figure prominently. When children have difficulty with abstract ideas, proportional thinking, and other developmental acquisitions on which mathematics depends, they are apt to struggle with mathematical reasoning and problem solving.

Without doubt, the most important factor affecting mathematics development in childhood and adolescence is formal education (e.g., Case & Okamoto, 1996; H. P. Ginsburg, Posner, & Russell, 1981). We offer the following suggestions for teachers who work with young people on mathematical concepts and tasks:

● *Teach numbers and counting in preschool and the primary grades.* A basic understanding of numbers and counting forms the foundation for virtually every aspect of mathematics. When young children haven't acquired these basics at home, teachers can often make up the difference. Activities and games involving counting, comparing quantities, adding, and subtracting are apt to be beneficial. For instance, regular practice in counting objects and comparing quantities with one another (e.g., determining which of three groups of apples has the *most* apples) leads to improved performance not only in these tasks but in other quantitative tasks as well (Case & Okamoto, 1996; Griffin et al., 1995).

● *At all age levels, use manipulatives and visual displays to tie mathematical concepts and procedures to concrete reality.* Concrete manipulatives (beans, blocks, Cuisinaire rods, toothpicks bundled in groups of 10 and 100, etc.) can often help children grasp the nature of addition, subtraction, place value, and fractions (Fujimura, 2001; Fuson & Briars, 1990; Greeno et al., 1996). Visual aids such as number lines and pictures of pizzas depicting various fractions can be helpful in the early elementary grades, and graphs and diagrams of geometric figures are useful for secondary students (Greeno et al., 1996; Schwartz, Yarushalmy, & Wilson, 1993). As noted in Chapter 6, children and adolescents alike benefit from concrete manipulatives and illustrations of abstract ideas.

● *As youngsters work on challenging problem-solving tasks, provide materials and strategies they can use to ease the load on working memory.* Complex mathematical tasks and problems—those within a child's zone of proximal development—often put a strain on working memory. Fortunately, Western cultures have devised a variety of mechanisms for easing the burden. For children in the early elementary grades, such mechanisms may simply be pencil and paper for keeping track of quantities, calculations, and other information. And once children have mastered basic math facts and understand the logic behind arithmetic operations, they might use calculators or computers while working with large numbers or cumbersome number sets.

● *Encourage children to invent, use, and defend their own strategies.* As we've seen, young children often invent strategies (e.g., the *min* strategy) for adding and subtracting objects well before they have formal instruction in addition and subtraction. Rather than ignore strategies children have developed on their own, teachers should encourage those that seem to be effective. As children acquire more efficient strategies over time, they will gradually abandon their earlier ones (Geary, 1994; Siegler, 1989).

Also beneficial is specifically asking children to reflect on and explain in writing why they solved a problem as they did (Carr & Biddlecomb, 1998; Johanning, D'Agostino, Steele, & Shumow, 1999). As an example, Figure 10-9 shows 8-year-old Noah's explanation of how he solved the problem 354 − 298.

Strategy development does not have to be a solitary activity, however. Group discussions can often enhance children's mathematical understandings (e.g., Carr & Biddlecomb, 1998; Kline & Flowers, 1998; Lampert, Rittenhouse, & Crumbaugh, 1996). At the second-grade level, students might develop and justify their own strategies for adding two- and three-digit numbers (J. Hiebert & Wearne, 1996). At the high school level, they might work in groups to derive their own set of geometric theorems (Healy, 1993).

● *When youngsters consistently make errors, identify and address the flaws in their reasoning.* Children and adolescents don't always invent or use effective strategies, of course.

Connecting Concepts ————
Chapter 6 describes Vygotsky's concept of *zone of proximal development*.

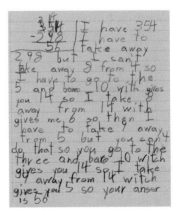

Figure 10-9

Noah's explanation of what he did when he solved the problem 354 − 298

When adding fractions, they may add both the numerators and denominatiors—for example, concluding that ¼ + ⅔ = ⅗ (Byrnes, 1996). When simplifying an algebraic equation, they may add or subtract unknowns inappropriately—for instance, concluding that $3xy - 3x = y$ (Kieran, 1989). And in some cases they may simply make careless errors. In the "Simplifying a Fraction" exercise that follows, see if you can figure out where one eighth grader went wrong.

INTERPRETING CHILDREN'S ARTIFACTS AND ACTIONS   Simplifying a Fraction

Fourteen-year-old Nora gets a score of 49 percent on an eighth-grade math test, revealing that she responded to only about half of the test problems correctly. In one item she was asked to convert the improper fraction −⁷⁴⁄₈ to a mixed number. Her work provides only minimal clues as to how she might have approached the problem, but her final answer, −3¾, was incorrect. Take a few minutes to speculate on how Nora might have gone wrong.

Test item and Nora's work

$$-\frac{74}{8}\ \frac{27}{4}$$

Nora's final answer

$$-3\frac{3}{4}$$

Nora's first step apparently was to divide both numerator and denominator by 2. This led to a denominator of 4 and *should* have led to a numerator of 37 rather than 27. Perhaps she miscalculated when she divided 74 by 2, or perhaps she carelessly recorded 27 instead of 37. Yet ²⁷⁄₄ converts to 6¾, not 3¾, so Nora made at least one more error as well. One possibility is that Nora divided 27 by the original denominator 8—this would give her the whole number 3—and combined the remainder of 3 with her denominator of 4. Such an analysis suggests that Nora applies mathematical procedures without giving them much thought and perhaps does not understand the logic underlying these procedures. Furthermore, Nora appears to need guidance both in keeping better track of her steps in a problem-solving task and in double-checking her work to be sure it makes sense—two aspects of the metacognitive aspect of mathematics we spoke of earlier.

Science

As scientists observe physical and biological phenomena in nature, they use certain strategies (formulating and testing hypotheses, separating and controlling variables, etc.) to conduct systematic investigations, and they form theories to explain their findings. Development in science, then, involves both theory building and acquisition of scientific reasoning skills. It also involves advancements in epistemological beliefs about science.

Children's Theories about the Physical and Biological Worlds

———— Connecting Concepts
Recall our discussion of *theory theory* and *nativism* in Chapter 7.

In studying children's growing understandings of scientific phenomena, many developmental theorists take a *theory theory* approach, suggesting that children construct (rather than absorb) their knowledge and beliefs about physical and biological phenomena. Some theorists are also *nativists,* arguing that infants' brains are neurologically "preprogrammed" with some basic knowledge about their world, or at least with some preliminary dispositions to interpret events in certain ways. For example, even young infants (i.e., those between 2 and 5 months old) seem to know that an object maintains its existence and shape as it moves, that two objects cannot occupy the same space at the same time, and that one object can influence another object only when the two come into contact (Baillargeon, 1994, 2004; Spelke, 1994). Researchers have not tested such understandings in newborns, however, partly because newborns' limited visual acuity would make it difficult to do so. Thus it is possible that young infants' early experiences, rather than biologically built-in preprogramming, are the source of their knowledge about physical objects.

One important step in early theory building is making a distinction between biological and nonbiological entities. By the time infants are 6 months old, most have some awareness that people and other animals move in ways that nonliving things do not (Cohen & Cashon, 2006). For example, human beings walk with a rhythmic motion quite different from the movements of inanimate objects that are pushed or thrown. By age 3 or 4, children know that humans and other animals, but not nonliving objects, can move *themselves* and that living and nonliving entities "grow" in different ways (Jipson & Callanan, 2003; Massey & Gelman, 1988). At about age 4, children also realize that two living creatures in the same category, even if they look quite different, are apt to share many characteristics—for instance, that a blackbird has more in common with a flamingo (because both are birds) than it does with a bat (S. A. Gelman & Markman, 1986). And by the middle elementary school years, children understand that both plants and animals are defined largely by their genetic heritage and internal makeup—for instance, that round, reddish fruits that come from pear trees must be pears rather than apples (see Chapter 7).

Infants' early understandings of nonliving physical objects (e.g., the idea that two objects cannot occupy the same space at the same time) are consistent with classical principles of physics. As children get older and gain more experience with the physical world, they construct increasingly elaborate, but usually fairly concrete, theories about physical entities. Many school-age children view all physical phenomena either as actual substances (i.e., touchable "things" that have specific, although possibly changeable, locations) or as properties of those substances (Reiner, Slotta, Chi, & Resnick, 2000). This **substance schema** can be quite useful in explaining many everyday events (e.g., holding a ball, touching a hot stove). Yet children and adolescents tend to apply it inappropriately to such phenomena as light, heat, fire, and force, which in and of themselves have little or no substance (Reiner et al., 2000). For example, children are likely to think of *force* as something that a pitched ball "contains," rather than as the initial impetus for the ball's motion. And they are apt to think of *heat* as something that can "flow" from one object to another.

Another idea that children acquire quite early but eventually misapply is the concept of *gravity*. At 3 or 4 months of age, children have some understanding that objects fall down (never up) when there is nothing to support them (Baillargeon, 1994). This "downward" view of gravity works quite well on a small scale. But imagine the situation depicted in Figure 10-10. A rock is dropped at the equator, at the entrances to two tunnels that go through the earth. Tunnel A comes out at the equator on the opposite side of the earth. Tunnel B comes out at the South Pole. Into which tunnel will the rock fall? Many middle school students say that the rock will fall into Tunnel B, apparently thinking that gravity always pulls something "down." They respond in this way even if they have explicitly learned that gravity pulls objects toward the center of the earth (Pulos, 1997).

To some degree, children's not-quite-right theories undoubtedly reflect a limited ability to think about abstract ideas. Even though these theories don't always jibe with scientific explanations, they almost certainly reflect children's genuine desire to make sense of their experiences.

Scientific Reasoning Skills

As noted in Chapter 7, even in the first year of life, children seem predisposed to identify cause-and-effect relationships in the world around them. But children's ability to think as scientists appears much later, and then only gradually. **Scientific reasoning** encompasses a number of cognitive processes, including planning an investigation, analyzing evidence, and drawing appropriate conclusions (Kuhn & Franklin, 2006). Taken together, such processes are often called the *scientific method*. Common to all of them is a conscious intention to acquire new knowledge and explanations and to evaluate their worth.

Planning and conducting a scientific investigation requires abilities first introduced in Chapter 6: formulating hypotheses and then separating and controlling variables while testing those hypotheses. Such abilities emerge gradually over the course of middle childhood and adolescence. Formulating hypotheses depends on at least two things that change with age: (a) the ability to think about abstract and potentially contrary-to-fact ideas, and (b) a knowledge base that can help a person generate a *variety* of ideas. The ability to separate

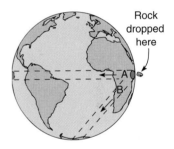

Rock dropped here

Figure 10-10

If a rock is dropped into a hole near the equator, into which of the two tunnels will it fall?

Connecting Concepts
Chapter 2 discusses the scientific method as an important tool in acquiring knowledge about child and adolescent development.

substance schema
General view of all physical phenomena as being either touchable substances or properties of those substances.

scientific reasoning
Cognitive processes central to conducting scientific research and interpreting findings appropriately.

and control variables seems to depend partly on children's working memory capacity, which increases somewhat with age (Bullock & Ziegler, 1999). Elementary school children can often distinguish between experiments that do and do not control variables appropriately, yet they are apt to have trouble controlling variables in their *own* experiments—a task that requires them to keep track of several things simultaneously (Barchfeld, Sodian, Thoermer, & Bullock, 2005; Bullock & Ziegler, 1999; Metz, 2004).

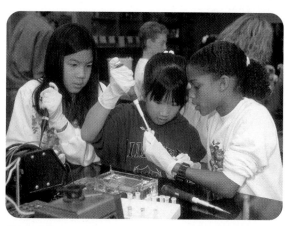

Although adolescents are better able to separate and control variables than elementary school children, even they occasionally have difficulty doing so (Barchfeld et al., 2005; Kuhn et al., 1988). Furthermore, in their hypothesis testing, they tend to focus on and test hypotheses they think are correct and to ignore hypotheses that, in their minds, are *in*correct (Byrnes, 1996). Such *try-to-prove-what-I-already-believe* thinking reflects the *confirmation bias* we spoke of in Chapter 7.

Confirmation bias appears not only when adolescents test hypotheses but also when they analyze and interpret their data (Klaczynski, 2000; Kuhn et al., 1988; Schauble, 1990). In general, they tend to overlook results that conflict with their favorite hypotheses. And they often try to explain away unexpected results that they *can't* ignore. For example, when students in a high school science lab observe results that contradict what they expected to happen, they might complain that "Our equipment isn't working right" or "I can never do science anyway" (Minstrell & Stimpson, 1996, p. 192). Even high school graduates and many college students are apt to think in such "unscientific" ways (Byrnes, 1996; Kuhn & Franklin, 2006).

Although they are eager investigators, children and adolescents often have trouble evaluating the quality of their evidence.

Metacognition in Science

Ultimately, growing children must discover that science is, like other disciplines, a dynamic body of ideas that will continue to evolve over time as new data come in. They must also be able to reflect on and critically evaluate their own beliefs and theories. And, of course, they must be willing to change their views in the face of disconfirming evidence. Such understandings, abilities, and dispositions emerge only gradually over childhood and adolescence (Barchfeld et al., 2005; Elder, 2002; Kuhn & Pearsall, 2000). Giuliana, an eighth grader, reveals beliefs and attitudes about science that are fairly sophisticated for her age-group:

> I think nothing is true. You can say about the Egyptians, for example, that once such and such was believed, but now there's another truth, we aren't sure of anything. We weren't there at the time of the Egyptians, and so we can only hypothesize about it. Historians rely on documents, studies, findings, but I really don't know how true it is what they say. We can say it's true now, but tomorrow another scientist may say "I've found another document that proves something else" and then we'll have two different things and we'll no longer know which is true and which is false. When the atom was discovered, it was considered the smallest particle, but now the quark's been discovered. What we believed before, now we don't believe anymore because the quark is smaller. Perhaps in fifty years' time an even smaller particle will turn up and then we'll be told that what we believed in before was false. It's really something to do with progress. (Mason, 2003, p. 223)

Youngsters' epistemological beliefs about the nature of science will undoubtedly affect the approaches they take (mentally) when they study science. For example, in the "Memory: Early Adolescence" video clip on Observation CD 1, 12-year-old Colin seems to view science largely as a collection of facts he needs to memorize. When asked what things are really hard to remember, he says this:

> I think long things like science and stuff where you have to remember a lot of stuff and stuff that really isn't . . . you really wouldn't want to remember it that much.

Observe Colin's epistemological beliefs about science in the "Memory: Early Adolescence" clip on Observation CD 1.

Students who believe that "knowing" science means understanding how various concepts and principles fit together and using those concepts and principles to explain everyday phenomena are going to study and learn more effectively than students who think that learning science means remembering isolated facts (M. C. Linn et al., 1996). And students who recognize that scientific theories will inevitably change over time are more likely to evaluate theories (including their own) with a critical eye (Bereiter, 1994; Kuhn, 1993, 2001a; M. C. Linn et al., 1996).

The Developmental Trends table "Science at Different Age Levels" presents examples of scientific knowledge and reasoning you are apt to see in infancy, childhood, and adolescence.

DEVELOPMENTAL TRENDS

Science at Different Age Levels

Age	What You Might Observe	Diversity	Implications
Infancy (Birth–2) 	• Knowledge of a few basic principles of physics (e.g., two objects cannot occupy the same space at the same time) • Emerging awareness that humans and animals are fundamentally different from nonliving things • Increasing ability to infer cause-effect relationships	• Infants with sensory impairments (e.g., blindness, hearing loss) are more limited in the scientific phenomena they can observe.	• Put infants and toddlers in contexts in which they can safely explore and experiment with physical objects. • Let toddlers interact with small, gentle animals (e.g., rabbits, Cocker spaniels) under your close supervision.
Early Childhood (2–6)	• Increasing differentiation between living and nonliving things (e.g., they "grow" differently) • Increasing understanding that members of a biological category (e.g., *birds*) share many characteristics in common despite differences in appearance • Naive beliefs about the solar system (e.g., the earth is flat)	• Children in some cultures (e.g., Japanese children) are more likely to think of plants and nonliving objects as having "minds." • Children who grow up in inner-city environments may have little exposure to life cycles (e.g., calves being born, trees losing leaves in the fall and growing blossoms in the spring).	• Read simple nonfiction picture books that depict wild and domesticated animals. • Take children to zoos, farms, arboretums, and other sites where they can see a variety of animals and plants. • Talk with children about natural phenomena, pointing out the physical properties of objects (e.g., some objects float and others sink).
Middle Childhood (6–10)	• Intuitive understanding that biological entities are defined by their genetic heritage and internal makeup • Tendency to think of all physical phenomena as having physical and potentially touchable substance • Some ability to discriminate between valid and invalid tests of hypotheses	• Children differ considerably in their early exposure to scientific ideas (e.g., through family visits to natural history museums and access to age-appropriate science books). • Some children are apt to view supernatural forces (e.g., God, the devil) as being largely responsible for hurricanes and other natural disasters.	• Have children conduct simple experiments with familiar materials; for example, have them raise sunflowers with varying amounts of light and water. • Obtain computer programs that let students "explore" human anatomy or "dissect" small animals.
Early Adolescence (10–14)	• Some ability to think abstractly about scientific phenomena and to separate and control variables • Formulation and testing of hypotheses influenced by existing beliefs (confirmation bias) • Some tendency to misapply scientific concepts (e.g., thinking that gravity pulls objects toward the South Pole)	• Especially in adolescence, boys tend to have more positive attitudes toward science than girls. Girls are more likely than boys to underestimate their science abilities. • Influences of religion on beliefs about natural phenomena (e.g., evolution) become especially noticeable in early adolescence.	• Have young adolescents explore individual interests in science fair projects, scaffolding their efforts at forming hypotheses and controlling irrelevant variables. • Provide scientific explanations that are sufficiently concrete that young adolescents can understand and apply them.
Late Adolescence (14–18)	• Increasing ability to understand abstract scientific concepts • Increasing ability to separate and control variables • Continuing confirmation bias in experimentation and interpretation of results • Increasing awareness that science is a dynamic and changing (rather than static) discipline	• Boys and girls perform similarly on relatively easy science tasks; boys sometimes have the advantage on more challenging tasks. • Boys are more likely to aspire to careers in science. • Cultures that place high value on honoring authority figures tend to promote simplistic epistemological beliefs about science (e.g., that scientific findings should not be questioned).	• Increasingly introduce abstract explanations for phenomena; for example, introduce the idea that heat results from molecules colliding at a certain rate. • To increase girls' interest and involvement in science, occasionally form same-gender groups in science labs and activities.

Sources: Baillargeon, 1994; Bandura, Barbaranelli, Caprara, & Pastorelli, 2001; Barchfeld et al., 2005; Bullock & Ziegler, 1999; Cohen & Cashon, 2006; Eccles, 1989; E. M. Evans, 2001; Flavell et al., 2002; S. A. Gelman & Markman, 1986; Hatano & Inagaki, 1996; Jipson & Callanan, 2003; Keil, 1989; Klaczynski, 2000; Kuhn & Franklin, 2006; O. Lee, 1999; Lee-Pearce et al., 1998; M. C. Linn & Muilenburg, 1996; Massey & Gelman, 1988; Metz, 2004; Nakazawa et al., 2001; Penner, 2003; Pomerantz, Altermatt, & Saxon, 2002; Pulos, 1997; Qian & Pan, 2002; Reiner et al., 2000; M. B. Rowe, 1978; Schauble, 1990; Spelke, 1994; Tamburrini, 1982; Vosniadou, 1991; B. Y. White & Frederiksen, 1998; Wigfield et al., 1996.

Diversity in Science Development

For a variety of reasons, children and adolescents in any single age-group are apt to differ considerably in their science development. Youngsters with sensory impairments (e.g., blindness, hearing loss) may have fairly limited opportunities to observe certain scientific phenomena firsthand. For example, a child who is blind may be unaware that wood changes in size and color when it burns (M. B. Rowe, 1978). Youngsters with strong visual-spatial skills should have an easier time imagining and understanding interrelationships among objects in space (Friedman, 1994). For instance, children who can easily picture and manipulate objects in their minds can better grasp the idea that the moon revolves around the earth while the earth simultaneously revolves around the sun.

Gender differences.   As is true for math, science has traditionally been regarded as a "male" domain. Most prominent scientists are males, and men are more likely than women to be portrayed in educational materials about science (Eisenberg et al., 1996). Perhaps as a result, boys tend to like science more than girls do, and they are more likely than girls to aspire to careers in science (Bandura et al., 2001; Nakazawa et al., 2001). This is true even though girls often perform at a similar level to boys on measures of science achievement (Penner, 2003; Wigfield et al., 1996).

All-girl science classes with female teachers seem to enhance girls' achievement and aspirations in science (MacLean, Sasse, Keating, Stewart, & Miller, 1995; Shapka & Keating, 2003). Perhaps such classes convey the message that science is "for" females as much as it is for males. Of course, placing girls in a female-only environment is not the only way to inspire girls in science. Offering effective instruction, engaging activities, and ample encouragement about scientific careers are key elements of any science-friendly environment and may be especially important for girls (e.g., Burkam, Lee, & Smerdon, 1997).

Cultural differences.   Cultural beliefs and practices clearly influence children's scientific knowledge and reasoning skills. For example, Japanese children are more likely than European American children to think of plants (e.g., a tree, a blade of grass) and certain nonliving objects as having some sort of "mind" that thinks (Hatano & Inagaki, 1996). And cultural differences in schooling may influence youngsters' epistemological beliefs about the nature of science. For example, schools in China tend to encourage respect for authority figures and to downplay differences of opinion among experts. Possibly as a result, high school students in China are more likely than U.S. students to believe that science is simple rather than complex—that it involves discrete facts rather than interrelationships and unresolved issues (Qian & Pan, 2002).

Religion also comes into play when youngsters develop their theories about the world. For instance, in the upper elementary grades, some children are apt to think that supernatural forces (e.g., God, the devil) are largely responsible for natural disasters such as hurricanes (O. Lee, 1999). And adolescents' acceptance or nonacceptance of Darwin's theory of evolution is closely connected to what their religion has taught them about how human beings and other living creatures came into being (E. M. Evans, 2001; Southerland & Sinatra, 2003).

Promoting Development in Science

In the first few years of life, children's science "education" is usually limited to informal experiences. At this point, perhaps the best strategy is simply to provide objects and experiences—building blocks, sand piles, field trips to farms and zoos, and so on—that help children acquire general knowledge on which more formal science instruction can later build.

Once children reach kindergarten or first grade, the curriculum typically includes some science topics. As we've seen, children's abstract and hypothetical reasoning capabilities and their ability to separate and control variables are fairly limited in the elementary grades. Perhaps for this reason, elementary school teachers focus most science instruction on descriptions of natural phenomena rather than on explanations of why those phenomena occur (Byrnes, 1996). Yet even at the elementary level, it is probably coun-

Field trips to farms and zoos in the preschool and early elementary years can enrich children's knowledge about the animal kingdom.

terproductive to portray science as primarily a collection of facts. By having students engage in simple experiments almost from the very beginning of the science curriculum, teachers convey the message that science is an ongoing, dynamic process of unraveling the mysteries of our world.

At the middle school level, students' increasing ability to think about abstract ideas makes it possible to address some of the abstract causal mechanisms that underlie natural phenomena. Even so, middle school teachers may not want to introduce ideas completely removed from students' everyday, concrete experiences (M. C. Linn et al., 1996; Reiner et al., 2000). For instance, when teaching eighth graders about heat, teachers may have better success if they talk about heat as something that "flows" from one object to another rather than as something that involves molecules moving and colliding with one another at a certain rate. Although the heat-flow model is, from a physical science perspective, not entirely accurate, students can effectively apply it to a wide variety of everyday situations. For instance, they can use it to explain why a bathtub filled with warm water heats the air around it, why packing food in ice helps keep it cold, and why using a wooden spoon is safer than using a metal one to stir hot spaghetti sauce (M. C. Linn & Muilenburg, 1996).

When students reach high school, they are more likely to have acquired the scientific knowledge and reasoning skills they need to begin thinking in truly abstract ways about natural phenomena (M. C. Linn et al., 1996). Nevertheless, teachers should continue to engage students in frequent hands-on science activities, not only through systematic laboratory experiments but also through informal, exploratory activities that relate scientific concepts and principles to everyday experiences. Secondary students in general, but especially females, are likely to achieve at higher levels when they have regular hands-on experiences with the phenomena they are studying (Burkam et al., 1997).

Several additional instructional strategies can be helpful for a wide variety of age-groups:

● *Engage students regularly in authentic scientific investigations.* Many school lab activities are little more than cookbook recipes: Students are given specific materials and instructions to follow step by step (see Figure 10-11). Such activities can certainly help make scientific phenomena more concrete for students. However, they are unlikely to encourage youngsters to engage in thinking processes (formulating and testing hypotheses, separating and controlling variables, and so on) that characterize true scientific reasoning (Keil & Silberstein, 1996; Padilla, 1991; J. Singer, Marx, Krajcik, & Chambers, 2000). So in addition, teachers should give students many opportunities to conduct investigations in which the procedures and outcomes are not necessarily predetermined. For instance, teachers might ask students to address such questions as "Does one fast-food restaurant provide more meat in a hamburger than others?" or "Is the local drinking water really safe to drink?" (Padilla, 1991; J. Singer et al., 2000).

Youngsters may need some scaffolding for such activities, however. For instance, a teacher might do the following:

- Present situations in which only two or three variables need to be controlled.
- Use familiar situations that have relevance to students' lives.
- Ask students to identify several possible hypotheses about cause-effect relationships before beginning to experiment.
- Provide regular guidance, hints, and feedback regarding the need to control variables and evaluate observations objectively.
- Ask questions that encourage students to make predictions and reflect appropriately on their observations (e.g., "What do you think will happen?" "What is your evidence?" "Do you see things that are inconsistent with what you predicted?"). (Byrnes, 1996; S. Carey, Evans, Honda, Jay, & Unger, 1989; Kuhn et al., 1988; Minstrell & Stimpson, 1996)

● *Provide age-appropriate explanations for physical and biological phenomena.* Although youngsters can discover a great deal through their own experimentation, they also need to learn the concepts, principles, and theories that scientists use to make sense of the

Figure 10-12

In this drawing of the water cycle, 9-year-old Trisha shows her understanding that various phenomena in nature are interrelated.

world (recall our discussion of Vygotsky's theory in Chapter 6). Ideally, they should pull the things they learn into integrated, meaningful bodies of knowledge. Often teachers can make interrelationships concrete for students by presenting diagrams, flowcharts, or three-dimensional models. Also helpful is asking students themselves to organize what they're learning, as 9-year-old Trisha has done in her depiction of the water cycle shown in Figure 10-12.

● *Actively work to promote conceptual change.* Existing misconceptions probably interfere with children's and adolescents' development in science more than in any other academic discipline. Thanks to confirmation bias, youngsters are apt to seek out information that confirms, rather than contradicts, what they currently believe. Chapter 7 identifies several strategies for promoting conceptual change. Perhaps one of the most effective approaches is to give students opportunities to discuss competing perspectives within a classroom environment that communicates the message, "It's OK to make errors and change our minds" (Minstrell & Stimpson, 1996).

Development in Other Content Domains

In their studies of children's development in academic subject areas, researchers have focused largely on reading, writing, mathematics, and science. Yet they have also learned a few things about children's development in history, geography, art, and music. We now look briefly at trends in each of these domains.

History

Connecting Concepts

You will learn more about this *autobiographical self* in Chapter 12.

Children's first awareness of history typically involves their *own* history. Sometime between ages 2 and 4, children begin to recall past events in their own lives and to understand that they exist *in time,* with a past and a future as well as a present (Bauer, 2006; Howe, 2003). As their improving language skills allow an increasing exchange of ideas with family members and playmates, they gradually expand their sense of history to include other people whom they know well.

Children's knowledge of history on a broader scale emerges largely as a result of formal instruction beginning in the elementary school years. In the elementary grades, children's understanding of history tends to be concrete and simplistic. For example, they may conceptualize the birth of the United States as resulting from a single, specific event (e.g., the Boston Tea Party) or as involving nothing more than constructing new buildings and towns (Ormrod, Jackson, Kirby, Davis, & Benson, 1999).

One source of difficulty for elementary school children is a limited ability to understand historical time. They might refer to events that happened "a long, long time ago" or "in the old days" but tell you that such events happened in 2004. And they tend to lump historical events into two general categories: those that happened very recently and those that happened many years ago. In Figure 10-13 we once again show you the first of four essays presented in the opening case study in Chapter 7. As a second grader, the essay's author obviously has little sense of how long a time span "2000 days" is. In the early grades, then, history instruction should probably focus on students' own personal histories and on events that have occurred locally and in the recent past (Byrnes, 1996).

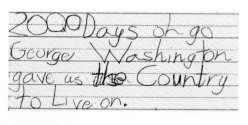

Figure 10-13

As shown in this response to the question *How did the United States become a country?,* second graders have only a limited ability to understand historical time.

At around age 10, children acquire some ability to put historical events in sequence and to attach them to particular time periods (Barton & Levstik, 1996). Accordingly, systematic history instruction usually begins in fourth or fifth grade. Yet when children first study history, they have little personal knowledge and experiences on which to build. They haven't lived in most of the time periods they study, nor have they seen most of the locations they learn about. What they *can* build on, however, is their knowledge of human beings. Children can better understand historical events when they discover that historical figures had particular goals, motives, and personalities—in other words, that people in history were, in many respects, just ordinary folks (Brophy & VanSledright, 1997; Yeager et al., 1997). Figure 10-14 shows 10-year-old Kaitlyn's attempt to view events in the early 1600s as a Native American woman might have. Following are several additional strategies that can help children and adolescents gain a "human" understanding of history:

Connecting Concepts ———————
Such strategies can foster *perspective taking,* which we examine more closely in Chapter 12.

- Assign works of fiction that realistically depict people living in particular times and places.
- Role-play family discussions that focus on making decisions during critical times in history (e.g., deciding whether to send a teenage son off to war).
- Have "journalists" (two or three students) interview people (other students) who "participated" in various ways in a historical event. (Brophy & Alleman, 1996; Brophy & VanSledright, 1997)

Unfortunately, many history textbooks for elementary and secondary students describe historical events in a very matter-of-fact way, communicating the message that "This is what happened" (Britt et al., 1994; Paxton, 1999; Wineburg, 1994). In reality, historians often don't know exactly how particular events occurred. Instead, they construct a reasonable interpretation of events after looking at a variety of historical documents that provide varying perspectives of what transpired (Leinhardt & Young, 1996; Seixas, 1996; Wineburg, 1994). The idea that history is often as much a matter of perspective and opinion as it is a matter of fact is a fairly abstract notion that students may not be able to fully comprehend until late adolescence (Byrnes, 1996; Seixas, 1996). Even so, students can benefit from reading multiple accounts of events, including primary historical sources (diaries, letters, newspaper articles, etc.), as early as fourth grade (Afflerbach, VanSledright, & Dromsky, 2003).

At its core, history is very much a culturally transmitted body of knowledge. Furthermore, different cultural groups are likely to put their own "spin" on historical events. For example, adolescents with a Japanese heritage are likely to have a very different perspective on President Truman's decision to bomb Hiroshima than adolescents with English or French ancestors. European American students tend to view American history as being guided by principles of freedom and democracy, whereas African American students are more likely to view American history as being marked by racism and violation of human rights (T. Epstein, 2000). And teens with different religious backgrounds may see events of the twentieth century (e.g., the banning of school prayer in American public schools) as reflecting either social progress, on the one hand, or moral decline, on the other (Mosborg, 2002).

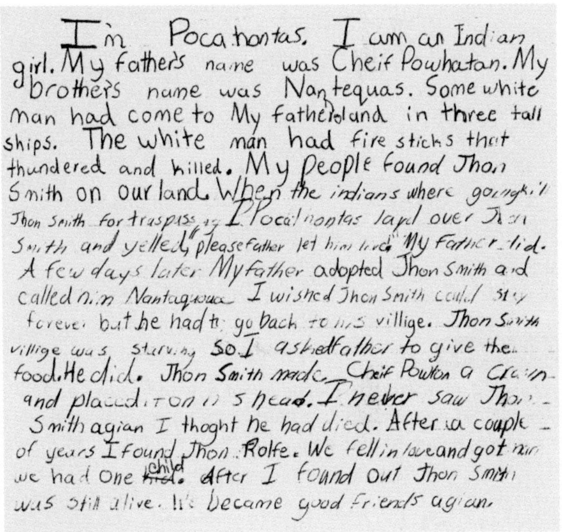

Figure 10-14

In this history assignment, 10-year-old Kaitlyn takes on the perspective of Pocahontas to describe events in the early 1600s.

Geography

The discipline of geography is concerned not only with where various natural features and cultural groups are located but also with why and how they got there. For instance, geographers study how rivers and mountain ranges end up where they do, why people are more likely to settle in some locations than in others, and how people in various locations make a living.

An essential cognitive tool in geography is, of course, the *map.* Maps are commonplace in some cultures, nonexistent in others. Even in a "map-rich" society, children have varying degrees of experience with geography and maps. For instance, children whose families travel extensively tend to have greater appreciation of distance, more familiarity with diverse landscapes, and a better understanding of how maps are used (Trawick-Smith, 2003).

Central to geographical thinking is an understanding that maps depict the arrangement and characteristics of particular locations. By age 3 or 4, children have some ability to recognize relationships between simple graphics and the physical locations that the graphics represent (J. Huttenlocher et al., 1999). Over the next several years, children can increasingly use maps to identify locations in their immediate surroundings (Blades & Spencer, 1987). Children in the early elementary grades tend to take what they see on a map quite literally, however (Gardner et al., 1996; Liben & Downs, 1989b). For example, they may think that lines separating states and countries are actually painted on the earth or that an airport denoted by a picture of an airplane has only one plane. Young children also have trouble maintaining a sense of scale and proportion when interpreting maps (Liben & Downs, 1989b). For instance, they might deny that a road could actually be a road because it's "too skinny for two cars to fit on" or insist that mountains depicted on a three-dimensional relief map can't possibly be mountains because "they aren't high enough."

As children get older, and especially as they reach adolescence, they become more proficient in dealing with the symbolic and proportional nature of maps (Forbes et al., 1999). Yet many adolescents have a simplistic epistemological belief about geography as a discipline. Typically, they conceive of geography as being little more than the names and locations of various countries, capital cities, rivers, mountain ranges, and so on—perhaps, in part, because teachers often present geography this way (Bochenhauer, 1990). Adolescents rarely reflect on why various locations have the physical features they do or on how the economic and cultural practices of various social groups might be partly the result of their physical environment.

A major goal of any geography curriculum must be to foster an understanding of the symbolic nature of maps. Eventually youngsters must learn, too, that different maps are drawn to different scales, reflecting various proportions between graphic representation and reality (Liben & Downs, 1989b). One effective strategy is to ask children to create their *own* maps, perhaps of their neighborhoods or of their entire country (Forbes et al., 1999; Gregg & Leinhardt, 1994a). Teachers and other adults might also ask youngsters to look for patterns in what they see and to speculate about why those patterns exist (Gregg & Leinhardt, 1994b; Liben & Downs, 1989a). For example, in the task presented in Figure 10-15, high school students must apply a basic geographic principle—that, historically, people who lived near large bodies of water had an easier time transporting goods to distant markets—in order to understand why Chicago had the prominence that it did. Ultimately, children and adolescents become more proficient geographers when they not only know *what is where* but also understand *why it is where it is.*

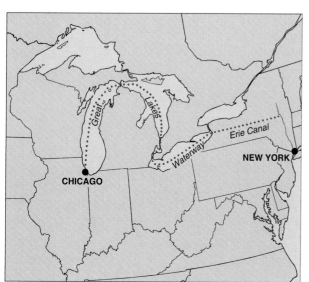

Why did Chicago become the major railroad center of the American Midwest in the middle of the nineteenth century?

Figure 10-15

By asking children to speculate about why things are located where they are, teachers can promote more sophisticated epistemological beliefs about geography.

Art

As early as age 2, some children begin to represent their experiences on paper—for instance, by making a series of dots to mimic how an animal hops (Matthews, 1999; Winner, 2006). They also begin to experiment with geometric figures, especially lines and circles, as illustrated in 2½-year-old Tina's scribbles in Figure 4-10 (p. 113). At age 3, their repertoire of shapes expands to include squares, rectangles, triangles, crosses, and Xs, and they soon begin combining such shapes to create pictures (Beaty, 1998; Golomb, 2004; R. Kellogg, 1967). Many of their early drawings are of people, which might initially consist of a circle (depicting either a head or a head plus body) with a few facial features (e.g., eyes, mouth) within it and four lines (two arms, two legs) extending from it. With age, preschoolers increasingly add features—perhaps hair, hands, fingers, and feet—to their human figures. Piece A in Figure 10-16 is one example.

Sometime around age 4, children begin to combine drawings of several objects to create pictures of groups or nature scenes. Initially, they may scatter things haphazardly around the page, but eventually placement of objects on the page is somewhat consistent with everyday reality. For example, in the scene depicted in Piece B in Figure 10-16, grass appears at the bottom of the page, the tree appropriately grows up from the ground, and traditionally "high" things (bird, sun, clouds) are near the top. Notice how the sky (depicted by the blue at the very top) is restricted to a small space above everything else. The tendency to depict sky as a separate entity at the top of the page is quite common in 5- and 6-year-olds (Golomb, 2004).

In the elementary grades, children become capable of producing a wide variety of shapes and contours, and their drawings and paintings become more detailed, realistic,

a.

b.

c.

d.

e.

Figure 10-16

Developmental progressions in children's art are clearly seen in these pieces by (A) Corey at age 5, (B) Corey at age 6, (C) Trisha at age 11, (D) Elizabeth at age 14, and (E) Joey at age 17.

and appropriately proportional (N. R. Smith et al., 1998; Winner, 2006). By the upper elementary grades, children represent depth in their drawings (Braine, Schauble, Kugelmass, & Winter, 1993). For example, in Piece C in Figure 10-16, 11-year-old Trisha has drawn the fence "behind" the house and barn, with the three hills "behind" one another and the fence. Notice how, in contrast to Piece B, the sky in Piece C fills up all of the "unoccupied" space.

Some children draw and paint very little once they reach adolescence, especially if art is not a regular part of the school curriculum, and so their artistic skills may progress very little beyond this point (Moran & Gardner, 2006; Winner, 2006). Those who continue to create art refine their abilities to show texture, depth, perspective, and spatial relationships (see Pieces D and E in Figure 10-16) (N. R. Smith et al., 1998; Willats, 1995). They may also try to convey mood and emotion by selectively using various shapes, hues, and intensities of color (N. R. Smith et al., 1998).

When a culture neither values nor encourages art, children's art skills emerge slowly if at all (Gordon, 2004; Trawick-Smith, 2003). But when drawing implements are readily available to children—as they are in many cultures—certain universals in artistic development appear in the preschool years (Case & Okamoto, 1996; Golomb, 2004; R. Kellogg, 1967). Young children worldwide draw their early "people" in much the same manner that 5-year-old Corey did in Piece A in Figure 10-16. They are also apt to draw houses as squares with

Figure 10-17

Young children in a variety of industrialized cultures draw houses in much the same way that 4-year-old Kaitlyn did here.

———————— Connecting Concepts
Chapter 9 describes infant-directed speech in more detail.

smaller, internal squares depicting windows, doors, and perhaps chimneys (see Figure 10-17). And they begin to compose more complex pictures (such as that in Piece B in Figure 10-16) in the same sequence and at approximately the same ages regardless of their cultural background.

Other aspects of artistic development are more culture-specific. For example, if children receive extensive instruction in artistic techniques, as many children do in Japan and China, their drawings are more elaborate, detailed, and true-to-life (Alland, 1983; Case & Okamoto, 1996). And by the middle elementary grades, some children begin to mimic popular images in their local cultural environment, such as the drawings they see in comic books and children's magazines (B. Wilson, 1997; Winner, 2006).

Even with little instruction, however, some children appear to have a natural talent for art (Winner, 1996). In fact, some children with autism show exceptional proficiency and precision in their drawings at a very early age despite significant delays in their overall cognitive development (Treffert & Wallace, 2002). One characteristic of autism we mentioned in Chapter 7—an inability to screen out sensory information—may very well be at the root of such talent. Children may be more inclined to capture the details in what they see when they have trouble *ignoring* those details (Grandin & Johnson, 2005).

Music

Human beings of all ages clearly enjoy music. For instance, 6-month-olds pay more attention to their mothers when Mom is singing, rather than talking, to them (Nakata & Trehub, 2004). Lively songs sung by Mom help keep infants on an even keel, perking them up a bit if they seem low on energy but soothing them if they are overly aroused (Shenfield, Trehub, & Nakata, 2003). Even the way that most parents talk to their infants—a style known as *infant-directed speech*—has a singsongy quality to it, with considerable repetition and greater variation in pitch than is true for normal speech.

Just as young infants can hear subtle differences in spoken language that adults don't hear (see Chapter 9), so, too, do they pick up on subtle changes in music that adults don't notice. For example, when a melody changes slightly (say, by a note or two within the same key), 8-month-olds are more likely than adults to notice the difference (Trainor & Trehub, 1992). But as youngsters grow older, and especially as they progress through the preschool and early elementary school years, they increasingly perceive patterns (melodies, keys, complex rhythms, etc.) rather than individual notes (Gromko & Poorman, 1998; Winner, 2006).

Children also gain considerable proficiency in singing during the early childhood years (Winner, 2006). At around age 2, they begin to repeat some of the song lyrics they hear. They soon add a rhythmic structure and up-and-down "melody" of sorts. By the time they are 5 or 6, most can sing a recognizable tune and keep it largely within the same key and meter. For most youngsters, further development in singing comes largely from explicit voice training (Winner, 2006). Formal instruction is typically necessary for children to gain proficiency in playing a musical instrument as well (D. J. Elliott, 1995).

Another important aspect of musical development is **music literacy,** the ability to read and understand musical notation. As early as age 4, children can, when asked, invent ways to represent musical sounds with objects—for instance, using large, heavy objects to represent loud notes and smaller objects to represent softer notes (Gromko, 1996). At about the same age, they can also invent strategies for representing music on paper. For instance, they may make small circles or mountain "peaks" for high notes and make larger circles or "valleys" for lower pitches (Gromko, 1994, 1996, 1998). Standard musical notation is, of course, a cultural creation, and so children must be instructed in its interpretation. Youngsters' ability to read music can enhance their ability to hear and remember the subtle nuances of a musical piece (Gromko & Poorman, 1998). Essentially, written music provides an alternative means through which children and adolescents can store music in long-term memory.

Virtually all cultures have some form of music, and the types of music with which children grow up certainly affect their musical preferences (Winner, 2006). But within any single culture, children have varying abilities to hear and appreciate music. About 4 percent of children in any age-group have *amusia* (or tone deafness), an inability to detect the small changes in pitch that are common in melodies. Such youngsters show little or no improvement in their perception of musical tones despite instruction and practice, suggesting that the ability to hear music *as* music may have a biological basis (Gardner et al., 1996; Hyde &

music literacy
Ability to read and understand musical notation.

Peretz, 2004). In contrast, some children not only hear, but can also *remember*, subtle differences in pitch. Although most people can remember the relative pitches of notes in a melody, individuals with **absolute pitch** can also recall the *exact* pitch of a note they have repeatedly heard in, say, a popular song or soundtrack (Shellenberg & Trehub, 2003). Absolute pitch is more common in infants and preschoolers than in older children or adults, so possibly children lose this ability if everyday demands in their culture don't require it (Saffran & Griepentrog, 2001; Winner, 2006). For example, absolute pitch is more common in people who speak Asian languages such as Chinese and Vietnamese, in which spoken sounds have differing meanings depending on their pitch (D. Deutsch, Henthorn, & Dolson, 2004). It is also more common in children who begin music lessons before age 7 (Takeuchi & Hulse, 1993).

The ability to *produce* music seems to be a product of both nature and nurture as well (D. J. Elliott, 1995; Treffert & Wallace, 2002). Some children with autism have exceptional instrumental talent. For example, after watching a movie on television one evening, 14-year-old Leslie Lemke sat down at the family piano and played Tchaikovsky's Piano Concerto no. 1, which had been a sound track for portions of the movie. He had never heard the concerto before that night, yet his rendition was flawless. Lemke is now a world-renowned pianist, even though he has autism and mental retardation, is blind, and has never had a piano lesson (Treffert & Wallace, 2002).

The Basic Developmental Issues table "Developmental Progressions in the Content Domains" summarizes how our three general themes—nature and nurture, universality and diversity, and qualitative and quantitative change—play out in the various subject areas we've examined in this chapter.

Using Content Area Standards to Guide Instruction

Formal instruction in the content domains must, of course, take into account the knowledge and abilities that children and adolescents are likely to have at various ages. Within the past two or three decades, numerous discipline-specific professional groups have compiled comprehensive lists of topics and skills that they believe to be appropriate for different grade levels. Such lists, known as content area **standards,** are often used to guide instruction and assessment from kindergarten or first grade through high school. Table 10-1 lists Web sites at which you can find standards for a variety of content domains.

In the United States an additional source of guidance comes from standards created by state departments of education and, in some cases, local school districts. As a result of the No Child Left Behind Act of 2001, all 50 states now have standards for reading, writing, and mathematics, and will soon have standards for science as well. The No Child Left Behind legislation, sometimes known simply as "NCLB," mandates that school districts annually assess students in grades 3–8 to determine whether students are making "adequate yearly progress" in meeting state-determined standards. Schools that do not show progress are subject to sanctions and corrective actions (such as administrative restructuring), and students have the option of attending another public school at the school district's expense. Research on the effects of the legislation on children's learning and development is still in progress, but one thing is clear: Because their livelihood depends on their students' test scores, teachers spend more time on reading, writing, math, and science—subject areas that are or soon will be annually assessed—and less time on social studies, art, music, and other disciplines (Jacob, 2003; Siskin, 2003).

Existing standards are certainly useful in helping teachers focus instruction on important educational goals in various content domains. When teachers establish clear instructional goals and target instruction toward achieving those goals, all children, and especially those who struggle academically, are likely to make good academic progress (Hamre & Pianta, 2005). We worry, however, that many existing standards are based on topics and skills that are *typically taught* at various grade levels, rather than on developmental research regarding what youngsters can reasonably accomplish at different ages. We worry, too, that some lists of standards are so lengthy that teachers may provide only fragmented, superficial "coverage" of topics rather than designing lessons that foster elaboration, comprehension monitoring, and other effective cognitive and metacognitive processes.

absolute pitch
Ability to recall the precise pitch of a particular note in music.

standards
In education, general statements regarding the knowledge and skills that students should gain and the characteristics that their accomplishments should reflect.

BASIC DEVELOPMENTAL ISSUES

Developmental Progressions in the Content Domains

Issue	Reading and Writing	Math and Science	History and Geography	Art and Music
Nature and Nurture	Although children appear to have a biological predisposition to learn spoken language (see Chapter 9), facility with *written* language is largely the result of exposure to printed materials. Nature can interfere with normal literacy development, however: Some children with biologically based disabilities have unusual difficulty learning to read and write.	Within the first few months of life, infants notice differences in quantity and appear to understand certain basic principles of physics (e.g., that no two objects can occupy the same space at the same time). Some theorists speculate that such early acquisitions reflect neurologically "preprogrammed" knowledge. By and large, however, children's knowledge of numbers and scientific phenomena develops through informal experiences and formal instruction.	The bodies of knowledge and cognitive tools that children acquire in history and geography are the result of nurture, as provided by both formal instruction in school and informal experiences within the family (trips to historical sites, use of maps on subway systems, etc.). However, maturational processes may dictate when children become able to think about historical time and understand the symbolic nature of maps.	Hereditary and maturational factors play some role in artistic and musical development. In the preschool years, children's ability to draw depends largely on maturation of fine motor skills. Furthermore, most children seem to have an inborn appreciation for music from birth. And some children show exceptional talent in art or music even without formal instruction. For the most part, however, development in art and music is the result of training and practice.
Universality and Diversity	Phonological awareness facilitates reading development even when written language is *not* based on how words are pronounced. However, children learn to read and write more easily when words have highly regular and predictable spelling patterns. Children's literacy development also depends on the extent to which their families and cultural groups model and encourage reading and writing.	Although children worldwide have some awareness of quantity and amount, their precision in measuring and comparing quantities depends on the number concepts and operations that their culture provides. Asian children seem to be especially adept in mathematics, in part because Asian languages make the structure of the base-10 number system more obvious. Children's basic scientific knowledge (e.g., knowing that animals are fundamentally different from human-made objects) is similar worldwide, but their understandings of many natural phenomena (e.g., the origins of species) differ depending on their cultural and religious upbringings.	Because children's knowledge of history and geography is largely the product of the environment and culture in which they have been raised, universal acquisitions have not been identified. In industrialized societies, history is formally taught in school, and maps are widely used to aid navigation. In other cultures, however, children's knowledge of history comes from hearing stories from their elders, and people navigate largely by locating distinctive landmarks in the physical terrain.	Virtually all cultures have some form of art and music. Artistic styles and musical patterns differ considerably from culture to culture, however, and children's development in these areas varies accordingly. For instance, although preschoolers' drawings tend to be quite similar across cultures (e.g., early drawings of people may consist of circles with rudimentary facial features and four lines extending outward to represent limbs), by middle childhood their artwork begins to mimic the styles and images they see in their environment.
Qualitative and Quantitative Change	Reading and writing skills show many qualitative changes over time. For instance, children gradually shift their primary focus from word identification to comprehension (in reading), gradually switch from knowledge telling to knowledge transforming (in writing), and increasingly incorporate metacognitive processes in their efforts (in both reading and writing). Literacy development is quantitative in the sense that children become able to recognize and spell more and more words each year, and basic reading and writing skills become increasingly automatized.	As children get older, they acquire more knowledge about mathematical and scientific concepts and principles—a progression that reflects quantitative change. In addition, they acquire more complex and sophisticated—and qualitatively different—ways of thinking about math and science. For example, elementary school children increasingly rely on retrieval (rather than counting objects or fingers) to solve addition and subtraction problems, and adolescents gain new reasoning skills (e.g., separating and controlling variables) in their scientific experimentation.	A good deal of development in history and geography is quantitative, in that children acquire more information about historical events and geographical locations. Qualitative changes are seen in how children *think* about history and geography. For example, with appropriate instruction children gradually begin to realize that knowledge of history is comprised not only of what *did* happen but also of varying perspectives of what *might have* happened. And as children gain proportional reasoning, they become better able to understand the various scales with which maps are constructed.	Many qualitative changes are seen in art and music development. For example, children's drawings gradually address composition (e.g., creating an organized scene rather than a random collection of objects), perspective, and texture. And in the preschool years, their songs begin to reflect a consistent rhythm and key. Quantitative change is seen in such things as children's increasing knowledge of musical notation and increasing automaticity in playing a musical instrument.

TABLE 10-1

Web Sites with Standards for Various Academic Disciplines

Content Domain	Organization	Internet Address	Once you get there . . . [a]
Civics and government	Center for Civic Education	http://www.civiced.org	Select *Resource Materials* from the Publications menu.
English and language arts	National Council of Teachers of English	http://www.ncte.org	Select *Standards* from the Quick Links menu.
Foreign language	American Council on the Teaching of Foreign Languages	http://www.actfl.org	Select the standards document from the Publications menu.
Geography	National Council for Geographic Education	http://www.ncge.org	Select *Geography Standards* from the Geography menu.
Health, physical education, and dance	National Association for Sport and Physical Education	http://www.aahperd.org/naspe	Click on *Standards & Guidelines* in the Quick Links box.
History	National Center for History in the Schools	http://www.sscnet.ucla.edu/nchs	Click on *Standards (Online).*
Information literacy	American Association of School Librarians	http://www.ala.org/aasl	Click on *Issues & Advocacy* and then on *Information Literacy.*
Mathematics	National Council of Teachers of Mathematics	http://www.nctm.org	Click on *NCTM Standards.*
Music	National Association for Music Education	http://www.menc.org	Click on *National Standards.*
Reading	International Reading Association	http://www.reading.org	Type "standards for the English language arts" in the Search box.
Science	National Academy of Sciences	http://www.nap.edu	Type "National Science Education Standards" in the *Find* box.
Visual arts	National Art Education Association[b]	http://artsedge.kennedy-center.org/teach/standards	

[a]These steps worked for us when this book was in production in February 2006. Given the dynamic nature of many Web sites, you may find that you have to do something different to locate the standards on some of the sites.
[b]The NAEA site does not list the standards; however, you can find them at the site to the right.

Furthermore, if teachers rely exclusively on content area standards, they are apt to neglect other, equally important domains, such as the development of general learning strategies, social skills, and emotional well-being. This is *not* to say that teachers must choose between strong academic standards and students' social-emotional growth. Effective teachers pursue both sets of objectives by integrating existing local, state, national, and international standards with other, nonacademic agendas. In the final case, one teacher sets and meets some very ambitious goals indeed.

Connecting Concepts ——————
Chapter 1 discusses the need to address the full spectrum of children's needs in the physical, cognitive, and social-emotional domains.

Case Study: Beating the Odds

James A. Garfield Senior High School is located in a low-income neighborhood in East Los Angeles, California. In the 1980s, many of the students' parents had immigrated from Mexico, had limited formal education, and spoke little or no English. Garfield had a high dropout rate, in part because apathetic teachers and frequent violence on campus (often between rival gangs) gave students little reason to stay in school.

Despite such circumstances, math teacher Jaime Escalante, himself an immigrant from Bolivia, was convinced that many Garfield students had the ability to achieve at high levels. To prove his point, he urged students in his calculus class to take the Advanced Placement (AP) calculus test, an instrument developed by the Educational Testing Service (ETS) to assess the extent to which students had achieved at a level equivalent to that in an introductory college calculus course. Scores on the test range from 1 to 5, with 3 being a "pass" and most colleges offering college credit for scores of 3, 4, and 5.

(continued)

During the 1981–1982 school year, Mr. Escalante had 18 students (10 boys and 8 girls, all with Mexican heritage) in his calculus class. He required all class members (and their parents as well) to sign contracts in which they promised to attend class, pay attention, try hard, and do all assigned homework. Throughout the school year, teacher and students worked intensively, not only during class time, but also before school, after school, and on Saturdays. During study sessions, Mr. Escalante continually drilled students in basic calculus procedures, presented a wide variety of challenging problems to solve, and encouraged students to help one another. In the last few weeks before the AP calculus test, most of the students devoted themselves almost exclusively to calculus, withdrawing from girlfriends, boyfriends, hobbies, and after-school jobs to prepare for the exam. (One student even took his textbook into the bathroom with him.) The class became a close-knit group, with teacher and classmates offering support and encouragement as needed. Mr. Escalante often reminded his students of what their dedication might bring them: "You want to make your parents proud. You want to make your school proud. Think how good it will feel if you go to college and know you did the calculus AP. It isn't everybody who can do that" (Mathews, 1988, p. 14).

On May 19, the 18 students took the test under the supervision of the school counselor. Although they struggled with a few items, for the most part they were well prepared for the test and found it easier than they had expected. In fact, they performed at such high levels (and in some cases their answers were so similar) that ETS accused 12 of them of cheating. These students were vindicated when, on August 31 (this time under the watchful eye of ETS employees), the 12 accused students retook the test and all earned a score of 3 or higher.

At least 15 of the 18 students went on to college, many earned bachelor's degrees, and several attended graduate school. Mr. Escalante's 1981–1982 calculus class eventually produced teachers, accountants, medical technicians, and an aerospace engineer.[a]

- In what ways did nurture clearly play a role in the students' mathematical achievement? How might nature also have been involved?
- The calculus class consisted of 10 boys and 8 girls. Are these numbers consistent or inconsistent with research related to gender differences in mathematics?
- ETS employees based their suspicions about cheating partly on the similarity of answers they saw in students' responses. What other explanation for the similarity might there be?

Once you have answered these questions, compare your responses with those presented in the appendix.

[a]Case based on Mathews, 1988; Menéndez, 1988.

Summary

Reading Development

When toddlers and preschoolers have multiple and varied experiences with reading and writing materials and activities, they learn a great deal about the nature of written language. For instance, they learn that spoken language is represented in consistent ways and that different kinds of printed materials serve different purposes. Such knowledge, known as *emergent literacy,* provides an important foundation for the reading and writing skills that children acquire once they begin school.

Skilled reading involves knowing letter-sound correspondences, recognizing letters and words quickly and automatically, constructing meaning from the words on the page, and metacognitively regulating the reading process. Phonological awareness (hearing the distinct sounds within spoken words), word identification skills, and the automatic recognition of many common words typically emerge in the early and middle elementary school years. Reading comprehension and metacognitive strategies continue to develop throughout childhood and adolescence.

Some children with sensory impairments or learning disabilities have more difficulty learning to read than their nondisabled peers. Researchers have also found gender, socioeconomic, ethnic, and cross-linguistic differences in reading development. Strategies for fostering reading development include teaching parents strategies for effective storybook reading, promoting children's phonological awareness, providing many opportunities to read authentic literature, and engaging children and adolescents in discussions about what they read.

Writing Development

To become skillful writers, children and adolescents must not only master handwriting and spelling but must also discover how to communicate their thoughts clearly; learn conventions of capitalization, punctuation, and syntax; and metacognitively regulate the entire writing effort. Handwriting is usually mastered in the elementary grades, but other aspects of writing continue to develop throughout the school years. For example, in the middle school and high school years, many youngsters gradually abandon a *knowledge-telling* approach to writing (in which they write ideas in whatever order the ideas come to mind) in favor of a *knowledge-transforming* approach (in which they conscientiously try to communicate their ideas to the reader). Self-evaluation and editing skills also improve during adolescence.

To a considerable degree, children's writing development is dependent on their general intellectual development, but some children have difficulty writing despite normal cognitive development in other areas. Gender and cultural differences in writing development have also been observed. Teachers and other adults can promote writing development by introducing preschoolers to simple writing activities (e.g., making alphabet letters, using pseudowriting in pretend play), assigning authentic writing tasks in the elementary and secondary grades, scaffolding youngsters' writing efforts, and requiring writing in all areas of the school curriculum.

Mathematics Development

Children have some awareness of quantity in the first year of life, but they learn to count only if their culture provides the cognitive tools (e.g., number words) that make counting possible. Often they learn to perform simple mathematical operations (e.g., adding and subtracting small numbers) on their own, but formal instruction is necessary for acquisition of complex concepts and procedures. For optimal mathematical development, children should truly understand (rather than simply memorize) mathematical procedures and discover that there is often more than one correct way to solve a problem.

Some children have learning disabilities that impede their ability to automatize math facts and solve simple math problems, and others have little exposure to numbers and counting before they begin school. Gender and cultural differences in mathematics have been observed as well. Concrete manipulatives and visual aids often facilitate children's mathematical development, especially in the preschool and elementary years, and tools that reduce the load on working memory (e.g., paper and pencil, calculators) can enhance youngsters' mathematical problem-solving abilities once basic facts and skills have been mastered and automatized.

Science Development

Although children are possibly "prewired" with some basic knowledge of physics, by and large they acquire scientific knowledge through their informal experiences and formal instruction. As early as the preschool years, they begin to form theories (sometimes accurate, sometimes not) about cause-effect relationships in their physical worlds and about categories of living creatures. Their ability to reason as scientists do (e.g., formulating and testing hypotheses, interpreting evidence) continues to improve in adolescence, but even many high school students have difficulty analyzing their data objectively.

Children's individual abilities (e.g., visual-spatial skills) and disabilities (e.g., blindness) affect their development in science, as do gender stereotypes and cultural beliefs. Authentic scientific investigations, age-appropriate explanations, and intentional efforts to bring about conceptual change can all enhance youngsters' scientific understandings and reasoning skills.

Development in Other Domains

Such domains as history, geography, art, and music have received less attention in developmental research, but researchers are finding some trends in these areas. For instance, children in the early elementary grades are apt to have difficulty understanding the nature of historical time, and they may not appreciate that some historical "knowledge" is a matter of perspective rather than fact. Geographical reasoning requires understanding the symbolic and proportional nature of maps, which emerges gradually over the elementary and middle school years.

Art and music are found in virtually all cultures, but the specific *forms* that art and music take differ considerably from one society to another. Some universals are seen, to be sure—for instance, infants around the world seem to enjoy music, and children's early drawings of people are similar regardless of where they grow up—but advanced art and music abilities are largely dependent on instruction and practice.

Using Content Area Standards

Groups of subject-matter experts in various academic disciplines have developed content area standards describing topics they believe to be appropriate for study at various grade levels. State departments of education and many local school districts have also created standards to guide instruction, especially in reading, writing, math, and science. Such standards provide useful guidance when teachers plan lessons for their own classrooms. Teachers must remember, however, that standards tend to be focused almost exclusively on academic achievement and neglect accomplishments in other areas (e.g., social skills, work habits) that may be equally important for students' long-term development.

Applying Concepts in Child Development

Development in the content domains proceeds according to the same principles that characterize cognitive development in general. One key principle is that *early acquisitions provide a foundation on which later development can build.* The table on the following page describes the behaviors of children and adolescents at five different age levels, identifies later knowledge and skills that might build on their behaviors, and offers implications for adults working with each age-group. Apply what you've learned in this chapter to fill in the empty cells in the table. When you're done, compare your responses with those in Table 10-1 in the *Study Guide and Reader.*

APPLYING CONCEPTS IN CHILD DEVELOPMENT

Identifying Building Blocks for Later Acquisitions in the Content Areas

Age	A Youngster's Experience	Developmental Concepts *Identifying Knowledge and Skills on Which Later Acquisitions Can Build*	Implications *Helping Youngsters Acquire a Solid Foundation in the Content Domain*
Infancy (Birth–2) 	As she sits in her highchair, 14-month-old Selena keeps throwing the toys that are on her tray. She seems upset when she no longer has the toys, yet as soon as her caregiver returns them to the tray, she throws them again.	By continually seeing objects move in particular directions (away from her and down to the floor), Selena is learning that certain actions lead to predictable results. Her observations in this and similar circumstances will provide a knowledge base to which she can later relate such concepts as *force*, *momentum*, and *gravity*.	
Early Childhood (2–6) 	As 5-year-old Rico builds a Lego house, he tells his teacher that he needs more red Legos. Seeing an opportunity for Rico to practice addition, the teacher says, "I see you have three red ones already. If I give you two more, how many red ones will you have altogether?" Rico counts three and then two more on his fingers and then happily responds, "Five!"		Encourage children to use any invented mathematical strategies that yield accurate results. Teach children more efficient strategies, and encourage automaticity for basic math facts, but allow children to use their previously acquired, more concrete strategies until they feel comfortable with the new ones.
Middle Childhood (6–10) 	Seven-year-old Leila's second-grade class is studying the *ight* "family" in spelling this week, so Leila is learning how to spell such words as *fight*, *tight*, and *bright*. In one assignment Leila writes a short story she calls "The Bright Nightlight," in which she uses as many *ight* words as she can.	Through repeated practice, Leila is gradually automatizing the *ight* spelling pattern. By automatizing basic spelling and grammatical rules, Leila will be able to focus more effectively on (i.e., she can devote more working memory capacity to) composition skills and effective communication in her writing.	Provide a variety of activities in which children can automatize basic reading, writing, and math skills. Such activities are typically more effective when they are authentic and motivating in their own right.
Early Adolescence (10–14)	A middle school history teacher asks students to "write a biography of a person in history as a real person who has both strengths and weaknesses." In a biography of Franklin Delano Roosevelt, 13-year-old Jesse describes Roosevelt's struggle with polio and determination to hide the severity of his disability when running for president.	By understanding that historical figures were in most respects just ordinary human beings (who were perhaps in extraordinary circumstances), Jesse will be able to apply his general knowledge of human thoughts, motives, and emotions to make sense of history—that is, to understand why historical events unfolded in particular ways.	Encourage youngsters to draw on what they know about human nature to understand why various historical figures acted as they did.
Late Adolescence (14–18) 	As her high school literature class discusses Carl Sandburg's poem "The Road and the End," 15-year-old Zia discovers that reasonable people may interpret the same information in distinctly different ways.	Zia may be able to apply her newly acquired understanding to other domains in addition to poetry. For instance, she can now more easily understand that scientists might formulate two or more different theories to explain a particular phenomenon. She may also realize that eye witnesses at an historical event might give divergent and possibly contradictory reports on what happened.	

Key Concepts

emergent literacy (p. 358)
phonological awareness (p. 359)
sight vocabulary (p. 360)
story schema (p. 361)

dyslexia (p. 364)
invented spelling (p. 370)
knowledge telling (p. 371)
knowledge transforming (p. 371)

part-whole principle (p. 375)
visual-spatial ability (p. 381)
substance schema (p. 385)
scientific reasoning (p. 385)

music literacy (p. 394)
absolute pitch (p. 395)
standards (p. 395)

Companion
Website

Now go to our Companion Website at www.prenhall.com/mcdevitt to assess your understanding of chapter content with a Practice Quiz, apply what you've learned in Essay Questions, and broaden your knowledge with links to related Developmental Psychology Web sites.

Emotional Development

chapter 11

Case Study: Merv

Case Study: Merv

Erikson's Theory of Psychosocial Development

Attachment

Emotion

Temperament and Personality

Case Study: The Girly Shirt

Summary

Applying Concepts in Child Development

When Merv looks back at her childhood, she faces some painful memories. Her father had been an alcoholic, and her mother had been regularly preoccupied with her own troubles. Neither parent took adequate care of Merv or her six brothers and sisters. Merv's parents frequently fought, and they often struck Merv and their other children. Food, shoes, clothing, and basic school supplies were scarce. And sadly, neighborhood parents considered Merv and her brothers and sisters to be dirty and unworthy playmates for their own children (Werner & Smith, 2001).

Remarkably, Merv beat the odds. Now in her forties, Merv is a productive, well-adjusted woman who works as a parent educator and has been married since age 16 to "a pretty neat guy . . . a schoolteacher" (Werner & Smith, 2001, pp. 100–101). Merv and her husband are raising their seven children in a manner that is gentle and loving. Merv also remains close to her own brothers and sisters. She leads a happy, fulfilled life.

What qualities were present in Merv's childhood that helped her ultimately become a well-adjusted, productive person? Merv credits four childhood experiences with making her strong. First of all, Merv learned to work hard:

> "As children, we took care of the yard, the house, the clothes, each other, and the cars. We did everything. My father cooked when there was something to cook, and my mother simply coped. . . . When things got rough, I learned to dig in my heels and say, 'How am I going to make this happen?' versus 'This is too hard, I quit.'" (Werner & Smith, 2001, pp. 95–96)[a]

Second, Merv had "caring and supportive people" to guide and nurture her (Werner & Smith, 2001, p. 96). Merv thrived on the care she received from her grandmother Kahaunaele. During Merv's visits to Kahaunaele's house, Kahaunaele showered Merv with love, bathed the girl, and combed the tangles out of Merv's long hair. Having had one leg amputated years before, Kahaunaele had some discomfort when she moved around, yet she disregarded her own pain and inconvenience when it came to reassuring Merv. Here's one of Merv's poignant memories of Kahaunaele:

> "I remember waking up at night with nightmares and crying, and being afraid, looking for someone to care for me. My vision, that I will never forget, is this woman [Kahaunaele] crawling on her hands and knees down the hall to come and make sure that I was okay. . . . Then, when I was all right and settled and feeling better, she would crawl back to her room." (p. 98)

Love from her grandmother was supplemented with kindness from several teachers and school staff. Merv's principal once said to her, "You are Hawaiian and you can be anything you choose to be" (p. 98). Merv was forever grateful for these words of encouragement.

Third, Merv received a good education. When she was 12 years old, she accepted an invitation to attend a prestigious school on another Hawaiian island. At the Kamehameha School, Merv was well cared for, and she progressed academically. However, at 16, Merv became pregnant, married the father of her baby, and was expelled from school. Merv was soon allowed to return when a school counselor went "out on a major limb" for her, having realized that she was "not a bad student. She just made a mistake" (Werner & Smith, 2001, p. 100). Merv learned from the school that it is possible to make good choices in life:

> "Going away to Kamehameha . . . helped me make some choices that I never knew I could. All around me in my neighborhood was alcoholism and abuse. . . . When I went away [to the school], I realized that it wasn't the way it had to be . . . I realized that I could make choices." (p. 100)

(continued)

Finally, Merv learned to trust that there is goodness in the world. Merv now sees hope as a vital quality for all young people, and notes that inspiration can be found in a variety of places:

"Somewhere, someplace down the line, somebody had taught me, 'There is somebody greater than us who loves you.' And that is my hope and my belief. Whatever that translates for you—a belief in God, a belief in a religion, a goal, a dream, something that we can hang on to. As adults, we need to give our young people hope and something to hang on to. As young people, we need to find our own." (Werner & Smith, 2001, p. 101)

[a]Reprinted from *Journeys from Childhood to Midlife: Risk, Resilience, and Recovery,* by Emmy E. Werner and Ruth S. Smith. Copyright © 2001 by Cornell University. Used by permission of the publisher, Cornell University Press.

Every child needs to be loved. Merv's own parents neglected her, but fortunately several other people cherished her and tended to her needs. Her grandmother adored her, her brothers and sisters formed lasting bonds with her, and her teachers and other school staff educated and supported her as she grew. In this chapter you will find that warm, sensitive care is the mainstay of children's first relationships. When caregivers are kind and responsive, children begin to trust these caregivers and to gain confidence in their own abilities. You will also learn that good relationships help children express their emotions productively and blossom into healthy, one-of-a-kind personalities. Finally, you will see that educators can contribute immensely to the emotional development of youngsters, as they did for Merv.

Erikson's Theory of Psychosocial Development

In the last few chapters, you learned that many changes take place in children's cognitive abilities—in their memory capacity, reasoning skills, language competencies, academic concepts, and so forth. Equally momentous transformations occur in the social-emotional domain. To give you an overview of these significant social-emotional changes, we begin with Erikson's theory of psychosocial development.

Lessons Learned from Life's Challenges

Erik Erikson was a *psychodynamic theorist* who believed that people grow from life's challenges. Specifically, Erikson suggested that people experience eight "crises," in the form of **psychosocial stages,** as they progress from birth to old age (Erikson, 1963, 1972). He called these eight levels *psychosocial* stages because the various challenges refer to qualitatively different concerns about oneself (*psycho-*) and relationships with other people (*-social*). Erikson observed that when individuals constructively address these eight challenges, they gain lasting personal assets, but when their efforts fall short, they are apt to dwell on their social-emotional problems. As they move from stage to stage, people build on the assets and deficits they have previously acquired.

Using life experience and a capacity for introspection, human beings navigate through each of the unfolding challenges. Let's look at the potential outcomes of the eight stages.

Trust versus mistrust (infancy). According to Erikson, infants' primary developmental task is to learn whether or not they can trust other people. When caregivers can be depended on to feed a hungry stomach, change an uncomfortable diaper, and provide affection at regular intervals, an infant learns *trust*—that others are consistently dependable. When caregivers ignore the infant's needs, are inconsistent in their attention, or are abusive, the infant learns *mistrust*—that the world is an unpredictable and dangerous place.

————Connecting Concepts
The cognitive benefits of *challenge* are summarized in Chapter 6. *Psychodynamic theories* are introduced in Chapter 1.

Developing a trusting relationship with a parent or other caregiver is the child's first social-emotional task.

psychosocial stages
In Erikson's theory, eight periods of life that involve age-related challenges.

Autonomy versus shame and doubt (toddler years).   As toddlers gain better control of their muscles, they become capable of satisfying some of their own needs. Toddlers learn to feed, wash, and dress themselves, and to use the toilet. When parents and other caregivers encourage self-sufficient behavior, toddlers develop *autonomy,* a sense of being able to handle many problems on their own. But when caregivers demand too much too soon, refuse to let children perform tasks of which they are capable, or ridicule early attempts at self-sufficiency, children may instead develop *shame and doubt* about their inability to conduct themselves appropriately.

Initiative versus guilt (preschool years).   If all goes well, children spend their infancy and toddler years learning that the world is a good place, people love them, and they can make things happen. Children are now ready to face Erikson's third psychosocial stage. With a growing drive for independence, preschoolers begin to have their own ideas about activities they want to pursue; for example, they may undertake simple art projects, make houses and roadways in the sandbox, or share fantasies about being superheroes with other children. When adults encourage such efforts, children develop *initiative,* an energetic drive to undertake activities independently. When adults discourage such activities, children may instead develop *guilt* about acting inappropriately or having indecent feelings.

Industry versus inferiority (elementary school years).   When they reach elementary school, children are expected to master many new skills, and they soon learn that they can gain recognition from adults through their academic assignments, athletic accomplishments, artistic performances, participation in community activities, and so on. When children complete projects and are praised for their accomplishments, they demonstrate *industry,* a pattern of working hard, gaining mastery in tool use, and persisting at lengthy tasks. But when children are ridiculed or punished for their efforts or when they find that they cannot meet adults' expectations, they may develop feelings of *inferiority* about their own abilities.

Identity versus role confusion (adolescence).   As they make the transition from childhood to adulthood, adolescents wrestle with questions of who they are and how they fit into the adult world. Values learned during childhood are now reassessed in light of a new sexual drive and the desire to be true to oneself. Initially, youths experience *role confusion*—mixed feelings about the specific ways in which they fit into society—and may experiment with a variety of actions and attitudes (e.g., affiliating with a few separate groups of friends, trying several distinct sports and hobbies, and learning about the views of various political groups). In Erikson's view, most adolescents eventually achieve a sense of *identity* regarding who they are and where their lives are headed.

Children derive a sense of accomplishment from their success on concrete tasks.

Intimacy versus isolation (young adulthood).   Once people have established their identities, they are ready to make commitments to one or more other individuals. They become capable of *intimacy*—that is, they form close, reciprocal relationships with others (e.g., through marriage or close friendships) and willingly make the sacrifices and compromises that such relationships require. When people cannot form intimate relationships (perhaps because of their reluctance or inability to forgo satisfaction of their own needs), a sense of *isolation* may result.

Generativity versus stagnation (middle age).   During middle age, the primary developmental tasks are contributing to society and guiding future generations. When an individual makes a contribution, perhaps by raising a family or by working toward the betterment of society, a sense of *generativity,* or productivity, results. In contrast, an individual who is self-centered and unable or unwilling to help others develops a feeling of *stagnation*—dissatisfaction with lack of production.

Integrity versus despair (retirement years).   According to Erikson, the final developmental task is a retrospective one, as individuals look back on their lives. They develop feelings of contentment and *integrity* if they believe they have led a happy, productive life. Alternatively, they may develop a sense of *despair* if they look back on a life of disappointments and unachieved goals.

For Erikson, successful progress through each stage is not an absolute accomplishment but rather a matter of degree. In other words, people advance at each stage when they develop *more* of the positive tendency and *less* of the negative tendency. In fact, Erikson believed that having modest deficits, balanced with adequate assets, helps people to act sensibly with the opportunities and threats they face in daily life. For example, a young boy who has learned to trust his parents is somewhat hopeful when meeting a new teacher, yet having also known a few grouchy and short-tempered grown-ups, the boy is cautious until he gets to know the teacher better. Because his optimism is tempered with restraint, the boy is ready to form healthy relationships. In contrast, with too much of a deficit—for example, when uneasiness outweighs peace of mind—a tipping point is reached, and a person becomes unhappy, isolated, and socially impaired.

Contemporary Perspectives on Erikson's Theory

Three strengths of Erikson's theory make it a compelling framework of human development. First, Erikson argued convincingly that important changes occur *throughout* the lifespan. Thanks in part to Erikson's theory, developmentalists now accept that catalysts for growth—a change in routine, an opportunity for a different kind of relationship, new desires, and a multitude of other factors—surface at every age. Second, Erikson focused on truly significant social-emotional developments, including forming trusting relationships with other people and carving out one's identity. Finally, Erikson's stages reflect the idea that development is a dynamic synthesis of nature, nurture, and a person's own motivation to make sense of life (Côté, 2005; Lerner, 2002). Erikson's integrative model fits nicely with the contemporary view that developmental changes are complex blends of several interacting factors.

These contributions notwithstanding, Erikson's theory has some serious limitations. For one thing, Erikson's observations of the human condition were largely anecdotal (Crain, 2000). The systematic research findings that have accumulated since Erikson formulated his theory indicate that his stages are probably not completely accurate descriptions of what happens at each age level. For instance, Erikson believed that most people achieve a sense of identity by the end of adolescence. But more recent evidence indicates that even by the high school years, only a small minority of young people in mainstream Western cultures have begun to think seriously about the eventual role they will play in society and the lifelong goals they wish to pursue (S. L. Archer, 1982; Durkin, 1995; Marcia, 1988). Also problematic is the fact that Erikson based his stages on observations of *men* alone. Contemporary theorists find that contrary to Erikson's sequence, many women focus on intimacy at the same time as, and in some cases before, they dwell on their own identity (Josselson, 1988). Finally, Erikson may have underestimated just how differently cultural groups think about particular assets and age levels. For example, many cultures intentionally discourage self-assertiveness (*autonomy*) in young children, sometimes as a way of protecting them from the very real dangers of their environments and at other times with the goal of deepening ties to family members (X. Chen, Rubin, & Sun, 1992; Harwood, Miller, & Irizarry, 1995; G. J. Powell, 1983). You can see a summary of the research on each of Erikson's stages in Table 11-1.

——————— Connecting Concepts

Chapter 12 describes young people's search for identity in greater detail.

Despite the gaping holes in Erikson's theory, this framework does offer a valuable perspective on human life. As we mentioned earlier, Erikson's framework has several strong points, and it offers the additional advantage to educators of inspiring optimism about young people's potential for positive growth. Most educators agree with Erikson that youngsters can usually find the inner strength they need to transform life's challenges into such worthwhile assets as a healthy self-confidence, a commitment to productive social values, and a solid work ethic. Although Erikson failed to provide detailed information about how to cultivate social-emotional skills and attributes in youngsters, other developmental scholars have taken up this cause, and we summarize their research in the remainder of this book. The developmental focus of Erikson's first stage, a trusting relationship with caregivers, has been thoroughly examined by researchers, and we look at this topic now.

		TABLE 11-1	Developmental Research Related to Erikson's Stages

Stage	Age	Research
Trust vs. Mistrust	Birth to 1 year	Developmental investigations support Erikson's assertion that learning to trust others is a fundamental need for infants (Ainsworth, Blehar, Waters, & Wall, 1978; Bowlby, 1988). However, whereas Erikson indicated that infancy was a critical time for having a first trusting relationship, recent research indicates that children sometimes get second chances. For example, when children receive *un*responsive care during early infancy, their first attachments are likely to be *in*secure, but if their later care is warm and sensitive, the children may develop trusting relationships.
Autonomy vs. Shame and Doubt	1 to 3 years	Evidence supports Erikson's conclusion that toddlers have a strong will to exert themselves and practice emerging skills without restriction. For example, toddlers are motivated to handle objects, walk on their own, and explore a home's forbidden areas. Yet not every culture agrees with Erikson that autonomy is a virtue: Some groups see young children's drive for independence as an immature impulse that must be tempered (T. A. Dennis, Cole, Zahn-Waxler, & Mizuta, 2002).
Initiative vs. Guilt	3 to 5 years	Erikson aptly portrayed preschool-aged children as radiating a sense of purpose. Research confirms that young children show initiative in imaginative play, enthusiastic conversations, and effortful engagement with toys. With his attention on shame, doubt, and guilt in young children, Erikson also paved the way for contemporary research on these emotions. For example, developmental studies indicate that young children tend to feel distressed when they break a rule or fail to live up to a standard (Kagan, 1984; Kochanska, 1993).
Industry vs. Inferiority	6 to 10 years	Erikson saw middle childhood as a period for gaining confidence in completing demanding tasks proficiently. Cross-cultural research indicates that adults routinely assign chores to children in this age range, reflecting widespread agreement that elementary-school aged children can act responsibly. But research also indicates that children compare their own abilities to those of peers, paying special attention to their relative proficiency in domains that they personally value, and they may lose confidence if they see themselves coming up short relative to others (Harter, 1999).
Identity vs. Role Confusion	10 to 20 years	Erikson's focus on identity has spawned a lot of research. Studies generally confirm Erikson's assertion that young people actively engage in soul searching related to who they are, what they believe in, and where they are going (Marcia, 1980, 1988). The tendency to wrestle with identity issues extends for a longer period than Erikson proposed, however. Researchers have also suggested that for girls and women, a focus on intimacy (the next stage in Erikson's model) may occur simultaneously with or precede the focus on identity (Josselson, 1988).
Intimacy vs. Isolation	Young adulthood	Research evidence confirms that taking part in intimate relationships is a typical concern of the young adult years. However, some critics suggest that being closely connected with others is a human quality that transcends any single time period (Gilligan, 1982). Furthermore, the early adult years are more complex than is captured in Erikson's primary focus on intimacy. For example, young adults frequently struggle also with identity concerns, career prospects and, in many cases, family matters, including the rearing of their own children.
Generativity vs. Stagnation	Middle age	During middle age, most adults organize their lives such that they give back to the next generation, as Erikson proposed. One common critique of Erikson's theory is that he believed that men were primarily concerned with their careers and women with parenting their children. Yet in mainstream Western culture today, career and family are frequently serious concerns for both men and women (Peterson & Stewart, 1996).
Integrity vs. Despair	Retirement years	Looking back on one's life is an important task for many older adults, and Erikson was on the mark in this regard (R. N. Butler, 1963; Haight, 1992). However, older adults tackle many other developmental tasks, including finding ways to cope with losses and make the best of their later years (Baltes, 1997). In other words, many older adults live in the present as well as the past.

Attachment

Human beings of all ages seem to have a fundamental need to feel socially connected to, and loved and respected by, other people. In other words, they have a **need for relatedness** (Connell, 1990; Furrer & Skinner, 2003; Honig, 2002). Across the lifespan, this need is fulfilled with social bonds of various types, including friendships, romantic ties, marital partnerships, and family relationships.

The child's first bond, called an **attachment,** is an enduring emotional tie that unites the child to one or more caregivers and has far-reaching effects on the child's development (Ainsworth, 1973). In the last few decades, the dominant theoretical perspective on

need for relatedness
Fundamental need to feel socially connected to, and loved and respected by, other people.

attachment
An enduring emotional tie uniting one person to another.

caregiver-infant relationships has been **ethological attachment theory,** a perspective originally suggested by John Bowlby (1951, 1958), fleshed out by Mary Ainsworth (1963, 1973; Ainsworth et al., 1978), and tested and refined by many contemporary psychologists. Ethological attachment theory suggests that the human capacity for close relationships evolved over millions of years of human history. Attachment theorists speculate that severe environmental conditions in our ancestors' past made it necessary for small children to stay close to and learn all they could from their parents. Obviously, the parents also had to be inclined to nurture and protect their children. These mutually close ties helped children to survive their infancy and to be motivated to imitate how parents hunted, gathered crops, used tools, and interacted with others. This capacity for attachment, then, was presumably passed down from generation to generation.

In today's world, attachments can be seen in infants' crying, clinging, and crawling toward parents and other caregivers when distressed. Under less stressful conditions, infants show affection with snuggles, smiles, and cooing. However, what develops in infants is not simply a collection of discrete behaviors, such as crying and smiling, but also an underlying system of relating to parents. This system has two important elements. First, infants learn to use their parents as a *safe haven*. Infants depend on parents for protection from harm and for soothing comfort when feelings of hunger, fatigue, or fear escalate to unmanageable levels. Infants also use parents as a *secure base*. Infants relax in the presence of their parents and go about crawling here and there, glancing back now and then for reassuring looks from parents.

It takes time, maturation, and experience before infants are able to use caregivers as a safe haven and secure base. Let's see how their attachments develop.

Developmental Course of Children's Attachments

In the process of forming attachments, infants learn a lot about themselves, their caregivers, and interpersonal relationships. For example, a baby slowly develops expectations about shared routines ("When Grandma says, 'Peek a boo,' I hide my eyes and we both laugh"), beliefs about other people's trustworthiness ("Mommy takes care of me"), emotional connections ("I love my Daddy"), and a sense of self ("People love me; I am loveable"). To end up with this coherent system of expectations, infants must first gain considerable social experience.

Birth to 2 months.   Newborn infants are indiscriminately social—they watch and listen to all people in their vicinity. Their first gestures seem reflexive and unintentional, as when a newborn baby turns toward a human face or looks away when overstimulated. But infants are quick learners and by about the second month, they recognize familiar people through their faces, voices, and smells. Nevertheless, infants treat adults in an equal opportunity fashion, allowing anyone with the right touch to comfort them (Schaffer, 1996).

Two to 6 months.   From the second to the sixth month after birth, infants begin to learn that they cannot count on just anyone for affection and attention, but instead must turn to the few people who regularly care for them. By the third month, infants recognize and smile selectively at people they know best (Camras, Malatesta, & Izard, 1991). During interactions between infants and caregivers, adults carry most of the burden for initiating and maintaining the social exchange. For example, caregivers notice when a baby is alert and calm, use this occasion to extend a friendly greeting, and wait for the baby to make a simple response that they treat as the baby's turn in the interaction. With experience, infants learn the rhythms of interaction and come to enjoy playful exchanges with caregivers, such as counting toes or singing during a diaper change. Toward the end of this period, infants continue to accept comfort from unfamiliar adults, although nature is about to put the breaks on their spontaneity.

Seven months to 2 years.   At about 7 months, infants show full-fledged attachments to one person or a small number of people, including, perhaps, a mother, father, grandparent, professional caregiver, or some combination of these and other individuals. Attachments can be seen when infants reach out to be picked up by familiar caregivers; protest when separated from them; and wriggle, coo, and show unmistakable looks of recognition when particular caregivers walk into the room.

─────── Connecting Concepts
In Chapter 1 you learned that human genes dispose children to adapt effectively to their environment.

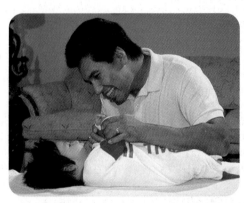

The attachments that infants form with parents and other primary caregivers provide a foundation for later relationships.

ethological attachment theory
Theoretical perspective that emphasizes the benefits to children, particularly protection from harm and a secure base from which to explore the environment, derived from close bonds wih caregivers.

During this period, infants also begin to show intense fears. Just as infants are learning to crawl and are motivated to explore, nature activates a useful fear of the unknown. As you might guess, the preferred antidote to scary things is direct contact with familiar caregivers. When puzzling phenomena appear out of nowhere, such as a barking dog (woof!) or a jack-in-the-box's loud, unexpected effect (pop!), infants demand reassurance (now!).

Adults unknown to the baby likewise now trigger fearful reactions. In the latter half of the first year of life and well into the second year, an unfamiliar adult often incites fear—**stranger anxiety**—in infants (Mangelsdorf, Shapiro, & Marzolf, 1995). This fear often intensifies into a red-faced, tearful, arm-flapping demand for the safe haven of a familiar caregiver. Of course, not all strangers will provoke this kind of reaction, but it is common for infants to become wary of unfamiliar people at this time.

The latter part of infancy is not simply about fright and flight, however. Infants increasingly engage in pleasant interactions with caregivers, as they become active partners in social interchanges. Children begin to take turns in a conversation, as you can see in 16-month-old Corwin's interchanges with his mother in the "Literacy: Infancy" video clip on Observation CD 2. Corwin's vocalizations are simple, but they serve nicely as contributions to the exchange.

Early childhood.   In early childhood young children who have enjoyed loving care from parents now actively reciprocate with affectionate gestures of their own. For example, children often create "love notes" to their parents, as you can see in the following "I Love Mommy" exercise.

Observe Corwin taking turns in a conversation with his mother in the "Literacy: Infancy" clip on Observation CD 2.

INTERPRETING CHILDREN'S ARTIFACTS AND ACTIONS
I Love Mommy

Three-year-old Ivy and 4-year-old Alex prepared these notes (at left and right, respectively) for their mothers. As you examine the notes, consider what the two children are trying to communicate and the cultural symbols they use to represent their feelings.

These two notes communicate the children's simple, heartfelt affection for their moms. Ivy and Alex have chosen the same graphic device, a stacks of hearts, to represent the depth of their feelings for their mothers. Hearts are a common symbol of love in mainstream Western culture. Young children often choose other devices as well, such as drawing themselves holding hands with a loved one.

As they did in their infant days, young children continue to use familiar caregivers as a safe haven, particularly when they are sick, scared, or distressed. However, urgent protests

stranger anxiety
Fear of unfamiliar adults in the latter half of the first year and into the second year of life.

over separations are fewer now, and stranger anxiety also has become less intense, possibly because children are finally convinced that their parents *will* return to get them at the end of the day, and in the meantime, warm, reliable teachers will protect them (Main & Cassidy, 1988; Schaffer, 1996). Increasingly, children also find that peers can play a supportive role in their daily lives. Particularly when they have enjoyed loving relationships with parents, young children play happily with peers in parents' absence (Howes, 1999).

Middle childhood and adolescence.   As they grow, youngsters venture farther away but still maintain close ties with family members. Youngsters expect parents to keep tabs on them, to celebrate their successes, and to be there when needed. Routine separations (such as going to school each day or to summer camp for a week) generally induce little of the anxiety associated with late-infancy separations, although a few elementary school children continue to be anxious before and during separations. When relationships with parents are seriously disrupted, perhaps because of divorce or death, youngsters do tend to become angry, aggressive, or physically ill, and they may withdraw from their customary activities (Pribilsky, 2001).

As they progress through adolescence, youngsters remain attached to parents and siblings, but family relationships change. Adolescents now prefer to receive their affection behind the scenes, and they also become increasingly close to friends and romantic partners (Mayseless, 2005). At this age peers offer reassurance to one another when times are tough, providing a new kind of safe haven, one that permits equal participation and reciprocal obligations. Adolescents do not usually renounce their ties to parents, but they do strengthen connections with peers and prepare (consciously or not) for their inevitable departure from the family nest.

The developmental course of attachments we have outlined is one that assumes a trusting relationship with parents and parental figures. As we now see, most caregivers earn the trust of their children, but in unfortunate exceptions a few caregivers do not.

Attachments to family members continue to be important during middle childhood and adolescence.

Individual Differences in Children's Attachments

If you look around at young children you know, you may notice variations in how they respond when afraid, hurt, or upset. Some children seek and find comfort in the reassuring arms of caregivers; some are clingy and fretful; and others want to be left alone, denying that anything is (ever) wrong.

To study such differences in the laboratory, Ainsworth created a mildly stressful situation for 1-year-old infants. First, a mother and her infant were brought to a playroom and left alone. A stranger (a research assistant) soon entered the room and attempted to play with the baby. After 3 minutes, the mother left the room, leaving the baby alone with the stranger. Subsequently, the mother returned and the stranger departed, leaving mother and baby together. Next, mother departed and baby was alone; the stranger returned at this point. Finally, the mother returned and the stranger departed (Ainsworth et al., 1978). This sequence, commonly known as the *Strange Situation,* has become a classic research tool for assessing attachment in young children.

In the Strange Situation, attention is focused primarily on the child's behavior. Observers rate the child's attempts to seek contact with a caregiver, the physical proximity of the child to the caregiver, the child's resistance to or avoidance of the caregiver, and the child's level of distress. From such ratings, the child is given one of several classifications:

secure attachment
Attachment classification in which children use attachment figures as a source of comfort in times of distress and as a secure base from which to explore.

insecure-avoidant attachment
Attachment classification in which children appear somewhat indifferent to attachment figures.

- Infants who exhibit **secure attachment** seem to use caregivers as a secure base. When caregivers are present, infants actively explore new toys and surroundings. When caregivers return after leaving the room, infants smile at or talk to them, move over to greet them, or in other ways seek proximity to them. About 65 percent of infants from typical middle-class Western backgrounds are classified as securely attached (R. A. Thompson, 1998).
- Infants who exhibit **insecure-avoidant attachment** seem oblivious to a caregiver's presence. They fail to greet the caregiver upon his or her return and may even look away. Instead, they go about their business independently, and they are somewhat

superficial in their interactions with toys. About 20 percent of children participating in Strange Situation studies are classified as insecure-avoidant (R. A. Thompson, 1998).

- Infants who exhibit **insecure-resistant attachment** seem preoccupied with their caregivers, but they are not easily comforted during reunions. When caregivers return, these infants remain distressed and angry; they may rush to parents and other caregivers yet quickly struggle to be released. Insecure-resistant infants comprise about 15 percent of participants in Strange Situation studies (R. A. Thompson, 1998).

- More serious problems in attachment, which were not part of Ainsworth's original classification, have subsequently been identified. For example, a **disorganized and disoriented attachment** style has been documented (Main & Solomon, 1986, 1990). Infants in this group lack a coherent way of responding to stressful events. These infants may be calm and contented one minute yet, without provocation, become angry the next minute. They may interrupt their own actions midstream, for example by crawling toward caregivers and then suddenly freezing with apprehension. In addition, a very few children show *no* attachment behaviors or exhibit other extremely serious problems, such as displaying fear of caregivers rather than being comforted by them. Such serious problems frequently call for intervention by trained professionals. Only a small minority of children show a disorganized and disoriented attachment, no attachment, or other serious attachment problem.

The Observation Guidelines table "Assessing Young Children's Attachment Security" summarizes how children with particular kinds of attachments might act. In observing children, teachers and caregivers should be careful that they not take any single response from a child too seriously—that they instead look for patterns of behavior over time. We turn now to how attachments originate, expand from a single person to multiple caregivers, and affect long-term adjustment.

Origins of Attachment Security

What factors lead to different patterns of attachment? Research has shown that the quality of the caregiver-child relationship, the cultural setting, and the child's own behavior each play a role.

Quality of caregiver-child relationship.   The relationship between a caregiver and child is the most powerful factor in attachment security. When caregivers are sensitive and responsive to young children, protect them, and provide for their needs, children are inclined to develop secure attachments (J. S. Chisholm, 1996; Lamb, 2005; NICHD Early Child Care Research Network, 1997). Caregivers who are sensitive and responsive show these qualities:

- *They consistently respond to infants' needs.* Caregivers establish routines for feeding, diapering, and holding infants. They do not run to every whimper, but they are faithfully available when infants express genuine needs (Cassidy & Berlin, 1994). Caregivers who fail to show this quality may be neglectful or available only occasionally; others are callous to infants' feelings.

- *They regularly express affection.* Caregivers dote on babies by caressing them, holding them gently, looking into their eyes, talking to them, and expressing tenderness and warmth. Caregivers who fail to show this quality may be withdrawn or even hostile and rejecting.

- *They permit babies to influence the pace and direction of their mutual interactions.* Caregivers let infants take the lead on occasion. They carefully note where infants are looking, notice their body posture, and recognize when infants want to interact (Isabella & Belsky, 1991; D. N. Stern, 1977). Caregivers learn to act in synchrony with infants, letting them take a turn in an interaction by smiling, moving their hands, or babbling. Caregivers who fail to show this quality may be overly intrusive, perhaps to the point that babies look away from them, cry, or try to go to sleep. Other caregivers may fail to notice or respond to infants' bids for affection—for example, they may ignore infants' attempts to make eye contact.

Study Guide and Reader ———————
To learn more about serious attachment problems in children, see Supplementary Reading 11-1.

insecure-resistant attachment
Attachment classification in which children are preoccupied with their attachment figures but gain little comfort from them when distressed.

disorganized and disoriented attachment
Attachment classification in which children lack a single coherent way of responding to attachment figures.

OBSERVATION GUIDELINES

Assessing Young Children's Attachment Security

Characteristic	Look For	Example	Implication
Secure Attachment	• Active, intentional exploration of the environment in the presence of the caregiver • Protest at being separated from a caregiver; ability to be soothed when the caregiver returns • Initial wariness of strangers, with subsequent acceptance if reassured by the caregiver	Luis cries when his father drops him off at the child care center in the morning. After a few minutes, he settles down and crawls to a familiar and affectionate caregiver who is beginning to become another attachment figure for him.	It is natural for young children to resist separation from family members. Help them establish a routine of saying good-bye in the morning, and give them extra attention during this transition. Reassure parents and other family members by describing children's individual ways of settling down and the activities children typically turn to when they relax.
Insecure-Avoidant Attachment	• Superficial exploration of the environment • Indifference to a caregiver's departure; failure to seek comfort upon the caregiver's return • Apparent discomfort around strangers, but without an active resistance to their overtures	Jennifer walks around her new child care center with a frown on her face. She parts easily with her mother, and after a short time she seems to adjust to her new environment. Jennifer glances up when her mother comes at the end of the day, but she doesn't seem overjoyed about her mother's return.	Independence from parents is often a sign of children's familiarity with child care or preschool settings. For children who seem at ease with separation, support them throughout the day. When children appear indifferent to family members, form your own affectionate relationships with these children, knowing that such relationships could become children's first secure ones.
Insecure-Resistant Attachment	• Exceptional clinginess and anxiety with caregiver • Agitation and distress at the caregiver's departure; continued crying or fussing after the caregiver returns • Apparent fear of strangers; tendency to stay close to caregiver in new situation	Irene tightly clutches her mother as the two enter the preschool building, and she stays close by as her mother signs her in for the morning. She is quite upset when her mother leaves yet finds little comfort in the mother's return a few hours later.	If children appear anxious when they enter a new child care or preschool setting, give them extra time to part from their parents. Sometimes a "comfort" object from home (a teddy bear or blanket) can help. Be patient and reassuring as you interact with these children, knowing that they may eventually form a secure attachment to you.
Disorganized and Disoriented Attachment or Other Serious Attachment Problem	• Unpredictable emotional responses • Cautious approaches to familiar caregiver • By end of first year, failure to contact caregiver when distressed • Reckless exploration and no use of caregiver as secure base • Reversed roles, with excessive concern about caregiver • No signs of attachment to family members or other familiar caregivers, or fear of them • Indiscriminately friendly behavior with no preferential actions toward family members • Signs of overwhelming grief after the death of a primary caregiver	Myles seems lost at school. He arrives hungry, walks aimlessly for some time, and eventually sits to play with blocks. He is aggressive with his peers, and his teacher sees bruises on his arms.	Provide special attention and monitoring to children who seem disorganized and disoriented in their attachment. Be on the lookout for signs of abuse, and be ready to seek advice from authorities. Remember that these children are *not* doomed to serious lifelong problems, but you must work hard to establish positive, trusting relationships with them.

Sources: Ainsworth et al., 1978; Greenberg, 1999; Main & Solomon, 1986, 1990; R. A. Thompson, 1998; Zeanah, 2000.

Cultural setting. A second factor affecting children's attachments is the cultural setting (Rothbaum, Weisz, Pott, Miyake, & Morelli, 2000). Cultures differ appreciably in their value for a close, exclusive relationship between parents and infants. Here are two examples:

- In some studies with Japanese children, a high proportion of children displayed behaviors that researchers interpreted as insecure-resistant attachment. Many Japanese infants became quite upset when mothers left the room, perhaps because Japanese people emphasize physical closeness, intimacy, and strong mother-child bonds (Miyake, Chen, & Campos, 1985; Takahashi, 1990). In Japan, infants' separation from mother is not common, babysitters are rare, and when mothers leave their children, it is often with grandparents (Saarni, Mumme, & Campos, 1998).

- In northern Germany, many infants display behaviors that, on the surface, indicate insecure-avoidant attachment (K. E. Grossmann, Grossmann, Huber, & Wartner, 1981). These babies do not fret much when their mothers leave the playroom, nor do they move frantically toward mothers when they return. Mothers regularly leave infants at home alone or outside supermarkets as the mothers do brief errands. The time alone is not lengthy, but it happens often enough to be routine. These children seem to grow accustomed to getting along on their own, at least for brief periods of time.

These cultural examples suggest that children get a general sense of how often their parents come and go. When separation is rare, infants may expect parents to always be present. When parents must leave, these infants are overwhelmed with distress, a state fueled by parents' own anxiety over the separation. In contrast, when parents leave infants routinely, infants learn to get on by themselves for the time being. Thus different cultural groups help infants to develop trusting relationships in ways that are not always validly assessed by the Strange Situation. However, these normal cultural variations should be distinguished from circumstances *within* cultures in which parents are harsh, abusive, apathetic, or neglectful, and in which infants learn to withdraw, fear primary caregivers, or let negative emotions intensify into uncontrolled outcries.

Children's contributions.   A third factor affecting the security of children's attachment is the children themselves. Children actively participate in their relationships with caregivers by making their needs known, relaxing when comforted, and reciprocating with affection.

Children's dispositions may also play a small part in the types of attachments they form. Through their unique ways of handling stress and relating to others, children influence the manner in which caregivers respond to them. Whereas some fuss a lot when scared, others protest less adamantly. Perhaps those who are prone to be fearful and irritable are more difficult to care for, and those who are even-tempered and sociable invite positive interactions. However, differences in infants' behaviors play only a minor role in attachment security. Most parents are generally able to be sensitive to a wide range of dispositions in children.

Similarly, for most children with disabilities, their special circumstances may play only a small role in the kinds of attachments they form. For example, babies who are premature, show developmental delays, and are unusually fussy tend to develop secure attachments as long as their individual needs are met sensitively (van IJzendoorn, Goldberg, Kroonenberg, & Frenkel, 1992). Likewise, many babies with chromosomal or genetic disorders form secure attachments with parents who provide responsive and attentive care (E. A. Carlson, Sampson, & Sroufe, 2003). Some children with neurological disorders do behave in ways that test the patience of even the most nurturing of parents, however, and in such cases the guidance and support of professionals may be helpful (E. A. Carlson et al., 2003).

Connecting Concepts
Chapter 3 describes the development of children with chromosomal irregularities and genetic defects.

Multiple Attachments

Because women physically bear children and often do most of the feeding, bathing, and diapering, early research examined *mothers* as primary attachment figures (Ainsworth et al., 1978; Bowlby 1969/1982). This emphasis is understandable, but fathers can be equally passionate parents, waking in the night to feed children, cheering them when they first walk and talk, and advocating for them when the rest of the world lets them down.

When two parents are present in the home, infants frequently show a preference for one parent to begin with and soon thereafter include the second parent as an attachment figure. Both parents are likely to instill secure attachments when they sensitively respond to children's needs and are present in children's lives for an extended time (Howes, 1999). Nevertheless, mothers and fathers sometimes go about expressing their warmth in slightly different ways. For example, in a study comparing styles of parents with 1- to 2-year-olds, mothers spent more time caring for infants while fathers spent more time with infants in pretend play (Kazura, 2000). A playful style, when sensitive and challenging, seems to spur infants on to explore their physical and social environment (K. Grossmann et al., 2002). You can observe a father's tender and playful style with his 7-month-old daughter in the "Emotional Development: Infancy" video clip on Observation CD 2.

Observe Madison and her father interact playfully and affectionately in the "Emotional Development: Infancy" clip on Observation CD 2.

Many infants form close bonds with their older siblings.

Contemporary research on attachment examines the nurturing bonds that children form with other people in addition to parents (Howes, 1999). Children in Kenya, for instance, are cared for extensively by older siblings and protest loudly when separated from them (Weisner, 1997). In other cultures, including the Israeli kibbutzim, children spend considerable time in settings with adults who are not members of their families (J. F. Jackson, 1986, 1993; van IJzendoorn, Sagi, & Lambermon, 1992). Such networks of nurturing adults have important benefits for children, who can rely on many trustworthy individuals for affectionate care (Howes, 1999). Also, as children's needs change, access to multiple caregivers provides options for different kinds of support (C. B. Fisher et al., 1998). For example, a 1-year-old crawls to Grandma when a stranger enters the family home; at 6, the same child now seeks advice from his uncle as he faces bullies on the playground; and at 14, the youth has heart-to-heart talks with Dad about career options.

Children also routinely form attachments to employed caregivers and teachers in child care centers and classrooms. Secure attachments with these figures, as with parents, depend upon sensitive care, sustained relationships, and emotional investment (Howes, 1999). Unfortunately, long-term relationships are not possible when employees come and go. Under conditions of employee change, new caregivers must be patient as children slowly learn to trust them (Barnas & Cummings, 1994).

Attachment Security and Later Development

A secure attachment during infancy predicts later positive long-term outcomes in youngsters. In Western cultures, children who have been securely attached as infants tend to become relatively independent, empathic, socially competent preschoolers, especially in comparison with children who have been insecurely attached (Kestenbaum, Farber, & Sroufe, 1989; Sroufe, 1983; Vaughn, Egeland, Sroufe, & Waters, 1979). In middle childhood and adolescence, they tend to be self-confident, adjust easily to school environments, establish productive relationships with teachers and peers, and do well at classroom tasks (Elicker, Englund, & Sroufe, 1992; Sroufe, Carlson, & Shulman, 1993; Urban, Carlson, Egeland, & Sroufe, 1991). It is important to note that not all of these patterns apply to children in non-Western cultures. As you learned earlier in this chapter, caregivers in Japan encourage infants to rely on immediate family members. For Japanese children, close and affectionate relationships with caregivers may be more likely to lead to dependence on caregivers' benevolence and a desire to act harmoniously with others than to independence from caregivers and sociability with people outside the family (Rothbaum et al., 2000).

Attachment theorists believe that a secure attachment sets the stage for later relationships and helps children form positive, self-fulfilling expectations about other people. As children gain experience with primary caregivers, they begin to form an understanding, or *mental representation,* of what relationships with other people are like (Bowlby, 1969/1982, 1973; R. M. Ryan, Stiller, & Lynch, 1994). Their understanding of "typical" relationships is largely unconscious but nevertheless influential in directing how they relate to other individuals, including teachers (Maier, Bernier, Pekrun, Zimmermann, & Grossmann, 2004; R. M. Ryan et al., 1994). Secure children expect other people to be trustworthy, and they give second chances to those who initially let them down—actions that feed and sustain healthy interpersonal ties. In contrast, children with insecure attachments may form mental representations—and expectations—of other people as untrustworthy (Main, 1995). If you've ever visited a preschool, perhaps you know what we're talking about. Some children, curious and affectionate, flock to you with books and puzzles in hand, assuming you will want to join them in their chosen activities (we certainly urge you to do so!). In making these social overtures, children convey their expectations: "Unfamiliar adults find me likeable." Such positive expectations are not universal, however, as you might expect from our previous discussion of individual differences in attachment security. A few children may look at you suspiciously, not because they're shy, but because they wonder, "What harm might you cause me?"

Although attachment theorists initially suggested that an infant's early attachments to primary caregivers (especially the mother) set the tone for *all* future relationships (e.g., Bowlby, 1973), more recent research has shown otherwise. As Merv's experience in the opening case study reveals, the kinds of bonds children form with their mothers do not firmly dictate the kinds of bonds they make with other caregivers. Furthermore, as youngsters grow older, their attachments to peers—perhaps to best friends and, eventually, to romantic partners—may be significantly different from those they have previously formed with parents (M. W. Baldwin, Keelan, Fehr, Enns, & Koh-Rangarajoo, 1996; La Guardia, Ryan, Couchman, & Deci, 2000). Apparently, growing children and adolescents form not one mental representation (based solely on their early attachment to a primary caregiver), but several mental representations of what interpersonal relationships are like (M. W. Baldwin et al., 1996).

Originally secure bonds and positive mental representations of relationships may also change as a result of stressful events. For instance, children who initially form secure attachments but later live through one or more traumatic events (perhaps parents get divorced, a family member dies or suffers a debilitating illness, or the children are physically or sexually abused by a family member) may have difficulty forming good relationships as adolescents or adults (Lewis, Feiring, & Rosenthal, 2000; E. Waters, Merrick, Treboux, Crowell, & Albersheim, 2000; Weinfield, Sroufe, & Egeland, 2000).

Children's adaptability in their close relationships has implications for practitioners outside the family. We now look at what teachers and caregivers can do to support children's attachments.

Implications of Attachment Research

As we have seen, infant attachments provide the foundation for later relationships. This foundation can be rebuilt if it's shaky, and it must occasionally be bolstered if, despite a solid beginning, it later weakens in the face of adverse circumstances (R. A. Thompson, 1998). In essence, secure attachment is like a multivitamin: It increases the chances of, but does not guarantee, good health. Conversely, a child with an early insecure attachment may, with love and guidance, become a happy, productive adult. Drawing from attachment literature, we offer these recommendations for adults who work with children and adolescents:

● *Care for young children in a warm and sensitive manner.* Although family members are usually the recipients of children's first attachments, young children often form close bonds with employed caregivers. As you might expect, the recipe for good care of infants is the same in a child care center as it is at home—affection, attention, and reliable care from familiar people. The Development and Practice feature "Offering Warm and Sensitive Care to Infants and Toddlers" illustrates such high-quality care.

● *Give children time to adjust to you.* It takes time for infants to form bonds with new caregivers, although the particular difficulties infants face may depend partly on the quality of their relationship with parents. For example, infants who are securely attached to parents usually need time to adjust to an unfamiliar caregiver's unique personality and style of responding to them. In the meantime, caregivers will need to offer lots of comfort when infants protest separations from parents. Infants who have not yet experienced sensitive care may feel anxious or withdrawn before they are able to conclude that a new adult can be trusted. While children are adjusting, practitioners can be affectionate, meet the children's needs, empathize with their feelings, and celebrate their accomplishments. In fact, children without prior secure attachments to parents often benefit immensely when other caregivers act consistently and lovingly (Howes & Ritchie, 1998; NICHD Early Child Care Research Network, 1997).

Children often form strong attachments to caregivers who sensitively care for them over an extended time.

● *Model affectionate caregiving for family members.* Parents who maltreat their children were often maltreated themselves as children (Egami, Ford, & Crum, 1996). They may not know what it feels like to have affectionate relationships with children. One of the most effective tactics family educators can take with insensitive parents is to *show* them—in person or through videotapes—how eagerly infants devour affectionate gestures, especially during such routine games as playing peekaboo and sharing simple nursery rhymes (Bakermans-Kranenburg, van IJzendoorn, & Juffer, 2003). Caregivers and educators can demonstrate how they return a baby's smiles, vocalizations, and eye contact and hold the baby tenderly. They also can point out the signals infants give to indicate that they are not ready to play (e.g., averting a gaze) or have had enough (e.g., pouting). Finally, family educators might ask parents to practice relaxing together on the couch or carrying small

DEVELOPMENT AND PRACTICE

Offering Warm and Sensitive Care to Infants and Toddlers

- Give warm and responsive care, meeting infants' needs in a timely fashion.

  An infant program has one caregiver for every three infants so that no child has to be left unattended for very long. When it is impossible to tend immediately to the needs of individual children, the caregiver reassures children that their needs are important and that she will provide care as soon as possible.

- Respond positively to newly developed abilities.

  Caregivers in one center celebrate milestones as they notice them, including new teeth, advances in crawling, first steps, and first words. They share their admiration with family members but are sensitive to the desire of parents and other family members to be among the first to witness the accomplishment: "Raj is getting ready to walk, isn't he!"

- Be polite but matter-of-fact when referring to infants' bodies.

  The director of an infant program trains staff members to use neutral terms for body functions. For example, she asks a new teacher not to use the term "stinky baby," but instead to make a simple statement that an infant's diaper needs to be changed.

- Set limits and redirect unacceptable behavior in a firm, but gentle way.

  The director of an infant-toddler program reminds teachers that their role is one of a *nurturer* who helps children learn self-control rather than an *authority figure* who doles out punishments. Concretely, he suggests, "Tell children what they *can* do instead of telling them what they can*not* do. For example, you might say, 'Walk inside, please. Run outside.'"

- Structure group infant care so that infants can form and maintain stable relationships with caregivers.

  An infant-toddler program is arranged into separate rooms so that each caregiver has a small number of infants with whom to form close relationships. Toddler teachers make a point to visit the infant room occasionally, so that they get to know children who will soon be moving to their room. In another center, caregivers arrange groups of children that stay together; as the infants outgrow the "Infant Room," for example, they "graduate" together to the "Toddler Room," and their caregiver goes with them.

infants in snuggly carriers close to the chest (Anisfeld, Casper, Nosyce, & Cunningham, 1990; A. F. Lieberman, Weston, & Pawl, 1991).

● *Encourage parents to watch their children's play.* Practitioners can encourage parents to watch their children carefully and notice what the children attend to and enjoy. Babies can learn a great deal by simply looking at their fingers, sucking on their toes, and listening to voices. When parents appreciate the significance of infants' spontaneous learning, they are more inclined to affirm and extend it ("Look at that mirror, Abigail! Is it shiny? Do you see yourself?").

● *Encourage parents to think about how infants and children understand events.* Infants can be mysterious—even exasperating—creatures. Parents do not always understand what makes their babies "tick" ("Why does Mike keep jumping out of his crib? Every time he does this, he gets hurt. What is he *thinking*?"). Professionals can casually share ideas about infants' motives, feelings, and understandings to help parents appreciate how babies might view the world ("Mike is one determined little guy, isn't he? He really wants to explore his environment!"). When parents reflect on how infants feel and construe events, attachments tend to be more secure (Koren-Karie, Oppenheim, Dolev, Sher, & Etzion-Carasso, 2002).

● *When parents divorce, help children remain attached to both parents.* Many divorced parents share custody of children, making it likely that children will maintain attachments to both parents. Teachers can help by sending home duplicate copies of newsletters and correspondence to both parents' homes. Family educators and counselors can advise parents on practical issues that may arise when children move back and forth between two households. For example, they can talk with parents about ways in which children of different ages handle rotations between two households (J. B. Kelly & Lamb, 2000).

● *Acknowledge and encourage multiple attachments.* In the child care center and at school, children may talk about a variety of people in their lives—brothers and sisters, aunts and uncles, grandparents, and neighbors. Teachers and other practitioners can encourage children to invite these individuals to school events and orientation meetings.

● *Promote social bonds in children of all ages.* Developmental researchers tend to emphasize attachments in infancy, but close bonds are a lifelong human need. During childhood and adolescence, youngsters want to belong to the various communities in which they spend time—families, classrooms, clubs, and sports teams, for example. Adults can foster ties with and among young people by giving them chances to become involved, work together in projects, and so forth.

Adults can promote bonds in young people of all ages.

● *Support families when parents experience distress.* Parental discord and other family stresses decrease the likelihood that parents have the energy to attend to infants' needs. To help avert the serious attachment problems that may result (Rutter & O'Connor, 1999), practitioners can share information with families about local agencies that provide assistance. For example, parents who have been out of work for a long time may appreciate hearing about local employment agencies and charitable organizations, provided that such information is presented privately and tactfully.

● *Offer a range of services when children are placed with new families.* When children are removed from families because of maltreatment or neglect, children frequently form healthy bonds with new caregivers (K. Chisholm, Carter, Ames, & Morison, 1995; Howes & Segal, 1993; Marcovitch et al., 1997). However, professionals who work with children and their new families should not leave this adjustment to chance. Instead, they can prepare the new families to recognize and meet the children's individual needs. For example, a foster family might be advised to expect temper tantrums from an 8-year-old child who has recently joined the family. Family members can learn to communicate their expectations for controlled behavior, follow through with agreed-upon consequences when rules are violated, and persist in showing love even though the child has not yet learned to reciprocate with affection.

● *Encourage sympathetic dispositions in children.* Some children who have had few affectionate relationships have poorly developed social skills and so may, in many people's eyes, be difficult children to like. They may appear self-centered and unconcerned about others' distress—for example, they may hit a child who has gotten hurt rather than offer sympathy (Volling, 2001). To help a child who seems uncaring, you can model the appropriate reactions when someone is hurt, talk about the hurt person's feelings, and encourage the child to offer help and show sympathy.

● *Address the needs of both parents and infants when parents struggle with unmet emotional needs.* When mothers are emotionally depressed, they may be unresponsive toward their infants, or hostile and intrusive (Teti, Gelfand, Messinger, & Isabella, 1995). In turn, infants may become chronically sad and withdrawn. Professional intervention that guides these mothers to address their own unresolved emotional needs may be a necessary step before mothers are able to use an involved, affectionate parenting style (Benoit & Parker, 1994; Main, Kaplan, & Cassidy, 1985). During the period in which a parent receives mental health treatment, the other parent or another family member may be able to pick up the slack and provide children with loving attention.

● *Seek professional guidance when attachment problems are serious.* When infants fail to develop healthy attachments, there are many things practitioners can do informally to help infants and their families. However, some attachment problems are so serious that families require the services of a counselor, psychologist, or social worker (Booth & Koller, 1998; V. A. Brown, 2002; Levy & Orlans, 2000). Thus it is important for practitioners to be alert for signs of deeply troubled infant-family relationships. You should definitely seek professional guidance when you suspect a serious problem—for instance, when a distressed child never seeks comfort from a familiar caregiver, shows fear of a family member, or displays some other highly unusual style of responding to family members (see indicators of serious attachment problems in the Observations Guidelines table "Assessing Young Children's Attachment Security" on p. 412).

In their relationships with attachment figures, young children learn to express their pleasure, distress, and other feelings. Expressing emotions is an important development in its own right and the focus of our next discussion.

Emotion

Emotions (sometimes referred to as *affective states*) are the feelings, both physiological and psychological, that people have in response to events that are personally relevant to their needs and goals (J. J. Campos, Frankel, & Camras, 2004). Emotions energize thinking and acting in ways that are often adaptive to the circumstances (Goleman, 1995; Saarni et

emotion
Affective response to an event that is personally relevant to one's needs and goals.

al., 1998). For example, *sadness* may lead a child to find comfort from others and reassess whether a goal is possible; *anger* may spur a child to try a new tactic or abandon an unrealistic goal; and *happiness* may prompt a child to share positive feelings with others and pursue a similar pleasurable experience in the future (Saarni et al., 1998). These and other emotions are described in the Observation Guidelines table "Assessing the Emotions of Children and Adolescents."

Developmental Changes in Emotions

The ways that youngsters express, understand, and cope with emotions change with age and experience. Emotional development is characterized by these specific trends:

● *Infants begin life with a few basic emotions and gradually add new feelings.* *Contentment, interest,* and *distress* are shown within the first 6 months of life (Emde, Gaensbauer, & Harmon, 1976; Hiatt, Campos, & Emde, 1979; Lewis, 2000; Stenberg & Campos, 1990). Hungry babies most certainly feel pleasure when they begin to feed (Lewis, 2000). A small smile may occur when infants are relaxed, happy, or enchanted with animated people. Infants show interest by watching objects carefully, inspecting their own body parts, mouthing fingers and toes, and tilting their heads to listen closely to the fine points of speech and music. Newborns exposed to a loud and sudden noise express distress, usually by crying; they do the same when hunger, fatigue, and discomfort mount.

As they mature, infants add to these basic emotions. Simple distress can become true *anger* when infants' desires are obstructed: Daddy does not come immediately to pick baby up, and Mommy does not indulge baby's desire to press buttons on the DVD player. Infants show their anger vividly by crying, thrashing, and looking directly, with accusation, at caregivers. Infants tend to show *fear* during the second half of the first year. This new emotion is evident in the stranger anxiety we examined earlier as a sign of attachment. Animals and objects that move in unexpected ways also often scare infants.

● *Infants respond to other people's emotions.* A basic ability to detect emotions in others is present even in infancy (Caron, Caron, & MacLean, 1988; Haviland & Lelwica, 1987; G. M. Schwartz, Izard, & Ansul, 1985). This is illustrated by the **emotional contagion** of babies: When one starts crying, others soon join in (Eisenberg, 1992; Hatfield, Cacioppo, & Rapson, 1994). By 3 months, infants imitate the happy, sad, and angry faces their mothers make (Haviland & Lelwica, 1987). At about the same time, infants react to the emotional expressions of caregivers in meaningful ways. For example, researchers once used particular facial expressions with 4-month-old infants in a peekaboo game (Montague & Walker-Andrews, 2001). All infants were familiar with the game from having played it with parents, but the researchers changed it, sometimes displaying angry, sad, or fearful expressions along with the expected happy expressions. Infants who watched *sad* expressions progressively looked away, as if they wanted to shield themselves from this emotion. Infants who watched *fearful* expressions increased attention to the adult's face and then gradually looked less, as if they wanted to learn more but then had enough. Infants who watched *angry* expressions increased their looking and maintained this interest, as if they were organizing internal processes needed for self-defense (Montague & Walker-Andrews, 2001). When caregivers violate infants' expectations for a particular emotional expression—perhaps by showing no smiles after a period of social play—infants also react. Between 3 and 9 months, they may respond to a parent's deadpan face by smiling, crying, looking away, and using self-soothing behaviors such as sucking their thumbs (T. Field, Vega-Lahr, Scafidi, & Goldstein, 1986; G. A. Moore, Cohn, & Campbell, 2001; Tronick, Als, Adamson, Wise, & Brazelton, 1978).

● *Children learn to guide their actions on the basis of other people's emotional expressions.* In the first year or two of life, children also show an inclination to monitor the emotions of others, particularly parents and trusted caregivers. Infants show *social referencing* toward the end of their first year: They watch their parents' faces, especially in the presence of a novel or puzzling phenomenon (Boccia & Campos, 1989; Sorce, Emde, Campos, & Klinnert, 1985). For instance, a 2-year-old girl may glance at Mommy's face when a new babysitter enters the house. By determining whether Mommy is smiling or frowning, the little girl gains a sense of how to respond to the babysitter.

——————— Connecting Concepts
Social referencing is introduced in Chapter 7.

---

emotional contagion
Tendency for infants to cry spontaneously when they hear other infants crying.

OBSERVATION GUIDELINES

Assessing the Emotions of Children and Adolescents

Characteristic	Look For	Example	Implication
Happiness	• Smiles • Laughter • Spontaneity	Paul, age 17, chatters with his friends during his school's end-of-the-year athletic field day. He is happy about having schoolwork over and looks forward to his summer job and paychecks.	Happiness helps people enjoy life and seek similar pleasurable experiences. Help children and adolescents find appropriate outlets to express their joy, and celebrate with them. Encourage them to talk about things they are happy about.
Anger	• Frowns and angry expressions • Possible retaliation toward the target of anger	Aranya, age 14, is furious that she wasn't admitted into an elective course, whereas her two closest friends *were*. Aranya is angry with her teacher, who she thinks dislikes her.	Anger helps people deal with obstacles to their goals, often spurring them to try new tactics. Help youngsters express their anger appropriately and determine how they can redirect their energy toward new solutions.
Fear	• Scared face • Withdrawal from circumstances • Physiological responses, such as sweating	Tony, age 2½, sits on his mat, eyes wide, body tense. He stares at a new poster of a clown in his preschool classroom. On this particular day, he becomes downright scared; he runs to his teacher and buries his head in her lap.	Fear occurs when people feel threatened and believe that their physical safety and psychological well-being are potentially at stake. Fear motivates people to flee, escape from harm, seek reassurance, and perhaps fight back. Help children articulate their fears. Offer reassurance.
Sadness	• Sad expression • Crying • Pouting • Being quiet • Possible withdrawal from a situation	Greta, age 15, sits quietly on a bench near her locker. With her head hung low, she rereads the letter from a cheerleading organization. She has not been admitted to the prestigious cheerleading summer camp.	People are sad when they realize they cannot attain a desired goal or when they experience a loss, such as a friend moving to a distant city. Sadness causes some people to reassess their goals. Reassure children, help them express their sadness, and encourage them to consider ways to deal with sad feelings.
Disgust	• Wrinkled nose • Remarks such as "Phew!" • Withdrawal from the source of displeasure	Norton, age 8, looks skeptically at the meal he has just purchased in the school cafeteria. He wrinkles his nose and averts his gaze from the "tuna melt" on his plate.	Disgust occurs when people encounter food, smells, and sights they find repulsive. Disgust is nature's way of getting people to be wary of something that is potentially troublesome or threatening to their health. Respect children's feeling of disgust, but also encourage them to reflect on why they might have this reaction.
Anxiety	• Frequent worrying • Excessive fidgeting, hand wringing, or nail biting • Avoidance of source of anxiety	Tanesha, age 16, has to give an oral presentation to her class. She has spent time preparing but is worried that, when she is standing all by herself in front of the group, she might get so nervous that she forgets everything she wants to say.	As long as it is not excessive, anxiety can spur people to take steps to avoid problems and achieve valued goals. Teach youngsters strategies that keep anxiety at a manageable level, as well as strategies that help them achieve their goals.
Shame	• Signs of embarrassment • Attempts to withdraw from a situation • Looking down and away from other people	Luke, age 9, is stunned. He's just had an accident, urinating on the floor. He had felt a bit antsy beforehand but wasn't aware that he needed to go to the bathroom. Now 20 pairs of eyes are glued on him.	When children feel ashamed, they are aware of other people's standards for behavior and know they are not meeting these standards. Shame motivates children to try harder. Shame works only when it comes from within; adults should never intentionally ridicule students. Help children redirect their behavior so they can meet their own standards.
Guilt	• Sad expression • May appear self-conscious • May show concern for a person who has been harmed	A. J., age 12, regrets bad-mouthing his friend Pete to other classmates. A. J. sinks down low in his chair, feeling remorse for what he said behind Pete's back and for Pete's sadness.	Guilt occurs when people do something that violates their own standards. It leads people to right the wrong. More generally, it causes people to behave in socially appropriate ways that protect others from harm. Help children express their feelings and realize that they can behave differently next time.
Pride	• Happy expression • Desire to show off work and accomplishments to other people	Jacinda, age 5, is beaming. For the last 20 minutes, she's painstakingly pasted sequins, stars, and feathers onto a mask. Her final product is a colorful, delicately adorned creation. She is happy with her work, as is evident from her ear-to-ear grin.	People are proud when they earn others' respect and meet their own goals. Pride fosters continued commitment to behaving appropriately and achieving high standards. Pride motivates people to share their accomplishments with others. Encourage children to identify things that make them proud. Share in their joy when they accomplish something meaningful for them.

Source: Adaptive functions of emotions based on material in Saarni et al., 1998.

——————— **Study Guide and Reader**
Supplementary Reading 11-2 describes
how children detect and understand
other people's emotions.

ALEX 5

Connor 13

Figure 11-1

Drawings of basic emotional expressions by Alex (age 5) and Connor (age 13)

——————— **Connecting Concepts**
Emotional regulation is one aspect of
self-regulation, which is discussed in
Chapter 13.

self-conscious emotion
Affective state that reflects awareness of
a community's social standards (e.g.,
pride, guilt, shame).

emotional regulation
Strategies to manage affective states.

● *Children learn to reflect on emotions.* As children grow older, they become thoughtful about emotions. As early as age 2 or 3, they talk about emotions that they and others experience ("Daniel got mad and pushed me"), and they realize that emotions are connected to people's desires ("Kurt loves to go down the slide and was really mad when he didn't get a turn") (Bretherton, Fritz, Zahn-Waxler, & Ridgeway, 1986; Dunn, Bretherton, & Munn, 1987; Wellman, Harris, Banerjee, & Sinclair, 1995). By middle childhood, they realize that their interpretations of a situation determine how they feel about it and that other people may have different interpretations and, as a result, different feelings ("Arlene feels bad because she thinks I don't like her") (P. L. Harris, 1989). Children also learn to connect words for emotions (*happy, sad, angry,* etc.) with particular facial expressions and with conditions under which these emotions may be elicited. In the drawings in Figure 11-1, two boys, ages 5 and 13, both show considerable knowledge of how different emotions might be reflected differently in people's facial expressions.

By the upper elementary grades, children begin to realize that emotional expressions do not always reflect people's true feelings (Selman, 1980). For instance, a 9-year-old may observe his teacher's cheerful demeanor yet realize she just lost her brother to cancer and is probably sad inside. During the end of middle childhood and the beginning of adolescence, children also understand that people can have ambivalent feelings (S. K. Donaldson & Westerman, 1986; Harter & Whitesell, 1989). For instance, a 12-year-old girl may love her father but be angry with him for moving out of the house; she may like going to see him during custodial visits but not like the feelings of turmoil the visits evoke in her.

● *Children expand their repertoire of basic emotions to include self-conscious emotions.* Simple emotions such as fear, anger, and pleasure in infancy are joined by **self-conscious emotions** in early childhood. These are affective states that reflect awareness of social standards and other people's concerns about these standards (Lewis, 1993, 1995). Self-conscious emotions include guilt, shame, embarrassment, and pride. Teresa recalls early displays of guilt in both of her sons. As toddlers and preschoolers, the boys would often respond angrily when misbehavior resulted in their being sent to their room or having a privilege taken away. Occasionally they'd swat at her or stomp out of the room. However, they'd often return a few minutes later, looking at her face for signs of sadness and affectionately rubbing her arm as they apologized.

● *Children and adolescents gradually learn to regulate their emotions.* **Emotional regulation** refers to the management of affective states (J. J. Campos et al., 2004; R. A. Thompson, 1994). Children gradually acquire a constellation of strategies that help them cope with their feelings and deal with stressful situations (E. M. Brenner & Salovey, 1997).

As newborns, infants need help when they feel hungry, tormented, or fearful. Most can count on caregivers to help them find relief. But soon infants also learn to soothe themselves to some extent: They may suck on a thumb, avert their gaze from a stranger, or crawl away (Mangelsdorf, Shapiro, & Marzolf, 1995). Of course, they continue to depend as well on caregivers to help them manage uncomfortable feelings. Without such support, infants may develop unhealthy emotional habits. For example, when parents habitually leave crying babies alone for extended periods, the babies may grow increasingly agitated when they cry, a pattern that makes it difficult later for parents to calm them down (Eisenberg, Cumberland, & Spinrad, 1988).

As children grow, experience a range of emotionally significant events, and observe role models, they acquire more coping strategies (Saarni et al., 1998). They may observe their parents controlling anger physically yet expressing it verbally: "I'm angry that you promised to make dinner but didn't do it!" They may then use a similar strategy in dealing with peer conflicts: "You said you would meet me at four o'clock but you never showed up. Where were you?!" In Figure 11-2 you can see 7-year-old Miguel's drawing and comments about being angry. He wrote about trying to cope with his anger, indicating that he is learning to control his temper. Youngsters who appropriately control and express their emotions are those most likely to be popular with peers (Fabes et al., 1999). In the "Emotional Development: Middle Childhood" video clip on Observation CD 2, it is apparent that 10-year-old Daniel has learned the value of expressing anger in socially appropriate ways:

Interviewer:	What kinds of things make kids your age angry?
Daniel:	Not getting what you want, even though it's, there's no real good explanation for not getting it. At school, I guess reading some sorts of books that I don't like. They don't like teachers yelling at 'em. Or they don't like listening sometimes.
Interviewer:	What are some things kids do when they're angry?
Daniel:	Frowning, maybe crying, pouting, back talking.
Interviewer:	What things are hard for kids when they get angry?
Daniel:	Calming themselves down. Of course, then you can go back to reading comic books and playing video games.

Children also become better able to appraise advantages and disadvantages of particular coping strategies. For instance, a 14-year-old may observe a best friend becoming entangled in a fight or an intoxicated neighbor heading for her car with keys in hand; in such circumstances the teenager quickly identifies a range of possible solutions and considers the potential benefits and disadvantages of each one. Sometimes children's appraisals of emotionally charged events enable them to deal directly with a problem—for instance, by confronting a peer. At other times, when they cannot change the situation, they instead try to deal with their emotions. For example, a child might alleviate anxiety about an upcoming classroom test by reminding himself that he has done well in the past on such examinations.

Children of different ages tend to seek out different kinds of people when they need reassurance in times of sadness or anger. In general, younger children are more inclined to go to adults (especially parents, other family members, and teachers), whereas older children and adolescents are more likely to seek support of peers (Rossman, 1992). You can observe this developmental difference as 4-year-old Zoe and 13-year-old Crystal talk about how children deal with sadness in the "Emotional Development" video clips for early childhood and early adolescence, on Observation CD 2:

Zoe:	They're angry sometimes. . . . I cry. . . . I don't know. . . . Have something to eat. . . . Tell the teacher. Have something to drink.
Crystal:	Cry on somebody's shoulder or lean, like lean on somebody. For someone to comfort them. The counselor, or their friend, or a teacher [could help]. . . . They could calm 'em down or to let them tell what's wrong.

Zoe believes her teacher will provide the necessary comfort. Crystal, too, realizes that social support is desirable, but she mentions both adults and peers as people who can be helpful.

A final component of emotional regulation is determining when to express emotions publicly. Children gradually learn to curb their emotional reactions in ways that are socially acceptable and will help them maintain good relationships with others (P. M. Cole, 1986). For example, many preschoolers understand that rules of politeness discourage them from revealing their true feelings when disappointed by a gift from a well-meaning relative. And by elementary school, many youngsters (boys especially) believe they should not show sadness, as 15-year-old Greg explains in the "Emotional Development: Late Adolescence" video clip on Observation CD 2:

Interviewer:	What are some things that kids do when they're sad?
Greg:	Cry, or like if you're a guy, you don't show it. . . . Eat, or just go with their really good friends and have them talk to them.

● *Concern for others' feelings is an important emotional response that develops with age, especially when encouraged by adults.* **Empathy** is the capacity to experience the same feelings as another person, who perhaps may be in pain or distress (Damon, 1988; Eisenberg, 1982; Hoffman, 1991). You can hear 14-year-old Brendan express empathic concern as he talks about caring for injured birds in the "Neighborhood: Early Adolescence" video clip

Figure 11-2
Seven-year-old Miguel drew and commented on his efforts to express anger appropriately. He wrote, "I try not to hit and shout."

Listen to Daniel describe how peers deal with anger in the "Emotional Development: Middle Childhood" clip on Observation CD 2.

Listen to Zoe and Crystal talk about being consoled by other people in the "Emotional Development" clips for early childhood and early adolescence, on Observation CD 2.

Listen to Greg explain how adolescents cope with sadness in the "Emotional Development: Late Adolescence" clip on Observation CD 2.

empathy
Capacity to experience the same feelings as another person, especially when the feeling is pain or distress.

Listen to Brendan express empathic concern for injured birds in the "Neighborhood: Early Adolescence" clip on Observation CD 2.

Despite gains in emotional regulation, adolescents can be emotionally volatile on occasion.

on Observation CD 2. When asked by the interviewer how he would improve his neighborhood if he could, Brendan replies that he would clean up the trash and "take all the birds that can't fly into your houses and take care of 'em until they're nursed back to health." Young people tend to be capable of such empathic responses when their parents have previously been warm and responsive to them (Zhou et al., 2002).

● *Adolescence brings new anxieties and pressures.* Adolescents tend to be more emotionally volatile than younger children: They more often report feeling lonely, embarrassed, or anxious, and they have more extreme mood swings (Arnett, 1999). The hormonal changes that accompany puberty may account for some of this volatility. And as young teenagers undergo rapid, uncontrollable physical changes, they may feel self-conscious and awkward, perhaps even alienated from their own bodies (Rudlin, 1993).

Environmental factors can magnify adolescents' emotional volatility (Arnett, 1999). The teenage years usher in new situations and problems that young people haven't encountered before. As they grow more independent, they may find their needs and desires conflicting with those of parents and other authority figures (Arnett, 1999). Concerns about fitting in at school, completing homework, and achieving good grades intensify during adolescence (Phelan et al., 1994). Peers themselves can be a source of aggravation due to inevitable conflicts that arise in social groups. Occasionally, adolescents intentionally ridicule one another, and when this happens, adolescents targeted with insulting remarks may feel humiliated and angry (Elison & Harter, in press). Many such factors come into play for even the most "normal" adolescents, but some have additional challenges—perhaps living in poverty, experiencing ongoing family conflict, or being abused by a family member—that they must deal with (Cicchetti & Toth, 1998; Rutter & Garmezy, 1983).

Not surprisingly, many (though by no means all) adolescents perceive their lives as being quite stressful, particularly in industrialized Western countries (Arnett, 1999; Masten, Neemann, & Andenas, 1994). Some adolescents believe that the problems they face exceed their capabilities to cope effectively, but most find the resources they need to confront pressures in their lives (Masten et al., 1994). Adolescents may turn to their peers for understanding, or perhaps for distraction from their troubles. They may also express their frustrations through poetry and art. For example, early in his senior year of high school, 17-year-old Jeff felt "locked in" by the combined pressures of a demanding course load, impending due dates for college applications, and his role as confidant for several troubled friends. Late one night, he put his schoolwork aside to create the picture shown in Figure 11-3. Because he had trouble drawing human figures, he combined two favorite things—a soft drink can and black-and-white cowhide—to represent himself. As you can see, a cage and gigantic boulder hold him in, and so he cannot join in as his peers (represented by other soft drink cans) frolic freely in the distance.

Group Differences in Emotions

All children progress developmentally in their expression and control of emotions. To some degree, their developmental pathways are influenced by group membership—by gender, family and culture, and socioeconomic status.

Gender differences.   On average, male and female babies are similar in emotional states; any gender differences are subtle and situation-dependent (Eisenberg et al., 1996). After the age of 2, however, consistent gender differences emerge. For instance, boys show more anger than girls beginning in the preschool years, and girls more often report feeling sad, fearful, and guilty beginning in the elementary grades (Eisenberg et al., 1996). Girls also respond more negatively to failures, to such an extent that their subsequent performance may suffer (Dweck, 2000). And some girls are inclined to dwell on their problems rather than taking action or distracting themselves, a ruminating style that is a risk factor for becoming depressed (Nolen-Hoeksema, Morrow, & Fredrickson, 1993). As early as elementary school, boys begin to put on a self-confident front when they feel vulnerable (Eisenberg et al., 1996; Sadker & Sadker, 1994). This style, too, has its disadvantages, especially when boys feel pressured to live up to unrealistic standards of personal strength.

Biology may be a source of some gender differences in emotions; for instance, rising hormonal levels at puberty are associated with increases in moodiness and depression in girls, but with aggressiveness and rebelliousness in boys (Buchanan, Eccles, & Becker, 1992;

Susman, Inoff-Germain, et al., 1987). Yet many theorists suspect that differences in socialization are a more significant cause of gender differences in emotional responding (Durkin, 1995; Eisenberg et al., 1996; Sadker & Sadker, 1994). For instance, parents are more likely to discourage overt anger in daughters than in sons (Birnbaum & Croll, 1984; Malatesta & Haviland, 1982). Parents are apt to discourage sons from expressing emotions yet may encourage daughters to talk about their feelings (J. H. Block, 1979; Eisenberg et al., 1996). At school, many teachers prefer the passive, compliant nature that girls are more likely to exhibit (R. E. Bennett, Gottesman, Rock, & Cerullo, 1993; Pollack, 1998). Consider, for example, Pollack's (1998) observations of a fourth-grade classroom:

Figure 11-3

Drawing himself as a cow-patterned soda can, 17-year-old Jeff dramatically depicts how the pressures in his life prevent him from doing the things he would like to do.

> [O]n several occasions I had observed the fourth-grade class of Ms. Callahan. She was particularly skillful, modern, and warm in her approach, universally beloved by her students. I have every reason to believe that Ms. Callahan was a teacher who would want both boys and girls to derive all they could from the classroom experience.
>
> On this visit, some boys and girls who had been organized into "teams" were working together on a writing project about friendship. Adult volunteers were consultants for these teams and were helping them with their computer skills. I was surprised to see that instead of focusing on the writing project, Ms. Callahan's attention was almost entirely taken up by disciplining the boys. Several lively boys were making a commotion in one corner near the computer. Ms. Callahan cautioned them about making too much noise, and told them to return to their desks and wait their turns. With long faces, the boys meandered across the room and slumped into their seats. A moment later one of the boys could not resist calling out about something. Ms. Callahan gave him a stern second warning. "I don't want to have to caution you again," Ms. Callahan said. "If I do, you're heading for the principal's office."
>
> I had observed the class before, and now I noticed that two of the more creative male students—Robert and Shawn—were not in evidence. I asked Ms. Callahan if they were sick that day.
>
> "No," she explained. "Robert is too excitable for the group process. He's working on an entirely different project." She pointed him out—sitting alone on the floor, tucked out of view, banished from the team endeavor.
>
> "And where's Shawn?" I inquired.
>
> "He was telling inappropriate jokes about Albert Einstein earlier in the day and distracting the entire class. So, he's sitting outside working on his spelling," Ms. Callahan sighed. "Some kids just seem unable to fit into this more quiet team-based teaching."
>
> I wish I had asked her what those jokes about Albert Einstein were, but I was too concerned about her attitude toward these boys. She clearly felt that they could not "fit in" and that they were "unable" to participate appropriately, when I knew (as she did) that these were bright boys with a lot to offer. Although I doubt that Ms. Callahan would agree, I think the prevailing method in class that day was structured around the way girl students prefer to work, and that boys were at a disadvantage. (pp. 240–241)[1]

Obviously, both boys and girls have emotional needs. Being careful not to stereotype the sexes, concerned educators can watch for occasions when girls and boys use styles of emotional regulation that make matters worse for them. For example, adults can watch for times when girls are ruminating over problems and can help these girls work through their feelings, actively tackle the problems, and then get on with life. Similarly, when boys seem to be trying hard to brush off a significant personal loss, adults can acknowledge that the event is, in fact, likely to be upsetting but the boys can take proactive steps to cope with their distress.

Family and cultural differences.   Earlier we suggested that some differences in children's attachment-related behaviors are the result of how parents in different cultures care for their babies. Cultural differences in socialization practices continue throughout childhood, resulting in noticeable differences in emotional responding. For instance, in China and Japan, many children are raised to be shy and restrained, whereas in Zambia, smiling and sociability are apt to be the norm (X. Chen et al., 1992; Hale-Benson, 1986; D. Y. F. Ho, 1986, 1994; Rothbaum et al., 2000). Girls in India are more likely than British girls to be deferential and

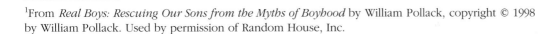

[1]From *Real Boys: Rescuing Our Sons from the Myths of Boyhood* by William Pollack, copyright © 1998 by William Pollack. Used by permission of Random House, Inc.

Families within a culture or ethnic group can differ markedly from one another in emotional expression.

controlled, and to hide negative feelings such as anger and sadness, especially in the presence of adults (Joshi & MacLean, 1994).

Cultures also differ in how they deal with specific emotions, such as anger (Saarni, 2000). For example, some !Kung families in Botswana accept children's tantrums toward parents but discourage aggression toward peers. Some working class families in the United States encourage aggression toward peers who themselves have caused injury. Many families in Japan ask children to focus on how others feel when the children break social rules (Conroy, Hess, Azuma, & Kashiwagi, 1980; Konner, 1972; P. Miller & Sperry, 1987).

Yet families within any single culture can differ markedly in how they socialize children's emotional expression. In one study with families in England, researchers listened to conversations among 3-year-old children, their mothers, and their older siblings; some children *never* mentioned emotions during an hour-long conversation at home, whereas one child mentioned emotions more than 27 times (Dunn, Brown, & Beardsall, 1991). On average, mothers were more likely to talk about feelings than were the children. When they occur, family "lessons" about emotions may help children to understand how emotions operate. For example, in another study 6-year-old U.S. children explained complex emotions more effectively when their parents had previously talked with them about why people behave as they do (J. R. Brown & Dunn, 1996).

Socioeconomic differences.   Children from low-income families are slightly more prone to emotional difficulties than are children from middle-income families (Caspi, Taylor, Moffitt, & Plomin, 2000; McLoyd, 1998a). Environmental factors are almost certainly the primary reasons for this difference. Children living in impoverished circumstances have more than their share of reasons to feel sad, fearful, and angry. For instance, they may not know where their next meal is coming from, and they are more likely to encounter violence and drug addiction in their neighborhoods. Their parents have limited resources (and sometimes limited energy) to address their needs and may discipline inconsistently (McLoyd, 1998a). Furthermore, many children from low-income backgrounds, particularly those with histories of learning problems, have few positive interactions with teachers at school (R. M. Clark, 1983).

The emotional stresses of middle- and high-income backgrounds can also be substantial, however. For example, some middle-income parents project their own aspirations onto their children. They may expect children to follow unrealistic developmental timetables, such as cooperatively sharing toys with peers at 18 months and reading at 3 years. When children do not measure up, parents may become critical, overly directive, and controlling (Hyson, Hirsh-Pasek, Rescorla, Cone, & Martell-Boinske, 1991). Youngsters may worry about parental expectations, particularly when they think they are not measuring up.

Teachers in particular are in a strategic position to encourage constructive emotional responses in children. We now consider some strategies that adults can use to promote children's emotional development.

Promoting Children's Emotional Development

Emotions are an important part of children's everyday lives, yet many adults are uneasy in dealing with them (Sylvester, 1995). We propose that educators can promote emotional development if they consider emotions as *competencies*—that is, as valuable skills that can improve over time. We offer these suggestions for promoting children's abilities in emotional expression:

● ***Help crying infants find comfort.***   Caregivers can do several things to help infants in distress. First, they can strive to give timely reassurance—not always immediately, as they may sometimes have other demands, but not so late that crying escalates into turbulent agitation. Second, caregivers can allow and encourage actions used by infants to reduce stress. Searching for a favorite blanket, putting a finger in the mouth, tugging at an ear with a gentle hand—these are positive signs that infants are learning to soothe themselves. Third, caregivers can consciously invite a baby to join them in a calm state by showing baby a smiling face, holding baby close to the chest, rubbing baby gently, and trying to breathe in a shared rhythm (Gonzalez-Mena, 2002). Fourth, caregivers can investigate why an infant is crying and

———————— Connecting Concepts
Chapter 5 describes the influences of low-income environments in more depth.

———————— Connecting Concepts
Chapter 4 explains that crying is an important physiological response that infants use to express their discomfort.

try to meet the unfilled need or remove the painful stimulus. Finally, caregivers should try to stay calm and not take it personally—infants sometimes cry despite the most sensitive care.

● *Create an atmosphere of warmth, acceptance, and trust.* Children learn most effectively when they have positive emotions—for instance, when they feel secure, happy, or excited about an activity (Boekaerts, 1993; Isen, Daubman, & Gorgoglione, 1987; Oatley & Nundy, 1996). And they are more likely to confide in an adult about troublesome issues if they know that the adult will continue to respect them no matter what they may reveal about themselves in heart-to-heart conversations.

● *Encourage young people to express their feelings.* Children and adolescents can better deal with their feelings when they are aware of what their feelings *are.* Some teachers successfully incorporate discussions about feelings into everyday classroom routines. For example, when Teresa's son Connor was in first grade, his teacher ended each day with "circle time." She asked the children to hold hands and communicate how they felt about their day: one squeeze for happy, two squeezes for sad, three squeezes for bored, and so on. They took turns and, without words, communicated how they felt; all eyes were glued on the single hand doing the squeezing. This simple exercise gave the children a chance to reflect on, and then communicate, their basic emotional states.

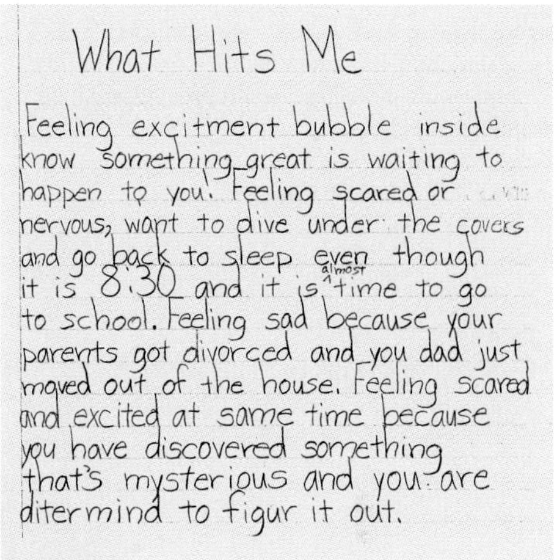

● *Consider using a research-based curriculum for fostering emotional development.* To have a significant impact on children's emotional expression, adults need systematic ways to educate children about their feelings (Raver, 2002). One illustration of a comprehensive emotional education program is the *Promoting Alternative Thinking Strategies* (PATHS) curriculum (Greenberg, Kusche, Cook, & Quamma, 1995). Sixty lessons in second- and third-grade classrooms focus on self-control, emotions, and problem solving. Children are taught that all feelings are okay, some feelings are comfortable and others uncomfortable, feelings can help children learn what to do in certain situations, and some ways of dealing with feelings are better than others. Children keep a record of their feelings and use a poster showing a traffic signal as a guide to regulating their responses to feelings. Teachers encourage children to refer to the steps on the poster: to stop and calm down (red), to slow down and consider the options (yellow), and to try a plan (green). This program has been shown to increase emotional understanding and to decrease problem behaviors in children with a range of ability levels (Greenberg, Domitrovich, & Bumbarger, 2000).

● *Offer age-appropriate outlets for emotional expression.* When they are young, children can find safe outlets for emotional expression in play. Through fantasy play with peers, children often work out their fears and anger (Kohlberg & Fein, 1987). For older children, writing about feelings, perhaps in essays or journals shared only with a teacher or counselor, can provide a confidential outlet. In the essay in Figure 11-4, 10-year-old Shea describes her growing awareness of the various emotions she experiences. In the journal entry in Figure 11-5, 8-year-old Noah—ordinarily a happy, energetic student—reveals how upset he is about his parents' divorce.

● *Discuss emotions experienced by characters in literature and history.* Stories provide an occasion to talk about emotional states. We have found in our own experience that children in the elementary grades are able to make sensible inferences about characters' emotional states. For instance, in *Frog and Toad Are Friends* (Lobel, 1979), a book suitable for 4- to 8-year-olds, Frog waits impatiently to play with his hibernating friend, Toad, and plays a trick on him to get him up early. The story provides a forum for discussions about feelings that may arise between friends, such as anger at being teased (Solomon, Watson, Battistich, Schaps, & Delucchi, 1992). Older children and adolescents can read firsthand historical accounts to find tales of inequities and hostilities and can talk about how people dealt with various strong emotions.

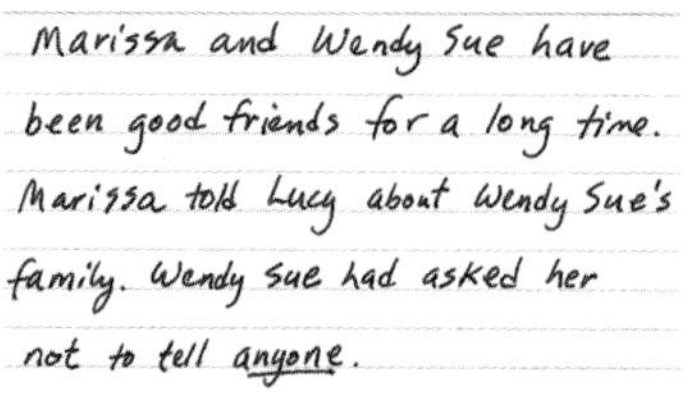

● *Ask children to guess what emotions people may feel in particular scenarios.* Children can practice analyzing situations and considering how those involved might feel. In Figure 11-6 you can see one situation that an elementary school counselor asks children to pretend they face. Adults can guide children to see that anger, fear, guilt, and other feelings are reasonable reactions to particular circumstances. In addition, they can ask children to think about how they might act when they have such uncomfortable feelings.

What Hits Me

Feeling excitment bubble inside know something great is waiting to happen to you. Feeling scared or nervous, want to dive under the covers and go back to sleep even though it is 8:30 and it is almost time to go to school. feeling sad because your parents got divorced and you dad just moved out of the house. Feeling scared and excited at same time because you have discovered something that's mysterious and you are determind to figur it out.

Figure 11-4

In this "What Hits Me" essay, 10-year-old Shea describes her experiences with various emotions.

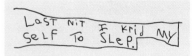

last nit I kried my self to slep.

Figure 11-5

In this journal entry, 8-year-old Noah reveals his sadness about his parents' recent divorce.

Marissa and Wendy Sue have been good friends for a long time. Marissa told Lucy about Wendy Sue's family. Wendy Sue had asked her not to tell anyone.

Figure 11-6

Counselors can ask children to pretend they are characters in particular situations, such as this one, and can help them talk about how they might feel and respond.

Idea courtesy of Sally Tossey, Columbus, Ohio.

How Can a Conslr Help I Do not Even know Him

Figure 11-7

Anxious about going to summer camp, 10-year-old Andy explained his feelings in a series of yellow sticky notes. Andy was especially concerned about sleeping away from home and missing his family. He also commented that the rules "stink." In this excerpt, Andy wonders how an unfamiliar counselor can help.

Adults can help relieve children's anxiety by talking through problems in a warm, supportive manner.

— **Connecting Concepts**

Persistent and pervasive perceptions of uncontrollability result in *learned helplessness,* discussed in Chapter 13.

---

anxiety

Emotional state characterized by worry and apprehension.

● *Take cultural differences into account.* Some cultures encourage open expression of feelings, whereas others actively discourage emotional expressiveness. Adults working with children from diverse cultures must continually be mindful of such differences when interpreting children's emotional expressions (or lack thereof).

● *Help children keep anxiety at a manageable level.* **Anxiety** is an emotional state characterized by worry and apprehension, often about future events with unknown outcomes. Children who are anxious may experience such physiological symptoms as muscle tension and headaches and have trouble concentrating. The brief note in Figure 11-7 reveals 10-year-old Andy's feelings of anxiety and dread about going to summer camp.

Educators can do a variety of things to help keep anxiety at a manageable level. For instance, when teachers assign oral reports, they can encourage students to create index cards or other memory "crutches." Before giving an important test (such as the standardized tests that many school districts require), they can administer a practice test that gives students a general idea of what to expect. And, in general, they should communicate realistic expectations for classroom performance and provide the support students need to *meet* those expectations.

● *Pay attention to your own emotions.* Practitioners who work with children and families often find themselves frustrated by the people they serve (B. Davis, 2001). Teachers may become angry about rude children, apathetic parents, unrealistic external mandates, and inadequate resources to schools. Frustration and anger are natural emotions, but they must be handled with care. Exploding on the nearest bystander or retreating into personal despair are *not* good ideas; counting to 10 and finding another professional to talk with *can* be helpful in preserving a teacher's mental health and in gaining ideas about productive tactics for addressing difficult problems.

● *Model appropriate ways of dealing with negative emotions.* Youngsters often struggle with how to deal with anger, fear, and sadness; they can benefit from seeing adults express these emotions appropriately. Teresa vividly remembers how her fifth-grade teacher expressed anger: Rather than raising her voice, she lowered it to a whisper. The teacher's approach worked well: Students sensed her disappointment, responded with concern and guilt, and tried to make amends. Educators can enhance the benefits of modeling controlled, honest emotional reactions by offering an explanation: "I'm really angry now. Let's talk this out when we've both calmed down."

Some children have such strong emotions that simply talking about feelings and modeling appropriate coping skills are not enough to ease their distress. We now look at serious emotional problems that some youngsters have, as well as at strategies that educators can use with these youngsters.

Emotional Problems in Children and Adolescents

Some children and adolescents have more than their share of negative emotional experiences, to the point where their quality of life and ability to tackle everyday problems are disrupted. Other youngsters have trouble handling intense emotions, showing emotions in culturally acceptable ways, coping with mixed emotions, or responding appropriately to other people's emotional displays (P. M. Cole, Michel, & Teti, 1994). Children with serious emotional problems can benefit from interventions from mental health professionals, but they also need support at school and in other daily activities.

As you might expect, emotional problems are affected by both nurture and nature. Many emotional problems are believed to result from environmental factors, such as child abuse, inconsistent parenting practices, stressful living conditions, exposure to violence, and family drug or alcohol abuse (H. C. Johnson & Friesen, 1993; G. R. Patterson, DeBaryshe, & Ramsey, 1989; Shaffer, 1988). We got a sense of the impact of adverse environmental conditions earlier in the chapter when we examined attachment problems. Yet early relationships with caregivers are not the only environmental source of emotional difficulty. Perhaps, instead, as children grew they did not learn any strategies for keeping angry feelings in check, and so they lash out at the slightest provocation. Or possibly unfavorable circumstances in their lives seem so overwhelming and uncontrollable that they sink into a deep depression. At the same time, biological causes, such as inherited predispositions, chemical imbalances, brain injuries, and illnesses, can also contribute to emotional problems (Hallowell, 1996; H. C. Johnson & Friesen, 1993). Overall, it appears that no single factor entirely accounts for serious emotional difficulties, except in extreme conditions (Cicchetti & Toth, 1998).

Three emotional-behavioral disorders are fairly common in children and adolescents: depression, anxiety disorder, and conduct disorder. We look at each of these conditions and then formulate some recommendations for working with youngsters who have ongoing emotional problems.

Depression.   People with **depression** feel exceptionally sad, discouraged, and hopeless; they may also feel restless, sluggish, helpless, worthless, or guilty (American Psychiatric Association, 1994; Seligman, 1991). Seriously depressed individuals may have trouble concentrating, lose interest in their usual activities, have little appetite, and have difficulty sleeping (American Psychiatric Association, 1994; Hertel, 1994). In children and adolescents, irritability is often more evident than sadness. Other common characteristics of depression in young people include complaints about physical pain, withdrawal from social relationships, significant substance abuse, and talk of suicide. A variation of depression, *bipolar disorder,* occurs when individuals experience periods of extreme elation as well as periods of deep depression.

The specific symptoms of depression vary somewhat from culture to culture. The American Psychiatric Association provides several examples of how depression might manifest itself in different cultures:

> Complaints of "nerves" and headaches (in Latino and Mediterranean cultures), of weakness, tiredness, or "imbalance" (in Chinese and Asian cultures), of problems of the "heart" (in Middle Eastern cultures), or of being "heartbroken" (among Hopi). (American Psychiatric Association, 1994, p. 324)

Many instances of depression and bipolar disorder probably have biological, and possibly genetic, roots (Cicchetti, Rogosch, & Toth, 1997; Griswold & Pessar, 2000). These conditions tend to run in families, are often foreshadowed by temperamental moodiness and insecure attachment, and may reflect chemical imbalances (Cicchetti et al., 1997; Griswold & Pessar, 2000). Yet environmental factors may also play a role in depression; for instance, the death of a loved one, mental illness or marital conflict in parents, child maltreatment, poverty, and inadequate schools may bring about or worsen depressive symptoms (Cicchetti et al., 1997). When individuals succumb to extreme stress with a depressive episode, the event may alter their neurological chemistry, making it more likely that they will suffer another depressive episode in the future (Akiskal & McKinney, 1973; Antelman & Caggiula, 1977; Siever & Davis, 1985).

Before adolescence, depression and bipolar disorder are rare. Their prevalence increases during adolescence; for instance, 5 percent to 10 percent of teenagers have one or more major depressive episodes (Cicchetti et al., 1997). During childhood, depression rates are approximately equal for boys and girls, but by age 16, rates are considerably higher for girls than for boys, perhaps because girls are more likely to ruminate on their problems (Cicchetti et al., 1997; Eisenberg et al., 1996; Nolen-Hoeksema, 1987).

How might depression emerge in the life of a child? Let's consider Billy, a 5-year-old boy who's just entered kindergarten. His single mother suffers from depression and gives him little attention. She occasionally gives in to his persistent demands, but at other times she vacillates between indifference and explosive anger. When Billy first comes to school, he clings anxiously to her. When she leaves, he is irritable and tired, and he has trouble focusing on activities and interacting with peers. He is not diagnosed with depression for another 10 years, when he now shows classic symptoms—missing school, sleeping irregularly, abusing alcohol, and feeling sad much of the time. Billy exemplifies two of the vulnerability factors for depression: a possible genetic predisposition to a moody temperament (inherited from his mother) and an insecure attachment to his mother (the outcome of inconsistent and sometimes harsh parenting).

Youths with serious depression or bipolar disorder are at risk for committing suicide. Depressed individuals who contemplate suicide often believe that they face problems they cannot solve or have extreme emotional pain they wish to end (D. Miller, 1994). Approximately 15 percent of individuals with a major depressive disorder die by their own hand (American Psychiatric Association, 1994).

depression
Emotional condition characterized by significant sadness, discouragement, hopelessness and, in children, irritability.

The overwhelming despair and high frequency of suicide that characterize depression make it a condition that educators must take seriously. Through their daily contact with youngsters, teachers have numerous opportunities to observe fluctuations in mood and performance and so may spot cases of possible depression in children. (Friends and family, though they may have closer ties to youngsters, may not comprehend how serious the problem is or may possibly deny its existence.) Educators will want to offer emotional reassurance to young people who appear troubled, but they should consult with principals and counselors if they suspect depression or another serious emotional disturbance.

Anxiety disorders.   In its milder forms, anxiety is a common and very "normal" emotion. But some people, including some children and adolescents, worry excessively and find it difficult to control their worrisome thoughts and feelings; in other words, they have an **anxiety disorder** (American Psychiatric Association, 1994). Children with a *generalized anxiety disorder* tend to worry excessively about a wide variety of things—including their academic achievement, their performance in sports, and potential catastrophic events such as wars or hurricanes. Some individuals have more specific anxiety disorders—perhaps worrying excessively about gaining weight, having a serious illness, being away from family and home, or feeling embarrassed in public (American Psychiatric Association, 1994).

Anxiety disorders tend to run in families (American Psychiatric Association, 1994; Last, Hersen, Kazdin, Francis, & Grubb, 1987). Furthermore, children with anxiety disorders are more susceptible to other emotional difficulties, such as serious depression (Mattison, 1992). There are hints in the research that family environment may play a role in the onset of anxiety disorders, but more investigation is needed (Famularo, Kinscherff, & Fenton, 1992; Mattison, 1992).

Conduct disorder.   When children and adolescents display a chronic pattern of misbehavior and show little shame or guilt about their wrongdoings, they are sometimes identified as having a **conduct disorder.** Youngsters who display a conduct disorder ignore the rights of others in ways that are unusual for their age. Common symptoms include aggression toward people and animals (e.g., initiating physical fights, forcing someone into sexual activity, torturing animals), destruction of property (e.g., setting fires, painting graffiti), theft and deceitfulness (e.g., breaking into cars, lying about shoplifting so as not to be caught), and serious violations of rules (e.g., ignoring reasonable curfews, being truant from school) (American Psychiatric Association, 1994). Approximately 2 percent to 6 percent of school-age youths could be classified as having a conduct disorder, with rates being three or four times higher for boys than for girls (Kazdin, 1997).

It is important to note that one or two antisocial acts do not necessarily indicate a serious emotional problem. Conduct disorders are more than a matter of "kids being kids" or "sowing wild oats." Instead, they represent deep-seated and persistent disregard for the rights and feelings of others. Youths with conduct disorders tend to see the world through conflict-colored glasses, for example by always assuming that others have hostile intentions toward them (Crick & Dodge, 1994).

Conduct disorder is manifested somewhat differently depending on youngsters' gender and age when the behavior problems first appear. Among young people with conduct disorder, boys are more likely to engage in theft and aggression; girls are apt to engage in sexual misbehavior. Conduct disorder is especially serious (and likely to foreshadow adjustment problems in the adult years) when it is manifested even before adolescence begins (Barrett, 2005). Youngsters who exhibit conduct disorders beginning in childhood are likely to have many problems in adulthood, including antisocial and criminal behavior, frequent changes in employment, high divorce rates, little participation in families and community groups, and early death (Kazdin, 1997). In contrast, conduct disorders that don't emerge until adolescence are often the result of affiliation with peers who engage in delinquent behavior; as young people mature and find new social contacts, the delinquent acts tend to stop.

As is true for the emotional disorders we've previously considered, biology may be *partly* to blame for conduct disorders. For instance, children and adolescents with conduct disorders may have difficulty inhibiting aggressive impulses, perhaps as a result of brain damage or other neurological abnormalities (Dempster & Corkill, 1999; Gladwell, 1997; Kazdin, 1997). Family environments may be influential as well: Conduct disorders are more common when children's

---

——— **Connecting Concepts**

This *hostile attributional bias* is examined in Chapter 12.

---

anxiety disorder
Chronic emotional condition characterized by excessive, debilitating worry.

conduct disorder
Chronic emotional condition characterized by lack of concern for the rights of others.

parents provide little affection, are highly critical, and unpredictably administer harsh physical punishment (Blackson et al., 1999; DeKlynen, Speltz, & Greenberg, 1998; Kazdin, 1997; G. R. Patterson et al., 1989; Webster-Stratton & Hammond, 1999). Tragically, some school environments contribute to the problem. Conduct disorders are more frequently observed in situations where teachers have low expectations for students, provide little encouragement or praise for schoolwork, and put little effort into planning lessons (Kazdin, 1997).

Supporting youngsters with emotional problems.   Effective programs for youngsters with emotional disorders are usually individualized. Without such adaptations, schools and other settings are difficult places for youths with serious emotional problems. As a telling statistic, fewer than half of students with serious emotional problems graduate from high school (Bassett et al., 1996; Koyanagi & Gaines, 1993). Teachers, psychologists, and special education professionals can collaboratively design support systems. In addition, educators can consider these strategies:

● ***Show an interest in the well-being of all children and adolescents.*** Many youngsters with emotional disorders have few positive and productive ties with individuals outside of school, and so their relationships with caring professionals may become all the more important (S. C. Diamond, 1991). The many "little things" educators do each day—greeting youngsters warmly, expressing concern when they seem worried, and lending a ready ear when they want to share their ideas or frustrations—can make a world of difference (S. C. Diamond, 1991).

● ***Teach social skills.*** Many children and adolescents with emotional problems have difficulty maintaining friendships (Asher & Coie, 1990; Cartledge & Milburn, 1995; Schonert-Reichl, 1993). Practicing effective social skills, such as saying something friendly to a peer, seems to improve peer relationships for these youngsters (e.g., Gillham, Reivich, Jaycox, & Seligman, 1995).

Connecting Concepts —————
Chapter 12 offers suggestions for fostering social skills.

● ***Provide extra structure for youngsters who have high levels of anxiety.*** One especially effective strategy is to communicate expectations for performance in clear and concrete terms. Highly anxious youngsters perform better in well-structured environments, such as classrooms with explicit expectations for academic achievement and social behavior (Hembree, 1988; Stipek, 1993; Tobias, 1977). When they know what to expect and how they will be evaluated, these young people are more inclined to relax, enjoy themselves, and learn.

● ***Set reasonable limits for behavior.*** All children need to learn that certain actions—aggression, destruction of property, stealing, and so on—are unacceptable. Establishing rules for appropriate behavior and imposing consequences (e.g., loss of privileges) for infractions provide the structure and guidance many children need to keep undesirable behaviors in check (R. Turnbull et al., 2004).

● ***Give children and adolescents a sense that they have some control.*** Some young people, especially those who consistently defy authority figures, often behave even less appropriately when people try to control them. With such youngsters, it is important that practitioners not get into power struggles, situations where only one person "wins" and the other inevitably loses. Instead, adults might create situations in which children conform to expectations yet also know they have some control over what happens to them. For instance, students in a classroom can learn techniques for observing and monitoring their own actions (Kern, Dunlap, Childs, & Clark, 1994). They can also be given choices (within reasonable limits) about how to proceed in particular situations (Knowlton, 1995).

Connecting Concepts —————
Chapter 13 explains that having some control over their lives enhances youngsters' intrinsic motivation to learn and achieve. Chapter 13 also describes strategies for helping youngsters self-monitor their behaviors.

● ***Be alert for signs that a child or adolescent may be contemplating suicide.*** Seriously depressed youngsters often give signs that they may be thinking about taking their own lives. Such warning signs include the following (Jensen, 2005; Kerns & Lieberman, 1993):

- Signs of depression and helplessness
- Sudden withdrawal from social relationships (possibly after being rejected by peers or breaking up with a boyfriend or girlfriend)
- Disregard for personal appearance
- Serious health problems (e.g., a debilitating injury from an accident or a chronic condition resulting from an eating disorder)
- A dramatic personality change
- A sudden elevation in mood
- A preoccupation with death and morbid themes

BASIC DEVELOPMENTAL ISSUES

Attachment and Emotional Development

Issue	Attachment	Emotional Development
Nature and Nurture	Young human beings are biologically predisposed to form close bonds with their parents and other primary caregivers, but they are more likely to form attachments to such individuals when they are treated in a sensitive and responsible fashion. Parents, in turn, are by nature predisposed to care for their offspring, but they learn specific ways of caring for their children from other family members and from the community and culture in which they live.	The full range of emotions is made possible by human genetic instructions; the brain is wired to experience anger, joy, fear, and so on. Genetic factors also affect individual differences in temperament (e.g., activity level, irritability, and ways of responding to new stimuli). Nurture affects ways in which emotions are expressed. Children learn to control expression of negative emotions by observing other people and practicing various ways of dealing with emotional experiences.
Universality and Diversity	The predisposition to form close social-emotional bonds is universal. Moreover, socially sensitive care is the universal trigger for forming healthy attachments. However, not all children form secure attachments to their caregivers, and different environments place distinct demands on children. For example, being clingy and demanding may help infants who live in an environment with scarce resources. Similarly, being able to negotiate multiple relationships may enhance adjustment when numerous caregivers are present during the early years.	All children experience such basic emotions as happiness, sadness, anger, and fear. The tendency for emotional states to energize particular kinds of responses (e.g., fleeing in response to fear) is also universal. But substantial diversity is present in how children regulate their emotions (e.g., when trying to conceal their true feelings). Some children are more likely than others to respond to situations in a positive, upbeat fashion.
Qualitative and Quantitative Change	The development of attachments largely reflects quantitative change: Children gradually become more active as social partners, initiating conversations and other exchanges, taking turns to keep interactions going, and so on. Qualitative change occurs when young children, who have previously met strangers with no protest, suddenly display stranger anxiety. During this phase, they are anxious around people they do not know and show a clear preference for attachment figures.	Children gradually gain knowledge and skills for assessing others' emotions. By watching facial expressions, listening to voice tones, and drawing inferences from behaviors, children learn how others express and control emotions. They also reflect on their own emotional states. However, the emergence of self-conscious emotions (pride, guilt, embarrassment, etc.) represents a qualitative change in development. As children become more aware of societal standards, they learn how these standards apply to themselves, are motivated (usually) to adhere to them, and feel ashamed or guilty when they realize they don't meet expectations.

Adults must always be alert for signs that a youngster is seriously depressed. If they suspect that a young person is contemplating suicide, they should seek trained help immediately.

- Serious problems at school, home, or in the community (e.g., expulsion from school, death of a friend, pregnancy, or arrest for illegal behavior)
- Overt or veiled threats (e.g., "I won't be around much longer")
- Actions that indicate "putting one's affairs in order" (e.g., giving away prized possessions)
- Substance abuse
- Preference for certain kinds of music (e.g., heavy metal rock music with morbid themes)
- Efforts to obtain suicidal means (e.g., medications, ropes, or guns)

Adults must take these behaviors seriously, particularly if they see more than one. Educators should show genuine caring and concern for potentially suicidal youngsters, and they should also seek trained help from a school psychologist or counselor *immediately* (McCoy, 1994).

The Basic Developmental Issues table "Attachment and Emotional Development" shows how attachments and emotions draw from nature and nurture, show universality and diversity, and exhibit qualitative and quantitative change. As you have learned, nature furnishes children with inclinations to form attachments and express emotions, and nurture translates these abstract capacities into real-life relationships and abilities. In the final section of this chapter, we reveal how individual differences in emotional responding, first manifested during infancy as distinct temperaments, are slowly integrated into well-defined personalities.

Temperament and Personality

Visit any group of children—perhaps in a room at a local child care center, a classroom at school, or an after-school program—and you are bound to notice dramatic differences in individual children's energy, mood, spontaneity, and attention to academic tasks. Such variations reflect differences in children's *temperaments* and *personalities*.

Temperament and personality are related concepts. As noted in Chapter 1, *temperament* refers to a child's typical ways of responding to events and novel stimulation and of regulating impulses (Kagan, 1998; Rothbart & Bates, 1998). Individual differences in temperament are present even in infancy. For example, some infants are fussy and demanding; others are cheerful and easy to care for. Temperament has a genetic basis, as we shall see, but it also is very much affected by children's relationships and experiences.

As children grow older, they develop distinctive ways of behaving, thinking, and feeling. That is, they develop unique **personalities.** Temperament surely affects personality: A child who is timid relates to people and events differently than one who is socially confident. But personality includes more than temperament. Personality is affected by children's intellectual interests and the many habits they learn while growing up—for example, their traditions for fulfilling family obligations, strategies for dealing with stressful situations, styles of managing belongings, and preferences for spending leisure time.

Both temperament and personality help us understand how individual children respond to emotions, form relationships, and act within schools and other group settings. Temperament may be especially helpful to consider when children are infants and toddlers; personality may be more useful as youngsters move through their childhood and adolescent years. Let's look more closely at both concepts and then consider their relevance for educators.

Elements of Temperament and Personality

Temperament and personality are each comprised of constellations of relatively independent dimensions. Individual children may have a lot, a little, or an in-between amount of each attribute.

Temperament. Developmental scholars have suggested that temperament has a variety of dimensions. Much of the initial work on temperament was done with infants, and as a result, there are some well-developed categories for describing how infants express themselves. For example, infants can be rated relatively high or low (or somewhere in the middle) on the six dimensions described in the Observation Guidelines table "Noticing Temperament in Infants and Toddlers."

Recently researchers have identified a simpler way to look at temperament that seems to be strongly supported by the research. Mary Rothbart and her colleagues have identified three dimensions of temperament in children (Rothbart, 2004a, 2004b; Rothbart, Ahadi, Hershey, & Fisher, 2001):

- Children who score high on *extraversion/surgency* show high levels of optimistic anticipation, impulsivity, activity, and sensation seeking, and they smile and laugh often.
- Children who score high on *negative affectivity* frequently are fearful, shy, frustrated, sad, uncomfortable, and not easily soothed.
- Children who show high levels of *effortful control* are proficient in strategically focusing and shifting their attention, are sensitive to perceptual stimuli, and seek out low-intensity pleasures (those that do not entail risk taking).

These three dimensions have implications for educators and other practitioners. For example, a child high on *extraversion/surgency* may need help channeling energy into a few constructive outlets. A child high on *negative affectivity* may need quiet support in gradually joining a busy group. And a child low on *effort control* may need help focusing on classroom lessons.

Growing evidence suggests that temperament has a genetic basis. For example, identical twins reared in different homes often have similar temperaments (Henderson, 1982; Rothbart & Bates, 1998; Tellegren et al., 1988). Yet nature dictates not full-blown features but rather behavioral *predispositions* that are modified by experience (Kagan, 1998; R. A. Thompson, 1998). For example, shy children have more opportunities to interact with other

personality
Characteristic way a person behaves, thinks, and feels.

OBSERVATION GUIDELINES

Noticing Temperament in Infants and Toddlers

Characteristic	Look For	Example	Implication
Activity Level	*High activity level* • Squirms a lot • As infant, wiggles while getting diaper changed • As toddler, loves to run, climb, jump, and explore *Low activity level* • Sits in high chair contentedly and watches the world go by • Sits quietly on own and plays with toys	Two-year-old Brenda is constantly on the move. Her caregiver finds he can more easily change her diaper if he cleans her bottom and then lets her stand, allowing her to help fasten the tabs on the new diaper.	For infants and toddlers with a *high activity level*, provide many opportunities for safe exploration of the environment. Create challenges in the environment, such as a safe obstacle course with a favorite toy at the end. Encourage children to dance to music. Incorporate movement into quiet activities; for example, while reading a book, encourage children to flip and touch the pages. For children with *low activity level,* slow down to their pace and then invite more active play.
Sensitivity to Physical Input	*High sensitivity* • Withdraws from bright lights • Cries when music is loud *Low sensitivity* • Doesn't mind new stimulation • Doesn't pay much attention until stimulation is extreme	Angela reacts strongly to sudden changes, so her caregiver puts a new portable mobile in her lap and lets her get used to it before showing her how the mobile can be turned on to play music.	For *highly sensitive* children, keep the environment calm—dim the lights, play music quietly, and shield them from chaotic social events. For *less sensitive* children, watch for the kind of stimulation they crave. For example, if they like active social games, engage them in peekaboo or roll a ball on the floor and give them a turn.
Emotional Intensity	*High emotional intensity* • Is fearful and cautious with new people and experiences • Shows dramatic displays of anger, sadness *Low emotional intensity* • Is quiet and does not fuss much • Shows more interest when emotional exchanges are fairly intense	Habib is a very outgoing, passionate toddler. He laughs hard, cries hard, and has dramatic temper tantrums. His caregiver is patient with him and helps him verbalize his negative feelings when they seem to get out of control.	For children who are *emotionally intense*, empathize with their strong feelings, and suggest appropriate ways to express them ("I can see you're angry. Remember, don't bite. Say 'No!' instead"). Help children who are *less emotionally intense* to articulate their feelings ("You look sad; can you tell me how you're feeling?").
Sociability	*High sociability* • Smiles at new people • Enjoys playing in large groups • Is somewhat independent of caregivers *Low sociability* • Doesn't interact with new people unless it is clear they are friendly and in other ways safe • Prefers to play with one other child • Stays close to familiar adult in new social situation	Tony is shy around other people, especially adults not in his immediate family. He would rather sit and play alone than join in an active group of toddlers climbing outside. His caregiver occasionally helps him join in on enjoyable interactions with other children.	For children who show *high sociability,* encourage this disposition. Also encourage them to sit and do quiet activities on their own. For children who show *low sociability,* let them warm up to new people slowly. For example, hold a child in your arms when meeting a new person; sit near the child when he or she ventures to play with an unfamiliar peer; and offer reassurance in new settings ("Let's go visit the preschool room and see what they do in there—they have an awesome slide").
Adaptability	*Ease with change* • Has an easy time with transitions, such as moving inside after outdoor play • Notices changes in environment, such as new furniture, with interest but no concern *Difficulty with change* • Resists new objects and experiences, such as new cups with a different kind of lid • Acts out during transitions between activities • Is suspicious of new people	Thomas frets when going to bed at night. He acts out whenever the routine changes at school. When going somewhere new, he demands continual attention from a trusted adult. His caregiver gives him plenty of warning when a change in routine is expected and talks to him about novel events before they happen.	When children show *ease with change,* continue to make their world challenging, but also predictable. With children who have *difficulty with change,* establish routines so that children know what to expect from day to day, advise them when there is a departure from a regular routine ("Our nap time will be a little late today because we have a special visitor"), give them warning about a change ("When I turn off the light, it will be time to pick up toys"), and give choices when possible ("Would you prefer to build blocks or go to dramatic play?").
Persistence	*High persistence* • Can wait patiently while drink or bottle is being prepared • Shows tolerance for frustration *Low persistence* • Wants comfort immediately • Gets frustrated easily	Rosemary shows no tolerance for frustration. When she is hungry, she wants her meal *now!* When completing puzzles, she gets angry when pieces don't fit immediately into the proper slots.	For *highly persistent* children, explain what you are doing to meet their needs ("I'm slicing up these apples for a healthy snack") and comment on their progress toward goals ("You are working hard on that puzzle!"). For children who show *little persistence,* offer comfort when they are frustrated ("Can I sit with you while you do that?"), help them to consider other ways to reach their desired goal ("What if you turned the puzzle piece around like this?"), and encourage them to break up difficult tasks into smaller, more manageable parts.

Sources: Based on observational indicators of temperament and recommendations for dealing with them in Zero to Three: National Center for Infants, Toddlers, and Families, 2002. For basic distinctions in temperaments, see A. Thomas & Chess, 1977.

children—and thus they may overcome shyness—if they attend preschool rather than remain at home until kindergarten or first grade.

In addition, parents, teachers, and peers may intentionally cultivate certain ways of responding. In other words, children's temperaments are the targets of *socialization* (Harwood et al., 1995). For instance, Japanese parents do much to keep their babies pacified and quiet, in part out of regard for a cultural ideal of harmony and in part out of consideration for neighbors who live on the other sides of thin walls. Japanese mothers therefore talk infrequently, speak softly, and gently stroke their babies (Miyake, Campos, Kagan, & Bradshaw, 1986). In contrast, American mothers talk to infants frequently and in an expressive and evocative manner, perhaps in efforts to stimulate cognitive development and strengthen the caregiver-infant relationship (e.g., Trainor et al., 2000).

Research on temperament also suggests some stability over time. We therefore can, to some degree, predict children's later social behaviors and their later emotional problems from their temperaments (Caspi, 1998; Kagan, 1998; Rothbart & Bates, 1998; A. Thomas & Chess, 1977). For example, children who are inhibited and fearful as young children tend to become fairly anxious adolescents and adults (Caspi, 1998). Children who freely show negative affect (e.g., fussiness, frequent anger) in the early years are more likely to show negative affect (e.g., depression, anxiety) later in life (Caspi, 1998). This stability is undoubtedly due both to genetic factors and to persistent characteristics of children's environments (such as affectionate families and harsh neighborhoods consistently promoting and undermining children's well-being, respectively).

Personality.   Over time, a child integrates biologically based emotional tendencies with his or her experiences, relationships, and intellectual interests. The result is a distinctive and somewhat stable personality. For example, a child may be passionate about finding order in the material world. As a 4-year-old, he has an insatiable curiosity for dinosaurs; as an 8-year-old, he is fascinated with space and aeronautics; as a 12-year-old, he learns all he can about bridges and buildings; as a 16-year-old, he becomes an expert in computers; and as a young man, he prepares for a career in civil engineering.

Despite their relative stability, children's personalities can change slightly over time and in response to the demands of particular situations. Thus a 12-year-old girl may be highly sociable—talking frequently, smiling at others, and befriending many peers—but find it difficult to make new friends when her family moves across the country and she encounters a new group of peers with different customs and values. The demands of particular settings can likewise affect which aspects of complex personalities children reveal. For instance, a child may be spontaneous and cheerful on the playground and distracted and agitated in the classroom.

Recognizing that personality changes somewhat over time and across situations, psychologists have nevertheless found five dimensions of personality to be notably stable:

- *Extraversion* (being socially outgoing)
- *Agreeableness* (being warm and sympathetic)
- *Conscientiousness* (being persistent and organized)
- *Neuroticism* (being anxious and fearful)
- *Openness* (being curious and imaginative)

These five dimensions were originally identified in adults, but they also characterize children (Caspi, 1998; Digman, 1989; John, 1990; John, Caspi, Robins, Moffitt, & Stouthamer-Loeber, 1994; McCrae, Costa, & Busch, 1986). The stability of these dimensions is due partly to genetics and partly to the consistency of children's environments and the perpetuating qualities of children's social-emotional functioning (e.g., irritable children provoke other people to be punitive and aggressive, increasing the probability for children's future hostile actions). The traits of extraversion and neuroticism appear to be especially strongly affected by genetic factors (Loehlin, 1992).

The Developmental Trends table "Emotional and Personal Development at Different Age Levels" encapsulates what you have learned about children's attachment, emotional qualities, and temperaments and personalities. By now it will be abundantly clear to you that children benefit when educators and other adults treat them sensitively and with appreciation for their individual qualities. In the final section, we turn to practical strategies you can use as you work with children with varied temperaments and personalities.

Connecting Concepts
In Chapter 5 you learned that socialization involves systematic efforts by other people and institutions to prepare youngsters to act in ways valued by society.

This mother comforts her baby in a peaceful and soothing manner—an approach that may partly explain the baby's quiet and subdued mood.

Study Guide and Reader
An approach to personality that is based on children's orientation toward rules is described in Supplementary Reading 11-3.

Emotional and Personal Development at Different Age Levels

Age	What You Might Observe	Diversity	Implications
Infancy (Birth–2) 	• Attachment behaviors (seeking contact with caregiver when afraid, hurt, or hungry) • Distress at separation from caregiver • Increasing repertoire of ways to communicate feelings; crying and smiling gradually supplemented with laughter, hand gestures, and words • Beginning ability to soothe self by sucking thumb, hugging favorite blankets, pulling on ear, and so on	• Some children have multiple attachments and move easily from one caregiver to another, whereas other children may have one strong attachment and strongly protest separation from the attachment figure. • Some cultures encourage small children to express all their feelings, including anger and sadness. Other cultures place harmony above self-expression and discourage infants and toddlers from expressing certain feelings; instead, they teach restraint (Camras et al., 1998).	• Model appropriate emotions, and remain calm when infants and toddlers cry and shout. • Be responsive and sensitive to the needs of infants—they are learning to trust you as you help them satisfy their needs. • Seek professional guidance when you encounter infants who appear to have serious attachment problems. • Take infants' separation distress seriously, and provide them with lots of reassurance. • Help parents and other family members cope with their infants' separation distress. Encourage them to watch their infants through one-way mirrors, if available.
Early Childhood (2–6) 	• Desire to be close to parents when afraid, hurt, or uncertain • Wide variety of emotions (e.g., happiness, sadness, fear, anger, disgust) • Emergence of self-conscious emotions (e.g., pride, guilt)	• Children vary in the number of close attachments they form, the extent to which they find reassurance in these attachment figures, and their responses to strangers. Some cling tightly to caregivers, others venture confidently to explore new environments and check out strangers. • Children vary in how they express their emotions. Some are very controlled, especially in masking anger and sadness. Others are more expressive.	• Realize that young children may initially be cautious or fearful in a new classroom or other group; they will become more confident as they begin to form attachments to their teachers or other group leaders. • Be patient in establishing relationships with young children; some may form attachments quickly, but others may take several weeks or months before trusting adults outside the home. • Teach appropriate ways of handling negative emotions. Encourage children to "use their words" rather than pushing or hitting when angry.
Middle Childhood (6–10) 	• Increasing number of bonds with people outside the family, including peers, teachers, and other adults • Increasing ability to regulate emotions	• Children are emotionally affected by major family disruptions (e.g., divorce of parents, death or illness). Changes in family membership may temporarily undermine children's security. • Some children have strong role models for emotional regulation (e.g., a parent may work out negative feelings and conflicts in productive ways).	• Incorporate discussions of emotional states into the curriculum; for example, address the feelings of characters in literature and history. • Model appropriate ways of expressing feelings. • Respect cultural differences in regulating emotions.
Early Adolescence (10–14) 	• Frequent fluctuations in mood, partly as a result of hormonal changes • Careful regulation of emotions (e.g., hiding joy about a good grade in order to appear "cool" to peers)	• Adolescents differ in the extent to which they strive to conform to typical gender differences in emotional regulation. • Some adolescents tend to internalize their stresses (e.g., experiencing depression or anxiety); others respond with overt behaviors (e.g., being violent, breaking the law).	• Be a supportive listener when young people want to share their anxieties. • Keep in mind that some moodiness is normal in the middle school grades. However, talk with parents or the school counselor about the emotional well-being of youngsters who seem especially troubled.
Late Adolescence (14–18) 	• Seeking emotional intimacy with same-sex and opposite-sex peers • Continued attachments to parents, but with strong preferences for affection to be demonstrated in private rather than in public • Increasing ability to be comforted by peers when distressed	• For some adolescents, relationships with parents are full of conflict and offer little emotional support. • Some adolescents use drugs and alcohol to cope with negative emotions. • Some adolescents (girls especially) ruminate over life's challenges. • Some adolescents (boys especially) may project the impression that difficult experiences do not bother them.	• When adolescents are in minor conflicts with their parents, help them understand that most parents truly want the best for their children and behave accordingly (albeit sometimes punitively or coercively); refer them to a school counselor when relationships with parents are extremely poor. • Ask adolescents to reflect on the emotional experiences of fictional characters and historical figures. • Refer adolescents to counselors when they appear depressed or unhappy.

Helping Children to Be Themselves

Teachers can plan lessons and activities that address the varied temperaments and personalities of youngsters in their care. Here are some specific suggestions:

● *Identify the kinds of temperaments that you naturally prefer, as well as those that push your buttons.* Many teachers prefer to work with children who are curious, happy to be at school, and inclined to follow directions, work hard, and act cooperatively, intelligently, cautiously, and efficiently (Keogh, 2003; Wentzel, 2000). Teachers tend to find it less rewarding to work with children who are easily distracted, angry or irritable, disruptive, and assertive. When teachers come to realize that they automatically (and often unconsciously) respond in certain ways to particular temperaments, they can take the first steps toward holding their biases in check and accepting the inevitability of a broad range of temperaments in children.

● *Adjust to young children's stylistic ways of responding to the world.* Infant caregivers often look after active babies who love to crawl around their environment, sway to music, and squirm in their high chairs (A. Thomas & Chess, 1977; Zero to Three, 2002). To meet the needs of active infants, caregivers may permit them to explore and move often. In contrast, infants who show a lower activity level may sit contently and let the world come to them. Caregivers may sit quietly with them, talk softly about pictures in a book, and acknowledge their focus on toys.

● *Consider children's temperaments when forming groups.* Teachers can often help children who are shy or impulsive by pairing them with peers who might compensate for their limitations. For example, a first-grade teacher might plan a Halloween activity of making "dirt" cake, knowing she can count on one boy to be methodical in measuring cocoa and other ingredients. She pairs him with another boy who will attack the project enthusiastically, but without restraint; together, they might make a good combination. Because there is never any guarantee that temperamentally dissimilar children will work effectively together, you also need to monitor the evolving dynamics of such groups once you form them.

● *Allow children to apply their natural strengths, but also encourage them to try out new strategies for learning.* Permitting children to choose from among a few specified options is an important way to respect children's individuality. For instance, children might be asked to report on a book they have read, choosing from an array of defined options—a written analysis, poster, or oral presentation. Yet children are naturally inclined to remain in their comfort zone, and they can benefit from occasional practice of their less developed talents. For example, a child who has trouble concentrating may be taught to use attention-focusing strategies, and a child who chooses books impulsively might be asked to prepare a checklist of desirable features (that includes favorite topics, for instance) to refer to when selecting a new book at the library.

Connecting Concepts
Chapter 7 describes instructional strategies for helping children with difficulties in attention and learning.

● *Communicate your expectations about acceptable behaviors.* When adults make expectations explicit and consistently enforce compliance, children with many kinds of temperaments and personalities benefit (Keogh, 2003). Children who are apprehensive about doing the right thing can be assured that they are indeed acting in an acceptable manner. Children who are inclined to act impulsively can be reminded of rules, consequences for misbehavior, and strategies that they can use to keep track of their behaviors.

● *Set up routines that youngsters can follow.* A predictable schedule in the day is very important to children. Children adjust to activities when they know what to expect—for example, that when they arrive at school in the morning, they are to place their backpacks and jackets in pre-assigned places, go straight to their desks, and begin working on the daily worksheet. Of course, some variation is inevitable and desirable, but familiar routines help everyone adjust to daily activities. Children also need to be advised of the procedural rules of a classroom, such as how to line up or disperse for lunch, and the circumstances under which they can sharpen their pencils, use the restroom, and ask for assistance.

● *Help children to cope with changes in routines.* Children with some temperaments and personalities—for instance, those who are timid or irritable—may find alterations to routines

———————— Connecting Concepts
Children with autism may find changes
in routine especially unsettling (see
Chapter 7).

particularly difficult. To help these and other children, educators can tell youngsters ahead of time about anticipated modifications regarding school personnel, schedules, or rules. To illustrate, elementary school children can be introduced to a substitute teacher the week before their regular teacher departs for an extended family leave. Middle school adolescents can be shown the blueprints for a new auditorium before the existing structure is leveled, and high school students should receive a copy of a new code of conduct for their school. When changes can *not* be anticipated ahead of time, children appreciate hearing as soon as possible about changes to routines, especially those changes that may affect them personally.

● *Physically arrange the classroom to minimize disruptions and noise.* Defined pathways between desks and protected space in high-traffic areas can minimize tussles among children who are easily frustrated or lacking in social skills. In addition, highly sensitive children may be overwhelmed by the chaos of the classroom and appreciate the relief of spending some time in a quieter setting. For example, children who are sensitive to sensory stimuli might occasionally be allowed to complete lessons in the school library.

● *Make appropriate adjustments for children who show unusually high or low levels on one or more personality dimensions.* Children with exceptional levels on particular personality dimensions stand out from other children. These children need to be accepted for who they are, but they often also benefit from special accommodations that guide their learning, peer relationships, emotional expression, and motivation to follow rules. Let's consider how educators might adjust to some unusually high or low levels of the personality dimensions we introduced earlier.

Extraversion: Extraverted children are active, assertive, emotionally expressive, talkative, enthusiastic, and socially outgoing. Extraverted children often appreciate opportunities to work on projects with peers. Teachers can also intersperse opportunities for physical movement around quiet activities to give these children needed exercise and occasionally provide a public forum (such as a dramatic performance) for self-expression. In contrast, children who are shy may benefit from private conversations with teachers and friendly invitations from peers and playground supervisors to join in a game.

Agreeableness: Agreeable children are warm, responsive, generous, kind, sympathetic, and trusting. Children who are agreeable may be pleased when adults and other children notice and comment on their cooperative spirit. Children who are less prone to be pleasant may benefit if teachers coach them to compliment other children, share toys, offer comfort to others in distress, and voice opinions without putting people down.

Conscientiousness: Conscientious children are attentive, persistent in activities, organized, and responsible. Teachers can admire the persistence and organization shown by these children and point out how their style pays off in well-designed work products. Children who set lower standards and fail to complete tasks can be taught to set appropriate goals, to resist counterproductive urges, and to monitor their own progress toward goals.

Neuroticism: Neurotic children are anxious, fearful, lacking in confidence, and self-pitying. Children who are overly anxious and fearful may need support in dealing with negative feelings. They also need encouragement to try challenging and potentially anxiety-arousing tasks they might otherwise avoid. Children who are relaxed and confident thrive when given continuous support from adults. No one is self-assured all the time, however, and adults can express extra support when normally confident children face momentous losses, personal failures, or traumatic events.

Openness: Children who are open are curious, artistic, exploring, and imaginative. Children who are particularly open intellectually need to exercise their budding skills in many contexts. Those who are less driven to explore art, literature, history, and the scientific world may need to be shown the intrigue and beauty of these and other fields.

● *Recognize the complexity of children's personalities.* Within individual children, the various dimensions of temperament and personality combine in a myriad of ways that can both delight and tax adults. For example, a teacher may have one child who is socially outgoing but a bit anxious and not terribly agreeable; another child who is self-confident and conscientious, but somewhat conforming and slow to exercise her imagination; another who worries constantly and craves approval from adults but is quietly curious and thoughtful; and many more other children, each with an individual profile. Ultimately, every child has special needs when it comes to temperament and personality.

Showing sensitivity to children's unique temperaments and personalities goes a long way toward nurturing children's psychological health. Teachers can go only so far, however. Adults should be supportive, but the children themselves must also take steps to cope with daily hassles and significant life challenges. In the final case, a conflict occurs among peers, and a child has the opportunity to face up to his difficulty in regulating emotions.

Case Study: The Girly Shirt

Eight-year-old Tim caused quite a disruption in class this morning. His teacher, Amy Fox, isn't quite sure why things got out of hand, and so she is meeting with Tim while the rest of the class is at lunch to learn what happened.

Ms. Fox:	Things got out of control in class this morning, didn't they, Tim?
Tim:	I guess they did.
Ms. Fox:	Tell me what happened.
Tim:	John and Steven were teasing me about my shirt. They really made me mad.
Ms. Fox:	They were teasing you about your *shirt*? What did they say?
Tim:	That it's too pink. That it's a "girly" color.
Ms. Fox:	Really? I don't think it's too "girly" at all. In fact, I rather like that color on you. But anyway, you say the boys teased you about it. What did you do then?
Tim:	I yelled at them. Then when you gave me that dirty look, they kept on laughing, and so I kept on yelling.
Ms. Fox:	I see. John and Steven were certainly wrong to tease you about your clothes. I'll speak to them later. But right now I'm concerned about how you reacted to the situation. You were so loud that the class couldn't possibly continue with the lesson.
Tim:	I know. I'm sorry.
Ms. Fox:	I appreciate your apology, Tim. And I'd like to make sure that the next time someone hurts your feelings—maybe intentionally, maybe not—you don't blow up the way you did today. Let's come up with a plan for how you might keep your temper under better control.

- Considering what you have learned about trends in emotional development, is Tim's reaction typical for his age?
- What kind of plan might be effective in helping Tim control his anger?

Once you have answered these questions, compare your responses with those presented in the appendix.

Summary

Erikson's Theory

Erikson proposed that psychosocial characteristics emerge over the course of eight stages (the first beginning in infancy and the last occurring in old age). Erikson blazed many trails for later developmental scholars, yet the prolific research inspired by his work has revealed that his theory does not accurately describe emotional development in some cultures, nor does it adequately account for the interplay of identity and intimacy.

First Attachments

Ideally, children's first attachments are close and enduring bonds between themselves and their caregivers. Sensitive and responsive attention is the necessary ingredient for the formation of secure attachments, but children also contribute by returning affection. Secure attachments in the early years lead to positive social-emotional outcomes later on. However, attachments manifest themselves somewhat differently in different cultures, and the nature of people's attachments can and often does change over time.

Emotional Development

Emotions have adaptive functions for children, helping them decide how to act. Children and adolescents become increasingly able to regulate their emotions in ways that are both socially acceptable and personally effective. Individual differences in emotional functioning are the result of both biology (e.g., temperament and gender-specific hormones) and environment (e.g., socialization by parents, peers, and culture). Dealing with youngsters' emotions is an important aspect of teaching and

working with children and adolescents. Adults can do many things to promote the emotional well-being of youngsters and should remain especially alert to the needs of young people with serious emotional needs (e.g., depression, anxiety disorders, and conduct disorders).

Temperament and Personality

Children are born with dispositions to respond to the world and express their emotions in certain ways. These constitutional inclinations, called temperaments, are also affected by experience and social relationships. As children grow, they integrate their temperamental dimensions with their intellectual interests, habits, and other experiences to acquire distinctive personalities. Teachers and other practitioners can help children enormously when they make accommodations for children's unique temperaments and personalities.

Applying Concepts in Child Development

In this chapter you learned about core elements of children's social-emotional development—their first attachments to caregivers, their emotional expression, and their unique temperaments and personalities. The following table describes behaviors that youngsters at five different age levels exhibit. For each of these behaviors, the table identifies one or more relevant social-emotional qualities, offers an implication for working with children of that age-group, or both. Apply what you've learned about attachment, emotions, temperament, and personality to fill in the empty cells in the table. When you're done, compare your responses with those in Table 11-1 in the *Study Guide and Reader*.

APPLYING CONCEPTS IN CHILD DEVELOPMENT	Nurturing Youngsters' Emotional Development		
Age	A Youngster's Experience	**Developmental Concepts** *Identifying Emotional Qualities*	**Implications** *Nurturing Emotional Development*
Infancy (Birth–2)	Edel is a healthy 1-year-old girl with Down syndrome. Her mother is going back to work and enrolls Edel in a child care center. During the first few weeks, when Edel is first dropped off in the morning, she clings to her mother and cries loudly as her mother leaves. When her mother returns in the afternoon, Edel is usually sitting quietly and mouthing and handling toys. Upon noticing her mother, Edel crawls to her, demands to be picked up, and snuggles into her arms.		Be especially reassuring to infants when they first enter your care. Hold them gently, pamper them when they cry, and look after them with utmost sensitivity. Expect them to protest separations from parents, realizing that they eventually will form attachments to you.
Early Childhood (2–6)	Mr. Bono notices that one of his preschool students, Phyllis, seems somewhat anxious at school. Phyllis appears timid and shy, and she stands on the fringes of group activities. She does not interact easily with other children and has no regular friends in the class. With a change in routine, such as missing story time because of a fire drill or having to stay inside during a bitter snow day, Phyllis is obviously upset.	As with all children, Phyllis has her own unique *temperament* and a budding *personality*. Depending on the particular constellation of temperamental or personality characteristics being considered, Phyllis might be described as emotionally intense, showing negative affectivity, or having an inclination toward neuroticism.	When children seem timid, shy, and nervous, offer them reassurance that everything is fine. Provide them with a well-structured learning environment, and when possible, give advance notice of changes in regular activities. When children have trouble making friends, help them ease into social groups.

(continued)

APPLYING CONCEPTS IN CHILD DEVELOPMENT

Nurturing Youngsters' Emotional Development (continued)

Age	A Youngster's Experience	Developmental Concepts *Identifying Emotional Qualities*	Implications *Nurturing Emotional Development*
Middle Childhood (6–10)	A third-grade teacher returns children's graded mathematics assignments. Most children did well on the assignment, but two children, Brenda and Billy, had trouble keeping their attention on the task and so received low grades for their work. When Brenda receives her low grade, she cries and broods over the poor score for the remainder of the day. Billy, on the other hand, smiles when he gets the assignment back, says, "Oh well," but he later gets in trouble during recess for disruptive behavior.	Brenda and Billy seem to exhibit typical *gender differences in emotions.* Brenda responds negatively to her poor performance and frets about it all day. Billy seems to deny that there is a problem, but his disruptive behavior later in the day may be a sign that he is, in fact, trying to put on a self-confident front to mask his disappointment.	
Early Adolescence (10–14)	Thirteen-year-old Adam has confronted many hardships in his life, including his parents' divorce, economic poverty, and the death of a baby sister. Despite facing adversity, Adam is a reasonably happy and healthy young man. When he is sad or anxious, he makes a point to go for a ride on his bicycle and talk openly about his feelings with his parents and close friends. Sometimes when he feels particularly stressed, he goes to the movies with a friend or drops in to the neighborhood youth center to play pool.	Adam seems reasonably well adjusted, perhaps due in part to the fact that he has learned a range of helpful techniques for *emotional regulation.*	Teach and encourage effective ways of regulating emotions. When adolescents are particularly troubled, remind them of the strategies that have helped them in the past, including expressing feelings to others, exercising, and distracting themselves with enjoyable activities.
Late Adolescence (14–18)	Seventeen-year-old Nate broke up with his steady girlfriend. He appears despondent and tells his father and friends that he can't bear it anymore. He says he feels terrible, drinks alcohol excessively, and searches the Internet for Web sites about suicide.	Nate is showing some warning signs that he might be at risk for *suicide.* None of these indicators is definitive, but collectively they do suggest he is in serious trouble and needs immediate attention.	

Key Concepts

psychosocial stages (p. 404)
need for relatedness (p. 407)
attachment (p. 407)
ethological attachment theory (p. 408)
stranger anxiety (p. 409)

secure attachment (p. 410)
insecure-avoidant attachment (p. 410)
insecure-resistant attachment (p. 411)

disorganized and disoriented attachment (p. 411)
emotion (p. 417)
emotional contagion (p. 418)
self-conscious emotion (p. 420)
emotional regulation (p. 420)

empathy (p. 421)
anxiety (p. 426)
depression (p. 427)
anxiety disorder (p. 428)
conduct disorder (p. 428)
personality (p. 431)

Companion Website

Now go to our Companion Website at www.prenhall.com/mcdevitt to assess your understanding of chapter content with a Practice Quiz, apply what you've learned in Essay Questions, and broaden your knowledge with links to related Developmental Psychology Web sites.

Development of Self and
Social Understanding

chapter 12

Case Study: Kellen

As a preschooler, Kellen was, as his mother Christine puts it, "really active" and difficult to manage. He sometimes opened the car door when it was in motion. He often bit people when he was frustrated. He showed little if any improvement in kindergarten. On the wall of the kindergarten classroom was a "good behavior" chart listing every child's name. The girls had lots of stickers beside their names, the boys had fewer, and Kellen had none. "He really knows how to push my buttons," the teacher said.

When his classmates moved on to first grade, Kellen remained in kindergarten for a second year. Midway through the school year, Kellen's teacher bluntly told Christine, "I think there's something wrong with your son." At the teacher's recommendation, a child psychologist conducted an in-depth evaluation. An intelligence test yielded an overall IQ of 135, a score reflecting high general intelligence. But Kellen's verbal skills lagged far behind his nonverbal skills, indicating that he faced certain challenges in school learning tasks. The psychologist concluded that Kellen had both attention-deficit hyperactivity disorder and a "language-based disability."

With medication, Kellen's behavior improved considerably. His high intelligence was evident in his ability to create complex structures with Legos and other construction toys. Yet when his second-grade classmates were reading fluently—and despite his second-grade teacher's report that "He's doing great!"—Kellen could barely read at all. Intensive instruction in letter-sound relationships and other basic literacy skills helped, but Kellen continued to struggle with both reading and writing throughout the elementary grades. Kellen was repeatedly frustrated that he could not do things that classmates did easily. Rather than bite other people, as he had when he was younger, he chewed on his shirt sleeves and collars, and he felt uncomfortable around many of his peers. In Christine's words, Kellen had "big anxiety issues."

In fifth grade Kellen moved on to middle school, where his classwork quickly deteriorated. Although he received specialized instruction in reading and spelling several times a week, he no longer used the cursive writing he had finally mastered the year before. His teachers consistently downplayed his poor performance with such comments as "He was probably just having a bad day" and "He's doing enough to get by." At home Kellen became increasingly irritable and soon stopped doing his homework. One day Christine found him curled up in a ball under his desk, crying and saying, "I can't do this anymore!" Alarmed, she took him to a psychiatrist, who concluded that Kellen had dyslexia and a "clinically significant anxiety disorder directly related to educational difficulties." Two follow-up evaluations by language and reading specialists confirmed the dyslexia diagnosis.

"No one had ever used the word *dyslexia* before," Christine recalls. Armed with this new information, she and her husband looked for an educational setting for Kellen that could address both his strengths and his weaknesses. Eventually, they found a small private school about an hour away. Most of the students at the school had high IQ scores; some also had learning disabilities. After Kellen's parents hired an attorney, the local school district reluctantly agreed to pick up the school's tuition costs.

In sixth grade at the new school, each day was tightly structured. Kellen showed dramatic improvement in virtually every area. He earned all As in math and science. He began writing in cursive again. His teachers taught him how to organize his assignments in folders and a backpack, and so he rarely forgot to do his homework. His self-esteem skyrocketed, and he became more outgoing with adults and peers alike. "He's a different kid now," his mother said at the end of his sixth-grade year.[a]

[a]We thank an anonymous friend for sharing her son's story. The names Kellen and Christine are pseudonyms.

Case Study: Kellen

Sense of Self

Social Cognition

Interpersonal Behaviors

Case Study: Gang Mediation

Summary

Applying Concepts in Child Development

Children's beliefs and feelings about who they are as people have a significant influence on their behavior, school achievement, and emotional well-being. When Kellen saw his peers' reading performance far surpass his own, his increasing frustration eventually escalated into an emotional crisis. When he later discovered that with the right structure and strategies he could be academically successful, he gained the self-confidence he needed not only to work hard at school but also to interact effectively with others.

As the opening case so clearly illustrates, teachers' actions can have a significant influence on children's self-perceptions. Sometimes this influence is a positive one, as was true for the sixth-grade teachers who taught Kellen how to organize his schoolwork. But it can also be a negative one, as was the case for the kindergarten teacher whose good behavior chart so explicitly communicated her poor opinions of Kellen's behavior. In this chapter we look at how and what children think both about themselves and about the people around them and how such perceptions affect their interpersonal behaviors and general social-emotional development. We also look at how teachers and other adults can enhance children's and adolescents' self-perceptions and help youngsters interact effectively with others.

Sense of Self

Children's knowledge, beliefs, judgments, and feelings about themselves are collectively known as **sense of self.** Particular elements of this sense of self go by a variety of names, including self-concept, self-esteem, self-worth, and self-efficacy. In general, one's *self-concept* addresses the question *"Who am I?"* It includes knowledge and beliefs about one's own characteristics, strengths, and weaknesses ("I get high grades in school," "My nose is a bit crooked"). The terms *self-esteem* and *self-worth* address the question *"How good am I as a person?"* They include judgments and feelings about one's own value and worth (e.g., "I am proud of my academic record," "I hate my crooked nose!"). However, we urge you not to agonize over how self-concept, self-esteem, and self-worth differ, because their meanings overlap quite a bit, and so they are often used interchangeably (Byrne, 2002; Harter, 1999; Pintrich & Schunk, 2002).

In contrast to the other three terms, *self-efficacy* addresses the question *"How well can I do such-and-such?"* In other words, it refers to children's beliefs about their competence in a specific domain or activity—perhaps in reading, drawing, or rap music. To some extent, youngsters' specific self-efficacies for various tasks and activities contribute to their more general sense of self (Bong & Skaalvik, 2003).

Effects of Children's Sense of Self

Children's sense of self serves several important functions (Harter, 1999). It helps children make sense of and organize the things that happen to them ("Other kids keep asking me to join their teams, so I must be good at sports"). It motivates them to engage in behaviors to which others might respond favorably ("If I'm nice to Russell, maybe he'll ask me to play with him"). It influences their reactions to events ("I'm really frustrated that I'm not reading as well as my classmates"). It allows them to envision the various *future selves* they might become (see Figure 12-1). And once they begin to look seriously at a particular future self, it helps them make choices appropriate for their goals ("If I want to become a veterinarian, then I should take a biology class").

Many psychologists believe that human beings have a basic need to think of themselves as competent, likeable, and worthy individuals—that is, to achieve and maintain a positive sense of self-worth (Covington, 1992; Deci & Ryan, 1992; R. White, 1959). Most children do seem to focus more on what they do well than on what they do poorly, and so they are predisposed to think well of themselves (Fischer, 2005; Jacobs, Lanza, Osgood, Eccles, & Wigfield, 2002). Often they downplay areas that give them trouble (e.g., "Math is dumb"). They may also explain their shortcomings in ways that enable them to maintain a positive sense of self. In the "Memory: Middle Childhood" video clip on

Study Guide and Reader
Youngsters not only strive to understand themselves and other people, but also work hard to make sense of the society in which they live (see Supplementary Reading 12-1).

Figure 12-1

In these spontaneously created drawings, 10-year-old Alex envisions a variety of possible *future selves,* some realistic and others more fanciful.

sense of self
Knowledge, beliefs, judgments, and feelings about oneself as a person.

Observation CD 1, you can see 10-year-old David give a healthy, upbeat spin on why he doesn't recall as many words as he expects to. He predicts that he might recall 12 out of 12 words but actually recalls only 3. Here is David's positive interpretation:

David: Okay, shirt, carrot, bed. I'm sorry, I can't remember the rest of it. It's just, I don't know. My brain was turned off right now. I use it a lot during school hours so then I just like to relax. . . .

Interviewer: What did you do to remember the ones that you remembered?

David: Even though I said 12, I was just trying to challenge myself a little.

In the "Memory: Middle Childhood" clip on Observation CD 1, hear David put a positive spin on why he didn't remember as many words as he had predicted.

Curiously, youngsters occasionally do things that actually *undermine* their chances of success—a phenomenon known as **self-handicapping.** Self-handicapping takes a variety of forms, including the following:

- *Reducing effort:* Putting forth an obviously insufficient amount of effort to succeed
- *Setting unattainably high goals:* Working toward goals that even the most capable individuals couldn't achieve
- *Taking on too much:* Assuming so many responsibilities that no one could possibly accomplish them all
- *Procrastinating:* Putting off a task until success is virtually impossible
- *Cheating:* Presenting others' work as one's own
- *Using alcohol or drugs:* Taking substances that will inevitably reduce performance (E. M. Anderman, Griesinger, & Westerfield, 1998; Covington, 1992; D. Y. Ford, 1996; Riggs, 1992; Urdan, Ryan, Anderman, & Gheen, 2002)

It might seem paradoxical that youngsters who want to be successful would actually try to undermine their own success. But if they believe they are unlikely to succeed no matter what they do—and especially if failure will reflect poorly on their intelligence and ability—they increase their chances of *justifying* the failure and thereby protecting their self-worth (Covington, 1992; Riggs, 1992; Urdan et al., 2002). Self-handicapping is seen as early as fifth grade and becomes increasingly common in the high school and college years (Urdan, 2004; Urdan & Midgley, 2001; Wolters, 2003).

Unfortunately, some children encounter failure so often or find themselves failing in so many domains that it becomes extremely difficult to maintain a positive sense of self. As a fifth grader, Kellen could not overlook the fact that he was doing poorly at school. He suffered a great deal of emotional distress as a result.

Children tend to behave in ways that mirror their self-perceptions (Bong & Skaalvik, 2003; Caldwell, Rudolph, Troop-Gordon, & Kim, 2004; Valentine, DuBois, & Cooper, 2004). Those who see themselves as "good students" are more apt to pay attention in class, use effective learning strategies, and tackle challenging tasks and problems, whereas those who believe they are "poor students" are apt to misbehave in class, study infrequently, and avoid difficult subject matter. Children who see themselves as friendly and likable are apt to seek the company of classmates and perhaps run for student council, whereas those who believe they are disliked may keep to themselves or behave aggressively toward peers.

As you can see, a positive sense of self is optimal for children's development. Yet children's self-perceptions must also take reality into account. When children assess themselves fairly accurately, they are in a good position to choose age-appropriate activities and work toward achievable goals (Baumeister, Campbell, Krueger, & Vohs, 2003; Harter, 1999). A slightly inflated self-assessment can be beneficial as well, in that it encourages children to set their sights on challenges that, with effort, they can possibly surmount (Bandura, 1997; D. Phillips & Zimmerman, 1990). However, a sense of self that is *very* overinflated may reflect an unhealthy need to feel superior to others—a need that children may strive to meet through bullying peers and other antisocial behaviors (Baumeister et al., 2003). And as you might guess, children who routinely *under*estimate their ability avoid the many challenges that are apt to enhance their cognitive, social, and physical growth (Assor & Connell, 1992; D. Phillips & Zimmerman, 1990).

Factors Influencing Sense of Self

Just as children largely self-construct their understandings of the world around them (see Chapters 6 and 7), so, too, do they self-construct their understandings of who they are as people. To a considerable degree, they base their self-perceptions on their own past behaviors and

self-handicapping
Action that undermines one's own success as a way of protecting self-worth during difficult tasks.

performance (Damon, 1991; Marsh, 1990a; Marsh, Trautwein, Lüdtke, Köller, & Baumert, 2005). Children are more likely to believe they have an aptitude for mathematics if they have been successful in past math classes. They are more apt to see themselves as likable individuals if they have previously been able to establish and maintain friendly relationships with peers. Kellen's low self-esteem was due in large part to his consistently poor performance in reading, writing, and other literacy-based tasks. A second grader named Tom, who (like Kellen) had dyslexia, once described how he felt when struggling with reading in first grade:

> I falt like a losr. Like nobad likde me. I was afrad then kais wod tec me. Becacz I wased larning wale . . . I dan not whet to raed. I whoe whte to troe a book it my mom.
>
> *(I felt like a loser. Like nobody liked me. I was afraid that kids would tease me. Because I wasn't learning well . . . I did not want to read. I would want to throw a book at my mom.)*
> (N. F. Knapp, 1995, p. 9)

Other people also influence children's sense of self, and in several ways. First, adults and peers communicate messages about children's strengths, limitations, and overall worth through both words and behaviors. Such lessons begin in infancy and continue throughout childhood and adolescence. When caregivers regularly give infants nurturance and affection, infants learn not only that their caregivers can be loving but also that they themselves are worthy of being loved (Bretherton, 1991). Parents who accept children as they are— applauding children's abilities and taking *in*abilities in stride—are likely to have children with high self-esteem. Parents who punish children for things they cannot do, without also praising them for things done well, are apt to have children with low self-esteem (Harter, 1983, 1999). Teachers foster a more positive sense of self when they have high yet realistic expectations for children's performance and offer support to help children attain challenging goals (Dweck, 2000; M. J. Harris & Rosenthal, 1985). Meanwhile, peers communicate information about children's social and athletic competence, perhaps by seeking out a child's companionship or ridiculing a child in front of others (Dweck, 2000; Harter, 1999).

Peers contribute to children's sense of self in a second way as well: They provide information about what children "should" be able to do. How children evaluate themselves often depends on how their own performance compares to that of their peers (Guay, Boivin, & Hodges, 1999; Marsh & Hau, 2003). Children who see themselves achieving at higher levels than age-mates in certain domains usually develop a more positive sense of self than those who, like Kellen, consistently find themselves falling short.

Finally, membership in one or more groups can influence children's sense of self, especially in adolescence (Durkin, 1995; Lave & Wenger, 1991; Wigfield et al., 1996). If you think back to your own school years, perhaps you can recall taking pride in something your entire class accomplished, feeling good about a community service project completed through an extracurricular club, or reveling in the state championship earned by one of your school's athletic teams. In general, youngsters are more likely to have high self-esteem if they are members of a successful group (Phinney, 1989; Wigfield et al., 1996).

Children take into consideration the many messages they get about "desirable" and "undesirable" qualities and behaviors and reflect on what such messages mean about their own abilities and self-worth. Oftentimes, how children *interpret* other people's responses to them is more influential than what others actually say or do. For example, in the personal reflection presented in Figure 12-2 , Leslie perceives Georgia's actions to be personal slights and attempts to make her look foolish, despite Georgia's actual intentions to be friendly and accommodating.

So far our discussion has focused primarily on the effects of children's experiences— that is, the effects of environment—on their self-perceptions. Biology also has an impact, although usually indirectly. Inherited temperaments, physical skills, cognitive abilities, and physical and cognitive *dis*abilities all contribute to children's successes and failures in social, athletic, and academic pursuits. Physical appearance makes a difference as well: Adults and peers alike respond more favorably to children who are physically attractive (e.g., Harter, Whitesell, & Junkin, 1998).

General Trends in Children's Sense of Self

Children's physical, cognitive, and social abilities change with age, and their perceptions of themselves shift accordingly. Researchers have observed the following developmental trends in sense of self:

———— Connecting Concepts

Early relationships with caregivers also provide an important foundation for emotional development (see the discussion of *attachment* in Chapter 11).

We were playing freeze tag one day at recess. Leslie got tagged and asked me to step on her shadow before anyone else. I stepped on Becca's shadow before I stepped on Leslie's and got mad. I told Leslie to stop being so selfish and bratty. She took it extremely personally and stormed off, told a teacher, and called her mom.

I later apologized and we became friends again. I invited her to my birthday and she came but I could tell she felt uncomfortable. So, I decided to do makeovers. I was playing around with lipsticks and accidentally messed up on Leslie's makeover, but laughed because I knew it could be fixed. She ran to see the "damage" in the mirror, started to cry, and called her mom and left.

From then on, I've never really understood her and we've never been close. We see each other and say "hi" in the halls, but that's it.

Figure 12-2

In this reflective essay, 13-year-old Georgia expresses dismay that her friend Leslie misinterpreted several of her behaviors.

LUANN   **BY GREG EVANS**

Many adolescents encounter unrealistic self-evaluation criteria in magazines and other popular media.
LUANN: © GEC Inc./Dist. by United Feature Syndicate, Inc.

● *Children construct increasingly multifaceted understandings of who they are.* Children in the early elementary grades tend to distinguish between two general aspects of themselves: how competent they are in daily activities and how well they are liked by family and friends. As they grow older, they make finer and finer discriminations (Davis-Kean & Sandler, 2001; Harter, 1999). In the upper elementary grades, they realize that they may be more or less competent in their academic work, athletic activities, classroom behavior, likability among peers, and physical attractiveness. By adolescence, they also have general self-perceptions about their ability to make friends, their competence at adultlike work tasks, and their romantic appeal. Each of these domains may have a greater or lesser influence on youngsters' overall sense of self. In general, youngsters have high self-esteem when they evaluate themselves as being strong in domains that are most important to them. For some, academic achievement may be the overriding factor, whereas for others popularity with peers may be more influential. For many children and adolescents around the world, physical attractiveness contributes heavily to overall self-esteem (D. Hart, 1988; Harter, 1999).

● *As children grow older, their feelings of self-worth increasingly depend on peers' behaviors and opinions.* In the early years, parents and other family members are key players in shaping children's sense of self. As children spend more time away from home, however, they become more aware of and concerned about what nonfamily members—and especially peers—think of them (Harter, 1999). With this shift may come changes in the criteria by which youngsters evaluate themselves. Whereas parents often express approval for good behavior and high academic achievement, peers tend to favor children who are physically attractive, athletically skillful, and fun to be with (Harter, 1999).

● *Most youngsters gradually internalize criteria by which to evaluate themselves.* Just as children internalize many of the cognitive strategies they first use in social interactions, so, too, do they internalize other people's criteria for evaluating performance and overall worth (Burton & Mitchell, 2003; Harter, 1999). As they adopt such criteria, their self-esteem is increasingly based on self-judgments rather than others' judgments. For example, a boy whose parents regularly praise him for his high grades is likely to begin judging *himself* by the grades he earns. You can see such internalization in an interview with 15-year-old Greg in the "Intrinsic Motivation: Late Adolescence" video clip on Observation CD 3:

Study Guide and Reader
Supplementary Reading 12-2 offers additional insights about the nature and importance of sense of self in early childhood.

Connecting Concepts
The discussion of Vygotsky's theory in Chapter 6 introduced you to the process of internalization.

Interviewer:	What are the things that make you want to do well in school?
Greg:	My parents. [*Both laugh.*]
Interviewer:	Okay.
Greg:	My parents mostly. . . . And myself . . . sometimes.
Interviewer:	Okay. How do your parents influence you wanting to do well in school?
Greg:	I don't know. They did well so they want me to. . . .
Interviewer:	You said that sometimes you also want to do well for you. Can you tell me more about that?
Greg:	'Cause, I mean, you feel better if you get all As than Cs or Fs.

Yet the standards that youngsters adopt are not always realistic or beneficial. For instance, a girl whose friends place a premium on fashion-magazine standards for thinness may think

In the "Intrinsic Motivation: Late Adolescence" clip on Observation CD 3, observe how Greg has internalized his parents' standards for academic performance.

———————— Connecting Concepts
See Chapter 4 for more information
about eating disorders.

she is "fat" even when she is dangerously underweight—a misperception commonly seen in youngsters who have eating disorders (Attie et al., 1990).

Despite the general trend toward greater dependence on self-evaluation, some youngsters remain heavily dependent on others' opinions well into adolescence. They may be so preoccupied with peer approval that they base their own sense of self-worth largely on what their peers think—or at least on what *they think* their peers think—of them (Dweck, 2000; Harter, 1999; Harter, Stocker, & Robinson, 1996). Teenagers who have such **contingent self-worth** are often on an emotional roller coaster, feeling elated one day and devastated the next, depending on how friends and classmates have recently treated them.

● *Youngsters gradually integrate their many self-perceptions into general abstractions of who they are.* Young children tend to define themselves in terms of specific, concrete, easily observable characteristics and behaviors. As they grow older, they begin to pull these characteristics and behaviors into more general, abstract conceptions (D. Hart, 1988; Harter, 1988; Rosenberg, 1986). For examples of how children's self-perceptions change with age, try the following exercise, "Comparing Self-Descriptions."

INTERPRETING CHILDREN'S ARTIFACTS AND ACTIONS   Comparing Self-Descriptions

When her children were younger, Jeanne once asked them to describe themselves. As you read their self-descriptions, identify one or more developmental trends in their responses.

Jeff (age 6): I like animals. I like making things. I do good in school. I'm happy. Blue eyes. Yellow hair. Light skin.

Alex (age 9): I have brown hair, brown eyes. I like wearing short-sleeved shirts. My hair is

curly. I was adopted. I was born in Denver. I like all sorts of critters. The major sport I like is baseball. I do fairly well in school. I have a lizard, and I'm going to get a second one.

Tina (age 12): I'm cool. I'm awesome. I'm way cool. I'm twelve. I'm boy crazy. I go to Brentwood Middle School. I'm popular with my fans. I play viola. My best friend is Lindsay. I have a gerbil named Taj. I'm adopted. I'm beautiful.

Notice how Jeff and Alex talked mostly about how they looked, how they behaved, and what they liked. In contrast, Tina described several abstract qualities—cool, awesome, boy crazy, popular, beautiful—that she had apparently derived from her many experiences over time. Notice, too, how both boys mentioned their performance in school. Tina focused more on social and physical qualities than on academic achievement (or, we might add, modesty). As we've seen, social acceptance and physical appearance are often a high priority in the minds of young adolescents.

● *Sense of self becomes more stable over time.* Children with positive self-perceptions in the early years tend to have positive self-perceptions in later years as well. Conversely, children who think poorly of themselves in elementary school also tend to have low self-esteem in high school (Marsh & Craven, 1997; O'Malley & Bachman, 1983; Savin-Williams & Demo, 1984). As children get older, their self-perceptions become increasingly stable, probably for several reasons:

- They usually behave in ways consistent with what they believe about themselves, and their behaviors are apt to produce reactions from others that confirm their self-concepts.
- They tend to seek out information that confirms what they already believe. Those with positive self-perceptions are more likely to seek out positive feedback, whereas some with negative self-perceptions may actually look for information about their weaknesses (S. Epstein & Morling, 1995; Swann, 1997).
- They seldom put themselves in situations where they believe they won't succeed, minimizing the chances of discovering that they *can* succeed in a domain about which they've been pessimistic. For instance, if a middle school student believes he's a poor athlete and so refuses to go out for the baseball team, he may never learn that, in fact, he has the potential to become a good player.
- Many factors that contribute to self-esteem—inherited abilities and disabilities, parents' behaviors, physical attractiveness, and so on—remain relatively stable throughout childhood (O'Malley & Bachman, 1983).

contingent self-worth
Overall sense of self that is highly
dependent on others' opinions.

This is not to say that once children acquire an unfavorable sense of self, they will always think poorly of themselves. Quite the contrary can be true, especially when circumstances change significantly (Marsh & Craven, 1997). We saw this situation in the opening case study. After a history of repeated failures, Kellen began experiencing regular success at his new school. In his mother's words, he became "a different kid."

Changing Nature of the Self Over Childhood and Adolescence

The developmental trends just listed reflect gradual changes in sense of self over time. We now look at unique aspects of self-perceptions at five age levels: infancy, early childhood, middle childhood, early adolescence, and late adolescence.

Infancy (birth–age 2).   The first elements of children's sense of self appear in infancy. Through repeated physical experiences, babies discover that they have bodies that bring them discomfort (through hunger, fatigue, and injury) and pleasure (through feeding, sucking thumbs, and snuggling in the arms of caregivers). Possibly, too, babies' protests at being separated from caregivers reflect an emerging and uneasy insight that they exist separately from the people on whom they depend.

In the first year, infants' increasing ability to imitate other people's facial expressions nourishes their early sense of self (Collie & Hayne, 1999; Meltzoff, 1990). In order to mimic others—older brother opening his mouth wide, Aunt Mei Lin smiling broadly, Dad playfully sticking out his tongue—they must to some degree realize that they and the people they're looking at are separate entities. Late in the first year, activities involving joint attention come into play as well. When Mommy and baby examine a toy together, baby shifts her gaze between toy and Mommy's face. Baby begins to learn that she has a sense of "we-ness" with her mother but also is a being separate from Mom (Emde & Buchsbaum, 1990).

Connecting Concepts
See Chapter 7 for more on the importance of joint attention.

In the second year, infants begin to recognize themselves in the mirror. In a clever study of self-recognition, babies 9 to 24 months were placed in front of a mirror (Lewis & Brooks-Gunn, 1979). Their mothers then wiped their faces, leaving a red mark on their noses. Older infants, especially those 15 months or older, touched their noses when they saw their reflections, as if they understood that the reflected images belonged to them.

Once young children develop a firm sense of themselves, they find it easier to share with others.

Early childhood (ages 2–6).   In early childhood, acquisition of language and other cognitive abilities makes many advancements possible. Once children begin to talk, their self-awareness becomes much more obvious. Toddlers begin to refer to themselves by the pronouns *I* and *me,* and at ages 2 and 3 exclamations of "Mine!" are common (Levine, 1983; Lewis & Brooks-Gunn, 1979). Learning about what is *mine* is a natural part of development and is probably a precursor to sharing.

Another acquisition that depends on cognitive development is the **autobiographical self,** a mental "history" of important events in one's life. On average, children remember few if any events that occurred before age 3½, and their recall of events before age 2 is virtually nonexistent. Children's early recollections are usually sparse, fragmented snippets that don't hang together in any meaningful way. Memories for events become increasingly detailed and integrated during the preschool years, especially if children discuss their experiences with other people (Fivush & Nelson, 2004; M. L. Howe, 2003). This ever-expanding personal history becomes an important part of how children conceptualize who they are as people (Bauer, 2006).

Connecting Concepts
See Chapters 6 and 7 for more discussion on how conversations about present and past events enhance children's memory for the events.

Young children see themselves largely in terms of obvious physical characteristics and simple psychological traits (Damon & Hart, 1988; Harter, 1999). (Recall that 6-year-old Jeff had "blue eyes" and was "happy.") As they learn from caregivers what things are "good" and "bad," they begin to apply these standards in evaluating themselves (Dweck, 2000; J. Kagan, 1981). Often they feel bad when they don't measure up. For instance, a 5-year-old may become quite frustrated when he discovers he can't spread peanut butter on bread as neatly as his father does.

By and large, however, most young children have positive self-concepts and high self-esteem. Often they believe that they are more capable than they really are and that they can easily overcome initial failures (Harter, 1999; Lockhart, Chang, & Story, 2002; Paris & Cunningham, 1996). Such optimism is perhaps due to their tendency to base self-assessments on their continuing improvements in "big boy" and "big girl" activities. Their overconfidence is probably beneficial for their development, in that it motivates them to try and persist at challenging tasks (Bjorklund & Green, 1992; Pintrich & Schunk, 2002).

autobiographical self
Mental "history" of events important in one's life.

Song of Myself

```
I am Shea
Above me are the bright colored leaves on the trees
Below me are seeds waiting to become flowers next spring
Before me are years to come full of new things to be learned
Behind me are memories I've forgotten
All around me are my friends lending me a helping hand
I see children having fun
I smell the sweet scent of flowers
I hear the birds talking to each other
I feel the fur of a helpless baby bunny
I move like wind as I run through the grass
I am old like the planets who have been here from the beginning
I am young like a seed waiting to sprout
I am the black of a panda's patches
I am the gold of the sun
I am the green of a cat's eye
I am the many colors of the sunset
I am a parrot, kangaroo, tiger, turtle
I am kind, responsible, pretty, smart
I think, plan, help, research
I give ideas to people that need them
I fear lightning
I believe that we all are equal
I remember my dreams
I dream of bad things as well as the good
I do not understand why some people pollute the Earth
I am Shea, a child of honesty
May I walk in peace
```

Figure 12-3

Shea's *Song of Myself.* Shea and her classmates were given "stems" to guide their writing (e.g., "Above me . . . ," "I feel . . . ," "I am . . . ," and "I dream . . .").

─────────── **Connecting Concepts**

In Chapter 14 you'll learn more about the many challenges associated with moving from elementary school to a middle school or junior high.

imaginary audience
Belief that one is the center of attention in any social situation.

personal fable
Belief held by many adolescents that they are unique beings invulnerable to normal risks and dangers.

Middle childhood (ages 6–10).   During middle childhood, children tend to see themselves in more complex physical and psychological terms. Consider the many domains 9-year-old Shea addresses in her *Song of Myself,* presented in Figure 12-3. Among other things, Shea describes herself as "kind, responsible, pretty, smart . . . a child of honesty."

Elementary school children are usually aware that they have both strengths and weaknesses, that they do some things well and other things poorly (Harter et al., 1998; Marsh & Craven, 1997; Wigfield, 1994). As they progress through the elementary school grades, they have many opportunities to compare themselves with others (as Kellen did) and become cognitively more able to *make* such comparisons. Most youngsters observe some of their peers outshining them at least some of the time, and so their self-assessments typically decline from the overconfidence of the preschool years to levels that are more accurate (Chapman, Tunmer, & Prochnow, 2000; Marsh & Hau, 2003; Wigfield, Tonks, & Eccles, 2004). Generally, however—perhaps because they have so many domains to consider as they look for strengths—most children maintain reasonable positive self-esteem during the elementary school years (Wigfield & Eccles, 1994).

Early adolescence (ages 10–14).   In the opening case study, Kellen's academic performance and general mental health dropped dramatically when, as a fifth grader, he began middle school. A drop in self-esteem often occurs at about the time that youngsters move from elementary school to middle school or junior high school; this drop tends to be more pronounced for girls (Marsh, 1990b; Robins & Trzesniewski, 2005; Simmons & Blyth, 1987). The physiological changes of puberty may be one factor in the decline. Self-evaluations depend increasingly on beliefs about appearance and popularity, and boys and girls alike tend to think of themselves as being somewhat less attractive once they reach adolescence (Cornell et al., 1990; D. Hart, 1988; Harter et al., 1998). Changes in the school environment, such as disrupted friendships, more superficial teacher-student relationships, more rigorous academic standards, and so on, probably also have a negative impact (Eccles & Midgley, 1989).

Also with early adolescence come two new phenomena that have implications for sense of self. First, youngsters become more cognitively able to reflect on how others see them (Harter, 1999). They may initially go to extremes in this respect, to the point where they think that in any social situation, everyone else's attention is focused squarely on them (Elkind, 1981a; Lapsley, 1993; R. M. Ryan & Kuczkowski, 1994). This self-centered aspect of the young adolescent's sense of self is sometimes called the **imaginary audience.** Because they believe they are the center of attention, teenagers (girls especially) are often preoccupied with their physical appearance and can be quite self-critical. Extreme sensitivity to embarrassment, when coupled with inadequate social skills, leads some adolescents to respond to harsh words or other humiliating circumstances with undue violence (Lowry, Sleet, Duncan, Powell, & Kolbe, 1995).

A second noteworthy phenomenon in early adolescence is the **personal fable** (introduced in Chapter 4). Young teenagers often believe they are completely unlike anyone else (Elkind, 1981a; Lapsley, 1993). They are apt to think their own feelings are unique—that the people around them have never experienced such emotions. Hence they may insist that no one else, least of all parents and teachers, can possibly know how they feel. Furthermore, they may believe that they are not susceptible to the normal dangers of life—that they are somehow invulnerable and immortal. Thus many adolescents take seemingly foolish risks, such as driving at high speeds, experimenting with drugs, or having unprotected sexual intercourse (see Chapter 4).

Teachers and other adults must do everything possible to prevent adolescents from engaging in behaviors that may compromise health and well-being. Yet adults should keep in mind that both the personal fable and the imaginary audience appear to serve important functions in youngsters' developmental progress. The personal fable—in particular, the sense of invulnerability—may encourage young people to venture out into the world and try new things (Bjorklund & Green, 1992; Lapsley, 1993). The imaginary audience keeps youngsters "connected"

A frequently observed phenomenon in early adolescence is the *personal fable:* Young teenagers often believe that they are so unique that no one else can possibly understand their thoughts and feelings.
© Zits Partnership. Reprinted with permission of King Features Syndicate.

to their larger social context. Because they continually are considering how others might judge their actions, they are more apt to behave in ways that their society will view favorably (Lapsley, 1993; R. M. Ryan & Kuczkowski, 1994). At some point, both phenomena apparently outlive their purposes, as they slowly decline in late adolescence (Lapsley, 1993; Lapsley et al., 1988).

Late adolescence (ages 14–18).   As their worlds expand, teenagers have a greater variety of social experiences with a greater variety of people. With their increasing ability to reflect on their own behaviors, they may realize that they take on different personalities with parents, teachers, friends, and romantic partners. Thus their sense of self may include multiple self-perceptions that are somewhat contradictory (D. Hart, 1988; Harter, 1999; Wigfield et al., 1996). The contradictions can be a source of confusion, as one ninth grader revealed:

> I really don't understand how I can switch so fast from being cheerful with my friends, then coming home and feeling anxious, and then getting frustrated and sarcastic with my parents. Which one is the *real* me? (Harter, 1999, p. 67)

As high school students wrestle with the question *Who is the real me?,* they gradually broaden their sense of self to accommodate their variability (Harter, 1988, 1999). For instance, they may resolve their self-perceptions of being both "cheerful" and "depressed" by concluding that they are "moody," or they may explain their inconsistent behaviors in different situations by concluding that they are "flexible" or "open-minded."

In the process of reconciling their "multiple selves," older adolescents make progress toward establishing a sense of **identity,** a self-constructed definition of who they are, what they find important, what they believe, and what they want to do in life. But before adolescents achieve a true sense of their adult identity, most need considerable time to explore career options, political views, religious affiliations, and so on. One psychologist (Marcia, 1980, 1991) has observed four distinct patterns of behavior that may characterize an adolescent's search for identity:

Connecting Concepts ——————
Identity formation plays a key role in Erik Erikson's theory (see Chapter 11).

- *Identity diffusion.* The adolescent has made no commitment to a particular career path or ideological belief system. Possibly there has been some haphazard experimentation with particular roles or beliefs, but the adolescent has not yet embarked on a serious exploration of issues related to self-definition.
- *Foreclosure.* The adolescent has made a commitment to an occupation and a particular set of beliefs. The choices have been made without much deliberation or exploration of other possibilities; rather, they have been based largely on what others (especially parents) have prescribed.
- *Moratorium.* The adolescent has no strong commitment to a particular career or set of beliefs but is actively exploring and considering a variety of professions and ideologies.
- *Identity achievement.* The adolescent has previously gone through a period of moratorium and emerged with a clear choice regarding occupation and commitment to political and religious beliefs.

identity
Self-constructed definition of who one is, what things one finds important, what one believes, and what goals one wants to accomplish in life.

Foreclosure—identity choice without prior exploration—rules out potentially more productive alternatives, and identity diffusion leaves young people without a clear sense of direction.

Being in moratorium can be an uncomfortable experience for some adolescents, but it is often an important step in forming a healthy identity (Berzonsky, 1988; Marcia, 1988).

For most older high school students, then, the search for identity is hardly complete. Even so, their self-esteem has largely recuperated from the unsettling experiences of the middle school and early high school years (Harter, 1999). Several developmental advancements contribute to this rebound in sense of self. Most older adolescents have acquired the social skills they need to get along well with others. They have resolved many of the apparent inconsistencies in their self-perceptions. They have considerable autonomy to choose activities at which they are likely to be successful. And they are increasingly judging themselves based on their *own* (rather than other people's) standards. You can see some of these factors at work in the essay presented in the following exercise, "Hermit Crab."

INTERPRETING CHILDREN'S ARTIFACTS AND ACTIONS

Hermit Crab

As an assignment for one of her 11th-grade classes, 17-year-old "Kiley" (a pseudonym) wrote the essay shown here. As you read the essay, identify factors that seem to have contributed to Kiley's positive sense of self. (We have blanked out the name of Kiley's school but have left spelling and grammar errors intact.)

It was during high school that I discovered who I was. Freshman and sophomore year I was a hermit crab, slowly trying to change to a new shell. I was eager to make the process yet I was yearning for something to hold on to help ease the way. For me my path of stepping stones was the _____ High School music department.

When I walked into chorus my freshman year, I was petrified. I felt like I was involved in a cult of some sort. Everyone either seemed extremely friendly or in love with the music department. I have to admit that at first I thought that the music department was pretty lame. Everyday I would walk in and see everyone hugging their friends or people crying on each other's shoulders, what was this? Everyone seemed so dependent on each other. I had my thoughts of quitting; I didn't know a lot of people and wasn't excited at the thought of making friends with them either, but I stuck it out, singing has always been my passion and I wasn't about to never perform again. This is who I was, I wasn't about to let some crazy group of people intimidate me.

By the middle of my sophomore year I was a full time band geek; besides the fact that I wasn't even in the band. I finally let my walls cave in and let the music department be my second home. I loved it. I could come in during the middle of a bad school day and always find a friend, always have someone their for me. The seniors in the rest of the school always seemed so big, so intimidating, but when I walked through the doors of the music department everyone was equal; there were no judgments and everyone felt welcome.

The music department changed me. I am no longer shy or timid but I am me to the fullest extent of the word. I now have the ability to walk into a group of people and make friends instantly. The music department helped me realize that performing is my passion, it's what I love; it's who I am. I am now ready to go out and show the world what I am made of. Throughout high school nothing else has made such a lasting impression on me, I am not going to sit back one day as a mother and tell my children about my freshman PE class; my only eventful memories are contained within the walls of the music department. . . .

The music department has given me the strength to move on. When I am nervous I know I can always think back to my _____ years, and the confidence that slowly grew with the help of loving arms. I may be unsure about the future but I am excited. I will always remember the friends I made, the confidence I earned, and the love I shared within the four years; or better yet the four solid walls of the _____ High School music department.

As she began high school, Kiley had electives in her class schedule, and this autonomy enabled her to sign up for a class (chorus) in which she could showcase one of her talents (singing). Kiley initially balked at the hugging and crying she saw in other students, but she eventually reinterpreted such behaviors as being supportive—and so self-enhancing and confidence building—rather than "dependent." Furthermore, Kiley internalized some of her peers' standards for behavior, including the importance of being friendly and outgoing. In the music department, then, Kiley consistently received the positive messages so important for a healthy sense of self.

Even as older adolescents move rapidly toward independence, their attachments to family members, especially parents, continue to play a significant role in their sense of self. Adolescents who have strong emotional bonds with parents tend to have higher self-esteem and function at more mature levels (Josselson, 1988; R. M. Ryan & Lynch, 1989). Parental bonds should not be overly restrictive or protective, however; parents best foster adolescents' personal growth by gradually releasing the apron strings (Lapsley, 1993; R. M. Ryan & Lynch, 1989). Adolescents who feel alienated from their parents are more susceptible to the opinions of others; that is, they are more likely to have the *contingent self-worth* described earlier. They also have more difficulty establishing a sense of identity (Josselson, 1988; Marcia, 1988; R. M. Ryan & Kuczkowski, 1994).

Diversity in Sense of Self

The various factors that influence sense of self—quality of relationships with parents and other caregivers, teacher and peer behaviors, inherited characteristics and abilities, and so on—all lead to considerable diversity among youngsters at any particular age level. Gender and ethnic background also contribute to variability in children's sense of self.

Gender differences.   An important component of most youngsters' sense of self is their gender. By age 2½, most children know that they are a "boy" or a "girl" (Etaugh, Grinnell, & Etaugh, 1989; Lippa, 2002). But it may be 2 or 3 more years before they fully understand that this state is permanent—that boys do not become girls if they grow their hair long and wear ribbons, and that girls do not become boys if they cut their hair short and wear boys' clothes (Bem, 1989; DeLisi & Gallagher, 1991). As children become increasingly aware of the typical characteristics and behaviors of boys, girls, men, and women, they begin to pull their knowledge together into self-constructed understandings, or **gender schemas,** of "what males are like" and "what females are like." These gender schemas become part of their sense of self and provide guidance for how they themselves should behave—how they should dress, what toys they should play with, what interests and academic subject areas they should pursue, and so on (Bem, 1981; C. L. Martin, 2000; C. L. Martin & Halverson, 1987).

With the onset of puberty, being "male" or "female" takes on new meaning. Many youngsters show an upsurge in gender-specific interests beginning in adolescence (Galambos, Almeida, & Petersen, 1990). For example, at age 13, Teresa's son Connor displayed a newfound interest in American football—definitely a rough, "manly" sport—and joined the middle school football team. To affirm their masculinity or femininity, many adolescents also begin to shy away from behaviors more closely associated with the opposite sex. For instance, in the "Emotional Development: Late Adolescence" clip on Observation CD 2, 15-year-old Greg responds to the question "What are some things that kids do when they're sad?" by saying, "Cry . . . if you're a guy, you don't show it." And we authors both recall that, as adolescent girls, we had mixed feelings about mathematics. Although math was something we were good at, we thought of it as a "masculine" domain that would somehow make us look less feminine. (Fortunately, our interest rekindled in college, where we felt freer to "be ourselves" and not conform to sex-role stereotypes.) Even girls who have grown up in more recent and seemingly more open-minded decades tend to have less interest in subject areas that are traditionally masculine—for instance, in mathematics, science, and sports (T. J. L. Chandler & Goldberg, 1990; Wigfield et al., 1996).

Not only do behaviors and interests seem to differ by gender, but boys' and girls' self-confidence and overall sense of self-worth also differ. Beginning in the upper elementary or middle school grades, boys have a higher overall sense of self-worth than girls. This gender difference appears to be due to boys' tendency to *over*estimate their abilities and possibly also to girls' tendency to *under*estimate theirs (D. A. Cole, Martin, Peeke,

Connecting Concepts —————
Chapter 11 describes the nature of attachments to parents during adolescence.

Connecting Concepts —————
Not all adolescents develop a heterosexual identity, as you will discover in the discussion of sexual orientation in Chapter 14.

Listen to Greg express his belief that boys often hide their emotions in the "Emotional Development: Late Adolescence" clip on Observation CD 2.

gender schema
Self-constructed body of beliefs about the traits and behaviors of males or females.

Seroczynski, & Fier, 1999; Dweck, 2000; Harter, 1999). Girls also have more difficulty taking criticism and failure in stride (Dweck, 2000).

Additional gender differences exist in the specific areas of strength and weakness that students perceive in themselves (Binns, Steinberg, Amorosi, & Cuevas, 1997; J. H. Block, 1983; D. A. Cole et al., 2001). On average, boys see themselves as being better athletes, and they have greater self-confidence in their ability to control the world and solve problems. Girls are more apt to judge themselves as being well behaved in school and competent and considerate in social relationships. Beginning in middle childhood, girls rate their physical appearance less favorably than boys do, and they are more preoccupied with how they look, reflecting the imaginary audience phenomenon described earlier (D. A. Cole et al., 2001; Harter, 1999; R. Stein, 1996). At school, both boys and girls tend to rate themselves higher in academic areas that are stereotypically "appropriate" for their gender (Eccles et al., 1998; Herbert et al., 2003; Marsh, 1989). Especially in math and science—stereotypically masculine domains—boys evaluate themselves more highly than girls do, even when no true differences in achievement exist (Eccles, 1989; Herbert et al., 2003; E. Rowe, 1999).

Of course, there are individual differences in how strictly children adhere to sex-role stereotypes. **Androgynous** youngsters show both feminine and masculine attributes. For instance, they might be nurturing with friends (a stereotypically feminine characteristic) yet assertive in classroom activities (a stereotypically masculine characteristic) (Bem, 1977). Children, adolescents, and adults who relax sex-role boundaries are more apt to pursue counterstereotypical interests and career paths (Liben & Bigler, 2002). These individuals also tend to be fairly well adjusted, perhaps because they have more choices in the standards by which they evaluate themselves and perhaps because others respond favorably to their wide range of skills and behaviors (Piche & Plante, 1991; D. E. Williams & D'Alessandro, 1994).

Heredity, environment, and self-socialization in gender differences.
Biology clearly has some influence on how boys and girls behave. The brain is permanently marked "male" or "female" by subtle differences in anatomy in prenatal development (Arnold & Gorski, 1984). At puberty, gender differences increase as rising hormones activate gender-specific brain structures that previously were quiet (Ruble & Martin, 1998). In boys, for example, these rising hormones are associated with increased aggression—a stereotypically male characteristic (more about this point later in the chapter).

The environment, too, plays a role by encouraging children to think about males and females in particular ways. Family, peers, and the broader community often reinforce children for "staying within bounds" and punish them (e.g., by ridicule or exclusion) when they violate accepted gender roles (Pipher, 1994; Ruble & Martin, 1998). For example, a boy who cries after breaking his arm may be called a "sissy," and a girl who excels in mathematics might be teased for being a "math geek." Other people also influence children's gender schemas through the typical roles they play in society (backhoe operators are almost always men), the preferences and priorities they express ("How do you like this shade of lipstick?"), and the behaviors they model and encourage ("Why don't you gals go shopping while we watch the football game?") (Ruble & Martin, 1998; Tennenbaum & Leaper, 2002).

Yet by the time children reach elementary school, much of the pressure to act "appropriately" for their gender comes from within rather than from others (Bem, 1981; Bussey & Bandura, 1992; C. L. Martin, 2000; C. L. Martin & Halverson, 1987). This tendency for children and adolescents to conform to their own ideas about what behaviors are appropriate for themselves is known as **self-socialization.** For example, when teachers actively encourage children to engage in non-gender-stereotypical activities (boys playing with dolls, girls playing with toy cars, etc.), the children may comply for a short time, but they soon revert to their earlier, more gender-typical ways (Lippa, 2002). Self-socialization is also evident in one woman's recollection of her childhood:

> [In our home] it was OK, even feminine, not to be good in math. It was even cute. And so I locked myself out of a very important part of what it is to be a human being, and that is to know all of oneself. I just locked that part out because I didn't think that was an appropriate thing for me to do. . . . [But] it was not OK for the men to not do well in math. It was *not* OK for them to not take calculus. It was not manly. . . .
>
> Another thing that affected me greatly happened when I went to a foreign country. One day I decided that I was going to build a sandbox for my little boy. I went in to get the wood and they told me, "Oh, no! You cannot buy wood. You have to have your

Connecting Concepts

Chapter 5 describes a variety of ways in which parents are apt to socialize their sons and daughters differently.

androgyny
Tendency to have some characteristics that are stereotypically female (e.g., nurturance) and others that are stereotypically male (e.g., assertiveness).

self-socialization
Tendency to integrate personal observations and others' input into self-constructed standards for behavior and to choose actions consistent with those standards.

husband's permission before you can purchase wood." That was a very big shock to me. But it was a shock that helped me see the insidiousness of what had happened to me in the beginning. And it helped me to open my eyes. When I came back to my country I was very intolerant of what I had swallowed hook, line, and sinker. (Benita Balegh, in Weiss-glass, 1998, p. 160)

As happens to many young people, Benita's desire to fit society's definitions of gender roles changed as she grew. As a child, she learned and accepted sex-role stereotypes in the contexts of family and school. Later she rejected aspects of traditional gender roles that seemed inequitable. In general, as youngsters get older, they become increasingly open-minded about what activities and behaviors are appropriate for males and females (Trautner, 1992).

Ethnic and cultural differences.   Many children from ethnic minority groups have positive self-concepts and high self-esteem. In fact, researchers often find that, on average, minority youths have more favorable self-perceptions than European American youths (H. Cooper & Dorr, 1995; Spencer & Markstrom-Adams, 1990; H. W. Stevenson et al., 1990; van Laar, 2000).

Researchers sometimes have trouble getting a good read on ethnic differences in children's sense of self, however, for a couple of reasons. First, the relative emphasis on *self* versus *others* varies among ethnic groups. Some groups encourage children to take pride in the accomplishments of their families and communities, rather than in their own, individual achievements. Thus, for some children, sense of self includes a strong sense of connectedness with family and community (Banks & Banks, 1995; Harrison et al., 1990; Markus & Kitayama, 1991). Second, children from some ethnic groups (e.g., many children from Southeast Asia) are more willing to acknowledge their weaknesses—and so tend to be more self-effacing—than is true for other groups. For these children, admitting personal limitations is a sign of humility—a very desirable quality—rather than an indication of poor self-esteem (Brophy, 2004).

By the time children reach kindergarten or first grade, some are quite aware that they belong to a different "group" than many of their age-mates. By age 5, many can accurately classify themselves as being African, Mexican, Laotian, and so on (Sheets, 1999). A variety of characteristics may make them stand out in a crowd, including their skin color, facial features, and language. Parents and other family members may also give them labels—*Black, Chinese,* and so on—that communicate that they are "special" in some important way.

Initially, having one foot in mainstream Western society and the other in one's ethnic and cultural heritage can be a confusing state of affairs (C. R. Cooper, Jackson, Azmitia, Lopez, & Dunbar, 1995; Kiang & Harter, 2005; Tatum, 1997). Consider Alice, who migrated from China to the United States at age 8. Although she gained fluency in English fairly quickly, for several years she had trouble reconciling the Chinese and American aspects of herself:

> [A]t home my parents expect me to be not a traditional Chinese daughter . . . but they expect things because I was born in China and I am Chinese. And at school, that's a totally different story because you're expected to behave as an American. You know, you speak English in your school; all your friends speak English. You try to be as much of an American as you can. So I feel I'm caught somewhere in between. . . . I feel I can no longer be fully Chinese or fully American anymore. (Igoa, 1995, p. 85)

Such "multiple ethnic selves" enter into the mix that young people struggle with in adolescence. Happily, many teens from minority groups emerge with a strong **ethnic identity.** That is, they are aware and proud of their ethnic heritage and willingly adopt some of their ethnic group's behaviors (Phinney, 1989; Sheets & Hollins, 1999).

Occasionally youngsters' ethnic identities lead them to reject mainstream Western values (Nasir & Saxe, 2003). In some minority-group communities, peers may accuse high-achieving youngsters of "acting White," a label that essentially means "you're not one of us" (Cross, Strauss, & Fhagen-Smith, 1999; Graham, 1997; Steinberg, 1996). Consider what happened to the professional basketball player Kareem Abdul-Jabbar when, as a 9-year-old African American student, he enrolled in a new school:

> I got there and immediately found I could read better than anyone in the school. . . . When the nuns found this out they paid me a lot of attention, once even asking me, a fourth grader, to read to the seventh grade. When the kids found this out I became a target. . . . I got all A's and was hated for it; I spoke correctly and was called a punk. I had to learn a new language simply to be able to deal with the threats. I had good manners and was a good little boy and paid for it with my hide. (Abdul-Jabbar & Knobles, 1983, p. 16)

Especially in adolescence, much of the pressure to act "appropriately" for one's gender comes from within rather than from other people.

Connecting Concepts
Chapter 5 describes a variety of information sources from which youngsters draw as they construct their ethnic identities.

ethnic identity
Awareness of being a member of a particular ethnic or cultural group and willingness to adopt certain behaviors characteristic of that group.

Many children from minority groups incorporate a strong sense of ethnic identity into their sense of self.

But for the most part students with a strong and positive ethnic identity do *well* in school both academically and socially (Chavous et al., 2003; Spencer et al., 2001). Furthermore, pride in one's ethnic heritage can serve as an emotional "buffer" against the insults and discrimination that children and adolescents from minority groups sometimes encounter (see Chapter 5).

Not all young people from minority groups affiliate strongly with their ethnic and cultural heritage. The strength of their ethnic identity depends partly on how much their families and communities nurture it and partly on how much they "look" like a member of a particular racial or ethnic group (Dien, 1998; Herman, 2004; Thornton, Chatters, Taylor, & Allen, 1990). And some youngsters (especially those with multiple racial or cultural heritages) fluctuate in the strength of their ethnic identity depending on the context and situation (A. M. Lopez, 2003; Tatum, 1997; Yip & Fuligni, 2002). In addition, older adolescents may experiment with varying forms of an ethnic identity. Some teens, for instance, may initially adopt a fairly intense, inflexible, and perhaps hostile ethnic identity before eventually retreating to a more relaxed and open-minded one (Cross et al., 1999).

The Developmental Trends table "Sense of Self at Different Age Levels" summarizes changes in self-perceptions and self-understandings across infancy, childhood, and adolescence, as well as some of the diversity you are likely to see.

Enhancing Children's Sense of Self

As was true for Kellen's fifth-grade year in the opening case study, the interplay between self-esteem and behavior can create a vicious downward spiral: Poor self-esteem leads to less productive behavior, which leads to fewer successes, which perpetuates poor self-esteem. Yet simply telling youngsters that they are "good" or "smart" or "popular" is unlikely to make a dent in a poor sense of self (Damon, 1991; Marsh & Craven, 1997; Pajares, 1996). Such platitudes become meaningless when they contradict children's own observations—for instance, when Kellen's second-grade teacher said he was "doing great!" despite his obviously poor reading performance.

The following strategies are far more likely to have a genuine impact on children's sense of self:

● *Communicate a genuine interest in children's lives and well-being.* As children observe how adults treat them and hear what adults say to them, they wonder, "What do these things mean about me?" Youngsters often interpret harsh words and thoughtless actions as indications that adults do not like them, possibly because they are not worthy of love. We urge all adults, but especially teachers, parents, and other caregivers, to think carefully about what they say and do to and with children, being sure that their words and actions consistently communicate genuine caring and respect. Messages of caring and respect come in a variety of forms, including the following:

- Giving children a smile and warm greeting at the beginning of the day
- Complimenting children on a special talent, new skill, or exceptional effort
- Asking children to talk about important events in their lives (this strategy can also enhance their *autobiographical selves*)
- Being a good listener when children appear angry or upset
- Being well prepared for lessons and other activities with children
- Including children in decision making and in evaluations of their own performance
- Acknowledging that children can occasionally have an "off" day and not holding it against them
  (L. H. Anderman, Patrick, Hruda, & Linnenbrink, 2002; Certo, Cauley, & Chafin, 2002; H. A. Davis, 2003; H. A. Davis, Schutz, & Chambless, 2001)

● *Promote success on academic, social, and physical tasks.* Experiences with success are powerful catalysts for the development of a positive sense of self (Damon, 1991; Marsh & Craven, 1997). Thus teachers should gear assignments to youngsters' capabilities—for instance, by making sure that they have already mastered any necessary prerequisite knowledge and skills. However, success at very easy activities is unlikely to have much of an impact. Mastering the significant challenges in life—earning the hard-won successes that come only with effort and persistence—brings more enduring and resilient self-perceptions

DEVELOPMENTAL TRENDS

Sense of Self at Different Age Levels

Age	What You Might Observe	Diversity	Implications
Infancy (Birth–2)	• Increasing awareness that one is separate from one's caregivers (in the first year) • Increasing recognition of self in mirror (in the second year) • Appearance of first-person pronouns, such as *I, me, mine* (late in the second year)	• The quality of child-caregiver relationships influences infants' beliefs that they are worthy of love. • Infants' temperaments (e.g., whether they are irritable or easily comforted) affect some caregivers' ability and desire to give affection and care.	• Communicate affection by cuddling and talking to infants and by attending to their physical needs in a timely and consistent manner. • Talk with infants and toddlers about their bodily features and possessions ("Where's your nose?" "Here's your teddy bear!").
Early Childhood (2–6)	• Frequent use of *I, me,* and *mine,* especially at ages 2 and 3 • Emergence of an autobiographical self (beginning at age 3 or 4) • Concrete self-descriptions (e.g., "I'm a boy," "I'm pretty") • Overconfidence about what tasks can be accomplished	• Children whom others treat affectionately tend to develop a positive sense of self. Those who are rejected, ridiculed, or ignored have a harder time seeing themselves in positive terms. • Some children gain an emerging awareness that they belong to a particular racial or ethnic group (by age 5).	• Acknowledge children's possessions, but encourage sharing. • Engage children in joint retellings of recent events. • Don't disparage children's lofty ambitions ("I'm going to be President!"), but focus their efforts on accomplishable short-term goals.
Middle Childhood (6–10)	• Increasing discrimination among various aspects of oneself (e.g., among academic performance, athletic ability, and likability) • Increasing tendency to base sense of self on how one's own performance compares with that of peers • Increasing internalization of others' standards for performance (continues into adolescence) • Generally good self-esteem in most children	• Different children place greater or lesser importance on various domains (e.g., on academic performance vs. athletic prowess) in deriving their overall sense of self-worth. • In middle childhood, girls begin to evaluate their physical appearance less favorably than boys do.	• Praise children for their talents and accomplishments in numerous areas (e.g., in physical activities, social relationships, and specific academic subjects). • Help children find arenas in which they can be especially successful. • Teach hygiene and personal grooming habits that enhance children's physical attractiveness.
Early Adolescence (10–14)	• Increasing tendency to define oneself in terms of abstract rather than concrete characteristics • Possible drop in self-esteem after the transition to middle school or junior high • Heightened sensitivity to what others think of oneself (*imaginary audience*), leading to a preoccupation with physical appearance • Belief in oneself as overly unique (*personal fable*), leading to a sense of invulnerability and increased risk taking	• Drops in self-esteem, when sizable and not followed by a rebound, can signal a serious problem. • On average, youngsters increasingly base their self-perceived strengths on gender stereotypes (e.g., boys see themselves as good in math, girls see themselves as good in reading) even when actual achievement levels are similar. • Members of ethnic minority groups vary in the extent to which their ethnic status plays a role in their identity.	• When students are making the transition to middle school or junior high, be especially supportive and optimistic about their potential for success. • Be patient when adolescents show exceptional self-consciousness; give them strategies for presenting themselves well to others. • Show no tolerance for risk-taking behaviors that put youngsters' health and well-being in danger.
Late Adolescence (14–18)	• Decrease in the self-consciousness evident in early adolescence • Continuing risk-taking behavior, especially in males • Reflection about identity issues: Who am I? What do I believe? What course should my life take? • Reconciliation of many apparent contradictions in oneself	• Adolescents whose sense of self-worth continues to depend heavily on others' behaviors and opinions (those who have *contingent self-worth*) are more susceptible to mood swings and peer pressure. • Some adolescents willingly accept the professional goals and ideologies that their parents offer. Others engage in more soul-searching and exploration as they strive to develop their identity.	• Provide opportunities for adolescents to explore diverse belief systems and try on a variety of occupational "hats." • When discussing adverse consequences of risky behaviors, present the facts but don't make teens so anxious or upset that they can't effectively remember the information (i.e., avoid scare tactics). • Be on the lookout for teens whose self-worth seems especially dependent on peers' opinions; help them discover areas of talent that can contribute to a more stable sense of self-worth.

(Dweck, 2000; Eisenberger, 1992; Winne, 1995a). Thus teachers and other practitioners are most likely to bolster youngsters' sense of self when they assign challenging tasks and provide the structure and support (the scaffolding) youngsters need to accomplish the tasks successfully. They should also help young people keep the little "failures" along the way in perspective: Mistakes are an inevitable part of learning something new (Clifford, 1990; Eccles & Wigfield, 1985).

● *Focus children's attention on their own improvement rather than on how their peers perform.* Youngsters are likely to be optimistic about their chances of future success if they see they are making regular progress—if they continually make gains through effort and practice. They are *un*likely to be optimistic if, like Kellen, they focus their attention on how their age-mates are surpassing them (Deci & Ryan, 1992; Krampen, 1987; Stipek, 1996).

● *Be honest about children's shortcomings, but also provide the guidance and support children need to deal with and possibly overcome them.* The popular educational literature often overrates positive self-esteem as a target for intervention, sometimes to the point where it becomes the *only* target (Dweck, 2000; Harter, 1998). Certainly we want children and adolescents to feel good about themselves, but we also want them to work hard, learn a lot, and get along with peers.

Furthermore, youngsters are more likely to be successful over the long run if they come to grips with their areas of weakness. Adults do youngsters a disservice when they pretend that problems don't exist, as some of Kellen's teachers did in the opening case. If adults provide only positive feedback—and especially if they provide inflated evaluations of children's performance—some children may be unaware of areas that need improvement (Dweck, 2000; T. D. Little, Oettingen, Stetsenko, & Baltes, 1995; Paris & Cunningham, 1996). And when adults praise children for successes on very *easy* tasks, children may conclude that they are not capable of handling anything more difficult (Pintrich & Schunk, 2002).

Realistically, then, adults must give children negative as well as positive feedback. When feedback must include information about children's shortcomings, the best approach is to give it within the context of high (yet achievable) expectations for future performance (Deci & Ryan, 1985; Pintrich & Schunk, 2002). Following are examples of how a teacher might put a positive spin on negative feedback:

- "You're generally a very kind person, but you hurt Jenny's feelings by making fun of her new outfit. Perhaps you can think of a good way to make her feel better."
- "In the first draft of your research paper, many of your paragraphs don't lead logically to the ones that follow. A few headings and transitional sentences would make a world of difference. Let's find a time to discuss how you might use these techniques to improve the flow of your paper."
- "Your time in the 100-meter dash was not as fast as it could be. It's early in the season, though, and if you work on your endurance, I know you'll improve. Also, I think you might get a faster start if you stay low when you first come out of the starting blocks."

When children have long-standing difficulties in certain domains, discovering that their failures are due to a previously undiagnosed disability, such as dyslexia or ADHD, can help repair some of the damage to self-esteem. Such a discovery helps children make sense of *why* they can't perform certain tasks as well as their peers. It can also spur children and their teachers to identify effective coping strategies. In the following reflection, one young adolescent boy reveals how, in coming to terms with his dyslexia, he's acquired a healthy sense of self despite his disability:

Dyslexia is your brain's wired differently and there's brick walls for some things and you just have to work either around it or break it. I'm dyslexic at reading that means I need a little bit more help. If you have dyslexia the thing you have to find is how to get over the hump, the wall. Basically you either go around it and just don't read and get along in life without it or you break down the wall. (Zambo, 2003, p. 10)

● *Provide opportunities to explore a wide variety of activities and content domains.* Not all children and adolescents can achieve at superior levels in the classroom, nor can they all be superstars on the playing field. Youngsters are more likely to have a positive sense of self if they find an activity—perhaps singing, student government, or competitive jump-roping—in which they can shine (Harter, 1999). And by exploring many different fields and career options and beginning to zero in on a few possible career paths, young people take an important step toward forming a sense of their adult identity.

● *Consider the unique needs of girls and boys.* Many youngsters place little value on characteristics and abilities that they think are more "appropriate" for members of the opposite sex. In addition, they may place too much value on qualities they think they need to be "feminine" or "manly." Thus some teenage girls may strive for impossible standards of physical beauty. And some teenage boys may worry that they are maturing too slowly and lack the height and build of some of their classmates.

With these points in mind, teachers and other adults should probably use somewhat different tactics in nurturing the self-esteem of girls and boys. They might help girls identify realistic standards by which to judge their physical appearance. And given girls' tendency to react more negatively to failures, adults might encourage them to pat themselves on the back for their many successes, even those (and perhaps *especially* those) in traditionally male domains such as science and math. But boys, too, have special needs. Many boys are brought up to believe they should be "tough" and hide any feelings of self-doubt or inadequacy. Adults may want to take special pains to acknowledge a boy's "softer" sides—for instance, his compassion and skill in interacting with small children.

● *Communicate respect for diverse ethnic and cultural backgrounds.* Although most educators today are aware of the need to respect the diversity in children's backgrounds, they do not always know how best to show such regard. An important first step, of course, is *understanding* various ethnic and cultural groups—their traditions, values, priorities, and so on. Teachers must also realize that a child's native language or dialect can be very much a part of the child's sense of self, as this recollection from one Mexican American man illustrates:

> During my years of school, I experienced low expectations and hostile attitudes on the part of some teachers, administrators, and other students. I had difficulty assimilating into this unfamiliar environment. Continuously, I was made aware that speaking Spanish had bad consequences. I was also told many times that I should not speak Spanish because I used an incorrect form. Was the language I learned at home inferior? I had learned to express my love, desires, and fears in that language. Of course, my parents must have been a very bad influence by teaching me such language, this Tex-Mex. . . .
>
> Like all children, there were so many qualities that I brought with me to school that were valuable. I was eager to learn, eager to please, and eager to do a good job and feel right just like everyone. Instead, like so many other students with similar backgrounds, I was made to feel wrong, unintelligent, and inferior. My whole person was in jeopardy. (López del Bosque, 2000, pp. 3–4)

In addition to showing appreciation for children's native languages and dialects, educators can communicate respect for diverse groups through strategies such as these:

- Treat all children as full-fledged members of the classroom and community, rather than as exotic "curiosities" who live in a strange and separate world.
- Call children by their given names unless they specifically request otherwise (see Figure 12-4).
- Consistently look at historical and current events from diverse cultural perspectives—for instance, by considering American, European, Arabic, and African perspectives of recent events in the Middle East.

I had lots of friends back home, and I remember all of them, we used to play soccer together. I have also friends here now, well ... mostly classmates.

School is OK but there is one thing that bothers me. My name is Mohammed, no other. Here, my teacher calls me Mo, because there are five other kids with the same name. My friends sometimes call me M J, which is not too bad, but I wish they will call me by my real name. I like what my grandma called me: "Mamet" I like how she used to say it. One thing makes me really mad I have a pen pal called Rudy. He lives in Toronto. Once I showed his letter to my teacher and she said: "That is nice name." Now, all my friends call me Rudy. I hate it, because that's not me, that's not my name. My name is "MO-HA-MMED" Do you understand me?

Figure 12-4

For many children, their given name is an important part of their identity, as this reflection by a refugee child in Canada illustrates.
Excerpt from "Refugee Children in Canada: Searching for Identity," by A. M. Fantino and A. Colak, 2001, *Child Welfare, 80,* pp. 591–592, a publication of the Child Welfare League of America.

Connecting Concepts ————
See Chapter 9 for more on the importance of children's native languages and dialects.

Connecting Concepts ————
Such *multicultural education* is discussed in more depth in Chapter 5.

- Create situations in which youngsters from diverse backgrounds must collaborate to achieve success—for instance, through cooperative group activities or community service projects. (Banks & Banks, 1995; Branch, 1999; Fantino & Colak, 2001; Ladson-Billings, 1994; Oskamp, 2000; Wong, 1993)

In their efforts to be multiculturally sensitive, some well-meaning practitioners make the mistake of thinking of children as belonging exclusively to a particular ethnic or cultural group. Yet in this age of increasing multiracial and multicultural intermingling, many youngsters cannot easily be pigeonholed. Teachers must keep in mind that some of their students are apt to have a mixed ethnic or racial heritage, and many students from minority-group backgrounds want to be integral parts of both their local cultural groups and mainstream Western society (C. R. Cooper et al., 1995; A. M. Lopez, 2003; Root, 1999).

Not only do youngsters think a lot about who they themselves are, but they also spend considerable time trying to make sense of *other people*. We look at such social cognition now.

Social Cognition

As inherently social creatures, most children and adolescents spend much of their mental energy engaged in **social cognition,** speculating about what other people are thinking and feeling and choosing their behaviors toward others accordingly. Here we look at two important and interrelated aspects of social cognition: theory of mind and social information processing.

Theory of Mind

———————— Connecting Concepts
You can learn more about children's early theories about their physical and biological worlds in the discussions of *theory theory* and science development in Chapters 7 and 10, respectively.

Just as children construct theories about their physical and biological worlds, so, too, do they construct theories about the psychological world. More specifically, they develop a **theory of mind** that eventually encompasses complex understandings of people's mental and emotional states—thoughts, beliefs, feelings, motives, intentions, and so on. Their theory of mind enables them to interpret and predict the behaviors of important people in their lives and, as a result, to interact with those individuals more effectively (Flavell, 2000; Gopnik & Meltzoff, 1997; P. L. Harris, 2006). As you will see, a child's theory of mind changes considerably over the course of infancy, childhood, and adolescence.

Infancy (birth–age 2). Infants quickly discover that, unlike inanimate objects, people are active, expressive, and responsive (Poulin-Dubois, 1999). In the latter part of their first year, they also begin to realize that people have an "inner life" that objects do not. For instance, by about 9 or 10 months, infants show *intersubjectivity,* an awareness that a caregiver is looking at the same thing that they themselves are looking at. At about the same time or shortly thereafter, they acquire some awareness of **intentionality.** That is, they know that other people behave in order to accomplish certain goals, and they begin to draw inferences about people's intentions from such actions as reaching for, pointing at, and gazing at objects (D. A. Baldwin, 2000; Kuhlmeier, Wynn, & Bloom, 2003; Woodward & Sommerville, 2000).

———————— Connecting Concepts
Intersubjectivity and social referencing are both described in more detail in Chapter 7.

In the second year, infants become increasingly mindful of other people's mental states. For example, infants as young as 12 months show *social referencing,* looking at how an adult responds to a new object or event and then responding in a similar manner. At this point, then, they have some insights into other people's attentional focus and emotions (Moses, Baldwin, Rosicky, & Tidball, 2001).

By 18 months, children clearly know that their own actions influence other people's emotions and behaviors. For instance, they are more likely to offer an adult a food item that the adult has favorably reacted to before, even though they themselves dislike that kind of food (Repacholi & Gopnik, 1997).[1] In some cases they may even behave in ways that they know

social cognition
Process of thinking about how other people are likely to think, act, and react and choosing one's own interpersonal behaviors accordingly.

theory of mind
Awareness that people have an inner, psychological life (thoughts, beliefs, feelings, etc.).

intentionality
Engagement in an action congruent with one's purpose or goal.

---

[1]In Chapter 6 we saw evidence that preschoolers are not as egocentric as Piaget said they were. Here we see evidence that even toddlers can occasionally take another person's perspective.

will annoy or upset someone else (Dunn & Munn, 1985; Flavell, Miller, & Miller, 2002). For example, as a toddler, Jeanne's daughter Tina occasionally ran into the street and then looked tauntingly back at Mom as if to say, "Look at what I'm doing! I know this upsets you! Catch me if you can!"

Early childhood (ages 2–6). In the preschool years, children become increasingly aware of people's mental states. Beginning at age 2 (sometimes even earlier), they spontaneously use words that refer to desires and emotions (e.g., *want, feel sad*), and by age 2½ or 3, "cognitive" words such as *think* and *know* appear in their speech (Astington & Pelletier, 1996; Bartsch & Wellman, 1995; Bretherton & Beeghly, 1982; Flavell et al., 1995). By the time children are 3, they also realize that the mind is distinct from the physical world—that thoughts, memories, and dreams are not physical entities (Wellman & Estes, 1986; Woolley, 1995).

Yet preschoolers have very limited metacognitive awareness: They have trouble looking inward and describing the nature of their own thinking and knowledge. Furthermore, they may mistakenly assume that what *they* know is what other people know as well. Consider the following situation:

Connecting Concepts
The metacognitive awareness of both younger and older children is discussed in Chapter 7.

> Max puts a piece of chocolate in the kitchen cupboard and then goes out to play. While he is gone, his mother discovers the chocolate and moves it to a drawer. When Max returns later, where will he look for his chocolate? (based on Wimmer & Perner, 1983)

Max will look in the cupboard, of course, because that's where he thinks the chocolate is. However, 3-year-olds are quite certain he will look in the drawer, where the chocolate is actually located. Not until age 4 or 5 do children appreciate a *false belief*: They realize that circumstances may reasonably lead people to believe something different from what they themselves know to be true (Avis & Harris, 1991; Wellman et al., 2001; Wimmer & Perner, 1983).

Preschoolers are often eager to learn why people do the things they do, as this conversation between 2½-year-old Adam and his mother illustrates:

Adam: Why she write dat name?
Mother: Because she wanted to.
Adam: Why she wanted to?
Mother: Because she thought you'd like it.
Adam: I don't want to like it. (Wellman, Phillips, & Rodriquez, 2000, p. 908)

Inherent in Adam's question *Why she write dat name?* is an additional advancement in theory of mind: Preschoolers become increasingly aware of the relationship between other people's psychological states and behaviors. They understand that people's perceptions, emotions, and desires influence their actions, and they become increasingly adept at inferring people's mental states from behaviors and other events (Astington & Pelletier, 1996; Flavell, 2000; Wellman et al., 2000). For example, look at the two scenarios in Figure 12-5. *Which boy would like to swing?* Obviously the boy in the lower picture is the one who has an *intention* of using the swing. Most 5-year-olds correctly answer the question we've just asked you, but few 3-year-olds can (Astington, 1991).

Figure 12-5

Which boy would like to swing? Children who can correctly answer such questions can distinguish between intention and behavior.

From "Intention in the Child's Theory of Mind" by J. W. Astington. In *Children's Theories of Mind* (p. 168), by C. Moore & D. Frye, 1991, Hillsdale, NJ: Erlbaum, p. 168. Reprinted with permission of Lawrence Erlbaum Associates.

Middle childhood (ages 6–10). As children reach the elementary grades, they become capable of more sophisticated inferences about people's mental states. They realize that people's actions do not always reflect their true thoughts and feelings (Flavell et al., 2002; Gnepp, 1989; K. Lee et al., 2002). For example, a person may intentionally lie about a situation to mislead someone else. A person who appears happy may actually be sad.

Middle childhood heralds more complex understandings of the nature of thinking as well. In particular, children understand that people *interpret*

─────────── Connecting Concepts
The belief that learning is an active,
constructive process is an example of
an *epistemological belief* (see
Chapter 7).

an event, rather than simply "recording" it, and that others may interpret it differently than they themselves do (M. Chandler & Boyes, 1982; P. L. Harris, 2006). Furthermore, they are apt to take people's preexisting expectations and biases into account when interpreting what people say and do (Pillow & Henrichon, 1996). In other words, children in the elementary grades increasingly realize that thinking and learning are active, constructive processes (Flavell et al., 1995; Wellman, 1990).

Finally, children now begin to recognize that people's thoughts and feelings are often closely intertwined. Thus different thoughts about a situation lead to different feelings about it (Flavell, Flavell, & Green, 2001; P. L. Harris, 1989). For example, a 9-year-old might say, "Arlene feels bad because she thinks I don't like her. I *do* like her, though."

Early adolescence (ages 10–14).   As children move into early adolescence, they begin to appreciate that people can have mixed feelings about events and other individuals (S. K. Donaldson & Westerman, 1986; Flavell & Miller, 1998; Harter & Whitesell, 1989). And they realize that people may simultaneously have multiple, and possibly conflicting, intentions (M. J. Chandler, 1987). Young adolescents become increasingly thoughtful about such matters, and their ability to recognize the complexity of thoughts and emotions in themselves is correlated with their ability to recognize the same complexity in others (Bosacki, 2000).

In adolescence, youngsters also become more observant of the subtle nuances of other people's behaviors—the drooping shoulders, raised eyebrows, and so on. You can see this advancement in the "Emotional Development" module on Observation CD 2. In the "Middle Childhood" clip, 10-year-old Daniel shows an understanding that people often (but not always) reveal their emotions in their facial expressions and body language. For example, they may smile when happy, frown when angry, or walk with drooping shoulders when sad. In the "Early Adolescence" and "Late Adolescence" clips, 13-year-old Crystal and 15-year-old Greg are sensitive to even more subtle cues. For example, people may get "hyper" or "won't stop talking" when they're happy, may "hide their face" or "don't talk" when sad, or "don't want you to be around them" when angry.

Observe advancements in children's awareness of subtle behavioral cues in the "Emotional Development" clips for middle childhood, early adolescence, and late adolescence, on Observation CD 2.

Courtesy of their expanding reasoning abilities, working memory capacity, and social awareness, young adolescents also begin to engage in **recursive thinking** (Oppenheimer, 1986; Perner & Wimmer, 1985). That is, they can think about what other people might be thinking about them and eventually can reflect on other people's thoughts about themselves through multiple iterations (e.g., "You think that I think that you think . . ."). This is not to say that adolescents (or adults, for that matter) always use this capacity. In fact, thinking only about one's own perspective, without regard for the perspective of others, is a common phenomenon in the early adolescent years (recall our earlier discussion of the *imaginary audience*).

Late adolescence (ages 14–18).   Older adolescents can draw on a rich knowledge base derived from numerous social experiences, and so they become ever more skillful at drawing inferences about people's psychological characteristics, intentions, and needs (Eisenberg, Carlo, Murphy, & Van Court, 1995; Paget, Kritt, & Bergemann, 1984). In addition, they are more attuned to the complex dynamics—not only thoughts, feelings, and present circumstances, but also past experiences—that influence behavior (Flanagan & Tucker, 1999; Selman, 1980). And they realize that human beings are not always aware of why they act as they do (Selman, 1980). What we see emerging in the high school years, then, is a budding psychologist: an individual who can be quite astute in deciphering and explaining the motives and actions of others. Yet adults must remember that throughout childhood and adolescence, some youngsters are more perceptive than others, and their perceptiveness plays a significant role in their ability to interact effectively with other people (Astington & Pelletier, 1996).

recursive thinking
Thinking about what other people may be thinking about oneself, possibly through multiple iterations.

social perspective taking
Imagining what someone else might be thinking or feeling.

To truly understand and get along with other people, children must apply their growing theory of mind to step occasionally into other people's shoes and look at the world from other viewpoints. Such **social perspective taking** helps children to make sense of actions that might otherwise be puzzling. You can see one child's attempt at social perspective taking in the following exercise, "Bosnia."

INTERPRETING CHILDREN'S ARTIFACTS AND ACTIONS

Bosnia

As an assignment for her seventh-grade English class in 1995, 12-year-old Tosha wrote a fictional piece set in Bosnia, which at the time was in the midst of horrendous fighting between rival ethnic groups, with many thousands of innocent adults and children losing their lives. In her piece, Tosha takes the perspec-

tive of George Brown, a member of an international singing group that has traveled to Bosnia to bolster the spirits of American troops stationed there. As you read Tosha's essay, look for signs of social perspective taking and consider what they reveal about her theory of mind.

> As I sit and look outside through the ripps in our small, worn, beated tent I see an once beautiful land now wrecked with hatrid, war, and destruction. This once heavily forested area, now tree less. This once clear blue sky now gray with smog, smoke, and dust. This once happy place filled with people, buildings, and excitement is now deserted, empty, and dead. This place like many others is a war zone, a terrible place. Welcome to Bosnia.
>
> My name is George Brown and I am a member of the United Nations Peace Choir. I came to this horrible place to help, only to be completely helpless. Nothing I can do can change or stop whats going on and I'm stuck in the middle of the war. I spend my lonesome days writing to my wonderful wife Jane and my 2 darling little girls. I would love to go home but I can't. I am stuck in this horrible place until the war ends- leaving the camp grounds could be deadly. Even if I could go home I dont know if I'd want to, I would feel so horrible and guilty coming home with nothing accomplished. Do you know what it is like being stuck in the middle of something and watch everything wrong happen and
>
> not be able to do anything about it. I feel as though Ive failed my country, family, and fellow soldiers. I am a failure for sore.
>
> In recent letters I've recieved I've learned that today is thanksgiving. Thanks for what, I ask. I supose being alive should be good enough. I remember that in past years for thanksgiving I had mouth warming turkey, taste bud tickeling stuffing, purfect potatoes, scromptous cranberry sause, peas, corn, and homemade eggnog. I wonder what my familys eating now. For thanksgiving I'll get a piece of nameless meat along with leftours from various other dishes. My only pleasure this Thansgiving is the package of Swiss Chocolates my wife sent me and the silver crossed neelace I recived before I left. As I hold my neclace I say a silent prayer hoping for long sought peace.
>
> As I close my ears the familiar soond of gunshots race through my head. Why I repeatidly ask myself. Why?

In her composition Tosha captures many elements of what it might be like to be a man in a distant, war-torn country. For example, she describes his frustration ("Nothing I can do can change or stop whats going on"), loneliness ("my lonesome days writing to my wonderful wife Jane and my 2 darling little girls"), sadness ("I'll get a piece of nameless meat along with leftovers from various other dishes"), and commitment to a worthy cause ("I would feel so horrible and guilty coming home with nothing accomplished"). In the process Tosha reveals not only an understanding of diverse human emotions and motives but also a recognition that people can have mixed feelings about a situation. Many adolescents exhibit a similar awareness of the complexity of human nature.

Study Guide and Reader ————
Supplementary Reading 12-3 describes Robert Selman's early, groundbreaking theory of how social perspective taking changes with age.

Factors promoting development of a theory of mind. To some degree, development of a theory of mind probably depends on brain maturation and the advancements in executive functioning that accompany it (Andrews, Halford, Bunch, Bowden, & Jones, 2003; Carlson & Moses, 2001; Perner, Lang, & Kloo, 2002). Yet environmental factors are almost certainly involved as well. Discussions with adults about what people think, feel, want, and so on enhance children's awareness of thoughts and emotions as entities separate from physical reality (Jenkins, Turrell, Kogushi, Lollis, & Ross, 2003; Meins et al., 2003; Woolfe, Want, & Siegal, 2002). Parents who openly consider differing points of view during family discussions help children realize that multiple perspectives can legitimately exist (Astington & Pelletier, 1996). In the early years, sociodramatic play activities, in which children take on a variety of roles ("mommy," "doctor," etc.), can also help children imagine what people might think and feel in different contexts (P. L. Harris, 1989; Lillard, 1998; Rubin & Pepler, 1995).

Connecting Concepts ————
Executive functions are described in Chapters 4 and 7.

Social Information Processing

To interact effectively with other people, children must put their theory of mind and social perspective-taking ability to work in social situations. In particular, they engage in **social information processing:** They attend to and interpret various aspects of a situation and eventually choose what is, in their eyes, an appropriate response. Social information processing is similar to information processing in general. It involves selecting and paying *attention* to certain stimuli, making sense of those stimuli through *elaboration, storing* what has been learned in long-term memory, and *retrieving* previously acquired information and beliefs on relevant occasions.

From an information processing perspective, children go through several steps when they encounter, interpret, and respond to specific social situations (Dodge, 1986; Lemerise & Arsenio, 2000). To give life to these steps, imagine the following scenario:

> Audrey is sitting at a table across from her new friend Henry. A man walks into a room with a sad look on his face. He stumbles a bit and then sits beside Henry. The man smiles, picks up a cookie, takes a bite, drinks from a glass of milk, and puts the half-filled glass on the table. Henry looks up at the man, smiles, and knocks over the milk. The milk spills and splashes onto Audrey's shirt. What does Audrey do?

Audrey would engage in the following processes in her efforts to understand and respond to the situation:

1. *Attention and storage in memory.* Audrey would focus on certain aspects of the situation, including the other people's appearance, behavior, and apparent emotions, and store this information in working memory. She might be especially attentive to the spilling of the milk, as this event would be fast-moving and attention-getting. She might also look at the other people's facial expressions for clues about their feelings and possible motives.
2. *Interpretation.* Audrey would elaborate on what she's directly observed using what she knows and believes about human nature. She might wonder: Why did the man stumble? Why is he sad? Did Henry spill the milk by accident or on purpose? What will the man and Henry do next? She might also formulate tentative answers to these questions.
3. *Clarification of goals.* Audrey would examine her own motives and priorities and decide what she herself wants to gain from the situation. Does she want to maintain her friendship with Henry? Does she want to teach him a "lesson" for getting milk on her shirt? Does she want to make the man feel better? And how important is it that the man approves of her actions? Ultimately, she must decide which goal(s) are most important to achieve.
4. *Response search.* Audrey would draw on her past experiences to decide how to handle the situation. That is, she would search for and retrieve potentially useful responses from long-term memory. To deal with the spilled milk, she might consider a variety of possibilities—perhaps patiently cleaning up the spill, or perhaps retaliating against the "aggressor"—depending on which behaviors have been most useful in previous social experiences.
5. *Response decision.* After Audrey has identified two or more possible responses, she would weigh the benefits and drawbacks of each one. What would she gain and lose from cleaning up the mess? What would she gain and lose from retaliating? Perhaps she would ponder various alternatives for quite some time, or perhaps she would reach her conclusion quickly, with very little deliberation.
6. *Response enactment.* Once Audrey has settled on a course of action, she would make her response and observe its effects. For example, if she cleans up the mess (and perhaps asks Henry to be more careful), she might find that she maintains a productive relationship with him. If, instead, she retaliates, she might find herself embroiled in an escalating argument.

As you can see, social information processing is not confined to perception of and response to immediate social stimuli. It also draws on children's theory of mind and on their

Connecting Concepts
Components of information processing are described in more depth in Chapter 7.

social information processing
Series of cognitive steps used in understanding and responding to social events.

memories of past social events, and it involves deliberation and decision making. Furthermore, children's emotional states (e.g., whether they are happy, sad, or angry) affect their interpretations each step of the way, and their interpretations, in turn, affect their emotional reactions (Dodge, 1991; Lemerise & Arsenio, 2000).

The various components of social information processing clearly affect youngsters' ability to interact effectively with others. For example, imagine this conversation between two teenagers:

Jamie: Do you want to go skating with me on Saturday?
Pat: No, I can't. I'm busy on Saturday.

Does Pat really have a prior commitment on Saturday, or does Pat simply not want to spend time with Jamie? Adolescents who consistently interpret another's reluctance or refusal as a sign of personal rejection are apt to respond in counterproductive ways (G. Downey, Bonica, & Rincón, 1999; G. Downey, Lebolt, Rincón, & Freitas, 1998). And consider this situation:

> You and your friend just finished playing a board game. You had fun playing the game because you got to pick the game and it is your favorite. You really want to play the same game again, but your friend doesn't want to and says it's her [or his] turn to pick. (A. J. Rose & Asher, 1999, p. 73)

When adults understand how children and adolescents think about and interpret social situations, they can better help youngsters interact effectively with peers.

Children whose primary goal is to preserve the friendship in such a situation (e.g., "I would be trying to be fair") tend to have more friends than children who are primarily concerned with addressing their own needs (e.g., "I would be trying to keep my friend from pushing me around") (A. J. Rose & Asher, 1999, p. 71).

Social-Cognitive Bias and Prejudice

Thinking about social situations can involve a lot of mental "work." Accordingly, people often take mental "shortcuts" to ease the load on working memory and make their dealings with others more efficient (L. A. Brenner, Koehler, Liberman, & Tversky, 1996; Tversky & Kahneman, 1990). Many of these shortcuts reflect **social-cognitive biases,** predispositions to interpret or respond to social situations in particular ways. For example, some children, but not others, tend to believe that a single action reflects a person's typical behavior and personality (Dweck, 2000; Karafantis & Levy, 2004). Let's return to our earlier scenario involving Audrey, Henry, and the man. If Audrey is predisposed to think that a single behavior indicates how a person typically acts, she might assume that the man (who has a sad look) is a generally unhappy guy and that Henry (who spills the milk) is, by nature, clumsy or inconsiderate.

Some social-cognitive biases are a minor nuisance; they lead to small distortions in thinking but don't cause grave harm. Others, however, have serious consequences. For instance, children occasionally jump to hasty conclusions about others based on group membership (e.g., gender, ethnicity, sexual orientation, religious affiliation). In other words, they respond on the basis of a **stereotype,** a rigid, simplistic, and erroneous characterization of a particular group. Often a stereotype encompasses a host of negative attributes (e.g., "stingy," "lazy," "promiscuous") and leads children to exhibit negative attitudes, feelings, and behaviors—that is, **prejudice**—toward the group in question.

The roots of stereotypes and prejudice lie in the natural tendency of human beings to categorize their experiences. In their first few years, children learn that people belong to different groups, such as boys, girls, "Blacks," and "Whites," and many preschoolers can identify members of various ethnic groups (Aboud, 1988, 1993). As children are forming these social categories, they tend to favor their own group and to expect less desirable characteristics and behaviors from members of other groups, especially if the different groups are in some form of conflict with one another (Black-Gutman & Hickson, 1996; Pitner, Astor, Benbenishty, Haj-Yahia, & Zeira, 2003; Wilder & Shapiro, 1989).

On average, stereotypes and prejudice decrease as children move through the elementary grades (D. E. Carter, Detine-Carter, & Benson, 1995; F. H. Davidson, 1976; C. L. Martin, 1989). This decline is probably due to children's increasing awareness of the limits of social categories. Many children gradually begin to realize that people who share membership in a category (e.g.,

social-cognitive bias
Mental shortcut in thinking about other people or social events.

stereotype
Rigid, simplistic, and erroneous characterization of a particular group.

prejudice
Display of negative attitudes, feelings, and behaviors toward particular individuals because of their membership in a specific group.

"girls") are similar in some ways but very different in others. Yet other factors may work to maintain or strengthen stereotypes, and so some children show an increase in prejudice as they reach early adolescence (Black-Gutman & Hickson, 1996). Parents may encourage prejudice through both words and actions—for instance, by telling ethnic jokes, restricting playmates to same-race peers, or enrolling their children in schools with as little racial and ethnic diversity as possible (Ashmore & DelBoca, 1976; Branch, 1999). Popular images in television and other media—where males are often depicted as strong and aggressive, females appear to be weak and passive, and members of certain ethnic groups are consistently cast as "bad guys"—may also have an impact (Huston et al., 1992; Kimball, 1986; Signorielli & Lears, 1992).

By adolescence, and probably before, children who are victims of prejudice are well aware that others' treatment of them is discriminatory (Phinney & Tarver, 1988; R. D. Taylor, Casten, Flickinger, Roberts, & Fulmore, 1994). Over time they acquire a variety of strategies— seeking the support and companionship of other group members, forming a positive ethnic identity, and so on—for coping with prejudice and discrimination (Swim & Stangor, 1998). Even so, young people who are daily victims of prejudice are more likely than their peers to become ill or depressed (Allison, 1998; Tatum, 1997).

— Connecting Concepts
Chapter 14 explores the effects of tele-vision and other media in more detail.

— Connecting Concepts
Strategies for coping with prejudice and discrimination are described in more detail in Chapter 5.

Diversity in Social Cognition

Both nurture and nature contribute to youngsters' growing abilities in social cognition. The effects of nurture sometimes reveal themselves in ethnic and cultural differences. The effects of nature are often evident in children with certain special needs.

Ethnic and cultural differences.   Children in a wide variety of cultures acquire a theory of mind, and often at similar ages (P. L. Harris, 2006). But *how much* children think about other people's thoughts and feelings depends, in part, on how much their culture encourages them to (Lillard, 1999). Some cultures frequently explain people's behaviors in terms of mental events, whereas others are more likely to focus on external circumstances. For example, in the United States, children who live in urban areas often refer to people's psychological states when explaining good and bad behaviors (e.g., "He helped me to catch bugs, because he and I like to catch bugs"). In contrast, children in rural areas are more likely to attribute people's behaviors to situational factors (e.g., "She helped me pick up my books, because if she didn't I would have missed the bus"). The latter approach is also common in many Southeast Asian cultures (Lillard, 1999; J. G. Miller, 1987).

Children with special needs.   Some children with disabilities seem to have a biological disadvantage in thinking about other people. Deficits in social cognition have been observed in many children with ADHD, mental retardation, or autism (Baron-Cohen, Tager-Flusberg, & Cohen, 1993; Leffert, Siperstein, & Millikan, 1999; Milch-Reich, Campbell, Pelham, Connelly, & Geva, 1999). Such deficits are virtually universal in children with Asperger syndrome, a condition that shares certain features with autism but is far less debilitating. Children who have Asperger syndrome have exceptional difficulty drawing accurate inferences from others' behaviors and body language and speculating about others' thoughts and emotions.

Other disabilities may hinder the development of social cognition indirectly by limiting children's experiences in certain areas. For example, when children have significant hearing impairments beginning at birth or soon thereafter, they miss out on many discussions about "thinking," "feeling," "wanting," and the like, and so their theory of mind may develop more slowly (C. C. Peterson, 2002).

Fostering the Development of Social Cognition

The theories and research findings just reviewed have several implications for teachers and other adults who work with children and adolescents:

● *Talk about psychological phenomena and other people's perspectives in age-appropriate ways.* Adults frequently talk with children about thoughts and feelings, and together they may speculate about what other people (e.g., children's peers, figures in historical and current events, or fictional characters) might be thinking and feeling. Adults should, of course, try to gear such discussions to children's cognitive and linguistic capabilities. For in-

Encouraging Social Perspective Taking

- Ask children to share their perceptions and interpretations with one another.

  A third-grade teacher finds several children arguing over why Serena tripped and fell during their game of tag. Meanwhile, Serena is crying. The teacher comforts Serena and then asks the children for their varying perspectives on what happened. He suggests that each of them may be partly right. He also urges them to be more careful when they play running games, as it is easy for children to bump one another accidentally in such activities.

- Encourage children to speculate about characters' thoughts, emotions, and motives in works of literature.

  As a teacher in a child care center reads a story to a group of young children, she occasionally stops to ask questions about what the different

characters might be thinking and feeling. For instance, while reading *The Berenstain Bears' Trouble with Pets* (Berenstain & Berenstain, 1990), she asks, "Why does the Bear family let Little Bird fly away?" and "How do you think Mama and Papa Bear feel when Lady makes a mess in the living room?"

- Ask children to consider the perspectives of people they don't know.

  During a discussion of a recent earthquake in South America, an eighth-grade social studies teacher asks students to imagine how people must feel when they lose their home and possessions so quickly and don't know whether their loved ones are dead or alive.

stance, preschoolers understand such straightforward feelings as *sad, disappointed,* and *angry* (Chalmers & Townsend, 1990; Wittmer & Honig, 1994). Adolescents have sufficient cognitive and social reasoning capabilities to consider abstract and complex psychological qualities (e.g., being *passive aggressive* or having an inner *moral compass*) and to speculate about people's feelings in catastrophic circumstances, such as the atrocities committed in Bosnia in the name of "ethnic cleansing" in the 1990s or the devastation caused by Hurricane Katrina in 2005 (Yeager et al., 1997).

● *Encourage children to look at situations from other people's perspectives.* Classrooms and other group situations provide many opportunities for children to look at the world as others do, and over time such opportunities enhance children's theory of mind and perspective-taking capabilities. The Development and Practice feature "Encouraging Social Perspective Taking" presents three common strategies.

● *Help children tune in to the nonverbal cues that can help them "read people's minds."* Some children (especially girls) readily pick up on the body language that reveals companions' thoughts and feelings (Bosacki, 2000; Deaux, 1984). Other children are less perceptive. The latter group can benefit from explicit instruction regarding signals they might look for— the furrowed brow that indicates confusion, the agitation that indicates frustration or impatience, the "silent treatment" that suggests anger, and so on (e.g., Minskoff, 1980).

● *Actively work to break down stereotypes and prejudice.* One effective strategy is to encourage children to see people as *individuals*—as human beings with their own unique strengths and weaknesses—rather than as members of particular groups (García, 1994; C. D. Lee & Slaughter-Defoe, 1995; Spencer & Markstrom-Adams, 1990). Even more effective is to increase interpersonal contacts among people from diverse groups (and ideally to create a sense that "we are all in this together"), perhaps through cooperative group activities, multischool community service projects, or pen pal relationships with children in distant locations (Devine, 1995; Koeppel & Mulrooney, 1992; Oskamp, 2000).

In addition, adults should challenge any stereotypes and prejudicial attitudes they encounter in children's speech or actions. For example, if a teenager talks about "lazy migrant workers," a teacher might respond by saying, "I occasionally hear students express that view. I wonder where that stereotype came from. Migrant workers are often up before dawn and picking produce until dusk. And many of them take other demanding jobs when the growing season is over." Notice how the teacher confronts the "lazy migrant worker" stereotype tactfully and matter-of-factly and does not assume that the teen's remark has malicious intent. Youngsters often thoughtlessly repeat the prejudicial remarks of others. Playing on their interest to appear tolerant and open-minded may be more effective than chastising them for attitudes they have not carefully thought through (Dovidio & Gaertner, 1999).

Productive interactions with peers of diverse backgrounds and races help children discover that every individual has unique qualities and that ethnic and racial stereotypes are rarely accurate.

Knowing what other people are apt to be thinking and feeling certainly enhances youngsters' effectiveness in social interactions. But social cognition alone is not enough. Children and adolescents also need to know how best to *behave* in their interactions with others. We turn to the development of such interpersonal behaviors now.

Interpersonal Behaviors

Children show social skills even in infancy.

As children grow older, they acquire an ever-expanding repertoire of **social skills,** strategies they use to interact effectively with others. Children vary considerably in their social competence. Some are courteous, know the right things to say in conversations, and willingly share and cooperate with peers. Others are less skilled, perhaps offending and alienating age-mates or perhaps feeling so anxious in social situations that they keep to themselves. Not surprisingly, young people's social skills affect the number and quality of their friendships, as well as their overall adjustment at school (Dishion, Andrews, & Crosby, 1995; Gottman, 1983; Pellegrini & Bohn, 2005).

Children develop social skills in large part through experience and practice with peers and adults (Gottman, 1986; Maccoby & Lewis, 2003). But they also acquire social skills by observing what adults and peers do in interactions with others. For instance, children's parents may model a variety of interpersonal styles—perhaps agreeable and respectful of others' needs, on the one hand, or hostile and aggressive, on the other (Dodge, Pettit, Bates, & Valente, 1995; Nix et al., 1999; Putallaz & Heflin, 1986).

Interpersonal Behaviors at Different Ages

Human beings acquire a wide variety of social skills in the first two decades of life. The unique aspects of infancy, childhood, and adolescence all offer important lessons and opportunities for practice.

Infancy (birth–age 2).   Interpersonal relationships begin with attachments to parents and other caregivers. In the second year, interactions with caregivers increasingly involve a common focus on external objects (once again recall our discussion of intersubjectivity and joint attention in Chapter 7). Infants who have regular contact with other small children often practice their emerging social skills with their peers. They may babble in response to one another, smile at another infant, or look where another child points (Eckerman, 1979; Mueller & Silverman, 1989). As toddlers, they may imitate one another, offer one another toys, and cooperate with and assist others in simple tasks and play activities (P. L. Harris, 2006; Howes, 1992; Howes & Matheson, 1992). Their developing language skills in the second year, as well as games with older children and adults (e.g., peekaboo, pat-a-cake, hide-and-seek), allow increasingly sustained and meaningful exchanges (W. C. Bronson, 1981).

Figure 12-6

Alex (age 5) and Davis (age 6) shared fantasies that guided them in drawing this picture together.

Early childhood (ages 2–6).   With the capacity for coordinating attention with others well established by age 2, young children interact more with age-mates, especially within the context of play activities. One early researcher identified six different kinds of behavior that preschool teachers and child care providers might observe in 2- to 5-year-olds (Parten, 1932). These categories, most of which reflect a continuum of increasing social interaction, are described in the Observation Guidelines table "Observing the Social Aspects of Young Children's Play." Younger and older preschoolers alike are apt to exhibit many or all of these behaviors at one time or another. However, most children become increasingly interactive and cooperative in play activities as they grow older (Gottman, 1983; Howes & Matheson, 1992).

Parallel play, though seemingly nonsocial, has a definite social function: Children use it as a way to learn more about peers' interests, initiate conversations, and find common ground on which they might play together (Bakeman & Brownlee, 1980; Gottman, 1983; Rubin, Bukowski, & Parker, 1998). Yet the imagination and social coordination that characterize the last category—cooperative play—make it an especially important activity of early childhood. In Figure 12-6 you can see the result of a coordinated effort between friends Alex (age 5) and Davis (age 6). As they worked on the picture, they continually listened to each other, built on each other's ideas, and drew from their many past experiences together.

social skills
Strategies used to interact effectively with others.

OBSERVATION GUIDELINES

Observing the Social Aspects of Young Children's Play

Characteristic	Look For	Example	Implication
Unoccupied Behavior	• Failure to engage in any activity, either with or without another individual • Aimless wandering • Quiet sitting and staring	During free-play time, Donald often retreats to a corner of the play yard, where he sits quietly either running his fingers through the dirt or staring off into space.	Try to engage the child with intriguing toys or other objects, or with a small-group activity. Consult with a specialist if unoccupied behavior is persistent and pervasive despite frequent attempts to engage the child.
Solitary Play	• Absorption in one's own playthings • Apparent lack of awareness of other children's presence	Although Laura and Erika are sitting next to each other in the sandbox, they are facing in opposite directions. Laura is digging a large hole ("to China," she says), and Erika is making "roads" with a toy bulldozer.	Keep in mind the value of children's independent play. On some occasions, present new toys or games that require the participation of two or more children.
Onlooker Behavior	• Unobtrusive observation of other children's play activities	As three of his classmates play "store," Jason quietly watches them from the side of the room.	Ask the child if he or she would like to play with the other children. If so, ask the others if the onlooker might join in.
Parallel Play	• Playing next to another child, but with little or no interaction • Similarities in the behaviors of two or more children who are playing independently but in close proximity	Naticia and Leo are both making "skyscrapers" with wooden blocks. Sometimes one child looks at what the other is doing, and occasionally one child makes a tower similar to the other's.	Comment that both children are doing something similar. Suggest an enjoyable activity that incorporates what both children are doing.
Associative Play	• Some talking and sharing of objects with another child • Occasional comments about what another child is doing	Several children are working at the same table creating different animals from Play-Doh. They occasionally ask for a particular color ("Gimme the red") or make remarks about others' creations ("You made a kitty just like I did").	Keep in mind that associative play is often a productive way for children to get to know one another better. Once children feel comfortable together, suggest an activity that would encourage cooperative behaviors.
Cooperative Play	• Active sharing of toys and coordination of activities • Taking on specific roles related to a common theme	Sheldon sets up a "doctor's office" and Jan comes to visit him with her teddy bear, who has a "sore throat." Sheldon puts a tongue depressor to the bear's mouth and instructs it to "Say aahh."	Provide a variety of toys and other objects that are best used in group play—balls, props for playing "house" and "store," and so on.

Source: First two columns based on Parten, 1932.

In one form of cooperative play, *sociodramatic play,* children assume complementary imagined roles and carry out a logical sequence of actions. In the following scenario, we see Eric and Naomi, long-time friends, assuming roles of husband and wife. Naomi is making plans to go shopping:

N: I'm buying it at a toy store, to buy Eric Fisher a record 'cause he doesn't have a . . .
E: What happened to his old one?
N: It's all broken.
E: How did it get all broken?
N: Ah, a robber stealed it, I think. That's what he said, a robber stealed it.
E: Did he see what the action was? You know my gun is in here, so could you go get my gun? It's right over there, back there, back there, not paper . . . did you get it?
N: Yes, I found the robbers right in the closet.
E: Good, kill 'em.
N: I killed em.
E: Already?
N: Yes, so quick they can't believe it. (Gottman, 1986, p. 191)

Sociodramatic play activities contribute in many ways to children's growing social competence. Children must coordinate their actions and perspectives, taking turns, sharing objects, and in other ways considering what a playmate is doing. They must agree on individual roles ("I'll be the warrior"; "Okay, I'll be the chief"), props ("The log can be our base"), and

Connecting Concepts ————
Sociodramatic play also promotes cognitive development (see Chapter 6).

rules and guidelines that govern actions ("We'll let Frances play, but she has to be the horse") (Garvey, 1990; Howes & Matheson, 1992). And underneath it all, they must be willing to share certain fantasies (Rubin et al., 1998).

In the process of doing such things, children develop skills in assertiveness, negotiation, and conflict resolution (Göncü, 1993; Gottman, 1986; Howes, 1992). For instance, they become increasingly skillful and polite in making requests. Whereas a 3-year-old is apt to be a bit bossy ("Give me the red one"; "You hafta . . ."), 5- and 6-year-olds are more likely to use hints and suggestions ("Would you like . . . ?" "Let's . . .") (Parkhurst & Gottman, 1986, p. 329). Through negotiating roles and story lines, they discover the advantages of compromise ("I want to be the Mommy, you're the baby"; "No, you were the Mommy last time, so it's *my* turn"; "Okay, but next time I get to be the Mommy"). And children learn how to give one another emotional support, perhaps by voicing approval for one another's actions ("That's pretty") or expressing sympathy for a playmate's distress ("Don't worry about that, it'll come off") (Gottman, 1983, p. 58).

In the "Physical Activity: Early Childhood" clip on Observation CD 1, observe Acadia and Cody coordinating their activities and resolving their differences.

In the "Physical Activity: Early Childhood" video clip on Observation CD 1, you can watch two 4-year-olds, Acadia and Cody, use a variety of strategies to nourish their relationship and prevent any differences of opinion from escalating. They make explicit reference to their friendship ("Let's go, Cody, my best friend"). They encourage one another to climb ("This is gonna be cool!"). They admit when they're wrong ("Silly me, I forget everything"). And eventually they come to agreement about which slide to go down ("Yeah. Let's do it"). Not all preschoolers are as skillful as Acadia and Cody, however. In some instances preschoolers cooperate more successfully when adults help them iron out their difficulties (Mize, Pettit, & Brown, 1995; Parke & Bhavnagri, 1989).

Middle childhood (ages 6–10).   Once children begin elementary school, opportunities to interact with peers increase considerably. At ages 6 through 12, children spend about 40 percent of their waking hours with peers—approximately twice as much time as they did in early childhood (Zarbatany, Hartmann, & Rankin, 1990). They also become aware that some ways of behaving are acceptable to peers, whereas other ways are not (Gottman & Mettetal, 1986; J. R. Harris, 1998). For example, in the following gossip session, 8-year-old Erica and Mikaila reveal their shared belief that tattling on others is inappropriate:

E: Katie's just a . . .
M: Tattletale.
E: Yeah, she tells on everything.
M: Yeah. (Gottman & Mettetal, 1986, p. 206; reprinted with permission of Cambridge University Press)

Figure 12-7

Ten-year-old Jacob drew a child getting into an argument with a friend and then coming to a mutually acceptable solution.

With their growing awareness of other people's opinions, most children become eager to behave in socially acceptable ways. They also become more concerned about equitably resolving conflicts and preserving friendships (Hartup, 1996; Newcomb & Bagwell, 1995). In Figure 12-7, 10-year-old Jacob reveals his awareness that arguing with friends can be unpleasant, but that disputes often can be resolved to everyone's satisfaction. Not all attempts to resolve conflicts are successful, of course. Most children discover that such strategies as sulking ("I'm going home!"), threatening ("I'm never gonna play with you again!"), and hitting ("Take that!") rarely work. Through experimentation with a variety of strategies and through their growing capacity for social perspective taking, most children become proficient at maintaining amicable relationships with their age-mates.

Whereas younger children are apt to get together in groups of two or three to engage in free-flowing fantasy, elementary school children often convene in larger groups and choose games and other activities that have established rules. Verbal contests (e.g., "Twenty Questions," "I Spy"), board games, and team sports are common (Corsaro, 1985; Hartup, 1984). At this age, rules take on a certain immutable quality: They are permanent fixtures that cannot be altered by whim, and failure to follow them constitutes cheating—a serious breach from what is good and civilized. In the following conversation with 10-year-old Ben, an adult asks if it would be possible to change the rules in a game of marbles. Ben agrees (somewhat unwillingly) that he could formulate new rules but has doubts about their legitimacy:

Ben: [I]t would be cheating.
Adult: But all your pals would like to [play with the new rule], wouldn't they?
Ben: Yes, they all would.
Adult: Then why would it be cheating?
Ben: Because I invented it: it isn't a rule! It's a wrong rule because it's outside of the rules. A fair rule is one that is in the game. (dialogue from Piaget, 1932/1960b, p. 55; format adapted)

Children learn a great deal from participating in rule-governed games. They discover how to use rules to their own advantage ("If I put another house on Boardwalk, you have to pay me double next time you land on it"). They learn how to form alliances with other children ("I'll run behind him, and then you pass me the ball over his head"). And they develop strategies for dealing with ambiguous situations ("It was *in?*" "Are you kidding? It was *out!*" "Okay, it's out, but next time *I* get to decide!"). Occasional bickering aside, the predominance of rule-governed activities in middle childhood seems to reflect children's growing motivation to learn and abide by the rules of society (DeVries, 1997).

Early adolescence (ages 10–14).   Once children reach puberty, they increasingly rely on their peers for emotional support as well as recreation (Levitt, Guacci-Franco, & Levitt, 1993; R. M. Ryan et al., 1994). Some begin to reveal their innermost thoughts to others, especially peers (Basinger, Gibbs, & Fuller, 1995; Levitt et al., 1993). But even as their tendency for self-disclosure expands, young adolescents become increasingly self-conscious about what others might think of them. To some degree, their age-mates are apt to exert **peer pressure,** strongly encouraging them to behave in certain ways and not to behave in others. Youngsters who have poor relationships with their families and those whose self-esteem is largely contingent on other people's opinions seem to be especially vulnerable to peer pressure (Erwin, 1993; Hacker & Bol, 2004; Rudolph, Caldwell, & Conley, 2005).

Yet self-socialization plays a significant role in young adolescents' motivation to conform. In other words, much of the motivation to conform to peers' standards for behavior probably comes from within rather than from outside (Hartup, 1983; R. E. Owens, 1996). As you should recall from our earlier discussion of the *imaginary audience,* young adolescents often overestimate other people's interest in their appearance and behavior. This heightened concern for how others evaluate them can lead them to closely imitate their peers' choices in dress, music, slang, and so on.

Young adolescents have a tendency to categorize other people, especially their peers. They are apt to pigeonhole classmates into such groups as "brains," "jocks," "skaters," and "geeks" (J. R. Harris, 1995; Pipher, 1994). A desire to be part of the "in" crowd can drive many young adolescents to do foolish things, as this reflection by one youngster reveals:

There's all this crap about being accepted into a group and struggling and making an effort to make friends and not being comfortable about your own self-worth as a human being. You're trying very hard to show everyone what a great person you are, and the best way to do that is if everyone else is drinking therefore they think that's the thing to do, then you might do the same thing to prove to them that you have the same values that they do and therefore you're okay. At the same time, the idea of peer pressure is a lot of bunk. What I heard about peer pressure all the way through school is that someone is going to walk up to me and say, "Here, drink this and you'll be cool." It wasn't like that at all. You go somewhere and everyone else would be doing it and you'd think, "Hey, everyone else is doing it and they seem to be having a good time—now why wouldn't I do this?" In that sense, the preparation of the powers that be, the lessons that they tried to drill into me, they were completely off. They had no idea what we are up against. (C. Lightfoot, 1992, p. 240)

Often, too, young adolescents begin to divide into racial or ethnic groups, even if they have previously mingled freely with one another in the elementary school grades. To some extent, such self-imposed segregation reflects youngsters' desires to affiliate with peers who, in their eyes, can better understand and deal with the overt and subtle forms of discrimination they sometimes face (Tatum, 1997).

peer pressure
Tactics used to encourage some behaviors and discourage others in age-mates.

In their desire to fit in with a certain group of peers, some teenagers lead "double lives," displaying one set of behaviors with their families and an entirely different set of behaviors at school. For instance, if they believe that their classmates view high academic achievement as uncool, they might do their homework faithfully at home each night yet feign disinterest in classroom activities, disrupt class with jokes or goofy behaviors, and express surprise at receiving high grades (B. B. Brown, 1993; Covington, 1992). Many young adolescents have trouble reconciling these different sides and may feel as if they are continually hiding their true selves (L. M. Brown, Tappan, & Gilligan, 1995; Harter, Bresnick, Bouchey, & Whitesell, 1997; Harter, Waters, & Whitesell, 1997).

Cognitive advancements make it possible for older adolescents to see their peers more as individuals than as members of particular groups, and so most increasingly associate with peers from diverse backgrounds.

Late adolescence (ages 14–18). Older adolescents spend almost half of their waking hours interacting with their peers (Csikszentmihalyi, 1995). They spend relatively little time with adults and very little time *exclusively* with an adult, such as a parent or teacher (Csikszentmihalyi, 1995; Csikszentmihalyi & Larson, 1984). In their efforts to develop a sense of identity, they often use their peers as a forum for self-exploration and self-understanding (Gottman & Mettetal, 1986). For instance, in the following dialogue, two girls struggle with their beliefs about premarital sexual intercourse as they discuss one girl's recent breakup with her boyfriend Randy:

A: [*joking*] I think you should take Randy to court for statutory rape.
B: I don't. I'm to the point of wondering what "that kind of girl" . . . I don't know about the whole scene.
A: The thing is . . .
B: It depends on the reasoning. And how long you've been going out with somebody.
A: Yeah, I'm satisfied with my morals.
B: As long as you're satisfied with your morals, that's cool.
A: Yeah, but other people . . .
B: And I'm pretty, I'm pretty sturdy in mine.
A: Yeah [*giggle*], I know that. Mine tend to bend too easily. (Gottman & Mettetal, 1986, p. 218; reprinted with the permission of Cambridge University Press)

A greater capacity for abstract thought allows older adolescents to think of other people as unique individuals rather than as members of specific groups. Older teens also become increasingly aware of the characteristics they share with people from diverse backgrounds. Perhaps as a result, ties to specific peer groups dissipate, hostilities between groups soften, and youngsters become more flexible about the people with whom they associate (B. B. Brown, Eicher, & Petrie, 1986; Gavin & Furman, 1989; Larkin, 1979; Shrum & Cheek, 1987). One recent graduate of a racially mixed high school put it this way:

Senior year was wonderful, when the black kids and the white kids got to be friends again, and the graduation parties where everyone mixed. . . . It was so much better. (Lewin, 2000, p. 20)

Social maturity is a long time in the making, however. High school seniors have far more sophisticated social skills than do preschoolers or fifth graders, but most have not completely mastered the tact and courtesy so essential for resolving delicate interpersonal matters. Human beings continue to develop and refine their social skills throughout adulthood and old age.

Development of Prosocial Behavior and Aggression

— **Connecting Concepts**
Children's inclinations to behave prosocially or aggressively are to some degree related to their beliefs about right and wrong. You will learn more about such *moral reasoning* in Chapter 13.

prosocial behavior
Action intended to benefit another person rather than oneself.

aggression
Action intentionally taken to hurt another either physically or psychologically.

Two kinds of interpersonal behaviors—prosocial behavior and aggression—have been the focus of considerable research. **Prosocial behavior** is an action intended to promote the well-being of another person, perhaps by sharing, teaching, or comforting. **Aggression** is an action intentionally taken to hurt another person either physically (e.g., hitting, shoving, or fighting) or psychologically (e.g., embarrassing, insulting, or ostracizing). Although prosocial behavior and aggression are at opposite ends of a helping-versus-hurting continuum, each has both biological and environmental origins. Here we look at the effects of biology and environment and at basic trends and principles that characterize the development of each kind of behavior.

Hereditary and other biological influences. From an evolutionary perspective, both prosocial and aggressive tendencies have enabled human beings to survive and flourish and so may be part of humans' genetic endowment (Coie & Dodge, 1998; Hoffman, 1981; Lorenz,

1966). Prosocial behavior promotes group cohesion, is critical for childrearing, and helps people live in harsh conditions. Some kinds of aggression, though antisocial in nature, also increase chances of survival. Squabbling and warfare cause people to spread apart (thereby improving people's chances of finding food and other essential resources), and in times of battle the strongest members of the species are those most likely to survive and give birth to future generations.

An evolutionary perspective of such behaviors is, of course, speculative at best. Twin studies provide more convincing evidence that both prosocial and aggressive behaviors have genetic origins. Monozygotic (identical) twins tend to be more similar than dizygotic (fraternal) twins with respect to altruistic behavior, empathy for others, and aggression (Ghodsian-Carpey & Baker, 1987; Rushton, Fulkner, Neal, Nias, & Eysenck, 1986; Zahn-Waxler, Robinson, & Emde, 1992).

The exact biological causes of prosocial behavior are largely unknown, but researchers have identified several possible biological bases of aggression. To some extent, aggressive behavior appears to be a product of the male hormone testosterone. On average, males are more aggressive than females, and after puberty, males with high testosterone levels tend to be more aggressive than males with lower levels (J. Archer, 1991; Susman, Inoff-Germain, et al., 1987). Other chemical substances in the brain—in particular, substances involved in transmitting messages from one neuron to another—also affect children's aggressive tendencies, perhaps by influencing children's ability to inhibit impulses to respond aggressively to provocation (Coie & Dodge, 1998). Children with damage to certain areas of the brain, especially an area of the cortex involved in planning and behavior control, also display heightened aggression (Pennington & Bennetto, 1993; Raine & Scerbo, 1991).

Environmental influences.

One influential environmental factor is the presence of prosocial and aggressive models in children's lives. Children who observe sympathetic and generous models tend to be more helpful than those without such models (R. Elliott & Vasta, 1970; C. R. Owens & Ascione, 1991; Yarrow, Scott, & Waxler, 1973). Likewise, children who observe aggressive models—whether the models are adults, peers, or fictional characters in the media—show greater-than-average aggression (C. A Anderson et al., 2003; N. E. Goldstein, Arnold, Rosenberg, Stowe, & Ortiz, 2001; Margolin & Gordis, 2004).

Reinforcement also plays a role in both prosocial and aggressive behavior. Over the short run, children engage in more prosocial behavior if they are rewarded (e.g., with candy or praise) for such behavior (J. H. Bryan, Redfield, & Mader, 1971; Eisenberg, Fabes, Carlo, & Karbon, 1992; Rushton & Teachman, 1978). However, tangible rewards such as candy appear counterproductive over the long run, perhaps because children begin to perform prosocial actions primarily to benefit themselves ("I gave her my candy because I knew Dad would give me an even bigger treat for sharing"), rather than to gain personal satisfaction from helping others (Eisenberg & Fabes, 1998; Szynal-Brown & Morgan, 1983). Aggressive behavior is often reinforced by its outcomes: It may enable children to gain desired objects or get revenge (Coie & Dodge, 1998; Crick & Dodge, 1996; Lochman, Wayland, & White, 1993). And some aggressive children find reinforcement in their victims' expressions of alarm and pain, perhaps because these children gain a sense of power when they see others squirm under their cruel treatment (Bandura, 1991).

Families and cultures affect children's prosocial and aggressive tendencies as well. Children are more likely to imitate their parents' prosocial behaviors when parents exhibit an authoritative parenting style—that is, when parents are warm and loving, hold high standards for behavior, and explain why certain behaviors are unacceptable (Eisenberg, 1995; Eisenberg & Fabes, 1998; Hoffman, 1988). Children also tend to be more prosocial when their parents (mothers as well as fathers) have work obligations outside the home and give them numerous responsibilities (e.g., taking care of younger siblings) to help keep the household going (Whiting & Whiting, 1975). Other family environments are breeding grounds for aggression. Authoritarian (rather than authoritative) parenting, especially when accompanied by frequent physical punishment or abuse, appears to foster aggression and other antisocial behavior, but so, too, does very permissive parenting (P. L. Harris, 2006; Straus, 2000; also see Chapter 5). And in some cultures, families may teach children that aggression is an appropriate means of resolving conflicts or maintaining one's honor (D. Cohen & Nisbett, 1994; E. Staub, 1995).

Schools provide additional contexts in which children can learn either prosocial or aggressive behaviors. For example, children and adolescents are more likely to engage in prosocial behaviors, as well as to integrate qualities such as compassion and altruism into their overall sense

Connecting Concepts ——————
A classic study of the effects of models on aggression is presented in the discussion of *experimental studies* in Chapter 2.

Connecting Concepts ——————
See Chapter 5 for more on authoritarian, authoritative, and permissive parenting styles.

of self, if teachers and other adults get them actively involved in public service to others (Youniss & Yates, 1999). Violent aggression at schools is rare, but milder forms—racial and sexual harassment, bullying, vandalization, and so on—are fairly common (Burstyn et al., 2001; DeVoe et al., 2003; Garbarino, Bradshaw, & Vorrasi, 2002). At a few high schools (fortunately, only a few), it is acceptable practice to threaten or fight with a peer who tries to steal one's boyfriend or girlfriend, or students may believe that acting aggressively is the only way to ensure that they don't become victims of someone *else's* aggression (K. M. Williams, 2001a, 2001b).

Sadly, many children and adolescents encounter aggression in their homes, schools, or communities at one time or another. A recent national survey in the United States found that more than 50 percent of youngsters ages 2 to 17 had, in the preceding 12 months, been victims of physical aggression, with the highest frequencies reported for children ages 6 to 12 (Finkelhor, Ormrod, Turner, & Hamby, 2005).

Development of prosocial behavior.   Even young infants seem to be attuned to others' distress, in that they may start to cry when they hear other babies crying (Simner, 1971). True prosocial behaviors—actions intended to help someone else—appear early in the second year (P. L. Harris, 2006; Farver & Branstetter, 1994; Zahn-Waxler, Radke-Yarrow, Wagner, & Chapman, 1992). For example, toddlers may spontaneously give adults or peers assistance with everyday tasks, and they are apt to offer their favorite blanket or teddy bear to someone who seems to be unhappy or in pain. As a general rule, children behave more prosocially—for instance, they become increasingly generous—as they grow older (Eisenberg, 1982; Rushton, 1980).

Age, of course, is not the only variable that determines whether children and adolescents act prosocially. Social perspective taking is also important. In the process of putting themselves in someone else's shoes, children must experience some of the other person's feelings—that is, they must have *empathy*. Many children who behave prosocially also feel **sympathy,** a genuine feeling of sorrow and concern about another person's problems or distress (Batson, 1991; Eisenberg, 1995; Eisenberg & Fabes, 1998). Early signs of empathy and sympathy, in the form of concerned facial expressions, appear at age 2 or even earlier (S. Lamb & Feeny, 1995; Zahn-Waxler, Radke-Yarrow, et al., 1992). However, a deep concern for others' needs emerges only gradually over time. Nancy Eisenberg and her colleagues have identified five different levels, or *orientations,* through which youngsters are apt to proceed over the course of childhood and adolescence. These orientations are described and illustrated in the Observation Guidelines table "Assessing Children's Prosocial Development." Children do not march through the orientations in a lock-step, level-by-level manner, however. Instead, their behavior is apt to reflect two or more orientations in any particular time period (Eisenberg, Miller, Shell, McNalley, & Shea, 1991). Generally, however, youngsters increasingly exhibit more advanced orientations as they grow older (Eisenberg et al., 1995).

Other factors come into play as well. For example, children are more likely to help another individual if they themselves have been the cause of the person's pain or distress (Eisenberg, 1995). They are also more likely to behave prosocially if others' misfortunes are the result of an accident, disability, or other uncontrollable circumstance, rather than the result of something they think people have brought upon themselves (Eisenberg & Fabes, 1998; Graham, 1997).

Finally, prosocial behaviors are more common when the benefits outweigh the costs—for instance, when children think the beneficiary might eventually do them a favor in return (Eisenberg, Fabes, Schaller, Carlo, & Miller, 1991; L. Peterson, 1980). For some youngsters, the benefits of prosocial actions are strictly internal: A feeling of personal satisfaction about helping someone else more than makes up for any loss of time or convenience (see the "empathic" and "internalized values" orientations in the Observation Guidelines table). Unfortunately, some children believe that *aggression* yields more benefits than prosocial actions, as we shall see now.

Development of aggression.   Aggression takes a variety of forms. **Physical aggression** is an action that can potentially cause bodily injury. Examples are hitting, pushing, fighting, and using weapons. **Relational aggression** is an action that can adversely affect friendships and other interpersonal relationships. Examples are name calling, spreading unflattering rumors, and ostracizing a peer from a desirable social group.

The capacity for aggression emerges fairly early. By the latter half of the first year, infants may show anger toward caregivers who prevent them from reaching desired objects (Sten-

---

———— Connecting Concepts

This "spread" of crying from one baby to another is known as *emotional contagion* (see Chapter 11).

———— Connecting Concepts

As you learned in Chapter 11, children's capacity for empathy increases with age.

Children tend to act more prosocially as they grow older. For example, they become increasingly empathic with age.

sympathy
Feeling of sorrow and concern about another's problems or distress.

physical aggression
Action that can potentially cause bodily injury.

relational aggression
Action that can adversely affect interpersonal relationships.

OBSERVATION GUIDELINES

Assessing Children's Prosocial Development

Characteristic	Look For	Example	Implication
Hedonistic Orientation (common in preschool and the early elementary grades)	• Tendency to help others only when one can simultaneously address one's own needs as well • Prosocial behaviors directed primarily toward familiar adults and peers	Several preschoolers are at a table drawing pictures. Peter is using the only black crayon at the table. Alaina asks him for the crayon so she can color her dog black, telling him, "I just need it for a second." Ignoring her, Peter continues to use the black crayon for several more minutes and then gives it to Alaina.	Point out that other people also have legitimate needs, and emphasize the importance of fairness and helping others. For example, ask children to be "reading buddies" for younger children, explaining that doing so will help them become better readers themselves.
Superficial Needs-of-Others Orientation (common in the elementary grades)	• Some willingness to help others even at personal sacrifice to oneself • Only superficial understanding of others' perspectives	During an annual holiday toy drive, many of the children in a third-grade class contribute some of their toys. They seem happy to do so, commenting that "Poor kids need toys too" and "This doll will be fun for somebody else to play with."	Commend youngsters for altruistic behaviors, and ask them to speculate on how their actions are apt to make others feel (e.g., "Can you imagine how these children must feel when they get your toys? Most of them escaped the flood with only the clothes on their backs. What must it be like to lose everything you own—your clothes, your books, your favorite toys—*everything*?!").
Stereotyped, Approval-Focused Orientation (seen in some elementary and secondary students)	• Tendency to behave prosocially as a means to gain others' approval • Simplistic, stereotypical views of what "good" and "bad" people do	When walking to school one day, Cari sees Stanley inadvertently stumble and drop his backpack in a puddle. She stops, asks him if he's okay, and helps him wipe off the backpack. As she describes the incident to her teacher later that morning, she says, "Maybe he'll be my friend now. Anyway, it's nice to help other people."	Provide numerous opportunities for youngsters to engage in prosocial activities. Choose activities that are apt to be enjoyable and in other ways rewarding in and of themselves.
Empathic Orientation (common in the secondary grades)	• Genuine empathy for other people's distress, even when one does not know the people personally • Willingness to help without regard for consequences for oneself	Members of a high school service club coordinate a schoolwide garage sale, with all proceeds going to a fund to help pay medical expenses of a classmate with a rare form of cancer. They spend several weekends collecting people's contributions to the sale, using their own money for the supplies they need to make the fund-raiser a success.	Alert youngsters to circumstances, both locally and around the globe, in which people's basic needs are not being met or in which basic human rights are being violated. Ask youngsters to brainstorm ways in which they might in some small way make a difference for people living in dire circumstances.
Internalized Values Orientation (seen in a small minority of high school students)	• Generalized concern for equality, dignity, human rights, and the welfare of society as a whole • Commitment to helping others integrated into one's overall sense of self	Franklin spends much of his free time working with Habitat for Humanity, which builds houses for low-income families. "This is as important as my schoolwork," he says. "It's the responsibility of all of us to help one another whenever we can."	Create opportunities—public service projects, fund-raisers, and so on—in which youngsters with an internalized-values orientation can share their enthusiasm for prosocial activities with their peers.

Sources: First two columns based on Eisenberg, 1982; Eisenberg et al., 1995; Eisenberg, Lennon, & Pasternack, 1986.

berg & Campos, 1990). As they approach their first birthday, they may swat at age-mates who take their toys (Caplan, Vespo, Pedersen, & Hay, 1991). Conflicts over possessions are fairly common during the preschool years (Jenkins, Bax, & Hart, 1980).

For most children, physical aggression declines after early childhood, partly because children learn to control their impulses and partly because they acquire better strategies for resolving conflicts (R. B. Cairns, Cairns, Neckerman, Ferguson, & Gariépy, 1989; Coie & Dodge, 1998; Loeber, 1982; Mischel, 1974). This developmental decline in aggression is not universal, however. Researchers have identified two distinct groups of aggressive children and adolescents (Crick & Dodge, 1996; Poulin & Boivin, 1999; Vitaro, Gendreau, Tremblay, & Oligny, 1998). Those who engage in **proactive aggression** deliberately initiate aggressive behaviors as a means of obtaining desired goals. Those who engage in **reactive aggression** act aggressively primarily in response to frustration or provocation. Of the two groups, children who

proactive aggression
Deliberate aggression against another as a means of obtaining a desired goal.

reactive aggression
Aggressive response to frustration or provocation.

exhibit proactive aggression are more likely to have difficulty maintaining friendships with others (Poulin & Boivin, 1999). They may also direct considerable aggression toward particular peers, and those who do so are often known as *bullies*. Their hapless victims often are children who are immature, anxious, friendless, and lacking in self-confidence—some also have disabilities—and so are relatively defenseless (L. Little, 2002b; Marsh, Parada, Yeung, & Healey, 2001; Pellegrini, Bartini, & Brooks, 1999).

Social cognition clearly plays a role in aggressive behavior. Aggressive children tend to have one or more of the following characteristics:

- *Poor perspective-taking ability.* Children who are highly aggressive tend to have limited ability to look at situations from other people's perspectives or to empathize with their victims (Coie & Dodge, 1998).
- *Misinterpretation of social cues.* Children who are either physically or relationally aggressive toward peers tend to interpret others' behaviors as reflecting hostile intentions, especially when such behaviors have ambiguous meanings. This **hostile attributional bias** is especially prevalent in children who are prone to *reactive* aggression (Crick & Dodge, 1996; Dodge et al., 2003; Orobio de Castro, Veerman, Koops, Bosch, & Monshouwer, 2002).
- *Prevalence of self-serving goals.* For most young people, establishing and maintaining interpersonal relationships is a high priority. For aggressive children, however, more self-serving goals—perhaps maintaining an inflated self-image, seeking revenge, or gaining power and dominance—often take precedence (Bender, 2001; Crick & Dodge, 1996; Pellegrini, 2002).
- *Ineffective social problem-solving strategies.* Aggressive children often have little knowledge of how to persuade, negotiate, or compromise, and so they resort to hitting, shoving, barging into play activities, and other ineffective strategies (Lochman & Dodge, 1994; Neel, Jenkins, & Meadows, 1990; D. Schwartz et al., 1998).
- *Beliefs about the appropriateness and effectiveness of aggression.* Many aggressive children believe that violence and other forms of aggression are acceptable ways of resolving conflicts and retaliating for others' misdeeds. For instance, they may believe they need to teach someone a "lesson." Those who display high rates of *proactive* aggression are also apt to believe that aggressive action will yield positive results—for instance, that it will enhance their social status. Aggressive children tend to associate with one another, thus confirming one another's beliefs that aggression is appropriate (Astor, 1994; Espelage, Holt, & Henkel, 2003; Farmer et al., 2002; Pellegrini & Bartini, 2000; E. Staub, 1995).

Children who are especially aggressive when they are young tend to be more aggressive in later years as well (C. A. Anderson et al., 2003; Kupersmidt & Coie, 1990; Ladd & Burgess, 1999). Furthermore, children who display proactive (but not reactive) aggression are at increased risk for engaging in delinquent activities later on (Vitaro et al., 1998). And the victims of aggression—whether it be physical or relational—are apt to have low self-esteem and possibly suffer from depression (Crick, Casas, & Nelson, 2002). For instance, after being the victim of relational aggression from close friends, 13-year-old Julie confides in her diary (we've changed the names of her friends but left her original spelling intact):

> I feel like I need to tell somebody whats going on. Umm well the topic is friends. OK well I start off with Sonja and Dana. They make me so mad sometimes. Today I went and sat down @ lunch then I got up for a sec. When I came back Sonja was sitting right next to where I was sitting so I sat down next to her. Then Sonja says "Julie you can't sit there I'm saving it for someone important." "Who?" "Dana." I had already kinda known it was Dana those two have been inseperable the last month or so. So me, being angry at Sonja, goes to sit on the other side. The whole time at lunch Sonja was talking about me. I am not afraid to say that I am jealous because I am and I have already told Dana and Sonja this twice and they don't really get the point. They are both really great friends and I don't want to lose them.

Julie ends by saying that Dana and Sonja are both "really great friends." Is she really willing to overlook their intentionally vindictive behavior? It is impossible to tell, but some children, such as Georgia's friend Leslie in Figure 12-2, are especially sensitive to teasing, ridicule, and social exclusion (Crick, Casas, & Nelson, 2002).

In his drawing of a superhero holding a weapon, 6-year-old Myron shows his understanding that aggression is a way of gaining power and dominance over others.

hostile attributional bias
Tendency to interpret others' behaviors as reflecting hostile or aggressive intentions.

BASIC DEVELOPMENTAL ISSUES

Comparing Prosocial Behavior and Aggression

Issue	Prosocial Behavior	Aggression
Nature and Nurture	The capacity for prosocial behavior appears to be a natural, inborn human characteristic, but individual children have unique genetic endowments (e.g., temperaments) that predispose them to varying degrees of altruism. Prosocial behavior is nurtured by affectionate caregiving, role modeling, reinforcement for prosocial actions, and explicit requests for children to consider the needs of others in unfortunate circumstances.	The capacity for aggression has a biological basis and is to some degree inherited. Aggressiveness in individual children is influenced by temperamental dispositions, hormone levels, and neurological structures in the brain. Yet the social environment influences how children express their aggressive impulses. Families, social institutions (e.g., schools), and communities may foster aggression either directly (e.g., through modeling and endorsement of aggression) or indirectly (e.g., through harsh punishment and unreasonable expectations).
Universality and Diversity	The capacity for prosocial behavior is universal in the human species. Furthermore, people in most cultures become increasingly prosocial as they get older. Significant diversity exists in the extent to which various cultural groups encourage prosocial activities (e.g., sharing, nurturing), as well as in children's exposure to adults who model prosocial behavior and articulate a commitment to caring for people in need.	Aggressive behavior is universal in human beings. Some general developmental sequences in aggressive expression, such as a gradual shift from physical aggression to verbal aggression, may also be universal. Substantial diversity is present in the ways that children and adolescents express aggression, in the amount of aggression young people encounter in their daily environments, and in the extent to which cultural groups condone aggression as a way of resolving conflict.
Qualitative and Quantitative Change	Qualitative changes may occur in children's understanding of why helping others is important and valuable. For instance, young children often give help primarily to gain rewards or approval, whereas older children and adolescents are more likely to have a genuine concern for people in need. Quantitative increases occur in children's knowledge of effective prosocial strategies and in their ability to carry out such strategies.	A gradual shift from physical aggression in early childhood to more verbal and relational forms of aggression in later years reflects qualitative change. The decline in physical aggression over childhood and adolescence reflects quantitative change.

Sources: Coie & Dodge, 1998; Eisenberg & Fabes, 1998.

In the Basic Developmental Issues table "Comparing Prosocial Behavior and Aggression," we describe similarities in, as well as differences between, these seemingly opposite forms of behavior.

Diversity in Interpersonal Behaviors

Youngsters' interpersonal behaviors tend to differ somewhat depending on their gender, their ethnic and cultural background, and (in some cases) their disabilities and other special educational needs.

Gender differences.   At the preschool level, you are apt to see gender differences in children's play activities (Gallahue & Ozmun, 1998; Gottman, 1986; Paley, 1984). In sociodramatic play, girls tend to enact scenarios that are relatively calm and sedate (e.g., playing house or school). In contrast, boys often introduce elements of adventure and danger (e.g., playing cops and robbers or fighting intergalactic battles).

As boys grow older, they continue to place high priority on physical action. Girls spend much more time simply talking—sharing personal concerns, telling secrets, offering emotional support, and so on (Berndt, 1992; G. P. Jones & Dembo, 1989; McCallum & Bracken, 1993). Girls tend to form closer and more intimate relationships with others and are more sensitive to the subtle, nonverbal messages (body language) that others communicate (J. H. Block, 1983; Deaux, 1984). On average, girls are slightly more kind and considerate, but in many circumstances boys do show their "softer" sides, displaying affection and sympathy appropriate for the occasion (Eisenberg & Fabes, 1998).

Girls tend to form closer, more intimate relationships with one another than boys do.

The most pronounced gender difference in children's interpersonal behaviors is in physical aggression. Beginning in the preschool years, boys are more physically aggressive than girls (Collaer & Hines, 1995; Eagly, 1987; Loeber & Stouthamer-Loeber, 1998). This greater inclination toward physical aggression is probably the result of both biological factors (recall the link between testosterone and aggression) and socialization (parents are more likely to allow aggression in sons than in daughters) (Collaer & Hines, 1995; Condry & Ross, 1985; Eisenberg et al., 1996). However, girls are often just as aggressive as boys in relational aggression—for example, by tattling, gossiping, and snubbing their peers (Crick, Grotpeter, & Bigbee, 2002; D. C. French, Jansen, & Pidada, 2002; Pellegrini, 2002).

━━━━━━━━━━ **Study Guide and Reader**
Although gossip is often a form of relational aggression, it serves an important social function for many youngsters (see Supplementary Reading 12-4).

Boys also tend to be more assertive than girls. For example, in mixed-sex work groups, they are apt to dominate activities and take charge of needed equipment, and they are more likely to get their way when group members disagree (Jovanovic & King, 1998). Such assertiveness may be nurtured in same-sex activity groups over the years, as boys' friendships typically involve more conflict and competition than girls' friendships do (Eisenberg et al., 1996). In contrast, girls are more likely to acquiesce to others' wishes, perhaps because they value group harmony more than boys do and so make frequent small concessions to keep the peace (P. M. Miller, Danaher, & Forbes, 1986).

Ethnic and cultural differences.

Children may have more or fewer opportunities to interact with peers depending on the culture in which they grow up. Unlike in North America, where most children come into frequent contact with age-mates at an early age, children in some cultures stay close to home and play primarily with parents and siblings, at least until they reach school age (Trawick-Smith, 2003; Whiting & Edwards, 1988). Children whose primary language is different from that of the larger society in which they live (e.g., as is true for non-English-speaking immigrants to an English-speaking country) also have limited opportunities to interact with age-mates (A. Doyle, 1982).

━━━━━━━━━━ **Connecting Concepts**
Conventions for carrying on conversations also differ from culture to culture (see the discussion of *sociolinguistic behaviors* in Chapter 9).

To some degree, different cultural groups also model and teach different interpersonal behaviors. For instance, children in China are encouraged to be shy, whereas those in Israel are encouraged to be assertive (X. Chen, Rubin, & Li, 1995; Krispin, Sternberg, & Lamb, 1992). Smiling is a sign of agreement and friendliness in almost any cultural group, but in a few cultures (e.g., in some Japanese American families) it may also indicate embarrassment (Eckman, 1972).

Cultures differ, too, in the degree to which they encourage competition or cooperation with others. In North America and western Europe, many people see competition as desirable (e.g., parents may enter their children in dance contests, high school teachers sometimes grade on a curve), and children are more likely to be praised for their individual achievements than for group success. In contrast, many other cultures (e.g., most Asian and Hispanic societies) place a high premium on loyalty, trust, cooperation, and prosocial behavior (Greenfield, 1994; P. B. Smith & Bond, 1994; Triandis, 1995).

Children with special needs.

On average, children and adolescents with high intelligence (e.g., youngsters whom school personnel have identified as gifted) have good social skills. However, a few youngsters with highly advanced intellectual abilities have trouble establishing and maintaining effective interpersonal relationships with age-mates because they are in some ways so *very* different from their peers (A. E. Gottfried, Fleming, & Gottfried, 1994; Keogh & MacMillan, 1996; Winner, 1997).

Many children with disabilities, too, have good interpersonal skills. But many others do not. Children with significant physical disabilities may have few opportunities to practice social skills with their peers. And children who have impaired social cognition—for instance, children with mental retardation or Asperger syndrome—usually have poor social skills as well (S. Greenspan & Granfield, 1992; Milch-Reich et al., 1999; R. Turnbull et al., 2004). Youngsters with chronic emotional and behavioral problems (e.g., conduct disorders) often have difficulty making and keeping friends, usually because of poor social problem-solving and other social skills (Asher & Coie, 1990; Cartledge & Milburn, 1995; DuPaul & Eckert, 1994).

In the Developmental Trends table "Social Cognition and Interpersonal Skills at Different Age Levels," we present characteristics and behaviors that teachers and other practitioners are likely to see in infants, children, and adolescents, as well as common forms of diversity in different age-groups.

DEVELOPMENTAL TRENDS

Social Cognition and Interpersonal Skills at Different Age Levels

Age	What You Might Observe	Diversity	Implications
Infancy (Birth–2) 	• Emerging awareness that other people have desires, goals, and intentions different from one's own • Increasing engagement with other infants (e.g., watching and touching them, vocalizing, smiling at them, imitating them) • Appearance of simple prosocial behaviors (e.g., offering a teddy bear to a crying child) in the second year • Anger at caregivers who frustrate efforts toward desired goals • Conflicts with peers about toys and other desired objects	• Infants who have frequent contact with age-mates (e.g., in group child care) tend to be more sociable. • Infants may be more inclined to show prosocial behaviors when caregivers model these behaviors. • Some children have "difficult" temperaments; they may be especially contrary in the second year, biting others or exhibiting frequent temper tantrums.	• Use words such as *like, want,* and *think* regularly in descriptions of yourself and children. • Allow infants to interact with one another under your guidance and protection. • Verbalize expressions of empathy and sympathy within earshot of other children. • Praise prosocial behaviors. • Set up the environment to reduce frustration and aggression; for instance, provide duplicates of favorite toys, and create separate areas for quiet play and active movement. • Explain to aggressive toddlers that some actions are unacceptable, and impose appropriate consequences (e.g., by placing a child in a short time-out).
Early Childhood (2–6) 	• Increasing use of "feeling" and "thinking" words (e.g., *want, sad, know*) • Growing realization that the mind does not always represent events accurately (e.g., that a person may have a false belief) • Growing ability to take others' perspectives, with some signs of empathy for people in distress • Increasing sharing and coordination of play activities (e.g., sociodramatic play) • Attempts to comfort people in distress, especially those whom children know well; comforting strategies not always effective • Some aggressive struggles with peers about possessions; increasing ability to inhibit aggressive impulses	• Children whose parents talk frequently about thoughts and feelings tend to have a more advanced theory of mind. • Children with certain cognitive impairments (e.g., Asperger syndrome) and those with reduced exposure to language as a result of hearing impairments tend to have a more limited theory of mind. • Children are more apt to behave prosocially if they are consistently reinforced for such behavior. • On average, boys are more physically aggressive than girls.	• Talk often about various people's thoughts, feelings, perspectives, and needs. • Recognize that selfish and territorial behaviors are common in early childhood. • Model sympathetic responses; explain what you are doing and why you are doing it. • Encourage children to give one another comfort when they can. • Praise any gentle, controlled, and constructive responses to frustration or provocation. • Comfort the victims of aggression, and administer appropriate consequences for the perpetrators. Explain why aggressive behavior cannot be tolerated.
Middle Childhood (6–10) 	• Recognition that people's actions do not always reflect their true thoughts and feelings • Growing realization that other people interpret (rather than simply remember) their experiences • Decrease in rigid stereotypes of particular groups of people (for most children) • Growing repertoire of conflict-resolution skills • Increasing empathy for unknown individuals who are suffering or needy • Increasing desire to help others as an objective in and of itself • Decrease in overt physical aggression, but with an increase in relational aggression and more covert antisocial behaviors (e.g., lying, stealing)	• Children with certain disabilities (e.g., ADHD, autism, mental retardation) are more apt to have difficulty making accurate inferences about people's motives and intentions. • Children whose families or communities consistently promote unflattering images of particular groups may continue to have strong prejudices. • Children whose parents value prosocial behavior are more likely to value it as well and to have genuine concern for others. • Some children consistently misinterpret peers' thoughts and motives (e.g., by interpreting accidents as deliberate attempts to cause harm). • Some children become increasingly aggressive in the elementary grades. • Some children are bullies who regularly victimize vulnerable children (e.g., those without friends or those with disabilities).	• Assist children in their attempts to resolve interpersonal conflicts by asking them to consider one another's perspectives and to develop a solution that addresses everyone's needs. • Draw attention to a comforted child's relief when another child helps ("Look how much better Sally feels now that you've apologized for hurting her feelings"). • Do not tolerate physical aggression or bullying. Make sure children understand rules for behavior, and follow through with appropriate consequences when children are aggressive. • Be on the lookout for children who seem to be frequent victims of others' aggression; help them form productive relationships with peers.

(continued)

DEVELOPMENTAL TRENDS	Social Cognition and Interpersonal Skills at Different Age Levels (continued)		
Age	**What You Might Observe**	**Diversity**	**Implications**
Early Adolescence (10–14) 	• Recognition that people may have multiple and possibly conflicting feelings and motives • Increasing sensitivity to body language and other nonverbal cues • Emerging ability to think recursively about one's own and others' thoughts • Decline in physical aggression • Frequent teasing and taunting of peers; emergence of sexual harassment	• Self-disclosure is more common in girls than in boys. • Beginning at puberty, increased testosterone levels in boys contribute to their more aggressive tendencies. • Some adolescents with social-emotional problems (e.g., those with conduct disorders) show deficits in empathy for others. • Bullying behavior in some youngsters may temporarily increase after the transition to middle school or junior high.	• Conduct discussions that require adolescents to look at controversial issues from multiple perspectives. • Do not tolerate ethnic jokes or other remarks that show prejudice toward a particular group. • Communicate that giving, sharing, and caring for others should be high priorities. • Keep a watchful eye on students' between-class and after-school activities; make it clear that physical aggression is *not* acceptable on school grounds.
Late Adolescence (14–18) 	• Recognition that people are products of their environment and that past events and present circumstances influence personality and behavior • Use of peer group as a forum for self-exploration and self-understanding • Increasing awareness that members of any single category of people (e.g., women, people with disabilities) can be very different from one another • For many, less motivation to engage in aggressive behavior, often as a result of forming more intimate and rewarding relationships with others	• Some high school students are exceptionally committed to making the world a better place (e.g., they may be active in Amnesty International, a group committed to preserving human rights around the world). • On average, youngsters who live in poor, violent neighborhoods are more apt to become aggressive. • Violence-prone adolescents often believe that hitting another person is reasonable retribution for unjust actions. • Substance abuse and sexual activity increase the probability of aggression.	• Talk about other people's complex (and sometimes conflicting) motives, perhaps while discussing contemporary issues, historical events, or works of fiction. • Encourage community service work so as to engender a commitment to helping others. Ask adolescents to reflect on their experiences through group discussions or written essays. • Assign autobiographies and other readings that depict individuals who have actively worked for the greater good of society. • Enforce prohibitions against bringing weapons to school and other settings.

Fostering Effective Interpersonal Skills

Teachers and other practitioners who work with young people in social settings have many opportunities to encourage good social skills and discourage inappropriate interpersonal behaviors. Following are strategies that researchers and experienced educators have found to be effective:

● *Teach specific social skills and social problem-solving strategies.* Through frequent interactions with adults and peers, many youngsters acquire effective social behaviors on their own. But many others—perhaps because of limited opportunities to interact with age-mates, poor role models at home, or a cognitive disability—know little about how to initiate conversations, exchange compliments, offer emotional support, or in other ways establish and maintain rewarding interpersonal relationships. Some also lack productive strategies for solving social problems. For example, they may barge into a game without asking if they can participate or respond to any provocation with aggression.

Teachers, counselors, and other adults can teach effective interpersonal behaviors both through explicit verbal instructions (e.g., see Figure 12-8) and through encouragement and modeling of desired behaviors. The Development and Practice feature "Teaching Social Skills" presents several useful strategies.

Yet adults must also give children some leeway in their social lives. Children sometimes benefit from a trial-and-error approach with social strategies. Following is one elementary school teacher's perspective on the advantages of letting children learn some social lessons on their own:

Figure 12-8

In this writing assignment, 9-year-old Mariel lists four strategies that her teacher has suggested for making a new friend.

DEVELOPMENT AND PRACTICE

Teaching Social Skills

- Explicitly teach skills that children may be lacking.

  A counselor who is working with several very shy and socially isolated high school students teaches them several ways to initiate and maintain conversations with others. "One thing you might do," he says, "is give a compliment about something you like about a person. Then you can follow up with a question to get the person talking. For example, you might say, 'I really liked what you said about protecting the rain forests in class the other day. I didn't realize how quickly the earth's rain forests were being destroyed. Have you read a lot about the topic?'" After describing several additional strategies, the counselor has the students work in pairs to practice each one.

- Ask children to brainstorm approaches to solving social dilemmas.

  A middle school teacher presents this situation to his class: "Imagine that one of your classmates comes up to you and asks if she can copy your homework. You don't want to let her do it—after all, she won't learn what her teacher wanted her to learn by copying someone else's work—but you also don't want to make her angry or upset. How might you refuse her request while also keeping her friendship?"

- Encourage children and adolescents to think carefully before acting in difficult social situations.

  A soccer coach finds that several of her 9- and 10-year-old players react impulsively to any provocation. For instance, they might hit or yell at a teammate who unintentionally bumps into them on the playing field. The coach teaches the athletes four steps to follow in such situations: (a) *Think* about what just happened, (b) *list* three different ways to respond, (c) *predict* what might happen for each response, and (d) *choose* the best response.

- Give concrete feedback about effective and ineffective interpersonal behaviors.

  During a cooperative learning activity, a high school teacher notices that the members of one cooperative group are getting increasingly angry. After briefly eavesdropping on their discussion, the teacher reminds them, "As we agreed yesterday, it's okay to criticize ideas, but it's *not* okay to criticize people."

- Communicate your concern for children who are hurt, and enlist the support of other children in caring for them.

  A preschool teacher sympathizes with a child who has skinned his knee. She brings out the first-aid kit and asks another child to find a bandage as she applies the antiseptic.

- Acknowledge children's good deeds.

  When a third-grade teacher notices a child helping a classmate who doesn't understand an assignment, she comments, "Thank you for helping Amanda, Jack. You're always ready to lend a hand!"

Before, when problems came up, I think I was very quick to intervene. Certainly, I asked the kids involved to express themselves "very briefly" about what had happened. But I was quick to judge, to comment, to advise, and to try to reconcile them, for instance, by saying, "Well, now you must be friends." Thus, the students themselves were not active in the problem solution. It was usually I who found the solutions and I who controlled the situation. Now I am not as quick to intervene. I ask the children to stop and think, and to express themselves about what happened, and I withdraw more and listen to them. Certainly it is more effective if they themselves face and solve the problems. Then the solution and the whole experience are more likely to stay with them. (Adalbjarnardottir & Selman, 1997, p. 421)

● *Label appropriate behaviors as they occur.* Teachers can heighten children's awareness of effective social skills by identifying and praising behaviors that reflect those skills (Vorrath, 1985; Wittmer & Honig, 1994). For example, a teacher might say, "Thank you for *sharing* your art materials so helpfully," or, "I think that you two were able to write a more imaginative short story by *cooperating* on the project." Researchers have found, too, that describing children as having desirable characteristics (generosity, empathy, etc.) has beneficial effects (Grusec & Redler, 1980; R. S. L. Mills & Grusec, 1989). For example, 8-year-olds who are told, "You're the kind of person who likes to help others whenever you can," are more likely to share their belongings with others later on.

● *Plan cooperative activities.* When youngsters participate in cooperative games rather than in competitive ones, aggressive behaviors tend to decrease (Bay-Hinitz, Peterson, & Quilitch, 1994). In cooperative learning activities, youngsters can practice help-giving, help-seeking, and conflict-resolution skills (Damon, 1988; Lickona, 1991; N. M. Webb & Farivar, 1994). Furthermore, cooperative tasks that require a number of different skills and abilities foster an appreciation for the various strengths that children with diverse backgrounds are likely to contribute (E. G. Cohen, 1994; E. G. Cohen & Lotan, 1995). Cooperative activities are usually most successful when children have a structure to follow (e.g., when each group member is given a specific role to perform) and are given some guidelines about appropriate group behavior (E. G. Cohen, 1994; Schofield, 1995; Webb & Palincsar, 1996).

● *Expose children to numerous models of prosocial behavior.* Adults teach by what they do as well as by what they say. When teachers and other adults model compassion and consideration for others, children are likely to emulate such behaviors. Ideally, children should come into contact with other prosocial models as well. For instance, preschool teachers might encourage children to watch age-appropriate television programs that model prosocial behavior (e.g., *Sesame Street, Barney and Friends*) (D. R. Anderson, 2003; Jordan, 2003). In the elementary and secondary grades, teachers might invite public servants or members of charitable organizations to talk with students about the many intangible rewards of community service work. Teachers can also make use of prosocial models in literature (Nucci, 2001). One good example is Harper Lee's *To Kill a Mockingbird,* set in the highly segregated and racially charged Alabama of the 1930s. In this novel a lawyer defends an African American man falsely accused of raping a white woman and exemplifies a willingness to fight for social justice in the face of strong social pressure to convict the man.

● *Provide opportunities for children and adolescents to make a difference in their community.* Both in school and out, young people should discover that their prosocial efforts can, in fact, have an impact. As an example, a mathematics teacher at an inner-city middle school consistently encouraged her students to identify problems in their community and work to solve them (Tate, 1995). One of her classes expressed concern about the 13 liquor stores located within 1,000 feet of their school, in part because of the alcoholics and drug dealers that the stores attracted. The students calculated the distance of each store from the school, gathered information about zoning restrictions and other regulations, identified potential violations, met with a local newspaper editor (who published an editorial describing the situation), and eventually met with state legislators and the city council. As a result of their efforts, city police monitored the liquor stores more closely, major violations were identified (leading to the closing of two stores), and the city council made it illegal to consume alcohol within 600 feet of the school (Tate, 1995).

● *Give concrete guidelines for behavior.* Children should consistently hear the message that they must be respectful and considerate of others. One way to communicate this message is to establish firm rules that prohibit physical aggression and possession of weapons. Behaviors that cause psychological harm—malicious gossip, prejudicial remarks, sexual harassment, intimidation, ostracism, and so on—must also be off-limits. And adults must consistently enforce these rules in the classroom, on the playground, in extracurricular activities, and elsewhere (Juvonen, Nishina, & Graham, 2000; Learning First Alliance, 2001).

● *Seek intensive intervention for youngsters with a history of aggression.* When left unchecked, children's and adolescents' aggressive tendencies sometimes escalate into serious violence (e.g., see Figure 12-9). For a variety of reasons, minor interventions are not always sufficient for youngsters who are predisposed to be physically aggressive. Typically, schools must work closely and collaboratively with other community agencies—perhaps mental health clinics, police and probation departments, and social services—to help exceptionally aggressive youngsters (Dwyer & Osher, 2000; Greenberg et al., 2003). Teachers are a vital component of this collaborative effort, offering insights about youngsters' strengths and weaknesses, communicating with parents about available services, and working with specialists to develop appropriate intervention strategies.

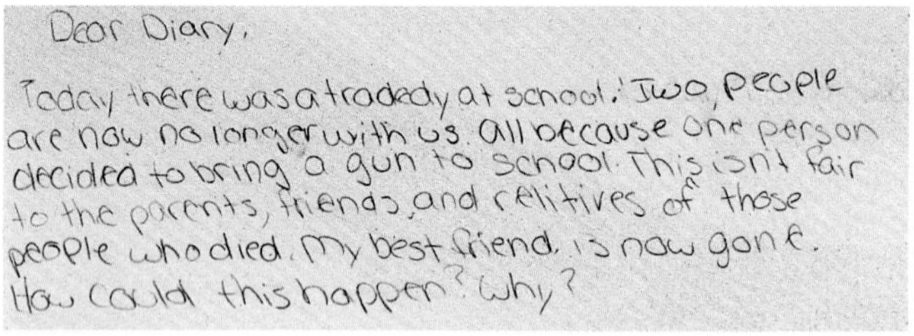

Teachers' frequent interactions with students also put them in an ideal position to identify those young people most in need of intensive intervention to get them back on track for social success. Especially after working with a particular age-group for a period of time, teachers acquire a good sense of what characteristics are and are not normal for that age level. Teachers should especially be on the lookout for the early warning signs of violence presented in Figure 12-10.

Although teachers must be ever vigilant for signs that a student may be planning to cause harm to others, it is essential that they keep several points in mind. First, despite recent media reports about school shootings, extreme violence is *very* rare in schools (DeVoe et al., 2003; Garbarino et al., 2002). Unreasonable paranoia about potential school violence will prevent a teacher from working effectively with students. Second, the great majority of students who exhibit one or a few of the warning signs in Figure 12-10 will *not* become violent. And most importantly, a teacher must *never* use the warning signs as a reason to unfairly accuse,

Dear Diary,

Today there was a tradedy at school. Two people are now no longer with us. All because one person decided to bring a gun to school. This isn't fair to the parents, friends, and relitives of those people who died. My best friend is now gone. How could this happen? Why?

Figure 12-9

Occasionally physical aggression at school has tragic consequences, as shown in one child's diary entry.

Experts have identified numerous warning signs that a child or adolescent may possibly be contemplating violent actions against others. Any one of them alone is unlikely to signal a violent attack, but you should consult with school administrators or specially trained professionals if you see several of them *in combination*.

Social withdrawal. Over time, a student interacts less and less frequently with teachers and with all or most peers.

Excessive feelings of isolation, rejection, or persecution. A student may directly or indirectly express the belief that he or she is friendless, disliked, or unfairly "picked on."

Rapid decline in academic performance. A student shows a dramatic change in academic performance and seems unconcerned about doing well. Cognitive and physical factors (e.g., learning disabilities, ineffective study skills, brain injury) have been ruled out as the cause of the decline.

Poor coping skills. A student has little ability to deal effectively with frustration, takes the smallest affront personally, and has trouble "bouncing back" after minor disappointments.

Lack of anger control. A student frequently responds with uncontrolled anger to even the slightest injustice and may misdirect anger at innocent bystanders.

Sense of superiority, self-centeredness, and lack of empathy. A student depicts himself or herself as "smarter" or in some other way better than peers, is preoccupied with his or her own needs, and has little regard for the needs of others.

Lengthy grudges. A student is unforgiving of others' transgressions, even after considerable time has elapsed.

Violent themes in drawings and written work. Violence predominates in a student's artwork, stories, and journal entries, and perhaps certain individuals (e.g., a parent or particular classmate) are regularly targeted in these fantasies. (Keep in mind that *occasional* violence in writing and art is not unusual, especially for boys.)

Intolerance of individual and group differences. A student shows intense disdain and prejudice toward people of a certain race, ethnicity, gender, sexual orientation, religion, or disability.

History of violence, aggression, and other discipline problems. A student has a long record of seriously inappropriate behavior extending over several years.

Association with violent peers. A student associates regularly with a gang or other antisocial peer group.

Inappropriate role models. A student may speak with admiration about Satan, Hitler, Osama bin Laden, or some other malevolent figure.

Excessive alcohol or drug use. A student who abuses alcohol or drugs may have reduced self-control. In some cases substance abuse signals significant mental illness.

Inappropriate access to firearms. A student has easy access to guns and ammunition and may regularly practice using them.

Threats of violence. A student has openly expressed an intent to harm someone else. *This warning sign alone requires immediate action.*

Figure 12-10

Early warning signs of violent behavior From *Educational Psychology: Developing Learners* (5th ed., p. 508, Figure 14.4), by Jeanne Ellis Ormrod, © 2006. Adapted by permission of Pearson Education, Inc., Upper Saddle River, NJ. Warning signs based on Dwyer, Osher, & Warger, 1998; O'Toole, 2000.

isolate, or punish a student (Dwyer, Osher, & Warger, 1998). These signs provide a means of getting youngsters help if they need it, not of excluding them from the education that all children and adolescents deserve.

● *Develop a peer mediation program.* Children and adolescents alike often benefit from **peer mediation** training that teaches them how to intervene effectively in their peers' interpersonal disputes (M. Deutsch, 1993; D. W. Johnson & Johnson, 1996, 2001; Schumpf, Crawford, & Usadel, 1991). In such training, youngsters learn how to help their peers resolve conflicts by asking opposing sides to express their differing points of view and then work together to devise a reasonable resolution. In one study (D. W. Johnson, Johnson, Dudley, Ward, & Magnuson, 1995), students in grades 2 through 5 were trained to help peers resolve interpersonal conflicts by asking the opposing sides to do the following:

1. Define the conflict (the problem).
2. Explain their own perspectives and needs.
3. Explain the *other* side's perspectives and needs.
4. Identify at least three possible solutions to the conflict.
5. Reach an agreement that addressed the needs of both parties.

Students took turns serving as mediator for their classmates, such that everyone had experience resolving the conflicts of others. As a result, the students more frequently resolved their *own* interpersonal conflicts in ways that addressed the needs of both parties, and they were less likely to ask for adult intervention, than students who had not had mediation training.

Peer mediation is most effective when youngsters of diverse ethnic backgrounds, socioeconomic groups, and achievement levels all serve as mediators. Furthermore, it is typically most useful for relatively small, short-term interpersonal problems (hurt feelings, conflicts over use of limited academic resources, etc.). Even the most proficient of peer mediators may be ill prepared to handle conflicts that reflect deep-seated and emotionally charged attitudes and behaviors, such as conflicts that involve sexual harassment or homophobia (Casella, 2001; K. M. Williams, 2001b).

Connecting Concepts ————
Can you explain the effectiveness of peer mediation using Vygotsky's concept of *internalization*?

peer mediation
Approach to conflict resolution in which one child or adolescent (the mediator) asks peers in conflict to express their differing viewpoints and then work together to identify an appropriate compromise.

A point made in Chapter 11 is worth repeating here: Human beings of all ages seem to have a fundamental *need for relatedness*—to feel socially connected to others. Acquiring the perspective-taking abilities and social skills that make productive interpersonal relationships possible can be very rewarding indeed, as the final case study illustrates.

Case Study: Gang Mediation

At Washington Middle School, many students belonged to one of several gangs that seemed to "rule the school." Fights among rival gangs were common, and non-gang members were frequent victims of harassment. School officials tried a variety of strategies to keep the gang-related behavior in check—mandating dress codes, conducting regular weapon searches, counseling or suspending chronic trouble makers, and so on—but without success.

In desperation, two school counselors suggested that the school implement a peer mediation program. The program began by focusing on the three largest gangs, which were responsible for most of the trouble on school grounds. Interpersonal problems involving two or more gangs would be brought to a mediation team, comprised of five school faculty members and three representatives from each of the three gangs. The team would abide by the following rules:

1. Really try to solve the problem.
2. No name-calling or put-downs.
3. No interrupting.
4. Be as honest as possible.
5. No weapons or acts of intimidation.
6. All sessions to be confidential until an agreement is reached or mediation is called off.
   (Sanchez & Anderson, 1990, p. 54)

All team members would have to agree to and sign off on any decisions that the team reached. However, participation in the process was voluntary, and students could withdraw at any time.

To lay the groundwork for productive discussions, faculty members of the mediation team met separately with each of the three gangs to establish feelings of rapport and trust and to explain how the mediation process would work. After considerable discussion and venting of hostile inter-group feelings, many gang members agreed to try the new approach. Meanwhile, the buzz throughout the student body was that "something unusual and special was happening" at Washington.

Mediation sessions were held in a conference room, with team members sitting around a large table so that they could maintain eye contact with one another. In the first session, common grievances were aired. Students agreed that they didn't like being put down or intimidated, that they worried about their physical safety, and that they all wanted one another's respect. Curiously, each gang also complained that the school administration showed preferential treatment for the *other* gangs. Through all of this, the students got one message loud and clear: They could speak freely and honestly at the meeting, without fear of reprisal from faculty members or other students.

In several additional meetings over the next 2 weeks, the team reached agreement that a number of behaviors would be unacceptable at school: There would be no put-downs, name calling, hateful stares, threats, shoving, or gang graffiti. After the final meeting, each gang was separately called into the conference room. Its representatives on the mediation team explained the agreement, and other members of the gang were asked to sign it. Despite some skepticism, most members of all three gangs signed the agreement.

A month later, it was clear that the process had been successful, at least in improving the school's social climate over the short term. Members of rival gangs nodded pleasantly to one another or gave one another a "high five" sign as they passed in the hall. Gang members no longer felt compelled to hang out in groups for safety's sake. Members of two of the gangs were seen playing soccer together one afternoon. And there had been no gang-related fights all month. (case described in Sanchez & Anderson, 1990)[a]

- Why do you think the mediation approach was successful when other approaches had failed? Drawing on what you've learned about social cognition and the development of interpersonal skills, identify at least three possible reasons.

Once you have answered this question, compare your response with that presented in the appendix.

Summary

Sense of Self

Children's *sense of self* includes their beliefs about who they are as people (self-concept), their judgments and feelings about their value and worth (self-esteem, self-worth), and their beliefs about their ability to be successful in various domains (self-efficacy). Most children tend to interpret events in ways that allow them to maintain a positive self-image. Realistic self-perceptions, or perhaps self-perceptions that are just slightly inflated, are optimal, in that they encourage children to set their sights on potentially achievable challenges.

To a considerable degree, children's sense of self is based on their own prior successes and failures. Yet other people also play a role, either by treating children in ways that communicate high or low regard, or (in the case of peers) by demonstrating the kinds of things children "should" be able to do at a certain age. Membership in various groups (e.g., athletic teams, ethnic groups) also has an impact, as do gender, physical appearance, disabilities, and other inherited characteristics.

With age, children construct increasingly complex and multifaceted understandings of who they are as people. In the early years their self-perceptions are fairly simplistic, concrete, and categorical (e.g., "I have brown eyes," "I'm a boy"). But as they acquire the capacity for abstract thought, their self-descriptions increasingly include general, abstract qualities (e.g., "thoughtful," dependable"). In adolescence they also begin to wrestle with who they ultimately want to become as human beings.

Social Cognition

As children grow older, they become more attuned to and interested in the mental lives of those around them. In the process of developing a *theory of mind*, they gradually learn that people have thoughts, feelings, and motives different from their own and that these thoughts, feelings, and motives can be complex and at times contradictory. They also become increasingly skilled in taking the perspectives of others: They can imagine how other people must think and feel and begin to empathize with those who are suffering or in need.

To some degree, social cognition encompasses elements of cognition more generally. For instance, it involves storing information about social events in working memory, interpreting (elaborating on) such events using one's existing knowledge base, and retrieving possible responses from long-term memory. Unfortunately, youngsters' existing "knowledge" may include rigid stereotypes about certain groups of people, leading them to act toward members of those groups in prejudicial ways.

Classrooms and other group settings are important contexts in which children and adolescents develop increasing awareness of other people's needs and perspectives. Teachers and other adults can foster greater awareness and knowledge in numerous ways—for instance, by talking frequently about people's thoughts and feelings, exposing youngsters to multiple and equally legitimate perspectives about complex topics and events, and confronting inaccurate and counterproductive stereotypes.

Interpersonal Behaviors

Interpersonal behaviors begin in infancy, when children show an interest in other people and make simple social gestures. Youngsters continue to acquire and refine their social skills (e.g., cooperation, negotiation, conflict resolution) throughout childhood and adolescence, especially as they spend more and more of their time with peers rather than adults. Schools, child-care settings, and other group environments provide important contexts in which effective interpersonal skills develop and can be nurtured.

Most children become increasingly prosocial and less aggressive over the years, with such changes being partly the result of their growing capacity for perspective taking, empathy, and sympathy. However, some children and adolescents display troublesome levels of physical or psychological aggression, perhaps as a result of disabilities, aggressive role models at home or in the community, or counterproductive social information processing. These youngsters often need planned interventions to get them on the road to more productive relationships with others.

Applying Concepts in Child Development

In this chapter you learned a great deal about how children and adolescents think about themselves and other people. The following table presents five examples of youngsters' understanding of themselves or others. For each example, the table presents one or more relevant developmental principles, offers an implication for working with youngsters in that age-group, or both. Apply what you've learned about the development of sense and social cognition to fill in the empty cells in the table. When you're done, compare your responses with those in Table 12-1 in the *Study Guide and Reader*.

APPLYING CONCEPTS IN CHILD DEVELOPMENT	Determining How Children Are Thinking About Themselves and Others		
Age	**A Youngster's Experience**	**Developmental Concepts** *Identifying Youngsters' Existing Understandings of Self or Others*	**Implications** *Promoting Development in Sense of Self and Social Cognition*
Infancy (Birth–2)	When 18-month-old Marvin sees his reflection in the mirror, he rubs his cheek to wipe off the lipstick his mother left when kissing him good-bye earlier in the day.	Marvin understands that he is a physical entity separate from the objects and people around him. Furthermore, he recognizes his image in the mirror, indicating that he has some awareness of his own appearance.	Help infants and toddlers learn about their physical selves not only by holding them in front of mirrors but also by showing them photographs of themselves and talking with them about various body parts ("Show me your nose!", "Did you fall and hurt your knee?").
Early Childhood (2–6)	Arriving early at preschool one morning, 3-year-old Kesia helps her teacher reorganize the art supplies. At the teacher's instruction, she moves the colored markers from a bookshelf to the bottom drawer of a cabinet. Later she is quite surprised when her friend Darla looks for the markers on the shelf. "They're in the drawer, silly!" she exclaims.	Like Kesia, young preschoolers often mistakenly assume that other people know what they themselves know. Not until age 4 or 5 do children appreciate that others may have *false beliefs* based on prior learning experiences.	
Middle Childhood (6–10)	When a classmate accidentally brushes past him on the way to the pencil sharpener, Douglas angrily shouts, "You *meant* to do it! I'll get you for that!"	Douglas is exhibiting a *hostile attributional bias*, a tendency to interpret ambiguous (and possibly accidental) behaviors as having malicious intent. Such a bias is often seen in aggressive children.	Help children interpret social situations in accurate and productive ways. For instance, role-play situations in which a person's behavior is ambiguous, then have children brainstorm possible interpretations, responses, and long-term outcomes.
Early Adolescence (10–14)	Soon after beginning junior high school, 13-year-old Robert begins dressing as he sees some of his peers do—for instance by wearing oversized pants that hang low on his hips and balloon around his legs. And when he sees a few older boys secretly smoking cigarettes in a far corner of the schoolyard, he asks if he can "take a drag."		Expose youngsters to a wide variety of models of "acceptable" behavior, with particular emphasis on peers who maintain a "cool" image while engaging in healthful and productive activities.

(continued)

APPLYING CONCEPTS IN CHILD DEVELOPMENT	Determining How Children Are Thinking About Themselves and Others (continued)		
Age	A Youngster's Experience	**Developmental Concepts** *Identifying Youngsters' Existing Understandings of Self or Others*	**Implications** *Promoting Development in Sense of Self and Social Cognition*
Late Adolescence (14–18) 	As a 15-year-old, Rita is quite proud of her Puerto Rican heritage. She belittles certain extracurricular activities at her school, especially athletics and the National Honor Society, saying that they are "entirely too White" for her.	On the road to forming an *ethnic identity,* some adolescents may, like Rita, initially adopt a rigid, inflexible one that rejects the perceived values of other ethnic groups. Eventually, however, she is apt to become more open-minded about behaviors that are acceptable for her. In general, youngsters with a strong ethnic identity have high self-esteem.	

Key Concepts

sense of self (p. 442)
self-handicapping (p. 443)
contingent self-worth (p. 446)
autobiographical self (p. 447)
imaginary audience (p. 448)
personal fable (p. 448)
identity (p. 449)
gender schema (p. 451)

androgyny (p. 452)
self-socialization (p. 452)
ethnic identity (p. 453)
social cognition (p. 458)
theory of mind (p. 458)
intentionality (p. 458)
recursive thinking (p. 460)
social perspective taking (p. 460)

social information processing (p. 462)
social-cognitive bias (p. 463)
stereotype (p. 463)
prejudice (p. 463)
social skills (p. 466)
peer pressure (p. 469)
prosocial behavior (p. 470)

aggression (p. 470)
sympathy (p. 472)
physical aggression (p. 472)
relational aggression (p. 472)
proactive aggression (p. 473)
reactive aggression (p. 473)
hostile attributional bias (p. 474)
peer mediation (p. 481)

Companion Website

Now go to our Companion Website at www.prenhall.com/mcdevitt to assess your understanding of chapter content with a Practice Quiz, apply what you've learned in Essay Questions, and broaden your knowledge with links to related Developmental Psychology Web sites.

Development of Motivation and Self-Regulation

chapter 13

Case Study: Derrika

Case Study: Derrika

Motivation

Self-Regulation

**Moral Reasoning
    and Behavior**

Case Study: Spencer

Summary

**Applying Concepts in Child
    Development**

In a study conducted in the Chicago public schools, Roderick and Camburn (1999) investigated the academic progress of students who had recently made the transition from relatively small elementary or middle schools to much larger high schools. Many students in their research sample experienced considerable difficulty making the transition from eighth to ninth grade, as the case of Derrika illustrates:

> Derrika liked to be challenged and felt her eighth-grade teachers cared and made her work. Derrika entered high school with plans to go to college and felt that her strong sense of self would get her through: "Nobody stops me from doing good because I really wanna go to college. . . . Nobody in my family's been to college . . . so I want to be the first person to go to college and finish."
>
> Derrika began having problems in eighth grade. Despite average achievement scores and previously high grades, she ended eighth grade with a C average and failed science. In high school, her performance deteriorated further. At the end of the first semester, Derrika received Fs in all her major subjects, had 20 absences, almost 33 class cuts for the last two periods of the day, and had been suspended for a food fight. Derrika is vague in explaining her performance, except for biology, in which she admits, "I don't never get up on time." She feels that her elementary school teachers were better because, "If you don't want to learn, they are going to make you learn," while her current teachers think, "If you fail, you just fail. It ain't our fault. You're the one that's dumb." (Roderick & Camburn, 1999, p. 304)

I n elementary school Derrika was off to a good start. And she now seems truly motivated to finish school and go to college. But something has gone terribly wrong. If Derrika's perceptions are accurate, perhaps part of the problem is that her teachers have little concern about whether she succeeds or fails. But Derrika herself is also a part of the problem: She doesn't always get up in time for her first-period biology class, and even when she *is* up, she doesn't always attend her classes. And her suspension for a food fight is almost certainly something she could have avoided.

So how do we reconcile this apparent discrepancy between Derrika's long-term goals (to do well in school and go to college) and her behaviors in ninth grade (cutting class, misbehaving in the cafeteria)? As you will discover in this chapter, motivation is not a simple "switch" that children turn on and off at will. Rather, it is the result of many internal factors—ability to delay gratification, self-perceptions, multiple (and possibly conflicting) goals, explanations for success and failure, and so on—that build up gradually over time. Furthermore, even the most motivated of young people cannot stay focused on a long-term target unless they have strategies to *keep* themselves focused even in the face of tempting alternatives—in other words, unless they are capable of self-regulation. As we discuss motivation and self-regulation in this chapter, we identify a variety of ways in which teachers can help youngsters like Derrika accomplish their goals and persevere on the path to long-term success.

Motivation

In general, **motivation** energizes, directs, and sustains behavior: It gets people moving, points them in a particular direction, and keeps them going. Virtually all children and adolescents are

motivation
State that energizes, directs, and
sustains behavior.

Observe infants' and toddlers' intrinsic motivation to learn about their physical world in the "Cognitive Development" clips for infancy and early childhood (Observation CD 1) and the "Emotional Development" clip for infancy (Observation CD 2).

———————— Connecting Concepts
Basic principles underlying behaviorist theories are described in Chapter 1.

———————— Study Guide and Reader
Supplementary Reading 13-1 explains why many psychologists think that a need for physical cuddling may be biologically built in.

extrinsic motivation
Motivation provoked by the external consequences that certain behaviors bring.

intrinsic motivation
Motivation resulting from personal characteristics or inherent in the task being performed.

reinforcer
Consequence of a response that leads to an increased frequency of that response.

primary reinforcer
Stimulus or event that satisfies a built-in biological need.

secondary reinforcer
Stimulus or event that becomes reinforcing over time through its association with one or more other reinforcers.

delay of gratification
Forgoing small immediate rewards for larger ones at a future time.

motivated in one way or another. One may be keenly interested in academic subject matter and seek out challenging coursework, participate actively in classroom discussions, complete assignments diligently, and earn high grades. Another may be more concerned about social affairs, interacting with peers frequently, participating in numerous extracurricular activities, and chatting incessantly with friends on the phone or Internet. Still another may be focused on athletics, excelling in physical education classes, playing or watching sports most afternoons and weekends, and working out daily in hopes of making the varsity soccer team. And yet another, perhaps because of an undetected learning disability, poor social skills, or a seemingly uncoordinated body, may be interested primarily in *avoiding* academics, social situations, or athletic activities.

Sometimes children and adolescents have **extrinsic motivation:** They are motivated to either attain or avoid certain consequences in the outside world. For instance, they may study to get good grades, pick up litter to gain an adult's praise, or lie about a misdeed ("I didn't do it, *she* did!") to avoid being punished. At other times youngsters have **intrinsic motivation:** They are motivated by factors within themselves or inherent in a task they are performing. For instance, they might read a book simply for the pleasure it brings, practice soccer skills in order to become a better player, or return a wallet to its owner as a way of being true to an internal moral code. Both extrinsic and intrinsic motivation can spur children to acquire new knowledge and skills and engage in productive behaviors. But as you will discover shortly, intrinsic motivation is optimal for children's development over the long run.

In the following sections we look at how extrinsic consequences—in particular, rewards and punishments—are apt to affect children's behavior. We then consider a variety of forms that intrinsic motivation might take.

Effects of Extrinsic Rewards and Punishments

Human beings of all ages usually behave in ways that bring desired results. In an early theory of learning known as *operant conditioning,* the behaviorist B. F. Skinner proposed that children learn and engage primarily in behaviors that lead to certain consequences, which he called **reinforcers** (e.g., Skinner, 1953, 1968). From Skinner's perspective, most of children's behaviors are those that are currently being reinforced or have often been reinforced in the past. For instance, Miguel might practice the piano regularly if his parents continually praise him for his efforts. Brigita might throw frequent temper tantrums if she's learned that tantrums are the only way she can get special toys or privileges. Peter might misbehave in class if doing so gains him the attention of his teacher and classmates. The last of these examples illustrates an important point: Reinforcers are not always what we would typically think of as "rewards." The attention Peter gets for his misbehavior may seem unpleasant—Peter's teacher may scold him for acting out, or his classmates might shake their heads in disgust—but if Peter's misbehaviors increase as a result, then the attention is indeed a reinforcer.

In early infancy, children are largely concerned with **primary reinforcers**—such as food, drink, warmth, and physical cuddling—which satisfy built-in biological needs. Over time, children begin to associate certain other consequences with primary reinforcers. For example, a child might learn that praise from Mother often comes with a special candy treat or discover that a good grade frequently leads to a hug from Father. Through such associations, consequences such as praise, good grades, money, trophies, and attention (sometimes even in the form of a scolding) become reinforcing in their own right. That is, they become **secondary reinforcers.** Because secondary reinforcers are consequences that children *learn* to appreciate, the effectiveness of any one of them will differ considerably from one child to the next.

As children grow older, they become better able to **delay gratification:** They can forgo small, immediate reinforcers for the larger rewards that their long-term efforts may bring down the road (e.g., L. Green, Fry, & Myerson, 1994; Rotenberg & Mayer, 1990; Vaughn, Kopp, & Krakow, 1984). For example, a 3-year-old is apt to choose a small toy she can have now over a larger and more attractive toy she cannot have until tomorrow. In contrast, an 8-year-old is usually willing to wait a day or two for a more appealing item. Many adolescents can delay gratification for weeks at a time. For instance, as a 16-year-old, Jeanne's son Jeff worked long hours stocking shelves at the local grocery store (hardly a rewarding activity!) to earn enough money to pay half the cost of a $400-a-night limousine for his high school prom. Some children and adolescents are better able to delay gratification than others, however, and those who can are less likely to yield to temptation, more carefully plan their future actions, and achieve at higher levels at school (Durkin, 1995; Shoda, Mischel, & Peake, 1990; Veroff, McClelland, & Ruhland, 1975).

Whereas children are likely to behave in ways that lead to reinforcement, they are *un*likely to behave in ways that lead to punishment. Punishment of undesirable responses, especially when combined with reinforcement of desired responses, can bring about lasting improvements in children's behavior (e.g., R. V. Hall et al., 1971; Walters & Grusec, 1977). For example, when teachers and therapists work with children who have serious behavioral problems, they may award points (reinforcement) for desired behaviors and take away points (punishment) for misbehaviors. After a certain time interval (perhaps at the end of the day or week), children can exchange the points they've accumulated for small toys or privileges. Taking away previously earned points for unacceptable behavior (a strategy called *response cost*) can be quite effective in bringing about behavior change (K. D. O'Leary & O'Leary, 1972). Many other forms of punishment are *not* effective, however, especially those that model aggression or inflict physical or psychological harm (G. A. Davis & Thomas, 1989; Straus, 2000; J. E. Walker & Shea, 1999).

Children are motivated not only by the consequences they experience themselves but also by the consequences their *peers* experience. When they see another child being reinforced for doing something, they are apt to behave similarly—a phenomenon known as **vicarious reinforcement.** And when they see a peer being punished for a particular behavior, they are less likely to behave in the same way—a phenomenon known as **vicarious punishment.** For example, by watching the consequences that their peers experience, children might learn that being elected to a student government office brings status and popularity, that acting out in class gets the teacher's attention, or that unsportsmanlike conduct on the playing field results in being benched during the next game.

Development of Intrinsic Motivation

Although extrinsic motivation can certainly promote successful learning and productive behavior, intrinsic motivation has numerous advantages over extrinsic motivation. Intrinsically motivated children are eager to learn classroom material, willingly tackle assigned tasks, use effective learning strategies (e.g., organization and elaboration), and are likely to achieve at high levels. In contrast, extrinsically motivated children may have to be enticed or prodded, are apt to study classroom topics only superficially (e.g., by using rehearsal), and are often interested in performing only easy tasks and meeting minimal classroom requirements (A. E. Gottfried, Fleming, & Gottfried, 2001; Renninger, Hidi, & Krapp, 1992; Spaulding, 1992).

Several factors appear to underlie intrinsic motivation, as the following principles reveal:

● *Children seem to have a genetic predisposition to explore their environment.* Following in Jean Piaget's footsteps, many developmental theorists believe that children are naturally curious about their world and actively seek out information to help them make sense of it (e.g., Callanan & Oakes, 1992; Lieberman, 1993; Raine, Reynolds, & Venables, 2002). Even as infants, children are constantly experimenting to discover the properties of various objects and the outcomes of various actions. Later, as children gain proficiency in their native language, their seemingly incessant questions (e.g., "How do they make statues?" "Why does it rain sometimes?") are an additional means through which they try to satisfy their curiosity about the world around them (Callanan & Oakes, 1992, p. 218; Kemler Nelson, Egan, & Holt, 2004).

● *Children strive for consistency in their understandings of the world.* Jean Piaget suggested that another key factor driving a child's learning and development is *disequilibrium,* an inconsistency between new information and what the child already believes to be true. According to Piaget, disequilibrium causes mental discomfort and spurs the child to integrate, reorganize, or in some cases replace existing schemes to accommodate to the new information. Like Piaget, many contemporary developmental theorists believe that beginning early in life, human beings have an innate need for consistency and coherence among the things they learn (e.g., M. B. Bronson, 2000; Sinatra & Pintrich, 2003).

Study Guide and Reader
Supplementary Reading 13-2 describes another form of reinforcement—one in which an unpleasant stimulus is removed—that is known as *negative reinforcement*. Readers should be aware that negative reinforcement is *not* a synonym for *punishment*. Supplementary Reading 13-3 discusses punishment and offers guidelines for using it effectively when working with children.

Connecting Concepts
Learning strategies such as organization, elaboration, and rehearsal are described in Chapter 7.

Connecting Concepts
Piaget's concept of disequilibrium is discussed in more depth in Chapter 6.

vicarious reinforcement
Phenomenon in which a child increases a certain response after seeing someone else reinforced for that response.

vicarious punishment
Phenomenon in which a child decreases a certain response after seeing someone else punished for that response.

──────────── Connecting Concepts
Learn more about the need to feel
competent in the discussion of *sense of
self* in Chapter 12.

● *Children tend to choose activities at which they think they can be successful.* Some psychologists propose that an important source of intrinsic motivation is an innate need to feel *competent*—to believe that one can deal effectively with one's environment (Deci & Ryan, 1992; Jacobs, Lanza, Osgood, Eccles, & Wigfield, 2002). A need for competence pushes children to develop effective ways of dealing with various environmental circumstances and thus increases their chances of survival. It may be one important reason that we human beings have, over the course of time, been able to adapt successfully to many different habitats (R. White, 1959).

As you learned in Chapter 12, children increasingly distinguish among various aspects of themselves, and they soon discover that they are good at some things and not so good at others. To maintain and enhance their sense of competence, children are apt to choose and persist at activities for which they have high **self-efficacy**—that is, activities at which they believe they can be successful (Bandura, 1982, 1997). For example, in the "Intrinsic Motivation: Early Adolescence" video clip on Observation CD 3, 12-year-old Claudia reveals high self-efficacy for mathematics when she explains why math is her favorite subject: "I don't know, it just . . . I'm good at it and . . . it's just, I like it better than the other subjects."

Once youngsters have high self-efficacy for a task or activity, they eagerly seek out challenges that can further enhance their ability and self-efficacy. In the "Intrinsic Motivation" video clips for middle childhood and late adolescence on Observation CD 3, 9-year-old Elena and 15-year-old Greg both express their desire for challenge at school:

In the "Intrinsic Motivation" clips for middle childhood, early adolescence, and late adolescence, notice the importance of self-efficacy, challenge, and self-determination.

Interviewer:	What do you like best about school?
Elena:	I like PEAK [a program for students identified as gifted]. It's this thing where you go to this program. It's for smart kids who have, like, good ideas for stuff you could do. And so they make it more challenging for you in school. So instead of third-grade math, you get fourth-grade math.
Interviewer:	What do teachers do that encourage you to do well at school?
Greg:	[S]ome of them kind of make it a competition, like class rank and stuff. . . . And that makes you want to. . . . And the challenge. If it's a really hard class, then I . . . will usually try harder in harder classes.

● *Children also prefer activities for which they have some autonomy.* In general, children are more intrinsically motivated when they have a **sense of self-determination**, a belief that they have some choice and control regarding the things they do and the direction their lives take (Deci & Ryan, 1985, 1992; Ng, Kenney-Benson, & Pomerantz, 2004). For instance, a child who thinks, "I *want* to do this" or "I'd *find it useful* to do that" has a high sense of self-determination. In contrast, a child who thinks, "I *must* do this" or "*My teacher wants* me to do that" is thinking that someone or something else is directing the course of events. Consider 14-year-old Alicia's comment about required reading in the "Literacy: Late Adolescence" video clip on Observation CD 2:

I really don't like it when the reading's required. I can't read books if they're required. I just avoid reading them because they don't seem very interesting. And even after you read them, even though they might be interesting, they're not as interesting as if you picked them up by yourself.

Developmental trends in intrinsic motivation.   The nature of youngsters' intrinsic motivation changes in several ways over the course of childhood and adolescence:

● *As children grow older, their interests become increasingly stable.* When we say that children have *interest* in a particular topic or activity, we mean that they find the topic or activity intriguing and rewarding in and of itself. Interest, then, is one form of intrinsic motivation. Psychologists distinguish between two general types of interest (Renninger et al., 1992). **Situational interest** is evoked by something in the environment—something that is perhaps new, unusual, or surprising. In contrast, **personal interest** comes from within the child and is largely unrelated to immediate circumstances.

In infancy and early childhood, interests are mostly situational and short-lived: Young children are readily attracted to novel, attention-getting stimuli for, say, a few seconds or min-

self-efficacy
Belief that one is capable of executing certain behaviors or reaching certain goals.

sense of self-determination
Belief that one has some choice and control regarding the future course of one's life.

situational interest
Interest evoked temporarily by something in the environment.

personal interest
Long-term, relatively stable interest in a particular topic or activity.

Age 8

Age 11

Age 17

Figure 13-1

In these drawings Joey shows his long-term personal interest in drawing the human form.

utes. By the middle to upper elementary grades, however, many children have personal interests—perhaps in reptiles, ballet, or outer space—that persist over a period of time (Eccles et al., 1998; L. Nagy, 1912). As an example of an enduring personal interest, look at Joey's drawings in Figure 13-1. Joey displayed an exceptional interest in art beginning at age 3. Throughout his childhood and adolescence, he had a strong interest in drawing the human form and, later, in fashion design. (Joey's self-portrait at age 17 appears in Figure 10-16 in Chapter 10.)

● *Children and adolescents increasingly pursue activities that they perceive to be valuable for themselves.* A task or activity has **value** when children believe there are direct or indirect benefits in performing it (Dweck & Elliott, 1983; Feather, 1982; Wigfield & Eccles, 2000). Some activities are valued because they are associated with certain personal qualities. For example, a boy who wants to be smart and thinks that smart people do well in school will place a premium on academic success. Other activities have high value because they are seen as means to desired goals. For example, much as she disliked mathematics, Jeanne's daughter Tina struggled through math classes throughout high school because many colleges require 4 years of math. Still other activities are valued simply because they bring pleasure and enjoyment (Eccles & Wigfield, 1985; Eccles [Parsons], 1983).

In the elementary grades, children primarily choose activities that they perceive to be interesting and enjoyable. As they reach adolescence and proceed through the secondary grades, however, they increasingly choose activities that, in their minds at least, will be instrumental in helping them achieve their goals (Eccles et al., 1998; Wigfield et al., 2004).

In contrast, children tend *not* to value activities that seem to require more effort than they're worth. For instance, a teenager who would ideally like to get straight As in school may begin to downplay the importance of As if she finds that they require forgoing much of her social life. Children may also *de*value activities that they associate with frequent frustration and failure ("I don't see why I need to do these stupid geometry proofs!") and that may lessen their sense of competence.

● *Over time, children internalize the motivation to engage in certain activities.* As children grow older, most begin to adopt some of the priorities and values of the people around them. Such **internalized motivation** typically develops gradually, perhaps in the sequence depicted in Figure 13-2 (Deci & Ryan, 1995). Initially, youngsters may engage in some activities primarily because of the external consequences that result. For instance, students may do schoolwork to gain the approval of adults or to avoid being punished for poor grades. Gradually, however, they internalize the "pressure" to perform the activities and begin to see the activities as important in their own right. Such internalization of values is most likely to occur if adults who espouse those values (parents, teachers, etc.) provide a warm, supportive, and structured environment yet also offer enough autonomy in decision making that learners have a sense of self-determination about their actions (R. M. Ryan, Connell, & Grolnick, 1992; R. M. Ryan & Deci, 2000).

1. External regulation. Children may initially be motivated to behave (or not to behave) in certain ways based primarily on the external consequences that follow behaviors; that is, children are extrinsically motivated.

2. Introjection. Children begin to behave in ways that gain the approval of others, partly as a way of protecting and enhancing their sense of self. They feel guilty when they violate certain standards for behavior but do not fully understand the rationale behind these standards.

3. Identification. Children begin to regard certain behaviors as being personally important or valuable to themselves.

4. Integration. Children integrate certain behaviors into their overall system of motives and values. In essence, these behaviors become a central part of their sense of self.

Figure 13-2

Possible sequence in which *internalized motivation* develops.
Based on Deci & Ryan, 1995.

value
Belief that a particular activity has direct or indirect benefits.

internalized motivation
Adoption of behaviors that others value, whether or not one's environment reinforces those behaviors.

—————————— Connecting Concepts
Chapter 14 describes the many challenges adolescents face as they make the transition from elementary to secondary school.

● *Intrinsic motivation for learning school subject matter declines during the school years.* Young children are often eager and excited to learn new things at school. But sometime between grades 3 and 9, children become less intrinsically motivated, and more *extrinsically* motivated, to learn and master classroom topics. Their intrinsic motivation may be especially low after they make the often anxiety-arousing transition from elementary school to a secondary-school format (Eccles & Midgley, 1989; Harter, 1992, 1996; J. M. T. Walker, 2001).

This decline in intrinsic motivation for academic subject matter is probably due to several factors. As children move through the grade levels, evidence mounts that they are not necessarily as competent as some of their peers, and they may shy away from activities for which they have low self-efficacy (Harter, 1992, 1996). Frequent reminders of the importance of good grades for promotion, graduation, and college admission may undermine their sense of self-determination (Deci & Ryan, 1992; Harter, Whitesell, & Kowalski, 1992). In addition, as youngsters grow older, they become more able to set and strive for long-term goals and begin to evaluate school subjects in terms of their relevance or *non*relevance to such goals, rather than in terms of intrinsic appeal. And they may grow increasingly bored and impatient with highly structured, repetitive activities (Battistich, Solomon, Kim, Watson, & Schaps, 1995; Larson, 2000). The following interview with high school student Alfredo illustrates this last point:

> Adult: Do you think your classes are interesting?
> Alfredo: Some of them are. But some of them are boring. You go to the same class every day and you just do the same type of work every day. Like biology, I like [the teacher of this] class. She's about the only one I like. And last year I had the same problem. The only class I liked last year was science. . . . We used to do different things every day . . . but like classes like Reading, you go inside, read a story with the same person every day. That's boring.
> Adult: That's boring? So will you just not show up?
> Alfredo: No, I'll go but I won't do nothing sometimes. (dialogue from Way, 1998, p. 198)

Despite the average downward trend in intrinsic motivation, some youngsters remain genuinely interested in academic subject matter throughout the school years. Furthermore, virtually all children and adolescents have intrinsic motivation for *some* activities—perhaps for skateboarding, cheerleading, or playing video games. The Observation Guidelines table "Recognizing Intrinsic Motivation in Children's Behaviors" lists characteristics and behaviors to look for.

Development of Goals

—————————— Connecting Concepts
In Piaget's theory, goal-directed behavior is an acquisition of the *sensorimotor stage* (see Chapter 6).

As infants develop their motor skills (reaching, grabbing, crawling, etc.), they become increasingly capable of getting things they want, such as toys, food on the high chair tray, or Dad's eyeglasses on the bedside table. Furthermore, they become increasingly capable of setting and working toward particular goals ("I want that toy, and I intend to get it!"). As you may recall from Chapter 6, Piaget proposed that infants begin to engage in such *goal-directed behavior* in the latter part of their first year. But in fact, infants show signs of goal directedness well before this. For example, when one end of a string is attached to a 2-month-old baby's foot and the other end is attached to a mobile, at some point the baby realizes that foot motion makes the mobile move (Rovee-Collier, 1999). The infant begins to shake his or her foot more vigorously, apparently as a way to accomplish a particular goal: to gain a more interesting visual display.

Many psychologists believe that human beings are purposeful by nature: People set goals for themselves and choose behaviors they think will help them achieve those goals (e.g., Dweck & Elliott, 1983; A. Kaplan, 1998; Locke & Latham, 1994). Some goals ("I want to finish reading my dinosaur book") are short-term and transitory. Others ("I want to be a paleontologist") are long-term and relatively enduring.

Children and adolescents typically have a wide variety of goals. Being happy and healthy, doing well in school, gaining popularity with peers, bringing honor to the family, having a rewarding career, and finding a long-term mate are just a few of the many possi-

OBSERVATION GUIDELINES

Recognizing Intrinsic Motivation in Children's Behaviors

Characteristic	Look For	Example	Implication
Inquisitiveness	• Eagerness to explore and learn • Fascination with objects, other people, or both • Frequent and thoughtful questions • Lack of concern about external rewards for learning	Jamie often takes great interest in the new toys he finds at his infant care center. He is especially drawn to objects that come apart and can be reassembled in various ways.	Pique children's curiosity with puzzling situations, unusual phenomena, and opportunities to explore the physical world. Make sure their environment is safe for exploration.
High Self-Efficacy	• Obvious pleasure in mastering tasks • Eagerness to tackle challenging topics and activities • Willingness to take risks and make mistakes	Luana delights in trying to solve the brainteasers that her math teacher occasionally assigns for extra credit.	Give children the academic and social support they need to succeed at challenging tasks. Use evaluation procedures that encourage risk taking and allow for occasional mistakes.
Autonomy	• Pursuit of self-chosen activities • Willingness to engage in tasks that are only minimally structured	Mark, Reggie, and Cynthia form a rock band and practice together every chance they get. They actively seek out "gigs" both at school and in the community.	Provide opportunities for children to pursue self-chosen activities. Give them only as much structure as they need to be successful and achieve instructional goals.
Effective Learning Strategies	• Focus on making sense of subject matter, rather than on rote memorization of facts • Persistence in trying to solve difficult problems and understand complex ideas	At home, Lenesia reads an assigned chapter in her geography textbook. Despite reading the section on mountain formation several times, she is confused about how folded mountains form and so asks her teacher to explain the process in class the next day.	In both instruction and assessment activities, emphasize genuine understanding and integration of the subject matter, rather than rote memorization of isolated facts.
Long-Term Interests	• Consistent selection of a particular topic when choices are given • Frequent initiation of activities in a particular domain	Whenever his after-school group goes to the local library, Connor looks for books about military battleships and aircraft.	Relate instructional subject matter to children's interests and needs. Give them occasional choices about the topics they study and write about.
Priorities	• Consistent pursuit of certain activities over other alternatives • Apparent adoption of other people's values (e.g., a strong work ethic, the importance of maintaining a well-organized work space) as one's own	Audrey is clearly frustrated when unexpected events at home prevent her from doing a homework assignment as thoroughly as she'd like. "Even though I got an A," she says later, "I didn't do as well as I *could* have if I'd had more time."	Encourage activities that will be in youngsters' best interest over the long run. Do so in a warm, supportive environment in which youngsters have input into decision making.

bilities (M. E. Ford, 1996; Schutz, 1994). Among these various goals are certain *core goals* that drive much of what youngsters do (Schutz, 1994). For instance, those who attain high levels of academic achievement typically make classroom learning a high priority. Those who achieve at lower levels are often more concerned with social relationships (Wentzel & Wigfield, 1998; Wigfield et al., 1996). We look now at the nature of children's achievement and social goals, and also at their long-term future aspirations.

Achievement goals. In a case study in a middle school math class (D. K. Meyer, Turner, & Spencer, 1997), a teacher asks her students to apply geometry concepts to aerodynamics, and more specifically to kite design. Students experiment with a variety of kite shapes and sizes and then design kites using what they have learned. One student, Sara, approaches the task as an engineer might: She is keenly interested in creating an aerodynamic kite and realizes that doing so will take time and patience. Sara redesigns her kite three times to make it as aerodynamic as possible. After the project, she summarizes her results:

> I wasn't completely successful, because I had a few problems. But I realized that most scientists, when they try experiments, well, they're not always right. . . . [I]f I can correct myself on [errors] then I don't really mind them that much. I mean, everybody learns from their mistakes. I know I do. . . . I think mistakes are actually good, to tell you the truth. (D. K. Meyer et al., 1997, p. 511)

As children get older, they become increasingly concerned with performance goals (such as impressing peers), sometimes at the expense of mastering school subject matter.

Another student, Amy, sticks with a single design throughout the project even though she has trouble getting her kite to fly. Later Amy reflects on her performance:

I knew from the start what shape I wanted. Once I had the materials it was very easy to make the kite. . . . [T]here wasn't enough wind for the kites to fly. . . . I don't like to make challenges for myself, to make goals. I just like to do it as I go along. . . . I like to do well for [the teacher] and my parents, and myself, I guess. . . . [I]f it doesn't affect my grade, whether I do this or not, if I totally fail and do everything wrong, if it doesn't affect my grade, then I'll [take risks]. (D. K. Meyer et al., 1997, pp. 510, 512)

Both Sara and Amy want to do well on the kite project—in other words, they have *achievement goals*—but for different reasons. In particular, Sara has a **mastery goal:** She wants to acquire new knowledge and skills related to kites and their construction, and to do so she must inevitably make a few mistakes. Meanwhile, Amy has a **performance goal:** She wants to look good and receive favorable judgments from others and so tries to avoid mistakes if possible (Ames, 1992; Dweck & Elliott, 1983; Nicholls, 1984).

To the extent that children and adolescents have mastery goals, they engage in the very activities that will help them learn: They pay attention at school, study in effective ways (e.g., by elaborating on new ideas), and learn from their mistakes. Furthermore, they have a healthy perspective about learning, effort, and failure: They realize that learning is a process of trying hard and persevering even after temporary setbacks (E. M. Anderman & Maehr, 1994; Blazevski, McEvoy, & Pintrich, 2003; Dweck & Elliott, 1983). In contrast, children with performance goals may be so concerned about how others evaluate them that they stay away from challenging tasks that would help them master new skills (Dweck, 1986; Urdan, 1997). Often they exert only the minimal effort needed to achieve desired performance outcomes, and so they may learn only a fraction of what their teachers can offer them (Brophy, 1987; Dowson & McInerney, 2001).

Mastery and performance goals are not necessarily mutually exclusive. On many occasions children may simultaneously have *both* kinds of goals. However, the relative prevalence of the two types of goals changes with age. Most young children seem to be primarily concerned with mastery goals. But by the time they reach second grade, they begin to show signs of having performance goals as well, and such goals become increasingly prevalent as they move into middle school and high school (Eccles & Midgley, 1989; Elliot & McGregor, 2000; Nicholls, Cobb, Yackel, Wood, & Wheatley, 1990). The greater emphasis on performance goals at older ages is probably due partly to youngsters' increasing awareness of how their performance compares with that of peers and partly to an increasing focus on grades and other evaluations at the upper grade levels (Eccles et al., 1998; Nicholls et al., 1990).

Social goals.   As you learned in Chapter 11, human beings seem to have a basic *need for relatedness*—that is, they want to feel socially connected with, and to secure the love and respect of, other people. For infants and toddlers, this need is reflected in early efforts to engage other people through crying, smiling, eye contact, and imitation, as well as in the close attachments they form with one or more caregivers (e.g., Striano, 2004). For many school-age children and adolescents, it may be reflected in the high priority they put on socializing with friends, sometimes at the expense of finishing chores, schoolwork, or other assigned tasks (W. Doyle, 1986; Wigfield, Eccles, Mac Iver, Reuman, & Midgley, 1991). In an interview in the "Intrinsic Motivation: Late Adolescence" clip on Observation CD 3, 15-year-old Greg reveals the importance of social relationships in his life at school:

In the "Intrinsic Motivation: Late Adolescence" clip on Observation CD 3, notice that social connections are a priority for Greg.

Interviewer:	What do you like best about school?
Greg:	Lunch.
Interviewer:	Lunch?
Greg:	All the social aspects. . . . Just friends and cliques. . . .

Like Greg, many high school students find the nonacademic aspects of school to be the most enjoyable and rewarding parts of the day (Certo et al., 2002).

Consistent with their need for relatedness, children and adolescents are apt to have a variety of **social goals,** perhaps including the following:

- Forming and maintaining friendly or intimate relationships with other people
- Gaining other people's approval

mastery goal
Desire to acquire additional knowledge or master new skills (also known as a *learning goal*).

performance goal
Desire to look good and receive favorable judgments from others.

social goal
Goal related to establishing or maintaining relationships with other people.

- Becoming part of a cohesive, mutually supportive group
- Achieving status and prestige within a peer group
- Meeting social obligations and keeping interpersonal commitments
- Assisting and supporting others, and ensuring their welfare (Berndt & Keefe, 1996; Dowson & McInerney, 2001; M. E. Ford, 1996; Hicks, 1997; Schutz, 1994)

Young people's social goals affect their behavior and performance in the classroom and other group settings. For instance, if they are seeking friendly relationships with peers or are concerned about others' welfare, they may eagerly engage in such activities as cooperative learning and peer tutoring (Dowson & McInerney, 2001). If they want to gain adults' attention and approval, they are apt to strive for good grades and in other ways shoot for performance goals (Hinkley, McInerney, & Marsh, 2001). A desire for peer approval can lead to a focus on performance goals as well, especially if youngsters are concerned about making a good impression (L. H. Anderman & Anderman, 1999). And if youngsters are seeking the approval of *low-achieving* peers, they may exert little effort in their studies (Berndt, 1992; B. B. Brown, 1993; Steinberg, 1996).

Future aspirations. Children and adolescents often set long-term goals for themselves, in part by envisioning possible *future selves* they might become (Harter, 1999; Oyserman & Markus, 1993). For instance, they may hope to go to college (as Derrika does in the opening case study), and they may want to get married, raise a family, or have a career in a certain field. Young children set such goals with little thought and may change them frequently—perhaps wanting to be a firefighter one week and professional basketball player the next. But by middle to late adolescence, many (though by no means all) reach some tentative and relatively stable decisions about the life and career paths they want to pursue (Marcia, 1980). To a considerable degree, the goals that adolescents set for themselves are related to their self-efficacy for being successful in various roles and careers (Bandura et al., 2001).

Coordinating multiple goals. Most children and adolescents simultaneously have numerous and varied goals that they must juggle in one way or another. Sometimes they find activities that allow them to achieve several goals simultaneously. For instance, they might satisfy both achievement goals and social goals by forming a study group to prepare for an exam. But at other times they may believe they have to abandon one goal to satisfy another (McCaslin & Good, 1996; Phelan et al., 1994). For example, youngsters who want to do well in school may choose not to perform at their best so that they can maintain relationships with peers who don't value academic achievement. Students with mastery goals in particular subject areas may find that the multiple demands of school coerce them into focusing on performance goals (e.g., getting good grades) rather than studying the subject matter as thoroughly as they'd like. Brian, a junior high school student, expresses his ambivalence about striving for performance goals over mastery goals:

> I sit here and I say, "Hey, I did this assignment in five minutes and I still got an A+ on it." I still have a feeling that I could do better, and it was kind of cheap that I didn't do my best and I still got this A. . . . I think probably it might lower my standards eventually, which I'm not looking forward to at all. . . . I'll always know, though, that I have it in me. It's just that I won't express it that much. (S. Thomas & Oldfather, 1997, p. 119)

Teachers' instructional strategies and grading practices influence the extent to which their students have mastery goals at school and successfully juggle such goals with their social goals and performance goals. For example, students are more likely to strive for mastery goals when assignments entice them to learn new skills (thus encouraging a focus on mastery), when they have occasional group projects (thus helping them also meet their social goals), and when evaluation criteria allow for risk taking and mistakes (thus helping them meet their performance goals). Students are unlikely to strive for mastery goals when assignments ask little of them (consider Brian's concern about low standards), when their teachers insist that they compete with one another for resources or high test scores, and when any single failure has a significant impact on final grades.

Development of Attributions

In the opening case study, Derrika believes her elementary school teachers were largely responsible for her academic success ("If you don't want to learn, they are going to make you

Connecting Concepts Children's possible future selves are part of their *sense of self* (see Chapter 12).

learn"). She thinks her high school teachers are to blame for her recent failures yet also acknowledges that her teachers think *she* is to blame ("If you fail, you just fail. It ain't our fault. You're the one that's dumb") (Roderick & Camburn, 1999, p. 304).

The various explanations people have for their successes and failures—or in some cases for the successes and failures of others—are **attributions.** Children form a variety of attributions about the causes of events in their lives. That is, they come up with reasons for why they do well or poorly on classroom assignments, why they are popular or have trouble making friends, why they are skilled athletes or total klutzes, and so on. They may attribute their successes and failures to such factors as aptitude or ability (how smart or proficient they are), effort (how hard they're trying), other people (how well an instructor teaches or how much other children like them), task difficulty (how easy or hard something is), luck, mood, illness, fatigue, or physical appearance. Such attributions differ from one another in three general ways (B. Weiner, 1986, 2000):

"And remember, kids: If you play to the best of your ability and still lose the game, just blame it all on the umpire."

By blaming the umpire for a loss, children can more easily maintain a sense of competence. However, such external attributions are counterproductive when the true causes for success and failure are actually internal and within children's control.

- *Internal versus external.* Children may attribute the causes of events to factors within themselves (*internal* things) or to factors outside themselves (*external* things).
- *Stable versus unstable.* Children may believe that events are due either to *stable* factors, which probably won't change much in the near future, or to *unstable* factors, which can vary from one occasion to the next.
- *Controllable versus uncontrollable.* Children may attribute events to *controllable* factors over which they (or perhaps other people) have influence, or to *uncontrollable* factors, which neither they nor other people in their lives can change.

Children's attributions are self-constructed *interpretations* that don't always reflect reality. In general, children tend to attribute their successes to internal causes (e.g., high ability, hard work) and their failures to external causes (e.g., bad luck, behaviors of others) (Marsh, 1990a; Whitley & Frieze, 1985). By patting themselves on the back for the things they do well and putting the blame elsewhere for poor performance, they can maintain a sense of competence (Clifford, 1990; Paris & Byrnes, 1989). Yet youngsters are most likely to be successful over the long run when they attribute successes and failures alike to *internal and controllable factors*—that is, to things they are doing or might do differently.

Researchers have observed several developmental trends in children's attributions:

● **Children increasingly distinguish among various attributions.** Up until age 5 or 6, children don't clearly discriminate among the possible causes—effort, ability, luck, task difficulty, and so on—of their successes and failures (Eccles et al., 1998; Nicholls, 1990). Especially troublesome is the distinction between effort and ability, which they gradually get a better handle on over time (Nicholls, 1990):

- At about age 6, children begin to recognize that effort and ability are separate qualities. At this point they believe that people who try hardest are those who have the greatest ability, and that effort is the primary determiner of successful outcomes.
- At about age 9, they begin to understand that effort and ability can compensate for each other, that people with less ability may have to exert greater effort to achieve the same outcomes as their more able peers.
- By about age 13, children clearly differentiate between effort and ability. They realize that people differ both in their inherent ability to perform a task and in the amount of effort they exert. They also realize that a lack of ability sometimes precludes success no matter how much effort a person puts forth—that some people simply don't have what it takes to accomplish certain tasks.

attribution
Belief about the cause of one's success or failure.

incremental view of ability
Belief that ability can and does improve with effort and practice.

entity view of ability
Belief that ability is a "thing" that is relatively permanent and unchangeable.

● **Many children increasingly attribute their successes and failures to stable, uncontrollable characteristics, rather than to effort.** Children have varying ideas of what *ability* is. Some have an **incremental view** of ability, thinking that they will almost certainly become proficient in an activity if they try hard and persevere. Others have an **entity view** of ability, believing that their capacity to perform various tasks is an inherited trait or is in some other way beyond their control (Dweck, 2000; Dweck & Leggett, 1988).

In the elementary grades, children tend to attribute their successes to effort and hard work, and so they are usually relatively optimistic about their chances for success and may work harder when they fail. By adolescence, however, they are apt to attribute success and failure more to a fairly stable ability that is beyond their control. To some degree, then, children move from an incremental view of ability in the elementary years to an entity view in adolescence (Dweck, 2000; Lockhart et al., 2002; Nicholls, 1990). Probably for this reason, adolescents are more discouraged by temporary setbacks than elementary school children are (Eccles & Wigfield, 1985; Pressley, Borkowski, & Schneider, 1987). And if they believe that their own low ability makes mastery of a topic or skill impossible, they may increasingly focus on performance goals (A. Kaplan, Middleton, Urdan, & Midgley, 2002).

Yet there are individual differences here: Some young people continue to hold an incremental view throughout high school. And others gradually discover the importance of hard work and effective learning strategies as they move through the high school grades (see Chapter 7). High school students who have an incremental view of ability are more likely to have mastery goals and seek out challenges to enhance their competence in various domains (Dweck & Leggett, 1988).

● *As they get older, children and adolescents become more aware of the reactions that different attributions elicit.* Adults are often sympathetic and forgiving when children fail because of something beyond their control (illness, lack of ability, etc.) but frequently get angry when children fail simply because they didn't try very hard. By the time children reach fourth grade, most are aware of this fact and so may express attributions that are likely to elicit a favorable reaction (Juvonen, 2000). For instance, a child who knows very well that she did poorly on a school assignment because she didn't put forth her best effort may distort the truth, telling her teacher that she doesn't "understand this stuff" or "wasn't feeling well."

Children also become more adept at tailoring their attributions for the ears of their peers. Generally speaking, fourth graders believe that their peers value diligence and hard work, and so they are likely to say that they did well on an assignment because they worked hard. In contrast, many eighth graders believe that their peers will disapprove of those who exert much effort on academic tasks, and so they often prefer to convey the impression that they aren't working very hard—for instance, that they didn't study very much for an important exam (Howie, 2002; Juvonen, 2000).

● *Children gradually develop predictable patterns of attributions and expectations for future performance.* When young people have frequent success in new endeavors, they gain confidence that they can master a variety of tasks. They attribute their accomplishments to their own ability and effort and have an *I can do it* attitude known as a **mastery orientation.** Yet other youngsters, especially those who encounter a consistent string of failures, become increasingly pessimistic about their chances for future success. They develop an *I can't do it* attitude known as **learned helplessness.**

Even when children with a mastery orientation and those with learned helplessness initially have equal ability, those with a mastery orientation behave in ways that lead to higher achievement over the long run. In particular, they set ambitious goals, seek out new challenges, and persist in the face of obstacles. Children with learned helplessness behave quite differently. Because they underestimate their ability, they set goals they can easily accomplish, avoid challenges that might enhance their learning and development, and respond to failure in counterproductive ways (e.g., giving up quickly) that almost guarantee future failure (Dweck, 2000; Graham, 1989; C. Peterson, 1990; Seligman, 1991).

Occasionally preschoolers develop learned helplessness about a particular activity if they consistently fail at it, and they may conclude that they are "bad" children overall (Burhans & Dweck, 1995; Dweck, 2000). By age 5 or 6, a few children begin to show a general inclination toward learned helplessness that persists over time; for instance, they express little confidence about tackling challenging tasks and quickly abandon tasks at which they initially struggle (Ziegert, Kistner, Castro, & Robertson, 2001). By and large, however, children rarely exhibit extreme forms of learned helplessness before age 8, perhaps because they still believe that success is due largely to their own efforts (Eccles et al., 1998; Lockhart et al., 2002; Paris & Cunningham, 1996).

Feelings of helplessness are more common in adolescence. For instance, some middle schoolers believe they have no control over things that happen to them and are at a loss for

Connecting Concepts
As Chapter 7 points out, some adolescents' *epistemological beliefs* increasingly include a recognition that learning requires practice and good strategies.

mastery orientation
General belief that one is capable of accomplishing challenging tasks, accompanied by an intent to master such tasks.
learned helplessness
General belief that one is incapable of accomplishing tasks and has little or no control of the environment.

strategies that might get them on the road to success (Paris & Cunningham, 1996; C. Peterson, Maier, & Seligman, 1993). If you read the opening case study once again, you might get the impression that Derrika feels helpless about her poor academic performance. Although she admits that she doesn't always get up on time for her biology class, she offers no suggestions about how she might improve her situation.

Origins of attributions.   To some extent, children's attributions are the result of their previous success and failure experiences (Covington, 1987; Hong, Chiu, & Dweck, 1995). Those who usually succeed when they give a task their best shot are likely to believe that success is due to internal factors such as effort or high ability. Those who frequently fail despite considerable effort are likely to believe that success is due to something beyond their control—perhaps to a lack of genetic potential or to such external factors as luck or an adult's arbitrary and capricious judgments.

But children also pick up on other people's beliefs about why they have done well or poorly. In the opening case, Derrika detects low-ability attributions on the part of her high school teachers ("You're the one that's dumb"). Teachers, parents, and other adults communicate their interpretations of children's successes and failures in a variety of ways. Sometimes attributions are quite explicit, as the following statements illustrate:

- "That's wonderful. Your hard work has really paid off, hasn't it?" (*effort*)
- "You did it! You're so smart!" (*fairly stable ability*)
- "Hmmm, maybe this just isn't something you're good at." (*ability once again*)
- "Maybe you're just having a bad day." (*luck*)

The "Environments: Late Adolescence" video clip on Observation CD 1 depicts a poster that says, "Responsibility: Being accountable for your own actions, able to answer for your own conduct and obligations." Such a message clearly suggests that students should attribute their behaviors to internal and controllable causes.

At other times, adults' messages are more subtle. For example, when adults criticize and express anger about children's poor performance, they imply that children have the ability to master the task and simply aren't trying hard enough. When they instead express pity, they imply that low ability is the reason for the failure (Graham, 1997; Pintrich & Schunk, 2002; B. Weiner, 1984). Adults communicate low ability, too, when they praise easy successes, provide unneeded assistance on easy tasks, or encourage children to abandon challenging ones (Hokoda & Fincham, 1995; Schunk & Pajares, 2004; Stipek, 1996). As children get older, they become increasingly attuned to such subtle messages (Barker & Graham, 1987).

In the "Environments: Late Adolescence" clip of Observation CD 1, observe a message that encourages internal, controllable attributions for school behavior.

Children's attributions will inevitably influence the extent to which they are intrinsically or extrinsically motivated. Internal, controllable attributions should enhance children's sense of self-efficacy and self-determination—their beliefs that they can be successful in certain activities and have some control over the general course of their lives—and so should increase their intrinsic motivation. When youngsters have little or no sense of control over their successes and failures or over their lives more generally, consistent use of extrinsic reinforcers—praise, special privileges, points toward a desired object, and so on—may sometimes be necessary to help them learn that their actions *do* affect the things that happen to them.

Attributions, then, are an important source of diversity in youngsters, as indicated in the Basic Developmental Issues table "Contrasting Extrinsic and Intrinsic Motivation." We now look more closely at diversity in motivation.

Diversity in Motivation

Children and adolescents at any single age level can differ considerably in their responses to particular reinforcers (especially secondary reinforcers), as well as in their intrinsic motivation, long-term goals, and attributions. Such diversity is due largely to differences in young people's environments and past experiences.

Yet some diversity in motivation is due to biology. Sometimes biology has a direct impact on motivation. For example, when children encounter a new situation, temperamental differences influence their inclinations either to be intrigued by and explore their surroundings or, in contrast, to cling to a caregiver for security (Keogh, 2003). At other times

BASIC DEVELOPMENTAL ISSUES — Contrasting Extrinsic and Intrinsic Motivation

Issue	Extrinsic Motivation	Intrinsic Motivation
Nature and Nurture	Primary reinforcers satisfy basic, inborn biological needs (e.g., hunger, thirst). Secondary reinforcers acquire their reinforcing effects through regular association with primary reinforcers in a child's environment.	Children appear to have an innate curiosity about their world. Their needs to feel competent and resolve apparent inconsistencies may also be inborn. Other factors that contribute to intrinsic motivation, such as self-determination, interest-arousing situations, and values depend largely on environmental conditions.
Universality and Diversity	By and large, primary reinforcers are universal around the world. Secondary reinforcers (e.g., praise) are *learned* reinforcers, and so their effectiveness differs from child to child.	Innate sources of motivation, such as curiosity and the need for competence, are universal, as is the goal-directed nature of human behavior. Yet children have diverse interests, values, and goals. They also form different attributions for the things that happen to them, and such attributions influence their intrinsic motivation for particular activities.
Qualitative and Quantitative Change	Children increasingly learn to delay gratification, a trend that reflects quantitative change. Occasionally children respond differently to certain reinforcers than they have previously—a shift that reflects a qualitative change. For instance, a child who responds favorably to a teacher's praise in the elementary grades may later, as an adolescent, work hard to *avoid* teacher praise, perhaps for fear of being ridiculed as "teacher's pet."	Children internalize some of the priorities and values of people around them, reflecting qualitative change. But for many youngsters, intrinsic motivation for learning academic subject matter declines over the school years, reflecting quantitative change.

biology's effects are indirect. This is the case, for instance, when disabilities limit what children can do. Many children with significant physical disabilities have little sense of autonomy and self-determination because they must depend heavily on other people to help them meet their needs and achieve their goals (Sands & Wehmeyer, 1996). And children with cognitive disabilities (e.g., mental retardation or an undiagnosed learning disability) may show signs of learned helplessness about classroom tasks if their past efforts have repeatedly met with failure (Deshler & Schumaker, 1988; B. Jacobsen, Lowery, & DuCette, 1986; Seligman, 1975).

Most diversity in children's motivation reflects idiosyncratic differences in children's environments and inherited characteristics. Yet some variation reflects common differences between males and females and among members of distinct cultural groups.

Gender differences. Historically, boys have had more ambitious career aspirations than girls (Deaux, 1984; Lueptow, 1984). In recent years, many girls—especially those in Western countries—have also begun to set their sights on challenging professions (Bandura et al., 2001; Lapan, Tucker, Kim, & Kosciulek, 2003). Often, however, boys and girls alike focus on careers that are stereotypically "appropriate" for their gender, in part because they have higher self-efficacy for such careers (Bandura et al., 2001; Liben, Bigler, & Krogh, 2002; Olneck, 1995).

Not only do boys have higher self-efficacy for stereotypically male professions, but they also evaluate themselves more favorably overall (see Chapter 12). Gender differences in attributions may at least partly explain boys' greater self-confidence. Some researchers have observed a tendency for boys to attribute their successes to a fairly stable ability and their failures to lack of effort, thus displaying the attitude that *I know I can do this if I work at it.* Girls tend to show the reverse pattern: They attribute their successes to effort and their failures to lack of ability, believing that *I don't know whether I can keep on doing it, because I'm not very good at this type of thing.* When encountering failure, then, boys are apt to have an incremental view of ability and girls are apt to have an entity view. Gender differences in attributions, which can appear even when youngsters' previous achievement levels have been

Connecting Concepts ——————
Chapter 12 describes gender differences in *sense of self* in more detail.

equal, are most often observed in stereotypically male domains such as mathematics and sports (Dweck, 2000; Fennema, 1987; Stipek, 1984; Vermeer et al., 2000).

Cultural differences.   Children and adolescents everywhere are naturally curious about their physical world and about the society in which they live. But some aspects of intrinsic motivation vary from culture to culture. For example, the amount and forms that autonomy and self-determination take differ considerably from group to group (d'Ailly, 2003; Rogoff, 2003). Adults in some Native American communities give children far more independence and autonomy, and do so at an earlier age, than do many adults in mainstream Western culture (Deyhle & LeCompte, 1999). In contrast, many African American adults give children *less* autonomy than the average American adult, apparently as a way of ensuring children's safety in potentially hostile environments (Hale-Benson, 1986; McLoyd, 1998b).

Children and adolescents from many ethnic and cultural groups place high value on getting a good education (Brophy, 2004; Fuligni & Hardway, 2004). However, youngsters from some minority groups may have low self-efficacy about their chances for future academic and professional success, perhaps as a result of low teacher expectations or widespread discrimination practices (Eccles et al., 1998; Fordham & Ogbu, 1986). Youngsters from different ethnic backgrounds may also define "academic success" differently, and their achievement goals vary accordingly. On average, Asian American students shoot for higher grades than students in other ethnic groups, in part because they believe their parents would be angry if they got grades lower than A− (Steinberg, 1996). Even so, Asian American students, and African American students as well, may be more focused on mastery goals (they truly want to learn and understand what they are studying) than European American students (Freeman, Gutman, & Midgley, 2002; Qian & Pan, 2002). And students raised in cultures that value group achievement over individual achievement (e.g., many Native American, Mexican American, Southeast Asian, and Pacific Islander cultures) tend to focus their mastery goals not on how much they alone can improve, but instead on how much they and *others* (perhaps classmates or siblings) can improve (A. Kaplan, 1998).

Cultural differences are also seen in the particular careers that youngsters shoot for and the particular activities that youngsters value. For instance, in China and Japan, children are encouraged to achieve and work in domains perceived to be especially helpful to the common good (e.g., science), rather than to pursue domains that are a good fit with their own talents and interests (Wigfield et al., 2004).

Finally, attributions for academic tasks and activities differ somewhat from culture to culture. For example, adolescents from Asian backgrounds tend to attribute their academic achievement to effort rather than ability, perhaps because Asian parents and teachers actively nurture such a belief (Hess, Chang, & McDevitt, 1987; Lillard, 1997; B. Weiner, 2004). Another common finding is a higher-than-average frequency of learned helplessness in children and adolescents of color (Graham, 1989; Holliday, 1985). Racial prejudice may be one factor here: Children begin to believe that, because of the color of their skin, they have little chance of academic success no matter *what* they do (van Laar, 2000; B. Weiner, 2004). We suspect that youngsters of color are more likely to acquire learned helplessness about academic tasks when they perceive their teachers and other school personnel to be treating different students differently on the basis of race or ethnicity.

The Developmental Trends table "Motivation at Different Age Levels" identifies motivational characteristics and kinds of motivational diversity you are likely to see in different age-groups.

Motivating Children and Adolescents

When children and adolescents find themselves in supportive environments, the vast majority of them are quite motivated to acquire the knowledge and skills that will serve them in good stead in their personal and professional lives. Yet simple pep talks ("I know you can do it if you try!") are not terribly helpful in motivating youngsters, especially for the long run (Brophy, 2004). The following strategies are far more effective:

● *Focus on promoting intrinsic (rather than extrinsic) motivation.* Externally imposed consequences—praise, money, good grades, and so on—often bring about desired

──────── Connecting Concepts
You will learn more about the effects of teacher expectations in Chapter 14.

DEVELOPMENTAL TRENDS

Motivation at Different Age Levels

Age	What You Might Observe	Diversity	Implications
Infancy (Birth–2) 	• Curiosity about objects and people • Enthusiasm for exploring the environment • Some goal-directed behavior as early as 3 months • Little or no need for praise, especially in the first year; greater appreciation of praise after age 1	• Temperament and culture influence children's willingness to explore and experiment with their physical environment. • Attachment security influences children's willingness to explore (see Chapter 11). • Children with disabilities may show less interest in exploration than their nondisabled peers.	• Create a predictable, affectionate environment in which children feel comfortable exploring and trying new things. • Provide new and unusual objects that pique children's curiosity. • Identify objects and events that can capture the interest of children with disabilities.
Early Childhood (2–6) 	• Preference for small, immediate rewards over larger, delayed ones • Overconfidence about one's ability to perform new tasks • Rapidly changing, situation-dependent interests • Focus on obtaining the approval of adults more than that of peers • Focus on mastery (rather than performance) goals • Little understanding of the likely causes of successes and failures	• Differences in desire for social interaction are evident as early as age 3 or 4. • Children who begin school without basic knowledge of colors, shapes, letters, or numbers may see obvious differences between their own abilities and those of peers, setting the stage for poor self-efficacy in certain academic domains. • Learned helplessness occasionally appears as early as age 4 or 5, especially after a history of failure.	• Praise (or in some other way reinforce) desired behaviors as soon as they occur. • Provide a wide variety of potentially interesting toys, puzzles, storybooks, props for dramatic play, and other equipment. • Provide the guidance and support children need in order to experience success more often than failure.
Middle Childhood (6–10) 	• Increasing ability to delay gratification • Increasing awareness of how one's performance compares with that of peers; more realistic assessment of abilities • Increasing prevalence of performance goals • Increasing distinction between effort and ability as possible causes of success and failure; tendency to attribute successes to hard work	• As a result of low self-efficacy, children with a history of learning problems have less intrinsic motivation to learn academic subject matter. • Girls who are gifted may be reluctant to do their best because of concerns about appearing unfeminine or surpassing peers. • Children of color and children with disabilities are more likely to develop learned helplessness about their ability to achieve academic success.	• Communicate that with appropriate effort and support, *all* children can master basic knowledge and skills in academic subject matter. • Focus children's attention on the progress they are making, rather than on how their performance compares to that of their peers. • Stress the importance of learning for the intrinsic pleasure it brings; downplay the importance of grades and other external evaluations.
Early Adolescence (10–14) 	• Declining sense of competence, often accompanying the transition to middle school or junior high • Increasing interest in social activities; increasing concern about gaining approval of peers • Decline in intrinsic motivation to learn school subject matter; increasing focus on performance goals • Increasing belief that skill is the result of stable factors (e.g., inherited ability) rather than effort and practice • Increasing motivation to learn and achieve in stereotypically gender-appropriate domains	• Girls have a stronger desire to interact frequently with peers. • Some adolescents, girls especially, believe that demonstrating high achievement can interfere with popularity. • Adolescents from some ethnic groups (e.g., those from many Asian cultures) continue to place high value on adult approval. • On average, adolescents from lower socioeconomic backgrounds show less interest in academic achievement than those from middle and upper socioeconomic backgrounds. • Some individuals develop a general sense of learned helplessness about achieving academic success.	• Evaluate adolescents on the basis of how well they are achieving instructional objectives, not on how well their performance compares with that of their classmates. • Assign cooperative group projects that allow adolescents to socialize, display their unique talents, and contribute to the success of the group. • When youngsters exhibit a pattern of failure, provide the support they need to begin achieving consistent success.

(continued)

DEVELOPMENTAL TRENDS

Motivation at Different Age Levels (continued)

Age	What You Might Observe	Diversity	Implications
Late Adolescence (14–18) 	• Ability to postpone immediate pleasures in order to gain long-term rewards • Increasing stability of interests and priorities • Increasing focus on the utilitarian value of activities • Tendency to attribute successes and failures more to ability than to effort • Some tentative decisions about career paths	• Girls work harder on school assignments, and are also more likely to graduate, than boys. • Adolescents from Asian cultures often attribute their successes and failures to effort rather than ability. • Many teens have career aspirations that are stereotypically gender-appropriate. • Adolescents from low socioeconomic groups have lower academic aspirations and are at greater risk for dropping out of school.	• Point out the relevance of various academic content domains for adolescents' long-term goals. • Design assignments in which adolescents apply academic content to real-world adult tasks and problems. • Allow teens to pursue personal interests within the context of particular academic domains.

Sources: Bandura et al., 2001; L. A. Bell, 1989; J. H. Block, 1983; Burhans & Dweck, 1995; H. Cooper & Dorr, 1995; Deaux, 1984; Deshler & Schumaker, 1988; Dien, 1998; Durkin, 1995; Dweck, 1986, 2000; Eccles & Midgley, 1989; Eccles et al., 1998; Fewell & Sandall, 1983; Graham, 1989; L. Green et al., 1994; Halpern, 1992; Harter, 1992, 1996; Jacobs et al., 2002; B. Jacobsen et al., 1986; Juvonen, 2000; Lieberman, 1993; Lillard, 1997; Linder, 1993; Lockhart et al., 2002; McCall, 1994; Nicholls, 1990; F. Pajares & Valiante, 1999; Paris & Cunningham, 1996; Peak, 1993; C. Peterson, 1990; Portes, 1996; Rotenberg & Mayer, 1990; Rovee-Collier, 1999; Sadker & Sadker, 1994; Schultz & Switzky, 1990; Seligman, 1991; Vaughn et al., 1984; Wigfield et al., 1991; Ziegert et al., 2001.

Children learn more effectively when they are intrinsically rather than extrinsically motivated.

changes in children's behavior. Such reinforcers have disadvantages, however. Although they provide a source of extrinsic motivation, they can undermine children's *intrinsic* motivation, especially when children perceive them to be controlling, manipulative, or in some other way limiting their autonomy and sense of self-determination (Deci & Ryan, 1987). Furthermore, they may communicate the message that assigned tasks are unpleasant chores (why else would a reinforcer be necessary?), rather than activities to be carried out and enjoyed for their own sake (Hennessey, 1995; Stipek, 1993).

Ideally, teachers and other adults should focus children's attention not on the external consequences of their efforts but on the internal pleasures—the feelings of enjoyment, satisfaction, and pride—that their accomplishments bring. Adults can also increase children's intrinsic motivation for learning new topics and skills using strategies such as these (Brophy, 2004):

• Piquing children's curiosity with new and intriguing objects
• Incorporating fantasy, adventure, or suspense into activities
• Creating disequilibrium by presenting puzzling phenomena
• Getting children physically involved with a topic (e.g., through role playing or hands-on experimentation)
• Relating important skills and subject matter to children's interests and goals
• Offering choices when several alternatives will be equally effective in helping children acquire desired skills
• Identifying areas in which each child can be especially successful

In addition, adults should communicate their own enthusiasm for a topic or activity, as 12-year-old Claudia points out in the "Intrinsic Motivation: Early Adolescence" video clip on Observation CD 3:

Hear Claudia describe environmental factors affecting her motivation in the "Intrinsic Motivation: Early Adolescence" clip on Observation CD 3.

Interviewer: What do teachers do that encourages you to do well?
Claudia: Like, when they kind of sound enthusiastic. They don't just teach everything, they have a little fun with it, too.
Interviewer: Why do you think that helps?
Claudia: So they . . . we can stay focused.

Interviewer: What kinds of things do you think make it hard for kids to pay attention at school?

Claudia: If the teacher's not sure what they're doing, or they just keep playing movies over and over.

● *Enhance children's self-efficacy for mastering important knowledge and skills.* One important way to enhance children's self-efficacy in a particular domain is, of course, to help them achieve success in the domain—for instance, by tailoring instruction to their existing ability levels, scaffolding their efforts, and so on. Another effective approach is to show them *other people's* successes. When children see peers of similar age and ability successfully accomplish a task, they are more likely to believe that they, too, can accomplish it. In one study (Schunk & Hanson, 1985), elementary school children having trouble with subtraction were given 25 subtraction problems to complete. Children who had seen another student successfully complete the problems got an average of 19 correct, whereas those who saw a teacher complete the problems got only 13 correct, and those who saw no model at all solved only 8.

Adult models, too, can enhance children's self-efficacy, especially if the adults have characteristics and backgrounds similar to children's own. For instance, young people from ethnic minority groups benefit from observing successful minority adults, and youngsters with disabilities become more optimistic about their own futures when they meet adults successfully coping with and overcoming disabilities (Pang, 1995; L. E. Powers, Sowers, & Stevens, 1995).

● *Maintain children's sense of self-determination when describing rules and giving instructions.* Every classroom needs a few rules and procedures to ensure that children act appropriately and activities run smoothly. Furthermore, teachers and other adults must often impose guidelines and restrictions about how children carry out assigned tasks. The trick is to present these rules, procedures, guidelines, and restrictions without communicating an intention to *control* children's behavior and thereby undermining their sense of self-determination. Instead, adults should present them as *information*—for instance, as conditions that can help children accomplish important goals and objectives (Deci, 1992; Koestner, Ryan, Bernieri, & Holt, 1984). Following are examples:

- "We can make sure everyone has an equal chance to speak and be heard if we listen without interrupting and if we raise our hands when we want to contribute to the discussion."
- "I'm giving you a particular format to follow when you do your math homework. If you use this format, it will be easier for me to figure out which concepts you understand and which ones you need more help with."
- "Let's remember that other children will be using the same paints and brushes later today, so we need to make sure everything we use now is still in tip-top shape when we're done. It's important, then, that we rinse the brushes in water and wipe them on a paper towel before we switch to a new color. We should also clean the brushes thoroughly when we're done painting."

● *Encourage children to shoot for specific goals.* Often children respond more favorably to goals they set for themselves than to goals others have set for them (Wentzel, 1999), possibly because self-chosen goals help them maintain a sense of self-determination. Yet many children (younger ones especially) often have trouble conceptualizing a "future" that is abstract and perhaps many years down the road (Bandura, 1997; Husman & Freeman, 1999). They may initially respond more favorably to short-term, concrete goals—perhaps learning a certain number of math facts or irregular French verbs in a given week, getting the next belt in karate, or earning a merit badge in a scout troop (Bandura & Schunk, 1981; Brophy, 2004; Schunk & Rice, 1989). By setting and working for a series of short-term goals, children get regular feedback about the progress they are making, acquire a greater sense of self-efficacy that they can master new skills, and achieve at higher levels (Kluger & DeNisi, 1998; Page-Voth & Graham, 1999; Schunk, 1996). In Figure 13-3, 10-year-old Amaryth describes goals she set for herself in athletics and academics,

Figure 13-3

Children are often more motivated when they have specific goals to shoot for. Here 10-year-old Amaryth describes how she worked toward goals on the soccer field and in the classroom.

as well as how she worked to achieve her goals. Her teacher awarded her a Goal Medal for successfully meeting her goals.

As children reach adolescence, their increasing capacity for abstract thought allows them to envision and work toward long-term goals—perhaps making a varsity sports team, gaining admission to a prestigious college, or having a career in journalism. The following exercise, "Kiley's Goals," presents the aspirations of one young woman who seems to have a good idea of what she wants to accomplish in life.

INTERPRETING CHILDREN'S ARTIFACTS AND ACTIONS — Kiley's Goals

At age 15, Kiley identified the 10 goals shown here for one of her 10th-grade teachers. As you look at her goals, think about how valuable they are apt to be in motivating her and helping her choose activities and focus her efforts.

> **Goals (10)**
> 1. get good grades throughout h/s
> 2. go to acting school
> 3. perform on broadway
> 4. act on small TV show
> 5. raise a family
> 6. get a house with a big backyard near the beach
> 7. go to Europe
> 8. keep all my teeth
> 9. have a lot of family + friends
> 10. die at an old age

Connecting Concepts
This is the same Kiley whose essay appears in the "Hermit Crab" exercise in Chapter 12.

Like many teenagers, Kiley has goals related to her professional life (becoming a successful actress), her personal life (raising a family, owning a home), and her physical well-being (keeping her teeth, having a long and healthy life). By and large, her goals are long-term, fairly abstract ones that should help her focus her efforts. But sometimes teenagers' abstract goals are so vague that they are of little use in guiding day-to-day decision making. This is the case, for example, with the goal "get good grades throughout [high school]." How high must Kiley's grades be in order to be "good"? And what specific steps should she take in the short run to achieve those grades? Consider, too, the goal "die healthy at an old age." What must Kiley do to increase her odds of being healthy at, say, age 80? Children and adolescents alike are apt to set more useful goals when their teachers initially scaffold their efforts, perhaps by providing examples of concrete criteria toward which to strive. For example, rather than striving for "good grades," Kiley might work toward improving specific skills in writing, math, and music. Rather than hoping to "die healthy at an old age," she might identify physical activities that will build her strength and stamina.

Kiley is clearly aiming high in her aspirations. Yet perhaps as a result of low self-efficacy or limited financial resources, many other adolescents set their sights quite low or in some other way limit their future options. Teachers and other adults should not only encourage these young people to think ambitiously but also convince them that high goals are achievable. For instance, when encouraging girls to consider stereotypically masculine career paths, adults might provide examples of women who have led successful and happy lives in those careers. When encouraging teens from low-income families to think about going to college, they might assist with filling out scholarship applications and scheduling appointments with college financial aid officers.

● *Encourage mastery goals as well as (ideally even more than) performance goals.* To some degree, performance goals are inevitable in today's schools and in society at large. Children and adolescents will invariably look to their peers' performance as one criterion for evaluating their own performance, and many aspects of the adult world (gaining admission to college, seeking employment, working in private industry, etc.) are inherently competitive in nature. Yet adults do youngsters a disservice when they focus attention on "looking good"

DEVELOPMENT AND PRACTICE

Helping Children Meet Their Social Goals

- Continually communicate the message that you like and respect the young people with whom you are working.

  A second-grade teacher tells a student that she saw his karate exhibition at the local mall over the weekend. "You were great!" she says. "How many years have you been studying karate?"

- Plan learning tasks that involve social interaction.

  A sixth-grade social studies teacher incorporates classroom debates, small-group discussions, and cooperative learning tasks into each month's lesson plans.

- Get youngsters involved in large projects in which they must all work toward the common good.

  The eighth graders at one middle school are sharply divided into "popular" and "unpopular" groups, and some students are routinely bullied or excluded from social interaction. The school music teacher suggests that a production of the musical *You're a Good Man, Charlie Brown* become a project for the entire class. All 92 eighth graders are either in the cast or working on costumes, scenery, or lighting. The sheer ambitiousness of the project and the fact that the class's efforts will eventually be on public display instill a cohesiveness and class spirit among the students, with formerly popular and unpopular students working collaboratively and respectfully with one another (M. Thompson & Grace, 2001).

- Teach strategies that enable youngsters to present themselves well to others.

  As fourth graders prepare for upcoming oral reports on their small-group science projects, their teacher offers suggestions for capturing their audience's interest. "You might present a puzzling question your classmates would really like to know the answer to," she says. "Or you might show them something that will surprise them. Hands-on activities are good, too. For example, perhaps you can think of a short, simple experiment they might conduct to arrive at the same conclusion *you* did."

- Give praise in private when peers do not seem to value high achievement.

  A high school English teacher reads a particularly creative story written by a young man who, she knows, is quite concerned about maintaining his "cool" image. On the second page of his story (which the student's classmates are unlikely to see), she writes, "This is great work, Tony! I think it's good enough to enter into the state writing contest. Can we meet before or after school some day this week to talk more about the contest?"

- Respect individual differences.

  A child care provider notices that some of the young children in his care have a greater need for social contact than others. Some children really seem to enjoy sociodramatic play activities, while others are more interested in manipulating and experimenting with physical objects. Although he interacts with all of the children regularly, he is careful not to interrupt when children are happily and productively engrossed in either interactive or solitary play activities.

and surpassing peers. When adults instead explain how certain knowledge and skills will be useful down the road, highlight ongoing progress, and acknowledge that effective learning requires exerting effort and making mistakes, they are emphasizing mastery goals that will enhance learning and achievement over the long run (Bong, 2001; Brophy, 2004; Urdan, Ryan, Anderman, & Gheen, 2002).

● *Downplay the seriousness of failures.* Children and adolescents are more apt to accept responsibility for their failures—and therefore to learn from them—if adults don't make a big deal of them (Katkovsky, Crandall, & Good, 1967; N. E. Perry & Winne, 2004). For instance, teachers might give students numerous opportunities to improve assignments and overall class grades (Ames, 1992). In some instances adults may also find it appropriate to focus children's attention on the *processes* they use to tackle assigned tasks and solve problems, rather than on the final outcome of their efforts (Schunk & Swartz, 1993; Stipek & Kowalski, 1989). For example, a teacher may occasionally give an assignment with instructions like these:

> It doesn't matter at all how many you get right. In fact, these problems are kind of hard. I'm just interested in learning more about what [you] think about while [you're] working on problems like these. I want you to focus on the problem and just say out loud whatever you're thinking while you're working—whatever comes into your head. (Stipek & Kowalski, 1989, p. 387)

● *Help youngsters meet their social goals.* One of the reasons older children and adolescents focus so much on performance goals is that making a good impression will help them gain the respect and companionship of their peers. They encounter most of their peers at school and in other large-group situations, and so they will naturally make social goals a high priority in these settings. The Development and Practice feature "Helping Children Meet Their Social Goals" suggests several ways in which educators can address youngsters' social needs within the context of academic instruction and other learning activities.

● *Give encouraging messages about the causes of successes and failures.* When commenting on children's successes, probably the best approach is to attribute the successes partly to a relatively stable ability and partly to such controllable factors as effort and learning strategies (Schunk, 1990; B. Weiner, 1984). In this way, adults provide assurance that children are certainly capable of succeeding but remind them that continued success also requires work and perseverance. For example, a teacher might say:

- "You've done very well. Obviously you're good at this, and you've been trying very hard to get better."
- "Your project shows a lot of talent and a lot of hard work."

When identifying possible causes for failures, however, adults should focus primarily on effort and better strategies—attributions that are internal, unstable, and controllable—and they should usually give such feedback in private (Brophy, 2004; Dweck, 2000). Following are examples:

- "The more you practice, the better you will get."
- "Perhaps you need to study a little bit each night rather than waiting until the night before. And let's talk about how you might also study *differently* than you did last time."

When children's failures are consistently attributed to lack of effort or ineffective strategies, rather than to low ability or uncontrollable external factors, and when increased effort or new strategies do, in fact, produce success, children often work harder, persist longer in the face of failure, and seek help when they need it (Dweck & Elliott, 1983; Eccles & Wigfield, 1985; Graham, 1991; Robertson, 2000).

The most effective feedback—no matter whether it commends successes or identifies weaknesses—also maintains children's sense of self-determination. More specifically, it provides information about children's performance but doesn't convey a desire to control their behavior (Brophy, 2004; Burnett, 2001; Deci, 1992). For example, in complimenting a student who has written a good persuasive essay, a teacher might say, "Your arguments are well organized, easy to follow, and quite convincing" (emphasis is on what the student has done well), rather than saying, "Good job in adhering to my guidelines and suggestions" (emphasis is on following the teacher's instructions). And in admonishing students for off-task behavior during a cooperative learning activity, a teacher might ask, "Are you three going to have time to work on your project tonight if you don't finish it during class?" (emphasis is on students' own time management concerns), rather than saying, "How many times do I have to remind this group to *get to work*?" (emphasis is on keeping the students under control).

● *Use extrinsic reinforcers when necessary.* Despite adults' best efforts, children sometimes have little interest in acquiring knowledge or skills critical for their later success in life. On such occasions adults may have to provide extrinsic reinforcers—not only praise but perhaps also free time, grades, special privileges, or points toward a small prize—to encourage learning or desired behaviors. How can adults use such reinforcers without undermining children's intrinsic motivation? One effective strategy is to reinforce children not simply for doing something but for doing it *well*. Another is to communicate that an extrinsic reinforcer is merely a concrete acknowledgment of significant progress or achievement—an accomplishment about which children should feel very proud (Brophy, 2004; Cameron, 2001).

When adults give reinforcement in a group situation, they should make sure that all children have a reasonable opportunity to earn it. For instance, they should be careful that in their attempts to improve the behavior of some children, they don't ignore other, equally deserving children. Furthermore, they should take into account the fact that a few children may have exceptional difficulty performing particular behaviors through no fault of their own. Consider the case of a young immigrant girl who had to adjust very quickly from a 10:00–5:00 school day in Vietnam to a 7:45–3:45 school day in the United States:

[E]very week on Friday after school, the teacher would give little presents to kids that were good during the week. And if you were tardy, you wouldn't get a present. . . . I would never get one because I would always come to school late, and that hurt at first. I had a terrible time. I didn't look forward to going to school. (Igoa, 1995, p. 95)

When using concrete reinforcers, adults should help children delay gratification for longer and longer periods. For example, even 4- and 5-year-olds can learn to delay gratification for a few hours if their preschool teachers tell them that rewards for

When used strategically and temporarily, extrinsic reinforcement can help children acquire foundational skills.

DEVELOPMENT AND PRACTICE

Encouraging and Supporting Students at Risk

- Make the curriculum relevant to students' lives and needs.

  A junior high school science teacher shows students how basic principles of sound reveal themselves in rock music. On one occasion the teacher brings in a guitar and explains why holding down a string at different points along the neck of the guitar creates different frequencies and thus different notes.

- Use students' strengths to promote high self-efficacy in certain domains.

  A low-income, inner-city elementary school forms a singing group (the "Jazz Cats") for which students must try out. The group performs at a variety of community events, and the students enjoy considerable visibility for their talent. Group members exhibit increased self-esteem, improvement in other school subjects, and greater teamwork and leadership skills (Jenlink, 1994).

- Provide extra support for academic success.

  At the beginning of class each day, a middle school teacher distributes a general outline that students can use to guide their note taking. She also writes two or three questions on the board that students should be able to answer at the end of the lesson.

- Communicate optimism about students' chances for long-term personal and professional success.

  A mathematics teacher at a low-income inner-city high school recruits students to participate in an intensive math program. The teacher and stu-

dents work on evenings, Saturdays, and vacations, and all of them later pass the Advanced Placement calculus exam (see the final case study in Chapter 10).

- Show students that they are personally responsible for their successes.

  A teacher says to a student, "Your essay about recent hate crimes in the community is very powerful. You've given the topic considerable thought, and you've clearly mastered some of the techniques of persuasive writing that we've talked about this semester. I'd like you to think seriously about submitting your essay to the local paper for its editorial page. Can we spend some time during lunch tomorrow fine-tuning the grammar and spelling?"

- Get students involved in extracurricular activities.

  A teacher encourages a student with a strong throwing arm to go out for the school baseball team and introduces the student to the baseball coach. The coach, in turn, expresses his enthusiasm for having the student join the team and asks several current team members to help him feel at home during team practices.

- Involve students in school policy and management decisions.

  At an inner-city high school, students and teachers hold regular "town meetings" to discuss issues of fairness and justice and establish rules for appropriate behavior. Meetings are democratic, with students and teachers alike having one vote apiece, and the will of the majority is binding (A. Higgins, 1995).

desired behaviors (e.g., sharing toys with other children) will be coming later in the day (S. A. Fowler & Baer, 1981). Teaching children effective waiting strategies—perhaps frequently reminding themselves, "If I wait a little longer, I will get a bigger cookie," or perhaps engaging in activities that get their minds off an upcoming reward—also enhances their ability to delay gratification (Binder, Dixon, & Ghezzi, 2000; Dixon & Cummings, 2001).

● *Be especially attentive to the needs of students at risk.* In the opening case study, Derrika is showing early warning signs that she may not acquire the academic skills she will need to be successful in the adult world. In other words, Derrika is a **student at risk.** Many students at risk drop out before high school graduation, and many others graduate without basic skills in reading or mathematics (National Assessment of Educational Progress, 1985; Slavin, 1989). Such individuals are often ill-equipped to make productive contributions to their families, communities, or society at large.

Some students at risk have special educational needs, such as learning disabilities. Others may have cultural backgrounds that don't mesh easily with the dominant culture at school. Still others may come from home environments in which academic success is neither supported nor encouraged.

Children and adolescents at risk come from all socioeconomic levels, but youngsters of economically poor, single-parent families are especially likely to leave school before high school graduation (Steinberg, Blinde, & Chan, 1984). Boys are more likely to drop out than girls, and African Americans, Hispanic Americans, and Native Americans have higher dropout rates than other groups (L. S. Miller, 1995; Roderick & Camburn, 1999). Students at risk often have a long history of low academic achievement, ineffective learning strategies, low self-esteem, poor relationships with teachers, and little sense of an emotional bond with their school (Belfiore & Hornyak, 1998; Christenson & Thurlow, 2004; Finn, 1989; Garnier, Stein, & Jacobs, 1997; V. E. Lee & Burkam, 2003).

Students at risk are a diverse group of individuals with a diverse set of needs and motives, but the motivational strategies we've listed in the preceding pages are critical for most of them. The Development and Practice feature "Encouraging and Supporting Students at Risk" offers additional suggestions. However, even the most motivated of youngsters will not succeed in the secondary grades unless they also know how to take charge of their own behavior. We turn to the development of such *self-regulation* now.

student at risk
Student who has a high probability of failing to acquire the minimal academic skills necessary for success in the adult world.

Self-Regulation

In the opening case study, Derrika has trouble getting herself out of bed for her first-period biology class, and she all too willingly cuts her afternoon classes. Her failing grades suggest that, in general, Derrika doesn't have the habits and skills—the self-discipline, if you will—that will keep her on a path to the college education she ultimately wants.

As you've seen, children and adolescents have a greater sense of self-determination and are more intrinsically motivated when they can make choices about what they do and so can direct the course of their lives to some degree. But making *wise* choices requires **self-regulation,** which includes capabilities such as the following:

- *Impulse control:* Resisting sudden urges to engage in forbidden or counterproductive behaviors
- *Emotional regulation:* Expressing emotions in a socially appropriate manner and controlling them in ways that facilitate goal attainment
- *Self-socialization:* Forming beliefs about society's standards for behavior and voluntarily acting in accordance with those standards
- *Goal setting:* Identifying and striving for valued, self-chosen goals
- *Delaying gratification:* Putting off small, immediate rewards in anticipation of larger rewards at a later time
- *Self-motivation:* Creating conditions that make a task more engaging or rewarding
- *Self-regulated learning:* Directing and monitoring one's own attention and learning strategies in ways that promote effective cognitive processing

——————— Connecting Concepts
Learn more about *emotional regulation, self-socialization,* and *self-regulated learning* in Chapters 11, 12, and 7, respectively.

As you discovered in Chapter 7, children who regulate their own learning are more academically successful than those who do not. Self-regulation is important in social relationships as well. Children who can control their emotional reactions and other behaviors have better social skills and are more popular with peers (M. B. Bronson, 2000; Fabes et al., 1999; Patrick, 1997).

Developmental Trends in Self-Regulation

Young children have considerable difficulty controlling their own behavior. Parents often complain about the terrible twos, a period between the second and third birthdays when children are mobile enough to get into almost anything and make quite a fuss when they don't get their own way.[1] Self-regulation requires several capabilities that are only beginning to emerge in young children. For instance, children must anticipate the consequences of various courses of action. They must also inhibit thoughts and behaviors that are unlikely to be productive. And they must have sufficient working memory capacity to think about what they want to do, how they might do it, and perhaps why they *shouldn't* do it. Such capabilities depend, in part, on neurological maturation in the early years (Biemiller et al., 1998; Blair, 2002; M. B. Bronson, 2000; Dempster & Corkill, 1999).

As you've already learned in Chapters 7 and 11, children become increasingly able to regulate their learning and emotional responses as they grow older. Researchers have identified three additional developmental trends in self-regulation:

● *Children increasingly talk their way, and eventually think their way, through situations and tasks.* Self-talk and, later, inner speech seem to be key mechanisms through which children become able to regulate their behavior. As children acquire language skills, they begin to talk themselves through new challenges ("To tie my shoe, I need to put one lace over and then under the other; then I need to make a loop . . ."). Children gradually internalize their self-talk, first whispering to themselves and eventually just *mentally* telling themselves what they should do (Berk, 1994; Biemiller et al., 1998; Schimmoeller, 1998; Schutz & Davis, 2000).

——————— Connecting Concepts
For more on self-talk and inner speech, see the discussion of Vygotsky's theory in Chapter 6.

self-regulation
Directing and controlling one's own actions.

[1]The terrible twos may to some extent be a cultural phenomenon. When children are strongly encouraged to control their feelings even as toddlers, as is true in Chinese and Japanese cultures, the twos don't necessarily stand out as a difficult period (D. Y. F. Ho, 1994).

● *External rules and restrictions gradually become internalized.* Children can comply with simple requests and restrictions by the time they are 12 to 18 months old (Kaler & Kopp, 1990; Kopp, 1982). As they become increasingly verbal, they begin to use self-talk to prevent themselves from engaging in prohibited behaviors even when caregivers are absent—for instance, saying "no" or "can't" to themselves as they begin to reach for an electric outlet (Kochanska, 1993). By age 3 or 4, many children are acquiring flexible strategies for regulating their own behavior in accordance with adult rules and prohibitions. For example, if they are asked to wait for a short time (e.g., 15 minutes), they might invent games or sing to themselves to pass the time more quickly (Mischel & Ebbesen, 1970). If a playmate has an enticing toy, they may turn away and engage in an alternative activity as a way of lessening the temptation to grab the toy (Kopp, 1982). Children who have such strategies are better able to resist temptation (Mischel, Shoda, & Rodriguez, 1989).

During the preschool, elementary, and secondary school years, children and adolescents increasingly take ownership of society's rules and regulations (Deci & Ryan, 1995; Kochanska, Coy, & Murray, 2001). Possibly this ownership proceeds through the process of internalization of motivation portrayed earlier in Figure 13-2 (Deci & Ryan, 1995). The first sign of internalization (the *introjection* phase) is evident when children feel some internal pressure (e.g., guilt) to comply with rules and regulations. Later (at the *identification* phase), children start to perceive rules and other desired behaviors to be important or valuable to them personally. This phase is evident in an interview with 9-year-old Elena in the "Neighborhood: Middle Childhood" video clip on Observation CD 2:

In the "Neighborhood: Middle Childhood" clip on Observation CD 2, observe Elena's understanding that some laws are created to keep people safe.

> Interviewer: Neighborhoods and cities have lots of different laws. Why do you think people make these laws?
>
> Elena: For example, they closed this road because a lot of children were playing around here and some people just came zipping right through fast and fast and not going to the speed limit.
>
> Interviewer: What would it be like if we didn't have laws?
>
> Elena: If we didn't have these laws, by the time I step out of the door probably I would have a broken leg.

Finally (at the *integration* phase), rules and regulations become an integral part of children's sense of self. At this point, a teenage girl might define herself as being "law-abiding" or "concerned about others' welfare" and so strive to behave in ways consistent with her self-definition.

● *Self-evaluation becomes more frequent.* Infants and young toddlers do not seem to evaluate their own behavior, nor do they show much concern about how others evaluate it. In contrast, 2-year-olds often seek adults' approval for their actions (Stipek, Recchia, & McClintic, 1992). Sometime around age 3, children show the first signs of *self*-evaluation. For instance, they look happy when they're successful and sad when they fail (Heckenhausen, 1984, 1987).

As children move through the preschool, elementary, and middle school years, they show a marked increase in self-judgment (M. B. Bronson, 2000; van Kraayenoord & Paris, 1997). Their parents may praise certain behaviors and criticize others, their teachers give them frequent information about their academic performance, and their peers often let them know in no uncertain terms about the effectiveness of their social skills. Such feedback allows them to develop criteria by which they can more accurately judge their own actions. As their ability for self-reflection grows and they become increasingly concerned about others' perceptions, especially in adolescence, they look more closely at their own behavior and evaluate it in terms of how they think others will judge it (Dacey & Kenny, 1994; Lapsley, 1993; R. M. Ryan & Kuczkowski, 1994).

Connecting Concepts ――――――
Young adolescents often think other people are constantly observing and judging them (see the discussion of the *imaginary audience* phenomenon in Chapter 12).

Conditions That Foster Self-Regulation

Adults' parenting styles appear to influence the development of self-regulation. In general, *authoritative parenting* seems to be optimal. When parents, other caregivers, and teachers have warm and supportive relationships with children, set reasonable boundaries

Connecting Concepts ――――――
Chapter 5 explores the effects of parenting styles in more depth.

This girl's willingness to delay gratification—to save the freshly baked cookies for the school picnic—reflects her emerging self-regulation.

for behavior, and take everyone's needs into consideration, they create the conditions in which children learn to make appropriate choices and work toward productive goals (M. B. Bronson, 2000; Reeve, Bolt, & Cai, 1999; Zimmerman, 2004).

Children and adolescents are also more likely to become self-regulating when they have age-appropriate opportunities for independence (S. S. Feldman & Wentzel, 1990; I. W. Silverman & Ragusa, 1990; Zimmerman, 1998). They are most likely to benefit from such opportunities when they are taught the skills they need to productively direct their own behaviors and successfully overcome obstacles (Belfiore & Hornyak, 1998). Ideally, adults gradually release the apron strings over time, first providing considerable guidance but eventually giving only occasional suggestions and reminders as children show an ability to make good decisions (Mithaug & Mithaug, 2003; Stright, Neitzel, Sears, & Hoke-Sinex, 2001; Zimmerman, 2004).

Adults promote self-regulation in another way as well: by modeling self-regulating behaviors (M. B. Bronson, 2000; Zimmerman, 2004). In a classic study (Bandura & Mischel, 1965), fourth and fifth graders watched adult models make a series of choices between small, immediate rewards and more valuable, delayed ones (e.g., plastic chess pieces available that day versus wooden ones that they could have in 2 weeks). Some models chose the immediate rewards (e.g., saying, "Chess figures are chess figures. I can get much use out of the plastic ones right away," p. 701). Others chose the delayed rewards (e.g., saying, "The wooden chess figures are of much better quality, more attractive, and will last longer. I'll wait two weeks for the better ones," p. 701). Immediately after they had observed the models, and also on a second occasion several weeks later, the children themselves were asked to choose between small, immediate rewards and larger, delayed ones (e.g., a small plastic ball now or a much larger one in 2 weeks). The children were more likely to delay gratification if they had seen the model do likewise.

Diversity in Self-Regulation

To some extent children's ability to self-regulate their behavior appears to be a function of biology. Children with impulsive temperaments as toddlers or preschoolers tend to have trouble inhibiting inappropriate behaviors in the elementary grades (Eisenberg et al., 2004; Pfeifer, Goldsmith, Davidson, & Rickman, 2002). And children with biologically based disabilities—for instance, children with learning disabilities or mental illness—often have deficits in self-regulation (Siegel, 1999; Zimmerman, 2004).

Yet the environmental factors just identified, especially parenting behaviors and role models, also lead to considerable diversity in self-regulation. Perhaps as a result of such factors, children who grow up and attend school in low-income neighborhoods often don't acquire the basic self-regulating behaviors they need for success in secondary school (Roderick & Camburn, 1999; Wilson & Corbett, 2001). Consider the case of Anna who, like Derrika, is doing poorly in high school. Anna explains her poor performance in the first semester of ninth grade—mostly Ds and an F in science—this way:

> In geography, "he said the reason why I got a lower grade is 'cause I missed one assignment and I had to do a report, and I forgot that one." In English, "I got a C . . . 'cause we were supposed to keep a journal, and I keep on forgetting it 'cause I don't have a locker. Well I do, but my locker partner she lets her cousins use it, and I lost my two books there. . . . I would forget to buy a notebook, and then I would have them on separate pieces of paper, and I would lose them." And, in biology, "the reason I failed was because I lost my folder . . . it had everything I needed, and I had to do it again, and, by the time I had to turn in the new folder, I did, but he said it was too late . . . 'cause I didn't have the folder, and the folder has everything, all the work. . . . That's why I got an F." (Roderick & Camburn, 1999, p. 305)

Students like Anna, who seem absentminded about school assignments or unable to focus their efforts on productive goals, often benefit considerably from interventions designed to help them acquire self-regulation skills.

Promoting Self-Regulation

Children and adolescents are more likely to engage in self-regulating behaviors when they are intrinsically motivated to accomplish certain goals. To foster self-regulation, then, teachers and other adults must also foster intrinsic motivation—for example, by creating conditions in which youngsters have high self-efficacy and can maintain their sense of self-determination (M. B. Bronson, 2000). We offer the following recommendations:

● *Create an orderly and somewhat predictable environment.* Children are in a better position to make wise choices and direct their activities appropriately when they have some structure to guide them, know what to expect in the hours and days ahead, and can reasonably anticipate that certain behaviors will yield certain outcomes (e.g., M. B. Bronson, 2000). Communicating general guidelines for behavior, establishing regular routines for completing tasks and assignments, identifying the locations of items that children may need during the day (glue, hole punches, dictionaries, etc.)—all of these strategies can help children work productively with minimal guidance from adults.

● *Provide age-appropriate opportunities for choice and independence.* Older children and adolescents need frequent opportunities to make their own decisions and direct their own activities. Independent assignments, computer-based instructional programs, group projects, homework, and the like are clearly beneficial for these age-groups, especially when the activities are structured so that youngsters know how to proceed and understand the expectations for their performance (H. Cooper & Valentine, 2001; Corno & Mandinach, 2004; Zimmerman, 1998). When youngsters make poor choices, adults should offer constructive feedback that will nurture, rather than dampen, their enthusiasm for independence on future occasions.

Although young children inevitably require some adult supervision to keep them safe, they, too, benefit from having some choice and independence (e.g., N. E. Perry, VandeKamp, Mercer, & Nordby, 2002). However, caregivers and teachers must anticipate and minimize problems that are likely to arise when children make their own decisions. For instance, preschool and kindergarten teachers might create a few rules for taking turns and sharing materials, designate certain areas of the classroom for messy activities (e.g., painting, working with clay), and put potentially dangerous objects out of reach (M. B. Bronson, 2000).

Children with mental and physical disabilities may especially need opportunities for independence, as adults often monitor their behavior and well-being fairly closely (Sands & Wehmeyer, 1996). Independent activities should, of course, be tailored to children's unique characteristics and abilities. For example, a teacher might ask a student with mental retardation to take the daily attendance sheet to the office but remind her that as soon as she has done so, she should return immediately to class (Patton et al., 1996). Or a teacher might give a student who is blind a chance to explore the classroom before other students have arrived, locating various objects in the classroom (wastebasket, pencil sharpener, etc.) and identifying distinctive sounds (e.g., the buzz of a wall clock) that will help the student get his bearings (J. W. Wood, 1998).

● *Provide help and guidance when, but only when, children really need it.* Being self-regulating doesn't necessarily always mean doing something independently. It also involves knowing when assistance is needed and seeking it out (Karabenick & Sharma, 1994). Adult assistance often provides the scaffolding that children need to succeed at new and challenging tasks. Accordingly, adults should welcome any reasonable requests for help or guidance and not convey the message that children are "dumb" or bothersome for asking (R. S. Newman & Schwager, 1992).

In some instances even adolescents may initially need considerable structure to get them on the road to independence. For students like Derrika and Anna, after-school homework programs are often effective (Belfiore & Hornyak, 1998; Eilam, 2001; S. D. Miller, Heafner, Massey, & Strahan, 2003). In one approach (Belfiore & Hornyak, 1998), students report to a particular classroom at the end of the regular school day, where they find their homework assignments on a shelf. They learn to use a checklist such as that depicted in Figure 13-4, checking off steps they have completed. They also learn to administer **self-reinforcement,** giving themselves a reward (e.g., allowing themselves to play a board game or spend time on a computer) whenever they have completed all the steps. In addition, they learn problem-solving strategies for difficulties they might encounter (e.g., asking

self-reinforcement
Self-imposed pleasurable consequence for a desired behavior.

Figure 13-4

Daily checklist for homework completion.
From "Operant Theory and Application to Self-Monitoring in Adolescents" by P. J. Belfiore and R. S. Hornyak, 1998. In *Self-Regulated Learning: From Teaching to Self-Reflective Practice* (p. 190), by D. H. Schunk & B. J. Zimmerman (Eds.), New York: Guilford Press. Copyright 1998 by Guilford Press. Reprinted with permission.

STUDENT: _____	DATE: _____		
SUBJECT AREA: _____	GRADE: _____		
TEACHER: _____			

STEPS TO FOLLOW	YES	NO	NOTES
1. Did I turn in yesterday's homework?			
2. Did I write all homework assignments in my notebook?			
3. Is all homework in homework folder?			
4. Are all my materials to complete homework with me?			
5. BEGIN HOMEWORK?			
6. Are all homework papers completed?			
7. Did someone check homework to make sure it was completed?			
8. After checking, did I put all homework back in folder?			
9. Did I give this paper to teacher?			

a teacher for assistance when they can't find needed materials). Initially, a teacher monitors whether their checklists accurately reflect what they've accomplished, but eventually such monitoring is no longer necessary. And over time, as students acquire a sense of accomplishment about completing their homework each day, the self-imposed extrinsic reinforcers become less critical.

Sometimes, however, children ask for help when they really just want attention or companionship. For instance, if a 4-year-old asks for help on a puzzle, an astute preschool teacher might, after watching the child work at the puzzle, say, "I don't think you need help with this. But I can keep you company for a few minutes if you'd like" (M. B. Bronson, 2000).

● *To guide behavior, use suggestions and rationales, rather than direct commands, as much as possible.* Youngsters are more likely to internalize and follow guidelines for behavior when adults make suggestions about how to accomplish goals successfully and provide a rationale for why some behaviors are unacceptable (M. B. Bronson, 2000; Hoffman, 1975). Figure 13-5 shows how one fifth-grade teacher encourages self-regulation by using a handout that explains his expectations for behavior. The handout, distributed during an open house at school, also gives parents important information about how the teacher conducts his classroom.

Consistent with what we have learned about cognitive development, younger children respond more favorably to suggestions that are concrete rather than abstract. For example, to avoid incidents of bumping and pushing in the cafeteria, teachers at one school asked students to imagine they had "magic bubbles" around them. The students could keep their bubbles from "popping" if they kept a safe distance between themselves and others. This simple strategy resulted in fewer behavior problems at lunchtime (Sullivan-DeCarlo, DeFalco, & Roberts, 1998).

● *Teach specific self-regulation skills.* Children and adolescents become more self-regulating when they learn specific strategies for directing and evaluating their own behavior. Such strategies include the following:

• **Self-monitoring.** Children aren't always aware of how frequently they do something wrong or how infrequently they do something right. To help them focus on these things, adults can ask them to observe and record their own behavior. Such self-focused observation and recording often bring about significant improvements

self-monitoring
Process of observing and recording one's own behavior.

MY BROAD GOALS

- Plan and implement a balanced curriculum.

- Help students develop a repertoire of skills and styles of working (open-ended assignments/discrete assignments; collaboration/individual).

- Get students engaged in mental activity; emphasize learning and being a strategic thinker.

- Help students to be both organized and flexible, deal with a schedule, and set priorities for time and things done.

DISCIPLINE

Overarching Golden Rule
Treat others as you would like to be treated.

BASIC RULES

1. Be responsible for your own actions.
2. Use work time for school work; use recess time for play.
3. Appreciate other people; respect the rights of others.
4. Make your behavior appropriate for the situation.

I try to be fair and not play favorites. Everyone is valued and respected. I run the classroom to take care of everyone. The focus is on correcting the behaviors that need correcting so that we develop habit patterns of behavior that serve instructional goals.

My appeal: You've been taught at home for years how to behave. You have a good head—now use it.

Typical fifth-grade problems:

1. Cliques and excluding others—being angry at lunch, friends again after school. A problem especially with the girls.
2. Silliness and not setting boundaries for appropriate behavior, such as bringing recess into the classroom. A problem especially with the boys.
3. Too much undirected talk, talk across desks and across the room, especially during transition times.
4. Restroom problems—talking loudly in the hallways, messing around and loitering in the restrooms.
5. Whininess and sneakiness. Talk to me honestly and openly about problems.
6. "Romance" (going-with) talk or teasing. These are absolutely not allowed in the classroom.

Figure 13-5

A fifth-grade teacher's goals and expectations. In this handout, Michael Gee describes his expectations for students' behavior and encourages age-appropriate self-regulation.

Adapted with the permission of Michael Gee, Barrington Elementary School, Columbus, Ohio.

in children's academic and social behaviors (K. R. Harris, 1986; Mace & Kratochwill, 1988; Webber, Scheuermann, McCall, & Coleman, 1993).

- **Self-instructions.** Sometimes children simply need a reminder about how to respond in particular situations. By teaching them specific ways of talking themselves through these situations, adults give them a means through which they remind *themselves* about appropriate actions, thereby helping them to control their own behavior. Such a strategy is often effective in helping children with poor impulse control (Casey & Burton, 1982; Meichenbaum, 1985).

- **Self-motivation.** Children may also need strategies to keep themselves motivated during dull but important tasks. For example, they might consciously identify several reasons why completing an activity will help them over the long run. They might embellish a task in some way to make it more interesting. Or they might learn how to divide a lengthy task into a number of small pieces and then reinforce themselves after completing each one (Wolters, 2003).

- **Self-evaluation.** To become truly self-regulating, children must acquire appropriate criteria by which to judge their own behavior. For instance, teachers might ask students to reflect on their improvement ("What can we do that we didn't do before?") or to complete self-assessment instruments that show them what to look for

self-instructions
Specific directions that one gives oneself while performing a complex behavior; a form of *self-talk*.

self-motivation
Intentionally using certain strategies to keep oneself on task during a dull but important activity.

self-evaluation
Judging one's own performance in accordance with predetermined criteria.

in their own performance (Paris & Ayres, 1994; N. E. Perry et al., 2002). At the secondary school level (and perhaps even sooner), young people might even play a role in identifying the criteria by which their performance might reasonably be evaluated.

The following exercise, "Tears of Pearls," illustrates a strategy one sixth-grade teacher uses in her efforts to help her students become more self-regulating—something that will become especially important when they begin middle school the following year.

INTERPRETING CHILDREN'S ARTIFACTS AND ACTIONS

Tears of Pearls

When students in a sixth-grade class don't turn in homework assignments, a teacher intern insists that they write a 200-word essay explaining the missing homework and describing how they plan to be more diligent next time. In this essay, 11-year-old Alicia explains why she didn't turn in her analysis of the lyrics to the song "Tears of Pearls," by the Australian singing duo Savage Garden. As you read the essay, think about its possible benefits, and look for evidence of self-regulation in Alicia's study habits.

200 word essay

I am very sorry this happened. I feel guilty that I forgot to pass the assignment Tears of Pearls in. Every time in social studies I will make sure I passed in <u>all</u> my assignments so that this will not happen again. I understand how hard it is for you to keep track of two classes work and I think it is a good idea you are doing this. I wish I wasn't so forgetful. Hopefully this will not happen to me again. Every night I will check my social studies folder to make sure the homework is complete. Now all I have to do is get it to school and put it in the pass in box. It was complete but I just forgot to pass it in. Every night I do my homework and my mom checks it and it goes in my back pack but sometimes I just forget to give it to you. I'm sorry. I really am. It is sometimes hard for us kids sometimes too. It is sometimes hard for us kids to be prepared but I guess that's just something we'll have to learn before middle school! Oh and sometimes we're packed with homework and the next day its hard to get it back together and into your and Mrs. Copeland's hands as soon as possible (A.S.A.P.). Like I said it's hard for you too and I can understand, but sometimes things (other) things are hard for us too. For the third time im really am sorry

sincerly,
Alicia

Writing an essay of this kind has several potential advantages. First, by knowing why homework was turned in late, the teacher can help Alicia develop a better strategy for future homework assignments (e.g., Alicia might make a point to check her social studies folder as soon as she arrives at class each day). Second, in writing the essay, Alicia must engage in some degree of self-monitoring and self-evaluation. And third, Alicia must describe a future course of action (how she intends to get future assignments in on time) to someone else.

It is clear in Alicia's essay that she does have some ability to regulate her learning and behavior, albeit with assistance from her mother. In particular, she says, "Every night I do my homework and my mom checks it and it goes in my backpack." She also feels *guilt* about not getting her homework in on time, a reaction indicating that she is at least in the introjection phase of internalizing certain guidelines for behavior (look once again at Figure 13-2). Much as guilt is an unpleasant feeling, it can be an extremely powerful motivator in helping youngsters adhere to certain standards for behavior. It is especially important in moral reasoning and behavior, as you will discover shortly.

The Development and Practice feature "Teaching Self-Management Skills" illustrates a variety of self-management skills. Adults must, of course, monitor children's ability to use them and make adjustments accordingly.

DEVELOPMENT AND PRACTICE

Teaching Self-Management Skills

- **Have children observe and record their own behavior.**

  When a student has trouble staying on task during class activities, her teacher asks her to stop and reflect on her behavior every 10 minutes (with the aid of an egg timer) and determine whether she has been on task during each interval. The student uses the checklist shown below to record her observations. Within a couple of weeks, the student's on-task behavior has noticeably improved.

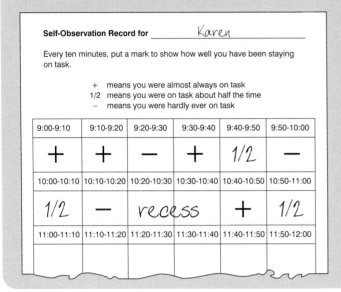

- **Teach children instructions they can give themselves as reminders of what they need to do.**

  A school counselor helps a fifth grader control his impulsive behavior on multiple-choice tests by having him mentally say to himself as he reads each question: "Read the entire question. Then look at each answer carefully and decide whether it is correct or incorrect. Then choose the answer that seems *most* correct."

- **Help children identify ways to embellish tedious tasks to make them more enjoyable and rewarding.**

  A third-grade teacher suggests that students practice writing the week's new spelling words at home every night. "That might not sound like much fun," she says, "but it's an important thing to do. Who can think of a way to make spelling practice more fun?" One student suggests cutting letters out of grocery store flyers and pasting them together to make the words. Another suggests trying to think of sentences that spell the words with first letters—for example, "*Eighty-nine overweight unicorns get hiccups*" spells *enough*.

- **Teach children to reinforce themselves for appropriate behavior.**

  A middle school teacher suggests that her students can develop more regular study habits by making a favorite activity—for example, shooting baskets, watching television, or calling a friend on the telephone—contingent on completing their homework first.

- **Encourage children to evaluate their own performance.**

  Early in the season, the coach of a boys' baseball team videotapes each boy as he practices batting, pitching, and fielding ground balls. The coach then models good form for each of these activities and lists several things the boys should look for as they watch themselves on tape.

Moral Reasoning and Behavior

One very important domain in which most children and adolescents become increasingly self-regulating is the moral domain. An aspect of social-emotional development, **moral development** involves acquiring standards about right and wrong, thinking more thoughtfully and abstractly about moral issues, and increasingly engaging in prosocial behaviors that reflect concern for other people's rights and needs.

Some early theorists (e.g., Sigmund Freud, Jean Piaget) suggested that young children base their decisions about right and wrong exclusively on what adults tell them to do and not do and on which behaviors adults reward and punish. Young children certainly do try out a wide variety of behaviors to see how their parents and other caregivers will respond. But developmental researchers have found that moral development is *not* simply a process of adopting other people's moral guidelines and teachings (Damon, 1988; A. Higgins, 1995; Turiel, 1998). Instead, youngsters construct their *own* standards about what is morally "right" and "wrong," and they often revisit and revise these standards over time. Furthermore, children's ability to think about complex moral issues depends on advancing cognitive capabilities, such as abstract thought and perspective-taking ability (Kurtines, Berman, Ittel, & Williamson, 1995; Nucci, 2001; Turiel, 1998).

Developmental Trends in Morality

Researchers have identified several developmental trends that characterize children's moral reasoning and behavior:

● ***Children begin using internal standards to evaluate behavior at a very early age.*** Children begin to apply their own standards for right and wrong even before age 2 (Dunn, 1988; Kochanska, Casey, & Fukumoto, 1995; S. Lamb, 1991). For example, infants and toddlers may wince, cover their eyes or ears, or cry when they witness an aggressive interaction. And

Connecting Concepts
See Chapter 12 for a discussion of how children's prosocial behaviors change with age.

Study Guide and Reader
Supplementary Reading 13-4 describes Piaget's theory of moral development.

moral development
Advancements in reasoning and behaving in accordance with culturally prescribed or self-constructed standards of right and wrong.

See evidence that Corwin has emerging internal standards in the "Intelligence: Infancy" clip on Observation CD 1.

———————— **Study Guide and Reader**
Supplementary Reading 13-5 describes circumstances in which young children's internal standards win out over an authority figure's instructions. Supplementary Reading 13-6 explores children's understanding of moral versus conventional transgressions in more depth.

———————— **Connecting Concepts**
Guilt and shame are examples of *self-conscious emotions* (see Chapter 11).

moral transgression
Action that causes damage or harm or in some other way infringes on the needs and rights of others.

conventional transgression
Action that violates society's general guidelines (often unspoken) for socially acceptable behavior.

guilt
Feeling of discomfort when one inflicts damage or causes someone else pain or distress.

shame
Feeling of embarrassment or humiliation after failing to meet certain standards for moral behavior.

distributive justice
Beliefs about what constitutes people's fair share of a valued commodity.

many toddlers distinguish between what's "good" and "bad" and what's "nice" and "naughty." For instance, they may look at a broken object and say "uh-oh!" (J. Kagan, 1984; S. Lamb & Feeny, 1995). In the "Intelligence: Infancy" video clip on Observation CD 1, 16-month-old Corwin shows concern ("uh-oh!") when his block tower falls down.

Sometime around age 3, children know that causing psychological harm, such as fear or embarrassment, is inappropriate. And by age 4, most children understand that causing physical harm to another person is wrong regardless of what authority figures might tell them and regardless of what consequences certain behaviors may or may not bring to themselves (Helwig, Zelazo, & Wilson, 2001; Laupa & Turiel, 1995; Smetana, 1981).

● *Children increasingly distinguish between moral and conventional transgressions.* Mainstream Western culture discourages some behaviors—**moral transgressions**—because they cause damage or harm, violate human rights, or run counter to basic principles of equality, freedom, or justice. It discourages other behaviors—**conventional transgressions**—because, although not unethical, they violate widely held understandings about how one should act (e.g., children shouldn't talk back to adults or burp at meals). Conventional transgressions are usually specific to a particular culture. For instance, although burping is frowned upon in mainstream Western culture, people in some cultures burp as a compliment to the cook. In contrast, many moral transgressions are universal across cultures (Nucci, 2001; Turiel, 2002).

Even preschoolers realize that not all actions are "wrong" in the same way and that violations of moral standards are more serious than other transgressions (Nucci & Weber, 1995; Turiel, 1983; Yau & Smetana, 2003). Children's awareness of social conventions is minimal in early childhood but increases throughout the elementary school years (Helwig & Jasiobedzka, 2001; Laupa & Turiel, 1995; Nucci & Nucci, 1982). However, children and adults do not always agree about which behaviors constitute moral transgressions, which ones fall into the conventional domain, and which ones are simply a matter of personal choice. For instance, whereas adults typically view drug use as a moral transgression, teenagers often think it is acceptable as long as it doesn't hurt other people (M. W. Berkowitz, Guerra, & Nucci, 1991; Nucci, 2001).

● *Children's capacity to respond emotionally to others' harm and distress increases over the school years.* Certain emotions tend to accompany and evoke moral actions, and these emotions emerge gradually as children grow older. Children begin to show signs of **guilt**—a feeling of discomfort when they know that they have inflicted damage or caused someone else pain or distress—as early as 22 months, and those who show it at a young age are less likely to misbehave later on (Kochanska, Gross, Lin, & Nichols, 2002). By the time children reach the middle elementary grades, most of them occasionally feel **shame:** They feel embarrassed or humiliated when they fail to meet the standards for moral behavior that either they or others have established (Damon, 1988; Harter, 1999; Hoffman, 1991).[2] Both guilt and shame, though unpleasant emotions, are good signs that children are developing a sense of right and wrong and will work hard to correct their misdeeds (Eisenberg, 1995; Harter, 1999; Narváez & Rest, 1995).

Guilt and shame emerge when children believe they have done something wrong. In contrast, *empathy* and *sympathy* motivate moral behavior even in the absence of wrongdoing. As you learned in Chapter 12, these emotions emerge in early childhood and continue to develop throughout middle childhood and adolescence. In the primary grades, children show empathy mostly for people they know, such as friends and classmates. But by the upper elementary school grades, they may also begin to feel empathy for people they *don't* know—perhaps for the poor, the homeless, or those in catastrophic circumstances (Damon, 1988; Eisenberg, 1982; Hoffman, 1991).

● *Children's understanding of fairness evolves throughout early and middle childhood.* The ability to share with others depends on children's sense of **distributive justice,** their

———————————
[2]As you learned in Chapter 11, Erik Erikson suggested that shame may appear in the toddler years if adults try to impose unrealistic expectations on youngsters' behaviors. As a general rule, however, shame appears in the elementary years, as children become more cognitively able to consider how their behaviors might be consistent or inconsistent with how they would like themselves to be (Harter, 1999).

beliefs about what constitutes everyone's fair share of a valued commodity (food, toys, playground equipment, etc.). Children's notions of distributive justice change over time (Damon, 1977, 1980; Nucci, 2001). In the preschool years, their beliefs about what's fair are based on their own needs and desires; for instance, it would be perfectly "fair" to give oneself a large handful of candy and give others smaller amounts. In the early elementary grades, children base their judgments about fairness on strict equality: A desired commodity is divided into equal portions. Sometime around age 8, children begin to take merit and special needs into account. For instance, they may think that people who contribute more to a group's efforts should reap a greater portion of the group's rewards and that people who are exceptionally poor might be given more resources than others.

● *With age, reasoning about moral issues becomes increasingly abstract and flexible.* Consider the following situation:

> In Europe, a woman was near death from a rare form of cancer. There was one drug that the doctors thought might save her, a form of radium that a druggist in the same town had recently discovered. The druggist was charging $2,000, ten times what the drug cost him to make. The sick woman's husband, Heinz, went to everyone he knew to borrow the money, but he could only get together about half of what the drug cost. He told the druggist that his wife was dying and asked him to sell it cheaper or let him pay later. But the druggist said no. So Heinz got desperate and broke into the man's store to steal the drug for his wife. (Kohlberg, 1984, p. 186)

Should Heinz have stolen the drug? What would you have done if you were Heinz? Which is worse, stealing something that belongs to someone else or letting another person die a preventable death, and why?

The story of Heinz and his dying wife is an example of a **moral dilemma,** a situation in which two or more people's rights or needs may be at odds and for which there is no clear-cut right or wrong solution. Following are three boys' responses to Heinz's dilemma. We have given the boys fictitious names so that we can talk about them more easily.

> *Andrew (a fifth grader):* Maybe his wife is an important person and runs a store, and the man buys stuff from her and can't get it any other place. The police would blame the owner that he didn't save the wife. He didn't save an important person, and that's just like killing with a gun or a knife. You can get the electric chair for that. (Kohlberg, 1981, pp. 265–266)

> *Blake (a high school student):* If he cares enough for her to steal for her, he should steal it. If not he should let her die. It's up to him. (Kohlberg, 1981, p. 132)

> *Charlie (a high school student):* In that particular situation Heinz was right to do it. In the eyes of the law he would not be doing the right thing, but in the eyes of the moral law he would. If he had exhausted every other alternative I think it would be worth it to save a life. (Kohlberg, 1984, pp. 446–447)

Each boy offers a different reason to justify why Heinz should steal the lifesaving drug. Andrew bases his decision on the possible advantages and disadvantages of stealing or not stealing the drug for Heinz alone. He does not consider the perspective of the dying woman at all. Blake, too, takes a self-serving view, proposing that the decision to either steal or not steal the drug depends on how much Heinz loves his wife. Only Charlie considers the value of human life in justifying why Heinz should break the law.

After obtaining hundreds of responses to moral dilemmas, one groundbreaking cognitive-developmental psychologist, Lawrence Kohlberg, proposed that the development of moral reasoning is characterized by a sequence of six stages grouped into three general *levels* of morality: preconventional, conventional, and postconventional (Colby, Kohlberg, Gibbs, & Lieberman, 1983; Kohlberg, 1963, 1976, 1984) (see Table 13-1). **Preconventional morality** is the earliest and least mature form of moral reasoning, in that a child has not yet adopted or internalized society's conventions regarding what is right or wrong—hence the label *preconventional.* Andrew's response to the Heinz dilemma is a good example of preconventional, Stage 1 thinking, in that he considers the consequences of Heinz's actions only for Heinz himself. Kohlberg also classified Blake's response as a preconventional, Stage 2 response. Blake is beginning to recognize the importance of saving someone else's life, but the decision to do so ultimately depends on whether or not Heinz loves his wife. In other words, his decision depends on *his* feelings alone.

Study Guide and Reader
You can find more information about Kohlberg's levels and stages in Supplementary Reading 13-4.

moral dilemma
Situation in which there is no clear-cut answer regarding the morally right thing to do.

preconventional morality
A lack of internalized standards about right and wrong; making decisions based on what is best for oneself, without regard for others' needs and feelings.

TABLE 13-1	Kohlberg's Three Levels and Six Stages of Moral Reasoning		
Level	**Age Range**	**Stage**	**Nature of Moral Reasoning**
Level I: Preconventional Morality	Seen in preschool children, most elementary school students, some junior high school students, and a few high school students	Stage 1: Punishment-avoidance and obedience	People make decisions based on what is best for themselves, without regard for others' needs or feelings. They obey rules only if established by more powerful individuals; they may disobey if they aren't likely to get caught. "Wrong" behaviors are those that will be punished.
		Stage 2: Exchange of favors	People recognize that others also have needs. They may try to satisfy others' needs if their own needs are also met ("You scratch my back, I'll scratch yours"). They continue to define right and wrong primarily in terms of consequences to themselves.
Level II: Conventional Morality	Seen in a few older elementary school students, some junior high school students, and many high school students (Stage 4 typically does not appear until the high school years)	Stage 3: Good boy/good girl	People make decisions based on what actions will please others, especially authority figures and other individuals with high status (e.g., teachers, popular peers). They are concerned about maintaining relationships through sharing, trust, and loyalty, and they take other people's perspectives and intentions into account when making decisions.
		Stage 4: Law and order	People look to society as a whole for guidelines about right or wrong. They know rules are necessary for keeping society running smoothly and believe it is their "duty" to obey them. However, they perceive rules to be inflexible; they don't necessarily recognize that as society's needs change, rules should change as well.
Level III: Postconventional Morality	Rarely seen before college (Stage 6 is extremely rare even in adults)	Stage 5: Social contract	People recognize that rules represent agreements among many individuals about appropriate behavior. Rules are seen as potentially useful mechanisms that can maintain the general social order and protect individual rights, rather than as absolute dictates that must be obeyed simply because they are "the law." People also recognize the flexibility of rules; rules that no longer serve society's best interests can and should be changed.
		Stage 6: Universal ethical principle	Stage 6 is a hypothetical, "ideal" stage that few people ever reach. People in this stage adhere to a few abstract, universal principles (e.g., equality of all people, respect for human dignity, commitment to justice) that transcend specific norms and rules. They answer to a strong inner conscience and willingly disobey laws that violate their own ethical principles.

Sources: Colby & Kohlberg, 1984; Colby et al., 1983; Kohlberg, 1976, 1984, 1986; Reimer, Paolitto, & Hersh, 1983; Snarey, 1995.

conventional morality
Acceptance of society's conventions regarding right and wrong; behaving to please others or to live up to society's expectations for appropriate behavior.

postconventional morality
Behaving in accordance with self-developed abstract principles regarding right and wrong.

Conventional morality is characterized by an acceptance of society's conventions regarding right and wrong. At this level, an individual obeys rules and follows society's norms even when there are no consequences for obedience or disobedience. Adherence to rules and conventions is somewhat rigid, however, and a rule's appropriateness or fairness is seldom questioned. In contrast, people who exhibit **postconventional morality** view rules as useful but changeable mechanisms created to maintain the general social order and protect human rights, rather than as absolute dictates that must be obeyed without question. They live by their own abstract principles about right and wrong—principles that typically include such basic human rights as life, liberty, and justice. They may disobey rules inconsistent with their principles, as we see in Charlie's Stage 5 response to the Heinz dilemma: "In the eyes of the law he would not be doing the right thing, but in the eyes of the moral law he would."

A great deal of research on moral development has followed on the heels of Kohlberg's work. Some of it supports Kohlberg's sequence of moral reasoning: Generally speaking, children and adolescents seem to make advancements in the order that Kohlberg proposed (Boom, Brugman, & van der Heijden, 2001; Colby & Kohlberg, 1984; Snarey, 1995; Stewart &

Pascual-Leone, 1992). Nevertheless, contemporary psychologists have identified several weaknesses in Kohlberg's theory. For one thing, Kohlberg included both moral issues (e.g., causing harm) and social conventions (e.g., having rules to help society run smoothly) into his views of morality, but as we have seen, children view these two domains differently. Furthermore, he largely overlooked one very important aspect of morality: that of *helping and showing compassion for* (as well as respecting the rights of) others (Gilligan, 1982, 1987). Kohlberg also underestimated young children, who, as we discovered earlier, acquire some internal standards of right and wrong long before they begin kindergarten or first grade. Finally, Kohlberg largely overlooked situational factors that youngsters take into account when deciding what's morally right and wrong in specific contexts (Rest, Narváez, Bebeau, & Thoma, 1999). For example, children are more apt to think of lying as immoral if it causes someone else harm than if it has no adverse effect—that is, if it is just a "white lie" (Turiel, Smetana, & Killen, 1991).

Many contemporary developmental psychologists believe that moral reasoning involves general *trends* rather than distinct stages. It appears that children and adolescents gradually acquire several different standards that guide their moral reasoning and decision making in different situations. Such standards include the need to address one's own personal interests, a desire to abide by society's rules and conventions and, eventually, an appreciation for abstract ideals regarding human rights and society's overall needs (Rest et al., 1999). With age, youngsters increasingly apply more advanced standards, but even a fairly primitive one—satisfying one's own needs without regard for others—may occasionally take precedence (Rest et al., 1999; Turiel, 1998).

● *As children get older, they increasingly behave in accordance with self-chosen moral standards.* Children's moral behaviors are correlated with their moral reasoning (Blasi, 1980; Eisenberg, Zhou, & Koller, 2001; Reimer et al., 1983). For example, children and adolescents who, from Kohlberg's perspective, reason at higher stages are less likely to cheat or insult others, more likely to help people in need, and more likely to disobey orders that would cause someone harm (F. H. Davidson, 1976; Kohlberg, 1975; Kohlberg & Candee, 1984; P. A. Miller, Eisenberg, Fabes, & Shell, 1996).

Yet the correlation between moral reasoning and moral behavior is not an especially strong one. Children's perspective-taking ability and emotions (shame, guilt, empathy) also influence their decisions to behave morally or otherwise (Batson, 1991; Damon, 1988; Eisenberg et al., 2001). Children's personal needs and goals typically come into play as well. For instance, although children may want to do the right thing, they may also be concerned about whether others will approve of their actions and about what positive or negative consequences might result. Children are more apt to behave in accordance with their moral standards if the benefits are high ("Will other people like me better?") and the personal costs are low ("How much will I be inconvenienced?") (M. L. Arnold, 2000; Batson & Thompson, 2001; Narváez & Rest, 1995).

The Developmental Trends table "Moral Reasoning and Behavior at Different Age Levels" describes advancements you are likely to see in infancy, childhood, and adolescence.

Factors Affecting Moral Development

Some prominent members of mainstream Western culture (e.g., politicians, religious leaders, and newspaper columnists) have suggested that society is in a sharp moral decline. Yet evidence does not necessarily support this idea. In fact, some indicators reveal *improvements* in people's moral behaviors (Turiel, 1998, 2002). In the United States, for example, crime rates have gone down in the past few years, and volunteerism in charities and public service organizations has increased considerably (Ladd, 1999; Turiel, 2002).

Developmental researchers have identified several factors associated with the development of moral reasoning and behavior: general cognitive development, interactions with peers, use of reasons and rationales, moral issues and dilemmas, and sense of self.

General cognitive development.   Let's return once again to Charlie's response to the Heinz dilemma: "In the eyes of the law he would not be doing the right thing, but in the eyes of the moral law he would." Advanced moral reasoning—thoughtful reasoning about moral law

Moral Reasoning and Behavior at Different Age Levels

Age	What You Might Observe	Diversity	Implications
Infancy (Birth–2)	• Reactions of distress when witnessing aggressive behavior • Acquisition of some standards for behavior (e.g., saying "uh-oh!" after knocking over and breaking an object)	• In the second year, children begin to label objects and events in ways that reflect culture-specific standards (e.g., *good, bad, dirty, boo boo*). • Some toddlers begin to show distress about certain behaviors (e.g., damaging a valuable object) late in the second year.	• Consistently discourage behaviors that cause harm or distress to others (e.g., hitting or biting peers). • Acknowledge undesirable events (e.g., spilled milk or a broken object), but don't communicate that children are somehow inadequate for having caused them.
Early Childhood (2–6)	• Some awareness that behaviors causing physical or psychological harm are morally wrong • Guilt for some misbehaviors (e.g., damaging a valuable object) • Greater concern for one's own needs than for those of others; complaining "It's not fair" when one's own needs aren't met	• Some cultures emphasize early training in moral values; for example, in many Hispanic communities, a child who is *bien educado* (literally, "well educated") knows right from wrong and behaves accordingly. • Children who show greater evidence of guilt about transgressions are more likely to adhere to rules for behavior. • At ages 2 and 3, girls are more likely to show guilt than boys; boys catch up at about age 4.	• Make standards for behavior very clear. • When children misbehave, give reasons why such behaviors are unacceptable, focusing on the harm and distress they have caused others (see the discussion on *induction* in the upcoming section "Use of Reasons and Rationales").
Middle Childhood (6–10)	• Sense of distributive justice increasingly taking into account people's differing contributions, needs, and special circumstances (e.g., people with disabilities might get a larger share) • Increasing empathy for unknown individuals who are suffering or needy • Feelings of shame as well as guilt for moral wrongdoings	• Some cultures place greater emphasis on ensuring individuals' rights and needs, whereas others place greater value on the welfare of the community as a whole. • Children whose parents explain why certain behaviors are unacceptable show more advanced moral development.	• Talk about how rules enable classrooms and other group situations to run more smoothly. • Present simple moral dilemmas similar to circumstances children might encounter themselves (e.g., "What should a girl do when she has forgotten her lunch money and finds a dollar bill on the floor under a classmate's desk?").
Early Adolescence (10–14)	• Some tendency to think of rules and conventions as standards that should be followed for their own sake • Tendency to believe that distressed individuals (e.g., the homeless) are entirely responsible for their own fate	• Sometime around puberty, some youngsters begin to incorporate moral traits into their overall sense of self. • Youngsters' religious beliefs (e.g., their beliefs in an afterlife) influence their judgments about what behaviors are morally right and wrong.	• Involve adolescents in group projects that will benefit their school or community. • Encourage adolescents to think about how society's laws and practices affect people in need (e.g., the poor, the sick, the elderly). • When imposing discipline for moral transgressions, point out harm caused to others (doing so is especially important when youngsters have deficits in empathy and moral reasoning).
Late Adolescence (14–18)	• Understanding that rules and conventions help society run more smoothly • Increasing concern about doing one's duty and abiding by the rules of society as a whole rather than simply pleasing certain authority figures • Genuine empathy for people in distress • Belief that society has an obligation to help those in need	• For some older adolescents, high moral values are a central part of their overall identity; these individuals often show a strong commitment to helping those less fortunate than themselves. • Adolescents who have less advanced moral reasoning—especially those who focus on their own needs almost exclusively (i.e., preconventional reasoners)—are more likely to engage in antisocial activities.	• Explore moral issues in social studies, science, and literature. • Give teenagers a political voice in decision making about rules at school and elsewhere.

Sources: M. Chandler & Moran, 1990; Damon, 1988; Eisenberg, 1982; Eisenberg & Fabes, 1998; Eisenberg et al., 1986; Farver & Branstetter, 1994; C. A. Flanagan & Faison, 2001; Gibbs, 1995; D. Hart & Fegley, 1995; Helwig & Jasiobedzka, 2001; Helwig et al., 2001; Hoffman, 1975, 1991; Kochanska et al., 1995; Kochanska et al., 2002; Kohlberg, 1984; D. L. Krebs & Van Hesteren, 1994; Kurtines et al., 1995; S. Lamb & Feeny, 1995; Laupa & Turiel, 1995; Nucci, 2001; Nucci & Weber, 1995; Rushton, 1980; Schonert-Reichl, 1993; Smetana & Braeges, 1990; Triandis, 1995; Turiel, 1983, 1998; Yates & Youniss, 1996; Yau & Smetana, 2003; Youniss & Yates, 1999; Zahn-Waxler, Radke-Yarrow, et al., 1992.

and about such ideals as equality, justice, and basic human rights—requires considerable reflection about abstract ideas (Kohlberg, 1976; Turiel, 2002). Thus, moral development depends to some extent on cognitive development. For instance, children who are intellectually gifted are, on average, more likely than their peers to think about moral issues and to work hard to address injustices in the local community or the world at large (L. K. Silverman, 1994).

Yet cognitive development does not *guarantee* moral development. It is quite possible to think abstractly about academic subject matter and yet reason in a self-centered, "preconventional" manner (Kohlberg, 1976; L. K. Silverman, 1994). In other words, cognitive development is a necessary but insufficient condition for moral development.

Interactions with peers. Children learn many moral lessons in their interactions with agemates. When infants and toddlers interact at home or in child care settings, such lessons begin quite early. Interactions among very young children should be monitored closely, as they often involve physical contact and a potential for physical harm. When adults scold children for aggressive actions and suggest alternative ways to resolve conflicts, children begin to develop an awareness of appropriate and inappropriate ways to treat others.

Beginning in the preschool years and continuing through adolescence, issues related to sharing, cooperation, and negotiation emerge in youngsters' group activities (Damon, 1981, 1988; Turiel, 1998). Conflicts frequently arise as a result of physical harm, disregard for another's feelings, or mistreatment of possessions (Dunn & Munn, 1987; Killen & Nucci, 1995). In order to learn to resolve interpersonal conflicts successfully, children must begin to look at situations from others' perspectives, show consideration for others' feelings and possessions, and try to satisfy others' needs in addition to their own (Killen & Nucci, 1995).

Use of reasons and rationales. Certainly it is important to impose consequences for harmful actions and other immoral behaviors. However, punishment by itself often focuses children's attention primarily on their own hurt and distress (Hoffman, 1975; Nucci, 2001). Children are more likely to make gains in moral development when they think about the harm and distress that certain behaviors have caused for *others*. Giving children reasons that certain behaviors are unacceptable, with a focus on other people's perspectives, is known as **induction** (Hoffman, 1970, 1975). Following are examples:

- "Having your hair pulled the way you just pulled Mai's can really be painful."
- "You probably hurt John's feelings when you call him names like that."
- "This science project you've just ridiculed may not be as fancy as yours, but I know that Michael spent many hours working on it and is quite proud of what he's done."

Giving children reasons about why specific rules are necessary and holding them accountable for their transgressions can help promote their moral development.

Consistent use of induction in disciplining children, especially when accompanied by *mild* punishment for misbehavior—for instance, insisting that children make amends for their wrongdoings—appears to promote compliance with rules and foster the development of empathy, compassion, and altruism (G. H. Brody & Shaffer, 1982; Hoffman, 1975; Nucci, 2001; Rushton, 1980). In contrast, power-assertive techniques (e.g., "Do this because I say so!") are relatively *in*effective in promoting moral development (Damon, 1988; Kochanska et al., 2002; Nucci, 2001; Zhou et al., 2002).

Moral issues and dilemmas. Kohlberg proposed that children develop morally when they are challenged by moral dilemmas they cannot adequately deal with at their current stage of moral reasoning—in other words, when they encounter situations that create disequilibrium. Although most contemporary developmental psychologists reject Kohlberg's idea of discrete stages, they have confirmed his view that disequilibrium spurs moral development. For instance, discussions of controversial topics and moral issues appear to promote the development of moral reasoning, especially when children are exposed to reasoning that's slightly more advanced than their own (DeVries & Zan, 1996; Power, Higgins, & Kohlberg, 1989; Schlaefli, Rest, & Thoma, 1985).

Sense of self. Children are more likely to engage in moral behavior when they think they are actually capable of helping other people—in other words, when they have high self-efficacy about their ability to make a difference (Narváez & Rest, 1995). Furthermore, in

---

induction
The act of explaining why a certain behavior is unacceptable, usually with a focus on the pain or distress that someone has caused another.

adolescence some youngsters begin to integrate a commitment to moral values into their overall sense of *identity* (M. L. Arnold, 2000; Blasi, 1995; Nucci, 2001). They think of themselves as moral, caring individuals and place a high priority on acting in accordance with this self-perception. Their acts of altruism and compassion are not limited to their friends and acquaintances but also extend to the community at large. In one study (D. Hart & Fegley, 1995), researchers conducted in-depth interviews with inner-city Hispanic and African American teenagers who demonstrated an exceptional commitment to helping others (by volunteering many hours at Special Olympics, a neighborhood political organization, a nursing home, etc.). These teens did not necessarily display more advanced moral reasoning (as defined by Kohlberg's stages) than others their age, but they were more likely to describe themselves in terms of moral traits and goals (e.g., helping others) and to mention certain ideals toward which they were striving.

Diversity in Moral Development

The factors just described can lead to considerable diversity in the moral values and behaviors that young people acquire. Some disabilities also impact moral development; for instance, children with a *conduct disorder* show a general disregard for the rights and feelings of others. In addition, moral development may be somewhat different for youngsters of different genders and cultural backgrounds, as you will see now.

——————— Connecting Concepts
Chapter 11 describes conduct disorders in more detail.

Gender differences.   On average, girls are more likely than boys to feel guilt, shame, and empathy—emotions associated with moral behavior (Alessandri & Lewis, 1993; Zahn-Waxler & Robinson, 1995). Girls' greater tendency to feel shame may be related to their general tendency to attribute failures to internal, personal qualities. In other words, girls are more likely than boys to take personal responsibility for their misdeeds (Alessandri & Lewis, 1993).

Although girls and boys may feel somewhat different about situations with moral implications, do they also *reason* differently? In presenting a variety of moral dilemmas to young adults of both genders, Kohlberg found that females reasoned, on average, at Stage 3, whereas males were more likely to reason at Stage 4 (Kohlberg & Kramer, 1969). But psychologist Carol Gilligan has argued that Kohlberg's stages do not adequately describe female moral development (Gilligan, 1982, 1987; Gilligan & Attanucci, 1988). In particular, Gilligan has suggested that Kohlberg's stages reflect a **justice orientation**—an emphasis on fairness and equal rights—which characterizes males' moral reasoning. In contrast, she has proposed, females are socialized to take a **care orientation** toward moral issues— that is, to focus on interpersonal relationships and take responsibility for others' well-being. The following dilemma can elicit either a justice orientation or a care orientation:

Are girls more likely than boys to be socialized to take care of others? Carol Gilligan suggests that they are, but other researchers have found no significant differences in the care orientations of males and females.

The Porcupine Dilemma:

A group of industrious, prudent moles have spent the summer digging a burrow where they will spend the winter. A lazy, improvident porcupine who has not prepared a winter shelter approaches the moles and pleads to share their burrow. The moles take pity on the porcupine and agree to let him in. Unfortunately, the moles did not anticipate the problem the porcupine's sharp quills would pose in close quarters. Once the porcupine has moved in, the moles are constantly being stabbed. The question is, what should the moles do? (D. T. Meyers, 1987, p. 141, adapted from Gilligan, 1985)

People with a justice orientation are apt to look at this situation in terms of someone's rights being violated. They might point out that the burrow belongs to the moles, and so the moles can legitimately throw the porcupine out. If the porcupine refuses to leave, the moles might rightfully harm him, perhaps even kill him. In contrast, people with a care orientation are likely to show compassion and caring when dealing with the porcupine. For instance, they might suggest that the moles cover the porcupine with a blanket so his quills won't annoy anyone (D. T. Meyers, 1987).

Gilligan has raised a good point: Males and females are often socialized quite differently, as you discovered in Chapters 5, 11, and 12. Furthermore, by including compassion for other human beings as well as respect for others' rights, she has broadened our conception of what morality encompasses (Durkin, 1995; L. J. Walker, 1995). However, most re-

justice orientation
Focus on individual rights in moral decision making.

care orientation
Focus on nurturance and concern for others in moral decision making.

search studies do not find major gender differences in moral reasoning (Eisenberg et al., 1996; Nunner-Winkler, 1984; L. J. Walker, 1991). Minor differences (usually favoring females) sometimes emerge in early adolescence but disappear by late adolescence (Basinger, Gibbs, & Fuller, 1995; Eisenberg et al., 1996). Furthermore, males and females typically incorporate both justice and care into their moral reasoning, applying different orientations (sometimes one, sometimes the other, sometimes both) to different moral problems (Rothbart, Hanley, & Albert, 1986; Smetana, Killen, & Turiel, 1991; L. J. Walker, 1995). Such findings are sufficiently compelling that Gilligan herself has acknowledged that both justice and care orientations are frequently seen in males and females alike (L. M. Brown, Tappan, & Gilligan, 1995; Gilligan & Attanucci, 1988).

Ethnic and cultural differences.   Different cultural groups have somewhat different standards regarding which behaviors are "right" and which are "wrong." For example, in mainstream Western culture, lying to avoid punishment for inappropriate behavior is considered wrong, but it is a legitimate way of saving face in certain other cultures (Triandis, 1995). Some cultures emphasize the importance of being considerate of other people (e.g., "Please be quiet so that your sister can study"), whereas others emphasize the importance of tolerating inconsiderate behavior (e.g., "Please try not to let your brother's radio bother you when you study") (Fuller, 2001; Grossman, 1994). And whereas many people in mainstream Western societies believe that males and females should have equal rights and opportunities, many Hindu people in India believe that a woman's obedience to her husband is integral to the social and moral order, and so a husband is justified in beating his wife if she disobeys him (Nucci, 2001; Shweder, Mahapatra, & Miller, 1987).

Culture-specific religious beliefs sometimes enter into children's moral reasoning. Consider such simple behaviors as eating chicken and getting a haircut. Although these behaviors have no moral implications in mainstream Western culture, they can have dire consequences in Hindu culture. Some Hindu groups believe that if a family's eldest son eats chicken or gets a haircut soon after his father's death, he is preventing his father from having eternal salvation (Shweder et al., 1987).

Cultural differences almost certainly affect the degree to which children, boys and girls alike, acquire justice or care orientations toward morality (Markus & Kitayama, 1991; J. G. Miller, 1997; Shweder, Much, Mahapatra, & Park, 1997). At the same time, we must be careful not to overgeneralize about differences in moral reasoning across cultural groups. Most cultures place value on both individual rights and concern for others (Turiel, 1998; Turiel, Killen, & Helwig, 1987). Furthermore, moral decision making within any culture is often situation-specific, calling for justice in some situations, compassion in other situations, and a balance between the two in still others (Turiel, 1998; Turiel et al., 1987).

Promoting Moral Development

Clearly children's moral reasoning and behavior are important components of their overall social-emotional development. Yet superficial attempts to build character—giving youngsters lectures about morally appropriate behavior, having them read stories with moral messages, or publicly rewarding them for displaying certain virtues—have little or no impact on moral development (Narváez, 2002; Nucci, 2001; Turiel, 1998). In fact, giving concrete reinforcers for moral actions may actually *undermine* moral development, in much the same way that extrinsic rewards undermine intrinsic motivation more generally (Nucci, 2001).

Several other strategies can definitely promote more advanced moral reasoning and behavior, however. Research findings point to the following recommendations for teachers, parents, and other adults who work regularly with children and adolescents:

● ***Clarify which behaviors are acceptable and which are not, and help children understand the reasons for various regulations and prohibitions.*** Adults must make it crystal clear that some behaviors (e.g., shoving, making racist remarks, bringing weapons to school) will not be acceptable under any circumstances. Adults should also explain that some behaviors may be quite appropriate in certain situations yet inappropriate in others. For example, copying a classmate's work may be permissible when a student is in the process of learning but is unacceptable (it constitutes fraud) during tests and other assessments of what a student has already learned (Thorkildsen, 1995).

Study Guide and Reader ————
Supplementary Reading 13-7 provides additional information about Gilligan's theory.

Adults should accompany any disciplinary actions or discussions of rules with explanations about why certain behaviors cannot be tolerated, with a particular emphasis on potential or actual physical or psychological harm (recall our earlier discussion of *induction*). For example, a preschool teacher might say, "If we throw the blocks, someone may get hurt. Jane can come back to the block area when she is ready to use the blocks for building" (M. B. Bronson, 2000, p. 206). Similarly, an elementary school teacher might remind students, "We walk when we are in line so nobody gets bumped or tripped" (M. B. Bronson, 2000, p. 205). Adults might also ask children to describe to one another exactly how they feel when they're the victims of certain misbehaviors or to speculate about how they would feel in a situation where someone else has been victimized (Doescher & Sugawara, 1989; Hoffman, 1991). And adults should certainly encourage children to make amends for misdeeds (Nucci, 2001). For instance, a middle school teacher might say, "I'm sure you didn't mean to hurt Jamal's feelings, but he's pretty upset about what you said. Why don't you think about what you might do or say to make him feel better."

● *Engage children in discussions about moral issues.* Moral issues and dilemmas often arise in conjunction with inappropriate behaviors (e.g., aggression, theft) that occur at school and in other group settings. One effective way of encouraging productive discussions about such issues is through *peer mediation* sessions in which youngsters in conflict try to understand one another's needs and perspectives. Another effective approach is a *just community,* in which students and their teachers hold regular "town meetings" to discuss recent interpersonal conflicts and moral violations and to establish rules that can help students be more productive and socially responsible (e.g., A. Higgins, 1995; Power et al., 1989).

Moral issues arise in classroom subject matter as well. For instance, an English class might debate whether Hamlet was justified in killing Claudius to avenge the murder of his father. A social studies class might wrestle with the inhumane treatment that millions of people suffered during the Holocaust of World War II (see Figure 13-6). A science class might discuss the ethical issues involved in using laboratory rats to study the effects of cancer-producing agents.

Teachers and other adults can do several things to ensure that discussions about moral issues promote children's moral development (Nucci, 2001; Reimer et al., 1983). First, they should create a trusting and nonthreatening atmosphere in which children feel free to express their ideas without censure or embarrassment. Second, they can help children identify all aspects of a dilemma, including the needs and perspectives of the various individuals involved. Third, they can encourage children to explore the underlying bases for their thinking—that is, to clarify and examine the principles that their moral judgments reflect.

In discussions about misdeeds and moral issues, adults must also help youngsters understand the diverse perspectives that some of their peers may bring to the conversation. They might encourage children to look at moral dilemmas from several different angles, perhaps considering the extent to which justice, care, social conventions, and personal choice are all involved (Nucci & Weber, 1991). For example, although classmates who deface their school building with graffiti might believe they are engaging in creative self-expression (personal choice), they are also breaking a rule (convention), disregarding other students' rights to study and learn in a clean and attractive setting (justice), and thumbing their nose to the needs of those around them (care).

● *Challenge children's moral reasoning with slightly more advanced reasoning.* Kohlberg's stages (Table 13-1) provide a useful framework for identifying moral arguments likely to create disequilibrium for youngsters. In particular, Kohlberg suggested that teachers offer reasoning that is one stage above a child's reasoning. For example, imagine that a teenage boy who is concerned primarily about gaining peer approval (Stage 3) often lets a popular cheerleader copy his homework. His teacher might present law-and-order logic (Stage 4), suggesting that homework assignments are designed to help students learn more effectively and so all students should complete them without others' assistance. If adults present arguments too much higher than children's current reasoning, however, children will have trouble understanding

——————— **Connecting Concepts**
See Chapter 12 for more information about peer mediation.

——————— **Study Guide and Reader**
Supplementary Reading 13-8 presents an example of a just community in action.

I tried to get the feeling of deep Sadness and Sorrow into my Picture. I whant the viewer to feel the emotion of what it was like for a Jew. I didn't add any color becaus for a Jew ther life was gray dull and very Painfall, that is what I want the viewer to feel.

My Picture is titled
    A Jewish life

Figure 13-6

Children's moral beliefs influence their interpretations of and reactions to school subject matter. Here Cody tries to imagine and capture the feelings of Jewish people during World War II in a seventh-grade unit on the Holocaust.

the logic and so will probably not experience the disequilibrium that will encourage them to reflect on and reconsider their thinking (Boom et al., 2001; Narváez, 1998).

● *Get children and adolescents actively involved in community service.* As you've learned, youngsters are more likely to adhere to strong moral principles when they have high self-efficacy for helping others and when they have integrated a commitment to moral ideals into their overall sense of identity. Such self-perceptions don't appear out of the blue, of course. Children are more likely to have high self-efficacy for particular behaviors (including moral ones) when they have the guidance, support, and feedback they need to carry out those behaviors successfully. And they are more likely to integrate moral values into their overall sense of self when they become actively involved in service to others even before they reach puberty (Nucci, 2001; Youniss & Yates, 1999). Through ongoing community service activities—food and clothing drives, visits to homes for the elderly, community clean-up efforts, and so on—children and adolescents alike learn that they have the skills and the responsibility for helping those less fortunate than themselves and in other ways making the world a better place in which to live. In the process, they also begin to think of themselves as concerned, compassionate, and moral citizens (Nucci, 2001; Youniss & Yates, 1999).

Case Study: Spencer

Eight-year-old Spencer is the tallest student in his second-grade class. At almost five feet in height, he's even an inch taller than Ms. Quintero, his teacher. Most days he seems to enjoy being at school, because this is the only place where he sees other children. Yet his classmates dislike him because of his erratic behavior and poor social skills. "He's like a roller coaster," Ms. Quintero says. "One day he's an angel, sweet, gentle, and helpful. But the next day he might throw his desk across the room. He'll scream, cry, punch, and bully other kids. Once he put a 'hate note' in a classmate's backpack. Another time he threatened to urinate on a classmate in the boys' restroom."

Ms. Quintero describes Spencer's academic performance as "mediocre." He has trouble following directions that involve more than one or two steps. He doesn't ask for help when he needs it; instead, he acts out. And he's quite forgetful about things he needs to bring to and from school, such as his lunchbox and his jacket.

For several months Ms. Quintero has been trying to get Spencer's behavior under control, but with little success. Sometimes he seems to like her negative feedback, but at other times he resents and personalizes it ("You hate me!"). Ms. Quintero seeks the principal's assistance but gets none. For instance, when she describes Spencer's bullying behaviors, the principal's response is simply, "The other kids need to toughen up."

Nor are Spencer's parents any help. His mother and father, who are divorced, share custody of Spencer. Ms. Quintero can always tell at which home Spencer has spent the previous night. After a night at his father's, "He's off the wall from lack of sleep. He talks about sex, because his dad listens to a lot of rap music." After a night at his mother's, "He hates school, hates his teachers. He's a bully, and he doesn't put any effort into his schoolwork." Mother clearly fuels his counterproductive behaviors. "Watch out for those evil teachers at school," she tells him. "You only need to look out for yourself." And she accuses Ms. Quintero of incompetence, screaming, "You're killing the spirit of my child!"

Spencer blames his teachers whenever he has trouble learning. So, too, does his mother. When Spencer brings home poor report cards, "Mom goes ballistic," Ms. Quintero says. "His previous teachers changed his grades to please her. In fact, two of them actually quit because of Spencer and his mom."

Somehow Ms. Quintero makes it through the school year, but in April she tells the principal she won't be returning the following fall. Spencer, meanwhile, is promoted to third grade.[a]

● What motives and goals does Spencer seem to have?
● What evidence do you see that Spencer has poor self-regulation skills?
● How would you characterize Spencer's moral development?

(continued)

- What factors in Spencer's environment have probably contributed to his behavior problems? Might biological factors also be playing a role?
- Is the principal's attitude toward Spencer's bullying behaviors appropriate? Why or why not?
- What changes in Spencer's environment might help him acquire more productive behaviors?

Once you have answered these questions, compare your responses with those presented in the appendix.

[a]We thank an anonymous colleague for this case. The names Spencer and Ms. Quintero are pseudonyms.

Summary

Motivation

Motivation energizes, directs, and sustains behavior. It can be either extrinsic (evoked largely by the external consequences that certain behaviors will bring) or intrinsic (emanating from characteristics within a person or inherent in a task being performed). Children who are intrinsically motivated use more effective learning strategies and achieve at higher levels.

One key source of extrinsic motivation is the extent to which either primary reinforcers (things that satisfy built-in biological needs) or secondary reinforcers (things that have become reinforcing through frequent association with other reinforcing consequences) follow behaviors. With age, children become increasingly able to forgo small, immediate rewards in favor of larger, delayed ones. An additional source of extrinsic motivation is punishment: Children tend to avoid behaviors that have previously led to unpleasant consequences either for themselves or for others.

Intrinsic motivation takes a variety of forms. Some forms, such as curiosity about intriguing events, a feeling of discomfort (disequilibrium) about apparent inconsistencies in the world, and a general need to feel competent and autonomous, may be innate. Others, such as personal interests, values, and mastery goals, may be related to children's environmental circumstances and to their earlier successes with certain kinds of tasks. Most children gradually internalize some of the priorities and values of parents, teachers, and other influential adults in their lives, especially if the adults create an authoritative climate that balances structure and guidance with some autonomy in decision making.

Among the important factors influencing intrinsic motivation are the attributions children make regarding their successes and failures at particular tasks. Children are most optimistic when they attribute both successes and failures to internal factors that they can control (e.g., amount of effort and use of good strategies). Ultimately, some children acquire a general *I can do it* attitude (a mastery orientation), whereas others acquire an *I can't do it even if I try* attitude (learned helplessness).

By and large, children's motivation to tackle certain tasks and pursue certain activities (or perhaps *not* to get involved with such tasks and activities) depends on a number of factors—self-efficacy, sense of self-determination, attributions, and so on—that develop over a lengthy period of time. Thus, children's motivation in any particular situation is not something they can easily turn on or turn off at will. Yet teachers, parents, and other adults can do many things to enhance youngsters' motivation to engage in productive activities. Piquing youngsters' curiosity and interest, helping them be successful in their efforts to master new skills, enhancing their sense of autonomy, and encouraging them to set and strive for specific goals are just a few of the many possibilities.

Self-Regulation

With age and experience, most children and adolescents become increasingly able to control and direct their own behavior and learning. They more effectively restrain their impulses and emotional reactions, internalize the rules and restrictions that adults have imposed, and increasingly evaluate their own behavior. Nevertheless, many high school students don't regulate their own behaviors very effectively. Adults promote self-regulation through authoritative parenting and classroom management, in which they establish definite guidelines for behavior while also attending to children's needs, listening to children's ideas and perspectives, and providing a reasonable rationale for any requests. Adults can also model self-regulating behaviors, give children age-appropriate opportunities for independence, and teach specific self-management skills.

Moral Reasoning and Behavior

An ability to distinguish between right and wrong emerges early in life and continues to develop over time. Infants are clearly uncomfortable when they witness others being hurt. Most preschoolers have some awareness that actions that cause significant physical or psychological harm are wrong even if an authority figure tells them otherwise. As children get older, they gain an increasing understanding of fairness and an increasing capacity to feel guilt, shame, and empathy about moral wrongdoings. As they make advancements in cognitive development, and especially as they become capable of abstract thought, they reason about moral issues and dilemmas in more sophisticated ways, and they are more likely to behave in accordance with general moral principles. Even at the high school level, however, youngsters do not always take the moral high road, as personal needs and self-interests often enter into their moral decisions.

To some degree, different cultures foster different moral values, but virtually all cultural groups recognize the importance of fairness, justice, and concern for others. Adults can promote young people's moral development by explaining why certain behaviors are unacceptable (in that they cause harm or distress to another or jeopardize another's rights and needs), engaging youngsters in discussions about moral issues and dilemmas, exposing them to diverse and slightly more advanced moral perspectives, and getting them actively involved in service to others.

Applying Concepts in Child Development

In this chapter you learned that motivation takes many forms and that virtually all children and adolescents are motivated in one way or another. The following table describes behaviors of youngsters at five different age levels. For each youngster the table identifies motives that may be at work, offers suggestions for encouraging productive behavior, or both. Apply what you've learned about motivation to fill in the empty cells in the table. When you're done, compare your responses with those in Table 13-1 in the *Study Guide and Reader*.

APPLYING CONCEPTS IN CHILD DEVELOPMENT	Observing Motivation in Youngsters' Behaviors		
Age	A Youngster's Experience	Developmental Concepts *Identifying Motivational Phenomena*	Implications *Motivating Productive Behaviors*
Infancy (Birth–2)	Now that she can easily crawl from place to place, 9-month-old Regina is into everything. Her child care provider once found her trying to stick a couple of house keys into an electrical outlet. And all the cleaning supplies under the sink are a particular source of interest.		Make infants' and toddlers' environments safe for exploration. For example, put plastic plugs in electrical outlets and child-proof safety latches on cabinet doors.
Early Childhood (2–6)	When her mother returns to work after a lengthy maternity leave, 3½-year-old Laura begins attending an all-day preschool. Laura's teachers find her behavior to be a challenge from the very first day. "She shows no patience or self-restraint," one teacher says. "When she wants something, she wants it *now,* and she'll throw a tantrum if she doesn't get it. If I immediately go to her, I can usually calm her down. But I never know when she might explode again."	Like many young children, Laura shows an inability to *delay gratification.* Her teacher is possibly *reinforcing* her tantrums with immediate attention. Perhaps Laura's mother or other caregivers have previously reinforced such tantrums, giving Laura little reason to learn to control her impulses or acquire other self-regulation skills.	Reinforce young children for appropriate behaviors (e.g., give a child one-on-one attention when she is engaged in a productive activity). Impose mild punishments for inappropriate behaviors (e.g., place an unruly child in a short "time-out" situation in which she gets no attention from others). Also teach strategies for delaying gratification (e.g., suggest that a child repeatedly tell herself, "I can play with the toy longer if I wait for my turn").
Middle Childhood (6–10)	After years of struggling with basic reading skills, 10-year-old Kellen becomes increasingly irritable and soon stops doing his homework. One day his mother finds him curled up under his desk, crying and saying, "I can't do this anymore." Mother takes him to a psychiatrist, who concludes that Kellen has dyslexia. (This is the same Kellen whose story appears at the beginning of Chapter 12.)		Give children the guidance and support they need to be successful. Seek the advice of specialists when children show unusual delays in acquiring certain skills. Do *not* dismiss chronic problems as being just a "phase" that children will "grow out of."

(continued)

APPLYING CONCEPTS IN CHILD DEVELOPMENT

Observing Motivation in Youngsters' Behaviors (continued)

Age	A Youngster's Experience	Developmental Concepts *Identifying Motivational Phenomena*	Implications *Motivating Productive Behaviors*
Early Adolescence (10–14) 	During his third-period class, a middle school teacher often sees 12-year-old JoBeth passing notes to one or more of her classmates. Inevitably, the other students giggle after reading what she has written. Before class one day, the teacher takes JoBeth aside and tells her, "This note passing has to stop. It's getting to be a distraction to the entire class." JoBeth looks down sheepishly. "I'm sorry, Mr. Roberts," she says. "I'm just trying to make the other kids like me. Jeremy Smith tells jokes all the time, and he's one of the most popular kids in the school."	JoBeth's desire for popularity reflects a *social goal*. In observing Jeremy's success telling jokes, JoBeth is experiencing *vicarious reinforcement,* which leads to an increase in her own joke-telling behavior.	
Late Adolescence (14–18) 	Even as a preschooler, Emmanuel showed a keen interest in basketball, and throughout his childhood and early adolescence he spent many hours playing basketball with his friends at a nearby Boys' Club. Since beginning high school, he's twice tried out for the varsity high school team, but without success. "I'm just too short," he reasons. "Anyway, it's probably better that I focus on my schoolwork, which will help me get into a good college."	Emmanuel has a *personal interest* in basketball. However, his failure in making the varsity team decreases his *self-efficacy* for the sport. He places less *value* on it and instead turns his attention to academic achievement, which he perceives to be more useful in helping him achieve his long-term goal of attending a prestigious college.	Incorporate teenagers' personal interests into academic subject matter. Provide outlets through which *all* youngsters can pursue interest areas that are apt to promote their physical and psychological well-being (e.g., create nonselective intramural programs for all who want to participate in team sports).

Key Concepts

motivation (p. 487)
extrinsic motivation (p. 488)
intrinsic motivation (p. 488)
reinforcer (p. 488)
primary reinforcer (p. 488)
secondary reinforcer (p. 488)
delay of gratification (p. 488)
vicarious reinforcement (p. 489)
vicarious punishment (p. 489)
self-efficacy (p. 490)
sense of self-determination (p. 490)

situational interest (p. 490)
personal interest (p. 490)
value (p. 491)
internalized motivation (p. 491)
mastery goal (p. 494)
performance goal (p. 494)
social goal (p. 494)
attribution (p. 496)
incremental view (of ability) (p. 496)
entity view (of ability) (p. 496)
mastery orientation (p. 497)

learned helplessness (p. 497)
student at risk (p. 507)
self-regulation (p. 508)
self-reinforcement (p. 511)
self-monitoring (p. 512)
self-instructions (p. 513)
self-motivation (p. 513)
self-evaluation (p. 513)
moral development (p. 515)
moral transgression (p. 516)
conventional transgression (p. 516)

guilt (p. 516)
shame (p. 516)
distributive justice (p. 516)
moral dilemma (p. 517)
preconventional morality (p. 517)
conventional morality (p. 518)
postconventional morality (p. 518)
induction (p. 521)
justice orientation (p. 522)
care orientation (p. 522)

Now go to our Companion Website at www.prenhall.com/mcdevitt to assess your understanding of chapter content with a Practice Quiz, apply what you've learned in Essay Questions, and broaden your knowledge with links to related Developmental Psychology Web sites.

Peers, Schools, and Society

chapter 14

Case Study: Sharing at the Zoo

Case Study: Sharing at the Zoo

Peers

Schools

Society

Case Study: Aaron and Cole

Summary

Applying Concepts in Child Development

On a bright day in May, kindergarten teacher Pamela Bradshaw took her class on a field trip to the zoo. The visit went well, but as it was wrapping up, Pamela began to worry about getting the children back to school on time. The children and parent volunteers were not yet fully assembled, and Pamela still had to squeeze in a birthday celebration before they could leave the zoo. Feeling pressured as she stood at the zoo's gate, Pamela was baffled when 6-year-old Patrick asked her about "sharing," the class's version of show-and-tell. Here's how Pamela recalls the events:

"What about sharing?" he [Patrick] asked. . . .

Patrick wanted to share?—surely he could see that there was no way. He just had to be kidding. . . .

Patrick asked again. . . .

If time was normally limited, and tremendously limited for a trip to the zoo, on this particular day it was impossibly limited. Already Mary's dad held out a Tupperware container that held precious birthday cupcakes Mary had waited all day—all year—to present. I called Mary to me, positioning her before the handful of gathered children for her Happy Birthday song. If the children were ready to sing, we might still have just enough time to buckle seat belts and drive across the valley. . . .

I was dumbfounded . . . that Patrick insisted on sharing at the zoo. Under the pressure of watching the time and gathering the group, I had held off his question. Now I had to explain the simple facts to him.

"Patrick," I began as I kneeled to be at eye level with him, "there won't be time for sharing today. Could you maybe bring your sharing back on Monday instead?"

Patrick's face answered what he didn't verbalize. His anxious expression was transformed to one of total dismay before I could convince him with reasons. Patrick was usually so happy-go-lucky, so willing to go with the flow, that I had to wonder what could make this sharing so important to him. Only then did I remember that his family needed to leave about a week before school ended to begin their summer jobs in Wyoming. This was, in fact, his last day at school, his last chance to share, his last opportunity to be a member of this bonded group.

"Oh Patrick, I forgot!"

He looked at me hopefully, as if I could manufacture more time. . . . One more glance at his face made the decision for me.

"You can share after we sing to Mary," I told him.

And he did, producing a plastic "frilled lizard" from his backpack, explaining its origins, then calling for the ritual questions or comments from his classmates.

Even with the jostling and shouting crowd surrounding them, the children raised their hands. Patrick called on kids whose faces were smeared with chocolate cupcake icing; Patrick's frilled lizard, for the most part, was the focus of their attention. I checked my watch again, and just as I was hopeful that we could still make it through the exit turnstile and back to school in time, I was surprised to hear Patrick shout, "Next sharer!"

According to custom, it was indeed Patrick's privilege to choose the next child for sharing time, but I smiled, knowing that only a child such as Patrick, aware that this was his last day, would remember to bring an item to the zoo for sharing. The other children who routinely took their turns on Thursdays wouldn't want to lug something around for three hours.

There on the bright patch of lawn, four kindergarteners tossed aside half-eaten cupcakes as their hands shot up, each competing for Patrick's attention while trying to unzip backpacks with the other hand. My jaw must have dropped as I watched them push aside their water bottles and crumpled lunch bags for the item they had indeed lugged around the zoo for three hours.

(continued)

While I caught up with my own astonishment, Patrick quickly chose Will. Before I could move, Will stood to tell the group about his "Nintendo guy" with a clear voice....

In spite of the noise, the commotion, and their own weariness at the zoo, my kindergarteners conducted and participated in their own independent sharing circle. I stood in awe of their vitality and strong sense of purpose. I was proud to see how integrated they were with one another. (Bradshaw, 2001, pp. 108–110)[a]

[a]From "What About Sharing?" by P. Bradshaw, in B. Rogoff, C. G. Turkanis, and L. Bartlett (Eds.), *Learning Together: Children and Adults in a School Community* (pp. 108–110), 2001, New York: Oxford University Press. Copyright 2001 Barbara Rogoff et al. Used by permission of Oxford University Press, Inc.

A s children grow, they spend an increasing amount of time in social groups outside the family—with peers, in schools, and in other community settings. Children learn a lot from participating in these groups, including how to get along with others and how welcome they are—or are not—in particular settings. In the opening case study, Patrick and the other children learned that they belonged in Pamela's kindergarten—and it belonged to them. Pamela had consistently fostered a productive classroom environment, and as a result, the children enjoyed kindergarten, made good academic progress, invested in the classroom customs, and listened respectfully to one another. In this chapter you will find that peers and teachers are catalysts for children's growth and that other elements of society, including the media and after-school programs, also strongly influence the lives of youngsters. You will also see that teachers and other adults can facilitate healthy relationships among peers, create productive learning environments at school, and help children and adolescents make good choices in society.

Peers

Throughout this book we have discussed many ways in which adults influence children and adolescents. *Peers,* people of approximately the same age and position within a social group, make equally important contributions to youngsters' development, especially in the social-emotional domain. In the next few pages, we examine the functions of peer relationships, the factors that affect acceptance by peers, the nature of close friendships and larger social groups, and the qualities of adolescents' romantic relationships and sexual behaviors.

Functions of Peer Relationships

Companionship with peers is one of children's top priorities. In fact, recess and lunch breaks are among children's favorite school activities because these occasions permit interactions with peers (B. B. Brown, 1993; W. Doyle, 1986). Away from school as well, boys and girls frequently choose to spend precious free time with friends. From a developmental standpoint, peer relationships serve multiple functions:

● *Peers offer emotional support.* The presence of familiar peers helps children relax in new environments and cope with any ridicule and physical aggression from other children (Asher & Parker, 1989; D. Ginsburg, Gottman, & Parker, 1986; Pellegrini & Bartini, 2000; D. Schwartz, McFadyen-Ketchum, Dodge, Pettit, & Bates, 1999; Wentzel, 1999). Although some youngsters adjust quite successfully on their own, as a general rule children and adolescents who have

Peers are longed-for companions beginning in early childhood. Art by Madison, age 7.

peers to turn to in times of trouble or uncertainty have higher self-esteem, fewer emotional problems (such as depression), and higher school achievement (Buhrmester, 1992; Guay et al., 1999; Levitt et al., 1999; R. M. Ryan, Stiller, & Lynch, 1994).

● *Peers serve as partners for practicing social skills.* When children interact with their peers, they enter social exchanges on a more or less equal footing: No single individual has absolute power or authority. By satisfying their own needs while also maintaining productive relationships with others, children acquire skills in perspective taking, persuasion, negotiation, compromise, and self-control (Creasey, Jarvis, & Berk, 1998; Gottman, 1986b; Selman, 2003; Sutton-Smith, 1979).

Connecting Concepts
The development of children's *social skills* is discussed in Chapter 12.

● *Peers socialize one another.* Children and adolescents socialize one another in several ways (Erwin, 1993; D. Ginsburg et al., 1986; J. R. Harris, 1998; A. M. Ryan, 2000). Peers define options for leisure time, perhaps jumping rope in a vacant lot, getting together in a study group, or smoking cigarettes on the corner. They offer new ideas and perspectives, whether demonstrating how to do an "Ollie" on a skateboard or presenting potent arguments for becoming a vegetarian. They serve as role models, showing what is possible and what is admirable. Peers reinforce one another for acting in ways deemed appropriate for their age, gender, ethnic group, and cultural background. And they sanction one another for stepping beyond acceptable bounds, often through ridicule, gossip, or ostracism.

Adolescents find it reassuring to talk with peers about everday challenges and experiences.

● *Peers contribute to a sense of identity.* Association with a particular group of peers helps children and adolescents decide who they are and who they want to become. For instance, when Jeanne's son Alex was in middle school, he and his friends were avid skateboarders and spent long hours at a local skateboard ramp practicing and refining their technique. Alex proudly labeled himself a "skater" and wore the extra-large T-shirts and wide-legged pants that conveyed this identity.

Connecting Concepts
Chapter 12 describes the development of identity in greater detail.

● *Peers help one another make sense of their lives.* During daily conversations, children share ideas that help one another interpret confusing and troubling events. For example, children may talk about similar experiences in dealing with a difficult teacher or being punished by parents. Such informally instructive conversations occur throughout childhood but take on special significance during adolescence, when teenagers are changing rapidly and appreciate reassurance from peers who are facing similar challenges (Seltzer, 1982).

Peer Acceptance

The functions of peer relationships just described operate for most youngsters, and especially for youngsters who are reasonably well regarded by peers. The resulting benefits are substantial. By and large, children who believe that peers view them favorably achieve at higher levels academically, have higher self-esteem, are happier at school, exhibit fewer problem behaviors, and have better school attendance records (Guay et al., 1999; Harter, 1996; D. F. Reese & Thorkildsen, 1999; Wentzel, 1999).

Developmental researchers often examine peer acceptance by asking children in a classroom or other setting to confidentially nominate individual children with whom they would like to interact and others whom they would prefer to avoid. Researchers then collect these nominations and classify the children into one of five groups: *popular, rejected, neglected, controversial,* and *average.* The researchers subsequently compare the typical social features of children in the five groups.

Children who are well liked by numerous peers are considered **popular.** However, we have to be clear about the qualities represented by the term *popularity* in the peer acceptance literature. When researchers ask children to identify classmates they would most like to do something with, the children don't necessarily choose those whom they and their teachers perceive to be the most "popular" members of the student body (Lafontana & Cillessen, 1998; Parkhurst & Hopmeyer, 1998). When we talk about *popular children* in terms of peer acceptance, we are describing young people who are well liked, kind, and trustworthy—those who may or may not hold obvious high-status positions such as head cheerleader or

popular children
Children whom many peers like and perceive to be kind and trustworthy.

football quarterback. Children who are well accepted by peers typically have good social skills. For instance, they know how to initiate and sustain conversations, are sensitive to the subtle social cues that others give them, and adjust their behaviors to changing circumstances. They also tend to be quite prosocial, often helping, sharing, cooperating, and empathizing with others (Caprara, Barbaranelli, Pastorelli, Bandura, & Zimbardo, 2000; Crick & Dodge, 1994; Wentzel & Asher, 1995).

Children who are frequently selected for exclusion by peers are known as **rejected children.** Rejected children often have poor social skills—for example, they may continually try to draw attention to themselves and may also be impulsive and disruptive in the classroom (Asher & Renshaw, 1981; Pellegrini et al., 1999; Putallaz & Heflin, 1986). Many, but not all, aggressive children are also rejected, probably in part because they place a higher priority on acquiring objects and gaining power over others than on maintaining congenial interpersonal relationships (Dodge, Bates, & Pettit, 1990; Ladd & Burgess, 1999; Patrick, 1997). Some rejected children appear to peers to be immature, insensitive, inattentive, strange, or moody; such children often become victims of other children's bullying behaviors (Bierman, 2004). Rejected children's tendency to alienate others leaves them few opportunities to develop the social skills they so desperately need, and they consequently feel lonely and unhappy (Bullock, 1993; Coie & Cillessen, 1993).

The third group of children researchers have identified is neglected children. **Neglected children** are those whom age-mates rarely select as peers they would either most like or least like to do something with (Asher & Renshaw, 1981). Neglected children tend to be quiet and keep to themselves. Some prefer to be alone, others may simply not know how to go about making friends, and still others may be quite content with the one or two close friends that they have (Guay et al., 1999; Rubin & Krasnor, 1986). Neglected status is often only a temporary situation; children categorized as neglected at one time are not always so categorized in follow-up assessments.

The fourth category, **controversial children,** refers to youngsters who are very well liked by some of their peers and intensely disliked by others. And in the fifth group are children who, for lack of a better term, are known simply as *average;* some peers like them and others don't, but without the intensity of feelings shown for popular, rejected, or controversial children and without the invisibility of neglected children.

Because of its important effects on the development of children and adolescents, peer acceptance is an important quality for adults to monitor. In the Observation Guidelines table "Noticing Children's Level of Peer Acceptance," we present common characteristics of popular, rejected, neglected, controversial, and average children, and we suggest some basic strategies for supporting children of varying levels of peer acceptance. A little later on, we offer more detailed recommendations for fostering relationships among children.

Friendships

Healthy friendships come in many forms. Some are brief liaisons; others last a lifetime. Some are relatively casual; others are deep and intimate. Some children have many friends; others invest steadfastly in a few close ones. Despite their varied types, friendships have four common qualities that distinguish them from other kinds of peer relationships:

● *Friendships are voluntary relationships.* Children often spend time with peers strictly through happenstance: Perhaps they ride the same school bus, are members of the same class, or join the same sports team. In contrast, children *choose* their friends. Two or more youngsters remain friends as long as they continue to enjoy one another's company and can successfully resolve their differences.

● *Friendships are powered by shared routines.* Friends find activities that are mutually meaningful and enjoyable, as can be seen in 10-year-old Joseph's essay on the many good times, as well as some difficult times, he has had with his friend Brian (Figure 14-1). Over time, friends acquire a common set of experiences that enable them to share certain perspectives on life (Gottman, 1986b; Suttles, 1970). As a result, they can easily communicate

Figure 14-1

Ten-year-old Joseph explains that he has shared many experiences with his friend Brian.

rejected children

Children whom many peers identify as being unfavorable social partners.

neglected children

Children whom peers rarely select as someone they would most like or least like to do something with.

controversial children

Children whom some peers really like and other peers strongly dislike.

OBSERVATION GUIDELINES

Noticing Children's Level of Peer Acceptance

Characteristic	Look For	Example	Implication
Popular Children	• Good social and communication skills • Sensitivity and responsiveness to others' wishes and needs • Willingness to assimilate into ongoing activities • Signs of leadership potential	On the playground, 8-year-old Daequan moves easily from one group to another. Before joining a conversation, he listens to what others are saying and adds an appropriate comment. He doesn't draw much attention to himself but is well liked by most of his classmates.	Use popular children as leaders when trying to change other children's behavior. For example, when starting a recycling program, ask a well-regarded youngster to help get the program off the ground.
Rejected Children	• For some, high rates of aggression; for others, immature, anxious, or impulsive behavior • Disruptive behavior in class • Unwillingness of other children to play or work with them • In some cases, appearance to other children of being strange and annoying	Most children dislike 10-year-old Terra. She frequently calls other children insulting nicknames, threatens to beat them up, and noisily intrudes into their private conversations.	Help rejected children learn basic social skills, such as how to initiate a conversation. Place them in cooperative groups with children who are likely to be accepting. With aggressive children, give appropriate consequences and teach self-regulatory strategies for controlling impulses. Publicly compliment all youngsters (including rejected children) on things they do well. When rejected children fail to respond to informal interventions, consult counselors.
Neglected Children	• Tendency to be relatively quiet; little or no disruptive behavior • Fewer-than-average interactions with age-mates but possible friendships with one or two peers • For some, anxiety about interacting with others • Possible temporary nature of neglected status	Fourteen-year-old Sedna is initially shy and withdrawn at her new school. Later in the year, however, she seems to be happier and more involved in school activities.	Identify group activities in which neglected children might feel comfortable and be successful. Arrange situations in which shy children with similar interests can get to know one another.
Controversial Children	• Acceptance by some peers, rejection by others • Possible aggression and disruptive behavior in some situations, yet helpfulness, cooperation, and social sensitivity in others	Thirteen-year-old Marcus is usually charming and cheerful, but occasionally he makes jokes at someone else's expense. His sunny personality impresses many classmates, yet his biting humor offends others.	Let controversial children know in no uncertain terms when their behaviors are inappropriate, but acknowledge their effective social skills as well.
Average Children	• Tendency to be liked by some peers but disliked by others • Average interpersonal skills (e.g., average levels of prosocial behavior and aggression) • Ability to find a comfortable social niche	Five-year-old Joachim doesn't draw much attention to himself. He's made a few friends in kindergarten and seems to get along fairly well with them, but he sometimes has trouble handling disagreements.	Help average children refine their emerging social skills. Encourage them to be tactful, honest, and kind with peers and others.

Sources: Bierman, 2004; Coie & Dodge, 1988; Coie & Kupersmidt, 1983; Dodge, 1983; Dodge, Coie, & Brakke, 1982; Dodge, Schlundt, Schocken, & Delugach, 1983; Newcomb & Bukowski, 1984; Newcomb, Bukowski, & Pattee, 1993; Putallaz & Gottman, 1981; Rubin, Bukowski, & Parker 1998.

about many topics. Children talk, smile, and laugh more often with friends than with non-friends; they also engage in more complex fantasy play with friends (J. G. Parker, 1986).

● *Friendships are reciprocal relationships.* In the time they spend together, friends address one another's needs (J. L. Epstein, 1986; Rubin et al., 1998). Although friends take on slightly different roles in their relationship, generally they are equal partners. For example, one friend may instigate fun activities, and the other friend may be an especially sympathetic listener, with both styles reflecting the children's mutual regard.

● *Friendships ensure ongoing, dependable sources of support.* Friends help each other cope with stressful events by providing emotional support (Berndt & Keefe, 1995; D. Gins-

Today Miranda walked me to school and she is going to walk me back. Miranda is my best friend we met egether afther lunch. Miranda is teching me lot's of things she the best friend any boty cwold have.

Figure 14-2

Seven-year-old Jessica recognizes the value of a good friend.

Listen to 17-year-old Paul talk about resolving conflicts with friends in the "Friendship: Late Adolescence" clip on Observation CD 3.

berg et al., 1986). In Figure 14-2, 7-year-old Jessica reveals her emerging understanding of the importance of a good friend in her life. Because friends have an emotional investment in their relationship, they work hard to look at situations from each other's point of view and to resolve disputes that threaten to be divisive. As a result, they develop enhanced perspective-taking and conflict resolution skills (Basinger, Gibbs, & Fuller, 1995; DeVries, 1997). In the "Friendship: Late Adolescence" video clip on Observation CD 3, 17-year-old Paul expresses an ability to adapt his conflict resolution skills to the different perspectives of male and female friends. Paul reports:

Normally with my guy friends, we just get over it. I mean, there's no working it out, you just like fine, whatever, you know, and we get over it. Girlfriends, you gotta like talk to them and work it out slowly, and apologize for whatever you did wrong. [*He and the interviewer laugh.*] There's a whole process.

Characteristics of friendships at different ages.   Years ago, Jeanne asked her three children, "What are friends for?" Here are their responses:

Jeff (age 6):   To play with.
Alex (age 9):   Friends can help you in life. They can make you do better in school. They can make you feel better.
Tina (age 12):   To be your friend and help you in good times and bad times. They're there so you can tell secrets. They're people that care. They're there because they like you. They're people you can trust.

Like Jeff, young children describe friends primarily as recreational companions; thus, their understandings of friendship are simple and concrete. As children reach the upper elementary grades, they, like Alex, begin to understand that friends can help and depend on one another. Adolescents, like Tina, begin to share their innermost secrets with friends (Berndt, 1992; Damon, 1977; Gottman & Mettetal, 1986; G. P. Jones & Dembo, 1989; Youniss, 1980). As we look more closely at the nature of friendship across the five developmental periods, we see that friendships begin with mutual enjoyment and gradually reflect such additional characteristics as loyalty, trust, compromise, and intimacy (Selman, 1980, 2003).

Infancy (birth–2).   Primitive relationships among peers evolve slowly during infancy. In the beginning, social interests are fleeting, and infants are as likely to crawl over one another as to initiate social contact. Yet as infants grow and become familiar with one another, they smile and watch one another's faces and actions. For example, when Teresa's son Connor was 9 months old, he became friendly with Patrick, another boy of the same age at his child care center. The two boys established familiar play routines, often laughing and chasing one another as they crawled around the room. Although they weren't yet speaking, and they certainly didn't swap secrets, they were clearly attuned to each other's behaviors. Such social interests solidify, and in their second year, toddlers make social overtures more consistently, carry on complex interactions, and display positive emotions with children whom they know (Howes, 1988).

Early childhood (ages 2–6).   In the preschool years children infuse language, fantasy, and play into social interactions with familiar peers. When 3- and 4-year-olds interact with children they have gotten to know (rather than with children who are strangers), they are more likely to offer social greetings and carry on a conversation, engage in complex play, and exhibit good social skills (Charlesworth & LaFreniere, 1983; A. Doyle, 1982; Hinde, Titmus, Easton, & Tamplin, 1985). Figure 14-3 shows a picture drawn by 4-year-old Dana of herself and her friend, Dina. The two girls met in child care and became close companions. Afterwards, they moved to separate towns but happily renewed their friendship when given the chance at summer camp.

Of course, early friendships also provide opportunities for disagreements and arguments (Hartup & Laursen, 1991). In the process of working through conflicts with friends, children learn to assert themselves while showing their regard for friends. You can observe a young child's desire to resolve conflict by listening to 6-year-old Ying-Yu in the "Friendship: Early

DANA DINA

Figure 14-3

Four-year-old Dana drew a picture of herself and her friend Dina. The two girls met in child care and became good friends.

Childhood" video clip on Observation CD 3 as she describes how she responds to an argument with a friend: "I let them choose. My friends choose first and then me 'cause I think that's the helpful thing to do."

In the "Friendship: Early Childhood" clip on Observation CD 3, listen to 6-year-old Ying-Yu talk about resolving conflicts with friends.

Middle childhood (ages 6–10).   During the elementary school years, children continue to act differently with friends than with peers who are not friends. For example, with friends they are more likely to express their feelings and to speculate about one another's emotional states (Newcomb & Bagwell, 1995; Newcomb & Brady, 1982). At this age friends develop a sense of loyalty to one another, and many of them, girls especially, use self-disclosure as a strategy for maintaining a friendship (Buhrmester, 1996; Diaz & Berndt, 1982). Friendships are more stable in middle childhood than in earlier years, and children are more deliberate in selecting playmates with qualities similar to their own (Berndt & Hoyle, 1985; Rubin, Lynch, Coplan, Rose-Krasnor, & Booth, 1994). Youngsters typically choose friends of their own gender, perhaps in part because same-gender peers are more likely to share interests and pastimes (Gottman, 1986b; Kovacs, Parker, & Hoffman, 1996; Maccoby, 1990).

Early adolescence (ages 10–14).   Differences in relationships between friends and nonfriends intensify during early adolescence (Basinger et al., 1995; J. G. Parker & Gottman, 1989). Many young adolescents let down their guard and reveal their weaknesses and vulnerabilities to close friends, even as they may try to maintain a demeanor of competence and self-confidence in front of other age-mates. Adolescents also experience and confront feelings of possessiveness and jealousy about friends (Rubin et al., 1998). Gradually, young adolescents learn that friendships don't have to be exclusive, and friendship pairs converge into larger groups (Rubin et al., 1998).

Close friendships in the elementary and middle school years are typically between children of the same gender. Art by Andres, age 10.

Late adolescence (ages 14–18).   Older adolescents tend to be quite selective in their choice of friends (J. L. Epstein, 1986). Gone are the days when they run out of fingers as they count off their "close" friends. Instead, older teenagers tend to nurture relationships with a few friends that they keep for some time, perhaps throughout their lives. Having such friendships enhances their self-esteem (Berndt, 1992; Berndt & Hoyle, 1985). Older adolescents frequently turn to friends for emotional support in times of trouble or confusion, and they are likely to engage in lengthy discussions about personal problems and possible solutions (Asher & Parker, 1989; Buhrmester, 1992, 1996; Newcomb & Bagwell, 1995; J. G. Parker & Gottman, 1989; Seltzer, 1982). As they exchange their tales of trials and tribulations, adolescent friends often discover that they aren't as unique as they once thought (Elkind, 1981a).

Connecting Concepts
Young adolescents' belief that they are unlike anyone else is known as the *personal fable,* a concept discussed in Chapters 4 and 12.

Fostering friendships and other productive peer relationships.   Group environments for children—classrooms, schools, after-school programs, and so forth—are excellent settings for fostering children's friendships and other constructive peer relationships. Thoughtful intervention is particularly important for youngsters who are socially isolated or rejected by their peers. We offer the following suggestions:

● *Help young children ease into social groups.* Young children who are shy or new to a community can benefit from gentle intercession by teachers and caregivers. In the following anecdote, Mrs. Kusumoto, a Japanese preschool teacher, skillfully models desired behaviors and helps one child, Fumiko, enter a group of peers:

> Mrs. Kusumoto helps Fumiko put a cha-cha-cha tape in the portable cassette player, and calls a second girl to come over and join them on a small stage made of blocks. The two girls and Mrs. Kusumoto stand on the stage, singing and shaking their maracas. Then Mrs. Kusumoto steps down and faces them, singing along and encouraging them to continue. After a few minutes she attempts to melt away. The girls continue singing briefly, but when the song ends the second girl runs off, leaving Fumiko alone and unoccupied. She looks for Mrs. Kusumoto and begins following her around again. Mrs. Kusumoto approaches a small group of girls who are playing house, asking them: "Would you like to invite this girl over for dinner? After giving the concert, she is very hungry." One of the girls nods silently. Fumiko smiles and enters the

One effective way to foster productive peer relationships in children is to encourage them to pursue shared goals in cooperative groups.

"house." She stands there uncertainly, saying nothing. Mrs. Kusumoto inquires, "Fumiko-chan. Have you had your dinner? Why don't you join us? Don't you want something to eat? It looks good." Fumiko nods and the girls bring her a couple [of] dishes of clay "food." Mrs. Kusumoto looks on briefly, then moves quietly out of the scene. (Holloway, 2000, pp. 100–101)

● *Set up situations in which youngsters can enjoy friendly interactions with one another.* Teachers can do many simple things to encourage children to get to know one another. For example, teachers can arrange structured cooperative learning activities that require all group members to share equal responsibility, and they can provide play equipment such as balls and climbing structures that lend themselves to coordinated group activities (Banks, 1994; S. S. Martin, Brady, & Williams, 1991; Schofield, 1995; Slavin, 1990). They can also ask youngsters to read to a peer with a visual impairment, sign to a child with a hearing loss, tutor a classmate with a learning disability, or take notes for a child with a physical impairment. In addition, teachers can acknowledge the mutual benefits of children's helpful gestures ("Thanks, Jamie, for helping Branson—he really appreciated your assistance, and you seemed to learn a lot yourself by explaining the assignment to him").

● *Minimize or eliminate barriers to social interaction.* Children and adolescents are less likely to interact with peers when physical, linguistic, or social barriers stand in the way. For example, Jeanne recalls a junior high school student who could not negotiate the cafeteria steps with her wheelchair and frequently ended up eating lunch alone. Educators can be on the lookout for such physical impediments to interaction and campaign for their removal. They can also teach groups of youngsters who speak different languages (including American Sign Language) some basic vocabulary and simple phrases in one another's native tongues. And at a deeper level, educators must actively address the prejudices and tensions that sometimes separate diverse ethnic groups.

──────── Connecting Concepts
Strategies to address prejudice in children are examined in Chapter 12.

● *Cultivate children's empathy for peers with special needs.* Some children feel resentment or anger because of inappropriate behaviors they believe a peer with special needs should be able to control (Juvonen, 1991; Juvonen & Weiner, 1993). Consequently, they are less likely to be tolerant of children with cognitive difficulties or emotional and behavioral disorders than they are of children with obvious physical disabilities (Madden & Slavin, 1983; Ysseldyke & Algozzine, 1984). Teachers and other practitioners must help nondisabled children understand the difficulties that peers may have as a result of a disability. At the same time, perhaps through paired or small-group activities, they can show nondisabled youngsters that peers with disabilities have many of the same talents, thoughts, feelings, and desires that they have (D. Staub, 1998).

──────── Study Guide and Reader
To learn more about how to promote the social inclusion of children with special needs, refer to Supplementary Reading 14-1 in the *Study Guide and Reader.*

● *Provide the specific kinds of support rejected children need most.* An important first step in helping rejected children is to determine the reasons that other children find them unpleasant to be around. Some rejected children are aggressive, have limited social skills, and use coercive behaviors to get their way (Bierman, 2004). Other rejected children have trouble asserting their desires and opinions, and peers may occasionally call them names and victimize them (Salmivalli & Isaacs, 2005). Once educators understand exactly what is missing from rejected children's repertoires of social skills, they can take the next step and address these needs.

──────── Connecting Concepts
You saw one teacher help change a rejected child's reputation in the opening case study in Chapter 1.

● *Help change the reputations of rejected children.* Unfortunately, bad reputations often live on long after people's behavior has changed for the better. Even after children show dramatic improvements in social behavior, peers may continue to dislike and reject them (Bierman, Miller, & Staub, 1987; Juvonen & Hiner, 1991; Juvonen & Weiner, 1993). For example, in the case of formerly aggressive children, the perception of many peers is "once a bully, always a bully." To improve children's reputations, adults can create structured cooperative learning groups and extracurricular activities in which children can use their newly developed social skills. In one way or another, adults must help previously annoying and abrasive children show peers that they now can be good playmates.

● *Encourage a general feeling of respect for others.* Adults who effectively promote friendships among diverse groups of children are often those who consistently communicate that all members of their community deserve respect as human beings (A. P. Turnbull, Pereira, & Blue-Banning, 2000). Fernando Arias, a high school vocational education teacher, put it this way:

> In our school, our philosophy is that we treat everybody the way we'd like to be treated. . . . Our school is a unique situation where we have pregnant young ladies who go to our school. We have special education children. We have the regular kids, and we have the drop-out recovery program . . . we're all equal. We all have an equal chance. And we have members of every gang at our school, and we hardly have any fights, and there are close to about 300 gangs in our city. We all get along. It's one big family unit it seems like. (A. P. Turnbull et al., 2000, p. 67)

● *Encourage children to be honest and diplomatic during conflicts with friends.* When children argue with friends, they often find it difficult to express their personal feelings *and* accept the validity of their friends' perspectives. Role playing can be a useful way to give children practice with resolving disagreements. For instance, one fifth-grade teacher, Mrs. Burgos, asked her students to interpret a dispute between characters in a novel. During class Mrs. Burgos asked two girls, Marisol and Rosario, to simulate the conflict. In the scenario Marisol has been assigned a desirable part in the school's dramatic production of a Thanksgiving story but has not told her good friend Rosario about this honor. It takes extended discussion before the girls fully acknowledge both their perspectives:

> Marisol: I think that you're just jealous because I got the best part and you couldn't get the part that you wanted to get.
> Rosario: That's not true, I'm not jealous. I'm just mad at you because you didn't tell me.
> Marisol: I just changed my mind when I went home and thought about it all over.
> Rosario: Yeah, but best friends is for to share and tell secrets.
> Marisol: When I went to look for you, you didn't want to talk to me or nothing.
> Rosario: Because I was mad at you. (Selman, 2003, p. 205)

● *Be a backup system when relationships with peers aren't going well.* Disruptions in peer relationships—perhaps because of interpersonal conflicts or a friend's relocation to a distant city—can trigger emotional distress in youngsters (Wentzel, 1999). Warm, supportive adults can lessen the pain in such circumstances, and ongoing gestures of affection can also bolster the spirits of other children who, for whatever reasons, have no close friends (Guay et al., 1999; Wentzel, 1999). Such sympathetic overtures may be especially important for children who have little support at home and might otherwise turn to deviant peer groups for attention (Parks, 1995).

Social Groups

In middle childhood children are motivated to interact with peers at school and in their neighborhoods. Adolescents are even more inclined to congregate with peers. As a result of their expanding social life, youngsters come into contact with many peers and begin to form larger social groups that regularly fraternize (Eisenberg et al., 1996; Gottman & Mettetal, 1986). Initially, these groups are comprised of single-sex friendships, but in adolescence they often include both boys and girls (Gottman & Mettetal, 1986; J. R. Harris, 1995).

Youngsters' social groups vary considerably in size, function, and character. However, many have the following attributes:

● *Group members develop a common culture.* A social group works out a general set of rules (often unspoken), expectations, and interpretations—a **peer culture** that influences how group members behave (P. Davidson & Youniss, 1995; J. R. Harris, 1998; M. S. Knapp & Woolverton, 1995). This shared culture gives group members a sense of community, belonging, and identity. Within a school the array of groups can be quite complex, as 14-year-old Connor shows in his representation of the groups of students he perceived during his freshman year in high school (see Figure 14-4).

peer culture
General set of rules, expectations, and interpretations that influence how members of a particular peer group behave.

● *Group members socialize one another to follow the group's norms.* Group members encourage conformity by reinforcing behaviors that are appropriate in the eyes of the group and discouraging behaviors that are not (Clasen & Brown, 1985; Dishion, Spracklen, Andrews, & Patterson, 1996). Youngsters also pressure themselves to adopt the group's shared norms and values, that is, they *self-socialize* (Gottman & Mettetal, 1986; Kindermann, 1993). Fortunately, many peer groups embrace productive and prosocial behaviors, such as honesty, fairness, cooperation, academic achievement, and a sense of humor (Damon, 1988; Kindermann, 1993; McCallum & Bracken, 1993). Some others, however, encourage less worthy behaviors, such as threatening and pushing classmates around, and discourage scholastic endeavors, perhaps making fun of "brainy" students or endorsing cheating, cutting class, and skipping school (Berndt, 1992; B. B. Brown, 1993; M. S. Knapp & Woolverton, 1995; Lowry, Sleet, Duncan, Powell, & Kolbe, 1995).

——————— Connecting Concepts
Self-socialization is described in more detail in Chapter 12.

● *Group members influence youngsters more strongly in some areas of life than others.* Young people rarely accept a peer's suggestions without question (B. B. Brown, 1990). Instead, they typically evaluate what peers ask them to do and may consider advice they have previously received from people outside the peer group. Peer groups are particularly influential in matters of style—for example, in dress, music, and social activities. In contrast, parents, teachers, and other significant adults continue to be influential in most young people's views about education, morality, religion, and careers (J. R. Harris, 1998; Hartup, 1983; Sewald, 1986).

● *Group members have a sense of unity as a group.* Once youngsters gel as a group, they prefer other group members over nonmembers, and they develop feelings of loyalty to individuals within the group. In some cases they also develop feelings of hostility and rivalry toward members of other groups (J. R. Harris, 1995, 1998; Sherif, Harvey, White, Hood, & Sherif, 1961). Such feelings toward *out-groups* are particularly intense when two or more groups must actively compete for status or resources, as rival athletic teams and adolescent gangs often do.

Figure 14-4

Fourteen-year-old Connor diagrammed the groups of students he observed during his freshman year in high school. In his inner circle he labeled the different groups (e.g., preps, jocks, gamers) and in the outer circle he described each one (e.g., "wear nice clothes and usually cocky," "athletic, usually wear letter jackets," "Nintendo is a large part in their lives").

● *Dominance hierarchies emerge within the group.* When children's groups continue for any length of time, a pecking order, or **dominance hierarchy,** gradually evolves (Strayer, 1991). Some group members rise to the top, leading the way and making decisions for the entire group. Other group members are followers: They look to those around them for guidance about how to behave and assume lesser roles in the group's activities. Sometimes these less dominant individuals find unique niches within the group, perhaps becoming the clown, daredevil, or brain of the group.

Once youngsters reach puberty, social groups become a particularly prominent feature of their social worlds. Developmental researchers have described three group phenomena that are significant during the adolescent years: cliques, subcultures, and gangs.

Cliques. **Cliques** are moderately stable friendship groups of perhaps 3 to 10 individuals; they provide the basis for many voluntary social interactions during adolescence (Crockett, Losoff, & Peterson, 1984; J. L. Epstein, 1986; Kindermann, McCollom, & Gibson, 1996). Clique boundaries tend to be fairly rigid and exclusive (some people are in, others are out), and membership in various cliques affects social status and dominance with peers (Wigfield et al., 1996). In early adolescence, cliques are usually comprised of a single sex; in later adolescence, cross-sex cliques become increasingly common (J. L. Epstein, 1986).

Although most middle school and high school students have friends, a smaller number of them belong to cliques (J. L. Epstein, 1986). Thus, the emergence of cliques in early ado-

dominance hierarchy
Relative standing of group members in terms of such qualities as leadership and social influence.

clique
Moderately stable friendship group of perhaps 3 to 10 members.

lescence heightens young people's concerns about acceptance (Gavin & Furman, 1989). Young adolescents wonder about their social standing: "Who likes me?" "Will I be popular at my new school?" "Why didn't Sal invite me to his party?" When they occasionally leave one clique to join another, they are apt to engender feelings of betrayal, hurt, and jealousy in the friends they leave behind (Kanner, Feldman, Weinberger, & Ford, 1987; Rubin et al., 1998). Late in high school, adolescents feel freer to move in and out of groups, and suspicion and rivalry among groups dissipate (see Chapter 12).

Subcultures. Some adolescents affiliate with a well-defined **subculture,** a group that resists a powerful dominant culture by adopting a significantly different way of life (J. S. Epstein, 1998). Such a group may be considerably larger than a clique and does not always have the tight-knit cohesiveness and carefully drawn boundaries of a clique. Instead, it is defined by common values, beliefs, and behavior patterns. Some subcultures are relatively benign; for instance, a middle school skateboarders' subculture may simply espouse a particular mode of dress. Other subcultures, such as those that endorse racist and anti-Semitic behaviors (e.g., skinheads) or who practice Satanic rituals, can be worrisome (C. C. Clark, 1992).

Some adolescent subcultures, like this one, are distinguished by relatively superficial characteristics, such as mode of dress or preference for a particular kind of music. Other subcultures that endorse dangerous and violent behaviors are more worrisome.

Adolescents are more likely to affiliate with subcultures when they feel alienated from the dominant culture, whether that of their school or of the larger society, and want to distinguish themselves from it in some way (C. C. Clark, 1992; J. R. Harris, 1998). They also tend to develop subcultures when they are pessimistic or apathetic about their future (J. S. Epstein, 1998).

Gangs. A **gang** is a cohesive social group characterized by initiation rites, distinctive colors and symbols, alleged ownership of a specific territory, feuds with one or more rival groups, and criminal activity (A. Campbell, 1984; Jensen, 2005). Gangs have well-defined dominance hierarchies, strict rules, and stiff penalties for breaking them.

In recent decades the appeal of gangs has become widespread, and membership has grown substantially, especially in lower-income inner-city areas but also in suburbs and rural areas (Parks, 1995; Valdez, 2000). In a recent survey of U.S. adolescents, 7 percent of boys and 4 percent of girls reported that they were members of a gang (Gottfredson & Gottfredson, 2001).

Adolescents, and sometimes younger children as well, affiliate with gangs for a variety of reasons. Joining a gang enables young people to demonstrate their loyalty to friends, gain recognition for accomplishments, obtain financial rewards (through criminal activities), receive missing emotional support, please family members already in the gang, and gain protection from victimization (A. Campbell, 1984; C. C. Clark, 1992; Jensen, 2005; Parks, 1995; Simons, Whitbeck, Conger, & Conger, 1991).

In some instances gang members endorse prosocial behaviors, such as caring for one another and encouraging one another's self-expression (Moje, 2000). But generally speaking, gangs do more harm than good. High rates of using and selling drugs, carrying destructive weapons, and intimidating peers make gangs a serious concern to law enforcement officers, community leaders, and educators (Jensen, 2005; Parks, 1995).

Based on the available research, the following recommendations may be of help to educators and others who work in communities where youth gangs are present:

● *Nurture children's abilities.* When youngsters feel cared for by teachers and are confident in their own academic abilities, they are more likely to remain in school, avoid criminal activity, and resist the pressures of gangs (Jensen, 2005). A variety of programs aim to cultivate children's skills and optimism about being successful in mainstream society. *Gang prevention programs* include early childhood curricula that prepare young children with emergent literacy skills and a healthy self-confidence; school-based initiatives that focus on safety, resistance to gangs, and meaningful school experiences; and after-school programs, such as Boys and Girls Clubs of America (Howell, 2000; D. Peterson & Esbensen, 2004).

● *Watch for signs that youngsters may be involved with a gang.* Youths affiliated with a gang broadcast their allegiance to the group by wearing certain colors on clothing and bandanas; displaying gang symbols on jewelry and tattoos; performing particular hand signals or handshakes; creating graffiti and symbols on walls, notebooks, and class assignments; and

subculture
Group that resists the ways of the dominant culture and adopts its own norms for behavior.

gang
Cohesive social group characterized by initiation rites, distinctive colors and symbols, territorial orientation, feuds with rival groups, and criminal activity.

using certain words and mannerisms (Howell, 2000). When teachers suspect that a young person is in a gang, they should consult with their principals and school counselors about appropriate responses.

● *Protect youngsters from the intimidation of gang members.* Children and adolescents deserve to feel safe at school. Therefore, teachers and other school staff need to work hard to establish safe school climates with clear rules and enforced consequences for acts of violence and intimidation. Many schools prohibit gang signals and markings, and some schools employ extreme measures, such as security guards, metal detectors, and locker checks (Howell & Lynch, 2000). When drastic measures must be taken, they should be accompanied by extra efforts to preserve students' basic rights and convey a general sense of respect for students' integrity and goodwill. After all, most students are *not* gang members and should certainly not be treated as if they were.

● *Seek help from the experts.* Gangs are a sufficiently serious problem that they merit multipronged strategies from collaborative teams of professionals. Teachers, principals, and school counselors often find they are most productive in addressing gang-related problems when they enlist the support of law enforcement and community officials. Police and community leaders can also advise educators about intervention and suppression programs in their area. *Intervention programs* entice youths to leave gangs and to forgo criminal activities by offering job training, adult mentoring, gang mediation, and counseling (Howell, 2000). *Suppression programs* try to reduce gang activities through weapon seizures and arrests for gang-related incidents near schools.

Romance and Sexuality

Awareness of romantic relationships first develops in early childhood. Many children, especially those living in traditional two-parent families, believe that getting married and having children is a normal, perhaps inevitable, part of growing up. They sometimes act out their fantasies in play, as this episode involving Eric and Naomi illustrates:

E: Hey, Naomi, I know what we can play today.
N: What?
E: How about, um, the marry game. You like that.
N: Marry?
E: How about baker or something? How about this. Marry you? OK, Naomi, you want to pretend that?
N: Yes.
E: OK, Naomi, do you want to marry me?
N: Yeah.
E: Good, just a minute, Naomi, we don't have any marry place.
N: We could pretend this is the marry place.
E: Oh, well, pretend this, ah, there'll have to be a cake.
N: The wedding is here first.
E: OK, but listen to this, we have to have a baby, oh, and a pet.
N: This is our baby. (Gottman, 1986b, p. 157)

Consistent with what we have learned about cognitive abilities at this age, young children's understandings of courtship and marriage are simple and concrete. For example, in the preceding scenario, the children focus on having a "marry place" and wedding cake. Nevertheless, by pretending to get married, young children anticipate their eventual entry into romantic relationships.

As children grow, they gradually expand on their ideas about what it means to participate in romantic relationships. For instance, prior to puberty some children practice courtship behaviors (Elkind, 1981b). Girls vie for the attention of boys, use cosmetics, and choose clothing and hairstyles that make them look older and (they think) prettier. Boys, meanwhile, flaunt whatever manly airs they can muster. Both sexes pay close heed to the romantic activities of those around them and absorb the many romantic images they see in the media (Connolly & Goldberg, 1999; Larson, Clore, & Wood, 1999).

As young people reach adolescence, romance is increasingly on their minds and is a frequent topic of conversation (B. B. Brown, Feiring, & Furman, 1999). The biological changes associated with puberty usher in sexual desires as well (Larson et al., 1999). Furthermore, in most Western cultures, social pressures mount to tempt, perhaps even push, young adolescents into dating and some degree of sexual activity (Larson et al., 1999; B. C. Miller & Benson, 1999).

——————— **Connecting Concepts**
Chapter 12 offers strategies for discouraging aggressive behavior at school.

——————— **Connecting Concepts**
A mediation program for gang members is described in Chapter 12.

Most preschoolers are curious about courtship and marriage. Here Teresa's son Alex (age 5) depicts his parents getting married.

Romantic relationships benefit adolescents in several ways. Being in a relationship fulfills needs for companionship, affection, and security and may significantly enhance social status with peers (W. A. Collins & Sroufe, 1999; Furman & Simon, 1999; B. C. Miller & Benson, 1999). Such relationships also provide opportunities for young people to experiment with new interpersonal behaviors and examine previously unexplored aspects of their own identity (Furman & Simon, 1999). With time and experience, many young people become adept at capturing and maintaining the affections of romantic partners.

At the same time, romantic relationships can wreak havoc on adolescents' emotions (Larson et al., 1999). Already somewhat prone to moodiness, adolescents can find it exciting and frustrating to enter (and exit) romantic liaisons with one another. The emotional highs and lows that come with romance—the roller coaster ride between exhilaration and disappointment—can cloud judgment, trigger depression, and distract young people from schoolwork (Larson et al., 1999).

Fortunately, most adolescents enter the world of romance slowly and cautiously (B. B. Brown, 1999; Connolly & Goldberg, 1999). Initially, their romances often exist more in their minds than in reality, as the following conversation between two young teenage girls illustrates:

A: How's Lance [*giggle*]? Has he taken you to a movie yet?
B: No. Saw him today but I don't care.
A: Didn't he say anything to you?
B: Oh . . .
A: Lovers!
B: Shut up!
A: Lovers at first sight! [*Giggle.*]
B: [*Giggle.*] Quit it! (Gottman & Mettetal, 1986, p. 210; reprinted with the permission of Cambridge University Press)

Young adolescents' romantic thoughts may also involve crushes on people who are out of reach—perhaps favorite teachers, movie idols, or rock stars (B. B. Brown, 1999; B. C. Miller & Benson, 1999). Slowly, young people become more comfortable in spending time with peers of the opposite sex (B. B. Brown et al., 1999; B. C. Miller & Benson, 1999). These opposite-gender peers often become targets of desire. Eventually, many adolescents broaden their social worlds in two ways—by dating and by experiencing sexual intimacy. Some of them also wrestle with new feelings about members of their own sex.

Dating.   In the middle school years, young adolescents' forays into dating may initially consist of little more than being identified as a couple in the eyes of peers. For instance, in their seventh-grade year, Jeanne's daughter Tina and her friends often talked about their various "boyfriends." Although the girls described themselves as "going out" with this boy or that, in fact they never actually dated any of them.

Eventually, however, most adolescents do venture out on actual dates with one or more peers. Early dating partners are often chosen because of their physical attractiveness or social status, and dating relationships tend to be short-lived and involve only superficial interaction (B. B. Brown, 1999; W. A. Collins & Sroufe, 1999; G. Downey, Bonica, & Rincón, 1999). As teenagers move into the high school years, some begin to form more long-term, intimate relationships (B. B. Brown, 1999; Connolly & Goldberg, 1999). At this point their choices of dating partners depend more on personality characteristics and compatibility; peers' judgments are less influential.

As they participate in romantic relationships, adolescents draw from their prior social experiences with family and friends (Bigelow, Tesson, & Lewko, 1999; W. A. Collins & Sroufe, 1999; Leaper & Anderson, 1997). For instance, adolescents who have secure attachments with family members are more likely to have successful dating experiences, perhaps because they have greater self-confidence, better social skills, and more experience in trusting relationships. Similarly, adolescents who are accustomed to a balanced give-and-take in decision making at home may use this same style with romantic partners, negotiating what movie to see, which party to attend, and so on. Conversely, teens who have repeatedly seen family violence may bring physical aggression into disagreements with dating partners—hitting, pushing, or in other ways violating them (Wolfe & Wekerle, 1997). They may also tolerate and rationalize aggressive behavior from partners ("He didn't mean it," "She was drunk," "He'll outgrow it").

Connecting Concepts —————
As Chapters 4 and 11 point out, the hormonal changes of puberty can trigger volatile moods in young people.

Sexual intimacy.   Both genders have some capacity for sexual arousal even before puberty (Conn & Kanner, 1940; Langfeldt, 1981). Children and preadolescents occasionally look at or touch one another in private places and play games (e.g., strip poker) that have sexual overtones (Dornbusch et al., 1981; Katchadourian, 1990). Except in cases of sexual abuse, however, sexuality before adolescence lacks the erotic features present in later development.

During puberty nature ensures that young people gain both the physical structures and the impetus to become sexually active. Although sexual maturation is a natural process, it is not a simple matter to address. No one knows how best to handle adolescent sexuality—not parents, not teachers, and certainly not adolescents themselves (Katchadourian, 1990). Many adults ignore the topic, assuming (or perhaps hoping) it's not yet relevant for adolescents. Even teenagers who have good relationships with their parents have few chances to talk about sex (Brooks-Gunn & Furstenberg, 1990; R. M. C. Leite, Buoncompagno, Leite, & Mergulhao, 1995). And when parents and teachers do broach the topic of sexuality, they often raise it in conjunction with problems, such as irresponsible behavior, substance abuse, disease, and unwanted pregnancy.

Adolescents, meanwhile, must come to terms with their emerging sexuality, either on their own or in collaboration with trusted peers. They must learn to accept their changing bodies, cope with unanticipated feelings of sexual arousal and desire, and try to reconcile the conflicting messages they get from various sources—home, school, religious groups, peers, the media—about whether and under what circumstances varying degrees of sexual intimacy are appropriate (Brooks-Gunn & Paikoff, 1993).

For many adolescents sexual intimacy goes hand in hand with, and is a natural outgrowth of, long-term romantic relationships (Graber, Britto, & Brooks-Gunn, 1999; B. C. Miller & Benson, 1999). For many others, however, it is something that should be saved for the "right moment," perhaps for marriage. And for a few, sexual intimacy is an activity completely separate from romantic involvement. For these individuals it may be a means of enhancing image and social status with peers, exploring possible sexual orientations, gaining others' attention and affection, or simply experiencing physical pleasure (W. A. Collins & Sroufe, 1999; L. M. Diamond, Savin-Williams, & Dubé, 1999).

Adolescents' intimate experiences sometimes add to their confusion about sexuality. Consider these varying recollections about a first kiss (Alapack, 1991):

> The experience was so gentle that I was in awe. I walked back to my cabin on weak knees. My girlfriends told me I was blushing furiously. I felt lightheaded, but oh so satisfied. (p. 58)

> I found myself mentally stepping back, thinking: "no rockets, fireworks, music or stars." I had to fake enjoyment, humor him. But I felt nothing! Later I sat on my bed and contemplated becoming a nun! (p. 60)

> He kissed me violently and pawed me over. When I started to cry, he let me go . . . I didn't want it to count. I wanted to wipe it off as I rubbed off the saliva. I couldn't. It couldn't be reversed; I couldn't be unkissed again. And the moisture, I could feel it, smell it, even though it was wiped. It made me nauseous. I felt like I was going to throw up. (p. 62)

These varied accounts have little in common, except perhaps a sense of discovery. Other first intimacies also reflect such variability: Some teens are moved by tenderness and shared pleasure, but others are disappointed, repulsed, or confused (Carns, 1973; Sorensen, 1983).

Most adolescents gradually add to their repertoire of sexual behaviors. As you might recall from Chapter 4, a sizable minority of adolescents (approximately 4 in 10) try sexual intercourse during the high school years. Typically, adolescents initiate sexual intercourse only after several years of experience with less intimate contacts (DeLamater & MacCorquodale, 1979; Udry, 1988).

For quite a few adolescents, sexual activity has unintended physical consequences, including pregnancy and infection. Unfortunately, adolescents may hold beliefs that exacerbate their vulnerability. For example, many teenagers do not consider oral or anal sexual contact to be "real" sex, and they believe (incorrectly) that sexually transmitted infections are not possible with such contact (Remez, 2000). Even when adolescents are aware that such consequences are possible, they sometimes discount these risks because they feel invulnerable or are impaired by drugs or alcohol.

— Connecting Concepts
Personal fable—a belief that one is unlike others and invulnerable to common dangers—is examined in Chapters 4 and 12. This belief seems to contribute to risky sexual behaviors.

sexual orientation
Particular sex(es) to which an individual is romantically and sexually attracted.

Sexual orientation.   By **sexual orientation** we mean the particular sex(es) to which an individual is romantically and sexually attracted. A small but significant percentage of adolescents find themselves sexually attracted to their own gender, either instead of or in addition to the opposite gender. Although it has been difficult to establish precise figures, researchers have estimated that 5 percent to 10 percent of the adult population may be gay, lesbian, or bisexual (Durby, 1994; C. J. Patterson, 1995).

The causes of sexual orientation remain uncertain, but many theorists suspect that both genetic and environmental factors contribute (Byne, 1997; De Cecco & Parker, 1995; Money, 1988; Savin-Williams & Diamond, 1997). Some evidence for a genetic component comes from twin studies: Monozygotic (identical) twins are more similar in their sexual orientation than dizygotic (fraternal) twins (Bailey & Pillard, 1997; Gabard, 1999). Nevertheless, even monozygotic twins are not always the same. For male twins, if one is homosexual, the other has a 50-50 chance of being so; for female twins, the probability is a bit lower. Other researchers have observed subtle differences between homosexual and heterosexual individuals in certain brain structures, and some investigators suggest that variations in hormones circulating in the prenatal environment may initiate a cascade of physiological effects that ultimately influence sexual orientation (Bailey & Pillard, 1997; Money, 1987).

Regardless of the exact blend of nature and nurture that determines sexual orientation, this important aspect of sexuality does not appear to be a voluntary decision. Many homosexual and bisexual young people recall feeling "different" from peers in their childhood days yet do not fully understand this feeling (D. A. Anderson, 1994; Savin-Williams, 1995). Adolescence is a particularly confusing time for them, as they struggle to form an identity while feeling different and isolated from peers (Morrow, 1997; C. J. Patterson, 1995). When their attractions to same-gender peers become stronger, they may initially work hard to ignore or discount such sentiments. At an older age, they may begin to accept some aspects of their homosexuality, and later still they may "come out" and identify fully and openly with other gay and lesbian individuals. In the following Interpreting Children's Artifacts and Actions feature, "This Is Who I Am," consider the challenges that one young man faced when considering his homosexuality.

Connecting Concepts
Chapter 3 describes biological differences between monozygotic and dizygotic twins.

INTERPRETING CHILDREN'S ARTIFACTS AND ACTIONS

This Is Who I Am

After a year of college, 19-year-old Michael wrote the following essay. As you read it, speculate about the factors that initially made it difficult for him to accept his homosexuality and feel good about himself.

As long as I can remember, I always felt a little different when it came to having crushes on other people. When I was in elementary school I never had crushes on girls, and when I look back on that time now, I was probably most attracted to my male friends. I participated in some of the typical "boy" activities, like trading baseball cards and playing video games, but I was never very interested in rough sports. I often preferred to play with the girls in more role-playing and cooperative games. Of course, I didn't understand much about sex or gender roles at the time. I just figured I would become more masculine and develop feelings for the opposite sex after going through puberty.

To my dismay, middle school and the onset of puberty only brought more attention to my lack of interest in girls. The first time I thought about being gay was when I was in 6th grade, so I was probably 11 or 12 years old at the time. But in my mind, being gay was not an option and I began to expend an incredible amount of energy repressing my developing homosexual urges. In 7th grade, I had my first experience with major depression. Looking back on it, I am almost positive that being gay was the immediate cause of the depression. . . . When I finally recovered from the episode a few months later, I did my best to move on with my life and forget about my problems with sexuality. I continued to repress my feelings through high school, a task that became more and more difficult as the years went by. I never really dated any girls and my group of friends in high school was highly female. When I was 16, a junior in

high school, I had another more severe bout of depression. . . . I continued to be ashamed of my feelings and refused to even tell my psychologist about concerns over my sexuality. After finally emerging from my depression, I came to somewhat of an agreement with myself. I decided that I would simply put my conflict on hold, hoping it would resolve itself. Unfortunately, I still held on to the hope that it would resolve itself in heterosexuality and I remained distraught by my feelings. I finally came out during my freshman year at [college] with the support of my friends and an extremely accepting social environment.

Having exposure to the homosexual lifestyle in college is what finally made me realize that I could have a normal life and that I would not have to compromise my dreams because of it. Even though my high school was relatively liberal and very supportive of different backgrounds, there was very little discussion about homosexuality, even in health class. We had visibly gay teachers, but it was rarely openly talked about. I think the reason it took me so long to accept my sexuality was simply because I had no exposure to it while growing up. It angers me that people refer to homosexuality as a lifestyle choice because I had no choice over my sexuality. I spent seven years of my life denying my homosexuality, and believe me, if there had ever been a choice between gay or straight during that time, I would have chosen straight in a second. Today I can't imagine my life without being gay and I would never choose to be straight.

Essay used with permission.

As Michael's experience suggests, the road to self-acceptance for a gay youth can be a rocky one, and anger and depression are common along the way (Elia, 1994; C. J. Patterson, 1995). The fact that no one talked openly about homosexuality made it difficult for Michael to accept the validity of his own feelings. The resulting emotional toll that Michael experienced was substantial—he became seriously depressed. Happily, Michael eventually entered a supportive social climate, which fostered his self-acceptance.

Michael's experience raises the issue of how homosexuality and bisexuality are addressed at school. When the topic of homosexuality comes up in the school curriculum, it is usually within the context of acquired immune deficiency syndrome (AIDS) and other risks (Malinsky, 1997). Among their peers adolescents with a homosexual or bisexual orientation are frequently harassed and occasionally become the victims of hate crimes (Elze, 2003; R. A. Friend, 1993; Savin-Williams, 1995). Under such circumstances gay, lesbian, and bisexual youths are often "silent, invisible, and fearful" (M. B. Harris, 1997, p. xxi), and a higher-than-average proportion drop out of school (Elia, 1994).

Despite these social hardships, most gay and lesbian youths are psychologically and socially healthy and find the social support they need (Savin-Williams, 1989; Savin-Williams & Ream, 2003). For example, one lesbian girl, Elise, joined a local support group with the help of her mother. Elise found contact with other gay and lesbian adolescents to be very reassuring:

> I was so happy to realize that—oh wow, it's very difficult to describe the feeling—realizing, feeling completely completely alone and then realizing that other people know exactly where you're at or what you're going through. I mean it was amazing. (Herr, 1997, p. 60)

Addressing adolescents' sexuality.   When young people reach puberty, the intrigue of romance seeps into their social environments, and they become preoccupied with who harbors secret yearnings for whom, whether the targets of desire reciprocate the affection, and which friends have progressed to various points along the continuum of sexual exploration. Teachers often find this undercurrent of romantic desire distracting but cannot squash the instincts that energize adolescent bodies. Teachers can, however, be supportive in the following ways:

● *Remember how you felt as an adolescent.* If romance was not a part of your own adolescence, we suspect that you longed for it or found yourself fantasizing about someone. If you dated occasionally or frequently, the depth of sentiments from your first experiences undoubtedly left a trace (we wager you can remember your first date, first kiss, first rejection). Distracting as they might be, romantic desires are a natural, healthy part of coming-of-age.

● *Expect diversity in adolescents' romantic relationships.* Teenagers' romantic activities will, to some degree, reflect the cultural norms of the surrounding community. Yet within any given culture, individual differences are sizable. Some young people attract a series of steady admirers, whereas others may be inexperienced in, possibly even indifferent to, the world of romance. And a small percentage of adolescents will have yearnings for members of their own sex.

● *Make information about human sexuality easily available.* A conventional belief has held that education about human sexuality is the prerogative of parents and has no place in schools. Typically, if sex education is a part of the school curriculum at all, it focuses on the biological aspects of sexual intercourse and offers little information to help teens make sense of their conflicting thoughts and feelings about physical intimacy. Furthermore, adolescents' participation in a sex education curriculum usually requires parents' approval, and many parents are loath to give it. Less controversial alternatives include making literature about a variety of related issues accessible at school libraries and letting adolescents know that school counselors and nurses are always willing to talk with them about matters of health and sexuality.

● *Create a supportive environment for all young people.* To adults the romantic bonds and breakups of adolescents often seem trivial, but they may cause considerable stress in teenagers. For instance, adolescents may feel deep humiliation after rejection from an elusive suitor or a profound sense of loss as a long-term relationship ends (Kaczmarek & Back-

Adults who are open-minded and supportive can help adolescents navigate the highs and lows of romance.

SEXUAL HARASSMENT: IT'S NO JOKE!

■ **Sexual harassment is unwanted and unwelcomed sexual behavior** which interferes with your right to get an education or to participate in school activities. In school, sexual harassment may result from someone's words, gestures or actions (of a sexual nature) that make you feel uncomfortable, embarrassed, offended, demeaned, frightened, helpless or threatened. If you are the target of sexual harassment, it may be very scary to go to school or hard to concentrate on your school work.

■ **Sexual harassment can happen once, several times, or on a daily basis.**

■ **Sexual harassment can happen any time and anywhere** in school—in hallways or in the lunchroom, on the playground or the bus, at dances or on field trips.

■ **Sexual harassment can happen to anyone!** Girls and boys both get sexually harassed by other students in school.

■ **Agreement isn't needed.** The target of sexual harassment and the harasser do not have to agree about what is happening; sexual harassment is defined by the girl or boy who is targeted. The harasser may tell you that he or she is only joking, but if their words, gestures or actions (of a sexual nature) are making you uncomfortable or afraid, then you're being sexually harassed. You do not have to get others, either your friends, teachers or school officials, to agree with you.

■ **No one has the right to sexually harass another person!** School officials are legally responsible to guarantee that all students, you included, can learn in a safe environment which is free from sexual harassment and sex discrimination. If you are being sexually harassed, your student rights are being violated. Find an adult you trust and tell them what's happening, so that something can be done to stop the harassment.

■ **Examples of sexual harassment in school:**
  • touching, pinching, and grabbing body parts
  • being cornered
  • sending sexual notes or pictures
  • writing sexual graffiti on desks, bathroom walls or buildings
  • making suggestive or sexual gestures, looks, jokes, or verbal comments (including "mooing," "barking" and other noises)
  • spreading sexual rumors or making sexual propositions
  • pulling off someone's clothes
  • pulling off your own clothes
  • being forced to kiss someone or do something sexual
  • attempted rape and rape

REMEMBER: SEXUAL HARASSMENT IS SERIOUS AND AGAINST THE LAW!

Figure 14-5

Example of how teachers and school counselors might describe sexual harassment in language that children and adolescents understand.
Originally appeared as "Stop Sexual Harassment in Schools," by N. Stein, May 18, 1993, *USA Today*. Copyright 1993 by Nan Stein. Reprinted with permission of the author.

lund, 1991). In such situations teachers and counselors can help adolescents sort through their feelings and look forward with optimism to brighter days and new relationships (Larson et al., 1999).

In addition, educators must make sure that adolescents with diverse sexual orientations feel welcome, respected, and safe at school. Teachers and other school personnel should prohibit verbal insults about sexual orientation and can listen sympathetically to youths who feel alienated or ostracized in the school environment because of their sexual orientation (Elze, 2003; Morrow, 1997).

● *Describe sexual harassment and indicate why it is prohibited.* **Sexual harassment** is any action that a target can reasonably construe as hostile, humiliating, or sexually offensive (Sjostrom & Stein, 1996). It is a form of discrimination and therefore is prohibited by federal and state laws. Sexual harassment can be a problem at the late elementary, middle school, and high school levels, and children and adolescents must know that it will not be tolerated. They should be informed that under no circumstances may they degrade one another—by words, gestures, or actions—with regard to physical traits or sexual orientation. An example of a description of sexual harassment, appropriate for students at varying grade levels, appears in Figure 14-5.

● *Make appropriate referrals when necessary.* Teachers occasionally learn unexpectedly about aspects of youngsters' personal lives. For instance, students may tell teachers they are pregnant, have a pregnant girlfriend, have been raped or sexually abused, or suspect they've contracted a sexually transmitted infection. Educators need to be prepared to make appropriate referrals to counselors and other officials and to encourage adolescents to talk with family members.

As you have learned, peer relationships change considerably over the childhood years. In the Developmental Trends table "Peer Relationships at Different Age Levels," you can review typical features and variations in peer relationships during the developmental periods and consider their implications for supporting youngsters of various ages.

sexual harassment
Form of discrimination in which a target individual perceives another's actions or statements to be hostile, humiliating, or offensive, especially pertaining to physical appearance or sexual matters.

DEVELOPMENTAL TRENDS

Peer Relationships at Different Age Levels

Age	What You Might Observe	Diversity	Implications
Infancy (Birth–2) 	• Growing interest in other infants in the same child care setting • Beginning attempts to make contact with familiar infants, such as looking at their faces and smiling at them • In second year, side-by-side play with awareness of one another's actions	• Some infants have not had social experiences with other children in their families or in child care; they may need time to adjust to the presence of other children. • Security of attachment to caregivers may affect children's interaction style with peers. • Infants who are temperamentally inclined to be shy, fearful, or inhibited may be wary of other children.	• Place small babies side by side when they are calm and alert. • Talk about what children are doing (e.g., "Look at Willonda shaking that toy; let's go watch how she makes the beads spin"). • Supervise small children to prevent them from hurting one another. When they accidentally bump into others, redirect them to a different path (e.g., "Come this way, Tammy. Chloe doesn't like it when you bump into her.").
Early Childhood (2–6) 	• Increasing frequency and complexity of interactions with familiar peers • Developing preference for play activities with particular peers • Formation of rudimentary friendships based on proximity and easy access (e.g., formation of friendships with neighbors and preschool classmates) • Involved conversations and imaginative fantasies with friends	• Children with prior social experiences may find it easier to make friends in a new preschool or child care center. • Children with sociable and easy-going temperaments tend to form and keep friends more easily than children who are shy, aggressive, anxious, or highstrung.	• Help shy children gain entry into groups, especially if they have previously had limited social experiences. • When necessary, help children resolve conflicts with friends, but encourage them to identify solutions that benefit everyone and let them do as much of the negotiation as possible.
Middle Childhood (6–10) 	• Concern about being accepted by peers • Tendency to assemble in larger groups than in early childhood • Less need for adult supervision than in early childhood • Outdoor peer groups structured with games and sports • Increase in gossip as children show concern over friends and enemies • Some social exclusiveness, with friends being reluctant to have others join in their activities • Predominance of same-gender friendships (especially after age 7)	• Boys tend to play in larger groups than girls do. • Some children are temperamentally cautious and timid; they may stand at the periphery of groups and show little social initiative. • Some children are actively rejected by peers, perhaps because they are perceived as odd or have poor social skills.	• Supervise children's peer relationships from a distance; intervene when needed to defuse an escalating situation. • Tactfully facilitate the entry of isolated and rejected children into ongoing games, cooperative learning groups, and informal lunch groups. • Teach rejected children how to interact pleasantly with peers.
Early Adolescence (10–14) 	• Variety of contexts (e.g., competitive sports, extracurricular activities, parties) in which to interact with peers • Heightened concern about acceptance and popularity among peers • Fads and conformity in dress and communication styles in peer groups • Same-gender cliques, often restricted to members of a single ethnic group • Increasing intimacy, self-disclosure, and loyalty among friends • New interest in members of the opposite sex; for gay and lesbian youths, new dimensions of interest in the same sex • For some, initiation of dating, often within the context of group activities	• Some young adolescents are very socially minded; others are more quiet and reserved. • Some young adolescents become involved in gangs and other delinquent social activities. • A few young adolescents are sexually active. • A small percentage begin to construct an identity as a gay or lesbian individual. • Gossiping and social exclusion may continue in some groups.	• Make classrooms, schools, and other settings friendly, affirming places for all adolescents. Create an atmosphere of acceptance and respect for diverse kinds of students. Do not tolerate name calling, insensitive remarks, or sexual harassment. • Provide appropriate places for adolescents to hang out before and after school. • Identify mechanisms (e.g., cooperative learning groups, public service projects) through which teenagers can fraternize productively as they work toward academic or prosocial goals. • On some occasions decide which youngsters will work together in groups; on other occasions let them choose their work partners. • Sponsor after-school activities (e.g., in sports, music, or academic interest areas).

(continued)

DEVELOPMENTAL TRENDS

Peer Relationships at Different Age Levels (continued)

Age	What You Might Observe	Diversity	Implications
Late Adolescence (14–18) 	• Emerging understanding that relationships with numerous peers do not necessarily threaten close friendships • Increasing dependence on friends for advice and emotional support, with adults remaining important in such matters as educational choices and career goals • Less cliquishness toward the end of high school; greater tendency to affiliate with larger, less exclusive crowds • Increasing amount of time spent in mixed-gender groups • Many social activities unsupervised by adults • Emergence of committed romantic couples, especially in the last two years of high school	• Some teenagers have parents who continue to monitor their whereabouts; others have little adult supervision. • Adolescents' choices of friends and social groups affect their leisure activities, risk-taking behaviors, and attitudes about schoolwork. Some adolescents, known as thrill-seekers, actively seek out risky activities. • Teens who find themselves attracted to same-gender peers face additional challenges in constructing their adult identities, especially if others are not accepting.	• In literature and history, assign readings with themes of psychological interest to adolescents (e.g., loyalty among friends, self-disclosure of feelings, and vulnerability). • Encourage adolescents to join extracurricular activities, and in other ways make them feel an integral part of their school. • Sponsor dances and other supervised social events that give adolescents opportunities to socialize.

Schools

You have learned in this book that teachers and other practitioners can nurture children and adolescents by providing age-appropriate instruction, adequate physical activity, good nutrition, affectionate care, clear rules, and appropriate discipline. When educators integrate such effective practices into productive environments at school, youngsters truly stand to gain. Let's now consider three characteristics of schools that make them developmentally enriching environments for children and adolescents: a sense of community, affirming socialization messages, and sensitivity to developmental transitions.

The School as a Community

In our introductory case study, Pamela established a productive learning environment by being warm and sympathetic, respectful of children, and knowledgeable about age-appropriate activities. The result was that children listened politely to one another and felt bonded to their kindergarten group. In other words, they functioned well together as a *community*.

Educators foster a **sense of community** in schools when students, teachers, and other school staff have shared goals, support one another's efforts, and believe that everyone makes an important contribution (Hom & Battistich, 1995; D. Kim, Solomon, & Roberts, 1995; Lickona, 1991; Osterman, 2000). When schools cultivate a sense of community, students are more likely to exhibit prosocial behavior, express positive attitudes about school, be intrinsically motivated to learn, and achieve at high levels. Furthermore, a sense of community is associated with lower rates of disruptive classroom behavior, emotional distress, truancy, violence, drug use, and dropping out (Hom & Battistich, 1995; D. Kim et al., 1995; Osterman, 2000).

A sense of community is the outgrowth of hard work by teachers, other school staff, families, and students themselves. Teachers can do their part to cultivate a sense of community when they attend to three factors: (a) the climate of the classroom, (b) instructional methods, and (c) school traditions.

Classroom climate.   To begin with, teachers can foster a sense of community when they establish a warm, supportive atmosphere in the classroom, show that they care for children,

Connecting Concepts
Chapter 5 refers to *community* as children's local neighborhood and surrounding vicinity. Here we note that schools also function as communities because teachers and students interact as groups over an extended time period.

sense of community
In a classroom or school, a collection of widely shared beliefs that students, teachers, and other staff have common goals, support one another's efforts, and make important contributions to everyone's success.

and express their support for children's learning. Children are apt to thrive personally and academically when their classrooms exhibit the following features:

- Teachers communicate genuine caring, respect, and support for all students.
- Students feel both physically and psychologically safe; for instance, they know that they can make mistakes without being ridiculed by their teacher or classmates and that they can seek help from others when they need it.
- Teachers adopt an *authoritative* approach to instruction and classroom management, setting clear guidelines for behavior but, in the process, also considering students' needs and involving students in decision making.
- Teachers provide sufficient order and structure to guide classroom assignments and procedures.
- Teachers give students opportunities to engage in appropriate self-chosen and self-directed activities.

Connecting Concepts
Authoritative parenting and the importance of self-directed activities are discussed in Chapters 5 and 13, respectively.

Classrooms that reflect these characteristics are, in general, productive ones: Students are motivated to learn new skills, perceive themselves as being reasonably capable, and achieve at high academic levels (G. A. Davis & Thomas, 1989; deCharms, 1984; Roderick & Camburn, 1999; A. M. Ryan & Patrick, 2001; Scott-Little & Holloway, 1992; Wentzel, 1999; Wentzel & Wigfield, 1998). When other aspects of children's lives trouble them—for instance, when children's family relationships are strained, children live in dangerous and economically disadvantaged neighborhoods, or the community has recently experienced a natural disaster—perceived support from teachers is especially important in helping youngsters feel safe, competent, valued, and understood (E. P. Smith, Boutte, Zigler, & Finn-Stevenson, 2004).

Study Guide and Reader
To learn more about how teachers can support children during times of trouble and tragedy, refer to Supplementary Reading 14-2 in the *Study Guide and Reader*.

Instructional methods. Teachers can also promote a sense of community by using engaging instructional methods and encouraging children to help one another. Teaching methods that encourage children's active learning and cooperation tend to be effective in instilling positive attitudes about school (E. P. Smith et al., 2004). In one model, children form a **community of learners,** a classroom arrangement in which students help one another achieve a common learning goal. A community of learners has characteristics such as these:

- All students are active participants in classroom activities.
- Discussion and collaboration among two or more students are common occurrences and play a key role in learning.
- Diversity in students' interests and rates of progress is expected and respected.
- Students and teacher coordinate their efforts at helping one another learn; no one has exclusive responsibility for teaching others.
- Everyone is a potential resource for the others; different individuals are likely to serve as resources on different occasions, depending on the topics and tasks at hand. (In some cases students may "major" in a particular topic and become local experts on it.)
- The teacher provides some guidance and direction for classroom activities, but students may also contribute to such guidance and direction.
- Students regularly critique one another's work.
- The process of learning is emphasized as much as, and sometimes more than, the finished product. (A. L. Brown & Campione, 1994, 1996; Campione, Shapiro, & Brown, 1995; Prawat, 1992; Rogoff, 1994; Rogoff, Matusov, & White, 1996)

Connecting Concepts
Chapter 6 describes several cognitive benefits of regular peer interaction during instruction.

The outcomes of community-of-learning groups are often quite positive, especially when teachers encourage children to abide by age-appropriate rules for interaction. These groups tend to promote fairly complex thinking processes (A. L. Brown & Campione, 1994) and are highly motivating for students. For instance, students in these groups often insist on going to school even when they are ill, and they are disappointed when summer vacation begins (Rogoff, 1994).

community of learners
A classroom in which teacher(s) and students actively and collaboratively work to help one another learn.

School traditions. Teachers can also foster a sense of community by encouraging children to participate actively in school activities and day-to-day operations. Schools that operate as true communities encourage everyone to work together as cooperative and productive citizens (Battistich, Solomon, Kim, Watson, & Schaps, 1995; Battistich, Solomon, Watson, & Schaps, 1997; A. L. Brown & Campione, 1994). Several strategies are helpful in creating this positive school spirit:

- Soliciting students' ideas about school activities, such as how Valentine's Day might be observed
- Creating mechanisms through which students can help make the school run smoothly and efficiently (e.g., assigning various helper roles to classrooms and individual students on a rotating basis)
- Emphasizing prosocial values in school codes of conduct, in newsletters, and on bulletin boards
- Providing public recognition of students' contributions to the overall success of the classroom and school
- Creating schoolwide traditions that are fun for youngsters and their families, such as carnivals and field days (D. Kim et al., 1995; Lickona, 1991; Osterman, 2000)

This poster in a middle school corridor (shown in the "Environments: Early Adolescence" clip on Observation CD 1) illustrates one important element of classroom climate: the feeling that one is physically and psychologically safe at school.

Socialization in Schools

Beginning early in their lives, most children learn that there are certain things that they can or should do and other things that they definitely should not do. For example, many parents teach young children not to hit other children and to show politeness by saying "please" and "thank you." Although teachers value some of these same behaviors, they also introduce their own expectations about how children should behave as pupils.

Connecting Concepts ————
As you learned in Chapter 5, *socialization* is the process by which other people encourage youngsters to exhibit behaviors valued in society.

School values.   Teachers begin to socialize children the moment children enter school. For example, teachers typically expect and encourage behaviors such as these:

- Showing respect for authority figures
- Controlling impulses
- Following instructions
- Completing assigned tasks in a timely manner
- Working independently
- Helping and cooperating with classmates
- Striving for academic excellence

Teachers' often-unstated expectations for such behaviors are sometimes known as the *hidden curriculum* of the classroom (Anyon, 1988; Chafel, 1997; P. W. Jackson, 1988). Some customs and values are considered hidden because teachers firmly expect them to be followed but rarely talk about them. A teacher's hidden curriculum may or may not be consistent with sound developmental and educational principles. For example, as the following dialogue between a teacher and several students illustrates, a teacher may emphasize just getting the right answer, doing tasks in a particular way, and getting things done as quickly as possible:

Teacher:	I will put some problems on the board. You are to divide.
Child:	We got to divide?
Teacher:	Yes.
Several children:	[*Groan*] Not again, Mr. B., we done this yesterday.
Child:	Do we put the date?
Teacher:	Yes. I hope we remember we work in silence. You're supposed to do it on white paper. I'll explain it later.
Child:	Somebody broke my pencil. [*Crash*—a child falls out of his chair.]
Child:	[*Repeats*] Mr. B., somebody broke my *pencil!*
Child:	Are we going to be here all morning? (Anyon, 1988, p. 367)

In this situation the teacher presents math problems merely as things that need to be done—not as tasks that might actually have some benefit—and the children clearly have little interest in the assignment.

To help children adjust to the values of a classroom and school, teachers can do two things:

● *Uncover the hidden curriculum.* Children come to school with their own ways of talking and acting and do not automatically decipher teacher's expectations for how children are

Teachers can help students see their schoolwork as activities to achieve important knowledge and skills, not just as things to get done.

supposed to communicate in groups, ask for help, express their confusion, and so forth. In general, children find it easier to act in acceptable ways when teachers explain their expectations and post important rules of behavior on a bulletin board or disseminate them in simple handouts.

● *Consider what children inadvertently learn about school.* In the dialogue about a math assignment, children learned that school was tedious and coercive. We strongly suspect these were *not* the messages the teacher intended to send. Because no teacher is perfect and children can easily interpret lessons and interactions differently than the teacher planned, it is good practice to monitor what children say and do during lessons. From such information teachers can gain insights into ways they might occasionally need to redirect their efforts in order to improve instruction, management, and morale.

Connecting Concepts
Chapter 2 offers recommendations for gathering data from children.

Effects of teacher expectations.   As we have seen, teachers have expectations of how their students should behave in the classroom. But teachers also form expectations about how individual students are likely to perform. In many instances teachers size up their students fairly accurately: They know which ones need help with reading skills, which ones have short attention spans, which ones have trouble working together in the same cooperative group, and so on, and they can adapt their instruction and assistance accordingly (Goldenberg, 1992; Good & Brophy, 1994; Good & Nichols, 2001).

But teachers occasionally make inaccurate assessments. For instance, teachers often underestimate the abilities of students who

- Are physically unattractive
- Misbehave frequently in class
- Speak in dialects other than Standard English
- Are members of ethnic minority groups
- Are recent immigrants
- Come from low-income backgrounds (Banks & Banks, 1995; R. E. Bennett, Gottesman, Rock, & Cerullo, 1993; M. S. Knapp & Woolverton, 1995; McLoyd, 1998b; J. Oakes & Guiton, 1995; Ritts, Patterson, & Tubbs, 1992)

Teachers with low expectations for certain students offer them fewer opportunities for speaking in class, ask them easier questions, give less feedback about their responses, and present them with few, if any, challenging assignments (Babad, 1993; Good & Brophy, 1994; Graham, 1990; Rosenthal, 1994). In contrast, teachers with high expectations for students create a warmer classroom climate, interact with students more frequently, provide more opportunities for students to respond, and give more positive feedback. These teachers also present more course material and more challenging topics.

Connecting Concepts
Teachers' expectations and behaviors significantly influence children's sense of self (see Chapter 12).

Most children and adolescents are well aware of their teachers' differential treatment of individual students and use that treatment to draw inferences about their own and others' abilities (R. Butler, 1994; Good & Nichols, 2001; Weinstein, 1993). When teachers repeatedly give children low-ability messages, children may begin to see themselves as their teachers see them. Furthermore, students' behavior may mirror their self-perceptions. For example, students may exert little effort on academic tasks, or they may frequently misbehave in class (Marachi, Friedel, & Midgley, 2001; Murdock, 1999). In some cases, then, teachers' expectations may lead to a **self-fulfilling prophecy:** What teachers expect students to achieve becomes what students actually do achieve.

Communicating high expectations.   A characteristic consistently found in effective schools is high expectations for student performance (M. Phillips, 1997; Roderick & Camburn, 1999). Even if students' initial academic performance is low, educators and other professionals must remember that cognitive abilities and skills can and do change over time, especially when the environment is conducive to growth. We suggest two strategies to help teachers maintain a realistic yet optimistic outlook on what young people can accomplish:

● *Learn more about students' backgrounds and home environments.* Adults are most likely to develop low expectations for students' performance when they have rigid stereotypes about students from certain ethnic or socioeconomic groups (McLoyd, 1998b; Reyna, 2000). Such stereotypes are often the result of ignorance about students' home environments

self-fulfilling prophecy
Phenomenon in which an adult's expectations for a child's performance bring about that level of performance.

and cultures (K. Alexander et al., 1987). Education is the key here: Teachers and other school personnel must learn as much as they can about students' backgrounds and local communities. With a clear picture of students' families, activities, and values, educators are far more likely to think of students as *individuals*—each with a unique set of talents and skills—than as stereotypical members of a particular group.

● *Collaborate with colleagues to maximize academic success on a schoolwide basis.* Educators are more likely to have high expectations for students when they are confident in their own ability to help students achieve academic and social success (Ashton, 1985; Weinstein, Madison, & Kuklinski, 1995). Consider the case of one inner-city high school. For many years teachers at the school believed that their low-achieving students, most of whom were from low-income families, were simply unmotivated to learn. The teachers also saw themselves, their colleagues, and school administrators as ineffective in helping these students succeed. To counteract such tendencies, the school faculty began holding regular 2-hour meetings in which they

- Read research related to low-achieving and at-risk students
- Explored various hypotheses about why their students were having difficulty
- Developed, refined, and evaluated innovative strategies for helping their students succeed
- Established a collaborative atmosphere in which, working together, they could take positive action

Such meetings helped the teachers form higher expectations for their students' achievement and a better understanding of what they themselves could do to help the students achieve (Weinstein et al., 1995).

Transitions to New Schools

Entering a new school requires youngsters to adjust to unfamiliar peers and teachers, new academic expectations, and novel activities in a new building. Although a new elementary and secondary school both require these adjustments, in other respects the two environments present distinct challenges to youngsters.

Elementary school.   Children typically begin school at the age of 5 or 6, when society declares them "ready" for serious learning. In reality children have been learning steadily since birth, and schools build on this knowledge. For instance, children who have been encouraged to listen to stories and use complex language at home or in preschool have a solid foundation for a school's literacy curriculum. Likewise, children who have had many constructive experiences with peers are prepared for a classroom's social environment. In general, children who have participated in preschool tend to make good social adjustments and perform at reasonably high levels in first grade (W. S. Barnett, 1996; Consortium of Longitudinal Studies, 1983; Entwisle & Alexander, 1999).

In addition to adjusting to the personalities of new teachers and peers, children must also adapt to the regulatory atmosphere of the classroom. Elementary classrooms tend to be more formal and regimented than the cozy settings of family, child care, and preschool. As a result, when children first enter elementary school, one of their challenges is learning and following the policies and procedures of the "big kids" school (Corsaro & Molinari, 2005). Here's how first grader Sofia described school rules to her mother and an interviewer:

Mother:	Do you know the rules? What are the rules in first grade?
Sofia:	You cannot run in the corridors, you cannot hurt anyone, you have to raise your hand before talking, you cannot lose toys.
Interviewer:	You know all the rules!
Sofia:	Then you cannot walk around, you cannot shout in the bathroom.
Interviewer:	You know everything.
Mother:	And then? Perhaps you must wait your turn.
Sofia:	And then, then, you have to be silent, write the date. That's all. (Corsaro & Molinari, 2005, pp. 74–75).

Of course, there is more to school than restrictions, and most children eventually settle in and enjoy the warmth, nurturance, and safety of their classrooms. To help children adjust

Connecting Concepts ———————
When school environments are appropriately encouraging and supportive, the vast majority of children and adolescents are motivated to master school subject matter (see Chapter 13).

Connecting Concepts ———————
Families differ in the degree to which they prepare children for formal academic learning (see Chapters 5 and 10).

to elementary school and their new classrooms, teachers generally spend time establishing routines and offering lots of reassurance during those initial days (and sometimes weeks or months) when children feel uneasy. Many teachers and schools also offer orientations and encourage children and families to visit their classrooms before school begins (Corsaro & Molinari, 2005). We authors recall that all of our children had elementary teachers who invited them to visit their classrooms in the spring or summer when student placements were announced and who also sent the children friendly letters before the school year began.

To ease children's adjustment, elementary teachers give careful consideration to those children who begin the year lacking age-typical intellectual and social skills. These children most certainly *are* ready to learn, but they may need individualized services to succeed academically. For example, kindergarten children who have had little exposure to books at home can begin to master essential literacy skills at school, listening regularly to simple stories in small groups, perhaps with the help of a parent volunteer or teacher's aide. Without focused enrichment and supportive relationships with teachers, however, children who begin school with cognitive delays are likely to fall further behind (Hamre & Pianta, 2005).

In the elementary grades, each child is one of 15 to 30 students whom a teacher gets to know fairly well. Eventually, most children adjust favorably and develop proficiency in basic academic and social skills. Youngsters will draw from these resources when they move into secondary school environments.

Secondary schools.   There are often two major transitions at the secondary level. First, beginning at grade 5, 6, or 7, many students move from elementary to either middle school or junior high school. Second, at grade 9 or 10, students move from middle or junior high school to high school. And as they progress through these upper grade levels, students attend separate classes, each with its own teacher. The three secondary configurations—middle, junior high, and high school—have distinctive features but share qualities that distinguish them from elementary schools. A typical secondary school is unlike an elementary school in these ways:

- The school is larger and has more students.
- Teacher-student relationships are more superficial and less personal than they were in elementary school.
- There is more whole-class instruction, with less individualized instruction that takes into account each student's particular needs.
- Classes are less socially cohesive; students may not know their classmates very well and may be reluctant to call on peers for assistance.
- Competition among students (e.g., for popular classes or spots on an athletic team) is more common, especially in high school.
- Students have more independence and responsibility for their own learning; for instance, they sometimes have relatively unstructured assignments to be accomplished over a 2- or 3-week period and must take the initiative to seek help if they are struggling.
- Standards for assigning grades are more rigorous, so students may earn lower grades than they did in elementary school. Grades are often assigned on a comparative basis, with only the highest-achieving students getting As and Bs. (Eccles & Midgley, 1989; Harter, 1996; Hine & Fraser, 2002; Roderick & Camburn, 1999; Wentzel & Wigfield, 1998; Wigfield et al., 1996)

Many educators lament the apparent mismatch between the secondary environment and the needs of adolescents. At a time when adolescents are self-conscious, uncertain, and confronted with tumultuous changes in their bodies and social circumstances, they have relationships with teachers that are superficial, shallow, and sometimes adversarial. For many students secondary school environments lead to less self-confidence about academic subject matter, lower overall self-esteem, and considerable anxiety. Some students withdraw emotionally from the school environment—a disengagement that may eventually result in their dropping out of school and participating in delinquent activities (Eccles & Midgley, 1989; Seidman, Aber, & French, 2004; Urdan & Maehr, 1995; Wigfield et al., 1996).

Certainly, many dedicated secondary teachers are warm and supportive in their interactions with individual students, but teachers serve dozens and sometimes hundreds of stu-

---

Connecting Concepts

By the age of 5 or 6, virtually *all* children are ready to learn, but children vary in the particular kinds of instruction they need in order to achieve academic success (Chapter 6).

Connecting Concepts

The opening case in Chapter 13 illustrates how quickly an adolescent's academic performance can deteriorate after the transition from elementary to secondary school.

- Make contact with children before the beginning of school.

  In April a kindergarten teacher invites prospective students and their parents to come to an orientation in her classroom. The teacher arranges for snacks to be served and reserves time for a brief presentation and for independent exploration of the room.

- Provide a means through which every student can feel a part of a small, close-knit group.

  In September a ninth-grade math teacher establishes *base groups* of three or four students, who provide support and assistance to one another throughout the school year. At the beginning or end of every class period, the teacher gives students in the base groups 5 minutes to help one another with homework assignments.

- Find time to meet one-on-one with every student.

  Early in the school year, while his classes are working on a variety of cooperative learning activities, a middle school social studies teacher

schedules individual appointments with each of his students. In these meetings he searches for common interests that he and his students share and encourages the students to seek him out whenever they need help with academic or personal problems. Throughout the semester he continues to touch base with individual students (often during lunch or before or after school) to see how they are doing.

- Give children and adolescents the extra support that some may need to master subject matter and study skills.

  A high school implements a homework hotline staffed by a teacher and a group of honor students, and teachers in the school make a point of encouraging students to keep up with their work (McCarthy & Kuh, 2005).

dents every year, making it virtually impossible to establish close relationships with all of them. One strategy that many high schools are now using is to have every teacher take responsibility for a small group of students whom the teacher gets to know individually. A second and related strategy is to separate out groups of students within the school building. These groups, sometimes known as *houses* or *schools within schools,* permit a reasonably small group of youngsters to become familiar with one another and with a few teachers (Seidman et al., 2004). Units of students may take some classes together, and they are sometimes located in separate areas of the school.

Fortunately, many secondary schools are finding ways to welcome entering students and personalize the learning environments as students settle into classes. Students who make a smooth adjustment to secondary school are more likely to be successful there and, as a result, are more likely to graduate from high school (Roderick & Camburn, 1999; Wigfield et al., 1996). The Development and Practice feature "Easing School Transitions" illustrates several strategies for helping youngsters adjust to new schools.

Society

As you have learned, youngsters acquire many skills, beliefs, and attitudes during ongoing interactions with adults and other children in their families and schools. Other individuals and institutions in **society**—the large group of people who live in a particular region and share certain customs—also influence children's development. We now examine society's services, media, and interactive technologies as social contexts for the development of children and adolescents.

Services for Children and Adolescents

In the following sections we examine the services offered by society to children and adolescents when they are not in school. We focus on child care, early intervention programs, after-school programs and activities, and religious and philosophical affiliations for young people.

Child care. Many young children are in the care of adults other than their parents for a significant portion of the week. Children are attended to in a variety of settings, from family homes to commercial buildings, and by caregivers who differ in experience, education, and dedication to children. Such variations raise concerns about the degree to which children are cared for in a manner that is affectionate, safe, and age appropriate (Brauner, Gordic, & Zigler, 2004).

Advocates for high standards in child care have two primary ways of defining quality. *Structural measures* include such objective indicators as caregivers' training and experience,

Connecting Concepts
Chapter 5 describes the kinds of child care that parents use when they work outside the home.

society
A very large group of people who live in a particular region and share certain customs.

Young children often benefit from experiences in high-quality child care—that is, settings in which caregivers are sensitive and have appropriate training, child-staff ratios are low, and caregivers focus on children's individual needs.

Connecting Concepts
Many infants easily form secure attachments to multiple caregivers (see Chapter 11).

child-caregiver ratios, staff turnover, and number and complexity of toys and equipment (M. E. Lamb, 1998; Sims, Hutchins, & Taylor, 1997). For example, early childhood specialists recommend that the child-caregiver ratio be no more than three infants or six toddlers for each adult (Bredekamp & Copple, 1997). *Process measures* of quality, which reflect children's social and cognitive experiences in child care, include measures of child-caregiver relationships, child-peer interactions, and developmentally appropriate activities (Harms & Clifford, 1980; Sims et al., 1997). For example, the schedules of activities in a toddler room might be fairly predictable from day to day but also flexible enough to be guided by children's individual and changing needs (Bredekamp & Copple, 1997). Thus, toddlers might be offered two snacks over the span of the morning, even though only a few choose to eat twice.

In reality, indicators of structure and process are closely related. Numerous studies show that lower child-staff ratios, smaller group sizes, and more caregiver education are associated with good child-caregiver interactions (e.g., Howes, Smith, & Galinsky, 1995; NICHD Early Child Care Research Network, 2002a; D. Phillips, Mekos, Scarr, McCartney, & Abbott-Shim, 2001). Conversely, when caregivers have too many children to care for, their style of interacting with individual children tends to become rushed and mechanical.

In general, research confirms that child care in high-quality settings has beneficial effects on children's development. For example, infants and small children typically enjoy secure attachments to employed caregivers who are warm, sensitive, and persistently involved in the children's care (Barnas & Cummings, 1994; Raikes, 1993). In addition, high-quality child care has been shown to enhance children's cognitive, language, and social development, with the greatest benefits occurring for children whose home environments are inattentive or unstimulating (Andersson, 1989; T. Field, 1991; T. Field, Masi, Goldstein, Perry, & Parl, 1988; Howes, 1988; M. E. Lamb, 1998; Ramey, 1992; Scarr, 1997, 1998; Scott-Little & Holloway, 1992). Moreover, high-quality care that is culturally sensitive can be a constructive influence, not only on children but also on their families and the community (Dahlberg, Moss, & Pence, 1999).

Children who spend long hours in child care from an early age do face risks, however. Exposure to child care at a young age and for long hours seems to trigger slight increases in children's aggression and noncompliance (Belsky & Eggebeen, 1991; NICHD Early Child Care Research Network, 2002b, 2005). These effects are not always seen and, when they are, are smaller for high-quality than for low-quality care (Bagley, 1989; Clarke-Stewart, 1989; Hegland & Rix, 1990).

Early childhood intervention programs. High-quality educational environments for young children have positive effects on children's intellectual growth and may be particularly beneficial for children from low-SES backgrounds (Brooks-Gunn, 2003; M. E. Lamb, 1998; McLoyd, 1998a; Ramey & Ramey, 1998; Scarr, 1998). **Early childhood intervention programs** typically combine an educational focus with other supports for children and their families, such as medical care, social services, and parenting guidance.

In the United States the best-known model of early childhood intervention is Project *Head Start*. Established under federal legislation, Head Start was designed for 3- to 5-year-old low-income children and their families. Since 1965 it has served millions of children, many of them from single-parent homes. A typical Head Start program includes preschool, health screening and referrals, mental health services, nutrition education, family support services, and parent involvement in decision making (McLoyd, 1998a; Washington & Bailey, 1995).

Many investigations have examined the effectiveness of Head Start and similar early childhood intervention programs. Children from these programs score higher on measures of cognitive ability and achieve at higher levels in school, but such advantages often disappear by the upper elementary grades (V. Lee, Brooks-Gunn, Schnur, & Liaw, 1990; McKey et al., 1985; McLoyd, 1998b; Ramey & Ramey, 1998). Nonetheless, other long-term benefits have been observed: Low-income children who attend Head Start or similar preschool programs are less likely to require special educational services and more likely to graduate from high

early childhood intervention program
Program designed to foster basic intellectual, social-emotional, and physical development in infants and young children whose heads of family are burdened by economic poverty or other debilitating life circumstances.

school than are similar children with no preschool experience (Lazar, Darlington, Murray, Royce, & Snipper, 1982; McLoyd, 1998a; Schweinhart & Weikart, 1983; Washington & Bailey, 1995). Longer and more intensive programs (e.g., 2 or more years of full-time preschool rather than a single year of part-time schooling), as well as programs in which teachers are well trained and parents are actively involved, yield the greatest benefits (Ramey & Ramey, 1998; Ripple, Gilliam, Chanana, & Zigler, 1999).

Some educators suggest that quality care and education should be more universally available and should start earlier than age 3. One model program, the Carolina Abecedarian Project, offers services to children of economically poor families beginning in infancy (F. A. Campbell & Ramey, 1994, 1995; Horacek, Ramey, Campbell, Hoffman, & Fletcher, 1987). Rigorous research suggests that children who have attended the early intervention program have higher intelligence scores from age 1½ until age 15 and are less likely to require special educational services than are those who have had no early intervention. In general, children from economically disadvantaged families make the most progress when interventions begin early (ideally in infancy) and continue throughout the school years (Brooks-Gunn, 2003; Ramey & Ramey, 1998; A. Reynolds, 1994; Washington & Bailey, 1995; E. Zigler & Muenchow, 1992).

After-school programs and extracurricular activities.   Another way in which communities contribute to young people's development is through the programs they offer before and after school and during the summer—clubs, sports leagues, dance and martial arts lessons, scout troops, and so on. Twelve-year-old Colin gives a sense of his rich learning experiences, made possible by his community, in the "After School: Early Adolescence" video clip on Observation CD 3:

Listen to 12-year-old Colin describe what he does outside school in the "After School: Early Adolescence" clip.

Interviewer:	So you play basketball?
Colin:	Yeah. Yeah.
Interviewer:	What other . . . is that your favorite sport?
Colin:	I like basketball and track about the same.
Interviewer:	Do you play any other sports?
Colin:	Yeah. I play, basically, I play football, baseball, hockey. . . .
Interviewer:	Wow. What do you like about sports?
Colin:	Well, they're fun and just something to do.
Interviewer:	What kinds of hobbies do you have?
Colin:	I like coin collecting and . . . I garden and I try to take sign language and really do sign language. Yeah.
Interviewer:	So what kinds of clubs do you belong to?
Colin:	I belong to . . . well, I used to belong to 4-H. And I'm in the chess club, Boy Scouts, and sign language club.

A growing body of research indicates that participation in structured after-school and summer activities fosters children's cognitive and social-emotional development. For instance, academically oriented programs appear to cultivate positive feelings about school, better school attendance, higher grades and achievement test scores, better classroom behavior, greater conflict resolution skills, and decreased tension with family members (Charles A. Dana Center, 1999; H. Cooper, Charlton, Valentine, & Muhlenbruck, 2000; Dryfoos, 1999; Vandell & Pierce, 1999). Nonacademic programs, too, seem to have benefits. For instance, high school students who participate in their school's extracurricular activities are more likely than nonparticipants to achieve at high levels and graduate from high school. They are also less likely to smoke, use alcohol or drugs, join gangs, engage in criminal activities, or become teenage parents (Biddle, 1993; H. Cooper, Valentine, Nye, & Lindsay, 1999; Donato et al., 1997; Eppright, Sanfacon, Beck, & Bradley, 1998; Zill, Nord, & Loomis, 1995). Joining a club or team at school may give students a productive peer group with which to associate and thereby indirectly promote greater investment in school (H. Cooper et al., 1999; Zill et al., 1995).

Effective after-school programs typically offer a variety of activities through which young people can pursue their individual interests and develop their unique talents. Art by Brandon, age 11.

After-school and summer programs vary in their focus and services, yet most espouse a commitment to providing caring adult-child relationships. In addition, effective programs include these general features:

- A variety of activities, including recreation, academic and cultural enrichment, and opportunities for pursuit of individual interests
- Chances for meaningful participation in authentic activities, such as building a fort, reading to younger children, or registering voters
- Opportunities for success, perhaps in domains in which youngsters have previously unrecognized talents
- Positive interactions with both adults and peers
- Structure and clear limits, with youngsters' active participation in planning and rule setting
- High regard and respect for young people's diverse cultural beliefs and practices (C. R. Cooper, Denner, & Lopez, 1999; Kerewsky & Lefstein, 1982; Lefstein & Lipsitz, 1995)

Directions: This form is to be used by the classroom teacher and after-school tutor to share information about an individual student's homework assignments and study habits. For each homework assignment, the teacher fills out the information in column one and gives the form to the tutor. After assisting the student, the tutor fills out the information in column two and returns the form to the teacher.

Today's Date:	
Student's Name:	
Teacher's Name:	
Tutor's Name:	
Completed by teacher.	**Completed by tutor.**
The homework for today is:	This student: ❑ Completed the homework easily and independently. ❑ Had difficulty *understanding* what was asked in the homework. ❑ Had difficulty *completing* the homework. ❑ Had difficulty *focusing* on the assignment.
Please pay special attention to:	This student required: ❑ No help with the assignment. ❑ A little help. ❑ Occasional help. ❑ A great deal of help. ❑ See comments on back.
This homework should take _____ minutes to complete.	The homework took _____ minutes to complete.

Figure 14-6

A homework sharing tool. Daytime teachers and after-school teachers who tutor children can use this form to communicate about homework. *From Beyond the Bell: A Toolkit for Creating Effective After-School Programs* (2nd ed., p. 105), by Judith G. Caplan, Carol K. McElvain, and Katie E. Walter, 2001, Naperville, IL: NCREL. Copyright 2001 by the North Central Regional Educational Laboratory. All rights reserved. Reprinted by permission.

At the elementary level, after-school programs often provide supervision, academic support, and recreational activities for children of working parents. Many programs are delivered in school buildings, sometimes by school authorities and at other times with the cooperation of private vendors, community organizations, or government agencies (Dryfoos, 1999; National Center for Education Statistics, 1997). When after-school programs help children with homework, regular communication between classroom teachers and after-school caregivers can align instructional objectives across the two environments (Caplan, McElvain, & Walter, 2001). Face-to-face meetings and two-way written forms, such as the one shown in Figure 14-6, are often effective means of coordinating educational objectives. In some cases schools become a hub of activities offering not only programs for school-age children but also care for younger children and assistance to families with nutrition and mental health needs (Finn-Stevenson & Stern, 1996; B. M. Stern & Finn-Stevenson, 1999).

At the secondary level, most out-of-school programs take the form of school-affiliated *extracurricular activities,* such as athletic teams, performing arts groups, debating societies, and organizations for school leadership and school spirit. These school-based activities provide young people with an opportunity to gain skills and spend productive time with peers. Additional programs are offered in the community and are especially appealing when they provide contact with caring adults and friendly peers. In one study 75 percent of 10- to 18-year-olds who attended one of four inner-city sites of Boys and Girls Clubs of America described the setting as being like a home to them (Deutsch & Hirsch, 2001). Sixteen-year-old Sammy described his feelings about his club:

> Some people do not have any home. I have been granted the gift of having two homes: my home and the Boys and Girls Club. [The club] allows me to express myself mentally, verbally, physically, and artistically. (p. 1)

service learning
Activity that promotes learning and skill development through volunteerism or community service.

Giving back to the community is another worthwhile after-school activity for young people. Community service projects provide an opportunity for **service learning,** in which youngsters gain practical skills and increased self-confidence while assisting other people and contributing to the betterment of their community (Sheckley & Keeton, 1997; Stukas, Clary, & Snyder, 1999). Fifteen-year-old Connor volunteered to become the football coach for his seven-year-old brother's team when none of the team parents were able to do so. Following is his description of what the experience meant to him:

DEVELOPMENT
AND PRACTICE

DEVELOPMENT AND PRACTICE — Enhancing Students' Before- and After-School Experiences

- Help children navigate transitions between school and after-school care.

  After school a kindergarten teacher walks outside with children to make sure that each child successfully connects with family members or car pool drivers, gets on the appropriate bus or van, or begins walking home.

- Sponsor after-school clubs in your school.

  A middle school offers several clubs for students to participate in after school. Popular options include a Hispanic cultures club, several athletic teams, an honor society, a band, a community service group, and the yearbook staff.

- Inform parents and other family members about nonschool programs in the area.

  At a parent-teacher-student conference, a middle school teacher describes clubs and sports programs available at the school, as well as recreational and service opportunities in the local community.

- Establish a team of school personnel and after-school providers to ensure that after-school programs use resources appropriately and meet children's physical, social-emotional, and academic needs.

  Two teachers, the principal, and the director of an after-school program meet regularly to discuss space, resources, and ways that the after-school program can give children needed rest, relaxation, snacks, and tutoring.

[I learned] just how to be a leader and a lot about football. You have to be nice to the little kids and when they make a good play, you gotta tell them about it and when they make a bad play, you gotta *not* tell them about it. I had fun doing it.

Many adolescents also structure their free time with part-time jobs. Having a part-time job with limited hours (e.g., no more than 15 to 20 hours per week) seems generally beneficial. Adolescents can gain experience in getting to work on time, following the requirements of a position, being courteous in a business setting, and managing money. With limited work hours, adolescents still have adequate time to study and can stay involved in school activities (Charner & Fraser, 1988; Mortimer, Shanahan, & Ryu, 1994; Steinberg, Brown, Cider, Kaczmarek, & Lazzaro, 1988).

We cannot be definite about the specific effects of extracurricular activities and after-school programs because youngsters who choose to participate in these services may be different from youngsters who decide not to take advantage of them. Nonetheless, because of the potential—and, we suggest, likely—benefits of extracurricular activities and after-school programs, they merit investment of time, energy, and financial resources until social scientists can determine their effects with more certainty. The Development and Practice feature "Enhancing Students' Before- and After-School Experiences" suggests strategies for educators and other practitioners to help young people make good use of their nonschool time.

Connecting Concepts
Community service can also promote youngsters' moral development (see Chapter 13).

After-school activities can foster young people's skills and dispositions to help others and serve the community.

Religious and philosophically based groups.   Some community organizations socialize children and adolescents to adhere to certain values and belief systems. For example, children often participate with their families in churches, synagogues, mosques, temples, and other religious and philosophically based congregations (Roehlkepartain & Patel, 2006).

From their participation in religious and philosophical communities, youngsters can gain not only a defined outlook on life but also supportive relationships with adults outside their family. Religious and philosophical orientations also provide ways to think about social responsibility. In Figure 14-7 you can see that children holding distinct beliefs share a disposition to care for other people. Unfortunately, a few youngsters also develop an attitude of intolerance to people who do not share their beliefs, and a very small number of young people maltreat others, justifying their actions as attempts to eradicate "evil" forces or "restore justice" for their community (Wagener & Malony, 2006).

As with all aspects of development, children's spiritual and philosophical convictions evolve over time. Initially, the trust that children establish with parents predisposes them to accept their parents' beliefs (Fowler, 1981; Fowler & Dell, 2006). As children grow older, they make sense of religious doctrine and philosophical positions in accordance with their current reasoning abilities. In Figure 14-8 nine-year-old Noah describes himself as both Jewish and Christian, primarily because his mother and father are, respectively, Jewish and

Figure 14-7

Children use their religious and philosophical beliefs to help interpret life's meaning and obligations.

Excerpts from *The Spiritual Life of Children* by Robert Coles. Copyright © 1990 by Robert Coles. Reprinted by permission of Houghton Mifflin Company. All rights reserved.

Thirteen-year-old Sajid, a Muslim boy from London, reflects on Allah's teachings as explained to him by his father:

> Either you give to the poor, to your neighbor, or you risk lots of trouble when you die …[My father] said I should still try to be very good in school, in all that I do; but I should help my friends, too. You should be generous; you should give help to others. (Coles, 1990, pp. 240–41)

Seven-year-old Fred describes the Christian values he has learned, and his 6-year-old brother, Ray, draws a nativity scene.

Jesus teaches me: *To love, how to love, to take care of other people, to make care of the poor.*

Eleven-year-old Sylvia comes from an agnostic family and articulates her beliefs:

> I didn't say there's nothing out there; I know there is a lot to live for. I love my family, and I love my friends. I love it when we go to a new place on a trip, and I can see new people, and you can stand there—like up in Vermont or New Hampshire—and look at all the land, for miles (if you're up a mountain), and the trees, and you're nearer the clouds. (Coles, 1990, p. 299)

Five-year-old Lindsey has drawn a picture of Buddha. Her drawing and commentary are posted to an online Buddhist Web site:

If you look in the triangle, it will make you gooder …because there are people doing nice things in there. And thinking about it will make you nice. First when you look it is just scribble—but if you look closer (that is why the Buddha is closing one eye) you can seem [sic] them being nice. (The Online Buddhist Family Center, 2003; http://www.idsl.net/heather/onlinebuddhistcenter/welcome.html). Reprinted with permission of Heather K. Woollard.

On Yom Kippur, 12-year-old Maggie prepares for her Bat Mitzvah and learns moral lessons from her Rabbi:

The rabbi explained that the point of our coming together for Yom Kippur was to think about what we had done wrong in the past year and to think about our relationships with each other, with friends and family. She said that sometimes the services get boring and that's when we're meant to think about who we are as people and how to help in our communities.

Figure 14-8

In middle childhood, children's notions of religion are fairly concrete. Here 9-year-old Noah conceptualizes Christmas and Hanukkah as a time for getting presents.

Christian; and he focuses on the concrete advantages of his affiliations. Adolescents, in contrast, tend to take a critical stance toward their religion, accepting some of its tenets, becoming skeptical of others, and grasping the underlying meanings of symbols and traditions.

In the United States the First Amendment to the Constitution requires that matters of church and state be kept separate. Public school teachers can certainly discuss religions within the context of history, culture, or other appropriate academic topics. But they cannot incorporate religious ideas or practices into classroom activities or school events in any way that shows a preference for one religion over another or even a preference for religion over atheism. Here are some suggestions for promoting tolerance of diverse religious and non-religious orientations:

● ***Become aware of religious diversity in your community.*** At a practical level, educators should think about religious holidays and observances whenever they schedule school events and meetings with families. Moreover, teachers must certainly avoid giving preferential treatment to youngsters from religious (or nonreligious) backgrounds similar to their own.

● ***Create a climate of religious tolerance.*** Just as teachers foster respect for diverse cultural backgrounds, so, too, they should foster respect for diverse religious beliefs. If young people are to work effectively in adult society, they must learn that people have the right to religious freedom, and no one should be demeaned or victimized because of religious or philosophical beliefs. Many school districts have policies that prohibit any name-calling that denigrates others' religious beliefs, practices, and affiliations.

● *Communicate respectfully with families when discussing controversial issues.* Parents and other community members often participate in decisions about school curricula and occasionally voice strong religious convictions about certain issues (e.g., the origins of the human species or the appropriateness of telling adolescents about birth control methods). Educators may or may not agree with perspectives raised in these discussions, but they can work hard to express their own opinions without discrediting anyone else's religious or nonreligious beliefs.

Television and the Interactive Technologies

Many children and adolescents regularly view television and use a growing collection of **interactive technologies**—computers, CD-ROMs, the Internet, video games, talking books, and cell phones. These media are widely used by youngsters, in part because of their accessibility. In a recent study the majority of U.S. families with children aged 2 to 17 years had a television, basic cable, video games, a computer, and Internet access in their homes (Woodard & Gridina, 2000). Contributing to the popularity of television and interactive technologies are their engaging qualities (such as colorful, fast-moving scenes), alluring themes (e.g., triumphing over bad guys or gyrating with teen idols), and interactive capabilities that enable youngsters to stay in touch with one another.

Content of programs and games. Bells and whistles may grab children's attention, but it is the *content* of media programs that sticks in their minds (Houston, 2004; Huston & Wright, 1998). Fortunately, many programs aired on television and built into interactive technologies have educationally worthwhile content. For example, educational television programs such as *Sesame Street, The Magic School Bus, Dora the Explorer, Blue's Clues, Between the Lions,* and *Bill Nye the Science Guy* teach children vocabulary, word recognition, reading concepts, and scientific principles (D. R. Anderson, 2003; A. B. Jordan, 2003; Linebarger, Kosanic, Greenwood, & Doku, 2004; Linebarger & Walker, 2005). Programs that model prosocial behaviors, such as the television programs *Mister Rogers' Neighborhood* and *Saved by the Bell* and the video game *Smurfs,* teach children social skills (D. R. Anderson, 2003; Chambers & Ascione, 2001; A. B. Jordan, 2003).

Unfortunately, developmentally counterproductive content coexists with, and potentially overshadows, socially responsible material in the media. For example, television programs and video games frequently contain stereotypical characters—for instance, women as airheads, men as brutes, and people with dark skin as thugs (Eisenberg et al., 1996; Huston et al., 1992). Such offensive portrayals are ridiculous distortions of reality but may prompt impressionable children to develop misconceptions about particular social groups (Huston & Wright, 1998). Similarly, when youngsters repeatedly view slender and athletically toned actors, actresses, and rock stars, they may develop a standard of physical attractiveness that is not realistic for their own body frame (D. R. Anderson, Huston, Schmitt, Linebarger, & Wright, 2001). In addition, advertisements on television and Internet Web sites may cultivate desires for particular cereals, fast food, clothing, toys, and digital devices—items that may or may not be in children's best interests (Buijzen & Valkenburg, 2003; S. Reese, 1996; Wartella, Caplovitz, & Lee, 2004).

The excessively violent and gruesomely realistic scenes of many television programs and video games are another concern. In fact, violence can be found in a large percentage of television programs and video games (C. A. Anderson et al., 2003; S. L. Smith & Donnerstein, 1998). Repeated exposure to violent acts on television seems to make children more aggressive and may be particularly harmful to those already predisposed to aggression (C. Anderson & Huesmann, 2005; Andison, 1977; Eron, 1980; Hearold, 1986; Huesmann, Moise-Titus, Podolski, & Eron, 2003; Paik & Comstock, 1994; Van der Voort & Valkenburg, 1994; W. Wood, Wong, & Chachere, 1991). For example, young children inclined to solve conflicts in physically aggressive ways are apt to watch programs with violent content and become more aggressive after viewing such programs. In addition, heavy viewing of televised violence may

interactive technology
Array of electronic, digitally based machines that are operated dynamically by a person whose commands determine emerging program sequences.

Children sometimes learn inappropriate lessons from television.

desensitize children to acts of violence; that is, children's repeated viewing of televised violence seems to erode children's empathic responses to victims of real violent acts. Violent video games also appear to increase child users' aggressive behavior and desensitize them to the suffering of actual victims of aggressive behavior (Cocking & Greenfield, 1996; Funk, Buchman, Jenks, & Bechtoldt, 2003; Gailey, 1993; Gentile & Anderson, in press; R. A. Irwin & Gross, 1995).

Television viewing.   On average, television viewing time increases rapidly during early childhood, continues to increase in middle childhood and early adolescence (reaching a peak of almost 4 hours a day), and then declines gradually after about age 14 (Comstock & Paik, 1991; Medrich, Roizen, Rubin, & Buckley, 1982; Timmer, Eccles, & O'Brien, 1985). Children vary greatly in their television viewing habits, however: Some are glued to their TV sets for several hours a day while others rarely, if ever, watch television. Developmental scholars, health practitioners, and educators are especially concerned about heavy-viewing children because of their high exposure to inappropriate content, low levels of physical activity, and diminished time for interactions with peers (e.g., Caroli, Argentieri, Cardone, & Masi, 2004).

Listen to Brent talk about video games in the "After School: Early Childhood" clip.

Video games.   Video games are a popular source of entertainment among American youths, especially boys between the ages of 5 and 12 (Huston & Wright, 1998). Video game systems can be found in many homes, where youngsters may spend numerous hours clutching a controller as they engage in virtual punching matches, motorcycle races, and explorations of mythical environments. Six-year-old Brent shows his enthusiasm for video games in the "After School: Early Childhood" video clip on Observation CD 3:

> I usually play video games. There's this army game and snowboard game and . . . and a game called "Smash Brothers." . . . They're cool.

The appeal of video games results largely from their use of strikingly effective instructional principles. Video games allow children to pursue a tangible goal, use flexible strategies, make steady progress, experience success, use increasingly advanced tools, and obtain personalized feedback at every step (Gentile & Gentile, 2005). Playing video games can become a habit, however, and overuse is a concern when it leads children to curtail their physical activity. Also, as we indicated earlier, youngsters who play video games are likely to select at least some games that contain violent content and inappropriate social stereotypes.

Gene drew this picture of his video game equipment from memory, showing his familiarity with the apparatus and a game's combat theme.

Nonetheless, video games have the potential to exert some positive influences on children. For instance, numerous nonviolent and creative video games are available, and youngsters can improve their spatial and visual-attention skills as a result of playing these games (e.g., C. A. Anderson, 2002; De Lisi & Wolford, 2002; Greenfield, DeWinstanley, Kilpatrick, & Kaye, 1996). Particular games, such as those with health-promotion themes, can teach children valuable skills in caring for themselves and managing their health conditions (D. A. Lieberman, 1997). In the following Interpreting Children's Artifacts and Actions feature, "Video Games: Good or Bad?" consider the advantages of video games that 12-year-old Corey cites in an essay he wrote for his middle school English class.

INTERPRETING CHILDREN'S ARTIFACTS AND ACTIONS

Video Games: Good or Bad?

As you read Corey's essay, consider the many benefits he associates with playing video games. Also, speculate about the validity of his rebuttal to the claims of many adults that video games make children violent.

Imagine the impossible, soaring to new heights, being unstoppable, without all the hard work! This is the world of video games, where nothing is impossible, and you can do anything. Unfortunately, most adults fail to understand the grandeur of gaming. They claim "we should not teach our children to be murderers". Most children, however, will know the games are fictional and know that these tasks should not be attempted. Besides all the nonsense over games, there are many benefits, too.

Video games help you manage problems in life. Some games have a simulation of life, where you need to buy a house, and pay off debt. This teaches you money skills that are necessary in life. Other games will teach you how to be a quick thinker by having you try to figure out how to get past a level. The games will also teach you to manage stress by having you try to beat a level with limited resources.

But besides helping you out with problems, video games are mainly a source for entertainment. Video games are really fun, in which you can do things that are impossible in real life. Instead of hearing or watching a story, you are playing the story. Also, when I am angry I can kill aliens on a game, which lifts my spirits, and no one is even hurt. Two-player games teach cooperation and turn taking. Video games are a great way to relax.

There are many things video games can do besides entertain. They can help with reaction time, by practicing and getting faster. Eyesight is improved by being able to focus faster and have eye hand coordination. You are more alert by having to react to anything. Video games will even help your academics because concentrating on a game will help you concentrate in real life.

So, as you can see, games are not just for entertainment, they are good for other things, too. Adults will hopefully consider giving video games a chance. So before you knock video games, give them a try.

Corey speaks from experience. He perceives many benefits from video games but concludes that their main advantage is providing enjoyable entertainment. Corey also suggests that video games teach users how to focus attention, think quickly, improve eye-hand coordination, manage money, and reduce stress. He finds adults' arguments about the disadvantages of video games, particularly the potential for increasing children's aggression, to be unrealistic. Corey is persuasive that video games can be beneficial in numerous ways, but his argument that games are "fictional" and unlikely to spur children to act violently is inconsistent with research on the issue. As we've seen, video games *can* lead children to act more violently. Perhaps they have little impact on Corey's behavior, but they can have considerable impact on other children.

Computers and the Internet.   Personal computers and other electronic devices seem to be just about everywhere these days. Computer technologies are changing the ways that adults communicate, make decisions, spend money, and entertain themselves. Children and adolescents follow suit and in many cases actually lead the pack.

Computers and the Internet have many uses in the classroom. Well-constructed software can give students a carefully structured curriculum that permits personalized lessons and steady feedback. The rich, dynamic environment of the Internet makes resources available from around the world. Through such mechanisms as electronic mail (e-mail), Web-based chat rooms, and electronic bulletin boards, computer technology enables students to communicate with peers, exchange perspectives, and build on one another's ideas (Fabos & Young, 1999; Hewitt & Scardamalia, 1996; Schachter, 2000). Technology also allows subject matter experts to be pulled occasionally into the discussion (A. L. Brown & Campione, 1996; Winn, 2002).

Outside the classroom (and sometimes within it), youngsters increasingly use the Internet for their own personal communications. As youngsters make the transition from childhood to adolescence, many supplement or even replace interests in electronic games with social communication by e-mail and in chat rooms and Internet-based group games (e.g., Multiuser Dungeons, known as MUDs) (Greenfield & Subrahmanyam, 2003; Hellenga, 2002). In a recent survey the majority of teens who spent time online created content for the Internet, such as their own Web pages (Lehnhart & Madden, 2005).

Research on social relationships enabled by the Internet is still quite new, but a preliminary case can be made for some positive effects. For example, a shy teenager who forms relationships with a few individuals through regular e-mail and chat room exchanges may learn to disclose personal information and express feelings of anger, fear, and frustration. Other adolescents may find like-minded individuals who support their interests and orientations (e.g., homosexuality). Adolescents may even experiment with different personalities at a time when they are wrestling with identity issues; for instance, some young people intentionally project older images or accentuate their physical attractiveness (Hellenga, 2002).

Some negative consequences are also possible, however. A teenager may withdraw from family and peers in favor of friends known only electronically. And this desire to stay connected electronically may lead to excessively long hours on the computer (Hellenga, 2002). Other youngsters develop bad habits, such as *flaming* (i.e., verbally ridiculing someone in a public electronic site), *trolling* in newsgroups (i.e., making an inflammatory remark to provoke an argument), *hacking* into secured sites to disrupt services or spread computer viruses, and plagiarizing the work of other people (Hellenga, 2002). Furthermore, adolescents who are regular users of the Internet often are sexually harassed or solicited (Finkelhor, Mitchell, & Wolak, 2000).

Implications of television and technology.   If utilized properly, electronic media and technologies have tremendous potential for educating children. We offer the following suggestions:

● ***Encourage parents to regulate children's television viewing.*** At meetings and school events and in newsletters, educators can encourage parents to set specific TV-viewing goals for their children. For instance, if parents find their children watching television many hours a day, they might want to set a 2-hour limit. Parents also may find it informative to watch television with their children. In the process they can discover how their children interpret what they watch and can provide a reality check when characters and story lines consistently violate norms for appropriate behavior ("Do you think people should really insult one another like that?").

● ***Advise parents of dangers on the Internet.*** Parents can familiarize themselves with Web sites their children visit and can consider using Internet filters or blocks. Parents can also talk with their children about who is on their buddy list for instant messaging communications and discourage any meetings with online acquaintances, in order to avoid exploitation by sexual predators. In addition, parents should learn common acronyms in contemporary use—for example, LOL, laugh out loud; PAW, parents are watching; A/S/L, age, sex, and location; IPN, I'm posting naked; OLL, online love; and WTGP, want to go private? (National Center for Missing and Exploited Children, 2004).

● ***Teach critical viewing skills.*** Practitioners can teach youngsters how to watch television with a critical eye. For example, preschool teachers can help young children understand that television commercials aim to persuade them to buy something, perhaps toys or hamburgers. Teachers and community leaders working with older children and adolescents can point out more subtle advertising ploys, such as the use of color, images (e.g., sexual symbols), and endorsements by famous actors and athletes. And with any medium—television, computers, books, magazines, and so on—adults can help young people become more aware of stereotypes and negative portrayals of men and women, ethnic groups, and various professions.

● ***Educate youngsters about the aggression they see on television and in video games.*** Educators and social scientists have had some success in persuading children that the glamorous, humorous, successful, and pervasive manner in which violence is shown on television is misleading (Rosenkoetter, Rosenkoetter, Ozretich, & Acock, 2004). For example, you can point out that, contrary to typical television scenes, violence is usually *not* an effective way to handle disagreements and often creates additional problems. You can also explain to children that violence is an eye-catching and unrealistic mechanism that television producers use to attract audiences and make money.

● ***Use televised movies and computer programs that build on instructional units.*** Some television programs and videos can make print content more concrete and understandable. For instance, when Teresa and a coleader guided a group of sixth and seventh graders in a Great Books discussion of George Bernard Shaw's play *Pygmalion,* everyone struggled to make sense of characters' dialects. Afterward, the group watched segments of *My Fair Lady,* a movie based on the play, and found the dialects much easier to understand.

BASIC DEVELOPMENTAL ISSUES — Social Contexts of Child Development

Issue	Influence of Peers, Schools, and Society
Nature and Nurture	Peers, schools, and society are powerful agents of *nurture* in children's lives. Peers offer children emotional support, a safe forum for polishing social skills, and reassuring perspectives on confusing and troubling events. Teachers communicate expectations about children's abilities, implement classroom traditions, organize learning groups, and cultivate children's sense of belonging at school. Society has institutions that care for children, technological systems that enable widespread communication, and media that transmit messages about expected behaviors. *Nature* provides a necessary foundation for children's social development with a biologically based desire to interact with other people. Nature's maturational changes are evident in children's evolving peer relationships—for example, increases in language and the ability to take the perspective of others enhance children's ability to resolve differences with peers. Finally, individual differences that derive partly from genes (e.g., temperament and some physical disabilities) can affect children's peer relationships and social acceptance.
Universality and Diversity	*Universality* is present in the benefits children experience from being liked by peers, having relationships with caring adults outside the family (e.g., teachers and child care providers), participating in a school setting where they are encouraged to achieve at high levels and feel that they belong, and having safe and interesting options for their free time. *Diversity* occurs in the particular social skills children develop, the extent to which peers find them likable social partners, the developmental suitability of children's environments (e.g., the quality of child care centers), and the degree to which young people engage in risky behaviors with peers (e.g., committing crimes with fellow gang members, engaging in unprotected sexual activities).
Qualitative and Quantitative Change	Children undergo several *qualitative* transformations in their social relationships. For example, children form associations with peers that are fleeting social exchanges during infancy, but these ties change into rich language-based and stable relationships during early and middle childhood and then into close friendships, cliques, and romantic relationships during adolescence. Other qualitative overhauls occur in youngsters' uses of particular technologies (e.g., initially preferring television and video games and later choosing electronic mail and chat rooms) and in the onset of sexual feelings for peers of opposite gender (or in some instances, same gender). Children also exhibit more gradual, *quantitative* changes in their peer relationships, styles of behaving in school, and uses of society's institutions and services. For example, children gradually refine their skills for interacting with peers, and once they adjust to a new school, children slowly learn to follow its rules and abide by its expectations.

● *Increase youngsters' familiarity and comfort with computers.* Although many middle- and upper-income families now have personal computers, many lower-income families cannot afford them. But as we look to the future, we anticipate that computer expertise, including Internet use, will be increasingly critical for everyone's success. Adults in many settings can find ways to incorporate computers and the Internet into lessons and activities. For instance, a preschool teacher might teach children how to play computer games that give practice in emergent literacy skills. An elementary school teacher might show students how to use online weather maps to track the path of a hurricane. And an after-school tutor might show young people how they can use the Internet to look up information needed for homework.

● *Teach young people to be critical users of the Internet.* Young people need to learn how to navigate through countless electronic sites. Because information is expanding exponentially on many significant topics, youngsters must learn (perhaps with the assistance of adults) to find, retrieve, organize, and evaluate information they find on the Internet. As young people begin to use the Internet for activities in classrooms and clubs, teachers should give guidance in evaluating the quality of information on the World Wide Web. For example, data provided by government agencies and well-known nonprofit organizations are fairly reliable, but opinion pieces on someone's personal Web page may not be.

● *Encourage use of a wide range of media.* Television is the primary medium, and in some cases the only medium, through which many children and adolescents gain news and information about their region and country. Ideally, youngsters should learn to use the many other media available to them—not only the Internet but also books, newspapers, and newsmagazines—to gain the knowledge and skills they will need in the adult world.

As you have learned, children grow up in a complex social world. The Basic Developmental Issues table "Social Contexts of Child Development" synthesizes the effects of peers, school, and society on children, from the perspective of nature and nurture, universality and diversity, and qualitative and quantitative change. Our final case study gives you one more chance to observe the benefits of children's friendships.

Case Study: Aaron and Cole

Aaron and Cole became friends when they were both students in Mr. Howard's fifth-grade class. Although Aaron was in most respects a typical fifth grader, Cole had significant developmental delays. Special educator Debbie Staub (1998) described Cole's special educational needs and his strengths as follows:

> Cole has limited expressive vocabulary and uses one- or two-word sentences. He does not participate in traditional academic tasks, although he is included with his typically developing schoolmates for the entire school day. Cole has a history of behavioral problems that have ranged from mild noncompliance to adult requests to serious aggressive and destructive behavior such as throwing furniture at others. In spite of his occasional outbursts, however, it is hard not to like him. Cole is like an eager toddler who finds wonder in the world around him. The boys he has befriended in Mr. Howard's class bring him great joy. He appreciates their jokes and harmless teasing. Cole would like nothing better than to hang out with his friends all day, but if he had to choose just one friend, it would be Aaron. (p. 76)[a]

Throughout their fifth- and sixth-grade years, Aaron was both a good friend and a caring mentor to Cole.

> Without prompting from adults, Aaron helped Cole with his work, included him at games at recess, and generally watched out for him. Aaron also assumed responsibility for Cole's behavior by explaining to Cole how his actions affected others. The following excerpt from a classroom observation illustrates Aaron's gentle way with Cole: "Cole was taking Nelle's [a classmate's] things out of her bag and throwing them on the floor. As soon as Aaron saw, he walked right over to Cole and started talking to him. He said, 'We're making a new rule—no being mean.' Then he walked with Cole to the front of the room and told him to tell another boy what the new rule was. Cole tapped the boy's shoulder to tell him but the boy walked away. Cole looked confused. Aaron smiled and put his hand on Cole's shoulder and told him, 'It's okay. Just remember the rule.' Then he walked Cole back to Nelle's stuff and quietly asked Cole to put everything back." (D. Staub, 1998, pp. 77–78)

But Aaron, too, benefited from the friendship, as his mother explained: "Our family has recently gone through a tough divorce and there are a lot of hurt feelings out there for everyone. But at least when Aaron is at school he feels good about being there and I think a big reason is because he has Cole and he knows that he is an important person in Cole's life" (D. Staub, 1998, pp. 90–91).

Dr. Staub observed that, despite their developmental differences, the boys' relationship was in many respects a normal one:

> I asked Mr. Howard once, "Do you think Cole's and Aaron's friendship looks different from others' in your class?" Mr. Howard thought for a moment before responding: "No, I don't think it looks that different. Well, I was going to say one of the differences is that Aaron sometimes tells Cole to be quiet, or 'Hey Cole, I gotta do my work!' But I don't know if that is any different than what he might say to Ben leaning over and interrupting him. I think I would say that Aaron honestly likes Cole and it's not because he's a special-needs kid." (D. Staub, 1998, p. 78)

Aaron and Cole remained close until Cole moved to a group home 30 miles away at the beginning of seventh grade.

(continued)

- In what ways did the friendship of Aaron and Cole promote each boy's social-emotional development?
- Was the boys' friendship a reciprocal one? Why or why not?

Once you have answered these questions, compare your responses with those presented in the appendix.

[a]Excerpts from *Delicate Threads: Friendships Between Children With and Without Special Needs in Inclusive Settings*, by D. Staub, 1998, Bethesda, MD: Woodbine House. Reprinted with permission.

Summary

Peers

Peers serve important functions in social-emotional development. Not only do they offer companionship, but peers create contexts for practicing social skills, making sense of social experiences, and shaping habits and ideas. Peer relationships change systematically throughout childhood and adolescence; for instance, activities tend to shift from simple gestures and imitation (infancy), to pretend play (early childhood), to structured group games (middle childhood), to social activities within cliques (early adolescence), and finally to larger, mixed-gender groups (late adolescence). Friendships are especially important peer relationships that provide emotional support and foster motivation to resolve conflicts in mutually satisfying ways.

Although preschoolers and elementary school children have some understanding of romantic relationships, young people do not appreciate the multifaceted nature of romance until they reach adolescence. As they go through puberty, they must come to terms with their changing bodies, sexual drives, and increasing sexual attraction to peers. Romances, either actual or imagined, can delight youngsters but also wreak havoc on their emotions. Some adolescents experiment with sexual intimacy with only limited information about the potential risks; others wrestle with sexual feelings for same-gender peers. As adolescents experience confusing new feelings, they certainly need and appreciate sensitivity and understanding on the part of educators.

Schools

Schools are powerful contexts of development for children and adolescents. Schools not only prepare youngsters with essential academic skills, but also serve as complex social environments that communicate to youngsters how welcome they are and how likely they are to succeed. Ideally, schools offer children a sense of community, deliver affirming messages about learning in general and individual abilities in particular, and support children as they transition into new academic environments.

Society

Society plays an important role through its provision of services to children. Many children spend time in child care settings that vary enormously in quality—from sensitive and developmentally appropriate to overcrowded and harsh. Child care has the potential to be a beneficial experience for children, and early childhood interventions—particularly those that begin during infancy and last for several years—can foster intellectual and social skills. After-school programs and extracurricular activities also bolster the development of youngsters, especially through stable, affectionate relationships with adults and peers and the many options for productive pastimes. Religious congregations and philosophically minded groups can heighten young people's sense of responsibility to the community, even as distinct doctrines challenge educators to treat all groups fairly and respectfully.

Many children and adolescents spend after-school hours watching television and playing or working on the computer. Television, computers, and other media have considerable potential to foster children's cognitive development, but their benefits have not yet been fully realized. Violent and stereotypic content in the media is a definite risk factor for young people, although some child consumers may be more susceptible to harmful effects than others.

Applying Concepts in Child Development

In this chapter you learned that children's social relationships with peers, teachers, and other adults in community institutions affect children's growing ability to get along with others. The following table describes the behaviors of youngsters at five different age levels, identifies concepts related to their peer acceptance, and offers suggestions for enhancing their inclusion as social partners. Apply what you've learned about peer relationships to fill in the empty cells in the table. When you're done, compare your responses with those in Table 14-1 in the *Study Guide and Reader*.

APPLYING CONCEPTS IN CHILD DEVELOPMENT

Fostering Children's Acceptance by Peers

Age	A Youngster's Experience	Developmental Concepts *Identifying Factors Affecting a Youngster's Acceptance by Peers*	Implications *Promoting Likability in Youngsters*
Infancy (Birth–2) 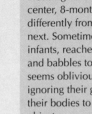	Noticing other infants in the child care center, 8-month-old Tyler reacts differently from one occasion to the next. Sometimes he smiles at other infants, reaches out to touch their faces, and babbles to them. At other times he seems oblivious to other infants, ignoring their gestures and crawling over their bodies to get to an interesting object.	Tyler is beginning to show an interest in other children. As is typical for his young age, Tyler's curiosity about peers is fleeting but will slowly blossom into a full-fledged desire to interact with peers. With continued opportunities and support from perceptive adults, Tyler is likely to develop *peer acceptance*.	Talk with infants and toddlers about the activities and emotional states you notice in other young children. For example, when a few children are in high chairs, comment on the food you are placing on each tray and everyone's reaction to it ("I guess Ben doesn't want green beans today, but look at how much Hana is enjoying them!"). Gently point out the effect when infants accidentally hurt another child ("Benny, please be careful. Soledad doesn't like it when you poke her eyes. Let's see if she likes having her arm rubbed instead").
Early Childhood (2–6) 	Five-year-old Finian and his family moved into a new community midway through his kindergarten year. Having now spent 2 months in his new kindergarten class, Finian typically stands quietly at the periphery of other children's social interactions. None of the children encourage him to join their play.	Like Finian, children who *transition to a new school* need considerable time to adjust to the school's people and customs. Finian has yet to find a social niche among his peers and has some of the qualities of *neglected children*. That is, he is quiet, keeps to himself, and is not sought after by peers to join their social groups.	
Middle Childhood (6–10) 	Eight-year-old Kia has no friends in school. Other children find her bossy and rude. For example, on the playground Kia walks up to a group of children who are quietly inspecting a shiny stone, shoves her way into the group, and demands that the children admire her new shoes, which she claims are far nicer than theirs. When the other children appear annoyed and try to move away from her, Kia grabs one girl, insisting that the two of them play on the monkey bars.		Identify and teach missing social skills to rejected children. In Kia's case it would be helpful to coach her in how to enter a social group. Kia could practice standing near other children, politely listening to the focus of their conversation, and then interjecting a comment that is relevant to the topic being discussed. Because rejected children generally have multiple social needs, consider offering ongoing support, including services from a school counselor or psychologist.
Early Adolescence (10–14) 	Twelve-year-old Frank is an energetic young man who takes his zeal for life into every setting he inhabits—his middle school classes, the school cafeteria, his after-school track team, and more. Frank has a good sense of humor but occasionally interrupts the class with off-color jokes and snide comments about peers. All the young people in his middle school know of Frank; many like him, but others find him abrasive, callous, and self-centered.	Frank shares the qualities of *socially controversial children*. He is well liked by some peers but avoided by others. Controversial children can be disruptive in some situations yet helpful, cooperative, and socially sensitive in others.	

(continued)

APPLYING CONCEPTS IN CHILD DEVELOPMENT

Fostering Children's Acceptance by Peers (continued)

Age	A Youngster's Experience	Developmental Concepts *Identifying Factors Affecting a Youngster's Acceptance by Peers*	Implications *Promoting Likability in Youngsters*
Late Adolescence (14–18) 	As a 15-year-old, Tara seems fairly happy with her social life. She has three close friends, all girls, and she and they increasingly interact with boys at school football games and school dances. Every now and then, Tara becomes annoyed with one of her friends, calls her names, or tries to exclude her from a social event; usually, however, Tara is kind-hearted and sensitive to her friends. Some students who are not Tara's friends think she's a bit snooty, but they do not perceive her to be overly objectionable.	In the parlance of social acceptance, Tara might be considered *average:* She is liked by some peers and moderately disliked by others. Children who are average in their likability tend to exhibit age-typical social skills, be reasonably concerned about other people's welfare, and show occasional lapses of tact and self-control.	Talk with young people about their social lives—how they get along with peers, who their friends are, and what trouble spots they encounter with peers. Acknowledge to average youngsters that they seem to exhibit a healthy social life, and encourage them to continue to develop their prosocial skills, such as being diplomatic with other people, while also continuing to look after their own needs.

Key Concepts

popular children (p. 533)
rejected children (p. 534)
neglected children (p. 534)
controversial children (p. 534)
peer culture (p. 539)

dominance hierarchy (p. 540)
clique (p. 540)
subculture (p. 541)
gang (p. 541)
sexual orientation (p. 544)

sexual harassment (p. 547)
sense of community (p. 549)
community of learners (p. 550)
self-fulfilling prophecy (p. 552)
society (p. 555)

early childhood intervention program (p. 556)
service learning (p. 558)
interactive technology (p. 561)

Now go to our Companion Website at www.prenhall.com/mcdevitt to assess your understanding of chapter content with a Practice Quiz, apply what you've learned in Essay Questions, and broaden your knowledge with links to related Developmental Psychology Web sites.

Appendix: Analyses of the Ending Case Studies

Included here are examples of how you might have answered the questions at the end of the case studies in Chapters 1–14.

CHAPTER 1: *LATISHA* (PP. 28–29)

In what ways do we see the contexts of family, school, neighborhood, and culture affecting Latisha's development?

Latisha is strongly influenced by the settings in which she lives. Latisha's mother offers the loving care and stable home environment Latisha needs to become an optimistic and productive citizen. Her mother also demonstrates a strong work ethic and exposes Latisha to the healing powers of modern medicine. Two men—Latisha's stepfather and an uncle—take an interest in her well-being as well. Prevailing dangers in the neighborhood obviously bother Latisha, but her family serves as a safe haven. In addition, school seems to be a nurturing environment for Latisha; she achieves at sufficiently high levels that she is able to consider becoming a doctor. Finally, Latisha seems to have absorbed some of the positive values of her culture, such as feeling obligated to help others.

Based on your own experiences growing up, what aspects of Latisha's development would you guess are probably universal? What aspects reflect diversity?

Latisha's natural human potential is nurtured by relationships and experiences. Like all other youngsters, Latisha can achieve her full potential only if she receives love, adequate nutrition, a clean and toxin-free environment, an opportunity for physical activity, and a reasonably challenging education. In other respects, however, Latisha's development is unique. She has a one-of-a-kind profile of individual traits and dispositions, and her particular genetic heritage probably contributes to her strong intellectual potential and her cheerful but cautious temperament. Every youngster's environment is ultimately distinctive as well; although Latisha's neighborhood is somewhat dangerous, fortunately her own family is affectionate and protective.

What clues do we have that Latisha's teachers can almost certainly have a positive impact on her long-term development and success?

Latisha is a well-intentioned student who likes school and most of her teachers, and she has a career goal that requires extensive education. These characteristics reflect favorably on Latisha's ability to benefit from instruction. To help her reach her career goal, her teachers might teach her to use effective study skills, encourage her interests in medicine, advise her to take challenging science and mathematics courses, and offer hands-on assistance when she is completing applications for college admission and financial aid.

CHAPTER 2: *THE STUDY SKILLS CLASS* (PP. 58–59)

What methods did Deborah use to collect her data? What were the potential strengths and limitations of each method?

Deborah conducted action research to learn why her 20 eighth-grade students were unmotivated and poorly behaved in the classroom. She observed the students' behavior and collected other information through questionnaires, interviews, and school records of grades and attendance. As sources of data, these methods tend to have the following advantages and disadvantages:

- *Observations* have the advantage of documenting actions that people may not be able or willing to articulate. However, it is not always clear whether actions are typical for a group, nor is it fully apparent what the actions mean. For example, might students be off-task if the work is too simple, difficult, tedious, or unrelated to their prior experiences? Furthermore, the presence of observers—in this case Deborah herself—is likely to affect the behaviors of those being observed, and observers' interpretations are often affected by their expectations.

- *Questionnaires* allow researchers to collect and analyze a lot of information from a fairly large group of people over a short period of time. However, questionnaires exceed some respondents' reading abilities and do not permit follow-up or probing. In addition, when respondents are not honest or when items are out of sync with respondents' ideas, the data that questionnaires yield can be misleading. It is not apparent from this case whether Deborah was sufficiently knowledgeable about her students to present them with meaningful questions and response choices.
- *Interviews* have the advantage of permitting respondents to describe their reasoning in depth, but they are time-consuming to conduct and require good rapport between interviewer and respondents. It is possible that the students were not candid with Deborah when answering her questions about school.
- *Records of grades and attendance* can be accurate measures of students' academic achievement and presence in school. However, grades are often affected by teachers' subjective impressions of students, and records of attendance do not reveal *why* students attend or miss school.

Deborah tentatively concluded that her own teaching led to the dramatic drop in grades from the second quarter to the third. Is her conclusion justified? Why or why not?

Deborah's conclusion that her teaching was responsible for the drop in grades is not justified. A range of factors can affect students' grades, including other things going on in students' lives. And even if Deborah's presence in the class precipitated students' academic decline, it would not be obvious which part of her teaching—such as her grading scheme, instructional methods, relationships with students, or some other aspect—was the primary factor.

CHAPTER 3: *UNDERSTANDING ADAM* (PP. 92–93)

Adam was eventually diagnosed with fetal alcohol syndrome *(FAS). What characteristics do children with FAS have?*

Children with fetal alcohol syndrome typically have mental retardation, delays in physical and motor development, and facial abnormalities. These children also tend to be impulsive and to exhibit other behavioral problems.

What conditions lead to FAS? In other words, how was it that Adam came to develop FAS?

Fetal alcohol syndrome can occur when a pregnant woman drinks alcohol, especially when she does so recurrently. Alcohol that circulates in the woman's body disrupts the growth of structures in the body and brain of the fetus. Based on the severity of Adam's symptoms and the fact that his birth mother died of acute alcohol poisoning, Adam was most likely exposed to consistently high levels of alcohol during his prenatal development.

Adam eventually learned many practical skills, such as how to read and hold down a simple job. What kinds of support would Adam have needed to achieve a good quality of life?

Like any child, Adam would have benefited from being in a loving family and receiving good nutrition, appropriate medical care, and opportunities for physical activity. As a result of his mental retardation and health problems, Adam would have needed many opportunities for practicing basic skills, such as tying his shoes and writing his name, and ongoing medical care to address his physical problems.

CHAPTER 4: *LUCY* (P. 142)

Lucy's illness delayed the onset of puberty. What other effects might her illness have had on her development relative to peers? As you ponder this question, consider her cognitive and social development as well as her physical development.

Lucy had leukemia, a disease that triggers the uncontrolled proliferation of white blood cells and is often treated with chemotherapy and radiation. Lucy's disease and invasive medical treatments delayed her progress through puberty, caused her hair loss, weakened her immune system, and may have impaired the functioning of her internal organs, such as her spleen. The illness also affected Lucy's social development. Lucy would have seemed unusual to peers—she appeared young and frail, had missed many important social events, and savored rather than resisted her family's protective gestures. The effects of the illness on her cognitive development are less clear, but her extended absences from school and her diminished energy would have made it difficult for her to keep up with increasingly challenging academic work.

In some respects, Lucy probably developed more quickly than most students her age. What particular strengths might Lucy have had as a result of having combated a life-threatening illness?

Lucy's life-threatening illness and hospital stays would have given her an advanced perspective on human physiology and medical care and may have transformed her long-term priorities and goals. Although Lucy is apt to remain fearful about her health, she can be proud of the resilience she has shown in the face of adversity.

As a teacher working with this age-group, what strategies might you use to ease Lucy's return to school?

Lucy's teachers might try one of several strategies:

- *Talk with Lucy's parents.* Lucy's parents can inform teachers about what to say about Lucy's condition to the other students; in fact, Lucy's teachers cannot tell other students *anything* about Lucy's illness without her parents' permission. Lucy's parents may also advise teachers of any remaining symptoms Lucy may have, such as nausea, and things teachers can do to help her, such as allowing her to snack on crackers during regular class time.
- *Prepare the other students for Lucy's return to school.* With permission from Lucy and her parents, teachers can explain to the other students what Lucy has been through and how they all can help her. For example, some students may need to be reassured that they will not catch leukemia from Lucy but that they can help her by shielding her from their sneezes and coughs, given her vulnerability to infection.
- *Encourage Lucy to take care of herself.* Children with chronic illnesses need to become conscientious in caring for themselves. They need to monitor their own symptoms, take prescribed medications on schedule, and carry out other health-protective measures, such as applying sunscreen when medications cause extreme sensitivity to sunlight.
- *Ease Lucy's reentry into school.* It can be difficult for children to return to school after lengthy hospitalizations or convalescence at home. Teachers can help returning students adjust to the classroom setting and engage once again in their schoolwork ("It is great to see you catching up with your math, Lucy! You're really starting to blaze through those problems").
- *Teach missing skills.* When students have been too weak to study, they naturally fall behind in their course work. Teachers can help students master missing concepts and skills so that students can return to a productive learning track.

CHAPTER 5: *FOUR-YEAR-OLD SONS* (P. 186)

How do the two mothers interpret their sons' questions differently? How might their interpretations help us to predict their disciplinary styles?

Elizabeth interprets Charles's questions as acts of defiance. She believes that Charles is trying to provoke her with his questions. In contrast, Joyce sees Peter's questions as an outgrowth of his natural curiosity. We might expect that Elizabeth discourages questioning from Charles and expects his immediate (and unquestioning) compliance. In contrast, we might expect that Joyce will actually encourage Peter's questioning by responding with patient and elaborate explanations and, in disciplinary situations, with reasons for following a certain course of action. In general, we might suspect that Elizabeth uses an authoritarian parenting style, whereas Joyce probably uses an authoritative one.

How might Elizabeth and Joyce have developed their particular parenting styles?

As they interact with their children, parents are affected by their cultural beliefs and previous experiences. It is possible that both Elizabeth and Joyce are using parenting styles that they themselves were exposed to as children; the two mothers might also be affected by predominant child-rearing techniques they see friends and other family members using. The surrounding community and its stressors can be influential as well. Elizabeth seems somewhat short-tempered, perhaps because of economic hardship or other problems in her life; Joyce appears to enjoy her interactions with her son.

What kinds of educational opportunities might these mothers create at home for their children? What might teachers do to encourage each mother's involvement at school?

Each mother would undoubtedly want her son to do well in school. The educational activities the two mothers provide at home may be different, however. Quite possibly, Elizabeth would provide information that she would expect Charles to accept at face value. In contrast, Joyce is likely to engage Peter in activities that capitalize on his natural curiosity (e.g., trips to the library, the zoo, and more) and to encourage him to think critically about his experiences. Teachers can encourage both mothers (and other family members as well) to become involved at school by inviting them to take part in school events and visit their children's classrooms, by asking them to share their talents at school, by encouraging them to read daily to their children, and so on. In addition, teachers might make a point of explaining their educational philosophy and disciplinary strategies so that families can understand the nature and purpose of the curriculum and classroom procedures.

CHAPTER 6: *ADOLESCENT SCIENTISTS* (PP. 227–228)

In what ways does Mr. Sowell scaffold the students' efforts during the lab activity?

He asks several questions that encourage the students to revise and reconsider their findings. He points out that they have simultaneously changed both length and weight and asks, "Why can't you come to a conclusion by looking at the two frequencies?" He guides them toward identifying an error in their reasoning and then asks, "Can you think of a way to redesign your experiments so that you're only changing weight?" In general, he guides them in their thinking but does not specifically tell them the correct answer.

With which one of Piaget's stages is the students' reasoning most consistent?

Their reasoning is consistent with Piaget's concrete operations stage, in which children have difficulty separating and controlling variables.

Use one or more of Piaget's ideas to explain why Marina persists in her belief that, despite evidence to the contrary, weight affects a pendulum's frequency.

Marina does not notice the inconsistency between what she has observed and what she believes to be true. In other words, she does not experience disequilibrium. Instead, she assimilates any new observations to her belief that weight is the most influential factor.

Drawing from current perspectives on Piaget's theory, identify a task for which the students might be better able to separate and control variables.

There are many possible answers to this question. In general, children are more likely to show formal operational reasoning with subject matter and tasks that are familiar to them. For example, you might present a task related to fishing (see Figure 6-3, on p. 202), growing sunflowers under varying conditions, or gaining proficiency in a particular athletic skill using various training regimens.

CHAPTER 7: *THE LIBRARY PROJECT* (PP. 271–272)

Initially, the intern realizes that her students will need some structure to complete the project successfully. In what ways do she and the librarian structure the assignment for the students?

The intern breaks the large project into several smaller pieces—gathering information at the library, writing rough drafts, and so on—and assigns each group member a particular topic to research. At the school library, the librarian locates appropriate resources, and the intern provides guidance as the students conduct their research. The following day the intern gives suggestions about how the students might effectively use an index to find the information they need.

What specific strategies do the students use as they engage in their library research? In what ways are their strategies less effective than an adult's might be?

The students are using the index to find the information they need and taking notes on facts and data that might be helpful. However, their use of the index is relatively inflexible (e.g., a student looking for information on *economy* doesn't think to look under *commerce, imports,* or *exports*), and the students copy excerpts from the resources verbatim rather than rephrasing, condensing, or summarizing. Adults would presumably be more flexible in their index use and note taking.

How does the students' prior knowledge (or lack thereof) influence the effectiveness of their strategies?

The students have less knowledge than adults about the topics they are researching (*economy, culture, religion,* etc.). Their relative lack of knowledge undoubtedly limits their ability to use an index effectively, make sense of what they read, identify the ideas most relevant to their research topics, and paraphrase and summarize what they've learned.

CHAPTER 8: *FRESH VEGETABLES* (PP. 310–311)

Did Steven have mental retardation? Why or why not?

It appears that Steven did *not* have mental retardation. Two characteristics must be present for a diagnosis of mental retardation: (a) significantly below-average general intelligence and (b) deficits in adaptive behavior. Although Steven's early IQ scores were low, the case revealed no evidence that he had deficits in adaptive functioning. Furthermore, he later earned a high grade point average in regular high school classes—an outcome that would be highly unlikely for a student with mental retardation.

The school psychologist recommended that Steven be placed in a special class for students with special needs. Was such a class an appropriate placement for Steven? Why or why not?

The class probably was appropriate as a short-term placement, although another option would have been to offer him enriching activities in the regular classroom. Whether Steven had mental retardation or not, his very limited knowledge and skills made it highly unlikely that he could initially succeed in a general education classroom without intensive instruction that addressed the areas in which he lagged behind his age-mates. Once Steven mastered basic skills in reading, writing, and mathematics, he became better able to tackle age-appropriate learning tasks.

CHAPTER 9: *BOARDING SCHOOL* (P. 353)

Why might Joseph prefer his native dialect to Standard English?

Joseph probably views his native dialect as an important part of his ethnic identity. Furthermore, he probably knows that his dialect is the preferred way of speaking in his local community and believes he can communicate most effectively when he uses it.

Is Joseph bilingual? Why or why not?

The answer to the question depends on one's definition of *bilingual.* Joseph can certainly speak both dialects fluently and knows the contexts in which he should use each one. However, both dialects are forms of English; they are not entirely different languages that have unique vocabularies, grammatical constructions, and so on. Perhaps a more accurate descriptor would be *bidialectical.*

The counselor told Joseph that he had "been cured." What beliefs about Joseph's native dialect does this statement reflect?

The counselor apparently believed that (a) Joseph's dialect was inferior to Standard English and (b) the dialect was a problem that needed to be corrected.

CHAPTER 10: *BEATING THE ODDS* (PP. 397–398)

In what ways did nurture clearly play a role in the students' mathematical achievement? How might nature also have been involved?

To a considerable degree, the students' achievement was the result of nurture: Mr. Escalante provided intensive instruction, to the point that students knew calculus thoroughly and probably had automatized basic skills. He also communicated high expectations for students' performance (the importance of doing so will become clear in Chapter 12's discussion of the development of a sense of self). From a nature perspective, the students' high ability levels were probably partly due to their genetic potential (see the discussion of hereditary influences on intelligence in Chapter 8). Also, visual-spatial ability plays a role in youngsters' mathematical reasoning; this ability appears to depend partly on certain sex-related hormones.

The calculus class consisted of 10 boys and 8 girls. Are these numbers consistent or inconsistent with research related to gender differences in mathematics?

Average gender differences in math ability tend to be fairly small, but boys show greater *variability* in math ability, especially in adolescence. The slightly higher number of boys might be expected, given research findings. (If you have some knowledge of statistics, you might realize that the small difference in the number of boys versus girls would not indicate a male advantage in mathematics unless a similar difference was observed consistently across many advanced math classes.)

ETS employees based their suspicions about cheating partly on the similarity of answers they saw in students' responses. What other explanation for the similarity might there be?

The students were all in the same class and so undoubtedly learned similar strategies for solving calculus problems. Furthermore, in their practice sessions, they may have solved many problems similar to those that appeared on the test and perhaps discussed the best approach for each one. If so, they would all have used similar approaches in solving the test problems.

CHAPTER 11: *THE GIRLY SHIRT* (P. 437)

Considering what you have learned about trends in emotional development, is Tim's reaction typical for his age?

Children in middle childhood are increasingly able to regulate their emotions, but their coping strategies are hardly foolproof. Children in the elementary years are affected by self-conscious emotions (e.g., shame), and Tim may have become furious because he felt embarrassed and humiliated by his classmates' thoughtless remarks and derisive laughter. Thus, Tim's angry outburst is probably not unusual for his age, but if he persists in making explosive outbursts, he is at risk for losing friends and having trouble concentrating on academic lessons.

What kind of plan might be effective in helping Tim control his anger?

Ms. Fox might, with Tim's help, formulate one or more plans to help Tim acquire skills for controlling his emotions. Together, they might target Tim's social-emotional skills and specifically focus on his ability to express his emotions productively. The plans might have a few objectives, such as (a) fostering Tim's social sensitivity and friendship skills so that he becomes a desirable social partner that other children genuinely care about; (b) helping Tim recognize and label his feelings as they occur (e.g., noticing when he is feeling happy, sad, embarrassed, disappointed, angry, ashamed, and so forth); and (c) asking Tim to follow a strategy for coping with unpleasant feelings such as anger (e.g., initially stopping to recognize that he is angered by another child's rude remark, taking a deep breath, and considering several actions and their consequences before responding). Because Tim's explosive anger might, unchecked, jeopardize his social standing among peers, become a detrimental habit, and disrupt the entire class, Ms. Fox will need to monitor his emotional expression. She can praise him when he shows restraint, and she can remove privileges from him (or apply another consequence) when he allows his temper to escalate.

CHAPTER 12: *GANG MEDIATION* (PP. 482–483)

Why do you think the mediation approach was successful when other approaches had failed? Drawing on what you've learned about social cognition and the development of interpersonal skills, identify at least three possible reasons.

Possible reasons include the following:

- The students were given concrete guidelines about acceptable and unacceptable interpersonal behaviors.

- Discussions with rival gang members probably promoted greater social perspective taking, including a better understanding of why rivals might act as they do and how rivals might interpret one another's behaviors. Because older adolescents are capable of recursive thinking, they should be able to think along these lines: "You think that I think that _____. But that's not how it is at all. Actually I think that _____."
- Many gang members probably had social-cognitive biases about rival gangs that led them to interpret rivals' behaviors as reflecting hostility. (That is, many students had a *hostile attributional bias*.) The mediation sessions possibly helped the students see one another as unique individuals, thereby breaking down their rigid stereotypes about rival gang members.
- Through the mediation sessions, students probably discovered alternative ways of processing social information. For instance, rather than interpret a rival gang member's facial expression as a hostile stare or an "attitude," a student might realize that the individual was simply deep in thought about a troubling personal matter.
- When members of rival gangs discussed a source of conflict, they may have acquired more effective social problem-solving skills (e.g., look at a situation from all sides and try to find a reasonable compromise that addresses everyone's needs).
- In conducting the mediation sessions, the counselors modeled effective interpersonal behaviors and social problem-solving skills.
- From a Vygotskian perspective, when the students used particular social strategies in the group situation (with the counselors' scaffolding), they may have gradually internalized these strategies and so eventually became capable of using them independently.

CHAPTER 13: *SPENCER* (PP. 525–526)

What motives and goals does Spencer seem to have?
Spencer's motives and goals include the following:

- Like all children, Spencer almost certainly has a basic need to feel competent. By putting the blame on his teachers (rather than on himself) when he has trouble learning—that is, by attributing his failures to external causes—he is able to maintain his sense of competence.
- Spencer appears to crave others' attention, sometimes without regard for the form the attention takes (notice how Spencer sometimes seems to enjoy Ms. Quintero's negative feedback). Throwing a desk, putting a hate note in a classmate's backpack, and threatening to urinate on another boy in the restroom are all behaviors that will gain him considerable attention. Such behaviors, then, are probably being reinforced.
- Spencer appears to enjoy being with other children, and on some occasions he is quite sweet and helpful in his interactions with Ms. Quintero. In other words, Spencer has a need for relatedness that manifests itself in a variety of social goals, such as having friendly interpersonal relationships and gaining other people's attention and approval. In some instances, however, it appears that his goals include gaining power and dominance over others—common goals among aggressive children (see Chapter 12).

What evidence do you see that Spencer has poor self-regulation skills?
Spencer's poor self-regulation is evident in the following ways:

- He seems unable to handle frustration, control his impulses, and regulate his emotions, as reflected in his frequent screaming and crying and, of course, in such actions as throwing his desk across the room.
- He doesn't know how to ask for help when he needs it.
- He doesn't have strategies for helping himself remember to bring important items (e.g., a jacket, his lunchbox) to and from school.

How would you characterize Spencer's moral development?
Spencer's moral development appears to be behind schedule. Unlike most 8-year-olds, he shows no concern about causing other people physical or psychological harm. From Kohlberg's perspective Spencer would be classified as being at Stage 1: He has regard only for his own needs.

What factors in Spencer's environment have probably contributed to his behavior problems? Might biological factors also be playing a role?

Spencer's environment has almost certainly contributed to his behavior problems. It appears that outside Ms. Quintero's classroom Spencer suffers no consequences for inappropriate behavior. Furthermore, his mother encourages him to look out for himself, and her external attributions for his poor classroom performance ("You're killing the spirit of my child!") may encourage him to take no responsibility for his actions. And Spencer often gets what he wants when Mom intervenes (e.g., by insisting that her son be given better grades).

Yet biology, too, is likely to be involved. Spencer gets little sleep at his father's house and so is often "off the wall" at school the following day. In addition, Spencer has trouble following directions involving more than one or two steps, indicating a possible cognitive disability (e.g., attention-deficit hyperactivity disorder or a learning disability).

Is the principal's attitude toward Spencer's bullying behaviors appropriate? Why or why not?

It certainly is *not* appropriate. All children have a right to feel safe at school, and they can perform at their best only when they *do* feel safe. Furthermore, because Spencer apparently has few social skills and because his aggressive behaviors often lead to reinforcement (e.g., gaining attention), an active and perhaps intensive intervention is in order.

What changes in Spencer's environment might help him acquire more productive behaviors?

The following are examples of changes that should make a difference:

- Ensuring consistency at school and at home regarding (a) expectations for behavior and (b) consequences for misbehavior
- Providing explicit instruction in social skills
- Reinforcing prosocial behaviors
- Administering consequences for inappropriate actions that are definitely punishing rather than reinforcing (e.g., Ms. Quintero's attention may be reinforcing rather than punishing Spencer's aggression; perhaps short time-outs would be more effective)
- Accompanying punishment with explanations about why certain behaviors are inappropriate (i.e., use of *induction*)
- Teaching self-regulation skills (e.g., strategies for coping with frustration)

CHAPTER 14: *AARON AND COLE* (PP. 566–567)

In what ways did the friendship of Aaron and Cole promote each boy's social-emotional development?

Aaron and Cole's friendship gave both boys mutual encouragement and support. Other benefits differed slightly for the two boys. During the time Aaron's parents were getting divorced, Aaron felt sad, confused, and vulnerable. Cole helped Aaron feel needed and appreciated. Aaron also displayed leadership among his classmates by serving as a positive role model who interacted patiently and inclusively with a peer with a disability. Cole benefited from the reassurance, acceptance, and guidance he received from Aaron. Cole also was included in certain social groups because of Aaron's intercession.

Was the boys' friendship a reciprocal one? Why or why not?

The friendship between the two boys was reciprocal in that they both entered the association voluntarily and enjoyed its benefits. Although the two boys had different abilities and social standings, they each felt affection for the other.

absolute pitch Ability to recall the precise pitch of a particular note in music.

accommodation Process of dealing with a new event by either modifying an existing scheme or forming a new one.

acculturation Process of taking on the customs and values of a new culture.

action research Systematic study of an issue or problem by a teacher or other practitioner, with the goal of bringing about more productive outcomes for children.

actual developmental level Upper limit of tasks that a child can successfully perform independently.

adaptive behavior Behavior related to daily living skills and appropriate conduct in social situations.

addiction Physical and psychological dependence on a substance, such that increasing quantities must be taken to produce the desired effect and withdrawal produces adverse physiological and psychological effects.

African American English Dialect of some African American communities that includes pronunciations, grammatical constructions, and idioms different from those of Standard English.

aggression Action intentionally taken to hurt another either physically or psychologically.

alleles Genes located at the same point on corresponding (paired) chromosomes and related to the same physical characteristic.

androgyny Tendency to have some characteristics that are stereotypically female (e.g., nurturance) and others that are stereotypically male (e.g., assertiveness).

anorexia nervosa Eating disorder in which a person eats little or nothing for weeks or months and seriously jeopardizes health.

anxiety Emotional state characterized by worry and apprehension.

anxiety disorder Chronic emotional condition characterized by excessive, debilitating worry.

apprenticeship Mentorship in which a novice works intensively with an expert to learn how to accomplish complex tasks in a particular domain.

appropriation Gradual adoption of (and perhaps also adaptation of) other people's ways of thinking and behaving for one's own purposes.

assessment Task that children complete and researchers use to make judgments of children's understandings and skills.

assimilation Form of acculturation in which a person totally embraces a new culture, abandoning a previous culture in the process. Also, in Piaget's theory, process of dealing with a new event in a way that is consistent with an existing scheme (see Chapter 6).

attachment An enduring emotional tie uniting one person to another.

attention-deficit hyperactivity disorder (ADHD) Disability characterized by inattention, by hyperactivity and impulsive behavior, or by all three characteristics.

attribution Belief about the cause of one's success or failure.

authentic activity Instructional activity similar to one that a child might eventually encounter in the outside world.

authoritarian style Parenting style characterized by strict expectations for behavior and rigid rules that children are expected to obey without question.

authoritative style Parenting style characterized by emotional warmth, high expectations and standards for behavior, consistent enforcement of rules, explanations regarding the reasons behind these rules, and the inclusion of children in decision making.

autism Disability characterized by infrequent social interaction, little awareness of one's own and others' thoughts, communication impairments, repetitive behaviors, narrowly focused interests, and a strong need for a predictable environment.

autobiographical self Mental "history" of events important in one's life.

automatization Process of becoming able to respond quickly and efficiently while mentally processing or physically performing certain tasks.

axon Armlike part of a neuron that sends information to other neurons.

babbling Repeating certain consonant-vowel syllables over and over (e.g., "mamamama"); common in the latter half of the first year.

behaviorism and social learning theory Theoretical perspective that focuses on environmental stimuli and learning processes that lead to behavioral change.

bicultural orientation Form of acculturation in which a person is familiar with two cultures and selectively draws from the values and traditions of one or both cultures depending on the context.

bilingual education Approach to second-language instruction in which students are instructed in academic subject areas in their native language while simultaneously being taught to speak and write in the second language.

bilingualism Knowing and speaking two languages fluently.

biological theory Theoretical perspective that emphasizes genetic factors and physiological structures and functions of the body and brain.

blended family Family created when one parent-child(ren) family combines with another parent figure and any children in his or her custody; also, the structure that emerges when a parent already with a child remarries and has another child with the new spouse.

bulimia Eating disorder in which a person, in an attempt to be thin, eats a large amount of food and then purposefully purges it from the body by vomiting or taking laxatives.

canalization Tight genetic control of a particular aspect of development.

care orientation Focus on nurturance and concern for others in moral decision making.

central conceptual structure Integrated network of concepts and cognitive processes that forms the basis for much of one's thinking, reasoning, and learning in a specific content domain.

central executive Component of the human information processing system that oversees the flow of information throughout the system.

cephalocaudal trend Vertical ordering of motor skills and physical development; order is head first to feet last.

child development Study of the persistent, cumulative, and progressive changes in the physical, cognitive, and social-emotional development of children and adolescents.

child maltreatment Adverse treatment of a child in the form of neglect, physical abuse, sexual abuse, or emotional abuse.

chromosome Rodlike structure that resides in the nucleus of every cell of the body and contains genes that guide growth and development; each chromosome is made up of DNA.

class inclusion Recognition that an object simultaneously belongs to a particular category and to one of its subcategories.

clinical method Procedure in which an adult probes a child's reasoning about a task or problem, tailoring questions in light of what the child has previously said or done in the interview.

clique Moderately stable friendship group of perhaps 3 to 10 members.

codominance Situation in which the two genes of an allele pair, although not identical, both have some influence on a characteristic.

cognition The various mental activities in which a person engages.

cognitive apprenticeship Mentorship in which an expert and a novice work together on a challenging task and the expert suggests ways to think about the task.

cognitive development Systematic changes in reasoning, concepts, memory, and language.

cognitive-developmental theory Theoretical perspective that focuses on major transformations to the underlying structures of thinking.

cognitive process theory Theoretical perspective that focuses on the precise nature of human mental operations.

cognitive strategy Specific mental process that people use to acquire or manipulate information.

cognitive tool Concept, symbol, strategy, or other culturally constructed mechanism that helps people think more effectively.

colic Persistent crying by infants; it is most prevalent in the first 3 months of life.

community The local neighborhood and surrounding vicinity of a child and his or her family.

community of learners A classroom in which teacher(s) and students actively and collaboratively work to help one another learn.

comprehension monitoring Process of checking oneself to make sure one understands what one is studying.

conceptual change Revision of one's knowledge and understanding of a topic in response to new information about the topic.

conduct disorder Chronic emotional condition characterized by lack of concern for the rights of others.

conservation Realization that if nothing is added or taken away, amount stays the same regardless of any alterations in shape or arrangement.

constructivism Theoretical perspective proposing that learners construct a body of knowledge and beliefs, rather than absorbing information at face value.

context The broad social environments, including family, schools and community services, neighborhoods, culture, ethnicity, and society at large, that influence children's development.

contingent self-worth Overall sense of self that is highly dependent on others' opinions.

control group A group of participants in a research study who do not receive the treatment under investigation; often used in an experimental study.

controversial children Children whom some peers really like and other peers strongly dislike.

conventional morality   Acceptance of society's conventions regarding right and wrong; behaving to please others or to live up to society's expectations for appropriate behavior.

conventional transgression   Action that violates society's general guidelines (often unspoken) for socially acceptable behavior.

cooing   Making and repeating vowel sounds (e.g., "ooooo"); common in early infancy.

coparents   The two (or more) parents who share responsibility for rearing their children.

co-regulated learning   Process through which an adult and child share responsibility for directing various aspects of the child's learning.

correlation   Extent to which two variables are related to each other, such that when one variable increases, the other either increases or decreases in a somewhat predictable fashion.

correlational feature   Characteristic present in many instances of a concept but not essential for concept membership.

correlational study   Research study that explores relationships among variables.

correlation coefficient   A statistic that indicates the nature of the relationship between two variables.

cortex   Part of the forebrain that houses conscious thinking processes (executive functions).

cross-sectional study   Research study in which the performance of individuals at different ages is compared.

crystallized intelligence   Knowledge and skills accumulated from one's prior experience, schooling, and culture.

cultural bias   Extent to which an assessment instrument offends or unfairly penalizes some individuals because of their ethnicity, gender, or socioeconomic status.

culture   Behaviors and belief systems that characterize a social group and provide a framework for how group members decide what is normal and appropriate.

culture shock   Sense of confusion that occurs when one encounters an environment with expectations for behavior very different from those in one's home environment.

defining feature   Characteristic that must be present in all instances of a concept.

delay of gratification   Forgoing small immediate rewards for larger ones at a future time.

dendrite   Branchlike part of a neuron that receives information from other neurons.

depression   Emotional condition characterized by significant sadness, discouragement, hopelessness and, in children, irritability.

developmentally appropriate practice   Instruction and other services adapted to the age, characteristics, and developmental progress of individual children.

developmental systems theory   Theoretical perspective that focuses on the multiple factors, including systems inside and outside children, that combine to influence children's development.

dialect   Form of a language characteristic of a particular geographic region or ethnic group.

differentiation   An increase from general to more specific functioning over the course of development.

disequilibrium   State of being unable to address new events with existing schemes.

disorganized and disoriented attachment   Attachment classification in which children lack a single coherent way of responding to attachment figures.

distributed intelligence   Thinking facilitated by physical objects and technology, social support, and concepts and symbols of one's culture.

distributive justice   Beliefs about what constitutes people's fair share of a valued commodity.

diversity   In a particular aspect of human development, the varied ways different individuals progress.

dizygotic twins   Twins that began as two separate zygotes and so are as genetically similar as two siblings conceived and born at different times.

DNA   A spiral-staircase shaped molecule that guides the production of proteins needed by the body for growth and development; short for *deoxyribonucleic acid.*

dominance hierarchy   Relative standing of group members in terms of such qualities as leadership and social influence.

dominant gene   Gene that overrides any competing instructions in an allele pair.

dynamic assessment   Systematic examination of how a child's knowledge or reasoning may change as a result of learning a specific task or performing it with adult guidance.

dyslexia   Inability to master basic reading skills in a developmentally typical time frame despite normal reading instruction.

early childhood intervention program   Program designed to foster basic intellectual, social-emotional, and physical development in infants and young children whose heads of family are burdened by economic poverty or other debilitating life circumstances.

egocentrism   Inability of a child in Piaget's preoperational stage to view situations from another person's perspective.

elaboration   Process of using prior knowledge to embellish on new information and thereby learn it more effectively.

embryo   During prenatal Weeks 2 through 8, the developing being that is in the process of forming major body structures and organs.

emergent literacy   Knowledge and skills that lay a foundation for reading and writing; typically develops in the preschool years from early experiences with written language.

emotion   Affective response to an event that is personally relevant to one's needs and goals.

emotional contagion   Tendency for infants to cry spontaneously when they hear other infants crying.

emotional regulation   Strategies to manage affective states.

empathy   Capacity to experience the same feelings as another person, especially when the feeling is pain or distress.

entity view of ability   Belief that ability is a "thing" that is relatively permanent and unchangeable.

epistemological beliefs   Beliefs regarding the nature of knowledge and knowledge acquisition.

equilibration   Movement from equilibrium to disequilibrium and back to equilibrium; a process that promotes the development of increasingly complex forms of thought and knowledge.

equilibrium   State of being able to address new events using existing schemes.

ethnic identity   Awareness of being a member of a particular ethnic or cultural group and willingness to adopt certain behaviors characteristic of that group.

ethnicity   Membership in a group of people with common ancestors and shared values, beliefs, and behaviors.

ethological attachment theory   Theoretical perspective that emphasizes benefits to children, particularly protection from harm and a secure base from which to explore the environment, derived from close bonds with caregivers.

executive functions   Purposeful and goal-directed intellectual processes (e.g., reasoning, decision making) made possible by higher brain structures.

expansion   Repetition of a child's short utterances in a more complete and grammatically correct form.

experimental study   Research study in which a researcher manipulates one aspect of the environment (a treatment), controls other aspects of the environment, and assesses the treatment's effects on participants' behavior.

expressive language   Ability to communicate effectively through speaking and writing.

extrinsic motivation   Motivation provoked by the external consequences that certain behaviors bring.

family   Two or more people who live together and are related by enduring factors such as birth, marriage, adoption, or long-term mutual commitment.

family structure   In a family with children, the family's makeup; specifically, the children in a family home and the adults who live with and care for the children.

fast mapping   Inferring a word's general meaning after a single exposure.

fetus   During prenatal Week 9 until birth, the developing being that is growing in size and weight and in sensory abilities, brain structures, and organs needed for survival.

figurative speech   Speech that communicates meaning beyond a literal interpretation of its words.

fine motor skills   Small, precise movements of particular parts of the body, especially the hands.

fluid intelligence   Ability to acquire knowledge quickly and thereby adapt effectively to new situations.

Flynn effect   Gradual increase in intelligence test performance observed in many countries over the past several decades.

forebrain   Part of the brain responsible for complex thinking, emotions, and motivation.

functionalism   Theoretical perspective of language development that emphasizes the purposes language serves for human beings.

g   General factor in intelligence that influences performance in a wide variety of tasks and content domains.

gamete   Reproductive cell that, in humans, contains 23 chromosomes rather than the 46 chromosomes present in other cells in the body; a male gamete (sperm) and a female gamete (ovum) join at conception.

gang   Cohesive social group characterized by initiation rites, distinctive colors and symbols, territorial orientation, feuds with rival groups, and criminal activity.

gender schema   Self-constructed body of beliefs about the traits and behaviors of males or females.

gene   Basic unit of heredity in a living cell; segments of genes are contained on chromosomes.

giftedness   Unusually high ability in one or more areas, to the point where children require special educational services to help them meet their full potential.

glial cell   Cell in the brain or other part of the nervous system that provides structural or functional support for one or more neurons.

goal-directed behavior   Intentional behavior aimed at bringing about an anticipated outcome.

grammatical word   Nonlexical word that affects the meanings of other words or the interrelationships among words in a sentence.

gross motor skills   Large movements of the body that permit locomotion through and within an environment.

growth spurt   Rapid increase in height and weight during puberty.

guided participation   Active engagement in adult activities, typically with considerable direction and structure from an adult or other more advanced individual; children are given increasing responsibility and independence as they gain experience and proficiency.

guilt   Feeling of discomfort when one inflicts damage or causes someone else pain or distress.

habituation   Changes in children's physiological responses to repeated displays of the same stimulus, reflecting loss of interest.

hindbrain   Part of the brain controlling the basic physiological processes that sustain survival.

holophrase   A single word used to express a complete thought; commonly observed in children's earliest speech.

hostile attributional bias   Tendency to interpret others' behaviors as reflecting hostile or aggressive intentions.

identity   Self-constructed definition of who one is, what things one finds important, what one believes, and what goals one wants to accomplish in life.

imaginary audience   Belief that one is the center of attention in any social situation.

immersion   Approach to second-language instruction in which students hear and speak that language almost exclusively in the classroom.

inclusion   Practice of educating all students, including those with severe and multiple disabilities, in neighborhood schools and general education classrooms.

incremental view of ability   Belief that ability can and does improve with effort and practice.

individual constructivism   Theoretical perspective that focuses on how people construct meaning from events on their own.

induction   The act of explaining why a certain behavior is unacceptable, usually with a focus on the pain or distress that someone has caused another.

infant-directed speech   Short, simple, high-pitched speech often used when talking to young children.

infantile amnesia   General inability to recall events that have occurred in the early years of life.

information processing theory   Theoretical perspective that focuses on the specific ways in which people mentally think about ("process") the information they receive.

inner speech   "Talking" to oneself mentally rather than aloud.

insecure-avoidant attachment   Attachment classification in which children appear somewhat indifferent to attachment figures.

insecure-resistant attachment   Attachment classification in which children are preoccupied with their attachment figures but gain little comfort from them when distressed.

integration   An increasing coordination of body parts over the course of development.

intelligence   Ability to apply past knowledge and experiences flexibly to accomplish challenging new tasks.

intelligence test   General measure of current cognitive functioning, used primarily to predict academic achievement over the short run.

intentionality   Engagement in an action congruent with one's purpose or goal.

interactive technology   Array of electronic, digitally based machines that are operated dynamically by a person whose commands determine emerging program sequences.

internalization   In Vygotsky's theory, the gradual evolution of external, social activities into internal, mental activities.

internalized motivation   Adoption of behaviors that others value, whether or not one's environment reinforces those behaviors.

intersubjectivity   Awareness of shared understandings and perceptions that provide the foundation for social interaction.

interview   Data collection technique that obtains self-report data through face-to-face conversation.

intrinsic motivation   Motivation resulting from personal characteristics or inherent in the task being performed.

invented spelling   A child's early, self-constructed word spelling, which may reflect only some of the word's phonemes.

IQ score   Score on an intelligence test, determined by comparing one's performance with the performance of same-age peers.

IRE cycle   Adult-child interaction pattern marked by adult initiation, child response, and adult evaluation; in Western cultures such a pattern is often seen in instructional settings.

joint attention   Phenomenon in which two people (e.g., a child and caregiver) simultaneously focus on the same object or event, monitor each other's attention, and coordinate their responses.

justice orientation   Focus on individual rights in moral decision making.

knowledge base   One's knowledge about specific topics and the world in general.

knowledge telling   Writing down ideas in whatever order they come to mind, with little regard for communicating the ideas effectively.

knowledge transforming   Writing ideas in such a way as to intentionally help the reader understand them.

language acquisition device   Biologically built-in mechanism hypothesized to facilitate language learning.

learned helplessness   General belief that one is incapable of accomplishing tasks and has little or no control of the environment.

learning disability   Significant deficit in one or more cognitive processes, to the point where special educational services are required.

learning strategy   Specific mental process used in acquiring new information.

left hemisphere   Left side of the cortex; largely responsible for sequential reasoning and analysis, especially in right-handed people.

level of potential development   Upper limit of tasks that a child can successfully perform with the assistance of a more competent individual.

lexical word   Word that in some way represents an aspect of one's physical, social, or psychological world.

longitudinal study   Research study in which the performance of a single group of people is tracked over a period of time.

long-term memory   Component of memory that holds knowledge and skills for a relatively long period of time.

mastery goal   Desire to acquire additional knowledge or master new skills (also known as a *learning goal*).

mastery orientation   General belief that one is capable of accomplishing challenging tasks, accompanied by an intent to master such tasks.

maturation   Genetically guided changes that occur over the course of development.

mediated learning experience   Discussion between an adult and a child in which the adult helps the child make sense of an event they have mutually experienced.

meiosis   The process of cell reproduction and division by which gametes are formed.

menarche   First menstrual period in an adolescent female.

mental retardation   Disability marked by significantly below-average general intelligence and deficits in adaptive behavior.

metacognition   Knowledge and beliefs about one's own cognitive processes, as well as efforts to regulate those cognitive processes to maximize learning and memory.

metacognitive awareness   Extent to which one is able to reflect on the nature of one's own thinking processes.

metalinguistic awareness   Extent to which one consciously understands and thinks about the nature of language.

midbrain   Part of the brain that coordinates communication between the hindbrain and forebrain.

mitosis   The process of cell duplication by which chromosomes are preserved and a human being or other biological organism can grow.

monozygotic twins   Twins that began as a single zygote and so share the same genetic makeup.

moral development   Advancements in reasoning and behaving in accordance with culturally prescribed or self-constructed standards of right and wrong.

moral dilemma   Situation in which there is no clear-cut answer regarding the morally right thing to do.

moral transgression   Action that causes damage or harm or in some other way infringes on the needs and rights of others.

motivation   State that energizes, directs, and sustains behavior.

multicultural education   Education that regularly includes the perspectives and experiences of numerous cultural groups.

music literacy   Ability to read and understand musical notation.

myelination   The growth of a fatty sheath around neurons that allows them to transmit messages more quickly.

narrative   Verbal account of a temporal sequence of events that are logically interconnected; a story.

native language   The first language a child learns.

nativism   Theoretical perspective proposing that some knowledge is biologically built-in and present at birth or soon thereafter.

naturalistic study   Research study in which individuals are observed in their natural environment.

nature   Inherited characteristics and tendencies that affect development.

need for relatedness   Fundamental need to feel socially connected to, and loved and respected by, other people.

neglected children   Children whom peers rarely select as someone they would most like or least like to do something with.

neo-Piagetian theory   Theoretical perspective that combines elements of Piaget's theory with more contemporary research findings and suggests that development in specific content domains is often stagelike in nature.

neuron   Cell that transmits information to other cells; also called nerve cell.

niche-picking   Tendency to actively seek out environments that match one's inherited abilities.

nurture   Environmental conditions that affect development.

obesity   Condition in which a person weighs at least 20 percent more than what is optimal for good health.

object permanence   Realization that objects continue to exist even when they are out of sight.

observation   Data collection technique whereby a researcher carefully observes and documents the behaviors of participants in a research study.

operation   In Piaget's theory, an organized and integrated system of logical thought processes.

organization   Process of identifying interrelationships among pieces of information as a way of learning them more effectively.

overgeneralization   Too broad a meaning for a word, such that it is used in situations to which it doesn't apply.

overregularization   Use of a syntactic rule in situations where an exception to the rule applies.

parenting style   General pattern of behaviors that a parent uses to nurture and guide his or her children.

part-whole principle   Idea that any single number can be broken into two or more smaller numbers, and that any two or more numbers can be combined to form a larger number; central to children's understanding of addition and subtraction.

peer culture   General set of rules, expectations, and interpretations that influence how members of a particular peer group behave.

peer mediation   Approach to conflict resolution in which one child or adolescent (the mediator) asks peers in conflict to express their differing viewpoints and then work together to identify an appropriate compromise.

peer pressure   Tactics used to encourage some behaviors and discourage others in age-mates.

perception   Interpretation of stimuli that the body has sensed.

performance goal   Desire to look good and receive favorable judgments from others.

permissive style   Parenting style characterized by emotional warmth but few expectations or standards for children's behavior.

personal fable   Belief held by many adolescents that they are unique beings invulnerable to normal risks and dangers.

personal interest   Long-term, relatively stable interest in a particular topic or activity.

personality   Characteristic way a person behaves, thinks, and feels.

personal space   Personally and culturally preferred distance between two people during social interaction.

phonemes   Smallest units of a spoken language that signify differences in meaning.

phonological awareness   Ability to hear the distinct sounds within words.

phonology   The sound system of a language; how words sound and are produced.

physical aggression   Action that can potentially cause bodily injury.

physical development   Physical and brain growth and age-related changes in motor skills.

physiological measure   Direct assessment of physical development or physiological functioning.

playing the dozens   Friendly, playful exchange of insults, common in some African American communities; also called *joaning or sounding.*

polygenic inheritance   Situation in which many genes combine in their influence on a particular characteristic.

popular children   Children whom many peers like and perceive to be kind and trustworthy.

postconventional morality   Behaving in accordance with self-developed abstract principles regarding right and wrong.

pragmatics   Conventions and strategies used in effective and socially acceptable verbal interactions.

preconventional morality   A lack of internalized standards about right and wrong; making decisions based on what is best for oneself, without regard for others' needs and feelings.

prejudice   Display of negative attitudes, feelings, and behaviors toward particular individuals because of their membership in a specific group.

premature infant   Infant born early (before 37 weeks of prenatal growth) and sometimes with serious medical problems.

prenatal development   Growth that takes place between conception and birth.

primary reinforcer   Stimulus or event that satisfies a built-in biological need.

proactive aggression   Deliberate aggression against another as a means of obtaining a desired goal.

prosocial behavior   Action intended to benefit another person rather than oneself.

proximodistal trend   Inside-outside ordering of motor skills and physical development; order is inside first and outside last.

psychodynamic theory   Theoretical perspective that focuses on how early experiences and internal conflicts affect social and personality development.

psychosocial stages   In Erikson's theory, eight periods of life that involve age-related challenges.

puberty   Physiological changes that occur during adolescence and lead to reproductive maturation.

qualitative change   Relatively dramatic developmental change that reflects considerable reorganization or modification of functioning.

quantitative change   Developmental change that involves a series of minor, trendlike modifications.

quasi-experimental study   Research study in which one or more experimental treatments are administered but in which random assignment to groups is not possible.

questionnaire   Data collection technique that obtains self-report data through a paper-pencil inventory.

reactive aggression   Aggressive response to frustration or provocation.

receptive language   Ability to understand the language one hears or reads.

recessive gene   Gene that influences growth and development primarily when the other gene in the allele pair is identical to it.

reciprocal teaching   Approach to teaching reading in which students take turns asking teacherlike questions of their classmates.

recursive thinking   Thinking about what other people may be thinking about oneself, possibly through multiple iterations.

reflex   Automatic motor response to stimuli.

rehearsal   Attempt to learn and remember information by repeating it over and over.

reinforcer   Consequence of a response that leads to an increased frequency of that response.

rejected children   Children whom many peers identify as being unfavorable social partners.

rejection   Form of acculturation in which a person refuses to learn or accept any customs and values from a new cultural environment.

relational aggression   Action that can adversely affect interpersonal relationships.

reliability   Extent to which a data collection technique yields consistent, dependable results—results that are only minimally affected by temporary and irrelevant influences.

resilience   Ability of some youngsters (often enhanced with environmental support) to thrive despite adverse environmental conditions.

right hemisphere   Right side of the cortex; largely responsible for simultaneous processing and synthesis, especially in right-handed people.

rough-and-tumble play   Playful physical "fighting" typical in early and middle childhood.

sample   The specific participants in a research study; their performance is often assumed to indicate how a larger population of individuals would perform.

scaffolding   Support mechanism, provided by a more competent individual, that helps a child successfully perform a task within his or her zone of proximal development.

schema   Tightly integrated set of ideas about a specific object or situation.

scheme   In Piaget's theory, an organized group of similar actions or thoughts that are used repeatedly in response to the environment.

schizophrenia   A psychiatric condition characterized by irrational ideas and disorganized thinking.

scientific method   Multistep process of answering a carefully defined research question by using critical thinking and analysis of the evidence.

scientific reasoning   Cognitive processes central to conducting scientific research and interpreting findings appropriately.

script   Schema that involves a predictable sequence of events related to a common activity.

secondary reinforcer   Stimulus or event that becomes reinforcing over time through its association with one or more other reinforcers.

secure attachment   Attachment classification in which children use attachment figures as a source of comfort in times of distress and as a secure base from which to explore.

selective adoption   Form of acculturation in which a person assumes some customs of a new culture while also retaining some customs of a previous culture.

self-conscious emotion   Affective state that reflects awareness of a community's social standards (e.g., pride, guilt, shame).

self-efficacy   Belief that one is capable of executing certain behaviors or reaching certain goals.

self-evaluation   Judging one's own performance in accordance with predetermined criteria.

self-fulfilling prophecy   Phenomenon in which an adult's expectations for a child's performance bring about that level of performance.

self-handicapping   Action that undermines one's own success as a way of protecting self-worth during difficult tasks.

self-instructions   Specific directions that one gives oneself while performing a complex behavior; a form of *self-talk.*

self-monitoring   Process of observing and recording one's own behavior.

self-motivation   Intentionally using certain strategies to keep oneself on task during a dull but important activity.

self-regulated learning   Directing and controlling one's own cognitive processes in order to learn successfully.

self-regulation   Directing and controlling one's own actions.

self-reinforcement   Self-imposed pleasurable consequence for a desired behavior.

self-report   Data collection technique whereby participants are asked to describe their own characteristics and performance.

self-socialization   Tendency to integrate personal observations and others' input into self-constructed standards for behavior and to choose actions consistent with those standards.

self-talk   Talking to oneself as a way of guiding oneself through a task.

semantic bootstrapping   Using knowledge of word meanings to derive knowledge about syntactic categories and structures.

semantics   The meanings of words and word combinations.

sensation   Physiological detection of stimuli in the environment.

sense of community   In a classroom or school, a collection of widely shared beliefs that students, teachers, and other staff have common goals, support one another's efforts, and make important contributions to everyone's success.

sense of self   Knowledge, beliefs, judgments, and feelings about oneself as a person.

sense of self-determination   Belief that one has some choice and control regarding the future course of one's life.

sensitive period   A period in development when certain environmental experiences have a more pronounced influence than is true at other times.

sensory register   Component of memory that holds incoming information in an unanalyzed form for a very brief time (2–3 seconds or less).

service learning   Activity that promotes learning and skill development through volunteerism or community service.

sexual harassment   Form of discrimination in which a target individual perceives another's actions or statements to be hostile, humiliating, or offensive, especially pertaining to physical appearance or sexual matters.

sexual orientation   Particular sex(es) to which an individual is romantically and sexually attracted.

shame   Feeling of embarrassment or humiliation after failing to meet certain standards for moral behavior.

sight vocabulary   Words that a child can immediately recognize while reading.

situational interest   Interest evoked temporarily by something in the environment.

social cognition   Process of thinking about how other people are likely to think, act, and react and choosing one's own interpersonal behaviors accordingly.

social-cognitive bias   Mental shortcut in thinking about other people or social events.

social constructivism   Theoretical perspective that focuses on people's collective efforts to impose meaning on the world.

social-emotional development   Systematic changes in emotions, self-concept, motivation, social relationships, and moral reasoning and behavior.

social goal   Goal related to establishing or maintaining relationships with other people.

social information processing   Series of cognitive steps used in understanding and responding to social events.

socialization   Systematic efforts by other people and by institutions to prepare youngsters to act in ways deemed by society to be appropriate and responsible.

social perspective taking   Imagining what someone else might be thinking or feeling.

social referencing   Looking at someone else (e.g., a caregiver) for clues about how to respond to a particular object or event.

social skills   Strategies used to interact effectively with others.

society   A very large group of people who live in a particular region and share certain customs.

sociocognitive conflict   Situation in which one encounters and has to wrestle with ideas and viewpoints different from one's own.

sociocultural theory   Theoretical perspective that focuses on children's learning of tools and communication systems through practice in meaningful tasks with other people.

sociodramatic play   Play in which children take on roles and act out a scenario of events.

socioeconomic status (SES)   One's general standing in an economically stratified society, encompossing family income, type of job, and education level.

sociolinguistic behaviors   Social and culturally specific conventions that govern appropriate verbal interaction.

specific ability test   Test designed to assess a specific cognitive skill or the potential to learn and perform in a specific content domain.

speech and communication disorders   Disability characterized by abnormalities in producing or understanding spoken language, to the point where special educational services are required.

spermarche   First ejaculation in an adolescent male.

stage   A period of development characterized by a qualitatively distinct way of behaving or thinking.

stage theory   Theory that describes development as involving a series of qualitatively distinct changes.

Standard English   Form of English generally considered acceptable in school (as reflected in textbooks, grammar instruction, etc.) and in the media.

standards   In education, general statements regarding the knowledge and skills that students should gain and the characteristics that their accomplishments should reflect.

state of arousal   Physiological condition of sleepiness or wakefulness.

stereotype   Rigid, simplistic, and erroneous characterization of a particular group.

stereotype threat   Reduction in performance (often unintentional) as a result of a belief that one's group typically performs poorly.

story schema   Knowledge of the typical elements and sequence of a narrative.

stranger anxiety   Fear of unfamiliar adults in the latter half of the first year and into the second year of life.

student at risk   Student who has a high probability of failing to acquire the minimal academic skills necessary for success in the adult world.

subculture   Group that resists the ways of the dominant culture and adopts its own norms for behavior.

substance schema   General view of all physical phenomena as being either touchable substances or properties of those substances.

sudden infant death syndrome (SIDS)   Death of an infant in the first year of life, typically during sleep, that cannot be explained by a thorough medical examination; it peaks between birth and 4 months.

symbol   Mental entity that represents an external object or event, often without reflecting its perceptual and behavioral qualities.

symbolic thought   Ability to represent and think about external objects and events in one's mind.

sympathy   Feeling of sorrow and concern about another's problems or distress.

synapse   Junction between two neurons.

synaptic pruning   A universal process in brain development whereby many previously formed synapses wither away, especially if they have not been used frequently.

synaptogenesis   A universal process in brain development whereby many new synapses appear, typically in the first 3½ years of life.

syntax   Rules used to put words together into sentences.

telegraphic speech   Short, grammatically incomplete sentences that include lexical (rather than grammatical) words almost exclusively; common in toddlers.

temperament   A child's characteristic ways of responding to emotional events, novel stimuli, and personal impulses.

teratogen   Potentially harmful substance that can cause damaging effects during prenatal development.

test   Instrument designed to assess knowledge, understandings, abilities, or skills in a consistent fashion across individuals.

theory   Organized system of principles and explanations regarding a particular phenomenon.

theory of mind   Awareness that people have an inner, psychological life (thoughts, beliefs, feelings, etc.).

theory theory   Theoretical perspective proposing that children construct increasingly integrated and complex understandings of physical and mental phenomena.

undergeneralization   Overly restricted meaning for a word, excluding some situations to which the word applies.

uninvolved style   Parenting style characterized by a lack of emotional support and a lack of standards regarding appropriate behavior.

universality   In a particular aspect of human development, the commonalities seen in the way virtually all individuals progress.

validity   Extent to which a data collection technique actually assesses what the researcher intends for it to assess.

value   Belief that a particular activity has direct or indirect benefits.

vicarious punishment   Phenomenon in which a child decreases a certain response after seeing someone else punished for that response.

vicarious reinforcement   Phenomenon in which a child increases a certain response after seeing someone else reinforced for that response.

visual-spatial ability   Ability to imagine and mentally manipulate two- and three-dimensional figures.

wait time   The length of time a teacher pauses, after either asking a question or hearing a student's comment, before saying something.

working memory   Component of memory that enables people to actively think about and process a small amount of information.

zone of proximal development (ZPD)   Range of tasks that one cannot yet perform independently but can perform with the help and guidance of others.

zygote   Cell formed when a male sperm joins with a female ovum; with healthy genes and nurturing conditions in the uterus, it may develop into a fetus and be born as a live infant.

References

Abdul-Jabbar, K., & Knobles, P. (1983). *Giant steps: The autobiography of Kareem Abdul-Jabbar.* New York: Bantam.

Abi-Nader, J. (1993). Meeting the needs of multicultural classrooms: Family values and the motivation of minority students. In M. J. O'Hair & S. J. Odell (Eds.), *Diversity and teaching: Teacher education yearbook I.* Fort Worth, TX: Harcourt Brace Jovanovich.

Abma, J. C., Martinez, G. M., Mosher, W. D., & Dawson, B. S. (2004). Teenagers in the United States: Sexual activity, contraceptive use, and childbearing, 2002. *Vital and Health Statistics, 23*(24), 1–48.

Aboud, F. E. (1988). *Children and prejudice.* Oxford, England: Blackwell.

Aboud, F. E. (1993). The developmental psychology of racial prejudice. *Transcultural Psychiatric Research Review, 30,* 229–242.

Adalbjarnardottir, S., & Selman, R. L. (1997). "I feel I have received a new vision": An analysis of teachers' professional development as they work with students on interpersonal issues. *Teaching and Teacher Education, 13,* 409–428.

Adam, E. K. (2004). Beyond quality: Parental and residential stability and children's adjustment. *Current Directions in Psychological Science, 13*(5), 210–213.

Adams, G. R., Gullotta, T. P., & Markstrom-Adams, C. (1994). *Adolescent life experiences* (3rd ed.). Pacific Grove, CA: Brooks/Cole.

Adams, M. J. (1990). *Beginning to read: Thinking and learning about print.* Cambridge, MA: MIT Press.

Adams, R. J. (1987). An evaluation of color preference in early infancy. *Infant Behavior and Development, 10,* 143–150.

Adamson, L. B., & Bakeman, R. (1991). The development of shared attention during infancy. In R. Vasta (Ed.), *Annals of child development* (Vol. 8, pp. 1–41). London: Kingsley.

Adamson, L. B., & McArthur, D. (1995). Joint attention, affect, and culture. In C. Moore & P. J. Dunham (Eds.), *Joint attention: Its origins and role in development* (pp. 205–221). Hillsdale, NJ: Erlbaum.

Afflerbach, P., VanSledright, B., & Dromsky, A. (2003, April). *Reading and thinking like historians: Investigating a 4th grade performance assessment.* Paper presented at the annual meeting of the American Educational Research Association, Chicago.

Agency for Toxic Substances and Disease Registry. (1999, June). *ToxFAQs™ for lead.* Retrieved January 19, 2003, from http://www.atsdr.cdc.gov/tfacts13.html

Ainsworth, M. D. S. (1963). The development of infant-mother interaction among the Ganda. In B. M. Foss (Ed.), *Determinants of infant behavior* (Vol. 2, pp. 67–104). New York: Wiley.

Ainsworth, M. D. S. (1973). The development of infant-mother attachment. In B. Caldwell & H. Ricciuti (Eds.), *Review of child development research* (Vol. 3, pp. 1–94). Chicago: University of Chicago Press.

Ainsworth, M. D. S., Blehar, M. C., Waters, E., & Wall, S. (1978). *Patterns of attachment.* Hillsdale, NJ: Erlbaum.

Aitchison, J. (1996). *The seeds of speech: Language origin and evolution.* Cambridge, England: Cambridge University Press.

Akhtar, N., Carpenter, M., & Tomasello, M. (1996). The role of discourse novelty in early word learning. *Child Development, 67,* 635–645.

Akhtar, N., Jipson, J., & Callanan, M. A. (2001). Learning words through overhearing. *Child Development, 72,* 416–430.

Akiskal, H. S., & McKinney, W. T. (1973). Depressive disorders: Toward a unified hypothesis. *Science, 162,* 20–29.

Alapack, R. (1991). The adolescent first kiss. *Humanistic Psychologist, 19,* 48–67.

Aldridge, M. A., Stillman, R. D., & Bower, T. G. R. (2001). Newborn categorization of vowel-like sounds. *Developmental Science, 4,* 220–232.

Alessandri, S. M., & Lewis, M. (1993). Parental evaluation and its relation to shame and pride in young children. *Sex Roles, 29,* 335–343.

Alessi, N. E., Krahn, D., Brehm, D., & Wittekindt, J. (1989). Prepubertal anorexia nervosa and major depressive disorder. *Journal of the American Academy of Child and Adolescent Psychiatry, 28,* 380–384.

Alexander, K., Entwisle, D., & Thompson, M. (1987). School performance, status relations, and the structure of sentiment: Bringing the teacher back in. *American Sociological Review, 52,* 665–682.

Alexander, P. A., Graham, S., & Harris, K. R. (1998). A perspective on strategy research: Progress and prospects. *Educational Psychology Review, 10,* 129–154.

Alfassi, M. (1998). Reading for meaning: The efficacy of reciprocal teaching in fostering reading comprehension in high school students in remedial reading classes. *American Educational Research Journal, 35,* 309–332.

Alland, A. (1983). *Playing with form.* New York: Columbia University Press.

Allison, K. W. (1998). Stress and oppressed social category membership. In J. K. Swim & C. Stangor (Eds.), *Prejudice: The target's perspective* (pp. 149–170). San Diego, CA: Academic Press.

Almeida, D. M., Wethington, E., & Chandler, A. L. (1999). Daily transmission of tensions between marital dyads and parent-child dyads. *Journal of Marriage and the Family, 61,* 49–61.

Als, H., Lawhon, G., Duffy, F. H., McAnulty, G. B., Gibes-Grossman, R., & Blickman, J. G. (1994). Individualized developmental care for the very low-birth-weight preterm infant. Medical and neurofunctional effects. *Journal of the American Medical Association, 272,* 853–858.

Alvermann, D. E., & Moore, D. W. (1991). Secondary school reading. In R. Barr, M. L. Kamil, P. B. Mosenthal, & P. D. Pearson (Eds.), *Handbook of reading research* (Vol. II). New York: Longman.

Alvermann, D. E., Young, J. P., Green, C., & Wisenbaker, J. M. (1999). Adolescents' perceptions and negotiations of literacy practices in after-school read and talk clubs. *American Educational Research Journal, 36,* 221–264.

Ambrose, D., Allen, J., & Huntley, S. B. (1994). Mentorship of the highly creative. *Roeper Review, 17,* 131–133.

American Academy of Pediatrics. (2005). Breast-feeding and the use of human milk. *Pediatrics, 115,* 496–506.

American Academy of Pediatrics Committee on Nutrition. (1998). Soy protein-based formulas: Recommendations for use in infant feeding. *Pediatrics, 101,* 148–153.

American Academy of Pediatrics Committee on Nutrition. (1999). Iron fortification of infant formulas. *Pediatrics, 104,* 119–123.

American Academy of Pediatrics Committee on Pediatric AIDS and Committee on Adolescence. (2001). Adolescents and human immunodeficiency virus infection: The role of the pediatrician in prevention and intervention. *Pediatrics, 107,* 188–190.

American Academy of Pediatrics Committee on Pediatric AIDS and Committee on Infectious Diseases. (1999). Issues related to human immunodeficiency virus transmission in schools, child care, medical settings, home, and community. *Pediatrics, 104,* 318–324.

American Academy of Pediatrics Committee on Sports Medicine and Fitness. (2000). Intensive training and sports specialization in young athletes. *Pediatrics, 106,* 154–157.

American Academy of Pediatrics Committee on Sports Medicine and Fitness and Committee on Injury and Poison Prevention. (2000). Swimming programs for infants and toddlers. *Pediatrics, 105,* 868–870.

American Academy of Pediatrics Task Force on Infant Sleep Position and Sudden Infant Death Syndrome. (2000). Changing concepts of sudden infant death syndrome: Implications for infant sleeping environment and sleep position. *Pediatrics, 105,* 650–656.

American Association on Mental Retardation. (1992). *Mental retardation: Definition, classification, and systems of supports* (9th ed.). Washington, DC: Author.

American Obesity Association. (2005). *Childhood obesity.* Retrieved June 19, 2005, from www.obesity.org/subs/childhood/prevalence.shtml

American Psychiatric Association. (1994). *Diagnostic and statistical manual of mental disorders* (4th ed.). Washington, DC: Author.

American Psychological Association. (2002). *Ethical principles of psychologists and code of conduct.* Retrieved October 8, 2004, from http://www.apa.org/ethics/code2002.html#8

American Speech-Language-Hearing Association. (1993). Definitions of communication disorders and variations. *ASHA, 35*(Suppl. 10), 40–41.

Ames, C. (1984). Competitive, cooperative, and individualistic goal structures: A cognitive-motivational analysis. In R. Ames & C. Ames (Eds.), *Research on motivation in education: Vol. 1. Student motivation.* San Diego, CA: Academic Press.

Ames, C. (1992). Classrooms: Goals, structures, and student motivation. *Journal of Educational Psychology, 84,* 261–271.

Amirkhanian, Y. A., Tiunov, D. V., & Kelly, J. A. (2001). Risk factors for HIV and other sexually transmitted diseases among adolescents in St. Petersburg, Russia. *Family Planning Perspectives, 33,* 106–112.

Anastasi, A., & Urbina, S. (1997). *Psychological testing* (7th ed.). Upper Saddle River, NJ: Prentice Hall.

Anderman, E. M., & Maehr, M. L. (1994). Motivation and schooling in the middle grades. *Review of Educational Research, 64,* 287–309.

Anderman, E. M., Griesinger, T., & Westerfield, G. (1998). Motivation and cheating during early adolescence. *Journal of Educational Psychology, 90,* 84–93.

Anderman, L. H., & Anderman, E. M. (1999). Social predictors of changes in students' achievement goal orientation. *Contemporary Educational Psychology, 25,* 21–37.

Anderman, L. H., Patrick, H., Hruda, L. Z., & Linnenbrink, E. A. (2002). Observing classroom goal structures to clarify and expand goal theory. In C. Midgley (Ed.), *Goals, goal structures, and patterns of adaptive learning* (pp. 243–278). Mahwah, NJ: Erlbaum.

Anderson, C., & Huesmann, L. R. (2005). The evidence that media violence stimulates aggression in young viewers remains "unequivocal." *Observer, 18*(10), 7.

Anderson, C. A. (2002). *Video game suggestions from Dr. Craig A. Anderson.* Retrieved November 22, 2005, from http://www.psychology.iastate.edu/faculty/caa/VG_recommendations.html

Anderson, C. A., Berkowitz, L., Donnerstein, E., Huesmann, L. R., Johnson, J. D., Linz, D., et al. (2003). The influence of media violence on youth. *Psychological Science in the Public Interest, 4,* 81–110.

Anderson, D. A. (1994). Lesbian and gay adolescents: Social and developmental considerations. *The High School Journal, 77* (1,2), 13–19.

Anderson, D. R. (2003). The Children's Television Act: A public policy that benefits children. *Applied Developmental Psychology, 24,* 337–340.

Anderson, D. R., Huston, A. C., Schmitt, K. L., Linebarger, D. L., & Wright, J. C. (2001). Early childhood television viewing and adolescent behavior: The recontact study. *Monographs of the Society for Research in Child Development, 66*(1, Serial No. 264).

Anderson, J. C. (1983). *The architecture of cognition.* Cambridge, MA: Harvard University Press.

Anderson, L. W., & Pellicer, L. O. (1998). Toward an understanding of unusually successful programs for economically disadvantaged students. *Journal of Education for Students Placed at Risk, 3,* 237–263.

Anderson, R. C., Nguyen-Jahiel, K., McNurlen, B., Archodidou, A., Kim, S.-Y., Reznitskaya, A., et al. (2001). The snowball phenomenon: Spread of ways of talking and ways of thinking across groups of children. *Cognition and Instruction, 19,* 1–46.

Anderson, R. C., Shirey, L., Wilson, P., & Fielding, L. (1987). Interestingness of children's reading materials. In R. Snow & M. Farr (Eds.), *Aptitude, learning, and instruction: III. Conative and affective process analyses.* Hillsdale, NJ: Erlbaum.

Andersson, B. E. (1989). Effects of public day care: A longitudinal study. *Child Development, 60,* 857–866.

Andison, F. S. (1977). TV violence and viewer aggression: Accumulation of study results 1956–1976. *Public Opinion Quarterly, 41,* 314–331.

Andrews, G., Halford, G. S., Bunch, K. M., Bowden, D., & Jones, T. (2003). Theory of mind and relational complexity. *Child Development, 74,* 1476–1499.

Andrews, J. F., & Mason, J. M. (1986). Childhood deafness and the acquisition of print concepts. In D. B. Yaden, Jr., & S. Templeton (Eds.), *Metalinguistic awareness and beginning literacy: Conceptualizing what it means to read and write.* Portsmouth, NH: Heinemann.

Anglin, J. M. (1977). *Word, object, and conceptual development.* New York: Norton.

Anisfeld, E., Casper, V., Nosyce, M., & Cunningham, N. (1990). Does infant carrying promote attachment? An experimental study of the effects of increased physical contact on the development of attachment. *Child Development, 61,* 1617–1627.

Annett, R. D. (2004). Asthma. In R. T. Brown (Ed.), Handbook of pediatric psychology in school settings (pp. 149–167). Mahwah, NJ: Erlbaum.

Antelman, S., & Caggiula, A. (1977). Norepinephrine-dopamine interactions and behavior. *Science, 195,* 646–651.

Antequera, F., & Bird, A. (1993). Number of CpG islands and genes in human and mouse. *Proceedings of the National Academy of Sciences of the United States of America, 90,* 11995–11999.

Anthony, J. L., Lonigan, C. J., & Dyer, S.M. (1996, April). *The development of reading comprehension: Listening comprehension or basic language processes?* Paper presented at the annual meeting of the American Educational Research Association, New York.

Anyon, J. (1988). Social class and the hidden curriculum of work. In G. Handel (Ed.), *Childhood socialization.* New York: Aldine de Gruyter.

Aparicio, S. A. (2000). How to count . . . human genes. *Nature Genetics, 25,* 129–130.

Archer, J. (1991). The influence of testosterone on human aggression. *British Journal of Psychology, 82,* 1–28.

Archer, S. L. (1982). The lower age boundaries of identity development. *Child Development, 53,* 1551–1556.

Arcus, D. M. (1991). *Experiential modification of temperamental bias in inhibited and uninhibited children.* Unpublished doctoral dissertation, Harvard University, Cambridge, MA.

Arnett, J. J. (1999). Adolescent storm and stress, reconsidered. *American Psychologist, 54,* 317–326.

Arnold, A. P., & Gorski, R. A. (1984). Gonadal steroid induction of structural sex differences in the central nervous system. *Annual Review of Neuroscience, 7,* 413–442.

Arnold, M. L. (2000). Stage, sequence, and sequels: Changing conceptions of morality, post-Kohlberg. *Educational Psychology Review, 12,* 365–383.

Aronson, S. R., & Huston, A. C. (2004). The mother-infant relationship in single, cohabiting, and married families: A case for marriage? *Journal of Family Psychology, 18*(1), 5–18.

Arsenio, W. F., & Lemerise, E. A. (2004). Aggression and moral development: Integrating social information processing and moral domain models. *Child Development, 75,* 987–1002.

Artman, L., & Cahan, S. (1993). Schooling and the development of transitive inference. *Developmental Psychology, 29,* 753–759.

Asai, S. (1993). In search of Asia through music: Guidelines and ideas for teaching Asian music. In T. Perry & J. W. Fraser (Eds.), *Freedom's plow: Teaching in the multicultural classroom.* New York: Routledge.

Asante, M. K. (1991). Afrocentric curriculum. *Educational Leadership, 24*(4), 28–31.

Ashcraft, M. H. (1982). The development of mental arithmetic: A chronometric approach. *Developmental Review, 2,* 212–236.

Asher, S. R., & Coie, J. D. (Eds.). (1990). *Peer rejection in childhood.* Cambridge, England: Cambridge University Press.

Asher, S. R., & Parker, J. G. (1989). Significance of peer relationship problems in childhood. In B. H. Schneider, G. Attili, J. Nadel, & R. P. Weissberg (Eds.), *Social competence in developmental perspective.* Dordrecht, Netherlands: Kluwer.

Asher, S. R., & Renshaw, P. D. (1981). Children without friends: Social knowledge and social skill training. In S. R. Asher & J. M. Gottman (Eds.), *The development of children's friendships* (pp. 273–296). Cambridge, England: Cambridge University Press.

Ashmead, D. H., Davis, D. L., Whalen, T., & Odom, R. D. (1991). Sound localization and sensitivity to interaural time differences in human infants. *Child Development, 62,* 1211–1226.

Ashmore, R., & DelBoca, F. (1976). Psychological approaches. In P. A. Katz (Ed.), *Elimination of racism.* New York: Pergamon.

Ashton, P. (1985). Motivation and the teacher's sense of efficacy. In C. Ames & R. Ames (Eds.), *Research on motivation in education: Vol. 2. The classroom milieu.* San Diego, CA: Academic Press.

Aslin, R. N. (1993). Perception of visual direction in human infants. In C. E. Granrud (Ed.), *Visual perception and cognition in infancy.* Hillsdale, NJ: Erlbaum.

Aslin, R. N., Saffran, J. R., & Newport, E. L. (1998). Computation of conditional probability statistics by 8-month-old infants. *Psychological Science, 9,* 321–324.

Asmussen, L., & Larson, R. (1991). The quality of family time among adolescents in single-parent and married-parent families. *Journal of Marriage and the Family, 53,* 1021–1030.

Assor, A., & Connell, J. P. (1992). The validity of students' self-reports as measures of performance affecting self-appraisals. In D. H. Schunk & J. L. Meece (Eds.), *Student perceptions in the classroom.* Hillsdale, NJ: Erlbaum.

Astington, J. W. (1991). Intention in the child's theory of mind. In C. Moore & D. Frye (Eds.), *Children's theories of mind* (pp. 157–172). Hillsdale, NJ: Erlbaum.

Astington, J. W., & Pelletier, J. (1996). The language of mind: Its role in teaching and learning. In D. R. Olson & N. Torrance (Eds.), *The handbook of education and human development: New models of learning, teaching and schooling* (pp. 593–619). Cambridge, MA: Blackwell.

Astor, R. A. (1994). Children's moral reasoning about family and peer violence: The role of provocation and retribution. *Child Development, 65,* 1054–1067.

Astuti, R., Solomon, G. E. A., & Carey, S. (2004). Constraints on conceptual development. *Monographs of the Society for Research in Child Development, 69*(3, Serial No. 277).

Atkinson, M. (1992). *Children's syntax: An introduction to principles and parameters theory.* Oxford, England: Blackwell.

Attie, I., & Brooks-Gunn, J. (1989). Development of eating problems in adolescent girls: A longitudinal study. *Developmental Psychology, 25,* 70–79.

Attie, I., Brooks-Gunn, J., & Petersen, A. (1990). A developmental perspective on eating disorders and eating problems. In M. Lewis & S. M. Miller (Eds.), *Handbook of developmental psychopathology* (pp. 409–420). New York: Plenum Press.

Atwater, E. (1996). *Adolescence.* Upper Saddle River, NJ: Prentice Hall.

Au, K. H. (1980). Participation structures in a reading lesson with Hawaiian children: Analysis of a culturally appropriate instructional event. *Anthropology and Education Quarterly, 11,* 91–115.

Au, K. H., & Mason, J. (1981). Social organizational factors in learning to read: The balance of rights hypothesis. *Reading Research Quarterly, 17,* 115–152.

Au, T. K., & Glusman, M. (1990). The principle of mutual exclusivity in word learning: To honor or not to honor? *Child Development, 61,* 1474–1490.

Ausubel, D. P., Novak, J. D., & Hanesian, H. (1978). *Educational psychology: A cognitive view* (2nd ed.). New York: Holt, Rinehart & Winston.

Avis, J., & Harris, P. L. (1991). Belief-desire reasoning among Baka children: Evidence for a universal conception of mind. *Child Development, 62,* 460–467.

Babad, E. (1993). Teachers' differential behavior. *Educational Psychology Review, 5,* 347–376.

Bagley, C. (1989). Aggression and anxiety in day-care graduates. *Psychological Reports, 64,* 250.

Bahrick, L. E., Gogate, L. J., & Ruiz, I. (2002). Attention and memory for faces and actions in infancy: The salience of actions over faces in dynamic events. *Child Development, 73,* 1629–1643.

Bailey, J. M., Bobrow, D., Wolfe, M., & Mikach, S. (1995). Sexual orientation of adult sons of gay fathers. *Developmental Psychology, 31,* 124–129.

Bailey, J. M., & Pillard, R. C. (1997). The innateness of homosexuality. In M. R. Walsh (Ed.), *Women, men, and gender: Ongoing debates* (pp. 184–187). New Haven, CT: Yale University Press.

Baillargeon, R. (1994). How do infants learn about the physical world? *Current Directions in Psychological Science, 3,* 133–140.

Baillargeon, R. (2004). Infants' physical worlds. *Current Directions in Psychological Science, 13,* 89–94.

Bakari, R. (2000). *The development and validation of an instrument to measure preservice teachers' attitudes toward teaching African American students.* Unpublished doctoral dissertation, University of Northern Colorado, Greeley.

Bakeman, R., & Brownlee, J. R. (1980). The strategic use of parallel play: A sequential analysis. *Child Development, 51,* 873–878.

Baker, C. (1993). *Foundations of bilingual education and bilingualism.* Clevedon, England: Multilingual Matters.

Baker, L., Scher, D., & Mackler, K. (1997). Home and family influences on motivations for reading. *Educational Psychologist, 32,* 69–82.

Bakermans-Kranenburg, M. J., van IJzendoorn, M. H., & Juffer, F. (2003). Less is more: Meta-analyses of sensitivity and attachment interventions in early childhood. *Psychological Bulletin, 129,* 195–215.

Baldwin, D. A. (1993). Early referential understanding: Infants' ability to recognize referential acts for what they are. *Developmental Psychology, 29,* 832–843.

Baldwin, D. A. (2000). Interpersonal understanding fuels knowledge acquisition. *Current Directions in Psychological Science, 9,* 40–45.

Baldwin, M. W., Keelan, J. P. R., Fehr, B., Enns, V., & Koh-Rangarajoo, E. (1996). Social-cognitive conceptualization of attachment working models: Availability and accessibility effects. *Journal of Personality and Social Psychology, 71,* 94–109.

Baltes, P. B. (1997). On the incomplete architecture of human ontogeny: Selection, optimization, and compensation as a foundation of developmental theory. *American Psychologist, 52,* 366–380.

Baltes, P. B., Reese, H. W., & Lipsitt, L. P. (1980). Life-span developmental psychology. *Annual Review of Psychology, 31,* 65–110.

Bandura, A. (1982). Self-efficacy mechanism in human agency. *American Psychologist, 37,* 122–147.

Bandura, A. (1986). *Social foundations of thought and action: A social cognitive theory.* Englewood Cliffs, NJ: Prentice Hall.

Bandura, A. (1991). Social cognitive theory of moral thought and action. In W. M. Kurtines & J. L. Gewirtz (Eds.), *Handbook of moral behavior and development: Vol. 1. Theory.* Hillsdale, NJ: Erlbaum.

Bandura, A. (1997). *Self-efficacy: The exercise of control.* New York: Freeman.

Bandura, A., Barbaranelli, C., Caprara, G. V., & Pastorelli, C. (2001). Self-efficacy beliefs as shapers of children's aspirations and career trajectories. *Child Development, 72,* 187–206.

Bandura, A., & Mischel, W. (1965). Modification of self-imposed delay of reward through exposure to live and symbolic models. *Journal of Personality and Social Psychology, 2,* 698–705.

Bandura, A., Ross, D., & Ross, S. A. (1963). Imitation of film-mediated aggressive models. *Journal of Abnormal and Social Psychology, 66,* 3–11.

Bandura, A., & Schunk, D. H. (1981). Cultivating competence, self-efficacy, and intrinsic interest through proximal self-motivation. *Journal of Personality and Social Psychology, 41,* 586–598.

Bank, S. (1992). Remembering and reinterpreting sibling bonds. In F. Boer & J. Dunn (Eds.), *Children's sibling relationships: Developmental and clinical issues.* Hillsdale, NJ: Erlbaum.

Banks, J. A. (1994). *An introduction to multicultural education.* Needham Heights, MA: Allyn & Bacon.

Banks, J. A. (1995). Multicultural education: Historical development, dimensions, and practice. In J. A. Banks & C. A. M. Banks (Eds.), *Handbook of research on multicultural education.* New York: Macmillan.

Banks, J. A., & Banks, C. A. M. (Eds.). (1995). *Handbook of research on multicultural education.* New York: Macmillan.

Barab, S. A., & Plucker, J. A. (2002). Smart people or smart contexts? Cognition, ability, and talent development in an age of situated approaches to knowing and learning. *Educational Psychologist, 37,* 165–182.

Barchfeld, P., Sodian, B., Thoermer, C., & Bullock, M. (2005, April). *The development of experiment generation abilities from primary school to late adolescence.* Poster presented at the biennial meeting of the Society for Research in Child Development, Atlanta, GA.

Barga, N. K. (1996). Students with learning disabilities in education: Managing a disability. *Journal of Learning Disabilities, 29,* 413–421.

Barker, G. P., & Graham, S. (1987). Developmental study of praise and blame as attributional cues. *Journal of Educational Psychology, 79,* 62–66.

Barkley, R. A. (1998). *Attention-deficit hyperactivity disorder: A handbook for diagnosis and treatment* (2nd ed.). New York: Guilford Press.

Barnas, M. V., & Cummings, E. M. (1994). Caregiver stability and toddlers' attachment-related behaviors towards caregivers in day care. *Infant Behavior and Development, 17,* 141–147.

Barnett, J. E. (2001, April). *Study strategies and preparing for exams: A survey of middle and high school students.* Paper presented at the annual meeting of the American Educational Research Association, Seattle, WA.

Barnett, W. S. (1996). Long-term effects of early childhood programs on cognitive and school outcomes. *The Future of Children, 5*(3), 25–50.

Baron-Cohen, S., Tager-Flusberg, H., & Cohen, D. J. (1993). *Understanding other minds: Perspectives from autism.* Oxford, England: Oxford University Press.

Barr, H. M., Streissguth, A. P., Darby, B. L., & Sampson, P. D. (1990). Prenatal exposure to alcohol, caffeine, tobacco, and aspirin: Effects on fine and gross motor performance in 4-year-old children. *Developmental Psychology, 26,* 339–348.

Barr, R. (1999, April). *The role of siblings in the development of imitation.* Paper presented at the biennial meeting of the Society for Research in Child Development, Albuquerque, NM.

Barrett, J. G. (2005). Conduct disorders. In C. B. Fisher & R. M. Lerner (Eds.), *Encyclopedia of applied developmental science* (Vol 1., pp. 294–295). Thousand Oaks, CA: Sage.

Barringer, C., & Gholson, B. (1979). Effects of type and combination of feedback upon conceptual learning by children: Implications for research in academic learning. *Review of Educational Research, 49,* 459–478.

Barron, R. W. (1998). Proto-literate knowledge: Antecedents and influences on phonological awareness and literacy. In C. Hulme & R. M. Joshi (Eds.), *Reading and spelling: Development and disorders.* Mahwah, NJ: Erlbaum.

Bartlett, E. J. (1982). Learning to revise: Some component processes. In M. Nystrand (Ed.), *What writers know: The language, process, and structure of written discourse.* New York: Academic Press.

Barton, K. C., & Levstik, L. S. (1996). "Back when God was around and everything": Elementary children's understanding of historical time. *American Educational Research Journal, 33,* 419–454.

Bartsch, K., & Wellman, H. M. (1995). *Children talk about the mind.* New York: Oxford University Press.

Basinger, K. S., Gibbs, J. C., & Fuller, D. (1995). Context and the measurement of moral judgment. *International Journal of Behavioral Development, 18,* 537–556.

Bassett, D. S., Jackson, L., Ferrell, K. A., Luckner, J., Hagerty, P. J., Bunsen, T. D., et al. (1996). Multiple perspectives on inclusive education: Reflections of a university faculty. *Teacher Education and Special Education, 19,* 355–386.

Basso, K. (1972). To give up on words: Silence in western Apache culture. In P. Giglioli (Ed.), *Language and social context.* New York: Penguin Books.

Basso, K. H. (1984). Stalking with stories: Names, places, and moral narratives among the Western Apache. In E. M. Bruner & S. Plattner (Eds.), *Text, play and story: The construction and reconstruction of self and society* (pp. 19–55). Washington, DC: American Ethnological Society.

Bates, E., & MacWhinney, B. (1987). Competition, variation, and language learning. In B. MacWhinney (Ed.), *Mechanisms of language acquisition.* Hillsdale, NJ: Erlbaum.

Bates, J. E., Viken, R. J., Alexander, D. B., Beyers, J., & Stockton, L. (2002). Sleep and adjustment in preschool children: Sleep diary reports by mothers relate to behavior reports by teachers. *Child Development, 73,* 62–74.

Batshaw, M. L., & Shapiro, B. K. (1997). Mental retardation. In M. L. Batshaw (Ed.), *Children with disabilities* (4th ed.). Baltimore: Brookes.

Batson, C. D. (1991). *The altruism question: Toward a social-psychological answer.* Hillsdale, NJ: Erlbaum.

Batson, C. D., & Thompson, E. R. (2001). Why don't moral people act morally? Motivational considerations. *Current Directions in Psychological Science, 10,* 54–57.

Battistich, V., Solomon, D., Kim, D., Watson, M., & Schaps, E. (1995). Schools as communities, poverty levels of student populations, and students' attitudes, motives, and performance: A multilevel analysis. *American Educational Research Journal, 32,* 627–658.

Battistich, V., Solomon, D., Watson, M., & Schaps, E. (1997). Caring school communities. *Educational Psychologist, 32,* 137–151.

Bauer, P. J. (2002). Long-term recall memory: Behavioral and neuro-developmental changes in the first 2 years of life. *Current Directions in Psychological Science, 11,* 137–141.

Bauer, P. J. (2006). Event memory. In W. Damon, R. M. Lerner (Series Eds.), D. Kuhn, & R. Siegler (Vol. Eds.), *Handbook of child psychology: Vol. 1. Cognition, perception, and language* (6th ed.). New York: Wiley.

Bauer, P. J., & Dow, G. A. (1994). Episodic memory in 16- and 20-month-old children: Specifics not generalized, but not forgotten. *Developmental Psychology, 30,* 403–417.

Bauer, P. J., & Mandler, J. M. (1990). Remembering what happened next: Very young children's recall of event sequences. In R. Fivush & J. A. Hudson (Eds.), *Knowing and remembering in young children* (pp. 9–29). Cambridge, England: Cambridge University Press.

Baumeister, R. F., Campbell, J. D., Krueger, J. I., & Vohs, K. D. (2003). Does high self-esteem cause better performance, interpersonal success, happiness, or healthier lifestyles? *Psychological Science in the Public Interest, 4*(1), 1–44.

Baumrind, D. (1967). Child care practices anteceding three patterns of preschool behavior. *Genetic Psychology Monographs, 75,* 43–88.

Baumrind, D. (1971). Current patterns of parental authority. *Developmental Psychology Monographs, 4*(1, Pt. 2).

Baumrind, D. (1980). New directions in socialization research. *American Psychologist, 35,* 639–652.

Baumrind, D. (1982). An explanatory study of socialization effects on Black children: Some Black-White comparisons. *Child Development, 43,* 261–267.

Baumrind, D. (1989). Rearing competent children. In W. Damon (Ed.), *Child development today and tomorrow.* San Francisco: Jossey-Bass.

Baumrind, D. (1991). Parenting styles and adolescent development. In R. Lerner, A. C. Petersen, & J. Brooks-Gunn (Eds.), *The encyclopedia of adolescence.* New York: Garland Press.

Baydar, N., Brooks-Gunn, J., & Furstenberg, F. F., Jr. (1993). Early warning signs of functional illiteracy: Predictors in childhood and adolescence. *Child Development, 64,* 815–829.

Bay-Hinitz, A. K., Peterson, R. F., & Quilitch, H. R. (1994). Cooperative games: A way to modify aggressive and cooperative behaviors in young children. *Journal of Applied Behavior Analysis, 27,* 435–446.

Bayley, N. (2005). *Bayley Scales of Infant Development* (3rd ed.). San Antonio, TX: Psychological Corporation.

Beal, C. R. (1996). The role of comprehension monitoring in children's revision. *Educational Psychology Review, 8,* 219–238.

Bearison, D., & Levey, L. (1977). Children's comprehension of referential communication: Decoding ambiguous messages. *Child Development, 48,* 716–720.

Bearison, D. J. (1998). Pediatric psychology and children's medical problems. In W. Damon (Series Ed.), I. E. Sigel, & K. A. Renninger (Vol. Eds.), *Handbook of child psychology: Vol. 4. Child psychology in practice* (5th ed., pp. 635–711). New York: Wiley.

Beaty, J. J. (1998). *Observing development of the young child* (4th ed.). Upper Saddle River, NJ: Merrill/Prentice Hall.

Beauboeuf-LaFontant, T. (1999). A movement against and beyond boundaries: "Politically relevant teaching" among African American teachers. *Teachers College Record, 100,* 702–723.

Beaudry, M., Dufour, R., & Marcoux, S. (1995). Relation between infant feeding and infections during the first six months of life. *Journal of Pediatrics, 126,* 191–197.

Bebko, J. M., Burke, L., Craven, J., & Sarlo, N. (1992). The importance of motor activity in sensorimotor development: A perspective from children with physical handicaps. *Human Development, 35*(4), 226–240.

Beck, I. L., McKeown, M. G., Sinatra, G. M., & Loxterman, J. A. (1991). Revising social studies text from a text-processing perspective: Evidence of improved comprehensibility. *Reading Research Quarterly, 26,* 251–276.

Beck, M. (1999). *Expecting Adam: A true story of birth, rebirth, and everyday magic.* New York: Random House.

Beeman, M. J., & Chiarello, C. (1998). Complementary right- and left-hemisphere language comprehension. *Current Directions in Psychological Science, 7,* 2–8.

Beirne-Smith, M., Ittenbach, R., & Patton, J. R. (1998). *Mental retardation* (5th ed.). Upper Saddle River, NJ: Merrill/Prentice Hall.

Belenky, M. F., Bond, L. A., & Weinstock, J. S. (1997). *A tradition that has no name: Nurturing the development of people, families, and communities.* New York: Basic Books.

Belenky, M. F., Clinchy, B. M., Goldberger, N. R., & Tarule, J. M. (1986). *Women's ways of knowing: The development of self, voice, and mind.* New York: Basic Books.

Belfiore, P. J., & Hornyak, R. S. (1998). Operant theory and application to self-monitoring in adolescents. In D. H. Schunk & B. J. Zimmerman (Eds.), *Self-regulated learning: From teaching to self-reflective practice.* New York: Guilford Press.

Bell, L. A. (1989). Something's wrong here and it's not me: Challenging the dilemmas that block girls' success. *Journal for the Education of the Gifted, 12,* 118–130.

Bell, N., Grossen, M., & Perret-Clermont, A. (1985). Sociocognitive conflict and intellectual growth. In M. W. Berkowitz (Ed.), *Peer conflict and psychological growth.* San Francisco: Jossey-Bass.

Bell, P., & Linn, M. C. (2002). Beliefs about science: How does science instruction contribute? In B. K. Hofer & P. R. Pintrich (Eds.), *Personal epistemology: The psychology of beliefs about knowledge and knowing* (pp. 321–346). Mahwah, NJ: Erlbaum.

Bell, R. Q. (1988). Contributions of human infants to caregiving and social interaction. In G. Handel (Ed.), *Childhood socialization* (pp. 103–122). New York: Aldine de Gruyter.

Belsky, J., & Eggebeen, D. (1991). Early and extensive maternal employment and young children's socioemotional development: Children of the National Longitudinal Survey of Youth. *Journal of Marriage and the Family, 53*(4), 1083–1098.

Belsky, J., Gilstrap, B., & Rovine, M. (1984). The Pennsylvania Infant and Family Development Project, I: Stability and change in mother-infant and father-infant interaction in a family setting at one, three, and nine months. *Child Development, 55,* 692–705.

Belzer, M. E., Rogers, A. S., Camarca, M., Fuschs, D., Peralta, L., Tucker, D., et al. (2001). Contraceptive choices in HIV infected and HIV at-risk adolescent females. *Journal of Adolescent Health, 29*(Suppl. 3), 93–100.

Bem, S. L. (1977). On the utility of alternative procedures for assessing psychological androgyny. *Journal of Consulting and Clinical Psychology, 45,* 196–205.

Bem, S. L. (1981). Gender schema theory: A cognitive account of sex typing. *Psychological Review, 88,* 354–364.

Bem, S. L. (1989). Genital knowledge and gender constancy in preschool children. *Child Development, 60,* 649–662.

Benbow, C. P., Lubinski, D., Shea, D. L., & Eftekhari-Sanjani, H. (2000). Sex differences in mathematical reasoning ability at age 13: Their status 20 years later. *Psychological Science, 11,* 474–480.

Bender, G. (2001). Resisting dominance? The study of a marginalized masculinity and its construction within high school walls. In J. N. Burstyn, G. Bender, R. Casella, H. W. Gordon, D. P. Guerra, K. V. Luschen, et al., *Preventing violence in schools: A challenge to American democracy* (pp. 61–77). Mahwah, NJ: Erlbaum.

Bendixen, L. D., & Rule, D. C. (2004). An integrative approach to personal epistemology: A guiding model. *Educational Psychologist, 39,* 69–80.

Benes, F. (2001, May–June). Modern myelination: The brain at midlife. *Harvard Magazine, 103,* 9.

Bennett, G. K., Seashore, H. G., & Wesman, A. G. (1982). *Differential Aptitude Tests.* San Antonio, TX: Psychological Corporation.

Bennett, R. E., Gottesman, R. L., Rock, D. A., & Cerullo, F. (1993). Influence of behavior perceptions and gender on teachers' judgments of students' academic skill. *Journal of Educational Psychology, 85,* 347–356.

Benoit, D., & Parker, K. C. (1994). Stability and transmission of attachment across three generations. *Child Development, 65,* 1444–1456.

Benton, S. L. (1997). Psychological foundations of elementary writing instruction. In G. D. Phye (Ed.), *Handbook of academic learning: Construction of knowledge.* San Diego, CA: Academic Press.

Benware, C., & Deci, E. L. (1984). Quality of learning with an active versus passive motivational set. *American Educational Research Journal, 21,* 755–765.

Bereiter, C. (1994). Implications of postmodernism for science, or, science as progressive discourse. *Educational Psychologist, 29,* 3–12.

Bereiter, C., & Scardamalia, M. (1987). *The psychology of written composition.* Hillsdale, NJ: Erlbaum.

Berenstain, S., & Berenstain, J. (1990). *The Berenstain bears' trouble with pets.* New York: Random House.

Berk, L. E. (1994). Why children talk to themselves. *Scientific American, 271,* 78–83.

Berkowitz, M. W., Guerra, N., & Nucci, L. (1991). Sociomoral development and drug and alcohol abuse. In W. M. Kurtines & J. L. Gewirtz (Eds.), *Moral behavior and development: Vol. 3. Application.* Hillsdale, NJ: Erlbaum.

Berliner, D. C. (2005, April). *Ignoring the forest, blaming the trees: Our impoverished view of educational reform.* Paper presented at the annual meeting of the American Educational Research Association, Montreal, Canada.

Bermejo, V. (1996). Cardinality development and counting. *Developmental Psychology, 32,* 263–268.

Berndt, T. J. (1992). Friendship and friends' influence in adolescence. *Current Directions in Psychological Science, 1,* 156–159.

Berndt, T. J., & Hoyle, S. G. (1985). Stability and change in childhood and adolescent friendships. *Developmental Psychology, 21,* 1007–1015.

Berndt, T. J., & Keefe, K. (1995). Friends' influence on adolescents' adjustment to school. *Child Development, 66,* 1312–1329.

Berndt, T. J., & Keefe, K. (1996). Friends' influence on school adjustment: A motivational analysis. In J. Juvonen & K. R. Wentzel (Eds.), *Social motivation: Understanding children's school adjustment* (pp. 248–278). Cambridge, England: Cambridge University Press.

Berninger, V. W., Fuller, F., & Whitaker, D. (1996). A process model of writing development across the life span. *Educational Psychology Review, 8,* 193–218.

Bertenthal, B. I. (1993). Perception of biomechanical motions by infants: Intrinsic image and knowledge-based constraints. In C. E. Granrud (Ed.), *Visual perception and cognition in infancy* (pp. 175–214). Hillsdale, NJ: Erlbaum.

Bertenthal, B. I., Campos, J. J., & Kermoian, R. (1994). An epigenetic perspective on the development of self-produced locomotion and its consequences. *Current Directions in Psychological Science, 3,* 140–145.

Bertenthal, B. I., & Pinto, J. (1993). Complementary processes in the perception and production of human movements. In E. Thelen & L. Smith (Eds.), *Dynamic approaches to development: Vol. 2. Applications.* Cambridge, MA: Bradford Books.

Berzonsky, M. D. (1988). Self-theorists, identity status, and social cognition. In D. K. Lapsley & F. C. Power (Eds.), *Self, ego, and identity: Integrative approaches* (pp. 243–261). New York: Springer-Verlag.

Best, D. L., & Ornstein, P. A. (1986). Children's generation and communication of mnemonic organizational strategies. *Developmental Psychology, 22,* 845–853.

Bialystok, E. (1994a). Representation and ways of knowing: Three issues in second language acquisition. In N. C. Ellis (Ed.), *Implicit and explicit learning of languages.* London: Academic Press.

Bialystok, E. (1994b). Towards an explanation of second language acquisition. In G. Brown, K. Malmkjær, A. Pollitt, & J. Williams (Eds.), *Language and understanding.* Oxford, England: Oxford University Press.

Bialystok, E. (2001). *Bilingualism in development: Language, literacy, and cognition.* Cambridge, England: Cambridge University Press.

Bialystok, E., & Senman, L. (2004). Executive processes in appearance-reality tasks: The role of inhibition of attention and symbolic representation. *Child Development, 75,* 562–579.

Bibace, R., & Walsh, M. E. (1981). Children's conceptions of illness. In R. Bibace & M. E. Walsh (Eds.), *New directions for child development: Children's conceptions of health, illness, and bodily functions* (pp. 31–48). San Francisco: Jossey-Bass.

Biddle, S. J. (1993). Children, exercise and mental health. *International Journal of Sport Psychology, 24,* 200–216.

Biemiller, A., Shany, M., Inglis, A., & Meichenbaum, D. (1998). Factors influencing children's acquisition and demonstration of self-regulation on academic tasks. In D. H. Schunk & B. J. Zimmerman (Eds.), *Self-regulated learning: From teaching to self-reflective practice* (pp. 203–224). New York: Guilford Press.

Bierman, K. L. (2004). *Peer rejection: Developmental processes and intervention strategies.* New York: Guilford Press.

Bierman, K. L., Miller, C. L., & Staub, S. D. (1987). Improving the social behavior and peer acceptance of rejected boys: Effect of social skill training with instructions and prohibitions. *Journal of Consulting and Clinical Psychology, 55,* 194–200.

Bigelow, B. J., Tesson, G., & Lewko, J. H. (1999). The contextual influences of sibling and dating relations on adolescents' personal relations and their close friends, dating partners, and parents: The Sullivan-Piaget-Hartup hypothesis considered. In J. A. McLellan & M. J. V. Pugh (Eds.), The role of peer groups in adolescent social identity: Exploring the importance of stability and change. *New directions for child and adolescent development* (No. 84, pp. 71–86). San Francisco: Jossey-Bass.

Bijeljac-Babic, R., Bertoncini, J., & Mehler, J. (1993). How do 4-day-old infants categorize multisyllable utterances? *Developmental Psychology, 29,* 711–721.

Binder, L. M., Dixon, M. R., & Ghezzi, P. M. (2000). A procedure to teach self-control to children with attention deficit hyperactivity disorder. *Journal of Applied Behavior Analysis, 33,* 233–237.

Binns, K., Steinberg, A., Amorosi, S., & Cuevas, A. M. (1997). *The Metropolitan Life survey of the American teacher 1997: Examining gender issues in public schools.* New York: Louis Harris and Associates.

Birnbaum, D. W., & Croll, W. L. (1984). The etiology of children's stereotypes about sex differences in emotionality. *Sex Roles, 10,* 677–691.

Bishop, S. J., Murphy, J. M., Hicks, R., Quinn, S. D., Lewis, P. D., Grace, M. P., et al. (2001). The youngest victims of maltreatment: What happens to infants in a court sample? *Child Maltreatment, 6,* 243–249.

Bivens, J. A., & Berk, L. E. (1990). A longitudinal study of the development of elementary school children's private speech. *Merrill-Palmer Quarterly, 36,* 443–463.

Bjorklund, D. F. (1987). How age changes in knowledge base contribute to the development of children's memory: An interpretive review. *Developmental Review, 7,* 93–130.

Bjorklund, D. F. (2003). Evolutionary psychology from a developmental systems perspective: Comment on Lickliter and Honeycutt (2003). *Psychological Bulletin, 129*(6), 836–841.

Bjorklund, D. F., & Brown, R. D. (1998). Physical play and cognitive development: Integrating activity, cognition, and education. *Child Development, 69,* 604–606.

Bjorklund, D. F., & Coyle, T. R. (1995). Utilization deficiencies in the development of memory strategies. In F. E. Weinert & W. Schneider (Eds.), *Research on memory development: State of the art and future directions.* Hillsdale, NJ: Erlbaum.

Bjorklund, D. F., & Green, B. L. (1992). The adaptive nature of cognitive immaturity. *American Psychologist, 47,* 46–54.

Blachford, S. L. (2002). *The Gale encyclopedia of genetic disorders.* Detroit, MI: Gale Group.

Black, M. M., Hutcheson, J. J., Dubowitz, H., & Berenson-Howard, J. (1994). Parenting style and developmental status among children with non-organic failure to thrive. *Journal of Pediatric Psychology, 19,* 689–707.

Black-Gutman, D., & Hickson, F. (1996). The relationship between racial attitudes and social-cognitive development in children: An Australian study. *Developmental Psychology, 32,* 448–456.

Blackson, T. C., Butler, T., Belsky, J., Ammerman, R. T., Shaw, D. S., & Tarter, R. E. (1999). Individual traits and family contexts predict sons' externalizing behavior and preliminary relative risk ratios for conduct disorder and substance use disorder outcomes. *Drug and Alcohol Dependence, 56,* 115–131.

Blades, M., & Spencer, C. (1987). Young children's strategies when using maps with landmarks. *Journal of Environmental Psychology, 7,* 201–217.

Blair, C. (2002). School readiness: Integrating cognition and emotion in a neurobiological conceptualization of children's functioning at school entry. *American Psychologist, 57,* 111–127.

Blakemore, C. (1976). The conditions required for the maintenance of binocularity in the kitten's visual cortex. *Journal of Physiology, 261,* 423–444.

Blasi, A. (1980). Bridging moral cognition and moral action: A critical review of the literature. *Psychological Bulletin, 88,* 593–637.

Blasi, A. (1995). Moral understanding and the moral personality: The process of moral integration. In W. M. Kurtines & J. L. Gewirtz (Eds.), *Moral development: An introduction.* Boston: Allyn & Bacon.

Blazevski, J. L., McEvoy, A. P., & Pintrich, P. R. (2003, April). *The relation of achievement goals to cognitive regulation, persistence, and achievement.* Paper presented at the annual meeting of the American Educational Research Association, Chicago.

Bleeker, M. M., & Jacobs, J. E. (2004). Achievement in math and science: Do mothers' beliefs matter 12 years later? *Journal of Educational Psychology, 96,* 97–109.

Block, J. H. (1979). Another look at sex differentiation in the socialization behaviors of mothers and fathers. In J. Sherman & F. L. Denmark (Eds.), *Psychology of women: Future of research.* New York: Psychological Dimensions.

Block, J. H. (1983). Differential premises arising from differential socialization of the sexes: Some conjectures. *Child Development, 54,* 1335–1354.

Block, N. (1999). How heritability misleads about race. In A. Montagu (Ed.), *Race and IQ* (expanded ed., pp. 444–486). New York: Oxford University Press.

Bloom, B. S. (1964). *Stability and change in human characteristics.* New York: Wiley.

Bloom, K., Russell, A., & Wassenberg, K. (1987). Turn taking affects the quality of infant vocalizations. *Journal of Child Language, 14,* 211–227.

Bloom, L., & Lahey, M. (1978). *Language development and language disorders.* New York: Wiley.

Bloom, L., & Tinker, E. (2001). The intentionality model and language acquisition. *Monographs of the Society for Research in Child Development, 66*(4, Serial No. 267).

Blyth, D. A., Simmons, R. G., & Zakin, D. F. (1985). Satisfaction with body image for early adolescent females: The impact of pubertal timing within different school environments. *Journal of Youth and Adolescence, 14,* 207–225.

Boccia, M., & Campos, J. J. (1989). Maternal emotional signals, social referencing, and infants' reactions to strangers. In N. Eisenberg (Ed.), *New directions for child development* (Vol. 44, pp. 25–49). San Francisco: Jossey-Bass.

Bochenhauer, M. H. (1990, April). *Connections: Geographic education and the National Geographic Society.* Paper presented at the annual meeting of the American Educational Research Association, Boston.

Bodrova, E., & Leong, D. J. (1996). *Tools of the mind: The Vygotskian approach to early childhood education.* Upper Saddle River, NJ: Merrill/Prentice Hall.

Boekaerts, M. (1993). Being concerned with well-being and with learning. *Educational Psychologist, 28,* 149–167.

Bogin, B. (1988). *Patterns of human growth.* Cambridge, England: Cambridge University Press.

Bohannon, J. N., MacWhinney, B., & Snow, C. (1990). No negative evidence revisited: Beyond learnability, or who has to prove what to whom. *Developmental Psychology, 26,* 221–226.

Bong, M. (2001). Between- and within-domain relations of academic motivation among middle and high school students: Self-efficacy, task-value, and achievement goals. *Journal of Educational Psychology, 93,* 23–34.

Bong, M., & Skaalvik, E. M. (2003). Academic self-concept and self-efficacy: How different are they really? *Educational Psychology Review, 15,* 1–40.

Boom, J., Brugman, D., & van der Heijden, P. G. M. (2001). Hierarchical structure of moral stages assessed by a sorting task. *Child Development, 72,* 535–548.

Booth, P. B., & Koller, T. J. (1998). Training parents of failure-to-attach children. In J. M. Briesmeister & C. E. Schaefer (Eds.), *Handbook of parent training: Parents as co-therapists for children's behavior problems* (2nd ed., pp. 308–342). New York: Wiley.

Borkowski, J. G., Bisconti, T., Willard, C. C., Keogh, D. A., Whitman, T. L., & Weed, K. (2002). The adolescent as parent: Influences on children's intellectual, academic, and socioemotional development. In J. G. Borkowski, S. L. Ramey, & M. Bristol-Power (Eds.), *Parenting and the child's world: Influences on academic, intellectual, and social-emotional development* (pp. 161–184). Mahwah, NJ: Erlbaum.

Borkowski, J. G., & Burke, J. E. (1996). Theories, models, and measurements of executive functioning. In G. R. Lyon & N. A. Krasnegor (Eds.), *Attention, memory, and executive function* (pp. 235–261). Baltimore: Brookes.

Bornstein, M. (1989). Information processing (habituation) and stability in cognitive development. *Human Development, 32,* 129–136.

Bornstein, M. H., & Cote, L. R., with Maital, S., Painter, K., Park, S., Pascual, L., Pêcheux, M., Ruel, J., et al. (2004). Cross-linguistic analysis of vocabulary in young children: Spanish, Dutch, French, Hebrew, Italian, Korean, and American English. *Child Development, 75,* 1115–1139.

Bornstein, M. H., Haynes, O. M., Pascual, L., Painter, K. M., & Galperin, C. (1999). Play in two societies: Pervasiveness of process, specificity of structure. *Child Development, 70,* 317–331.

Bortfeld, H., & Whitehurst, G. J. (2001). Sensitive periods in first language acquisition. In D. B. Bailey, Jr., J. T. Bruer, F. J. Symons, & J. W. Lichtman (Eds.), *Critical thinking about critical periods* (pp. 173–192). Baltimore: Brookes.

Bosacki, S. L. (2000). Theory of mind and self-concept in preadolescents: Links with gender and language. *Journal of Educational Psychology, 92,* 709–717.

Botvin, G. J., & Scheier, L. M. (1997). Preventing drug abuse and violence. In D. K. Wilson, J. R. Rodrigue, & W. C. Taylor (Eds.), *Health-promoting and health-compromising behaviors among minority adolescents* (pp. 55–86). Washington, DC: American Psychological Association.

Bouchard, T. J. (2004). Genetic influence on human psychological traits. *Current Directions in Psychological Science, 13,* 148–151.

Bouchard, T. J., & McGue, M. (1981). Familial studies of intelligence: A review. *Science, 212,* 1056.

Bouchard, T. J., Jr. (1997). IQ similarity in twins reared apart: Findings and responses to critics. In R. J. Sternberg & E. L. Grigorenko (Eds.), *Intelligence, heredity, and environment* (pp. 126–160). Cambridge, England: Cambridge University Press.

Boutte, G. S., & McCormick, C. B. (1992). Authentic multicultural activities: Avoiding pseudomulticulturalism. *Childhood Education, 68*(3), 140–144.

Bowey, J. (1986). Syntactic awareness and verbal performance from preschool to fifth grade. *Journal of Psycholinguistic Research, 15,* 285–308.

Bowlby, J. (1951). *Maternal care and mental health.* Geneva, Switzerland: World Health Organization.

Bowlby, J. (1958). The nature of the child's tie to his mother. *International Journal of Psycho-Analysis, 39,* 350–373.

Bowlby, J. (1969/1982). *Attachment and loss: Vol. 1. Attachment* (2nd ed.). New York: Basic Books.

Bowlby, J. (1973). *Attachment and loss: Vol. 2. Separation: Anxiety and anger.* New York: Basic Books.

Bowlby, J. (1988). *A secure base: Parent-child attachment and healthy human development.* New York: Basic Books.

Bowman, B. T. (1989). Educating language-minority children: Challenges and opportunities. *Phi Delta Kappan, 71,* 118–120.

Boykin, A. W. (1994). Harvesting talent and culture: African-American children and educational reform. In R. J. Rossi (Ed.), *Schools and students at risk: Context and framework for positive change.* New York: Teachers College Press.

Brabham, E. G., & Lynch-Brown, C. (2002). Effects of teachers' reading-aloud styles on vocabulary acquisition and comprehension of students in the early elementary grades. *Journal of Educational Psychology, 94,* 465–473.

Bracken, B. A., & McCallum, R. S. (1998). *Universal Nonverbal Intelligence Test.* Itasca, IL: Riverside.

Bracken, B. A., McCallum, R. S., & Shaughnessy, M. F. (1999). An interview with Bruce A. Bracken and R. Steve McCallum, authors of the Universal Nonverbal Intelligence Test (UNIT). *North American Journal of Psychology, 1,* 277–288.

Bracken, B. A., & Walker, K. C. (1997). The utility of intelligence tests for preschool children. In D. P. Flanagan, J. L. Genshaft, & P. L. Harrison (Eds.), *Contemporary intellectual assessment: Theories, tests, and issues* (pp. 484–502). New York: Guilford Press.

Bradley, L., & Bryant, P. (1991). Phonological skills before and after learning to read. In S. A. Brady & D. P. Shankweiler (Eds.), *Phonological processes in literacy.* Hillsdale, NJ: Erlbaum.

Bradley, R. H., & Caldwell, B. M. (1984). The relation of infants' home environments to achievement test performance in first grade: A follow-up study. *Child Development, 55,* 803–809.

Bradley, R. H., Corwyn, R. F., McAdoo, H., & Coll, C. (2001). The home environments of children in the United States: Part I. Variations by age, ethnicity, and poverty status. *Child Development, 72,* 1844–1867.

Bradshaw, P. (2001). What about sharing? In B. Rogoff, C. G. Turkanis, & L. Bartlett (Eds.), *Learning together: Children and adults in a school community* (pp. 108–120). New York: Oxford University Press.

Braine, L. G., Schauble, L., Kugelmass, S., & Winter, A. (1993). Representation of depth by children: Spatial strategies and lateral biases. *Developmental Psychology, 29,* 466–479.

Brainerd, C. J. (2003). Jean Piaget, learning research, and American education. In B. J. Zimmerman & D. H. Schunk (Eds.), *Educational psychology: A century of contributions* (pp. 251–287). Mahwah, NJ: Erlbaum.

Bramlett, M. D., & Mosher, W. D. (2002). Cohabitation, marriage, divorce, and remarriage in the United States. National Center for Health Statistics. *Vital and Health Statistics, 23*(22).

Branch, C. (1999). Race and human development. In R. H. Sheets & E. R. Hollins (Eds.), *Racial and ethnic identity in school practices: Aspects of human development* (pp. 7–28). Mahwah, NJ: Erlbaum.

Brannon, M. E. (2002). The development of ordinal numerical knowledge in infancy. *Cognition, 83,* 223–240.

Brauner, J., Gordic, B., & Zigler, E. (2004). Putting the child back into child care: Combining care and education for children ages 3–5. *Social Policy Report, 18* (Society for Research in Child Development).

Brazelton, T. B., Koslowski, B., & Main, M. (1974). The origins of reciprocity: The early mother-infant interaction. In M. Lewis & L. A. Rosenblum (Eds.), *The origins of behavior: The effect of the infant on its caregiver* (pp. 49–76). New York: Wiley.

Brazelton Institute. (2000). *The Neonatal Behavioral Assessment Scale (Revised).* Boston: Children's Hospital.

Bredekamp, S., & Copple, C. (Eds.). (1997). *Developmentally appropriate practice in early childhood programs* (3rd ed.). Washington, DC: National Association for the Education of Young Children.

Brenner, E. M., & Salovey, P. (1997). Emotion regulation during childhood: Developmental, interpersonal, and individual considerations. In P. Salovey & D. J. Sluyter (Eds.), *Emotional development and emotional intelligence: Educational implications* (pp. 168–195). New York: Basic Books.

Brenner, L. A., Koehler, D. J., Liberman, V., & Tversky, A. (1996). Overconfidence in probability and frequency judgments: A critical examination. *Organizational Behavior and Human Decision Processes, 65,* 212–219.

Bretherton, I. (1991). Pouring new wine into old bottles: The social self as internal working model. In M. R. Gunnar & L. A. Sroufe (Eds.), *Self processes and development: The Minnesota Symposia on Child Development* (Vol. 23, pp. 1–42). Hillsdale, NJ: Erlbaum.

Bretherton, I., & Beeghly, M. (1982). Talking about internal states: The acquisition of an explicit theory of mind. *Developmental Psychology, 18,* 906–921.

Bretherton, I., Fritz, J., Zahn-Waxler, C., & Ridgeway, D. (1986). Learning to talk about emotions: A functionalist perspective. *Child Development, 57,* 529–548.

Bridges, L. J., Connell, J. P., & Belsky, J. (1988). Similarities and differences in infant-mother and infant-father interaction in the Strange Situation: A component process analysis. *Developmental Psychology, 24,* 92–100.

Brinton, B., & Fujiki, M. (1984). Development of topic manipulation skills in discourse. *Journal of Speech and Hearing Research, 27,* 350–358.

Bristol, M. M., Cohen, D. J., Costello, E. J., Denckia, M., Eckberg, T. J., Kallen, R., et al. (1996). State of the science in autism: Report to the National Institutes of Health. *Journal of Autism and Developmental Disorders, 26,* 121–154.

Britt, M. A., Rouet, J-F., Georgi, M. C., & Perfetti, C. A. (1994). Learning from history texts: From causal analysis to argument models. In G. Leinhardt, I. L. Beck, & C. Stainton (Eds.), *Teaching and learning in history.* Hillsdale, NJ: Erlbaum.

Brody, G. H. (2004). Siblings' direct and indirect contributions to child development. *Current Directions in Psychological Science, 13,* 124–126.

Brody, G. H., & Shaffer, D. R. (1982). Contributions of parents and peers to children's moral socialization. *Developmental Review, 2,* 31–75.

Brody, G. H., Stoneman, Z., & McCoy, J. K. (1994). Forecasting sibling relationships in early adolescence from child temperament and family processes in middle childhood. *Child Development, 65,* 771–784.

Brody, N. (1985). The validity of tests of intelligence. In B. B. Wolman (Ed.), *Handbook of intelligence.* New York: Wiley.

Brody, N. (1992). *Intelligence.* New York: Academic Press.

Brody, N. (1997). Intelligence, schooling, and society. *American Psychologist, 52,* 1046–1050.

Brodzinsky, D. M. (1993). Long-term outcomes in adoption. *The Future of Children, 3*(1), 153–166.

Bronfenbrenner, U. (1979). *The ecology of human development: Experiments by nature and design.* Cambridge, MA: Harvard University Press.

Bronfenbrenner, U. (1999). Is early intervention effective? Some studies of early education in familial and extra-familial settings. In A. Montagu (Ed.), *Race and IQ* (expanded ed., pp. 343–378). New York: Oxford University Press.

Bronfenbrenner, U. (2001). The bioecological theory of human development. In N. J. Smelser & P. B. Baltes (Eds.), *International encyclopedia of the social and behavioral sciences* (Vol. 10, pp. 6963–6970). New York: Elsevier.

Bronfenbrenner, U. (2005). *Making human beings human: Bioecological perspectives on human development.* Thousand Oaks, CA: Sage.

Bronfenbrenner, U., Alvarez, W. F., & Henderson, C. R., Jr. (1984). Working and watching: Maternal employment status and parents' perceptions of their three-year-old children. *Child Development, 55,* 1362–1379.

Bronson, M. B. (2000). *Self-regulation in early childhood: Nature and nurture.* New York: Guilford Press.

Bronson, W. C. (1981). Toddlers' behaviors with agemates: Issues of interaction, cognition, and affect. *Monographs of Infancy, 1,* 127.

Brooks-Gunn, J. (1989). Pubertal processes and the early adolescent transition. In W. Damon (Ed.), *Child development today and tomorrow* (pp. 155–176). San Francisco: Jossey-Bass.

Brooks-Gunn, J. (2003). Do you believe in magic? What we can expect from early childhood intervention programs. *Social Policy Report, 17*(1). Ann Arbor, MI: Society for Research in Child Development.

Brooks-Gunn, J., & Duncan, G. J. (1997). The effects of poverty on children. *The Future of Children: Children and Poverty, 7*(2), 55–71.

Brooks-Gunn, J., & Furstenberg, F. F. (1990). Coming of age in the era of AIDS: Puberty, sexuality, and contraception. *Milbrank Quarterly, 68* (Suppl. 1), 59–84.

Brooks-Gunn, J., Klebanov, P. K., & Duncan, G. J. (1996). Ethnic differences in children's intelligence test scores: Role of economic deprivation, home environment, and maternal characteristics. *Child Development, 67,* 396–408.

Brooks-Gunn, J., & Paikoff, R. L. (1992). Changes in self-feelings during the transition toward adolescence. In H. R. McGurk (Ed.), *Childhood social development: Contemporary perspectives* (pp. 63–97). Hillsdale, NJ: Erlbaum.

Brooks-Gunn, J., & Paikoff, R. L. (1993). "Sex is a gamble, kissing is a game": Adolescent sexuality and health promotion. In S. G. Millstein, A. C. Petersen, & E. O. Nightingale (Eds.), *Promoting the health of adolescents: New directions for the twenty-first century* (pp. 180–208). New York: Oxford University Press.

Brophy, J. E. (1987). Synthesis of research on strategies for motivating students to learn. *Educational Leadership, 45*(2), 40–48.

Brophy, J. E. (2004). *Motivating students to learn* (2nd ed.). Mahwah, NJ: Erlbaum.

Brophy, J. E., & Alleman, J. (1996). *Powerful social studies for elementary students.* Fort Worth, TX: Harcourt Brace.

Brophy, J. E., & VanSledright, B. (1997). *Teaching and learning history in elementary schools.* New York: Teachers College Press.

Brown, A. L., & Campione, J. C. (1994). Guided discovery in a community of learners. In K. McGilly (Ed.), *Classroom lessons: Integrating cognitive theory and classroom practice.* Cambridge, MA: MIT Press.

Brown, A. L., & Campione, J. C. (1996). Psychological theory and the design of innovative learning environments: On procedures, principles, and systems. In L. Schauble & R. Glaser (Eds.), *Innovations in learning: New environments for education.* Mahwah, NJ: Erlbaum.

Brown, A. L., & Palincsar, A. S. (1987). Reciprocal teaching of comprehension strategies: A natural history of one program for enhancing learning. In J. Borkowski & J. D. Day (Eds.), *Cognition in special education: Comparative approaches to retardation, learning disabilities, and giftedness.* Norwood, NJ: Ablex.

Brown, A. L., Susser, E. S., Butler, P. D., Andrews, R. R., Kauffman, C. A., & Gorman, J. M. (1996). Neurobiological plausibility of prenatal nutritional deprivation as a risk factor for schizophrenia. *Journal of Nervous and Mental Disease, 184,* 71–85.

Brown, B. (1999). Optimizing expression of the common human genome for child development. *Current Directions in Psychological Science, 8,* 37–41.

Brown, B. B. (1990). Peer groups and peer culture. In S. S. Feldman & G. R. Elliott (Eds.), *At the threshold: The developing adolescent* (pp. 171–196). Cambridge, MA: Harvard University Press.

Brown, B. B. (1993). School culture, social politics, and the academic motivation of U.S. citizens. In T. M. Tomlinson (Ed.), *Motivating students to learn: Overcoming barriers to high achievement.* Berkeley, CA: McCutchan.

Brown, B. B. (1999). "You're going out with *who?*" Peer group influences on adolescent romantic relationships. In W. Furman, B. B. Brown, & C. Feiring (Eds.), *The development of romantic relationships in adolescence* (pp. 291–329). Cambridge, England: Cambridge University Press.

Brown, B. B., Eicher, S. A., & Petrie, S. (1986). The importance of peer group ("crowd") affiliation in adolescence. *Journal of Adolescence, 9,* 73–96.

Brown, B. B., Feiring, C., & Furman, W. (1999). Missing the love boat: Why researchers have shied away from adolescent romance. In W. Furman, B. B. Brown, & C. Feiring (Eds.), *The development of romantic relationships in adolescence* (pp. 1–16). Cambridge, England: Cambridge University Press.

Brown, J. D., & Siegel, J. D. (1988). Exercise as a buffer of life stress: A prospective study of adolescent health. *Health Psychology, 7,* 341–353.

Brown, J. R., & Dunn, J. (1996). Continuities in emotion understanding from three to six years. *Child Development, 67,* 789–802.

Brown, J. S., Collins, A., & Duguid, P. (1989). Situated cognition and the culture of learning. *Educational Researcher, 18*(1), 32–42.

Brown, J. V., Bakeman, R., Coles, C. D., Platzman, K. A., & Lynch, M. E. (2004). Prenatal cocaine exposure: A comparison of 2-year-old children in parental and nonparental care. *Child Development, 75,* 1282–1295.

Brown, L. M. (1998). *Raising their voices: The politics of girls' anger.* Cambridge, MA: Harvard University Press.

Brown, L. M., Tappan, M. B., & Gilligan, C. (1995). Listening to different voices. In W. M. Kurtines & J. L. Gewirtz (Eds.), *Moral development: An introduction.* Boston: Allyn & Bacon.

Brown, R. (1973). *A first language: The early stages.* Cambridge, MA: Harvard University Press.

Brown, R., & Hanlon, C. (1970). Derivational complexity and order of acquisition in child speech. In J. R. Hayes (Ed.), *Cognition and the development of language.* New York: Wiley.

Brown, R. D., & Bjorklund, D. F. (1998). The biologizing of cognition, development, and education: Approach with cautious enthusiasm. *Educational Psychology Review, 10,* 355–373.

Brown, R. T., Reynolds, C. R., & Whitaker, J. S. (1999). Bias in mental testing since *Bias in Mental Testing.* *School Psychology Quarterly, 14,* 208–238.

Brown, V. A. (2002). *Child welfare case studies.* Boston, MA: Allyn & Bacon.

Brownell, M. T., Mellard, D. F., & Deshler, D. D. (1993). Differences in the learning and transfer performance between students with learning disabilities and other low-achieving students on problem-solving tasks. *Learning Disabilities Quarterly, 16,* 138–156.

Brown-Mizuno, C. (1990). Success strategies for learners who are learning disabled as well as gifted. *Teaching Exceptional Children, 23*(1), 10–12.

Bruck, M., & Ceci, S. J. (1997). The suggestibility of young children. *Current Directions in Psychological Science, 6,* 75–79.

Bruer, J. T. (1997). Education and the brain: A bridge too far. *Educational Researcher, 26*(8), 4–16.

Bruer, J. T. (1999). *The myth of the first three years: A new understanding of early brain development and lifelong learning.* New York: Free Press.

Bruer, J. T., & Greenough, W. T. (2001). The subtle science of how experience affects the brain. In D. B. Bailey, Jr., J. T. Bruer, F. J. Symons, & J. W. Lichtman (Eds.), *Critical thinking about critical periods* (pp. 209–232). Baltimore: Brookes.

Bruner, J. S. (1966). *Toward a theory of instruction.* Cambridge, MA: Harvard University Press.

Bruner, J. S. (1972). The nature and uses of immaturity. *American Psychologist, 27,* 687–708.

Bruner, J. S. (1983). The acquisition of pragmatic commitments. In R. M. Golinkoff (Ed.), *The transition from prelinguistic to linguistic communication* (pp. 27–42). Hillsdale, NJ: Erlbaum.

Bruner, J. S., & Sherwood, V. (1976). Early rule structure: The case of "peekaboo." In R. Harre (Ed.), *Life sentences* (pp. 55–62). London: Wiley.

Bruni, M. (1998). *Fine-motor skills in children with Down syndrome: A guide for parents and professionals.* Bethesda, MD: Woodbine House.

Bryan, J. H., Redfield, J., & Mader, S. (1971). Words and deeds concerning altruism and subsequent reinforcement power of the model. *Child Development, 42,* 1501–1508.

Bryan, T., Burstein, K., & Bryan, J. (2001). Students with learning disabilities: Homework problems and promising practices. *Educational Psychologist, 36,* 167–180.

Bryant, A. L., & Zimmerman, M. A. (1999, April). *Adolescent substance use and school apathy: A developmental perspective examining motivational, peer, and family factors.* Paper presented at the biennial meeting of the Society for Research in Child Development, Albuquerque, NM.

Bryant, J. B. (2001). Language in social contexts: Communicative competence. In J. B. Gleason (Ed.), *The development of language* (pp. 167–209). Boston: Allyn & Bacon.

Bryant, P., Nunes, T., & Aidinis, A. (1999). Different morphemes, same spelling problems: Cross-linguistic developmental studies. In M. Harris & G. Hatano (Eds.), *Learning to read and write: A cross-linguistic perspective.* Cambridge, England: Cambridge University Press.

Bryson, S. E. (1997). Epidemiology of autism: Overview and issues outstanding. In D. J. Cohen & F. R. Volkmar (Eds.), *Handbook of autism and pervasive developmental disorders* (2nd ed.). New York: Wiley.

Buchanan, C. M. (1991). Pubertal status in early adolescent girls: Relations to moods, energy, and restlessness. *Journal of Early Adolescence, 11,* 185–200.

Buchanan, C. M., Eccles, J. S., & Becker, J. B. (1992). Are adolescents the victims of raging hormones? Evidence for activational effects of hormones on moods and behaviors at adolescence. *Psychological Bulletin, 111,* 62–107.

Buchoff, T. (1990). Attention deficit disorder: Help for the classroom teacher. *Childhood Education, 67*(2), 86–90.

Budwig, N. (1995). *A developmental-functionalist approach to child language.* Mahwah, NJ: Erlbaum.

Bugental, D. B., & Goodnow, J. J. (1998). Socialization processes. In W. Damon (Series Ed.) & N. Eisenberg (Vol. Ed.), *Handbook of child psychology: Vol. 3. Social, emotional, and personality development* (5th ed., pp. 389–462). New York: Wiley.

Buhrmester, D. (1992). The developmental courses of sibling and peer relationships. In F. Boer & J. Dunn (Eds.), *Children's sibling relationships: Developmental and clinical issues.* Hillsdale, NJ: Erlbaum.

Buhrmester, D. (1996). Need fulfillment, interpersonal competence, and the developmental contexts of friendship. In W. M. Bukowski, A. F. Newcomb, & W. W. Hartup (Eds.), *The company they keep: Friendship during childhood and adolescence* (pp. 158–185). New York: Cambridge University Press.

Buijzen, M., & Valkenburg, P. M. (2003). The effects of television advertising on materialism, parent-child conflict, and unhappiness: A review of research. *Applied Developmental Psychology, 24,* 437–456.

Bullock, J. R. (1993). Children's loneliness and their relationships with family and peers. *Family Relations, 42,* 46–49.

Bullock, M., & Ziegler, A. (1999). Scientific reasoning: Developmental and individual differences. In F. E. Weinert & W. Schneider (Eds.), *Individual development from 3 to 12: Findings from the Munich longitudinal study.* New York: Cambridge University Press.

Burhans, K. K., & Dweck, C. S. (1995). Helplessness in early childhood: The role of contingent worth. *Child Development, 66,* 1719–1738.

Burkam, D. T., Lee, V. E., & Smerdon, B. A. (1997). Gender and science learning early in high school: Subject matter and laboratory experiences. *American Educational Research Journal, 34,* 297–331.

Burnett, P. (2001). Elementary students' preferences for teacher praise. *Journal of Classroom Interaction, 36,* 16–23.

Burnett, R. E., & Kastman, L. M. (1997). Teaching composition: Current theories and practices. In G. D. Phye (Ed.), *Handbook of academic learning: Construction of knowledge.* San Diego, CA: Academic Press.

Burns, C. E., Brady, M. A., Dunn, A. M., & Starr, N. B. (2000). *Pediatric primary care: A handbook for nurse practitioners* (2nd ed.). Philadelphia: Saunders.

Burstyn, J. N., Bender, G., Casella, R., Gordon, H. W., Guerra, D. P., Luschen, K. V., et al. (2001). *Preventing violence in schools: A challenge to American democracy.* Mahwah, NJ: Erlbaum.

Burton, L. M. (1992). Black grandparents rearing children of drug addicted parents: Stressors, outcomes, and social service needs. *The Gerontologist, 32,* 744–751.

Burton, S., & Mitchell, P. (2003). Judging who knows best about yourself: Developmental change in citing the self across middle childhood. *Child Development, 74,* 426–443.

Bush, P. J., Zuckerman, A. E., Taggert, V. S., Theiss, P. K., Peleg, E. O., & Smith, S. A. (1989). Cardiovascular risk factor prevention in Black school children: The 'Know Your Body' evaluation project. *Health Education Quarterly, 16,* 215–227.

Bussey, K., & Bandura, A. (1992). Self-regulatory mechanisms governing gender development. *Child Development, 63,* 1236–1250.

Butler, D. L., & Winne, P. H. (1995). Feedback and self-regulated learning: A theoretical synthesis. *Review of Educational Research, 65,* 245–281.

Butler, R. (1994). Teacher communication and student interpretations: Effects of teacher responses to failing students on attributional inferences in two age groups. *British Journal of Educational Psychology, 64,* 277–294.

Butler, R. N. (1963). The life review: An interpretation of reminiscence in the aged. *Psychiatry, 26,* 65–76.

Butterfield, E. C., & Ferretti, R. P. (1987). Toward a theoretical integration of cognitive hypotheses about intellectual differences among children. In J. G. Borkowski & J. D. Day (Eds.), *Cognition in special children: Approaches to retardation, learning disabilities, and giftedness.* Norwood, NJ: Ablex.

Byne, W. (1997). Why we cannot conclude that sexual orientation is primarily a biological phenomenon. *Journal of Homosexuality, 34,* 73–80.

Byrne, B. M. (2002). Validating the measurement and structure of self-concept: Snapshots of past, present, and future research. *American Psychologist, 57,* 897–909.

Byrne, B. M., & Shavelson, R. J. (1986, April). *On gender differences in the structure of adolescent self-concept.* Paper presented at the annual meeting of the American Educational Research Association, San Francisco.

Byrnes, J. P. (1996). *Cognitive development and learning in instructional contexts.* Boston: Allyn & Bacon.

Byrnes, J. P. (2001). *Minds, brains, and learning: Understanding the psychological and educational relevance of neuroscientific research.* New York: Guilford Press.

Côté, J. E. (2005). Erikson's theory. In C. B. Fisher & R. M. Lerner (Eds.), *Encyclopedia of applied developmental science* (Vol. 1, pp. 406–409). Thousand Oaks, CA: Sage.

Caetanno, R. (1987). Acculturation and drinking patterns among U.S. Hispanics. *British Journal of Addiction, 82,* 789–799.

Cain, K., & Oakhill, J. (1998). Comprehension skill and inference-making ability: Issues of causality. In C. Hulme & R. M. Joshi (Eds.), *Reading and spelling: Development and disorders.* Mahwah, NJ: Erlbaum.

Cairns, H. S. (1996). *The acquisition of language* (2nd ed.). Austin, TX: Pro-Ed.

Cairns, R. B., Cairns, B. D., Neckerman, H. J., Ferguson, L. L., & Gariépy, J.-L. (1989). Growth and aggression: 1. Childhood to early adolescence. *Developmental Psychology, 25,* 320–330.

Caldwell, M. S., Rudolph, K. D., Troop-Gordon, W., & Kim, D. (2004). Reciprocal influences among relational self-views, social disengagement, and peer stress during early adolescence. *Child Development, 75,* 1140–1154.

Calfee, R. C., & Masuda, W. V. (1997). Classroom assessment as inquiry. In G. D. Phye (Ed.), *Handbook of classroom assessment: Learning, achievement, and adjustment.* San Diego, CA: Academic Press.

Callanan, M. A., & Oakes, L. M. (1992). Preschoolers' questions and parents' explanations: Causal thinking in everyday activity. *Cognitive Development, 7,* 213–233.

Cameron, C. A., Hunt, A. K., & Linton, M. J. (1996). Written expression as recontextualization: Children write in social time. *Educational Psychology Review, 8,* 125–150.

Cameron, J. (2001). Negative effects of reward on intrinsic motivation—a limited phenomenon: Comment on Deci, Koestner, and Ryan (2001). *Review of Educational Research, 71,* 29–42.

Campbell, A. (1984). *The girls in the gang: A report from New York City.* New York: Basil Blackwell.

Campbell, D. T., & Stanley, J. C. (1963). Experimental and quasi-experimental designs for research on teaching. In N. L. Gage (Ed.), *Handbook of research on teaching* (pp. 171–246). Chicago: Rand McNally.

Campbell, D. W., Eaton, W. O., McKeen, N. A., & Mitsutake, G. (1999, April). *The rise and fall of motor activity: Evidence of age-related change from 7 to 14 years.* Paper presented at the biennial meeting of the Society for Research in Child Development, Albuquerque, NM.

Campbell, F. A., & Ramey, C. T. (1994). Effects of early intervention on intellectual and academic achievement: A follow-up study of children from low-income families. *Child Development, 65,* 684–698.

Campbell, F. A., & Ramey, C. T. (1995). Cognitive and school outcomes for high-risk African-American students at middle adolescence: Positive effects of early intervention. *American Educational Research Journal, 32,* 742–772.

Campbell, L., Campbell, B., & Dickinson, D. (1998). *Teaching and learning through multiple intelligences* (2nd ed.). Boston: Allyn & Bacon.

Campbell, T. F., Dollaghan, C. A., Rockette, H. E., Paradise, J. L., Feldman, H. M., Shriberg, L. D., et al. (2003). Risk factors for speech delay of unknown origin in 3-year-old children. *Child Development, 74,* 346–357.

Campione, J. C., Shapiro, A. M., & Brown, A. L. (1995). Forms of transfer in a community of learners: Flexible learning and understanding. In A. McKeough, J. Lupart, & A. Marini (Eds.), *Teaching for transfer: Fostering generalization in learning.* Mahwah, NJ: Erlbaum.

Campos, J. J., Bertenthal, B. I., & Kermoian, R. (1992). Early experiences and emotional development: The emergence of wariness of heights. *Psychological Science, 3,* 61–64.

Campos, J. J., Frankel, C. B., & Camras, L. (2004). On the nature of emotion regulation. *Child Development, 75,* 377–394.

Campos, R., Antunes, C. M., Raffaelli, M., Halsey, N., Ude, W., Greco, M., et al. (1994). Social networks and daily activities of street youth in Belo Horizonte, Brazil. *Child Development, 65,* 319–330.

Camras, L. A., Malatesta, C., & Izard, C. (1991). The development of facial expressions in infancy. In R. S. Feldman & B. Rime (Eds.), *Fundamentals of nonverbal behavior: Studies in emotion and social interaction* (pp. 73–105). New York: Cambridge University Press.

Camras, L. A., Oster, H., Campos, J., Campos, R., Ujiie, T., Miyake, K., et al. (1998). Production of emotional and facial expressions in European American, Japanese, and Chinese infants. *Developmental Psychology, 34,* 616–628.

Cancellaro, C. A. (2001). *Pregnancy stories: Real women share the joys, fears, thrills, and anxieties of pregnancy from conceptions to birth.* Oakland, CA: New Harbinger.

Canfield, R. L., & Smith, E. G. (1996). Number-based expectations and sequential enumeration by 5-month-old infants. *Developmental Psychology, 32,* 269–279.

Capelli, C. A., Nakagawa, N., & Madden, C. M. (1990). How children understand sarcasm: The role of context and intonation. *Child Development, 61,* 1824–1841.

Caplan, J. G., McElvain, C. K., & Walter, K. E. (2001). *Beyond the bell: A tool kit for creating after-school programs* (2nd ed.). Naperville, IL: North Central Regional Educational Laboratory.

Caplan, M., Vespo, J. E., Pedersen, J., & Hay, D. F. (1991). Conflict over resources in small groups of 1- and 2-year-olds. *Child Development, 62,* 1513–1524.

Caplow, T., Bahr, H. M., Chadwick, B. A., Hill, R., & Williamson, M. H. (1982). *Middletown families.* Minneapolis: University of Minnesota Press.

Caprara, G. V., Barbaranelli, C., Pastorelli, C., Bandura, A., & Zimbardo, P. G. (2000). Prosocial foundations of children's academic achievement. *Psychological Science, 11,* 302–306.

Capron, C., & Duyme, M. (1989). Assessment of effects of socio-economic status on IQ in a full cross-fostering study. *Nature, 340,* 552–554.

Cardelle-Elawar, M. (1992). Effects of teaching metacognitive skills to students with low mathematics ability. *Teaching and Teacher Education, 8,* 109–121.

Carey, S. (1978). The child as word learner. In M. Halle, J. Bresnan, & G. Miller (Eds.), *Linguistic theory and psychological reality.* Cambridge, MA: MIT Press.

Carey, S. (1985). *Conceptual change in childhood.* Cambridge, MA: MIT Press.

Carey, S., & Bartlett, E. (1978). Acquiring a single new word. *Papers and Reports on Child Language Development, 15,* 17–29.

Carey, S., Evans, R., Honda, M., Jay, E., & Unger, C. (1989). "An experiment is when you try it and see if it works": A study of grade 7 students' understanding of the construction of scientific knowledge. *International Journal of Science Education, 11,* 514–529.

Carlson, E. A., Sampson, M. C., & Sroufe, L. A. (2003). Implications of attachment theory and research for developmental-behavioral pediatrics. *Journal of Developmental and Behavioral Pediatrics, 24,* 364–379.

Carlson, N. R. (1999). *Foundations of physiological psychology.* Boston: Allyn & Bacon.

Carlson, S. M., & Moses, L. J. (2001). Individual differences in inhibitory control and children's theory of mind. *Child Development, 72,* 1032–1053.

Carns, D. (1973). Talking about sex: Notes on first coitus and the double sexual standard. *Journal of Marriage and the Family, 35,* 677–688.

Caroli, M., Argentieri, L., Cardone, M., & Masi, A. (2004). Role of television in childhood obesity prevention. *International Journal of Obesity, 28,* S105–S108.

Caron, A. J., Caron, R. F., & MacLean, D. J. (1988). Infant discrimination of naturalistic emotional expressions: The role of face and voice. *Child Development, 59,* 604–616.

Carpenter, M., Nagell, K., & Tomasello, M. (1998). Social cognition, joint attention, and communicative competence from 9 to 15 months of age. *Monographs of the Society for Research in Child Development, 63*(4, Serial No. 255). Chicago: University of Chicago Press.

Carr, M., & Biddlecomb, B. (1998). Metacognition in mathematics from a constructivist perspective. In D. J. Hacker, J. Dunlosky, & A. C. Graesser (Eds.), *Metacognition in educational theory and practice* (pp. 69–91). Mahwah, NJ: Erlbaum.

Carr, M., & Schneider, W. (1991). Long-term maintenance of organizational strategies in kindergarten children. *Contemporary Educational Psychology, 16,* 61–72.

Carraher, T. N., Carraher, D. W., & Schliemann, A. D. (1985). Mathematics in the streets and in the schools. *British Journal of Developmental Psychology, 3,* 21–29.

Carroll, J. B. (1992). Cognitive abilities: The state of the art. *Psychological Science, 3,* 266–270.

Carter, D. E., Detine-Carter, S. L., & Benson, F. W. (1995). Interracial acceptance in the classroom. In H. C. Foot, A. J. Chapman, & J. R. Smith (Eds.), *Friendship and social relations in children* (pp. 117–143). New Brunswick, NJ: Transaction.

Carter, K. R. (1991). Evaluation of gifted programs. In N. Buchanan & J. Feldhusen (Eds.), *Conducting research and evaluation in gifted education: A handbook of methods and applications.* New York: Teachers College Press.

Carter, K. R., & Ormrod, J. E. (1982). Acquisition of formal operations by intellectually gifted children. *Gifted Child Quarterly, 26,* 110–115.

Cartledge, G., & Milburn, J. F. (1995). *Teaching social skills to children and youth: Innovative approaches* (3rd ed.). Needham Heights, MA: Allyn & Bacon.

Casanova, U. (1987). Ethnic and cultural differences. In V. Richardson-Koehler (Ed.), *Educator's handbook: A research perspective.* White Plains, NY: Longman.

Case, R. (1985). *Intellectual development: Birth to adulthood.* Orlando, FL: Academic Press.

Case, R., & Mueller, M. P. (2001). Differentiation, integration, and covariance mapping as fundamental processes in cognitive and neurological growth. In J. L. McClelland & R. S. Siegler (Eds.), *Mechanisms of cognitive development: Behavioral and neural perspectives* (pp. 185–219). Mahwah, NJ: Erlbaum.

Case, R., & Okamoto, Y., (1996). The role of central conceptual structures in the development of children's thought. *Monographs of the Society for Research in Child Development, 61*(1–2, Serial No. 246).

Case, R., Okamoto, Y., Henderson, B., & McKeough, A. (1993). Individual variability and consistency in cognitive development: New evidence for the existence of central conceptual structures. In R. Case & W. Edelstein (Eds.), *The new structuralism in cognitive development: Theory and research on individual pathways.* Basel, Switzerland: Karger.

Casella, R. (2001). The cultural foundations of peer mediation: Beyond a behaviorist model of urban school conflict. In J. N. Burstyn, G. Bender, R. Casella, H. W. Gordon, D. P. Guerra, K. V. Luschen, et al. *Preventing violence in schools: A challenge to American democracy* (pp. 159–179). Mahwah, NJ: Erlbaum.

Case-Smith, J. (1996). Fine motor outcomes in preschool children who receive occupational therapy services. *American Journal of Occupational Therapy, 50,* 52–61.

Casey, B. J. (2001). Disruption of inhibitory control in developmental disorders: A mechanistic model of implicated frontostriatal circuitry. In J. L. McClelland & R. S. Siegler (Eds.), *Mechanisms of cognitive development: Behavioral and neural perspectives* (pp. 327–349). Mahwah, NJ: Erlbaum.

Casey, B. J., Giedd, J. N., & Thomas, K. M. (2000). Structural and functional brain development and its relation to cognitive development. *Biological Psychology, 54,* 241–257.

Casey, B. M., McIntire, D. D., & Leveno, K. J. (2001). The continuing value of the Apgar score for the assessment of newborn infants. *New England Journal of Medicine, 344,* 467–471.

Casey, W. M., & Burton, R. V. (1982). Training children to be consistently honest through verbal self-instructions. *Child Development, 53,* 911–919.

Caspi, A. (1998). Personality development across the life course. In W. Damon (Series Ed.) & N. Eisenberg (Vol. Ed.), *Handbook of child psychology: Vol. 3. Social, emotional, and personality development* (5th ed., pp. 311–388). New York: Wiley.

Caspi, A., Taylor, A., Moffitt, T. E., & Plomin, R. (2000). Neighborhood deprivation affects children's mental health: Environmental risks identified in a genetic design. *Psychological Science, 11,* 338–342.

Cassidy, M., & Berlin, L. J. (1994). The insecure/ ambivalent pattern of attachment: Theory and research. *Child Development, 65,* 971–991.

Catania, J. A., Coates, T. J., Stall, R., Turner, H., Peterson, J., Hearst, N., et al. (1992). Prevalence of AIDS-related risk factors and condom use in the United States. *Science, 258,* 1101–1106.

Cattell, R. B. (1963). Theory of fluid and crystallized intelligence: A critical experiment. *Journal of Educational Psychology, 54,* 1–22.

Cattell, R. B. (1980). The heritability of fluid, g_f, and crystallised, g_f, intelligence, estimated by a least squares use of the MAVA method. *British Journal of Educational Psychology, 50,* 253–265.

Cattell, R. B. (1987). *Intelligence: Its structure, growth, and action.* Amsterdam: North-Holland.

Cazden, C. B. (1968). The acquisition of noun and verb inflections. *Child Development, 39,* 433–448.

Cazden, C. B. (1976). Play with language and meta-linguistic awareness: One dimension of language experience. In J. Bruner, A. Jolly, & K. Sylva (Eds.), *Play: Its role in development and evolution.* New York: Basic Books.

Ceci, S. J. (2003). Cast in six ponds and you'll reel in something: Looking back on 25 years of research. *American Psychologist, 58,* 855–864.

Ceci, S. J., & Roazzi, A. (1994). The effects of context on cognition: Postcards from Brazil. In R. J. Sternberg & R. K. Wagner (Eds.), *Mind in context: Interactionist perspectives on human intelligence.* Cambridge, England: Cambridge University Press.

Ceci, S. J., Rosenblum, T. B., & Kumpf, M. (1998). The shrinking gap between high- and low-scoring groups: Current trends and possible causes. In U. Neisser (Ed.), *The rising curve: Long-term gains in IQ and related measures* (pp. 287–302). Washington, DC: American Psychological Association.

Ceci, S. J., & Williams, W. M. (1997). Schooling, intelligence, and income. *American Psychologist, 52,* 1051–1058.

Center for the Future of Children. (1993). Adoption: Overview and major recommendations. *The Future of Children, 3*(1), 4–15.

Center for the Future of Children. (1997). Executive summary: Children and poverty. *The Future of Children, 7*(2), 1–7.

Centers for Disease Control and Prevention. (1996). *Youth risk behavior surveillance—United States, 1995.* Atlanta: U.S. Department of Health and Human Services, Centers for Disease Control and Prevention. Retrieved from http://cdc.gov/mmwr/PDF/ss/ss4504.pdf

Centers for Disease Control and Prevention. (1997). *Pediatric nutrition surveillance: 1997 Executive summary.* Atlanta: U.S. Department of Health and Human Services, Centers for Disease Control and Prevention.

Centers for Disease Control and Prevention. (2002, Fall). *Planning for physical activity* (a BAM! Body and Mind Teacher's Corner resource). Retrieved January 19, 2003, from http://www.bam.gov/teachers/activities/planning.htm

Centers for Disease Control and Prevention. (2004). *Youth risk behavior surveillance—United States, 2003.* Atlanta: Author.

Centers for Disease Control and Prevention. (2005a). *Guidelines for effective school health education to prevent the spread of AIDS.* Retrieved June 19, 2005, from http://www.cdc.gov/HealthyYouth .sexualbehaviors/guidelines/guidelines.htm

Centers for Disease Control and Prevention. (2005b). *Making it happen: School nutrition success stories.* Retrieved May 25, 2005, from http://www.cdc.gov/HealthyYouth/nutrition/Making-It-Happen/success.htm.

Centers for Disease Control and Prevention. (2005c). *Nutrition and the health of young people.* Atlanta: Author.

Centers for Disease Control and Prevention. (2005d). QuickStats: Total and primary cesarean rate and vaginal birth after previous cesarean (VBAC) rate— United States, 1989–2003. *Morbidity and Mortality Weekly Report, 54*(2), 46.

Certo, J., Cauley, K. M., & Chafin, C. (2002, April). *Students' perspectives on their high school experience.* Paper presented at the annual meeting of the American Educational Research Association, New Orleans, LA.

Chafel, J. A. (1991). The play of children: Developmental processes and policy implications. *Child & Youth Care Forum, 20,* 115–132.

Chafel, J. A. (1997). Schooling, the hidden curriculum, and children's conceptions of poverty. *Social Policy Report: Society for Research in Child Development, 11*(1), 1–18.

Chall, J. S. (1996). *Stages of reading development* (2nd ed.). Fort Worth, TX: Harcourt, Brace.

Chalmers, J., & Townsend, M. (1990). The effects of training in social perspective taking on socially maladjusted girls. *Child Development, 61,* 178–190.

Chambers, J. H., & Ascione, F. R. (2001). The effects of prosocial and aggressive videogames on children's donating and helping. *Journal of Genetic Psychology, 148*(4), 499–505.

Chambliss, M. J. (1998, April). *Children as thinkers composing scientific explanations.* Paper presented at the annual meeting of the American Educational Research Association, San Diego, CA.

Champagne, A. B., & Bunce, D. M. (1991). Learning-theory-based science teaching. In S. M. Glynn, R. H. Yeany, & B. K. Britton (Eds.), *The psychology of learning science.* Hillsdale, NJ: Erlbaum.

Chan, C., Burtis, J., & Bereiter, C. (1997). Knowledge building as a mediator of conflict in conceptual change. *Cognition and Instruction, 15,* 1–40.

Chandler, M., & Boyes, M. (1982). Social-cognitive development. In B. Wolman (Ed.), *Handbook of developmental psychology.* Upper Saddle River, NJ: Prentice Hall.

Chandler, M., & Moran, T. (1990). Psychopathy and moral development: A comparative study of delinquent and nondelinquent youth. *Development and Psychopathology, 2,* 227–246.

Chandler, M. J. (1987). The Othello effect: Essay on the emergence and eclipse of skeptical doubt. *Human Development, 30,* 137–159.

Chandler, T. J. L., & Goldberg, A. D. (1990). The academic All-American as vaunted adolescent role-identity. *Sociology of Sport Journal, 7,* 287–293.

Chang, H., & Trehub, S. (1977). Infants' perception of temporal grouping in auditory patterns. *Child Development, 48,* 1666–1670.

Chao, R. K. (1994). Beyond parental control and authoritarian parenting style: Understanding Chinese parenting through the cultural notion of training. *Child Development, 65,* 1111–1119.

Chao, R. K. (2000). Cultural explanations for the role of parenting in the school success of Asian-American children. In R. D. Taylor & M. C. Wang (Eds.), *Resilience across contexts: Family, work, culture, and community* (pp. 333–363). Mahwah, NJ: Erlbaum.

Chapman, J. W., Tunmer, W. E., & Prochnow, J. E. (2000). Early reading-related skills and performance, reading self-concept, and the development of academic self-concept: A longitudinal study. *Journal of Educational Psychology, 92,* 703–708.

Charity, A. H., Scarborough, H. S., & Griffin, D. M. (2004). Familiarity with school English in African American children and its relation to early reading achievement. *Child Development, 75,* 1340–1356.

Charles A. Dana Center. (1999). *Hope for urban education: A study of nine high-performing, high-poverty, urban elementary schools.* Washington, DC: U.S. Department of Education, Planning and Evaluation Service.

Charlesworth, W. R., & LaFreniere, P. (1983). Dominance, friendship, and resource utilization in preschool children's groups. *Ethology and Sociobiology, 4,* 175–186.

Charner, I., & Fraser, B. S. (1988). *Youth and work: What we know, what we don't know, and what we need to know.* Washington, DC: Commission on Work, Family, and Citizenship. (ERIC Document Service No. ED 292 980)

Chase-Lansdale, P. L., & Brooks-Gunn, J. (1994). Correlates of adolescent pregnancy and parenthood. In C. B. Fisher & R. M. Lerner (Eds.), *Applied developmental psychology* (pp. 207–236). New York: McGraw-Hill.

Chase-Lansdale, P. L., Brooks-Gunn, J., & Zamsky, E. S. (1994). Young African-American multigenerational families in poverty: Quality of mothering and grandmothering. *Child Development, 65,* 373–393.

Chasnoff, I. J., Burns, K. A., Burns, W. J., & Schnoll, S H. (1986). Prenatal drug exposure: Effects on neonatal and infant growth and development. *Neurobehavioral Toxicology & Teratology, 8,* 357–362.

Chassin, L., Curran, P. J., Hussong, A. M., & Colder, C. R. (1996). The relation of parent alcoholism to adolescent substance use: A longitudinal follow-up study. *Journal of Abnormal Psychology, 105,* 70–80.

Chavez, A., Martinez, C., & Soberanes, B. (1995). Effects of early malnutrition on late mental and behavioral performance. *Developmental Brain Dysfunction, 8,* 90–102.

Chavkin, N. F. (Ed.). (1993). *Families and schools in a pluralistic society.* Albany: State University of New York Press.

Chavous, T. M., Bernat, D. H., Schmeelk-Cone, K., Caldwell, C. H., Kohn-Wood, L., & Zimmerman, M. A. (2003). Racial identity and academic attainment among African American adolescents. *Child Development, 74,* 1076–1090.

Chazan-Cohen, R., Jerald, J., & Stark, D. R. (2001). A commitment to supporting the mental health of our youngest children. *Zero to Three, 22*(1), 4–12.

Chen, X., Anderson, R. C., Li, W., Hao, M., Wu, X., & Shu, H. (2004). Phonological awareness of bilingual and monolingual Chinese children. *Journal of Educational Psychology, 96,* 142–151.

Chen, X., Rubin, K. H., & Li, Z. (1995). Social functioning and adjustment in Chinese children. *Developmental Psychology, 31,* 531–539.

Chen, X., Rubin, K. H., & Sun, Y. (1992). Social reputation and peer relationships in Chinese and Canadian children: A cross-cultural study. *Child Development, 63,* 1336–1343.

Chen, Z., Sanchez, R. P., & Campbell, T. (1997). From beyond to within their grasp: The rudiments of analogical problem solving in 10- and 13-month-olds. *Developmental Psychology, 33,* 790–801.

Chi, M. T. H. (1978). Knowledge structures and memory development. In R. S. Siegler (Ed.), *Children's thinking: What develops?* Hillsdale, NJ: Erlbaum.

Chinn, C. A., & Brewer, W. F. (1993). The role of anomalous data in knowledge acquisition: A theoretical framework and implications for science instruction. *Review of Educational Research, 63,* 1–49.

Chisholm, J. S. (1996). The evolutionary ecology of attachment organization. *Human Nature, 1,* 1–37.

Chisholm, K., Carter, M. C., Ames, E. W., & Morison, S. J. (1995). Attachment security and indiscriminately friendly behavior in children adopted from Romanian orphanages. *Development and Psychopathology, 7,* 283–297.

Chomsky, C. S. (1969). *The acquisition of syntax in children from 5 to 10.* Cambridge, MA: MIT Press.

Chomsky, N. (1959). Review of B. F. Skinner's *Verbal Behavior. Language, 35,* 26–58.

Chomsky, N. (1965). *Aspects of the theory of syntax.* Cambridge, MA: MIT Press.

Chomsky, N. (1972). *Language and mind* (enlarged ed.). San Diego, CA: Harcourt Brace Jovanovich.

Chomsky, N. (1976). *Reflections on language.* London: Temple Smith.

Christenson, S. L., & Thurlow, M. L. (2004). School dropouts: Prevention, considerations, interventions, and challenges. *Current Directions in Psychological Science, 13,* 36–39.

Christie, J. F., & Johnsen, E. P. (1983). The role of play in social-intellectual development. *Review of Educational Research, 53,* 93–115.

Chu, Y.-W. (2000). *The relationships between domain-specific self-concepts and global self-esteem among adolescents in Taiwan.* Unpublished doctoral dissertation, University of Northern Colorado, Greeley.

Chukovsky, K. (1968). *From two to five* (M. Morton, Trans.). Berkeley: University of California Press.

Cicchetti, D., Rogosch, F. A., & Toth, S. L. (1997). Ontogenesis, depressotypic organization, and the depressive spectrum. In S. S. Luthar, J. A. Burack, D. Cicchetti, & J. R. Weisz (Eds.), *Developmental psychopathology: Perspectives on adjustment, risk, and disorder* (pp. 273–313). Cambridge, England: Cambridge University Press.

Cicchetti, D., & Toth, S. L. (1998). Perspectives on research and practice in developmental psychopathology. In W. Damon (Series Ed.), I. E. Sigel & K. A. Renninger (Vol. Eds.), *Handbook of child psychology: Vol. 4. Child psychology in practice* (5th ed., pp. 479–583). New York: Wiley.

CJ Foundation for SIDS. (2002). *SIDS information.* Retrieved January 19, 2003, from http://www.cjsids.com/sids.htm

Clark, B. (1997). *Growing up gifted* (5th ed.). Upper Saddle River, NJ: Merrill/Prentice Hall.

Clark, C. C. (1992). Deviant adolescent subcultures: Assessment strategies and clinical interventions. *Adolescence, 27*(106), 283–293.

Clark, E. V. (1971). On the acquisition of the meaning of "before" and "after." *Journal of Verbal Learning and Verbal Behavior, 10,* 266–275.

Clark, R. M. (1983). *Family life and school achievement: Why poor Black children succeed or fail.* Chicago: University of Chicago Press.

Clarke-Stewart, K. A. (1989). Infant day care: Maligned or malignant? *American Psychologist, 44,* 266–273.

Clasen, D. R., & Brown, B. B. (1985). The multidimensionality of peer pressure in adolescence. *Journal of Youth and Adolescence, 14,* 451–468.

Claude, D., & Firestone, P. (1995). The development of ADHD boys: A 12-year follow-up. *Canadian Journal of Behavioural Science, 27,* 226–249.

Claverie, J. M. (2001). Gene number: What if there are only 30,000 human genes? *Science, 291*(5507), 1255–1257.

Clifford, M. M. (1990). Students need challenge, not easy success. *Educational Leadership, 48*(1), 22–26.

Cochran, M. (1993). Personal networks in the ecology of human development. In M. Cochran, M. Larner, D. Riley, L. Gunnarsson, & C. R. Henderson, Jr. (Eds.), *Extending families: The social networks of parents and their children* (pp. 1–33). New York: Cambridge University Press.

Cochran-Smith, M., & Lytle, S. (1993). *Inside out: Teacher research and knowledge.* New York: Teachers College Press.

Cocking, R. R., & Greenfield, P. M. (1996). Introduction. In P. M. Greenfield & R. Cocking (Eds.), *Interacting with video* (pp. 3–7). Norwood, NJ: Ablex.

Cody, H., & Kamphaus, R. W. (1999). Down syndrome. In S. Goldstein & C. R. Reynolds (Eds.), *Handbook of neurodevelopmental and genetic disorders* (pp. 385–405). New York: Guilford Press.

Coe, J., Salamon, L., & Molnar, J. (1991). *Homeless children and youth.* New Brunswick, NJ: Transaction.

Cohen, D., & Nisbett, R. E. (1994). Self-protection and the culture of honor: Explaining Southern violence. *Personality and Social Psychology Bulletin, 20,* 551–567.

Cohen, E. G. (1994). Restructuring the classroom: Conditions for productive small groups. *Review of Educational Research, 64,* 1–35.

Cohen, E. G., & Lotan, R. A. (1995). Producing equal-status interaction in the heterogeneous classroom. *American Educational Research Journal, 32,* 99–120.

Cohen, L. B., & Cashon, C. H. (2006). Infant cognition. In W. Damon, R. M. Lerner (Series Eds.), D. Kuhn, & R. Siegler (Vol. Eds.), *Handbook of child psychology: Vol. 1. Cognition, perception, and language* (6th ed.). New York: Wiley.

Cohen, M. N. (1998, April 17). Culture, not race, explains human diversity. *The Chronicle of Higher Education,* p. B4.

Cohen, M. R. (1997). Individual and sex differences in speed of handwriting among high school students. *Perceptual and Motor Skills, 84*(3, Pt. 2), 1428–1430.

Cohen, R. J., & Swerdlik, M. E. (1999). *Psychological testing and assessment.* Mountain View, CA: Mayfield.

Coie, J. D., & Cillessen, A. H. N. (1993). Peer rejection: Origins and effects on children's development. *Current Directions in Psychological Science, 2,* 89–92.

Coie, J. D., & Dodge, K. A. (1988). Multiple sources of data on social behavior and social status. *Child Development, 59,* 815–829.

Coie, J. D., & Dodge, K. A. (1998). Aggression and antisocial behavior. In W. Damon (Series Ed.) & N. Eisenberg (Vol. Ed.), *Handbook of child psychology: Vol. 3. Social, emotional, and personality development* (pp. 779–862). New York: Wiley.

Coie, J. D., Dodge, K. A., Terry, R., & Wright, V. (1991). The role of aggression in peer relations: An analysis of aggression episodes in boys' play groups. *Child Development, 62,* 812–826.

Coie, J. D., & Kupersmidt, J. (1983). A behavioral analysis of emerging social status in boys' groups. *Child Development, 54,* 1400–1416.

Colby, A., & Kohlberg, L. (1984). Invariant sequence and internal consistency in moral judgment stages. In W. M. Kurtines & J. L. Gewirtz (Eds.), *Morality, moral behavior, and moral development.* New York: Wiley.

Colby, A., Kohlberg, L., Gibbs, J., & Lieberman, M. (1983). A longitudinal study of moral judgment. *Monographs of the Society for Research in Child Development, 48*(1–2, Serial No. 200).

Cole, D. A., Martin, J. M., Peeke, L. A., Seroczynski, A. D., & Fier, J. (1999). Children's over- and underestimation of academic competence: A longitudinal study of gender differences, depression, and anxiety. *Child Development, 70,* 459–473.

Cole, D. A., Maxwell, S. E., Martin, J. M., Peeke, L. G., Seroczynski, A. D., Tram, J. M., et al. (2001). The development of multiple domains of child and adolescent self-concept: A cohort sequential longitudinal design. *Child Development, 72,* 1723–1746.

Cole, M. (1990). Cognitive development and formal schooling: The evidence from cross-cultural research. In L. C. Moll (Ed.), *Vygotsky and education* (pp. 89–110). New York: Cambridge University Press.

Cole, M. (2006). Culture and cognitive development in phylogenetic, historical and ontogenetic perspective. In W. Damon, R. M. Lerner (Series Eds.), D. Kuhn, & R. Siegler (Vol. Eds.), *Handbook of child psychology: Vol. 1. Cognition, perception, and language* (6th ed.). New York: Wiley.

Cole, M., & Scribner, S. (1977). Cross-cultural studies of memory and cognition. In R. V. Kail & J. W. Hagen (Eds.), *Perspectives on the development of memory and cognition.* Hillsdale, NJ: Erlbaum.

Cole, P. M. (1986). Children's spontaneous control of facial expression. *Child Development, 57,* 1309–1321.

Cole, P. M., Michel, M. K., & Teti, L. O. (1994). The development of emotion regulation and dysregulation: A clinical perspective. *Monographs of the Society for Research in Child Development, 59*(2–3, Serial No. 240), 73–100.

Coles, R. (1990). *The spiritual life of children*. Boston: Houghton Mifflin.

Coley, R. L., & Chase-Lansdale, P. L. (1998). Adolescent pregnancy and parenthood. *American Psychologist, 53*, 152–166.

Coll, C. G., Crnic, K., Lamberty, G., Wasik, B. J., Jenkins, R., García, H. V., et al. (1996). An integrative model for the study of developmental competencies in minority children. *Child Development, 67*, 1891–1914.

Collaer, M. L., & Hines, M. (1995). Human behavioral sex differences: A role for gonadal hormones during early development? *Psychological Bulletin, 118*, 55–107.

Collie, R., & Hayne, H. (1999). Deferred imitation by 6- and 9-month-old infants: More evidence for declarative memory. *Developmental Psychobiology, 35*, 83–90.

Collier, V. P. (1989). How long? A synthesis of research on academic achievement in a second language. *TESOL Quarterly, 23*, 509–523.

Collier, V. P. (1992). The Canadian bilingual immersion debate: A synthesis of research findings. *Studies in Second Language Acquisition, 14*, 87–97.

Collingwood, T. R. (1997). *Helping at-risk youth through physical fitness programming*. Champaign, IL: Human Kinetics.

Collins, A., Brown, J. S., & Newman, S. E. (1989). Cognitive apprenticeship: Teaching the crafts of reading, writing, and mathematics. In L. B. Resnick (Ed.), *Knowing, learning, and instruction: Essays in honor of Robert Glaser*. Hillsdale, NJ: Erlbaum.

Collins, R. (1999). The adoption and foster care analysis and reporting system: Implications for foster care policy. In P. A. Curtis, G. D. Dale, & J. C. Kendall (Eds.), *The foster care crisis: Translating research into policy and practice* (pp. 45–59). Lincoln: University of Nebraska Press.

Collins, W. A. (1990). Parent-child relationships in the transition to adolescence: Continuity and change in interaction, affects, and cognition. In R. Montemayor, G. Adams, & T. Gullota (Eds.), *Advances in adolescent development* (Vol. 2). Beverly Hills, CA: Sage.

Collins, W. A., Maccoby, E. E., Steinberg, L., Hetherington, E. M., & Bornstein, M. H. (2000). Contemporary research on parenting: The case for nature and nurture. *American Psychologist, 55*, 218–232.

Collins, W. A., & Sroufe, L. A. (1999). Capacity for intimate relationships: A developmental construction. In W. Furman, B. B. Brown, & C. Feiring (Eds.), *The development of romantic relationships in adolescence* (pp. 125–147). Cambridge, England: Cambridge University Press.

Colombo, J. (1993). *Infant cognition: Predicting later intellectual functioning*. Newbury Park, CA: Sage.

Commons, M. L., Richards, F. A., & Armon, C. (Eds.). (1984). *Beyond formal operations*. New York: Praeger.

Comstock, G. (with Paik, H.). (1991). *Television and the American child*. San Diego, CA: Academic Press.

Condon, J. C., & Yousef, F. S. (1975). *An introduction to intercultural communication*. Indianapolis, IN: Bobbs-Merrill.

Condry, J. C., & Ross, D. F. (1985). Sex and aggression: The influence of gender label on the perception of aggression in children. *Child Development, 56*, 225–233.

Conel, J. L. (1939–1975). *Postnatal development of the human cerebral cortex* (Vols. 1–8). Cambridge, MA: Harvard University Press.

Conn, J., & Kanner, L. (1940). Spontaneous erections in childhood. *Journal of Pediatrics, 16*, 237–240.

Connell, J. P. (1990). Context, self, and action: A motivational analysis of self-system processes across the life span. In D. Cicchetti & M. Beeghly (Eds.), *The self in transition: Infancy to childhood*. Chicago: University of Chicago Press.

Connolly, J., & Goldberg, A. (1999). Romantic relationships in adolescence: The role of friends and peers in their emergence and development. In W. Furman, B. B. Brown, & C. Feiring (Eds.), *The development of romantic relationships in adolescence* (pp. 266–290). Cambridge, England: Cambridge University Press.

Conroy, M., Hess, R. D., Azuma, H., & Kashiwagi, K. (1980). Maternal strategies for regulating children's behavior: Japanese and American families. *Journal of Cross-Cultural Psychology, 11*, 153–172.

Consortium of Longitudinal Studies (Ed.). (1983). *As the twig is bent: Lasting effects of preschool programs*. Mahwah, NJ: Erlbaum.

Conte, R. (1991). Attention disorders. In B. Y. L. Wong (Ed.), *Learning about learning disabilities*. San Diego, CA: Academic Press.

Cook, V., & Newson, M. (1996). *Chomsky's universal grammar: An introduction* (2nd ed.). Oxford, England: Blackwell.

Cooney, J. B, & Ladd, S. F. (1992). The influence of verbal protocol methods on children's mental computation. *Learning and Individual Differences, 4*, 237–257.

Cooney, J. B., Swanson, H. L., & Ladd, S. F. (1988). Acquisition of mental multiplication skill: Evidence for the transition between counting and retrieval strategies. *Cognition and Instruction, 5*, 323–345.

Cooper, C. R., Denner, J., & Lopez, E. M. (1999, Fall). Cultural brokers: Helping Latino children on pathways toward success. *The Future of Children: When School Is Out, 9*, 51–57.

Cooper, C. R., Jackson, J. F., Azmitia, M., Lopez, E., & Dunbar, N. (1995). Bridging students' multiple worlds: African American and Latino youth in academic outreach programs. In R. F. Macias & R. G. Garcia-Ramos (Eds.), *Changing schools for changing students: An anthology of research on language minorities* (pp. 211–234). Santa Barbara: University of California Linguistic Minority Research Institute.

Cooper, H., Charlton, K., Valentine, J. C., & Muhlenbruck, L. (2000). Making the most of summer school: A meta-analytic and narrative review. *Monographs of the Society for Research in Child Development, 65*(1, Serial No. 260).

Cooper, H., & Dorr, N. (1995). Race comparisons on need for achievement: A meta-analytic alternative to Graham's narrative review. *Review of Educational Research, 65*, 483–508.

Cooper, H., & Valentine, J. C. (2001). Using research to answer practical questions about homework. *Educational Psychologist, 36*, 143–153.

Cooper, H., Valentine, J. C., Nye, B., & Lindsay, J. J. (1999). Relationships between five after-school activities and academic achievement. *Journal of Educational Psychology, 91*, 369–378.

Cooper, R. P., & Aslin, R. N. (1990). Preference for infant-directed speech in the first month after birth. *Child Development, 61*, 1584–1595.

Coopersmith, S. (1967). *The antecedents of self-esteem*. San Francisco: Freeman.

Cornell, D. G., Pelton, G. M., Bassin, L. E., Landrum, M., Ramsay, S. G., Cooley, M. R., et al. (1990). Self-concept and peer status among gifted program youth. *Journal of Educational Psychology, 82*, 456–463.

Corno, L., & Mandinach, E. B. (2004). What we have learned about student engagement in the past twenty years. In D. M. McInerney & S. Van Etten (Eds.), *Big theories revisited* (pp. 299–328). Greenwich, CT: Information Age.

Corsaro, W. A. (1985). *Friendship and peer culture in the early years*. Norwood, NJ: Ablex.

Corsaro, W. A., & Molinari, L. (2005). *I compagni: Understanding children's transition from preschool to elementary school*. New York: Teachers College Press.

Cossu, G. (1999). The acquisition of Italian orthography. In M. Harris & G. Hatano (Eds.), *Learning to read and write: A cross-linguistic perspective*. Cambridge, England: Cambridge University Press.

Cota-Robles, S., & Adams, M. (1999, April). *The role of puberty in non-violent delinquency among Anglo-American, Hispanic, and African American boys*. Paper presented at the biennial meeting of the Society for Research in Child Development, Albuquerque, NM.

Cottrol, R. J. (1990). America the multicultural. *American Educator, 14*(4), 18–21.

Council for Exceptional Children. (1995). *Toward a common agenda: Linking gifted education and school reform*. Reston, VA: Author.

Courage, M. L., & Adams, R. J. (1990). Visual acuity assessment from birth to three years using the acuity card procedure: Cross-sectional and longitudinal samples. *Optometry and Vision Science, 67*, 713–718.

Covington, M. V. (1987). Achievement motivation, self-attributions, and the exceptional learner. In J. D. Day & J. G. Borkowski (Eds.), *Intelligence and exceptionality*. Norwood, NJ: Ablex.

Covington, M. V. (1992). *Making the grade: A self-worth perspective on motivation and school reform*. Cambridge, England: Cambridge University Press.

Cowan, W. M. (1979). The development of the brain. *Scientific American, 241*, 106–117.

Cox, C. B. (2000). *Empowering grandparents raising grandchildren*. New York: Springer.

Craft, D. H. (1995). Visual impairments and hearing losses. In J. P. Winnick (Ed.), Adapted physical education and sport (2nd ed., pp. 143–166). Champaign, IL: Human Kinetics.

Craft, M. (1984). Education for diversity. In M. Craft (Ed.), *Educational and cultural pluralism*. London: Falmer Press.

Crago, M. B. (1988). *Cultural context in the communicative interaction of young Inuit children*. Unpublished doctoral dissertation, McGill University, Montreal, Canada.

Crago, M. B., Allen, S. E. M., & Hough-Eyamie, W. P. (1997). Exploring innateness through cultural and linguistic variation. In M. Gopnik (Ed.), *The inheritance and innateness of grammars*. New York: Oxford University Press.

Crago, M. B., Annahatak, B., & Ningiuruvik, L. (1993). Changing patterns of language socialization in Inuit homes. *Anthropology and Education Quarterly, 24*, 205–223.

Crain, W. (2000). *Theories of development: Concepts and applications* (4th ed.). Upper Saddle River, NJ: Prentice Hall.

Crawley, A. M., Anderson, D. R., Wilder, A., Williams, M., & Santomero, A. (1999). Effects of repeated exposures to a single episode of the television program *Blue's Clues* on the viewing behaviors and comprehension of preschool children. *Journal of Educational Psychology, 91*, 630–637.

Creasey, G. L., Jarvis, P. A., & Berk, L. E. (1998). Play and social competence. In O. N. Saracho & B. Spodek (Eds.), *Multiple perspectives on play in early childhood education*. Albany: State University of New York Press.

Crick, N. R., Casas, J. F., & Nelson, D. A. (2002). Toward a more comprehensive understanding of peer maltreatment: Studies of relational victimization. *Current Directions in Psychological Science, 11*, 98–101.

Crick, N. R., & Dodge, K. A. (1994). A review and reformulation of social information-processing mechanisms in children's social adjustment. *Psychological Bulletin, 115*, 74–101.

Crick, N. R., & Dodge, K. A. (1996). Social information-processing mechanisms in reactive and proactive aggression. *Child Development, 67*, 993–1002.

Crick, N. R., Grotpeter, J. K., & Bigbee, M. A. (2002). Relationally and physically aggressive children's intent attributions and feelings of distress for relational and instrumental peer provocation. *Child Development, 73*, 1134–1142.

Crockett, L., Losoff, M., & Peterson, A. C. (1984). Perceptions of the peer group and friendship in early adolescence. *Journal of Early Adolescence, 4*, 155–181.

Cromer, R. F. (1993). Language growth with experience without feedback. In P. Bloom (Ed.), *Language acquisition: Core readings.* Cambridge, MA: MIT Press.

Cross, W. E., Jr., Strauss, L., & Fhagen-Smith, P. (1999). African American identity development across the life span: Educational implications. In R. H. Sheets & E. R. Hollins (Eds.), *Racial and ethnic identity in school practices: Aspects of human development* (pp. 29–47). Mahwah, NJ: Erlbaum.

Crouter, A. C. (1994). Processes linking families and work: Implications for behavior and development in both settings. In R. D. Parke & S. G. Killam (Eds.), *Exploring family relationships with other social contexts.* Hillsdale, NJ: Erlbaum.

Crouter, A. C., & Bumpus, M. F. (2001). Linking parents' work stress to children's and adolescents' psychological adjustment. *Current Directions in Psychological Science, 10*, 156–159.

Crowley, K., & Jacobs, M. (2002). Building islands of expertise in everyday family activity. In G. Leinhardt, K. Crowley, & K. Knutson (Eds.), *Learning conversations in museums* (pp. 333–356). Mahwah, NJ: Erlbaum.

Csikszentmihalyi, M. (1995). Education for the twenty-first century. *Daedalus, 124*(4), 107–114.

Csikszentmihalyi, M., & Larson, R. (1984). *Being adolescent: Conflict and growth in the teenage years.* New York: Basic Books.

Cunningham, A. E., & Stanovich, K. E. (1997). Early reading acquisition and its relation to reading experience and ability. *Developmental Psychology, 33*, 934–945.

Cunningham, C. E., & Cunningham, L. J. (1998). Student-mediated conflict resolution programs. In R. A. Barkley (Ed.), *Attention-deficit hyperactivity disorder: A handbook for diagnosis and treatment* (2nd ed., pp. 491–509). New York: Guilford Press.

Cunningham, T. H., & Graham, C. R. (2000). Increasing native English vocabulary recognition through Spanish immersion: Cognate transfer from foreign to first language. *Journal of Educational Psychology, 92*, 37–49.

Curtiss, S. (1977). *Genie: A psycholinguistic study of a modern-day "wild child."* New York: Academic Press.

Cutforth, N. J. (1997). What's worth doing: Reflections of an after-school program in a Denver elementary school. *Quest, 49*, 130–139.

Dacey, J., & Kenny, M. (1994). *Adolescent development.* Madison, WI: William C. Brown.

Dahlberg, G., Moss, P., & Pence, A. (1999). *Beyond quality in early childhood education and care: Postmodern perspectives.* London: Falmer Press.

d'Ailly, H. (2003). Children's autonomy and perceived control in learning: A model of motivation and achievement in Taiwan. *Journal of Educational Psychology, 95*, 84–96.

Dale, P. S. (1976). *Language development: Structure and function* (2nd ed.). New York: Holt, Rinehart & Winston.

Daley, T. C., Whaley, S. E., Sigman, M. D., Espinosa, M. P., & Neumann, C. (2003). IQ on the rise: The Flynn effect in rural Kenyan children. *Psychological Science, 14*, 215–219.

Dalrymple, N. J. (1995). Environmental supports to develop flexibility and independence. In K. A. Quill (Ed.), *Teaching children with autism: Strategies to enhance communication and socialization.* New York: Delmar.

Damon, W. (1977). *The social world of the child.* San Francisco: Jossey-Bass.

Damon, W. (1980). Patterns of change in children's social reasoning: A two-year longitudinal study. *Child Development, 51*, 1010–1017.

Damon, W. (1981). Exploring children's social cognitions on two fronts. In J. M. Flavell & L. Ross (Eds.), *Social cognitive development: Frontiers and possible futures* (pp. 154–175). Cambridge, England: Cambridge University Press.

Damon, W. (1984). Peer education: The untapped potential. *Journal of Applied Developmental Psychology, 5*, 331–343.

Damon, W. (1988). *The moral child: Nurturing children's natural moral growth.* New York: Free Press.

Damon, W. (1991). Putting substance into self-esteem: A focus on academic and moral values. *Educational Horizons, 70*(1), 12–18.

Damon, W., & Hart, D. (1988). *Self-understanding in childhood and adolescence.* New York: Cambridge University Press.

DanceSafe. (2000a). *What is LSD?* Retrieved November 1, 2005, from http://www.dancesafe .org/documents/druginfo/lsd.php

DanceSafe. (2000b). *What is speed?* Oakland, CA: Author. Retrieved November 1, 2005, from http://www.dancesafe.org/documents/druginfo/ speed.php

Dannemiller, J. L., & Stephens, B. R. (1988). A critical test of infant pattern preference models. *Child Development, 59*, 210–216.

Danner, F. W., & Day, M. C. (1977). Eliciting formal operations. *Child Development, 48*, 1600–1606.

Darling-Hammond, L. (1995). Inequality and access to knowledge. In J. A. Banks & C. A. M. Banks (Eds.), *Handbook of research on multicultural education.* New York: Macmillan.

Davenport, E. C., Jr., Davison, M. L., Kuang, H., Ding, S., Kim, S., & Kwak, N. (1998). High school mathematics course-taking by gender and ethnicity. *American Educational Research Journal, 35*, 497–514.

Davidson, F. H. (1976). Ability to respect persons compared to ethnic prejudice in childhood. *Journal of Personality and Social Psychology, 34*, 1256–1267.

Davidson, P., & Youniss, J. (1995). Moral development and social construction. In W. M. Kurtines & J. L. Gewirtz (Eds.), *Moral development: An introduction.* Boston: Allyn & Bacon.

Davis, B. (2001). The restorative power of emotions in Child Protective Services. *Child and Adolescent Social Work Journal, 18*, 437–454.

Davis, G. A., & Rimm, S. B. (1998). *Education of the gifted and talented* (4th ed.). Boston: Allyn & Bacon.

Davis, G. A., & Thomas, M. A. (1989). *Effective schools and effective teachers.* Needham Heights, MA: Allyn & Bacon.

Davis, H. A. (2003). Conceptualizing the role and influence of student-teacher relationships on children's social and cognitive development. *Educational Psychologist, 38*, 207–234.

Davis, H. A., Schutz, P. A., & Chambless, C. B. (2001, April). *Uncovering the impact of social relationships in the classroom: Viewing relationships with teachers from different lenses.* Paper presented at the annual meeting of the American Educational Research Association, Seattle, WA.

Davis-Kean, P. E., & Sandler, H. M. (2001). A meta-analysis of measures of self-esteem for young children: A framework for future measures. *Child Development, 72*, 887–906.

Dawson, D. A. (1991). Family structure and children's health and well-being: Data from the 1988 National Health Interview Survey on Child Health. *Journal of Marriage and the Family, 53*, 573–584.

Dawson, G., Carver, L., Meltzoff, A. N., Panagiotides, H., McPartland, J., & Webb, S. J. (2002). Neural correlates of face and object recognition in young children with autism spectrum disorder, developmental delay, and typical development. *Child Development, 73*, 700–717.

Dawson, G., Munson, J., Estes, A., Osterling, J., McPartland, J., Toth, K., et al. (2002). Neurocognitive function and joint attention ability in young children with autism spectrum disorder versus developmental delay. *Child Development, 73*, 345–358.

Deal, L. W., Gomby, D. S., Zippiroli, L., & Behrman, R. E. (2000). Unintentional injuries in childhood: Analysis and recommendations. *Future of Children, 10*(1), 4–22.

Deater-Deakard, K., Dodge, K., Bates, J., & Pettit, G. (1996). Physical discipline among African American and European American mothers: Links to children's externalizing behaviors. *Developmental Psychology, 32*, 1065–1072.

Deaux, K. (1984). From individual differences to social categories: Analysis of a decade's research on gender. *American Psychologist, 39*, 105–116.

DeCasper, A. J., & Fifer, W. P. (1980). Of human bonding: Newborns prefer their mothers' voices. *Science, 208*, 1174–1176.

DeCasper, A. J., & Spence, M. J. (1986). Prenatal maternal speech influences newborns' perception of speech sounds. *Infant Behavior and Development, 9*, 133–150.

De Cecco, J. P., & Parker, D. A. (1995). The biology of homosexuality: Sexual orientation or sexual preference. *Journal of Homosexuality, 28*, 1–27.

deCharms, R. (1984). Motivation enhancement in educational settings. In R. Ames & C. Ames (Eds.), *Research on motivation in education: Vol. 1. Student motivation.* Orlando, FL: Academic Press.

Deci, E. L. (1992). The relation of interest to the motivation of behavior: A self-determination theory perspective. In K. A. Renninger, S. Hidi, & A. Krapp (Eds.), *The role of interest in learning and development.* Hillsdale, NJ: Erlbaum.

Deci, E. L., & Ryan, R. M. (1985). *Intrinsic motivation and self-determination in human behavior.* New York: Plenum Press.

Deci, E. L., & Ryan, R. M. (1987). The support of autonomy and the control of behavior. *Journal of Personality and Social Psychology, 53*, 1024–1037.

Deci, E. L., & Ryan, R. M. (1992). The initiation and regulation of intrinsically motivated learning and achievement. In A. K. Boggiano & T. S. Pittman (Eds.), *Achievement and motivation: A social-developmental perspective.* Cambridge, England: Cambridge University Press.

Deci, E. L., & Ryan, R. M. (1995). Human autonomy: The basis for true self-esteem. In M. H. Kernis (Ed.), *Efficacy, agency, and self-esteem.* New York: Plenum Press.

De Corte, E., Greer, B., & Verschaffel, L. (1996). Mathematics teaching and learning. In D. C. Berliner & R. C. Calfee (Eds.), *Handbook of educational psychology.* New York: Macmillan.

De Corte, E., Op't Eynde, P., & Verschaffel, L. (2002). "Knowing what to believe": The relevance of students' mathematical beliefs for mathematics education. In B. K. Hofer & P. R. Pintrich (Eds.), *Personal epistemology: The psychology of beliefs about knowledge and knowing* (pp. 297–320). Mahwah, NJ: Erlbaum.

de Jong, T., & van Joolingen, W. R. (1998). Scientific discovery learning with computer simulations of conceptual domains. *Review of Educational Research, 68*, 179–201.

DeKlynen, M., Speltz, M. L., & Greenberg, M. T. (1998). Fathering and early onset of conduct problems: Positive and negative parenting, father-son attachment, and the marital context. *Clinical Child and Family Psychology Review, 1*, 3–28.

Dekovic, M., & Janssens, J. M. (1992). Parents' child-rearing style and child's sociometric status. *Developmental Psychology, 28,* 925–932.

DeLain, M. T., Pearson, P. D., & Anderson, R. C. (1985). Reading comprehension and creativity in Black language use: You stand to gain by playing the sounding game! *American Educational Research Journal, 22,* 155–173.

DeLamater, J., & MacCorquodale, P. (1979). *Premarital sexuality: Attitudes, relationships, behavior.* Madison: University of Wisconsin Press.

De La Paz, S., Swanson, P. N., & Graham, S. (1998). The contribution of executive control to the revising by students with writing and learning difficulties. *Journal of Educational Psychology, 90,* 448–460.

Delgado-Gaitan, C. (1992). School matters in the Mexican-American home: Socializing children to education. *American Educational Research Journal, 29,* 495–513.

Delgado-Gaitan, C. (1994). Socializing young children in Mexican-American families: An intergenerational perspective. In P. M. Greenfield & R. R. Cocking (Eds.), *Cross-cultural roots of minority child development* (pp. 55–86). Hillsdale, NJ: Erlbaum.

DeLisi, R., & Gallagher, A. M. (1991). Understanding of gender stability and constancy in Argentinian children. *Merrill-Palmer Quarterly, 37,* 483–502.

De Lisi, R., & Golbeck, S. L. (1999). Implications of Piagetian theory for peer learning. In A. M. O'Donnell & A. King (Eds.), *Cognitive perspectives on peer learning* (pp. 3–37). Mahwah, NJ: Erlbaum.

De Lisi, R., & Wolford, J. I. (2002). Improving children's mental rotation accuracy with computer game playing. *Journal of Genetic Psychology, 16*(3), 272–282.

DeLisle, J. R. (1984). *Gifted children speak out.* New York: Walker.

DeLoache, J. S., Cassidy, D. J., & Brown, A. L. (1985). Precursors of mnemonic strategies in very young children's memory. *Child Development, 56,* 125–137.

DeLoache, J. S., Miller, K. F., & Rosengren, K. S. (1997). The credible shrinking room: Very young children's performance with symbolic and nonsymbolic relations. *Psychological Science, 8,* 308–313.

DeLoache, J. S., & Todd, C. M. (1988). Young children's use of spatial categorization as a mnemonic strategy. *Journal of Experimental Child Psychology, 46,* 1–20.

Demarest, R. J., & Charon, R. (1996). *An illustrated guide to human reproduction and fertility control.* New York: Parthenon.

DeMarie-Dreblow, D., & Miller, P. H. (1988). The development of children's strategies for selective attention: Evidence for a transitional period. *Child Development, 59,* 1504–1513.

deMarrais, K. B., Nelson, P. A., & Baker, J. H. (1994). Meaning in mud: Yup'ik Eskimo girls at play. In J. L. Roopnarine, J. E. Johnson, & F. H. Hooper (Eds.), *Children's play in diverse cultures.* Albany, NY: SUNY Press.

Dempster, F. N., & Corkill, A. J. (1999). Interference and inhibition in cognition and behavior: Unifying themes for educational psychology. *Educational Psychology Review, 11,* 1–88.

Denkla, M. B. (1986). New diagnostic criteria for autism and related behavioral disorders: Guidelines for research protocols. *Journal of the American Academy of Child Psychiatry, 25,* 221–224.

Dennis, T. A., Cole, P. M., Zahn-Waxler, C., & Mizuta, I. (2002). Self in context: Autonomy and relatedness in Japanese and U.S. mother-preschooler dyads. *Child Development, 73,* 1803–1817.

Dennis, W. (1960). Causes of retardation among institutionalized children: Iran. *Journal of Genetic Psychology, 96,* 47–59.

DeRidder, L. M. (1993). Teenage pregnancy: Etiology and educational interventions. *Educational Psychology Review, 5,* 87–107.

Deshler, D. D., & Schumaker, J. B. (1988). An instructional model for teaching students how to learn. In J. L. Graden, J. E. Zins, & M. J. Curtis (Eds.), *Alternative educational delivery systems: Enhancing instructional options for all students.* Washington, DC: National Association of School Psychologists.

Deutsch, D., Henthorn, T., & Dolson, M. (2004). Absolute pitch, speech, and tone language: Some experiments and a proposed framework. *Music Perception, 21,* 339–356.

Deutsch, M. (1993). Educating for a peaceful world. *American Psychologist, 48,* 510–517.

Deutsch, N. L., & Hirsch, B. J. (2001, April). *A place to call home: Youth organizations in the lives of inner city adolescents.* Paper presented at the biennial meeting of the Society for Research in Child Development, Minneapolis, MN.

DeVault, G., Krug, C., & Fake, S. (1996, September). Why does Samantha act that way: Positive behavioral support leads to successful inclusion. *Exceptional Parent,* 43–47.

de Villiers, J. (1995). Empty categories and complex sentences: The case of wh- questions. In P. Fletcher & B. MacWhinney (Eds.), *The handbook of child language* (pp. 508–540). Oxford, England: Blackwell.

Devine, P. G. (1995). Prejudice and out-group perception. In A. Tesser (Ed.), *Advanced social psychology.* New York: McGraw-Hill.

Devlin, B., Fienberg, S. E., Resnick, D. P., & Roeder, K. (1995). Galton redux: Intelligence, race, and society: A review of "The Bell Curve: Intelligence and Class Structure in American Life." *American Statistician, 90,* 1483–1488.

DeVoe, J. F., Peter, K., Kaufman, P., Ruddy, S. A., Miller, A. K., Planty, M., et al. (2003). *Indicators of school crime and safety: 2002* (NCES 2003-009/NCJ 196753). Washington, DC: U.S. Departments of Education and Justice.

DeVries, R. (1997). Piaget's social theory. *Educational Researcher, 26*(2), 4–17.

DeVries, R., & Zan, B. (1996). A constructivist perspective on the role of the sociomoral atmosphere in promoting children's development. In C. T. Fosnot (Ed.), *Constructivism: Theory, perspectives, and practice.* New York: Teachers College Press.

Dewey, K. G., Heinig, M. J., & Nommsen-Rivers, L. A. (1995). Differences in morbidity between breast-fed and formula-fed infants. *Journal of Pediatrics, 126,* 696–702.

Deyhle, D., & LeCompte, M. (1999). Cultural differences in child development: Navajo adolescents in middle schools. In R. H. Sheets & E. R. Hollins (Eds.), *Racial and ethnic identity in school practices: Aspects of human development* (pp. 123–139). Mahwah, NJ: Erlbaum.

Diagram Group. (1983). *The human body on file.* New York: Facts on File.

Diamond, L. M., Savin-Williams, R. C., & Dubé, E. M. (1999). Sex, dating, passionate friendships, and romance: Intimate peer relations among lesbian, gay, and bisexual adolescents. In W. Furman, B. B. Brown, & C. Feiring (Eds.), *The development of romantic relationships in adolescence* (pp. 175–210). Cambridge, England: Cambridge University Press.

Diamond, M., & Hopson, J. (1998). *Magic trees of the mind.* New York: Dutton.

Diamond, S. C. (1991). What to do when you can't do anything: Working with disturbed adolescents. *Clearing House, 64,* 232–234.

Diaz, R. M. (1983). Thought and two languages: The impact of bilingualism on cognitive development. In E. W. Gordon (Ed.), *Review of research in education* (Vol. 10). Washington, DC: American Educational Research Association.

Diaz, R. M., & Berndt, T. J. (1982). Children's knowledge of best friend: Fact or fancy? *Developmental Psychology, 18,* 787–794.

Diaz, R. M., & Klingler, C. (1991). Toward an explanatory model of the interaction between bilingualism and cognitive development. In E. Bialystok (Ed.), *Language processing in bilingual children.* Cambridge, England: Cambridge University Press.

Dickinson, D., Wolf, M., & Stotsky, S. (1993). Words move: The interwoven development of oral and written language. In J. B. Gleason (Ed.), *The development of language.* Boston: Allyn & Bacon.

Dick-Read, G. (1944). *Childbirth without fear.* New York: Harper & Brothers.

Dien, T. (1998). Language and literacy in Vietnamese American communities. In B. Pérez (Ed.), *Sociocultural contexts of language and literacy.* Mahwah, NJ: Erlbaum.

Digman, J. M. (1989). Five robust trait dimensions: Development, stability, and utility. *Journal of Personality, 57,* 195–214.

Diller, D. (1999). Opening the dialogue: Using culture as a tool in teaching young African American children. *The Reading Teacher, 52,* 820–828.

diSessa, A. A. (1996). What do "just plain folk" know about physics? In D. R. Olson & N. Torrance (Eds.), *The handbook of education and human development: New models of learning, teaching, and schooling.* Cambridge, MA: Blackwell.

Dishion, T. J., Andrews, D. W., & Crosby, L. (1995). Antisocial boys and their friends in early adolescence: Relationship characteristics, quality, and interactional process. *Child Development, 66,* 139–151.

Dishion, T. J., Spracklen, K. M., Andrews, D. W., & Patterson, G. R. (1996). Deviancy training in male adolescents' friendships. *Behavior Therapy, 27,* 373–390.

Dixon, M. R., & Cummings, A. (2001). Self-control in children with autism: Response allocation during delays to reinforcement. *Journal of Applied Behavior Analysis, 34,* 491–495.

Dodge, K. A. (1983). Behavioral antecedents of peer social status. *Child Development, 54,* 1386–1399.

Dodge, K. A. (1986). A social information-processing model of social competence in children. In M. Perlmutter (Ed.), *Minnesota symposia on child psychology: Vol. 18. Cognitive perspectives in children's social and behavioral development.* Hillsdale, NJ: Erlbaum.

Dodge, K. A. (1991). Emotion and social information processing. In J. Garber & K. A. Dodge (Eds.), *The development of emotion regulation and dysregulation.* Cambridge, England: Cambridge University Press.

Dodge, K. A., Bates, J. E., & Pettit, G. S. (1990). Mechanisms in the cycle of violence. *Science, 250,* 1678–1683.

Dodge, K. A., Coie, J. D., & Brakke, N. P. (1982). Behavior patterns of socially rejected and neglected preadolescents: The role of social approach and aggression. *Journal of Abnormal Child Psychology, 10,* 389–410.

Dodge, K. A., Lansford, J. E., Burks, V. S., Bates, J. E., Pettit, G. S., Fontaine, R., et al. (2003). Peer rejection and social information-processing factors in the development of aggressive behavior problems in children. *Child Development, 74,* 374–393.

Dodge, K. A., Pettit, G. S., Bates, J. E., & Valente, E. (1995). Social information processing patterns partially mediate the effect of early physical abuse on later conduct problems. *Journal of Abnormal Psychology, 104,* 632–643.

Dodge, K. A., Schlundt, D. G., Schocken, I., & Delugach, J. D. (1983). Social competence and children's social status: The role of peer group entry strategies. *Merrill-Palmer Quarterly, 29,* 309–336.

Doescher, S. M., & Sugawara, A. I. (1989). Encouraging prosocial behavior in young children. *Childhood Education, 65,* 213–216.

Donaldson, M. (1978). *Children's minds.* New York: Norton.

Donaldson, S. K., & Westerman, M. A. (1986). Development of children's understanding of ambivalence and causal theories of emotion. *Developmental Psychology, 22,* 655–662.

Donato, F., Assanelli, D., Chiesa, R., Poeta, M. L., Tomansoni, V., & Turla, C. (1997). Cigarette smoking and sports participation in adolescents: A cross-sectional survey among high school students in Italy. *Substance Use and Misuse, 32,* 1555–1572.

Donovan, C. A. (1999, April). *"Stories have a beginning, a middle, and an end. Information only has a beginning": Elementary school children's genre and writing development.* Paper presented at the annual meeting of the American Educational Research Association, San Diego, CA.

Dornbusch, S. M., Carlsmith, J. M., Gross, R. T., Martin, J. A., Jennings, D., Rosenberg, A., et al. (1981). Sexual development, age, and dating: A comparison of biological and social influences upon one set of behaviors. *Child Development, 52,* 179–185.

Dornbusch, S. M., Ritter, P. L., Leiderman, P. H., Roberts, D. F., & Fraleigh, M. J. (1987). The relation of parenting style to adolescent school performance. *Child Development, 58,* 1244–1257.

Dorris, M. (1989). *The broken cord.* New York: Harper & Row.

Dougherty, T. M., & Haith, M. M. (1997). Infant expectations and reaction time as predictors of childhood speed of processing and IQ. *Developmental Psychology, 33,* 146–155.

Dovidio, J. F., & Gaertner, S. L. (1999). Reducing prejudice: Combating intergroup biases. *Current Directions in Psychological Science, 8,* 101–105.

Downey, G., Bonica, C., & Rincón, C. (1999). Rejection sensitivity and adolescent romantic relationships. In W. Furman, B. B. Brown, & C. Feiring (Eds.), *The development of romantic relationships in adolescence* (pp. 148–174). Cambridge, England: Cambridge University Press.

Downey, G., Lebolt, A., Rincón, C., & Freitas, A. L. (1998). Rejection sensitivity and children's interpersonal difficulties. *Child Development, 69,* 1074–1091.

Downey, J. (2000, March). *The role of schools in adolescent resilience: Recommendations from the literature.* Paper presented at the International Association of Adolescent Health, Washington, DC.

Dowson, M., & McInerney, D. M. (2001). Psychological parameters of students' social and work avoidance goals: A qualitative investigation. *Journal of Educational Psychology, 93,* 35–42.

Doyle, A. (1982). Friends, acquaintances, and strangers: The influence of familiarity and ethnolinguistic background on social interaction. In K. H. Rubin & H. S. Ross (Eds.), *Peer relationships and social skills in childhood* (pp. 229–252). New York: Springer-Verlag.

Doyle, W. (1986). Classroom organization and management. In M. C. Wittrock (Ed.), *Handbook of research on teaching* (3rd ed.). New York: Macmillan.

Dryden, M. A., & Jefferson, P. (1994, April). *Use of background knowledge and reading achievement among elementary school students.* Paper presented at the annual meeting of the American Educational Research Association, New Orleans, LA.

Dryfoos, J. G. (1999, Fall). The role of the school in children's out-of-school time. *The Future of Children: When School Is Out, 9,* 117–134.

Dube, E. F. (1982). Literacy, cultural familiarity, and "intelligence" as determinants of story recall. In U. Neisser (Ed.), *Memory observed: Remembering in natural contexts.* San Francisco: Freeman.

Dube, M., Julien, D., Lebeau, E., & Gagnon, I. (2000). Marital satisfaction of mothers and the quality of daily interaction with their adolescents. *Canadian Journal of Behavioural Science, 32,* 18–28.

Dufresne, A., & Kobasigawa, A. (1989). Children's spontaneous allocation of study time: Differential and sufficient aspects. *Journal of Experimental Child Psychology, 47,* 274–296.

Duncan, G. J., Yeung, W. J., Brooks-Gunn, J., & Smith, J. R. (1998). How much does childhood poverty affect the life chances of children? *American Sociological Review, 63*(3), 406–423.

Duncan, P. D., Ritter, P. L., Dornbusch, S. M., Gross, R. T., & Carlsmith, J. M. (1985). The effects of pubertal timing on body image, school behavior, and deviance. *Journal of Youth and Adolescence, 14,* 227–235.

Dunham, P. J., Dunham, F., & Curwin, A. (1993). Joint-attentional states and lexical acquisition at 18 months. *Developmental Psychology, 29,* 827–831.

Dunn, J. (1984). *Sisters and brothers.* Cambridge, MA: Harvard University Press.

Dunn, J. (1988). *The beginnings of social understanding.* Cambridge, MA: Harvard University Press.

Dunn, J. (1993). Social interaction, relationships, and the development of causal discourse and conflict management. *European Journal of Psychology of Education, 8,* 391–401.

Dunn, J. (1996). Sibling relationships and perceived self-competence: Patterns of stability between childhood and early adolescence. In A. J. Sameroff & M. M. Haith (Eds.), *The five to seven year shift* (pp. 253–270). Chicago: University of Chicago Press.

Dunn, J., Bretherton, I., & Munn, P. (1987). Conversations about feeling states between mothers and their young children. *Developmental Psychology, 23,* 132–139.

Dunn, J., Brown, J., & Beardsall, L. (1991). Family talk about feeling states and children's later understanding of others' emotions. *Developmental Psychology, 27,* 448–455.

Dunn, J., & Munn, P. (1985). Becoming a family member: Family conflict and the development of social understanding in the second year. *Child Development, 56,* 480–492.

Dunn, J., & Munn, P. (1987). Development of justification in disputes with mother and sibling. *Developmental Psychology, 23,* 791–798.

DuPaul, G. J., & Eckert, T. L. (1994). The effects of social skills curricula: Now you see them, now you don't. *School Psychology Quarterly, 9,* 113–132.

Duran, B. J., & Weffer, R. E. (1992). Immigrants' aspirations, high school process, and academic outcomes. *American Educational Research Journal, 29,* 163–181.

Durand, V. M. (1998). *Sleep better: A guide to improving sleep for children with special needs.* Baltimore: Brookes.

Durby, D. D. (1994). Gay, lesbian, and bisexual youth. In T. DeCrescenzo (Ed.), *Helping gay and lesbian youth: New policies, new programs, new practice* (pp. 1–37). New York: Haworth Press.

Durkin, K. (1995). *Developmental social psychology: From infancy to old age.* Cambridge, MA: Blackwell.

Dweck, C. S. (1986). Motivational processes affecting learning. *American Psychologist, 41,* 1040–1048.

Dweck, C. S. (2000). *Self-theories: Their role in motivation, personality, and development.* Philadelphia: Psychology Press.

Dweck, C. S., & Elliott, E. S. (1983). Achievement motivation. In E. M. Hetherington (Ed.), *Handbook of child psychology: Vol. 4. Socialization, personality, and social development* (4th ed.). New York: Wiley.

Dweck, C. S., & Leggett, E. L. (1988). A social-cognitive approach to motivation and personality. *Psychological Review, 95,* 256–273.

Dwyer, K., & Osher, D. (2000). *Safeguarding our children: An action guide.* Washington, DC: U.S. Departments of Education and Justice, American Institutes for Research. Retrieved February 26, 2004, from http://www.ed.gov/pubs/edpubs.html

Dwyer, K., Osher, D., & Warger, C. (1998). *Early warning, timely response: A guide to safe schools.* Washington, DC: U.S. Department of Education. Retrieved February 26, 2004, from http://www.ed.gov/offices/OSERS/OSEP/earlywrn.html

Dykens, E. M., & Cassidy, S. B. (1999). Prader-Willi syndrome. In S. Goldstein & C. R. Reynolds (Eds.), *Handbook of neurodevelopmental and genetic disorders* (pp. 525–554). New York: Guilford Press.

Dyson, A. H. (1986). Children's early interpretations of writing: Expanding research perspectives. In D. B. Yaden, Jr., & S. Templeton (Eds.), *Metalinguistic awareness and beginning literacy: Conceptualizing what it means to read and write.* Portsmouth, NH: Heinemann.

Eacott, M. J. (1999). Memory for the events of early childhood. *Current Directions in Psychological Science, 8,* 46–49.

Eagly, A. H. (1987). *Sex differences in social behavior: A social-role interpretation.* Hillsdale, NJ: Erlbaum.

Eaton, W. O., & Enns, L. R. (1986). Sex differences in human motor activity level. *Psychological Bulletin, 100,* 19–28.

Eccles (Parsons), J. S. (1983). Expectancies, values, and academic behaviors. In J. T. Spence (Ed.), *Achievement and achievement motivation.* San Francisco: Freeman.

Eccles, J. S. (1989). Bringing young women to math and science. In M. Crawford & M. Gentry (Eds.), *Gender and thought: Psychological perspectives.* New York: Springer-Verlag.

Eccles, J. S., & Harold, R. D. (1993). Parent-school involvement during the early adolescent years. *Teachers College Record, 94,* 568–587.

Eccles, J. S., Jacobs, J., Harold, R., Yoon, K. S., Arbreton, A., & Freedman-Doan, C. (1993). Parents and gender-related socialization during the middle childhood and adolescent years. In S. Oskamp & M. Costanzo (Eds.), *Gender issues in contemporary society.* Newbury Park, CA: Sage.

Eccles, J. S., & Midgley, C. (1989). Stage-environment fit: Developmentally appropriate classrooms for young adolescents. In C. Ames & R. Ames (Eds.), *Research on motivation in education: Vol. 3. Goals and cognition.* San Diego, CA: Academic Press.

Eccles, J. S., & Wigfield, A. (1985). Teacher expectations and student motivation. In J. B. Dusek (Ed.), *Teacher expectancies.* Hillsdale, NJ: Erlbaum.

Eccles, J. S., Wigfield, A., & Schiefele, U. (1998). Motivation to succeed. In W. Damon (Series Ed.) & N. Eisenberg (Vol. Ed.), *Handbook of child psychology: Vol 3. Social, emotional, and personality development* (5th ed., pp. 1017–1095). New York: Wiley.

Echols, L. D., West, R. F., Stanovich, K. E., & Kehr, K. S. (1996). Using children's literacy activities to predict growth in verbal cognitive skills: A longitudinal investigation. *Journal of Educational Psychology, 88,* 296–304.

Eckerman, C. O. (1979). The human infant in social interaction. In R. Cairns (Ed.), *The analysis of social interactions: Methods, issues, and illustrations* (pp. 163–178). Hillsdale, NJ: Erlbaum.

Eckman, P. (1972). Universals and cultural differences in facial expressions of emotion. In J. K. Cole (Ed.), *Nebraska symposium on motivation*. Lincoln: University of Nebraska Press.

Edwards, C. P., Gandini, L., & Giovaninni, D. (1996). The contrasting developmental timetables of parents and preschool teachers in two cultural communities. In Harkness, B., & Super, C. (Eds.), *Parents' cultural belief systems* (pp. 270–288). New York: Guilford Press.

Edwards, P. A., & Garcia, G. E. (1994). The implications of Vygotskian theory for the development of home-school programs: A focus on storybook reading. In V. John-Steiner, C. P. Panofsky, & L. W. Smith (Eds.), *Sociocultural approaches to language and literacy: An interactionist perspective*. Cambridge, England: Cambridge University Press.

Eeds, M., & Wells, D. (1989). Grand conversations: An explanation of meaning construction in literature study groups. *Research in the Teaching of English, 23*, 4–29.

Egami, Y., Ford, D., & Crum, R. (1996). Psychiatric profile and sociodemographic characteristics of adults who report physically abusing or neglecting children. *The American Journal of Psychiatry, 153*, 921–930.

Ehri, L. C. (1991). Development of the ability to read words. In P. D. Pearson (Ed.), *Handbook of reading research* (Vol. II). New York: Longman.

Ehri, L. C. (1994). Development of the ability to read words: Update. In R. B. Ruddell, M. R. Ruddell, & H. Singer (Eds.), *Theoretical models and processes of reading* (4th ed.). Newark, DE: International Reading Association.

Ehri, L. C. (1998). Word reading by sight and by analogy in beginning readers. In C. Hulme & R. M. Joshi (Eds.), *Reading and spelling: Development and disorders*. Mahwah, NJ: Erlbaum.

Ehri, L. C., Nunes, S. R., Stahl, S. A., & Willows, D. M. (2001). Systematic phonics instruction helps students learn to read: Evidence from the National Reading Panel's meta-analysis. *Review of Educational Research, 71*, 393–447.

Ehri, L. C., & Robbins, C. (1992). Beginners need some decoding skill to read words by analogy. *Reading Research Quarterly, 27*, 12–27.

Eilam, B. (2001). Primary strategies for promoting homework performance. *American Educational Research Journal, 38*, 691–725.

Eilers, R. E., & Oller, D. K. (1994). Infant vocalizations and early diagnosis of severe hearing impairment. *Journal of Pediatrics, 124*, 199–203.

Eisenberg, N. (1982). The development of reasoning regarding prosocial behavior. In N. Eisenberg (Ed.), *The development of prosocial behavior*. New York: Academic Press.

Eisenberg, N. (1992). *The caring child*. Cambridge, MA: Harvard University Press.

Eisenberg, N. (1995). Prosocial development: A multifaceted model. In W. M. Kurtines & J. L. Gewirtz (Eds.), *Moral development: An introduction*. Boston: Allyn & Bacon.

Eisenberg, N. (1998). Introduction. In W. Damon (Series Ed.) & N. Eisenberg (Vol. Ed.), *Handbook of child psychology: Vol. 3. Social, emotional, and personality development* (5th ed., pp. 1–24). New York: Wiley.

Eisenberg, N., Carlo, G., Murphy, B., & Van Court, N. (1995). Prosocial development in late adolescence: A longitudinal study. *Child Development, 66*, 1179–1197.

Eisenberg, N., Cumberland, A., & Spinrad, T. L. (1988). Parental socialization of emotion. *Psychological Inquiry, 9*, 241–273.

Eisenberg, N., & Fabes, R. A. (1994). Mothers' reactions to children's negative emotions: Relations to children's temperament and anger behavior. *Merrill-Palmer Quarterly, 40*, 138–156.

Eisenberg, N., & Fabes, R. A. (1998). Prosocial development. In W. Damon (Series Ed.) & N. Eisenberg (Vol. Ed.), *Handbook of child psychology: Vol. 3. Social, emotional, and personality development* (pp. 701–778). New York: Wiley.

Eisenberg, N., Fabes, R. A., Carlo, G., & Karbon, M. (1992). Emotional responsivity to others: Behavioral correlates and socialization antecedents. In N. Eisenberg & R. A. Fabes (Eds.), *New directions in child development* (No. 55, pp. 57–73). San Francisco: Jossey-Bass.

Eisenberg, N., Fabes, R. A., Schaller, M., Carlo, G., & Miller, P. A. (1991). The relations of parental characteristics and practices to children's vicarious emotional responding. *Child Development, 62*, 1393–1408.

Eisenberg, N., Lennon, R., & Pasternack, J. F. (1986). Altruistic values and moral judgment. In N. Eisenberg (Ed.), *Altruistic emotion, cognition, and behavior*. Hillsdale, NJ: Erlbaum.

Eisenberg, N., Martin, C. L., & Fabes, R. A. (1996). Gender development and gender effects. In D. C. Berliner & R. C. Calfee (Eds.), *Handbook of educational psychology*. New York: Macmillan.

Eisenberg, N., Miller, P. A., Shell, R., McNalley, S., & Shea, C. (1991). Prosocial development in adolescence: A longitudinal study. *Developmental Psychology, 27*, 849–857.

Eisenberg, N., Spinrad, T. L., Fabes, R. A., Reiser, M., Cumberland, A., Shepard, S. A., et al. (2004). The relations of effortful control and impulsivity to children's resiliency and adjustment. *Child Development, 75*, 25–46.

Eisenberg, N., Zhou, Q., & Koller, S. (2001). Brazilian adolescents' prosocial moral judgment and behavior: Relations to sympathy, perspective taking, gender-role orientation, and demographic characteristics. *Child Development, 72*, 518–534.

Eisenberger, R. (1992). Learned industriousness. *Psychological Review, 99*, 248–267.

Ekelin, M., Crang-Svalenius, E., & Dykes, A. K. (2004). A qualitative study of mothers' and fathers' experiences of routine ultrasound examination in Sweden. *Midwifery, 20*, 335–344.

Elder, A. D. (2002). Characterizing fifth grade students' epistemological beliefs in science. In B. K. Hofer & P. R. Pintrich (Eds.), *Personal epistemology: The psychology of beliefs about knowledge and knowing* (pp. 347–363). Mahwah, NJ: Erlbaum.

Elia, J. P. (1994). Homophobia in the high school: A problem in need of a resolution. *Journal of Homosexuality, 77*(1), 177–185.

Elias, G., & Broerse, J. (1996). Developmental changes in the incidence and likelihood of simultaneous talk during the first two years: A question of function. *Journal of Child Language, 23*, 201–217.

Elicker, J., Englund, M., & Sroufe, L. A. (1992). Predicting peer competence and peer relationships in childhood from early parent-child relationships. In R. D. Parke & G. W. Ladd (Eds.), *Family-peer relationships: Modes of linkage* (pp. 77–106). Hillsdale, NJ: Erlbaum.

Elison, J., & Harter, S. (in press). Humiliation: Causes, correlates, and consequences. In J. L. Tracy, R. W. Robins, & J. P. Tangney (Eds.), *The self-conscious emotions: Theory and research*. New York: Guilford Press.

Elkind, D. (1981a). *Children and adolescents: Interpretive essays on Jean Piaget* (3rd ed.). New York: Oxford University Press.

Elkind, D. (1981b). *The hurried child: Growing up too fast too soon*. Reading, MA: Addison-Wesley.

Elkind, D. (1984). *All grown up and no place to go*. Reading, MA: Addison-Wesley.

Elkind, D. (1987). *Miseducation: Preschoolers at risk*. New York: Knopf.

Elliot, A. J., & McGregor, H. A. (2000, April). Approach and avoidance goals and autonomous-controlled regulation: Empirical and conceptual relations. In A. Assor (Chair), *Self-determination theory and achievement goal theory: Convergences, divergences, and educational implications*. Symposium conducted at the annual meeting of the American Educational Research Association, New Orleans, LA.

Elliott, D. J. (1995). *Music matters: A new philosophy of music education*. New York: Oxford University Press.

Elliott, R., & Vasta, R. (1970). The modeling of sharing: Effects associated with vicarious reinforcement, symbolization, age, and generalization. *Journal of Experimental Child Psychology, 10*, 8–15.

Elman, J., Bates, E., Johnson, M., Karmiloff-Smith, A., Parisi, D., & Plunkett, K. (1997). *Rethinking innateness*. Cambridge, MA: MIT Press.

Elze, D. E. (2003). Gay, lesbian, and bisexual youths' perceptions of their high school environments and comfort in school. *Children and Schools, 25*(4), 225–239.

Ember, C. R., & Ember, M. (1994). War, socialization, and interpersonal violence. *Journal of Conflict Resolution, 38*, 620–646.

Emde, R., Gaensbauer, T., & Harmon, R. (1976). *Emotional expression in infancy: A biobehavioral study* (Psychological Issues, Vol. 10, No. 37). New York: International Universities Press.

Emde, R. N., & Buchsbaum, H. (1990). "Didn't you hear my mommy?" Autonomy with connectedness in moral self-emergence. In D. Cicchetti & M. Beeghly (Eds.), *The self in transition: Infancy to adulthood* (pp. 35–60). Chicago: University of Chicago Press.

Emery, R. E., & Laumann-Billings, L. (1998). An overview of the nature, causes, and consequences of abusive family relationships. *American Psychologist, 53*, 121–135.

Emery, R. E., Laumann-Billings, L., Waldron, M. C., Sbarra, D. A., & Dillon, P. (2001). Child custody mediation and litigation: Custody, contact, and coparenting 12 years after initial dispute resolution. *Journal of Counseling and Clinical Psychology, 69*, 323–332.

Empson, S. B. (1999). Equal sharing and shared meaning: The development of fraction concepts in a first-grade classroom. *Cognition and Instruction, 17*, 283–342.

Endicott, K. (1992). Fathering in an egalitarian society. In B. S. Hewlett (Ed.), *Father-child relations: Cultural and biosocial contexts* (pp. 281–295). New York: Aldine de Gruyter.

Engle, P. L., & Breaux, C. (1998). Fathers' involvement with children: Perspectives from developing countries. *Social Policy Report: Society for Research in Child Development, 12*(1), 1–21.

English, D. J. (1998). The extent and consequences of child maltreatment. *The Future of Children: Protecting Children from Abuse and Neglect, 8*(1), 39–53.

Enkin, M., Keirse, M. J., Neilson, J., Crowther, C., Duley, L., Hodnett, E., et al. *A guide to effective care in pregnancy and childbirth* (3rd ed.). Oxford, England: Oxford University Press.

Entwisle, D. R., & Alexander, K. L. (1999). Early schooling and social stratification. In R. C. Pianta & M. J. Cox (Eds.), *The transition to kindergarten* (pp. 13–38). Baltimore: Brookes.

Eppright, T. D., Sanfacon, J. A., Beck, N. C., & Bradley, S. J. (1998). Sport psychiatry in childhood and adolescence: An overview. *Child Psychiatry and Human Development, 28*, 71–88.

Epstein, J. A., Botvin, G. J., Diaz, T., Toth, V., & Schinke, S. P. (1995). Social and personal factors in marijuana use and intentions to use drugs among inner city minority youth. *Journal of Developmental and Behavioral Pediatrics, 16*, 14–20.

Epstein, J. L. (1986). Friendship selection: Developmental and environmental influences. In E. Mueller & C. Cooper (Eds.), *Process and outcome in peer relationships* (pp. 129–160). New York: Academic Press.

Epstein, J. L. (1996). Perspectives and previews on research and policy for school, family, and community partnerships. In A. Booth & J. F. Dunn (Eds.), *Family-school links: How do they affect educational outcomes?* Mahwah, NJ: Erlbaum.

Epstein, J. S. (1998). Introduction: Generation X, youth culture, and identity. In J. S. Epstein (Ed.), *Youth culture: Identity in a postmodern world.* Malden, MA: Blackwell.

Epstein, L. H. (1990). Behavioral treatment of obesity. In E. M. Stricker (Ed.), *Handbook of behavioral neurobiology: Vol. 10. Neurobiology of food and fluid intake* (pp. 61–73). New York: Plenum Press.

Epstein, L. H., Wing, R. R., & Valoski, A. (1985). Childhood obesity. *Pediatric Clinics of North America, 32,* 363–379.

Epstein, S., & Morling, B. (1995). Is the self motivated to do more than enhance and/or verify itself? In M. H. Kernis (Ed.), *Efficacy, agency, and self-esteem.* New York: Plenum Press.

Epstein, T. (2000). Adolescents' perspectives on racial diversity in U.S. history: Case studies from an urban classroom. *American Educational Research Journal, 37,* 185–214.

Erikson, E. H. (1963). *Childhood and society* (2nd ed.). New York: Norton.

Erikson, E. H. (1972). *Eight ages of man.* In C. S. Lavatelli & F. Stendler (Eds.), *Readings in child behavior and child development.* San Diego, CA: Harcourt Brace Jovanovich.

Eron, L. D. (1980). Prescription for reduction of aggression. *American Psychologist, 35,* 244–252.

Eron, L. D. (1987). The development of aggressive behavior from the perspective of a developing behaviorism. *American Psychologist, 42,* 435–442.

Erwin, P. (1993). *Friendship and peer relations in children.* Chichester, England: Wiley.

Espelage, D. L., Holt, M. K., & Henkel, R. R. (2003). Examination of peer-group contextual effects on aggression during early adolescence. *Child Development, 74,* 205–220.

Etaugh, C., Grinnell, K., & Etaugh, A. (1989). Development of gender labeling: Effect of age of pictured children. *Sex Roles, 21,* 769–773.

Evans, E. M. (2001). Cognitive and contextual factors in the emergence of diverse belief systems: Creation versus evolution. *Cognitive Psychology, 42,* 217–266.

Evans, G. W. (2004). The environment of childhood poverty. *American Psychologist, 59,* 77–92.

Eysenck, M. W. (1992). *Anxiety: The cognitive perspective.* Hove, England: Erlbaum.

Fabes, R. A., Eisenberg, N., Jones, S., Smith, M., Guthrie, I., Poulin, R., et al. (1999). Regulation, emotionality, and preschoolers' socially competent peer interactions. *Child Development, 70,* 432–442.

Fabos, B., & Young, M. D. (1999). Telecommunication in the classroom: Rhetoric versus reality. *Review of Educational Research, 69,* 217–259.

Fabricius, W. V., & Hagen, J. W. (1984). Use of causal attributions about recall performance to assess metamemory and predict strategic memory behavior in young children. *Developmental Psychology, 20,* 975–987.

Fagan, J. F., & Singer, L. T. (1983). Infant recognition memory as a measure of intelligence. In L. P. Lipsitt (Ed.), *Advances in infancy research* (Vol. 2). Norwood, NJ: Ablex.

Fahrmeier, E. D. (1978). The development of concrete operations among the Hausa. *Journal of Cross-Cultural Psychology, 9,* 23–44.

Fairchild, H. H., & Edwards-Evans, S. (1990). African American dialects and schooling: A review. In A. M. Padilla, H. H. Fairchild, & C. M. Valadez (Eds.), *Bilingual education: Issues and strategies.* Newbury Park, CA: Sage.

Faks, D. K., Filcher, I., Masterpasqua, E., & Joseph, G. (1995). Lesbians choosing motherhood: A comparative study of lesbian and heterosexual parents and their children. *Developmental Psychology, 31,* 105–114.

Falbo, T. (1992). Social norms and the one-child family: Clinical and policy implications. In F. Boer & J. Dunn (Eds.), *Children's sibling relationships* (pp. 71–82). Hillsdale, NJ: Erlbaum.

Falbo, T., & Polit, D. (1986). A quantitative review of the only child literature: Research evidence and theory development. *Psychological Bulletin, 100,* 176–189.

Famularo, R., Kinscherff, R., & Fenton, T. (1992). Psychiatric diagnoses of maltreated children: Preliminary findings. *Journal of the American Academy of Child and Adolescent Psychiatry, 31,* 863–867.

Fantini, A. E. (1985). *Language acquisition of a bilingual child: A sociolinguistic perspective.* Clevedon, England: Multilingual Matters. (Available from the SIT Bookstore, School for International Training, Kipling Road, Brattleboro, VT 05302)

Fantino, A. M., & Colak, A. (2001). Refugee children in Canada: Searching for identity. *Child Welfare, 80,* 587–596.

Faraone, S. V., Biederman, J., Chen, W. J., Milberger, S., Warburton, R., & Tsuang, M. T. (1995). Genetic heterogeneity in attention-deficit hyperactivity disorder (ADHD): Gender, psychiatric comorbidity, and maternal ADHD. *Journal of Abnormal Psychology, 104,* 334–345.

Farber, B., Mindel, C. H., & Lazerwitz, B. (1988). The Jewish American family. In C. H. Mindel, R. W. Habenstein, & R. Wright (Eds.), *Ethnic families in America: Patterns and variations.* New York: Elsevier.

Farmer, T. W., Leung, M.-C., Pearl, R., Rodkin, P. C., Cadwallader, T. W., & Van Acker, R. (2002). Deviant or diverse peer groups? The peer affiliations of aggressive elementary students. *Journal of Educational Psychology, 94,* 611–620.

Farran, D. C. (2001). Critical periods and early intervention. In D. B. Bailey, Jr., J. T. Bruer, F. J. Symons, & J. W. Lichtman (Eds.), *Critical thinking about critical periods* (pp. 233–266). Baltimore: Brookes.

Farrar, M. J., & Goodman, G. S. (1992). Developmental changes in event memory. *Child Development, 63,* 173–187.

Farrell, M. M., & Phelps, L. (2000). A comparison of the Leiter-R and the Universal Nonverbal Intelligence Test (UNIT) with children classified as language impaired. *Journal of Psychoeducational Assessment, 18,* 268–274.

Farver, J. A. M., & Branstetter, W. H. (1994). Preschoolers' prosocial responses to their peers' distress. *Developmental Psychology, 30,* 334–341.

Fausel, D. F. (1986). Loss after divorce: Helping children grieve. *Journal of Independent Social Work, 1*(1), 39–47.

Feather, N. T. (1982). *Expectations and actions: Expectancy-value models in psychology.* Hillsdale, NJ: Erlbaum.

Federal Glass Ceiling Commission. (1995). *Good for business: Making full use of the nation's human capital. The environmental scan.* Washington, DC: U.S. Government Printing Office.

Federal Interagency Forum on Child and Family Statistics. (1999). *America's children: Key national indicators of well-being, 1999.* Washington, DC: U.S. Government Printing Office.

Federal Interagency Forum on Child and Family Statistics. (2004). *America's children in brief: Key national indicators of well-being, 2004.* Washington, DC: U.S. Government Printing Office.

Federal Interagency Forum on Child and Family Statistics. (2005). *America's children: Key national indicators of well-being, 2005.* Washington, DC: U.S. Government Printing Office.

Feigenson, L., Carey, S., & Hauser, M. (2002). The representations underlying infants' choice of more: Object files versus analog magnitudes. *Psychological Science, 13,* 150–156.

Feingold, A. (1993). Cognitive gender differences: A developmental perspective. *Sex Roles, 29,* 91–112.

Feinman, S. (1992). *Social referencing and the social construction of reality in infancy.* New York: Plenum Press.

Feldhusen, J. F. (1989). Synthesis of research on gifted youth. *Educational Leadership, 26*(1), 6–11.

Feldhusen, J. F., Van Winkle, L., & Ehle, D. A. (1996). Is it acceleration or simply appropriate instruction for precocious youth? *Teaching Exceptional Children, 28*(3), 48–51.

Feldman, R., Sussman, A. L., & Zigler, E. (2004). Parental leave and work adaptation at the transition to parenthood: Individual, marital, and social correlates. *Applied Developmental Psychology, 25,* 459–470.

Feldman, S. S., Gowen, L. K., & Fisher, L. (1998). Family relationships and gender as predictors of romantic intimacy in young adults: A longitudinal study. *Journal of Research on Adolescence, 8,* 263–286.

Feldman, S. S., & Wentzel, K. R. (1990). The relationship between parental styles, sons' self-restraint, and peer relations in early adolescence. *Journal of Early Adolescence, 10,* 439–454.

Feldman, S. S., & Wood, D. N. (1994). Parents' expectations for preadolescent sons' behavioral autonomy: A longitudinal study of correlates and outcomes. *Journal of Research on Adolescence, 4,* 45–70.

Felton, R. H. (1998). The development of reading skills in poor readers: Educational implications. In C. Hulme & R. M. Joshi (Eds.), *Reading and spelling: Development and disorders.* Mahwah, NJ: Erlbaum.

Fennema, E. (1987). Sex-related differences in education: Myths, realities, and interventions. In V. Richardson-Koehler (Ed.), *Educators' handbook: A research perspective.* White Plains, NY: Longman.

Fenson, L., Dale, P., Reznick, J., Bates, E., Thal, D., & Pethick, S. (1994). Variability in early communicative development. *Monographs of the Society for Research in Child Development, 59*(5, Serial No. 242), 1–173.

Fenson, L., Vella, D., & Kennedy, M. (1989). Children's knowledge of thematic and taxonomic relations at two years of age. *Child Development, 60,* 911–919.

Fernald, A. (1992). Human maternal vocalizations to infants as biologically relevant signals: An evolutionary perspective. In J. Barkow, L. Cosmides, & J. Tooby (Eds.), *Evolutionary psychology and the generation of culture.* New York: Oxford University Press.

Fernald, A., Swingley, D., & Pinto, J. P. (2001). When half a word is enough: Infants can recognize spoken words using partial phonetic information. *Child Development, 72,* 1003–1015.

Feuerstein, R. (1979). *The dynamic assessment of retarded performers: The Learning Potential Assessment Device, theory, instruments, and techniques.* Baltimore: University Park Press.

Feuerstein, R. (1980). *Instrumental enrichment: An intervention program for cognitive modifiability.* Baltimore: University Park Press.

Feuerstein, R. (1990). The theory of structural cognitive modifiability. In B. Z. Presseisen (Ed.), *Learning and thinking styles: Classroom interaction.* Washington, DC: National Education Association.

Feuerstein, R., Feuerstein, R., & Gross, S. (1997). The Learning Potential Assessment Device. In D. P. Flanagan, J. L. Genshaft, & P. L. Harrison (Eds.), *Contemporary intellectual assessment: Theories, tests, and issues* (pp. 297–313). New York: Guilford Press.

Fewell, R. R., & Sandall, S. R. (1983). Curricula adaptations for young children: Visually impaired, hearing impaired, and physically impaired. *Curricula in Early Childhood Special Education, 2*(4), 51–66.

Fiedler, E. D., Lange, R. E., & Winebrenner, S. (1993). In search of reality: Unraveling the myths about tracking, ability grouping and the gifted. *Roeper Review, 16*(1), 4–7.

Field, D. (1987). A review of preschool conservation training: An analysis of analyses. *Developmental Review, 7,* 210–251.

Field, S. L., Labbo, L. D., & Ash, G. E. (1999, April). *Investigating young children's construction of social studies concepts and the intersection of literacy learning.* Paper presented at the annual meeting of the American Educational Research Association, Montreal, Canada.

Field, T. (1991). Quality infant daycare and grade school behavior and performance. *Child Development, 62,* 863–870.

Field, T. (2001). Massage therapy facilitates weight gain in preterm infants. *Current Directions in Psychological Science, 10,* 51–54.

Field, T., Masi, W., Goldstein, D., Perry, S., & Parl, S. (1988). Infant daycare facilitates preschool behavior. *Early Childhood Research Quarterly, 3,* 341–359.

Field, T., Vega-Lahr, N., Scafidi, F., & Goldstein, S. (1986). Effects of maternal unavailability on mother-infant interactions. *Infant Behavior and Development, 9,* 473–478.

Field, T., Woodson, R., Greenberg, R., & Cohen, D. (1982). Discrimination and imitation of facial expressions by neonates. *Science, 218,* 179–181.

Fields, J. (2001, April). *Living arrangements of children: Fall 1996.* Current Population Reports, P70–74. Washington, DC: U.S. Census Bureau.

Fifer, W. P., & Moon, C. M. (1995). The effects of fetal experience with sound. In J. P. Lecanuet, W. P. Fifer, N. A. Krasnegor, & W. P. Smotherman (Eds.), *Fetal development: A psychobiological perspective.* Hillsdale, NJ: Erlbaum.

Finders, M., & Lewis, C. (1994). Why some parents don't come to school. *Educational Leadership, 51*(8), 50–54.

Finkelhor, D., Mitchell, K. J., & Wolak, J. (2000). *Online victimization: A report on the nation's youth.* Durham, NH: Crimes Against Children Research Center. Retrieved March 7, 2003, from http://www.unh.edu/ccrc/pdf/Victimization_Online _Survey.pdf

Finkelhor, D., Ormrod, R., Turner, H., & Hamby, S. L. (2005). The victimization of children and youth: A comprehensive, national survey. *Child Maltreatment, 10,* 5–25.

Finn, J. D. (1989). Withdrawing from school. *Review of Educational Research, 59,* 117–142.

Finn-Stevenson, M., & Stern, B. (1996). CoZi: Linking early childhood and family support services. *Principal, 75*(5), 6–10.

Fischer, K. (2005, April). Dynamic skill development and integration of motivation, emotion, and cognition. In D. Y. Dai (Chair), *Beyond cognitivism: Where are we now?* Symposium presented at the annual meeting of the American Educational Research Association, Montreal, Canada.

Fischer, K. W., & Bidell, T. (1991). Constraining nativist inferences about cognitive capacities. In S. Carey & R. Gelman (Eds.), *The epigenesis of mind: Essays on biology and cognition.* Hillsdale, NJ: Erlbaum.

Fischer, K. W., & Immordino-Yang, M. H. (2006). Cognitive development and education: From dynamic general structure to specific learning and teaching. In W. Damon, & R. M. Lerner (Series Eds.), D. Kuhn, & R. Siegler (Vol. Eds.), *Handbook of child psychology: Vol. 1. Cognition, perception, and language* (6th ed.). New York: Wiley.

Fischer, K. W., Knight, C. C., & Van Parys, M. (1993). Analyzing diversity in developmental pathways: Methods and concepts. In R. Case & W. Edelstein (Eds.), *The new structuralism in cognitive development: Theory and research on individual pathways.* Basel, Switzerland: Karger.

Fisher, C. B., & Brone, R. J. (1991). Eating disorders in adolescence. In R. M. Lerner, A. C. Petersen, & J. Brooks-Gunn (Eds.), *Encyclopedia of adolescence* (Vol. 1). New York: Garland.

Fisher, C. B., Jackson, J. F., & Villarruel, F. A. (1998). The study of African American and Latin American children and youth. In W. Damon (Series Ed.) & R. M. Lerner (Vol. Ed.), *Handbook of child psychology: Vol. 1. Theoretical models of human development* (5th ed., pp. 1145–1207). New York: Wiley.

Fisher, J. D., & Fisher, W. A. (1992). Changing AIDS-risk behavior. *Psychological Bulletin, 111,* 455–474.

Fitzgerald, J. (1987). Research on revision in writing. *Review of Educational Research, 57,* 481–506.

Fives, C. J., & Flanagan, R. (2002). A review of the Universal Nonverbal Intelligence Test (UNIT): An advance for evaluating youngsters with diverse needs. *School Psychology International, 23,* 425–448.

Fivush, R., Haden, C., & Adam, S. (1995). Structure and coherence of preschoolers' personal narratives over time: Implications for childhood amnesia. *Journal of Experimental Child Psychology, 60,* 32–56.

Fivush, R., Haden, C., & Reese, E. (1996). Remembering, recounting, and reminiscing: The development of autobiographical memory in social context. In D. C. Rubin (Ed.), *Remembering our past: Studies in autobiographical memory* (pp. 341–359). Cambridge, England: Cambridge University Press.

Fivush, R., & Nelson, K. (2004). Culture and language in the emergence of autobiographical memory. *Psychological Science, 15,* 573–577.

Flanagan, C. A., & Faison, N. (2001). Youth civic development: Implications of research for social policy and programs. *Social Policy Report of the Society for Research in Child Development, 15*(1), 1–14.

Flanagan, C. A., & Tucker, C. J. (1999). Adolescents' explanations for political issues: Concordance with their views of self and society. *Developmental Psychology, 35,* 1198–1209.

Flannery, D. J., Vazsonyi, A. T., Torquati, J., & Fridrich, A. (1994). Ethnic and gender differences in risk for early adolescent substance use. *Journal of Youth and Adolescence, 23,* 195–213.

Flavell, J. H. (1994). Cognitive development: Past, present, and future. In R. D. Parke, P. A. Ornstein, J. J. Rieser, & C. Zahn-Waxler (Eds.), *A century of developmental psychology* (pp. 569–587). Washington, DC: American Psychological Association.

Flavell, J. H. (1996). Piaget's legacy. *Psychological Science, 7*(4), 200–203.

Flavell, J. H. (2000). Development of children's knowledge about the mental world. *International Journal of Behavioral Development, 24*(1), 15–23.

Flavell, J. H., Flavell, E. R., & Green, F. L. (2001). Development of children's understanding of connections between thinking and feeling. *Psychological Science, 12,* 430–432.

Flavell, J. H., Friedrichs, A. G., & Hoyt, J. D. (1970). Developmental changes in memorization processes. *Cognitive Psychology, 1,* 324–340.

Flavell, J. H., Green, F. L., & Flavell, E. R. (1995). Young children's knowledge about thinking. *Monographs of the Society for Research in Child Development, 60*(1, Serial No. 243).

Flavell, J. H., Green, F. L., & Flavell, E. R. (2000). Development of children's awareness of their own thoughts. *Journal of Cognitive Development, 1,* 97–112.

Flavell, J. H., & Miller, P. H. (1998). Social cognition. In W. Damon (Series Ed.), D. Kuhn, & R. S. Siegler (Vol. Eds.), *Handbook of child psychology: Vol. 2. Cognition, perception, and language* (5th ed.). New York: Wiley.

Flavell, J. H., Miller, P. H., & Miller S. A. (2002). *Cognitive development* (4th ed.). Upper Saddle River, NJ: Prentice Hall.

Fleege, P. O., Charlesworth, R., & Burts, D. C. (1992). Stress begins in kindergarten: A look at behavior during standardized testing. *Journal of Research in Childhood Education, 7*(1), 20–26.

Flege, J. E., Munro, M. J., & MacKay, I. R. A. (1995). Effects of age of second-language learning on the production of English consonants. *Speech Communication, 16,* 1–26.

Fletcher, K. L., & Bray, N. W. (1996). External memory strategy use in preschool children. *Merrill-Palmer Quarterly, 42,* 379–396.

Flieller, A. (1999). Comparison of the development of formal thought in adolescent cohorts aged 10 to 15 years (1967–1996 and 1972–1993). *Developmental Psychology, 35,* 1048–1058.

Flynn, J. R. (1987). Massive IQ gains in 14 nations: What IQ tests really measure. *Psychological Bulletin, 101,* 171–191.

Flynn, J. R. (1991). *Asian Americans: Achievement beyond IQ.* Hillsdale, NJ: Erlbaum.

Flynn, J. R. (1999). Searching for justice: The discovery of IQ gains over time. *American Psychologist, 54,* 5–20.

Flynn, J. R. (2003). Movies about intelligence: The limitations of g. *Current Directions in Psychological Science, 12,* 95–99.

Forbes, M. L., Ormrod, J. E., Bernardi, J. D., Taylor, S. L., & Jackson, D. L. (1999, April). *Children's conceptions of space, as reflected in maps of their hometown.* Paper presented at the annual meeting of the American Educational Research Association, Montreal, Canada.

Ford, D. H., & Lerner, R. M. (1992). *Developmental systems theory: An integrative approach.* Newbury Park, CA: Sage.

Ford, D. Y. (1996). *Reversing underachievement among gifted Black students.* New York: Teachers College Press.

Ford, M. E. (1996). Motivational opportunities and obstacles associated with social responsibility and caring behavior in school contexts. In J. Juvonen & K. R. Wentzel (Eds.), *Social motivation: Understanding children's school adjustment* (pp. 126–153). Cambridge, England: Cambridge University Press.

Fordham, S., & Ogbu, J. U. (1986). Black students' school success: Coping with "the burden of 'acting White.'" *The Urban Review, 18,* 176–206.

Forehand, R., Biggar, H., & Kotchick, B. A. (1998). Cumulative risk across family stressors: Short- and long-term effects for adolescents. *Journal of Abnormal Child Psychology, 26,* 119–128.

Forehand, R., Wierson, M., Thomas, A. M., Fauber, R., Armistead, L., Kempton, T., et al. (1991). A short-term longitudinal examination of young adolescent functioning following divorce: The role of family factors. *Journal of Abnormal Child Psychology, 19,* 97–111.

Forgey, M. A., Schinke, S., & Cole, K. (1997). School-based interventions to prevent substance use among inner-city minority adolescents. In D. K. Wilson, J. R. Rodrigue, & W. C. Taylor (Eds.), *Health-promoting and health-compromising behaviors among adolescents* (pp. 251–267). Washington, DC: American Psychological Association.

Fowler, J. W. (1981). *Stages of faith: The psychology of human development and the quest for meaning.* San Francisco: Harper & Row.

Fowler, J. W., & Dell, M. L. (2006). Stages of faith from infancy through adolescence: Reflections on three decades of faith development theory. In E. C. Roehlkepartain, P. E. King, L. Wagener, & P. L. Benson (Eds.), *The handbook of spiritual development in childhood and adolescence* (pp. 34–45). Thousand Oaks, CA: Sage.

Fowler, S. A., & Baer, D. M. (1981). "Do I have to be good all day?" The timing of delayed reinforcement as a factor in generalization. *Journal of Applied Behavior Analysis, 14,* 13–24.

Francis, M., & McCutchen, D. (1994, April). *Strategy differences in revising between skilled and less skilled writers.* Paper presented at the annual meeting of the American Educational Research Association, New Orleans, LA.

Frank, A. (1967). *The diary of a young girl* (B. M. Mooyaart-Doubleday, Trans.). New York: Doubleday.

Frank, C. (1999). *Ethnographic eyes: A teacher's guide to classroom observation.* Portsmouth, NH: Heinemann.

Frederiksen, N. (1984). Implications of cognitive theory for instruction in problem solving. *Review of Educational Research, 54,* 363–407.

Freedman, B. A. (2003, April). *Boys and literacy: Why boys? Which boys? Why now?* Paper presented at the annual meeting of the American Educational Research Association, Chicago.

Freedman, K. (2001). The social reconstruction of art education: Teaching visual culture. In C. A. Grant & M. L. Gomez, *Campus and classroom: Making schooling multicultural* (2nd ed.). Upper Saddle River, NJ: Merrill/Prentice Hall.

Freeman, K. E., Gutman, L. M., & Midgley, C. (2002). Can achievement goal theory enhance our understanding of the motivation and performance of African American young adolescents? In C. Midgley (Ed.), *Goals, goal structures, and patterns of adaptive learning* (pp. 175–204). Mahwah, NJ: Erlbaum.

French, D. C., Jansen, E. A., & Pidada, S. (2002). United States and Indonesian children's and adolescents' reports of relational aggression by disliked peers. *Child Development, 73,* 1143–1150.

French, L., & Brown, A. (1977). Comprehension of "before" and "after" in logical and arbitrary sequences. *Journal of Child Language, 4,* 247–256.

Freund, L. (1990). Maternal regulation of children's problem-solving behavior and its impact on children's performance. *Child Development, 61,* 113–126.

Friedman, L. (1994, April). *The role of spatial skill in gender differences in mathematics: Meta-analytic evidence.* Paper presented at the annual meeting of the American Educational Research Association, New Orleans, LA.

Friend, R. A. (1993). Choices, not closets: Heterosexism and homophobia in schools. In L. Weis & M. Fine (Eds.), *Beyond silenced voices: Class, race, and gender in United States schools* (pp. 209–235). Albany, NY: SUNY Press.

Frost, J. L., Shin, D., & Jacobs, P. J. (1998). Physical environments and children's play. In O. N. Saracho & B. Spodek (Eds.), *Multiple perspectives on play in early childhood education.* Albany: State University of New York Press.

Fry, A. F., & Hale, S. (1996). Processing speed, working memory, and fluid intelligence. *Psychological Science, 7,* 237–241.

Fuchs, D., Fuchs, L. S., Mathes, P. G., & Simmons, D. C. (1997). Peer-assisted learning strategies: Making classrooms more responsive to diversity. *American Educational Research Journal, 34,* 174–206.

Fuchs, L. S., Fuchs, D., Prentice, K., Burch, M., Hamlett, C. L., Owen, R., et al. (2003). Enhancing third-grade students' mathematical problem solving with self-regulated learning strategies. *Journal of Educational Psychology, 95,* 306–315.

Fujimura, N. (2001). Facilitating children's proportional reasoning: A model of reasoning processes and effects of intervention on strategy change. *Journal of Educational Psychology, 93,* 589–603.

Fukkink, R. G., & de Glopper, K. (1998). Effects of instruction in deriving word meanings from context: A meta-analysis. *Review of Educational Research, 68,* 450–469.

Fuligni, A. J. (1998). The adjustment of children from immigrant families. *Current Directions in Psychological Science, 7,* 99–103.

Fuligni, A. J., & Hardway, C. (2004). Preparing diverse adolescents for the transition to adulthood. *The Future of Children, 14*(2), 99–119.

Fuller, M. L. (2001). Multicultural concerns and classroom management. In C. A. Grant & M. L. Gomez, *Campus and classroom: Making schooling multicultural* (pp. 109–134). Upper Saddle River, NJ: Merrill/Prentice Hall.

Funk, J. B., Buchman, D. D., Jenks, J., & Bechtoldt, H. (2003). Playing violent video games, desensitization, and moral evaluation in children. *Applied Developmental Psychology, 24,* 413–436.

Furman, W., & Simon, V. A. (1999). Cognitive representations of adolescent romantic relationships. In W. Furman, B. B. Brown, & C. Feiring (Eds.), *The development of romantic relationships in adolescence* (pp. 75–98). Cambridge, England: Cambridge University Press.

Furrer, C., & Skinner, E. (2003). Sense of relatedness as a factor in children's academic engagement and performance. *Journal of Educational Psychology, 95,* 148–162.

Furstenberg, F. F., Jr., & Cherlin, A. J. (1991). *Divided families: What happens to children when parents part.* Cambridge, MA: Harvard University Press.

Furstenberg, F. F., Jr., Nord, C., Peterson, J. L., & Zill, N. (1983). The life course of children and divorce: Marital disruption and parental conflict. *American Sociological Review, 48,* 656–668.

Fuson, K. C., & Briars, D. J. (1990). Using a base-ten blocks learning/teaching approach for first- and second-grade place-value and multidigit addition and subtraction. *Journal for Research in Mathematics Education, 21,* 180–206.

Fuson, K. C., & Hall, J. W. (1983). The acquisition of early word meanings: A conceptual analysis and review. In H. P. Ginsburg (Ed.), *Children's mathematical thinking.* New York: Academic Press.

Fuson, K. C., & Kwon, Y. (1992). Korean children's understanding of multidigit addition and subtraction. *Child Development, 63,* 491–506.

Futterman, D., Chabon, B., & Hoffman, N. D. (2000). HIV and AIDS in adolescents. *Pediatric Clinics of North America, 47,* 171–188.

Gabard, D. L. (1999). Homosexuality and the Human Genome Project: Private and public choices. *Journal of Homosexuality, 37,* 25–51.

Gable, S., Belsky, J., & Crnic, K. (1992). Marriage, parenting, and child development: Progress and prospects. *Journal of Family Psychology, 5,* 276–294.

Gailey, C. W. (1993). Mediated messages: Gender, class, and cosmos in home video games. *Journal of Popular Culture, 27*(1), 81–97.

Gaines, D. (1991). *Teenage wasteland: Suburbia's dead end kids.* New York: Pantheon.

Galaburda, A. M., & Rosen, G. D. (2001). Neural plasticity in dyslexia: A window to mechanisms of learning disabilities. In J. L. McClelland & R. S. Siegler (Eds.), *Mechanisms of cognitive development: Behavioral and neural perspectives* (pp. 307–323). Mahwah, NJ: Erlbaum.

Galambos, N. L., Almeida, D. M., & Petersen, A. C. (1990). Masculinity, femininity, and sex role attitudes in early adolescence: Exploring gender intensification. *Child Development, 61,* 1905–1914.

Galambos, N. L., & Maggs, J. L. (1991). Children in self-care: Figures, facts and fiction. In J. V. Verner & N. L. Galambos (Eds.), *Employed mothers and their children* (pp. 131–157). New York: Garland Press.

Gallagher, J. J. (1991). Personal patterns of underachievement. *Journal for the Education of the Gifted, 14,* 221–233.

Gallahue, D. L., & Ozmun, J. C. (1998). *Understanding motor development: Infants, children, adolescents, adults.* Boston: McGraw-Hill.

Gallimore, R., & Goldenberg, C. (2001). Analyzing cultural models and settings to connect minority achievement and school improvement research. *Educational Psychologist, 36,* 45–56.

Gallimore, R., & Tharp, R. (1990). Teaching mind in society: Teaching, schooling, and literate discourse. In L. C. Moll (Ed.), *Vygotsky and education: Instructional implications and applications of sociohistorical psychology.* Cambridge, England: Cambridge University Press.

Gallistel, C. R., Brown, A. L., Carey, S., Gelman, R., & Keil, F. C. (1991). In S. Carey & R. Gelman (Eds.), *Epigenesis of mind: Essays on biology and cognition.* Hillsdale, NJ: Erlbaum.

Gallistel, C. R., & Gelman, R. (1992). Preverbal and verbal counting and computation. *Cognition, 44,* 43–74.

Galotti, K. M., Komatsu, L. K., & Voelz, S. (1997). Children's differential performance on deductive and inductive syllogisms. *Developmental Psychology, 33,* 70–78.

Gambrell, L. B., & Bales, R. J. (1986). Mental imagery and the comprehension-monitoring performance of fourth- and fifth-grade poor readers. *Reading Research Quarterly, 21,* 454–464.

Garbarino, J., & Abramowitz, R. H. (1992). Sociocultural risk and opportunity. In J. Garbarino (Ed.), *Children and families in the social environment* (pp. 35–70). New York: Aldine de Gruyter.

Garbarino, J., Bradshaw, C. P., & Vorrasi, J. A. (2002). Mitigating the effects of gun violence on children and youth. *The Future of Children, 12*(2), 73–85.

García, E. E. (1994). *Understanding and meeting the challenge of student cultural diversity.* Boston: Houghton Mifflin.

García, E. E. (1995). Educating Mexican American students: Past treatment and recent developments in theory, research, policy, and practice. In J. A. Banks & C.A.M. Banks (Eds.), *Handbook of research on multicultural education.* New York: Macmillan.

Garcia Coll, C., Lamberty, G., Jenkins, R., McAdoo, H. P., Crnic, K., Wasik, B. H., et al. (1996). An integrative model for the study of developmental competencies in minority children. *Child Development, 67,* 1891–1914.

Gardner, H. (1983). *Frames of mind: The theory of multiple intelligences.* New York: Basic Books.

Gardner, H. (1993). *Multiple intelligences: The theory in practice.* New York: Basic Books.

Gardner, H. (1995). Reflections on multiple intelligences: Myths and messages. *Phi Delta Kappan, 77,* 200–209.

Gardner, H. (1999). *Intelligence reframed: Multiple intelligences for the 21st century.* New York: Basic Books.

Gardner, H. (2000a). A case against spiritual intelligence. *International Journal of the Psychology of Religion, 10*(1), 27–34.

Gardner, H. (2000b). *The disciplined mind: Beyond facts and standardized tests, the K–12 education that every child deserves.* New York: Penguin Books.

Gardner, H., & Hatch, T. (1990). Multiple intelligences go to school: Educational implications of the theory of multiple intelligences. *Educational Researcher, 18*(8), 4–10.

Gardner, H., Torff, B., & Hatch, T. (1996). The age of innocence reconsidered: Preserving the best of the progressive traditions in psychology and education. In D. R. Olson & N. Torrance (Eds.), *The handbook of education and human development: New models of learning, teaching and schooling* (pp. 28–55). Cambridge, MA: Blackwell.

Garner, R. (1987). Strategies for reading and studying expository texts. *Educational Psychologist, 22,* 299–312.

Garner, R. (1998). Epilogue: Choosing to learn or not-learn in school. *Educational Psychology Review, 10,* 227–237.

Garnier, H. E., Stein, J. A., & Jacobs, J. K. (1997). The process of dropping out of high school: A 19-year perspective. *American Educational Research Journal, 34,* 395–419.

Garrison, L. (1989). Programming for the gifted American Indian student. In C. J. Maker & S. W. Schiever (Eds.), *Critical issues in gifted education: Vol. 2. Defensible programs for cultural and ethnic minorities.* Austin, TX: Pro-Ed.

Garvey, C. (1990). *Play.* Cambridge, MA: Harvard University Press.

Garvey, C., & Berninger, G. (1981). Timing and turn taking in children's conversations. *Discourse Processes, 4,* 27–59.

Gaskins, S. (1999). Children's daily lives in a Mayan village: A case study of culturally constructed roles and activities. In A. Göncü (Ed.), *Children's engagement in the world: Sociocultural perspectives* (pp. 25–61). Cambridge, England: Cambridge University Press.

Gathercole, S. E., & Hitch, G. J. (1993). Developmental changes in short-term memory: A revised working memory perspective. In A. F. Collins, S. E. Gathercole, M. A. Conway, & P. E. Morris (Eds.), *Theories of memory.* Hove, England: Erlbaum.

Gauvain, M. (1999). Everyday opportunities for the development of planning skills: Sociocultural and family influences. In A. Göncü (Ed.), *Children's engagement in the world: Sociocultural perspectives* (pp. 173–201). Cambridge, England: Cambridge University Press.

Gauvain, M. (2001). *The social context of cognitive development.* New York: Guilford Press.

Gavin, L. A., & Fuhrman, W. (1989). Age differences in adolescents' perceptions of their peer groups. *Developmental Psychology, 25,* 827–834.

Geary, D. C. (1994). *Children's mathematical development: Research and practical applications.* Washington, DC: American Psychological Association.

Geary, D. C. (2006). Development of mathematical understanding. In W. Damon, R. M. Lerner (Series Eds.), D. Kuhn, & R. Siegler (Vol. Eds.), *Handbook of child psychology: Vol. 1. Cognition, perception, and language* (6th ed.). New York: Wiley.

Gelman, R., & Baillargeon, R. (1983). A review of some Piagetian concepts. In J. H. Flavell & E. M. Markman (Eds.), *Handbook of child psychology: Vol. 3. Cognitive development.* New York: Wiley.

Gelman, R., & Gallistel, C. R. (1978). *The child's understanding of number.* Cambridge, MA: Harvard University Press.

Gelman, S. A., & Kalish, C. W. (2006). Conceptual development. In W. Damon, R. M. Lerner (Series Eds.), D. Kuhn, & R. Siegler (Vol. Eds.), *Handbook of child psychology: Vol. 1. Cognition, perception, and language* (6th ed.). New York: Wiley.

Gelman, S. A., & Markman, E. M. (1986). Categories and induction in young children. *Cognition, 23,* 183–209.

Gelman, S. A., & Taylor, M. (1984). How two-year-old children interpret proper and common names for unfamiliar objects. *Child Development, 55,* 1535–1540.

Genesee, F. (1985). Second language learning through immersion: A review of U.S. programs. *Review of Educational Research, 55,* 541–561.

Gentile, D. A., & Anderson, C. A. (in press). Violent video games: The effects on youth, and public policy implications. In N. E. Dowd, D. G. Singer, & R. F. Wilson (Eds.), *Handbook of children, culture, and violence* (pp. 225–246). Thousand Oaks, CA: Sage.

Gentile, D. A., & Gentile, J. R. (2005, April). *Violent video games as exemplary teachers.* Paper presented at the biennial meeting of the Society for Research in Child Development, Atlanta, GA.

Gentry, R. (1982). An analysis of the developmental spellings in Gnys at Wrk. *The Reading Teacher, 36,* 192–200.

Gerber, M. (1998). *Dear parent: Caring for infants with respect.* Los Angeles: Resources for Infant Educators.

Gerken, L. (1994). Child phonology: Past research, present questions, future directions. In M. A. Gernsbacher (Ed.), *Handbook of psycholinguistics* (pp. 781–820). San Diego, CA: Academic Press.

Gershoff, E. T. (2002). Corporal punishment by parents and associated child behaviors and experiences: A meta-analytic and theoretical review. *Psychological Bulletin, 128,* 539–579.

Gershoff, E. T., Aber, J. L., & Raver, C. C. (2005). Child poverty in the United States: An evidence-based conceptual framework for programs and policies. In R. M. Lerner, F. Jacobs, & D. Wertlieb (Eds.), *Applied developmental science: An advanced textbook* (pp. 269–324). Thousand Oaks, CA: Sage.

Gesell, A. (1928). *Infancy and human growth.* New York: Macmillan.

Ghetti, S., & Alexander, K. W. (2004). "If it happened, I would remember it": Strategic use of event memorability in the rejection of false autobiographical events. *Child Development, 75,* 542–561.

Ghodsian-Carpey, J., & Baker, L. A. (1987). Genetic and environmental influences on aggression in 4- to 7-year-old twins. *Aggressive Behavior, 13,* 173–186.

Gibbs, J. C. (1995). The cognitive developmental perspective. In W. M. Kurtines & J. L. Gewirtz (Eds.), *Moral development: An introduction.* Boston: Allyn & Bacon.

Gibson, E. J., & Walk, R. D. (1960). The "visual cliff." *Scientific American, 202*(4), 64–71.

Gibson, J. J., (1979). *The ecological approach to visual perception.* Boston: Houghton-Mifflin.

Giedd, J. N., Blumenthal, J., Jeffries, N. O., Castellanos, F. X., Liu, H., Zijdenbos, A., et al. (1999). Brain development during childhood and adolescence: A longitudinal MRI study. *Nature Neuroscience, 2,* 861–863.

Giedd, J. N., Jeffries, N. O., Blumenthal, J., Castellanos, F. X., Vaituzis, A. C., Fernandez, T., et al. (1999). Childhood-onset schizophrenia: Progressive brain changes during adolescence. *Biological Psychiatry, 46,* 892–898.

Gilbert, M. J., & Cervantes, R. (1986). Patterns and practices of alcohol use among Mexican Americans: A comprehensive review. *Hispanic Journal of Behavioral Sciences, 8,* 1–60.

Gillam, R. B., & Johnston, J. R. (1992). Spoken and written language relationships in language/learning-impaired and normal achieving school-age children. *Journal of Speech and Hearing Research, 35,* 1303–1315.

Gillberg, I. C., & Coleman, M. (1996). Autism and medical disorders: A review of the literature. *Developmental Medicine and Child Neurology, 38,* 191–202.

Gillham, J. E., Reivich, K. J., Jaycox, L. H., & Seligman, M. E. P. (1995). Prevention of depressive symptoms in schoolchildren: Two-year follow-up. *Psychological Science, 6,* 343–351.

Gilligan, C. (1982). *In a different voice: Psychological theory and women's development.* Cambridge, MA: Harvard University Press.

Gilligan, C. F. (1985, March). Keynote address at the Conference on Women and Moral Theory, Stony Brook, NY.

Gilligan, C. F. (1987). Moral orientation and moral development. In E. F. Kittay & D. T. Meyers (Eds.), *Women and moral theory.* Totowa, NJ: Rowman & Littlefield.

Gilligan, C. F., & Attanucci, J. (1988). Two moral orientations. In C. F. Gilligan, J. V. Ward, & J. M. Taylor (Eds.), *Mapping the moral domain: A contribution of women's thinking to psychological theory and education.* Cambridge, MA: Center for the Study of Gender, Education, and Human Development (distributed by Harvard University Press).

Gilliland, H. (1988). Discovering and emphasizing the positive aspects of the culture. In H. Gilliland & J. Reyhner (Eds.), *Teaching the Native American.* Dubuque, IA: Kendall/Hunt.

Gillis, J. J., Gilger, J. W., Pennington, B. F., & DeFries, J. C. (1992). Attention deficit disorder in reading-disabled twins: Evidence for a genetic etiology. *Journal of Abnormal Child Psychology, 20,* 303–315.

Ginsberg, D., Gottman, J. M., & Parker, J. G. (1986). The importance of friendship. In J. M. Gottman & J. G. Parker (Eds.), *Conversations of friends: Speculations on affective development* (pp. 3–48). Cambridge, England: Cambridge University Press.

Ginsburg, G. P., & Kilbourne, B. K. (1988). Emergence of vocal alternation in mother-infant interchanges. *Journal of Child Language, 15,* 221–235.

Ginsburg, H. P., Posner, J. K., & Russell, R. L. (1981). The development of mental addition as a function of schooling and culture. *Journal of Cross-Cultural Psychology, 12,* 163–178.

Giordano, P. C., Cernkovich, S. A., & DeMaris, A. (1993). The family and peer relations of Black adolescents. *Journal of Marriage and the Family, 55,* 277–287.

Girotto, V., & Light, P. (1993). The pragmatic bases of children's reasoning. In P. Light & G. Butterworth (Eds.), *Context and cognition: Ways of learning and knowing.* Mahwah, NJ: Erlbaum.

Gladwell, M. (1997, Feb. 24 and Mar. 3). Crime and science: Damaged. *The New Yorker.*

Glick, J. (1975). Cognitive development in cross-cultural perspective. In F. Horowitz (Ed.), *Review of child development research* (Vol. 4). Chicago: University of Chicago Press.

Glucksberg, S., & Krauss, R. M. (1967). What do people say after they have learned to talk? Studies of the development of referential communication. *Merrill-Palmer Quarterly, 13,* 309–316.

Glynn, S. M., Yeany, R. H., & Britton, B. K. (Eds.). (1991). *The psychology of learning science.* Hillsdale, NJ: Erlbaum.

Gnepp, J. (1989). Children's use of personal information to understand other people's feelings. In C. Saarni & P. L. Harris (Eds.), *Children's understanding of emotion.* Cambridge, England: Cambridge University Press.

Gohm, C. L., Oishi, S., Darlington, J., & Diener, E. (1998). Culture, parental conflict, parental marital status, and the subjective well-being of young adults. *Journal of Marriage & the Family, 60,* 319–334.

Goldberg, E., & Costa, L. D. (1981). Hemisphere differences in the acquisition and use of descriptive systems. *Brain and Language, 14,* 144–173.

Goldenberg, C. (1992). The limits of expectations: A case for case knowledge about teacher expectancy effects. *American Educational Research Journal, 29,* 517–544.

Goldin-Meadow, S. (1997). When gestures and words speak differently. *Current Directions in Psychological Science, 6,* 138–143.

Goldin-Meadow, S. (2001). Giving the mind a hand: The role of gesture in cognitive change. In J. L. McClelland & R. S. Siegler (Eds.), *Mechanisms of cognitive development: Behavioral and neural perspectives* (pp. 5–31). Mahwah, NJ: Erlbaum.

Goldin-Meadow, S., & Mylander, C. (1993). Beyond the input given: The child's role in the acquisition of language. In P. Bloom (Ed.), *Language acquisition: Core readings.* Cambridge, MA: MIT Press.

Goldin-Meadow, S., Nusbaum, H., Kelly, S. D., & Wagner, S. (2001). Explaining math: Gesturing lightens the load. *Psychological Science, 12,* 516–522.

Goldsmith, H. H., & Gottesman, I. I. (1996). Heritable variability and variable heritability in developmental psychopathology. In M. F. Lenzenweger & J. J. Haugaard (Eds.), *Frontiers of developmental psychopathology* (pp. 5–43). New York: Oxford University Press.

Goldstein, A. P. (1999). Aggression reduction strategies: Effective and ineffective. *School Psychology Quarterly, 14,* 40–58.

Goldstein, N. E., Arnold, D. H., Rosenberg, J. L., Stowe, R. M., & Ortiz, C. (2001). Contagion of aggression in day care classrooms as a function of peer and teacher responses. *Journal of Educational Psychology, 93,* 708–719.

Goleman, D. (1995). *Emotional intelligence.* New York: Bantam Books.

Golinkoff, R. M., Hirsh-Pasek, K., Bailey, L., & Wenger, N. (1992). Young children and adults use lexical principles to learn new nouns. *Developmental Psychology, 28,* 99–108.

Golinkoff, R. M., Hirsh-Pasek, K., Mervis, C. B., Frawley, W. B., & Parillo, M. (1995). Lexical principles can be extended to the acquisition of verbs. In M. Tomasello & W. E. Merriman (Eds.), *Beyond names for things: Young children's acquisition of verbs.* Hillsdale, NJ: Erlbaum.

Gollnick, D. M., & Chinn, P. C. (2002). *Multicultural education in a pluralistic society* (6th ed.). Upper Saddle River, NJ: Merrill/Prentice Hall.

Golomb, C. (2004). *The child's creation of a pictorial world* (2nd ed.). Mahwah, NJ: Erlbaum.

Golombok, S., & Tasker, F. (1996). Do parents influence the sexual orientation of their children? Findings from a longitudinal study of lesbian families. *Developmental Psychology, 32,* 3–11.

Gomby, D. S., Culross, P. L., & Behrman, R. E. (1999). Home visiting: Recent program evaluations—Analysis and recommendations. *The Future of Children. Home Visiting: Recent Program Evaluations, 9*(1), 4–26.

Göncü, A. (1993). Development of intersubjectivity in the dyadic play of preschoolers. *Early Childhood Research Quarterly, 8,* 99–116.

Gonzalez-Mena, J. (2002). *The child in the family and the community* (3rd ed.). Upper Saddle River, NJ: Merrill/Prentice Hall.

Good, T. L., & Brophy, J. E. (1994). *Looking in classrooms* (6th ed.). New York: Harper Collins.

Good, T. L., McCaslin, M. M., & Reys, B. J. (1992). Investigating work groups to promote problem solving in mathematics. In J. Brophy (Ed.), *Advances in research on teaching: Vol. 3. Planning and managing learning tasks and activities.* Greenwich, CT: JAI Press.

Good, T. L., & Nichols, S. L. (2001). Expectancy effects in the classroom: A special focus on improving the reading performance of minority students in first-grade classrooms. *Educational Psychologist, 36,* 113–126.

Goodwyn, S. W., & Acredolo, L. P. (1998). Encouraging symbolic gestures: A new perspective on the relationship between gesture and speech. In J. M. Iverson & S. Goldin-Meadow (Eds.), *Nature and functions of gesture in children's communication.* San Francisco: Jossey-Bass.

Goodwyn, S. W., Acredolo, L. P., & Brown, C. A. (2000). Impact of symbolic gesturing on early language development. *Journal of Nonverbal Behavior, 24,* 81–103.

Gopnik, A., & Meltzoff, A. N. (1997). *Words, thoughts, and theories.* Cambridge, MA: MIT Press.

Gopnik, M. (Ed.). (1997). *The inheritance and innateness of grammars.* New York: Oxford University Press.

Gordon, P. (2004). Numerical cognition without words: Evidence from Amazonia. *Science, 306,* 496–499.

Gortmaker, S. L., Dietz, W. H., Sobol, A. M., & Wehler, C. A. (1987). Increasing pediatric obesity in the United States. *American Journal of Diseases of Children, 141,* 535–540.

Goswami, U. (1999). The relationship between phonological awareness and orthographic representation in different orthographies. In M. Harris & G. Hatano (Eds.), *Learning to read and write: A cross-linguistic perspective.* Cambridge, England: Cambridge University Press.

Gottfredson, G. D., & Gottfredson, D. C. (2001). *Gang problems and gang programs in a national sample of schools.* Ellicott City, MD: Gottfredson Associates.

Gottfried, A. E. (1990). Academic intrinsic motivation in young elementary school children. *Journal of Educational Psychology, 82,* 525–538.

Gottfried, A. E., Fleming, J. S., & Gottfried, A. W. (1994). Role of parental motivational practices in children's academic intrinsic motivation and achievement. *Journal of Educational Psychology, 86,* 104–113.

Gottfried, A. E., Fleming, J. S., & Gottfried, A. W. (2001). Continuity of academic intrinsic motivation from childhood through late adolescence: A longitudinal study. *Journal of Educational Psychology, 93,* 3–13.

Gottfried, A. W., Gottfried, A. E., Bathurst, K., & Guerin, D. W. (1994). *Gifted IQ: Early developmental aspects.* New York: Plenum Press.

Gottlieb, G. (1991). Experiential canalization of behavioral development: Theory. *Developmental Psychology, 27,* 4–13.

Gottlieb, G. (1992). *Individual development and evolution: The genesis of novel behavior.* New York: Oxford University Press.

Gottman, J. M. (1983). How children become friends. *Monographs of the Society for Research in Child Development, 48*(3, Serial No. 201).

Gottman, J. M. (1986). The world of coordinated play: Same- and cross-sex friendship in young children. In J. M. Gottman & J. G. Parker (Eds.), *Conversations of friends: Speculations on affective development* (pp. 139–191). Cambridge, England: Cambridge University Press.

Gottman, J. M., & Mettetal, G. (1986). Speculations about social and affective development: Friendship and acquaintanceship through adolescence. In J. M. Gottman & J. G. Parker (Eds.), *Conversations of friends: Speculations on affective development* (pp. 192–237). Cambridge, England: Cambridge University Press.

Gould, S. J. (1977). *Ontogeny and phylogeny.* Cambridge, MA: Harvard University Press.

Goyen, T. A., Lui, K., & Woods, R. (1998). Visual-motor, visual-perceptual, and fine-motor outcomes in very-low-birthweight children at 5 years. *Developmental Medicine and Child Neurology, 40,* 76–81.

Graber, J. A., Britto, P. R., & Brooks-Gunn, J. (1999). What's love got to do with it? Adolescents' and young adults' beliefs about sexual and romantic relationships. In W. Furman, B. B. Brown, & C. Feiring (Eds.), *The development of romantic relationships in adolescence* (pp. 364–395). Cambridge, England: Cambridge University Press.

Graesser, A., Golding, J. M., & Long, D. L. (1991). Narrative representation and comprehension. In R. Barr, M. L. Kamil, P. Mosenthal, & P. D. Pearson (Eds.), *Handbook of reading research* (Vol. II). New York: Longman.

Graham, S. (1989). Motivation in Afro-Americans. In G. L. Berry & J. K. Asamen (Eds.), *Black students: Psychosocial issues and academic achievement.* Newbury Park, CA: Sage.

Graham, S. (1990). Communicating low ability in the classroom: Bad things good teachers sometimes do. In S. Graham & V. S. Folkes (Eds.), *Attribution theory: Applications to achievement, mental health, and interpersonal conflict.* Hillsdale, NJ: Erlbaum.

Graham, S. (1991). A review of attribution theory in achievement contexts. *Educational Psychology Review, 3,* 5–39.

Graham, S. (1997). Using attribution theory to understand social and academic motivation in African American youth. *Educational Psychologist, 32,* 21–34.

Graham, S., Harris, K. R., & Fink, B. (2000). Is handwriting causally related to learning to write? Treatment of handwriting problems in beginning writers. *Journal of Educational Psychology, 92,* 620–633.

Graham, S., Schwartz, S. S., & MacArthur, C. A. (1993). Knowledge of writing and the composing process, attitude toward writing, and self-efficacy for students with and without learning disabilities. *Journal of Learning Disabilities, 26,* 237–249.

Graham, S., & Weintraub, N. (1996). A review of handwriting research: Progress and prospects from 1980 to 1994. *Educational Psychology Review, 8,* 7–87.

Grandin, T. (1995). *Thinking in pictures and other reports of my life with autism.* New York: Random House.

Grandin, T., & Johnson, C. (2005). *Animals in translation: Using the mysteries of autism to decode animal behavior.* New York: Simon & Schuster.

Grant, C. A., & Gomez, M. L. (2001). *Campus and classroom: Making schooling multicultural* (2nd ed.). Upper Saddle River, NJ: Merrill/Prentice Hall.

Graue, M. E., & Walsh, D. J. (1998). *Studying children in context.* Thousand Oaks, CA: Sage.

Green, L., Fry, A. F., & Myerson, J. (1994). Discounting of delayed rewards: A life-span comparison. *Psychological Science, 5,* 33–36.

Greenberg, M. T. (1999). Attachment and psychopathology in childhood. In J. Cassidy & P. R. Shaver (Eds.), *Handbook of attachment: Theory, research, and clinical applications* (pp. 469–496). New York: Guilford Press.

Greenberg, M. T., Domitrovich, C., & Bumbarger, B. (2000). *Preventing mental disorders in school-age children: A review of the effectiveness of prevention programs.* University Park, PA: Prevention Research Center for the Promotion of Human Development at Pennsylvania State University.

Greenberg, M. T., Kusche, C. A., Cook, E. T., & Quamma, J. P. (1995). Promoting emotional competence in school-aged children: The effects of the PATHS curriculum. *Development and Psychopathology, 7,* 117–136.

Greenberg, M. T., Weissberg, R. P., O'Brien, M. U., Zins, J. E., Fredericks, L., Resnik, H., et al. (2003). Enhancing school-based prevention and youth development through coordinated social, emotional, and academic learning. *American Psychologist, 58,* 466–474.

Greenfield, P. M. (1994). Independence and interdependence as developmental scripts: Implications for theory, research, and practice. In P. M. Greenfield & R. R. Cocking (Eds.), *Cross-cultural roots of minority child development.* Hillsdale, NJ: Erlbaum.

Greenfield, P. M. (1998). The cultural evolution of IQ. In U. Neisser (Ed.), *The rising curve: Long-term gains in IQ and related measures* (pp. 81–123). Washington, DC: American Psychological Association.

Greenfield, P. M., DeWinstanley, P., Kilpatrick, H., & Kaye, D. (1996). Action video games and informal education: Effects on strategies for dividing visual attention. In P. M. Greenfield & R. R. Cocking (Eds.), *Advances in applied developmental psychology: Vol. 11. Interacting with video* (pp. 187–205). Westport, CT: Ablex.

Greenfield, P. M., & Subrahmanyam, K. (2003). Online discourse in a teen chatroom: New codes and new modes of coherence in a visual medium. *Applied Developmental Psychology, 24,* 713–738.

Greenman, J., & Stonehouse, A. (1996). *Prime times: A handbook for excellence in infant and toddler care.* St. Paul, MN: Redleaf Press.

Greeno, J. G., Collins, A. M., & Resnick, L. B. (1996). Cognition and learning. In D. C. Berliner & R. C. Calfee (Eds.), *Handbook of educational psychology.* New York: Macmillan.

Greenough, W. T., & Black, J. E. (1992). Induction of brain structure by experience: Substrates for cognitive development. In M. R. Gunnar & C. A. Nelson (Eds.), *Developmental behavioral neuroscience. The Minnesota Symposium on Child Psychology* (Vol. 24, pp. 155–200). Mahwah, NJ: Erlbaum.

Greenough, W. T., Black, J. E., & Wallace, C. S. (1987). Experience and brain development. *Child Development, 58,* 539–559.

Greenspan, D. A., Solomon, B., & Gardner, H. (2004). The development of talent in different domains. In L. V. Shavinina & M. Ferrari (Eds.), *Beyond knowledge: Extracognitive aspects of developing high ability* (pp. 119–135). Mahwah, NJ: Erlbaum.

Greenspan, S., & Granfield, J. M. (1992). Reconsidering the construct of mental retardation: Implications of a model of social competence. *American Journal of Mental Retardation, 96,* 442–453.

Greenspan, S. I., & Meisels, S. (1996). Toward a new vision for the developmental assessment of infants and young children. In S. J. Meisels & E. Fenichel (Eds.), *New visions for the developmental assessment of infants and young children.* Washington, DC: Zero to Three.

Gregg, M., & Leinhardt, G. (1994a, April). *Constructing geography.* Paper presented at the annual meeting of the American Educational Research Association, New Orleans, LA.

Gregg, M., & Leinhardt, G. (1994b). Mapping out geography: An example of epistemology and education. *Review of Educational Research, 64,* 311–361.

Gresham, F. M., & MacMillan, D. L. (1997). Social competence and affective characteristics of students with mild disabilities. *Review of Educational Research, 67,* 377–415.

Griffin, S., Case, R., & Capodilupo, A. (1995). Teaching for understanding: The importance of the central conceptual structures in the elementary mathematics curriculum. In A. McKeough, J. Lupart, & A. Marini (Eds.), *Teaching for transfer: Fostering generalization in learning.* Mahwah, NJ: Erlbaum.

Griffin, S. A., Case, R., & Siegler, R. S. (1994). Rightstart: Providing the central conceptual prerequisites for first formal learning of arithmetic to students at risk for school failure. In K. McGilly (Ed.), *Classroom lessons: Integrating cognitive theory and classroom practice.* Cambridge, MA: MIT Press.

Griffith, P. L. (1991). Phonemic awareness helps first graders invent spellings and third graders remember correct spellings. *Journal of Reading Behavior, 23,* 215–233.

Griswold, K. S., & Pessar, L. F. (2000). Management of bipolar disorder. *American Family Physician, 62,* 1343–1356.

Grodzinsky, G. M., & Diamond, R. (1992). Frontal lobe functioning in boys with attention-deficit hyperactivity disorder. *Developmental Neuropsychology, 8,* 427–445.

Gromko, J. E. (1994). Children's invented notations as measures of musical understanding. *Psychology of Music, 22,* 136–147.

Gromko, J. E. (1996, April). *Theorizing symbolic development in music: Interpretive interactions with preschool children.* Paper presented at the Music Educators National Conference, Kansas City, MO.

Gromko, J. E. (1998). Young children's symbol use: Common principles and cognitive processes. *Update: Applications of Research in Music Education, 16*(2), 3–7.

Gromko, J. E. (2004). Predictors of music sightreading ability in high school wind players. *Journal of Research in Music Education, 52,* 6–15.

Gromko, J. E., & Poorman, A. S. (1998). Developmental trends and relationships in children's aural perception and symbol use. *Journal of Research in Music Education, 46,* 16–23.

Gronlund, N. E. (2004). *Writing instructional objectives for teaching and assessment* (7th ed.). Upper Saddle River, NJ: Merrill/Prentice Hall.

Gross, D., Fogg, L., Webster-Stratton, C., Garvey, C., Julion, W., & Grady, J. (2003). Parent training with multi-ethnic families of toddlers in day care in low-income urban communities. *Journal of Consulting and Clinical Psychology, 71,* 261–278.

Gross, R. H. (2004). Sports medicine in youth athletes. *Southern Medical Journal, 97,* 880.

Gross, R. T., & Duke, P. M. (1980). The effect of early versus late physical maturation in adolescent behavior. *Pediatric Clinics of North America, 27,* 71–77.

Grossman, H. L. (1994). *Classroom behavior management in a diverse society.* Mountain View, CA: Mayfield.

Grossmann, K., Grossmann, K. E., Fremmer-Bombik, E., Kindler, H., Scheuerer-Englisch, H., & Zimmermann, P. (2002). The uniqueness of the child-father attachment relationship: Fathers' sensitive and challenging play as a pivotal variable in a 16-year longitudinal study. *Social Development, 11*(3), 307–331,

Grossmann, K. E., Grossmann, K., Huber, F., & Wartner, U. (1981). German children's behavior toward their mothers at 12 months and their fathers at 18 months in Ainsworth's Strange Situation. *International Journal of Behavioral Development, 4,* 157–181.

Grusec, J. E., & Redler, E. (1980). Attribution, reinforcement, and altruism. *Developmental Psychology, 16,* 525–534.

Grych, J. H., & Finchman, F. D. (1997). Children's adaptation to divorce: From description to explanation. In S. A. Wolchik & I. N. Sandler (Eds.), *Handbook of children's coping: Linking theory to intervention* (pp. 159–193). New York: Plenum Press.

Guay, F., Boivin, M., & Hodges, E. V. E. (1999). Social comparison processes and academic achievement: The dependence of the development of self-evaluations on friends' performance. *Journal of Educational Psychology, 91,* 564–568.

Guberman, S. R. (1999). Supportive environments for cognitive development: Illustrations from children's mathematical activities outside of school. In A. Göncü (Ed.), *Children's engagement in the world: Sociocultural perspectives* (pp. 202–227). Cambridge, England: Cambridge University Press.

Guberman, S. R., Rahm, J., & Menk, D. W. (1998). Transforming cultural practices: Illustrations from children's game play. *Anthropology and Education Quarterly, 29,* 419–445.

Gulya, M., Rovee-Collier, C., Galluccio, L., & Wilk, A. (1998). Memory processing of a serial list by young infants. *Psychological Science, 9,* 303–307.

Gustafsson, J., & Undheim, J. O. (1996). Individual differences in cognitive functions. In D. C. Berliner & R. C. Calfee (Eds.), *Handbook of educational psychology.* New York: Macmillan.

Guthrie, B. J., Caldwell, C. H., & Hunter, A. G. (1997). Minority adolescent female health: Strategies for the next millennium. In D. K. Wilson, J. R. Rodrigue, & W. C. Taylor (Eds.), *Health-promoting and health-compromising behaviors among minority adolescents* (pp. 153–171). Washington, DC: American Psychological Association.

Guthrie, J. T., Cox, K. E., Anderson, E., Harris, K., Mazzoni, S., & Rach, L. (1998). Principles of integrated instruction for engagement in reading. *Educational Psychology Review, 10,* 177–199.

Guttmacher, S., Lieberman, L., Ward, D., Freudenberg, N., Radosh, A., & DesJarlais, D. (1997). Condom availability in New York City public high schools: Relationships to condom use and sexual behavior. *American Journal of Public Health, 87,* 1427–1433.

Hacker, D. J. (1995, April). *Comprehension monitoring of written discourse across early-to-middle adolescence.* Paper presented at the annual meeting of the American Educational Research Association, San Francisco.

Hacker, D. J., & Bol, L. (2004). Metacognitive theory: Considering the social-cognitive influences. In D. M. McInerney & S. Van Etten (Eds.), *Big theories revisited* (pp. 275–297). Greenwich, CT: Information Age.

Hacker, D. J., Bol, L., Horgan, D. D., & Rakow, E. A. (2000). Test prediction and performance in a classroom context. *Journal of Educational Psychology, 92,* 160–170.

Haenan, J. (1996). Piotr Gal'perin's criticism and extension of Lev Vygotsky's work. *Journal of Russian and East European Psychology, 34*(2), 54–60.

Hagen, J. W., & Stanovich, K. G. (1977). Memory: Strategies of acquisition. In R. V. Kail, Jr., & J. W. Hagen (Eds.), *Perspectives on the development of memory and cognition.* Hillsdale, NJ: Erlbaum.

Hagerman, R. J., & Lampe, M. E. (1999). Fragile X syndrome. In S. Goldstein & C. R. Reynolds (Eds.), *Handbook of neurodevelopmental and genetic disorders* (pp. 298–316). New York: Guilford Press.

Haight, B. K. (1992). Long-term effects of a structured life review process. *Journal of Gerontology: Psychological Sciences, 47,* 312–315.

Haight, W. L. (1999). The pragmatics of caregiver-child pretending at home: Understanding culturally specific socialization practices. In A. Göncü (Ed.), *Children's engagement in the world: Sociocultural perspectives* (pp. 128–147). Cambridge, England: Cambridge University Press.

Haith, M. M. (1990). Perceptual and sensory processes in early infancy. *Merrill-Palmer Quarterly, 36,* 1–26.

Haith, M. M., Hazan, C., & Goodman, G. S. (1988). Expectation and anticipation of dynamic visual events by 3.5-month-old babies. *Child Development, 59,* 467–479.

Hakes, D. T. (1980). *The development of metalinguistic abilities in children.* Berlin, Germany: Springer-Verlag.

Hale-Benson, J. E. (1986). *Black children: Their roots, culture, and learning styles.* Baltimore: Johns Hopkins University Press.

Halford, G. S. (1989). Cognitive processing capacity and learning ability: An integration of two areas. *Learning and Individual Differences, 1,* 125–153.

Halford, G. S., & Andrews, G. (2006). Reasoning and problem solving. In W. Damon, R. M. Lerner (Series Eds.), D. Kuhn, & R. Siegler (Vol. Eds.), *Handbook of child psychology: Vol. 2. Cognition, perception, and language* (6th ed.). New York: Wiley.

Hall, R. V., Axelrod, S., Foundopoulos, M., Shellman, J., Campbell, R. A., & Cranston, S. (1971). The effective use of punishment to modify behavior in the classroom. *Educational Technology, 11*(4), 24–26.

Hallenbeck, M. J. (1996). The cognitive strategy in writing: Welcome relief for adolescents with learning disabilities. *Learning Disabilities Research and Practice, 11,* 107–119.

Hallowell, E. (1996). *When you worry about the child you love.* New York: Simon and Schuster.

Halpern, D. F. (1992). *Sex differences in cognitive abilities* (2nd ed.). Hillsdale, NJ: Erlbaum.

Halpern, D. F. (1997). Sex differences in intelligence: Implications for education. *American Psychologist, 52,* 1091–1102.

Halpern, D. F. (2004). A cognitive-process taxonomy for sex differences in cognitive abilities. *Current Directions in Psychological Science, 13,* 135–139.

Halpern, D. F., & LaMay, M. L. (2000). The smarter sex: A critical review of sex differences in intelligence. *Educational Psychology Review, 12,* 229–246.

Hamers, J. H. M., & Ruijssenaars, A. J. J. M. (1997). Assessing classroom learning potential. In G. D. Phye (Ed.), *Handbook of academic learning: Construction of knowledge.* San Diego, CA: Academic Press.

Hamill, P. V., Drizd, T. A., Johnson, C. L., Reed, R. B., Roche, A. F., & Moore, W. M. (1979). Physical growth: National Center for Health Statistics percentiles. *American Journal of Clinical Nutrition, 32,* 607–629.

Hammer, D. (1994). Epistemological beliefs in introductory physics. *Cognition and Instruction, 12,* 151–183.

Hammer, D. (1997). Discovery learning and discovery teaching. *Cognition and Instruction, 15,* 485–529.

Hamre, B. K., & Pianta, R. C. (2005). Can instructional and emotional support in the first-grade classroom make a difference for children at risk for school failure? *Child Development, 76,* 949–967.

Hanley, J. R., Tzeng, O., & Huang, H.-S. (1999). Learning to read Chinese. In M. Harris & G. Hatano (Eds.), *Learning to read and write: A cross-linguistic perspective.* Cambridge, England: Cambridge University Press.

Hare, J. (1994). Concerns and issues faced by families headed by a lesbian couple. *Families in Society, 43,* 27–35.

Harms, T., & Clifford, R. M. (1980). *The early childhood environment rating scale.* New York: Teachers College Press.

Harris, C. R. (1991). Identifying and serving the gifted new immigrants. *Teaching Exceptional Children, 23*(4), 26–30.

Harris, J. R. (1995). Where is the child's environment? A group socialization theory of development. *Psychological Review, 102,* 458–489.

Harris, J. R. (1998). *The nurture assumption: Why children turn out the way they do.* New York: Free Press.

Harris, K. R. (1986). Self-monitoring of attentional behavior versus self-monitoring of productivity: Effects of on-task behavior and academic response rate among learning disabled children. *Journal of Applied Behavior Analysis, 19,* 417–423.

Harris, K. R., & Graham, S. (1992). Self-regulated strategy development: A part of the writing process. In M. Pressley, K. R. Harris, & J. T. Guthrie (Eds.), *Promoting academic competence and literacy in school.* San Diego, CA: Academic Press.

Harris, M. (1992). *Language experience and early language development: From input to uptake.* Hove, England: Erlbaum.

Harris, M., & Giannouli, V. (1999). Learning to read and spell in Greek: The importance of letter knowledge and morphological awareness. In M. Harris & G. Hatano (Eds.), *Learning to read and write: A cross-linguistic perspective.* Cambridge, England: Cambridge University Press.

Harris, M., & Hatano, G. (Eds.). (1999). *Learning to read and write: A cross-linguistic perspective.* Cambridge, England: Cambridge University Press.

Harris, M. B. (1997). Preface: Images of the invisible minority. In M. B. Harris (Ed.), *School experiences of gay and lesbian youth: The invisible minority* (pp. xiv–xxii). Binghamton, NY: Harrington Park Press.

Harris, M. J., & Rosenthal, R. (1985). Mediation of interpersonal expectancy effects: 31 meta-analyses. *Psychological Bulletin, 97,* 363–386.

Harris, N. G. S., Bellugi, U., Bates, E., Jones, W., & Rossen, M. (1997). Contrasting profiles of language development in children with Williams and Down syndromes. *Developmental Neuropsychology, 13,* 345–370.

Harris, P. L. (1989). *Children and emotion: The development of psychological understanding.* Oxford, England: Basil Blackwell.

Harris, P. L. (2006). Social cognition. In W. Damon, R. M. Lerner (Series Eds.), D. Kuhn, & R. Siegler (Vol. Eds.), *Handbook of child psychology: Vol. 2. Cognition, perception, and language* (6th ed.). New York: Wiley.

Harrison, A. O., Wilson, M. N., Pine, C. J., Chan, S. Q., & Buriel, R. (1990). Family ecologies of ethnic minority children. *Child Development, 61,* 347–362.

Hart, B., & Risley, T. R. (1995). *Meaningful differences in the everyday experiences of young American children.* Baltimore: Brookes.

Hart, D. (1988). The adolescent self-concept in social context. In D. K. Lapsley & F. C. Power (Eds.), *Self, ego, and identity: Integrative approaches* (pp. 71–90). New York: Springer-Verlag.

Hart, D., & Fegley, S. (1995). Prosocial behavior and caring in adolescence: Relations to self-understanding and social judgment. *Child Development, 66,* 1346–1359.

Hart, E. L., Lahey, B. B., Loeber, R., Applegate, B., & Frick, P. J. (1995). Developmental changes in attention-deficit hyperactivity disorder in boys: A four-year longitudinal study. *Journal of Abnormal Child Psychology, 23,* 729–750.

Harter, S. (1983). Developmental perspectives on the self-system. In P. M. Mussen (Series Ed.) & E. M. Hetherington (Vol. Ed.), *Handbook of child psychology: Vol. 4. Socialization, personality, and social development* (4th ed., pp. 275–385). New York: Wiley.

Harter, S. (1988). The construction and conservation of the self: James and Cooley revisited. In D. K. Lapsley & F. C. Power (Eds.), *Self, ego, and identity: Integrative approaches* (pp. 43–69). New York: Springer-Verlag.

Harter, S. (1992). The relationship between perceived competence, affect, and motivational orientation within the classroom: Processes and patterns of change. In A. K. Boggiano & T. S. Pittman (Eds.), *Achievement and motivation: A social-developmental perspective.* Cambridge, England: Cambridge University Press.

Harter, S. (1996). Teacher and classmate influences on scholastic motivation, self-esteem, and level of voice in adolescents. In J. Juvonen & K. Wentzel (Eds.), *Social motivation: Understanding children's school adjustment.* New York: Cambridge University Press.

Harter, S. (1998). The development of self-representations. In W. Damon (Series Ed.) & N. Eisenberg (Vol. Ed.), *Handbook of child psychology: Vol. 3. Social, emotional, and personality development* (5th ed., pp. 553–617). New York: Wiley.

Harter, S. (1999). *The construction of the self.* New York: Guilford Press.

Harter, S., Bresnick, S., Bouchey, H., & Whitesell, N. R. (1997). The development of multiple role-related selves during adolescence. *Development and Psychopathology, 9,* 835–853.

Harter, S., Stocker, C., & Robinson, N. S. (1996). The perceived directionality of the link between approval and self-worth: The liabilities of a looking glass self-orientation among young adolescents. *Journal of Research on Adolescence, 6,* 285–308.

Harter, S., Waters, P. L., & Whitesell, N. R. (1997). Lack of voice as a manifestation of false self-behavior among adolescents: The school setting as a stage upon which the drama of authenticity is enacted. *Educational Psychologist, 32,* 153–173.

Harter, S., & Whitesell, N. R. (1989). Developmental changes in children's understanding of single, multiple, and blended emotion concepts. In C. Saarni & P. Harris (Eds.), *Children's understanding of emotion* (pp. 81–116). Cambridge, England: Cambridge University Press.

Harter, S., Whitesell, N. R., & Junkin, L. J. (1998). Similarities and differences in domain-specific and global self-evaluations of learning-disabled, behaviorally disordered, and normally achieving adolescents. *American Educational Research Journal, 35,* 653–680.

Harter, S., Whitesell, N. R., & Kowalski, P. (1992). Individual differences in the effects of educational transitions on young adolescents' perceptions of competence and motivational orientation. *American Educational Research Journal, 29,* 777–807.

Hartmann, D. P., & George, T. P. (1999). Design, measurement, and analysis in developmental research. In M. H. Bornstein & M. E. Lamb (Eds.), *Developmental psychology: An advanced textbook* (4th ed., pp. 125–195). Mahwah, NJ: Erlbaum.

Hartup, W. W. (1983). Peer relations. In P. H. Mussen (Ed.), *Handbook of child psychology: Vol. IV. Socialization* (4th ed.). New York: Wiley.

Hartup, W. W. (1984). The peer context in middle childhood. In A. Collins (Ed.), *Development during middle childhood: The years from six to twelve.* Washington, DC: National Academy Press.

Hartup, W. W. (1996). The company they keep: Friendships and their developmental significance. *Child Development, 67,* 1–13.

Hartup, W. W., & Laursen, B. (1991). Relationships as developmental contexts. In R. Cohen & W. A. Siegel (Eds.), *Context and development* (pp. 253–279). Hillsdale, NJ: Erlbaum.

Harwood, R. L., Miller, J. G., & Irizarry, N. L. (1995). *Culture and attachment: Perceptions of the child in context.* New York: Guilford Press.

Haryu, E., & Imai, M. (2002). Reorganizing the lexicon by learning a new word: Japanese children's interpretation of the meaning of a new word for a familiar artifact. *Child Development, 73,* 1378–1391.

Hatano, G., & Inagaki, K. (1991). Sharing cognition through collective comprehension activity. In L. B. Resnick, J. M. Levine, & S. D. Teasley (Eds.), *Perspectives on socially shared cognition.* Washington, DC: American Psychological Association.

Hatano, G., & Inagaki, K. (1996). Cognitive and cultural factors in the acquisition of intuitive biology. In D. R. Olson & N. Torrance (Eds.), *The handbook of education and human development: New models of learning, teaching, and schooling.* Cambridge, MA: Blackwell.

Hatfield, E., Cacioppo, J. T., & Rapson, R. L. (1994). *Emotional contagion.* Cambridge, England: Cambridge University Press.

Hattie, J., Biggs, J., & Purdie, N. (1996). Effects of learning skills interventions on student learning: A meta-analysis. *Review of Educational Research, 66,* 99–136.

Haviland, J. M., & Lelwica, M. (1987). The induced affect response: 10-week-old infants' responses to three emotional expressions. *Developmental Psychology, 23,* 97–104.

Hawkins, F. P. L. (1997). *Journey with children: The autobiography of a teacher.* Niwot: University Press of Colorado.

Hawkins, R. P. (1989). The nature and potential of therapeutic foster care programs. In R. P. Hawkins & J. Breiling (Eds.), *Therapeutic foster care: Critical issues.* Washington, DC: Child Welfare League of America.

Hayes, C. D., & Hofferth, S. L. (1987). *Risking the future: Adolescent sexuality, pregnancy, and child-bearing* (Vol. 2). Washington, DC: National Academy Press.

Hayes, D. P., & Grether, J. (1983). The school year and vacations: When do students learn? *Cornell Journal of Social Relations, 17*(1), 56–71.

Hayne, H., Rovee-Collier, C., & Borza, M. (1991). Infant memory for place information. *Memory and Cognition, 19*, 378–386.

Hayslip, B., Jr. (1994). Stability of intelligence. In R. J. Sternberg (Ed.), *Encyclopedia of human intelligence* (Vol. 2). New York: Macmillan.

Healy, C. C. (1993). Discovery courses are great in theory, but . . . In J. L. Schwartz, M. Yerushalmy, & B. Wilson (Eds.), *The geometric supposer: What is it a case of?* Hillsdale, NJ: Erlbaum.

Hearold, S. (1986). A synthesis of 1,043 effects of television on social behavior. In G. Comstock (Ed.), *Public communication and behavior* (Vol. 1). New York: Academic Press.

Heath, S. B. (1980). Questioning at home and at school: A comparative study. In G. Spindler (Ed.), *The ethnography of schooling: Educational anthropology in action.* New York: Holt, Rinehart & Winston.

Heath, S. B. (1983). *Ways with words: Language, life, and work in communities and classrooms.* Cambridge, England: Cambridge University Press.

Heath, S. B. (1986). Taking a cross-cultural look at narratives. *Topics in Language Disorders, 7*(1), 84–94.

Heath, S. B. (1989). Oral and literate traditions among Black Americans living in poverty. *American Psychologist, 44*, 367–373.

Hecht, S. A., Close, L., & Santisi, M. (2003). Sources of individual differences in fraction skills. *Journal of Experimental Child Psychology, 86*, 277–302.

Heckenhausen, H. (1984). Emergent achievement behavior: Some early developments. In J. Nicholls (Ed.), *Advances in achievement motivation.* Greenwich, CT: JAI Press.

Heckenhausen, H. (1987). Emotional components of action: Their ontogeny as reflected in achievement behavior. In D. Girlitz & J. F. Wohlwill (Eds.), *Curiosity, imagination, and play.* Hillsdale, NJ: Erlbaum.

Hedges, L. V., & Nowell, A. (1995). Sex differences in mental test scores, variability, and numbers of high-scoring individuals. *Science, 269*, 41–45.

Hegarty, M., & Kozhevnikov, M. (1999). Types of visual-spatial representations and mathematical problem solving. *Journal of Educational Psychology, 91*, 684–689.

Hegland, S. M., & Rix, M. K. (1990). Aggression and assertiveness in kindergarten children differing in day care experiences. *Early Childhood Research Quarterly, 5*, 105–116.

Heibeck, T. H., & Markman, E. M. (1987). Word learning in children: An examination of fast mapping. *Child Development, 58*, 1021–1034.

Held, R. (1993). What can rates of development tell us about underlying mechanisms? In C. E. Granrud (Ed.), *Visual perception and cognition in infancy.* Hillsdale, NJ: Erlbaum.

Hellenga, K. (2002). Social space, the final frontier: Adolescents on the Internet. In J. T. Mortimer & R. W. Larson (Eds.), *The changing adolescent experience: Societal trends and the transition to adulthood* (pp. 208–249). Cambridge, England: Cambridge University Press.

Helwig, C. C., & Jasiobedzka, U. (2001). The relation between law and morality: Children's reasoning about socially beneficial and unjust laws. *Child Development, 72*, 1382–1393.

Helwig, C. C., Zelazo, P. D., & Wilson, M. (2001). Children's judgments of psychological harm in normal and noncanonical situations. *Child Development, 72*, 66–81.

Hembree, R. (1988). Correlates, causes, effects, and treatment of test anxiety. *Review of Educational Research, 58*, 47–77.

Hemphill, L., & Snow, C. (1996). Language and literacy development: Discontinuities and differences. In D. R. Olson & N. Torrance (Eds.), *The handbook of education and human development: New models of learning, teaching, and schooling.* Cambridge, MA: Blackwell.

Henderson, N. D. (1982). Human behavior genetics. *Annual Review of Psychology, 33*, 403–440.

Hennessey, B. A. (1995). Social, environmental, and developmental issues and creativity. *Educational Psychology Review, 7*, 163–183.

Henshaw, S. K. (1997). Teenager abortion and pregnancy statistics by state, 1992. *Family Planning Perspectives, 29*, 115–122.

Herbert, J., Stipek, D., & Miles, S. (2003, April). *Gender differences in perceptions of ability in elementary school students: The role of parents, teachers and achievement.* Paper presented at the annual meeting of the American Educational Research Association, Chicago.

Herman, M. (2004). Forced to choose: Some determinants of racial identification in multiracial adolescents. *Child Development, 75*, 730–748.

Herr, K. (1997). Learning lessons from school: Homophobia, heterosexism, and the construction of failure. In M. B. Harris (Ed.), *School experiences of gay and lesbian youth: The invisible minority* (pp. 51–64). Binghamton, NY: Harrington Park Press.

Herrnstein, R. J., & Murray, C. (1994). *The bell curve: Intelligence and class structure in American life.* New York: Free Press.

Hertel, P. T. (1994). Depression and memory: Are impairments remediable through attentional control? *Current Directions in Psychological Science, 3*, 190–193.

Hess, R. D., Chang, C. M., & McDevitt, T. M. (1987). Cultural variations in family beliefs about children's performance in mathematics: Comparisons among People's Republic of China, Chinese-American, and Caucasian-American families. *Journal of Educational Psychology, 79*, 179–188.

Hess, R. D., & Holloway, S. D. (1984). Family and school as educational institutions. In R. D. Parke, R. N. Emde, H. P. McAdoo, & G. P. Sackett (Eds.), *Review of child development research: Vol. 7. The family* (pp. 179–222). Chicago: University of Chicago Press.

Hess, R. D., & McDevitt, T. M. (1989). Family. In E. Barnouw (Ed.), *International encyclopedia of communications.* New York: Oxford University Press.

Hetherington, E. M. (1988). Family relations six years after divorce. In E. M. Hetherington & R. D. Parke (Eds.), *Contemporary readings in child psychology.* New York: McGraw-Hill.

Hetherington, E. M. (1989). Coping with family transitions: Winners, losers, and survivors. *Child Development, 60*, 1–14.

Hetherington, E. M. (1999). Social capital and the development of youth from nondivorced, divorced and remarried families. In C. W. Andrew & L. Brett (Eds.), *The Minnesota Symposia on Child Psychology: Vol. 30. Relationships as developmental contexts* (pp. 177–209). Mahwah, NJ: Erlbaum.

Hetherington, E. M., Bridges, M., & Insabella, G. M. (1998). What matters? What does not? Five perspectives on the association between marital transitions and children's adjustment. *American Psychologist, 53*, 167–184.

Hetherington, E. M., & Clingempeel, W. G. (1992). Coping with marital transitions: A family systems perspective. *Monographs of the Society for Research in Child Development, 57*(2–3, Serial No. 227).

Hetherington, E. M., Cox, M., & Cox, R. (1978). The aftermath of divorce. In J. H. Stevens, Jr., & M. Matthews (Eds.), *Mother-child father-child relationships.* Washington, DC: National Association for the Education of Young Children.

Hetherington, E. M., Henderson, S. H., Reiss, D., Anderson, E. R., Bridges, M., Chan, R. W., et al. (1999). Adolescent siblings in stepfamilies: Family functioning and adolescent adjustment. *Monographs of the Society for Research in Child Development, 64*(4, Serial No. 259).

Hetherington, E. M., & Stanley-Hagan, M. M. (1997). The effects of divorce on fathers and their children. In M. E. Lamb (Ed.), *The role of the father in child development* (pp. 191–211). New York: Wiley.

Hettinger, H. R., & Knapp, N. F. (2001). Potential, performance, and paradox: A case study of J.P., a verbally gifted, struggling reader. *Journal for the Education of the Gifted, 24*, 248–289.

Heuwinkel, M. K. (1998). *An investigation of preservice teachers' interactive assessment of student understanding in a traditional program and a professional development school.* Unpublished doctoral dissertation, University of Northern Colorado, Greeley.

Hewitt, J., & Scardamalia, M. (1996, April). *Design principles for the support of distributed processes.* Paper presented at the annual meeting of the American Educational Research Association, San Francisco.

Hiatt, S., Campos, J., & Emde, R. (1979). Facial patterning and infant emotional expression: Happiness, surprise, and fear. *Child Development, 50*, 1020–1035.

Hickey, D. T. (1997). Motivation and contemporary socio-constructivist instructional perspectives. *Educational Psychologist, 32*, 175–193.

Hickey, T. L., & Peduzzi, J. D. (1987). Structure and development of the visual system. In P. Salapatek & L. Cohen (Eds.), *Handbook of infant perception: Vol. 1. From sensation to perception.* New York: Academic Press.

Hicks, L. (1997). Academic motivation and peer relationships—How do they mix in an adolescent world? *Middle School Journal, 28*, 18–22.

Hidalgo, N. M., Siu, S., Bright, J. A., Swap, S. M., & Epstein, J. L. (1995). Research on families, schools, and communities: A multicultural perspective. In J. A. Banks & C. A. M. Banks (Eds.), *Handbook of research on multicultural education.* New York: Macmillan.

Hide, D. W., & Guyer, B. M. (1982). Prevalence of infant colic. *Archives of Disease in Childhood, 57*, 559–560.

Hiebert, E. H., & Fisher, C. W. (1992). The tasks of school literacy: Trends and issues. In J. Brophy (Ed.), *Advances in research on teaching: Vol. 3. Planning and managing learning tasks and activities.* Greenwich, CT: JAI Press.

Hiebert, E. H., & Raphael, T. E. (1996). Psychological perspectives on literacy and extensions to educational practice. In D. C. Berliner & R. C. Calfee (Eds.), *Handbook of educational psychology.* New York: Macmillan.

Hiebert, J., & Wearne, D. (1996). Instruction, understanding, and skill in multidigit addition and subtraction. *Cognition and Instruction, 14*, 251–283.

Higgins, A. (1995). Educating for justice and community: Lawrence Kohlberg's vision of moral education. In W. M. Kurtines & J. L. Gewirtz (Eds.), *Moral development: An introduction.* Boston: Allyn & Bacon.

Higgins, A. T., & Turnure, J. E. (1984). Distractibility and concentration of attention in children's development. *Child Development, 55*, 1799–1810.

Hill, J. P., Holmbeck, G. N., Marlow, L., Green, T. M., & Lynch, M. E. (1985). Menarchal status and parent-child relations in families of seventh-grade girls. *Journal of Youth and Adolescence, 14*, 301–316.

Hilliard, A., & Vaughn-Scott, M. (1982). The quest for the minority child. In S. G. Moore & C. R. Cooper (Eds.), *The young child: Reviews of research* (Vol. 3). Washington, DC: National Association for the Education of Young Children.

Hillier, L., Hewitt, K. L., & Morrongiello, B. A. (1992). Infants' perception of illusions in sound localization: Reaching to sounds in the dark. *Journal of Experimental Child Psychology, 53,* 159–179.

Hinde, R. A., Titmus, G., Easton, D., & Tamplin, A. (1985). Incidence of "friendship" and behavior with strong associates versus non-associates in preschoolers. *Child Development, 56,* 234–245.

Hine, P., & Fraser, B. J. (2002, April). *Combining qualitative and quantitative methods in a study of Australian students' transition from elementary to high school.* Paper presented at the annual meeting of the American Educational Research Association, New Orleans, LA.

Hinkley, J. W., McInerney, D. M., & Marsh, H. W. (2001, April). *The multi-faceted structure of school achievement motivation: A case for social goals.* Paper presented at the annual meeting of the American Educational Research Association, Seattle, WA.

Hinshaw, S. P., Zupan, B. A., Simmel, C., Nigg, J. T., & Melnick, S. (1997). Peer status in boys with and without attention-deficit hyperactivity disorder: Predictions from overt and covert antisocial behavior, social isolation, and authoritative parenting beliefs. *Child Development, 68,* 880–896.

Hirsh-Pasek, K., & Golinkoff, R. M. (1996). *The origins of grammar: Evidence from early language comprehension.* Cambridge, MA: MIT Press.

Hirsh-Pasek, K., Hyson, M., & Rescorla, L. (1990). Academic environments in preschool: Do they pressure or challenge young children? *Early Education and Development, 1*(6), 401–423.

Ho, C. S., & Fuson, K. C. (1998). Children's knowledge of teen quantities as tens and ones: Comparisons of Chinese, British, and American kindergartners. *Journal of Educational Psychology, 90,* 536–544.

Ho, D. Y. F. (1986). Chinese pattern of socialization: A critical review. In M. H. Bond (Ed.), *The psychology of Chinese people.* Oxford, England: Oxford University Press.

Ho, D. Y. F. (1994). Cognitive socialization in Confucian heritage cultures. In P. M. Greenfield & R. R. Cocking (Eds.), *Cross-cultural roots of minority child development.* Hillsdale, NJ: Erlbaum.

Ho, H.-Z., Hinckley, H. S., Fox, K. R., Brown, J. H., & Dixon, C. N. (2001, April). *Family literacy: Promoting parent support strategies for student success.* Paper presented at the annual meeting of the American Educational Research Association, Seattle, WA.

Hofer, B. K., & Pintrich, P. R. (1997). The development of epistemological theories: Beliefs about knowledge and knowing and their relation to learning. *Review of Educational Research, 67,* 88–140.

Hofer, B. K., & Pintrich, P. R. (Eds.). (2002). *Personal epistemology: The psychology of beliefs about knowledge and knowing.* Mahwah, NJ: Erlbaum.

Hoff, E. (2003). The specificity of environmental influence: Socioeconomic status affects early vocabulary development via maternal speech. *Child Development, 74,* 1368–1378.

Hoff, E., & Naigles, L. (2002). How children use input to acquire a lexicon. *Child Development, 73,* 418–433.

Hoff-Ginsberg, E. (1997). *Language development.* Pacific Grove, CA: Brooks/Cole.

Hoffman, M. L. (1970). Moral development. In P. H. Mussen (Ed.), *Carmichael's manual of child psychology* (Vol. 2). New York: Wiley.

Hoffman, M. L. (1975). Altruistic behavior and the parent-child relationship. *Journal of Personality and Social Psychology, 31,* 937–943.

Hoffman, M. L. (1981). Is altruism part of human nature? *Journal of Personality and Social Psychology, 40,* 121–137.

Hoffman, M. L. (1988). Moral development. In M. H. Bornstein & M. E. Lamb (Eds.), *Developmental psychology: An advanced textbook* (2nd ed.). Hillsdale, NJ: Erlbaum.

Hoffman, M. L. (1991). Empathy, social cognition, and moral action. In W. M. Kurtines & J. L. Gewirtz (Eds.), *Moral behavior and development: Vol. 1. Theory.* Hillsdale, NJ: Erlbaum.

Hoffman, M. L. (1994). Discipline and internalization. *Developmental Psychology, 30,* 26–28.

Hogan, K. (1997, March). *Relating students' personal frameworks for science learning to their cognition in collaborative contexts.* Paper presented at the annual meeting of the American Educational Research Association, Chicago.

Hokoda, A., & Fincham, F. D. (1995). Origins of children's helplessness and mastery achievement patterns in the family. *Journal of Educational Psychology, 87,* 375–385.

Holliday, B. G. (1985). Towards a model of teacher-child transactional processes affecting Black children's academic achievement. In M. B. Spencer, G. K. Brookins, & W. R. Allen (Eds.), *Beginnings: The social and affective development of Black children.* Hillsdale, NJ: Erlbaum.

Hollins, E. R. (1996). *Culture in school learning: Revealing the deep meaning.* Mahwah, NJ: Erlbaum.

Holloway, S. D. (2000). *Contested childhood: Diversity and change in Japanese preschools.* New York: Routledge.

Holloway, S. D., Fuller, B., Rambaud, M. F., & Eggers-Péirola, C. (1997). *Through my own eyes: Single mothers and the cultures of poverty.* Cambridge, MA: Harvard University Press.

Holmes, R. M. (1998). *Fieldwork with children.* Thousand Oaks, CA: Sage.

Hom, A., & Battistich, V. (1995, April). *Students' sense of school community as a factor in reducing drug use and delinquency.* Paper presented at the annual meeting of the American Educational Research Association, San Francisco.

Hong, Y., Chiu, C., & Dweck, C. S. (1995). Implicit theories of intelligence: Reconsidering the role of confidence in achievement motivation. In M. H. Kernis (Ed.), *Efficacy, agency, and self-esteem.* New York: Plenum Press.

Hong, Y., Morris, M. W., Chiu, C., & Benet-Martínez, V. (2000). Multicultural minds: A dynamic constructivist approach to culture and cognition. *American Psychologist, 55,* 709–720.

Honig, A. S. (2002). *Secure relationships: Nurturing infant/toddler attachment in early care settings.* Washington D.C.: National Association for the Education of Young Children.

Hoover-Dempsey, K. V., & Sandler, H. M. (1997). Why do parents become involved in their children's education? *Review of Educational Research, 67,* 3–42.

Hopkins, B., & Westra, T. (1998). Maternal handling and motor development: An intracultural study. Genetic, *Social and General Psychology Monographs, 14,* 377–420.

Horacek, H., Ramey, C., Campbell, F., Hoffman, K., & Fletcher, R. (1987). Predicting school failure and assessing early intervention with high-risk children. *American Academy of Child and Adolescent Psychiatry, 26,* 758–763.

Horn, J. L., & Noll, J. (1997). Human cognitive capabilities: Gf-Gc theory. In D. P. Flanagan, J. L. Genshaft, & P. L. Harrison (Eds.), *Contemporary intellectual assessment: Theories, tests, and issues* (pp. 53–91). New York: Guilford Press.

Hossain, Z., & Roopnarine, J. L. (1994). African American fathers' involvement with infants: Relationship to their functioning style, support, education, and income. *Infant Behavior and Development, 17,* 175–184.

Hossler, D., & Stage, F. K. (1992). Family and high school experience influences on the postsecondary educational plans of ninth-grade students. *American Educational Research Journal, 29,* 425–451.

Houston, A. (2004). In new media as in old, content matters most. *Social Policy Report, 18*(4), 4 (Society for Research in Child Development).

Howe, D. (1995). Adoption and attachment. *Adoption and Fostering, 19,* 7–15.

Howe, M. L. (2003). Memories from the cradle. *Current Directions in Psychological Science, 12,* 62–65.

Howell, J. C. (2000, August). *Youth gang programs and strategies.* Washington, DC: U.S. Department of Justice, Office of Juvenile Justice and Delinquency Prevention.

Howell, J. C., & Lynch, J. P. (2000). *Youth gangs in schools.* Washington, DC: U.S. Department of Justice, Office of Juvenile Justice and Delinquency Prevention.

Howes, C. (1988). The peer interactions of young children. *Monographs of the Society for Research in Child Development, 53*(1, Serial No. 217).

Howes, C. (1992). *The collaborative construction of pretend.* Albany: State University of New York Press.

Howes, C. (1999). Attachment relationships in the context of multiple caregivers. In J. Cassidy & P. R. Shaver (Eds.), *Handbook of attachment: Theory, research, and clinical applications* (pp. 671–687). New York: Guilford Press.

Howes, C., & Matheson, C. C. (1992). Sequences in the development of competent play with peers: Social and social-pretend play. *Developmental Psychology, 28,* 961–974.

Howes, C., & Ritchie, S. (1998). Changes in child-teacher relationships in a therapeutic preschool program. *Early Education and Development, 9,* 411–422.

Howes, C., & Segal, J. (1993). Children's relationships with alternative caregivers: The special case of maltreated children removed from their homes. *Journal of Applied Developmental Psychology, 17,* 71–81.

Howes, C., Smith, E., & Galinsky, E. (1995). *The Florida child care quality improvement study.* New York: Families and Work Institute.

Howie, J. D. (2002, April). *Effects of audience, gender, and achievement level on adolescent students' communicated attributions and affect in response to academic success and failure.* Paper presented at the annual meeting of the American Educational Research Association, New Orleans, LA.

Huang, M.-H., & Hauser, R. M. (1998). Trends in Black-White test-score differentials: II. The WORDSUM vocabulary test. In U. Neisser (Ed.), *The rising curve: Long-term gains in IQ and related measures* (pp. 303–332). Washington, DC: American Psychological Association.

Hubel, D., & Wiesel, T. (1965). Binocular interaction in striate cortex of kittens reared with artificial squint. *Journal of Neurophysiology, 28,* 1041–1059.

Huesmann, L. R., Moise-Titus, J., Podolski, C. L., & Eron, L. D. (2003). Longitudinal relations between children's exposure to TV violence and their aggressive and violent behavior in young adulthood: 1977–1992. *Developmental Psychology, 39*(2), 201–221.

Hughes, F. P. (1998). Play in special populations. In O. N. Saracho & B. Spodek (Eds.), *Multiple perspectives on play in early childhood education* (pp. 171–193). Albany: State University of New York Press.

Huizink, A. C., Mulder, E.J.H., & Buitelaar, J. K. (2004). Prenatal stress and risk for psychopathology: Special effects or induction of general susceptibility? *Psychological Bulletin, 130,* 115–142.

Hulme, C., & Joshi, R. M. (Eds.). (1998). *Reading and spelling: Development and disorders.* Mahwah, NJ: Erlbaum.

Humphreys, A. P., & Smith, P. K. (1987). Rough-and-tumble play, friendship, and dominance in school children: Evidence for continuity and change with age. *Child Development, 58,* 201–212.

Humphreys, L. G. (1992). What both critics and users of ability tests need to know. *Psychological Science, 3,* 271–274.

Hunt, D. E. (1981). Teachers' adaptation: "Reading" and "flexing" to students. In B. R. Joyce, C. C. Brown, & L. Peck (Eds.), *Flexibility in teaching: An excursion into the nature of teaching and training* (pp. 59–71). New York: Longman.

Hunt, E. (1997). Nature vs. nurture: The feeling of *vujà dé.* In R. J. Sternberg & E. L. Grigorenko (Eds.), *Intelligence, heredity, and environment* (pp. 531–551). Cambridge, England: Cambridge University Press.

Hunt, E., Streissguth, A. P., Kerr, B., & Olson, H. C. (1995). Mothers' alcohol consumption during pregnancy: Effects on spatial-visual reasoning in 14-year-old children. *Psychological Science, 6,* 339–342.

Huntsinger, C. S., Jose, P. E., Larson, S. L., Krieg, D. B., & Shaligram, C. (2000). Mathematics, vocabulary, and reading development in Chinese American and European American children over the primary school years. *Journal of Educational Psychology, 92,* 745–760.

Hurtes, K. P. (2002). Social dependency: The impact of adolescent female culture. *Leisure Sciences, 24,* 109–121.

Husman, J., & Freeman, B. (1999, April). *The effect of perceptions of instrumentality on intrinsic motivation.* Paper presented at the annual meeting of the American Educational Research Association, Montreal, Canada.

Hussong, A., Chassin, L., & Hicks, R. (1999, April). *The elusive relation between negative affect and adolescent substance use: Does it exist?* Paper presented at the biennial meeting of the Society for Research in Child Development, Albuquerque, NM.

Huston, A. C. (1983). Sex typing. In E. M. Hetherington (Ed.), *Handbook of child psychology: Vol. 4. Socialization, personality, and social development* (4th ed., pp. 387–467). New York: Wiley.

Huston, A. C., Donnerstein, E., Fairchild, H., Feshbach, N. D., Katz, P. A., Murray, J. P., et al. (1992). *Big world, small screen: The role of television in American society.* Lincoln: University of Nebraska Press.

Huston, A. C., & Wright, J. C. (1998). Mass media and children's development. In W. Damon (Series Ed.), I. E. Sigel & K. A. Renninger (Vol. Eds.), *Handbook of child psychology: Vol. 4. Child psychology in practice* (5th ed., pp. 999–1058). New York: Wiley.

Huttenlocher, J., Jordan, N. C., & Levine, S. C. (1994). A mental model for early arithmetic. *Journal of Experimental Psychology: General, 123,* 284–296.

Huttenlocher, J., Newcombe, N., & Vasilyeva, M. (1999). Spatial scaling in young children. *Psychological Science, 10,* 393–398.

Huttenlocher, P. R. (1979). Synaptic density in human frontal cortex: Developmental changes and effects of aging. *Brain Research, 163,* 195–205.

Huttenlocher, P. R. (1990). Morphometric study of human cerebral cortex development. *Neuropsychologia, 28,* 517–527.

Huttenlocher, P. R. (1993). Morphometric study of human cerebral cortex development. In M. H. Johnson (Ed.), *Brain development and cognition: A reader.* Cambridge, MA: Blackwell.

Huttenlocher, P. R., & De Courten, C. (1987). The development of synapses in striate cortex of man. *Human Neurobiology, 6,* 1–9.

Hyde, K. L., & Peretz, I. (2004). Brains that are out of tune but in time. *Psychological Science, 15,* 356–360.

Hynd, C. (1998). Conceptual change in a high school physics class. In B. Guzzetti & C. Hynd (Eds.), *Perspectives on conceptual change: Multiple ways to understand knowing and learning in a complex world* (pp. 27–36). Mahwah, NJ: Erlbaum.

Hyson, M. C., Hirsh-Pasek, K., Rescorla, L., Cone, J., & Martell-Boinske, L. (1991). Ingredients of parental "pressure" in early childhood. *Journal of Applied Developmental Psychology, 12*(3), 347–365.

Igoa, C. (1995). *The inner world of the immigrant child.* Mahwah, NJ: Erlbaum.

Inglis, A., & Biemiller, A. (1997, March). *Fostering self-direction in mathematics: A cross-age tutoring program that enhances math problem solving.* Paper presented at the annual meeting of the American Educational Research Association, Chicago.

International Human Genome Sequencing Consortium. (2004, October 21). Finishing the euchromatic sequence of the human genome. *Nature, 431,* 931–945.

Irujo, S. (1988). An introduction to intercultural differences and similarities in nonverbal communication. In J. S. Wurzel (Ed.), *Toward multiculturalism: A reader in multicultural education.* Yarmouth, ME: Intercultural Press.

Irwin, C. E., Jr., & Millstein, S. G. (1992). Biopsychosocial correlates of risk-taking behaviors during adolescence: Can the physician intervene? *Journal of Adolescent Health Care, 7*(Suppl. 6), 82S–96S.

Irwin, R. A., & Gross, A. M. (1995). Cognitive tempo, violent video games, and aggressive behavior in young boys. *Journal of Family Violence, 10,* 337–350.

Isabella, R. A., & Belsky, J. (1991). Interactional synchrony and the origins of infant-mother attachment: A replication study. *Child Development, 62,* 373–384.

Isen, A., Daubman, K. A., & Gorgoglione, J. M. (1987). The influence of positive affect on cognitive organization: Implications for education. In R. E. Snow & M. J. Farr (Eds.), *Aptitude, learning and instruction: Vol. 3. Cognitive and affective process analysis.* Hillsdale, NJ: Erlbaum.

Isolauri, E., Sutas, Y., Salo, M. K., Isosomppi, R., & Kaila, M. (1998). Elimination diet in cow's milk allergy: Risk for impaired growth in young children. *Journal of Pediatrics, 132,* 1004–1009.

Jacklin, C. N. (1989). Female and male: Issues of gender. *American Psychologist, 44,* 127–133.

Jackson, D. L., & Ormrod, J. E. (1998). *Case studies: Applying educational psychology.* Upper Saddle River, NJ: Merrill/Prentice Hall.

Jackson, J. F. (1986). Characteristics of Black infant attachment. *American Journal of Social Psychiatry, 6*(1), 32–35.

Jackson, J. F. (1993). Multiple caregiving among African Americans and infant attachment: The need for an emic approach. *Human Development, 35,* 87–102.

Jackson, P. W. (1988). The daily grind. In G. Handel (Ed.), *Childhood socialization.* New York: Aldine de Gruyter.

Jacob, B. A. (2003). Accountability, incentives, and behavior: The impact of high-stakes testing in the Chicago Public Schools. *Education Next, 3*(1). Retrieved March 10, 2004, from http://www.educationnext.org/unabridged/20031/jacob.pdf

Jacobs, J. E., Lanza, S., Osgood, D. W., Eccles, J. S., & Wigfield, A. (2002). Changes in children's self-competence and values: Gender and domain differences across grades one through twelve. *Child Development, 73,* 509–527.

Jacobsen, B., Lowery, B., & DuCette, J. (1986). Attributions of learning disabled children. *Journal of Educational Psychology, 78,* 59–64.

Jacobsen, L. K., Giedd, J. N., Berquin, P. C., Krain, A. L., Hamburger, S. D., Kumra, S., et al. (1997). Quantitative morphology of the cerebellum and fourth ventricle in childhood-onset schizophrenia. *American Journal of Psychiatry, 154,* 1663–1669.

Jacobsen, L. K., Giedd, J. N., Castellanos, F. X., Vaituzis, A. C., Hamburger, S. D., Kumra, S., et al, J. L. (1997). Progressive reduction of temporal lobe structures in childhood-onset schizophrenia. *American Journal of Psychiatry, 155,* 678–685.

Jacoby, R., & Glauberman, N. (Eds.). (1995). *The Bell Curve debate: History, documents, opinions.* New York: Random House.

Jalongo, M. R., Isenberg, J. P., & Gerbracht, G. (1995). *Teachers' stories: From personal narrative to professional insight.* San Francisco: Jossey-Bass.

James, D. K., Spencer, C. J., & Stepsis, B. W. (2002). Fetal learning: A prospective randomized controlled study. *Ultrasound in Obstetrics and Gynecology, 20,* 431–438.

Jaswal, V. K., & Markman, E. M. (2001). Learning proper and common names in inferential versus ostensive contexts. *Child Development, 72,* 768–786.

Jencks, C. M., & Mayer, S. (1990). The social consequences of growing up in a poor neighborhood: A review. In M. McGreary & L. Lynn (Eds.), *Concentrated urban poverty in America.* Washington, DC: National Academy.

Jenkins, J. M., Turrell, S. L., Kogushi, Y., Lollis, S., & Ross, H. S. (2003). A longitudinal investigation of the dynamics of mental state talk in families. *Child Development, 74,* 905–920.

Jenkins, S., Bax, M., & Hart, H. (1980). Behavior problems in preschool children. *Journal of Child Psychology and Psychiatry, 21,* 5–18.

Jenlink, C. L. (1994, April). *Music: A lifeline for the self-esteem of at-risk students.* Paper presented at the annual meeting of the American Educational Research Association, New Orleans, LA.

Jensen, M. M. (2005). *Introduction to emotional and behavioral disorders: Recognizing and managing problems in the classroom.* Upper Saddle River, NJ: Merrill Prentice Hall.

Jessor, R., & Jessor, S. L. (1977). *Problem behavior and psychosocial development: A longitudinal study of youth.* San Diego, CA: Academic Press.

Jimerson, S., Egeland, B., & Teo, A. (1999). A longitudinal study of achievement trajectories: Factors associated with change. *Journal of Educational Psychology, 91,* 116–126.

Jipson, J. L., & Callanan, M. A. (2003). Mother-child conversation and children's understanding of biological and nonbiological changes in size. *Child Development, 74,* 629–644.

Johanning, D. I., D'Agostino, J. V., Steele, D. F., & Shumow, L. (1999, April). *Student writing, post-writing group collaboration, and learning in pre-algebra.* Paper presented at the annual meeting of the American Educational Research Association, Montreal, Canada.

John, O. P. (1990). The "Big Five" factor taxonomy: Dimensions of personality in the natural language and in questionnaires. In L. Pervin (Ed.), *Handbook of personality: Theory and research* (pp. 66–100). New York: Guilford Press.

John, O. P., Caspi, A., Robins, R. W., Moffitt, T. E., & Stouthamer-Loeber, M. (1994). The "Little Five": Exploring the five-factor model of personality in adolescent boys. *Child Development, 65,* 160–178.

Johnson, D. W., & Johnson, R. T. (1996). Conflict resolution and peer mediation programs in elementary and secondary schools: A review of the research. *Review of Educational Research, 66,* 459–506.

Johnson, D. W., & Johnson, R. T. (2001, April). *Teaching students to be peacemakers: A meta-analysis.* Paper presented at the annual meeting of the American Educational Research Association, Seattle, WA.

Johnson, D. W., Johnson, R., Dudley, B., Ward, M., & Magnuson, D. (1995). The impact of peer mediation training on the management of school and home conflicts. *American Educational Research Journal, 32,* 829–844.

Johnson, H. C., & Friesen, B. (1993). Etiologies of mental and emotional disorders in children. In H. Johnson (Ed.), *Child mental health in the 1990s: Curricula for graduate and undergraduate.* Washington, DC: U.S. Department of Health and Human Services.

Johnson, J. S., & Newport, E. L. (1989). Critical period effects in second language learning: The influence of maturational state on acquisition of English as a second lanuage. *Cognitive Psychology, 21,* 60–99.

Johnson, M. H. (1998). The neural basis of cognitive development. In W. Damon (Series Ed.), D. Kuhn, & R. S. Siegler (Vol. Eds.), *Handbook of child psychology: Vol. 2. Cognition, perception, and language* (5th ed.). New York: Wiley.

Johnson, M. H. (1999). Developmental neuroscience. In M. H. Bornstein & M. E. Lamb (Eds.), *Developmental psychology: An advanced textbook* (4th ed., pp. 199–230). Mahwah, NJ: Erlbaum.

Johnson, M. H., & de Haan, M. (2001). Developing cortical specialization for visual-cognitive function: The case of face recognition. In J. L. McClelland & R. S. Siegler (Eds.), *Mechanisms of cognitive development: Behavioral and neural perspectives* (pp. 253–270). Mahwah, NJ: Erlbaum.

Johnson, M. H., & Morton, J. (1991). *Biology and cognitive development: The case of face recognition.* Oxford, England: Blackwell.

Johnston, J. R. (1997). Specific language impairment, cognition and the biological basis of language. In M. Gopnik (Ed.), *The inheritance and innateness of grammars.* New York: Oxford University Press.

Johnston, L. D., O'Malley, P. M., & Bachman, J. G. (2000). *The Monitoring the Future national results on adolescent drug use: Overview of the findings, 1999.* Bethesda, MD: National Institute on Drug Use. Retrieved from http://www.monitoringthefuture.org/pubs/keyfindings.pdf

Johnston, L. D., O'Malley, P. M., Bachman, J. G., & Schulenberg, J. E. (2005). *Monitoring the Future national results on adolescent drug use: Overview of key findings, 2004* (NIH Publication No. 05-5726). Bethesda, MD: National Institute on Drug Abuse.

Johnston, P., & Afflerbach, P. (1985). The process of constructing main ideas from text. *Cognition and Instruction, 2,* 207–232.

Johnston, T. D., & Edwards, L. (2002). Genes, interactions, and the development of behavior. *Psychological Review, 109,* 26–34.

Jones, D., & Christensen, C. A. (1999). Relationship between automaticity in handwriting and students' ability to generate written text. *Journal of Educational Psychology, 91,* 44–49.

Jones, G. P., & Dembo, M. H. (1989). Age and sex role differences in intimate friendships during childhood and adolescence. *Merrill-Palmer Quarterly, 35,* 445–462.

Jones, H. F. (1949). Adolescence in our society. In *Anniversary Papers of the Community Service Society of New York: The family in a democratic society* (pp. 70–82). New York: Columbia University Press.

Jordan, A. B. (2003). Children remember prosocial program lessons but how much are they learning? *Applied Developmental Psychology, 24,* 341–345.

Jordan, N. C., Hanich, L. B., & Kaplan, D. (2003). A longitudinal study of mathematical competencies in children with specific mathematics difficulties versus children with comorbid mathematics and reading difficulties. *Child Development, 74,* 834–850.

Joshi, M. S., & MacLean, M. (1994). Indian and English children's understanding of the distinction between real and apparent emotion. *Child Development, 65,* 1372–1384.

Josselson, R. (1988). The embedded self: I and Thou revisited. In D. K. Lapsley & F. C. Power (Eds.), *Self, ego, and identity: Integrative approaches* (pp. 91–106). New York: Springer-Verlag.

Jovanovic, J., & King, S. S. (1998). Boys and girls in the performance-based science classroom: Who's doing the performing? *American Educational Research Journal, 35,* 477–496.

Juel, C. (1991). Beginning reading. In R. Barr, M. Kamii, P. Mosenthal, & P. D. Pearson (Eds.), *Handbook of reading research* (Vol. II). New York: Longman.

Jusczyk, P. W. (1995). Language acquisition: Speech sounds and phonological development. In J. L. Miller & P. D. Eimas (Eds.), *Handbook of perception and cognition: Vol. 11. Speech, language, and communication.* Orlando, FL: Academic Press.

Jusczyk, P. W. (1997). Finding and remembering words: Some beginnings by English-learning infants. *Current Directions in Psychological Science, 6,* 170–174.

Jusczyk, P. W. (2002). How infants adapt speech-processing capacities to native-language structure. *Current Directions in Psychological Science, 11,* 15–18.

Jusczyk, P. W., & Aslin, R. N. (1995). Infants' detection of the sound patterns of words in fluent speech. *Cognitive Psychology, 29,* 1–23.

Juster, N. (1961). *The phantom tollbooth.* New York: Random House.

Juvonen, J. (1991). Deviance, perceived responsibility, and negative peer reactions. *Developmental Psychology, 27,* 672–681.

Juvonen, J. (2000). The social functions of attributional face-saving tactics among early adolescents. *Educational Psychology Review, 12,* 15–32.

Juvonen, J., & Hiner, M. (1991, April). *Perceived responsibility and annoyance as mediators of negative peer reactions.* Paper presented at the annual meeting of the American Educational Research Association, Chicago.

Juvonen, J., Nishina, A., & Graham, S. (2000). Peer harassment, psychological adjustment, and school functioning in early adolescence. *Journal of Educational Psychology, 92,* 349–359.

Juvonen, J., & Weiner, B. (1993). An attributional analysis of students' interactions: The social consequences of perceived responsibility. *Educational Psychology Review, 5,* 325–345.

Kaczmarek, M. G., & Backlund, B. A. (1991). Disenfranchised grief: The loss of an adolescent romantic relationship. *Adolescence, 26,* 253–259.

Kagan, J. (1981). *The second year: The emergence of self-awareness.* Cambridge, MA: Harvard University Press.

Kagan, J. (1984). *The nature of the child.* New York: Basic Books.

Kagan, J. (1998). Biology and the child. In W. Damon (Series Ed.) & N. Eisenberg (Vol. Ed.), *Handbook of child psychology: Vol. 3. Social, emotional, and personality development* (pp. 177–235). New York: Wiley.

Kagan, J. S. (1969). Inadequate evidence and illogical conclusions. *Harvard Educational Review, 39,* 274–277.

Kahl, B., & Woloshyn, V. E. (1994). Using elaborative interrogation to facilitate acquisition of factual information in cooperative learning settings: One good strategy deserves another. *Applied Cognitive Psychology, 8,* 465–478.

Kail, R. (1990). *The development of memory in children* (3rd ed.). New York: Freeman.

Kail, R. (1993). The role of a global mechanism in developmental change in speed of processing. In M. L. Howe & R. Pasnak (Eds.), *Emerging themes in cognitive development: Vol. 1. Foundations.* New York: Springer-Verlag.

Kail, R. V. (1998). *Children and their development.* Upper Saddle River, NJ: Prentice Hall.

Kaler, S. R., & Kopp, C. B. (1990). Compliance and comprehension in very young toddlers. *Child Development, 61,* 1997–2003.

Kamerman, S. B. (2000). Parental leave policies: An essential ingredient in early childhood education and care policies. *Social Policy Report, 14*(2). Ann Arbor, MI: Society for Research in Child Development.

Kanner, A. D., Feldman, S. S., Weinberger, D. A., & Ford, M. E. (1987). Uplifts, hassles, and adaptational outcomes in early adolescents. *Journal of Early Adolescence, 7,* 371–394.

Kaplan, A. (1998, April). *Task goal orientation and adaptive social interaction among students of diverse cultural backgrounds.* Paper presented at the annual meeting of the American Educational Research Association, San Diego, CA.

Kaplan, A., Middleton, M. J., Urdan, T., & Midgley, C. (2002). Achievement goals and goal structures. In C. Midgley (Ed.), *Goals, goal structures, and patterns of adaptive learning* (pp. 21–53). Mahwah, NJ: Erlbaum.

Kaplan, P. S., Goldstein, M. H., Huckeby, E. R., & Cooper, R. P. (1995). Habituation, sensitization, and infants' responses to motherese speech. *Developmental Psychobiology, 28,* 45–57.

Kapp-Simon, K., & Simon, D. J. (1991). Meeting the challenge: Social skills training for teens with special needs. *Connections: The Newsletter of the National Center for Youth and Disabilities, 2*(2), 1–5.

Karabenick, S. A., & Sharma, R. (1994). Seeking academic assistance as a strategic learning resource. In P. R. Pintrich, D. R. Brown, & C. E. Weinstein (Eds.), *Student motivation, cognition, and learning: Essays in honor of Wilbert J. McKeachie.* Hillsdale, NJ: Erlbaum.

Karafantis, D. M., & Levy, S. R. (2004). The role of children's lay theories about the malleability of human attributes in beliefs about and volunteering for disadvantaged groups. *Child Development, 75,* 236–250.

Kardash, C. A. M., & Howell, K. L. (1996, April). *Effects of epistemological beliefs on strategies employed to comprehend dual-positional text.* Paper presented at the annual meeting of the American Educational Research Association, New York.

Karmiloff-Smith, A. (1979). Language development after five. In P. Fletcher & M. Garman (Eds.), *Language acquisition: Studies in first language development.* Cambridge, England: Cambridge University Press.

Karmiloff-Smith, A. (1993). Innate constraints and developmental change. In P. Bloom (Ed.), *Language acquisition: Core readings.* Cambridge, MA: MIT Press.

Karpov, Y. V. (2003). Development through the lifespan. In A. Kozulin, B. Gindis, V. S. Ageyev, & S. M. Miller (Eds.), *Vygotsky's educational theory in cultural context* (pp. 138–155). Cambridge, England: Cambridge University Press.

Karpov, Y. V., & Haywood, H. C. (1998). Two ways to elaborate Vygotsky's concept of mediation: Implications for instruction. *American Psychologist, 53,* 27–36.

Katchadourian, H. (1990). Sexuality. In S. S. Feldman & G. R. Elliott (Eds.), *At the threshold: The developing adolescent* (pp. 330–351). Cambridge, MA: Harvard University Press.

Katkovsky, W., Crandall, V. C., & Good, S. (1967). Parental antecedents of children's beliefs in internal-external control of reinforcements in intellectual achievement situations. *Child Development, 38,* 765–776.

Katz, E. W., & Brent, S. B. (1968). Understanding connectives. *Journal of Verbal Learning and Verbal Behavior, 7,* 501–509.

Katz, L. F., & Gottman, J. M. (1991). Marital discord and child outcomes: A social psychophysiological approach. In J. Garber & K. A. Dodge (Eds.), *The development of emotion regulation and dysregulation.* Cambridge, England: Cambridge University Press.

Katz, L. F., & Low, S. M. (2004). Marital violence, co-parenting, and family-level processes in relation to children's adjustment. *Journal of Family Psychology, 18,* 372–382.

Kazdin, A. E. (1997). Conduct disorder across the lifespan. In S. S. Luthar, J. A. Burack, D. Cicchetti, & J. R. Weisz (Eds.), *Developmental psychopathology: Perspectives on adjustment, risk, and disorder* (pp. 248–272). Cambridge, England: Cambridge University Press.

Kazura, K. (2000). Fathers' qualitative and quantitative involvement: An investigation of attachment. *The Journal of Men's Studies, 9*(1), 41–57.

Kearins, J. M. (1981). Visual spatial memory in Australian aboriginal children of desert regions. *Cognitive Psychology, 13,* 434–460.

Kedesdy, J. H., & Budd, K. S. (1998). *Childhood feeding disorders: Biobehavioral assessment and intervention.* Baltimore: Brookes.

Keil, F. C. (1989). *Concepts, kinds, and cognitive development.* Cambridge, MA: MIT Press.

Keil, F. C. (1994). The birth and nurturance of concepts by domains: The origins of concepts of living things. In L. A. Hirschfeld & S. A. Gelman (Eds.), *Mapping the mind: Domain specificity in cognition and culture.* New York: Cambridge University Press.

Keil, F. C., & Silberstein, C. S. (1996). Schooling and the acquisition of theoretical knowledge. In D. R. Olson & N. Torrance (Eds.), *The handbook of education and human development: New models of learning, teaching, and schooling.* Cambridge, MA: Blackwell.

Kelemen, D. (1999). Why are rocks pointy? Children's preference for teleological explanations of the natural world. *Developmental Psychology, 35,* 1440–1452.

Kelemen, D. (2004). Are children "intuitive theists"?: Reasoning about purpose and design in nature. *Psychological Science, 15,* 295–301.

Kellogg, R. (1967). *The psychology of children's art.* New York: CRM–Random House.

Kellogg, R. T. (1994). *The psychology of writing.* New York: Oxford University Press.

Kelly, J. A. (1995). *Changing HIV risk behaviors: Practical strategies.* New York: Guilford Press.

Kelly, J. A., Murphy, D. A., Sikkema, K. J., & Kalichman, S. C. (1993). Psychological interventions to prevent HIV infection are urgently needed. *American Psychologist, 48,* 1023–1034.

Kelly, J. B., & Lamb, M. E. (2000). Using child development research to make appropriate custody and access decisions for young children. *Family and Conciliation Courts Review, 38*(3), 297–311.

Kemler Nelson, D. G., Egan, L. C., & Holt, M. B. (2004). When children ask, "What is it?" what do they want to know about artifacts? *Psychological Science, 15,* 384–389.

Kemper, S. (1984). The development of narrative skills: Explanations and entertainments. In S. Kuczaj (Ed.), *Discourse development: Progress in cognitive development research.* New York: Springer-Verlag.

Kemper, S., & Edwards, L. (1986). Children's expression of causality and their construction of narratives. *Topics in Language Disorders, 7L*(1), 11–20.

Kenneth, K., Smith, P. K., & Palermiti, A. L. (1997). Conflict in childhood and reproductive development. *Evolution and Human Behavior, 18,* 109–142.

Keogh, B. K. (2003). *Temperament in the classroom: Understanding individual differences.* Baltimore, MD: Brookes.

Keogh, B. K., & MacMillan, D. L. (1996). Exceptionality. In D. C. Berliner & R. C. Calfee (Eds.), *Handbook of educational psychology.* New York: Macmillan.

Kerewsky, W., & Lefstein, L. M. (1982). Young adolescents and their community: A shared responsibility. In L. M. Lefstein et al. (Eds.), *3:00 to 6:00 P.M.: Young adolescents at home and in the community.* Carrboro, NC: Center for Early Adolescence.

Kern, L., Dunlap, G., Childs, K. E., & Clark, S. (1994). Use of a classwide self-management program to improve the behavior of students with emotional and behavioral disorders. *Education and Treatment of Children, 17,* 445–458.

Kerns, L. L., & Lieberman, A. B. (1993). *Helping your depressed child.* Rocklin, CA: Prima.

Kestenbaum, R., Farber, E. A., & Sroufe, L. A. (1989). Individual differences in empathy among preschoolers: Relation to attachment history. In N. Eisenberg (Ed.), *Empathy and related emotional responses* (New Directions for Child Development, No. 44; pp. 51–64). San Francisco: Jossey-Bass.

Kiang, L., & Harter, S. (2005, April). *Integrated/fragmented selves in Chinese Americans: Do pieces of the personal puzzle fit?* Poster presented at the biennial meeting of the Society for Research in Child Development, Atlanta.

Kienberger-Jaudes, R., Ekwo, E., & Van Voorhis, J. (1995). Association of drug abuse and child abuse. *Child Abuse and Neglect, 19,* 531–543.

Kieran, C. (1989). The early learning of algebra: A structural perspective. In S. Wagner & C. Kieran (Eds.), *Research issues in the learning and teaching of algebra.* Reston, VA: National Council of Teachers of Mathematics.

Killen, M., & Nucci, L. P. (1995). Morality, autonomy, and social conflict. In M. Killen & D. Hart (Eds.), *Morality in everyday life: Developmental perspectives* (pp. 52–86). Cambridge, England: Cambridge University Press.

Killgore, W. D., Oki, M., & Yurgelun-Todd, D. A. (2001). Sex-specific developmental changes in amygdala responses to affective faces. *Neuroreport, 12,* 427–433.

Kim, D., Solomon, D., & Roberts, W. (1995, April). *Classroom practices that enhance students' sense of community.* Paper presented at the annual meeting of the American Educational Research Association, San Francisco.

Kim, U., & Choi, S. H. (1994). Individualism, collectivism, and child development: A Korean perspective. In P. M. Greenfield & R. R. Cocking (Eds.), *Cross-cultural roots of minority child development* (pp. 227–257). Hillsdale, NJ: Erlbaum.

Kimball, M. M. (1986). Television and sex-role attitudes. In T. M. Williams (Ed.), *The impact of television.* New York: Academic Press.

Kim-Cohen, J., Moffitt, T. E., Caspi, A., & Taylor A. (2004). Genetic and environmental processes in young children's resilience and vulnerability to socioeconomic deprivation. *Child Development, 75,* 651–668.

Kindermann, T. A. (1993). Natural peer groups as contexts for individual development: The case of children's motivation in school. *Developmental Psychology, 29,* 970–977.

Kindermann, T. A., McCollam, T. L., & Gibson, E., Jr. (1996). Peer networks and students' classroom engagement during childhood and adolescence. In J. Juvonen & K. R. Wentzel (Eds.), *Social motivation: Understanding children's school adjustment.* Cambridge, England: Cambridge University Press.

King, A. (1999). Discourse patterns for mediating peer learning. In A. M. O'Donnell & A. King (Eds.), *Cognitive perspectives on peer learning* (pp. 87–115). Mahwah, NJ: Erlbaum.

King, E. W. (1999). *Looking into the lives of children: A worldwide view.* Albert Park, Australia: James Nicholas.

Kingstone, A., Smilek, D., Ristic, J., Friesen, C. K., & Eastwood, J. D. (2003). Attention, researchers! It is time to take a look at the real world. *Current Directions in Psychological Science, 12,* 176–180.

Kirby, J. R., Parrila, R. K., & Pfeiffer, S. L. (2003). Naming speed and phonological awareness as predictors of reading development. *Journal of Educational Psychology, 95,* 453–464.

Kirschenbaum, R. J. (1989). Identification of the gifted and talented American Indian student. In C. J. Maker & S. W. Schiever (Eds.), *Critical issues in gifted education: Vol. 2. Defensible programs for cultural and ethnic minorities.* Austin, TX: Pro-Ed.

Kisilevsky, B. S., Hains, S. M. J., Lee, K., Xie, X., Huang, H., Ye, H. H., et al. (2003). Effects of experience on fetal voice recognition. *Psychological Science, 14,* 220–224.

Klaczynski, P. (2000). Motivated scientific reasoning biases, epistemological beliefs, and theory polarization: A two-process approach to adolescent cognition. *Child Development, 71,* 1347–1366.

Klaczynski, P. A. (2001). Analytic and heuristic processing influences on adolescent reasoning and decision-making. *Child Development, 72,* 844–861.

Klahr, D. (1982). Non-monotone assessment of monotone development: An information processing analysis. In S. Strauss & R. Stavy (Eds.), *U-shaped behavioral growth* (pp. 63–86). New York: Academic Press.

Klahr, D., & Robinson, M. (1981). Formal assessment of problem solving and planning processes in children. *Cognitive Psychology, 13,* 113–148.

Klassen, T. P., MacKay, J. M., Moher, D., Walker, A., & Jones, A. L. (2000). Community-based injury prevention interventions. *The Future of Children, 10*(1), 83–110.

Kline, K., & Flowers, J. (1998, April). *A comparison of fourth graders' proportional reasoning in reform and traditional classrooms.* Paper presented at the annual meeting of the American Educational Research Association, San Diego, CA.

Klinnert, M. D. (1984). The regulation of infant behavior by maternal facial expression. *Infant Behavior and Development, 7,* 447–465.

Klinnert, M. D., Emde, R. N., Butterfield, P., & Campos, J. J. (1986). Social referencing: The infant's use of emotional signals from a friendly adult with mother present. *Developmental Psychology, 22,* 427–434.

Kluger, A. N., & DeNisi, A. (1998). Feedback interventions: Toward the understanding of a double-edged sword. *Current Directions in Psychological Science, 7,* 67–72.

Knapp, M. S., & Woolverton, S. (1995). Social class and schooling. In J. A. Banks & C. A. M. Banks (Eds.), *Handbook of research on multicultural education.* New York: Macmillan.

Knapp, N. F. (1995, April). *Tom and Joshua: Two at-risk readers at home and at school.* Paper presented at the annual meeting of the American Educational Research Association, San Francisco, CA.

Knowlton, D. (1995). Managing children with oppositional behavior. *Beyond Behavior, 6*(3), 5–10.

Knudson, R. E. (1992). The development of written argumentation: An analysis and comparison of argumentative writing at four grade levels. *Child Study Journal, 22,* 167–181.

Kochanska, G. (1993). Toward a synthesis of parental socialization and child temperament in early development of conscience. *Child Development, 64,* 325–347.

Kochanska, G., Casey, R. J., & Fukumoto, A. (1995). Toddlers' sensitivity to standard violations. *Child Development, 66,* 643–656.

Kochanska, G., Coy, K. C., & Murray, K. T. (2001). The development of self-regulation in the first four years of life. *Child Development, 72,* 1091–1111.

Kochanska, G., Gross, J. N., Lin, M.-H., & Nichols, K. E. (2002). Guilt in young children: Development, determinants, and relations with a broader system of standards. *Child Development, 73,* 461–482.

Koenig, M. A., Clément, F., & Harris, P. L. (2004). Trust in testimony: Children's use of true and false statements. *Psychological Science, 15,* 694–698.

Koeppel, J., & Mulrooney, M. (1992). The Sister Schools Program: A way for children to learn about cultural diversity—when there isn't any in their school. *Young Children, 48*(1), 44–47.

Koestner, R., Ryan, R. M., Bernieri, F., & Holt, K. (1984). Setting limits in children's behavior: The differential effects of controlling versus informational styles on intrinsic motivation and creativity. *Journal of Personality, 52,* 233–248.

Kohlberg, L. (1963). Moral development and identification. In H. W. Stevenson (Ed.), *Child psychology: 62nd yearbook of the National Society for the Study of Education* (pp. 277–332). Chicago: University of Chicago Press.

Kohlberg, L. (1969). Stage and sequence: The cognitive-developmental approach to socialization. In D. A. Goslin (Ed.), *Handbook of socialization theory and research* (pp. 347–480). Chicago: Rand McNally.

Kohlberg, L. (1975). The cognitive-developmental approach to moral education. *Phi Delta Kappan, 57,* 670–677.

Kohlberg, L. (1976). Moral stages and moralization: The cognitive-developmental approach. In T. Lickona (Ed.), *Moral development and behavior: Theory, research, and social issues.* New York: Holt, Rinehart & Winston.

Kohlberg, L. (1981). *The philosophy of moral development: Moral stages and the idea of justice.* San Francisco: Harper & Row.

Kohlberg, L. (1984). *The psychology of moral development: The nature and validity of moral stages.* San Francisco: Harper & Row.

Kohlberg, L. (1986). A current statement on some theoretical issues. In S. Modgil & C. Modgil (Eds.), *Lawrence Kohlberg: Consensus and controversy.* Philadelphia: Falmer Press.

Kohlberg, L., & Candee, D. (1984). The relationship of moral judgment to moral action. In W. M. Kurtines & J. L. Gewirtz (Eds.), *Morality, moral behavior, and moral development.* New York: Wiley.

Kohlberg, L., & Fein, G. G. (1987). Play and constructive work as contributors to development. In L. Kohlberg (Ed.), *Child psychology and childhood education: A cognitive-developmental view* (pp. 392–440). New York: Longman.

Kohlberg, L., & Kramer, R. (1969). Continuities and discontinuities in childhood and adult moral development. *Human Development, 12,* 93–120.

Kohlberg, L., Levine, C., & Hewer, A. (1983). Moral stages: A current formulation and a response to critics. *Contributions to Human Development, 10,* 1–174.

Kohlberg, L., & Mayer, R. (1972). Development as the aim of education. *Harvard Educational Review, 42,* 449–496.

Kohn, M. L. (1977). *Class and conformity* (2nd ed.). Chicago: University of Chicago Press.

Kolb, B., & Fantie, B. (1989). Development of the child's brain and behavior. In C. R. Reynolds & E. F. Janzen (Eds.), *Handbook of clinical child neuropsychology* (pp. 17–40). New York: Plenum Press.

Kolb, B., & Whishaw, I. (1996). *Fundamentals of human neuropsychology* (3rd ed.). San Francisco: Freeman.

Konner, M. (1972). Aspects of the developmental ethology of a foraging people. In N. Blurton Jones (Ed.), *Ethological studies of child behavior* (pp. 285–304). Cambridge, England: Cambridge University Press.

Kontos, S., Raikes, H., & Woods, A. (1983). Early childhood staff attitudes toward their parent clienteles. *Child Care Quarterly, 12,* 45–58.

Kontos, S., & Wells, W. (1986). Attitudes of caregivers and the day care experience of families. *Early Childhood Research Quarterly, 1,* 47–67.

Kopp, C. B. (1982). Antecedents of self-regulation: A developmental perspective. *Developmental Psychology, 18,* 199–214.

Koren-Karie, N., Oppenheim, D., Dolev, S., Sher, E., & Etzion-Carasso, A. (2002). Mothers' insightfulness regarding their infants' internal experience: Relations with maternal sensitivity and infant attachment. *Developmental Psychology, 38*(4), 534–542.

Korkman, M., Autti-Raemoe, I., Koivulehto, H., & Granstroem, M. L. (1998). Neuropsychological effects at early school age of fetal alcohol exposure of varying duration. *Child Neuropsychology, 4,* 199–212.

Kornhaber, A. (1996). *Contemporary grandparenting.* Thousand Oaks, CA: Sage.

Kornhaber, M., Fierros, E., & Veenema, S. (2004). *Multiple intelligences: Best ideas from research and practice.* Boston: Allyn & Bacon.

Koskinen, P. S., Blum, I. H., Bisson, S. A., Phillips, S. M., Creamer, T. S., & Baker, T. K. (2000). Book access, shared reading, and audio models: The effects of supporting the literacy learning of linguistically diverse students in school and at home. *Journal of Educational Psychology, 92,* 23–36.

Kottler, J. A. (1997). *What's really said in the teachers' lounge: Provocative ideas about cultures and classrooms.* Thousand Oaks, CA: Corwin Press.

Kovacs, D. M., Parker, J. G., & Hoffman, L. W. (1996). Behavioral, affective, and social correlates of involvement in cross-sex friendship in elementary school. *Child Development, 67,* 2269–2286.

Kowal, A. K., Krull, J. L., & Kramer, L. (2004). How the differential treatment of siblings is linked with parent-child relationship quality. *Journal of Family Psychology, 18,* 658–665.

Koyanagi, C., & Gaines, S. (1993). *All systems failure: An examination of the results of neglecting the needs of children with serious emotional disturbance.* Alexandria, VA: National Mental Health Association.

Koza, J. E. (2001). Multicultural approaches to music education. In C. A. Grant & M. L. Gomez, *Campus and classroom: Making schooling multicultural* (2nd ed.). Upper Saddle River, NJ: Merrill/Prentice Hall.

Kozulin, A., & Falik, L. (1995). Dynamic cognitive assessment of the child. *Current Directions in Psychological Science, 4,* 192–196.

Kraemingk, K., & Paquette, A. (1999). Effects of prenatal alcohol exposure on neuropsychological functioning. *Developmental Neuropsychology, 15,* 111–140.

Krampen, G. (1987). Differential effects of teacher comments. *Journal of Educational Psychology, 79,* 137–146.

Krashen, S. D. (1996). *Under attack: The case against bilingual education.* Culver City, CA: Language Education Associates.

Krebs, D. L., & Van Hesteren, F. (1994). The development of altruism: Toward an integrative model. *Developmental Review, 14,* 103–158.

Krebs, P. L. (1995). Mental retardation. In J. P. Winnick (Ed.), *Adapted physical education and sport* (2nd ed., pp. 93–109). Champaign, IL: Human Kinetics.

Kreider, R. M. (2003). *Adopted children and stepchildren: 2000* (Census 2000 Special Reports, CENSR-6RV). Washington, DC: U.S. Department of Commerce, U.S. Census Bureau.

Kreutzer, M. A., Leonard, C., & Flavell, J. H. (1975). An interview study of children's knowledge about memory. *Monographs of the Society for Research in Child Development, 40*(1, Serial No. 159).

Krispin, O., Sternberg, K. J., & Lamb, M. E. (1992). The dimensions of peer evaluation in Israel: A cross-cultural perspective. *International Journal of Behavioral Development, 15,* 299–314.

Krivitski, E. C., McIntosh, D. E., Rothlisberg, B., & Finch, H. (2004). Profile analysis of deaf children using the Universal Nonverbal Intelligence Test. *Journal of Psychoeducational Assessment, 22,* 338–350.

Kroger, J. (2003). What transits in an identity status transition? *Identity: An International Journal of Theory and Research, 3,* 197–220.

Kroger, S. M., Schettler, T., & Weiss, B. (2005). Environmental toxicants and developmental disabilities. *American Psychologist, 60*(3), 243–255.

Kuhl, P. K., & Meltzoff, A. N. (1997). Evolution, nativism and learning in the development of language and speech. In M. Gopnik (Ed.), *The inheritance and innateness of grammars.* New York: Oxford University Press.

Kuhlmeier, V., Wynn, K., & Bloom, P. (2003). Attribution of dispositional states by 12-month-olds. *Psychological Science, 14,* 402–408.

Kuhn, D. (1993). Connecting scientific and informal reasoning. *Merrill-Palmer Quarterly, 39,* 74–103.

Kuhn, D. (1997). Constraints or guideposts? Developmental psychology and science education. *Review of Educational Research, 67,* 141–150.

Kuhn, D. (2001a). How do people know? *Psychological Science, 12,* 1–8.

Kuhn, D. (2001b). Why development does (and does not) occur: Evidence from the domain of inductive reasoning. In J. L. McClelland & R. S. Siegler (Eds.), *Mechanisms of cognitive development: Behavioral and neural perspectives* (pp. 221–249). Mahwah, NJ: Erlbaum.

Kuhn, D., Amsel, E., & O'Loughlin, M. (1988). *The development of scientific thinking skills.* San Diego, CA: Academic Press.

Kuhn, D., & Franklin, S. (2006). The second decade: What develops (and how)? In W. Damon, R. M. Lerner (Series Eds.), D. Kuhn, & R. Siegler (Vol. Eds.), *Handbook of child psychology: Vol. 1. Cognition, perception, and language* (6th ed.). New York: Wiley.

Kuhn, D., Garcia-Mila, M., Zohar, A., & Andersen, C. (1995). Strategies of knowledge acquisition. *Monographs of the Society for Research in Child Development, 60*(4, Whole No. 245).

Kuhn, D., & Pearsall, S. (2000). Developmental origins of scientific thinking. *Journal of Cognition and Development, 1,* 113–129.

Kuhn, D., Shaw, V., & Felton, M. (1997). Effects of dyadic interaction on argumentative reasoning. *Cognition and Instruction, 15,* 287–315.

Kuhn, D., & Weinstock, M. (2002). What is epistemological thinking and why does it matter? In B. K. Hofer & P. R. Pintrich (Eds.), *Personal epistemology: The psychology of beliefs about knowledge and knowing* (pp. 121–144). Mahwah, NJ: Erlbaum.

Kulberg, A. (1986). Substance abuse: Clinical identification and management. *Pediatrics Clinics of North America, 33,* 325–361.

Kulik, J. A., & Kulik, C. C. (1997). Ability grouping. In N. Colangelo & G. Davis (Eds.), *Handbook of gifted education* (2nd ed., pp. 230–242). Boston: Allyn & Bacon.

Kunzinger, E. L., III. (1985). A short-term longitudinal study of memorial development during early grade school. *Developmental Psychology, 21,* 642–646.

Kupersmidt, J. B., & Coie, J. D. (1990). Preadolescent peer status, aggression, and school adjustment as predictors of externalizing problems in adolescence. *Child Development, 61,* 1350–1362.

Kurtines, W. M., Berman, S. L., Ittel, A., & Williamson, S. (1995). Moral development: A co-constructivist perspective. In W. M. Kurtines & J. L. Gewirtz (Eds.), *Moral development: An introduction.* Boston: Allyn & Bacon.

Kurtines, W. M., & Gewirtz, J. L. (Eds.). (1991). *Moral behavior and development: Vol. 2. Research.* Hillsdale, NJ: Erlbaum.

LaBlance, G. R., Steckol, K. F., & Smith, V. L. (1994). Stuttering: The role of the classroom teacher. *Teaching Exceptional Children, 26*(2), 10–12.

Laboratory of Comparative Human Cognition. (1982). Culture and intelligence. In R. J. Sternberg (Ed.), *Handbook of human intelligence.* Cambridge, England: Cambridge University Press.

Ladd, E. C. (1999). *The Ladd report.* New York: Free Press.

Ladd, G. W., & Burgess, K. B. (1999). Charting the relationship trajectories of aggressive, withdrawn, and aggressive/withdrawn children during early grade school. *Child Development, 70,* 910–929.

Ladson-Billings, G. (1994). *The dreamkeepers: Successful teachers of African American children.* San Francisco: Jossey-Bass.

Lafontana, K. M., & Cillessen, A. H. N. (1998). The nature of children's stereotypes of popularity. *Social Development, 7,* 301–320.

LaFromboise, T., Hardin, L., Coleman, K., & Gerton, J. (1993). Psychological impact of biculturalism: Evidence and theory. *Psychological Bulletin, 114,* 395–412.

La Guardia, J. G., Ryan, R. M., Couchman, C. E., & Deci, E. L. (2000). Within-person variation in security of attachment: A self-determination theory perspective on attachment, need fulfillment, and well-being. *Journal of Personality and Social Psychology, 79,* 367–384.

Lajoie, S. P., & Derry, S. J. (Eds.). (1993). *Computers as cognitive tools.* Mahwah, NJ: Erlbaum.

Lamaze, F. (1958). *Painless childbirth.* London: Burke.

Lamb, M. E. (1976). Interactions between eight-month-old children and their fathers and mothers. In M. E. Lamb (Ed.), *The role of the father in child development* (pp. 307–327). New York: Wiley.

Lamb, M. E. (1998). Nonparental child care: Context, quality, correlates, and consequences. In W. Damon (Series Ed.), I. E. Sigel, & K. A. Renninger (Vol. Eds.), *Handbook of child psychology* (Vol. 4, pp. 73–133). New York: Wiley.

Lamb, M. E. (2005). Attachment, child-parent. In C. B. Fisher & R. M. Lerner (Eds.), *Encyclopedia of applied developmental science* (pp. 127–129). Thousand Oaks, CA: Sage.

Lamb, M. E., Chuang, S. S., & Cabrera, N. (2005). Promoting child adjustment by fostering positive paternal involvement. In R. M. Lerner, F. Jacobs, & D. Wertlieb (Eds.), *Applied developmental science: An advanced textbook* (pp. 179–200). Thousand Oaks, CA: Sage.

Lamb, M. E., Frodi, A. M., Hwang, C. P., Frodi, M., & Steinberg, J. (1982). Mother- and father-infant interactions involving play and holding in traditional and non-traditional Swedish families. *Developmental Psychology, 18,* 215–221.

Lamb, S. (1991). First moral sense: Aspects of and contributions to a beginning morality in the second year of life. In W. M. Kurtines & J. L. Gewirtz (Eds.), *Handbook of moral behavior and development: Vol. 2. Research.* Hillsdale, NJ: Erlbaum.

Lamb, S., & Feeny, N. C. (1995). Early moral sense and socialization. In W. M. Kurtines & J. L. Gewirtz (Eds.), *Moral development: An introduction.* Boston: Allyn & Bacon.

Lamborn, S. D., Mounts, N. S., Steinberg, L., & Dornbusch, S. M. (1991). Patterns of competence and adjustment among adolescents from authoritative, authoritarian, indulgent, and neglectful families. *Child Development, 62,* 1049–1065.

Lampert, M., Rittenhouse, P., & Crumbaugh, C. (1996). Agreeing to disagree: Developing sociable mathematical discourse. In D. R. Olson & N. Torrance (Eds.), *The handbook of education and human development: New models of learning, teaching, and schooling.* Cambridge, MA: Blackwell.

Landau, S., & McAninch, C. (1993). Young children with attention deficits. *Young Children, 48*(4), 49–58.

Landesman, S., & Ramey, C. (1989). Developmental psychology and mental retardation: Integrating scientific principles with treatment practices. *American Psychologist, 44,* 409–415.

Lane, D. M., & Pearson, D. A. (1982). The development of selective attention. *Merrill-Palmer Quarterly, 28,* 317–337.

Langacker, R. (1986). An introduction to cognitive grammar. *Cognitive Science, 10,* 1–40.

Lange, G., & Pierce, S. H. (1992). Memory-strategy learning and maintenance in preschool children. *Developmental Psychology, 28,* 453–462.

Langfeldt, T. (1981). Sexual development in children. In M. Cook & K. Howells (Eds.), *Adult sexual interest in children.* London: Academic Press.

Langlois, J. A., Rutland-Brown, W., & Thomas, K. E. (2004). *Traumatic brain injury in the United States: Emergency department visits, hospitalizations, and deaths.* Atlanta, GA: Centers for Disease Control and Prevention, National Center for Injury Prevention and Control.

Lanza, E. (1992). Can bilingual two-year-olds code-switch? *Journal of Child Language, 19,* 633–658.

Lapan, R. T., Tucker, B., Kim, S.-K., & Kosciulek, J. F. (2003). Preparing rural adolescents for post–high school transitions. *Journal of Counseling and Development, 81,* 329–342.

La Paro, K. M., & Pianta, R. C. (2000). Predicting children's competence in the early school years: A meta-analytic review. *Review of Educational Research, 70,* 443–484.

Lapsley, D. K. (1993). Toward an integrated theory of adolescent ego development: The "new look" at adolescent egocentrism. *American Journal of Orthopsychiatry, 63,* 562–571.

Lapsley, D. K., Jackson, S., Rice, K., & Shadid, G. (1988). Self-monitoring and the "new look" at the imaginary audience and personal fable: An ego-developmental analysis. *Journal of Adolescent Research, 3,* 17–31.

Lareau, A. (1989). *Home advantage: Social class and parental intervention in elementary education.* New York: Falmer Press.

Larkin, R. W. (1979). *Suburban youth in cultural crisis.* New York: Oxford University Press.

Larner, M. B., Stevenson, C. S., & Behrman, R. E. (1998). Protecting children from abuse and neglect: Analysis and recommendations. *The Future of Children: Protecting Children from Abuse and Neglect, 8*(1), 4–22.

Larson, R. W. (2000). Toward a psychology of positive youth development. *American Psychologist, 55,* 170–183.

Larson, R. W., Clore, G. L., & Wood, G. A (1999). The emotions of romantic relationships: Do they wreak havoc on adolescents? In W. Furman, B. B. Brown, & C. Feiring (Eds.), *The development of romantic relationships in adolescence* (pp. 19–49). Cambridge, England: Cambridge University Press.

Last, C. G., Hersen, M., Kazdin, A. E., Francis, G., & Grubb, H. J. (1987). Psychiatric illness in the mothers of anxious children. *American Journal of Psychiatry, 144,* 1580–1583.

Laupa, M., & Turiel, E. (1995). Social domain theory. In W. M. Kurtines & J. L. Gewirtz (Eds.), *Moral development: An introduction.* Boston: Allyn & Bacon.

Lautrey, J. (1993). Structure and variability: A plea for a pluralistic approach to cognitive development. In R. Case & W. Edelstein (Eds.), *The new structuralism in cognitive development: Theory and research on individual pathways.* Basel, Switzerland: Karger.

Lave, J. (1993). Word problems: A microcosm of theories of learning. In P. Light & G. Butterworth (Eds.), *Context and cognition: Ways of learning and knowing.* Hillsdale, NJ: Erlbaum.

Lave, J., & Wenger, E. (1991). *Situated learning: Legitimate peripheral participation.* Cambridge, England: Cambridge University Press.

Lazar, I., Darlington, R., Murray, H., Royce, J., & Snipper, A. (1982). Lasting effects of early education: A report from the Consortium for Longitudinal Studies. *Monographs of the Society for Research in Child Development, 47*(2–3, Serial No. 195).

Lazarus, R. S. (1991). *Emotion and adaptation.* New York: Oxford University Press.

Leakey, R. (1994). *The origin of humankind.* New York: Basic Books.

Leaper, C., & Anderson, K. J. (1997). Gender development and heterosexual romantic relationships during adolescence. In S. Shulman & W. A. Collins (Eds.), *New directions for child development:* No. 78. *Romantic relationships in adolescence: Development perspective* (pp. 85–103). San Francisco: Jossey-Bass.

Learning First Alliance. (2001). *Every child learning: Safe and supportive schools.* Washington, DC: Learning First Alliance and Association for Supervision and Curriculum Development.

Lee, C. D., & Slaughter-Defoe, D. T. (1995). Historical and sociocultural influences on African and American education. In J. A. Banks & C. A. M. Banks (Eds.), *Handbook of research on multicultural education.* New York: Macmillan.

Lee, K., Cameron, C. A., Doucette, J., & Talwar, V. (2002). Phantoms and fabrications: Young children's detection of implausible lies. *Child Development, 73,* 1688–1702.

Lee, O. (1999). Science knowledge, world views, and information sources in social and cultural contexts: Making sense after a natural disaster. *American Educational Research Journal, 36,* 187–219.

Lee, S. (1985). Children's acquisition of conditional logic structure: Teachable? *Contemporary Educational Psychology, 10,* 14–27.

Lee, V., Brooks-Gunn, J., Schnur, E., & Liaw, F. (1990). Are Head Start effects sustained? A longitudinal follow-up comparison of disadvantaged children attending Head Start, no preschool, and other preschool programs. *Child Development, 61,* 495–507.

Lee, V. E., & Burkam, D. T. (2003). Dropping out of high school: The role of school organization and structure. *American Educational Research Journal, 40,* 353–393.

Lee-Pearce, M. L., Plowman, T. S., & Touchstone, D. (1998). Starbase-Atlantis, a school without walls: A comparative study of an innovative science program for at-risk urban elementary students. *Journal of Education for Students Placed at Risk, 3,* 223–235.

Leffert, J. S., Siperstein, G. N., & Millikan, E. (1999). *Social perception and strategy generation: Two key social cognitive processes in children with mental retardation.* Paper presented at the biennial meeting of the Society for Research in Child Development, Albuquerque, NM.

Lefstein, L. M., & Lipsitz, J. (1995). *3:00 to 6:00 P.M.: Programs for young adolescents.* Minneapolis, MN: Search Institute.

Lehman, D. R., & Nisbett, R. E. (1990). A longitudinal study of the effects of undergraduate training on reasoning. *Developmental Psychology, 26,* 952–960.

Lehnhart, A., & Madden, M. (2005, November). *Teen content creators and consumers.* Washington, DC: Pew Internet and American Life Project.

Leichtman, M. D., & Ceci, S. J. (1995). The effects of stereotypes and suggestions on preschoolers' reports. *Developmental Psychology, 31,* 568–578.

Lein, L. (1975). Black American immigrant children: Their speech at home and school. *Council on Anthropology and Education Quarterly, 6,* 1–11.

Leinhardt, G. (1994). History: A time to be mindful. In G. Leinhardt, I. L. Beck, & C. Stainton (Eds.), *Teaching and learning in history.* Hillsdale, NJ: Erlbaum.

Leinhardt, G., & Young, K. M. (1996). Two texts, three readers: Distance and expertise in reading history. *Cognition and Instruction, 14,* 441–486.

Leite, R. M. C., Buoncompagno, E. M., Leite, A. C. C., & Mergulhao, E. A. (1995). Psychosexual characteristics of male university students in Brazil. *Adolescence, 30,* 363–380.

Leite, R. W., & McKenry, P. C. (2002). Aspects of father status and postdivorce father involvement with children. *Journal of Family Issues, 23,* 601–623.

Leiter, J., & Johnsen, M. C. (1997). Child maltreatment and school performance declines: An event-history analysis. *American Educational Research Journal, 34,* 563–589.

Lemanek, K. L. (2004). Adherence. In R. T. Brown (Ed.), *Handbook of pediatric psychology in school settings* (pp. 129–148). Mahwah, NJ: Erlbaum.

Lemerise, E. A., & Arsenio, W. (2000). An integrated model of emotion processes and cognition in social information processing. *Child Development, 72,* 107–118.

Lennon, R., Eisenberg, N., & Carroll, J. L. (1983). The assessment of empathy in early childhood. *Journal of Applied Developmental Psychology, 4,* 295–302.

Lennox, C., & Siegel, L. S. (1998). Phonological and orthographic processes in good and poor spellers. In C. Hulme & R. M. Joshi (Eds.), *Reading and spelling: Development and disorders.* Mahwah, NJ: Erlbaum.

Lerner, J. W. (1985). *Learning disabilities: Theories, diagnosis, and teaching strategies* (4th ed.). Boston: Houghton Mifflin.

Lerner, R. M. (1989). Developmental contextualism and the life-span view of person-context interaction. In M. Bornstein & J. S. Bruner (Eds.), *Interaction in human development* (pp. 217–239). Hillsdale, NJ: Erlbaum.

Lerner, R. M. (1998). Theories of human development: Contemporary perspectives. In W. Damon (Series Ed.) & R. M. Lerner (Vol. Ed.), *Handbook of child psychology: Vol. 1. Theoretical models of human development* (5th ed., pp. 1–24). New York: Wiley.

Lerner, R. M. (2002). *Concepts and theories of human development* (3rd ed.). Mahwah, NJ: Erlbaum.

Leslie, A. M. (1991). The theory of mind impairment in autism: Evidence for a modular mechanism of development? In A. Whiten (Ed.), *Natural theories of mind: Evolution, development and simulation of everyday mindreading.* Oxford, England: Blackwell.

Levine, L. (1983). Mine: Self-definition in 2-year-old boys. *Developmental Psychology, 19,* 544–549.

Levitt, M. J., Guacci-Franco, N., & Levitt, J. L. (1993). Convoys of social support in childhood and early adolescence: Structure and function. *Developmental Psychology, 29,* 811–818.

Levitt, M. J., Levitt, J. L., Bustos, G. L., Crooks, N. A., Santos, J. D., Telan, P., et al. (1999, April). *The social ecology of achievement in pre-adolescents: Social support and school attitudes.* Paper presented at the annual meeting of the American Educational Research Association, Montreal, Canada.

Levy, T. M., & Orlans, M. (2000). Attachment disorder and the adoptive family. In T. M. Levy et al. (Eds.), *Handbook of attachment interventions* (pp. 243–259). San Diego, CA: Academic Press.

Lewin, T. (2000, June 25). Growing up, growing apart: Fast friends try to resist the pressure to divide by race. *The New York Times,* pp. 1, 18–20.

Lewis, M. (1993). Self-conscious emotions: Embarrassment, pride, shame, and guilt. In M. Lewis & J. Haviland (Eds.), *The handbook of emotions* (pp. 563–573). New York: Guilford Press.

Lewis, M. (1995). Embarrassment: The emotion of self-exposure and evaluation. In J. Tangney & K. Fischer (Eds.), *Self-conscious emotions: The psychology of shame, guilt, embarrassment and pride* (pp. 198–218). New York: Guilford Press.

Lewis, M. (2000). The emergence of human emotions. In M. Lewis & J. M. Haviland-Jones (Eds.), *Handbook of emotions* (2nd ed., pp. 265–280). New York: Guilford Press.

Lewis, M., & Brooks-Gunn, J. (1979). *Social cognition and the acquisition of self.* New York: Plenum.

Lewis, M., Feiring, C., & Rosenthal, S. (2000). Attachment over time. *Child Development, 71,* 707–720.

Li, J. (2004). High abilities and excellence: A cultural perspective. In L. V. Shavinina & M. Ferrari (Eds.), *Beyond knowledge: Extracognitive aspects of developing high ability* (pp. 187–208). Mahwah, NJ: Erlbaum.

Liang, F., Holt, I., Pertea, G., Karamycheva, S., Salzberg, S. L., & Quackenbush, J. (2000). Gene index analysis of the human genome estimates approximately 120,000 genes. *Nature Genetics, 25,* 239–240.

Liben, L. S., & Bigler, R. S. (2002). The developmental course of gender differentiation: Conceptualizing, measuring, and evaluating constructs and pathways. *Monographs of the Society for Research in Child Development, 67*(2, Serial No. 269).

Liben, L. S., Bigler, R. S., & Krogh, H. R. (2002). Language at work: Children's gendered interpretations of occupational titles. *Child Development, 73,* 810–828.

Liben, L. S., & Downs, R. M. (1989a). Educating with maps: Part I, the place of maps. *Teaching Thinking and Problem Solving, 11*(1), 6–9.

Liben, L. S., & Downs, R. M. (1989b). Understanding maps as symbols: The development of map concepts in children. In H. W. Reese (Ed.), *Advances in child development and behavior* (Vol. 22). San Diego, CA: Harcourt Brace Jovanovich.

Liberman, A. M. (1998). Why is speech so much easier than reading and writing?. In C. Hulme & R. M. Joshi (Eds.), *Reading and spelling: Development and disorders.* Mahwah, NJ: Erlbaum.

Lichtenberger, E. O., & Kaufman, A. S. (2003). *Essentials of WPPSI-III assessment.* New York: Wiley.

Lickona, T. (1991). Moral development in the elementary school classroom. In W. M. Kurtines & J. L. Gewirtz (Eds.), *Moral behavior and development: Vol. 3. Application.* Hillsdale, NJ: Erlbaum.

Lidz, C. S. (1991). Issues in the assessment of preschool children. In B. A. Bracken (Ed.), *The psychoeducational assessment of preschool children* (2nd ed., pp. 18–31). Boston: Allyn & Bacon.

Lidz, C. S. (1997). Dynamic assessment approaches. In D. P. Flanagan, J. L. Genshaft, & P. L. Harrison (Eds.), *Contemporary intellectual assessment: Theories, tests, and issues* (pp. 281–296). New York: Guilford Press.

Lidz, C. S., & Gindis, B. (2003). Dynamic assessment of the evolving cognitive functions in children. In A. Kozulin, B. Gindis, V. S. Ageyev, & S. M. Miller (Eds.), *Vygotsky's educational theory in cultural context* (pp. 99–116). Cambridge, England: Cambridge University Press.

Lieberman, A. (1993). *The emotional life of the toddler.* New York: Free Press.

Lieberman, A. F., Weston, D. R., & Pawl, J. H. (1991). Preventive intervention and outcome with anxiously attached dyads. *Child Development, 62,* 199–209.

Lieberman, D. A. (1997). Interactive video games for health promotion: Effects on knowledge, self-efficacy, social support, and health. In R. L. Street, Jr., W. R. Gold, & T. R. Manning (Eds.), *Health promotion and interactive technology: Theoretical applications and future directions* (pp. 103–120). Mahwah, NJ: Erlbaum.

Light, J. G., & Defries, J. C. (1995). Comorbidity of reading and mathematics disabilities: Genetic and environmental etiologies. *Journal of Learning Disabilities, 28,* 96–106.

Light, P., & Butterworth, G. (Eds.). (1993). *Context and cognition: Ways of learning and knowing.* Hillsdale, NJ: Erlbaum.

Lightfoot, C. (1992). Constructing self and peer culture: A narrative perspective on adolescent risk taking. In L. T. Winegar & J. Valsiner (Eds.), *Children's development within social context: Vol. 2. Research and methodology* (pp. 229–245). Hillsdale, NJ: Erlbaum.

Lightfoot, D. (1999). *The development of language: Acquisition, change, and evolution.* Malden, MA: Blackwell.

Lillard, A. S. (1993). Pretend play skills and the child's theory of mind. *Child Development, 64,* 348–371.

Lillard, A. S. (1997). Other folks' theories of mind and behavior. *Psychological Science, 8,* 268–274.

Lillard, A. S. (1998). Playing with a theory of mind. In O. N. Saracho & B. Spodek (Eds.), *Multiple perspectives on play in early childhood education.* Albany: State University of New York Press.

Lillard, A. S. (1999). Developing a cultural theory of mind: The CIAO approach. *Current Directions in Psychological Science, 8,* 57–61.

Lin, C. C., & Fu, V. R. (1990). A comparison of child-rearing practices among Chinese, immigrant Chinese, and Caucasian-American parents. *Child Development, 61,* 429–433.

Lindberg, M. (1991). A taxonomy of suggestibility and eyewitness memory: Age, memory process, and focus of analysis. In J. L. Doris (Ed.), *The suggestibility of children's recollections.* Washington, DC: American Psychological Association.

Linder, T. W. (1993). *Transdisciplinary play-based assessment: A functional approach to working with young children.* Baltimore: Brookes.

Linebarger, D. L., Kosanic, A. Z., Greenwood, C. R., & Doku, N. S. (2004). Effects of viewing the television program *Between the Lions* on the emergent literacy skills of young children. *Journal of Educational Psychology, 96*(2), 297–308.

Linebarger, D. L., & Walker, D. (2005). Infants' and toddlers' television viewing and language outcomes. *American Behavioral Scientist, 48*(5), 624–645.

Linn, M. C., Clement, C., Pulos, S., & Sullivan, P. (1989). Scientific reasoning during adolescence: The influence of instruction in science knowledge and reasoning strategies. *Journal of Research in Science Teaching, 26,* 171–187.

Linn, M. C., & Hyde, J. S. (1989). Gender, mathematics, and science. *Educational Researcher, 18*(8), 17–19, 22–27.

Linn, M. C., & Muilenburg, L. (1996). Creating lifelong science learners: What models form a firm foundation? *Educational Researcher, 25*(5), 18–24.

Linn, M. C., Songer, N. B., & Eylon, B. (1996). Shifts and convergences in science learning and instruction. In D. C. Berliner & R. C. Calfee (Eds.), *Handbook of educational psychology.* New York: Macmillan.

Linn, R. L., & Miller, M. D. (2005). *Measurement and assessment in teaching* (9th ed.). Upper Saddle River, NJ: Merrill/Prentice Hall.

Linscheid, T. R., & Fleming, C. H. (1995). Anorexia nervosa, bulimia nervosa, and obesity. In M. C. Roberts (Ed.), *Handbook of pediatric psychology* (pp. 676–700). New York: Guilford Press.

Linver, M. R., Brooks-Gunn, J., & Kohen, D. E. (2002). Family processes as pathways from income to young children's development. *Developmental Psychology, 38,* 719–734.

Lippa, R. A. (2002). *Gender, nature, and nurture.* Mahwah, NJ: Erlbaum.

Lipson, M. Y. (1983). The influence of religious affiliation on children's memory for text information. *Reading Research Quarterly, 18,* 448–457.

Liss, M. B. (Ed.). (1983). *Social and cognitive skills: Sex roles and children's play.* San Diego, CA: Academic Press.

Little, L. (2000a, June). *Maternal discipline of children with Asperger-spectrum disorders.* Paper presented at the Youth and Victimization International Research Conference, Durham, NH.

Little, L. (2000b, June). *Peer victimization of children with Asperger-spectrum disorders.* Paper presented at the Youth and Victimization International Research Conference, Durham, NH.

Little, T. D., Oettingen, G., Stetsenko, A., & Baltes, P. B. (1995). Children's action-control beliefs about school performance: How do American children compare with German and Russian children? *Journal of Personality and Social Psychology, 69,* 686–700.

Littlewood, W. T. (1984). *Foreign and second language learning: Language-acquisition research and its implications for the classroom.* Cambridge, England: Cambridge University Press.

Lobel, A. (1979). *Frog and Toad are friends.* New York: HarperCollins.

Lochman, J. E., & Dodge, K. A. (1994). Social-cognitive processes of severely violent, moderately aggressive, and nonaggressive boys. *Journal of Consulting and Clinical Psychology, 62,* 366–374.

Lochman, J. E., Wayland, K. K., & White, K. J. (1993). Social goals: Relationship to adolescent adjustment and to social problem solving. *Journal of Abnormal Child Psychology, 21,* 1993.

Locke, E. A., & Latham, G. P. (1994). Goal setting theory. In H. F. O'Neil, Jr., & M. Drillings (Eds.), *Motivation: Theory and research.* Hillsdale, NJ: Erlbaum.

Locke, J. L. (1993). *The child's path to spoken language.* Cambridge, MA: Harvard University Press.

Lockhart, K. L., Chang, B., & Story, T. (2002). Young children's beliefs about the stability of traits: Protective optimism? *Child Development, 73,* 1408–1430.

Loeb, R. C., Horst, L., & Horton, P. J. (1980). Family interaction patterns associated with self-esteem in preadolescent girls and boys. *Merrill-Palmer Quarterly, 26,* 205–217.

Loeb, S., Fuller, B., Kagan, S. L., & Carrol, B. (2004). Child care in poor communities: Early learning effects of type, quality, and stability. *Child Development, 75,* 47–65.

Loeber, R. (1982). The stability of antisocial child behavior. *Annals of Child Development, 2,* 77–116.

Loeber, R., & Stouthamer-Loeber, M. (1998). Development of juvenile aggression and violence. *American Psychologist, 53,* 242–259.

Loehlin, J. C. (1992). *Genes and environment in personality development.* Newbury Park, CA: Sage.

Logan, K. R., Alberto, P. A., Kana, T. G., & Waylor-Bowen, T. (1994). Curriculum development and instructional design for students with profound disabilities. In L. Sternberg (Ed.), *Individuals with profound disabilities: Instructional and assistive strategies* (3rd ed.). Austin, TX: Pro-Ed.

Logsdon, B. J., Alleman, L. M., Straits, S. A., Belka, D. E., & Clark, D. (1997). *Physical education unit plans for grades 5–6* (2nd ed.). Champaign, IL: Human Kinetics.

Lombroso, P. J., & Sapolsky, R. (1998). Development of the cerebral cortex: XII. Stress and brain development: I. *Journal of the American Academy of Child and Adolescent Psychiatry, 37,* 1337–1339.

Long, M. (1995). The role of the linguistic environment in second language acquisition. In W. C. Ritchie & T. K. Bhatia (Eds.), *Handbook of language acquisition: Vol. 2. Second language acquisition.* San Diego, CA: Academic Press.

Long, T. J., & Long, L. (1982). *Latchkey children: The child's view of self care.* Washington, DC: Catholic University. (ERIC Document Reproduction Service No. ED211229)

Lonigan, C. J., Burgess, S. R., Anthony, J. L., & Barker, T. A. (1998). Development of phonological sensitivity in 2- to 5-year-old children. *Journal of Educational Psychology, 90,* 294–311.

Lopez, A. M. (2003). Mixed-race school-age children: A summary of census 2000 data. *Educational Researcher, 32*(6), 25–37.

Lopez, E. C. (1997). The cognitive assessment of limited English proficient and bilingual children. In D. P. Flanagan, J. L. Genshaft, & P. L. Harrison (Eds.), *Contemporary intellectual assessment: Theories, tests, and issues* (pp. 503–516). New York: Guilford Press.

López, G. R., Scribner, J. D., & Mahitivanichcha, K. (2001). Redefining parental involvement: Lessons from high-performing migrant-impacted schools. *American Educational Research Journal, 38,* 253–288.

López del Bosque, R. (2000). Sticks and stones: What words are to self-esteem. *Intercultural Development Research Association Newsletter, 27*(5), 4–7, 16.

Lorenz, K. (1966). *On aggression.* New York: Harcourt.

Losey, K. M. (1995). Mexican American students and classroom interaction: An overview and critique. *Review of Educational Research, 65,* 283–318.

Lou, Y., Abrami, P. C., Spence, J. C., Poulsen, C., Chambers, B., & d'Apollonia, S. (1996). Within-class grouping: A meta-analysis. *Review of Educational Research, 66,* 423–458.

Lovell, K. (1979). Intellectual growth and the school curriculum. In F. B. Murray (Ed.), *The impact of Piagetian theory: On education, philosophy, psychiatry, and psychology.* Baltimore: University Park Press.

Lovett, M. W., Lacerenza, L., Borden, S. L., Frijters, J. C., Steinbach, K. A., & De Palma, M. (2000). Components of effective remediation for developmental reading disabilities: Combining phonological and strategy-based instruction to improve outcomes. *Journal of Educational Psychology, 92,* 263–283.

Lovett, S. B., & Flavell, J. H. (1990). Understanding and remembering: Children's knowledge about the differential effects of strategy and task variables on comprehension and memorization. *Child Development, 61,* 1842–1858.

Lowry, R., Sleet, D., Duncan, C., Powell, K., & Kolbe, L. (1995). Adolescents at risk for violence. *Educational Psychology Review, 7,* 7–39.

Lucariello, J., Kyratzis, A., & Nelson, K. (1992). Taxonomic knowledge: What kind and when? *Child Development, 63,* 978–998.

Luckasson, R., Borthwick-Duffy, S., Buntinx, W. H. E., Coulter, D. L., Craig, E. M., Reeve, A., et al. (Eds.). (2002). *Mental retardation: Definition, classification, and systems of supports* (10th ed.). Washington, DC: American Association on Mental Retardation.

Lueptow, L. B. (1984). *Adolescent sex roles and social change.* New York: Columbia University Press.

Luna, B., Garver, K. E., Urban, T. A., Lazar, N. A., & Sweeney, J. A. (2004). Maturation of cognitive processes from late childhood to adulthood. *Child Development, 75,* 1357–1372.

Lupart, J. L. (1995). Exceptional learners and teaching for transfer. In A. McKeough, J. Lupart, & A. Marini (Eds.), *Teaching for transfer: Fostering generalization in learning.* Mahwah, NJ: Erlbaum.

Luster, L. (1992). *Schooling, survival, and struggle: Black women and the GED.* Unpublished doctoral dissertation, Stanford University, School of Education, Stanford, CA.

Luthar, S. S., & Latendresse, S. J. (2005). Children of the affluent: Challenges to well-being. *Current Directions in Psychological Science, 14,* 49–53.

Lutke, J. (1997). Spider web walking: Hope for children with FAS through understanding. In A. Streissguth & J. Kanter (Eds.), *The challenge of fetal alcohol syndrome: Overcoming secondary disabilities* (pp. 181–188). Seattle: University of Washington Press.

Lynd, R. S., & Lynd, H. M. (1929). *Middletown.* New York: Harcourt, Brace.

Lyon, G. R., & Krasnegor, N. A. (Eds.). (1996). *Attention, memory, and executive function.* Baltimore: Brookes.

Lyon, T. D., & Flavell, J. H. (1994). Young children's understanding of "remember" and "forget." *Child Development, 65,* 1357–1371.

Lytton, H., & Romney, D. M. (1991). Parents' differential socialization of boys and girls: A meta-analysis. *Psychological Bulletin, 109,* 267–296.

MacArthur, C., & Graham, S. (1987). Learning disabled students' composing with three methods: Handwriting, dictation, and word processing. *Journal of Special Education, 21,* 22–42.

Maccoby, E. E. (1980). *Social development: Psychological growth and the parent-child relationship.* New York: Harcourt Brace Jovanovich.

Maccoby, E. E. (1984). Middle childhood in the context of the family. In W. A. Collins (Ed.), *Development during middle childhood* (pp. 184–239). Washington, DC: National Academy Press.

Maccoby, E. E. (1990). Gender and relationships: A developmental account. *American Psychologist, 45,* 513–520.

Maccoby, E. E., & Hagen, J. W. (1965). Effects of distraction upon central versus incidental recall: Developmental trends. *Journal of Experimental Child Psychology, 2,* 280–289.

Maccoby, E. E., & Jacklin, C. N. (1974). *The psychology of sex differences.* Stanford, CA: Stanford University Press.

Maccoby, E. E., & Lewis, C. C. (2003). Less day care or different day care? *Child Development, 74,* 1069–1075.

Maccoby, E., & Martin, J. (1983). Socialization in the context of the family: Parent-child interaction. In P. H. Mussen (Series Ed.) & E. M. Hetherington (Vol. Ed.), *Handbook of child psychology: Vol. 4. Socialization, personality and social development* (4th ed., pp. 1–102). New York: Wiley.

MacDermid, S. M., Lee, M. D., & Smith, S. (2001). Forward into yesterday: Families and work in the 21st century. In K. J. Daly (Ed.), *Minding the time in family experience: Emerging perspectives and issues* (pp. 59–81). Amsterdam: Elsevier Science.

Mace, F. C., & Kratochwill, T. R. (1988). Self-monitoring. In J. C. Witt, S. N. Elliott, & F. M. Gresham (Eds.), *Handbook of behavior therapy in education.* New York: Plenum Press.

Mackey, W. C. (2001). Support for the existence of an independent man-to-child affiliative bond: Fatherhood as a biocultural invention. *Psychology of Men and Masculinity, 2,* 51–66.

Mackintosh, N. J. (1998). *IQ and human intelligence.* London: Oxford University Press.

MacLean, D. J., Sasse, D. K., Keating, D. P., Stewart, B. E., & Miller, F. K. (1995, April). *All-girls' mathematics and science instruction in early adolescence: Longitudinal effects.* Paper presented at the annual meeting of the American Educational Research Association, San Francisco.

MacWhinney, B., & Chang, F. (1995). Connectionism and language learning. In C. Nelson (Ed.), *Basic and applied perspectives on learning, cognition, and development: The Minnesota Symposia on Child Psychology* (Vol. 28). Mahwah, NJ: Erlbaum.

Madden, N. A., & Slavin, R. E. (1983). Mainstreaming students with mild handicaps: Academic and social outcomes. *Review of Educational Research, 53,* 519–569.

Madhubuti, H., & Madhubuti, S. (1994). *African-centered education.* Chicago: Third World Press.

Magnuson, K. A., Meyers, M. K., Ruhm, C. J., & Waldfogel, J. (2004). Inequality in preschool education and school readiness. *American Educational Research Journal, 41,* 115–157.

Maier, M. A., Bernier, A., Pekrun, R., Zimmermann, P., & Grossmann, K. E. (2004). Attachment working models as unconscious structures: An experimental test. *International Journal of Behavioral Development, 28*(2), 180–189.

Main, M. (1995). Recent studies in attachment: Overview, with selected implications for clinical work. In S. Goldberg, R. Muir, & J. Kerr (Eds.), *Attachment theory: Social, developmental, and clinical perspectives* (pp. 407–474). Hillsdale, NJ: Analytic Press.

Main, M., & Cassidy, J. (1988). Categories of response to reunion with the parent at age 6: Predictable from infant attachment classification and stable over a 1-month period. *Developmental Psychology, 24,* 415–426.

Main, M., Kaplan, N., & Cassidy, J. (1985). Security in infancy, childhood, and adulthood: A move to the level of representation. *Monographs of the Society for Research in Child Development, 50,* 66–104.

Main, M., & Solomon, J. (1986). Discovery of an insecure-disorganized/disoriented attachment pattern. In T. B. Brazelton & M. W. Yogman (Eds.), *Affective development in infancy* (pp. 95–124). Norwood, NJ: Ablex.

Main, M., & Solomon, J. (1990). Procedures for identifying infants as disorganized/disoriented during the Ainsworth Strange Situation. In M. T. Greenberg, D. Cicchetti, & E. M. Cummings (Eds.), *Attachment in the preschool years* (pp. 121–160). Chicago: University of Chicago Press.

Maker, C. J. (1993). Creativity, intelligence, and problem solving: A definition and design for cross-cultural research and measurement related to giftedness. *Gifted Education International, 9*(2), 68–77.

Maker, C. J., & Schiever, S. W. (Eds.). (1989). *Critical issues in gifted education: Vol. 2. Defensible programs for cultural and ethnic minorities.* Austin, TX: Pro-Ed.

Malatesta, C. Z., & Haviland, J. M. (1982). Learning display rules: The socialization of emotion expression in infancy. *Child Development, 53,* 991–1003.

Malinsky, K. P. (1997). Learning to be invisible: Female sexual minority students in America's public high schools. In M. B. Harris (Ed.), *School experiences of gay and lesbian youth: The invisible minority* (pp. 35–50). Binghamton, NY: Harrington Park Press.

Maller, S. J. (2000). Item invariance of four subtests of the Universal Nonverbal Intelligence Test across groups of deaf and hearing children. *Journal of Psychoeducational Assessment, 18,* 240–254.

Mallick, S. K., & McCandless, B. R. (1966). A study of catharsis of aggression. *Journal of Personality and Social Psychology, 4,* 591–596.

Malone, D. M., Stoneham, Z., & Langone, J. (1995). Contextual variation of correspondences among measures of play and developmental level of preschool children. *Journal of Early Intervention, 18,* 199–215.

Mandel, D. R., Jusczyk, P. W., & Pisoni, D. B. (1995). Infants' recognition of the sound patterns of their own names. *Psychological Science, 6,* 314–317.

Manderson, L., Tye, L. C., & Rajanayagam, K. (1997). Condom use in heterosexual sex: A review of research, 1985–1994. In J. Catalan, L. Sherr, et al. (Eds.), *The impact of AIDS: Psychological and social aspects of HIV infection* (pp. 1–26). Singapore: Harwood Academic.

Mandler, J. M., Fivush, R., & Reznick, J. S. (1987). The development of contextual categories. *Cognitive Development, 2,* 339–354.

Mangelsdorf, S. C., Shapiro, J. R., & Marzolf, D. (1995). Developmental and temperamental differences in emotion regulation in infancy. *Child Development, 66,* 1817–1828.

Manis, F. R. (1996). Current trends in dyslexia research. In B. J. Cratty & R. L. Goldman (Eds.), *Learning disabilities: Contemporary viewpoints.* Amsterdam: Harwood Academic.

Marachi, R., Friedel, J., & Midgley, C. (2001, April). "*I sometimes annoy my teacher during math*": *Relations between student perceptions of the teacher and disruptive behavior in the classroom.* Paper presented at the annual meeting of the American Educational Research Association, Seattle, WA.

Maratsos, M. (1998). Some problems in grammatical acquisition. In W. Damon (Series Ed.), D. Kuhn, & R. S. Siegler (Vol. Eds.), *Handbook of child psychology: Vol. 2. Cognition, perception, and language* (5th ed.). New York: Wiley.

Marcia, J. (1991). Identity and self-development. In R. M. Lerner, A. C. Petersen, & J. Brooks-Gunn (Eds.), *Encyclopedia of adolescence* (Vol. 1, pp. 529–533). New York: Garland.

Marcia, J. E. (1980). Identity in adolescence. In J. Adelson (Ed.), *Handbook of adolescent psychology.* New York: Wiley.

Marcia, J. E. (1988). Common processes underlying ego identity, cognitive/moral development, and individuation. In D. K. Lapsley & F. C. Power (Eds.), *Self, ego, and identity: Integrative approaches* (pp. 211–225). New York: Springer-Verlag.

Marcovitch, S., Goldberg, S., Gold, A., Washington, J., Wasson, C., Krekewich, K., et al. (1997). Determinants of behavioral problems in Romanian children adopted in Ontario. *International Journal of Behavioral Development, 20,* 17–31.

Marcus, G. F. (1996). Why do children say "breaked"? *Current Directions in Psychological Science, 5,* 81–85.

Marcus, G. F., Vijayan, S., Bandi Rao, S., & Vishton, P. M. (1999). Rule learning by seven-month-old infants. *Science, 283,* 77–80.

Margolin, G., & Gordis, E. B. (2004). Children's exposure to violence in the family and community. *Current Directions in Psychological Science, 13,* 152–155.

Markman, E. M. (1977). Realizing that you don't understand: A preliminary investigation. *Child Development, 48,* 986–992.

Markman, E. M. (1979). Realizing that you don't understand: Elementary school children's awareness of inconsistencies. *Child Development, 50,* 643–655.

Markman, E. M. (1989). *Categorization and naming in children: Problems of induction.* Cambridge, MA: MIT Press.

Markman, E. M. (1992). Constraints on word learning: Speculations about their nature, origins, and domain specificity. In M. R. Gunner & M. P. Maratsos (Eds.), *Modularity and constraints in language and cognition: The Minnesota Symposia on Child Development.* Hillsdale, NJ: Erlbaum.

Marks, J. (1995). *Human biodiversity: Genes, race, and history.* New York: Aldine de Gruyter.

Markus, H. R., & Kitayama, S. (1991). Culture and the self: Implications for cognition, emotion, and motivation. *Psychological Review, 98,* 224–253.

Marsh, H. W. (1989). Age and sex effect in multiple dimensions of self-concept: Preadolescence to early-adulthood. *Journal of Educational Psychology, 81,* 417–430.

Marsh, H. W. (1990a). Causal ordering of academic self-concept and academic achievement: A multiwave, longitudinal panel analysis. *Journal of Educational Psychology, 82,* 646–656.

Marsh, H. W. (1990b). A multidimensional, hierarchical model of self-concept: Theoretical and empirical justification. *Educational Psychology Review, 2,* 77–172.

Marsh, H. W., & Craven, R. (1997). Academic self-concept: Beyond the dustbowl. In G. D. Phye (Ed.), *Handbook of classroom assessment: Learning, achievement, and adjustment.* San Diego, CA: Academic Press.

Marsh, H. W., & Hau, K.-T. (2003). Big-fish-little-pond effect on academic self-concept: A cross-cultural (26-country) test of the negative effects of academically selective schools. *American Psychologist, 58,* 364–376.

Marsh, H. W., Parada, R. H., Yeung, A. S., & Healey, J. (2001). Aggressive school troublemakers and victims: A longitudinal model examining the pivotal role of self-concept. *Journal of Educational Psychology, 93,* 411–419.

Marsh, H. W., Trautwein, U., Lüdtke, O., Köller, O., & Baumert, J. (2005). Academic self-concept, interest, grades, and standardize test scores: Reciprocal effects models of causal ordering. *Child Development, 76,* 397–416.

Marshall, N. L. (2004). The quality of early child care and children's development. *Current Directions in Psychological Science, 13,* 165–168.

Martin, C. L. (1989). Children's use of gender-related information in making social judgments. *Developmental Psychology, 25,* 80–88.

Martin, C. L. (2000). Cognitive theories of gender development. In T. Eckes & H. Trautner (Eds.), *The developmental social psychology of gender* (pp. 91–121). Mahwah, NJ: Erlbaum.

Martin, C. L., & Halverson, C. F. (1987). The roles of cognition in sex role acquisition. In D. B. Carter (Ed.), *Current conceptions of sex roles and sex typing: Theory and research.* New York: Praeger.

Martin, S. S., Brady, M. P., & Williams, R. E. (1991). Effects of toys on the social behavior of preschool children in integrated and nonintegrated groups: Investigation of a setting event. *Journal of Early Intervention, 15,* 153–161.

Masataka, N. (1992). Pitch characteristics of Japanese maternal speech to infants. *Journal of Child Language, 19,* 213–224.

Mason, C. Y., & Jaskulski, T. (1994). HIV/AIDS prevention and education. In M. Agran, N. E. Marchand-Martella, & R. C. Martella (Eds.), *Promoting health and safety: Skills for independent living* (pp. 161–191). Baltimore: Brookes.

Mason, L. (2003). Personal epistemologies and intentional conceptual change. In G. M. Sinatra & P. R. Pintrich (Eds.), *Intentional conceptual change* (pp. 199–236). Mahwah, NJ: Erlbaum.

Massey, C. M., & Gelman, R. (1988). Preschoolers' ability to decide whether a photographed unfamiliar object can move itself. *Developmental Psychology, 24,* 307–317.

Massey, D. S., & Denton, N. A. (1993). *American apartheid: Segregation and the making of the underclass.* Cambridge, MA: Cambridge University Press.

Massimini, K. (2000). *Genetic disorders sourcebook* (2nd ed.). Detroit, MI: Omnigraphics.

Masten, A. S., Neemann, J., & Andenas, S. (1994). Life events and adjustment in adolescents: The significance of event independence, desirability, and chronicity. *Journal of Research on Adolescence, 4,* 71–97.

Masur, E. F., McIntyre, C. W., & Flavell, J. H. (1973). Developmental changes in apportionment of study time among items in a multitrial free recall task. *Journal of Experimental Child Psychology, 15,* 237–246.

Mathews, J. (1988). *Escalante: The best teacher in America.* New York: Henry Holt.

Matthews, J. (1999). *The art of childhood and adolescence: The construction of meaning.* London: Falmer Press.

Mattison, R. E. (1992). Anxiety disorders. In S. R. Hooper, G. W. Hynd, & R. E. Mattison (Eds.), *Child psychopathology: Diagnostic criteria and clinical assessment* (pp. 179–202). Hillsdale, NJ: Erlbaum.

Mayall, B., Bendelow, G., Barker, S., Storey, P., & Veltman, M. (1996). *Children's health in primary schools.* London: Falmer Press.

Mayer, D. L., & Dobson, V. (1982). Visual acuity development in infants and young children, as assessed by operant preferential looking. *Vision Research, 22,* 1141–1151.

Mayer, R. E. (1992). *Thinking, problem solving, cognition* (2nd ed.). New York: Freeman.

Mayer, R. E. (1998). Does the brain have a place in educational psychology? *Educational Psychology Review, 10,* 389–396.

Mayer, R. E. (2004). Should there be a three-strikes rule against pure discovery learning? *American Psychologist, 59,* 14–19.

Mayes, L. C., & Bornstein, M. H. (1997). The development of children exposed to cocaine. In S. S. Luthar, J. A. Burack, D. Cicchetti, & J. R. Weisz (Eds.), *Developmental psychopathology: Perspectives on adjustment, risk, and disorder* (pp. 166–188). Cambridge, England: Cambridge University Press.

Maynard, A. E. (2002). Cultural teaching: The development of teaching skills in Maya sibling interactions. *Child Development, 73,* 969–982.

Mayseless, O. (2005). Ontogeny of attachment in middle childhood: Conceptualization of normative changes. In K. A. Kerns & R. A. Richardson (Eds.), *Attachment in middle childhood* (pp. 1–23). New York: Guilford Press.

McAdoo, H. P., & Martin, A. (2005). Families and ethnicity. In R. M. Lerner, F. Jacobs, & D. Wertlieb (Eds.), *Applied developmental science: An advanced textbook* (pp. 141–154). Thousand Oaks, CA: Sage.

McAlpine, L. (1992). Language, literacy and education: Case studies of Cree, Inuit and Mohawk communities. *Canadian Children, 17*(1), 17–30.

McAlpine, L., & Taylor, D. M. (1993). Instructional preferences of Cree, Inuit, and Mohawk teachers. *Journal of American Indian Education, 33*(1), 1–20.

McBride-Chang, C., & Ho, C. S. (2000). Developmental issues in Chinese children's character acquisition. *Journal of Educational Psychology, 92,* 50–55.

McBride-Chang, C., & Kail, R. V. (2002). Cross-cultural similarities in the predictors of reading acquisition. *Child Development, 73,* 1392–1407.

McBride-Chang, C., & Treiman, R. (2003). Hong Kong Chinese kindergartners learn to read English analytically. *Psychological Science, 14,* 138–143.

McCall, R. B. (1993). Developmental functions for general mental performance. In D. K. Detterman (Ed.), *Current topics in human intelligence* (Vol. 3). Norwood, NJ: Ablex.

McCall, R. B. (1994). Academic underachievers. *Current Directions in Psychological Science, 3,* 15–19.

McCall, R. B., & Kagan, J. (1967). Stimulus-schema discrepancy and attention in the infant. *Journal of Experimental Child Psychology, 5,* 381–390.

McCall, R. B., Kennedy, C. B., & Applebaum, M. I. (1977). Magnitude of discrepancy and the distribution of attention in infants. *Child Development, 48,* 772–786.

McCall, R. B., & Mash, C. W. (1995). Infant cognition and its relation to mature intelligence. *Annals of Child Development, 4,* 27–56.

McCall, R. B., & Plemons, B. W. (2001). The concept of critical periods and their implications for early childhood services. In D. B. Bailey, Jr., J. T. Bruer, F. J. Symons, & J. W. Lichtman (Eds.), *Critical thinking about critical periods* (pp. 267–287). Baltimore: Brookes.

McCallum, R. S. (1991). The assessment of preschool children with the Stanford-Binet Intelligence Scale: Fourth Edition. In B. A. Bracken (Ed.), *The psychoeducational assessment of preschool children* (2nd ed., pp. 107–132). Boston: Allyn & Bacon.

McCallum, R. S. (1999). A "baker's dozen" criteria for evaluating fairness in nonverbal testing. *The School Psychologist, 53,* 41–60.

McCallum, R. S., & Bracken, B. A. (1993). Interpersonal relations between school children and their peers, parents, and teachers. *Educational Psychology Review, 5,* 155–176.

McCallum, R. S., & Bracken, B. A. (1997). The Universal Nonverbal Intelligence Test. In D. P. Flanagan, J. L. Genshaft, & P. L. Harrison (Eds.), *Contemporary intellectual assessment: Theories, tests, and issues* (pp. 268–280). New York: Guilford Press.

McCann, T. M. (1989). Student argumentative writing knowledge and ability at three grade levels. *Research in the Teaching of English, 23,* 62–72.

McCarthy, M., & Kuh, G. D. (2005, September 9). Student engagement: A missing link in improving high schools. *Teachers College Record.*

McCarty, T. L., & Watahomigie, L. J. (1998). Language and literacy in American Indian and Alaska Native communities. In B. Pérez (Ed.), *Sociocultural contexts of language and literacy.* Mahwah, NJ: Erlbaum.

McCaslin, M., & Good, T. L. (1996). The informal curriculum. In D. C. Berliner & R. C. Calfee (Eds.), *Handbook of educational psychology.* New York: Macmillan.

McCauley, R. N. (1987). The role of theories in a theory of concepts. In U. Neisser (Ed.), *Concepts and conceptual development: Ecological and intellectual factors in categorization.* Cambridge, England: Cambridge University Press.

McCloskey, M. (1983). Naïve theories of motion. In D. Genter & A. L. Stevens (Eds.), *Mental models* (pp. 299–324). Hillsdale, NJ: Erlbaum.

McCoy, K. (1994). *Understanding your teenager's depression.* New York: Perigee.

McCrae, R. R., Costa, P. T. Jr., & Busch, C. M. (1986). Evaluating comprehensiveness in personality systems: The California Q-Set and the five-factor model. *Journal of Personality, 54,* 430–446.

McCreary, M. L., Slavin, L. A., & Berry, E. J. (1996). Predicting problem behavior and self-esteem among African-American adolescents. *Journal of Adolescent Research, 11,* 216–234.

McCrink, K., & Wynn, K. (2004). Large-number addition and subtraction by 9-month-old infants. *Psychological Science, 15,* 776–781.

McCutchen, D. (1987). Children's discourse skill: Form and modality requirements of schooled writing. *Discourse Processes, 10,* 267–286.

McCutchen, D. (1996). A capacity theory of writing: Working memory in composition. *Educational Psychology Review, 8,* 299–325.

McDaniel, M. A., & Schlager, M. S. (1990). Discovery learning and transfer of problem-solving skills. *Cognition and Instruction, 7,* 129–159.

McDevitt, M., & Chaffee, S. H. (1998). Second chance political socialization: "Trickle-up" effects of children on parents. In T. J. Johnson, C. E. Hays, & S. P. Hays (Eds.), *Engaging the public: How government and the media can reinvigorate American democracy.* Lanhan, MD: Rowman & Littlefield.

McDevitt, T. M. (1990). Encouraging young children's listening skills. *Academic Therapy, 25,* 569–577.

McDevitt, T. M., & Ford, M. E. (1987). Processes in young children's communicative functioning and development. In M. E. Ford & D. H. Ford (Eds.), *Humans as self-constructing systems: Putting the framework to work* (pp. 145–175). Hillsdale, NJ: Erlbaum.

McDevitt, T. M., Spivey, N., Sheehan, E. P., Lennon, R., & Story, R. (1990). Children's beliefs about listening: Is it enough to be still and quiet? *Child Development, 61,* 713–721.

McDonnell, L. M., & Hill, P. T. (1993). *Newcomers in American schools: Meeting the educational needs of immigrant youth.* Santa Monica, CA: RAND.

McGowan, R. J., & Johnson, D. L. (1984). The mother-child relationship and other antecedents of childhood intelligence: A causal analysis. *Child Development, 55,* 810–820.

McGrew, K. S., Flanagan, D. P., Zeith, T. Z., & Vanderwood, M. (1997). Beyond *g:* The impact of *Gf-Gc* specific cognitive abilities research on the future use and interpretation of intelligence tests in the schools. *School Psychology Review, 26,* 189–210.

McGue, M., Bouchard, T. J., Jr., Iacono, W. G., & Lykken, D. T. (1993). Behavioral genetics of cognitive ability: A life-span perspective. In R. Plomin & G. E. McClearn (Eds.), *Nature, nurture, and psychology.* Washington, DC: American Psychological Association.

McGuigan, F., & Salmon, K. (2004). The time to talk: The influence of the timing of adult-child talk on children's event memory. *Child Development, 75,* 669–686.

McHale, J. P., & Rasmussen, J. L. (1998). Coparental and family group-level dynamics during infancy: Early family precursors of child and family functioning during preschool. *Development and Psychopathology, 10,* 39–59.

McHale, S. M., Bartko, W. T., Crouter, A. C., & Perry-Jenkins, M. (1990). Children's housework and psychosocial functioning: The mediating effects of parents' sex-role behaviors and attitudes. *Child Development, 61,* 1413–1426.

McKay, A. (1993). Research supports broadly-based sex education. *The Canadian Journal of Human Sexuality, 2*(2), 89–98.

McKenzie, J. K. (1993). Adoption of children with special needs. *The Future of Children, 3*(1), 26–42.

McKeough, A. (1995). Teaching narrative knowledge for transfer in the early school years. In A. McKeough, J. Lupart, & A. Marini (Eds.), *Teaching for transfer: Fostering generalization in learning.* Mahwah, NJ: Erlbaum.

McKey, R., Condelli, L., Ganson, H., Barrett, B., McConkey, C., & Plantz, M. (1985). *The impact of Head Start on children, families, and communities* (DHHS Publication No. OHDS 90-31193). Washington, DC: U.S. Government Printing Office.

McLane, J. B., & McNamee, G. D. (1990). *Early literacy.* Cambridge, MA: Harvard University Press.

McLoyd, V. C. (1990). The impact of economic hardship on black families and children: Psychological distress, parenting, and socioemotional development. *Child Development, 61,* 311–346.

McLoyd, V. C. (1998a). Children in poverty: Development, public policy, and practice. In W. Damon (Series Ed.), I. E. Sigel, & K. A. Renninger (Vol. Eds.), *Handbook of child psychology: Vol. 4. Child psychology in practice* (5th ed., pp. 135–208). New York: Wiley.

McLoyd, V. C. (1998b). Socioeconomic disadvantage and child development. *American Psychologist, 53,* 185–204.

McMahon, S. (1992). Book club: A case study of a group of fifth graders as they participate in a literature-based reading program. *Reading Research Quarterly, 27,* 292–294.

McNamara, D. S., & Healy, A. F. (1995). A generation advantage for multiplication skill training and nonword vocabulary acquisition. In A. F. Healy & L. E. Bourne, Jr. (Eds.), *Learning and memory of knowledge and skills: Durability and specificity.* Thousand Oaks, CA: Sage.

McNeill, D. (1966). Developmental psycholinguistics. In F. Smith & G. A. Miller (Eds.), *The genesis of language.* Cambridge, MA: MIT Press.

McNeill, D. (1970). *The acquisition of language: The study of developmental psycholinguistics.* New York: Harper & Row.

Medrich, E. A., Roizen, J. A., Rubin, V., & Buckley, S. (1982). *The serious business of growing up: A study of children's lives outside school.* Berkeley: University of California Press.

Mehan, H. (1979). *Social organization in the classroom.* Cambridge, MA: Harvard University Press.

Meichenbaum, D. (1977). *Cognitive-behavior modification: An integrative approach.* New York: Plenum Press.

Meichenbaum, D. (1985). Teaching thinking: A cognitive-behavioral perspective. In S. F. Chipman, J. W. Segal, & R. Glaser (Eds.), *Thinking and learning skills: Vol. 2. Research and open questions.* Hillsdale, NJ: Erlbaum.

Meichenbaum, D., & Goodman, J. (1971). Training impulsive children to talk to themselves: A means of developing self-control. *Journal of Abnormal Psychology, 77,* 115–126.

Meins, E., Fernyhough, C., Wainwright, R., Clark-Carter, D., Gupta, M. D., Fradley, E., et al. (2003). Pathways to understanding mind: Construct validity and predictive validity of maternal mind-mindedness. *Child Development, 74,* 1194–1211.

Meltzoff, A. N. (1990). Foundations for developing a concept of self: The role of imitation in relating self to other and the value of social mirroring, social modeling, and self practice in infancy. In D. Cicchetti & M. Beeghly (Eds.), *The self in transition: Infancy to childhood* (pp. 139–164). Chicago: University of Chicago Press.

Menéndez, R. (Director). (1988). *Stand and deliver* [Motion picture]. United States: Warner Studios.

Mennella, J. A., Jagnow, C. P., & Beauchamp, G. K. (2001). Prenatal and postnatal flavor learning by human infants. *Pediatrics, 107,* 88.

Menyuk, P., & Menyuk, D. (1988). Communicative competence: A historical and cultural perspective. In J. S. Wurzel (Ed.), *Toward multiculturalism: A reader in multicultural education.* Yarmouth, ME: Intercultural Press.

Mercer, C. D. (1997). *Students with learning disabilities* (5th ed.). Upper Saddle River, NJ: Merrill/Prentice Hall.

Mercer, C. D., Jordan, L., Allsopp, D. H., & Mercer, A. R. (1996). Learning disabilities definitions and criteria used by state education departments. *Learning Disabilities Quarterly, 19,* 217–231.

Merrill, P. F., Hammons, K., Vincent, B. R., Reynolds, P. L., Christensen, L., & Tolman, M. N. (1996). *Computers in education* (3rd ed.). Needham Heights, MA: Allyn & Bacon.

Mervis, C. B. (1987). Child-basic object categories and early lexical development. In U. Neisser (Ed.), *Concepts and conceptual development: Ecological and intellectual factors in categorization.* Cambridge, England: Cambridge University Press.

Merzenich, M. M. (2001). Cortical plasticity contributing to child development. In J. L. McClelland & R. S. Siegler (Eds.), *Mechanisms of cognitive development: Behavioral and neural perspectives* (pp. 67–95). Mahwah, NJ: Erlbaum.

Metz, K. E. (1995). Reassessment of developmental constraints on children's science instruction. *Review of Educational Research, 65,* 93–127.

Metz, K. E. (1997). On the complex relation between cognitive developmental research and children's science curricula. *Review of Educational Research, 67,* 151–163.

Metz, K. E. (2004). Children's understanding of scientific inquiry: Their conceptualizations of uncertainty in investigations of their own design. *Cognition and Instruction, 22,* 219–290.

Meyer, D. K., Turner, J. C., & Spencer, C. A. (1997). Challenge in a mathematics classroom: Students' motivation and strategies in project-based learning. *Elementary School Journal, 97,* 501–521.

Meyers, D. T. (1987). The socialized individual and individual autonomy: An intersection between philosophy and psychology. In E. F. Kittay and D. T. Meyers (Eds.), *Women and moral theory.* Totowa, NJ: Rowman & Littlefield.

Meyerstein, I. (2001). A systemic approach to fetal loss following genetic testing. *Contemporary Family Therapy, 23,* 385–402.

Michel, C. (1989). Radiation embryology. *Experientia, 45,* 69–77.

Micheli, L. J. (1995). Sports injuries in children and adolescents: Questions and controversies. *Clinics in Sports Medicine, 14,* 727–745.

Middleton, M. J. (1999, April). *Classroom effects on the gender gap in middle school students' math self-efficacy.* Paper presented at the annual meeting of the American Educational Research Association, Montreal, Canada.

Midgley, C., Feldlaufer, H., & Eccles, J. S. (1989). Change in teacher efficacy and student self- and task-related beliefs in mathematics during the transition to junior high school. *Journal of Educational Psychology, 81,* 247–258.

Milch-Reich, S., Campbell, S. B., Pelham, W. E., Jr., Connelly, L. M., & Geva, D. (1999). Developmental and individual differences in children's on-line representations of dynamic social events. *Child Development, 70,* 413–431.

Miller, B. C., & Benson, B. (1999). Romantic and sexual relationship development during adolescence. In W. Furman, B. B. Brown, & C. Feiring (Eds.), *The development of romantic relationships in adolescence* (pp. 99–121). Cambridge, England: Cambridge University Press.

Miller, D. (1994). Suicidal behavior of adolescents with behavior disorders and their peers without disabilities. *Behavioral Disorders, 20*(1), 61–68.

Miller, G. A., & Gildea, P. M. (1987). How children learn words. *Scientific American, 257,* 94–99.

Miller, J. G. (1987). Cultural influences on the development of conceptual differentiation in person description. *British Journal of Developmental Psychology, 5,* 309–319.

Miller, J. G. (1997). A cultural-psychology perspective on intelligence. In R. J. Sternberg & E. L. Grigorenko (Eds.), *Intelligence, heredity, and environment* (pp. 269–302). Cambridge, England: Cambridge University Press.

Miller, K. (1989). Measurement as a tool for thought: The role of measuring procedures in children's understanding of quantitative invariance. *Developmental Psychology, 25,* 589–600.

Miller, K. F., Smith, C. M., Zhu, J., & Zhang, H. (1995). Preschool origins of cross-national differences in mathematical competence: The role of number-naming systems. *Psychological Science, 6,* 56–60.

Miller, L. S. (1995). *An American imperative: Accelerating minority educational advancement.* New Haven, CT: Yale University Press.

Miller, N., & Maruyama, G. (1976). Ordinal position and peer popularity. *Journal of Personality and Social Psychology, 33,* 123–131.

Miller, P., & Seier, W. (1994). Strategy utilization deficiencies in children: when, where, and why. In H. Reese (Ed.), *Advances in child development and behavior* (Vol. 25). New York: Academic Press.

Miller, P., & Sperry, L. L. (1987). The socialization of anger and aggression. *Merrill-Palmer Quarterly, 33,* 1–31.

Miller, P. A., Eisenberg, N., Fabes, R. A., & Shell, R. (1996). Relations of moral reasoning and vicarious emotion to young children's prosocial behavior toward peers and adults. *Developmental Psychology, 32,* 210–219.

Miller, P. J. (1982). *Amy, Wendy, and Beth: Learning language in South Baltimore.* Austin: University of Texas Press.

Miller, P. J., & Goodnow, J. J. (1995). Cultural practices: Toward an integration of culture and development. In J. J. Goodnow & P. J. Miller (Eds.), *Cultural practices as contexts for development* (New Directions for Child Development, No. 67; pp. 5–16). San Francisco, CA: Jossey-Bass.

Miller, P. M., Danaher, D. L., & Forbes, D. (1986). Sex-related strategies of coping with interpersonal conflict in children aged five to seven. *Developmental Psychology, 22,* 543–548.

Miller, S. D., Heafner, T., Massey, D., & Strahan, D. B. (2003, April). *Students' reactions to teachers' attempts to create the necessary conditions to promote the acquisition of self-regulation skills.* Paper presented at the annual meeting of the American Educational Research Association, Chicago.

Miller-Jones, D. (1989). Culture and testing. *American Psychologist, 44,* 360–366.

Mills, G. E. (2003). *Action research: A guide for the teacher researcher* (2nd ed.). Upper Saddle River, NJ: Merrill/Prentice Hall.

Mills, R. S. L., & Grusec, J. E. (1989). Cognitive, affective, and behavioral consequences of praising altruism. *Merrill-Palmer Quarterly, 35,* 299–326.

Minami, M., & McCabe, A. (1996). Compressed collections of experiences: Some Asian American traditions. In A. McCabe (Ed.), *Chameleon readers: Some problems cultural differences in narrative structure pose for multicultural literacy programs* (pp. 72–97). New York: McGraw-Hill.

Minskoff, E. H. (1980). Teaching approach for developing nonverbal communication skills in students with social perception deficits: II. Proxemic, vocalic, and artifactual cues. *Journal of Learning Disabilities, 13,* 203–208.

Minstrell, J., & Stimpson, V. (1996). A classroom environment for learning: Guiding students' reconstruction of understanding and reasoning. In L. Schauble & R. Glaser (Eds.), *Innovations in learning: New environments for education.* Mahwah, NJ: Erlbaum.

Mischel, W. (1974). Processes in delay of gratification. In L. Berkowitz (Ed.), *Advances in experimental social psychology* (Vol. 7, pp. 249–292). New York: Academic Press.

Mischel, W., & Ebbesen, E. (1970). Attention in delay of gratification. *Journal of Personality and Social Psychology, 16,* 329–337.

Mischel, W., Shoda, Y., & Rodriguez, M. L. (1989). Delay of gratification in children. *Science, 244,* 933–938.

Mitchell, A. (1998). African American teachers: Unique roles and universal lessons. *Education and Urban Society, 31,* 104–122.

Mithaug, D. K., & Mithaug, D. E. (2003). Effects of teacher-directed versus student-directed instruction on self-management of young children with disabilities. *Journal of Applied Behavior Analysis, 36,* 133–136.

Mitru, G., Millrood, D., & Mateika, J. H. (2002). The impact of sleep on learning and behavior of adolescents. *Teachers College Record, 104,* 704–726.

Miura, I. T., Okamoto, Y., Vlahovic-Stetic, V., Kim, C. C., & Han, J. H. (1999). Language supports for children's understanding of numerical fractions: Cross-national comparisons. *Journal of Experimental Child Psychology, 74,* 356–365.

Miyake, K., Campos, J., Kagan, J., & Bradshaw, D. (1986). Issues in socioemotional development in Japan. In H. Azuma, K. Hakuta, & H. Stevenson (Eds.), *Kodomo: Child development and education in Japan* (pp. 238–261). San Francisco: Freeman.

Miyake, K., Chen, S.-J., & Campos, J. J. (1985). Infant temperament, mother's mode of interaction, and attachment in Japan: An interim report. In I. Bretherton & E. Waters (Eds.), Growing points of attachment theory and research. *Monographs of the Society for Research in Child Development, 50*(1–2, Serial No. 209), 276–297.

Mize, J., Pettit, G. S., & Brown, E. G. (1995). Mothers' supervision of their children's peer play: Relations with beliefs, perceptions, and knowledge. *Developmental Psychology, 31,* 311–321.

Mohatt, G., & Erickson, F. (1981). Cultural differences in teaching styles in an Odawa school: A sociolinguistic approach. In H. T. Trueba, G. P. Guthrie, & K. H. Au (Eds.), *Culture and the bilingual classroom: Studies in classroom ethnography.* Rowley, MA: Newbury House.

Moje, E. B. (2000). "To be part of the story": The literacy practices of gangsta adolescents. *Teachers College Record, 102*(3), 651–690.

Money, J. (1987). Sin, sickness, or status? Homosexual gender identification and psychoneuroendocrinology. *American Psychologist, 42,* 384–399.

Money, J. (1988). *Gay, straight, and in-between: The sexology of erotic orientation.* New York: Oxford University Press.

Montagu, A. (1999a). Introduction. In A. Montagu (Ed.), *Race and IQ* (expanded ed., pp. 1–18). New York: Oxford University Press.

Montagu, A. (Ed.). (1999b). *Race and IQ* (expanded ed.). New York: Oxford University Press.

Montague, D. P. F., & Walker-Andrews, A. S. (2001). Peekaboo: A new look at infants' perceptions of emotion expressions. *Developmental Psychology, 37,* 826–838.

Montemayor, R. (1982). The relationship between parent-adolescent conflict and the amount of time adolescents spend with parents, peers, and alone. *Child Development, 53,* 1512–1519.

Montemayor, R. (1983). Parents and adolescents in conflict. *Journal of Early Adolescence, 3,* 83–103.

Montgomery, D. (1989). Identification of giftedness among American Indian people. In C. J. Maker & S. W. Schiever (Eds.), *Critical issues in gifted education: Vol. 2. Defensible programs for cultural and ethnic minorities.* Austin, TX: Pro-Ed.

Moon, S. M., Feldhusen, J. F., & Dillon, D. R. (1994). Long term effects of an enrichment program based on the Purdue three-stage model. *Gifted Child Quarterly, 38,* 38–47.

Moore, G. A., Cohn, J. F., & Campbell, S. B. (2001). Infant affective responses to mother's still face at 6 months differentially predict externalizing and internalizing behaviors at 18 months. *Developmental Psychology, 37,* 706–714.

Moore, K. L., & Persaud, T. V. N. (2003). *Before we are born: Essentials of embryology and birth defects* (6th ed.). Philadelphia: W. B. Saunders.

Moore, K. L., Persaud, T. V. N., & Shiota, K. (2000). *Color atlas of clinical embryology.* Philadelphia: Saunders.

Moore, S. M., & Rosenthal, D. A. (1991). Condoms and coitus: Adolescents' attitudes to AIDS and safe sex behavior. *Journal of Adolescence, 14,* 211–227.

Moorehouse, M. J. (1991). Linking maternal employment patterns to mother-child activities and children's school competence. *Developmental Psychology, 27,* 295–303.

Moran, C. E., & Hakuta, K. (1995). Bilingual education: Broadening research perspectives. In J. A. Banks & C. A. M. Banks (Eds.), *Handbook of research on multicultural education.* New York: Macmillan.

Moran, S., & Gardner, H. (2006). Extraordinary achievements: A developmental and systems analysis. In W. Damon (Series Ed.), D. Kuhn, & R. Siegler (Vol. Eds.), *Handbook of child psychology: Vol. 1. Cognition, perception, and language* (6th ed.). New York: Wiley.

Morgan, M. (1985). Self-monitoring of attained subgoals in private study. *Journal of Educational Psychology, 77,* 623–630.

Morris, D. (1977). *Manwatching: A field guide to human behaviour.* New York: Abrams.

Morris, D., Tyner, B., & Perney, J. (2000). Early steps: Replicating the effects of a first-grade reading intervention program. *Journal of Educational Psychology, 92,* 681–693.

Morrongiello, B. A., Fenwick, K. D., Hillier, L., & Chance, G. (1994). Sound localization in newborn human infants. *Developmental Psychobiology, 27,* 519–538.

Morrow, S. L. (1997). Career development of lesbian and gay youth: Effects of sexual orientation, coming out, and homophobia. In M. B. Harris (Ed.), *School experiences of gay and lesbian youth: The invisible minority* (pp. 1–15). Binghamton, NY: Harrington Park Press.

Mortimer, J. T., Shanahan, M., & Ryu, S. (1994). The effects of adolescent employment on school-related orientation and behavior. In R. K. Silbereisen & E. Todt (Eds.), *Adolescence in context: The interplay of family, school, peers and work in adjustment.* New York: Springer-Verlag.

Mosborg, S. (2002). Speaking of history: How adolescents use their knowledge of history in reading the daily news. *Cognition and Instruction, 20,* 323–358.

Moses, L., Baldwin, D. A., Rosicky, J. G., & Tidball, G. (2001). Evidence for referential understanding in the emotions domain at twelve and eighteen months. *Child Development, 72,* 718–735.

Mueller, E., & Silverman, N. (1989). Peer relations in maltreated children. In D. Cicchetti & V. Carlson (Eds.), *Child maltreatment: Theory and research on the causes and consequences of child abuse and neglect* (pp. 529–579). New York: Cambridge University Press.

Mühlnickel, W., Elbert, T., Taub, E., & Flor, H. (1998). Reorganization of auditory cortex in tinnitus. *Proceedings of the National Academy of Sciences, USA, 95,* 10340–10343.

Mullen, M. K., & Yi, S. (1995). The cultural context of talk about the past: Implications for the development of autobiographical memory. *Cognitive Development, 10,* 407–419.

Munro, E. (2001). Empowering looked-after children. *Child and Family Social Work, 6,* 129–137.

Munroe, R. L., & Munroe, P. J. (1992). Fathers in children's environments: A four culture study. In B. S. Hewlett (Ed.), *Father-child relations: Cultural and biosocial contexts* (pp. 213–230). New York: Aldine de Gruyter.

Murdock, T. B. (1999). The social context of risk: Status and motivational predictors of alienation in middle school. *Journal of Educational Psychology, 91,* 62–75.

Murphy, D. A., Durako, S. J., Moscicki, A. B., Vermund, S. H., Ma, Y., Schwarz, D. F., et al. (2001). No change in health risk behaviors over time among HIV infected adolescents in care: Role of psychological distress. *Journal of Adolescent Health, 29*(Suppl. 3), 57–63.

Muter, V. (1998). Phonological awareness: Its nature and its influence over early literacy development. In C. Hulme & R. M. Joshi (Eds.), *Reading and spelling: Development and disorders.* Mahwah, NJ: Erlbaum.

Naegele, J. R., & Lombroso, P. J. (2001). Genetics of central nervous system developmental disorders. *Child and Adolescent Psychiatric Clinics of North America, 10,* 225–239.

Nagy, L. (1912). *Psychologie des kindlichen Interesses.* Leipzig, Germany: Nemnich.

Nagy, W. E., Berninger, V., Abbott, R., Vaughan, K., & Vermeulen, K. (2003). Relationship of morphology and other language skills to literacy skills in at-risk second-grade readers and at-risk fourth-grade writers. *Journal of Educational Psychology, 95,* 730–742.

Nagy, W. E., Herman, P. A., & Anderson, R. C. (1985). Learning words from context. *Reading Research Quarterly, 20,* 233–253.

Nakata, N., & Trehub, S. E. (2004). Infants' responsiveness to maternal speech and singing. *Infant Behavior and Development, 27,* 455–464.

Nakazawa, C., Takahira, S., Muramatsu, Y., Kawano, G., Fujiwara, C., Takahashi, M., et al. (2001, April). *Gender issues in mathematics, science and technology.* Paper presented at the annual meeting of the American Educational Research Association, Seattle, WA.

Namy, L. L., & Waxman, S. R. (2002). Patterns of spontaneous production of novel words and gestures within an experimental setting in children ages 1;6 and 2;2. *Journal of Child Language, 29,* 911–921.

Narváez, D. (1998). The influence of moral schemas on the reconstruction of moral narratives in eighth graders and college students. *Journal of Educational Psychology, 90,* 13–24.

Narváez, D. (2002). Does reading moral stories build character? *Educational Psychology Review, 14,* 155–171.

Narváez, D., & Rest, J. (1995). The four components of acting morally. In W. M. Kurtines & J. L. Gewirtz (Eds.), *Moral development: An introduction.* Boston: Allyn & Bacon.

Nasir, N. S., & Saxe, G. B. (2003). Ethnic and academic identities: A cultural practice perspective on emerging tensions and their management in the lives of minority students. *Educational Researcher, 32*(5), 14–18.

Nation, K., & Hulme, C. (1998). The role of analogy in early spelling development. In C. Hulme & R. M. Joshi (Eds.), *Reading and spelling: Development and disorders.* Mahwah, NJ: Erlbaum.

National Assessment of Educational Progress. (1985). *The reading report card: Progress toward excellence in our schools; trends in reading over four national assessments, 1971–1984.* Princeton, NJ: Author.

National Association of Secondary School Principals (NASSP). (2004). *Breaking ranks II: Strategies for leading high school reform.* Reston, VA: Author.

National Campaign to Prevent Teen Pregnancy. (2005a). *Teenage pregnancy rates in the United States, 1972–2000.* Retrieved June 22, 2005, from http://www.teenpregnancy.org/resources/data/national.asp

National Campaign to Prevent Teen Pregnancy. (2005b). *United States birth rates for teens, 15–19.* Retrieved June 22, 2005, from http://www.teenpregnancy.org/resources/data/brates.asp

National Center for Education Statistics. (1997). *Issue brief: Schools serving family needs: Extended-day programs in public and private schools.* Washington, DC: U.S. Department of Education.

National Center for Education Statistics. (1999, August). *Snapshots of public schools in the United States: Results from the Schools and Staffing Survey.* Washington, DC: Author.

National Center for Education Statistics. (2003). *Percentage of high school completers ages 16–24 who were enrolled in college the October after completing high school, by type of institution, family income, and race/ethnicity: October 1972–96.* Washington, DC: Author. Retrieved February 24, 2003, from http://nces.ed.gov/quicktables/Detail.asp?Key5147

National Center for Missing and Exploited Children. (2004). *HDOP: Help delete online predators.* Retrieved November 20, 2005, from http://www.missingkids.com/adcouncil

National Council for Accreditation of Teacher Education. (2000). *Program standards for elementary teacher preparation.* Retrieved from http://www.ncate.org/elemstds.pdf

National Human Genome Research Institute. (2003). *From the blueprint to you* (NIH Publication No. 03–5377). Betheseda, MD: National Institutes of Health.

National Joint Committee on Learning Disabilities. (1994). Learning disabilities: Issues on definition, a position paper of the National Joint Committee on Learning Disabilities. In *Collective perspectives on issues affecting learning disabilities: Position papers and statements.* Austin, TX: Pro-Ed.

National Middle School Association (NMSA). (2003). *This we believe: Successful schools for young adolescents.* Columbus, OH: Author.

National Research Council. (1993a). *Losing generations: Adolescents in high risk settings.* Washington, DC: National Academy of Sciences.

National Research Council. (1993b). *Understanding child abuse and neglect.* Washington, DC: National Academy Press.

National Research Council. (1999). *How people learn: Brain, mind, experience, and school.* Washington, DC: Author.

NCSS Task Force on Ethnic Studies Curriculum Guidelines. (1992). Curriculum guidelines for multicultural education. *Social Education, 56,* 274–294.

Neel, R. S., Jenkins, Z. N., & Meadows, N. (1990). Social problem-solving behaviors and aggression in young children: A descriptive observational study. *Behavioral Disorders, 16,* 39–51.

Neff, J. A., Hoppe, S. K., & Perea, P. (1987). Acculturation and alcohol use: Drinking patterns and problems among Anglo- and Mexican-American male drinkers. *Hispanic Journal of Behavioral Sciences, 9,* 151–181.

Neisser, U. (1998a). Introduction: Rising test scores and what they mean. In U. Neisser (Ed.), *The rising curve: Long-term gains in IQ and related measures* (pp. 3–22). Washington, DC: American Psychological Association.

Neisser, U. (Ed.). (1998b). *The rising curve: Long-term gains in IQ and related measures.* Washington, DC: American Psychological Association.

Neisser, U., Boodoo, G., Bouchard, T. J., Boykin, A. W., Brody, N., Ceci, S. J., et al. (1996). Intelligence: Knowns and unknowns. *American Psychologist, 51,* 77–101.

Nelson, C. A. (1995). The ontogeny of human memory: A cognitive neuroscience perspective. *Developmental Psychology, 31,* 723–738.

Nelson, C. A. (1999). Neural plasticity and human development. *Current Directions in Psychological Science, 8,* 42–45.

Nelson, C. A. (2005, April). *Brain development and plasticity: Examples from the study of early institutional rearing.* Invited address at the Developmental Science Teaching Institute at the biennial meeting of the Society for Research in Child Development, Atlanta.

Nelson, C. A. (2006). Neural bases of cognitive development. In W. Damon, R. M. Lerner (Series Eds.), D. Kuhn, & R. Siegler (Vol. Eds.), *Handbook of child psychology: Vol. 1. Cognition, perception, and language* (6th ed.). New York: Wiley.

Nelson, C. A., & Fivush, R. (2004). The emergence of autobiographical memory: A social cultural developmental theory. *Psychological Review, 111,* 486–511.

Nelson, K. (1973). Structure and strategy in learning to talk. *Monographs of the Society for Research in Child Development, 38*(1–2, Serial No. 149).

Nelson, K. (Ed.). (1986). *Event knowledge: Structure and function in development.* Hillsdale, NJ: Erlbaum.

Nelson, K. (1996a). *Language in cognitive development: The emergence of the mediated mind.* Cambridge, England: Cambridge University Press.

Nelson, K. (1996b). Memory development from 4 to 7 years. In A. J. Sameroff & M. M. Haith (Eds.), *The 5 to 7 shift* (pp. 141–160). Chicago: University of Chicago Press.

Nelson, K. (1997). Event representations then, now, and next. In P. van den Broek, P. J. Bauer, & T. Bourg (Eds.), *Developmental spans in event representation and comprehension: Bridging fictional and actual events* (pp. 1–26). Mahwah, NJ: Erlbaum.

Neville, H. J., & Bavelier, D. (2001). Variability of developmental plasticity. In J. L. McClelland & R. S. Siegler (Eds.), *Mechanisms of cognitive development: Behavioral and neural perspectives* (pp. 271–287). Mahwah, NJ: Erlbaum.

Newcomb, A. F., & Bagwell, C. L. (1995). Children's friendship relations: A meta-analysis review. *Psychological Bulletin, 117,* 306–347.

Newcomb, A. F., & Brady, J. E. (1982). Mutuality in boys' friendship relations. *Child Development, 53,* 392–395.

Newcomb, A. F., & Bukowski, W. M. (1984). A longitudinal study of the utility of social preference and social impact sociometric classification schemes. *Child Development, 55,* 1434–1447.

Newcomb, A. F., Bukowski, W. M., & Pattee, L. (1993). Children's peer relations: A meta-analytic review of popular, rejected, controversial, and average sociometric status. *Psychological Bulletin, 113,* 99–128.

Newcombe, N., & Huttenlocher, J. (1992). Children's early ability to solve perspective-taking problems. *Developmental Psychology, 28,* 635–643.

Newcombe, N. S. (2002). The nativist-empiricist controversy in the context of recent research on spatial and quantitative development. *Psychological Science, 13,* 395–401.

Newcombe, N. S., Drummey, A. B., Fox, N. A., Lie, E., & Ottinger-Albergs, W. (2000). Remembering early childhood: How much, how, and why (or why not). *Current Directions in Psychological Science, 9,* 55–58.

Newman, L. S. (1990). Intentional and unintentional memory in young children: Remembering vs. playing. *Journal of Experimental Child Psychology, 50,* 243–258.

Newman, R. S., & Schwager, M. T. (1992). Student perceptions and academic help seeking. In D. Schunk & J. Meece (Eds.), *Student perceptions in the classroom.* Hillsdale, NJ: Erlbaum.

Newport, E. L. (1990). Maturational constraints on language learning. *Cognitive Science, 14,* 11–28.

Newson, J., & Newson, E. (1975). Intersubjectivity and the transmission of culture: On the origins of symbolic functioning. *Bulletin of the British Psychological Society, 28,* 437–446.

Ng, F. F., Kenney-Benson, G. A., & Pomerantz, E. M. (2004). Children's achievement moderates the effects of mothers' use of control and autonomy support. *Child Development, 75,* 764–780.

Nguyen, S. P., & Murphy, G. L. (2003). An apple is more than just a fruit: Cross-classification in children's concepts. *Child Development, 74,* 1783–1806.

NICHD Early Child Care Research Network. (1997). The effects of infant child care on infant-mother attachment security: Results of the NICHD study of early child care. *Child Development, 68,* 860–879.

NICHD Early Child Care Research Network. (2002a). Child care structure→process→outcome: Direct and indirect effects of child care quality on young children's development. *Psychological Science, 13*(3), 199–206.

NICHD Early Child Care Research Network. (2002b). Early child care and children's development prior to school entry: Results from the NICHD study of early child care. *American Educational Research Journal, 39*(1), 133–164.

NICHD Early Child Care Research Network. (2005). Early child care and children's development in the primary grades: Follow-up results from the NICHD study of early child care. *American Educational Research Journal, 43*(3), 537–570.

Nicholls, J. G. (1984). Conceptions of ability and achievement motivation. In R. Ames & C. Ames (Eds.), *Research on motivation in education: Vol. 1. Student motivation.* San Diego, CA: Academic Press.

Nicholls, J. G. (1990). What is ability and why are we mindful of it? A developmental perspective. In R. J. Sternberg & J. Kolligian (Eds.), *Competence considered.* New Haven, CT: Yale University Press.

Nicholls, J. G., Cobb, P., Yackel, E., Wood, T., & Wheatley, G. (1990). Students' theories of mathematics and their mathematical knowledge: Multiple dimensions of assessment. In G. Kulm (Ed.), *Assessing higher order thinking in mathematics.* Washington, DC: American Association for the Advancement of Science.

Nichols, M. L., & Ganschow, L. (1992). Has there been a paradigm shift in gifted education? In N. Coangelo, S. G. Assouline, & D. L. Ambroson (Eds.), *Talent development: Proceedings from the 1991 Henry B. and Jocelyn Wallace National Research Symposium on Talent Development.* New York: Trillium.

Nichols, P. D., & Mittelholtz, D. J. (1997). Constructing the concept of aptitude: Implications for the assessment of analogical reasoning. In G. D. Phye (Ed.), *Handbook of academic learning: Construction of knowledge.* San Diego, CA: Academic Press.

Nicolson, S., & Shipstead, S. G. (2002). *Through the looking glass: Observations in the early childhood classroom* (3rd ed.). Upper Saddle River, NJ: Merrill/Prentice Hall.

Nieto, S. (1995). *Affirming diversity* (2nd ed.). White Plains, NY: Longman.

Nilsson, D. E., & Bradford, L. W. (1999). Neurofibromatosis. In S. Goldstein & C. R. Reynolds (Eds.), *Handbook of neurodevelopmental and genetic disorders* (pp. 350–367). New York: Guilford Press.

Nippold, M. A. (1988). The literate lexicon. In M. A. Nippold (Ed.), *Later language development: Ages nine through nineteen.* Boston: Little, Brown.

Niven, C. A. (1992). *Psychological care for families: Before, during and after birth.* Oxford, England: Butterworth-Heinemann.

Nix, R. L., Pinderhughes, E. E., Dodge, K. A., Bates, J. E., Pettit, G. S., & McFadyen-Ketchum, S. A. (1999). The relation between mothers' hostile attribution tendencies and children's externalizing behavior problems: The mediating role of mothers' harsh discipline practices. *Child Development, 70,* 896–909.

Noffke, S. (1997). Professional, personal, and political dimensions of action research. *Review of Research in Education, 22,* 305–343.

Nolen-Hoeksema, S. (1987). Sex differences in unipolar depression: Evidence and theory. *Journal of Personality and Social Psychology, 101,* 259–282.

Nolen-Hoeksema, S., Morrow, J., & Fredrickson, B. L. (1993). Response styles and the duration of episodes of depressed moods. *Journal of Abnormal Psychology, 102,* 20–28.

Nomura, Y., Fifer, W., & Brooks-Gunn, J. (2005). *The role of perinatal factors for risk of co-occurring psychiatric and medical disorders in adulthood.* Paper presented at the biennial meeting of the Society for Research in Child Development, Atlanta, GA.

Nucci, L. P. (2001). *Education in the moral domain.* Cambridge, England: Cambridge University Press.

Nucci, L. P., & Nucci, M. S. (1982). Children's social interactions in the context of moral and conventional transgressions. *Child Development, 53,* 403–412.

Nucci, L. P., & Weber, E. K. (1991). The domain approach to values education: From theory to practice. In W. M. Kurtines & J. L. Gewirtz (Eds.), *Handbook of moral behavior and development: Vol. 3. Application* (pp. 251–266). Hillsdale, NJ: Erlbaum.

Nucci, L. P., & Weber, E. K. (1995). Social interactions in the home and the development of young children's conceptions of the personal. *Child Development, 66,* 1438–1452.

Nunner-Winkler, G. (1984). Two moralities? A critical discussion of an ethic of care and responsibility versus an ethic of rights and justice. In W. M. Kurtines & J. L. Gewirtz (Eds.), *Morality, moral behavior, and moral development.* New York: Wiley.

Oakes, J., & Guiton, G. (1995). Matchmaking: The dynamics of high school tracking decisions. *American Educational Research Journal, 32,* 3–33.

Oakes, L. M., Kannass, K. N., & Shaddy, D. J. (2002). Developmental changes in endogenous control of attention: The role of target familiarity on infants' distraction latency. *Child Development, 73,* 1644–1655.

Oakes, L. M., & Rakison, D. H. (2003). Issues in the early development of concepts and categories: An introduction. In D. H. Rakison & L. M. Oakes (Eds.), *Early category and concept development: Making sense of the blooming, buzzing confusion* (pp. 3–23). Oxford, England: Oxford University Press.

Oakhill, J., Cain, K., & Yuill, N. (1998). Individual differences in children's comprehension skill: Toward an integrated model. In C. Hulme & R. M. Joshi (Eds.), *Reading and spelling: Development and disorders.* Mahwah, NJ: Erlbaum.

Oatley, K., & Nundy, S. (1996). Rethinking the role of emotions in education. In D. R. Olson & N. Torrance (Eds.), *The handbook of education and human development: New models of learning, teaching, and schooling.* Cambridge, MA: Blackwell.

O'Boyle, M. W., & Gill, H. S. (1998). On the relevance of research findings in cognitive neuroscience to educational practice. *Educational Psychology Review, 10,* 397–409.

Ochs, E., & Schieffelin, B. (1995). The impact of language socialization on grammatical development. In P. Fletcher & B. MacWhinney (Eds.), *The handbook of child language.* Cambridge, MA: Blackwell.

Ogbu, J. U. (1992). Understanding cultural diversity and learning. *Educational Researcher, 21*(8), 5–14, 24.

Ogbu, J. U. (1994). From cultural differences to differences in cultural frames of reference. In P. M. Greenfield & R. R. Cocking (Eds.), *Cross-cultural roots of minority child development* (pp. 365–391). Hillsdale, NJ: Erlbaum.

Ogbu, J. U. (1999). Beyond language: Ebonics, proper English, and identity in a Black-American speech community. *American Educational Research Journal, 36,* 147–184.

Ogden, E. H., & Germinario, V. (1988). *The at-risk student: Answers for educators.* Lancaster, PA: Technomic.

O'Grady, W. (1997). *Syntactic development.* Chicago: University of Chicago Press.

O'Leary, K. D., & O'Leary, S. G. (Eds.). (1972). *Classroom management: The successful use of behavior modification.* New York: Pergamon Press.

O'Leary, S. G., & Vidair, H. B. (2005). Marital adjustment, child-rearing disagreements, and overreactive parenting: Predicting child behavior problems. *Journal of Family Psychology, 19,* 208–216.

Okagaki, L. (2001). Triarchic model of minority children's school achievement. *Educational Psychologist, 36,* 9–20.

Okagaki, L., & Sternberg, R. J. (1993). Parental beliefs and children's school performance. *Child Development, 64,* 36–56.

Oldfather, P., & West, J. (1999). *Learning through children's eyes: Social constructivism and the desire to learn.* Washington, DC: American Psychological Association.

Oliver, J. M., Cole, N. H., & Hollingsworth, H. (1991). Learning disabilities as functions of familial learning problems and developmental problems. *Exceptional Children, 57,* 427–440.

Olneck, M. R. (1995). Immigrants and education. In J. A. Banks & C. A. M. Banks (Eds.), *Handbook of research on multicultural education.* New York: Macmillan.

Olson, D. R. (1994). *The world on paper: The conceptual and cognitive implications of writing and reading.* New York: Cambridge University Press.

Olweus, D., Mattson, A., Schalling, D., & Low, H. (1988). Circulating testosterone levels and aggression in adult males: A causal analysis. *Psychosomatic Medicine, 42,* 253–269.

O'Malley, P. M., & Bachman, J. G. (1983). Self-esteem: Change and stability between ages 13 and 23. *Developmental Psychology, 19,* 257–268.

Oppenheimer, L. (1986). Development of recursive thinking: Procedural variations. *International Journal of Behavioral Development, 9,* 401–411.

O'Reilly, A. W. (1995). Using representations: Comprehension and production of actions with imagined objects. *Child Development, 66,* 999–1010.

Ormrod, J. E. (2004). *Human learning* (4th ed.). Upper Saddle River, NJ: Merrill/Prentice Hall.

Ormrod, J. E. (2006). *Educational psychology: Developing learners* (5th ed.). Upper Saddle River, NJ: Merrill/Prentice Hall.

Ormrod, J. E., Jackson, D. L., Kirby, B., Davis, J., & Benson, C. (1999, April). *Cognitive development as reflected in children's conceptions of early American history.* Paper presented at the annual meeting of the American Educational Research Association, Montreal, Canada.

Ornstein, P. A., & Haden, C. A. (2001). *Memory* development or the *development* of memory? *Current Directions in Psychological Science, 10,* 202–205.

Ornstein, R. (1997). *The right mind: Making sense of the hemispheres.* San Diego, CA: Harcourt Brace.

Orobio de Castro, B., Veerman, J. W., Koops, W., Bosch, J. D., & Monshouwer, H. J. (2002). Hostile attribution of intent and aggressive behavior: A meta-analysis. *Child Development, 73,* 916–934.

Ortony, A., Turner, T. J., & Larson-Shapiro, N. (1985). Cultural and instructional influences on figurative comprehension by inner city children. *Research in the Teaching of English, 19*(1), 25–36.

Osborne, J. W., & Simmons, C. M. (2002, April). *Girls, math, stereotype threat, and anxiety: Physiological evidence.* Paper presented at the annual meeting of the American Educational Research Association, New Orleans, LA.

Oser, C., & Cohen, J. (2003). *America's babies: The Zero to Three Policy Center data book.* Washington, DC: Zero to Three Press.

Oskamp, S. (Ed.). (2000). *Reducing prejudice and discrimination.* Mahwah, NJ: Erlbaum.

Osterman, K. F. (2000). Students' need for belonging in the school community. *Review of Educational Research, 70,* 323–367.

O'Toole, M. E. (2000). *The school shooter: A threat assessment perspective.* Quantico, VA: Federal Bureau of Investigation. Retrieved February 26, 2004, from http://www.fbi.gov/publications/school/school2.pdf

Owens, C. R., & Ascione, F. R. (1991). Effects of the model's age, perceived similarity, and familiarity on children's donating. *Journal of Genetic Psychology, 152,* 341–357.

Owens, R. E., Jr. (1995). *Language disorders: A functional approach to assessment and intervention* (2nd ed.). Boston: Allyn & Bacon.

Owens, R. E., Jr. (1996). *Language development* (4th ed.). Boston: Allyn & Bacon.

Oyserman, D., & Markus, H. R. (1993). The sociocultural self. In J. Suls (Ed.), *Psychological perspectives on the self* (Vol. 7, pp. 187–220). Mahwah, NJ: Erlbaum.

Padilla, M. J. (1991). Science activities, process skills, and thinking. In S. M. Glynn, R. H. Yeany, & B. K. Britton (Eds.), *The psychology of learning science.* Hillsdale, NJ: Erlbaum.

Paget, K. F., Kritt, D., & Bergemann, L. (1984). Understanding strategic interactions in television commercials: A developmental study. *Journal of Applied Developmental Psychology, 5,* 145–161.

Page-Voth, V., & Graham, S. (1999). Effects of goal setting and strategy use on the writing performance and self-efficacy of students with writing and learning problems. *Journal of Educational Psychology, 91,* 230–240.

Paik, H., & Comstock, G. (1994). The effects of television violence on antisocial behavior: A meta-analysis. *Communication Research, 21,* 516–546.

Paikoff, R. L., & Brooks-Gunn, J. (1991). Do parent-child relationships change during puberty? *Psychological Bulletin, 110,* 47–66.

Pajares, F. (1996). Self-efficacy beliefs in academic settings. *Review of Educational Research, 66,* 543–578.

Pajares, F., & Valiante, G. (1999). *Writing self-efficacy of middle school students: Relation to motivation constructs, achievement, gender, and gender orientation.* Paper presented at the annual meeting of the American Educational Research Association, Montreal, Canada.

Palermo, D. S. (1974). Still more about the comprehension of "less." *Developmental Psychology, 10,* 827–829.

Paley, V. G. (1984). *Boys and girls: Superheroes in the doll corner.* Chicago: University of Chicago Press.

Palincsar, A. S., & Brown, A. L. (1984). Reciprocal teaching of comprehension-fostering and comprehension-monitoring activities. *Cognition and Instruction, 1,* 117–175.

Palincsar, A. S., & Brown, A. L. (1989). Classroom dialogues to promote self-regulated comprehension. In J. Brophy (Ed.), *Advances in research on teaching* (Vol. 1). Greenwich, CT: JAI Press.

Palincsar, A. S., & Herrenkohl, L. R. (1999). Designing collaborative contexts: Lessons from three research programs. In A. M. O'Donnell & A. King (Eds.), *Cognitive perspectives on peer learning* (pp. 151–177). Mahwah, NJ: Erlbaum.

Pallotta, J., & Masiello, R. (Illustrator). (1992). *The icky bug counting book.* Watertown, MA: Charlesbridge.

Palmer, E. L. (1965). Accelerating the child's cognitive attainments through the inducement of cognitive conflict: An interpretation of the Piagetian position. *Journal of Research in Science Teaching, 3,* 324.

Pang, V. O. (1995). Asian Pacific American students: A diverse and complex population. In J. A. Banks & C. A. M. Banks (Eds.), *Handbook of research on multicultural education.* New York: Macmillan.

Panksepp, J. (1998). Attention deficit hyperactivity disorders, psychostimulants, and intolerance of childhood playfulness: A tragedy in the making? *Current Directions in Psychological Science, 7,* 91–98.

Panofsky, C. P. (1994). Developing the representational functions of language: The role of parent-child book-reading activity. In V. John-Steiner, C. P. Panofsky, & L. W. Smith (Eds.), *Sociocultural approaches to language and literacy: An interactionist perspective.* Cambridge, England: Cambridge University Press.

Papernow, P. (1988). Stepparent role development: From outsider to intimate. In W. R. Beer (Ed.), *Relative strangers* (pp. 54–82). Totowa, NJ: Rowman & Littlefield.

Papousek, M., & Papousek, H. (1996). Infantile persistent crying, state regulation, and interaction with parents: A systems view. In M. H. Bornstein & J. L. Genevro (Eds.), *Child development and behavioral pediatrics* (pp. 11–33). Mahwah, NJ: Erlbaum.

Paris, S. G., & Ayres, L. R. (1994). *Becoming reflective students and teachers with portfolios and authentic assessment.* Washington, DC: American Psychological Association.

Paris, S. G., & Byrnes, J. P. (1989). The constructivist approach to self-regulation and learning in the classroom. In B. J. Zimmerman & D. H. Schunk (Eds.), *Self-regulated learning and academic achievement: Theory, research, and practice.* New York: Springer-Verlag.

Paris, S. G., & Cunningham, A. E. (1996). Children becoming students. In D. C. Berliner & R. C. Calfee (Eds.), *Handbook of educational psychology.* New York: Macmillan.

Paris, S. G., & Upton, L. R. (1976). Children's memory for inferential relationships in prose. *Child Development, 47,* 660–668.

Parish, P. (1985). *Amelia Bedelia goes camping.* New York: William Morrow.

Parke, R. D., & Bhavnagri, N. P. (1989). Parents as managers of children's peer relationships. In D. Belle (Ed.), *Children's social networks and social supports.* New York: Wiley.

Parke, R. D., & Buriel, R. (1998). Socialization in the family: Ethnic and ecological perspectives. In W. Damon (Series Ed.) & N. Eisenberg (Vol. Ed.), *Handbook of child psychology: Vol. 3. Social, emotional, and personality development* (5th ed., pp. 463–552). New York: Wiley.

Parke, R. D., Coltrane, S., Duffy, S., Buriel, R., Dennis, J., Powers, J., et al. (2004). Economic stress, parenting, and child adjustment in Mexican American and European American families. *Child Development, 75,* 1632–1656.

Parke, R. D., Ornstein, P. A., Rieser, J. J., & Zahn-Waxler, C. (1994). The past as prologue: An overview of a century of developmental psychology. In R. D. Parke, P. A. Ornstein, J. J. Rieser, & C. Zahn-Waxler (Eds.), *A century of developmental psychology* (pp. 1–70). Washington, DC: American Psychological Association.

Parke, R. D., & Tinsley, B. R. (1981). The father's role in infancy: Determinants of involvement in caregiving and play. In M. E. Lamb (Ed.), *The role of the father in child development* (pp. 429–458). New York: Wiley.

Parke, R. D., & Tinsley, B. R. (1987). Family interaction in infancy. In J. D. Osofsky (Ed.), *Handbook of infant development* (pp. 429–458). New York: Wiley.

Parker, J. G. (1986). Becoming friends: Conversational skills for friendship formation in young children. In J. M. Gottman & J. G. Parker (Eds.), *Conversations of friends: Speculations on affective development* (pp. 103–138). Cambridge, England: Cambridge University Press.

Parker, J. G., & Gottman, J. M. (1989). Social and emotional development in a relational context: Friendship interaction from early childhood to adolescence. In T. J. Berndt & G. W. Ladd (Eds.), *Peer relations in child development* (pp. 95–131). New York: Wiley.

Parker, W. D. (1997). An empirical typology of perfectionism in academically talented children. *American Educational Research Journal, 34,* 545–562.

Parkhurst, J., & Gottman, J. M. (1986). How young children get what they want. In J. M. Gottman & J. G. Parker (Eds.), *Conversations of friends: Speculations on affective development* (pp. 315–345). Cambridge, England: Cambridge University Press.

Parkhurst, J. T., & Hopmeyer, A. (1998). Socio-metric popularity and peer-perceived popularity: Two distinct dimensions of peer status. *Journal of Early Adolescence, 18,* 125–144.

Parks, C. P. (1995). Gang behavior in the schools: Reality or myth? *Educational Psychology Review, 7,* 41–68.

Parten, M. B. (1932). Social participation among preschool children. *Journal of Abnormal and Social Psychology, 27,* 243–269.

Pascarella, E. T., & Terenzini, P. T. (1991). *How college affects students: Findings and insights from twenty years of research.* San Francisco: Jossey-Bass.

Passler, M., Isaac, W., & Hynd, G. W. (1985). Neuropsychological development of behavior attributed to frontal lobe functioning in children. *Developmental Neuropsychology, 1,* 349–370.

Pate, R. R., Long, B. J., & Heath, G. (1994). Descriptive epidemiology of physical activity in adolescents. *Pediatric Exercise Science, 6,* 434–447.

Patrick, H. (1997). Social self-regulation: Exploring the relations between children's social relationships, academic self-regulation, and school performance. *Educational Psychologist, 32,* 209–220.

Patterson, C. J. (1992). Children of lesbian and gay parents. *Child Development, 63,* 1025–1042.

Patterson, C. J. (1995). Sexual orientation and human development: An overview. *Developmental Psychology, 31,* 3–11.

Patterson, C. J., & Chan, R. W. (1997). Gay fathers. In M. E. Lamb (Ed.), *The role of the father in child development* (3rd ed., pp. 245–360). New York: Wiley.

Patterson, G. R. (1986). Performance models for anti-social boys. *American Psychologist, 41,* 432–444.

Patterson, G. R. (1995). Coercion as a basis for early age of onset for arrest. In J. McCord (Ed.), *Coercion and punishment in long-term perspectives* (pp. 81–105). New York: Cambridge University Press.

Patterson, G. R., DeBaryshe, B. D., & Ramsey, E. (1989). A developmental perspective on antisocial behavior. *American Psychologist, 44,* 329–335.

Patterson, G. R., & Reid, J. B. (1970). Reciprocity and coercion: Two facets of social systems. In C. Neuringer & J. Michael (Eds.), *Behavior modification in clinical psychology.* New York: Appleton-Century-Crofts.

Patton, J. R., Blackbourn, J. M., & Fad, K. (1996). *Exceptional individuals in focus* (6th ed.). Upper Saddle River, NJ: Merrill/Prentice Hall.

Pauen, S. (2002). Evidence for knowledge-based category discrimination in infancy. *Child Development, 73,* 1016–1033.

Paul, R. (1990). Comprehension strategies: Interactions between world knowledge and the development of sentence comprehension. *Topics in Language Disorders, 10,* 63–75.

Paus, T., Zijdenbos, A., Worsley, K., Collins, D. I., Blumenthal, J., Giedd, J. N., et al. (1999). Structural maturation of neural pathways in children and adolescents: in vivo study. *Science, 283,* 1908–1911.

Pawlas, G. E. (1994). Homeless students at the school door. *Educational Leadership, 51*(8), 79–82.

Paxton, R. J. (1999). A deafening silence: History textbooks and the students who read them. *Review of Educational Research, 69,* 315–339.

Pea, R. D. (1993). Practices of distributed intelligence and designs for education. In G. Salomon (Ed.), *Distributed cognitions: Psychological and educational considerations.* Cambridge, England: Cambridge University Press.

Peak, L. (1993). Academic effort in international perspective. In T. M. Tomlinson (Ed.), *Motivating students to learn: Overcoming barriers to high achievement.* Berkeley, CA: McCutchan.

Pearson, P. D., Hansen, J., & Gordon, C. (1979). The effect of background knowledge on young children's comprehension of explicit and implicit information. *Journal of Reading Behavior, 11,* 201–209.

Pederson, D. R., Rook-Green, A., & Elder, J. L. (1981). The role of action in the development of pretend play in young children. *Developmental Psychology, 17,* 756–759.

Pellegrini, A. D. (1996). *Observing children in their natural worlds: A methodological primer.* Mahwah, NJ: Erlbaum.

Pellegrini, A. D. (1998). Play and the assessment of young children. In O. N. Saracho & B. Spodek (Eds.), *Multiple perspectives on play in early childhood education.* Albany: State University of New York Press.

Pellegrini, A. D. (2002). Bullying, victimization, and sexual harassment during the transition to middle school. *Educational Psychologist, 37,* 151–163.

Pellegrini, A. D., & Bartini, M. (2000). A longitudinal study of bullying, victimization, and peer affiliation during the transition from primary school to middle school. *American Educational Research Journal, 37,* 699–725.

Pellegrini, A. D., Bartini, M., & Brooks, F. (1999). School bullies, victims, and aggressive victims: Factors relating to group affiliation and victimization in early adolescence. *Journal of Educational Psychology, 91,* 216–224.

Pellegrini, A. D., & Bjorklund, D. F. (1997). The role of recess in children's cognitive performance. *Educational Psychologist, 32,* 35–40.

Pellegrini, A. D., & Bohn, C. M. (2005). The role of recess in children's cognitive performance and school adjustment. *Educational Researcher, 34*(1), 13–19.

Pellegrini, A. D., & Horvat, M. (1995). A developmental contextualist critique of attention deficit hyperactivity disorder. *Educational Researcher, 24*(1), 13–19.

Pellegrini, A. D., & Smith, P. K. (1998). Physical activity play: Consensus and debate. *Child Development, 69,* 609–610.

Peña, E. (1993). Learning strategies checklist. In V. F. Gutiérrez-Clellan & E. Peña (2001), Dynamic assessment of diverse children: A tutorial. *Language, Speech and Hearing Services in Schools, 32,* 212–224.

Penner, A. M. (2003). International gender X item difficulty interactions in mathematics and science achievement tests. *Journal of Educational Psychology, 95,* 650–655.

Pennington, B. F., & Bennetto, L. (1993). Main effects of transactions in the neuropsychology of conduct disorder. Commentary on "The neuropsychology of conduct disorder." *Development and Psychopathology, 5,* 153–164.

Pérez, B. (Ed.). (1998). *Sociocultural contexts of language and literacy.* Mahwah, NJ: Erlbaum.

Perez-Granados, D. R., & Callanan, M. A. (1997). Parents and siblings as early resources for young children's learning in Mexican-descent families. *Hispanic Journal of Behavioral Sciences, 19,* 3–33.

Perfetti, C. A. (1985). Reading ability. In R. J. Sternberg (Ed.), *Human abilities: An information-processing approach.* New York: Freeman.

Perfetti, C. A. (1992). The representation problem in reading acquisition. In P. B. Gough, L. C. Ehri, & R. Treiman (Eds.), *Reading acquisition.* Hillsdale, NJ: Erlbaum.

Perfetti, C. A., & McCutchen, D. (1987). Schooled language competence: Linguistic abilities in reading and writing. In S. Rosenberg (Ed.), *Advances in applied psycholinguistics.* Cambridge, England: Cambridge University Press.

Perkins, D. N. (1992). *Smart schools: From training memories to educating minds.* New York: Free Press/Macmillan.

Perkins, D. N. (1995). *Outsmarting IQ: The emerging science of learnable intelligence.* New York: Free Press.

Perkins, D. N., & Grotzer, T. A. (1997). Teaching intelligence. *American Psychologist, 52,* 1125–1133.

Perkins, D. N., Tishman, S., Ritchhart, R., Donis, K., & Andrade, A. (2000). Intelligence in the wild: A dispositional view of intellectual traits. *Educational Psychology Review, 12,* 269–293.

Perner, J., Lang, B., & Kloo, D. (2002). Theory of mind and self-control: More than a common problem of inhibition. *Child Development, 73,* 752–767.

Perner, J., Ruffman, T., & Leekam, S. R. (1994). Theory of mind is contagious: You catch it from your sibs. *Child Development, 65,* 1228–1238.

Perner, J., & Wimmer, H. (1985). "John *thinks* that Mary *thinks* that . . . " Attribution of second-order beliefs by 5- to 10-year-old children. *Journal of Experimental Child Psychology, 39,* 437–471.

Perry, C. L., Luepker, R. V., Murray, D. M., Hearn, M. D., Halper, A., Dudvitz, B., et al. (1989). Parent involvement with children's health promotion: A one-year follow-up of the Minnesota Home Team. *Health Education Quarterly, 16,* 71–180.

Perry, M. (2000). Explanations of mathematical concepts in Japanese, Chinese, and U.S. first- and fifth-grade classrooms. *Cognition and Instruction, 18,* 181–207.

Perry, N. E. (1998). Young children's self-regulated learning and contexts that support it. *Journal of Educational Psychology, 90,* 715–729.

Perry, N. E., VandeKamp, K. O., Mercer, L. K., & Nordby, C. J. (2002). Investigating teacher-student interactions that foster self-regulated learning. *Educational Psychologist, 37,* 5–15.

Perry, N. E., & Winne, P. H. (2004). Motivational messages from home and school: How do they influence young children's engagement in learning? In D. M. McNerney & S. Van Etten (Eds.), *Big theories revisited* (pp. 199–222). Greenwich, CT: Information Age.

Perry, W. G., Jr. (1968). *Forms of intellectual and ethical development in the college years.* Cambridge, MA: President and Fellows of Harvard College.

Peters, A. M. (1983). *The units of language acquisition.* New York: Cambridge University Press.

Peterson, A. C., & Taylor, B. (1980). The biological approach to adolescence: Biological change and psychological adaptation. In J. Adelson (Ed.), *Handbook of adolescent psychology* (pp. 117–155). New York: Wiley.

Peterson, B. E., & Stewart, A. J. (1996). The antecedents and contexts of generativity motivation at midlife. *Psychology and Aging, 11*(1), 21–33.

Peterson, C. (1990). Explanatory style in the classroom and on the playing field. In S. Graham & V. S. Folkes (Eds.), *Attribution theory: Applications to achievement, mental health, and interpersonal conflict.* Hillsdale, NJ: Erlbaum.

Peterson, C., Maier, S. F., & Seligman, M. E. P. (1993). *Learned helplessness: A theory for the age of personal control.* New York: Oxford University Press.

Peterson, C. C. (2002). Drawing insight from pictures: The development of concepts of false drawing and false belief in children with deafness, normal hearing, and autism. *Child Development, 73,* 1442–1459.

Peterson, D., & Esbensen, F. A. (2004). The outlook is G.R.E.A.T.: What educators say about school-based prevention and the Gang Resistance Education and Training (G.R.E.A.T.) Program. *Evaluation Review, 28*(3), 218–245.

Peterson, L. (1980). Developmental changes in verbal and behavioral sensitivity to cues of social norms of altruism. *Child Development, 51,* 830–838.

Peterson, P. L. (1992). Revising their thinking: Keisha Coleman and her third-grade mathematics class. In H. H. Marshall (Ed.), *Redefining student learning: Roots of educational change.* Norwood, NJ: Ablex.

Petrill, S. A., & Wilkerson, B. (2000). Intelligence and achievement: A behavioral genetic perspective. *Educational Psychology Review, 12,* 185–199.

Pettit, G. S., Brown, E. G., Mize, J., & Lindsey, E. (1998). Mothers' and fathers' socializing behaviors in three contexts: Links with children's peer competence. *Merrill-Palmer Quarterly, 44,* 173–193.

Pettito, A. L. (1985). Division of labor: Procedural learning in teacher-led small groups. *Cognition and Instruction, 2,* 233–270.

Pettito, L. A. (1997). In the beginning: On the genetic and environmental factors that make early language acquisition possible. In M. Gopnik (Ed.), *The inheritance and innateness of grammars.* New York: Oxford University Press.

Pfeifer, M., Goldsmith, H. H., Davidson, R. J., & Rickman, M. (2002). Continuity and change in inhibited and uninhibited children. *Child Development, 73,* 1474–1485.

Phelan, P., Yu, H. C., & Davidson, A. L. (1994). Navigating the psychosocial pressures of adolescence: The voices and experiences of high school youth. *American Educational Research Journal, 31,* 415–447.

Phillips, D., Mekos, D., Scarr, S., McCartney, K., & Abbott-Shim, M. (2001). Within and beyond the classroom door: Assessing quality in child care centers. *Early Childhood Research Quarterly, 15,* 475–496.

Phillips, D., & Zimmerman, M. (1990). The developmental course of perceived competence and incompetence among competent children. In R. Sternberg & J. Kolligian (Eds.), *Competence considered* (pp. 41–66). New Haven, CT: Yale University Press.

Phillips, M. (1997). What makes schools effective? A comparison of the relationships of communitarian climate and academic climate to mathematics achievement and attendance during middle school. *American Educational Research Journal, 34,* 633–662.

Phinney, J. S. (1989). Stages of ethnic identity development in minority group adolescents. *Journal of Early Adolescence, 9,* 34–49.

Phinney, J. S. (1990). Ethnic identity in adolescents and adults: Review of research. *Psychological Bulletin, 108,* 499–514.

Phinney, J. S., & Tarver, S. (1988). Ethnic identity search and commitment in Black and White eighth graders. *Journal of Early Adolescence, 8,* 265–277.

Piaget, J. (1928). *Judgment and reasoning in the child* (M. Warden, Trans.). New York: Harcourt, Brace.

Piaget, J. (1929). *The child's conception of the world.* New York: Harcourt, Brace.

Piaget, J. (1952a). *The child's conception of number* (C. Gattegno & F. M. Hodgson, Trans.). London: Routledge & Kegan Paul.

Piaget, J. (1952b). *The origins of intelligence in children.* New York: International Universities Press.

Piaget, J. (1959). *The language and thought of the child* (3rd ed.; M. Gabain, Trans.). London: Routledge & Kegan Paul.

Piaget, J. (1960a). *The child's conception of physical causality* (M. Gabain, Trans.). Paterson, NJ: Littlefield, Adams.

Piaget, J. (1960b). *The moral judgment of the child* (M. Gabain, Trans.). Glencoe, IL: Free Press. (First published in 1932)

Piaget, J. (1985). *The equilibration of cognitive structures: The central problem of intellectual development.* Chicago: University of Chicago Press.

Piche, C., & Plante, C. (1991). Perceived masculinity, femininity, and androgyny among primary school boys: Relationships with the adaptation level of these students and the attitudes of the teachers towards them. *European Journal of Psychology of Education, 6,* 423–435.

Piirto, J. (1999). *Talented children and adults: Their development and education* (2nd ed.). Upper Saddle River, NJ: Merrill/Prentice Hall.

Pillow, B. H. (2002). Children's and adults' evaluation of the certainty of deductive inferences, inductive inferences, and guesses. *Child Development, 73,* 779–792.

Pillow, B. H., & Henrichon, A. J. (1996). There's more to the picture than meets the eye: Young children's difficulty understanding biased interpretation. *Child Development, 67,* 803–819.

Pinker, S. (1982). A theory of the acquisition of lexical interpretive grammars. In J. Bresnan (Ed.), *The mental representation of grammatical notions.* Cambridge, MA: MIT Press.

Pinker, S. (1984). *Language learnability and language development.* Cambridge, MA: Harvard University Press.

Pinker, S. (1987). The bootstrapping problem in language acquisition. In B. MacWhinney (Ed.), *Mechanisms of language acquisition.* Hillsdale, NJ: Erlbaum.

Pinker, S. (1997). Evolutionary biology and the evolution of language. In M. Gopnik (Ed.), *The inheritance and innateness of grammars.* New York: Oxford University Press.

Pinnegar, S. E. (1988, April). *Learning the language of practice from practicing teachers: An exploration of the term "with me."* Paper presented at the annual meeting of the American Educational Research Association, New Orleans, Louisiana.

Pintrich, P. R., & Schrauben, B. (1992). Students' motivational beliefs and their cognitive engagement in academic tasks. In D. Schunk & J. Meece (Eds.), *Students' perceptions in the classroom: Causes and consequences.* Hillsdale, NJ: Erlbaum.

Pintrich, P. R., & Schunk, D. H. (2002). *Motivation in education: Theory, research, and applications* (2nd ed.). Upper Saddle River, NJ: Merrill/Prentice Hall.

Pipher, M. (1994). *Reviving Ophelia: Saving the selves of adolescent girls.* New York: Putnam.

Pitner, R. O., Astor, R. A., Benbenishty, R., Haj-Yahia, M. M., & Zeira, A. (2003). The effects of group stereotypes on adolescents' reasoning about peer retribution. *Child Development, 74,* 413–425.

Plomin, R. (1989). Environment and genes: Determinants of behavior. *American Psychologist, 44,* 105–111.

Plomin, R., & DeFries, J. C. (1985). *Origins of individual differences in infancy.* New York: Academic Press.

Plomin, R., Fulker, D. W., Corley, R., & DeFries, J. C. (1997). Nature, nurture, and cognitive development from 1 to 16 years: A parent-offspring adoption study. *Psychological Science, 8,* 442–447.

Plomin, R., Owen, M. J., & McGuffin, P. (1994). The genetic basis of complex human behaviors. *Science, 24,* 1733–1739.

Plomin, R., & Petrill, S. A. (1997). Genetics and intelligence: What's new? *Intelligence, 24,* 53–77.

Plumert, J. M. (1994). Flexibility in children's use of spatial and categorical organizational strategies in recall. *Developmental Psychology, 30,* 738–747.

Pogrow, S., & Londer, G. (1994). The effects of an intensive general thinking program on the motivation and cognitive development of at-risk students: Findings from the HOTS program. In H. F. O'Neil, Jr., & M. Drillings (Eds.), *Motivation: Theory and research.* Hillsdale, NJ: Erlbaum.

Pollack, W. (1998). *Real boys: Rescuing our sons from the myths of boyhood.* New York: Henry Holt.

Pollitt, E., & Oh, S. (1994). Early supplemental feeding, child development and health policy. *Food & Nutrition Bulletin, 15,* 208–214.

Pomerantz, E. M., Altermatt, E. R., & Saxon, J. L. (2002). Making the grade but feeling distressed: Gender differences in academic performance and internal distress. *Journal of Educational Psychology, 94,* 396–404.

Poresky, R. H., Daniels, A. M., Mukerjee, J., & Gunnell, K. (1999, April). *Community and family influences on adolescents' use of alcohol and other drugs: An exploratory ecological analysis.* Paper presented at the biennial meeting of the Society for Research in Child Development, Albuquerque, NM.

Portes, P. R. (1996). Ethnicity and culture in educational psychology. In D. C. Berliner & R. C. Calfee (Eds.), *Handbook of educational psychology.* New York: Macmillan.

Posner, G. J., Strike, K. A., Hewson, P. W., & Gertzog, W. A. (1982). Accommodation of a scientific conception: Toward a theory of conceptual change. *Science Education, 66,* 211–227.

Poulin, F., & Boivin, M. (1999). Proactive and reactive aggression and boys' friendship quality in mainstream classrooms. *Journal of Emotional and Behavioral Disorders, 7,* 168–177.

Poulin-Dubois, D. (1999). Infants' distinction between animate and inanimate objects: The origins of naïve psychology. In P. Rochar (Ed.), *Early social cognition* (pp. 257–280). Mahwah, NJ: Erlbaum.

Powell, G. J. (1983). *The psychosocial development of minority children.* New York: Brunner/Mazel.

Powell, M. P., & Schulte, T. (1999). Turner syndrome. In S. Goldstein & C. R. Reynolds (Eds.), *Handbook of neurodevelopmental and genetic disorders* (pp. 277–297). New York: Guilford Press.

Power, F. C., Higgins, A., & Kohlberg, L. (1989). *Lawrence Kohlberg's approach to moral education.* New York: Columbia University Press.

Powers, L. E., Sowers, J. A., & Stevens, T. (1995). An exploratory, randomized study of the impact of mentoring on the self-efficacy and community-based knowledge of adolescents with severe physical challenges. *Journal of Rehabilitation, 61*(1), 33–41.

Pramling, I. (1996). Understanding and empowering the child as learner. In D. R. Olson & N. Torrance (Eds.), *The handbook of education and human development: New models of learning, teaching, and schooling.* Cambridge, MA: Blackwell.

Prawat, R. S. (1989). Promoting access to knowledge, strategy, and disposition in students: A research synthesis. *Review of Educational Research, 59,* 1–41.

Prawat, R. S. (1992). From individual differences to learning communities: Our changing focus. *Educational Leadership, 49*(7), 9–13.

Preedy, P. (1999). Meeting the educational needs of pre-school and primary aged twins and higher multiples. In A. C. Sandbank (Ed.), *Twin and triplet psychology: A professional guide to working with multiples* (pp. 70–99). London: Routledge.

Pressley, M. (1982). Elaboration and memory development. *Child Development, 53,* 296–309.

Pressley, M., Almasi, J., Schuder, T., Bergman, J., Hite, S., El-Dinary, P. B., et al. (1994). Transactional instruction of comprehension strategies: The Montgomery County Maryland SAIL program. *Reading and Writing Quarterly, 10,* 5–19.

Pressley, M., Borkowski, J. G., & Schneider, W. (1987). Cognitive strategies: Good strategy users coordinate metacognition and knowledge. In R. Vasta (Ed.), *Annals of child development* (Vol. 4). Greenwich, CT: JAI Press.

Pressley, M., El-Dinary, P. B., Marks, M. B., Brown, R., & Stein, S. (1992). Good strategy instruction is motivating and interesting. In K. A. Renninger, S. Hidi, & A. Krapp (Eds.), *The role of interest in learning and development.* Hillsdale, NJ: Erlbaum.

Pressley, M., & Hilden, K. (2006). Cognitive strategies: Production deficiencies and successful strategy instruction everywhere. In W. Damon, R. M. Lerner (Series Eds.), D. Kuhn, & R. Siegler (Vol. Eds.), *Handbook of child psychology: Vol. 2. Cognition, perception, and language* (6th ed.). New York: Wiley.

Pressley, M., Ross, K. A., Levin, J. R., & Ghatala, E. S. (1984). The role of strategy utility knowledge in children's strategy decision making. *Journal of Experimental Child Psychology, 38,* 491–504.

Pribilsky, J. (2001). Nervios and 'modern childhood': Migration and shifting contexts of child life in the Ecuadorian Andes. *Childhood, 8*(2), 251–273.

Price-Williams, D. R., Gordon, W., & Ramirez, M. (1969). Skill and conservation. *Developmental Psychology, 1,* 769.

Pritchard, R. (1990). The effects of cultural schemata on reading processing strategies. *Reading Research Quarterly, 25,* 273–295.

Proctor, R. W., & Dutta, A. (1995). *Skill acquisition and human performance.* Thousand Oaks, CA: Sage.

Pulkkinen, L. (1982). Self-control and continuity from childhood to adolescence. In P. B. Baltes & O. G. Brim (Eds.), *Life-span development and behavior* (Vol. 4). Orlando, FL: Academic Press.

Pulos, S. (1997). Adolescents' implicit theories of physical phenomena: A matter of gravity. *International Journal of Behavioral Development, 20,* 493–507.

Pulos, S., & Linn, M. C. (1981). Generality of the controlling variables scheme in early adolescence. *Journal of Early Adolescence, 1,* 26–37.

Purcell-Gates, V. (1995). *Other people's words: The cycle of low literacy.* Cambridge, MA: Harvard University Press.

Purdie, N., & Hattie, J. (1996). Cultural differences in the use of strategies for self-regulated learning. *American Educational Research Journal, 33,* 845–871.

Purdie, N., Hattie, J., & Douglas, G. (1996). Student conceptions of learning and their use of self-regulated learning strategies: A cross-cultural comparison. *Journal of Educational Psychology, 88,* 87–100.

Putallaz, M., & Gottman, J. M. (1981). Social skills and group acceptance. In S. R. Asher & J. M. Gottman (Eds.), *The development of children's friendships* (pp. 116–149). New York: Cambridge University Press.

Putallaz, M., & Heflin, A. H. (1986). Toward a model of peer acceptance. In J. M. Gottman & J. G. Parker (Eds.), *Conversations of friends: Speculations on affective development* (pp. 292–314). Cambridge, England: Cambridge University Press.

Qian, G., & Pan, J. (2002). A comparison of epistemological beliefs and learning from science text between American and Chinese high school students. In B. K. Hofer & P. R. Pintrich (Eds.), *Personal epistemology: The psychology of beliefs about knowledge and knowing* (pp. 365–385). Mahwah, NJ: Erlbaum.

Quinn, P. C. (2002). Category representation in young infants. *Current Directions in Psychological Science, 11,* 66–70.

Quinn, P. C. (2003). Concepts are not just for objects: Categorization of spatial relation information by young infants. In D. H. Rakison & L. M. Oakes (Eds.), *Early category and concept development: Making sense of the blooming, buzzing confusion.* Oxford, England: Oxford University Press.

Quittner, A. L., Modi, A. C., & Roux, A. L. (2004). Psychosocial challenges and clinical interventions for children and adolescents with cystic fibrosis: A developmental approach. In R. T. Brown (Ed.), *Handbook of pediatric psychology in school settings* (pp. 333–361). Mahwah, NJ: Erlbaum.

Radziszewska, B., & Rogoff, B. (1991). Children's guided participation in planning imaginary errands with skilled adult or peer partners. *Developmental Psychology, 27,* 381–389.

Raikes, H. (1993). Relationship duration in infant care: Time with high-ability teacher and infant-teacher attachment. *Early Childhood Research Quarterly, 8*(3), 309–325.

Raine, A., Reynolds, C., & Venables, P. H. (2002). Stimulation seeking and intelligence: A prospective longitudinal study. *Journal of Personality and Social Psychology, 82,* 663–674.

Raine, A., & Scerbo, A. (1991). Biological theories of violence. In J. S. Milner (Ed.), *Neuropsychology of aggression* (pp. 1–25). Boston: Kluwer Academic Press.

Rakic, P. (1995). Corticogenesis in human and nonhuman primates. In M. S. Gazzaniga (Ed.), *The cognitive neurosciences* (pp. 127–145). Cambridge, MA: MIT Press.

Rallison, M. L. (1986). *Growth disorders in infants, children, and adolescents.* New York: Churchill Livingstone.

Ramachandran, V. S., Rogers-Ramachandran, D., & Stewart, M. (1992). Perceptual correlates of massive cortical reorganization. *Science, 258,* 1159–1160.

Ramey, C. T. (1992). High-risk children and IQ: Altering intergenerational patterns. *Intelligence, 16,* 239–256.

Ramey, C. T., & Ramey, S. L. (1998). Early intervention and early experience. *American Psychologist, 53,* 109–120.

Ramsey, P. G. (1987). *Teaching and learning in a diverse world: Multicultural education for young children.* New York: Teachers College Press.

Ratner, H. H. (1984). Memory demands and the development of young children's memory. *Child Development, 55,* 2173–2191.

Raver, C. C. (2002). Emotions matter: Making the case for the role of young children's emotional development for early school readiness. *Social Policy Report of the Society for Research in Child Development, 16*(3), 1, 3–6, 8–10, 12–18.

Rayner, K., Foorman, B. R., Perfetti, C. A., Pesetsky, D., & Seidenberg, M. S. (2001). How psychological science informs the teaching of reading. *Psychological Science in the Public Interest, 2,* 31–74.

Rayport, S. G. (1992). Cellular and molecular biology of the neuron. In S. C. Yudofsky & R. E. Hales (Eds.), *The American Psychiatric Press textbook of neuropsychiatry* (2nd ed., pp. 3–28). Washington, DC: American Psychiatric Press.

Reese, D. F., & Thorkildsen, T. A. (1999, April). *Perceptions of exclusion among eighth graders from low-income families.* Paper presented at the annual meeting of the American Educational Research Association, Montreal, Canada.

Reese, L., Garnier, H., Gallimore, R., & Goldenberg, C. (2000). Longitudinal analysis of the antecedents of emergent Spanish literacy and middle-school English reading achievement of Spanish-speaking students. *American Educational Research Journal, 37,* 633–662.

Reese, S. (1996). KIDMONEY: Children as big business. *Technos Quarterly, 5*(4), 1–7. Retrieved November 21, 2005, at http://www.ait.net/technos/tq_05/4reesephp

Reeve, J., Bolt, E., & Cai, Y. (1999). Autonomy-supportive teachers: How they teach and motivate students. *Journal of Educational Psychology, 91,* 537–548.

Reich, P. A. (1986). *Language development.* Englewood Cliffs, NJ: Prentice Hall.

Reid, M. K., & Borkowski, J. G. (1987). Causal attributions of hyperactive children: Implications for training strategies and self-control. *Journal of Educational Psychology, 79,* 296–307.

Reid, N. (1989). Contemporary Polynesian conceptions of giftedness. *Gifted Education International, 6*(1), 30–38.

Reid, P. T. (1985). Sex-role socialization of Black children: A review of theory, family, and media influences. *Academic Psychology Bulletin, 7,* 201–212.

Reifman, A., Barnes, G. M., & Hoffman, J. H. (1999, April). *Physical maturation and problem behaviors in male adolescents: A test of peer and parent relations as mediators.* Paper presented at the biennial meeting of the Society for Research in Child Development, Albuquerque, NM.

Reimer, J., Paolitto, D. P., & Hersh, R. H. (1983). *Promoting moral growth: From Piaget to Kohlberg* (2nd ed.). White Plains, NY: Longman.

Reiner, M., Slotta, J. D., Chi, M. T. H., & Resnick, L. B. (2000). Naïve physics reasoning: A commitment to substance-based conceptions. *Cognition and Instruction, 18,* 1–34.

Reis, S. M. (1989). Reflections on policy affecting the education of gifted and talented students: Past and future perspectives. *American Psychologist, 44,* 399–408.

Remez, L. (2000). Oral sex among adolescents: Is it sex or is it abstinence? *Family Planning Perspectives, 32*(6), 298–304.

Renninger, K. A., Hidi, S., & Krapp, A. (Eds.). (1992). *The role of interest in learning and development.* Hillsdale, NJ: Erlbaum.

Renzulli, J. S., & Reis, S. M. (1986). The enrichment triad/revolving door model: A schoolwide plan for the development of creative productivity. In J. Renzulli (Ed.), *Systems and models for developing programs for the gifted and talented.* Mansfield Center, CT: Creative Learning Press.

Repacholi, B. M., & Gopnik, A. (1997). Early reasoning about desires: Evidence from 14- and 18-month-olds. *Developmental Psychology, 33,* 12–21.

Resnicow, K., Cross, D., & Wynder, E. (1991). The role of comprehensive school-based interventions. *Annals of the New York Academy of Sciences, 623,* 285–298.

Rest, J. R., Narváez, D., Bebeau, M., & Thoma, S. (1999). A neo-Kohlbergian approach: The DIT and schema theory. *Educational Psychology Review, 11,* 291–324.

Reyna, C. (2000). Lazy, dumb, or industrious: When stereotypes convey attribution information in the classroom. *Educational Psychology Review, 12,* 85–110.

Reynolds, A. (1994). Effects of a preschool plus follow-on intervention for children at risk. *Developmental Psychology, 30,* 787–804.

Reynolds, R. E., Taylor, M. A., Steffensen, M. S., Shirey, L. L., & Anderson, R. C. (1982). Cultural schemata and reading comprehension. *Reading Research Quarterly, 17,* 353–366.

Reznick, J. S., & Goldfield, B. A. (1992). Rapid change in lexical development in comprehension and production. *Developmental Psychology, 28,* 408–414.

Ricciuti, H. N. (1993). Nutrition and mental development. *Current Directions in Psychological Science, 2,* 43–46.

Rice, M., Hadley, P. A., & Alexander, A. L. (1993). Social biases toward children with speech and language impairments: A correlative causal model of language limitations. *Applied Psycholinguistics, 14,* 445–471.

Rice, M. L., Huston, A. C., Truglio, R., & Wright, J. (1990). Words from "Sesame Street": Learning vocabulary while viewing. *Developmental Psychology, 26,* 421–428.

Richards, J. E., & Turner, E. D. (2001). Extended visual fixation and distractibility in children from six to twenty-four months of age. *Child Development, 72,* 963–972.

Ridderinkhof, K. R., & van der Molen, M. (1995). A psychophysiological analysis of developmental differences in the ability to resist interference. *Child Development, 60,* 1040–1056.

Riggs, J. M. (1992). Self-handicapping and achievement. In A. K. Boggiano & T. S. Pittman (Eds.), *Achievement and motivation: A social-developmental perspective.* Cambridge, England: Cambridge University Press.

Rinehart, S. D., Stahl, S. A., & Erickson, L. G. (1986). Some effects of summarization training on reading and studying. *Reading Research Quarterly, 21,* 422–438.

Ripple, C. H., Gilliam, W. S., Chanana, N., & Zigler, E. (1999). Will fifty cooks spoil the broth? The debate over entrusting Head Start to the states. *American Psychologist, 54,* 327–343.

Rittle-Johnson, B., & Siegler, R. S. (1999). Learning to spell: Variability, choice, and change in children's strategy use. *Child Development, 70,* 332–348.

Rittle-Johnson, B., Siegler, R. S., & Alibali, M. W. (2001). Developing conceptual understanding and procedural skill in mathematics: An iterative process. *Journal of Educational Psychology, 93,* 346–362.

Ritts, V., Patterson, M. L., & Tubbs, M. E. (1992). Expectations, impressions, and judgments of physically attractive students: A review. *Review of Educational Research, 62,* 413–426.

Robbins, W. J., Brody, S., Hogan, A. G., Jackson, C. M., & Green, C. W. (Eds.). (1928). *Growth.* New Haven, CT: Yale University Press.

Roberts, D. F., Christenson, P., Gibson, W. A., Mooser, L., & Goldberg, M. E. (1980). Developing discriminating consumers. *Journal of Communication, 30,* 94–105.

Roberts, M. C., Brown, K. J., Boles, R. E., & Mashunkashey, J. O. (2004). Prevention of injuries: Concepts and interventions for pediatric psychology in the schools. In R. T. Brown (Ed.), *Handbook of pediatric psychology in school settings* (pp. 65–80). Mahwah, NJ: Erlbaum.

Robertson, J. S. (2000). Is attribution training a worthwhile classroom intervention for K–12 students with learning difficulties? *Educational Psychology Review, 12,* 111–134.

Robin, D. J., Berthier, N. E., & Clifton, R. K. (1996). Infants' predictive reaching for moving objects in the dark. *Developmental Psychology, 32,* 824–835.

Robins, R. W., & Trzesniewski, K. H. (2005). Self-esteem development across the lifespan. *Current Directions in Psychological Science, 14,* 158–162.

Robinson, T. N., & Killen, J. D. (1995). Ethnic and gender differences in the relationship between television viewing and obesity, physical activity, and dietary fat intake. *Journal of Health Education, 26*(Suppl. 2), S91–S98.

Robinson, T. R., Smith, S. W., Miller, M. D., & Brownell, M. T. (1999). Cognitive behavior modification of hyperactivity-impulsivity and aggression: A meta-analysis of school-based studies. *Journal of Educational Psychology, 91,* 195–203.

Rochat, P., & Bullinger, A. (1994). Posture and functional action in infancy. In A. Vyt, H. Bloch, & M. H. Bornstein (Eds.), *Early child development in the French tradition: Contributions from current research.* Hillsdale, NJ: Erlbaum.

Rochat, P., & Goubet, N. (1995). Development of sitting and reaching in 5- to 6-month-old infants. *Infant Behavior and Development, 18,* 53–68.

Roderick, M., & Camburn, E. (1999). Risk and recovery from course failure in the early years of high school. *American Educational Research Journal, 36,* 303–343.

Roehlkepartain, E. C., & Patel, E. (2006). Congregations: Unexamined crucibles for spiritual development. In E. C. Roehlkepartain, P. E. King, L. Wagener, & P. L. Benson (Eds.), *The handbook of spiritual development in childhood and adolescence* (pp. 324–336). Thousand Oaks, CA: Sage.

Roffwarg, H. P., Muzio, J. N., & Dement, W. C. (1966). Ontogenetic development of the human sleep-dream cycle. *Science, 152,* 604–619.

Rogoff, B. (1990). *Apprenticeship in thinking: Cognitive development in social context.* New York: Oxford University Press.

Rogoff, B. (1991). Social interaction as apprenticeship in thinking: Guidance and participation in spatial planning. In L. B. Resnick, J. M. Levine, & S. D. Teasley (Eds.), *Perspectives on socially shared cognition.* Washington, DC: American Psychological Association.

Rogoff, B. (1994, April). *Developing understanding of the idea of communities of learners.* Paper presented at the annual meeting of the American Educational Research Association, New Orleans, LA.

Rogoff, B. (1995). Observing sociocultural activity on three planes: Participatory appropriation, guided participation, and apprenticeship. In J. V. Wertsch, P. del Rio, & A. Alvarez (Eds.), *Sociocultural studies of mind.* Cambridge, England: Cambridge University Press.

Rogoff, B. (2003). *The cultural nature of human development.* Oxford, England: Oxford University Press.

Rogoff, B., Matusov, E., & White, C. (1996). Models of teaching and learning: Participation in a community of learners. In D. R. Olson & N. Torrance (Eds.), *The handbook of education and human development: New models of learning, teaching, and schooling.* Cambridge, MA: Blackwell.

Rogoff, B., Mistry, J., Göncü, A., & Mosier, C. (1993). Guided participation in cultural activity by toddlers and caregivers. *Monographs of the Society for Research in Child Development, 58*(8, Serial No. 236).

Rogoff, B., & Morelli, G. (1989). Perspectives on children's development from cultural psychology. *American Psychologist, 44,* 343–348.

Rohner, R. P., & Rohner, E. C. (1981). Parental acceptance-rejection and parental control: Cross-cultural codes. *Ethnology, 20,* 245–260.

Roid, G. (2003). *Stanford-Binet Intelligence Scales* (5th ed.). Itasca, IL: Riverside.

Rommetveit, R. (1985). Language acquisition as increasing linguistic structuring of experience and symbolic behavior control. In J. V. Wertsch (Ed.), *Culture, communication, and cognition: Vygotskian perspectives* (pp. 183–204). Cambridge, England: Cambridge University Press.

Rondal, J. A. (1985). *Adult-child interaction and the process of language acquisition.* New York: Praeger.

Root, M. P. P. (1999). The biracial baby boom: Understanding ecological constructions of racial identity in the 21st century. In R. H. Sheets & E. R. Hollins (Eds.), *Racial and ethnic identity in school practices: Aspects of human development* (pp. 67–89). Mahwah, NJ: Erlbaum.

Rose, A. J., & Asher, S. R. (1999). Children's goals and strategies in response to conflicts within a friendship. *Developmental Psychology, 35,* 69–79.

Rose, S. A. (1994). Relation between physical growth and information processing in infants born in India. *Child Development, 65,* 889–903.

Rose, S. A., & Feldman, J. F. (1995). Prediction of IQ and specific cognitive abilities at 11 years from infancy measures. *Developmental Psychology, 31,* 685–696.

Rosenberg, M. (1986). Self-concept from middle childhood through adolescence. In S. Suls & A. Greenwald (Eds.), *Psychological perspectives on the self* (Vol. 3, pp. 107–135). Hillsdale, NJ: Erlbaum.

Rosenkoetter, L. I., Rosenkoetter, S. E., Ozretich, R. A., & Acock, A. C. (2004). Mitigating the harmful effects of violent television. *Applied Developmental Psychology, 25,* 25–47.

Rosenshine, B., & Meister, C. (1992). The use of scaffolds for teaching higher-level cognitive strategies. *Educational Leadership, 49*(7), 26–33.

Rosenshine, B., & Meister, C. (1994). Reciprocal teaching: A review of the research. *Review of Educational Research, 64,* 479–530.

Rosenshine, B., Meister, C., & Chapman, S. (1996). Teaching students to generate questions: A review of the intervention studies. *Review of Educational Research, 66,* 181–221.

Rosenstein, D., & Oster, H. (1988). Differential facial responses to four basic tastes in newborns. *Child Development, 59,* 1555–1568.

Rosenthal, R. (1994). Interpersonal expectancy effects: A 30-year perspective. *Current Directions in Psychological Science, 3,* 176–179.

Rosser, R. (1994). *Cognitive development: Psychological and biological perspectives.* Boston: Allyn & Bacon.

Rossman, B. R. (1992). School-age children's perceptions of coping with distress: Strategies for emotion regulation and the moderation of adjustment. *Journal of Child Psychology and Psychiatry, 33,* 1373–1397.

Rotenberg, K. J., & Mayer, E. V. (1990). Delay of gratification in Native and White children: A cross-cultural comparison. *International Journal of Behavioral Development, 13,* 23–30.

Roth, K. J. (1990). Developing meaningful conceptual understanding in science. In B. F. Jones & L. Idol (Eds.), *Dimensions of thinking and cognitive instruction.* Hillsdale, NJ: Erlbaum.

Roth, K. J., & Anderson, C. (1988). Promoting conceptual change learning from science textbooks. In P. Ramsden (Ed.), *Improving learning: New perspectives.* London: Kogan Page.

Roth, W., & Bowen, G. M. (1995). Knowing and interacting: A study of culture, practices, and resources in a grade 8 open-inquiry science classroom guided by a cognitive apprenticeship metaphor. *Cognition and Instruction, 13,* 73–128.

Rothbart, M. K. (2004a). Commentary: Differentiated measures of temperament and multiple pathways to childhood disorders. *Journal of Clinical Child and Adolescent Psychology, 33*(1), 82–87.

Rothbart, M. K. (2004b). Temperament and the pursuit of an integrated developmental psychology. *Merrill Palmer Quarterly, 50*(4), 492–505.

Rothbart, M. K., Ahadi, S. A., & Evans, D. E. (2000). Temperament and personality: Origins and outcomes. *Journal of Personality and Social Psychology, 78*, 122–135.

Rothbart, M. K., Ahadi, S. A., Hershey, K., & Fisher, P. (2001). Investigations of temperament at three to seven years: The Children's Behavior Questionnaire. *Child Development, 72*, 1394–1408.

Rothbart, M. K., & Bates, J. E. (1998). Temperament. In W. Damon (Series Ed.) & N. Eisenberg (Vol. Ed.), *Handbook of child psychology: Vol. 3. Social, emotional, and personality development* (5th ed., pp. 105–176). New York: Wiley.

Rothbart, M. K., Hanley, D., & Albert, M. (1986). Gender differences in moral reasoning. *Sex Roles, 15*, 645–653.

Rothbaum, F., Weisz, J., Pott, M., Miyake, K., & Morelli, G. (2000). Attachment and culture: Security in the United States and Japan. *American Psychologist, 55*, 1093–1104.

Rovee-Collier, C. (1999). The development of infant memory. *Current Directions in Psychological Science, 8*, 80–85.

Rowe, D., Vazsonyi, A., & Flannery, D. (1994). No more than skin deep: Ethnic and racial similarity in developmental processes. *Psychological Review, 101*, 396–413.

Rowe, D. C., Almeida, D. M., & Jacobson, K. C. (1999). School context and genetic influences on aggression in adolescence. *Psychological Science, 10*, 277–280.

Rowe, D. C., Jacobson, K. C., & Van den Oord, E. J. C. G. (1999). Genetic and environmental influences on Vocabulary IQ: Parental education level as moderator. *Child Development, 70*, 1151–1162.

Rowe, D. W., & Harste, J. C. (1986). Metalinguistic awareness in writing and reading: The young child as curricular informant. In D. B. Yaden, Jr., & S. Templeton (Eds.), *Metalinguistic awareness and beginning literacy: Conceptualizing what it means to read and write.* Portsmouth, NH: Heinemann.

Rowe, E. (1999, April). *Gender differences in math self-concept development: The role of classroom interaction.* Paper presented at the annual meeting of the American Educational Research Association, Montreal, Canada.

Rowe, M. B. (1974). Wait-time and rewards as instructional variables, their influence on language, logic, and fate control: Part one—wait time. *Journal of Research in Science Teaching, 11*, 81–94.

Rowe, M. B. (1978). *Teaching science as continuous inquiry.* New York: McGraw-Hill.

Rowe, M. B. (1987). Wait-time: Slowing down may be a way of speeding up. *American Educator, 11*, 38–43, 47.

Rowland, T. W. (1990). *Exercise and children's health.* Champaign, IL: Human Kinetics.

Rubin, K., Fein, G., & Vandenberg, B. (1983). Play. In E. M. Hetherington (Ed.), *Handbook of child psychology: Vol. 4. Socialization, personality, and social development* (pp. 693–774). New York: Wiley.

Rubin, K. H., Bukowski, W., & Parker, J. G. (1998). Peer interactions, relationships, and groups. In W. Damon (Series Ed.) & N. Eisenberg (Vol. Ed.), *Handbook of child psychology: Vol. 3. Social, emotional, and personality development* (pp. 619–700). New York: Wiley.

Rubin, K. H., & Krasnor, L. R. (1986). Social-cognitive and social behavioral perspectives on problem solving. In M. Perlmutter (Ed.), *Minnesota symposia on child psychology: Vol. 19. Cognitive perspectives on children's social and behavioral development.* Hillsdale, NJ: Erlbaum.

Rubin, K. H., & Pepler, D. J. (1995). The relationship of child's play to social-cognitive growth and development. In H. C. Foot, A. J. Chapman, & J. R. Smith (Eds.), *Friendship and social relations in children* (pp. 209–233). New Brunswick, NJ: Transaction.

Rubin, K. H., Lynch, D., Coplan, R., Rose-Krasnor, L., & Booth, C. L. (1994). "Birds of a feather": Behavioral concordances and preferential personal attraction in children. *Child Development, 65*, 1778–1785.

Ruble, D. N., & Martin, C. L. (1998). Gender development. In W. Damon (Series Ed.) & N. Eisenberg (Vol. Ed.), *Handbook of child psychology: Vol. 3. Social, emotional, and personality development* (5th ed., pp. 933–1016). New York: Wiley.

Rudlin, C. R. (1993). Growth and sexual development: What is normal, and what is not? *Journal of the American Academy of Physician Assistants, 6*, 25–35.

Rudolph, K. D., Caldwell, M. S., & Conley, C. S. (2005). Need for approval and children's well-being. *Child Development, 76*, 309–323.

Ruff, H. A., & Lawson, K. R. (1990). Development of sustained, focused attention in young children during free play. *Developmental Psychology, 26*, 85–93.

Ruff, H. A., & Rothbart, M. K. (1996). *Attention in early development: Themes and variations.* New York: Oxford University Press.

Ruffman, T., Perner, J., Naito, M., Parkin, L., & Clements, W. A. (1998). Older (but not younger) siblings facilitate false belief understanding. *Developmental Psychology, 34*, 161–174.

Ruffman, T., Perner, J., Olson, D. R., & Doherty, M. (1993). Reflecting on scientific thinking: Children's understanding of the hypothesis-evidence relation. *Child Development, 64*, 1617–1636.

Ruhm, C. J. (1998, May). *Parental leave and child health* (NBER Working Paper No. W6554). Cambridge, MA: National Bureau of Economic Research.

Rumberger, R. W. (1995). Dropping out of middle school: A multilevel analysis of students and schools. *American Educational Research Journal, 32*, 583–625.

Rushton, J. P. (1980). *Altruism, socialization, and society.* Upper Saddle River, NJ: Prentice Hall.

Rushton, J. P., Fulkner, D. W., Neal, M. C., Nias, D. K. B., & Eysenck, H. J. (1986). Altruism and aggression: The heritability of individual differences. *Journal of Personality and Social Psychology, 50*, 1192–1198.

Rushton, J. P., & Teachman, G. (1978). The effects of positive reinforcement, attributions, and punishment on model induced altruism in children. *Personality and Social Psychology Bulletin, 4*, 322–325.

Russell, A., & Russell, G. (1994). Coparenting early school-age children: An examination of mother-father independence within families. *Developmental Psychology, 30*, 757–770.

Rutter, M., & Garmezy, N. (1983). Developmental psychopathology. In P. H. Mussen (Series Ed.) & E. M. Hetherington (Vol. Ed.), *Handbook of child psychology: Vol. 4. Socialization, personality, and social development* (4th ed., pp. 775–911). New York: Wiley.

Rutter, M., & O'Connor, T. G. (1999). Implications of attachment theory for child care policies. In J. Cassidy & P. R. Shaver (Eds.), *Handbook of attachment: Theory, research, and clinical applications* (pp. 823–844). New York: Guilford Press.

Rutter, M. L. (1997). Nature-nurture integration: The example of antisocial behavior. *American Psychologist, 52*, 390–398.

Ryan, A. M. (2000). Peer groups as a context for the socialization of adolescents' motivation, engagement, and achievement in school. *Educational Psychologist, 35*, 101–111.

Ryan, A. M., & Patrick, H. (2001). The classroom social environment and changes in adolescents' motivation and engagement during middle school. *American Educational Research Journal, 38*, 437–460.

Ryan, R. M., Connell, J. P., & Grolnick, W. S. (1992). When achievement is *not* intrinsically motivated: A theory of internalization and self-regulation in school. In A. K. Boggiano & T. S. Pittman (Eds.), *Achievement and motivation: A social-developmental perspective.* Cambridge, England: Cambridge University Press.

Ryan, R. M., & Deci, E. L. (2000). Self-determination theory and the facilitation of intrinsic motivation, social development, and well-being. *American Psychologist, 55*, 68–78.

Ryan, R. M., & Kuczkowski, R. (1994). The imaginary audience, self-consciousness, and public individuation in adolescence. *Journal of Personality, 62*, 219–237.

Ryan, R. M., & Lynch, J. H. (1989). Emotional autonomy versus detachment: Revisiting the vicissitudes of adolescence and young adulthood. *Child Development, 60*, 340–356.

Ryan, R. M., Stiller, J. D., & Lynch, J. H. (1994). Representations of relationships to teachers, parents, and friends as predictors of academic motivation and self-esteem. *Journal of Early Adolescence, 14*, 226–249.

Saarni, C. (2000). The social context of emotional development. In M. Lewis & J. M. Haviland-Jones (Eds.), *Handbook of emotions* (2nd ed., pp. 306–322). New York: Guilford Press.

Saarni, C., Mumme, D. L., & Campos, J. J. (1998). Emotional development: Action, communication, and understanding. In W. Damon (Editor-in-Chief) & N. Eisenberg (Vol. Ed.), *Handbook of child psychology: Vol. 3. Social, emotional, and personality development* (5th ed., pp. 237–309). New York: Wiley.

Sadeh, A., Gruber, R., & Raviv, A. (2002). Sleep, neurobehavioral functioning, and behavior problems in school-age children. *Child Development, 73*, 405–417.

Sadker, M. P., & Sadker, D. (1994). *Failing at fairness: How our schools cheat girls.* New York: Touchstone.

Sadler, T. W. (2000). *Hangman's medical embryology* (8th ed.). Philadelphia: Lippincott Williams & Wilkins.

Saffran, J. R. (2003). Statistical language learning: Mechanisms and constraints. *Current Directions in Psychological Science, 12*, 110–114.

Saffran, J. R., Aslin, R. N., & Newport, E. L. (1996). Statistical learning by 8-month-old infants. *Science, 274*, 1926–1928.

Saffran, J. R., & Griepentrog, G. J. (2001). Absolute pitch in infant auditory learning: Evidence for developmental reorganization. *Developmental Psychology, 37*, 74–85.

Salend, S. J., & Taylor, L. (1993). Working with families: A cross-cultural perspective. *Remedial and Special Education, 14*, 25–32, 39.

Salisbury, C. L., Evans, I. M., & Palombaro, M. M. (1997). Collaborative problem solving to promote the inclusion of young children with significant disabilities in primary grades. *Exceptional Children, 63*, 195–210.

Sallis, J. F. (1993). Epidemiology of physical activity and fitness in children and adolescents. *Critical Reviews in Food Science and Nutrition, 33*, 403–408.

Salmivalli, C., & Isaacs, J. (2005). Prospective relations among victimization, rejection, friendlessness, and children's self- and peer-perceptions. *Child Development, 76*, 1161–1171.

Saltz, E. (1971). *The cognitive bases of human learning.* Homewood, IL: Dorsey.

Sameroff, A. J., Seifer, R., Baldwin, A., & Baldwin, C. (1993). Stability of intelligence from preschool to adolescence: The influence of social and family risk factors. *Child Development, 64,* 80–97.

Sanchez, F., & Anderson, M. L. (1990). Gang mediation: A process that works. *Principal, 69*(5), 54–56.

Sands, D. J., & Wehmeyer, M. L. (Eds.). (1996). *Self-determination across the life span: Independence and choice for people with disabilities.* Baltimore: Brookes.

Sattler, J. M. (2001). *Assessment of children: Cognitive applications* (4th ed.). San Diego, CA: Author.

Savin-Williams, R. C. (1989). Gay and lesbian adolescents. *Marriage and Family Review, 14*(3–4), 197–216.

Savin-Williams, R. C. (1995). Lesbian, gay male, and bisexual adolescents. In R. D'Augelli & C. J. Patterson (Eds.), *Lesbian, gay, and bisexual identities over the lifespan: Psychological perspectives* (pp. 165–189). New York: Oxford University Press.

Savin-Williams, R. C., & Demo, D. H. (1984). Developmental change and stability in adolescent self-concept. *Developmental Psychology, 20,* 1100–1110.

Savin-Williams, R. C., & Diamond, L. M. (1997). Sexual orientation as a developmental context for lesbians, gays, and bisexuals: Biological perspectives. In N. L. Segal, G. E. Weisfeld, & C. C. Weisfeld (Eds.), *Uniting psychology and biology: Integrative perspectives on human development* (pp. 217–238). Washington, DC: American Psychological Association.

Savin-Williams, R. C., & Ream, G. L. (2003). Suicide attempts among sexual-minority male youth. *Journal of Clinical Child and Adolescent Psychology, 32*(4), 509–522.

Sawyer, R. J., Graham, S., & Harris, K. R. (1992). Direct teaching, strategy instruction, and strategy instruction with explicit self-regulation: Effects on the composition skills and self-efficacy of students with learning disabilities. *Journal of Educational Psychology, 84,* 340–352.

Saxe, G. B. (1981). Body parts as numerals: A developmental analysis of numeration among the Oksapmin in Papua New Guinea, *Child Development, 52,* 306–316.

Scardamalia, M., & Bereiter, C. (1986). Research on written composition. In M. C. Wittrock (Ed.), *Handbook of research on teaching* (3rd ed.). New York: Macmillan.

Scarr, S. (1992). Developmental theories for the 1990s: Development and individual differences. *Child Development, 63,* 1–19.

Scarr, S. (1993). Biological and cultural diversity: The legacy of Darwin for development. *Child Development, 64,* 1333–1353.

Scarr, S. (1997). Behavior-genetic and socialization theories of intelligence: Truce and reconciliation. In R. J. Sternberg & E. L. Grigorenko (Eds.), *Intelligence, heredity, and environment* (pp. 3–41). Cambridge, England: Cambridge University Press.

Scarr, S. (1998). American child care today. *American Psychologist, 53,* 95–108.

Scarr, S., & McCartney, K. (1983). How people make their own environments: A theory of genotype environment effects. *Child Development, 54,* 424–435.

Scarr, S., & Weinberg, R. A. (1976). IQ test performance of Black children adopted by White families. *American Psychologist, 31,* 726–739.

Schachter, J. (2000). Does individual tutoring produce optimal learning? *American Educational Research Journal, 37,* 801–829.

Schaffer, H. R. (1996). *Social development.* Cambridge, MA: Blackwell.

Schaie, K. W., & Willis, S. L. (2000). A stage theory model of adult cognitive development revisited. In R. L. Rubinstein, M. Moss, & M. H. Klebans (Eds.), *The many dimensions of aging* (pp. 175–193). New York: Springer.

Schauble, L. (1990). Belief revision in children: The role of prior knowledge and strategies for generating evidence. *Journal of Experimental Child Psychology, 49,* 31–57.

Schauble, L. (1996). The development of scientific reasoning in knowledge-rich contexts. *Developmental Psychology, 32,* 102–119.

Schellenberg, E. G. (2004). Music lessons enhance IQ. *Psychological Science, 15,* 511–514.

Scherer, N., & Olswang, L. (1984). Role of mothers' expansions in stimulating children's language production. *Journal of Speech and Hearing Research, 27,* 387–396.

Schimmoeller, M. A. (1998, April). *Influence of private speech on the writing behaviors of young children: Four case studies.* Paper presented at the annual meeting of the American Educational Research Association, San Diego, CA.

Schinke, S. P., Moncher, M. S., & Singer, B. R. (1994). Native American youths and cancer risk prevention. *Journal of Adolescent Health, 15,* 105–110.

Schlaefli, A., Rest, J. R., & Thoma, S. J. (1985). Does moral education improve moral judgment? A meta-analysis of intervention studies using the defining issues test. *Review of Educational Research, 55,* 319–352.

Schliemann, A. D., & Carraher, D. W. (1993). Proportional reasoning in and out of school. In P. Light & G. Butterworth (Eds.), *Context and cognition: Ways of learning and knowing.* Hillsdale, NJ: Erlbaum.

Schneider, W., & Lockl, K. (2002). The development of metacognitive knowledge in children and adolescents. In T. J. Perfect & B. L. Schwartz (Eds.), *Applied metacognition* (pp. 224–257). Cambridge, England: Cambridge University Press.

Schneider, W., Korkel, J., & Weinert, F. E. (1989). Domain-specific knowledge and memory performance: A comparison of high- and low-aptitude children. *Journal of Educational Psychology, 81,* 306–312.

Schneider, W., & Pressley, M. (1989). *Memory development between 2 and 20.* New York: Springer-Verlag.

Schneider, W., Roth, E., & Ennemoser, M. (2000). Training phonological skills and letter knowledge in children at risk for dyslexia: A comparison of three kindergarten intervention programs. *Journal of Educational Psychology, 92,* 284–295.

Schneider, W., & Shiffrin, R. M. (1977). Controlled and automatic human information processing: I. Detection, search, and attention. *Psychological Review, 84,* 1–66.

Schnur, E., Brooks-Gunn, J., & Shipman, V. C. (1992). Who attends programs serving poor children? The case of Head Start attendees and nonattendees. *Journal of Applied Developmental Psychology, 13,* 405–421.

Schoenfeld, A. H. (1988). When good teaching leads to bad results: The disasters of "well-taught" mathematics courses. *Educational Psychologist, 23,* 145–166.

Schoenfeld, A. H. (1992). Learning to think mathematically: Problem solving, metacognition, and sense making in mathematics. In D. A. Grouws (Ed.), *Handbook of research on mathematics teaching and learning.* New York: Macmillan.

Schofield, J. W. (1995). Improving intergroup relations among students. In J. A. Banks & C. A. M. Banks (Eds.), *Handbook of research on multicultural education.* New York: Macmillan.

Schommer, M. (1994a). An emerging conceptualization of epistemological beliefs and their role in learning. In R. Garner & P. A. Alexander (Eds.), *Beliefs about text and instruction with text.* Hillsdale, NJ: Erlbaum.

Schommer, M. (1994b). Synthesizing epistemological belief research: Tentative understandings and provocative confusions. *Educational Psychology Review, 6,* 293–319.

Schommer, M. (1997). The development of epistemological beliefs among secondary students: A longitudinal study. *Journal of Educational Psychology, 89,* 37–40.

Schonert-Reichl, K. A. (1993). Empathy and social relationships in adolescents with behavioral disorders. *Behavioral Disorders, 18,* 189–204.

Schoppe-Sullivan, S. J., Mangelsdorf, S. C., Frosch, C. A., & McHale, J. L. (2004). Associations between coparenting and marital behavior from infancy to the preschool years. *Journal of Family Psychology, 18,* 194–207.

Schratz, M. (1978). A developmental investigation of sex differences in spatial (visual-analytic) and mathematical skills in three ethnic groups. *Developmental Psychology, 14,* 263–267.

Schraw, G., Potenza, M. T., & Nebelsick-Gullet, L. (1993). Constraints on the calibration of performance. *Contemporary Educational Psychology, 18,* 455–463.

Schreibman, L. (1988). *Autism.* Newbury Park, CA: Sage.

Schroth, M. L. (1992). The effects of delay of feedback on a delayed concept formation transfer task. *Contemporary Educational Psychology, 17,* 78–82.

Schultz, G. F., & Switzky, H. N. (1990). The development of intrinsic motivation in students with learning problems: Suggestions for more effective instructional practice. *Preventing School Failure, 34*(2), 14–20.

Schumpf, F., Crawford, D., & Usadel, H. C. (1991). *Peer mediation: Conflict resolution in schools.* Champaign, IL: Research Press.

Schunk, D. H. (1990, April). *Socialization and the development of self-regulated learning: The role of attributions.* Paper presented at the annual meeting of the American Educational Research Association, Boston.

Schunk, D. H. (1996). Goal and self-evaluative influences during children's cognitive skill learning. *American Educational Research Journal, 33,* 359–382.

Schunk, D. H., & Hanson, A. R. (1985). Peer models: Influence on children's self-efficacy and achievement. *Journal of Educational Psychology, 77,* 313–322.

Schunk, D. H., & Pajares, F. (2004). Self-efficacy in education revisited: Empirical and applied evidence. In D. M. McNerney & S. Van Etten (Eds.), *Big theories revisited* (pp. 115–138). Greenwich, CT: Information Age.

Schunk, D. H., & Rice, J. (1989). Learning goals and children's reading comprehension. *Journal of Reading Behavior, 21,* 279–293.

Schunk, D. H., & Swartz, C. W. (1993). Goals and progress feedback: Effects on self-efficacy and writing achievement. *Contemporary Educational Psychology, 18,* 337–354.

Schunk, D. H., & Zimmerman, B. J. (1997). Social origins of self-regulatory competence. *Educational Psychologist, 32,* 195–208.

Schutz, P. A. (1994). Goals as the transactive point between motivation and cognition. In P. R. Pintrich, D. R. Brown, & C. E. Weinstein (Eds.), *Student motivation, cognition, and learning: Essays in honor of Wilbert J. McKeachie.* Hillsdale, NJ: Erlbaum.

Schutz, P. A., & Davis, H. A. (2000). Emotions and self-regulation during test taking. *Educational Psychologist, 35,* 243–256.

Schwartz, B. L., & Perfect, T. J. (2002). Introduction: Toward an applied metacognition. In T. J. Perfect & B. L. Schwartz (Eds.), *Applied metacognition* (pp. 1–11). Cambridge, England: Cambridge University Press.

Schwartz, D., Dodge, K. A., Coie, J. D., Hubbard, J. A., Cillessen, A. H., Lemerise, E. A., et al. (1998). Social-cognitive and behavioral correlates of aggression and victimization in boys' play groups. *Journal of Abnormal Child Psychology, 26,* 431–440.

Schwartz, D., McFadyen-Ketchum, S., Dodge, K. A., Pettit, G. S., & Bates, J. E. (1999). Early behavior problems as a predictor of later peer victimization: Moderators and mediators in the pathways of social risk. *Journal of Abnormal Child Psychology, 27*, 191–201.

Schwartz, G. M., Izard, C. E., & Ansul, S. E. (1985). The 5-month-old's ability to discriminate facial expressions of emotion. *Infant Behavior and Development, 8*(1), 65–67.

Schwartz, J. L., Yarushalmy, M., & Wilson, B. (Eds.). (1993). *The geometric supposer: What is it a case of?* Hillsdale, NJ: Erlbaum.

Schweinhart, L. J., & Weikart, D. (1983). The effects of the Perry Preschool Program on youths through age 15: A summary. In Consortium for Longitudinal Studies (Ed.), *As the twig is bent: Lasting effects of preschool programs* (pp. 71–101). Hillsdale, NJ: Erlbaum.

Scott-Jones, D. (1991). Black families and literacy. In S. B. Silvern (Eds.), *Advances in reading/language research: Literacy through family, community, and school interaction* (pp. 173–200). Greenwich, CT: JAI Press.

Scott-Little, M., & Holloway, S. (1992). Child care providers' reasoning about misbehaviors: Relation to classroom control strategies and professional training. *Early Childhood Research Quarterly, 7*, 595–606.

Seaton, E., Rodriguez, A., Jacobson, L., Taylor, R., Caintic, R., & Dale, P. (1999, April). *Influence of economic resources on family organization and achievement in economically disadvantaged African-American families.* Paper presented at the annual meeting of the American Educational Research Association, Montreal, Canada.

Segal, B. M., & Stewart, J. C. (1996). Substance use and abuse in adolescence: An overview. *Child Psychiatry and Human Development, 26*, 193–210.

Segal, N. L. (2000). Virtual twins: New findings on within-family environmental influences on intelligence. *Journal of Educational Psychology, 92*, 442–448.

Segal, N. L., & Russell, J. M. (1992). Twins in the classroom: School policy issues and recommendations. *Journal of Educational and Psychological Consultation, 3*, 69–84.

Seidman, E., Aber, J. L., & French, S. E. (2004). The organization of schooling and adolescent development. In K. I. Maton, C. J. Schellenbach, B. J. Leadbeater, & A. L. Solarz (Eds.), *Investing in children, youth, families, and communities: Strengths-based research and policy* (pp. 233–250). Washington, DC: American Psychological Association.

Seixas, P. (1996). Conceptualizing the growth of historical understanding. In D. R. Olson & N. Torrance (Eds.), *The handbook of education and human development: New models of learning, teaching, and schooling.* Cambridge, MA: Blackwell.

Seligman, M. E. P. (1975). *Helplessness: On depression, development, and death.* San Francisco: Freeman.

Seligman, M. E. P. (1991). *Learned optimism.* New York: Knopf.

Selman, R. L. (1980). *The growth of interpersonal understanding: Developmental and clinical analysis.* New York: Academic Press.

Selman, R. L. (2003). *The promotion of social awareness: Powerful lessons from the partnership of developmental theory and classroom practice.* New York: Russell Sage Foundation.

Seltzer, V. C. (1982). *Adolescent social development: Dynamic functional interaction.* Lexington, MA: Heath.

Semb, G. B., Ellis, J. A., & Araujo, J. (1993). Long-term memory for knowledge learned in school. *Journal of Educational Psychology, 85*, 305–316.

Semrud-Clikeman, M., & Hynd, G. W. (1991). Specific nonverbal and social skills deficits in children with learning disabilities. In J. E. Obrzut & G. W. Hynd (Eds.), *Neuropsychological foundations of learning disabilities: A handbook of issues, methods, and practice* (pp. 603–630). San Diego, CA: Academic Press.

Sénéchal, M., & LeFevre, J.-A. (2002). Parental involvement in the development of children's reading skill: A five-year longitudinal study. *Child Development, 73*, 445–460.

Sénéchal, M., Thomas, E., & Monker, J. (1995). Individual differences in 4-year-old children's acquisition of vocabulary during storybook reading. *Journal of Educational Psychology, 87*, 218–229.

Senghas, A., & Coppola, M. (2001). Children creating language: How Nicaraguan Sign Language acquired a spatial grammar. *Psychological Science, 12*, 323–328.

Serpell, R., Baker, L., & Sonnenschein, S. (2005). *Becoming literate in the city: The Baltimore Early Childhood Project.* Cambridge, England: Cambridge University Press.

Seuss, Dr. (1960). *One fish two fish red fish blue fish.* New York: Beginner Books.

Sewald, H. (1986). Adolescents' shifting orientation toward parents and peers: A curvilinear trend over recent decades. *Journal of Marriage and the Family, 48*, 5–13.

Shaffer, D. R. (1988). *Social and personality development* (2nd ed.). Pacific Grove, CA: Brooks/Cole.

Shanahan, T., & Tierney, R. J. (1990). Reading-writing connections: The relations among three perspectives. In J. Zutell & S. McCormick (Eds.), *Literacy theory and research: Analyses from multiple paradigms. Thirty-ninth yearbook of the National Reading Conference.* Chicago: National Reading Conference.

Shapiro, E. S., & Manz, P. H. (2004). Collaborating with schools in the provision of pediatric psychological services. In R. T. Brown (Ed.), *Handbook of pediatric psychology in school settings* (pp. 49–64). Mahwah, NJ: Erlbaum.

Shapka, J. D., & Keating, D. P. (2003). Effects of a girls-only curriculum during adolescence: Performance, persistence, and engagement in mathematics and science. *American Educational Research Journal, 40*, 929–960.

Share, D. L. (1995). Phonological recoding and self-teaching: Sine qua non of reading acquisition. *Cognition, 55*, 151–218.

Share, D. L., & Gur, T. (1999). How reading begins: A study of preschoolers' print identification strategies. *Cognition and Instruction, 17*, 177–213.

Shatz, M., & Gelman, R. (1973). The development of communication skills: Modifications in the speech of young children as a function of the listener. *Monographs of the Society for Research in Child Development, 38*(5, Serial No. 152).

Shavers, C. A. (2000). The interrelationships of exposure to community violence and trauma to the behavioral patterns and academic performance among urban elementary school-aged children. *Dissertation Abstracts International: Section B. The Sciences and Engineering, 61*(4-B), 1876.

Shavinina, L. V., & Ferrari, M. (2004). Extracognitive facets of developing high ability: Introduction to some important issues. In L. V. Shavinina & M. Ferrari (Eds.), *Beyond knowledge: Extracognitive aspects of developing high ability* (pp. 3–13). Mahwah, NJ: Erlbaum.

Shealy, C. N. (1995). From Boys Town to Oliver Twist: Separating fact and fiction in welfare reform and out-of-home placement of children and youth. *American Psychologist, 50*, 565–580.

Sheckley, B. G., & Keeton, M. T. (1997). Service learning: A theoretical model. In J. Schine (Ed.), *Service learning.* Chicago: National Society for the Study of Education.

Shedler, J., & Block, J. (1990). Adolescent drug use and psychological health. *American Psychologist, 45*, 612–630.

Sheehan, E. P., & Smith, H. V. (1986). Cerebral lateralization and handedness and their effects on verbal and spatial reasoning. *Neuropsychologia, 24*, 531–540.

Sheets, R. H. (1999). Human development and ethnic identity. In R. H. Sheets & E. R. Hollins (Eds.), *Racial and ethnic identity in school practices: Aspects of human development* (pp. 91–101). Mahwah, NJ: Erlbaum.

Sheets, R. H., & Hollins, E. R. (Eds.). (1999). *Racial and ethnic identity in school practices: Aspects of human development.* Mahwah, NJ: Erlbaum.

Sheffield, E., Stromswold, K., & Molnar, D. (2005, April). *Do prematurely born infants catch up?* Paper presented at the biennial meeting of the Society for Research in Child Development, Atlanta, GA.

Sheldon, A. (1974). The role of parallel function in the acquisition of relative clauses in English. *Journal of Verbal Learning and Verbal Behavior, 13*, 272–281.

Shellenberg, E. G., & Trehub, S. E. (2003). Good pitch memory is widespread. *Psychological Science, 14*, 262–266.

Shelley-Sireci, L. M., & Yanni, J. (2005, April). *Community attitudes toward adoption.* Paper presented at the biennial meeting of the Society for Research in Child Development, Atlanta, GA.

Shenfield, T., Trehub, S. E., & Nakata, T. (2003). Maternal singing modulates infant arousal. *Psychology of Music, 31*, 365–375.

Shenkin, S. D., Starr, J. M., & Deary, I. J. (2004). Birth weight and cognitive ability in childhood: A systematic review. *Psychological Bulletin, 130*, 989–1013.

Shepard, R. N., & Metzler, J. (1971). Mental rotation of three-dimensional objects. *Science, 171*, 701–703.

Sheridan, M. D. (1975). *Children's developmental progress from birth to five years: The Stycar Sequences.* Windsor, England: NFER.

Sherif, M., Harvey, O. J., White, B. J., Hood, W. R., & Sherif, C. (1961). *Inter-group conflict and cooperation: The Robbers Cave experiment.* Norman: University of Oklahoma Press.

Sherwen, L. N., Scoloveno, M. A., & Weingarten, C. T. (1999). *Maternity nursing: Care of the childbearing family* (3rd ed.). Stamford, CT: Appleton & Lange.

Sheveland, D. E. (1994, April). *Motivational factors in the development of independent readers.* Paper presented at the annual meeting of the American Educational Research Association, New Orleans, LA.

Shi, R., & Werker, J. F. (2001). Six-month-old infants' preference for lexical words. *Psychological Science, 12*, 70–75.

Shields, M. K., & Behrman, R. E. (2004). Children of immigrant families: Analysis and recommendations. *The Future of Children, 14*(2), 4–15.

Shoda, Y., Mischel, W., & Peake, P. K. (1990). Predicting adolescent cognitive and self-regulatory competencies from preschool delay of gratification: Identifying diagnostic conditions. *Developmental Psychology, 26*, 978–986.

Shonkoff, J. P. & Phillips, D. A. (Eds.). (2000). *From neurons to neighborhoods: The science of early childhood development.* Washington, DC: National Academy of Sciences.

Short, E. J., & Ryan, E. B. (1984). Metacognitive differences between skilled and less skilled readers: Remediating deficits through story grammar and attribution training. *Journal of Educational Psychology, 76*, 225–235.

Short, E. J., Schatschneider, C. W., & Friebert, S. E. (1993). Relationship between memory and metamemory performance: A comparison of specific and general strategy knowledge. *Journal of Educational Psychology, 85*, 412–423.

Shrum, W., & Cheek, N. H. (1987). Social structure during the school years: Onset of the degrouping process. *American Sociological Review, 52*, 218–223.

Shuell, T. J. (1996). Teaching and learning in a classroom context. In D. C. Berliner & R. C. Calfee (Eds.), *Handbook of educational psychology.* New York: Macmillan.

Shultz, T. R. (1974). Development of the appreciation of riddles. *Child Development, 45,* 100–105.

Shultz, T. R., & Horibe, F. (1974). Development of the appreciation of verbal jokes. *Developmental Psychology, 10,* 13–20.

Shweder, R. A., Goodnow, J., Hatano, G., LeVine, R. A., Markus, H., & Miller, P. (1998). The cultural psychology of development: One mind, many mentalities. In W. Damon (Series Ed.) & R. M. Lerner (Vol. Ed.), *Handbook of child psychology: Vol. 1. Theoretical models of human development* (5th ed., pp. 865–937). New York: Wiley.

Shweder, R. A., Mahapatra, M., & Miller, J. G. (1987). Culture and moral development. In J. Kagan & S. Lamb (Eds.), *The emergence of morality in young children* (pp. 1–83). Chicago: University of Chicago Press.

Shweder, R. A., Much, N. C., Mahapatra, M., & Park, L. (1997). The "big three" of morality (autonomy, community, and divinity) and the "big three" explanations of suffering. In A. Brandt & P. Rozin (Eds.), *Morality and health* (pp. 119–169). Stanford, CA: Stanford University Press.

Sidel, R. (1996). *Keeping women and children last: America's war on the poor.* New York: Penguin Books.

Siegel, D. J. (1999). *The developing mind: How relationships and the brain interact to shape who we are.* New York: Guilford Press.

Siegler, R. S. (1976). Three aspects of cognitive development. *Cognitive Psychology, 8,* 481–520.

Siegler, R. S. (1978). The origins of scientific reasoning. In R. S. Siegler (Ed.), *Children's thinking: What develops?* Hillsdale, NJ: Erlbaum.

Siegler, R. S. (1989). Mechanisms of cognitive growth. *Annual Review of Psychology, 40,* 353–379.

Siegler, R. S. (1994). Cognitive variability: A key to understanding cognitive development. *Current Directions in Psychological Science, 3,* 1–5.

Siegler, R. S. (1996). *Emerging minds: The process of change in children's thinking.* New York: Oxford University Press.

Siegler, R. S., & Alibali, M. W. (2005). *Children's thinking* (4th ed.). Upper Saddle River, NJ: Prentice Hall.

Siegler, R. S., & Jenkins, E. (1989). *How children discover new strategies.* Hillsdale, NJ: Erlbaum.

Siegler, R. S., & Richards, D. D. (1982). The development of intelligence. In R. J. Sternberg (Ed.), *Handbook of human intelligence.* Cambridge, England: Cambridge University Press.

Siegler, R. S., & Robinson, M. (1982). The development of numerical understandings. In H. W. Reese & L. P. Lipsitt (Eds.), *Advances in child development and behavior* (Vol. 16). New York: Academic Press.

Siegler, R. S., & Stern, E. (1998). Conscious and unconscious strategy discoveries: A microgenetic analysis. *Journal of Experimental Psychology: General, 127,* 377–397.

Siever, L., & Davis, K. (1985). Overview: Toward a dysregulation hypothesis of depression. *American Journal of Psychiatry, 142,* 1017–1031.

Sigman, M. (1995). Nutrition and child development: Food for thought. *Current Directions in Psychological Science, 4,* 52–55.

Sigman, M., & Whaley, S. E. (1998). The role of nutrition in the development of intelligence. In U. Neisser (Ed.), *The rising curve: Long-term gains in IQ and related measures* (pp. 155–182). Washington, DC: American Psychological Association.

Signorielli, N., & Lears, M. (1992). Children, television, and conceptions about chores: Attitudes and behaviors. *Sex Roles, 27,* 157–170.

Silk, J. S., Sessa, F. M., Morris, A. S., Steinberg, L., & Avenevoli, S. (2004). Neighborhood cohesion as a buffer against hostile maternal parenting. *Journal of Family Psychology, 18,* 135–146.

Silver, E. A., & Kenney, P. A. (1995). Sources of assessment information for instructional guidance in mathematics. In T. Romberg (Ed.), *Reform in school mathematics and authentic assessment.* Albany: State University of New York Press.

Silverman, I. W., & Ragusa, D. M. (1990). Child and maternal correlates of impulse control in 24-month-old children. *Genetic, Social, and General Psychology Monographs, 116,* 435–473.

Silverman, L. K. (1994). The moral sensitivity of gifted children and the evolution of society. *Roeper Review, 17*(2), 110–116.

Simmons, R. G., & Blyth, D. A. (1987). *Moving into adolescence: The impact of pubertal change in school context.* New York: Aldine de Gruyter.

Simner, M. L. (1971). Newborn's response to the cry of another infant. *Developmental Psychology, 5,* 136–150.

Simons, R. L., Lorenz, F. O., Wu, C. I., & Conger, R. D. (1993). Social network and marital support as mediators and moderators of the impact of stress and depression on parental behavior. *Developmental Psychology, 29,* 368–381.

Simons, R. L., Robertson, J. F., & Downs, W. R. (1989). The nature of the association between parental rejection and delinquent behavior. *Journal of Youth and Adolescence, 18,* 297–310.

Simons, R. L., Whitbeck, L. B., Conger, R. D., & Conger, K. J. (1991). Parenting factors, social skills, and value commitments as precursors to school failure, involvement with deviant peers, and delinquent behavior. *Journal of Youth and Adolescence, 20,* 645–664.

Simons-Morton, B. G., Baranowski, T., Parcel, G. S., O'Hara, N. M., & Matteson, R. C. (1990). Children's frequency of consumption of foods high in fat and sodium. *American Journal of Preventive Medicine, 6,* 218–227.

Simons-Morton, B. G., Taylor, W. C., Snider, S. A., & Huang, I. W. (1993). The physical activity of fifth-grade students during physical education classes. *American Journal of Public Health, 83,* 262–264.

Simons-Morton, B. G., Taylor, W. C., Snider, S. A., Huang, I. W., & Fulton, J. E. (1994). Observed levels of elementary and middle school children's physical activity during physical education classes. *Preventive Medicine, 23,* 437–441.

Simonton, D. K. (2001). Talent development as a multidimensional, multiplicative, and dynamic process. *Current Directions in Psychological Science, 10,* 39–42.

Sims, M. (1993). How my question keeps evolving. In Cochran-Smith, M., & Lytle, S. L. (Eds.), *Inside/outside: Teacher research and knowledge* (pp. 283–289). New York: Teachers College Press.

Sims, M., Hutchins, T., & Taylor, M. (1997). Classroom "culture" and children's conflict behaviours. *Early Child Development and Care, 134,* 43–59.

Sinatra, G. M., & Pintrich, P. R. (2003). The role of intentions in conceptual change learning. In G. M. Sinatra & P. R. Pintrich (Eds.), *Intentional conceptual change* (pp. 1–18). Mahwah, NJ: Erlbaum.

Singer, J., Marx, R. W., Krajcik, J., & Chambers, J. C. (2000). Constructing extended inquiry projects: Curriculum materials for science education reform. *Educational Psychologist, 35,* 165–178.

Singer, L. M., Burkowski, M., & Waters, E. (1985). Mother-infant attachment in adoptive families. *Child Development, 56,* 1543–1551.

Sinnott, J. D. (1998). *The development of logic in adulthood: Postformal thought and its applications.* New York: Plenum.

Sirois, S., Buckingham, D., & Shultz, T. R. (2000). Artificial grammar learning by infants: An auto-associator perspective. *Developmental Science, 3,* 442–456.

Sisk, D. A. (1989). Identifying and nurturing talent among American Indians. In C. J. Maker & S. W. Schiever (Eds.), *Critical issues in gifted education: Vol. 2. Defensible programs for cultural and ethnic minorities.* Austin, TX: Pro-Ed.

Siskin, L. S. (2003). Outside the core: Accountability in tested and untested subjects. In M. Carnoy, R. Elmore, & L. S. Siskin (Eds.), *The new accountability: High schools and high-stakes testing* (pp. 87–98). New York: RoutledgeFalmer.

Sitko, B. M. (1998). Knowing how to write: Metacognition and writing instruction. In D. J. Hacker, J. Dunlosky, & A. C. Graesser (Eds.), *Metacognition in educational theory and practice* (pp. 93–115). Mahwah, NJ: Erlbaum.

Sjostrom, L., & Stein, N. (1996). *Bully proof: A teacher's guide on teasing and bullying for use with fourth and fifth grade students.* Wellesley, MA: Wellesley College Center for Women.

Skinner, B. F. (1953). *Science and human behavior.* New York: Macmillan.

Skinner, B. F. (1957). *Verbal behavior.* New York: Appleton-Century-Crofts.

Skinner, B. F. (1968). *The technology of teaching.* New York: Appleton-Century-Crofts.

Slater, A. M., Mattock, A., & Brown, E. (1990). Size constancy at birth: Newborn infants' responses to retinal and real size. *Journal of Experimental Child Psychology, 49,* 314–322.

Slater, A. M., & Morison, V. (1985). Shape constancy and slant perception at birth. *Perception, 14,* 337–344.

Slavin, R. E. (1989). Students at risk of school failure: The problem and its dimensions. In R. E. Slavin, N. L. Karweit, & N. A. Madden (Eds.), *Effective programs for students at risk.* Needham Heights, MA: Allyn & Bacon.

Slavin, R. E. (1990). *Cooperative learning: Theory, research, and practice.* Upper Saddle River, NJ: Prentice Hall.

Sleeter, C. E., & Grant, C. A. (1991). Race, class, gender, and disability in current textbooks. In M. W. Apple & L. K. Christian-Smith (Eds.), *The politics of the textbook* (pp. 78–110). New York: Routledge.

Sleeter, C. E., & Grant, C. A. (1999). *Making choices for multicultural education: Five approaches to race, class, and gender* (3rd ed.). Upper Saddle River, NJ: Merrill/Prentice Hall.

Slonim, M. B. (1991). *Children, culture, ethnicity: Evaluating and understanding the impact.* New York: Garland.

Slusher, M. P., & Anderson, C. A. (1996). Using causal persuasive arguments to change beliefs and teach new information: The mediating role of explanation availability and evaluation bias in the acceptance of knowledge. *Journal of Educational Psychology, 88,* 110–122.

Smagorinsky, P. (2001). If meaning is constructed, what is it made from: Toward a cultural theory of reading. *Review of Educational Research, 71,* 133–169.

Smart, C., Neale, B., & Wade, A. (2001). *The changing experience of childhood: Families and divorce.* Cambridge, England: Polity.

Smetana, J. G. (1981). Preschool children's conceptions of moral and social rules. *Child Development, 52,* 1333–1336.

Smetana, J. G., & Braeges, J. L. (1990). The development of toddlers' moral and conventional judgments. *Merrill-Palmer Quarterly, 36,* 329–346.

Smetana, J. G., Killen, M., & Turiel, E. (1991). Children's reasoning about interpersonal and moral conflicts. *Child Development, 62,* 629–644.

Smith, C. L., Maclin, D., Houghton, C., & Hennessey, M. G. (2000). Sixth-grade students' epistemologies of science: The impact of school science experiences on epistemological development. *Cognition and Instruction, 18,* 349–422.

Smith, C., Maclin, D., Grosslight, L., & Davis, H. (1997). Teaching for understanding: A study of students' preinstruction theories of matter and a comparison of the effectiveness of two approaches to teaching about matter and density. *Cognition and Instruction, 15*, 317–393.

Smith, E. P., Boutte, G. S., Zigler, E., & Finn-Stevenson, M. (2004). Opportunities for schools to promote resilience in children and youth. In K. I. Maton, C. J. Schellenbach, B. J. Leadbeater, & A. L. Solarz (Eds.), *Investing in children, youth, families, and communities: Strengths-based research and policy* (pp. 213–231). Washington, DC: American Psychological Association.

Smith, H. L. (1998). Literacy and instruction in African American communities: Shall we overcome? In B. Pérez (Ed.), *Sociocultural contexts of language and literacy*. Mahwah, NJ: Erlbaum.

Smith, J. T. (1999). Sickle cell disease. In S. Goldstein & C. R. Reynolds (Eds.), *Handbook of neurodevelopmental and genetic disorders* (pp. 368–384). New York: Guilford Press.

Smith, L. (1994, February 16). Bad habits: Testament to the downward spiral of drugs and teen angst. *Los Angeles Times*, p. 1.

Smith, N. R., Cicchetti, L., Clark, M. C., Fucigna, C., Gordon-O'Connor, B., Halley, B. A., et al. (1998). *Observation drawing with children: A framework for teachers*. New York: Teachers College Press.

Smith, P. B., & Bond, M. H. (1994). *Social psychology across cultures: Analysis and perspectives*. Needham Heights, MA: Allyn & Bacon.

Smith, R. A., Martin, S. C., & Wolters, P. L. (2004). Pediatric and adolescent HIV/AIDS. In R. T. Brown (Ed.), *Handbook of pediatric psychology in school settings* (pp. 195–220). Mahwah, NJ: Erlbaum.

Smith, R. E., & Smoll, F. L. (1997). Coaching the coaches: Youth sports as a scientific and applied behavioral setting. *Current Directions in Psychological Science, 6*, 16–21.

Smith, S. L., & Donnerstein, E. (1998). Harmful effects of exposure to media violence: Learning of aggression, emotional desensitization, and fear. In R. G. Geen & E. Donnerstein (Eds.), *Human aggression: Theories, research, and implications for social policy* (pp. 167–202). New York: Academic Press.

Smitherman, G. (1994). "The blacker the berry the sweeter the juice": African American student writers. In A. H. Dyson & C. Genishi (Eds.), *The need for story: Cultural diversity in classroom and community*. Urbana, IL: National Council of Teachers of English.

Snarey, J. (1995). In a communitarian voice: The sociological expansion of Kohlbergian theory, research, and practice. In W. M. Kurtines & J. L. Gewirtz (Eds.), *Moral development: An introduction*. Boston: Allyn & Bacon.

Snow, C. E., & Ninio, A. (1986). The contracts of literacy: What children learn from learning to read books. In W. Teale & E. Sulzby (Eds.), *Emergent literacy: Writing and reading*. Norwood, NJ: Ablex.

Snow, C. W., & McGaha, C. G. (2003). *Infant development* (3rd ed.). Upper Saddle River, NJ: Prentice Hall.

Snowling, M. J., Gallagher, A., & Frith, U. (2003). Family risk of dyslexia is continuous: Individual differences in the precursors of reading skill. *Child Development, 74*, 358–373.

Society for Research in Child Development. (2004). *Ethical standards for research with children*. Retrieved September 9, 2004, from http://www.srcd.org/ethicalstandards.html

Solomon, D., Watson, M., Battistich, E., Schaps, E., & Delucchi, K. (1992). Creating a caring community: Educational practices that promote children's prosocial development. In F. K. Oser, A. Dick, & J. L. Patry (Eds.), *Effective and responsible teaching: The new synthesis*. San Francisco: Jossey-Bass.

Sonnenschein, S. (1988). The development of referential communication: Speaking to different listeners. *Child Development, 59*, 694–702.

Sophian, C., & Vong, K. I. (1995). The parts and wholes of arithmetic story problems: Developing knowledge in the preschool years. *Cognition and Instruction, 13*, 469–477.

Sorce, J. F., Emde, R. N., Campos, J., & Klinnert, M. D. (1985). Maternal emotional signaling: Its effects on the visual cliff behavior of 1-year-olds. *Developmental Psychology, 21*, 195–200.

Sorensen, R. (1983). *Adolescent sexuality in contemporary society*. New York: World Books.

South, D. (2003). What motivates unmotivated students? In G. Mills, *Action research: A guide for the teacher researcher* (2nd ed., pp. 1–2). Upper Saddle River, NJ: Merrill/Prentice Hall.

Southerland, S. A., & Sinatra, G. M. (2003). Learning about biological evolution: A special case of intentional conceptual change. In G. M. Sinatra & P. R. Pintrich (Eds.), *Intentional conceptual change* (pp. 317–345). Mahwah, NJ: Erlbaum.

Sowell, E. R., Delis, D., Stiles, J., & Jernigan, T. L. (2001). Improved memory functioning and frontal lobe maturation between childhood and adolescence: A structural MRI study. *Journal of the International Neuropsychological Society, 7*, 312–322.

Sowell, E. R., Thompson, P. M., Holmes, C. J., Jernigan, T. L., & Toga, A. W. (1999). In vivo evidence for post-adolescent brain maturation in frontal and striatal regions. *Nature Neuroscience, 2*, 859–861.

Sowell, E. R., Thompson, P. M., Rex, D., Kornsand, D., Tessner, K. D., Jernigan, T. L., et al. (2002). Mapping sulcal pattern asymmetry and local cortical surface gray matter distribution in vivo: Maturation in the perisylvian cortices. *Cerebral Cortex, 12*, 17–26.

Sowell, E. R., Thompson, P. M., Tessner, K. D., & Toga, A. W. (2001). Mapping continued brain growth and gray matter density reduction in dorsal frontal cortex: Inverse relationships during post-adolescent brain maturation. *Journal of Neuroscience, 21*, 8819–8829.

Spaulding, C. L. (1992). *Motivation in the classroom*. New York: McGraw-Hill.

Spearman, C. (1904). General intelligence, objectively determined and measured. *American Journal of Psychology, 15*, 201–293.

Spearman, C. (1927). *The abilities of man: Their nature and measurement*. New York: Macmillan.

Spelke, E. S. (1994). Initial knowledge: Six suggestions. *Cognition, 50*, 431–445.

Spelke, E. S. (2000). Core knowledge. *American Psychologist, 55*, 1233–1243.

Spelke, E. S., Breinlinger, K., Macomber, J., & Jacobson, K. (1992). Origins of knowledge. *Psychological Review, 99*, 605–632.

Spencer, M. B., & Markstrom-Adams, C. (1990). Identity processes among racial and ethnic minority children in America. *Child Development, 61*, 290–310.

Spencer, M. B., Noll, E., Stoltzfus, J., & Harpalani, V. (2001). Identity and school adjustment: Revisiting the "acting White" assumption. *Educational Psychologist, 36*, 21–30.

Sperling, M. (1996). Revisiting the writing-speaking connection: Challenges for research on writing and writing instruction. *Review of Educational Research, 66*, 53–86.

Spicker, H. H. (1992). Identifying and enriching: Rural gifted children. *Educational Horizons, 70*(2), 60–65.

Spinath, F. M., Price, T. S., Dale, P. S., & Plomin, R. (2004). The genetic and environmental origins of language disability and ability. *Child Development, 75*, 445–454.

Spivey, N. N. (1997). *The constructivist metaphor: Reading, writing, and the making of meaning*. San Diego, CA: Academic Press.

Sprafkin, C., Serbin, L. A., Denier, C., & Connor, J. M. (1983). Sex-differentiated play: Cognitive consequences and early interventions. In M. B. Liss (Ed.), *Social and cognitive skills: Sex roles and children's play*. San Diego, CA: Academic Press.

Sroufe, L. A. (1983). Infant-caregiver attachment and patterns of adaptation in preschool: The roots of maladaptation and competence. In M. Perlmutter (Ed.), *Development and policy concerning children with special needs. Minnesota Symposium on Child Psychology, 16*, 41–83. Hillsdale, NJ: Erlbaum.

Sroufe, L. A., Carlson, E., & Shulman, S. (1993). Individuals in relationships: Development from infancy through adolescence. In D. C. Funder, R. D. Parke, C. Tomlinson-Keasey, & K. Widaman (Eds.), *Studying lives through time: Personality and development* (pp. 315–342). Washington, DC: American Psychological Association.

Stack, C. B., & Burton, L. M. (1993). Kinscripts. *Journal of Comparative Family Studies, 24*, 157–170.

Stanley, J. C. (1980). On educating the gifted. *Educational Researcher, 9*(3), 8–12.

Stanovich, K. E. (2000). *Progress in understanding reading: Scientific foundations and new frontiers*. New York: Guilford Press.

Starr, E. J., & Lovett, S. B. (2000). The ability to distinguish between comprehension and memory: Failing to succeed. *Journal of Educational Psychology, 92*, 761–771.

Stattin, H., & Magnusson, D. (1989). The role of early aggressive behavior in the frequency, seriousness, and types of later crime. *Journal of Consulting and Clinical Psychology, 57*, 710–718.

Staub, D. (1998). *Delicate threads: Friendships between children with and without special needs in inclusive settings*. Bethesda, MD: Woodbine House.

Staub, E. (1995). The roots of prosocial and antisocial behavior in persons and groups: Environmental influence, personality, culture, and socialization. In W. M. Kurtines & J. L. Gewirtz (Eds.), *Moral development: An introduction*. Boston: Allyn & Bacon.

Staudt, M. M. (2001). Use of services prior to and following intensive family preservation services. *Journal of Child and Family Studies, 10*, 101–114.

Steele, C. M. (1997). A threat in the air: How stereotypes shape intellectual identity and performance. *American Psychologist, 52*, 613–629.

Steen, F., & Owens, S. A. (2000, March). *Implicit pedagogy: From chase play to collaborative world-making*. Paper presented at the Evolution and Social Mind Speaker Series, University of California at Santa Barbara.

Stein, N. (1993, May 18). Stop sexual harassment in schools. *USA Today*.

Stein, N. L. (1982). What's in a story: Interpreting the interpretations of story grammars. *Discourse Processes, 5*, 319–335.

Stein, N. L., & Glenn, C. G. (1979). An analysis of story comprehension in elementary school children. In R. O. Freedle (Eds.), *New directions in discourse processing* (Vol. 2). Norwood, NJ: Ablex.

Stein, R. (1996). Physical self-concept. In B. A. Bracken (Ed.), *Handbook of self-concept: Developmental, social, and clinical considerations* (pp. 374–394). New York: Wiley.

Steinberg, L. (1986). Latchkey children and susceptibility to peer pressure: An ecological analysis. *Developmental Psychology, 22*, 433–439.

Steinberg, L. (1996). *Beyond the classroom: Why school reform has failed and what parents need to do*. New York: Touchstone.

Steinberg, L., Blinde, P. L., & Chan, K. S. (1984). Dropping out among language minority youth. *Review of Educational Research, 54*, 113–132.

Steinberg, L., Brown, B. B., Cider, M., Kaczmarek, N., & Lazzaro, C. (1988). *Noninstructional influences on high school student achievement: The contributions of parents, peers, extracurricular activities, and part-time work*. Madison, WI: National Center on Effective Secondary Schools. (ERIC Document Reproduction Service No. ED 307 509)

Steinberg, L., Elmen, J., & Mounts, N. (1989). Authoritative parenting, psychosocial maturity, and academic success among adolescents. *Child Development, 60,* 1424–1436.

Steinberg, L., Lamborn, S., Darling, N., Mounts, S., & Dornbusch, S. (1994). Over time change in adjustment and competence among adolescents from authoritative, authoritarian, indulgent, and neglectful families. *Child Development, 65,* 754–770.

Steiner, H. H., & Carr, M. (2003). Cognitive development in gifted children: Toward a more precise understanding of emerging differences in intelligence. *Educational Psychology Review, 15,* 215–246.

Steiner, J. E. (1979). Human facial expression in response to taste and smell stimulation. In H. W. Reese & L. P. Lipsitt (Eds.), *Advances in child development and behavior* (Vol. 13). New York: Academic Press.

Stenberg, C. R., & Campos, J. J. (1990). The development of anger expressions in infancy. In N. L. Stein, B. Leventhal, & T. Trabasso (Eds.), *Psychological and biological approaches to emotion* (pp. 247–282). Hillsdale, NJ: Erlbaum.

Stern, B. M., & Finn-Stevenson, M. (1999). Preregistered for success: The Comer/Zigler initiative. In J. P. Comer, M. Ben-Avie, N. M. Haynes, & E. T. Joyner (Eds.), *Child by child: The Comer process for change in education* (pp. 63–77). New York: Teachers College Press.

Stern, D. N. (1977). *The first relationship: Mother and infant.* Cambridge, MA: Harvard University Press.

Stern, W. (1912). *Die psychologischen Methoden der Intelligenzprufung.* Leipzig, Germany: Barth.

Sternberg, R. J. (1985). *Beyond IQ: A triarchic theory of human intelligence.* Cambridge, England: Cambridge University Press.

Sternberg, R. J. (1996). Myths, countermyths, and truths about intelligence. *Educational Researcher, 25*(2), 11–16.

Sternberg, R. J. (1997). The concept of intelligence and its role in lifelong learning and success. *American Psychologist, 52,* 1030–1037.

Sternberg, R. J. (1998). Abilities are forms of developing expertise. *Educational Researcher, 27*(3), 11–20.

Sternberg, R. J. (2002). Raising the achievement of all students: Teaching for successful intelligence. *Educational Psychology Review, 14,* 383–393.

Sternberg, R. J. (2003). *Wisdom, intelligence, and creativity synthesized.* Cambridge, England: Cambridge University Press.

Sternberg, R. J. (2004). Culture and intelligence. *American Psychologist, 59,* 325–338.

Sternberg, R. J., & Detterman, D. K. (Eds.). (1986). *What is intelligence? Contemporary views on its nature and definition.* Norwood, NJ: Ablex.

Sternberg, R. J., Forsythe, G. B., Hedlund, J., Horvath, J. A., Wagner, R. K., Williams, W. M., et al. (2000). *Practical intelligence in everyday life.* Cambridge, England: Cambridge University Press.

Sternberg, R. J., & Grigorenko, E. L. (2000). Theme-park psychology: A case study regarding human intelligence and its implications for education. *Educational Psychology Review, 12,* 247–268.

Sternberg, R. J., & Wagner, R. K. (Eds.). (1994). *Mind in context: Interactionist perspectives on human intelligence.* Cambridge, England: Cambridge University Press.

Sternberg, R. J., & Zhang, L. (1995). What do we mean by giftedness? A pentagonal implicit theory. *Gifted Child Quarterly, 39,* 88–94.

Stevens, R. J., & Slavin, R. E. (1995). The cooperative elementary school: Effects of students' achievement, attitudes, and social relations. *American Educational Research Journal, 32,* 321–351.

Stevenson, H. C. (1995). Relationships of adolescent perceptions of racial socialization to racial identity. *Journal of Black Psychology, 21,* 49–70.

Stevenson, H. W., Chen, C., & Uttal, D. H. (1990). Beliefs and achievement: A study of Black, White, and Hispanic children. *Child Development, 61,* 508–523.

Stewart, L., & Pascual-Leone, J. (1992). Mental capacity constraints and the development of moral reasoning. *Journal of Experimental Child Psychology, 54,* 251–287.

Stewart, R. B. (1983). Sibling interaction: The role of the older child as teacher for the younger. *Merrill-Palmer Quarterly, 29,* 47–68.

Stiles, J., & Thal, D. (1993). Linguistic and spatial cognitive development following early focal brain injury: Patterns of deficit and recovery. In M. Johnson (Ed.), *Brain development and cognition.* Oxford, England: Blackwell.

Stipek, D. (2002). At what age should children enter kindergarten? A question for policy makers and parents. *Social Policy Report, 16,* 1, 3–16. Ann Arbor, MI: Society for Research in Child Development.

Stipek, D. J. (1984). Sex differences in children's attributions for success and failure on math and spelling tests. *Sex Roles, 11,* 969–981.

Stipek, D. J. (1993). *Motivation to learn: From theory to practice* (2nd ed.). Needham Heights, MA: Allyn & Bacon.

Stipek, D. J. (1996). Motivation and instruction. In D. C. Berliner & R. C. Calfee (Eds.), *Handbook of educational psychology.* New York: Macmillan.

Stipek, D. J., & Kowalski, P. S. (1989). Learned helplessness in task-orienting versus performance-orienting testing conditions. *Journal of Educational Psychology, 81,* 384–391.

Stipek, D. J., Recchia, S., & McClintic, S. M. (1992). Self-evaluation in young children. *Monographs of the Society for Research in Child Development, 57*(2, Serial No. 226).

St. James-Roberts, I., & Halil, T. (1991). Infant crying patterns in the first year of life: Normal community and clinical findings. *Journal of Child Psychology and Psychiatry, 32,* 951–968.

St. James-Roberts, I., & Plewis, I. (1996). Individual differences, daily fluctuations, and developmental changes in amounts of infant waking, fussiness, crying, feeding, and sleeping. *Child Development, 67,* 2527–2540.

Stolley, K. S. (1993). Statistics on adoption in the United States. *The Future of Children, 3*(1), 26–42.

Strauch, B. (2003). *The primal teen: What the new discoveries about the teenage brain tells us about our kids.* New York: Doubleday.

Straus, M. A. (2000). The benefits of never spanking: New and more definitive evidence. In M. A. Straus, *Beating the devil out of them: Corporal punishment by American families and its effects on children.* New Brunswick, NJ: Transaction Publications.

Strayer, F. F. (1991). The development of agonistic and affiliative structures in preschool play groups. In J. Silverberg & P. Gray (Eds.), *To fight or not to fight: Violence and peacefulness in humans and other primates.* Oxford, England: Oxford University Press.

Streigel-Moore, R., Silberstein, L. R., & Rodin, J. (1986). Toward an understanding of bulimia. *American Psychologist, 41,* 246–263.

Streissguth, A. P., Barr, H. M., Sampson, P. D., & Bookstein, F. L. (1994). Prenatal alcohol and offspring development: The first fourteen years. *Drug and Alcohol Dependence, 36,* 89–99.

Striano, T. (2004). Direction of regard and the still-face effects in the first year: Does intention matter? *Child Development, 75,* 468–479.

Stright, A. D., Neitzel, C., Sears, K. G., & Hoke-Sinex, L. (2001). Instruction begins in the home: Relations between parental instruction and children's self-regulation in the classroom. *Journal of Educational Psychology, 93,* 456–466.

Strike, K. A., & Posner, G. J. (1992). A revisionist theory of conceptual change. In R. A. Duschl & R. J. Hamilton (Eds.), *Philosophy of science, cognitive psychology, and educational theory and practice.* Albany: State University of New York Press.

Stringer, E., & Dwyer, R. (2005). *Action research in human services.* Upper Saddle River, NJ: Merrill/Prentice Hall.

Strozer, J. R. (1994). *Language acquisition after puberty.* Washington, DC: Georgetown University Press.

Stukas, A. A., Jr., Clary, E. G., & Snyder, M. (1999). Service learning: Who benefits and why. *Social Policy Report, Society for Research in Child Development, 13*(4), 1–19.

Subar, A. F., Heimendinger, J., Krebs-Smith, S. M., Patterson, B. H., Kessler, R., & Pivonka, E. (1992). *Five a day for better health: A baseline study of Americans' fruit and vegetable consumptions.* Rockville, MD: National Cancer Institute.

Sue, D. W. (1990). Culture-specific strategies in counseling: A conceptual framework. *Professional Psychology: Research and Practice, 21,* 424–433.

Sugar, W. A., & Bonk, C. J. (1998). Student role play in the World Forum: Analyses of an Arctic learning apprenticeship. In C. J. Bonk & K. S. King (Eds.), *Electronic collaborators: Learner-centered technologies for literacy, apprenticeship, and discourse.* Mahwah, NJ: Erlbaum.

Sugarman, S. (1983). *Children's early thought: Developments in classification.* New York: Cambridge University Press.

Suhr, D. D. (1999). *An investigation of mathematics and reading achievement of 5- through 14-year-olds using latent growth curve methodology.* Unpublished doctoral dissertation, University of Northern Colorado, Greeley.

Sullivan, F. M., & Barlow, S. M. (2001). Review of risk factors for sudden infant death syndrome. *Paediatric and Perinatal Epidemiology, 15,* 144–200.

Sullivan, L. W. (1987). The risks of the sickle-cell trait: Caution and common sense. *New England Journal of Medicine, 317,* 830–831.

Sullivan, P., & Knutson, J. F. (1998). The association between child maltreatment and disabilities in a hospital based epidemiological study. *Child Abuse and Neglect, 22,* 271–288.

Sullivan, R. C. (1994). Autism: Definitions past and present. *Journal of Vocational Rehabilitation, 4,* 4–9.

Sullivan-DeCarlo, C., DeFalco, K., & Roberts, V. (1998). Helping students avoid risky behavior. *Educational Leadership, 56*(1), 80–82.

Sulzby, E. (1985). Children's emergent reading of favorite storybooks: A developmental study. *Reading Research Quarterly, 20,* 458–481.

Sulzby, E. (1986). Children's elicitation and use of metalinguistic knowledge about *word* during literacy interactions. In D. B. Yaden, Jr., & S. Templeton (Eds.), *Metalinguistic awareness and beginning literacy: Conceptualizing what it means to read and write.* Portsmouth, NH: Heinemann.

Sund, R. B. (1976). *Piaget for educators.* Columbus, OH: Merrill.

Suskind, R. (1998). *A hope in the unseen: An American odyssey from the inner city to the Ivy League.* New York: Broadway Books.

Susman, E. J., Inoff-Germain, G., Nottelmann, E. D., Loriaux, D. L., Cutler, J., Gordon, B., et al. (1987). Hormones, emotional dispositions, and aggressive attributes in young adolescents. *Child Development, 58,* 1114–1134.

Susman, E. J., Nottelmann, E. D., Inoff-Germain, G. E., Dorn, L. D., Cutler, G. B., Jr., Loriaux, D. L., et al. (1985). The relation of development and social-emotional behavior in young adolescents. *Journal of Youth and Adolescence, 14,* 245–264.

Susman, E. J., Nottelmann, E. D., Inoff-Germain, G., Dorn, L. D., & Chrousos, G. P. (1987). Hormonal influences on aspects of psychological development during adolescence. *Journal of Adolescent Health Care, 8,* 492–504.

Suttles, G. D. (1970). Friendship as a social institution. In G. J. McCall, M. McCall, N. K. Denzin, G. D. Scuttles, & S. Kurth (Eds.), *Social relationships* (pp. 95–135). Chicago: Aldine de Gruyter.

Sutton-Smith, B. (Ed.). (1979). *Play and learning.* New York: Gardner Press.

Sutton-Smith, B. (1986). The development of fictional narrative performances. *Topics in Language Disorders, 7(1),* 1–10.

Svirsky, M. A., Robbins, A. M., Kirk, K. I., Pisoni, D. B., & Miyamoto, R. T. (2000). Language development in profoundly deaf children with cochlear implants. *Psychological Science, 11,* 153–158.

Swanborn, M. S. L., & de Glopper, K. (1999). Incidental word learning while reading: A meta analysis. *Review of Educational Research, 69,* 261–285.

Swann, W. B., Jr. (1997). The trouble with change: Self-verification and allegiance to the self. *Psychological Science, 8,* 177–180.

Swanson, H. L. (1993). An information processing analysis of learning disabled children's problem solving. *American Educational Research Journal, 30,* 861–893.

Swanson, H. L., & Lussier, C. M. (2001). A selective synthesis of the experimental literature on dynamic assessment. *Review of Educational Research, 71,* 321–363.

Swanson, H. L., Mink, J., & Bocian, K. M. (1999). Cognitive processing deficits in poor readers with symptoms of reading disabilities and ADHD: More alike than different? *Journal of Educational Psychology, 91,* 321–333.

Swim, J. K., & Stangor, C. (Eds.). (1998). *Prejudice: The target's perspective* (pp. 220–241). San Diego, CA: Academic Press.

Sylvester, R. (1995). *A celebration of neurosis: An educator's guide to the human brain.* Alexandria, VA: Association for Supervision and Curriculum Development.

Szynal-Brown, C., & Morgan, R. R. (1983). The effects of reward on tutor's behaviors in a cross-age tutoring context. *Journal of Experimental Child Psychology, 36,* 196–208.

Tager-Flusberg, H. (1993). Putting words together: Morphology and syntax in the preschool years. In J. Berko-Gleason (Ed.), *The development of language* (3rd ed.). Upper Saddle River, NJ: Merrill/Prentice Hall.

Takahashi, K. (1990). Are the key assumptions of the "Strange Situation" procedure universal? A view from Japanese research. *Human Development, 33,* 23–30.

Takeuchi, A. H., & Hulse, S. H. (1993). Absolute pitch. *Psychological Bulletin, 113,* 345–361.

Tallal, P. (2003). Language learning disabilities: Integrating research approaches. *Current Directions in Psychological Science, 12,* 206–211.

Tallman, I., Gray, L. N., Kullberg, V., & Henderson, D. (1999). The intergenerational transmission of marital conflict: Testing a process model. *Social Psychology Quarterly, 62,* 219–239.

Tamburrini, J. (1982). Some educational implications of Piaget's theory. In S. Modgil & C. Modgil (Eds.), *Jean Piaget: Consensus and controversy.* New York: Praeger.

Tamis-LeMonda, C. S., & Cabrera, N. (1999). Perspectives on father involvement: Research and policy. *Social Policy Report, 13*(2), 1–25.

Tannen, D. (1990). *You just don't understand: Talk between the sexes.* New York: Ballantine.

Tanner, J. M. (1990). *Foetus into man: Physical growth from conception to maturity* (Rev. ed.). Cambridge, MA: Harvard University Press.

Tate, W. F. (1995). Returning to the root: A culturally relevant approach to mathematics pedagogy. *Theory into Practice, 34,* 166–173.

Tatum, B. D. (1997). *Why are all the Black kids sitting together in the cafeteria? and other conversations about race.* New York: Basic Books.

Taylor, D., & Lorimer, M. (2002–2003). Helping boys succeed. *Educational Leadership, 60*(4), 68–70.

Taylor, J. M. (1994). *MDMA frequently asked questions list.* Retrieved from http://ibbserver.ibb.uu.nl/jboschma/ecstasy/xtc01

Taylor, M., Esbensen, B. M., & Bennett, R. T. (1994). Children's understanding of knowledge acquisition: The tendency for children to report that they have always known what they have just learned. *Child Development, 65,* 1581–1604.

Taylor, R. D., Casten, R., Flickinger, S. M., Roberts, D., & Fulmore, C. D. (1994). Explaining the school performance of African American adolescents. *Journal of Research on Adolescence, 4,* 21–44.

Taylor, R. D., & Roberts, D. (1995). Kinship support and maternal and adolescent well-being in economically disadvantaged African-American families. *Child Development, 66,* 1585–1597.

Taylor, S. M. (1994, April). *Staying in school against the odds: Voices of minority adolescent girls.* Paper presented at the annual meeting of the American Educational Research Association, New Orleans, LA.

Taylor, W. C., Beech, B. M., & Cummings, S. S. (1998). Increasing physical activity levels among youth: A public health challenge. In D. K. Wilson, J. R. Rodrigue, & W. C. Taylor (Eds.), *Health-promoting and health-compromising behaviors among minority adolescents* (pp. 107–128). Washington, DC: American Psychological Association.

Teale, W. H. (1978). Positive environments for learning to read: What studies of early readers tell us. *Language Arts, 55,* 922–932.

Teeter, P. A., & Semrud-Clikeman, M. (1997). *Child neuropsychology: Assessment and interventions for neurodevelopmental disorders.* Boston: Allyn & Bacon.

Tellegren, A., Lykken, D. T., Bouchard, T. J., & Wilcox, K. J. (1988). Personality similarity in twins reared apart and together. *Journal of Personality and Social Psychology, 54,* 1031–1039.

Tenenbaum, H. R., & Leaper, C. (2002). Are parents' gender schemas related to their children's gender-related cognitions? A meta-analysis. *Developmental Psychology, 38,* 615–630.

Tennyson, R. D., & Cocchiarella, M. J. (1986). An empirically based instructional design theory for teaching concepts. *Review of Educational Research, 56,* 40–71.

Terman, L. M. (1916). *The measurement of intelligence.* Boston: Houghton Mifflin.

Terman, L. M., & Merrill, M. A. (1972). *Stanford-Binet Intelligence Scale* (3rd ed.). Boston: Houghton Mifflin.

Teti, D. M., Gelfand, D., Messinger, D. S., & Isabella, R. (1995). Maternal depression and the quality of early attachment: An examination of infants, preschoolers and their mothers. *Developmental Psychology, 31,* 364–376.

Tharp, R. G. (1989). Psychocultural variables and constants: Effects on teaching and learning in schools. *American Psychologist, 44,* 349–359.

Tharp, R. G. (1994). Intergroup differences among Native Americans in socialization and child cognition: An ethnogenetic analysis. In P. M. Greenfield & R. R. Cocking (Eds.), *Cross-cultural roots of minority child development* (pp. 87–105). Hillsdale, NJ: Erlbaum.

Thelen, E., Corbetta, D., Kamm, K., Spencer, J. P., Schneider, K., & Zernicke, R. F. (1993). The transition to reaching: Mapping intention and intrinsic dynamics. *Child Development, 64,* 1058–1098.

Thelen, E., Corbetta, D., & Spencer, J. (1996). The development of reaching during the first year: The role of movement speed. *Journal of Experimental Psychology: Human Perception and Performance, 22,* 1059–1076.

Thelen, E., & Smith, L. B. (1998). Dynamic systems theories. In W. Damon (Series Ed.) & R. M. Lerner (Vol. Ed.), *Handbook of child psychology: Vol. 1. Theoretical models of human development* (5th ed., pp. 563–634). New York: Wiley.

Thiede, H., Romero, M., Bordelon, K., Hagan, H., & Murrill, C. S. (2001). Using a jail-based survey to monitor HIV and risk behaviors among Seattle area injection users. *Journal of Urban Health, 78,* 264–287.

Thomas, A., & Chess, S. (1977). *Temperament and development.* New York: Brunner/Mazel.

Thomas, J. R., & French, K. E. (1985). Gender differences across age in motor performance: A meta-analysis. *Psychological Bulletin, 98,* 260–282.

Thomas, J. W. (1993). Promoting independent learning in the middle grades: The role of instructional support practices. *Elementary School Journal, 93,* 575–591.

Thomas, S., & Oldfather, P. (1997). Intrinsic motivations, literacy, and assessment practices: "That's my grade. That's me." *Educational Psychologist, 32,* 107–123.

Thomas, S. P., Groër, M., & Droppleman, P. (1993). Physical health of today's school children. *Educational Psychology Review, 5,* 5–33.

Thompson, H., & Carr, M. (1995, April). *Brief metacognitive intervention and interest as predictors of memory for text.* Paper presented at the annual meeting of the American Educational Research Association, San Francisco.

Thompson, L. A., Fagan, J. F., & Fulker, D. W. (1991). Longitudinal prediction of specific cognitive abilities from infant novelty preference. *Child Development, 62,* 530–538.

Thompson, M., & Grace, C. O. (with L. J. Cohen). (2001). *Best friends, worst enemies: Understanding the social lives of children.* New York: Ballantine.

Thompson, P. M., Giedd, J. N., Woods, R. P., MacDonald, D., Evans, A. C., & Toga, A. W. (2000). Growth patterns in the developing brain detected by using continuum mechanical tensor maps. *Nature, 404,* 190–193.

Thompson, R. A. (1994a). Emotion regulation: A theme in search of a definition. *Monographs of the Society for Research in Child Development, 59*(2–3, Serial No. 240), 25–52.

Thompson, R. A. (1994b). The role of the father after divorce. *The Future of Children: Children and Divorce, 4*(1), 210–235.

Thompson, R. A. (1998). Early sociopersonality development. In W. Damon (Editor-in-Chief) & N. Eisenberg (Vol. Ed.), *Handbook of child psychology: Vol. 3. Social, emotional, and personality development* (5th ed., pp. 25–104). New York: Wiley.

Thompson, R. A., & Wyatt, J. M. (1999). Current research on child maltreatment: Implications for educators. *Educational Psychology Review, 11,* 173–201.

Thompson, R. F. (1975). *Introduction to physiological psychology.* New York: Harper & Row.

Thompson, R. H., McKerchar, P. M., & Dancho, K. A. (2004). The effects of delayed physical prompts and reinforcement on infant sign language acquisition. *Journal of Applied Behavior Analysis, 37,* 379–383.

Thorkildsen, T. A. (1995). Conceptions of social justice. In W. M. Kurtines & J. L. Gewirtz (Eds.), *Moral development: An introduction.* Boston: Allyn & Bacon.

Thorndike, R., Hagen, E., & Sattler, J. (1986). *Stanford-Binet Intelligence Scale* (4th ed.). Chicago: Riverside.

Thornton, M. C., Chatters, L. M., Taylor, R. J., & Allen, W. (1990). Sociodemographic and environmental correlates of racial socialization by Black parents. *Child Development, 61,* 401–409.

Thurstone, L. L., & Jeffrey, T. E. (1956). *FLAGS: A test of space thinking.* Chicago: Industrial Relations Center.

Tiedemann, J. (2000). Parents' gender stereotypes and teachers' beliefs as predictors of children's concept of their mathematical ability in elementary school. *Journal of Educational Psychology, 92,* 144–151.

Timlin-Scalera, R. M., Ponterotto, J. G., Blumberg, F. C., & Jackson, M. A. (2003). A grounded theory study of help-seeking behaviors among White male high school students. *Journal of Counseling Psychology, 50,* 339–350.

Timmer, S. G., Eccles, J., & O'Brien, K. (1985). How children use time. In F. T. Juster & F. P. Stafford (Eds.), *Time, goods, and well-being* (pp. 353–383). Ann Arbor, MI: Survey Research Center, Institute for Social Research.

Tincoff, R., & Jusczyk, P. W. (1999). Some beginnings of word comprehension in 6-month-olds. *Psychological Science, 10,* 172–175.

Tobias, S. (1977). A model for research on the effect of anxiety on instruction. In J. E. Sieber, H. F. O'Neil, Jr., & S. Tobias (Eds.), *Anxiety, learning, and instruction.* Hillsdale, NJ: Erlbaum.

Tomblin, J. B. (1997). Epidemiology of specific language impairment. In M. Gopnik (Ed.), *The inheritance and innateness of grammars.* New York: Oxford University Press.

Tompkins, G. E., & McGee, L. M. (1986). Visually impaired and sighted children's emerging concepts about written language. In D. B. Yaden, Jr., & S. Templeton (Eds.), *Metalinguistic awareness and beginning literacy: Conceptualizing what it means to read and write.* Portsmouth, NH: Heinemann.

Torney-Purta, J. (1994). Dimensions of adolescents' reasoning about political and historical issues: Ontological switches, developmental processes, and situated learning. In M. Carretero & J. F. Voss (Eds.), *Cognitive and instructional processes in history and the social sciences* (pp. 103–122). Mahwah, NJ: Erlbaum.

Torquati, J. C. (2002). Personal and social resources as predictors of parenting in homeless families. *Journal of Family Issues, 23,* 463–485.

Torrance, E. P. (1989). A reaction to "Gifted Black students: Curriculum and teaching strategies." In C. J. Maker & S. W. Schiever (Eds.), *Critical issues in gifted education: Vol. 2. Defensible programs for cultural and ethnic minorities.* Austin, TX: Pro-Ed.

Torrance, E. P. (1995). Insights about creativity: Questioned, rejected, ridiculed, ignored. *Educational Psychology Review, 7,* 313–322.

Torres-Guzmán, M. E. (1998). Language, culture, and literacy in Puerto Rican communities. In B. Pérez (Ed.), *Sociocultural contexts of language and literacy.* Mahwah, NJ: Erlbaum.

Tourniaire, F., & Pulos, S. (1985). Proportional reasoning: A review of the literature. *Educational Studies in Mathematics, 16,* 181–204.

Touwen, B. C. L. (1974). The neurological development of the infant. In J. A. Davis & J. Dobbing (Eds.), *Scientific foundations of pediatrics.* Philadelphia: Saunders.

Trainor, L. J., Austin, C. M., & Desjardins, R. N. (2000). Is infant-directed speech prosody a result of the vocal expression of emotion? *Psychological Science, 11,* 188–195.

Trainor, L. J., & Trehub, S. E. (1992). A comparison of infants' and adults' sensitivity to Western tonal structure. *Journal of Experimental Psychology: Human Perception and Performance, 19,* 615–626.

Trautner, H. M. (1992). The development of sex-typing in children: A longitudinal analysis. *German Journal of Psychology, 16,* 183–199.

Trawick-Smith, J. (2003). *Early childhood development: A multicultural perspective* (3rd ed.). Upper Saddle River, NJ: Merrill/Prentice Hall.

Treffert, D. A. (1989). *Extraordinary people: Understanding Savant syndrome.* New York: Harper & Row.

Treffert, D. A., & Wallace, G. L. (2002). Islands of genius. *Scientific American, 286*(6), 76–85.

Treiman, R. (1993). *Beginning to spell: A study of first-grade children.* New York: Oxford University Press.

Treiman, R. (1998). Beginning to spell in English. In C. Hulme & R. M. Joshi (Eds.), *Reading and spelling: Development and disorders.* Mahwah, NJ: Erlbaum.

Trelease, J. (1982). *The read-aloud handbook.* New York: Penguin Books.

Tremblay, L. (1999, April). *Acceleration hypothesis: A meta-analysis of environmental stressors impact on puberty onset.* Paper presented at the biennial meeting of the Society for Research in Child Development, Albuquerque, NM.

Trevarthen, C. (1980). The foundations of intersubjectivity: Development of interpersonal and cooperative understandings in infants. In D. R. Olson (Ed.), *The social foundations of language and thought* (pp. 316–342). New York: Norton.

Trevarthen, C., & Hubley, P. (1978). Secondary intersubjectivity: Confidence, confiding and acts of meaning in the first year. In A. Lock (Ed.), *Action, gesture, and symbol: The emergence of language.* London: Academic Press.

Triandis, H. C. (1995). *Individualism and collectivism.* Boulder, CO: Westview Press.

Tronick, E. Z., Als, H., Adamson, L., Wise, S., & Brazelton, B. (1978). The infants' response to entrapment between contradictory messages in face-to-face interaction. *American Academy of Child Psychiatry, 1,* 1–13.

Tronick, E. Z., Cohn, J., & Shea, E. (1986). The transfer of affect between mother and infant. In T. B. Brazelton & M. W. Yogman (Eds.), *Affective development in infancy* (pp. 11–25). Norwood, NJ: Ablex.

Trout, J. D. (2003). Biological specializations for speech: What can the animals tell us? *Current Directions in Psychological Science, 12,* 155–159.

Trueba, H. T. (1988). Peer socialization among minority students: A high school dropout prevention program. In H. T. Trueba & C. Delgado-Gaitan (Eds.), *School and society: Learning content through culture.* New York: Praeger.

Tse, L. (2001). *Why don't they learn English: Separating fact from fallacy in the U.S. language debate.* New York: Teachers College Press.

Tunmer, W. E., Pratt, C., & Herriman, M. L. (Eds.), (1984). *Metalinguistic awareness in children: Theory, research, and implications.* Berlin, Germany: Springer-Verlag.

Turiel, E. (1983). *The development of social knowledge: Morality and convention.* Cambridge, England: Cambridge University Press.

Turiel, E. (1998). The development of morality. In W. Damon (Series Ed.) & N. Eisenberg (Vol. Ed.), *Handbook of child psychology: Vol. 3. Social, emotional, and personality development* (pp. 863–932). New York: Wiley.

Turiel, E. (2002). *The culture of morality: Social development, context, and conflict.* Cambridge, England: Cambridge University Press.

Turiel, E., Killen, M., & Helwig, C. C. (1987). Morality: Its structure, function, and vagaries. In J. Kagan & S. Lamb (Eds.), *The emergence of morality in young children* (pp. 155–243). Chicago: University of Chicago Press.

Turiel, E., Smetana, J. G., & Killen, M. (1991). Social contexts in social cognitive development. In W. M. Kurtines & J. L. Gewirtz (Eds.), *Moral behavior and development: Vol. 2. Research.* Hillsdale, NJ: Erlbaum.

Turkheimer, E. (2000). Three laws of behavior genetics and what they mean. *Current Directions in Psychological Science, 9,* 160–164.

Turkheimer, E., Haley, A., Waldron, M., D'Onofrio, B., & Gottesman, I. I. (2003). Socioeconomic status modifies heritability of IQ in young children. *Psychological Science, 14,* 623–628.

Turnbull, A. P., Pereira, L., & Blue-Banning, M. (2000). Teachers as friendship facilitators: Respeto and personalismo. *Teaching Exceptional Children, 32*(5), 66–70.

Turnbull, R., Turnbull, A., Shank, M., & Smith, S. (2004). *Exceptional lives: Special education in today's schools* (4th ed.). Upper Saddle River, NJ: Merrill/Prentice Hall.

Turner, J. C. (1995). The influence of classroom contexts on young children's motivation for literacy. *Reading Research Quarterly, 30,* 410–441.

Turner, M. A., Freiberg, F., Godfrey, E., Herbig, C., Levy, D. K., & Smith, R. R. (2002). *All other things being equal: A paired testing study of mortgage lending institutions.* Washington, DC: Urban Institute.

Tversky, A., & Kahneman, D. (1990). Judgment under uncertainty: Heuristics and biases. In P. K. Moser (Ed.), *Rationality in action: Contemporary approaches* (pp. 171–188). New York: Cambridge University Press.

Tzuriel, D. (2000). Dynamic assessment of young children: Educational and intervention perspectives. *Educational Psychology Review, 12,* 385–435.

U.S. Census Bureau. (2000a). *Table FG1. Married Couple Family Groups, by Labor Force Status of Both Spouses, and Race and Hispanic Origin/1 of the Reference Person: March 2000.* Retrieved January 31, 2003, from http://www.census.gov/population/socdemo/hh-fam/p20-537/2000/tabFG1.txt

U.S. Census Bureau. (2000b). *Table FG5. One-Parent Family Groups with Own Children Under 18, by Labor Force Status, and Race and Hispanic Origin/1 of the Reference Person: March 2000.* Retrieved January 31, 2003, from http://www.census.gov/population/socdemo/hh-fam/p20-537/2000/tabFG5.txt

U.S. Census Bureau. (2003). *Historical Table. Primary Child Care Arrangements Used by Employed Mothers of Preschoolers: 1985 to 1999.* Retrieved January 31, 2003, from http://www.census.gov/population/socdemo/child/pp1-168/tabH-1.pdf

U.S. Census Bureau. (2005, February). *Detailed Table 1. Marital history for people 15 years old and over by age, sex, race and ethnicity: 2001.* Retrieved August 10, 2005 from http://www.census.gov/population/www/socdemo/marr-div/p70-97-tab01.html

U.S. Department of Education. (1993). *National excellence: A case for developing America's talent.* Washington, DC: Office of Educational Research and Improvement.

U.S. Department of Education. (1997). *To assure the free appropriate public education of all children with disabilities: Nineteenth annual report to Congress on the implementation of the Individuals with Disabilities Education Act.* Washington, DC: Author.

U.S. Department of Education, Office of Civil Rights. (1993). *Annual report to Congress.* Washington, DC: Author.

U.S. Department of Health and Human Services. (2000). *Child welfare outcomes 2000: Annual report.* Washington, DC: National Clearinghouse on Child Abuse and Neglect Information.

U.S. Department of Health and Human Services. (2001). *Prevention works! A practitioner's guide to achieving outcomes.* Rockville, MD: Author.

U.S. Department of Health and Human Services. (2004). *Child maltreatment 2002.* Washington, DC: U.S. Government Printing Office.

U.S. Drug Enforcement Administration. (2002). *Team up: A drug prevention manual for high school athletic coaches.* Washington, DC: U.S. Department of Justice Drug Enforcement Administration.

Uba, L., & Huang, K. (1999). *Psychology.* New York: Longman.

Udall, A. J. (1989). Curriculum for gifted Hispanic students. In C. J. Maker & S. W. Schiever (Eds.), *Critical issues in gifted education: Vol. 2. Defensible programs for cultural and ethnic minorities.* Austin, TX: Pro-Ed.

Udry, J. R. (1988). Biological predispositions and social control in adolescent sexual behavior. *American Sociological Review, 53*(5), 709–722.

Ulichny, P. (1994, April). *Cultures in conflict.* Paper presented at the annual meeting of the American Educational Research Association, New Orleans, LA.

Upchurch, D. M., & McCarthy, J. (1990). The timing of first birth and high school completion. *American Sociological Review, 55,* 224–234.

Urban, J., Carlson, E., Egeland, B., & Sroufe, L. A. (1991). Patterns of individual adaptation across childhood. *Development and Psychopathology, 3,* 445–460.

Urdan, T. (1997). Achievement goal theory: Past results, future directions. In M. L. Maehr & P. R. Pintrich (Eds.), *Advances in motivation and achievement* (Vol. 10). Greenwich, CT: JAI Press.

Urdan, T. (2004). Predicators of academic self-handicapping and achievement: Examining achievement goals, classroom goal structures, and culture. *Journal of Educational Psychology, 96,* 251–264.

Urdan, T., & Midgley, C. (2001). Academic self-handicapping: What we know, what more there is to learn. *Educational Psychology Review, 13,* 115–138.

Urdan, T., Ryan, A. M., Anderman, E. M., & Gheen, M. H. (2002). Goals, goal structures, and avoidance behaviors. In C. Midgley (Ed.), *Goals, goal structures, and patterns of adaptive learning* (pp. 55–83). Mahwah, NJ: Erlbaum.

Urdan, T. C., & Maehr, M. L. (1995). Beyond a two-goal theory of motivation and achievement: A case for social goals. *Review of Educational Research, 65,* 213–243.

Uttal, D. H., Marzolf, D. P., Pierroutsakos, S. L., Smith, C. M., Troseth, G. L., Scudder, K. V., et al. (1998). Seeing through symbols: The development of children's understanding of symbolic relations. In O. N. Saracho & B. Spodek (Eds.), *Multiple perspectives on play in early childhood education.* Albany: State University of New York Press.

Valdez, A. J. (2000). *Gangs: A guide to understanding street gangs* (3rd ed.). San Clemente, CA: LawTech.

Valentine, J. C., DuBois, D. L., & Cooper, H. (2004). The relation between self-beliefs and academic achievement: A meta-analytic review. *Educational Psychologist, 39,* 111–133.

Vandell, D. L., & Pierce, K. M. (1999, April). *Can after-school programs benefit children who live in high-crime neighborhoods?* Paper presented at the biennial meeting of the Society for Research in Child Development, Albuquerque, NM.

Van den Bergh, B. R. H., & Marcoen, A. (2004). High antenatal maternal anxiety is related to ADHD symptoms, externalizing problems, and anxiety in 8- and 9-year-olds. *Child Development, 75,* 1085–1097.

van den Broek, P., Bauer, P. J., & Bourg, T. (Eds.). (1997). *Developmental spans in event comprehension and representation: Bridging fictional and actual events.* Mahwah, NJ: Erlbaum.

van den Broek, P., Lynch, J. S., Naslund, J., Ievers-Landis, C. E., & Verduin, K. (2003). The development of comprehension of main ideas in narratives: Evidence from the selection of titles. *Journal of Educational Psychology, 95,* 707–718.

Van der Voort, T. H. A., & Valkenburg, P. M. (1994). Television's impact on fantasy play: A review of research. *Developmental Review, 14*(1), 227–251.

van Heteren, C. F., Boekkooi, P. F., Jongsma, H. W., & Nijhuis, J. G. (2001). Fetal habituation to vibroacoustic stimulation in relation to fetal states and fetal heart rate parameters. *Early Human Development, 61,* 135–145.

van Heteren, C. F., Boekkooi, P. F., Jongsma, H. W., & Nijhuis, J. G. (2000, September 30). Fetal learning and memory. *Lancet, 356,* 1169–1170.

van Hof-van Duin, J., & Mohn, G. (1986). The development of visual acuity in normal full-term and preterm infants. *Vision Research, 26,* 909–916.

Van Hoorn, J., Nourot, P. M., Scales, B., & Alward, K. R. (1999). *Play at the center of the curriculum* (2nd ed.). Upper Saddle River, NJ: Merrill/Prentice Hall.

van IJzendoorn, M. H., Goldberg, S., Kroonenberg, P. M., & Frenkel, O. J. (1992). The relative effects of maternal and child problems on the quality of attachment: A meta-analysis of attachment in clinical samples. *Child Development, 63,* 840–858.

van IJzendoorn, M. H., Sagi, A., Lambermon, M. (1992). The multiple caregiver paradox: Data from Holland and Israel. In R. C. Pianta (Ed.), *New directions for child development: No. 57. Beyond the parent: The role of other adults in children's lives* (pp. 5–27). San Francisco, CA: Jossey-Bass.

van Kraayenoord, C. E., & Paris, S. G. (1997). Children's self-appraisal of their work samples and academic progress. *Elementary School Journal, 97,* 523–537.

van Laar, C. (2000). The paradox of low academic achievement but high self-esteem in African American students: An attributional account. *Educational Psychology Review, 12,* 33–61.

Varela, R. E., Vernberg, E. M., Sanchez-Sosa, J. J., Riveros, A., Mitchell, M., & Mashunkashey, J. (2004). Parenting style of Mexican, Mexican American, and Caucasian-Non-Hispanic families: Social context and cultural influences. *Journal of Family Psychology, 18,* 651–657.

Vasquez, J. A. (1990). Teaching to the distinctive traits of minority students. *Clearing House, 63,* 299–304.

Vaughn, B. E., Egeland, B., Sroufe, L. A., & Waters, E. (1979). Individual differences in infant-mother attachment at twelve and eighteen months: Stability and change in families under stress. *Child Development, 50,* 971–975.

Vaughn, B. E., Kopp, C. B., & Krakow, J. B. (1984). The emergence and consolidation of self-control from eighteen to thirty months of age: Normative trends and individual differences. *Child Development, 55,* 990–1004.

Vega, W. A., Gil, A. G., Warheit, G. J., Zimmerman, R. S., & Apospori, E. (1993). Acculturation and delinquent behavior among Cuban American adolescents: Toward an empirical model. *American Journal of Community Psychology, 21,* 113–125.

Venter, J. C., et al. (2001). The sequence of the human genome. *Science, 291,* 1304–1351.

Ventura, S. J., & Tappel, S. M. (1985). Child bearing characteristics of U.S. and foreign born Hispanic mothers. *Public Health Reports, 100,* 647–652.

Vermeer, H. J., Boekaerts, M., & Seegers, G. (2000). Motivational and gender differences: Sixth-grade students' mathematical problem-solving behavior. *Journal of Educational Psychology, 92,* 308–315.

Vernon, P. A. (1993). Intelligence and neural efficiency. In D. K. Detterman (Ed.), *Current topics in human intelligence* (Vol. 3). Norwood, NJ: Ablex.

Veroff, J., McClelland, L., & Ruhland, D. (1975). Varieties of achievement motivation. In M. T. S. Mednick, S. S. Tangri, & L. W. Hoffman (Eds.), *Women and achievement: Social and motivational analyses.* New York: Halsted.

Vignau, J., Bailly, D., Duhamel, A., Vervaecke, P., Beuscart, R., & Collinet, C. (1997). Epidemiologic study of sleep quality and troubles in French secondary school adolescents. *Journal of Adolescent Health, 21,* 343–350.

Vitaro, F., Gendreau, P. L., Tremblay, R. E., & Oligny, P. (1998). Reactive and proactive aggression differentially predict later conduct problems. *Journal of Child Psychology and Psychiatry and Allied Disciplines, 39,* 377–385.

Voelkl, K. E., & Frone, M. R. (2000). Predictors of substance use at school among high school students. *Journal of Educational Psychology, 92,* 583–592.

Vogel, G. (1997). Cocaine wreaks subtle damage on developing brains. *Science, 278,* 38–39.

Volling, B. L. (2001). Early attachment relationships as predictors of preschool children's emotion regulation with a distressed sibling. *Early Education and Development, 12*(2), 185–207.

Vorhees, C. V., & Mollnow, E. (1987). Behavioral teratogenesis: Long-term influences on behavior from early exposure to environmental agents. In J. D. Osofsky (Ed.), *Handbook of infant development* (2nd ed., pp. 913–971). New York: Wiley.

Vorrath, H. (1985). *Positive peer culture.* New York: Aldine de Gruyter.

Vosniadou, S. (1991). Conceptual development in astronomy. In S. M. Glynn, R. H. Yeany, & B. K. Britton (Eds.), *The psychology of learning science.* Hillsdale, NJ: Erlbaum.

Vosniadou, S. (1994). Universal and culture-specific properties of children's mental models of the earth. In L. A. Hirschfeld & S. A. Gelman (Eds.), *Mapping the mind: Domain specificity in cognition and culture.* Cambridge, England: Cambridge University Press.

Vosniadou, S., & Brewer, W. F. (1987). Theories of knowledge restructuring in development. *Review of Educational Research, 57,* 51–67.

Vygotsky, L. S. (1962). *Thought and language* (E. Haufmann & G. Vakar, Eds. and Trans.). Cambridge, MA: MIT Press.

Vygotsky, L. S. (1978). *Mind in society: The development of higher psychological processes.* Cambridge, MA: Harvard University Press.

Vygotsky, L. S. (1987). Thinking and speech. In R. W. Rieber & A. S. Carton (Eds.), *The collected works of L. S. Vygotsky.* New York: Plenum Press.

Vygotsky, L. S. (1997). *Educational psychology.* Boca Raton, FL: St. Lucie Press.

Waddington, C. H. (1957). *The strategy of the genes.* London: Allyn & Bacon.

Wagener, L. M., & Malony, H. N. (2006). Spiritual and religious pathology in childhood and adolescence. In E. C. Roehlkepartain, P. E. King, L. Wagener, & P. L. Benson (Eds.), *The handbook of spiritual development in childhood and adolescence* (pp. 137–149). Thousand Oaks, CA: Sage.

Wagner, L. S., Carlin, P. L., Cauce, A. M., & Tenner, A. (2001). A snapshot of homeless youth in Seattle: Their characteristics, behaviors and beliefs about HIV protective strategies. *Journal of Community Health, 26,* 219–232.

Wagner, M. M. (1995). *The contributions of poverty and ethnic background to the participation of secondary school students in special education.* Washington, DC: U.S. Department of Education.

Wahlsten, D., & Gottlieb, G. (1997). The invalid separation of effects of nature and nurture: Lessons from animal experimentation. In R. J. Sternberg & E. L. Grigorenko (Eds.), *Intelligence, heredity, and environment* (pp. 163–192). Cambridge, England: Cambridge University Press.

Waisbren, S. E. (1999). Phenylketonuria. In S. Goldstein & C. R. Reynolds (Eds.), *Handbook of neurodevelopmental and genetic disorders* (pp. 433–458). New York: Guilford Press.

Walberg, H. J., & Paik, S. J. (1997). Home environments for learning. In H. J. Walberg & G. D. Haertel (Eds.), *Psychology and educational practice* (pp. 356–368). Berkeley, CA: McCrutchan.

Waldman, I. D., Weinberg, R. A., & Scarr, S. (1994). Racial-group differences in IQ in the Minnesota Transracial Adoption Study: A reply to Levin and Lynn. *Intelligence, 19,* 29–44.

Walker, J. E., & Shea, T. M. (1999). *Behavior management: A practical approach for educators* (7th ed.). Upper Saddle River, NJ: Merrill/Prentice Hall.

Walker, J. M. T. (2001, April). *A cross-sectional study of student motivation, strategy knowledge and strategy use during homework: Implications for research on self-regulated learning.* Paper presented at the annual meeting of the American Educational Research Association, Seattle, WA.

Walker, L. J. (1991). Sex differences in moral reasoning. In W. M. Kurtines & J. L. Gewirtz (Eds.), *Handbook of moral behavior and development: Vol. 2. Research* (pp. 333–364). Hillsdale, NJ: Erlbaum.

Walker, L. J. (1995). Sexism in Kohlberg's moral psychology? In W. M. Kurtines & J. L. Gewirtz (Eds.), *Moral development: An introduction.* Boston: Allyn & Bacon.

Wallander, J. L., Eggert, K. M., & Gilbert, K. K. (2004). Adolescent health-related issues. In R. T. Brown (Ed.), *Handbook of pediatric psychology in school settings* (pp. 503–520). Mahwah, NJ: Erlbaum.

Wallerstein, J. S. (1984). Children of divorce: The psychological tasks of the child. In S. Chess (Ed.), *Annual Progress in Child Psychiatry and Child Development* (pp. 263–280). Philadelphia: Brunner-Routledge.

Wallerstein, J. S., & Kelly, J. B. (1980). *Surviving the break-up: How children and parents cope with divorce.* New York: Basic Books.

Walters, G. C., & Grusec, J. E. (1977). *Punishment.* San Francisco: Freeman.

Walton, G. E., Bower, N. J. A., & Bower, T. G. R. (1992). Recognition of familiar faces by newborns. *Infant Behavior and Development, 15,* 265–269.

Wang, P. P., & Baron, M. A. (1997). Language and communication: Development and disorders. In M. L. Batshaw (Ed.), *Children with disabilities* (4th ed.). Baltimore: Brookes.

Want, S. C., & Harris, P. L. (2001). Learning from other people's mistakes: Causal understanding in learning to use a tool. *Child Development, 72,* 431–443.

Ward, R. A., & Spitze, G. (1998). Sandwiched marriages: The implications of child and parent relations for marital quality in midlife. *Social Forces, 77,* 647–666.

Warren, A. R., & McCloskey, L. A. (1993). Pragmatics: Language in social contexts. In J. Berko-Gleason (Ed.), *The development of language* (3rd ed.). New York: Macmillan.

Warren-Leubecker, A., & Bohannon, J. N. (1989). Pragmatics: Language in social contexts. In J. Berko-Gleason (Ed.), *The development of language* (2nd ed.). Upper Saddle River, NJ: Merrill/Prentice Hall.

Wartella, E., Caplovitz, A. G., & Lee, J. H. (2004). From Baby Einstein to Leapfrog, from Doom to The Sims, from instant messaging to Internet chat rooms: Public interest in the role of interactive media in children's lives. *Social Policy Report, 18*(4) (Society for Research in Child Development).

Warton, P. M., & Goodnow, J. J. (1991). The nature of responsibility: Children's understanding of "Your Job." *Child Development, 62,* 156–165.

Washington, V., & Bailey, U. J. O. (1995). *Project Head Start: Models and strategies for the twenty-first century.* New York: Garland.

Wasik, B. A., & Bond, M. A. (2001). Beyond the pages of a book: Interactive book reading and language development in preschool classrooms. *Journal of Educational Psychology, 93,* 243–250.

Wasik, B. A., Karweit, N., Burns, L., & Brodsky, E. (1998, April). *Once upon a time: The role of rereading and retelling in storybook reading.* Paper presented at the annual meeting of the American Educational Research Association, San Diego, CA.

Waters, E., Merrick, S., Treboux, D., Crowell, J., & Albersheim, L. (2000). Attachment security in infancy and early adulthood: A twenty-year longitudinal study. *Child Development, 71,* 684–689.

Waters, H. S. (1982). Memory development in adolescence: Relationships between metamemory, strategy use, and performance. *Journal of Experimental Child Psychology, 33,* 183–195.

Watson, J. (1928). *The psychological care of the infant and child.* New York: Norton.

Watson, R. (1996). Rethinking readiness for learning. In D. R. Olson & N. Torrance (Eds.), *The handbook of education and human development: New models of learning, teaching and schooling* (pp. 148–172). Cambridge, MA: Blackwell.

Waxman, S. R. (1990). Linguistic biases and the establishment of conceptual hierarchies: Evidence from preschool children. *Cognitive Development, 5,* 123–150.

Waxman, S. R. (2003). Links between object categorization and naming: Origins and emergence in human infants. In D. H. Rakison & L. M. Oakes (Eds.), *Early category and concept development: Making sense of the blooming, buzzing confusion* (pp. 213–241). Oxford, England: Oxford University Press.

Way, N. (1998). *Everyday courage: The lives and stories of urban teenagers.* New York: New York University Press.

Weaver, C. A., III, & Kintsch, W. (1991). Expository text. In R. Barr, M. L. Kamil, P. B. Mosenthal, & P. D. Pearson (Eds.), *Handbook of reading research* (Vol. II). New York: Longman.

Weaver-Hightower, M. (2003). The "boy turn" in research on gender and education. *Review of Educational Research, 73,* 471–498.

Webb, N. M., & Farivar, S. (1994). Promoting helping behavior in cooperative small groups in middle school mathematics. *American Educational Research Journal, 31,* 369–395.

Webb, N. M., & Palincsar, A. S. (1996). Group processes in the classroom. In D. C. Berliner & R. C. Calfee (Eds.), *Handbook of educational psychology.* New York: Macmillan.

Webber, J., Scheuermann, B., McCall, C., & Coleman, M. (1993). Research on self-monitoring as a behavior management technique in special education classrooms: A descriptive review. *Remedial and Special Education, 14,* 38–56.

Webster-Stratton, C., & Hammond, M. (1999). Marital conflict management skills, parenting style, and early-onset conduct problems: Processes and pathways. *Journal of Child Psychology & Psychiatry & Allied Disciplines, 40,* 917–927.

Wechsler, D. (2002). *Wechsler Preschool and Primary Scale of Intelligence–Third Edition.* San Antonio, TX: Psychological Corporation.

Wechsler, D. (2003). *Wechsler Intelligence Scale for Children* (4th ed.). San Antonio, TX: Psychological Corporation.

Weinberg, R. A. (1989). Intelligence and IQ: Landmark issues and great debates. *American Psychologist, 44,* 98–104.

Weiner, B. (1984). Principles for a theory of student motivation and their application within an attributional framework. In R. Ames & C. Ames (Eds.), *Research on motivation in education: Vol. 1. Student motivation.* San Diego, CA: Academic Press.

Weiner, B. (1986). *An attributional theory of motivation and emotion.* New York: Springer-Verlag.

Weiner, B. (2000). Intrapersonal and interpersonal theories of motivation from an attributional perspective. *Educational Psychology Review, 12,* 1–14.

Weiner, B. (2004). Attribution theory revisited: Transforming cultural plurality into theoretical unity. In D. M. McInerney & S. Van Etten (Eds.), *Big theories revisited* (pp. 13–29). Greenwich, CT: Information Age.

Weiner, L. (1999). *Urban teaching: The essentials.* New York: Teachers College Press.

Weinfield, N. S., Sroufe, L. A., & Egeland, B. (2000). Attachment from infancy to early adulthood in a high-risk sample: Continuity, discontinuity, and their correlates. *Child Development, 71,* 695–702.

Weinstein, R. S. (1993). Children's knowledge of differential treatment in school: Implications for motivation. In T. M. Tomlinson (Ed.), *Motivating students to learn: Overcoming barriers to high achievement.* Berkeley, CA: McCutchan.

Weinstein, R. S., Madison, S. M., & Kuklinski, M. R. (1995). Raising expectations in schooling: Obstacles and opportunities for change. *American Educational Research Journal, 32,* 121–159.

Weisner, T. S. (1997). Why ethnography and its findings matter. *Ethos, 25,* 177–190.

Weisner, T. S., & Gallimore, R. (1977). My brother's keeper: Child and sibling caregiving. *Current Anthropology, 18,* 169–190.

Weiss, M. J., & Hagen, R. (1988). A key to literacy: Kindergartners' awareness of the functions of print. *The Reading Teacher, 41,* 574–578.

Weissglass, J. (1998). *Ripples of hope: Building relationships for educational change.* Santa Barbara: Center for Educational Change in Mathematics and Science, University of California.

Wellman, H. M. (1990). *The child's theory of mind.* Cambridge, MA: MIT Press.

Wellman, H. M., Cross, D., & Watson, J. (2001). Meta-analysis of theory-of-mind development: The truth about false belief. *Child Development, 72,* 655–684.

Wellman, H. M., & Estes, D. (1986). Early understanding of mental entities: A reexamination of childhood realism. *Child Development, 57,* 910–923.

Wellman, H. M., & Gelman, S. A. (1998). Knowledge acquisition in functional domains. In W. Damon (Series Ed.), D. Kuhn, & R. S. Siegler (Vol. Eds.), *Handbook of child psychology: Vol. 2. Cognition, perception, and language* (5th ed., pp. 523–573). New York: Wiley.

Wellman, H. M., Harris, P. L., Banerjee, M., & Sinclair, A. (1995). Early understanding of emotion: Evidence from natural language. *Cognition and Emotion, 9,* 117–149.

Wellman, H. M., & Hickling, A. K. (1994). The mind's "I": Children's conception of the mind as an active agent. *Child Development, 65,* 1564–1580.

Wellman, H. M., Phillips, A. T., & Rodriguez, T. (2000). Young children's understanding of perception, desire, and emotion. *Child Development, 71,* 895–912.

Welsh, M. C. (1991). Rule-guided behavior and self-monitoring on the tower of Hanoi disk-transfer task. *Cognitive Development, 4,* 59–76.

Wentzel, K. R. (1999). Social-motivational processes and interpersonal relationships: Implications for understanding motivation at school. *Journal of Educational Psychology, 91,* 76–97.

Wentzel, K. R. (2000). What is it that I'm trying to achieve? Classroom goals from a content perspective. *Contemporary Educational Psychology, 25,* 105–115.

Wentzel, K. R., & Asher, S. R. (1995). The academic lives of neglected, rejected, popular, and controversial children. *Child Development, 66,* 754–763.

Wentzel, K. R., & Wigfield, A. (1998). Academic and social motivational influences on students' academic performance. *Educational Psychology Review, 10,* 155–175.

Werker, J. F., & Lalonde, C. E. (1988). Cross-language speech perception: Initial capabilities and developmental change. *Developmental Psychology, 24,* 672–683.

Werker, J. F., & Tees, R. C. (1999). Influences on infant speech processing: Toward a new synthesis. *Annual Review of Psychology, 50,* 509–535.

Werner, E. E., & Smith, R. S. (2001). *Journeys from childhood to midlife: Risk, resilience, and recovery.* Ithaca, NY: Cornell University Press.

Wertsch, J. V. (1984). The zone of proximal development: Some conceptual issues. *Children's learning in the zone of proximal development: New directions for child development* (No. 23). San Francisco: Jossey-Bass.

Wertsch, J. V., & Tulviste, P. (1994). Lev Semyonovich Vygotsky and contemporary developmental psychology. In R. D. Parke, P. A. Ornstein, J. J. Rieser, & C. Zahn-Waxler (Eds.), *A century of developmental psychology* (pp. 333–355). Washington, DC: American Psychological Association.

Whalen, C. K., Jamner, L. D., Henker, B., Delfino, R. J., & Lozano, J. M. (2002). The ADHD spectrum and everyday life: Experience sampling of adolescent moods, activities, smoking, and drinking. *Child Development, 73,* 209–227.

White, B. Y., & Frederiksen, J. R. (1998). Inquiry, modeling, and metacognition: Making science accessible to all students. *Cognition and Instruction, 16,* 3–118.

White, R. (1959). Motivation reconsidered: The concept of competence. *Psychological Review, 66,* 297–333.

Whitehurst, G. J., Arnold, D. S., Epstein, J. N., Angell, A. L., Smith, M., & Fischel, J. E. (1994). A picture book reading intervention in day care and home for children from low-income families. *Developmental Psychology, 30,* 679–689.

Whiting, B. B., & Edwards, C. P. (1988). *Children of different worlds.* Cambridge, MA: Harvard University Press.

Whiting, B. B., & Whiting, J. W. M. (1975). *Children of six cultures: A psycho-cultural analysis.* Cambridge, MA: Harvard University Press.

Whitley, B. E., Jr., & Frieze, I. H. (1985). Children's causal attributions for success and failure in achievement settings: A meta-analysis. *Journal of Educational Psychology, 77,* 608–616.

Wigfield, A. (1994). Expectancy-value theory of achievement motivation: A developmental perspective. *Educational Psychology Review, 6,* 49–78.

Wigfield, A., & Eccles, J. (2000). Expectancy-value theory of achievement motivation. *Contemporary Educational Psychology, 25,* 68–81.

Wigfield, A., Eccles, J., Mac Iver, D., Reuman, D., & Midgley, C. (1991). Transitions at early adolescence: Changes in children's domain-specific self-perceptions and general self-esteem across the transition to junior high school. *Developmental Psychology, 27,* 552–565.

Wigfield, A., & Eccles, J. S. (1994). Children's competence beliefs, achievement values, and general self-esteem: Change across elementary and middle school. *Journal of Early Adolescence, 14,* 107–138.

Wigfield, A., Eccles, J. S., & Pintrich, P. R. (1996). Development between the ages of 11 and 25. In D. C. Berliner & R. C. Calfee (Eds.), *Handbook of educational psychology.* New York: Macmillan.

Wigfield, A., Tonks, S., & Eccles, J. S. (2004). Expectancy value theory in cross-cultural perspective. In D. M. McNerney & S. Van Etten (Eds.), *Big theories revisited* (pp. 165–198). Greenwich, CT: Information Age.

Wiig, E. H., Gilbert, M. F., & Christian, S. H. (1978). Developmental sequences in perception and interpretation of ambiguous sentences. *Perceptual and Motor Skills, 46,* 959–969.

Wilcox, S. (1994). Struggling for a voice: An interactionist view of language and literacy in Deaf education. In V. John-Steiner, C. P. Panofsky, & L. W. Smith (Eds.), *Sociocultural approaches to language and literacy: An interactionist perspective.* Cambridge, England: Cambridge University Press.

Wilder, D. A., & Shapiro, P. N. (1989). Role of competition-induced anxiety in limiting the beneficial impact of positive behavior by an out-group member. *Journal of Personality and Social Psychology, 56,* 60–69.

Willats, J. (1995). An information-processing approach to drawing development. In C. Lange-Kuttner & G. V. Thomas (Eds.), *Drawing and looking: Theoretical approaches to pictorial representation in children* (pp. 27–43). New York: Harvester Wheatsheaf.

Willatts, P. (1990). Development of problem solving strategies in infancy. In D. F. Bjorklund (Ed.), *Children's strategies* (pp. 23–66). Hillsdale, NJ: Erlbaum.

Williams, D. (1996). *Autism: An inside-outside approach.* London: Kingsley.

Williams, D. E., & D'Alessandro, J. D. (1994). A comparison of three measures of androgyny and their relationship to psychological adjustment. *Journal of Social Behavior and Personality, 9,* 469–480.

Williams, E., & Radin, N. (1993). Parental involvement, maternal employment, and adolescents' academic achievement: An 11-year follow-up. *American Journal of Orthopsychiatry, 63,* 306–312.

Williams, G., Donley, C. R., & Keller, J. W. (2000). Teaching children with autism to ask questions about hidden objects. *Journal of Applied Behavior Analysis, 33,* 627–630.

Williams, J. (2004). Seizure disorders. In R. T. Brown (Ed.), *Handbook of pediatric psychology in school settings* (pp. 221–239). Mahwah, NJ: Erlbaum.

Williams, J., & Williamson, K. (1992). "I wouldn't want to shoot nobody": The out-of-school curriculum as described by urban students. *Action in Teacher Education, 14*(2), 9–15.

Williams, K. M. (2001a). "Frontin' it": Schooling, violence, and relationships in the 'hood. In J. N. Burstyn, G. Bender, R. Casella, H. W. Gordon, D. P. Guerra, K. V. Luschen, et al. *Preventing violence in schools: A challenge to American democracy* (pp. 95–108). Mahwah, NJ: Erlbaum.

Williams, K. M. (2001b). What derails peer mediation? In J. N. Burstyn, G. Bender, R. Casella, H. W. Gordon, D. P. Guerra, K. V. Luschen, et al. *Preventing violence in schools: A challenge to American democracy* (pp. 199–208). Mahwah, NJ: Erlbaum.

Williams, P. E., Weiss, L. G., & Rolfhus, E. L. (2003a). *WISC-IV technical report #2: Clinical validity.* San Antonio, TX: Harcourt Assessment. Retrieved September 6, 2005, from http://www.harcourtassessment.com

Williams, P. E., Weiss, L. G., & Rolfhus, E. L. (2003b). *WISC-IV technical report #2: Psychometric properties.* San Antonio, TX: Harcourt Assessment. Retrieved September 6, 2005, from http://www.harcourtassessment.com

Willig, A. C. (1985). A meta-analysis of selected studies on the effectiveness of bilingual education. *Review of Educational Research, 55,* 269–317.

Wills, T. A., McNamara, G., Vaccaro, D., & Hirky, A. E. (1996). Escalated substance use: A longitudinal grouping analysis from early to middle adolescence. *Journal of Abnormal Psychology, 105,* 166–180.

Wilson, B. (1997). Types of child art and alternative developmental accounts: Interpreting the interpreters. *Human Development, 40,* 155–168.

Wilson, B. L., & Corbett, H. D. (2001). *Listening to urban kids: School reform and the teachers they want.* Albany: State University of New York Press.

Wilson, D. K., Nicholson, S. C., & Krishnamoorthy, J. S. (1998). The role of diet in minority adolescent health promotion. In D. K. Wilson, J. R. Rodrigue, & W. C. Taylor (Eds.), *Health-promoting and health-compromising behaviors among minority adolescents* (pp. 129–151). Washington, DC: American Psychological Association.

Wilson, J. D., & Foster, D. W. (1985). *Williams textbook of endocrinology* (7th ed.). Philadelphia: Saunders.

Wilson, M. (1989). Child development in the context of the Black extended family. *American Psychologist, 44,* 380–383.

Wilson, S. M., Shulman, L. S., & Richert, A. E. (1987). "150 different ways" of knowing: Representations of knowledge in teaching. In J. Calderhead (Ed.), *Exploring teachers' thinking* (pp. 104–124). London: Cassell Educational.

Wimmer, H., Landerl, K., & Frith, U. (1999). Learning to read German: Normal and impaired acquisition. In M. Harris & G. Hatano (Eds.), *Learning to read and write: A cross-linguistic perspective.* Cambridge, England: Cambridge University Press.

Wimmer, H., Mayringer, H., & Landerl, K. (2000). The double-deficit hypothesis and difficulties in learning to read a regular orthography. *Journal of Educational Psychology, 92,* 668–680.

Wimmer, H., & Perner, J. (1983). Beliefs about beliefs: Representation and constraining function of wrong beliefs in young children's understanding of deception. *Cognition, 13,* 103–128.

Wineburg, S. S. (1994). The cognitive representation of historical texts. In G. Leinhardt, I. L. Beck, & C. Stainton (Eds.), *Teaching and learning in history.* Hillsdale, NJ: Erlbaum.

Winn, W. (2002). Current trends in educational technology research: The study of learning environments. *Educational Psychology Review, 14,* 331–351.

Winne, P. H. (1995a). Inherent details in self-regulated learning. *Educational Psychologist, 30,* 173–187.

Winne, P. H. (1995b). Self-regulation is ubiquitous but its forms vary with knowledge. *Educational Psychologist, 30,* 223–228.

Winner, E. (1988). *The point of words.* Cambridge, MA: Harvard University Press.

Winner, E. (1996). The rage to master: The decisive role of talent in the visual arts. In K. A. Ericcson (Ed.), *The road to excellence: The acquisition of expert performance in the arts, sciences, sports and games* (pp. 271–301). Mahwah, NJ: Erlbaum.

Winner, E. (1997). Exceptionally high intelligence and schooling. *American Psychologist, 52,* 1070–1081.

Winner, E. (2000). The origins and ends of giftedness. *American Psychologist, 55,* 159–169.

Winner, E. (2006). Development in the arts: Drawing and music. In W. Damon, R. M. Lerner (Series Eds.), D. Kuhn, & R. Siegler (Vol. Eds.), *Handbook of child psychology: Vol. 2. Cognition, perception, and language* (6th ed.). New York: Wiley.

Winsler, A., Díaz, R. M., Espinosa, L., & Rodriguez, J. L. (1999). When learning a second language does not mean losing the first: Bilingual language development in low-income, Spanish-speaking children attending bilingual preschool. *Child Development, 70,* 349–362.

Winsler, A., & Naglieri, J. (2003). Overt and covert verbal problem-solving strategies: Developmental trends in use, awareness, and relations with task performance in children aged 5 to 17. *Child Development, 74,* 659–678.

Winston, P. (1973). Learning to identify toy block structures. In R. L. Solso (Ed.), *Contemporary issues in cognitive psychology: The Loyola Symposium.* Washington, DC: V. H. Winston.

Wise, F., & Miller, N. B. (1983). The mental health of the American Indian child. In G. J. Powell (Ed.), *The psychosocial development of minority children.* New York: Brunner/Mazel.

Wittmer, D. S., & Honig, A. S. (1994). Encouraging positive social development in young children. *Young Children, 10*(5), 4–12.

Wodtke, K. H., Harper, F., & Schommer, M. (1989). How standardized is school testing? An exploratory observational study of standardized group testing in kindergarten. *Educational Evaluation and Policy Analysis, 11,* 223–235.

Wolf, M., & Bowers, P. G. (1999). The double-deficit hypothesis for the developmental dyslexias. *Journal of Educational Psychology, 91,* 415–438.

Wolfe, D. A., & Wekerle, C. (1997). Pathways to violence in teen dating relationships. In D. Cicchetti & S. L. Toth (Eds.), Developmental perspectives on trauma: Theory, research, and intervention. *Rochester Symposium on Developmental Psychology, 8,* 315–341. Rochester, NY: University of Rochester Press.

Wolff, P. G. (1966). The causes, controls, and organization of behavior in the neonate. *Psychological Issues, 5*(1, Serial No. 17).

Wolock, I., Sherman, P., Feldman, L. H., & Metzger, B. (2001). Child abuse and neglect referral patterns: A longitudinal study. *Children and Youth Services Review, 23,* 21–47.

Wolters, C. A. (2003). Regulation of motivation: Evaluating an underemphasized aspect of self-regulated learning. *Educational Psychologist, 38,* 189–205.

Wong, S. C. (1993). Promises, pitfalls, and principles of text selection in curricular diversification: The Asian-American case. In T. Perry & J. W. Fraser (Eds.), *Freedom's plow: Teaching in the multicultural classroom.* New York: Routledge.

Wood, A., & Wood, B. (2001). *Alphabet adventure.* New York: Scholastic Books.

Wood, D., Bruner, J. S., & Ross, G. (1976). The role of tutoring in problem-solving. *Journal of Child Psychology and Psychiatry, 17,* 89–100.

Wood, E., Willoughby, T., McDermott, C., Motz, M., Kaspar, V., & Ducharme, M. J. (1999). Developmental differences in study behavior. *Journal of Educational Psychology, 91,* 527–536.

Wood, J. W. (1998). *Adapting instruction to accommodate students in inclusive settings* (3rd ed.). Upper Saddle River, NJ: Merrill/Prentice Hall.

Wood, R. M., & Gustafson, G. E. (2001). Infant crying and adults' anticipated caregiving responses: Acoustic and contextual influences. *Child Development, 72,* 1287–1300.

Wood, W., Wong, F. Y., & Chachere, J. G. (1991). Effects of media violence on viewers' aggression in unconstrained social interaction. *Psychological Bulletin, 109,* 371–383.

Woodard, E. H., & Gridina, N. (2000). *Media in the home 2000: The fifth annual survey of parents and children.* Philadelphia: University of Pennsylvania, Annenberg Public Policy Center. Retrieved November 19, 2005, from http://www.annenbergpublicpolicycenter.org/02_reports_releases/report_by_category.htm#mediaandchild

Woodward, A. L., Markman, E. M., & Fitzsimmons, C. M. (1994). Rapid word learning in 13- and 18-month-olds. *Developmental Psychology, 30,* 553–566.

Woodward, A. L., & Sommerville, J. A. (2000). Twelve-month-old infants interpret action in context. *Psychological Science, 11,* 73–77.

Woolfe, T., Want, S. C., & Siegal, M. (2002). Signposts to development: Theory of mind in deaf children. *Child Development, 73,* 768–778.

Woolley, J. D. (1995). The fictional mind: Young children's understanding of pretense, imagination, and dreams. *Developmental Review, 15,* 172–211.

Wright, S. C., & Taylor, D. (1995). Identity and the language of the classroom: Investigating the impact of heritage versus second-language instruction on personal and collective self-esteem. *Journal of Educational Psychology, 87,* 241–252.

Wright, S. C., Taylor, D. M., & Macarthur, J. (2000). Subtractive bilingualism and the survival of the Inuit language: Heritage- versus second-language education. *Journal of Educational Psychology, 92,* 63–84.

Wynbrandt, J., & Ludman, M. D. (2000). *The encyclopedia of genetic disorders and birth defects* (2nd ed.). New York: Facts on File.

Wynn, K. (1990). Children's understanding of counting. *Cognition, 36,* 155–193.

Wynn, K. (1992). Addition and subtraction by human infants. *Nature, 358,* 749–750.

Wynn, K. (1995). Infants possess a system of numerical knowledge. *Current Directions in Psychological Science, 4,* 172–177.

Xu, F., & Spelke, E. S. (2000). Large number discrimination in 6-month-old infants. *Cognition, 74,* B1–B11.

Yaden, D. B., Jr., & Templeton, S. (Eds.). (1986). *Metalinguistic awareness and beginning literacy: Conceptualizing what it means to read and write.* Portsmouth, NH: Heinemann.

Yakovlev, P. I., & Lecours, A. R. (1967). The myelogenetic cycles of regional maturation of the brain. In A. Minkowski (Ed.), *Regional development of the brain in early life* (pp. 3–70). Oxford, England: Blackwell Scientific.

Yarrow, M. R., Scott, P. M., & Waxler, C. Z. (1973). Learning concern for others. *Developmental Psychology, 8,* 240–260.

Yates, M., & Youniss, J. (1996). A developmental perspective on community service in adolescence. *Social Development, 5,* 85–111.

Yau, J., & Smetana, J. G. (2003). Conceptions of moral, social-conventional, and personal events among Chinese preschoolers in Hong Kong. *Child Development, 74,* 647–658.

Yeager, E. A., Foster, S. J., Maley, S. D., Anderson, T., Morris, J. W., III, & Davis, O. L., Jr. (1997, March). *The role of empathy in the development of historical understanding.* Paper presented at the annual meeting of the American Educational Research Association, Chicago.

Yee, A. H. (1992). Asians as stereotypes and students: Misperceptions that persist. *Educational Psychology Review, 4,* 95–132.

Yip, T., & Fuligni, A. J. (2002). Daily variation in ethnic identity, ethnic behaviors, and psychological well-being among American adolescents of Chinese descent. *Child Development, 73,* 1557–1572.

Young, E. L., & Assing, R. (2000). Review of The Universal Nonverbal Intelligence Test. *Journal of Psychoeducational Assessment, 18,* 280–288.

Young, J. M., Howell, A. N., & Hauser-Cram, P. (2005, April). *Predictors of mastery motivation in children with disabilities born prematurely.* Paper presented at the biennial meeting of the Society for Research in Child Development, Atlanta, GA.

Young-Hyman, D. (2004). Diabetes and the school-age child and adolescent: Facilitating good glycemic control and quality of life. In R. T. Brown (Ed.), *Handbook of pediatric psychology in school settings* (pp. 169–193). Mahwah, NJ: Erlbaum.

Youniss, J. (1980). *Parents and peers in social development.* Chicago: University of Chicago Press.

Youniss, J. (1983). Social construction of adolescence by adolescents and their parents. In H. D. Grotevant & C. R. Cooper (Eds.), *Adolescent development in the family: New directions for child development* (No. 22). San Francisco: Jossey-Bass.

Youniss, J., & Yates, M. (1999). Youth service and moral-civic identity: A case of everyday morality. *Educational Psychology Review, 11,* 361–376.

Ysseldyke, J. E., & Algozzine, B. (1984). *Introduction to special education.* Boston: Houghton Mifflin.

Zahn-Waxler, C., Radke-Yarrow, M., Wagner, E., & Chapman, M. (1992). Development of concern for others. *Developmental Psychology, 28,* 126–136.

Zahn-Waxler, C., & Robinson, J. (1995). Empathy and guilt: Early origins of feelings of responsibility. In J. P. Tangney & K. W. Fischer (Eds.), *Self-conscious emotions: The psychology of shame, guilt, embarrassment, and pride* (pp. 143–173). New York: Guilford Press.

Zahn-Waxler, C., Robinson, J., & Emde, R. N. (1992). The development of empathy in twins. *Developmental Psychology, 28,* 1038–1047.

Zajonc, R. B., & Mullally, P. R. (1997). Birth order: Reconciling conflicting effects. *American Psychologist, 52,* 685–699.

Zambo, D. (2003, April). *Thinking about reading: Talking to children with learning disabilities.* Paper presented at the annual meeting of the American Educational Research Association, Chicago.

Zarbatany, L., Hartmann, D. P., & Rankin, D. B. (1990). The psychological function of preadolescent peer activities. *Child Development, 61,* 1067–1080.

Zeanah, C. H. (2000). Disturbances of attachment in young children adopted from institutions. *Journal of Developmental and Behavioral Pediatrics, 21,* 230–236.

Zelazo, P. D., Müller, U., Frye, D., & Marcovitch, S. (2003). The development of executive function in early childhood. *Monographs of the Society for Research in Child Development, 68*(3, Serial No. 274).

Zero to Three: National Center for Infants, Toddlers, and Families. (2002). *Temperament.* Retrieved January 16, 2003, from http://www.zerotothree.org/Archive/TEMPERAM.HTM

Zervigon-Hakes, A. (1984). Materials mastery and symbolic development in construction play: Stages of development. *Early Child Development and Care, 17,* 37–47.

Zhou, Q., Eisenberg, N., Losoya, S. H., Fabes, R. A., Reiser, M., Guthrie, I. K., et al. (2002). The relations of parental warmth and positive expressiveness to children's empathy-related responding and social functioning: A longitudinal study. *Child Development, 73,* 893–915.

Ziegert, D. I., Kistner, J. A., Castro, R., & Robertson, B. (2001). Longitudinal study of young children's responses to challenging achievement situations. *Child Development, 72,* 609–624.

Ziegler, J. C., Tan, L. H., Perry, C., & Montant, M. (2000). Phonology matters: The phonological frequency effect in written Chinese. *Psychological Science, 11,* 234–238.

Ziegler, S. G. (1987). Effects of stimulus cueing on the acquisition of groundstrokes by beginning tennis players. *Journal of Applied Behavior Analysis, 20,* 405–411.

Zigler, E. (2003). Forty years of believing in magic is enough. *Social Policy Report, 17*(1), 10.

Zigler, E., & Muenchow, S. (1992). *Head Start: The inside story of America's most successful educational experiment.* New York: Basic Books.

Zigler, E. F., & Finn-Stevenson, M. (1992). Applied developmental psychology. In M. H. Bornstein & M. E. Lamb (Eds.), *Developmental psychology: An advanced textbook.* Hillsdale, NJ: Erlbaum.

Zill, N. (1985, April). *Behavior and learning problems among adopted children: Findings from a national survey of child health.* Paper presented at the meeting of the Society for Research in Child Development, Toronto, Canada.

Zill, N., Nord, C., & Loomis, L. (1995, September). *Adolescent time use, risky behavior, and outcomes: An analysis of national data.* Rockville, MD: Westat.

Zimmerman, B. J. (1998). Developing self-fulfilling cycles of academic regulation: An analysis of exemplary instructional models. In D. H. Schunk & B. J. Zimmerman (Eds.), *Self-regulated learning: From teaching to self-reflective practice* (pp. 1–19). New York: Guilford Press.

Zimmerman, B. J. (2004). Sociocultural influence and students' development of academic self-regulation: A social-cognitive perspective. In D. M. McNerney & S. Van Etten (Eds.), *Big theories revisited* (pp. 139–164). Greenwich, CT: Information Age.

Zimmerman, B. J., & Risemberg, R. (1997). Self-regulatory dimensions of academic learning and motivation. In G. D. Phye (Ed.), *Handbook of academic learning: Construction of knowledge.* San Diego, CA: Academic Press.

Zuckerman, G. A. (1994). A pilot study of a ten-day course in cooperative learning for beginning Russian first graders. *Elementary School Journal, 94,* 405–420.

Zwaan, R. A., Langston, M. C., & Graesser, A. C. (1995). The construction of situation models in narrative comprehension: An event-indexing model. *Psychological Science, 6,* 292–297.

Photo Credits

Name Index

Abbott, R., 360
Abbott-Shim, M., 556
Abdul-Jabbar, K., 453
Aber, J. L., 184, 554
Abi-Nader, J., 175, 302
Abma, J. C., 132
Aboud, F. E., 463
Abramowitz, R. H., 155
Acock, A. C., 564
Acredolo, L. P., 336
Adalbjarnardottir, S., 479
Adam, E. K., 158
Adam, S., 248
Adams, G. R., 132
Adams, M. J., 359, 367
Adams, R. J., 90, 236, 237
Adamson, L., 418
Adamson, L. B., 260, 261
Afflerbach, P., 361, 364, 391
Agency for Toxic Substances and
    Disease Registry, 139
Ahadi, S. A., 7, 431
Aidinis, A., 370
Ainsworth, M. D. S., 17, 148, 407,
    408, 410, 412, 413
Aitchison, J., 317, 328, 331
Akhtar, N., 326
Akiskal, H. S., 427
Alapack, R., 544
Albersheim, L., 415
Albert, M., 523
Alberto, P. A., 140
Aldridge, M. A., 38, 332
Alessandri, S. M., 522
Alessi, N. E., 123
Alexander, A. L., 351
Alexander, D. B., 129
Alexander, K. L., 178, 299, 553
Alexander, K. W., 261
Alexander, P. A., 250
Alfassi, M., 219
Algozzine, B., 538
Alibali, M. W., 203, 241, 250,
    266, 282, 321, 332, 379
Alland, A., 394
Alleman, J., 391
Alleman, L. M., 115, 121
Allen, J., 308
Allen, S. E. M., 317
Allen, W., 454
Allison, K. W., 464
Allsopp, D. H., 268
Almeida, D. M., 7, 153, 451
Als, H., 89, 418
Altermatt, E. R., 387
Alvarez, W. F., 161
Alvermann, D. E., 362, 368
Alward, K. R., 220–221
Ambrose, D., 308
American Academy of Pediatrics
    (AAP), 119
American Academy of Pediatrics
    (AAP) Committee on
    Nutrition, 111, 121
American Academy of Pediatrics
    (AAP) Committee on Pediatric
    AIDS and Committee on
    Adolescence, 133
American Academy of Pediatrics
    (AAP) Committee on
    Pediatric AIDS and
    Committee on Infectious
    Diseases, 141

American Academy of Pediatrics
    (AAP) Committee on Sports
    Medicine and Fitness, 128
American Academy of Pediatrics
    (AAP) Committee on Sports
    Medicine and Fitness and
    Committee on Injury and
    Poison Prevention, 126
American Academy of Pediatrics
    (AAP) Task Force on Infant
    Sleep Position and Sudden
    Infant Death Syndrome,
    128, 129
American Association on Mental
    Retardation, 308
American Obesity
    Association, 122
American Psychiatric Association,
    268, 269, 427, 428
American Psychological
    Association, 34
American Speech-Language-
    Hearing Association, 350
Ames, C., 127, 494, 505
Ames, E. W., 417
Amirkhanian, Y. A., 133
Amorosi, S., 452
Amsel, E., 202
Anastasi, A., 288, 289, 290
Andenas, S., 422
Anderman, E. M., 443, 494,
    495, 505
Anderman, L. H., 454, 495
Andersen, C., 252
Anderson, C., 265, 561
Anderson, C. A., 265, 471, 474,
    561, 562
Anderson, D. A., 545
Anderson, D. R., 255, 480, 561
Anderson, J. C., 246
Anderson, K. J., 543
Anderson, L. W., 184, 185
Anderson, M. L., 482, 483n
Anderson, R. C., 242, 324, 350,
    367, 368
Andersson, B. E., 556
Andison, F. S., 561
Andrade, A., 302
Andrews, D. W., 466, 540
Andrews, G., 202, 224, 248, 461
Andrews, J. F., 364
Anglin, J. M., 325
Anisfeld, E., 416
Annahatak, B., 342
Annett, R. D., 139
Ansul, S. E., 418
Antelman, S., 427
Antequerra, F., 64
Anthony, J. L., 334, 359
Anyon, J., 551
Aparicio, S. A., 64
Apospori, E., 176
Applebaum, M. I., 238
Applegate, B., 268
Araujo, J., 217
Archer, J., 471
Archer, S. L., 406
Arcus, D. M., 7
Argentieri, L., 562
Armon, C., 202
Arnett, J. J., 422
Arnold, A. P., 452
Arnold, D. H., 471

Arnold, M. L., 519, 522
Aronson, S. R., 157
Arsenio, W., 462, 463
Artman, L., 203
Asai, S., 179
Asante, M. K., 178
Ascione, F. R., 471, 561
Ash, G. E., 361
Ashcraft, M. H., 376
Asher, S. R., 429, 463, 476, 532,
    534, 537
Ashmead, D. H., 237
Ashmore, R., 464
Ashton, P., 553
Aslin, R. N., 237, 318, 326, 332
Asmussen, L., 154
Assing, R., 288
Assor, A., 443
Astington, J. W., 253, 254, 459,
    460, 461
Astor, R. A., 463, 474
Astuti, R., 264
Atkinson, R. W., 318
Attanucci, J., 522, 523
Attie, I., 123, 446
Atwater, E., 132
Au, K. H., 341, 365
Au, T. K., 318, 319, 326
Austin, C. M., 323
Ausubel, D. P., 325
Autti-Raemoe, I., 81
Avenevoli, S., 150
Avis, J., 459
Ayres, L. R., 259, 513
Azmitia, M., 453
Azuma, H., 424

Babad, E., 552
Bachman, J. G., 132, 446
Backlund, B. A., 546–547
Baer, D. M., 507
Bagley, C., 556
Bagwell, C. L., 468, 537
Bahr, H. M., 37
Bahrick, L. E., 238
Bailey, J. M., 157, 545
Bailey, L., 326
Bailey, U. J. O., 294, 556, 557
Baillargeon, R., 201, 243, 263,
    264, 384, 385, 387
Bakari, R., 178, 179, 365
Bakeman, R., 84, 261, 466
Baker, C., 346, 348
Baker, J. H., 373
Baker, L., 358, 359
Baker, L. A., 471
Bakermans-Kranenburg, M. J., 415
Baldwin, A., 296
Baldwin, C., 296
Baldwin, D. A., 261, 319, 458
Baldwin, M. W., 415
Balegh, B., 453
Bales, R. J., 362
Baltes, P. B., 8, 18 407, 456
Bandi Rao, S., 330
Bandura, A., 13, 17, 18, 42, 43,
    162, 387, 388, 443, 452, 471,
    490, 495, 499, 502, 503,
    510, 534
Banerjee, M., 420
Bank, S., 165
Banks, C. A. M., 175, 180, 341,
    343, 453, 458, 552

Banks, J. A., 175, 179, 180, 181,
    341, 343, 453, 458, 538, 552
Barab, S. A., 304
Baranowski, T., 122
Barbaranelli, C., 387, 534
Barchfeld, P., 386, 387
Barga, N. K., 268
Barker, G. P., 498
Barker, S., 119
Barker, T. A., 359
Barkley, R. A., 268, 269
Barlow, S. M., 128
Barnas, M. V., 414, 556
Barnes, G. M., 117
Barnett, J. E., 248
Barnett, W. S., 553
Baron, M. A., 351
Baron-Cohen, S., 464
Barr, H. M., 114, 293
Barr, R., 165
Barrett, J. G., 428
Barringer, C., 327
Barron, R. W., 359
Bartini, M., 474, 532
Bartko, W. T., 175
Bartlett, E., 326
Bartlett, E. J., 371
Bartlett, L., 532n
Barton, K. C., 207, 208, 390
Bartsch, K., 459
Basinger, K. S., 469, 523, 536, 537
Bassett, D. S., 429
Basso, K., 340
Basso, K. H., 180
Bates, E., 320, 321, 330
Bates, J., 161
Bates, J. E., 73, 129, 431, 433,
    466, 532, 534
Bathurst, K., 162
Batshaw, M. L., 309
Batson, C. D., 472, 519
Battistich, E., 425
Battistich, V., 492, 549,
    550–551
Bauer, P. J., 241, 242, 261, 262,
    337, 390, 447
Baumeister, R. F., 443
Baumert, J., 444
Baumrind, D., 160, 161
Bavelier, D., 317
Bax, M., 473
Baydar, N., 183
Bay-Hinitz, A. K., 479
Bayley, N., 290, 297
Beal, C. R., 371, 372
Beardsall, L., 424
Bearison, D., 333
Bearison, D. J., 137
Beaty, J. J., 113, 392
Beauboeuf-LaFontant, T., 178
Beauchamp, G. K., 78
Beaudry, M., 119
Bebeau, M., 519
Bebko, J. M., 195
Bechtoldt, H., 562
Beck, I. L., 361
Beck, M., 309, 309n
Beck, N. C., 557
Becker, J. B., 422
Beech, B. M., 126
Beeghly, M., 459
Beeman, M. J., 317
Behrman, R. E., 137, 171, 184

Beirne-Smith, M., 310
Belenky, M. F., 166, 186
Belfiore, P. J., 507, 510, 511, 512
Belka, D. E., 115, 121
Bell, L. A., 502
Bell, N., 209
Bell, P., 260
Bell, R. Q., 164
Bellugi, U., 321
Belsky, J., 152, 153, 411, 556
Belzer, M. E., 135
Bem, S. L., 451, 452
Benbenishty, R., 463
Benbow, C. P., 298
Bendelow, G., 119
Bender, G., 474
Bendixen, L. D., 260
Benes, F., 106
Benet-Martínez, V., 176
Bennett, G. K., 382
Bennett, R. E., 423, 552
Bennett, R. T., 251
Bennetto, L., 471
Benoit, D., 417
Benson, B., 542, 543, 544
Benson, C., 390
Benson, F. W., 463
Benton, S. L., 373, 374
Benware, C., 217
Bereiter, C., 265, 371, 386
Berenson-Howard, J., 121
Berenstain, J., 465
Berenstain, S., 465
Bergemann, L., 460
Berk, L. E., 211, 508, 533
Berkowitz, M. W., 516
Berlin, L. J., 411
Berliner, D. C., 299
Berman, S., 515
Bermejo, V., 376
Bernardi, J. D., 242
Berndt, T. J., 475, 495, 535, 536,
    537, 540
Bernier, A., 414
Bernieri, F., 503
Berninger, G., 340
Berninger, V. W., 360, 371, 372
Berquin, P. C., 104
Berry, E. J., 177
Bertenthal, B. I., 237
Berthier, N. E., 372
Bertoncini, J., 236
Berzonsky, M. D., 450
Best, D. L., 256
Beyers, J., 129
Bhavnagri, N. P., 468
Bialystok, E., 318, 347, 348
Bibace, R., 137
Biddle, S. J., 557
Biddlecomb, B., 379, 381, 383
Bidell, T., 204
Biemiller, A., 217, 381, 508
Bierman, K. L., 534, 535, 538
Bigbee, M. A., 476
Bigelow, B. J., 543
Biggar, H., 153
Biggs, J., 255
Bigler, R. S., 176, 452, 499
Bijeljac-Babic, R., 236
Binder, L. M., 507
Binet, Alfred, 283–284, 287n
Binns, K., 452
Bird, A., 64

Birnbaum, D. W., 423
Bishop, S. J., 167
Bivens, J. A., 211
Bjorklund, D. F., 12, 17, 27, 108, 125, 126, 240, 241, 246, 252, 447, 448
Blachford, S. L., 71
Black, J. E., 108, 237
Black, M. M., 121
Blackbourn, J. M., 310
Black-Gutman, D., 463, 464
Blackson, T. C., 429
Blades, M., 391
Blair, C., 508
Blakemore, C., 8
Blasi, A., 519, 522
Blazevski, J. L., 494
Bleeker, M. M., 381
Blehar, M. C., 407
Bleiker, C., 377
Blinde, P. L., 507
Block, J., 131
Block, J. H., 423, 452, 475, 502
Block, N., 301
Bloom, B. S., 296
Bloom, K., 338
Bloom, L., 320, 351
Bloom, P., 458
Blue-Banning, M., 539
Blumberg, F. C., 53
Blumenthal, J., 107
Blyth, D. A., 117, 118, 448
Bobrow, D., 157
Boccia, M., 418
Bochenhauer, M. H., 392
Bocian, K. M., 270
Bodrova, E., 213
Boekaerts, M., 381, 425
Boekkooi, P. F., 38, 78
Bogin, B., 73
Bohannon, J. N., 317, 340
Bohn, C. M., 126, 270, 466
Boivin, M., 444, 473, 474
Bol, L., 253, 469
Boles, R. E., 140
Bolt, E., 510
Bond, L. A., 186
Bond, M. A., 349
Bond, M. H., 476
Bong, M., 442, 443, 505
Bonica, C., 463, 543
Bonk, C. J., 373
Bookstein, F. L., 293
Boom, J., 518, 525
Booth, C. L., 537
Booth, P. B., 417
Bordelon, K., 131
Borkowski, J. G., 157, 258, 309, 497
Bornstein, M., 38
Bornstein, M. H., 81, 175, 213, 292, 297, 324
Bortfeld, H., 317
Borza, M., 38
Bosacki, S. L., 460, 465
Bosch, J. D., 474
Botvin, G. J., 131, 134
Bouchard, T. J., 73, 291, 292
Bouchey, H., 470
Bourg, T., 262
Boutte, G. S., 179, 181, 550
Bowden, D., 461
Bowen, G. M., 216
Bower, N. J. A., 237
Bower, T. G. R., 38, 237
Bowers, P. G., 364
Bowey, J., 344
Bowlby, J., 17, 148, 407, 408, 413, 414
Bowman, B. T., 343
Boyes, M., 460
Boykin, A. W., 302
Brabham, E. G., 328
Bracken, B. A., 280, 284, 288, 290, 291, 475, 540
Bradford, L. W., 71

Bradley, L., 344
Bradley, R. H., 159, 162, 293
Bradley, S. J., 557
Bradshaw, C. P., 472
Bradshaw, D., 433
Bradshaw, P., 532n
Brady, J. E., 537
Brady, M. A., 69
Brady, M. P., 538
Braeges, J. L., 520
Braine, L. G., 393
Brainerd, C. J., 225
Brakke, N. P., 535
Bramlett, M. D., 153
Branch, C., 458, 464
Brannon, M. E., 374, 381
Branstetter, W. H., 472, 520
Brauner, J., 555
Bray, N. W., 310
Brazelton, B., 418
Brazelton, T. B., 238
Brazelton Institute, 290
Breaux, C., 152, 156
Bredekamp, S., 19, 121, 556
Brehm, D., 123
Breinlinger, K., 263–264
Brenner, E. M., 420
Brenner, L. A., 463
Brent, S. B., 325
Bresnick, S., 470
Bretherton, I., 420, 444, 459
Brewer, W. F., 264, 265
Briars, D. J., 383
Bridges, L. J., 152
Bridges, M., 154
Bright, J. A., 167
Brinton, B., 336
Bristol, M. M., 269
Britt, M. A., 259, 391
Britto, P. R., 544
Britton, B. K., 264
Brodsky, E., 335
Brody, G. H., 165, 521
Brody, N., 278, 279, 280, 288, 291, 292, 296, 299
Brody, S., 111
Brodzinsky, D. M., 156
Broerse, J., 346
Brone, R. J., 123
Bronfenbrenner, U., 16, 18, 89, 148, 150, 151, 161, 294
Bronson, M. B., 126, 253, 489, 508, 509, 510, 511, 512, 524
Bronson, W. C., 466
Brooks, F., 474
Brooks-Gunn, J., 89, 117, 123, 133, 156, 162, 173, 183, 184, 293, 294, 297, 299, 300, 447, 544, 556, 557
Brophy, J. E., 391, 453, 494, 500, 502, 503, 505, 506, 552
Brown, A., 334
Brown, A. L., 7, 17, 47, 100, 218, 219, 246, 550, 551, 563
Brown, B., 73
Brown, B. B., 470, 495, 532, 540, 542, 543, 559
Brown, C. A., 336
Brown, E., 236
Brown, E. G., 152, 468
Brown, J., 424
Brown, J. D., 125
Brown, J. H., 366
Brown, J. R., 424
Brown, J. S., 216
Brown, J. V., 84
Brown, K. J., 140
Brown, L. M., 107, 470, 523
Brown, R., 255, 316, 328, 329
Brown, R. D., 108, 125
Brown, R. T., 300
Brown, V. A., 417
Brownell, M. T., 74, 268
Brownlee, J. R., 466
Brown-Mizuno, C., 308
Bruck, M., 261

Bruer, J. T., 8, 105, 106, 108, 172, 238, 299, 317, 346, 347, 352
Brugman, D., 518
Bruner, J. S., 27, 206, 213, 215, 346
Bruni, M., 114
Bryan, J., 271
Bryan, J. H., 471
Bryan, T., 271
Bryant, A. L., 132
Bryant, J. B., 340
Bryant, P., 344, 370
Bryson, S. E., 269
Buchanan, C. M., 115, 422
Buchman, D. D., 562
Buchanan, T., 270
Buchsbaum, H., 447
Buckingham, D., 330
Buckley, S., 562
Budd, K. S., 123
Budwig, N., 320
Bugental, D. B., 64
Buhrmester, D., 533, 537
Buijzen, M., 561
Buitelaar, J. K., 81
Bukowski, W. M., 466, 535
Bullinger, A., 372
Bullock, J. R., 534
Bullock, M., 386, 387
Bumbarger, B., 425
Bumpus, M. F., 163
Bunce, D. M., 209
Bunch, K. M., 461
Buoncompagno, E. M., 544
Burgess, K. B., 474, 534
Burgess, S. R., 359
Burhans, K. K., 497, 502
Buriel, R., 156, 165, 175
Burkam, D. T., 388, 389, 507
Burke, J. E., 309
Burke, L., 195
Burnett, P., 506
Burnett, R. E., 374
Burns, C. E., 69, 71
Burns, K. A., 81
Burns, L., 335
Burns, W. J., 81
Burstein, K., 271
Burstyn, J. N., 472
Burtis, J., 265
Burton, L. M., 133, 156
Burton, R. V., 513
Burton, S., 445
Burts, D. C., 290
Busch, C. M., 433
Bush, P. J., 124
Bussey, K., 452
Butler, D. L., 254, 259
Butler, R., 552
Butler, R. N., 407
Butterfield, E. C., 309
Butterfield, P., 260
Butterworth, G., 217
Byne, W., 545
Byrne, B. M., 381, 442
Byrnes, J. P., 105, 207, 331, 361, 370, 372, 375, 378, 379, 381, 384, 386, 388, 389, 390, 391, 496

Cabrera, N., 152, 170
Cacioppo, J. T., 418
Caetanno, R., 176
Caggiula, A., 427
Cahan, S., 203
Cai, Y., 510
Cain, K., 362, 364
Cairns, B. D., 473
Cairns, H. S., 317, 318, 324, 328, 331
Cairns, R. B., 473
Caldwell, B. M., 162, 293
Caldwell, C. H., 118
Caldwell, M. S., 443, 469
Calfee, R. C., 220

Callanan, M. A., 165, 265, 326, 385, 387, 489
Camburn, E., 168, 487, 496, 507, 510, 550, 552, 554, 555
Cameron, C. A., 335, 371, 372
Cameron, J., 506
Campbell, A., 541
Campbell, B., 280
Campbell, D. T., 43
Campbell, D. W., 125
Campbell, F. A., 37, 294, 299, 557
Campbell, J. D., 443
Campbell, L., 280, 304
Campbell, S. B., 418, 464
Campbell, T., 255
Campbell, T. F., 351
Campione, J. C., 550, 551, 563
Campos, J. J., 237, 260, 412, 413, 417, 418, 420, 433, 472–473
Campos, R., 42
Camras, L. A., 408, 417
Cancellaro, C. A., 63
Candee, D., 519
Canfield, R. L., 374
Capelli, C. A., 333
Caplan, J. G., 558
Caplan, M., 473
Caplovitz, A. G., 561
Caplow, T., 37
Capodilupo, A., 375
Capron, C., 293
Caprara, G. V., 387, 534
Cardelle-Elawar, M., 379, 381
Cardone, M., 562
Carey, S., 7, 122, 201, 264, 324, 325, 326, 389
Carlin, P. L., 133
Carlo, G., 460, 471, 472
Carlsmith, J. M., 117
Carlson, E. A., 413, 414
Carlson, N. R., 69, 101, 102, 103, 104, 109, 128
Carlson, S. M., 461
Carns, D., 544
Caroli, M., 562
Caron, A. J., 418
Caron, R. F., 418
Carpenter, M., 260, 326
Carr, M., 255, 306, 362, 379, 381, 383
Carraher, D. W., 202, 217
Carraher, T. N., 217
Carrol, B., 294
Carroll, J. B., 278
Carroll, J. L., 201
Carroll, Lewis, 347
Carter, D. E., 463
Carter, K. R., 305, 306, 307
Carter, M. C., 417
Cartledge, G., 429, 476
Carver, L., 269
Casanova, U., 179, 350
Casas, J. F., 474
Case, R., 10, 17, 18, 184, 204, 374, 375, 377, 378, 381, 383, 393, 394
Case-Smith, J., 114
Casey, B. J., 106, 109, 268
Casey, B. M., 37
Casey, G., 515
Casey, W. M., 513
Cashon, C. H., 201, 237, 243, 263, 385, 387
Casper, V., 162
Caspi, A., 184, 424, 433
Cassidy, D. J., 246
Cassidy, J., 410, 417
Cassidy, M., 411
Cassidy, S. B., 71
Castellanos, F. X., 104
Casten, R., 464
Castro, R., 497
Catania, J. A., 133
Cattell, R. B., 279
Cauce, A. M., 133

Cauley, K. M., 454
Cazden, C. B., 344, 392
Ceci, S. J., 10, 261, 294, 295, 299, 301
Center for the Future of Children, 156, 183, 184
Centers for Disease Control and Prevention, 88, 119, 122, 123, 125, 127, 131, 132, 135, 137
Cernkovich, S. A., 177
Certo, J., 454, 494
Cerullo, F., 423, 552
Cervantes, R., 176
Chabon, B., 133
Chachere, J. G., 561
Chadwick, B. A., 37
Chafel, J. A., 108, 184, 213, 220, 551
Chaffee, S. H., 165
Chafin, C., 454
Chall, J. S., 361, 364, 365
Chalmers, J., 465
Chambers, J. C., 389
Chambers, J. H., 561
Chambless, C. B., 454
Chambliss, M. J., 374
Champagne, A. B., 209
Chan, C., 265
Chan, K. S., 507
Chan, R. W., 157
Chan, S. Q., 156
Chanana, N., 557
Chance, G., 236
Chandler, A. L., 153
Chandler, M., 460, 520
Chandler, M. J., 460
Chandler, T. J. L., 451
Chang, B., 447
Chang, C. M., 175, 500
Chang, F., 330
Chang, H., 38
Chao, R. K., 160, 161, 175
Chapman, J. W., 448
Chapman, M., 472
Chapman, S., 259
Charity, A. H., 350
Charles A. Dana Center, 557
Charlesworth, R., 290
Charlesworth, W. R., 536
Charlton, K., 557
Charner, I., 559
Charon, R., 86, 87, 88
Chase-Lansdale, P. L., 133, 156
Chasnoff, I. J., 81
Chassin, L., 131, 132
Chatters, L. M., 454
Chavez, A., 100
Chavkin, N. F., 162
Chavous, T. M., 454
Chazan-Cohen, R., 19
Cheek, N. H., 470
Chen, C., 178
Chen, S.-J., 412
Chen, X., 344, 406, 423, 476
Chen, Z., 255
Cherlin, A. J., 153, 154, 155
Chess, S., 297, 432, 433, 435
Chi, M. T. H., 243, 385
Chiarello, C., 317
Childs, K. E., 429
Chinn, C. A., 265
Chinn, P. C., 184, 350, 365
Chisholm, J. S., 411
Chisholm, K., 417
Chiu, C., 176, 498
Choi, S. H., 176
Chomsky, C. S., 325
Chomsky, N., 316, 317, 328, 346
Christensen, C. A., 370
Christenson, P., 335
Christenson, S. L., 507
Christian, S. H., 346
Christie, J. F., 213, 338, 344
Chrousos, G. P., 117
Chu, Y.-W., 114
Chuang, S. S., 152

Chukovsky, K., 324
Cicchetti, D., 422, 427
Cider, M., 559
Cillessen, A. H. N., 533, 534
CJ Foundation for SIDS, 128
Clark, B., 305, 307
Clark, C. C., 541
Clark, D., 115, 121
Clark, E. V., 330
Clark, R. M., 167, 424
Clark, S., 429
Clarke-Stewart, K. A., 556
Clary, E. G., 558
Clasen, D. R., 540
Claude, D., 268
Claverie, J. M., 64
Clement, C., 202
Clément, F., 335
Clements, W. A., 165
Clifford, M. M., 456, 496
Clifford, R. M., 556
Clifton, R. K., 372
Clinchy, B. M., 166
Clingempeel, W. G., 153, 154, 160
Clore, G. L., 542
Close, L., 379
Cobb, P., 494
Cocchiarella, M. J., 327
Cochran, M., 150
Cochran-Smith, M., 56
Cocking, R. R., 562
Cody, H., 71
Coe, J., 184
Cohen, D., 237, 471
Cohen, D. J., 464
Cohen, E. G., 479
Cohen, J., 81
Cohen, L. B., 201, 237, 243, 263, 385, 387
Cohen, M. N., 182
Cohen, M. R., 114
Cohen, R. J., 288
Cohn, J., 316
Cohn, J. F., 418
Coie, J. D., 44, 45, 429, 470, 471, 473, 474, 475, 476, 534, 535
Colak, A., 457, 458
Colby, A., 517, 518
Colder, C. R., 132
Cole, D. A., 451–452, 452
Cole, K., 134
Cole, M., 149, 203, 249, 294
Cole, N. H., 268
Cole, P. M., 407, 421, 426
Coleman, K., 176
Coleman, M., 269, 513
Coles, C. D., 84
Coles, Robert, 560
Coley, R. L., 133
Coll, C., 159
Coll, C. G., 35
Collaer, M. L., 476
Collie, R., 241, 447
Collier, V. P., 318, 347, 348
Collingwood, T. R., 134
Collins, A., 216, 220, 292
Collins, A. M., 381
Collins, R., 156
Collins, W. A., 173, 292, 295, 543, 544
Colombo, J., 297
Commons, M. L., 202
Comstock, G., 561, 562
Condon, J. C., 343
Condry, J. C., 476
Cone, J., 424
Conel, J. L., 105
Conger, K. J., 160, 541
Conger, R. D., 150, 160, 541
Conley, C. S., 469
Conn, J., 544
Connell, J. P., 152, 407, 443, 491
Connelly, L. M., 464

Connolly, J., 542, 543
Connor, J. M., 298–299
Conroy, M., 424
Consortium of Longitudinal Studies, 553
Conte, R., 268
Cook, E. T., 425
Cook, V., 316, 331
Cooney, J. B., 376, 381
Cooper, C. R., 453, 458, 558
Cooper, H., 443, 453, 502, 511, 557
Cooper, R. P., 318
Coopersmith, S., 160
Copland, R., 537
Copple, C., 19, 121, 556
Coppola, M., 320
Corbett, H. D., 54–55, 253, 510
Corbetta, D., 98
Corkill, A. J., 239, 268, 309, 428, 508
Corley, R., 292
Cornell, D. G., 448
Corno, L., 511
Corsaro, W. A., 468, 553, 554
Corwyn, R. F., 159
Cossu, G., 364
Costa, L. D., 103
Costa, P. T., Jr., 433
Cota-Robles, S., 117
Côté, J. E., 406
Cote, L. R., 324
Cottrol, R. J., 179
Couchman, C. E., 415
Council for Exceptional Children, 305
Courage, M. L., 90, 237
Covington, M. V., 308, 442, 443, 470, 498
Cowan, W. M., 104, 109
Cox, C. B., 156
Cox, M., 153
Cox, R., 153
Coy, K. C., 509
Coyle, T. R., 246
Craft, D. H., 140
Craft, M., 350
Crago, M. B., 278, 317, 342
Crain, W., 406
Crandall, V. C., 505
Craven, J., 195
Craven, R., 446, 447, 448, 454
Crawford, D., 481
Crawley, A. M., 255
Creasey, G. L., 533
Crick, N. R., 428, 471, 473, 474, 476, 534
Crnic, K., 153
Crockett, L. K., 540
Croll, W. L., 423
Cromer, R. F., 318
Crosby, L., 466
Cross, D., 124, 263
Cross, W. E., Jr., 453, 454
Crouter, A. C., 163, 175
Crowell, J., 415
Crowley, K., 191, 214
Crum, R., 415
Crumbaugh, C., 383
Csikszentmihalyi, M., 470
Cuevas, A. M., 452
Culross, P. L., 171
Cumberland, A., 420
Cummings, A., 507
Cummings, E. M., 414, 556
Cummings, S. S., 126
Cunningham, A. E., 358, 367, 447, 456, 497, 498, 502
Cunningham, C. E., 271
Cunningham, L. J., 271
Cunningham, N., 416
Cunningham, T. H., 347, 348
Curran, P. J., 132
Curtiss, S., 318
Curwin, A., 326
Cutforth, N. J., 33–34, 36

Dacey, J., 509
D'Agostino, J. V., 383
Dahlberg, G., 27, 556
d'Ailly, H., 500
Dale, P. S., 321, 331, 351
D'Alessandro, J. D., 452
Daley, T. C., 295
Dalrymple, N. J., 269, 271
Damon, W., 149, 209, 225, 421, 444, 447, 454, 479, 515, 516, 517, 519, 520, 521, 536, 540
Danaher, D. L., 476
DanceSafe, 132
Dancho, K. A., 338
Daniels, A. M., 131
Dannemiller, J. L., 237
Danner, F. W., 201
Darby, B. L., 114
Darling, N., 161
Darling-Hammond, L., 28
Darlington, J., 153
Darlington, R., 557
Darwin, C., 17
Daubman, K. A., 425
Davenport, E. C., Jr., 177, 381
Davidson, A. L., 343
Davidson, F. H., 463, 519
Davidson, P., 539
Davidson, R. J., 510
Davis, B., 426
Davis, D. L., 237
Davis, G. A., 297, 308, 489, 550
Davis, H., 265
Davis, H. A., 454, 508
Davis, J., 390
Davis, K., 427
Davis-Kean, P. E., 445
Dawson, B. S., 153
Dawson, D. A., 155
Dawson, G., 269
Day, M. C., 201
Deal, L. W., 137
Deary, I. J., 89
Deater-Deakard, K., 161
Deaux, K., 465, 475, 499, 502
DeBaryshe, B. D., 426
DeCasper, A. J., 78, 237, 241, 318
De Cecco, J. P., 545
deCharms, R., 550
Deci, E. L., 217, 415, 442, 456, 490, 491, 492, 502, 503, 506, 509
De Corte, E., 220, 374, 375, 379, 381
De Courten, C., 109
DeFalco, K., 512
DeFries, J. C., 68, 268, 292
de Glopper, K., 326, 328
de Haan, M., 237
de Jong, T., 205, 206
DeKlynen, M., 429
Dekovic, M., 160
DeLain, M. T., 350
Delamater, J., 118, 544
De La Paz, S., 374
DelBoca, F., 464
Delfino, R. J., 269
Delgado-Gaitan, C., 175, 176, 333, 341
Delis, D., 38, 106, 109
DeLisi, R., 451
De Lisi, R., 209, 562
DeLisle, J. R., 308
Dell, M. L., 559
DeLoache, J. S., 243, 246, 248, 249
Delucchi, K., 425
Delugach, J. D., 535
Demarest, R. J., 86, 87, 88
DeMarie-Dreblow, D., 239
DeMaris, A., 177
deMarrais, K. B., 373
Dembo, M. H., 475, 536
Dement, W. C., 129
Demo, D. H., 446

Dempster, F. N., 239, 268, 309, 428, 508
Denier, C., 298–299
DeNisi, A., 503
Denkla, M. B., 269
Denner, J., 558
Dennis, T. A., 407
Dennis, W., 121
Denton, N. A., 182
DeRidder, L. M., 117
Derry, S. J., 221
Deshler, D. D., 268, 499, 502
Desjardins, R. N., 323
Detine-Carter, S. L., 463
Detterman, D. K., 278
Deutsch, D., 395
Deutsch, M., 481
Deutsch, N. L., 558
DeVault, G., 74
de Villiers, J., 329
Devine, P. G., 465
Devlin, B., 293
DeVoe, J. F., 472, 480
DeVries, R., 469, 521, 536
Dewey, E. G., 119, 121
Dewey, J., 119, 121
DeWinstanley, P., 562
Deyhle, D., 500
Diamond, L. M., 544, 545
Diamond, M., 104, 105, 109
Diamond, R., 268
Diamond, S. C., 429
Díaz, R. M., 344, 347, 348, 349, 537
Diaz, T., 131
Dickinson, D., 280, 360, 372
Dick-Read, G., 86
Dien, T., 149, 372, 373, 454, 502
Diener, E., 542
Dietz, W. H., 122
Digman, J. M., 433
Diller, D., 179
Dillon, D. R., 308
Dillon, P., 154
diSessa, A. A., 264, 265
Dishion, T. J., 466, 540
Dixon, C. N., 366
Dixon, M. R., 507
Dobson, D. L., 90
Dodge, K., 161
Dodge, K. A., 44, 45, 428, 462, 463, 466, 470, 471, 474, 475, 532, 534, 535
Doescher, S. M., 524
Doherty, M., 201
Doku, N. S., 561
Dolev, A., 416
Dolson, M., 395
Domitrovich, C., 425
Donaldson, M., 201, 243, 332
Donaldson, S. K., 420, 460
Donato, F., 557
Donis, K., 302
Donley, C. R., 271
Donnerstein, E., 561
D'Onofrio, B., 295
Donovan, C. A., 371
Dorn, L. D., 117
Dornbusch, S. M., 117, 160, 161, 544
Dorr, N., 453, 502
Dorris, M., 93, 293
Doucette, J., 335
Dougherty, T. M., 279
Douglas, G., 253
Dovidio, J. F., 465
Dow, G. A., 242
Downey, G., 463, 543
Downey, J., 184, 185
Downs, R. M., 243, 392
Downs, W. R., 160
Dowson, M., 494, 495
Doyle, A., 347, 476, 536
Doyle, W., 494, 532
Dromsky, A., 391
Droppleman, P., 117
Drummey, A. B., 241

Dryden, M. A., 364
Dryfoos, J. G., 557, 558
Dube, E. F., 249
Dubé, E. M., 544
Dube, M., 153
DuBois, D. L., 443
Dubowitz, H., 121
DuCette, J., 499
Dudley, B., 481
Dufour, R., 119
Dufresne, A., 253
Duguid, P., 216
Duke, P. M., 117
Dunbar, N., 453
Dunbar, Paul Laurence, 368
Duncan, C., 448, 540
Duncan, G. J., 162, 183
Duncan, P. D., 117
Dunham, F., 326
Dunham, P. J., 326
Dunlap, G., 429
Dunn, A. M., 69
Dunn, J., 165, 420, 424, 459, 515, 521
DuPaul, G. J., 476
Duran, B. J., 175
Durand, V. M., 129
Durby, D. D., 545
Durkin, K., 118, 131, 406, 423, 444, 489, 502, 523
Dutta, A., 127
Duyme, M., 293
Dweck, C. S., 422, 444, 446, 447, 452, 456, 463, 491, 492, 494, 496, 497, 498, 500, 502, 506
Dwyer, K., 480, 481
Dwyer, R., 34
Dyer, S. M., 334
Dykens, E. M., 71
Dykes, A. K., 82
Dyson, A. H., 358

Eacott, M. J., 214, 243
Eagly, A. H., 476
Easton, D., 536
Eastwood, J. D., 260
Eaton, W. O., 121, 125
Ebbesen, E., 509
Eccles, J. S., 121, 162, 175, 299, 381, 387, 422, 442, 448, 452, 456, 490, 491, 492, 494, 496, 497, 500, 502, 506, 554, 562
Eccles (Parsons), J. S., 491
Echols, L. D., 296
Eckerman, C. O., 466
Eckert, T. L., 476
Eckman, P., 476
Edwards, C. P., 121, 184, 211, 476
Edwards, L., 66, 73, 337
Edwards, P. A., 299, 366
Edwards-Evans, S., 350
Eeds, M., 368
Eftekhari-Sanjani, H., 298
Egami, Y., 415
Egan, L. C., 265, 489
Egeland, B., 162, 414, 415
Eggebeen, D., 556
Eggers-Péirola, C., 171
Eggert, K. M., 118
Ehle, D. A., 307
Ehri, L. C., 359, 360, 364, 367
Eicher, S. A., 470
Eilam, B., 511
Eilers, R. E., 346
Eisenberg, N., 74, 121, 125, 164, 175, 201, 298, 299, 388, 418, 420, 421, 422, 423, 427, 456, 460, 471, 472, 473, 475, 476, 510, 516, 519, 520, 523, 539, 561
Eisenberger, R., 456
Ekelin, M., 82
Ekwo, E., 167
Elbert, T., 110
Elder, A. D., 386

Elder, J. L., 213
El-Dinary, P. B., 255
Elia, J. P., 546
Elias, G., 346
Elicker, J., 414
Elison, J., 422
Elkind, D., 17, 117, 201, 265, 294, 448, 537, 542
Elliot, A. J., 494
Elliott, D. J., 216, 394, 395
Elliott, E. S., 491, 492, 494, 506
Elliott, R., 471
Ellis, J. A., 217
Elman, J., 319
Elmen, J., 160
Elze, D. E., 546, 547
Ember, C. R., 45, 46
Ember, M., 45, 46
Emde, R. N., 260, 418, 447, 471
Emery, R. E., 154, 166
Empson, S. B., 202, 381
Endicott, K., 152
Engle, P. L., 152, 156
English, D. J., 166, 167
Englund, M., 414
Enkin, M., 88
Ennemoser, M., 367
Enns, L. R., 121, 125
Enns, V., 415
Entwisle, D., 178
Entwisle, D. R., 553
Eppright, T. D., 557
Epstein, J. A., 131
Epstein, J. L., 162, 167, 168, 535, 537, 540, 541
Epstein, J. S., 541
Epstein, L. H., 123
Epstein, S., 446
Epstein, T., 391
Erickson, F., 343
Erickson, L. G., 362
Erikson, E. H., 10, 13, 14, 17, 404–407, 516n
Eron, L. D., 45, 561
Erwin, P., 469, 533
Esbensen, B. M., 251
Esbensen, F. A., 541
Espelage, D. L., 474
Espinosa, L., 349
Espinosa, M. P., 295
Estes, D., 459
Etaugh, A., 451
Etaugh, C., 451
Etzion-Carasso, A., 416
Evans, D. E., 7
Evans, E. M., 264, 387, 388
Evans, G. W., 184
Evans, I. M., 140
Evans, R., 389
Eylon, B., 254
Eysenck, H. J., 471
Eysenck, M. W., 271

Fabes, R. A., 121, 164, 421, 471, 472, 475, 508, 519, 520
Fabos, B., 563
Fabricius, W. V., 249
Fad, K., 310
Fagan, J. F., 279, 299
Fahrmeier, E. D., 203
Fairchild, H. H., 350
Faison, N., 520
Fake, S., 74
Faks, D. K., 157
Falbo, T., 165
Falik, L., 288
Famularo, R., 428
Fantie, B., 107
Fantini, A. E., 315, 315n, 316, 320, 323, 324, 330, 332, 336, 340, 340n, 343, 346
Fantino, A. M., 457, 458
Faraone, S. V., 268
Farber, B., 343
Farber, E. A., 414
Farivar, S., 479

Farmer, T. W., 474
Farran, D. C., 294
Farrar, M. J., 242
Farrell, M. M., 288
Farver, J. A. M., 472, 520
Fausel, D. F., 154
Feather, N. T., 491
Federal Glass Ceiling Commission, 177
Federal Interagency Forum on Child and Family Statistics, 122, 178, 183
Feeny, N. C., 472, 516, 520
Fegley, S., 520, 522
Fehr, B., 415
Feigenson, L., 325
Fein, G., 213
Fein, G. G., 425
Feingold, A., 373
Feinman, S., 260
Feiring, C., 415, 542
Feldhusen, J. F., 307, 308
Feldlaufer, H., 299
Feldman, J. F., 279
Feldman, L. H., 167
Feldman, R., 163
Feldman, S. S., 132, 153, 510, 541
Felton, M., 259
Felton, R. H., 364, 366
Fennema, E., 500
Fenson, L., 248, 323, 346
Fenton, T., 428
Fenwick, K. D., 236
Ferguson, L. L., 473
Fernald, A., 318, 332
Ferrari, M., 307
Ferretti, R. P., 309
Feuerstein, R., 214, 288, 289, 309
Fewell, R. R., 502
Fhagen-Smith, P., 453
Fiedler, E. D., 308
Field, D., 202
Field, S. L., 361
Field, T., 89, 237, 418, 556
Fielding, L., 367
Fields, J., 152, 155, 156, 157, 165
Fienberg, S. E., 293
Fier, J., 451–452
Fierros, E., 280
Fifer, W., 89
Fifer, W. P., 237, 318, 346
Filcher, I., 157
Finch, H., 285
Fincham, F. D., 498
Finchman, F. D., 154
Finders, M., 168
Fink, B., 370
Finkelhor, D., 472, 564
Finn, J. D., 507
Finn-Stevenson, M., 301, 550, 558
Firestone, P., 268
Fischer, K. W., 18, 193, 204, 442
Fisher, C. B., 35, 123, 175, 176, 177, 414
Fisher, C. W., 220
Fisher, J. D., 133
Fisher, L., 153
Fisher, P., 431
Fisher, W. A., 133
Fitzgerald, J., 371
Fitzsimmons, C. M., 326
Fives, C. J., 288
Fivush, R., 241, 248, 261, 447
Flanagan, C. A., 460, 520
Flanagan, D. P., 278
Flanagan, R., 288
Flannery, D., 161
Flannery, D. J., 132
Flavell, E. R., 250, 251, 460
Flavell, J. H., 7, 8, 10, 17, 18, 201, 203, 213, 236, 242, 250, 251, 252, 264, 321, 332, 387, 458, 459, 460
Fleege, P. O., 290
Flege, J. E., 318

Fleming, C. H., 124
Fleming, J. S., 476, 489
Fletcher, K. L., 310
Fletcher, R., 557
Flickinger, S. M., 464
Flieller, A., 202, 203, 295
Flor, H., 110
Flowers, J., 383
Flynn, J. R., 177, 294, 295, 299, 301
Foorman, B. R., 332
Forbes, D., 476
Forbes, M. L., 242, 392
Ford, D., 415
Ford, D. H., 16
Ford, D. Y., 443
Ford, M. E., 318, 336, 337, 493, 495, 541
Fordham, S., 500
Forehand, R., 153, 154
Forgey, M. A., 134
Foster, D. W., 73
Fowler, J. W., 559
Fowler, S. A., 507
Fox, K. R., 366
Fox, N. A., 241
Fraleigh, M. J., 160
Francis, G., 428
Francis, M., 371
Frank, A., 116
Frank, C., 51, 51n
Frankel, C. B., 417
Franklin, S., 203, 243, 254, 385, 386, 387
Fraser, B. J., 554
Fraser, B. S., 559
Frawley, W. B., 326
Frederiksen, J. R., 206, 387
Frederiksen, N., 206
Fredrickson, B. L., 422
Freedman, B. A., 365
Freedman, K., 179
Freeman, B., 503
Freeman, K. E., 500
Freitas, A. L., 463
French, D. C., 476
French, K. E., 116, 121, 125
French, L., 334
French, S. E., 554
Frenkel, O. J., 413
Freud, A., 17
Freud, S., 13, 14, 17, 515
Freund, L., 262
Frick, P. J., 268
Fridrich, A., 132
Friebert, S. E., 252
Friedel, J., 552
Friedman, L., 388
Friedrichs, A. G., 251
Friend, R. A., 546
Friesen, B., 426, 427
Friesen, C. K., 260
Frieze, I. H., 496
Frith, U., 364
Fritz, J., 420
Frodi, A. M., 152
Frone, M. R., 134
Frosch, C. A., 152
Frost, J. L., 126, 221
Fry, A. F., 240, 279, 488
Frye, D., 240, 459
Fu, V. R., 161
Fuchs, D., 217
Fuchs, L. S., 217, 379
Fuhrman, W., 470, 541
Fujiki, M., 336
Fujimura, N., 202, 383
Fukkink, R. G., 326, 328
Fukumoto, A., 515
Fuligni, A. J., 176, 177, 454, 500
Fulker, D. W., 279, 292
Fulkner, D. W., 471
Fuller, B., 171, 294
Fuller, D., 469, 523, 536
Fuller, F., 371
Fuller, M. L., 523

Fulmore, C. D., 464
Fulton, J. E., 121
Funk, J. B., 562
Furman, W., 542, 543
Furrer, C., 407
Furstenberg, F. F., 544
Furstenberg, F. F., Jr., 153, 154, 155
Fuson, K. C., 374, 376, 381, 382, 383
Futterman, D., 133

Gabard, D. L., 545
Gable, S., 153
Gaensbauer, T., 418
Gaertner, S. L., 465
Gagnon, I., 153
Gailey, C. W., 562
Gaines, D., 182
Gaines, S., 429
Galaburda, A. M., 364
Galambos, N. L., 163, 451
Galinsky, E., 556
Gallagher, A., 364
Gallagher, A. M., 451
Gallagher, J. J., 307
Gallahue, D. L., 100, 101, 121, 125, 127, 128, 475
Gallimore, R., 165, 221, 364, 365, 366
Gallistel, C. R., 7, 375, 381
Galluccio, L., 241
Galotti, K. M., 243
Galperin, C., 175
Gambrell, L. B., 362
Gandini, L., 121
Ganschow, L., 308
Garbarino, J., 155, 472, 480
García, E. E., 175, 179, 180, 182, 341, 348, 465
Garcia, G. E., 299, 366
García Coll, C., 27, 177
Garcia-Mila, M., 252
Gardner, H., 7, 279, 280, 303, 304, 306, 308, 392, 393, 394
Gariépy, J.-L., 473
Garmezy, N., 422
Garner, R., 362, 373
Garnier, H., 364
Garnier, H. E., 507
Garrison, L., 180, 353
Garver, K. E., 240
Garvey, C., 340, 468
Gaskins, S., 215
Gathercole, S. E., 240, 246
Gauvain, M., 16, 17, 159, 213, 215, 217, 226, 260, 261, 262, 266, 269, 319
Gavin, L. A., 470, 541
Geary, D. C., 374, 375, 376, 379, 381, 383
Gee, M., 513
Gelfand, D., 417
Gelman, R., 7, 201, 243, 336, 375, 381, 385, 387
Gelman, S. A., 263, 264, 324, 326, 330, 385, 387
Gendreau, P. L., 473
Genesee, F., 348
Gentile, D. A., 562
Gentile, J. R., 562
Gentry, R., 370, 372
George, T. P., 41
Georgi, M. C., 259
Gerber, M., 121
Gerbracht, G., 4
Gerken, L., 332
Germinario, V., 184
Gershoff, E. T., 166, 184
Gerton, J., 176
Gertzog, W. A., 265
Gesell, A., 8, 12, 17
Geva, D., 464
Gewirtz, W. M., 10
Ghatala, E. S., 258
Gheen, M. H., 443, 505

Ghetti, S., 261
Ghezzi, P. M., 507
Ghodsian-Carpey, J., 471
Gholson, B., 327
Giannouli, V., 359
Gibbs, J. C., 469, 517, 520, 523, 536
Gibson, E., Jr., 540
Gibson, E. J., 237
Gibson, J. J., 237
Gibson, W. A., 335
Giedd, J. N., 104, 106, 107
Gil, A. G., 176
Gilbert, K. K., 118
Gilbert, M. F., 346
Gilbert, M. J., 176
Gildea, P. M., 324
Gilger, J. W., 268
Gill, H. S., 108, 298
Gillam, R. B., 370
Gillberg, I. C., 269
Gillham, J. E., 429
Gilliam, W. S., 557
Gilligan, C., 407, 470, 519, 522, 523
Gilligan, C. F., 522, 523
Gilliland, H., 180, 342, 343
Gillis, J. J., 268
Gilstrap, B., 152
Gindis, B., 288
Ginsburg, D., 532, 533, 535–536
Ginsburg, G. P., 338
Ginsburg, H. P., 383
Giordano, P. C., 177
Giovaninni, D., 121
Girotto, V., 202
Gladwell, M., 428
Glauberman, N., 300
Glenn, C. G., 361
Glick, J., 10
Glucksberg, S., 336
Glusman, A., 318, 319, 326
Glynn, J., 252
Glynn, S. M., 264
Gnepp, J., 459
Gogate, L. J., 238
Gohm, C. L., 153
Golbeck, S. L., 209
Goldberg, A., 542, 543
Goldberg, A. D., 451
Goldberg, E., 103
Goldberg, M. E., 335
Goldberg, S., 413
Goldberger, N. R., 166
Goldenberg, C., 364, 365, 366, 552
Goldfield, B. A., 349
Golding, J. M., 361
Goldin-Meadow, S., 244, 245, 352
Goldsmith, H. H., 73, 510
Goldstein, A. P., 14
Goldstein, D., 556
Goldstein, M. H., 318
Goldstein, N. E., 471
Goldstein, S., 418
Goleman, D., 417
Golinkoff, R. M., 317, 318, 326, 329
Gollnick, D. M., 184, 350, 365
Golomb, C., 392, 393
Golombok, S., 157
Gomby, D. S., 137, 171
Gomez, M. L., 180, 333, 341, 343
Göncü, A., 213, 224, 468
Gonzalez-Mena, J., 424
Good, S., 505
Good, T. L., 209, 221, 259, 262, 495, 552
Goodman, G. S., 239, 242
Goodman, J., 270
Goodnow, J. J., 64, 173, 178
Goodwyn, S. W., 336, 338, 346
Gopnik, A., 458
Gopnik, M., 317
Gordic, B., 555

Gordis, E. B., 471
Gordon, C., 361
Gordon, P., 382, 393
Gordon, W., 203
Gorgoglione, J. M., 425
Gorski, R. A., 452
Gortmaker, S. L., 122
Goswami, U., 359
Gottesman, I. I., 73, 295
Gottesman, R. L., 423, 552
Gottfredson, D. C., 541
Gottfredson, G. D., 541
Gottfried, A. E., 162, 476, 489
Gottfried, A. W., 162, 305, 306, 307, 476, 489
Gottlieb, G., 18, 66, 72, 292, 296
Gottman, J. M., 161, 466, 467, 468, 470, 475, 532, 533, 534, 535, 536, 537, 539, 540, 542, 543
Goubet, N., 372
Gould, S. J., 26
Gowen, L. K., 153
Goyen, T. A., 114
Graber, J. A., 544
Grace, C. O., 505
Graesser, A., 361
Graesser, A. C., 361
Graham, C. R., 347, 348
Graham, S., 178, 250, 369, 370, 372, 373, 374, 453, 472, 480, 497, 498, 500, 502, 503, 506, 552
Grandin, T., 269, 394
Granfield, J. M., 476
Grang-Svalenius, E., 82
Granstroem, M. L., 81
Grant, C. A., 178, 179, 180, 333, 341, 343
Graue, M. E., 54
Gray, L. N., 153
Green, B. L., 27, 240, 252, 447, 448
Green, C., 368
Green, C. W., 111
Green, F. L., 250, 251, 460
Green, L., 488, 502
Green, T. M., 118
Greenberg, M. T., 412, 425, 429, 480
Greenberg, R., 237
Greene, E., 249
Greenfield, P. M., 17, 278, 476, 562, 563
Greenman, J., 111, 112
Greeno, J. G., 381, 383
Greenough, W. T., 105, 108, 237
Greenspan, D. A., 306
Greenspan, S., 476
Greenspan, S. I., 297
Greenwood, C. R., 561
Greer, B., 220
Gregg, M., 220, 392
Gresham, F. M., 268
Grether, J., 368
Gridina, N., 561
Griepentrog, G. J., 395
Griesinger, T., 443
Griffin, D. M., 350
Griffin, S., 375, 377, 379, 381, 383
Griffin, S. A., 377
Griffith, P. L., 370
Grigorenko, E. L., 279
Grinnell, K., 451
Griswold, K. S., 427
Grodzinsky, G. M., 268
Groër, M., 117
Grolnick, W. S., 491
Gromko, J. E., 305, 394
Gronlund, N. E., 54
Gross, A. M., 562
Gross, D., 161
Gross, J. N., 516
Gross, R. H., 128
Gross, R. T., 117

Gross, S., 288
Grossen, M., 209
Grosslight, L., 265
Grossman, H. L., 523
Grossmann, K., 413
Grossmann, K. E., 413, 414
Grotpeter, J. K., 476
Grotzer, T. A., 304
Grubb, H. J., 428
Gruber, R., 129
Grusec, J. E., 479, 489
Grych, J. H., 154
Guacci-Franco, N., 469
Guay, F., 444, 533, 534, 539
Guberman, S. R., 210, 215, 217
Guerin, D. W., 162
Guerra, N., 516
Guiton, G., 552
Gulotta, T. P., 132
Gulya, M., 241
Gunnell, K., 131
Gur, T., 359, 360, 364
Gustafson, G. E., 111
Gustafsson, J., 288, 299
Guthrie, B. J., 118
Guthrie, J. T., 367
Gutman, L. M., 500
Guttmacher, S., 134
Guyer, B. M., 111

Hacker, D. J., 253, 362, 469
Haden, C., 248, 261
Haden, C. A., 260
Hadley, P. A., 351
Haenan, J., 213
Hagan, H., 131
Hagen, E., 284
Hagen, J. W., 239, 249
Hagen, R., 358
Hagerman, R. J., 69, 72
Haight, B. K., 407
Haight, W. L., 213
Haith, M. M., 237, 239, 279
Haj-Yahia, M. M., 463
Hakes, D. T., 344
Hakuta, K., 346, 348
Hale, S., 240, 279
Hale-Benson, J. E., 161, 333, 337, 339, 342, 343, 346, 423, 500
Haley, A., 295
Halford, G. S., 202, 224, 243, 248, 461
Halil, T., 111
Hall, J. W., 374, 381
Hall, R. V., 489
Hallenbeck, M. J., 373
Hallowell, E., 427
Halpern, D. F., 295, 298, 349, 381, 502
Halverson, C. F., 451, 452
Hamby, S. L., 472
Hamers, J. H. M., 289
Hamill, P. V., 99
Hammer, D., 205, 254
Hammond, M., 153, 429
Hamre, B. K., 395, 554
Han, J. H., 382
Hanesian, H., 325
Hanich, L. B., 379
Hanley, D., 523
Hanley, J. R., 366
Hanlon, C., 316
Hansen, J., 361
Hanson, A. R., 503
Hardin, L., 176
Hardway, C., 500
Hare, J., 158
Harmon, R., 418
Harms, T., 556
Harold, R. D., 162
Harpalani, V., 177
Harper, F., 290
Harris, C. R., 308
Harris, J. R., 153, 154, 164, 338, 468, 469, 533, 539, 540, 541

Harris, K. R., 250, 370, 373, 374, 513
Harris, M., 318, 322, 323, 324, 326, 351, 359, 364, 365, 372
Harris, M. B., 546
Harris, M. J., 444
Harris, N. G. S., 321
Harris, P. L., 255, 263, 269, 335, 420, 458, 459, 460, 461, 464, 466, 471, 472
Harrison, A. O., 156, 453
Harste, J. C., 360
Hart, B., 327, 349
Hart, D., 445, 446, 447, 448, 449, 520, 522
Hart, E. L., 268
Hart, H., 473
Harter, S., 114, 407, 420, 422, 442, 443, 444, 445, 446, 447, 448, 449, 450, 452, 453, 456, 457, 460, 470, 492, 495, 502, 516, 516n, 533, 554
Hartmann, D. P., 41, 468
Hartup, W. W., 468, 469, 536, 540
Harvey, O. J., 540
Harwood, R. L., 406, 433
Haryu, E., 326
Hatano, G., 209, 364, 365, 372, 387, 388
Hatch, T., 7
Hatfield, E., 418
Hattie, J., 249, 253, 255
Hau, K.-T., 444, 448
Hauser, M., 325
Hauser, R. M., 301
Hauser-Cram, P., 89
Haviland, J. M., 418, 423
Hawkins, F. P. L., 195, 360
Hawkins, R. P., 157
Hay, D. F., 473
Hayes, C. D., 117
Hayes, D. P., 368
Hayne, H., 38, 241, 447
Haynes, O. M., 175
Hayslip, B., Jr., 290
Haywood, H. C., 210, 225
Hazan, C., 239
Heafner, T., 511
Healey, J., 474
Healy, A. F., 205
Healy, C. C., 383
Hearold, S., 561
Heath, G., 125
Heath, S. B., 180, 300, 322, 332, 337, 342, 368
Hecht, S. A., 379
Heckenhausen, H., 509
Hedges, L. V., 298, 364, 372, 381
Heflin, A. H., 466, 534
Hegarty, M., 298, 381
Hegland, S. M., 556
Heibeck, T. H., 326
Heinig, M. J., 119, 121
Held, R., 237
Hellenga, K., 563, 564
Helwig, C. C., 516, 520, 523
Hembree, R., 429
Hemphill, L., 339, 370, 372
Henderson, B., 204, 377
Henderson, C. R., Jr., 161
Henderson, D., 153
Henderson, N. D., 73, 431
Henkel, R. R., 474
Henker, B., 269
Hennessey, B. A., 502
Hennessey, M. G., 259
Henrichon, A. J., 460
Henshaw, S. K., 133
Henthorn, P., 395
Herbert, J., 381, 452
Herman, M., 454
Herman, P. A., 324
Herr, K., 546
Herrenkohl, L. R., 257
Herriman, M. L., 344

Herrnstein, R., 299–300
Hersen, M., 428
Hersh, R. H., 518
Hershey, K., 431
Hertel, P. T., 427
Hess, R. D., 161, 162, 175, 424, 500
Hetherington, E. M., 153, 154, 155, 158, 160, 292
Hettinger, H. R., 308
Heuwinkel, M. K., 49
Hewer, A., 10
Hewett, J., 563
Hewitt, K. L., 237
Hewson, P. W., 265
Hiatt, S., 418
Hickey, D. T., 206, 220
Hickey, T. L., 237
Hickling, A. K., 251
Hicks, L., 495
Hicks, R., 131
Hickson, F., 463, 464
Hidalgo, N. M., 167, 171, 175
Hide, D. W., 111
Hidi, S., 271, 489
Hiebert, E. H., 220, 367, 368
Hiebert, J., 383
Higgins, A., 507, 515, 521, 524
Higgins, A. T., 239
Hilden, K., 248, 249
Hill, J. P., 118
Hill, P. T., 177
Hill, R., 37
Hilliard, A., 343
Hillier, L., 236, 237
Hinckley, H. S., 366
Hinde, R. A., 536
Hine, P., 554
Hiner, M., 538
Hines, M., 476
Hinkley, J. W., 495
Hinshaw, S. P., 160
Hirky, A. E., 132
Hirsch, B. J., 558
Hirsh-Pasek, K., 220, 317, 318, 326, 329, 424
Hitch, G. J., 240, 246
Ho, C. S., 366, 381, 382
Ho, D. Y. F., 249, 423, 508n
Ho, H.-Z., 366
Hodges, E. V. E., 444
Hofer, B. K., 253, 254
Hoff, E., 327, 349
Hofferth, S. L., 117
Hoff-Ginsburg, E., 347
Hoffman, J. H., 117
Hoffman, K., 557
Hoffman, L. W., 537
Hoffman, M. L., 161, 421, 470, 471, 512, 516, 520, 521, 524
Hoffman, N. D., 133
Hogan, A. G., 111
Hogan, K., 254
Hoke-Sinex, L., 510
Hokoda, A., 498
Holliday, B. G., 178, 500
Hollingsworth, H., 268
Hollins, E. R., 149, 175, 179, 453
Holloway, S., 550, 556
Holloway, S. D., 161, 171, 538
Holmbeck, G. N., 118
Holmes, C. J., 108
Holmes, R. M., 54
Holt, K., 503
Holt, M. B., 265, 489
Holt, M. K., 474
Hom, A., 549
Honda, M., 389
Hong, Y., 176, 178, 498
Honig, A. S., 407, 465, 479
Hood, W. R., 540
Hoover-Dempsey, K. V., 162, 167, 170, 183
Hopkins, B., 121
Hopkins, Betsy, 251

Hopmeyer, A., 533
Hoppe, S. K., 176
Hopson, J., 104, 105, 109
Horacek, H., 557
Horgan, D. D., 253
Horibe, F., 346
Horn, L. J., 280
Hornyak, R. S., 507, 510, 511, 512
Horst, L., 160
Horton, P. J., 160
Horvat, M., 270
Hossain, Z., 152
Hossler, D., 175
Hough-Eyamie, W. P., 317
Houghton, C., 259
Houston, A., 561
Howe, D., 156
Howe, M. L., 390, 447
Howell, A. N., 89
Howell, J. C., 541, 542
Howell, K. L., 254
Howes, C., 410, 413, 414, 415, 417, 466, 468, 536, 556
Howie, J. D., 497
Hoyle, S. G., 537
Hoyt, J. D., 251
Hruda, L. Z., 454
Huang, H.-S., 366
Huang, I. W., 121, 125
Huang, K., 103
Huang, M.-H., 301
Hubel, D. H., 8
Huber, F., 413
Hubley, P., 260
Huckeby, E. R., 318
Huesmann, L. R., 561
Hughes, F. P., 309
Huizink, A. C., 81
Hulme, C., 270, 364, 366, 370
Hulse, S. H., 395
Humphreys, A. P., 125
Humphreys, L. G., 296
Hunt, A. K., 371
Hunt, D. E., 49
Hunt, E., 81, 292
Hunter, A. G., 118
Huntley, S. B., 308
Huntsinger, C. S., 381
Hurtes, K. P., 50
Husman, J., 503
Hussong, A., 131
Hussong, A. M., 132
Huston, A. C., 157, 299, 464, 561, 562
Hutcheson, J. J., 121
Hutchins, T., 556
Huttenlocher, J., 201, 243, 376, 381, 391
Huttenlocher, P. R., 104, 105, 109
Hwang, C. P., 152
Hyde, J. S., 121, 125
Hyde, K. L., 394–395
Hynd, C., 206
Hynd, G. W., 103, 106
Hyson, M., 220
Hyson, M. C., 424

Iacono, W. G., 292
Ievers-Landis, C. E., 362
Igoa, C., 453, 506
Imai, M., 326
Immordino-Yang, M. H., 204
Inagaki, K., 209, 387, 388
Inglis, A., 217, 381
Inhelder, B., 17
Inoff-Germain, G., 117, 423, 471
Insabella, G. M., 154
International Human Genome Sequencing Consortium, 64
Irizarry, N. L., 406
Irujo, S., 180, 340, 342
Irwin, C. E., Jr., 117
Irwin, R. A., 562
Isaac, W., 106
Isaacs, J., 538

Isabella, R., 417
Isabella, R. A., 411
Isen, A., 425
Isenberg, J. P., 4
Isolauri, E., 121
Isosonppi, R., 121
Ittel, A., 515
Ittenbach, R., 310
Izard, C., 408
Izard, C. E., 418

Jacklin, C. N., 121, 298, 299
Jackson, C. M., 111
Jackson, D., 233, 371
Jackson, D. L., 129, 242, 311, 390
Jackson, J. F., 35, 175, 414, 453
Jackson, M. A., 53
Jackson, P. W., 551
Jackson, S., 118
Jacob, B. A., 395
Jacobs, J. E., 381, 442, 490, 502
Jacobs, J. K., 507
Jacobs, M., 191, 214
Jacobs, P. J., 126
Jacobsen, B., 499, 502
Jacobsen, L. K., 104
Jacobson, K., 263–264
Jacobson, K. C., 7
Jacoby, R., 300
Jagnow, C. P., 78
Jalongo, M. R., 3–4, 5, 13
James, D. K., 78
Jamner, L. D., 269
Jansen, E. A., 476
Janssens, J. M., 160
Jarvis, P. A., 533
Jasiobedzka, U., 516, 520
Jaskulski, T., 133
Jaswal, V. K., 326
Jay, E., 389
Jaycox, L. H., 429
Jefferson, P., 364
Jeffrey, T. E., 382
Jeffries, N. O., 104
Jencks, C. M., 150
Jenkins, E., 376, 381
Jenkins, J. M., 461
Jenkins, S., 473
Jenkins, Z. N., 474
Jenks, J., 562
Jenlink, C. L., 507
Jensen, M. M., 429, 541
Jerald, J., 19
Jernigan, T. L., 38, 39, 108
Jessor, R., 131
Jessor, S. L., 131
Jimerson, S., 162, 183, 365
Jipson, J., 326
Jipson, J. L., 385, 387
Johanning, D. I., 383
John, O. P., 433
Johnsen, E. P., 213, 338, 344
Johnsen, M. C., 166
Johnson, C., 269, 394
Johnson, D. L., 293
Johnson, D. W., 481
Johnson, H. C., 426, 427
Johnson, J. S., 318
Johnson, M. H., 38, 104, 105, 109, 237
Johnson, R., 481
Johnson, R. T., 481
Johnston, J. R., 351, 370
Johnston, L. D., 132
Johnston, P., 361, 364
Johnston, T. D., 66, 73
Jones, A. L., 139
Jones, D., 370
Jones, G. P., 475, 536
Jones, H. F., 117
Jones, T., 461
Jones, W., 321
Jongsma, H. W., 38, 78
Jordan, A. B., 480, 561
Jordan, L., 268
Jordan, N. C., 376, 379

Jose, P. E., 381
Joseph, G., 157
Joshi, M. S., 424
Joshi, L., 453
Joshi, R. M., 270, 364, 366
Josselson, R., 406, 407, 451
Jovanovic, J., 476
Juel, C., 359
Juffer, F., 415
Julien, D., 153
Junkin, L. J., 444
Jusczyk, P. W., 323, 325, 326, 332
Juster, N., 346
Juvonen, J., 480, 497, 502, 538

Kaczmarek, M. G., 546–547
Kaczmarek, N., 559
Kagan, J., 7, 38, 407, 431, 433, 447, 516
Kagan, J. S., 7
Kagan, S. L., 294
Kahl, B., 257
Kahneman, D., 463
Kail, R., 240, 243
Kail, R. V., 280, 309, 359
Kaila, M., 121
Kaler, S. R., 509
Kalichman, S. C., 133
Kalish, C. W., 263, 264, 324, 330
Kamerman, S. B., 163
Kamphaus, R. W., 71
Kana, T. G., 140
Kannass, K. N., 238
Kanner, A. D., 541
Kanner, L., 544
Kaplan, A., 492, 497, 500
Kaplan, D., 379
Kaplan, N., 417
Kaplan, P. S., 318
Kapp-Simon, K., 137, 141
Karabenick, S. A., 511
Karafantis, D. M., 463
Karbon, M., 471
Kardash, C. A. M., 254
Karmiloff-Smith, A., 318, 329, 331
Karpov, Y. V., 210, 213, 225
Karweit, N., 335
Kashiwagi, K., 424
Kastman, L. M., 374
Katchadourian, H., 544
Katkovsky, W., 505
Katz, E. W., 325
Katz, L. F., 153, 161
Kaufman, A. S., 290
Kaye, D., 562
Kazdin, A. E., 428, 429
Kazura, K., 413
Kearins, J. M., 249
Keating, D. P., 388
Kedesdy, J. H., 123
Keefe, K., 495, 535
Keelan, J. P., 415
Keeton, M. T., 558
Kehr, K. S., 296
Keil, F. C., 7, 263, 327, 387, 389
Kelemen, D., 264
Keller, J. W., 271
Kellogg, R., 113, 372, 392, 393
Kellogg, R. T., 371, 374
Kelly, J. A., 133
Kelly, J. B., 153, 416
Kelly, S. D., 244
Kemler Nelson, D. G., 265, 489
Kemper, S., 337
Kennedy, C. B., 238
Kennedy, J., 243
Kennedy, M., 248
Kenneth, K., 116
Kenney, P. A., 259
Kenney-Benson, G. A., 490
Kenny, M., 509
Keogh, B. K., 291, 305, 306, 308, 309, 435, 476, 498
Kerewsky, W., 558
Kermoian, R., 237
Kern, L., 429
Kerns, L. L., 429

Kerr, B., 81
Kestenbaum, R., 414
Kiang, L., 453
Kienberger-Jaudes, R., 167
Kieran, C., 384
Kilbourne, B. K., 338
Killen, J. D., 122
Killen, M., 519, 521, 523
Killgore, W. D., 107, 109
Kilpatrick, H., 562
Kim, C. C., 382
Kim, D., 443, 492, 549, 550, 551
Kim, S.-K., 499
Kim, U., 176
Kimball, M. M., 464
Kim-Cohen, J., 184
Kindermann, T. A., 540
King, A., 257
King, E. W., 175
Kingstone, A., 260
Kinscherff, R., 428
Kintsch, W., 361
Kirby, B., 390
Kirby, J. R., 359
Kirk, K. I., 352
Kirschenbaum, R. J., 175, 180, 302
Kisilevsky, B. S., 78, 241
Kistner, J. A., 497
Kitayama, S., 453, 523
Klaczynski, P., 387
Klaczynski, P. A., 202, 243, 386
Klahr, D., 194, 249
Klassen, T. P., 139
Klebanov, P. K., 162
Kline, K., 383
Klingler, C., 344, 348
Klinnert, M. D., 260, 418
Kloo, D., 461
Kluger, A. N., 503
Knapp, M. S., 185, 539, 540, 552
Knapp, N. F., 308, 444
Knight, C. C., 204
Knobles, P., 453
Knowlton, D., 429
Knudson, R. E., 371
Knutson, J. F., 167
Kobasigawa, A., 253
Kochanska, G., 407, 509, 515, 516, 520, 521
Koehler, D. J., 463
Koenig, M. A., 335
Koeppel, J., 465
Koestner, R., 503
Kogushi, Y., 461
Kohen, D. E., 184
Kohlberg, L., 10, 14, 17, 23, 164, 425, 517–519, 520, 521, 522, 524
Kohn, M. L., 163
Koh-Rangarajoo, E., 415
Koivulehto, H., 81
Kolb, B., 107, 317
Kolbe, L., 448, 540
Köller, O., 444
Koller, S., 519
Koller, T. J., 417
Komatsu, L. K., 243
Konner, M., 424
Kontos, S., 171
Koops, W., 474
Kopp, C. B., 488, 509
Koren-Karie, N., 416
Korkel, J., 243
Korkman, M., 81
Kornhaber, A., 156
Kornhaber, M., 280, 304
Kornsand, D., 39, 108
Kosanic, A. Z., 561
Kosciulek, J. F., 499
Koskinen, P. S., 368
Koslowski, B., 238
Kotchick, B. A., 153
Kottler, J. A., 179
Kovacs, D. M., 537

Kowal, A. K., 164
Kowalski, P., 492
Kowalski, P. S., 505
Koyanagi, C., 429
Koza, J. E., 179
Kozhevnikov, M., 298, 381
Kozulin, A., 288
Kraemingk, K., 81
Krahn, D., 123
Krajcik, J., 389
Krakow, J. B., 488
Kramer, L., 164
Kramer, R., 522
Krampen, G., 456
Krapp, A., 271, 489
Krashen, S. D., 349
Krasnegor, N. A., 240
Krasnor, L. R., 534
Kratochwill, T. R., 513
Krauss, R. M., 336
Krebs, D. L., 520
Krebs, P. L., 139
Kreider, R. M., 156
Kreutzer, M. A., 252
Krieg, D. B., 381
Krishnamoorthy, J. S., 124
Krispin, O., 476
Kritt, D., 460
Kroger, J., 10
Kroger, S. M., 139
Krogh, H. R., 499
Kroonenberg, P. M., 413
Krueger, J. I., 443
Krug, C., 74
Krull, J. L., 164
Kuczkowski, R., 448, 449, 451, 509
Kugelmass, S., 393
Kuh, G. D., 555
Kuhl, P. K., 317, 322
Kuhlmeier, V., 458
Kuhn, D., 202, 203, 206, 243, 252, 254, 255, 259, 260, 265, 302, 385, 386, 387, 389
Kuklinski, M. R., 553
Kulberg, A., 132
Kulik, C. C., 308
Kulik, J. A., 308
Kullberg, V., 153
Kumpf, M., 301
Kunzinger, E. L., III, 246
Kupersmidt, J., 535
Kupersmidt, J. B., 474
Kurtines, W. M., 10, 515, 520
Kusche, C. A., 425
Kwon, Y., 376, 381, 382
Kyratzis, A., 248

Labbo, L. D., 361
LaBlance, G. R., 351
Laboratory of Comparative Human Cognition, 278
Ladd, E. C., 519
Ladd, G. W., 474, 534
Ladd, S. F., 376, 381
Ladson-Billings, G., 178, 184, 350, 458
Lafontana, K. M., 533
LaFreniere, P., 536
LaFromboise, T., 176
La Guardia, J. G., 415
Lahey, B. B., 268
Lahey, M., 351
Lajoie, S. P., 221
Lalonde, C. E., 332
LaMay, M. L., 295, 298, 349, 381
Lamaze, F., 86
Lamb, M. E., 152, 411, 416, 476, 556
Lamb, S., 472, 515, 516, 520
Lambermon, M., 414
Lamborn, S. D., 160, 161
Lampe, M. E., 69, 72
Lampert, M., 383
Landau, S., 268

Landerl, K., 364
Landesman, S., 310
Lane, D. M., 239
Lang, B., 461
Langacker, R., 320
Lange, G., 255
Lange, R. E., 308
Langfeldt, T., 544
Langlois, J. A., 137
Langone, J., 309
Langston, M. C., 361
Lanza, E., 348
Lanza, S., 442, 490
Lapan, R. T., 499
La Paro, K. M., 291
Lapsley, D. K., 118, 448, 449, 451, 509
Lareau, A., 167
Larkin, R. W., 470
Larner, M. B., 167
Larson, R., 154, 470
Larson, R. W., 492, 542, 543, 547
Larson, S. L., 381
Larson-Shapiro, N., 333
Last, C. G., 428
Latendresse, S. J., 183
Latham, G. P., 492
Laumann-Billings, L., 154, 166
Laupa, M., 516, 520
Laursen, B., 536
Lautrey, J., 204
Lave, J., 215, 216, 220, 444
Lawson, K. R., 239
Lazar, I., 557
Lazar, N. A., 240
Lazarus, R. S., 271
Lazerwitz, B., 343
Lazzaro, C., 559
Leakey, R., 26
Leaper, C., 176, 452, 543
Learning First Alliance, 480
Lears, M., 464
Lebeau, E., 153
Lebolt, A., 463
LeCompte, M., 500
Lecours, A. R., 105, 106, 109
Lee, C. D., 465
Lee, H., 480
Lee, J. H., 561
Lee, K., 335, 459
Lee, M. D., 163
Lee, O., 264, 387, 388
Lee, S., 202
Lee, V., 556
Lee, V. E., 388, 507
Leekam, S. R., 165
Lee-Pearce, M. L., 185, 387
LeFevre, J.-A., 359
Leffert, J. S., 464
Lefstein, L. M., 558
Leggett, E. L., 496, 497
Lehman, D. R., 203
Lehnhart, A., 563
Leichtman, M. D., 261
Leiderman, P. H., 160
Lein, L., 340
Leinhardt, G., 220, 259, 391, 392
Leite, A. C. C., 544
Leite, R. M. C., 544
Leite, R. W., 154
Leiter, J., 166
Lelwica, M., 418
Lemanek, K. L., 139
Lemerise, E. A., 462, 463
Lennon, R., 201, 253, 473
Lennox, C., 370
Leonard, C., 252
Leong, D. J., 213
Lerner, J. W., 268
Lerner, Richard, 18
Lerner, R. M., 8, 16, 406
Leslie, A. M., 269
Leveno, K. J., 37
Levey, L., 333
Levin, J. R., 258
Levine, C., 10

Levine, L., 447
Levine, S. C., 376
Levitt, J. L., 469
Levitt, M. J., 469, 533
Levstik, L. S., 207, 208, 390
Levy, S. R., 463
Levy, T. M., 417
Lewin, T., 470
Lewis, C., 168
Lewis, C. C., 466
Lewis, M., 415, 418, 420, 447, 522
Lewko, J. H., 543
Li, J., 278
Li, Z., 476
Liang, F., 64
Liaw, F., 556
Liben, L. S., 176, 243, 392, 452, 499
Liberman, A. M., 358
Liberman, V., 463
Lichtenberger, E. O., 290
Lickona, T., 479, 549, 551
Lidz, C. S., 288, 291
Lie, E., 241
Lieberman, A., 489, 502
Lieberman, A. B., 429
Lieberman, A. F., 416
Lieberman, D. A., 562
Lieberman, M., 517
Light, J. G., 268
Light, P., 202, 217
Lightfoot, C., 469
Lightfoot, D., 316, 317, 331
Lillard, A. S., 213, 461, 464, 500, 502
Lin, C. C., 161
Lin, M.-H., 516
Lindberg, M., 243
Linder, T. W., 502
Lindsay, J. J., 557
Lindsey, E., 152
Linebarger, D. L., 561
Linn, M. C., 121, 125, 202, 254, 259, 260, 386, 387, 389
Linn, R. L., 300
Linnenbrink, E. A., 454
Linscheid, T. R., 124
Linton, M. J., 371
Linver, M. R., 184
Lippa, R. A., 175, 381, 451, 452
Lipsitt, L. P., 8
Lipsitz, J., 558
Lipson, M. Y., 242, 361
Liss, M. B., 298
Little, L., 167, 474
Little, T. D., 456
Littlewood, W. T., 322
Lobel, A., 425
Lochman, J. E., 471, 474
Locke, E. A., 492
Locke, J. L., 317, 318, 336, 343, 346, 351
Lockhart, K. L., 447, 497, 498, 502
Lockl, K., 252, 253
Loeb, R. C., 160
Loeb, S., 294, 303
Loeber, R., 268, 473, 476
Loehlin, J. C., 433
Logan, K. R., 140
Logsdon, B. J., 115, 121, 136
Lollis, S., 461
Lombroso, P. J., 73, 100
Londer, G., 260
Long, B. J., 125
Long, D. L., 361
Long, L., 163
Long, M., 347
Long, T. J., 163
Lonigan, C. J., 334, 359
Loomis, L., 557
Lopez, A. M., 454, 458
Lopez, E., 453
Lopez, E. C., 300
Lopez, E. M., 558

López, G. R., 174
López del Bosque, R., 457
Lorenz, F. O., 150
Lorenz, K., 17, 470–471
Lorimer, M., 365
Losey, K. M., 177, 180, 342
Losoff, M., 540
Lotan, R. A., 479
Lou, Y., 221
Lovell, K., 202
Lovett, M. W., 367
Lovett, S. B., 249, 252
Low, H., 117
Low, S. M., 153
Lowery, B., 499
Lowry, R., 448, 540
Loxterman, J. A., 361
Lozano, J. M., 269
Lubinski, D., 298
Lucariello, J., 248
Luckasson, R., 297
Ludman, M. D., 71
Lüdtke, O., 444
Lueptow, L. B., 298, 499
Lui, K., 114
Luna, B., 240
Lupart, J. L., 305, 308
Luria, A. R., 17
Lussier, C. M., 289
Luster, L., 177
Luthar, S. S., 183
Lutke, J., 110
Lykken, D. T., 73, 292
Lynch, D., 537
Lynch, J. H., 414, 451, 533
Lynch, J. P., 542
Lynch, J. S., 362
Lynch, M. E., 84, 118
Lynch-Brown, C., 328
Lynd, H. M., 37
Lynd, R. S., 37
Lyon, G. R., 240
Lyon, T. D., 251
Lytle, S., 56
Lytton, H., 175

MacArthur, C. A., 373
Macarthur, J., 348
Maccoby, E. E., 160, 173, 184, 239, 292, 298, 466, 537
MacCorquodale, P., 118, 544
MacDermid, S. M., 163
Mace, F. C., 513
Mac Iver, D., 494
MacKay, I. R. A., 318
MacKay, J. M., 139
Mackey, W. C., 152
Mackintosh, N. J., 291
Mackler, K., 358
MacLean, D. J., 388, 418
MacLean, M., 424
Maclin, D., 259, 265
MacMillan, D. L., 268, 291, 305, 306, 308, 309, 476
Macomber, J., 263–264
MacWhinney, B., 317, 320, 330
Madden, C. M., 333
Madden, M., 563
Madden, N. A., 538
Mader, S., 471
Madhubuti, H., 161, 178
Madhubuti, S., 161, 178
Madison, S. M., 553
Maehr, M. L., 494, 554
Maggs, J. L., 163
Magnuson, D., 481
Magnuson, K. A., 299
Magnusson, D., 117, 118
Mahapatra, M., 523
Mahitivanichcha, K., 174
Maier, M. A., 414
Maier, S. F., 498
Main, M., 238, 410, 411, 412, 414, 417
Maker, C. J., 305, 308
Malatesta, C., 408

Malatesta, C. Z., 423
Malinsky, K. P., 546
Maller, S. J., 285
Mallick, S. K., 14
Malone, D. M., 309
Malony, H. N., 559
Mandel, D. R., 332
Manderson, L., 135
Mandinach, E. B., 511
Mandler, J. M., 248, 261
Mangelsdorf, S. C., 152, 409, 420
Manis, F. R., 268
Manz, P. H., 137, 139, 141
Marachi, R., 552
Maratsos, M., 321
Marcia, J. E., 406, 407, 449, 450, 451, 495
Marcoen, A., 81
Marcoux, S., 119
Marcovitch, S., 240, 417
Marcus, G. F., 329, 330, 331
Margolin, G., 471
Markman, E. M., 253, 326, 361, 385, 387
Marks, J., 300
Marks, M. B., 255
Markstrom-Adams, C., 132, 453, 465
Markus, H. R., 453, 495, 523
Marlow, L., 118
Marsh, H. W., 444
Marshall, N. L., 299
Martell-Boinske, L., 424
Martin, A., 177
Martin, C. L., 121, 451, 452, 463
Martin, J., 160, 184
Martin, J. M., 451–452
Martin, S. C., 139
Martin, S. S., 538
Martinez, C., 100
Martinez, G. M., 132
Maruyama, G., 165
Marx, R. W., 389
Marzolf, D., 409, 420
Masataka, N., 338
Mash, C. W., 279
Mashunkashey, J. O., 140
Masi, A., 562
Masi, W., 556
Masiello, R., 380
Mason, C. Y., 133
Mason, J., 365
Mason, J. M., 364
Mason, L., 386
Massey, C. M., 385, 387
Massey, D., 511
Massey, D. S., 182
Massimini, K., 71
Masten, A. S., 422
Masterpasqua, E., 157
Masuda, W. V., 220
Masur, E. F., 252
Mateika, J. H., 129
Mathes, P. G., 217
Matheson, C. C., 466, 468
Mathews, J., 398, 398n
Matteson, R. C., 122
Matthews, J., 392
Mattison, R. E., 428
Mattock, A., 236
Mattson, A., 117
Matusov, E., 550
Mayall, B., 119, 125
Mayer, D. L., 90
Mayer, E. V., 488, 502
Mayer, R., 23
Mayer, R. E., 108, 202, 206
Mayer, S., 150
Mayes, L. C., 81, 297
Maynard, A. E., 217
Mayringer, H., 364
Mayseless, O., 410
McAdoo, H., 159
McAdoo, H. P., 177
McAlpine, L., 180, 350
McAninch, C., 268

McArthur, D., 260
McBride-Chang, C., 359, 364, 366
McCabe, A., 278
McCall, C., 513
McCall, R. B., 38, 238, 279, 290, 294, 296, 502
McCallum, R. S., 280, 284, 285, 288, 290, 299, 300, 475, 540
McCandless, B. R., 14
McCann, T. M., 371
McCarthy, J., 133
McCarthy, M., 555
McCartney, K., 8, 73, 295, 556
McCarty, T. L., 339, 348
McCaslin, M. M., 209, 259, 262, 495
McCauley, R. N., 263
McClelland, J. L., 378
McClelland, L., 489
McClintic, S. M., 509
McCloskey, L. A., 350
McCloskey, M., 264
McCollom, T. L., 540
McCormick, C. B., 179, 181
McCoy, J. K., 165
McCoy, K., 430
McCrae, R. R., 433
McCreary, M. L., 177
McCrink, K., 375, 381
McCutchen, D., 371
McDaniel, M. A., 205
McDevitt, M., 165
McDevitt, T. M., 162, 175, 253, 318, 333, 335, 336, 337, 346, 500
McDonnell, L. M., 177
McElvain, C. K., 558
McEvoy, A. P., 494
McFadyen-Ketchum, S., 532
McGaha, C. G., 91
McGee, L. M., 364
McGowan, R. J., 293
McGregor, H. A., 494
McGrew, K. S., 278, 288
McGue, M., 291, 292, 295, 296
McGuffin, P., 73
McGuigan, F., 241
McHale, J. L., 152
McHale, J. P., 153
McHale, S. M., 175
McInerney, D. M., 494, 495
McIntire, D. D., 37
McIntosh, D. E., 285
McIntyre, C. W., 252
McKay, A., 135
McKeen, N. A., 125
McKenry, P. C., 154
McKenzie, J. K., 157
McKeough, A., 204, 337, 339, 377
McKeown, M. G., 361
McKerchar, P. M., 338
McKey, R., 556
McKinney, W. T., 427
McKown, C., 301
McLane, J. B., 113, 357, 358, 360, 364, 365, 368, 369, 371, 372, 374
McLoyd, V. C., 150, 161, 178, 183, 184, 297, 299, 300, 309, 424, 500, 552, 556, 557
McMahon, S., 368
McNalley, S., 472
McNamara, D. S., 205
McNamara, J., 132
McNamee, G. D., 113, 357, 358, 360, 364, 365, 368, 369, 371, 372, 374
McNeill, D., 317, 328
Meadows, N., 474
Medrich, E. A., 562
Mehan, H., 342
Mehler, J., 236
Meichenbaum, D., 217, 220, 221, 270, 513
Meins, E., 461
Meisels, S., 297

Meister, C., 215, 219, 221, 259
Mekos, D., 556
Mellard, D. F., 268
Melnick, S., 160
Meltzoff, A. N., 317, 322, 447, 458
Menéndez, R., 398n
Menk, D. W., 210
Mennella, J. A., 78
Menyuk, D., 340
Menyuk, P., 340
Mercer, A. R., 268
Mercer, C. D., 268
Mercer, L. K., 511
Mergulhao, E. A., 544
Merrick, S., 415
Merrill, M. A., 297
Merrill, P. F., 221
Mervis, C. B., 326, 327
Merzenich, M. M., 319
Messinger, D. S., 417
Mettetal, G., 468, 470, 536, 539, 540, 543
Metz, K. E., 10, 201, 206, 386, 387
Metzger, B., 167
Metzler, J., 382
Meyer, D. K., 493, 494
Meyers, D. T., 522
Meyers, M. K., 299
Meyerstein, I., 79
Michel, C., 293
Michel, M. K., 426
Micheli, L. J., 128
Middleton, M. J., 381, 497
Midgley, C., 299, 443, 448, 492, 494, 497, 500, 502, 552, 554
Mikach, S., 157
Milburn, J. F., 429, 476
Milch-Reich, S., 464, 476
Miles, S., 381
Miller, B. C., 542, 543, 544
Miller, C. L., 538
Miller, D., 427
Miller, F. K., 388
Miller, G. A., 324
Miller, J. G., 203, 300, 406, 464, 523
Miller, K., 376, 381
Miller, K. F., 243, 381, 382
Miller, L. S., 177, 180, 184, 299, 507
Miller, M .D., 74, 300
Miller, N., 165
Miller, N. B., 175
Miller, P., 239, 424
Miller, P. A., 472, 519
Miller, P. H., 213, 239, 459, 460
Miller, P. J., 178, 326
Miller, P. M., 476
Miller, S. A., 213, 459
Miller, S. D., 511
Miller-Jones, D., 291
Millikan, E., 464
Millrood, D., 129
Mills, G. E., 56, 59
Mills, R. S. L., 479
Millstein, S. G., 117
Minami, M., 278
Mindel, C. H., 343
Mink, J., 270
Minskoff, E. H., 465
Minstrell, V., 206, 386, 389, 390
Mischel, W., 473, 489, 509
Mistry, J., 224
Mitchell, A., 178
Mitchell, K. J., 564
Mitchell, P., 445
Mithaug, D. E., 510
Mithaug, D. K., 510
Mitru, G., 129
Mitsutake, G., 125
Mittelholtz, D. J., 302
Miura, I. T., 382
Miyake, K., 412, 433
Miyamoto, R. T., 352

Mize, J., 152, 468
Mizuta, I., 407
Modi, A. C., 139
Moffitt, T. E., 184, 424, 433
Mohatt, G., 343
Moher, D., 139
Mohn, G., 90
Moise-Titus, J., 561
Moje, E. B., 541
Molinari, L., 553, 554
Mollnow, E., 293
Molnar, D., 89
Molnar, J., 184
Moncher, M. S., 124
Money, J., 545
Monker, J., 326
Monshouwer, H. J., 474
Montagu, A., 287n, 300
Montague, D. P. F., 418
Montant, M., 366
Montemayor, R., 37, 173
Montgomery, D., 340
Moon, C. M., 318, 346
Moon, S. M., 308
Moore, C., 459
Moore, D. W., 362
Moore, G. A., 418
Moore, K. L., 67, 68n, 71, 72, 75, 76, 77, 79, 80, 81, 82, 83, 85
Moore, S. M., 133
Moorehouse, M. J., 163
Mooser, L., 335
Moran, C. E., 346, 348
Moran, S., 308, 393
Moran, T., 520
Morelli, G., 342, 412
Morgan, M., 259
Morgan, R. R., 471
Morison, S. J., 417
Morison, V., 236
Morling, B., 446
Morris, A. S., 150
Morris, D., 213, 367
Morris, M. W., 176
Morrongiello, B. A., 236, 237
Morrow, J., 422
Morrow, S. L., 545, 547
Mortimer, J. T., 173, 559
Morton, J., 237
Mosborg, S., 391
Moses, L., 458
Moses, L. J., 461
Mosher, W. D., 132, 153
Mosier, C., 224
Moss, P., 27, 556
Mounts, N. S., 160
Mounts, S., 161
Much, N. C., 523
Mueller, E., 466
Mueller, M. P., 377, 378
Muenchow, S., 557
Muhlenbruck, L., 557
Mühlnickel, W., 110
Muilenburg, L., 387, 389
Mukerjee, J., 131
Mulder, E. J. H., 81
Mullally, P. R., 165
Mullen, M. K., 261
Müller, U., 240
Mulrooney, M., 465
Mumme, D. L., 413
Munn, P., 420, 459, 521
Munro, E., 55
Munro, M. J., 318
Munroe, P. J., 152
Munroe, R. L., 152
Munson, J., 269
Murdock, T. B., 184, 552
Murphy, B., 460
Murphy, D. A., 133, 135
Murphy, G. L., 248
Murray, Charles, 299–300
Murray, H., 557
Murray, K. T., 509
Murrill, C. S., 131
Muter, V., 359

Muzio, J. N., 129
Myerson, J., 488
Mylander, C., 352

Naegele, J. R., 100
Nagell, K., 260
Naglieri, J., 211
Nagy, L., 491
Nagy, W. E., 324, 360, 364
Naigles, L., 327
Naito, M., 165
Nakagawa, N., 333
Nakata, N., 394
Nakata, T., 394
Nakazawa, C., 387, 388
Namy, L. L., 336
Narváez, D., 516, 519, 521, 523, 525
Nasir, N. S., 453
Naslund, J., 362
Nation, K., 370
National Assessment of Educational Progress, 507
National Association of Secondary School Principals, 23
National Campaign to Prevent Teen Pregnancy, 133
National Center for Education Statistics, 182, 184, 558
National Center for Missing and Exploited Children, 564
National Council for Accreditation of Teacher Education, 21
National Human Genome Research Institute, 64
National Joint Committee on Learning Disabilities, 268
National Middle School Association, 22
National Research Council, 106, 109, 121, 166
NCSS Task Force on Ethnic Studies Curriculum Guidelines, 179
Neal, M. C., 471
Neale, B., 158, 158n
Nebelsick-Gullet, L., 259
Neckerman, H. J., 473
Neel, R. S., 474
Neemann, J., 422
Neff, J. A., 176
Neiss, M., 117
Neisser, U., 278, 279, 288, 290, 292, 293, 295, 296, 298, 299, 300, 301, 304
Neitzel, C., 510
Nelson, C. A., 104, 110, 241, 293
Nelson, D. A., 474
Nelson, K., 193, 211, 241, 242, 243, 248, 264, 319, 336, 338, 346, 349, 447
Nelson, P. A., 373
Neumann, C., 295
Neville, H. J., 317
Newcomb, A. F., 468, 535, 537
Newcombe, N. S., 201, 241, 243, 264
Newman, L. S., 246
Newman, R. S., 511
Newman, S. E., 216
Newport, E. L., 318, 326, 332, 351, 352
Newson, E., 214, 260
Newson, J., 214, 260
Newson, M., 316, 331
Ng, F. F., 490
Nguyen, S. P., 248
Nias, D. K. B., 471
NICHD Early Child Care Research Network, 294, 411, 415, 556
Nicholls, J. G., 494, 496, 497, 502
Nichols, K. E., 516
Nichols, M. L., 308

Nichols, P. D., 302
Nichols, S. L., 552
Nicholson, S. C., 124
Nicolson, S., 52, 53
Nieto, S., 348
Nigg, J. T., 160
Nijhuis, J. G., 38, 78
Nilsson, D. E., 71
Ningiuruvik, L., 342
Ninio, A., 358
Nippold, M. A., 324, 325, 333
Nisbett, R. E., 203, 471
Nishina, A., 480
Niven, C. A., 85
Nix, R. L., 466
Noffke, S., 57
Nolen-Hoeksema, S., 422, 427
Noll, E., 177
Noll, J., 280
Nommsen-Rivers, L. A., 119, 121
Nomura, Y., 89
Nord, C., 155, 557
Nordby, C. J., 511
Nosyce, M., 416
Nottelmann, E. D., 117
Nourot, P. M., 220–221
Novak, J. D., 325
Nowell, A., 298, 364, 372, 381
Nucci, L. P., 480, 515, 516, 517, 520, 521, 522, 523, 524, 525
Nucci, M. S., 516
Nundy, S., 425
Nunes, S. R., 367
Nunes, T., 370
Nunner-Winkler, G., 523
Nusbaum, H., 244
Nye, B., 557

Oakes, J., 552
Oakes, L. M., 224, 238, 265, 489
Oakhill, J., 362, 364
Oatley, K., 425
O'Boyle, M. W., 108, 298
O'Brien, K., 562
Ochs, E., 322
O'Connor, T. G., 156, 417
Odom, R. D., 237
Oettingen, G., 456
Ogbu, J. U., 177, 180, 297, 300, 301, 343, 350, 500
Ogden, E. H., 184
O'Grady, W., 316, 317, 321, 322, 323, 324, 328, 329, 330, 346
Oh, S., 293
O'Hara, N. M., 122
Oishi, S., 153
Okagaki, L., 175, 302, 382
Okamoto, Y., 10, 184, 204, 374, 377, 381, 382, 383, 393, 394
Oki, M., 107
Oldfather, P., 114, 495
O'Leary, K. D., 489
O'Leary, S. G., 153, 489
Oligny, P., 473
Oliver, J. M., 268
Oller, D. K., 346
Olneck, M. R., 499
O'Loughlin, M., 202
Olson, D. R., 7, 201
Olson, H. C., 81
Olswang, L., 331
Olweus, D., 117
O'Malley, P. M., 132, 446
Oppenheim, D., 416
Oppenheimer, L., 460
Op't Eynde, P., 379
O'Reilly, A. W., 213
Orlans, M., 417
Ormrod, J. E., 129, 242, 244, 249, 306, 311, 390, 481
Ormrod, R., 472
Ornstein, P. A., 10, 260
Ornstein, R., 317
Orobio de Castro, B., 474
Ortiz, C., 471
Ortony, A., 333, 334, 338, 346

Osborne, J. W., 301
Oser, C., 81
Osgood, D. W., 442, 490
Osher, D., 480, 481
Oskamp, S., 458, 465
Oster, H., 236
Osterman, K. F., 549, 551
O'Toole, M. E., 481
Ottinger-Albergs, W., 241
Owen, M. J., 73
Owens, C. R., 471
Owens, R. E., Jr., 211, 316, 322, 324, 325, 330, 331, 333, 334, 336, 337, 338, 340, 344, 346, 349, 350, 360, 361, 364, 370, 371, 469
Owens, S. A., 113
Oyserman, D., 495
Ozmun, J. C., 100, 101, 121, 125, 127, 128, 475
Ozretich, R. A., 564

Padilla, M. J., 389
Paget, K. F., 460
Page-Voth, V., 374, 503
Paik, H., 561, 562
Paik, S. J., 183
Paikoff, R. L., 117, 173, 544
Painter, K. M., 175
Pajares, F., 373, 454, 498, 502
Palermiti, A. L., 116
Palermo, D. S., 325
Paley, V. G., 475
Palincsar, A. S., 47, 149, 209, 217, 218, 219, 225, 257, 479
Pallotta, J., 380
Palmer, E. L., 206
Palombaro, M. M., 140
Pan, J., 387, 388, 500
Pang, V. O., 171, 179, 181, 503
Panksepp, J., 270
Panofsky, C. P., 358
Paolitto, D. P., 518
Papernow, P., 155
Papousek, H., 111
Papousek, M., 111
Paquette, A., 81
Parada, R. H., 474
Parcel, G. S., 122
Parillo, M., 326
Paris, S. G., 259, 358, 361, 447, 456, 496, 497, 498, 502, 509, 513
Park, L., 523
Parke, R. D., 10, 152
Parker, D. A., 545
Parker, J. G., 466, 532, 535, 537
Parker, K. C., 417
Parker, W. D., 306, 308
Parkhurst, J., 468, 533
Parkin, L., 165
Parks, C. P., 539, 541
Parl, S., 556
Parrila, R. K., 359
Parten, M. B., 466, 467
Pascarella, E. T., 202
Pascual, L., 175
Pascual-Leone, J., 518–519
Passler, M., 106
Pasternack, J. F., 473
Pastorelli, C., 387, 534
Pate, R. R., 125
Patel, E., 559
Patrick, H., 454, 508, 534, 550
Pattee, L., 535
Patterson, C. J., 157, 545, 546
Patterson, G. R., 73, 164, 426, 429, 540
Patterson, M. L., 552
Patton, J. R., 310, 351, 511
Pauen, S., 248
Paul, R., 332
Paus, T., 108, 109
Pavlov, Ivan, 17
Pawl, J. H., 416

Pawlas, G. E., 184, 186
Paxton, R. J., 391
Pea, R. D., 282, 304
Peak, L., 502
Peake, P. K., 489
Pearsall, S., 386
Pearson, D. A., 239
Pearson, P. D., 350, 361
Pedersen, J., 473
Pederson, D. R., 213
Peduzzi, J. D., 237
Peeke, L. A., 451–452
Pekrun, R., 414
Pelham, W. E., Jr., 464
Pellegrini, A. D., 39, 46, 53, 54, 121, 125, 126, 270, 291, 466, 474, 476, 532, 534
Pelletier, J., 253, 254, 459, 460, 461
Pellicer, L. O., 184, 185
Peña, E., 289
Pence, A., 27, 556
Penner, A. M., 381, 387, 388
Pennington, B. F., 268, 471
Pepler, D. J., 461
Perea, P., 176
Pereira, L., 539
Peretz, I., 394–395
Pérez, B., 179, 349, 358, 365
Perez-Granados, D. R., 165
Perfect, T. J., 251
Perfetti, C. A., 259, 332, 359, 361, 371
Perkins, D. N., 216, 282, 291, 302, 304, 305, 310
Perner, J., 165, 201, 459, 460, 461
Perney, J., 367
Perret-Clermont, A., 209
Perry, C., 366
Perry, C. L., 124
Perry, M., 381
Perry, N. E., 259, 505, 511, 513
Perry, S., 556
Perry, W. G., Jr., 253, 254
Perry-Jenkins, M., 175
Persaud, T. V. N., 67, 68n, 71, 72, 75, 76, 77, 79, 80, 81, 82, 85
Pesetsky, D., 332
Pessar, L. F., 427
Peters, A. M., 316, 326
Petersen, A., 123
Petersen, A. C., 451
Peterson, 498
Peterson, A. C., 118, 540
Peterson, B. E., 407
Peterson, C., 497, 498, 502
Peterson, D., 541
Peterson, J. L., 155
Peterson, L., 472
Peterson, P. L., 214, 215
Peterson, R. F., 479
Petrie, S., 470
Petrill, S. A., 7, 292, 296
Pettit, G., 161
Pettit, G. S., 152, 466, 468, 532, 534
Pettito, A. L., 212
Pettito, L. A., 317, 348, 351, 352
Pfeifer, M., 510
Pfeiffer, S. L., 359
Phelan, P., 343, 422, 495
Phelps, L., 288
Phillips, A. T., 459
Phillips, D., 443, 556
Phillips, D. A., 303
Phillips, M., 552
Phinney, J. S., 177, 444, 453, 464
Piaget, J., 8, 9, 10, 11, 14, 17, 192–209, 210, 211, 213, 214, 221, 222, 224, 225, 226, 228, 234, 236, 238, 242, 243, 244, 264, 265–266, 280, 336, 375, 458n, 469, 489, 492, 515
Pianta, R. C., 291, 395, 554
Piche, C., 452

Pidada, S., 476
Pierce, K. M., 557
Pierce, S. H., 255
Pierson, Greg, 19n
Piirto, J., 308, 364
Pillard, R. C., 545
Pillow, B. H., 243, 460
Pine, C. J., 156
Pinker, S., 318, 320, 326, 330
Pinnegar, S. E., 49
Pinto, J., 237
Pinto, J. P., 332
Pintrich, P. R., 121, 253, 254, 442, 447, 456, 489, 494, 498
Pipher, M., 116, 116n, 123, 124n, 132, 142, 173, 452, 469
Pisoni, D. B., 332, 352
Pitner, R. O., 463
Plante, C., 452
Platzman, K. A., 84
Plemons, B. W., 294
Plewis, I., 128
Plomin, R., 7, 17, 68, 73, 292, 295, 351, 424
Plowman, T. S., 185
Plucker, J. A., 304
Plumert, J. M., 248
Pogrow, S., 260
Polit, D., 165
Pollack, W., 97, 423, 423n
Pollitt, E., 293
Pomerantz, E. M., 387, 490
Ponterotto, J. G., 53
Poorman, A. S., 394
Poresky, R. H., 131
Portes, P. R., 177, 184, 299, 365, 502
Posner, G. J., 254, 265
Posner, J. K., 383
Potenza, M. T., 259
Pott, M., 412
Poulin, F., 473, 474
Poulin-Dubois, D., 458
Powell, G. J., 406
Powell, K., 448, 540
Powell, M. P., 71
Power, F. C., 521, 524
Powers, L. E., 503
Pramling, I., 54
Pratt, C., 344
Prawat, R. S., 265, 550
Preedy, P., 166
Pressley, M., 248, 249, 255, 258, 259, 362, 497
Pribilsky, J., 410
Price, T. S., 351
Price-Williams, D. R., 203
Pritchard, R., 242
Prochnow, J. E., 448
Proctor, R. W., 127
Pulkkinen, L., 160
Pulos, S., 202, 207, 385, 387
Purcell-Gates, V., 331, 350
Purdie, N., 249, 253, 255
Putallaz, M., 466, 534, 535

Qian, G., 387, 388, 500
Quamma, J. P., 425
Quilitch, H. R., 479
Quinn, P. C., 248, 325
Quittner, A. L., 139

Radin, N., 163
Radke-Yarrow, M., 472, 520
Radziszewska, B., 226
Rahm, J., 210
Raikes, H., 171, 556
Raine, A., 471, 489
Rajanayagam, K., 135
Rakic, P., 104, 109
Rakison, D. H., 224
Rakow, E. A., 253
Rallison, M. L., 122
Ramachandran, V. S., 110

Rambaud, M. F., 171
Ramey, C., 310, 557
Ramey, C. T., 37, 294, 299, 556, 557
Ramey, S. L., 556, 557
Ramirez, M., 203
Ramsey, E., 426
Ramsey, P. G., 181
Rankin, D. B., 468
Raphael, T. E., 367, 368
Rapport, Nancy S., 170
Rapson, R. L., 418
Rasmussen, J. L., 153
Ratner, H. H., 261
Raver, C. C., 184, 425
Raviv, A., 129
Rayner, K., 332, 361, 366
Rayport, S. G., 104
Ream, G. L., 546
Recchia, S., 509
Redfield, J., 471
Redler, E., 479
Reese, D. F., 533
Reese, E., 261
Reese, H. W., 8
Reese, L., 364
Reese, S., 561
Reeve, J., 510
Reich, P. A., 325, 328, 347
Reid, J. B., 164
Reid, M. K., 258
Reid, N., 175, 180, 302
Reid, P. T., 176
Reifman, A., 117
Reimer, J., 518, 519, 524
Reiner, M., 385, 387, 389
Reis, S. M., 305, 307
Reivich, K. J., 429
Remez, L., 544
Renninger, K. A., 271, 489, 490
Renshaw, P. D., 534
Renzulli, J. S., 305
Repacholi, B. M., 458
Rescorla, L., 220, 424
Resnick, D. P., 293
Resnick, L. B., 381, 385
Resnicow, K., 124
Rest, J., 516, 519, 521
Rest, J. R., 519, 521
Reuman, D. A., 494
Rex, D., 39, 108
Reyna, C., 552
Reynolds, A., 557
Reynolds, C., 489
Reynolds, C. R., 300
Reynolds, R. E., 242
Reys, B. J., 209
Reznick, J. S., 248, 349
Ricciuti, H. N., 293
Rice, J., 503
Rice, K., 118
Rice, M., 351
Rice, M. L., 326
Richards, D. D., 201
Richards, F. A., 202
Richards, J. E., 239
Richert, A. E., 49
Rickman, M., 510
Ridderinkhof, K. R., 238
Ridgeway, D., 420
Rieser, J. J., 10
Riggs, J. M., 443
Rimm, S. B., 297, 308
Rincón, C., 463, 543
Rinehart, S. D., 362
Ripple, C. H., 557
Risemberg, R., 253
Risley, T. R., 327, 349
Ristic, J., 260
Ritchhart, R., 302
Ritchie, S., 415
Rittenhouse, P., 383
Ritter, P. L., 117, 160
Rittle-Johnson, B., 370, 372, 379
Ritts, V., 552
Rix, M. K., 556

Roazzi, A., 10
Robbins, A. M., 352
Robbins, C., 360
Robbins, W. J., 111
Roberts, D., 156, 161, 464
Roberts, D. F., 160, 335
Roberts, M. C., 140, 141
Roberts, V., 512
Roberts, W., 549
Robertson, B., 497
Robertson, J. F., 160
Robertson, J. S., 506
Robin, D. J., 372
Robins, R. W., 433, 448
Robinson, J., 471, 522
Robinson, M., 249, 374
Robinson, N. S., 446
Robinson, T. N., 122
Robinson, T. R., 74
Rochat, P., 238
Rock, D. A., 423, 552
Roderick, M., 168, 487, 496, 507, 510, 550, 552, 554, 555
Rodin, J., 123
Rodriguez, J. L., 349
Rodriguez, M. L., 509
Rodriquez, T., 459
Roeder, K., 293
Roehlkepartain, E. C., 559
Roffwarg, H. P., 129
Rogers-Ramachandran, D., 110
Rogoff, B., 9, 10, 17, 149, 159, 203, 215, 216, 221, 224, 225, 226, 249, 295, 342, 500, 532n, 550
Rogosch, F. A., 427
Rohner, E. C., 160
Rohner, R. P., 160
Roid, G., 284
Roizen, J. A., 562
Rolfhus, E. L., 288
Romero, M., 131
Rommetveit, R., 260
Romney, D. M., 175
Rondal, J. A., 322
Rook-Green, A., 213
Roopnarine, J. L., 152
Root, M. P. P., 458
Rose, S. A., 279, 293
Rose, S. R., 463
Rose-Krasnor, L., 537
Rosen, G. D., 364
Rosenberg, J. L., 471
Rosenberg, M., 446
Rosenblum, T. B., 301
Rosengren, K. S., 243
Rosenkoetter, L. I., 564
Rosenkoetter, S. E., 564
Rosenshine, B., 215, 219, 221, 259
Rosenstein, D., 236
Rosenthal, D. A., 133
Rosenthal, R., 299, 444, 552
Rosenthal, S., 415
Rosicky, J. G., 458
Ross, D., 42, 43
Ross, D. F., 476
Ross, G., 215
Ross, H. S., 461
Ross, K. A., 258
Ross, S. A., 42, 43
Rossen, M., 321
Rosser, R., 201
Rossman, B. R., 421
Rotenberg, K. J., 488, 502
Roth, E., 367
Roth, K. J., 265
Roth, W., 216
Rothbart, M. K., 7, 73, 238, 431, 433, 523
Rothbaum, F., 412, 414, 423
Rothlisberg, B., 285
Rouet, J.-F., 259
Roux, A. L., 139
Rovee-Collier, C., 38, 241, 492, 502
Rovine, M., 152

Rowe, D., 161
Rowe, D. C., 7, 295
Rowe, D. W., 360
Rowe, E., 452
Rowe, M. B., 343, 387, 388
Rowland, T. W., 125, 126
Royce, J., 557
Rubin, K., 213
Rubin, K. H., 406, 461, 466, 468, 476, 534, 535, 537, 541
Rubin, V., 562
Ruble, D. N., 452
Rudlin, C. R., 127, 422
Rudolph, K. D., 443, 469
Ruff, H. A., 238, 239
Ruffman, T., 165, 201
Ruhland, D., 489
Ruhm, C. J., 163, 299
Ruijssenaars, A. J. J. M., 289
Ruiz, I., 238
Rule, D. C., 260
Rumberger, R. W., 177
Rushton, J. P., 471, 472, 520, 521
Russell, A., 161, 338
Russell, G., 161
Russell, J. M., 166
Russell, R. L., 383
Rutland-Brown, W., 137
Rutter, M., 156, 417, 422
Rutter, M. L., 7, 295
Ryan, A. M., 131, 443, 505, 533, 550
Ryan, E. B., 362
Ryan, R. M., 414, 415, 442, 448, 449, 451, 456, 469, 490, 491, 492, 502, 503, 509, 533
Ryu, S., 173, 559

Saarni, C., 413, 417–418, 419, 420, 424
Sadeh, A., 129
Sadker, D., 121, 126, 422, 423, 502
Sadker, M. P., 121, 126, 422, 423, 502
Sadler, T. W., 67, 68n, 77, 78, 83, 89
Saffran, J. R., 326, 330, 332, 395
Sagi, A., 414
Salamon, L., 184
Salend, S. J., 171
Salisbury, C. L., 140
Sallis, J. F., 125
Salmivalli, C., 538
Salmon, K., 241
Salo, M. K., 121
Salovey, P., 420
Salend, S. J., 171
Samuels, M. C., 413
Sameroff, A. J., 18, 296
Sampson, M. C., 413
Sampson, P. D., 114, 293
Sanchez, F., 482, 483n
Sanchez, R. P., 255
Sandall, S. R., 502
Sandler, H. M., 162, 167, 170, 183, 445
Sands, D. J., 499, 511
Sanfacon, J. A., 557
Santisi, M., 379
Santomero, A., 255
Sapolsky, R., 73
Sarlo, N., 195
Sasse, D. K., 388
Sattler, J. M., 280, 282, 284, 288, 290, 295, 296, 300
Savin-Williams, R. C., 446, 544, 545, 546
Sawyer, R. J., 373
Saxe, G. B., 453
Saxon, J. L., 387
Sbarra, D. A., 154
Scafidi, F., 418
Scales, B., 220–221
Scarborough, H. S., 350
Scardamalia, M., 371, 563
Scarr, S., 8, 17, 73, 164, 293, 295, 556

Rowe, D., 161
Scerbo, A., 471
Schachter, J., 563
Schaffer, H. R., 408, 410
Schaie, K. W., 202
Schaller, M., 472
Schaps, E., 425, 492, 550–551
Schatschneider, C. W., 252
Schauble, L., 202, 205, 386, 387, 393
Scheier, L. M., 131, 134
Schellenberg, E. G., 296
Scher, D., 358
Scherer, N., 331
Schettler, T., 139
Scheuermann, B., 513
Schiefele, U., 175
Schieffelin, B., 322
Schiever, S. W., 305, 308
Schimmoeller, M. A., 211, 508
Schinke, S. P., 124, 131, 134
Schlaefli, A., 521
Schlager, M. S., 205
Schliemann, A. D., 202, 217
Schlundt, D. G., 535
Schmitt, K. L., 561
Schneider, W., 243, 246, 248, 252, 253, 255, 367, 497
Schnoll, S. H., 81
Schnur, E., 294, 556
Schocken, I., 535
Schoenfeld, A. H., 379, 381
Schofield, J. W., 479, 538
Schommer, M., 253, 254, 259, 290
Schonert-Reichl, K. A., 429, 520
Schoppe-Sullivan, S. J., 152
Schratz, M., 299
Schraw, G., 259
Schreibman, L., 269
Schribner, S., 249
Schroth, M. L., 259
Schulenberg, J. E., 132
Schulte, T., 71
Schultz, G. F., 502
Schumaker, J. B., 499, 502
Schumpf, F., 481
Schunk, D. H., 252, 442, 447, 456, 498, 503, 505
Schutz, P. A., 454, 493, 495, 508
Schwager, M. T., 511
Schwartz, B. L., 251
Schwartz, D., 474, 532
Schwartz, G. M., 418
Schwartz, J. L., 383
Schwartz, S. S., 373
Schweinhart, L. J., 557
Scoloveno, M. A., 78
Scott, P. M., 471
Scott-Jones, D., 161
Scott-Little, M., 550, 556
Scribner, J. D., 174
Sears, K. G., 510
Seashore, H. G., 382
Seaton, E., 183
Seegers, G., 381
Segal, B. M., 131
Segal, J., 417
Segal, N. L., 166, 293
Seidenberg, M. S., 332
Seidman, E., 554, 555
Seier, W., 239
Seifer, R., 296
Seixas, J., 391
Seligman, M. E. P., 309, 427, 429, 497, 498, 499, 502
Selman, R. L., 420, 460, 479, 533, 536, 539
Seltzer, V. C., 533, 537
Semb, G. B., 217
Semrud-Clikeman, M., 81, 101, 103
Sénéchal, M., 326, 359
Senghas, A., 320
Senman, L., 348
Serbin, L. A., 298–299

Seroczynski, A. D., 451–452
Serpell, R., 358, 367
Sessa, F. M., 150
Seuss, Dr., 367
Sewald, H., 540
Shaddy, D. J., 238
Shadid, G., 118
Shaffer, D. R., 426, 521
Shaligram, C., 381
Shanahan, M., 173, 559
Shanahan, T., 372
Shank, M., 137, 268
Shany, M., 217
Shapiro, A. M., 550
Shapiro, B. K., 309
Shapiro, E. S., 137, 139, 141
Shapiro, J. R., 409, 420
Shapiro, P. N., 463
Shapka, J. D., 388
Share, D. L., 359, 360, 364, 367
Sharma, R., 511
Shatz, M., 336
Shaughnessy, M. F., 280
Shavelson, R. J., 381
Shavers, C. A., 44
Shavinina, L. V., 307
Shaw, George Bernard, 564
Shaw, V., 259
Shea, C., 472
Shea, D. L., 298
Shea, E., 316
Shea, T. M., 489
Shealy, C. N., 156
Sheckley, B. G., 558
Shedler, J., 131
Sheehan, E. P., 103, 253
Sheets, R. H., 453
Sheffield, E., 89
Sheldon, A., 330
Shell, R., 472, 519
Shellenberg, E. G., 395
Shelley-Sireci, L. M., 158
Shenfield, T., 394
Shenkin, S. D., 89
Shepard, R. N., 382
Sher, E., 416
Sheridan, M. D., 121
Sherif, C., 540
Sherif, M., 540
Sherman, P., 167
Sherwen, L. N., 78, 79, 81, 82, 83, 86, 88, 89
Sherwood, V., 213
Sheveland, D. E., 367
Shi, R., 324
Shields, M. K., 184
Shiffrin, R. M., 246
Shin, D., 126
Shiota, K., 76, 77
Shipman, V. C., 294
Shipstead, S. G., 52, 53
Shirey, L., 367
Shirey, L. L., 242
Shoda, Y., 489, 509
Shonkoff, J. P., 303
Short, E. J., 252, 362
Shrum, W., 470
Shuell, T. J., 265
Shulman, L. S., 49
Shulman, S., 414
Shultz, T. R., 330, 346
Shumow, L., 383
Shweder, R. A., 128, 149, 180, 523
Sidel, R., 184
Siegal, M., 461
Siegel, D. J., 110, 241, 510
Siegel, J. D., 125
Siegel, L. S., 370
Siegler, R. S., 17, 45, 201, 203, 241, 250, 266, 282, 321, 329, 332, 370, 372, 374, 376, 377, 378, 379, 381, 383
Siever, L., 427
Sigman, M. D., 100, 293, 295
Signorielli, N., 464

Sikkema, K. J., 133
Silberstein, C. S., 389
Silberstein, L. R., 123
Silk, J. S., 150
Silver, E. A., 259
Silverman, I. W., 510
Silverman, L. K., 306, 521
Silverman, N., 466
Simmel, C., 160
Simmons, C. M., 301
Simmons, D. C., 217
Simmons, R. G., 117, 118, 448
Simner, M. L., 472
Simon, D. J., 137, 141
Simon, V. A., 543
Simons, R. L., 150, 160, 541
Simons-Morton, B. G., 121, 122, 125
Simonton, D. K., 295
Sims, M., 56, 57, 556
Sinatra, G. M., 361, 388, 489
Sinclair, A., 420
Singer, B. R., 124
Singer, J., 389
Singer, L. M., 156
Singer, L. T., 299
Sinnott, J. D., 202
Siperstein, G. N., 464
Sirois, S., 330
Sisk, D. A., 340
Siskin, L. S., 395
Sitko, B. M., 374
Siu, S., 167
Sjostrom, L., 547
Skaalvik, E. M., 442, 443
Skinner, B. F., 12, 17, 316, 488
Skinner, E., 407
Slater, A. M., 236
Slaughter-Defoe, D. T., 465
Slavin, L. A., 177
Slavin, R. E., 221, 507, 538
Sleet, D., 448, 540
Sleeter, C. E., 178, 179
Slonim, M. B., 342, 343
Slotta, J. D., 385
Slusher, M. P., 265
Smagorinksy, P., 361
Smart, C., 158, 158n
Smerdon, B. A., 388
Smetana, J. G., 516, 519, 520, 523
Smilek, D., 260
Smith, C. L., 259, 265
Smith, C. M., 381
Smith, E., 556
Smith, E. G., 374
Smith, E. P., 550
Smith, H. L., 331, 333, 338, 346, 350
Smith, H. V., 103
Smith, J. R., 183
Smith, J. T., 71
Smith, L., 132
Smith, L. B., 16, 98, 237
Smith, N. R., 393
Smith, P. B., 476
Smith, P. K., 116, 121, 125
Smith, R. A., 139
Smith, R. E., 125
Smith, R. S., 403, 404
Smith, S., 137, 163, 268
Smith, S. L., 561
Smith, S. W., 74
Smith, V. L., 351
Smitherman, G., 372
Smoll, F. L., 125
Snarey, J., 518
Snider, S. A., 121, 125
Snipper, A., 557
Snow, C., 317, 339, 370, 372
Snow, C. E., 358
Snow, C. W., 91
Snowling, M. J., 364
Snyder, M., 558
Soberanes, B., 100
Sobol, A. M., 122

Society for Research in Child Development, 34
Sodian, B., 386
Solomon, B., 306
Solomon, D., 425, 492, 549, 550–551
Solomon, G. E. A., 264
Solomon, J., 411, 412
Sommerville, J. A., 458
Songer, N. B., 254
Sonnenschein, S., 336–337, 358
Sophian, C., 375
Sorce, J. F., 418
Sorensen, R., 544
South, D., 58–59
Southerland, S. A., 388
Sowell, E. R., 38, 39, 106, 108, 109, 110
Sowers, J. A., 503
Spaulding, C. L., 489
Spearman, C., 278–279
Spelke, E. S., 38, 263, 264, 374, 381, 384, 387
Speltz, M. L., 429
Spence, M. J., 78, 241
Spencer, C., 391
Spencer, C. A., 493
Spencer, C. J., 78
Spencer, J., 98
Spencer, M. B., 177, 294, 453, 454, 465
Sperling, M., 374
Sperry, L. L., 424
Spicker, H. H., 308
Spinath, F. M., 351
Spinrad, T. L., 420
Spitze, G., 153
Spivey, N., 253
Spivey, N. N., 331, 371, 372
Spracklen, K. M., 540
Sprafkin, C., 298–299
Sroufe, L. A., 413, 414, 415, 543, 544
Stack, C. B., 133, 156
Stage, F. K., 175
Stahl, S. A., 362, 367
Stangor, C., 464
Stanley, J. C., 43, 308
Stanley-Hagen, M. M., 153
Stanovich, K. E., 270, 296, 328, 359, 364, 366, 367, 368
Stanovich, K. G., 239
Stark, D. R., 19
Starr, E. J., 249
Starr, J. M., 89
Starr, N. B., 69
Stattin, H., 117, 118
Staub, D., 538, 566, 567n
Staub, E., 471, 474
Staub, S. D., 538
Staudt, M. M., 171
Steele, C. M., 297, 301
Steele, D. F., 383
Steen, F., 113
Steffensen, M. S., 242
Stein, J. A., 507
Stein, N., 547
Stein, N. L., 361
Stein, R., 452
Stein, S., 255
Steinberg, A., 452
Steinberg, J., 152
Steinberg, L., 150, 160, 161, 163, 292, 453, 495, 500, 507, 559
Steiner, H. H., 306
Steiner, J. E., 236
Stenberg, C. R., 418, 472–473
Stephens, B. R., 237
Stephenson, K. M., 377
Stepsis, B. W., 78
Stern, B. M., 558
Stern, D. N., 411
Stern, E., 45
Stern, W., 285
Sternberg, K. J., 476

Sternberg, R. J., 175, 278, 279, 280, 281, 282, 288, 289, 301, 302, 304, 305
Stetsenko, A., 456
Stevens, R. J., 221
Stevens, T., 503
Stevenson, H. C., 161
Stevenson, H. W., 178, 453
Stewart, A. J., 407
Stewart, B. E., 388
Stewart, J. C., 131
Stewart, L., 518–519
Stewart, M., 110
Stewart, R. B., 165
Stiles, J., 38, 317
Stiller, J. D., 414, 533
Stillman, R. D., 38
Stimpson, J., 206, 386, 389, 390
Stipek, D., 224, 291, 381
Stipek, D. J., 429, 456, 498, 500, 502, 505, 509
St. James-Roberts, I., 111, 128
Stocker, C., 446
Stockton, L., 129
Stolley, K. S., 156
Stoltzfus, J., 177
Stoneham, Z., 309
Stonehouse, A., 111
Stonehouse, Anne, 112
Stoneman, Z., 165
Storey, P., 119
Story, R., 253
Story, T., 447
Stotsky, S., 360
Stouthamer-Loeber, M., 476
Stowe, R. M., 471
Strahan, D. B., 511
Straits, S. A., 115, 121
Strauch, B., 106, 107
Straus, M. A., 471, 489
Strauss, S., 453
Strayer, F. F., 540
Streigel-Moore, R., 123
Streissguth, A. P., 81, 114, 293, 309
Striano, T., 494
Stright, A. D., 510
Strike, K. A., 254, 265
Stringer, E., 34
Stromswold, K., 89
Strozer, J. R., 317, 347, 348
Stukas, A. A., Jr., 558
Subar, A. F., 122
Subrahmanyam, K., 563
Sue, D. W., 342
Sugar, W. A., 373
Sugarman, S., 248
Sugawara, A. I., 524
Suhr, D. D., 45
Sullivan, F. M., 128
Sullivan, L. W., 69
Sullivan, P., 167, 202
Sullivan, R. C., 269
Sullivan-DeCarlo, C., 512
Sulzby, E., 360, 369
Sun, Y., 406
Sund, R. B., 200
Suskind, R., 147–148, 154, 154n
Susman, E. J., 117, 423, 471
Sussman, A. L., 163
Sutas, Y., 121
Suttles, G. D., 534
Sutton-Smith, B., 213, 337, 533
Svirsky, M. A., 352
Swanborn, M. S. L., 328
Swann, W. B., Jr., 446
Swanson, H. L., 268, 270, 289, 364, 376
Swanson, P. N., 374
Swap, S. M., 167
Swartz, C. W., 505
Sweeney, J. A., 240
Swerdlik, M. E., 288
Swim, J. K., 464
Swingley, D., 332
Switzky, H. N., 502

Sylvester, R., 424
Szynal-Brown, C., 471

Tager-Flusberg, H., 330, 464
Takahashi, K., 412
Takeuchi, A. H., 395
Tallal, P., 351
Tallman, I., 153
Talwar, V., 335
Tamburrini, J., 202, 387
Tamis-LeMonda, C. S., 170
Tamplin, A., 536
Tan, L. H., 366
Tannen, D., 349
Tanner, J. M., 69, 72, 99, 121
Tappan, M. B., 470, 523
Tappel, S. M., 176
Tarule, J. M., 166
Tarver, S., 464
Tasker, F., 157
Tate, W. F., 480
Tatum, B. D., 350, 453, 454, 464, 469
Taub, E., 110
Taylor, A., 184, 424
Taylor, B., 118
Taylor, D., 348, 365
Taylor, D. M., 180, 348
Taylor, J. M., 132
Taylor, L., 171
Taylor, M., 251, 326, 556
Taylor, M. A., 242
Taylor, R. D., 156, 161, 464
Taylor, R. J., 454
Taylor, S. L., 242
Taylor, S. M., 185
Taylor, W. C., 121, 125, 126
Teachman, G., 471
Teale, W. H., 358
Tees, R. C., 332
Teeter, P. A., 81, 101, 103
Tellegren, A., 73, 431
Templeton, S., 344, 364, 372
Tenenbaum, H. R., 176
Tennenbaum, H. R., 452
Tenner, A., 133
Tennyson, R. D., 327
Teo, A., 162
Terenzini, P. T., 202
Terman, L. M., 285, 287n, 297
Terry, R., 44, 45
Tessner, K. D., 39, 108
Tesson, G., 543
Teti, D. M., 417
Teti, L. O., 426
Thal, D., 317
Tharp, R., 221
Tharp, R. G., 180, 343
Thelen, E., 16, 18, 98, 237
Thiede, H., 131
Thoermer, C., 386
Thoma, S., 519
Thoma, S. J., 521
Thomas, A., 297, 432, 433, 435
Thomas, E., 326
Thomas, J. R., 116, 121, 125
Thomas, J. W., 252
Thomas, K. E., 137
Thomas, K. M., 106
Thomas, M. A., 489, 550
Thomas, S., 495
Thomas, S. P., 117
Thompson, E. R., 519
Thompson, H., 362
Thompson, L. A., 279
Thompson, M., 178, 505
Thompson, P. M., 39, 108, 109
Thompson, R. A., 154, 155, 166, 167, 184, 410, 411, 412, 415, 420, 431
Thompson, R. F., 101
Thompson, R. H., 338, 346
Thorkildsen, T. A., 523, 533
Thorndike, R., 284, 297
Thornton, M. C., 454
Thurlow, M. L., 507

Thurstone, L. L., 382
Tidball, G., 458
Tiedemann, J., 381
Tierney, R. J., 372
Timlin-Scalera, R. M., 53, 54
Timmer, S. G., 562
Tincoff, R., 323
Tinker, E., 320
Tinsley, B. R., 152
Tishman, S., 302
Titmus, G., 536
Tiunov, D. V., 133
Tobias, S., 429
Todd, C. M., 248, 249
Toga, A. W., 39, 108
Tomasello, M., 260, 326
Tomblin, J. B., 351
Tompkins, G. E., 364
Tonks, S., 448
Torff, B., 7
Torney-Purta, J., 263
Torquati, J., 132
Torquati, J. C., 170
Torrance, E. P., 184, 186, 302, 305
Torres-Guzmán, M. E., 180, 342, 348
Tossey, Sally, 425
Toth, S. L., 422, 427
Toth, V., 131
Touchstone, D., 185
Tourniaire, F., 207
Touwen, B. C. L., 111
Townsend, M., 465
Trainor, L. J., 323, 394, 433
Trautner, H. M., 453
Trautwein, U., 444
Trawick-Smith, J., 180, 211, 337, 341, 342, 364, 365, 372, 391, 393, 476
Treboux, D., 415
Treffert, D. A., 269, 394, 395
Trehub, S., 38
Trehub, S. E., 394, 395
Treiman, R., 364, 370, 374
Trelease, J., 364
Tremblay, L., 116
Tremblay, R. E., 473
Trevarthen, C., 260
Triandis, H. C., 10, 180, 476, 520, 523
Tronick, E. Z., 316, 418
Troop-Gordon, W., 443
Trout, J. D., 321
Trueba, H. T., 184
Trzesniewski, K. H., 448
Tse, L., 349
Tubbs, M. E., 552
Tucker, B., 499
Tucker, C. J., 460
Tulviste, P., 9
Tunmer, W. E., 344, 448
Turiel, E., 515, 516, 519, 520, 521, 523
Turkanis, C. G., 532n
Turkheimer, E., 292, 295
Turnbull, A. P., 137, 268, 539
Turnbull, R., 137, 139, 268, 269, 305, 308, 309, 310, 350, 351, 364, 372, 373, 429, 476
Turner, E. D., 239
Turner, H., 472
Turner, J. C., 367, 493
Turner, M. A., 177
Turner, T. J., 333
Turnure, J. E., 239
Turrell, S. L., 461
Tversky, A., 463
Tye, L. C., 135
Tyner, B., 367
Tzeng, O., 366
Tzuriel, D., 288, 289

Uba, L., 103
Udall, A. J., 308
Udry, J. R., 544
Ulichny, P., 179, 181

Undheim, J. O., 288, 299
Unger, C., 389
Upchurch, D. M., 133
Upton, L. R., 361
Urban, J., 414
Urban, T. A., 240
Urbina, S., 288, 289, 290
Urdan, T. C., 443, 494, 497, 505, 554
Usadel, H. C., 481
U.S. Census Bureau, 153, 163
U.S. Department of Education, 184, 305
U.S. Department of Education, Office of Civil Rights, 177, 309
U.S. Department of Health and Human Services, 56, 157, 167
U.S. Drug Enforcement Administration, 134, 135
Uttal, D. H., 178, 243

Vaccaro, D., 132
Valdez, A. J., 541
Valente, E., 466
Valentine, J. C., 443, 511, 557
Valiante, G., 373, 502
Valkenburg, P. M., 561
Valoski, A., 123
Van Court, N., 460
VandeKamp, K. O., 511
Vandell, D. L., 557
Vandenberg, B., 213
Van den Bergh, B. R. H., 81
van den Broek, P., 262, 362
Van den Oord, E. J. C. G., 7
van der Heijden, P. G. M., 518
van der Molen, M., 238
Van der Voort, T. H. A., 561
Vanderwood, M., 278
Van Hesteren, F., 520
van Heteren, C. F., 38, 78
van Hof-van Duin, J., 90
Van Hoorn, J., 220–221
van IJzendoorn, M. H., 413, 414, 415
van Joolingen, W. R., 205, 206
van Kraayenoord, C. E., 509
van Laar, C., 453, 500
Van Parys, M., 204
VanSledright, B., 391
Van Voorhis, J., 167
Van Winkle, L., 307
Varela, R. E., 177
Vasilyeva, M., 243
Vasquez, J. A., 302
Vasta, R., 471
Vaughan, K., 360
Vaughn, B. E., 414, 488, 502
Vaughn-Scott, M., 343
Vazsonyi, A., 161
Vazsonyi, A. T., 132
Veenema, S., 280
Veerman, J. W., 474
Vega, W. A., 176
Vega-Lahr, N., 418
Vella, D., 248
Veltman, M., 119
Venables, P. H., 489
Venter, J. C., 64
Ventura, S. J., 176
Verduin, K., 362
Vermeer, H. J., 381, 500
Vermeulen, K., 360
Vernon, P. A., 279
Veroff, J., 489
Verschaffel, L., 220, 379
Vespo, J. E., 473
Vidair, H. B., 153
Vignau, J., 129
Vijayan, S., 330
Viken, R. J., 129
Villarruel, F. A., 35, 175
Vishton, P. M., 330
Vitaro, F., 473
Vlahovic-Stetic, V., 382
Voelkl, K. E., 134

Voelz, S., 243
Vogel, G., 293, 309
Vohs, K. D., 443
Volling, B. L., 417
Vong, K. I., 375
Vorhees, C. V., 293
Vorrasi, J. A., 472
Vorrath, H., 479
Vosniadou, S., 264, 265, 387
Vygotsky, L., 15, 17, 45, 192, 209–221, 222, 224, 225, 226, 234, 257, 260, 262, 266, 288, 294, 307

Waddington, C. H., 72
Wade, A., 158, 158n
Wagener, L. M., 559
Wagner, E., 472
Wagner, L. S., 133
Wagner, M. M., 309
Wagner, R. K., 282
Wagner, S., 244
Wahlsten, D., 292
Waisbren, S. E., 71
Walberg, H. J., 183
Waldfogel, J., 299
Waldman, I. D., 293
Waldron, M., 295
Waldron, M. C., 154
Walk, R. D., 237
Walker, A., 139
Walker, D., 561
Walker, J. E., 489
Walker, J. M. T., 492
Walker, K. C., 290, 291
Walker, L. J., 523
Walker-Andrews, A. S., 418
Wall, S., 407
Wallace, C. S., 108
Wallace, G. L., 394, 395
Wallander, J. L., 118, 139
Wallerstein, J. S., 153, 154
Walsh, D. J., 54
Walter, K. E., 558
Walters, G. C., 489
Walton, G. E., 237
Wang, P. P., 351
Want, S. C., 255, 461
Ward, M., 481
Ward, R. A., 153
Warger, C., 481
Warheit, G. J., 176
Warren, A. R., 350
Warren-Leubecker, A., 340
Wartella, E., 561
Wartner, U., 413
Warton, P. M., 173
Washington, V., 294, 556, 557
Wasik, B. A., 335, 349
Wassenberg, K., 338
Watahomigie, L. J., 339, 348
Waters, E., 156, 407, 414, 415
Waters, H. S., 252
Waters, P. L., 470
Watson, J., 48, 263
Watson, J. B., 17
Watson, M., 425, 492, 550–551
Watson, R., 7, 224
Waxler, C. Z., 471
Waxman, S. R., 326, 336
Way, N., 492
Wayland, K. K., 471
Waylor-Bowen, T., 140
Wearne, D., 383
Weaver, C. A., III, 361
Weaver-Hightower, M., 365, 373
Webb, N. M., 149, 209, 217, 225, 479
Webber, J., 513
Weber, E. K., 516, 520, 524
Webster-Stratton, C., 153, 429
Wechsler, D., 284, 290, 297
Weffer, R. E., 175
Wehler, C. A., 122
Wehmeyer, M. L., 499, 511
Weikart, D., 557

Weinberg, R. A., 293, 295
Weinberger, D. A., 541
Weiner, B., 496, 498, 500, 505, 538
Weiner, L., 179
Weinert, F. E., 243
Weinfield, N. S., 415
Weingarten, C. T., 78
Weinstein, R. S., 301, 552, 553
Weinstock, J. S., 186
Weinstock, M., 260
Weintraub, N., 369, 370, 372
Weisner, T. S., 165, 414
Weiss, B., 139
Weiss, L. G., 288
Weiss, M. J., 358
Weissglass, J., 453
Weisz, J., 412
Wekerle, C., 543
Wellman, H. M., 17, 250, 251, 263, 420, 459, 460
Wells, D., 368
Wells, W., 171
Wenger, E., 215, 216, 444
Wenger, N., 326
Wentzel, K. R., 435, 493, 503, 510, 532, 533, 534, 539, 550, 554
Werker, J. F., 332
Werker, J. R., 324
Werner, E. E., 403, 404
Wertsch, J. V., 17, 9, 213
Wesman, A. G., 382
West, J., 114
West, R. F., 296
Westerfield, G., 443
Westerman, M. A., 420, 460
Weston, D. R., 416
Westra, T., 121
Wethington, E., 153
Whalen, C. K., 269
Whalen, T., 237
Whaley, S. E., 293, 295
Wheatley, G., 494
Whishaw, I., 317
Whitaker, D., 371
Whitaker, J. S., 300
Whitbeck, L. B., 160, 541
White, B. J., 540
White, B. Y., 206, 387
White, C., 550
White, K. J., 471
White, R., 442, 490
Whitehurst, G. J., 317, 359, 366
Whitesell, N. R., 420, 444, 460, 470, 492
Whiting, B. B., 184, 211, 471, 476
Whiting, J. W. M., 471
Whitley, B. E., Jr., 496
Wiesel, T., 8
Wigfield, A., 121, 126, 175, 364, 365, 387, 388, 442, 444, 448, 449, 451, 456, 490, 491, 493, 494, 497, 500, 502, 506, 540, 550, 554, 555
Wiig, E. H., 346
Wilcox, K. J., 73
Wilcox, S., 352
Wilder, A., 255
Wilder, D. A., 463
Wilk, A., 241
Wilkerson, B., 7, 292, 296
Willats, J., 393
Willatts, P., 249
Williams, D., 269
Williams, D. E., 452
Williams, E., 163
Williams, G., 271
Williams, J., 29, 139
Williams, K. M., 472, 481
Williams, M., 255
Williams, P. E., 288
Williams, R. E., 538
Williams, W. M., 294
Williamson, K., 29

Williamson, M. H., 37
Williamson, S., 515
Willig, A. C., 348
Willis, S. L., 202
Willows, D. M., 367
Wills, T. A., 132
Wilson, B., 383, 394
Wilson, B. L., 54–55, 253, 510
Wilson, D. K., 124
Wilson, J. D., 73
Wilson, M., 156, 516
Wilson, M. N., 156
Wilson, P., 367
Wilson, S. M., 49
Wimmer, H., 364, 459, 460
Winebrenner, S., 308
Wineburg, S. S., 391
Wing, R. R., 123
Winn, W., 563
Winne, P. H., 252, 254, 259, 456, 505
Winner, E., 269, 305, 306, 307, 308, 334, 368, 392, 393, 394, 395, 476
Winsler, A., 211, 349
Winston, P., 327
Winter, A., 393
Wise, F., 175
Wise, S., 418
Wisenbaker, J. M., 368
Wittekindt, J., 123
Wittmer, D. S., 465, 479
Wodtke, K. H., 290
Wolak, J., 564
Wolf, M., 360, 364
Wolfe, D. A., 543
Wolfe, M., 157
Wolff, P., 91, 128
Wolford, J. I., 562
Wolock, I., 167
Woloshyn, V. E., 257
Wolters, C. A., 252, 443, 513
Wolters, P. L., 139
Wong, F. Y., 561
Wong, S. C., 458
Wood, A., 361
Wood, B., 361
Wood, D., 215, 221
Wood, D. N., 132
Wood, E., 257
Wood, G. A., 542
Wood, J. W., 511
Wood, R. M., 111
Wood, T., 494
Wood, W., 561
Woodard, E. H., 561
Woods, A., 171
Woods, R., 114
Woodson, R., 237
Woodward, A. L., 326, 458
Woolfe, T., 461
Woolley, J. D., 459
Woolverton, S., 185, 539, 540, 552
Wright, J. C., 561, 562
Wright, S. C., 348
Wright, V., 44, 45
Wu, C. I., 150
Wyatt, J. M., 166, 167, 184
Wynbrandt, J., 71
Wynder, E., 124
Wynn, K., 374, 375, 381, 458

Xu, F., 38, 374, 381

Yackel, E., 494
Yaden, D. B., Jr., 344, 364, 372
Yakolev, P. I., 105, 106, 109
Yanni, J., 158
Yarrow, M. R., 471
Yarushalmy, M., 383
Yates, M., 472, 520, 525
Yau, J., 516, 520
Yeager, E. A., 391, 465
Yeany, R. H., 264
Yee, A. H., 175
Yeung, A. S., 474

Yeung, W. J., 183
Yi, S., 261
Yip, T., 454
Young, E. L., 288
Young, J. M., 89
Young, J. P., 368
Young, K. M., 391
Young, M. D., 563
Young-Hyman, D., 139
Youniss, J., 173, 472, 520, 525, 536, 539

Yousef, F. S., 343
Ysseldyke, J. E., 538
Yu, H. C., 343
Yuill, N., 362
Yurgelun-Todd, D. A., 107

Zahn-Waxler, C., 10, 407, 420, 471, 472, 520, 522
Zajonc, R. B., 165
Zakin, D. F., 118
Zambo, D., 456

Zamsky, E. S., 156
Zan, B., 521
Zarbatany, L., 468
Zeanah, C. H., 412
Zeira, A., 463
Zeith, T. Z., 278
Zelazo, P. D., 240, 516
Zero to Three, 435
Zervigon-Hakes, A., 213
Zhang, H., 381
Zhang, L., 305

Zhou, Q., 422, 519, 521
Zhu, J., 381
Ziegert, D. I., 497, 502
Ziegler, A., 386, 387
Ziegler, J. C., 366
Ziegler, S. G., 221
Zigler, E., 163, 294, 550, 555, 557
Zigler, E. F., 301
Zill, N., 155, 156, 557
Zimbardo, P. G., 534

Zimmerman, B. J., 253, 510, 511
Zimmerman, M., 443
Zimmerman, M. A., 132
Zimmerman, R. S., 176
Zimmermann, P., 414
Zippiroli, L., 137
Zohar, A., 252
Zuckerman, G. A., 259
Zummerman, B. J., 252
Zupan, B. A., 160
Zwaan, R. A., 361

Subject Index

Absolute pitch, 395
Abstract thought
  cognitive-developmental theories
    and, 14
  formal operations stage and, 200, 202
  goals and, 504
  history and, 391
  intelligence tests and, 300
  interpersonal behaviors and, 470
  listening comprehension and, 334
  mathematics and, 375, 383
  middle childhood and, 201, 208
  moral development and, 515, 521
  observations of, 207
  organization and, 248
  science and, 385
Abstract words, 325
Academic achievement
  after-school programs and, 557
  birth order and, 165
  child maltreatment and, 166
  culture and, 177–178
  elaboration and, 248
  epistemological beliefs and, 254
  giftedness and, 306, 308
  intelligence and, 278
  IQ scores and, 288, 291, 296, 298
  late adolescence and, 22
  learning disabilities and, 268
  motivation and, 491, 492, 493, 495, 500
  parenting styles and, 160
  peer pressure and, 470
  peer relationships and, 533
  reading and, 364
  school environment and, 549
  second-language learning and, 347
  sense of self and, 445
  social groups and, 540
  socioeconomic status and, 185, 299
  students at risk and, 260, 507
  teacher expectations and, 299, 552, 553
Accommodation
  definition of, 194
  Piaget's cognitive development theory
    and, 194, 195
Acculturation, 176
Achievement goals, 493–494, 495
Acquired immune deficiency syndrome
  (AIDS), 81, 131, 132, 137
Action research
  data collection and, 56–57
  definition of, 56
Active gene-environment relation, 73
Activity level, observation of, 432
Actual developmental level, 212
Adaptability, observation of, 432
Adaptation, 277, 278, 281
Adapted Physical Activity Council, 140
Adaptive behavior, 308
Addiction, 131–132
Adolescence. *See also* Early adolescence;
  Late adolescence
  art and, 393
  attachment and, 410, 414, 415, 416
  attention-deficit hyperactivity disorder
    and, 268–269
  attributions and, 497
  brain development and, 39, 106–108,
    109, 116
  comprehension monitoring and, 253
  conduct disorder and, 428–429
  crystallized intelligence and, 279
  depression and, 427
  divorce and, 154

eating disorders and, 123
eating habits and, 122
emotional development, 405, 420–421,
  422, 425
emotional regulation and, 421
epistemological beliefs and, 253, 255
extracurricular activities and, 557
families and, 158
formal operations stage and, 201, 202
gender and, 298, 451, 523
handwriting and, 370
history and, 391
identity and, 405, 406
inferences and, 243
Internet use and, 564
language development and, 323, 324,
  329, 330, 333, 335, 337–338, 340
learned helplessness and, 497–498
learning disabilities and, 268
learning strategies and, 246, 252, 255
maps and, 392
mathematics and, 375, 378–379, 381, 383
metacognitive strategies and, 255, 257
metalinguistic awareness and, 344
moral development and, 516, 522, 523
motivation and, 488–489, 491, 492–493,
  494, 504
organization and, 248
peer relationships and, 50, 532–533,
  539, 540–541
personalities and, 431
physical activity and, 125
Piaget's cognitive development theory
  and, 205, 207
play and, 213
reading development and, 366
reciprocal influences and, 164
religion and, 560
rest and sleep, 129, 130
romantic relationships and, 542–543
science and, 385, 386, 389
second-language learning and, 347
self-handicapping and, 443
self-regulation and, 509, 511
sense of self and, 444, 445, 446
sexual intimacy and, 544
sexual orientation and, 545
social cognition and, 465
social information processing and, 463
socialization and, 533
sociolinguistic behaviors and, 343
theory theory and, 264
transition to secondary schools and,
  554–555
writing and, 370, 371
Adolescent parents, 157
Adoption
  family structure and, 152, 156, 158
  foster care and, 157
Adoption studies, 292, 293
Adult activities, participation in, 215–217
Adults and adulthood
  attention of infants and, 238
  attributions and, 497, 498
  brain development and, 38, 39
  child maltreatment and, 166
  children's interacting with, 341
  collaborative use of cognitive strategies
    and, 262
  and communities, 150
  conduct disorder and, 428
  co-regulated learning and, 262
  crystallized intelligence and, 279
  emotional development and, 405–406

language development and, 316, 318,
  319, 322–323, 326
listening to children and, 53–55
metacognitive awareness and, 251
moral development and, 515, 516,
  523–525
motivation and, 502
obesity and, 123
postformal stage and, 202
problem-solving strategies and, 255
second-language learning and, 347
self-regulation and, 510
sense of self and, 444, 454
social construction of meaning and,
  214, 261
social construction of memory and, 261
social skills and, 466, 470
stereotypes and, 465
substance abuse and, 131
theory theory and, 265
Vygotsky's cognitive development
  theory and, 209, 210, 212, 214, 215,
  225, 226
Advertisements, 561, 564
Advisors, early adolescence and, 22
Affective states, 417
Africa, 249, 278
African American English, 349
African Americans
  academic achievement and, 177
  African-centered schools and, 178, 365
  culture and, 302
  dialects and, 349–350
  discrimination and, 177
  families and, 153, 177
  figurative language and, 333–334,
    337–338
  gender and, 176
  history and, 391
  intelligence and, 299, 300, 301
  moral development and, 522
  motivation and, 301, 500
  parenting styles and, 161
  playing the dozens and, 337
  reading and, 365
  schemas and, 242
  sociolinguistic behaviors and, 340, 341,
    342, 343
  students at risk and, 507
After-school programs, 43, 557–559, 565
Aggression
  child care and, 556
  child maltreatment and, 166
  conduct disorder and, 428
  correlational studies and, 44
  cross-sectional studies of, 45
  culture and, 424
  definition of, 470
  developmental issues of, 475
  development of, 472–475
  experimental studies and, 42–44
  family structure and, 153
  gender and, 422, 452, 471, 476
  interpersonal behaviors and, 470–475
  intervention for, 480–481
  longitudinal studies of, 45
  moral development and, 515, 521
  naturalistic studies and, 45–46
  nature/nurture and, 8, 73, 475
  parenting styles and, 160, 471
  peer relationships and, 532, 534, 538
  physical aggression, 472, 476, 480,
    532, 543
  proactive aggression, 473–474

psychodynamic theories and, 14
puberty and, 117, 471
punishment and, 471, 489
reactive aggression, 473–474
relational aggression, 472, 474, 476
rest and sleep, 129
romantic relationships and, 543
social cognition and, 474
television and, 561–562, 564
video games and, 562, 564
violence and, 44, 472, 480, 561–562
Agreeableness, 433, 436
Alcohol
  attention-deficit hyperactivity disorder
    and, 269
  brain development and, 104, 110,
    113–114
  families and, 426
  fetal alcohol syndrome, 81, 92–93, 110,
    293, 309
  health-compromising behavior and,
    131–132, 134
  intelligence and, 293
  late adolescence and, 118
  puberty and, 117
  self-handicapping and, 443
  as teratogen, 79, 81, 84
Alice's Adventures in Wonderland
  (Carroll), 347
Alleles, 68–69
Ambivalence, 420
Amelia Bedelia Goes Camping
  (Parish), 344
American Alliance for Health, Physical
  Education, Recreation and Dance, 140
American Athletic Association for the
  Deaf, 140
American Educational Research
  Association, 46
American Psychological Association, 46
American Sign Language, 317, 348, 352,
  364, 538
Amniocentesis, 83
Amusia, 394
Analgesics, 88
Analytical intelligence, 281
Androgyny, 452
Anecdotal records, 52, 53
Anesthetics, 88
Angelman syndrome, 70
Anger, 418, 419, 420–421, 422, 424, 425,
  426, 472, 546
Anorexia nervosa, 123–124
Anxiety
  definition of, 426
  emotional development and, 419,
    422, 426
  emotional problems and, 428, 429
  exceptionalities in information
    processing and, 271
  family environment and, 153
  stranger anxiety, 409, 410, 418
  temperament and, 433
Anxiety disorders, 428, 429
Apgar scale, 37, 290
Apprenticeships, 216
Appropriation, 212
Aptitude tests, 288
Arithmetic operations, 375–378
Art, 392–394, 395, 396, 422
Articulation
  apprenticeships and, 216
  speech and communication disorders
    and, 350

Asian Americans
　academic achievement and, 161, 175
　attributions and, 500
　depression and, 427
　families and, 153, 175
　family communication and, 171
　giftedness and, 308
　intelligence and, 299
　interpersonal behaviors and, 476
　language development and, 333
　mathematics and, 381–382
　motivation and, 500
　parenting styles and, 160–161
　sociolinguistic behaviors and, 342
Asperger syndrome, 269, 464, 476
Assessments. See also Observations
　as data collection technique, 37–38
　definition of, 37
　developmental assessments, 290
　distortions of information and, 41
　dynamic assessment, 288–289
　interpreting children's artifacts and
　　actions and, 55–56
　of reasoning skills, 38
　self-assessment, 443, 447, 448
　varying conditions and, 220
Assimilation
　culture and, 176
　definition of, 176, 194
　Piaget's cognitive development theory
　　and, 194
Associations, research design and, 44, 47
Associative play, 467
Athletics. See Organized sports
Attachments
　attachment security and later
　　development, 414–415, 543
　attachment security origins, 411–413
　child care and, 414, 556
　definition of, 407
　depression and, 427
　developmental course of, 408–410
　developmental issues and, 430
　disorganized and disoriented, 411
　emotional development and, 407–417
　implications of research on, 415–417
　individual differences in, 410–411
　infant-caregiver relationship and, 18,
　　408–409, 411, 415
　insecure-avoidant, 410
　insecure-resistant, 411
　interpersonal behaviors and, 466
　multiple attachments, 413–414, 416
　observation of, 412
　secure, 410
Attention
　developmentally appropriate practice
　　and, 245
　developmental trends in, 238–239
　distractions and, 238–239, 244
　effortful control and, 431
　exceptionalities in information
　　processing and, 270
　information processing theory and,
　　236, 261
　interdependence of, 255
　joint attention, 260, 447
　language development and, 318, 319
　learning disabilities and, 268
　mental retardation and, 309
　metacognition and, 258
　observation of, 267
　as reinforcer, 488
　self-perception and, 443
　self-regulated learning and, 252
　social information processing and, 462
Attention-deficit hyperactivity disorder,
　268–269, 271, 308, 464
Attitudes towards books, 360
Attributions
　controllable attributions, 496, 505–506
　culture and, 500
　definition of, 496
　development of, 495–498
　gender and, 499
　origins of, 498
　uncontrollable attributions, 496

Audience
　composition skills and, 371, 373
　imaginary audience, 448–449, 452,
　　460, 469
Australia, 249
Authentic activities
　after-school programs and, 558
　biological theories and, 12
　definition of, 220
　literacy and, 359
　reading and, 359, 366–367
　science and, 389
　sociocultural theories and, 15–16
　writing and, 373
Authoritarian style
　aggression and, 471
　definition of, 160
Authoritative style
　definition of, 160
　effectiveness of, 161
　prosocial and aggressive behavior, 471
　self-regulation and, 509–510
　teachers' use of, 550
Authority figures, behavior towards, 180
Autism
　art and, 394
　definition of, 269
　giftedness and, 308
　music and, 395
　predictability of surroundings and, 271
　social cognition and, 464
Autobiographical self, 447, 454
Automatization
　definition of, 240
　dyslexia and, 364
　language development and, 318, 319
　observation of, 267
　practice and, 246, 367
　reading and, 240, 366–367
　spelling and, 370
　word recognition and, 360, 367
　working memory and, 240
　writing and, 369, 370, 371
Autonomy
　autonomy versus shame and doubt
　　stage, 405, 406, 407
　culture and, 406, 500
　motivation and, 490, 493, 499, 502
Average children (peer acceptance), 533,
　534, 535
Axons, 100–101, 102, 104

Babbling, 317, 336, 351, 466
Barney & Friends, 480
Bayley Scales of Infant Development
　(Bayley), 290
Before-school programs, 559
Behaviorism, 12, 13
Behaviorism and social learning theory
　definition of, 12
　emphasis of, 12–13
　theoretical positions of, 17
Behaviors. See also Health-compromising
　　behaviors; Interpersonal behaviors;
　　Prosocial behavior; Sociolinguistic
　　behaviors
　culture and, 149
　emotional problems and, 429
　goal-directed behavior, 196, 492
　guidelines for, 435, 480, 523–524, 550
　inhibition of unproductive
　　thoughts/behaviors, 236, 240, 268,
　　508, 509, 510
　labeling appropriate behaviors, 479
　neural activity and, 296
Behaviors with books, 360
Beliefs. See also Epistemological beliefs
　aggression and, 474
　culture and, 149, 180
　false beliefs, 459
　mathematics and, 379
　religious beliefs, 559
　theory theory and, 263
Bell Curve, The (Herrnstein & Murray),
　299–300
Between the Lions, 561
Bias. See also Prejudice; Stereotypes

confirmation bias, 386
cultural bias, 178–179, 300, 302
family communication and, 171
hostile attributional bias, 474
reading comprehension and, 360
research studies and, 48
social-cognitive biases, 463–464
temperament and, 435
theory of mind and, 460
thinking/reasoning skills and, 243
Bicultural orientation, 176
Bilingual education, 348–349
Bilingualism, 344, 346, 347–348, 350, 352
Bill Nye the Science Guy, 561
Bioecological perspective, 16
Biological theories
　definition of, 12
　theoretical positions of, 17
Bipolar disorder, 427
Birth
　birth process, 86–88
　caregivers' sensitivity to newborn and,
　　90–92
　case studies, 63
　complications and interventions in,
　　88–89
　complications of, 104, 309
　preparation for, 85–86
Birth defects, 78–79
Birth order, 165, 307
Bisexuals, 545, 546
Black English Vernacular, 349
Blacks. See African Americans
Blastocyst, 75, 76
Blended families, 155
Blindness. See Visual impairments
Blue's Clues, 255, 561
Bodily-kinesthetic intelligence, 280
Body language
　gender and, 475
　social cognition and, 464, 465
Bosnia, 460–461, 465
Botswana, 424
Boys and Girls Clubs of America, 541, 558
Brain. See also Cortex
　aggression and, 471
　attention and, 238
　autism and, 269
　conduct disorder and, 428
　developmental changes in,
　　104–108, 109
　development of, 38, 39, 100–110,
　　113–114, 116, 118, 128, 204, 238, 461
　hemispheres of, 103, 106, 306–307
　injuries to, 137, 139, 427
　learning disabilities and, 268
　perceptual development and, 237
　prenatal development and, 77–78, 81
　research on, 108, 110
　sensitive periods and, 72, 108, 110
　speech and communication disorders
　　and, 351
　structures and functions of, 101–104
Braxton Hicks contractions, 86
Brazil, 340, 382
Breastfeeding, 119, 121
Breathing, 111
Broca's area, 317, 318
Bulimia, 123–124
Bullying behavior, 443, 472, 474, 534

Canalization, 72
Cardinal principle, 375
Caregivers. See also Professional practice
　attachment and, 414, 466
　babies at risk and, 89
　child care and, 556
　crying and, 49, 111, 411, 424–425
　emotional development and, 418
　family structure and, 158
　infant-caregiver relationship, 18, 19,
　　238, 404–405, 408–409, 411, 415,
　　420, 433, 435, 444
　intersubjectivity and, 260
　nonverbal cues and, 50
　sense of self and, 454
　sensitivity to newborn infants, 90–92

siblings as, 163, 165
sudden infant death syndrome
　and, 128
Caregiver speech, 322
Care orientation, 522, 523
Carolina Abecedarian Project, 557
Case studies, as form of naturalistic
　study, 45
Causal relationships
　formal operations stage and, 200
　goal-directed behavior and, 196
　long-term memory and, 242
　physical environment and, 195
　play and, 213
　research design and, 42–44, 47
　science and, 389
　theory theory and, 263
Cells, 64, 65, 75, 99
Central conceptual structures
　definition of, 204
　number and, 377–378
Central executive
　attention-deficit hyperactivity disorder
　　and, 268
　definition of, 236
　developmental trends in, 239–240
　information processing theory and, 236
Cephalocaudal trends, 111
Cesarean delivery, 88
Challenging tasks
　awareness of thought and, 250
　cognitive apprenticeship and, 216
　learned helplessness and, 497
　memory limitations and, 252
　Piaget's cognitive development theory
　　and, 222
　scaffolding and, 221
　self-efficacy and, 490
　sense of self and, 443, 447, 456
　Vygotsky's cognitive development
　　theory and, 211, 212, 219–220, 222,
　　252, 262
Chase play, 113
Chat rooms, 563, 564
Checklists, 52–53, 54
Child abuse
　adoption and, 156
　brain development and, 110
　child maltreatment, 166
　emotional problems and, 426
　foster care and, 156, 157
　sleep problems and, 129
Child care
　attachment, 414, 556
　moral development and, 521
　parents' employment and, 163
　services for children and, 555–556
Child development
　basic issues in, 6–12
　case studies, 3–4, 28–29
　definition of, 4
　developmental periods, 18–23
　eclectic approach to, 16, 18
　as field of inquiry, 4–5, 6
　professional practice and, 23, 26–28
　theories of, 12–18
Childhood. See also Early childhood;
　Middle childhood
　attachments and, 416
　brain development and, 38, 39, 109
　conduct disorder and, 428–429
　crystallized intelligence and, 279
　depression and, 427
　eating habits and, 121–122, 123
　motivation and, 492–493
　peer relationships and, 532–533
　personality and, 431
　physical development and, 110–119
　sense of self and, 444
　socialization and, 533
Child maltreatment, 166–167, 169, 183
Children with special needs. See also
　Exceptionalities
　adoption and, 156
　case studies, 92–93
　child maltreatment and, 167
　empathy for, 538

interpersonal behaviors and, 476
language development and, 321–322
motivation and, 503
self-regulation and, 511
sexually transmitted infections and, 133
social cognition and, 464
China, 249, 278, 366, 388, 394, 423, 427, 476, 500, 508n
Choices
information processing theory and, 244
self-regulation and, 511
Chorionic villus sampling (CVS), 82–83
Chromosome abnormalities, 69, 70, 72, 79, 82, 83, 89, 413
Chromosomes, 64, 65, 66, 67, 68, 68n, 75
Chronic illnesses, 137
Cigarette smoking
attention-deficit hyperactivity disorder and, 269
health-compromising behavior and, 131, 134
late adolescence and, 118
peer relationships and, 533
prenatal development and, 81, 84
puberty and, 117
sudden infant death syndrome and, 128
Circuits, of neurons, 101, 103
Class inclusion, 193, 199, 201
Classroom climate
routines and, 435–436, 554
self-regulation and, 511
sense of community and, 549–550
Cleft palate, 72
Clinical method, 192–193, 206
Cliques, 540–541
Closed-ended questions, 54
Coaches and coaching, 216
Cocaine, 81, 110, 132
Codominance, 69
Cognition. See also Metacognition; Social cognition
definition of, 191
Cognitive apprenticeships, 216
Cognitive development. See also Cognitive processes; Intelligence; Language development; Literacy; Piaget's cognitive development theory; Vygotsky's cognitive development theory
case studies, 191, 227–228
critique of contemporary approaches to, 265–266
definition of, 5
developmental trends, 4, 24–25
infancy and, 19, 38, 198
information processing theory and, 236
language development and, 320, 348
maturation and, 192, 204
metacognitive development and, 255
moral development and, 515, 519, 521
nature/nurture and, 11
physiological measures of, 38
qualitative/quantitative change and, 11
universality/diversity and, 9, 11
Cognitive-developmental theories
definition of, 14
theoretical positions of, 17
Cognitive modeling, 220
Cognitive processes
case studies, 233–234, 271–272
content domain standards and, 395
facilitation of, 244–245
information processing theory and, 203, 234–246
intelligence tests and, 300
interdependence with metacognitive processes, 255
language development and, 318, 319
learning disabilities and, 268
metacognition and, 255
observation of, 267
triarchic theory and, 281–282
Cognitive process theories
definition of, 14
emphasis of, 14–15
theoretical positions of, 17

Cognitive strategies
collaborative use of, 262
definition of, 246
developmental trends in, 256–257
dynamic assessment and, 289
intelligence and, 304
interdependence of, 255
learning strategies and, 246, 248–249
modeling of, 255, 257, 262
observation of, 305
as overlapping waves, 250
problem-solving strategies and, 249–250
promoting development of, 255, 257–260
Cognitive tools
acquisition of, 218
appropriation of, 212
of cultures, 180, 210–211, 225
definition of, 211
Cohabiting families, 157
Cohesive composition, 371
Cohorts, 45
Cohort-sequential design, 45
Colic, 111
Collaborative learning, 257
Collectivism, 180
Color discrimination, 236
Communities
children's and adolescents' health compromising behaviors and, 133–135
community involvement and, 480, 522, 525, 558–559
definition of, 149
developmental issues and, 151
family income and, 182–183
gender and, 452
influence of, 174–182
knowledge of, 242
resources of, 182–184
role of, 149–150
sense of self and, 453, 454
social systems and, 151
types of, 182
Community of learners, 550
Community service activities, 480, 522, 525, 558–559
Community services
aggression and, 480
assessment strategies and, 56
Community violence, 44
Competence
emotional development and, 424
motivation and, 490, 496
sense of self and, 445
social competence, 281, 466, 467
Competition, 476
Composition skills, 370–371, 373
Comprehension monitoring
content domain standards and, 395
definition of, 253
effectiveness of learning strategies and, 255
modeling of, 255
promotion of, 258–259
Computer metaphors, 234
Computers, 177, 561, 563–564, 565
Conception, 67
Conceptual change, 265, 390
Conclusions
ethical conduct and, 57
of research studies, 46–48
Concrete operations stage, 197, 199–200, 203
Concrete thought, 207
Concrete words, 325
Conduct disorder, 428–429, 476, 522
Confidentiality, 34, 55, 58
Confirmation bias, 386
Conflict resolution
aggression and, 473
family structure and, 153, 155
friendships and, 536–537, 539
interpersonal behaviors and, 468, 479
moral development and, 521
peer mediation programs and, 481, 524
play and, 213

Confucianism, 160
Conscientiousness, 433, 436
Conservation
cognitive tools and, 211
concrete operations stage and, 199
cultural effects on, 203
definition of, 199
experiences and, 207
gestures and, 245
preoperational stage and, 201
Conservation of liquid, 199
Conservation of number, 199, 375
Conservation of weight, 200
Constructivism
definition of, 194
individual constructivism, 194
information processing theory and, 234
Piaget's cognitive development theory and, 194, 234
reading comprehension and, 361
social constructivism, 194, 215
Content domains. See also Mathematics; Reading; Science; Writing
art, 392–394
case studies, 357, 397–398
developmental progressions in, 396
differential development in, 266
epistemological beliefs and, 254
formal operational thought and, 202
geography, 391–392
history, 390–391
intelligence and, 278
middle childhood and, 21
moral development and, 524
motivation and, 492
music, 394–395
neo-Piagetian theories and, 204
Piaget's clinical method and, 206
sense of self and, 457
specific ability tests and, 288
standards in, 395, 397
writing and, 374
Contentment, 418
Contexts. See also Communities; Culture; Ethnic minority groups; Families; Media; Neighborhoods; Religion and religious groups; Socioeconomic status
case studies and, 531–532
definition of, 5
developmental issues of, 565
developmental systems theories and, 16
distributed intelligence and, 282
intelligence and, 278
language development and, 332–333
moral development and, 519
naturalistic studies and, 45–46, 47
triarchic theory and, 281
Contingent self-worth, 446, 451
Contrary-to-fact ideas, formal operations stage and, 201, 208
Control groups, 42, 42n
Controllable attributions, 496, 505–506
Controversial children (peer acceptance), 533, 534, 535
Controversial issues, 561
Conventional morality, 518
Conventional transgressions, 516
Cooing, 336
Cooperation
culture and, 302, 476
family structure and, 153
play and, 213, 466, 467
Cooperative activities
interpersonal behaviors and, 479
peer relationships and, 495, 538
Cooperative play, 213, 466, 467
Coparents, 152–153, 154
Coping, 177, 464
Core goals, 493
Co-regulated learning, 262
Correlational features, 327
Correlational studies
advantages/disadvantages of, 47
conclusions of, 46–47
definition of, 44
intelligence and, 278

Correlation coefficients, 44
Correlations, definition of, 44
Cortex. See also Brain
adolescence and, 106, 107, 108, 116
aggression and, 471
attention and, 238
and central executive, 240
definition of, 102
early childhood and, 237
infancy and, 105
middle childhood and, 106
prenatal development and, 104
specialization within, 103
Counselors and counseling, 55, 425
Counting, 374–375
Covert self-instruction, 220
Creative intelligence, 281
Critical listening, 335
Critical periods, environmental factors and, 8
Cross-cultural comparisons, 47
Crossing-over of genetic material, 66, 67
Cross-linguistic differences, reading and, 365–366
Cross-sectional studies, 45, 47
Crying
caregivers' interpretation of, 49, 111, 411, 424–425
emotional contagion and, 418
emotional regulation and, 420
language development and, 323
physical development and, 111
prosocial behavior and, 472
Crystallized intelligence, 279, 283
Cultural bias, 178–179, 300, 302
Culture. See also Ethnic minority groups; Sociocultural theories
art and, 393–394
attachment security and, 412–413, 414
automatization and, 240
cognitive development and, 203, 210
cognitive tools and, 180, 210–211, 225
conventional transgressions and, 516
definition of, 149
depression and, 427
developmental issues of, 151
diversity and, 179, 181
dynamic assessment, 289
eating habits and, 124
emotional development and, 423–424, 426
Erikson's psychosocial development theory and, 406
of ethnic minority groups, 174
families and, 149, 169, 175
gender and, 175–176
guided participation and, 159, 214–215
intelligence and, 278, 304
intelligence tests and, 300, 302
interpersonal behaviors and, 476
intersubjectivity and, 261
language development and, 317, 321, 332, 333
learning strategies and, 249, 260
long-term memory and, 240
mathematics and, 381–382
moral development and, 516, 519, 523
motivation and, 500
multiple intelligences and, 280
music and, 394
narratives and, 337
parenting styles and, 161
peer relationships and, 533
prosocial and aggressive behavior, 471
puberty and, 118
qualitative/quantitative change and, 10, 151
reading and, 365
rest and sleep and, 128
romantic relationships and, 546
schemas and scripts and, 242
science and, 388
sense of self and, 453–454, 457
social construction of memory and, 261
social systems and, 151
sociolinguistic behaviors and, 340–344
students at risk and, 507

Culture, *continued*
    subcultures, 541
    teacher expectations and, 553
    temperament and, 433
    theory of mind and, 464
    theory theory and, 264
    universality/diversity and, 9, 151
    Vygotsky's cognitive development
        theory and, 210–211, 224, 226
    writing and, 373
Culture shock, 343
Curiosity, 305, 489, 502
Cystic fibrosis (CF), 71, 137

Data collection
    accuracy in, 40, 46
    action research and, 56–57
    collecting information in schools,
        48–49
    distortions in, 40, 41
    ethical conduct and, 48–49, 57–58
    interpreting assessments and, 55–56
    listening to children and, 53–55
    multiple collection techniques, 42, 49
    observations and, 38–40, 49–53
    scientific method and, 35
    techniques of, 36–42
Dating, 542, 543
Decision making
    central executive and, 236
    moral development and, 519
    social information processing and, 463
Defining features, 326–327
Definitions, 327
Delay of gratification, 488–489, 506–507,
    508, 510
Delinquency, 474
Dendrites, 101, 102, 105
Depression
    definition of, 427
    gay youth and, 546
    gender and, 422, 427
    nature/nurture and, 426
    peer relationships and, 533
    romantic relationships and, 543
    suicide and, 427–428, 429, 430
    victims of aggression and, 474
Depth perception, 237
Desensitization, 562
Despair, 405–406, 407
Developmental assessments, 290
Developmental domains, organization of, 5
Developmental immaturity, 26–27
Developmentally appropriate practice
    attention and, 245
    before- and after-school programs
        and, 559
    commitment to, 27–28
    conducting research as teacher, 57
    cultural and ethnic differences and, 179
    definition of, 23
    discovery learning and, 206
    elementary/secondary school transition
        and, 555
    family communication and, 174
    giftedness and, 308
    hearing impairments and, 352
    infant stimulation, 238
    listening skills and, 334
    mental retardation and, 310
    newborn infants' needs and, 90
    phonological awareness and letter
        recognition, 361
    physical needs of adolescents, 118
    physical needs of infants and
        children, 115
    preparing for, 23, 26–27
    professional practice and, 27–28
    reading comprehension and, 362
    scaffolding challenging tasks and, 221
    self-management skills and, 515
    social goals and, 505
    social perspective taking and, 465
    social skills and, 479
    speech and communication disorders
        and, 351
    students at risk and, 507

Developmental periods. *See also*
    Adolescence; Adults and adulthood;
    Childhood; Early adolescence; Early
    childhood; Infancy; Late adolescence;
    Middle childhood
    child development and, 18–23
    developmentally appropriate practice
        and, 23, 26–28
Developmental strengths, 23
Developmental studies, 45, 47
Developmental systems theories, 16, 18
Developmental trends
    accomplishments and diversity of,
        24–25
    in attention, 238–239
    in central executive, 239–240
    children's capabilities and needs and,
        10–11
    chronic health conditions, 138–139
    cognitive development and, 4, 24–25
    in cognitive strategies, 256–257
    emotional and personal development
        and, 434
    epistemological beliefs and, 253, 254
    field of child development and, 4
    in information processing abilities, 247
    in IQ scores, 296–298
    in language development, 323–347
    in long-term memory, 240–243
    in mathematics, 380–381
    in metacognition, 256–257
    in moral development, 515–519, 520
    in motivation, 501–502
    in peer relationships, 548–549
    perception and, 236–238
    physical development and, 4, 24–25,
        120–121
    prenatal development and, 85
    in reading, 363–364
    in science, 387
    in self-regulation, 508–509
    in sensation, 236–238
    in sense of self, 455
    in social cognition and interpersonal
        skills, 477–478
    thinking/reasoning skills, 223,
        243–244
    in working memory, 239–240
    in writing, 372
Dialects, 338, 349–350, 552, 564
Differentiation
    brain and, 102
    definition of, 99
    physical development and, 99, 100
Disabilities. *See also* Children with special
    needs; Learning disabilities
    babies at risk and, 92
    motivation and, 499
    peer relationships and, 141
    physical disabilities, 139–140, 195, 308,
        444, 476, 499, 511
    poverty and, 183
    sense of self and, 444, 446, 456
    sleep problems and, 129
Discovery learning, 206
Discrimination
    culture and, 177, 178–179
    intelligence and, 300–301
    interpersonal behaviors and, 469
    sexual harassment as, 547
Discriminatory practices, 300–301
Disequilibrium
    challenge and, 222
    definition of, 195
    moral development and, 521,
        524–525
    motivation and, 201, 208, 489
    social interaction and, 224
    sociocognitive conflict and, 209
Disgust, 419
Disorganized and disoriented attachment,
    411, 412
Dispositions, intelligence tests and, 302
Distractions, 238–239, 244
Distress, 418
Distributed intelligence, 282, 283, 304
Distributive justice, 516–517

Diversity. *See also* Ethnic minority groups;
    Gender; Socioeconomic status;
    Universality/diversity
    culture and, 179, 181
    definition of, 8
    developmentally appropriate practice
        and, 27
    of developmental trends, 24–25
    early adolescence and, 21
    families and, 157–159
    families' concerns about child
        development, 172–173
    in interpersonal behaviors, 475–476
    in knowledge base, 241
    in language development, 349–350
    in mathematics development, 379,
        381–382
    in moral development, 522–523
    in motivation, 498–500
    physical activity and, 126–127
    physical development and, 120–121
    prenatal development and, 85
    in reading development, 364–366
    religion and, 560
    romantic relationships and, 546
    in science development, 388
    in self-regulation, 510
    sense of self and, 451–454
    in social cognition, 464
    in sociolinguistic behaviors, 343–344
    in writing development, 373
Divorce
    attachment and, 416
    family structure and, 152, 153–154
    teachers' support for, 158
Dizygotic twins, 68, 291, 471, 545
DNA, 64, 65, 75
Dominance hierarchies, 540, 541
Dominant genes, 69
Dora the Explorer, 561
Down syndrome, 69, 70, 113, 139, 291,
    309, 321–322
Drugs
    brain development and, 110
    chromosome abnormalities and, 69
    families and, 426
    gangs and, 541
    health-compromising behavior and,
        131–132, 134, 135
    intelligence and, 293
    late adolescence and, 118
    moral transgressions and, 516
    school environment and, 549
    self-handicapping and, 443
    as teratogens, 79, 81, 84
Duchenne muscular dystrophy, 71
Dynamic assessment, 288–289
Dyslexia, 364, 456

Early adolescence
    after-school programs and, 557
    child maltreatment and, 166
    chronic health conditions in, 138
    cognitive strategies and, 256
    developmental features of, 21–22
    developmentally appropriate practice
        and, 26
    elaboration and, 248
    emotional development and,
        421–422, 434
    families' concerns about, 173
    friendships and, 537
    information processing abilities
        and, 247
    intelligence tests and, 297
    interpersonal behaviors and,
        469–470, 478
    language skills and, 345
    mathematics and, 380
    metacognitive awareness and, 251, 256
    moral development and, 520
    motivation and, 501, 502–503
    peer relationships and, 21, 469,
        540–541, 548
    physical development and, 21–22, 25,
        114–118, 121
    prejudice and, 464

professional viewpoints on, 22
    reading and, 363
    romantic relationships and, 542
    science and, 387
    sense of self and, 448–449, 455
    social cognition and, 478
    television viewing and, 562
    theory of mind and, 460
    thinking and reasoning skills, 223
    writing and, 372
Early childhood
    aggression and, 473
    art and, 392
    attachment and, 409–410
    attention and, 239
    brain development and, 105
    chronic health conditions in, 138
    cognitive strategies and, 256
    developmentally appropriate practice
        and, 26
    distributive justice and, 517
    elaboration and, 248
    emotional development and, 19, 405,
        420, 421, 422, 434
    families' concerns about, 172
    friendships and, 536–537
    gender and, 451, 475
    geography and, 391
    history and, 390
    information processing abilities
        and, 247
    intelligence tests and, 289–291, 297
    interpersonal behaviors and, 466–468,
        475, 477
    language development and, 19, 72,
        323, 324, 329–330, 331, 332, 336,
        337, 340
    language skills and, 345
    learned helplessness and, 497
    long-term memory and, 241
    mathematics and, 374–375, 376, 377,
        380, 383
    metacognitive awareness and, 250,
        251, 256
    metalinguistic awareness and, 344
    moral development and, 516, 516n,
        519, 520, 524
    motivation and, 488, 490–491, 494, 501
    music and, 394
    organization and, 248, 249
    peer relationships and, 548
    phonological awareness and, 359
    physical activity and, 125
    physical development and, 19, 24,
        111–114, 120
    Piaget's cognitive development theory
        and, 205, 207
    play and, 213, 220–221, 536
    problem-solving strategies and, 249
    professional viewpoints on, 19–20
    reading and, 359, 363
    reciprocal influences and, 164
    rest and sleep, 129
    romantic relationship awareness
        and, 542
    science and, 385, 387, 388
    self-regulation and, 508, 508n, 509,
        511, 512
    sense of self and, 447, 455
    social cognition and, 465, 477
    stereotypes and, 463
    television viewing and, 562
    theory of mind and, 459
    theory theory and, 264
    thinking and reasoning skills, 223
    visual perception and, 237
    Vygotsky's cognitive development
        theory and, 211
    writing and, 369, 370, 372, 373
Early childhood intervention programs,
    556–557
Early intervention
    early childhood intervention programs,
        556–557
    intelligence and, 292, 294, 303, 557
    research in, 37
Early-maturing boys, 117

Early-maturing girls, 117
Eating disorders, 123–124, 446
Eating habits. *See also* Nutrition
  infancy and, 113, 119–120, 121
  observation guidelines, 136
  physical development and, 119,
    121–125
  promoting better eating habits, 124–125
Ebonics, 349
Ecstasy (drug), 132
Education. *See also* Schools
  bilingual education, 348–349
  family's involvement in, 162, 167, 168
  multicultural education, 179, 181, 458
  sex education, 546
Effortful control, 431
Egocentrism
  definition of, 198
  language development and, 336
  observation of, 207
  preoperational stage and, 198–199, 201,
    207n, 224
  theory of mind and, 458, 458n
Elaboration
  content domain standards and, 395
  definition of, 248
  epistemological beliefs and, 255
  as learning strategy, 248–249, 252,
    257, 258
  long-term memory and, 236
  modeling of, 255
  social information processing and, 462
Elementary schools, transitions to,
  553–554
E-mail, 170, 563, 564
Embarrassment, 420, 422, 516
Embryonic period, 81
Embryos, 75, 76, 85
Emergent literacy, 358–359, 365
Emotional abuse, 166
Emotional contagion, 418, 430
Emotional development. *See also*
  Emotions
  attachments and, 407–417
  case studies, 403–404, 437
  developmental changes in emotions,
    418, 420–422
  developmental issues in, 430
  developmental trends in, 434
  Erikson's psychosocial development
    theory and, 404–407
  group differences in emotions, 422–424
  problems in, 426–430
  promotion of, 424–426
  temperament and personality, 431–437
Emotional disorders, 72, 308
Emotional intensity, observation of, 432
Emotional regulation
  definition of, 420
  modeling of, 420–421, 426
  self-regulation and, 508
  stress and, 424
Emotional support, 532–533, 535–536, 537
Emotions
  brain development and, 107, 118
  definition of, 417
  developmental changes in, 418,
    420–422
  emotional problems and, 426–430
  group differences in, 422–424
  moral development and, 516, 519
  observation guidelines, 419
  physical development and, 116
  romantic relationships and, 543
  self-conscious emotions, 114, 420
  social information processing and, 463
  theory of mind and, 459, 460
Empathic orientation, 473
Empathy
  for children with special needs, 538
  definition of, 421
  emotional development and, 421–422
  gender and, 522
  modeling of, 422
  moral development and, 516, 519, 521
  peer acceptance and, 534
  prosocial behavior and, 471, 472

Employment
  of parents, 163, 169
  part-time employment, 559
Entity view of ability, 496, 497
Environmental factors. *See also*
  Nature/nurture
  assessment of, 55–56
  automatization and, 240
  behaviorism and, 13
  bioecological perspective and, 16
  children's natural tendencies
    affecting, 8
  critical periods and, 8
  depression and, 427
  distributed intelligence and, 282
  emotional development and, 422,
    424, 426
  exceptionalities in information
    processing and, 271
  fluid intelligence and, 279
  gender and, 452
  genetic expression influenced by, 64,
    65, 66, 73–74
  giftedness and, 307
  home environments, 292, 293–294, 309,
    507, 552–553
  infancy and, 19
  influence of, 74
  information processing theory and,
    234–235
  intelligence and, 73, 292–296
  interaction with heredity, 7, 68,
    73–74, 295
  learning strategies and, 249
  mathematics and, 381
  mental retardation and, 310
  motivation and, 499
  poverty and, 183
  prosocial and aggressive behavior,
    471–472
  self-regulation and, 510
  sexual orientation and, 545
  theory of mind and, 461
  timing of environmental exposure and,
    7–8
Epidural analgesia, 88
Epistemological beliefs
  definition of, 253
  developmental changes in, 253, 254
  geography and, 392
  interdependence of, 255
  interviews with children and, 258
  metacognition and, 253–255
  observation of, 267
  promoting development of, 259–260
  science and, 386, 388
Equilibration, 195–196
Equilibrium, 195
Erikson's psychosocial development theory
  contemporary perspectives on, 406
  developmental research related to, 407
  identity and, 10, 14, 405, 406, 407
  psychosocial stages of, 10, 404–406
  resolution of internal struggles and, 13
Ethical conduct
  data collection and, 48–49, 57–58
  experimental studies and, 42, 42n, 43n
  research methods and, 34–35
Ethnic identity
  coping mechanisms and, 177, 464
  definition of, 177, 453
  motivation and, 301
  sense of self and, 453–454
Ethnicity
  definition of, 174
  race compared to, 175
Ethnic minority groups
  challenges for, 176–177
  cultural bias and, 178–179, 300, 302
  culture of, 174
  gender and, 299
  intelligence and, 299–301
  interpersonal behaviors and, 469, 476
  language development and, 349–350
  literacy and, 365
  moral development and, 523
  motivation and, 500

peer mediation and, 481
peer relationships and, 533, 538
percentages of children belonging
  to, 178
reading and, 365
research methods and, 35
sense of self and, 453, 457–458
social cognition and, 464
stereotypes and, 301
teacher expectations and, 178, 552
Ethnographies, 45
Ethological attachment theory, 408
Etiquette, 343, 344
European Americans
  academic achievement and, 177
  culture and, 240
  families and, 153
  gender and, 175
  history and, 391
  intelligence and, 299–300
  motivation and, 500
  science and, 388
  sociolinguistic behaviors and, 341–342
Evocative gene-environment relation, 73
Evolution, concept of, science and, 388
Evolutionary perspectives
  perceptual development and, 237
  prosocial and aggressive behavior, 471
Examples, in semantic development, 327
Exceptionalities. *See also* Children with
  special needs
  attention-deficit hyperactivity disorder
    and, 268–269, 271
  autism and, 269, 271
  giftedness and, 305–308
  in information processing, 267–271
  in intelligence, 304–310
  in language development, 350–352
  learning disabilities and, 268
  mental retardation and, 308–310
  professional practice and, 269–271
Executive functions
  definition of, 102
  information processing theory and, 236
  mental retardation and, 309
  theory of mind and, 461
Expansion, definition of, 331
Expectations
  attachment security and, 414
  attributions and, 497–498
  child maltreatment and, 167
  emotional development and, 418
  mathematics and, 381
  observations and, 40
  of parents, 424
  physical activity and, 126
  of research participants, 40
  school environment and, 551–553
  self-regulation and, 512
  sense of self and, 456
  socioeconomic status and, 185
  of teachers, 178, 185, 299, 426, 429,
    435, 444, 465, 512, 551–553
  theory of mind and, 460
Expecting Adam (Beck), 309
Experiences
  conservation and, 207
  effects of, 202–203
  fluid intelligence and, 279
  mediated learning experiences, 214
  perceptual development and, 237
  Piaget's cognitive development theory
    and, 224–225
  talking with children about, 262
  triarchic theory and, 281
  Vygotsky's cognitive development
    theory and, 224–225
  working memory and, 240
Experimental studies
  advantages/disadvantages of, 47
  conclusions of, 46
  definition of, 42
  research design and, 42–44, 42n, 43n
Experimentation
  motivation and, 502
  Piaget's cognitive development theory
    and, 205–206, 225

sensorimotor stage and, 198
Vygotsky's cognitive development
  theory and, 225
Exploration, apprenticeships and, 217
Exploration of objects, 198
Exploratory play, 222
Expressive language, 322
Extended families, 155–156
External attributions, 496
External regulation, 492
Extracurricular activities, 157, 488, 538,
  557, 558–559
Extraversion, 433, 436
Extraversion/surgency, 431
Extrinsic motivation
  academic achievement and, 492
  appropriate use of, 489, 500, 502,
    506–507
  attributions and, 498
  definition of, 488
  developmental issues of, 499
  self-regulation and, 512
Eye contact, 318, 341–342, 411, 415

Facial expressions, 237, 250, 340, 420,
  447, 462, 472
Faded, overt self-guidance, 220
Failures, 496, 498, 499, 505–506
Fairness, 516–517, 522
Fallopian tubes, 75
False beliefs, 459
Familiarity, attention and, 238
Families. *See also* Parents
  anxiety disorders and, 428
  case studies, 147–148, 186
  children's influences on families,
    163–166
  conduct disorder and, 428–429
  definition of, 148
  developmental issues in, 151
  diversity in family structure, 157–159
  emotional development and, 423–424
  extended families, 155–156
  families' influences on children,
    159–163, 169
  family processes, 159–174
  foster care and, 156–157
  gender and, 452
  income of, 182–183
  as little schoolhouses, 161–162
  observations of, 169
  parents' employment and, 163
  prosocial and aggressive behavior
    and, 471
  risk factors in, 166–167
  sense of self and, 445, 451, 453, 454
  siblings and, 155, 165–166
  socialization and, 148–149, 159
  social systems and, 151
  stress and, 417
  structure of, 152–159
  teachers' partnerships with, 167–174
Family educators, 56, 84
Family structure, 152–159
Fast mapping, 326
Fathers. *See also* Parents
  attachment and, 413
  divorce and, 154
  family structure and, 152–153
  prenatal development and, 84
  teachers' communication with,
    158, 170
Fear, 418, 419, 422, 425, 426, 433, 516
Feedback
  computer software and, 563
  goals and, 503
  language development and, 317,
    328, 331
  metacognition and, 255, 258
  moral development and, 525
  self-determination and, 506
  self-evaluation and, 259
  self-regulation and, 509, 511
  sense of self and, 446, 456
  sociolinguistic behaviors and, 343
  teacher expectations and, 552
Feelings, expression of, 425

Fetal alcohol syndrome (FAS), 81, 92–93, 110, 293, 309
Fetal period, 81
Fetoscope, 83
Fetuses, 38, 77–78, 83–84, 85, 90
Figurative speech, 333–334, 335, 337–338
Fine motor skills, 111, 113, 114
First Amendment, 560
First Choice program, 134
First stage of labor, 86–87
Flaming, 564
Fluency, 350
Fluid intelligence, 279, 283
Flynn effect, 292, 294–295
Forebrain, 101–102
Foreclosure, identity and, 449
Formal operations stage, 197, 200–201, 202, 203
Formal schooling
    intelligence and, 292, 294
    learning strategies and, 249
    mathematics and, 383
    metalinguistic awareness and, 344
    Vygotsky's cognitive development theory and, 210, 294
Foster care, 156–157, 158, 159, 167, 294, 417
Fragile X syndrome, 69, 71
France, 283–284
Fraternal twins, 68, 291, 471, 545
Friendships, 468, 534–539. See also Peer relationships
Frog and Toad Are Friends (Lobel), 425
Functionalism
    definition of, 320
    language development and, 320, 321, 324
Future aspirations, 495
Future selves, 442, 495

g
    definition of, 279
    intelligence theories compared to, 283
    IQ scores and, 279
    theoretical perspective of, 278–279
Gametes, 66, 67
Gang prevention programs, 541
Gangs, 482–483, 541–542
Gardner's multiple intelligences, 279–280, 283, 288, 303–304
Gay parents, 156, 157, 158
Gay youth, 545, 546
Gender
    aggression and, 422, 452, 471, 476
    conduct disorder and, 428
    depression and, 422, 427
    divorce and, 154
    emotional development and, 422–423
    Erikson's psychosocial development theory and, 406
    fine motor skills and, 114
    friendships and, 537
    giftedness and, 308
    intelligence tests and, 298–299
    interpersonal behaviors and, 475–476
    language development and, 349
    mathematics and, 381, 451, 500
    moral development and, 522–523
    motivation and, 499–500, 504
    organized sports and, 126, 175, 451, 500
    peer relationships and, 452, 533
    physical activity and, 125, 126
    physical development and, 99, 114
    puberty and, 115–116, 451, 452
    reading and, 365
    reproductive cells and, 68
    romantic relationships and, 542
    science and, 388, 451
    sense of self and, 448, 451–453, 457
    socialization and, 175–176, 476, 522–523
    stereotypes of, 452
    students at risk and, 507
    video games and, 562
    writing and, 373
Gender schemas, 451, 452

General factor, intelligence and, 278–279
Generalized anxiety disorder, 428
Generativity versus stagnation stage, 405, 407
Genes
    definition of, 64
    dominant/recessive genes, 69
    influence of, 72–73
    structure and operation of, 64–65
Genetic counseling, 78–79
Genetic disorders, 64, 69, 70–71, 78–79, 413
Genetics. See also Heredity
    attention-deficit hyperactivity disorder and, 268
    autism and, 269
    biological theories and, 12
    children's natural tendencies affecting, 8, 12
    chromosomal and genetic disorders, 69, 70–71
    depression and, 427
    developmental issues of, 79
    environmental factors influencing, 64, 65, 66, 73–74
    formation of reproductive cells and, 66–68
    individual traits and, 68–69, 72
    influence of genes, 66, 72–73
    mental retardation and, 309
    nature/nurture and, 74, 79
    sense of self and, 444
    sexual orientation and, 545
    speech and communication disorders and, 351
    structure and operation of genes and, 64–65
    temperament and, 6–7, 431, 444
Geography, 391–392, 396
Germany, 413
Germ cells, 66
Gestures, 243–244, 245, 318, 336, 338, 339
Giftedness
    characteristics of children with, 305–308
    definition of, 305
    interpersonal behaviors and, 476
    moral development and, 521
    reading and, 364
    states' criteria for, 304n
Glial cells, 101
Goal-directed behavior
    definition of, 196
    motivation and, 492
Goals
    achievement goals, 493–494, 495
    development of, 492–495
    health-compromising behaviors and, 134
    mastery goals, 494, 495, 497, 500, 504–505
    modeling of goal setting, 255
    moral development and, 519, 522
    motivation and, 487, 492–495, 502, 503–504
    multiple goals, 495
    performance goals, 494, 495, 497, 504–505
    self-handicapping and, 443
    self-regulated learning and, 252, 253
    self-regulation and, 508, 513
    self-serving goals, 474
    social goals, 494–495, 505
    social information processing and, 462, 463
    social learning theory and, 13
Grammatical rules, 328, 370
Grammatical words, 324, 325, 328
Grandparents, 155–156, 158, 163
Gravity, 385
Great Britain, 423–424
Gross motor skills, 111, 112–113, 114
Group activities, 209, 218, 435, 444, 479, 495, 511
Group discussions, 368, 383, 524
Group play, 222
Growth spurts, 114, 115–116, 118

Guatemala, 73, 224
Guidance
    self-guidance, 220
    self-regulation and, 511–512
Guided participation
    culture and, 159, 214–215
    definition of, 159, 215
Guilt
    conduct disorder and, 428
    definition of, 516
    depression and, 427
    emotional development and, 419, 420, 422
    gender and, 522
    initiative versus guilt stage and, 405, 407
    moral development and, 516, 519

Habituation, definition of, 38
Hacking, 564
Handwriting, 114, 370
Happiness, 418, 419
Heads of family, 148, 157, 158. See also Parents
Head Start, 294, 556–557
Health care, 183
Health-compromising behaviors
    long-term goals and, 134
    observation guidelines, 136
    organized sports and, 128
    physical development and, 131–135
    prevention of, 133–135, 448
Health hazards, 137, 139
Hearing loss/impairments, 351–352, 364, 464
Hedonistic orientation, 473
Hemispheres, of brain, 103, 106, 306–307
Heredity. See also Genetics
    fluid intelligence and, 279
    giftedness and, 306–307
    intelligence and, 73, 291–292, 295
    interaction with environmental factors, 7, 68, 73–74, 295
    prosocial and aggressive behavior, 470–471
    sensitive periods and, 72
Heroin, 81
Hidden curriculum, 551–552
Hierarchical stages, 9
High-interest literature, 367
Hindbrain, 101, 102
Hispanic Americans
    academic achievement and, 177
    bilingualism and, 348
    depression and, 427
    ethnicity of, 174–175
    families and, 153, 175
    intelligence and, 299, 300, 301
    language development and, 333
    moral development and, 522
    motivation and, 301, 500
    prosocial behavior and, 476
    puberty and, 118
    reading and, 365
    sense of self and, 457
    sociolinguistic behaviors and, 341, 342, 343
    students at risk and, 507
Historical time, 207, 208, 390
History, 390–391, 396
Holophrase, 328
Home environments. See also Families; Parents
    intelligence and, 292, 293–294
    mental retardation and, 309
    students at risk and, 507
    teacher expectations and, 552–553
Homeless families, 170, 185–186
Home visiting programs, 171, 174
Homework completion, 162, 511, 512
Homophobia, 481
Homosexual parents, 156, 157, 158
Homosexuals, 545, 546
Hostile attributional bias, 474
Housing, 183
Human immunodeficiency virus (HIV), 79, 81, 121, 131, 133, 135, 157

Huntington disease (HD), 71
Hurricane Katrina, 465
Hyperactivity, 268–269, 270
Hypothesis testing, 200, 385, 386, 389
Hypothetical ideas, formal operations stage and, 200, 201, 202

Idealism, 201, 207
Identical twins, 68, 291, 431, 471, 545
Identification phase of internalized motivation, 492, 509
Identity. See also Ethnic identity; Sense of self
    definition of, 449
    Erikson's psychosocial development theory and, 10, 14, 405, 406, 407
    establishing, 449–450
    moral development and, 522
    peer relationships and, 470, 533
    romantic relationships and, 543
Identity achievement, 449
Identity diffusion, 449
Identity versus role confusion stage, 405, 407
Imaginary audience
    definition of, 448
    interpersonal behaviors and, 448–449, 469
    self-perception and, 452
    theory of mind and, 460
Imitation
    interpersonal behaviors and, 466
    language development and, 316
    sense of self and, 447
    sensorimotor stage and, 198
    sociolinguistic behaviors and, 343
Immersion, definition of, 348
Immigrants, 552
Impulse control, 508
Impulsivity, 268–269, 270, 271
Inanimate objects
    infants' attention and, 238
    science and, 385
    theory of mind and, 458
    theory theory and, 263, 264
Inclusion, 140
Incremental view of ability, 496, 497
Independence, self-regulation and, 510, 511
Independent learning, 259
India, 224, 423–424
Individual constructivism, 194
Individualism, 180
Individual variability within groups, 298
Inducing labor, 88
Induction, 521, 524
Industry versus inferiority stage, 405, 407
Infancy
    aggression and, 472–473
    attachments and, 408–414, 494
    attention and, 238–239, 318, 431
    babies at risk, 88–89, 92
    brain development and, 104–105, 109, 128
    caregivers' sensitivity to newborn infants, 90–92
    causal relationships and, 385
    child maltreatment and, 166
    choices and, 244
    chronic health conditions in, 138
    cognitive development and, 19, 38, 198
    cognitive strategies and, 255, 256
    developmental features of, 18–19
    developmentally appropriate practice and, 26
    eating habits and, 113, 119–120, 121
    emotional development and, 404–405, 418, 420, 434
    families' concerns about, 172
    friendships and, 536
    information processing abilities and, 247
    intelligence tests and, 289–291, 297
    interpersonal behaviors and, 466, 477
    intersubjectivity and, 260
    IQ scores and, 279, 296

language development and, 72, 316, 317, 318, 322, 323, 324, 325–326, 327, 328, 330, 332, 336, 338, 343, 349
language skills and, 345
long-term memory and, 241
mathematics and, 374, 380
metacognition and, 256
moral development and, 515, 520, 521
motivation and, 488, 489, 490–491, 492, 501
music and, 394
needs and services plan for, 111, 112
peer relationships and, 548
physical activity and, 126
physical development and, 19, 24, 98, 111, 113, 120
Piaget's cognitive development theory and, 196, 205, 206–207
play and, 213
problem-solving strategies, 249
professional viewpoints on, 19
prosocial behavior and, 472
reading and, 359, 363
rest and sleep, 113, 128–129
schemes and, 243
science and, 384–385, 387
self-regulation and, 509
sense of self and, 444, 447, 455
sensory and perceptual capabilities and, 236–237
social cognition and, 458–459, 477
social interaction and, 262
social referencing and, 260–261
social stimuli and, 237, 260
stimulation for infants, 237, 238
temperament and, 431, 432, 433
theory of mind and, 458–459
theory theory and, 263–264
thinking and reasoning skills, 223
Vygotsky's cognitive development theory, 211
writing and, 372
Infant-caregiver relationship
attachment and, 18, 408–409, 411, 415
attention and, 238
autonomy versus shame and doubt stage and, 405
emotional regulation and, 420
quality of, 19
sense of self and, 444
temperament and, 433, 435
trust versus mistrust stage and, 404
Infant-directed speech, 322–323, 325, 394
Infantile amnesia, 241
Inferences
integration of knowledge and, 241
language development and, 326, 327
learning strategies and, 257
logic and, 243
observation and, 50–52
reading comprehension and, 361–362
social cognition and, 464
teacher expectations and, 552
theory of mind and, 458, 460
Inferiority, 405, 407
Infinity, 200, 201
Informal interactions, 210
Information processing
developmental trends in, 247
exceptionalities in, 267–271
infancy and, 247
social information processing, 462–463
social interaction and, 262
speed of, 279, 291
Information processing theory
attention and, 236, 261
cognitive processes and, 203, 234–246
cognitive strategies and, 250
critique of, 266
definition of, 234
key ideas in, 234–236
language development and, 318–319, 320, 321
model of human information processing system, 234, 235
neo-Piagetian theories and, 203, 265–266

semantics and, 320
sociocultural element of, 260–262
Inhalants, 132
Inhibition of unproductive thoughts/behaviors
attention-deficit hyperactivity disorder and, 268
central executive and, 236, 240
self-regulation and, 508, 509, 510
Initiative versus guilt stage, 405, 407
Injuries, 119, 125, 128, 137, 139, 141, 427
Inner speech
cognitive development and, 224
collaborative learning and, 257
definition of, 211
self-regulation and, 508
Inquisitiveness, observation of, 305, 493
Insecure-avoidant attachment, 410–411, 412, 413
Insecure-resistant attachment, 411, 412
Instructional strategies
cognitive process theories and, 15
community of learners and, 550
goals and, 495
second language and, 348–349
social constructivism and, 215
Integration
definition of, 99
of knowledge, 241–242
physical development and, 99, 100
Integration phase of internalized motivation, 492, 509
Integrity versus despair stage, 405–406, 407
Intelligence
case studies, 277, 310–311
Cattell's fluid and crystallized intelligence, 279
conceptions of, 277–278
critique of current perspectives on, 301–302
definition of, 278
developmental trends in IQ scores, 296–298
distributed intelligence, 282, 283, 304
early intervention and, 292, 294, 303, 557
environmental factors and, 73, 292–296
exceptionalities in, 304–310
Gardner's multiple intelligences, 279–280, 283, 288, 303–304
group differences in, 298–301
hereditary influences on, 73, 291–292, 295
implications of theories and research, 302–304
measurement of, 278, 283–291
nature/nurture and, 73, 295–296
observation of, 305
Spearman's g, 278–279, 283
Sternberg's triarchic theory, 281–282, 283, 288
theoretical perspectives of, 278–283
Intelligence quotient scores. See IQ scores
Intelligence tests
correlation studies of, 278
critique of, 301–302
cultural bias in, 300, 302
definition of, 284
dynamic assessment, 288–289
early childhood and, 289–291, 297
general intelligence tests, 284–288
group differences in, 298–301
infancy and, 289–291, 297
reliability and, 287–288, 290
specific ability tests, 288
validity and, 287–288, 290
Intentionality, 458
Interactive technologies
computers and the Internet, 563–565
content of programs and games, 561–562
definition of, 561
implications of, 564–565
video games, 562–563
Interest
emotional development and, 418

high-interest literature, 367
motivation and, 490–491, 493
Internal attributions, 496
Internalization
definition of, 211
moral development and, 515–516
Internalized motivation, 491, 492, 509
Internalized values orientation, 473
International adoption, 156
Internet, 561, 563–564, 565
Interpersonal behaviors
aggressive behavior and, 470–475
case studies, 482–483
developmental trends in, 477–478
diversity in, 475–476
early adolescence and, 469–470, 478
early childhood and, 466–468, 475, 477
fostering effective skills, 478–482
imaginary audience and, 448–449, 469
infancy and, 466, 477
late adolescence and, 470, 478
middle childhood and, 468–469, 477
prosocial behavior and, 470–472
romantic relationships and, 543
Interpersonal intelligence, 280
Interpersonal relationships. See also Peer relationships; Romantic relationships; Social interaction
attachment and, 414, 415
central conceptual structures and, 204
Erikson's psychosocial development theory and, 406
intersubjectivity and, 260–261
language development and, 320
moral development and, 522
Interpretation
attributions and, 496
ethical guidelines for, 57
infants' sensory and perceptual capabilities and, 236
of IQ scores, 301–302
peer relationships and, 533
social information processing and, 462, 463
theory of mind and, 459–460
Interpreting children's artifacts and actions
adolescents' risky behavior and, 107
arithmetic errors and, 376–377
assessments and, 55–56
attachment and, 409
brain development and, 106–107
children's stories, 20
children's views on thinking and, 258
epistemological beliefs and, 254–255
experimentation and, 225
families' influence on children, 162
figurative speech and, 335
giftedness and, 306
goals and, 504
homosexuality and, 545–546
information processing difficulties and, 270
listening to children and, 53
multiple intelligences and, 303–304
observations and, 50
physical activity and, 127–128
Piaget's stages and, 208
pseudowriting and, 369
self-perception and, 446
self-regulation and, 514
sense of self and, 450–451
simplifying fractions and, 384
social perspective taking and, 461
ultrasound examinations and, 82
video games and, 563
vocabulary development and, 323–324
Interrupting as a cultural difference, 342–343
Intersubjectivity
autism and, 269
definition of, 260
interpersonal relationships and, 260–261
language development and, 319
observation of, 267
theory of mind and, 458

Intervention programs (gangs), 542. See also Early intervention
Interviews
children's views on thinking and, 258
as data collection technique, 36–37
definition of, 36
interviewing skills, 54
Piaget's cognitive development theory and, 193
Intimacy
intimacy versus isolation stage, 405, 407
sexual intimacy, 118, 544
Intrapersonal intelligence, 280
Intrinsic motivation
attributions and, 498
culture and, 500
definition of, 488
developmental issues of, 499
development of, 489–492
observation guidelines, 493
Piaget's cognitive development theory and, 193
promotion of, 500, 502–503
school environment and, 549
self-regulation and, 510, 511
Introjection phase of internalized motivation, 492, 509
Invented spellings, 370
IQ scores
accuracy of, 287n, 303
adoption studies and, 292, 293
age and, 290–291
definition of, 287
developmental trends in, 296–298
distribution of, 287, 287n
environmental factors and, 291, 293, 294
gender and, 298
giftedness and, 305
heredity and, 295
information processing speed and, 279, 291
intelligence tests and, 284, 285, 287–288
interpretation of, 301–302
mental retardation and, 301, 322
percentage in different ranges, 287, 287n
predictive nature of, 296, 298
socioeconomic status and, 299, 300
stability of, 296, 298
twin studies and, 291–292, 292n, 293
IRE cycle, 342
Irregular verbs, 331
Isolation, 405, 407
Israel, 414, 476

Japan, 249, 332, 366, 388, 394, 412–413, 414, 423, 424, 433, 500, 508n
Jewish Americans, 343
Joint attention, 260, 447
Joint custody, 154
Junior high schools, 554
Just community, 524
Justice orientation, 522, 523

Kapauku, 45–46
Kenya, 414
Klinefelter syndrome, 70
Knowledge
epistemological beliefs and, 253, 259–260
integration of, 241–242
long-term memory and, 240, 241
motivation and, 320
Piaget's cognitive development theory and, 192, 201
prior knowledge, 183, 201, 202–203, 214, 244, 278, 279
triarchic theory and, 282
of written language's purpose, 360
Knowledge base
definition of, 241
interdependence of, 255
language development and, 334
learning and, 243, 264
reading comprehension and, 361

Knowledge telling, definition of, 371
Knowledge transforming, definition of, 371
Kohlberg's moral development theory
    conventional morality and, 518
    moral dilemmas and, 517, 518, 521, 522
    postconventional morality and, 518
    preconventional morality and, 517
    stage progression and, 519
    stages and, 14, 517, 518, 521, 524

Language acquisition device, 317
Language comprehension, 322
Language development
    case studies, 315, 353
    cognitive development and, 320, 348
    critiquing theories of, 320–323
    developmental trends in, 323–347
    diversity in, 349–350
    early theories of, 316–317
    exceptionalities in, 350–352
    functionalism and, 320, 321, 324
    information processing theory and, 318–319, 320, 321
    interpersonal behaviors and, 466
    listening skills and, 331–335
    long-term memory and, 241
    meaning and, 317, 318, 319–320, 322, 324–327, 330–331, 333–334
    metalinguistic awareness and, 340, 344, 346–347
    nativism and, 317–318, 319, 320, 321
    Piaget's cognitive development theory and, 200, 224
    pragmatics and, 316, 340–344
    preoperational stage and, 197
    right hemisphere and, 103, 317
    second language development, 318, 319, 344, 346, 347–349
    semantic development, 316, 323–328
    sensitive periods and, 72, 317–318, 319
    sociocultural theory and, 319–320
    sociolinguistic behaviors and, 340–344
    speaking skills and, 335–340
    syntactic development, 316, 328–331
    theoretical perspectives of, 316–323
    trends in, 323–347
    Vygotsky's cognitive development theory, 211, 224
Language production, 322
Late adolescence
    chronic health conditions in, 139
    cognitive strategies and, 257
    developmental features of, 22
    developmentally appropriate practice and, 26
    developmental strengths and, 31
    elaboration and, 248–249
    emotional development and, 421, 434
    families' concerns about, 173
    fluid intelligence and, 279
    friendships and, 537
    gender and, 451
    information processing abilities and, 247
    intelligence tests and, 297
    interpersonal behaviors and, 470, 478
    language skills and, 346
    mathematics and, 381
    metacognitive awareness and, 251, 257
    moral development and, 520
    motivation and, 502
    peer relationships and, 22, 470, 536, 549
    physical development and, 25, 118, 121
    professional viewpoints, 23
    reading and, 364
    science and, 387
    sense of self and, 449–451, 454, 455
    social cognition and, 478
    theory of mind and, 460
    thinking and reasoning skills, 223
    writing and, 372
Late-maturing boys, 117
Late-maturing girls, 117
Leadership, observation of, 305
Lead exposure, 79, 139, 293, 309

Leading questions, 261
Learned helplessness, 497–498, 499, 500
Learning ability
    forebrain and, 102
    intelligence and, 278
    observation of, 305
    prenatal development and, 78
    spontaneous learning and, 108
Learning disabilities
    chronic illnesses and, 141
    definition of, 268
    Fragile X syndrome and, 69, 72
    giftedness and, 308
    reading and, 268, 364
    self-regulation and, 510
    students at risk and, 507
Learning strategies
    definition of, 246
    evaluating effectiveness of, 252, 258
    inferences and, 257
    interdependence of, 255
    learning disabilities and, 268
    mathematics and, 383
    mental retardation and, 309
    metacognition and, 246, 248–249
    modeling of, 255
    motivation and, 489, 493, 497
    observation of, 267
    self-regulated learning and, 252–253
    sense of self and, 443
    students at risk and, 507
Left hemisphere
    definition of, 103
    language development and, 317
Lesbian parents, 156, 157, 158
Lesbian youth, 545, 546
Level of potential development
    definition of, 212
    dynamic assessment and, 288
Lexical words
    definition of, 324
    language development and, 324–325, 328
Libraries, in literacy development, 358, 368
Linguistic intelligence, 280
Listening skills, 219, 331–335
Listening to children, data collection and, 53–55
Literacy
    emergent literacy, 358–359, 365
    music literacy, 394
Literature-based curriculum, 346–347, 368
Lobes (in the brain), 103
Logic
    concrete operational stage and, 199, 200
    information processing theory and, 243
    integration of knowledge and, 241
    Piaget's cognitive development theory and, 199, 200, 201, 202, 243
    preoperational stage and, 199
    prior knowledge and, 201, 202
Logical-mathematical intelligence, 280
Longitudinal studies
    advantages/disadvantages of, 47
    definition of, 45
Long-term memory
    capacity of, 236, 241
    definition of, 235
    developmental trends in, 240–243
    information processing theory and, 235–236
    social information processing and, 462
    working memory and, 236
Low-achieving peers, 495
Lysergic acid diethylamide (LSD), 132

Magic School Bus, The, 561
Magnetic resonance imaging (MRI), 38, 39, 108
Manipulatives, 383
Maps, 391–392
Marijuana, 81, 132
Mastery goals, 494, 495, 497, 500, 504–505
Mastery orientation, 497
Mathematical reasoning skills, 200, 207

Mathematics
    advanced problem-solving procedures, 378–379
    basic arithmetic operations, 375–378
    concepts and principles of, 375
    developmental progressions in, 396
    developmental trends in, 380–381
    diversity in, 379, 381–382
    gender and, 381, 451, 500
    metacognition in, 379, 384
    number sense and counting, 374–375
    promoting development in, 382–384
Maturation
    biological theories and, 12
    brain development and, 103, 106, 204, 238, 461
    cognitive development and, 192, 204
    definition of, 7
    different rates of, 98–99
    genetic expression and, 65, 72
    language development and, 318
    perceptual development and, 237
    puberty and, 116
    qualitative/quantitative change and, 10
    self-regulation and, 508
    sexual maturation, 118, 119, 128
    theory of mind and, 461
Meaning
    language development and, 317, 318, 319–320, 322, 324–327, 330–331, 333–334
    metalinguistic awareness and, 344, 346–347
    reading and, 366–367
    social construction of, 214–215, 261, 358
    Vygotsky's cognitive development theory and, 210, 224
    writing and, 369
Media
    reading and, 368
    romantic relationships and, 542
    television and interactive technologies, 561–565
Mediated learning experiences, 214
Mediation
    as means of resolving peer conflicts, 481, 482–483, 524
    in Vygotsky's theory, 210
Meiosis
    chromosome abnormalities and, 69
    definition of, 66
    process of, 66, 67, 68, 68n
Memory. See also Long-term memory; Working memory
    information processing theory and, 234, 235
    interdependence of, 255
    metacognitive awareness and, 250, 251–252
    sense of self and, 447
    social construction of, 261
Menarche, 115
Mental age, 285
Mental representations, 414, 415
Mental retardation
    brain development and, 104
    characteristics of children with, 308–310
    chromosome abnormalities and, 69
    definition of, 308
    fetal alcohol syndrome and, 293
    Fragile X syndrome and, 72
    gender and, 298
    interpersonal behaviors and, 476
    IQ scores and, 301, 322
    language development and, 321
    learning disabilities distinguished from, 268
    professional practice and, 309–310
    reading and, 364
    sexually transmitted infections and, 133
    social cognition and, 464
    states' criteria for, 304n
Metacognition
    central executive and, 240
    content domain standards and, 395

definition of, 246
developmental trends in, 256–257
epistemological beliefs and, 253–255
intelligence tests and, 302
interdependence with cognitive processes, 255
learning strategies and, 246, 248–249
in mathematics, 379, 384
mental retardation and, 309
metacognitive awareness, 250–252
observation of, 267, 305
problem-solving strategies and, 249–250, 255, 258
promoting development of, 255, 257–260
in reading, 362, 367
in science, 386
self-regulated learning and, 252–253
triarchic theory and, 282
writing and, 371
Metacognitive awareness
    definition of, 250
    interdependence of, 255
    late adolescence and, 251, 257
    metacognition and, 250–252
    middle childhood and, 251, 256
Metalinguistic awareness
    definition of, 344
    language development and, 340, 344, 346–347
    second language development and, 344, 346, 347, 348
    sign language and, 352
    theory of mind and, 459
Metaphors, computer metaphors, 234
Methamphetamine (speed), 132
Methylene dioxymethamphetamine (MDMA), 132
Mexico, 203, 217
Microgenetic methods, 45
Midbrain, 101, 102
Middle childhood
    after-school programs and, 558
    art and, 392–393, 394
    attachment and, 410, 414
    attention and, 239
    attributions and, 496, 497
    brain development and, 106, 108
    chronic health conditions in, 138
    cognitive strategies and, 256
    comprehension monitoring and, 253
    developmental features of, 20–21
    developmentally appropriate practice and, 26
    emotional development and, 405, 420, 421, 422, 425, 434
    empathy and, 516
    epistemological beliefs and, 253
    families' concerns about, 173
    friendships and, 537
    geography and, 391–392
    history and, 390–391
    information processing abilities and, 247
    intelligence tests and, 297
    interpersonal behaviors and, 468–469, 477
    language development and, 323, 324, 325, 329–330, 333, 336, 337–338, 340
    language skills and, 345
    learning disabilities and, 268
    learning strategies and, 246, 252
    mathematics and, 375, 377–379, 380, 383
    metacognitive awareness and, 251, 256
    metalinguistic awareness and, 344
    moral development and, 516, 516n, 520, 524
    motivation and, 488, 491, 494, 501, 503
    music and, 394
    organization and, 248
    peer relationships and, 21, 468, 548
    phonological awareness and, 359
    physical activity and, 125, 126
    physical development and, 25, 114, 120
    Piaget's cognitive development theory and, 205, 207

play and, 213
problem-solving strategies and, 249
professional viewpoints on, 21
reading and, 363, 366
reciprocal influences and, 164
rehearsal and, 246
rest and sleep, 129
science and, 385, 386, 387, 388–389
second-language learning and, 347
self-handicapping and, 443
self-regulation and, 509, 511
sense of self and, 442–443, 445, 448, 455
social cognition and, 477
stereotypes and, 463–464
strategy development and, 250
television viewing and, 562
theory of mind and, 459–460
theory theory and, 264–265
thinking/reasoning skills, 21, 223
Vygotsky's cognitive development theory and, 211
word recognition and, 360
writing and, 370, 371, 372
Middle East, 427, 457
Middle schools, 554
Mind, theory of. *See* Theory of mind
Minority groups. *See* Ethnic minority groups
Misconceptions, 205, 264–265, 328, 379
Mister Rogers' Neighborhood, 561
Mistrust, 404, 407
Mitosis, 75
Modeling
aggression and, 471
apprenticeships and, 216
attachment security and, 415–416, 417
cognitive strategies and, 255, 257, 262
communities and, 150
conflict resolution and, 153
emotional regulation and, 420–421, 426
empathy and, 422
fathers and, 152
interpersonal behaviors and, 476
language development and, 316–317
motivation and, 503
parents' employment and, 163
peer relationships and, 533
prosocial behavior and, 471, 479–480
reading and, 368
self-regulation and, 510
siblings and, 165
socialization and, 149
socioeconomic status and, 186
Moderate correlations, 44
Monozygotic twins, 68, 291, 471, 545
Moral compass, 465
Moral development
aggression and, 515, 521
case studies, 525–526
definition of, 515
developmental trends in, 515–519, 520
diversity in, 522–523
factors affecting, 487, 519, 521–522
Kohlberg's theory of, 14, 517–519, 521, 522, 524
language development and, 320
promotion of, 523–525
prosocial behavior and, 515
Moral dilemmas, 517, 518, 521, 522, 524
Moral traits, 522
Moral transgressions, 516
Moratorium, identity and, 449–450
Motherese, 322
Mothers. *See also* Parents
adolescent mothers, 157
attachment and, 413, 414, 417
birth preparation and, 85–86
emotional development and, 424
employment and, 163
family structure and, 152–153
prenatal development and, 83–84
temperament and, 433
Motivation. *See also* Extrinsic motivation; Intrinsic motivation
attributions and, 495–498
case studies, 487

definition of, 487
developmental trends in, 501–502
disequilibrium and, 201, 208, 489
diversity in, 498–500
early intervention and, 294
ethnic minority groups and, 500
extrinsic rewards and punishments, 488–489, 523
goals and, 487, 492–495, 502, 503–504
interpersonal behaviors and, 469
IQ scores and, 296, 301
language development and, 318, 320
Piaget's cognitive development theory and, 193
promoting motivation, 500, 502–507
sense of self and, 442
social cognitive theory and, 13
Motor skills
adolescence and, 108
biological theories and, 12
differentiation and, 99
early childhood and, 111–113
fine motor skills, 111, 113, 114
genetics influence on, 72
gross motor skills, 111, 112–113, 114
infancy and, 111, 113, 207
learning disabilities and, 268
middle childhood and, 21
motivation and, 492
nature/nurture and, 130
physical development and, 98
qualitative/quantitative change and, 100, 130
universality/diversity and, 8, 130
MUDs (Multiuser Dungeons), 563
Multicultural education, 179, 181, 458
Multiethnic children, 175, 181, 454, 458
Multiple attachments, 413–414, 416
Multiple-clause sentences, 330
Multiple goals, 495
Multiple hypotheses, 49
Multiple intelligences
children's individual strengths and, 304
intelligence theories compared to, 283
interpreting children's artifacts and actions, 303–304
specific ability tests and, 288
theoretical perspective of, 279–280
Multiuser Dungeons (MUDs), 563
Music, 394–395, 396
Musical intelligence, 280
Music literacy, 394
Myelination, 105, 106, 107, 108, 240
My Fair Lady, 564

Narratives
definition of, 337
language development and, 337, 339
social construction of memory and, 261
story schemas and, 361
writing and, 370
National Association for the Education of Young Children, 19
National Consortium for Physical Education and Recreation for Individuals with Disabilities, 140
National Middle School Association (NMSA), 22
Native Americans
academic achievement and, 177
bilingualism and, 348
cultural perspective of, 240, 302
depression and, 427
families and, 175
family communication and, 171
intelligence and, 278, 302
motivation and, 500
reading and, 365
sociolinguistic behaviors and, 340, 341, 342, 343
students at risk and, 507
writing and, 373
Native language
automatization and, 319
bilingual education and, 348–349
definition of, 316
phonemes of, 332

Nativism
children's theories about physical world and, 384
definition of, 264, 317
language development and, 317–318, 319, 320, 321
theory theory and, 264
Naturalistic studies, 45–46, 47
Naturalist intelligence, 280
Nature
definition of, 6
developmental systems theories and, 16
Nature/nurture
aggression and, 8, 73, 475
attachment and, 430
brain development and, 104
child development theories and, 17–18
cognitive development and, 11
communities and, 151
content domains and, 396
contexts and, 565
culture and, 151
as developmental issue, 4, 6–8, 10
emotional development and, 430
emotional problems and, 426
Erikson's psychosocial development theory and, 406
families and, 151
genetics and, 74, 79
information processing theory and, 266
intelligence and, 73, 295–296
intelligence theories and, 283
language development theories and, 321
motivation and, 499
music and, 395
obesity and, 123
perceptual development and, 237
physical development and, 11, 98, 130
Piaget and Vygotsky contrasted, 226
prenatal development and, 79
prosocial behavior and, 475
sexual orientation and, 545
social-emotional development and, 11
temperament and, 6–7, 431
theory theory and, 266
twin studies and, 68
Need for relatedness, 407, 482, 494
Negative affectivity, 431, 433
Negative correlations, 44
Negative numbers, 200, 201, 207
Neglected children (peer acceptance), 533, 534, 535
Neighborhoods
discrimination and, 177
influence of, 182
maps of, 392
parenting styles and, 161
peer relationships and, 539
self-regulation and, 510
Neonatal Behavioral Assessment Scale (Brazelton Institute), 290
Neo-Piagetian theories
central conceptual structures and, 204, 377–378
definition of, 203
information processing theory and, 203, 265–266
key ideas in, 203–204
Neural activity, 296
Neural tube defects, 83
Neurofibromatosis, 70
Neurons, 75, 100–101, 102, 104
Neuroticism, 433, 436
Nicaragua, 318
Niche-picking, 295, 307
Nicotine, 81
No Child Left Behind Act of 2001, 395
Nonexamples, in semantic development, 327
Nonverbal cues, 50, 465
Norms, 540
Note taking, modeling of, 255
Number, central conceptual structures and, 204
Number sense, 374–375

Nurture. *See also* Nature/nurture
definition of, 7
developmental systems theories and, 16
Vygotsky's cognitive development theory and, 210
Nutrition. *See also* Eating habits
environmental/hereditary interaction and, 73, 74
intelligence and, 292, 293, 295, 300
mental retardation and, 309
physical development and, 99–100, 119
poverty and, 183
promoting better eating habits, 124–125
puberty and, 116, 119

Obesity, 122–123
Object permanence, 196, 201
Observations
attachment security assessment, 412
cognitive development and, 198
of cultural practices and beliefs, 180
data collection and, 38–40, 49–53
definition of, 38
distortions of information and, 41
emergent literacy and, 360
emotions and, 419
family conditions and, 169
of general characteristics, 51
health behaviors assessment, 136
indicators of health in newborns, 91
inferences and, 50–52
intelligence and, 305
intelligence tests used with, 291
intrinsic motivation and, 493
of metacognition, 267, 305
naturalistic studies and, 46
of peer acceptance, 535
physical development in infancy and, 113
physical well-being and, 136
of play activities, 222, 467
of prosocial behavior, 473
of sociolinguistic behaviors, 341
of temperament, 432
thinking/reasoning skills and, 207
types of, 52–53
One Fish Two Fish Red Fish Blue Fish (Seuss), 367
One-one principle, 375
Onlooker behavior, 467
Only children, 165, 307
Open adoption, 156
Openness, 433, 436
Operant conditioning, 488
Operations
definition of, 193
Piaget's cognitive development theory and, 193–194
Opioids, 88
Oral language skills, 305, 335–340
Order-irrelevance principle, 375
Organization
definition of, 248
epistemological beliefs and, 255
knowledge integration and, 241
as learning strategy, 246, 248
long-term memory and, 236
Organized sports
cognitive development and, 213
diversity and, 127
as extracurricular activities, 558
gender and, 126, 175, 451, 500
injuries and, 128
interpersonal behaviors and, 468
motivation and, 488
parents and, 125, 163
physical activity and, 125–126
transition to secondary schools and, 554
Orientations, of prosocial behavior, 472, 473
Out-groups, 540
Ova, 66, 67, 68, 68n, 75
Ovaries, 75, 76
Overgeneralization, 324

Overlapping talk, 365
Overlapping waves, strategy development
    as, 250
Overregularization, 329
Overt, external guidance, 220
Overt self-guidance, 220

Pacific Islanders
    motivation and, 500
    reading and, 365
    sociolinguistic behaviors and, 341,
        342, 343
Paper-pencil tests, 55
Papua New Guinea, 382
Parallel play, 466, 467
Parent discussion groups, 170
Parenting styles
    aggression and, 160, 471
    definition of, 160
    factors affecting, 164
    observation of, 168, 169
    types of, 159–161
Parents. See also Families; Fathers;
    Mothers
    adolescent parents, 157
    adoptive parents, 156, 158
    after-school programs and, 558
    attachments and, 408–410, 415, 416,
        417, 466
    attributions and, 498
    babies at risk and, 89, 92
    bilingualism and, 348
    bioecological perspective and, 16
    birth preparation and, 85–86
    care for newborn and, 90–92
    communities and, 150
    conduct disorder and, 429
    content domains and, 358
    coparents, 152–153, 154
    crying and, 111
    divorced parents, 152, 153–154
    eating habits and, 122
    emergent literacy and, 358
    emotional development and, 423, 424
    emotional regulation and, 420
    employment of, 163, 169
    language development and, 322–323
    organized sports and, 125, 163
    prenatal development and, 83–84
    reading to children and, 162, 358, 366
    religion and, 559–560, 561
    self-regulation and, 509, 510
    sense of self and, 445, 449, 451,
        453, 454
    sex education and, 546
    single parents, 152, 154–155
    socioeconomic status and, 299
    sociolinguistic behaviors and, 342
    stepparents, 155
    television viewing time and, 564
    theory of mind and, 461
    theory theory and, 265
    therapeutic foster parents, 156–157
    ultrasound examinations and, 82
Parent-teacher-student conferences, 168
Part-time employment, 559
Part-whole principle, 375
Passive aggressive, 465
Passive gene-environment relation, 73
Passive sentences, 329–330
Peer culture, 539
Peer mediation, 481, 482–483, 524
Peer pressure, 469–470
Peer relationships
    adolescence and, 50, 532–533, 539,
        540–541
    attachments and, 410, 414, 415
    attributions and, 497
    bilingualism and, 348
    birth order and, 165
    case studies, 566–567
    chronic illnesses and, 137
    conduct disorder and, 428
    correlational studies and, 44
    developmental trends in, 548–549
    disabilities and, 141
    divorce and, 154

early adolescence and, 21, 469,
    540–541, 548
elementary/secondary transition
    and, 553
emotional development and, 422
emotional regulation and, 421
extracurricular activities and, 558
friendships and, 468, 534–539
functions of, 532–533
gender and, 452, 533
health-compromising behavior and,
    131, 134
late adolescence and, 22, 470, 536, 549
middle childhood and, 21, 468, 548
moral development and, 521
motivation and, 504–505
nature/nurture and, 565
neighborhoods and, 539
obesity and, 123, 124
observations of peer acceptance, 535
peer acceptance and, 533–534
personalities and, 436
physical activity and, 127–128
Piaget's cognitive development theory
    and, 209, 225
reading and, 368
romantic relationships, 542–547
second-language learning and, 347
sense of self and, 443, 444, 445,
    446, 449
social construction of meaning and,
    214–215
social groups and, 539–542
socialization and, 533
social skills and, 466, 509, 533, 534,
    538, 543
sociolinguistic behaviors and, 340, 343
speech and communication disorders
    and, 351
teen dialects and, 338
Vygotsky's cognitive development
    theory and, 211–212
Peer tutoring, 495
Perception. See also Self-perception
    definition of, 90
    depth perception, 237
    developmental trends in, 236–238
    information processing theory and, 234
    organization and, 248
    of physical environment, 195
    sensitive periods and, 72
    visual perception, 108, 237
Performance goals, 494, 495, 497, 504–505
Permissive style
    aggression and, 471
    definition of, 160
Persistence, observation of, 432
Personal fable
    definition of, 117, 448
    late adolescence and, 118, 449
Personal interest, 490, 491
Personalities
    complexities of, 436–437
    definition of, 431
    environment/heredity interaction and, 73
    forebrain and, 102
    individual differences in, 433
    psychodynamic theories and, 13
Personal space, 341, 342
Perspective taking
    aggression and, 474
    moral development and, 515, 519,
        521, 524
    peer relationships and, 533, 536
    play and, 213
    social cognition and, 464–465
    social interaction and, 224
    social perspective taking, 460–461, 465,
        468, 472
    theory of mind and, 458–459, 458n
Peru, 340
Phantom Tollbooth, The (Juster), 346–347
Phenylkentonuria (PKU), 71
Phenytoin, 81
Phonemes
    definition of, 332
    metalinguistic awareness and, 344

phonological awareness and, 359
    spelling and, 370
Phonological awareness
    definition of, 359
    dyslexia and, 364
    language development and, 316, 318
    reading and, 359, 366
    spelling and, 370
Phonology, definition of, 316
Physical abuse, 166
Physical activity. See also Organized sports
    accommodating disabilities and,
        139–140
    encouraging of, 126–128
    observation guidelines, 136
    physical development and, 125–128
    television viewing time and, 562
Physical aggression, 472, 476, 480,
    532, 543
Physical appearance
    chat rooms and, 564
    gender and, 452, 457
    interpersonal behaviors and, 469
    media and, 561
    sense of self and, 444, 445, 446, 448
    teacher expectations and, 552
Physical development. See also Brain;
    Genetics; Motor skills
    case studies, 97, 142
    definition of, 5
    developmental trends and, 4, 24–25,
        120–121
    early adolescence and, 21–22, 25,
        114–118, 121
    early childhood and, 19, 24,
        111–114, 120
    eating habits and, 119, 121–125
    health-compromising behaviors and,
        131–135
    infancy and, 19, 24, 98, 111, 113, 120
    late adolescence and, 25, 118, 121
    middle childhood and, 25, 114, 120
    nature/nurture and, 11, 98, 130
    physical activity and, 125–128
    physical well-being and, 119–136,
        140–141
    physiological measures of, 38
    principles of, 98–100
    qualitative/quantitative change and, 11,
        100, 101, 130
    rest and sleep, 128–130
    sensitive periods and, 72
    special physical needs, 136–141
    universality/diversity and, 9, 11, 98, 130
Physical disabilities, 139–140, 195, 308,
    444, 476, 499, 511
Physical environment
    children's physical world theories and,
        263–265, 384–385
    nature/nurture and, 130
    Piaget's cognitive development theory
        and, 194–195, 205–206, 225
    play and, 213
Physical growth, physical development
    and, 114, 115–116, 118
Physical world, children's theories of,
    263–265, 384–385
Physiological measures, 38, 41
Piaget's cognitive development theory
    applying ideas of, 205–209
    cognitive-developmental theories
        and, 14
    constructivism and, 194, 234
    contemporary theories compared to, 266
    current perspectives on, 201–203
    interviews and, 193
    key ideas in, 193–196
    language development and, 200, 224
    moral development and, 515
    schemes and, 193, 196, 242, 243
    stages of cognitive development, 9, 14,
        196–201, 203, 206–208, 236
    stimuli and, 238
    studies of, 201
    universality/diversity and, 10, 196, 203
    Vygotsky compared to, 210, 211, 213,
        214, 221–222, 224–226

Placenta, 75
Place value, 207, 208, 376
Planning
    brain development and, 110
    central executive and, 236, 240
Play
    attention and, 239
    cooperative play, 213, 466, 467
    early childhood and, 213, 220–221, 536
    fantasy play and, 425, 542
    fathers and, 413
    gender and, 475
    interpersonal behaviors and, 466, 475
    mental retardation and, 309
    metalinguistic awareness and, 344
    observation guidelines, 222, 467
    pretend play, 113, 197–198, 413
    rough-and-tumble play, 125, 175
    sociodramatic play, 213, 461,
        467–468, 475
    symbolic thought and, 197–198, 222
    Vygotsky's cognitive development
        theory and, 212–213, 220–221
Playing the dozens, 337
Political systems, 165
Polygenic inheritance, 69
Polynesia, 302
Popular children (peer acceptance),
    533–534, 535
Popularity, 44, 448, 541
Population, research methods and, 35
Positive correlations, 44
Postconventional morality, 518
Postnatal development
    intelligence and, 292, 293, 300
    neurological development and, 293
Poverty. See also Socioeconomic status
    challenges of, 183–184
    coping mechanisms and, 177
    depression and, 427
Practical intelligence, 281, 308
Practice, 245–246
Prader-Willi syndrome, 70
Pragmatics, 316, 340–344, 350
Preconventional morality, 517, 518, 521
Predispositions, 431
Pregnancy, 78–79, 132, 133, 157, 544
Prejudice
    breaking down, 465
    definition of, 463
    learned helplessness and, 500
    peer relationships and, 538
    social cognition and, 463–464
Premature infants, 88–89, 92, 167
Prenatal development
    case studies, 92–93
    changes in brain during, 104, 109
    definition of, 74
    developmental issues of, 79
    developmental trends and, 85
    environmental factors and, 72
    gender and, 452
    intelligence and, 292, 300
    medical care and, 78–79, 81–82, 83, 84
    parents and, 83–84
    perception and, 90
    phases of prenatal growth, 75–78
    sensitive periods in, 73, 79, 80
Preoperational stage, 196–199, 201
Prepared childbirth classes, 86
Prescription medications, 132
Pretend play
    fathers and, 413
    motor skills and, 113
    preoperational stage and, 197–198
    sensorimotor stage and, 198
Pride, 419, 420
Primary reinforcers, definition of, 488
Priorities, motivation and, 493
Prior knowledge, 183, 201, 202–203, 214,
    244, 278, 279
Private speech, 211
Proactive aggression, 473–474
Problem solving
    aggression and, 474
    formal operations stage and, 200, 202
    learning disabilities and, 268

mathematics and, 379, 383
metacognition and, 249–250, 255, 258
modeling of, 255
observation of, 305
Piaget's clinical method and, 206
practical problem-solving ability, 281
scaffolding and, 257, 262
self-regulation and, 511–512
social problem-solving strategies, 478–479
thinking/reasoning skills and, 243–244
zone of proximal development and, 212
Process measures, of child care, 556
Professional organizations, 28
Professional practice
    accomplishments and diversity at different age levels, 24
    attachment security and, 415–417, 416
    child development and, 23, 26–28
    child maltreatment and, 167
    cognitive processes and, 244–245
    developmentally appropriate practice, 27–28
    diverse family structures and, 157–159
    early adolescence and, 22
    early childhood and, 19–20
    eating habits and, 124–125
    emotional development and, 424–426, 428
    emotional problems and, 429–430
    ethnic minority groups and, 178–179, 181–182
    friendships and, 537–539
    geography and, 392
    giftedness and, 307–308
    health-compromising behaviors and, 133–135
    infancy and, 19
    information processing and social interaction, 262
    information processing exceptionalities and, 269–271
    intelligence and, 302–304
    interpersonal skill promotion and, 478–482
    language development and, 327–328, 331
    late adolescence and, 23
    listening comprehension and, 334–335
    mathematics development and, 382–384
    mental retardation and, 309–310
    metacognitive and strategic development, 255, 257–260
    metalinguistic development and, 346–347
    middle childhood and, 21
    moral development and, 523–525
    motivation and, 500, 502–507
    newborn infants' needs, 90–92
    physical activity and, 126–128
    physical development and, 126–128
    physical well-being and, 140–141
    Piaget's cognitive development theory and, 205–209
    prenatal development and, 83–84
    reading development promotion, 366–368
    rest and sleep needs, 129–130
    science development and, 388–390
    self-regulation and, 510–515
    sense of self and, 454, 456–458
    social cognition development and, 464–466
    socioeconomic status and, 184–186
    sociolinguistic behaviors and, 343–344
    speaking skills and, 338–340
    television and technology, 564–565
    temperaments and personality development, 435–437
    theory of mind and, 461
    theory theory and, 265
    Vygotsky's cognitive development theory and, 218–221
    writing development and, 373–374
Promoting Alternative Thinking Strategies (PATHS), 425

Pronunciation, 336, 347, 349
Proportional reasoning
    art and, 393
    children's behavior and, 207
    formal operations stage and, 202
    maps and, 392
    mathematics and, 375, 379, 383
Prosocial behavior
    definition of, 470
    developmental issues of, 475
    development of, 472, 473
    gangs and, 541
    interpersonal behaviors and, 470–472
    modeling of, 471, 479–480
    moral development and, 515
    observation of, 473
    peer acceptance and, 534
    school environment and, 549, 551
    social groups and, 540
Proximodistal trends, 111
Pseudowriting, 369
Psychodynamic theories
    definition of, 13
    emphasis of, 13–14
    theoretical positions of, 17
Psychological harm, 516, 524
Psychosocial stages
    definition of, 404
    Erikson's psychosocial stages, 404–406
Puberty
    aggression and, 117, 471
    biological theories and, 12
    definition of, 114
    emotional development and, 422–423
    gender and, 115–116, 451, 452
    genetics and, 65
    physical development and, 21–22, 114–118
    romantic relationships and, 542, 546
    sense of self and, 448
    sexual intimacy and, 544
Punishment
    aggression and, 471, 489
    extrinsic rewards and punishments, 488–489, 523
    influence of, 13
    moral development and, 521
    parents' discipline and, 160, 161
    reinforcement and, 489
    vicarious punishment, 489
Pygmalion (Shaw), 564

Qualitative change, definition of, 9
Qualitative/quantitative change
    aggression and, 475
    attachment and, 430
    child development theories and, 17–18
    cognitive-developmental perspective and, 11
    communities and, 151
    content domains and, 396
    contexts and, 565
    culture and, 10, 151
    as developmental issue, 9–10, 11
    emotional development and, 430
    families and, 151
    genetics and, 79
    information processing theory and, 266
    intelligence theories and, 283
    language development theories and, 321
    motivation and, 499
    physical development and, 11, 100, 101, 130
    Piaget and Vygotsky contrasted, 226
    prenatal development and, 79
    prosocial behavior and, 475
    social-emotional development and, 11
    theory theory and, 266
Quantitative change, definition of, 9
Quasi-experimental studies, 43–44, 46
Questionnaires, 37
Questions
    interviewing skills and, 54
    language development and, 329
    leading questions, 261
    observation of, 341

sociolinguistic behavior and, 342
wait time and, 342–343, 344
why and how questions, 265, 489
Quinceañeras, 118

Race. See also African Americans; Ethnic minority groups
    ethnicity compared to, 175
    intelligence and, 299–301
    interpersonal behaviors and, 469, 470
    lack of biological basis for, 300
    research methods and, 35
    sense of self and, 458
    subcultures and, 541
Racial harassment, 472
Randomness, experimental studies and, 42
Rating scales, 52, 53, 54
Reactive aggression, 473–474
Readiness
    gestures and, 245
    Piaget/Vygotsky compared, 222, 224
    school readiness tests, 291
Reading
    authentic reading activities, 359, 366–367
    automatization and, 240, 366–367
    constructivism and, 361
    developmental progressions in, 396
    developmental trends in, 363–364
    diversity in, 364–366
    emergent literacy and, 358–359
    interactive technologies and, 561
    language development and, 328
    learning disabilities and, 268, 364
    metacognition in, 362, 367
    metalinguistic awareness and, 344
    parents reading to children, 162, 358, 366
    phonological awareness and, 359, 366
    promoting reading development, 366–368
    reading comprehension and, 47–48, 218, 219, 240, 360–362
    reciprocal teaching and, 47–48, 218–219, 362
    socioeconomic status and, 365
    speech and communication disorders and, 351
    Standard English and, 350
    word recognition and, 359–360
Reading comprehension, 47–48, 218, 219, 240, 360–362
Reasoning skills. See also Thinking/reasoning skills
    assessment of, 38
    cognitive-developmental theories and, 14
    mathematical reasoning skills, 200, 207
    proportional reasoning, 202, 207, 375, 379, 383, 392, 393
    scientific reasoning skills, 200, 207, 385–386, 389
Receptive language, 322, 350
Recessive genes, 69
Reciprocal influences, 164
Reciprocal relationships, 535
Reciprocal teaching
    definition of, 218
    reading instruction and, 47–48, 218–219, 362
Recursive thinking, 460
Reflection, apprenticeships and, 216
Reflexes, 91, 111, 196
Rehearsal
    culture and, 249
    definition of, 246
    epistemological beliefs and, 255
    as learning strategy, 246, 248, 258
    limitations of, 257, 258
    long-term memory and, 236
Reinforcement
    language development and, 316–317
    prosocial and aggressive behavior, 471
    self-reinforcement, 511
    vicarious reinforcement, 489
Reinforcers
    children's responses to, 488
    definition of, 488

extrinsic motivation and, 488–489, 498, 500, 502, 506–507, 512, 523
    moral development and, 523
    primary and secondary reinforcers, 488
Rejected children (peer acceptance), 533, 534, 535, 538
Rejection (culture), 176
Relatedness, need for, 407, 482, 494
Relational aggression, 472, 474, 476
Relaxation techniques, 86
Reliability
    assessments and, 55
    in data collection, 40, 46, 48, 49
    definition of, 40
    dynamic assessment and, 289
    intelligence tests and, 287–288, 290
Religion and religious groups, 388, 391, 559–561
Religious tolerance, 560–561
Repetition of gratifying actions, 198, 206–207
Reproductive cells
    chromosomes of, 65, 66
    formation of, 66–68
Research design
    associations and, 44, 47
    causal relationships and, 42–44, 47
    developmental studies and, 45, 47
    natural contexts and, 45–46, 47
    strengths and weaknesses of, 46, 47
Research methods
    analyzing developmental research, 36–48
    brain development and, 108, 110
    case studies, 33–34, 58–59
    conducting research in schools and, 48–58
    data collection techniques, 36–42, 48–49
    evaluation of, 46–48
    principles of, 34–36
    research designs, 42–46, 47
Research participants, 35–36, 40, 48
Resilience, definition of, 184
Respect, 539
Response cost, 489
Response decision, 462
Response enactment, 462
Response search, 462
Responses to questions, 341
Rest and sleep
    infancy and, 113, 128–129
    observation guidelines, 136
    physical development and, 128–130
Retrieving information, 234, 462
Reviving Ophelia (Pipher), 116
Rewards. See also Reinforcers
    extrinsic rewards and punishments, 488–489, 523
    influence of, 13
    moral development and, 523
    prosocial behavior and, 471
    reinforcers as, 488
Right hemisphere
    definition of, 103
    giftedness and, 306–307
    language development and, 103, 317
Risky behaviors, 107, 117, 118, 119, 448, 544
Role confusion, 405, 407
Role taking, play and, 213, 222
Romania, 293–294
Romantic relationships
    attachment and, 415
    dating and, 543
    early childhood awareness of, 542
    sense of self and, 449
    sexual intimacy and, 544
    sexual orientation and, 544–545
    teachers addressing adolescents' sexuality, 546–547
Rough-and-tumble play, 125, 175
Rules
    for acceptable behaviors, 435, 480, 523–524, 550
    dialects and, 349–350
    emotional problems and, 429

Rules, *continued*
  family structure and, 155
  gangs and, 541
  grammatical rules, 328, 370
  middle childhood and, 21, 468–469
  moral development and, 518, 521, 524
  parenting styles and, 160, 161
  play and, 213, 468
  problem-solving strategies and, 249–250
  self-determination and, 503
  self-regulation and, 509, 511
  syntactic rules, 328, 330, 331, 370
  writing and, 370
Running records, 52
Rural areas, communities of, 182

Sadness, 418, 419, 421, 422, 426
Samples
  conclusions and, 48
  definition of, 35
Saved by the Bell, 561
Scaffolding
  acquisition of teaching skills and, 217
  apprenticeships and, 216
  challenging tasks and, 221
  collaborative learning and, 257
  co-regulated learning and, 262
  definition of, 215
  exceptionalities in information
    processing and, 271
  independent learning and, 259
  motivation and, 503
  reciprocal teaching and, 219
  science and, 389
  self-regulation and, 511
  self-talk and, 220
  sense of self and, 456
  writing and, 374
Schemas
  definition of, 242
  gender schemas, 451, 452
  integration of knowledge and, 242
  language development and, 318, 334
  long-term memory and, 242
  story schemas, 361
  substance schemas, 385
Schemes
  definition of, 193
  schemas compared to, 242
  sensorimotor stage and, 196, 243
Schizophrenia, 103, 104
School psychologists, 110, 429
School readiness tests, 291
Schools. *See also* Academic achievement;
  Formal schooling
  conducting research in, 48–58
  eating habits and, 122, 124
  effects of school environment, 5
  elementary/secondary school
    transition, 448, 492, 553–555
  gangs and, 542
  health-compromising behaviors and,
    133–135
  nature/nurture and, 565
  partnerships with families and, 167–174
  poverty and, 184
  prosocial and aggressive behavior,
    471–472
  religion in, 560
  sense of community in, 549–551
  socialization and, 551–553
Schools within schools, 555
School traditions, 550–551
School values, 551–552
Science
  children's theories and, 263–265,
    384–385
  developmental progressions in, 396
  developmental trends in, 387
  diversity in, 388
  gender and, 388, 451
  interactive technology and, 561
  metacognition in, 386
  moral development and, 524
  promoting development in, 388–390
  scientific reasoning skills, 200, 207,
    385–386, 389

Scientific method
  cognitive processes and, 385
  definition of, 35
Scientific reasoning, definition of, 385
Scientific reasoning skills, 200, 207,
  385–386, 389
Scripts
  definition of, 242
  integration of knowledge and, 242
  language development and, 318, 334
  long-term memory and, 242
Secondary reinforcers, 488
Secondary schools, transitions to, 448,
  492, 554–555
Second language development
  language development and, 318, 319,
    344, 346, 347–349
  metalinguistic awareness and, 344, 346,
    347, 348
  sensitive periods and, 318, 319, 347
  syntactic development and, 318, 347
Second stage of labor, 87
Secure attachment, 410, 412
Selective adoption (culture), 176
Self, sense of. *See* Sense of self
Self-care, 163
Self-concept, issues of, 442
Self-conscious emotions
  definition of, 420
  physical development and, 114
Self-control, 110, 533
Self-determination
  culture and, 500
  goals and, 503–504
  motivation and, 490, 491, 492, 498, 502,
    503, 506
  rules and, 503
  school environment and, 550
  self-regulation and, 511
Self-disclosure, 537
Self-efficacy
  attributions and, 498
  definition of, 490
  gender and, 499
  issues of, 442
  moral development and, 521, 525
  motivation and, 490, 492, 493, 495, 503
  self-regulation and, 511
Self-esteem
  early intervention and, 294
  elementary/secondary school transition
    and, 448
  enhancing sense of self and, 454, 456
  ethnic minority groups and, 453
  factors influencing, 444, 450, 451
  issues of, 442
  parenting styles and, 160
  peer pressure and, 469
  peer relationships and, 533, 537
  physical development and, 114
  self-judgments and, 445–446, 447
  students at risk and, 507
  transition to secondary schools
    and, 554
  victims and, 474
Self-evaluation
  definition of, 513
  gender and, 499
  promotion of, 258–259
  self-regulation and, 509, 513–514
  sense of self and, 444, 445–446, 447, 448
Self-fulfilling prophecy, 552
Self-handicapping, 443
Self-improvement
  physical activity and, 127–128
  sense of self and, 456
Self-instructions, 513
Self-judgment, 445–446, 447, 509
Self-management, 515
Self-monitoring
  definition of, 512
  promotion of, 258–259
  self-regulation and, 512–513
Self-motivation, 508, 513
Self-perception
  changes in, 446
  children's behavior mirroring, 443

contradictions in, 449, 450
factors influencing, 444
gender and, 452
multifaceted understandings of, 445
teachers' influence on, 442, 552
Self-recognition, 447
Self-regulated learning
  definition of, 252
  interdependence of, 255
  metacognition and, 252–253
  observation of, 267
  self-regulation and, 508
  social interaction and, 262
  strategic development and, 258–259
Self-regulation
  central executive and, 236
  conditions fostering, 509–510
  definition of, 508
  developmental trends in, 508–509
  diversity in, 510
  moral development and, 515
  promotion of, 510–515
Self-reinforcement, 511
Self-reports
  as data collection technique, 36–37
  definition of, 36
  distortions of information and, 41
  limitations of, 37
Self-serving goals, 474
Self-socialization, 452–453, 469, 508, 540
Self-talk
  cognitive development and, 224
  definition of, 211
  exceptionalities in information
    processing and, 270
  scaffolding and, 220
  self-regulated learning and, 252
  self-regulation and, 508, 509
  sign language and, 352
Self-worth, 442, 443, 444, 445, 446, 451
Semantic bootstrapping, 330
Semantics
  definition of, 316
  language development and, 320
  semantic development, 323–328, 334
  sensory impairments and, 351–352
  speech and communication disorders
    and, 350
Sensation
  definition of, 90
  developmental trends in, 236–238
  information processing theory and, 234
Sense of community, 184, 549–551
Sense of self
  case studies, 441
  changing nature of, 447–451
  definition of, 442
  developmental trends in, 455
  diversity in, 451–454
  effects of, 442–443
  enhancement of, 454, 456–458
  factors influencing, 443–444
  general trends in, 444–447
  moral development and, 521–522
  peer relationships and, 443, 444, 445,
    446, 449
Sense of self-determination, 490, 491,
  492, 498
Sensitive periods
  brain development and, 72, 108, 110
  definition of, 8
  language development and, 72,
    317–318, 319
  in prenatal development, 73, 79, 80
  second language development and,
    318, 319, 347
Sensitivity to physical input, observation
  of, 432
Sensorimotor stage, 196, 197, 201, 243
Sensory impairments
  hearing loss/impairments, 351–352,
    364, 464
  language development and, 351–352
  science development and, 388
  visual impairments, 351, 364, 388, 511
Sensory register, 235, 236
Sentence structure, 331

Serious injuries, 137, 139
Service learning, 558
Sesame Street, 480, 561
Sex education, 546
Sex-role stereotypes, 452, 453
Sexual abuse, 166, 544
Sexual activity
  dating and, 542
  health-compromising behavior and,
    131, 132–135
  late adolescence and, 22
  risky behavior and, 117, 119, 544
  sexual intimacy and, 118, 544
Sexual harassment, 472, 480, 481, 547, 564
Sexually transmitted infections (STIs), 132,
  133, 134–135, 166, 544
Sexual maturation, 118, 119, 128
Sexual orientation, 544–545, 547
Sexual predators, 564
Shame
  autonomy versus shame and doubt
    stage, 405, 406, 407
  conduct disorder and, 428
  definition of, 516
  emotional development and, 419, 420
  gender, 522
  moral development and, 516, 516n, 519
Shared routines, 534–535
Short-term memory, 235, 235n. *See also*
  Working memory
Siblings
  acquisition of teaching skills and, 217
  attachments and, 410, 416
  blended families and, 155
  as caregivers, 163, 165
  influences of, 165–166
  prosocial behavior and, 471
Sickle cell disease, 69, 71, 82
Sight vocabulary, 360
Sign language
  American Sign Language, 317, 348, 352,
    364, 538
  language development and, 320
  sensory impairments and, 351–352
Silence
  intelligence and, 278
  sociolinguistic behaviors and, 340–341
Single-gene defects, 69, 70–71, 72
Single parents, 152, 154–155
Situational interest, 490
Sleep, 113, 128–130, 136
Small-group learning, 257
Smurfs, 561
Sociability, observation of, 432
Social cognition
  aggression and, 474
  definition of, 458
  developmental trends in, 477–478
  diversity in, 464
  fostering development of, 464–466
  social-cognitive bias and prejudice,
    463–464
  social information processing and,
    462–463
  theory of mind and, 458–462
Social-cognitive biases, definition of, 463
Social cognitive theory, motivation and, 13
Social competence, 281, 466, 467
Social construction of meaning, 214–215,
  261, 358
Social construction of memory, 261
Social constructivism, 194, 215
Social conventions, 516, 519, 524
Social cues, 474, 534
Social-emotional development. *See also*
  Emotional development; Interpersonal
  behaviors; Moral development;
  Motivation; Self-regulation
  cognitive process theories and, 15
  definition of, 5
  developmental issues and, 11
  developmental trends, 4, 24–25
  language development and, 320
  universality/diversity and, 9, 11
Social goals, 494–495, 505
Social groups
  depictions of, 561

peer relationships and, 539–542
teachers' facilitating of, 537–538
Social information processing, 462–463
Social intelligence, 308
Social interaction. *See also* Interpersonal
behaviors; Peer relationships; Social
skills
autism and, 269
eliminating barriers to, 538
enhancing information processing
through, 262
Internet use and, 563–564
language development and, 318, 319
Piaget's cognitive development theory
and, 195, 197, 199, 224, 225–226
self-regulated learning and, 262
Vygotsky's cognitive development
theory and, 211–212, 218, 224,
225–226
Socialization
definition of, 148
families and, 148–149, 159
gender differences and, 175–176, 476,
522–523
peer relationships and, 533
political socialization, 165
reciprocal influences on, 164
schools and, 551–553
self-socialization, 452–453
temperament and, 433
Social learning theory
children's beliefs and goals and, 13
definition of, 12
Social perspective taking
definition of, 460
encouragement of, 465
interpersonal behaviors and, 468
prosocial behavior and, 472
theory of mind and, 460–461
Social referencing
definition of, 260
emotional development and, 418
infancy and, 260–261
theory of mind and, 458
Social skills
child maltreatment and, 166
continued development of, 470
definition of, 466
emotional problems and, 429
environmental factors and, 72
exceptionality in information
processing and, 271
interactive technologies and, 561
observation of, 305
parenting styles and, 160
peer relationships and, 466, 509, 533,
534, 538, 543
play and, 213, 536
self-regulation and, 508
sense of self and, 450
teaching of, 478, 479
Social stimuli, 237, 260
Social systems, 151
Social workers and social work, 56
Society. *See also* Socialization
awareness of social conventions and,
516, 519
definition of, 555
moral development and,
517–518, 519
nature/nurture and, 565
services for children and adolescents
and, 555–561
television and interactive technologies,
561–565
Society for Research in Child
Development, 46
Sociocognitive conflict, definition of, 209
Sociocultural theories. *See also* Culture
definition of, 15
emphasis of, 15–16
language development and,
319–320, 321
semantics and, 320
theoretical positions of, 17
Vygotsky's cognitive development
theory and, 15, 209, 260

Sociodramatic play
definition of, 213
gender and, 475
interpersonal behaviors and, 467–468
theory of mind and, 461
Socioeconomic status. *See also* Poverty
adoption and, 156
computers and, 565
definition of, 182
dialects and, 350
early childhood intervention programs
and, 556
eating habits and, 121–122, 124, 125
emotional development and, 424
families and, 182–183
intelligence and, 294, 299, 300
language development and, 349
literacy and, 365
peer mediation and, 481
professional practice and, 184–186
reading and, 365
research methods and, 35
self-regulation and, 510
sociolinguistic behaviors and, 342
teacher expectations and, 552
teenage pregnancy and, 133
Sociolinguistic behaviors
definition of, 340
language development and, 340–344
observations of, 341
parents and, 342
peer relationships and, 340, 343
professional practice and, 343–344
Solitary play, 467
Sounds, locating source of, 236
Southeast Asians, 341, 453, 464, 500
Spatial intelligence, 280
Spatial relationships
central conceptual structures and, 204
language development and, 325
learning strategies and, 249
Speaking skills, language development
and, 335–340
Spearman's *g*, 278–279, 283
Special educators, 56, 110, 429
Special Olympics, 522
Special physical needs
physical activity and, 127
physical development, 136–141
Specific ability tests, 288
Specific factors, intelligence and, 279
Specific language impairments, 350–351
Speech and communication disorders
definition of, 350
language development and, 350–351
Speech-language pathologists, 344
Speed (methamphetamine), 132
Spelling, 370
Sperm, 66, 67, 68, 68n, 75
Spermarche, 115
Spina bifida, 72
Spontaneous learning, 108
Sports. *See* Organized sports
Stable attributions, 496
Stages
cognitive-developmental theories
and, 14
definition of, 9, 9n
Erikson's psychosocial development
theory and, 10, 404–406
Kohlberg's moral development theory
and, 14, 517, 518, 521, 524
neo-Piagetian theories and, 204
Piaget's cognitive development theory
and, 9, 14, 196–201, 203,
206–208, 236
Vygotsky's cognitive development
theory and, 213–214
Stage theories, 9–10
Stagnation (in Erikson's theory), 405, 407
Standard English
definition of, 349
dialects and, 349, 350
Standards
for child care, 555–556
of content domains, 395, 397
moral development and, 515–516, 519

Stanford-Binet Intelligence Scales, 284,
288, 290
States of arousal, 90–91
Stepparents, 155
Stereotyped, approval-focused
orientation, 473
Stereotypes
breaking down, 465
definition of, 463
of gender, 452
interactive technologies and, 561
social cognition and, 463–464
teacher expectations and, 465, 552
video games and, 562
Stereotype threat, definition of, 301
Sternberg's triarchic theory, 281–282,
283, 288
Stimuli, attention and, 238, 239
Storing information, 234, 462
Storybook reading skills, 366
Storyknifing, 373
Story schemas, 361
Stranger anxiety, 409, 410, 418
Strange Situation, 410–411, 413
Strategies, thinking/reasoning skills and,
243–244
Stress
adolescent mothers and, 157
attachment security and, 410–411, 413,
415
birth and, 85–86
distress, 418
emotional development and, 422, 426
emotional regulation and, 424
environmental/hereditary interaction
and, 73, 74
families and, 417
poverty and, 183
prenatal development and, 81, 84, 104
rest and sleep, 130
romantic relationships and, 543
Strong correlations, 44
Structural measures, of child care, 555–556
Structures, in fictional and nonfictional
texts, 361
Students at risk, 260, 268, 507
Subcultures, 541
Substance abuse. *See also* Alcohol; Drugs
depression and, 427
families and, 166, 167
foster care and, 156, 157
health-compromising behavior and,
131–132
mental retardation and, 309
risky behavior and, 119
socioeconomic status and, 183
suicide and, 430
Substance schemas, 385
Suburban communities, 182
Success
motivation and, 490, 495, 496, 498, 502,
503, 505–506
sense of self and, 454, 456
Sudden infant death syndrome (SIDS), 128
Suicide, 427–430
Superficial needs-of-others
orientation, 473
Suppression programs (gangs), 542
Symbolic thought
definition of, 196
play and, 197–198, 222
preoperational stage and, 196–198
Symbols
definition of, 243
language development and, 320
literacy and, 358
maps and, 392
Piaget's cognitive development theory
and, 196
Sympathy
definition of, 472
moral development and, 516
prosocial behavior and, 472
Synapses, 101, 102, 103, 104, 105
Synaptic pruning
brain development and, 105, 106, 108
definition of, 105

Synaptogenesis, definition of, 105
Syntax
definition of, 316
dialects and, 349
language development and, 316,
318, 321
nativism and, 320
second language development and,
318, 347
sensory impairments and, 351
sign language and, 320
speech and communication disorders
and, 350
syntactic development, 328–331, 334
writing and, 370
Synthesis, left hemisphere and, 103

Taiwan, 278, 366
Talkativeness
intelligence and, 278
sociolinguistic behaviors and, 340–341
Task complexity, 217
Tay-Sachs disease, 71, 82
Teachers. *See also* Developmentally
appropriate practice; Observations;
Professional practice
adolescents' sexuality and, 546–547
aggression and, 480–481
attributions and, 498
bioecological perspective and, 16
computers and, 565
depression and, 428
elementary/secondary transition and,
553–555
emotions of, 426
expectations of, 177, 185, 299, 426,
429, 435, 444, 465, 512, 551–553
family communication and, 158, 168,
170, 171
gangs and, 541–542
IRE cycle and, 342
listening to children and, 53–55
partnerships with families and,
167–174
religious tolerance and, 560–561
self-regulation and, 509
sense of community in schools and,
549–551
sense of self and, 442, 444, 449
siblings and, 165–166
television viewing skills and, 564
wait time and, 341, 342–343, 344
Teaching skills, acquisition of, 217
Teenage pregnancy, 133, 157, 544
Teen dialects, 338
Telegraphic speech
definition of, 328
expanding on, 331
Television
harmfulness of, 45
implications of, 564–565
viewing time, 561, 562, 564
Temperament
attachment security and, 413
attention and, 239
bioecological perspective and, 16
definition of, 6
depression and, 427
individual differences in, 431, 433
motivation and, 498–499
nature/nurture and, 6–7, 431
observation of, 432
parenting styles and, 164
preferences in, 435
self-regulation and, 510
Teratogens, 79, 80, 81, 84, 104, 293
Testosterone, 116, 471, 476
Tests. *See also* Intelligence tests
advantages/disadvantages of, 55
aptitude tests, 288
as data collection technique, 37–38
definition of, 37
distortions of information and, 41
ethical guidelines and, 57
school readiness tests, 291
specific ability tests, 288
of thinking/reasoning skills, 38

Thalassemia (Cooley's anemia), 71
Theories. *See also* specific theories
    definition of, 12
Theory of mind
    definition of, 458
    diversity in, 464
    factors promotion development of, 461
    perspective taking and, 458–459, 458n
    social cognition and, 458–462
    social information processing and, 462
Theory theory
    critique of, 266
    definition of, 263
    physical world theories, 263–265, 384–385
Therapeutic foster parents, 156–157
Thinking/reasoning skills. *See also*
    Abstract thought; Concrete thought;
    Symbolic thought
    cognitive-developmental theories and, 14
    cognitive process theories and, 15
    community of learners and, 550
    developmentally appropriate practice and, 27
    developmental trends in, 223, 243–244
    familiar content and tasks and, 208–209
    language development and, 211, 318, 319
    middle childhood and, 21, 223
    moral development and, 517–519
    neo-Piagetian theories and, 204
    observation of, 207
    sociocultural theories and, 15
    tests and assessments of, 38
Third stage of labor, 87, 88
Thought. *See also* Abstract thought;
    Concrete thought; Symbolic thought
    metacognitive awareness and, 250, 251
Through the Looking Glass (Carroll), 347
Time concepts, 180, 211
Time management, modeling of, 255
To Kill a Mockingbird (Lee), 480
Tools
    cognitive tools, 180, 210–211, 212, 218, 225
    for writing, 373
Topic depth, composition skills and, 370–371
Toxic substances, 72, 81, 183, 292, 293, 309
Transitions
    to elementary schools, 553–554
    family transitions, 158
    Piaget's cognitive development theory and, 196
    to secondary schools, 448, 492, 554–555
Treatments, 42, 42n
Triarchic theory, 281–282, 283, 288
Trolling, 564
Trust versus mistrust stage, 404, 407
Turner syndrome, 70
Turn taking, 213, 316, 338, 343, 467, 511

Twins, 68, 166
Twin studies
    attention-deficit hyperactivity disorder and, 268
    intelligence and, 291–292, 292n, 293
    nature/nurture and, 68
    prosocial and aggressive behavior, 471
    sexual orientation and, 545
    temperament and, 431

Ultrasound examination, 81–82
Umbilical cord, 75
Uncontrollable attributions, 496
Undergeneralization, 324
Uninvolved style, 160, 161, 166
Universal Grammar, 317
Universality, definition of, 8
Universality/diversity. *See also* Diversity
    aggression and, 475
    attachment and, 430
    child development theories and, 17–18
    cognitive development and, 9, 11
    communities and, 151
    content domains and, 396
    contexts and, 565
    culture and, 9, 151
    as developmental issue, 1, 8–9, 10
    emotional development and, 430
    Erikson's psychosocial development theory and, 10
    families and, 151
    genes and, 64
    genetics and, 79
    guided participation and, 159
    information processing theory and, 266
    intelligence theories and, 283
    language development theories and, 321
    motivation and, 499
    physical development and, 9, 11, 98, 130
    Piaget and Vygotsky contrasted, 226
    Piaget's cognitive development theory and, 10, 196, 203
    prenatal development and, 79
    prosocial behavior and, 475
    research methods and, 35
    social-emotional development and, 9, 11
    theory theory and, 266
    Vygotsky's cognitive development theory and, 211
Universal Nonverbal Intelligence Test (UNIT), 284–285, 286, 288, 300
Unoccupied behavior, 467
Unstable attributions, 496
Urban areas, communities of, 182
U.S. Association for Blind Athletes, 140
U.S. Census Bureau, 152
U.S. Drug Enforcement Agency, 134

Validity
    assessments and, 55
    data collection and, 40, 46, 48, 49

definition of, 40
    dynamic assessment and, 289
    intelligence tests and, 287–288, 290
Value, definition of, 491
Valued activities, 180
Variables, separation and control of, 200, 201, 202, 385–386, 389
Verbal ability
    gender and, 298, 349
    triarchic theory and, 281
Vicarious punishment, 489
Vicarious reinforcement, 489
Victims, 471, 472, 474, 524, 546
Video games, 492, 561, 562–563, 564
Vietnam, 506
Violence
    aggression and, 44, 472, 480, 561–562
    emotional problems and, 426
    school environment and, 549
    television and, 561–562
    video games and, 561, 562, 563
    warning signs of, 481
Visual acuity, 236, 237, 384
Visual aids, 383
Visual cliff, 237
Visual focusing, 236
Visual impairments, 351, 364, 388, 511
Visual perception, 108, 237
Visual-spatial ability, 381, 388, 562
Vocabulary development, 323–324, 360, 366, 561
Vygotsky's cognitive development theory
    applying ideas of, 218–221
    challenging tasks and, 211, 212, 219–220, 222, 252, 262
    contemporary theories compared to, 266
    current perspectives on, 213–217
    dynamic assessment and, 288
    formal schooling and, 210, 294
    key ideas in, 209–221
    language development, 211, 224
    Piaget compared to, 210, 211, 213, 214, 221–222, 224–226
    sociocultural theories and, 15, 209, 260

Wait time, 341, 342–343, 344
Weak correlations, 44
Weapons, possession of, 480
Web sites/pages, 170, 563, 565
Wechsler Intelligence Scale for Children (Wechsler), 284, 285, 288, 290
Wechsler Preschool and Primary Scale of Intelligence (Wechsler), 290
Wernicke's area, 317, 318
"We Wear the Mask" (Dunbar), 368
Wheelchair Sports USA, 140
Whites. *See* European Americans
Why and how questions, 265, 489
Williams syndrome, 321–322
WISC-IV (Wechsler), 284, 285, 288, 290

Women. *See also* Gender
    employment of, 163
    as single parents, 155
Word endings, 329
Word order, 329, 330
Word recognition, 359–360, 561
Working memory
    attention and, 236
    capacity of, 235, 240, 245, 258, 268, 386, 508
    definition of, 235
    developmental trends in, 239–240
    gestures and, 244
    information processing theory and, 235, 235n
    language development and, 318
    listening comprehension and, 334
    long-term memory and, 236
    mathematics and, 383
    mental retardation and, 309
    neo-Piagetian theories and, 204
    reading comprehension and, 362, 364
    science and, 386
    self-regulation and, 508
    social information processing and, 462
    writing and, 369
WPPSI-III (Wechsler), 290
Writing
    authentic writing activities, 373
    children's early efforts at, 368–369
    composition skills and, 370–371, 373
    developmental progressions in, 396
    developmental trends in, 372
    diversity in, 373
    emotional expression and, 425
    handwriting and, 114, 370
    metacognition in, 371
    physical development and, 113
    promoting writing development, 373–374
    speech and communication disorders and, 351
    spelling and, 370
    syntax and grammatical rules, 370

X-chromosome-linked disorders, 69, 82
X chromosomes, 68

Y chromosomes, 68

Zambia, 423
Zone of proximal development (ZPD)
    adult activities and, 216, 217
    assessments and, 220
    challenging tasks and, 212, 219–220, 222
    definition of, 212
    giftedness and, 307
    mathematics and, 383
    readiness and, 224
    scaffolding and, 215
    social interaction and, 224
Zygotes, 67, 68, 69, 75, 76, 79, 85